OXFORD REFERENCE

THE CONCISE
OXFORD DICTIONARY OF
THE CHRISTIAN
CHURCH

Edited by
ELIZABETH A. LIVINGSTONE

Oxford   New York
OXFORD UNIVERSITY PRESS

Oxford University Press, Walton Street, Oxford OX2 6DP

Oxford New York Toronto
Delhi Bombay Calcutta Madras Karachi
Petaling Jaya Singapore Hong Kong Tokyo
Nairobi Dar es Salaam Cape Town
Melbourne Auckland

and associated companies in
Berlin Ibadan

Oxford is a trade mark of Oxford University Press

First published in hardback and paperback 1977
Paperback reprinted with corrections 1980, 1986, 1987, 1990

British Library Cataloguing in Publication Data
The concise Oxford dictionary of
the Christian Church.—2nd ed. abridged.
1. Church—Dictionaries
I. Livingstone, Elizabeth Anne
II. Oxford dictionary of the Christian Church
260'.3   BV600.2   77 30192
ISBN 0–19–283014–7

Printed in Great Britain by
Richard Clay Ltd, Bungay, Suffolk

PREFACE

In 1939 Dr. G. F. J. Cumberlege commissioned two fairly young Librarians of Pusey House in Oxford to produce quite quickly what he envisaged as a handy *Oxford Companion to the Christian Religion*. Eighteen years later his successor published *The Oxford Dictionary of the Christian Church*, edited by F. L. Cross, who had meantime become the Lady Margaret Professor of Divinity in the University of Oxford. This quickly became a standard reference book; it provides, as Gregory the Great said of Scripture, water in which lambs may walk and elephants may swim. The aim of the present work is to offer basic information for the lambs who do not need, and perhaps cannot afford, the elephants' swimming-pools. It seeks in most cases to answer the questions who or what; for further information and for lists of books in which the subject may be pursued, the reader is referred to the corresponding article in the parent volume, and especially the second edition of 1974, on which this abridgement is based. Unless otherwise stated, Biblical references are to the Authorized Version.

It is my pleasant duty to acknowledge and offer thanks to the many people who have given me help and guidance in a variety of ways. There are too many to name them all, but I am particularly indebted to the Rev. Prof. J. Macquarrie, the Rev. J. O. Mills, O.P., and Dr. P. H. Rousseau, who supplied material for new entries or the revision of existing ones; to Mr. D. Bevan, the Rev. J. D. Crichton, the Rev. Canon D. L. Edwards, Mr. B. J. T. Hanson, the Rev. Dom Daniel Rees, O.S.B., and the Very Rev. Dr. K. T. Ware, who answered my questions on matters in their various spheres of expertise; to the Librarian of Downside, who graciously allowed me to use the community library whenever I asked, and to Miss J. K. F. Swinyard of Wells Public Library whose helpfulness far exceeded the bounds of duty; to Miss F. M. Williams and Miss A. Pickles, who both read the first proofs; to the Rev. Canon P. M. Martin, who checked the Hebrew and helped me in many other ways; and to the staff of the Oxford University Press who laboured unstintingly on the book.

E.A.L.

ABBREVIATIONS

(A) The most common abbreviations, used throughout the book

Abp.	Archbishop
acc.	according
AV	Authorized Version (i.e. King James Version, 1611)
BCP	Book of Common Prayer
Bl.	Blessed
Bp.	Bishop
BVM	Blessed Virgin Mary
Card.	Cardinal
C of E	Church of England
cent.	century
Ep.	Epistle
Emp.	Emperor
fl.	*floruit* (Lat., 'flourished')
LXX	Septuagint
MS.	manuscript
NEB	New English Bible (NT, 1961; OT and Apocrypha, 1970)
NT	New Testament
OT	Old Testament
Patr.	Patriarch
RC	Roman Catholic
RSV	Revised Standard Version (NT, 1946; OT, 1952; Apocrypha, 1957)
RV	[English] Revised Version (NT, 1881; OT, 1885; Apocrypha, 1895)
sc.	*scilicet* (Lat., 'namely')
tr.	translation
Ven.	Venerable
Vulg.	Vulgate

An asterisk (*) preceding a word indicates a relevant article in the *Dictionary* under that (or a closely similar) heading.

(B) Biblical Books (given in the order of the AV)

(Names used in the Vulgate and/or derived versions are given in brackets where they differ substantially from those of the AV)

OLD TESTAMENT

Gen.	Genesis
Exod.	Exodus
Lev.	Leviticus
Num.	Numbers
Deut.	Deuteronomy
Jos.	Joshua

Jgs.	Judges
Ruth	Ruth
1, 2 Sam, (1, 2 Reg.)	1, 2 Samuel (1, 2 Regum or Reigns)
1, 2 Kgs. (3, 4 Reg.)	1, 2 Kings (3, 4 Regum or Reigns)
1, 2 Chron. (1, 2 Paralip.)	1, 2 Chronicles (1, 2 Paralipomenon)
Ez. (1 Esd.)	Ezra (1 Esdras)
Neh. (2 Esd.)	Nehemiah (2 Esdras)
Est.	Esther
Job	Job
Pss.	Psalms
Prov.	Proverbs
Eccles.	Ecclesiastes
Song of Songs (Cant.)	Song of Songs (Canticles)
Is. (Es.)	Isaiah (Esaias)
Jer.	Jeremiah
Lam.	Lamentations
Ezek.	Ezekiel
Dan.	Daniel
Hos.	Hosea
Joel	Joel
Am.	Amos
Obad.	Obadiah
Jon.	Jonah
Mic.	Micah
Nah.	Nahum
Hab.	Habakkuk
Zeph. (Soph.)	Zephaniah (Sophonias)
Hag.	Haggai
Zech.	Zechariah
Mal.	Malachi

APOCRYPHA

1, 2 Esd. (3, 4 Esd.)	1, 2 Esdras (3, 4 Esdras)
Tob.	Tobit
Judith	Judith
Rest of Est.	Rest of Esther
Wisd. Sol.	Wisdom of Solomon
Ecclus. (Sirach)	Ecclesiasticus (Sirach)
Bar.	Baruch
S. of III Ch.	Song of the Three Children
Sus.	Susanna
Bel	Bel and the Dragon
Pr. Man.	Prayer of Manasses
1, 2 Macc.	1, 2 Maccabees

NEW TESTAMENT

Mt.	Matthew
Mk.	Mark
Lk.	Luke
Jn.	John
Acts	Acts of the Apostles

Rom.	Romans
1, 2 Cor.	1, 2 Corinthians
Gal.	Galatians
Eph.	Ephesians
Phil.	Philippians
Col.	Colossians
1, 2 Thess.	1, 2 Thessalonians
1, 2 Tim.	1, 2 Timothy
Tit.	Titus
Philem.	Philemon
Heb.	Hebrews
Jas.	James
1, 2 Pet.	1, 2 Peter
1, 2, 3 Jn.	1, 2, 3 John
Jude	Jude
Rev. (Apoc.)	Revelation (Apocalypse)

A

AARON. In Hebrew tradition *Moses' brother. He was assigned to Moses as his assistant (Ex. 4: 14), and later he and his descendants were appointed priests (Ex. 28 f.). His authority was miraculously confirmed by the budding rod (Num. 17: 1–8). In Christian theology he is a *type of Christ.

ABAILARD. See Abelard.

ABBA. The Aramaic word for 'Father', used by Christ.

ABBÉ. A French term, originally restricted to the *abbot of a monastery, but in modern times applied to secular clerics in general.

ABBESS. The superior of certain communities of nuns following the *Benedictine rule, though the title is extended to the superiors of orders of *canonesses and (esp.) to those of the Second *Franciscan Order. The earliest known use dates from 514. Except in the Franciscan Order, the office is held for life.

ABBO, St. (c. 945–1004), or **Abbon**, Abbot of *Fleury from 988. He supported the *Cluniac reform and was killed in a revolt occasioned by the reform of the priory of La Réole in Gascony. His correspondence is a valuable source for the relations between France and the Papacy. He also wrote on logic, mathematics, and astronomy, and an Epitome of the Lives of the Popes.

ABBOT. In the W. Church it is the official title of the superior of a (usually large) religious house belonging to one of the orders of the *Benedictine family or to certain orders of the *Canons regular. Acc. to the Rule of St. *Benedict, the abbot is to be regarded as the father of his monastic family and has far-reaching powers in the government of his house. He is elected, normally for life, by the monks of his abbey. The superior of certain prominent monasteries has the name of 'Archabbot', and the presiding abbot of a *Congregation is often known as the 'Abbot President' or 'Abbot General'. Since 1893 the Benedictine Order has had an 'Abbot Primate', who presides over the whole order.

ABBOT OF MISRULE. See Misrule, Lord of.

ABBOT, EZRA (1819–84), American Biblical scholar. A *Unitarian by belief, from 1856 he held posts at Harvard University. He was one of the original members of the American NT Revision Company in charge of the RV, and his judgement was influential.

ABBOT, GEORGE (1562–1633), Abp. of *Canterbury from 1611. His *Puritan sympathies had brought him into conflict with the rising party of *High Churchmen, but his defence of hereditary monarchy against J. *Overall in 1606 gained him royal favour. As archbishop he encouraged *James I's attempt to secure the dismissal of C. *Vorstius, and he ensured that England was represented at the Synod of *Dort (1618). The strong line which he took over the Essex nullity suit (1616) won him respect and a temporary popularity. In 1621 he accidentally shot a gamekeeper and his position was considered to have become irregular; the king decided in his favour and he resumed his duties. He crowned *Charles I but had little influence in his reign.

ABBREVIATOR. A former official of the Roman chancery, whose principal duty was the preparation of letters and writs for the *collation of Church dignities. He was so named from the excessive abbreviations employed in papal documents.

ABEL. Acc. to Gen. 4: 2 the second son of *Adam and *Eve. He was killed by his brother Cain, who was jealous that Abel's sacrifice had been accepted, whereas his own was rejected. In Christian tradition he is regarded as a type of Christ because of the innocence of his life, his accepted sacrifice, and his violent death.

ABELARD, PETER (1079–1142), more correctly **Abailard,** philosopher and theologian. He lectured at *Paris until his career was cut short in 1118 by the tragic issue of his love-affair with Héloïse. He retired to the abbey of *St.-Denis. Attacks were made on the orthodoxy of his teaching on the Trinity, and he was condemned unheard at the Council of *Soissons (1121). His outspoken criticism of the legends of St. *Dionysius made it necessary for him to leave St.-Denis and he established an oratory called the Paraclete near Troyes. In 1125 he became abbot of St.-Gildas. He resumed his teaching in Paris c. 1136. St. *Bernard of Clairvaux denounced his teaching and several propositions from his writings were condemned at the Council of *Sens in 1140. Abelard was eventually reconciled to St. Bernard.

Abelard's extensive works include *Sic et Non,* a collection of apparently conflicting excerpts from Scripture and the Fathers intended to stimulate his readers to resolve the seeming contradictions; *Theologia Summi Boni,* in which he applied his dialectical principles to the doctrine of the Trinity; a commentary on Romans expounding his view of the *Atonement; and several well-known hymns, among them 'O quanta qualia' ('O what the joy and the glory must be'). His philosophical and theological doctrines were largely determined by his early interest in the problem of *universals, and he evolved a position between the extreme *Realism of *William of Champeaux and the crude *Nominalism of *Roscellinus. In ethics he held that sin consisted solely in contempt for the wishes of God; this emphasis on intention led to a practical ignoring of the distinction between good and evil acts, and also assisted him towards an exemplarist theory of the Atonement, acc. to which the suffering Christ was our supreme example, but little more. In his application of reason to the deepest mysteries of the faith, he showed a daring which was bound to incur the censure of his contemporaries, though his distrust of authority has been exaggerated.

ABELITES, also **Abelians** and **Abelonians.** A small N. African sect whose members, while admitting marriage, lived in continence after the alleged example of *Abel. It is known only from St. *Augustine.

ABERCIUS, Inscription of. The Greek epitaph of Abercius Marcellus, Bp. of Hieropolis (d. *c.* 200), now in the *Lateran Museum. Apparently set up by Abercius over his future tomb, it testifies to the universality of the *Eucharist. The 'Life of Abercius', which incorporates the text of the inscription and attributes to Abercius a 'Book of Teaching', is much later (probably late 4th cent.).

ABGAR, Legend of. A legend ascribes to Abgar V (4 B.C.–A.D. 50), King of *Edessa, an exchange of letters with the Lord. The king, being ill, asked Christ to visit and heal him; in reply the Lord promised that after His Ascension He would send a disciple to cure the king and preach the Gospel to his people. Acc. to the 'Pilgrimage of *Etheria', the letter of Christ was preserved at Edessa.

ABJURATION. The act of renouncing any idea, person, or thing to which one has previously held. Acc. to W. *canon law it is an external retraction, made before witnesses, of errors contrary to Catholic faith and unity. Some form of abjuration is commonly required when Christians are received from one Church into another, while the Greek Church also has set forms of abjuration for converts from Judaism and Islam.

ABJURATION, Oath of. An oath renouncing the Stuart dynasty and the temporal power of the Pope, imposed in 1701 on all who took civil, military, or spiritual office. It was replaced in 1858 by a new form of the Oath of *Allegiance.

ABLUTIONS. (1) The washing of fingers and *chalice by the celebrant after the Communion in the Eucharist. (2) In the RC Church the rinsing of the mouth with wine after the reception of the Bl. Sacrament by the new priests in the Ordination Mass, customary until 1968, and a similar rinsing with water formerly common at the Communion of the Sick. A similar custom exists in the E., where in many places communicants receive unconsecrated wine after Communion in the Liturgy.

ABORTION. The practice of abortion has been consistently condemned by Christian moralists, though Christian opinion is divided on the legitimacy of abortion for therapeutic reasons. In English law it was permitted only when considered necessary to save the mother's life until the 1967 Abortion Act allowed wider grounds for terminating a pregnancy. Catholic moral theologians commonly hold that any abortion as an end in itself is unlawful and the 1967 Act largely exempts conscientious objectors from the need to participate in the treatment authorized.

ABRAHAM (or **Abram**), Hebrew patriarch (prob. *c* .1700 B.C.). His life is described in Gen. 11: 26–25: 18. Born in Ur in Chaldaea, under Divine inspiration he went to Haran and then to Canaan. God promised him a son by his wife Sarah and an innumerable posterity. After the birth of *Isaac, Abraham's faith was put to a severe test by a command to sacrifice his son. When he showed his readiness for this act of obedience, a ram was substituted, and he was rewarded by a formal renewal of God's promises.

The Church recognized in Abraham a spiritual ancestor on account of his faith and his obedience in leaving his homeland. His sacrifice furnished a model of perfect submission to the will of God and came to prefigure the death of Christ.

ABRAHAM, Apocalypse of. An apocryphal writing, perhaps dating from the 1st cent. A.D. It describes *Abraham's conversion from idolatry and a series of visions seen by him in the heavens. It shows Christian influence, but the opening part is based on Jewish traditions.

ABRAHAM, Testament of. An apocryphal Gk. writing, dating perhaps from the 2nd cent. A.D. *Abraham, taken to heaven by the Archangel *Michael, has a vision of the two roads leading to hell and paradise; he is brought back to earth and finally borne by the Angel of Death to paradise. In some versions it is supplemented by 'Testaments' of Isaac and Jacob.

ABRAHAM ECCHELLENSIS (1600–1664), *Maronite scholar. A Lebanese by birth, he spent most of his life in Paris and Rome. He published important works on Oriental languages, incl. an edition of 84 spurious *Nicene Canons (1645) and Syriac and Arabic versions of 3 Macc. and of Ruth for the Paris *Polyglot.

ABSOLUTION. The formal act of a priest or bishop pronouncing the forgiveness of sins by Christ to those who are qualified by penitence to receive it. The traditional Catholic doctrine is that this forgiveness is normally imparted on earth by means of the ordained ministry, though this belief is commonly denied among Protestants. The indicative form of absolution ('I absolve you') is used in the W. for individuals; the precatory form, in which the priest formally prays that God will absolve an individual or congregation, is used for absolutions in the course of the liturgy and in the E. also for individuals. See also *Penance.

ABSOLUTIONS OF THE DEAD. The title given to the service in the RC Church formerly said after the *Requiem Mass before the body was taken from the church. It consisted of prayers for the departed soul and the aspersing and censing of the body. In 1969 it was replaced by a final commendation, which includes a short address, aspersing and censing of the body, a collect, and a chant.

ABSTINENCE. A penitential practice, consisting in abstaining from the use of certain kinds of food. Both in E. and W. the *Friday abstinence in commemoration of the *Passion was observed from early times. It was attacked by the Reformers as contrary to the Gospels.

Among RCs abstinence from flesh-meat has traditionally been observed on nearly all Fridays and certain other occasions. By the Apostolic Constitution *Paenitemini (1966) the number of penitential days was reduced and episcopal conferences were empowered to substitute for abstinence other forms of penance. In the E. Church the practice is more rigid. There are about 150 days of abstinence in the year, and fish, eggs, milk, cheese, oil, and wine, as well as meat, are forbidden. See also *Fasts and Fasting.

ABUNA. The Patriarch of the *Abyssinian Church.

ABYSSINIAN CHURCH. See *Ethiopian Church*.

ACACIAN SCHISM. A temporary schism (482–519) between Rome and the East which began while Acacius was Patr. of Constantinople (471–89). It arose out of the *Henoticon.

ACACIUS OF CAESAREA (d. 366), *Arian theologian. He succeeded *Eusebius in the see of *Caesarea (in Palestine) in 340, but was pronounced deposed by the Council of *Sardica (343). In 359 he proposed a *Homoean Creed at the Council of *Seleucia. He signed the Creed of *Nicaea in 363 but returned to Arianism and was deposed in 365. His followers ('Acacians') were a distinct and important theological party between 357 and 361.

ACARIE, Mme (1566–1618), 'Mary of the Incarnation', foundress of the *Carmelites of the Reform in France. Barbe Jeanne Avrillot, though anxious to enter the cloister, in 1584 married Pierre Acarie, Vicomte de Villemore. After reading a life of St. *Teresa, she persuaded Mlle de Longueville to obtain the king's consent and assisted in establishing the Carmel of Paris in 1603. After her husband's death (1613) she was herself professed. She was the subject of ecstasies and the recipient of visions.

ACATHISTUS (Gk., 'not sitting', because it was sung standing), a famous Greek liturgical hymn in honour of the BVM. The text is based on the Gospel narrative of the Nativity. The authorship has been variously assigned.

ACCEPTANTS. Those who 'accepted' the bull '*Unigenitus' (1713) in the *Jansenist controversy. See also *Appellants*.

ACCESSION SERVICE, The. The form of prayer for use on the anniversary of the accession of the reigning British sovereign, printed at the end of the BCP.

ACCIDENT. In medieval philosophy, an entity whose essential nature it is to inhere in another entity as a subject ('ens in alio'). It is thus contrasted with a substance ('ens per se'). The term has played an important part in Eucharistic doctrine, since the *Schoolmen evolved the theory of 'accidents without a subject' to elucidate the mystery of the Presence. The concept was used to explain how, after the changing of the substances of the bread and wine into those of the Body and Blood of Christ, the accidents of the former, e.g. quantity, colour, &c., continued to exist and be perceptible by the senses. See also *Transubstantiation*.

ACCIDIE (Gk. for 'negligence', 'indifference'). By the 4th cent. the word had become a technical term in Christian asceticism, signifying a state of restlessness and inability either to work or to pray. It is accounted one of the '*Seven Deadly Sins'.

ACCOMMODATION. In theology, the adaptation of a text or teaching to altered circumstances. The word is used: (1) Esp. by RCs to connote the giving to a text of Scripture a meaning not intended by the writer, e.g. the reference of Pharaoh's words 'Go unto Joseph' (Gen. 41: 55) to the Lord's foster father. (2) By 18th-cent. liberal German theologians to expound the mode of Divine communication through the Bible. Thus Christ's words or assumptions about the authorship of parts of the OT, or about the Messianic character of certain prophecies, are explained as the deliberate adjustment of His ideas to contemporary Judaism. (3) In a more general sense of the teaching by Christians of only part of the truth for the sake of prudence, or of the modification of the form of Christian teaching to secure its more ready acceptance. A notable instance of accommodation in this sense was the practice of *Jesuit missionaries in *China of using the word *t'ien* for God and of allowing converts to continue in practices akin to ancestorworship.

ACELDAMA. 'The field of blood', a piece of land near Jerusalem, so named (1) acc. to Mt. 27: 8, because it was bought with the price of the Lord's blood; but (2) acc. to Acts 1: 18 f., because it was the scene of *Judas' end.

ACOEMETAE (literally 'sleepless ones'). A celebrated body of Orthodox monks. Abbot Alexander established at *Constantinople (c. 400) a religious house whose monks were to observe absolute poverty, do no manual work, and keep up perpetual psalmody in alternating choirs. The monks were subsequently transferred to the modern Tchiboukli, where they were first called 'Acoemetae'. They defended orthodoxy against the *Monophysites, but later fell into the *Nestorian heresy, for which they were excommunicated by Pope John II in 534.

ACOLYTE. One of the two remaining *Minor Orders in the RC Church. They are first mentioned in Rome in 251. Acolytes, who are specially dedicated to the service of the altar, came, with the *subdeacon, to absorb most of the functions of the other Minor Orders at Mass and Baptism. Since 1972 the acolyte may be a layman.

ACQUAVIVA, C. See *Aquaviva, C.*

ACT, Human. In moral theology the term denotes the free and voluntary action of a human being done with knowledge and attention. To such acts alone can moral praise or blame be accorded.

ACTA APOSTOLICAE SEDIS. From 1909 the official gazette of the *Vatican.

ACTA SANCTORUM. The celebrated series of lives of the saints, arranged in the order of their feasts in the ecclesiastical year, which was begun by the *Bollandists in the 17th cent. By 1925 it had reached 10 Nov.

ACTION. A name once applied to the whole Mass and later restricted to the *Canon of the Mass as the ultimate sacrificial action.

ACTION FRANÇAISE. A French political movement begun in 1898 and soon associated with the writer Charles Maurras. Though a freethinker himself, he regarded Catholicism as essential to French civilization. He attacked the methods of 19th-cent. democracy and preached a monarchist crusade. Many RCs sympathized with the movement, which became associated with French patriotism in the 1914–18 War. In 1926 *Pius XI forbade the co-operation of RCs and placed its newspaper, *L'Action Française*, on the *Index. The movement revived and flourished under the Vichy government of 1940–4.

ACTION SERMON. Among Scottish *Presbyterians, the sermon preached before the administration of the *Lord's Supper.

ACTON, J. See *Ayton, J.*

ACTON, JOHN EMERICH EDWARD DALBERG, first Baron Acton (1834–1902), politician and RC historian. In 1859 he became editor of the RC *Rambler*; under the threat of a Papal veto he suspended it in 1864. He sought to resist the movement towards *Ultramontanism in the RC Church.

In 1869 he went to Rome to organize resistance to the definition of Papal *Infallibility at the *Vatican Council, collaborating with J. J. I. von *Döllinger in publishing the series of letters under the signature '*Quirinus'. His later years were devoted to encouraging the study of history; from 1895 he was Regius Professor of Modern History at Cambridge.

ACTS OF THE APOSTLES, The. The fifth Book of the NT, recording the early development of the Church. It is generally admitted to be the work of St. *Luke (q.v.). Its composition has been variously dated, but most critics incline to a date between 70 and 85. The so-called 'We-sections' (16: 10–17; 20: 5–15; 21: 1–18; 27: 1–28: 16) are generally believed to have come from the author's own travel diary, revealing him as a witness of the events described.

The Book traces the progress of Christianity from *Jerusalem to Rome. 1: 1–6: 7 describes the Jerusalem Church and the preaching of St. *Peter; 6: 8–9: 31 the extension of the Church in Palestine; 9: 32–12: 24 the extension to *Antioch; 12: 25–16: 5 St. *Paul's mission to Galatia and the Council of Jerusalem; 16: 6–19: 20 the evangelization of Macedonia, Greece and the Roman province of Asia; and 19: 21 to the end the extension of the Church to Rome and Paul's journey there as a prisoner. The Book emphasizes the Divine origin of Christianity. The Apostles affirm that Jesus is the Messiah, proclaimed such by His Resurrection. Belief in the Divinity of Christ is implicit (e.g. 20: 28), and the Trinitarian dogma is there in germ, though the Personality of the Holy Spirit is not yet recognized. Acc. to Acts the Church from the beginning had her own rites of Baptism for the remission of sins (2: 38) and of the 'breaking of bread' (2: 42) (the term employed for the *Eucharistic rite). It seems to have been governed at first by the Apostles, to whom the 'Seven' were added later (6: 1–6), as well as *presbyters and *bishops, the latter two evidently not yet distinguished. The picture of the Church given in Acts is generally regarded as reliable.

ACTS OF THE MARTYRS. The most reliable accounts of early Christian martyrdoms are those (few) which follow the official reports of the trials. The so-called 'Passions' were written by Christian authors and based on eye-witness accounts; later versions were often embellished with miraculous material. A third category belong to the realm of legend, with probably no historical kernel whatever.

ACTS OF Sts. PAUL AND THECLA, ACTS OF St. PETER, &c. See *Paul and Thecla, Acts of; Peter, Acts of,* &c.

ACTUAL SIN. A sin which is the outcome of a free personal act of the human will. In Christian theology it is contrasted with *Original Sin. See also *Sin*.

ADALBERT OF BREMEN (*c.* 1000–72), Abp. of Bremen-Hamburg from 1045. He was an energetic promoter of missionary activities, esp. in the Nordic countries, and in 1053 *Leo IX nominated him Papal Vicar and Legate to the Nordic Nations. His last years were darkened by the invasion of pagan Wends who destroyed Hamburg in 1071–2.

ADAM. In traditional theology, the first man. There are two accounts of his creation in Genesis. Acc. to the Priestly editor (*P), he was created on the sixth day, made in the image and likeness of God, commanded to multiply, and given dominion over the earth (1: 26–30). The Yahwist (*J) account, which is more anthropomorphic, assigns his creation to the time when the earth was still void (2: 5–7); he then describes the creation of *Eve, Adam's work in the garden of *Eden, his *Fall and expulsion. Traditional theology has utilized the Scriptural statements about Adam in its doctrine of man and his relation to God. See also *Second Adam*.

ADAM OF MARSH (d. *c.* 1258), English theologian. Becoming a *Franciscan in 1232/3, from *c.* 1247 he was regent of the Franciscan house of studies in *Oxford. Apart from his work as a scholar, he exercised great influence on English political and social life. His learning gained him the title of 'Doctor Illustris'.

ADAM OF ST.-VICTOR (d. between 1177 and 1192), *sequence writer. Prob. a Breton, *c.* 1130 he entered the abbey of St.-Victor (see *Victorines*). His fame rests on the large number of sequences, including some of the earliest and finest, ascribed to him. Various prose works have also been attributed to him.

ADAM, KARL (1878–1966), German Catholic theologian. He combined a liberal and modern outlook with full Catholic orthodoxy, exercising wide influence over a lay public. His best-known work was *Das Wesen des Katholizismus* (1924; Eng. tr., 1929).

ADAMANTIUS (4th cent.), Greek anti-*Gnostic writer. His *De recta in Deum fide* takes the form of a dialogue first with two disciples of *Marcion and then with followers of *Bardesanes and *Valentinus.

ADAMITES. A small early Christian sect who aimed at returning to man's primitive innocence by the practice of nudity.

ADAMNAN, St. (*c.* 625–704), also **Adomnan** and, in Ireland, **Eunam**, abbot of *Iona from 679. On his last visit to *Ireland he caused the Synod of Tara (697) to adopt a law forbidding women and children to be made prisoners of war, called after him the 'Canon of Adamnan'. His Life of St. *Columba is of great historical value. He also wrote *De Locis Sanctis*, an account of a pilgrimage by Arculf, a bishop of Gaul, to Palestine.

ADAMSON, PATRICK (1537–92), Abp. of St. Andrews from 1576. He became involved in controversy with the *Presbyterian party. He won the support of *James VI (I), but his disfavour with the *General Assembly increased and his *Declaration of the King's Majesty's Intention in the late Acts of Parliament* (1585) provoked much hostility. His character and opinions were attacked at the Synod of Fife (1586), which excommunicated him.

ADDAI. The traditional founder of the Church at *Edessa. In Syriac tradition he was one of the 72 (or 70) disciplines of Lk. 10: 1. Acc. to the 'Doctrine of *Addai' he was sent by St. *Thomas the Apostle to heal King *Abgar.

ADDAI, The Doctrine of. A Syriac writing which describes how King *Abgar was brought into contact with Christ and *Addai was sent to *Edessa to convert him. It prob. dates from *c.* 400 but seems to depend on older sources.

ADDAI AND MARI, Liturgy of. The Syriac liturgy which is still the normal rite of the *Nestorian Christians. It was prob. composed *c*. 200 for the Syriac-speaking Church at *Edessa, which looked back to Addai and his disciple, Mari, as its founders.

ADELARD OF BATH (12th cent.), English *Scholastic philosopher. In his main work, *De Eodem et Diverso*, he developed a theory of the Liberal Arts and also tried to reconcile the *Platonic and *Aristotelian doctrines of *universals, holding that the universal and the particular were identical, and distinct only in our mode of apprehending them.

ADESTE FIDELES. Anonymous Christmas hymn, prob. written in the 17th or 18th cent., of French or German authorship. The common Eng. tr. is 'O come, all ye faithful'.

ADHÉMAR DE MONTEIL (d. 1098), Bp. of Le Puy from some time between 1080 and 1087. In 1095 *Urban II summoned the Council of *Clermont from Le Puy and made Adhémar his representative on the First *Crusade. Adhémar played an important part in the Crusaders' operations and councils until his death.

ADHERENTS. In the Church of *Scotland, baptized persons who, although non-communicants, are intimately connected with the congregation.

ADIAPHORISTS. A party in German Protestantism which held that certain rules and actions are matters of indifference. The first controversy on the subject broke out in connection with the *Leipzig Interim (1548). One side declared certain Catholic practices such as *Confirmation and Extreme *Unction, the Mass without Transubstantiation and the Veneration of *Saints 'adiaphora', i.e. matters on which concessions might be made without prejudice to Protestant doctrine. The other side stressed the dangers to integral *Lutheranism in these concessions. The controversy was ended only by the Formula of *Concord (1577), which ruled that in times of persecution concessions should not be made, but otherwise ceremonies not commanded or forbidden by Scripture might be altered according to the decisions of individual Churches. Another controversy broke out in the late 17th cent. between the *Piet-

ists, who declared all worldly pleasures such as theatres to be sinful, and the orthodox Lutherans, who held them to be indifferent and therefore permitted.

AD LIMINA APOSTOLORUM (Lat., 'to the thresholds of the Apostles'). Pilgrimages 'ad Limina Apostolorum', *sc*. to the tombs of St. *Peter and St. *Paul in Rome, were popular in the Middle Ages. In modern times the term ordinarily denotes the visits which RC bishops are required to pay to Rome to venerate the tombs of the Apostles and to report to the Pope on the state of their dioceses.

ADMONITION TO PARLIAMENT, The (1572). A widely read manifesto demanding a non-episcopal constitution for the English Church. It was issued anonymously, but responsibility for it was probably correctly attributed to two *Puritan clergymen, J. *Field and Thomas Wilcox. It was defended in the *Second Admonition*, ascribed to T. *Cartwright.

ADO, Martyrology of. The *martyrology compiled in 858 by St. Ado (*c*. 800–75), later Abp. of Vienne. Its plan and arrangement were the model for later martyrologies.

ADOMNAN, St. See *Adamnan, St.*

ADONAI. Hebrew Divine name; see *Tetragrammaton*. In the Christian Liturgy the term is applied to Christ in one of the *O-Antiphons.

ADOPTIANISM. (1) The heresy, originating in Spain in the 8th cent., acc. to which Christ in His humanity is only the adoptive Son of God. *Elipandus, Abp. of Toledo, upheld a distinction between the *Logos, as the true natural and eternal Son of God, and Christ, the adoptive Son, who is Son only metaphorically, because the Word 'adopted' the humanity, thereby attaching the sonship to the nature rather than to the Person of Christ. He was supported by the Spanish bishops, esp. *Felix of Urgel, but after he died the heresy disappeared. It was revived in a modified form in the 12th cent. by *Abelard, *Gilbert de la Porrée, and others.

(2) The term (usually spelt 'Adoptionism') has also been used of the heretical stream in early Greek theology which regarded Christ as a man gifted with Divine

powers.

ADORATION. In strict terminology 'adoration' denotes an act of worship due to God alone. In early times the word was sometimes used loosely to include the veneration paid to persons and objects of a sacred character. After the *Iconoclastic Controversy a distinction came to be accepted between '*latria', the adoration of God, and *'dulia', the veneration of created beings. The chief act of adoration in Christian worship is the offering of sacrifice; it is usually accompanied by such secondary acts as prayers of praise, protestation, &c. The adoration paid to the Bl. Sacrament depends on the doctrine of the *Real Presence.

ADORO TE DEVOTE. Eucharistic hymn, attributed to St. *Thomas Aquinas, though the authorship has been contested. The common Eng. tr. is 'Thee we adore, O hidden Saviour'.

ADRIAN I, IV, VI. See *Hadrian I, IV, VI.*

ADVENT (Lat. *Adventus*, 'coming', i.e. of Christ). The ecclesiastical season immediately before *Christmas. In the W. it begins on the Sunday nearest St. *Andrew's Day (30 Nov.); in the E. in the middle of Nov. It is observed as a penitential season, in preparation not only for Christmas but also for the *Second Coming of Christ at the Last Day. The first day of Advent (Advent Sunday) begins the ecclesiastical year.

ADVENTISTS. Various groups which hold in common that the *Second Coming of Christ is imminent. As a denomination they date from 1831, originating in the U.S.A. The original body, the 'Evangelical Adventists', have died out; the chief denominations are now the 'Second Advent Christians' and the '*Seventh Day Adventists'.

ADVERTISEMENTS, Book of. The abbreviated title of a book issued by Abp. M. *Parker in 1556. Among other things it ordered the use of the *surplice at the Eucharist and kneeling at the reception of Communion. It is disputed whether this book is to be understood as the 'other order' mentioned in the 1559 Act of *Uniformity. See *Ornaments Rubric.*

ADVOWSON. The right of appointing a clergyman to a parish or other ecclesiastical benefice. Advowsons may be held by the diocesan bishop or by some other person (known as the 'patron'). A patron, who may be an individual or a corporation, clerical or lay, presents the candidate to the bishop for *institution and *induction; the latter may for due cause reject the nomination. The exercise of advowson in the C of E is governed by English civil law.

AEGIDIUS. The Latin form of *Giles.

A.E.G.M. See *Anglican Evangelical Group Movement.*

AELFRIC (*c.* 955–*c.* 1020), the 'Grammarian'. He entered the *Benedictine abbey at *Winchester under *Ethelwold; in 987 he was transferred to the newly founded abbey at Cerne Abbas, and in 1005 he became first Abbot of Eynsham. He wrote three sets of homilies in English; the second series gained notoriety at the time of the Reformation because they were supposed to have maintained a doctrine of the Eucharist incompatible with *Transubstantiation; the third series was on the 'Lives of the Saints'. His greatest claim to fame was his provision of books of literary merit for the rural clergy in their own language.

AELIA CAPITOLINA. The new city which the Emp. Hadrian built *c.* 130 on the site of *Jerusalem (destroyed A.D. 70).

AELRED, St. See *Ailred, St.*

AENEAS OF GAZA (d. 518), Christian *Neoplatonist. In his 'Theophrastus' he defended the immortality of the soul and the resurrection of the body, but rejected such tenets of *Platonism as conflicted with orthodox Christian doctrine.

AENEAS SILVIUS PICCOLOMINI. See *Pius II.*

AERIUS (4th cent.), presbyter of Pontus. He was originally an associate of *Eustathius, Bp. of Sebaste, but later they quarrelled. He taught that the observance of *Easter was a Jewish superstition; that prescribed fasts were wrong; and that it is useless to pray and give alms for the dead. His followers (Aerians) appear to have died out soon after his death.

AETERNI PATRIS (1879). The encyclical of *Leo XIII commending to the Church the study of philosophy, and esp. the work of St *Thomas Aquinas.

AETIUS (d. *c*. 370), *Arian sophist. He was a dialectician at *Alexandria and was made a bishop by the Arians. He and his followers (*Anomoeans) asserted the total unlikeness of the Son and the Father. His *Syntagmation* is preserved by *Epiphanius.

AFFECTIVE PRAYER. A stage in the development of prayer at which less use of the intellect and imagination is made than by beginners, and the soul is chiefly engaged in making acts of the will, to unite itself to God.

AFFINITY. In *moral theology, relationship created by marriage. It arises from a valid marriage, whether consummated or not, and is held to form an impediment to subsequent marriage between one party and certain blood relations of the other. In the C of E the sphere of affinity is regulated by the 'Table of *Kindred and Affinity'.

AFFIRMATION. In English civil law, a solemn declaration in place of an *oath made by those who have conscientious objection to being sworn, either because of their religious conviction or because they have no religious belief. It may be administered only when the oath is refused.

AFFUSION (occasionally, **Infusion**). The method of *baptism now ordinarily practised in the W. Church whereby water is poured over the head of the candidate. It did not become general until the Middle Ages, *immersion and *submersion being the usual methods in earlier times. See also *Aspersion*.

AFRICA. See *Ethiopian Church*; *South Africa, Christianity in*; *U.M.C.A.*; *West Africa, Christianity in*; and the 2 following entries.

AFRICA, The Church in Roman. It is not known how Christianity reached Roman 'Africa' (roughly Tripoli, Tunisia, Algeria, and Morocco), but by the end of the 2nd cent. the Church was organized and widespread. Persecution under the Emp. *Decius (250) temporarily weakened the Church,

leading to controversy over the readmission of lapsed members and to the *Novatianist schism. The 4th cent. saw the struggle with *Donatism, the rise of St *Augustine, the growth of *monasticism, and a series of African Councils, whose canons were incorporated into both E. and W. *canon law. Such achievements were ended by the Vandal invaders (429), whose *Arian kings normally repressed Catholic Christianity. The reconquest (534) under *Justinian restored orthodoxy, but the Arab conquest at the end of the 7th cent. reduced to a shadow the Church that had bred so many martyrs and thinkers.

AFRICAN INDEPENDENT CHURCHES. Small indigenous Churches, esp. numerous in *South Africa. The earliest was founded in 1872. Some are doctrinally similar to the mission Churches, having seceded primarily in reaction to White domination, but of increasing significance are those with *pentecostal origins or characteristics. These conform to African thought patterns and owe much of their success to their emphasis on healing and exorcism. There is disagreement about how specifically Christian some of these 'Churches' are; the best known, the Kimbanguist Church of Zaïre (founded by Simon Kimbangu, 1889–1951), was admitted to the *World Council of Churches in 1969.

AFRICANUS, SEXTUS JULIUS. See *Julius Africanus, Sextus.*

AGABUS, St., prophet mentioned in Acts (11: 28 and 21: 10). In the E. Church he is held to be one of the seventy mentioned in Lk. 10: 1.

AGAPE. (1) A Greek word for 'love', believed to have been coined by the Biblical writers from a cognate verb, in order to avoid the sensual associations of the ordinary Greek noun ἔρως (eros); it is used to describe the love of God or of Christ, or the love of Christians for one another. It was usually translated into Latin by 'caritas', hence the original meaning of 'charity' in English. See also *Love*.

(2) The term is applied also to the common religious meal which seems to have been in use in the early Church in close relation to the Eucharist.

AGAPEMONE, Church of the, English sect. It was founded by H. J. Prince (1811–99), who, as a curate in Somerset, started a revivalist movement. He and his rector left the C of E and in 1849 opened the 'agapemone' in the village of Spaxton; his followers believed Prince to be a Divine being and their licentiousness led to grave scandal. The sect disappeared at the beginning of the 20th cent.

AGAPETUS, St. (d. 536), Pope from 535. A defender of orthodoxy, he deposed Anthimus, the *Monophysite Patr. of Constantinople, and consecrated *Mennas as his successor.

AGATHA, St. A virgin martyred at Catania in Sicily. Her name occurs in the traditional *Canon of the Roman Mass and two early churches at Rome were dedicated to her. The 6th-cent. Acts of her martyrdom are legendary.

AGATHANGELOS. The reputed first historian of *Armenia, who professes to be the author of the Life of St. *Gregory the Illuminator (d. 332) and his contemporary. 'Agathangelos' may be only a pseudonym of an Armenian Christian proclaiming to his countrymen the 'good tidings' of their conversion.

AGATHIAS (c. 532–c. 582), poet and historian. He practised as an advocate at *Constantinople. His history is the chief authority for the years 552–8. It is doubtful if he was a Christian.

AGATHO (c. 577–681), Pope from 678. In 680 he held a council at Rome against the *Monothelites. He also took up the cause of *Wilfrid of York against *Theodore, Abp. of Canterbury.

AGDE, Council of (506). A council held at Agde in S. France under the presidency of *Caesarius of Arles; 47 genuine canons are preserved.

AGE, Canonical. The age, fixed by *canon law, at which a person becomes capable of undertaking special duties, &c. The term is used esp. in connection with *ordination.

AGE OF REASON. The normal age at which a child may be supposed to be capable

of discerning right from wrong and therefore of being responsible for his conduct.

AGENDA (Lat., 'things to be performed'). The term has been used for matters of religious practice as opposed to those of belief; for the central part of the Eucharist; and for prescribed forms of service.

AGGIORNAMENTO (Ital., 'renewal'). A word connected with the pontificate of *John XXIII, denoting esp. a fresh presentation of the faith.

AGIOS O THEOS (Gk., 'Holy God'). A Greek anthem which has survived untranslated in the Roman *Good Friday liturgy.

AGNELLUS OF PISA, Bl. (1194–1235), founder of the English *Franciscan Province. He was received into the Franciscan Order by St. *Francis. In 1224 he was sent to England. He soon established friaries at *Canterbury and *Oxford; he engaged R. *Grosseteste to teach in the latter, which rapidly became a famous centre of learning.

AGNELLUS, ANDREAS (805–c. 846), historian of *Ravenna. His *Liber Pontificalis Ecclesiae Ravennatis* traces the history of the see from St. *Apollinaris to his own age. It embodies valuable information, esp. about contemporary buildings and customs.

AGNES, St. The legends of her martyrdom vary and nothing certain is known about the date or manner of her death. A basilica was built at Rome on the site of her remains c. 350, and her name occurs in the traditional *Canon of the Roman Mass. In art she is represented by a lamb, doubtless because of the similarity between 'agnus' (Lat., 'lamb') and 'Agnes', and the *pallium, made from the wool of two lambs, is blessed on her feast (21 Jan.).

AGNOETAE. A *Monophysite sect whose members attributed ignorance to the human soul of Christ. Founded by Themistius, a 6th-cent. deacon of *Alexandria, they are also known as 'Themistians'.

AGNOSTICISM. The doctrine that only material phenomena can be the subject of real knowledge and that all knowledge of such entities as a Divine Being and a supernatural world is impossible.

AGNUS DEI (Lat., 'Lamb of God'). (1) The formula opening with these words recited by the priest in the Latin liturgy shortly before the Communion. The use of a lamb as a symbol for Christ is based on Jn. 1: 29. (2) A wax medallion bearing the figure of a lamb, blessed by the Pope in the first year of his pontificate and every 7th year afterwards.

AGOBARD (c. 769–840), Abp. of Lyons from 816. He was a versatile scholar. His theological writings, which were mostly directed against the *Adoptianist heresy, included a treatise against *Felix of Urgel; he also attacked the liturgical speculations of *Amalarius of Metz and belief in magic and witchcraft.

AGONIZANTS. A religious order devoted to the needs of the sick and dying. It was founded by St. *Camillus de Lellis in 1586.

AGRAPHA ('unwritten [sayings]'). A name given to the sayings of Christ not recorded in the four canonical Gospels. One occurs in Acts (20: 35), others in the *apocryphal Gospels, esp. the Gospel of *Thomas.

AGRICOLA, JOHANN (c. 1494–1566), German Protestant reformer. A pupil and follower of M. *Luther, for a time he became a supporter of *Antinomianism. In 1540 he moved to Berlin, where he published a recantation which few except Luther refused to accept, Johann II, Elector of Brandenburg, appointed him *General-Superintendent, and he was associated in the preparation of the *Augsburg Interim of 1548.

AGRIPPA VON NETTESHEIM, HEINRICH CORNELIUS (1486–1535), scholar and adventurer. From c. 1518 he interested himself in the Reformation, and in his later years he was associated with *Hermann of Wied. He became historiographer to *Charles V in 1529, and in the next years published his two main works. The *De Occulta Philosophia* (1531), which was prob. completed c. 1510, tries to establish the mutual interrelation of all things, the knowledge of which constitutes the true science or 'magic' known only to the chosen few. This knowledge is based on nature, Revelation, and the mystic sense of Scripture. The *De Incertitudine* (1530) is hostile

to all science and scholarship. Confining truth to the Bible, it attacks *Scholasticism and many institutions of the Church.

AHIKAR LEGEND. A story which tells of a Grand Vizier of Sennacherib, Ahikar the Wise, against whom his adopted son plotted and received retribution. It is held to have influenced the Book of *Tobit.

AIDAN, St. (d. 651), monk of *Iona and Bp. of *Lindisfarne. He was sent from Iona at the request of *Oswald, King of Northumbria, and consecrated Bishop in 635. He established his headquarters at Lindisfarne and made long journeys to the mainland; the practices he taught were those of the *Celtic Church.

AILRED, St. (1109–67), also 'Aelred', the 'Bernard of the North', Abbot of *Rievaulx. The son of a Saxon priest, he entered the *Cistercian house at Rievaulx c. 1133, became Abbot of Revesby in 1143 and Abbot of Rievaulx in 1147. His extensive spiritual writings show similarity of interest and attitude with those of St. *Bernard of Clairvaux and *William of St.-Thierry; his devotion is marked by a strong attachment to the suffering humanity of Christ. His works include the *Speculum Caritatis, De Spirituali Amicitia,* and a life of *Edward the Confessor.

AISLE. The extension of the *nave of a church made by piercing its side walls with a series of arches and building an extension with a separate and lower roof. The word is often, but quite wrongly, used of a gangway up the centre of the nave or elsewhere.

AKIBA or **AQIBA** (c. 50–132). An influential Jewish Rabbi, he supported the revolt of *Bar-Cochba and was burnt alive by the Romans.

AKSUM. See *Axum.*

ALACOQUE, St. MARGARET MARY. See *Margaret Mary Alacoque, St.*

ALAN OF LILLE (d. 1203), poet, theologian, and preacher. He prob. studied and taught at Paris c. 1150–c. 1185. Later he moved to the South of France and towards the end of his life entered the abbey of *Cîteaux. His early theological writings include the incomplete *Summa Quoniam homines*, a number of unpublished **quaestiones*, the *Regulae caelestis iuris*, in which he tries to state theological truths in a series of rules or axioms, and the allegorical poem *Anticlaudianus* (1182–3). He later compiled a dictionary of Biblical terms with literal, moral, and allegorical interpretations, an *Ars praedicandi*, and a *Liber poenitentialis*, the earliest medieval manual for confessors.

ALANE, A. See *Alesius, A.*

ALAPA. Acc. to W. usage, the light blow formerly delivered by the bishop on the cheek of those being confirmed.

ALARIC (*c.* 370–410), Visigothic chief. He served in the Imperial army but, disappointed of his hopes of a more important position, he determined to conquer a kingdom for himself. He besieged Rome in 408, 409, and 410, entering the city on 24 Aug. 410. This event was the immediate occasion of St. **Augustine's City of God.*

À LASCO, J. See *Laski, J.*

ALB. A white linen garment, reaching from the neck to the ankles, with tight-fitting sleeves and held in at the waist by a girdle, worn by the ministers at Mass.

ALBAN, St. The first British martyr. A pagan of Verulamium (now **St. Albans), he was converted and baptized by a fugitive priest whom he sheltered. When the Emperor sent soldiers to search for the priest, Alban disguised himself in the priest's cloak, was arrested, and condemned to death. His martyrdom has traditionally been connected with the **Diocletianic persecution (*c.* 305), but he may have suffered under Septimius Severus (*c.* 209).

ALBAN, St., and SERGIUS, St., Fellowship of. An organization founded in 1928 which aims at promoting understanding between Christians, esp. between the Anglican and Orthodox Churches.

ALBANIA, Christianity in. Christianity prob. reached Albania at an early date, but with the fall of the W. Empire in the 5th and 6th cents. its influence was largely destroyed. In the Dark Ages the Illyrians, who became known as Albanians, were made

subject to the Byzantine court and so to Eastern Orthodoxy (840) and later to Slav invaders. The Turks finally subjugated Albania in 1521; there was subsequently much apostasy. In 1913 Albania became independent and its Orthodox Church became **autocephalous in 1922.

ALBERT OF BRANDENBURG (1490–1545), Cardinal Abp. and Elector of Mainz. In 1517 he was charged with the publication in Saxony and Brandenburg of the **indulgence for **St. Peter's, Rome; he secured the services of J. **Tetzel to preach it. A man of liberal views and a friend of the humanists, in its early stages he favoured the Reformation. He gradually changed his attitude and from 1525 he was a resolute defender of the Papacy.

ALBERT OF PRUSSIA (1490–1568). The last Grand Master of the **Teutonic Order and first Hohenzollern Duke of Prussia. He was converted to Protestantism and in 1525 succeeded in making Prussia a hereditary duchy. A strict form of **Lutheranism was established in his dominions.

ALBERTUS MAGNUS, St. (*c.* 1200–80), **Dominican theologian, philosopher, and scientist. He taught in various Dominican houses in Germany before he was sent to **Paris (*c.* 1241); he may have begun his work on **Aristotle here. In 1248 he was summoned to **Cologne, where he set up a new Dominican **studium generale. In 1256 he went to the Papal Court to defend the interests of the friars against the secular masters of Paris. In Rome he held a disputation on the unity of the intellect, directed against the views of **Averroes. In 1260, at the Pope's insistence, he was consecrated Bp. of Ratisbon, where the administration was in disorder; after two years he was allowed to resign and return to Cologne. He went to Paris in 1277 at the height of the Averroist controversy to try to avert the condemnation of the Aristotelian doctrines held by himself and his pupil, St. **Thomas Aquinas.

He taught at a time when theologians were beginning to realize that Aristotle and the Arabic philosophers could not be ignored, and the most significant part of his work is the commentaries or paraphrases on Aristotle. They cover almost the whole Aristotelian corpus and some pseudepigrapha such as the **Liber de Causis. He aimed at making the physics, metaphysics, and mathematics of Aristotle intelligible to the Latins. Acclaim came to him from his con temporaries. In theology his influence was smaller, though his work was one of the main sources of the *Compendium theologicae veritatis* of Hugh Ripelin which circulated widely, often under Albert's name. He was canonized and proclaimed a '*Doctor of the Church' in 1931.

ALBIGENSES. Heretics who flourished in S. France in the 12th and 13th cents. They were a branch of the *Cathari. They held that Christ was an angel with a phantom body, who thus did not suffer or rise again; His redemptive work consisted only in His teaching. Rejecting the Sacraments and believing that all matter was evil, they held a moral doctrine of extreme rigorism, condemning marriage and the use of all animal products. They distinguished two classes, the 'perfect', who received the 'consolamentum', i.e. baptism of the Holy Spirit by imposition of hands, and kept the precepts in all their rigour, and the ordinary 'believers', who were allowed to lead normal lives but promised to receive the 'consolamentum' when in danger of death.

The Albigenses were condemned by successive councils from 1165 onwards, but the heresy spread. *Innocent III launched against them a *Crusade, which was conducted with much cruelty. In 1233 *Gregory IX charged the Dominican *Inquisition with the final extirpation of the heresy, of which no trace remained by the end of the 14th cent.

ALBRIGHT BRETHREN, See *Evangelical Church*.

ALCUIN (*c.* 735–804), the inspirer of the *Carolingian Renaissance. He attended and taught in the cathedral school at *York. After meeting *Charlemagne in 781, he became his adviser in religious and educational matters. He established a palace library and, becoming Abbot of Tours in 796, set up an important library and school there. He produced educational manuals, poetry, and an attack on the *Adoptianist heresy of *Felix of Urgel; he also revised the lectionary in Gaul, put together a *Sacramentary, and composed 18 *votive masses.

ALDHELM, St. (d. 709), Abbot of *Mal mesbury and first Bp. of *Sherborne. He took a prominent part in the reforming movement initiated by Abp. *Theodore and *Hadrian the African; he founded some monasteries and several churches. Much of his Latin writing survives.

ALEANDER, GIROLAMO (1480–1542), humanist scholar. *Leo X appointed him one of two Papal envoys commissioned to present M. *Luther with the Bull '*Exsurge Domine' and to negotiate with the Emperor for support against him. At the Diet of *Worms (1521) he denounced Luther and demanded his condemnation without trial. In 1524 he was made Abp. of Brindisi and in 1538 a cardinal.

ALEMBERT, J. LE R. D'. See *D'Alembert, J. Le R.*

ALEPH (א) . The first letter of the Hebrew alphabet. Textual critics use it to denote the *Codex Sinaiticus.

ALESIUS, ALEXANDER (1500–65), also **Aless** or **Alane,** Scottish *Lutheran divine. As a canon of St. Andrews, he was selected to confute Patrick *Hamilton, but was won over by his arguments and steadfastness at the stake (1528). Soon afterwards he preached a sermon attacking the morals of the clergy. He was imprisoned but escaped to Germany. For a short time he was lecturer in divinity at Cambridge; in 1540 he became professor of theology at Frankfurt-on-Oder. He wrote many exegetical and controversial works.

ALEXANDER, St. (d. 328), Bp. of *Alexandria from 313. He was concerned in putting down the *Melitian and Arian schisms. He excommunicated *Arius, one of his presbyters, *c.* 321, and took a leading part in the Council of *Nicaea.

ALEXANDER II (d. 1073), 'Anselm of Lucca', Pope from 1061. Elected with the backing of Hildebrand (later *Gregory VII), he was enthroned without receiving the support of the Emp. *Henry IV, who had an antipope (Honorius II) elected. He tried to realize the ideals of the reforming party, legislating on *simony, clerical *celibacy, freedom of episcopal elections, and forbidding lay *investiture, and taking strong action to enforce these measures. His blessing was given to *William I's invasion of

England (1066).

ALEXANDER III (d. 1181), Pope from 1159. During the 17-year schism occasioned by the establishment of an antipope (Victor IV) supported by the Emp. *Frederick I, Alexander lived mainly in France. Here he came into contact with Henry II of England over the *Becket affair. Though embarrassed by the archbishop, he was firm in imposing penance for his murder. In 1179 he assembled the Third *Lateran Council, which vested the right of electing a Pope in a two-thirds majority of the cardinals. Alexander was a considerable scholar and canonist.

ALEXANDER V (c. 1339–1410), Pope from 1409. Peter of Candia (Crete) became a *Franciscan and lectured at Paris; from 1386 he held a succession of bishoprics. At the Council of *Pisa he was unanimously elected to fill the Papal chair presumed vacant; he died 10 months later.

ALEXANDER VI (1431–1503), Pope from 1492. Rodrigo Borgia's election was secured largely through bribery. The most notable acts of his pontificate were the series dividing the New World between *Spain and *Portugal (1493–4), his prosecution and execution of G. *Savonarola (1498), the crusade against the Moors (1499–1500), and the *Jubilee of 1500. A man of immoral life, he was an astute politician and a patron of artists.

ALEXANDER VII (1599–1667), Pope from 1655. As a theologian he held strongly anti-*Jansenist views, and to make Jansenist subterfuge impossible, in 1656 he condemned the five propositions from the *Augustinus in the sense C. *Jansen meant them. In this he was supported by *Louis XIV, but later, when Louis seized *Avignon and Venaissin, Alexander had to sign the humiliating peace of Pisa (1664). In 1665 and 1666 he condemned several *Probabilist propositions, though not the system as a whole.

ALEXANDER VIII (1610–91), Pope from 1689. He effected a reconciliation with Louis XIV, who in 1690 returned *Avignon and Venaissin. In 1690 he condemned the Four *Gallican Articles of 1682 and 31 propositions of C. *Jansen. He also condemned

the doctrine of Philosophical Sin.

ALEXANDER OF HALES (c. 1186–1245), the 'Doctor Irrefragabilis'. He studied arts and theology at *Paris, becoming a doctor c. 1220/1. He took the fateful step of using the Sentences of *Peter Lombard, instead of the Bible, as the basic text for his lectures on theology. In 1236 he joined the *Franciscan Order, but retained his chair. He is regarded as the founder of the Franciscan school of theology, but the Summa theologica which goes under his name is only partly his.

ALEXANDER OF LYCOPOLIS (3rd cent.), writer against *Manichaeism. He praises the simplicity and efficacy of Christian philosophy and contrasts it with the illogical and contradictory doctrines of Manichaeism. It is uncertain whether he was a Christian.

ALEXANDER NATALIS. See Natalis, A.

ALEXANDER, MICHAEL SOLOMON (1799–1845), first Anglican bishop in *Jerusalem (from 1841). A German orthodox Jew, he came to England in 1820 and was baptized in 1825. On his ordination in 1827 he joined the London Society for Promoting Christianity among the Jews, and from 1832 he was Professor of Hebrew at *King's College, London.

ALEXANDRIA. A very important city in the Roman Empire, Alexandria in Egypt was a centre of both Hellenism and Judaism. The foundation of the Church is traditionally ascribed to St. *Mark. It won fame as a centre of Christian thought through the *Catechetical School under *Clement and *Origen, and in the 4th–5th cent. through its bishops *Athanasius and *Cyril. Its ecclesiastical importance was later eclipsed by *Constantinople, further reduced by the adherence of the population to the *Monophysites, and virtually destroyed by the Persian and Arab invasions of the 7th cent.

ALEXANDRIAN THEOLOGY. The Alexandrian writers stressed the transcendence of God, the essential Godhead of all Three Persons, and the Divine Nature of the Incarnate Christ; hence their opposition to the characteristically *Antiochene heresies, which overemphasized the humanity of

Christ. The Alexandrians, however, in their desire to maintain that the distinction between the Persons of the Trinity was more than functional, came near to *tritheism, and in their emphasis on the Divinity of Christ the less orthodox (e.g. *Apollinaris) refused to believe in His true humanity. *Monophysitism and *Monothelitism are extreme forms of the Alexandrian school of thought.

In their exegesis of Scripture the Alexandrians were drawn to mystical and *allegorical exposition, in contrast with the literal and historical method of Antioch. See also *Alexandria*.

ALFRED THE GREAT (849–99), King of Wessex from 871. Apart from his defeat of the Danes, which contributed to the maintenance of Christianity in England, he is memorable for his promotion of ecclesiastical reform and the revival of learning. With a band of scholars he translated into English a number of popular Latin works, incl. the 'Dialogues' and 'Pastoral Rule' of *Gregory the Great. He founded two monastic communities and seems to have contemplated considerable subdivision of dioceses.

ALITURGICAL DAYS. Days on which the Eucharist may not be celebrated. In the RC Church *Good Friday and *Holy Saturday are the only such days; there are many more in the E. Church.

ALL SAINTS' DAY. The feast, now kept in the W. on 1 Nov., to celebrate all Christian saints, known or unknown. It was apparently originally kept on the first Sunday after *Pentecost, as it still is in the E. Its observance on 1 Nov. dates from the time of Gregory III (d. 741), who on that day dedicated a chapel in the basilica of St. Peter to 'All the Saints'.

ALL SOULS' DAY. The commemoration of the souls of the faithful departed on 2 Nov., the day after *All Saints' Day. Its observance became universal through the influence of *Odilo of Cluny (d. 1049).

ALLATIUS, LEO (1587/8–1669), Greek RC theologian. He was custodian of the *Vatican library from 1661. In a number of books he tried to show the unity in essential doctrine of the Orthodox and RC Churches.

ALLEGIANCE, Oath of. The oath of allegiance to the British Sovereign taken by clergy of the C of E at their ordination to the diaconate and to the priesthood and on admission to a benefice.

ALLEGORY. A mode of speech in which one thing is understood by another. The allegorical interpretation of Scripture is a particular method of exegesis which was practised in the Palestinian Rabbinical schools; it was also applied to the OT by the NT writers, the word itself being used by St. *Paul (Gal. 4: 24). The allegories which the NT writers found in the OT were held to contain a prophetic announcement of future events. Thus the relations between the Church and the Synagogue were seen as prefigured in the story of Isaac and Ishmael. This method of interpretation was developed and carried to excess by the School of *Alexandria. It was practised throughout the Middle Ages and is to some extent still used in the RC Church; it was denounced by the Reformers and is avoided by most Protestants.

ALLELUIA (Heb., 'Praise ye Yah'), liturgical expression of praise. It occurs in the Bible (e.g. in Pss. 111-17) and it was early taken into the liturgy of the Church. In the W. it is omitted from the Mass and Office during Lent, and as an expression of joy it is used especially frequently in *Paschaltide.

ALLELUYATIC SEQUENCE. A name popularly given to the hymn 'Cantemus cuncti melodium' ('The strain upraise of joy and praise') on account of its frequent repetition of 'Alleluia'. The hymn dates from about the 9th cent.

ALLEN, WILLIAM (1532–94), Cardinal from 1587. Forced to flee from England in 1565, he concentrated on training RC mission priests for the conversion of England; he founded colleges at *Douai (1568), Rome (1575–8), and Valladolid (1589). The *Douai version of the Bible was produced under his inspiration.

ALLESTREE, RICHARD (1619–81), Anglican divine. Under the Commonwealth he helped to continue C of E services in a private house; from 1663 to 1679 he was Regius Professor of Divinity at Oxford. He is the most probable author of 'The *Whole Duty of Man'.

ALLIES, THOMAS WILLIAM (1813–1903), theologian. He was closely associated with the leaders of the *Oxford Movement, but after the *Gorham Judgement he joined the RC Church, for which he became a prominent apologist.

ALMERY. An obsolete form of the word '*Aumbry'.

ALMONER. An officer, usually in holy orders, who has the duty of distributing alms.

ALMUCE (or Amice). An item of ecclesiastical dress, usually a cape lined with fur, worn in some religious orders.

ALOGI. A group of heretics in Asia Minor (c. A.D. 170). They seem to have opposed *Montanism and to have ascribed Jn. and Rev. to *Cerinthus.

ALOYSIUS GONZAGA, St. (1568–91), patron of RC youth. After a few years at court he entered the *Jesuit novitiate in 1585. He died at the age of 23, a victim of his labours among the plague-stricken at Rome.

ALPHA AND OMEGA (A and Ω). The first and last letters of the Greek alphabet, used to denote God's eternity and infinitude.

ALPHEGE, St. (954–1012), Abp. of *Canterbury from 1006. He was murdered by the Danes because he would not ransom himself at the expense of his poor tenants, and was therefore regarded as a martyr.

ALPHONSUS LIGUORI, St. (1696–1787), founder of the *Redemptorists and moral theologian. Alfonso Maria dei Liguori practised at the bar before he was ordained in 1726. He became a close friend of Tomaso Falcoia, from whom he took over the direction of some nuns at Scala, near Amalfi. In 1732 he founded the 'Congregation of the Most Holy Redeemer' or 'Redemptorists' for men in a nearby hospice. In 1762 he reluctantly accepted the see of Sant'Agata dei Goti, which he resigned in 1775. His last years were clouded by severe spiritual trials.

Alphonsus sought to commend the Gospel to a sceptical age by gentle and direct methods, believing that the rigorism of the contemporary confessional repelled rather than won back sinners. He set out his ideals in his celebrated *Theologia Moralis* (1753–5). In the debate on how far it is allowable to follow any 'probable' opinion in matters of conduct, he developed a system known as '*Equiprobabilism' (q.v.). His devotional writings were popular, though their exuberance made them a target of criticism.

ALTAR. The word was used of the Eucharistic table from early times. It was disliked by the Reformers, who associated it with the doctrine of the *sacrifice of the Mass.

The earliest altars were doubtless of wood, being tables in private houses, and it was perhaps the custom of celebrating the Eucharist on the tombs of the martyrs which led to the introduction of stone altars. It was long customary to have only one altar in a church, but in the W. the custom of saying private Masses caused others to be added. Altars were long placed against the E. wall, but in recent times the earlier free-standing position has been widely adopted.

ALTAR LIGHTS. The custom of placing on the altar two candles flanking an altar cross is attested c. 1175. The number of candles used has varied. In the C of E their legality was contested in the 19th cent., but allowed in 1890.

ALTAR RAILS. Rails to protect the altar from profanation were widely introduced in English churches in the early years of *Elizabeth I, when the *rood screens and their protecting doors were removed. Disliked by the *Puritans, they came back at the Restoration in 1660.

ALTERNATIVE SERVICES. The Prayer Book (Alternative and Other) Services Measure, 1965, provided that for a limited period the services of the C of E might follow forms sanctioned by the *Church Assembly (later by the General *Synod) as well as the BCP. It was repealed by the *Church of England (Worship and Doctrine) Measure, 1974, which allows the use of such services on a permanent basis. After 3 series of separate services had been used experimentally, the complete Alternative Service Book (1980) was authorized. In modern English, it includes 2 forms of Eucharistic rite, (optional) short forms of Morning and Evening Prayer, and a *Calendar with many new names.

ALUMBRADOS (also **Illuminati**, 'enlightened'). A loosely knit 16th-cent. Spanish group, whose members lived a retired life of prayer and contemplation. Some of them were certainly spiritually unbalanced and were treated severely by the *Inquisition.

AMALARIUS OF METZ (c. 780–850/1), liturgical scholar. A prominent figure in the *Carolingian Renaissance, in 835 he was appointed to administer the see of Lyons after the deposition of Abp. *Agobard. His De ecclesiasticis officiis, which was partly an attempt to further the fusion of Roman and *Gallican liturgical practices, exercised great influence in the Middle Ages.

AMALRIC (d.c. 1207), scholastic philosopher. He taught at *Paris. He maintained that God was the one essence underlying all created beings and that those who remain in the love of God cannot sin. His theses were condemned in 1210.

AMANA SOCIETY. A small Christian sect, also known as the Community of True Inspiration. It originated in Germany in 1714. A large part of the body sailed to America in 1842 and settled at Amana, Iowa, where a small communistic body survives.

AMANDUS, St. (d. c. 675), Apostle of Flanders. In 628, having been consecrated Bishop without a fixed see, he began active missionary work in Flanders and Carinthia. He founded two monasteries at Ghent and one at Elnon, near Tournai, of which he was Abbot; it was afterwards known as St.-Amand.

AMBO. A raised platform in a Christian *basilica, from which the Scriptures could be read and other public parts of the liturgy conducted. After the 14th cent. ambos were replaced by pulpits, but in some places they have been reintroduced in modern times.

AMBROSE, St. (c. 339–97), Bp. of Milan and one of the four traditional *Doctors of the Church. About 370 he became governor of Aemilia-Liguria, with his seat at Milan. In 374, on the death of the *Arian bishop, *Auxentius, the Catholic laity insisted that Ambrose should succeed him, though he had not yet been baptized. After baptism and ordination he devoted himself to the study of theology under *Simplicianus. As bishop he was famous as a preacher and was an outstanding upholder of orthodoxy. He defended the Church against the civil power and excommunicated the Emp. *Theodosius for a massacre (390). Apart from the *De Sacramentis (q.v.), his most notable work was a treatise on Christian ethics. He also wrote several well-known Latin hymns; his letters are full of historical interest.

AMBROSE, ISAAC (1604–64), English *Puritan divine. He was ordained priest before 1627 and held various cures. In 1641 he became a *Presbyterian; he served on the committee for the ejection of 'scandalous and ignorant ministers and school-masters' and was himself ejected from Garstang in 1662. After an illness he determined to write a devotional description of what the Lord had done for his soul: Looking unto Jesus (1658).

AMBROSIAN RITE. The rite used in the old archiepiscopal province of Milan, and one of the few non-Roman rites which survive in the RC Church. It differs from the Roman rite in a number of minor points, e.g. the *Offertory comes before and not after the Creed.

AMBROSIANA. The Ambrosian Library at Milan, founded c. 1605 by Federico Borromeo, and one of the first great libraries open to the public without distinction.

AMBROSIASTER. The name given (first by D. *Erasmus) to the author of a set of Latin commentaries on the 13 Epp. of St. *Paul, ascribed in all the manuscripts but one, and by most medieval authors, to St. *Ambrose. This ascription is now universally denied and a number of people have been suggested as the author.

AMBULATORY. The 'walking-space' created when an apsidal sanctuary in certain churches of the Norman period is surrounded by continuous *aisles.

A.M.D.G. The initial letters of 'Ad Maiorem Dei Gloriam', 'to the greater glory of God'.

AMEN. A Hebrew word meaning 'verily',

used to express assent at the end of religious formulas, esp. prayers.

AMERICANISM. A movement among American RCs at the end of the 19th cent., which aimed at adapting the external life of the Church to supposed modern cultural ideals. Its adherents stressed the 'active' virtues (humanitarianism, &c.), and urged the Church to minimize the points of difference between RCs and other Christians. It was condemned in 1899.

AMES, WILLIAM (1576–1633), English *Calvinist theologian. At Cambridge he became an extreme *Puritan. He took a prominent part in the *Remonstrant controversies in Holland and in 1622 he became professor of theology at Franeker. His chief work, *De Conscientia* (1632), is one of the few Protestant treatises on *casuistry and was long held in high repute for its incisive decisions.

AMIATINUS, CODEX. See *Codex Amiatinus*.

AMICE. A square or oblong linen cloth, with strings attached, which in the W. Church may be worn round the neck by the priest when celebrating the Eucharist and by other ministers who wear the *alb.

AMMON, St. (d. *c.* 350) (also **Amum**), a celebrated Egyptian hermit. He is mentioned by St. *Athanasius in his life of St. *Antony.

AMMONIAN SECTIONS. Divisions found in the margins of nearly all Latin and Greek MSS. of the Gospels, devised to illustrate the parallelism between corresponding passages in different Gospels. They were formerly attributed to *Ammonius Saccas, but are more prob. the work of *Eusebius of Caesarea.

AMMONIUS SACCAS (*c.* 175–242), an Alexandrian, reputed to be the founder of *Neoplatonism. He was highly regarded as a teacher and appears to have influenced *Plotinus.

AMOS, Book of. The first in time of the canonical prophets of the OT, Amos was a herdsman and dresser of sycamore trees, who exercised his ministry in Israel between 760 and 750 B.C.. At a time of prosperity, when the accumulation of wealth was leading to injustice and oppression of the poor, he urged the importance of social justice and the threat of coming judgement. The 'Day of the Lord', to which the Hebrews looked forward as the beginning of a Golden Age, would be a day of justice when Israel would be humiliated and receive the reward of iniquity.

AMPHILOCHIUS, St. (*c.* 340–95), Bp. of Iconium from 373. A cousin of .*Gregory Nazianzus, he was present at a Council of Iconium (376) in which the Divinity of the Holy Spirit was defended and in 390 he was head of the Council of Side which excommunicated the *Messalians. His *Iambics for Seleucus* contains a list of books of the Bible, important for the history of the *Canon.

AMPLEFORTH ABBEY, N. Yorks. An English *Benedictine Abbey, founded in 1802 with a nucleus of monks from Dieulouard in Lorraine, who claimed continuity with the pre-Reformation Benedictines of *Westminster Abbey.

AMPULLA. A globular vessel for holding liquid. The term is used of: (1) bottle-shaped vessels, usually of glass, found at tombs in the *catacombs, and previously thought to contain the blood of martyrs; (2) vessels of baked clay used to preserve oil from lights burnt in *martyria; (3) vessels used for the sacramental oils. The most famous is the 'Sainte Ampoule', supposed to have been brought by a dove at the prayers for St. *Remigius for the baptism of *Clovis in 496. It was preserved at *Reims and used in the coronation of French kings.

AMSDORF, NIKOLAUS VON (1483–1565), *Lutheran theologian. A canon of *Wittenberg, he joined M. *Luther in 1517. He later became a leader of the intransigent Lutheran party against the *Adiaphorists. His teaching that good works were not only useless but actually harmful was criticized in the Formula of *Concord (1577).

AMSTERDAM ASSEMBLY, The (1948). The Assembly of Church leaders in Amsterdam which formally constituted the '*World Council of Churches'.

ANABAPTISTS. The comprehensive designation of various groups who refused to allow their children to be baptized and re-established the baptism of believers. The main groups were: (1) Thomas *Münzer and the *Zwickau Prophets, who appeared at *Wittenberg in 1521. (2) The Swiss Bretheren, who re-introduced believers' baptism as the basis of Christian fellowship at Zürich in 1525; they preached non-resistance and rejected Christian participation in the magistracy. (3) Communities which found asylum in Moravia and, under the leadership of Jacob Hutter (d. 1536), established settlements based on community of property. Their descendants, known as 'Hutterites', survive in the U.S.A. (4) Melchiorites or Hoffmanites, i.e. Anabaptists influenced by Melchior *Hoffmann, mainly in NW. Germany and the Low Countries. (5) A group of Anabaptist refugees in Münster who in 1533–5 attempted to establish a Kingdom of Saints; their excesses brought disrepute on the movement. (6) The *Mennonites (q.v.).

The Anabaptists were denounced by M. *Luther, H. *Zwingli, and J. *Calvin and persecuted by both RCs and Protestants. There were Anabaptists in England as early as 1534. They prob. influenced the early *Separatists and *Brownists.

ANACLETUS, St. (1st cent.), Bp. of Rome. He is prob. to be identified with 'Cletus'. He followed St. *Linus (the successor of St *Peter) and preceded St. *Clement of Rome.

ANALOGY. A method of predication whereby concepts derived from a familiar object are made applicable to a relatively unknown object in virtue of some similarity between two otherwise dissimilar objects. Thus it is by 'analogy' that it is possible for the human intellect to speak of the 'justice' of God, for, though God's justice is not totally unlike justice encountered in human experience, it is not identical with it.

ANALOGY OF RELIGION, The (1736). J. *Butler's famous book was addressed to enquirers who, while conscious of order and regularity in nature, were unconvinced of the claims of religion. It sought to establish the analogy and conformity of Natural and Revealed Religion to what is observable in nature. Although it makes no direct refer-ence to the *Deists, it did more to discredit the movement than the vast body of polemical literature which sought to grapple with its upholders directly.

ANAMNESIS. The commemoration of the Passion, Resurrection, and Ascension of Christ, which in most liturgies is included in the Eucharistic *Canon after the Words of *Institution.

ANAPHORA. The central prayer in the Eucharistic liturgy, containing the *Consecration, the *Anamnesis, and the Communion.

ANASTASIA, St. (c. 304), martyr. Her name occurs in the traditional *Canon of the Roman Mass. She was apparently martyred at Sirmium in Pannonia, whence her relics were translated by *Gennadius to *Constantinople. From here her cultus spread to the church in Rome near the Imperial Palace known as the *titulus Anastasiae* (perhaps from its founder); the dedication was then understood of the Sirmian saint.

ANASTASIS (Gk., 'resurrection'). The term is used both of the resurrection of Christ and of that of mankind in general. Early churches were dedicated to the Anastasis (of Christ) at *Jerusalem and *Constantinople.

ANASTASIUS, St. (d. c. 700), Abbot of the monastery of St. Catherine on Mt. *Sinai. He is believed to have attacked *Monophysitism at *Alexandria as early as 640 and it is chiefly against this heresy that his most important work, the *Hodegos* (*Guide*) is directed.

ANASTASIUS BIBLIOTHECARIUS (9th cent.), scholar. He was the best Greek scholar of his age in the W. and became Papal librarian (hence his title). He attended the final session of the Eighth *Oecumenical Council (867) and in 871 translated its Acts into Latin. In 873 he translated those of the Seventh Council (787).

ANATHEMA. The word means 'separated' or 'accursed'. It was used several times by St. *Paul. At the Council of *Elvira (c. 306) offenders were anathematized and anathematization soon became the regular procedure against heretics. From the 6th cent. it was distinguished from *excommunication;

whereas the latter involved only exclusion from the worship and sacraments of the Church, the former was complete separation from the body of the faithful. In practice the distinction lost its meaning, apart from the solemn ceremony used for anathemas in the RC Church.

ANATOLIUS, St. (d. *c.* 282), Bp. of Laodicea from 268. A teacher and senator of *Alexandria before his consecration, he was a man of great learning. His writings included a treatise on the date of *Easter and a work on the Elements of Arithmetic.

ANCHORITE (*m.*), **ANCHORESS** (*f.*). A person who withdraws from the world to live a solitary life of silence, prayer, and mortification. The word is used esp. of one who lives in strictly confined quarters (his 'cell').

ANCIENT OF DAYS. A designation of God found in Dan. 7 (AV and RV).

ANCREN(E) RIWLE (or **Ancrene Wisse**), 'Rule' or 'Guide for Anchoresses', written in English, *c.* 1200, in the W. Midlands, for a small group of young women recluses, by a gifted and highly educated cleric, as yet unidentified. It exists in several versions and was widely copied.

ANCYRA (also **Angora**, now Ankara, Turkey). Among the more important early Church synods held here were those of: (1) 314, which dealt with the reconciliation of the lapsed and those who had committed other offences; and (2) 358. A council of *Semi-Arians who asserted that the Son was 'like in substance' to the Father.

ANDREW, St., *Apostle. He was the brother of St. *Peter, and several incidents are recorded of him in the Gospels. *Eusebius states that he later went to Scythia. The tradition of the form of St. Andrew's cross (like a Greek X) cannot be traced earlier than the 13th cent. Since *c.* 750 he has been regarded as the patron saint of *Scotland. See the following entry.

ANDREW, Acts of St. An apocryphal book, of which there is an epitome by *Gregory of Tours. It depicts the apostle imprisoned at Patras in Greece. The 'Martyrdom of St. Andrew', a variant text of part of the work, describes his death by crucifixion, but

without mention of the 'St. Andrew's cross' (see previous entry).

ANDREW OF CRETE, St. (*c.* 660–740), theologian. He became Abp. of Gortyna in Crete *c.* 692. He wrote many hymns, notably a series of *canons, a form of composition which he is said to have invented. A number of homilies also survive.

ANDREW OF ST.-VICTOR (d. 1175), Biblical exegete. A canon of St.-Victor in Paris, he became Abbot of Wigmore in Herefordshire. In his commentaries he used Jewish sources and concentrated on the literal sense of Scripture to an extent not found elsewhere in the Middle Ages.

ANDREWES, LANCELOT (1555–1626), Bp. successively of *Chichester (from 1605), *Ely (1609), and *Winchester (1619). He took a leading part in the *Hampton Court Conference (1604) and was one of the translators of the AV. He was held in high esteem by *James I. When the King's defence of the Oath of Allegiance was attacked by St. Robert *Bellarmine, Andrewes wrote a vigorous and able reply, and in 1617 he accompanied James to Scotland in an attempt to persuade the Scots to accept episcopacy. Theologically he was one of the main influences in the formation of a distinctively Anglican theology, which, in reaction from the rigidity of *Puritanism, was to be reasonable in outlook and Catholic in tone. In his lifetime his fame rested on his preaching; the first collection of his sermons was publd. in 1629. They are characterized by verbal conceits, a minute and (to modern feeling) overworked analysis of the text, and constant Greek and Latin quotations. His famous *Preces Privatae*, a collection of devotions gradually compiled for his own use, was publd. in 1648.

ANGEL. In the Bible angels are represented as an innumerable multitude of beings intermediate between God and man (e.g. Gen. 32: 1 f.). They form the heavenly court (Is. 6), and particular angels are mentioned as performing God's commands for nations and individuals (e.g. Dan. 10: 13 and 12: 1). Acc. to Christ's teaching they are spiritual beings (Mt. 22: 30); they enjoy the vision of God in heaven (Mt. 18: 10), and will accompany Him at His Second Coming (Mt. 16: 27); the NT writers represent Him as surrounded by angels at the most important points in His life.

In the first centuries of the Church interest in angels was comparatively peripheral; it largely centred on the question of angelic orders raised by the two enumerations in Eph. 1: 21 and Col. 1: 16. Their number and order were fixed by *Dionysius the Pseudo-Areopagite's *Celestial Hierarchies*, where they are arranged in three hierarchies of three choirs each, in the order of Seraphim, Cherubim, and Thrones; Dominations, Virtues, and Powers; and Principalities, Archangels, and Angels. Only the last two choirs have an immediate mission to men. In the Middle Ages there was a great deal of speculation and controversy over detailed points, e.g. their substantiality, form, and nature. In general Catholic Christianity teaches the existence of angels and enjoins a cult similar to that given to the saints. Protestants have shrunk from definition. See also *Guardian Angels*.

ANGELA OF FOLIGNO, Bl. (*c.* 1248–1309), Umbrian mystic. After the death of her husband, she became a *Franciscan tertiary. The account of her frequent visions, taken down by dictation and circulated as *Liber Visionum et Instructionum*, reflects early Franciscan piety at its highest.

ANGELA MERICI, St. (1474–1540), foundress of the *Ursulines. After a period of blindness, in 1535 she founded at Brescia a religious community of women, which she named after her patron, St. *Ursula.

ANGELIC DOCTOR, The. A title applied to St. *Thomas Aquinas.

ANGELIC HYMN. Another name for the *Gloria in excelsis*.

ANGELICO, Fra (1387–1455), Fra Angelico Giovanni da Fiesole, painter. He joined the *Dominican Order in 1407. Some of his greatest pictures are at Cortona, whither he fled during the *Great Schism. In middle life he undertook the decoration of the convent of San Marco at Florence and the frescoes in two chapels in the *Vatican.

ANGELS OF THE CHURCHES. The angels of the seven Churches mentioned in Rev. 1–3.

ANGELUS. In the W. Church, the devotion consisting in the repetition three times daily (early morning, noon, and evening) of three *Ave Marias with versicle and a collect as a memorial of the Incarnation. A bell is rung three times for each Ave and nine times for the collect.

ANGELUS SILESIUS (1624–77) (**Johann Scheffler**), mystical poet and controversialist. The son of a *Lutheran Polish noble, he became a RC in 1653. His chief fame lies in his mystical poems *Heilige Seelenlust* (1657) and *Der Cherubinische Wandersmann* (1675; 1st ed., with different title, 1657).

ANGLICAN AND EASTERN CHURCHES ASSOCIATION. The present name of a body founded in 1864 to pray for the reunion of the Orthodox Church and the Anglican Communion.

ANGLICAN CHANT. The music of the Psalms as widely used in the Anglican Communion. It consists of a tune in barred music, harmonized, in which the first part of each half-verse is sung on a reciting note, and the concluding words fitted to a tune in metrical rhythm.

ANGLICAN COMMUNION. The Church in communion with, and recognizing the leadership of, the see of *Canterbury. It consists of the *Church of England (the only part still retaining State Establishment), the Church of *Ireland, the Church in *Wales, the Episcopal Church in *Scotland, the (*Protestant) Episcopal Church in the U.S.A., the Anglican Churches of *Canada, *Australia, Papua New Guinea, and the Southern Cone of America, the Churches of the Provinces of the *West Indies, *New Zealand, *South Africa, *West Africa, Central Africa, Tanzania, Kenya, *Burma, Melanesia, the Indian Ocean, Nigeria, Uganda, and of Burundi, Rwanda and Zaïre, the Nippon Sei Ko Kwai (*Japan), the Chung Hua Sheng Kung Hui (*China), the Episcopal Churches of *Brazil and in *Jerusalem and the Middle East, the Province of the Episcopal Church of the Sudan, the Council of the Church of East Asia, the South Pacific Anglican Council, the Anglican Council of South America, and various dioceses under the Abp. of Canterbury's jurisdiction.

For the first 250 years after the Reformation, the Anglican Communion, except for the Episcopal Church in Scotland (disestablished under William III), consisted solely of the State Church of England, Ireland, and Wales. Priests working overseas were placed under the jurisdiction of the Bp. of London. After the consecration of S. *Seabury by the Scottish bishops, an Act of Parliament was passed in 1786 which made possible the consecration in England of bishops for sees abroad. The Protestant Episcopal Church of the United States of America came into being as an autonomous body in communion with the see of Canterbury. Bishoprics were then established in other parts of the British Empire. Provincial organization began in 1835 and gradually complete independence both of the State and of the jurisdiction of Canterbury was secured by those dioceses with provincial organization. Other dioceses, though free from State establishment, depend directly on Canterbury. Outside the British Empire a few Anglican dioceses were founded, e.g. in China and Japan.

Anglican bishops meet periodically as a body at the *Lambeth Conferences (q.v.). The 1968 Conference initiated the establishment of an Anglican Consultative Council, which was to meet every two years; its first meeting was held in 1971.

ANGLICAN EVANGELICAL GROUP MOVEMENT. An association of Anglican clergy and laity who held *Liberal Evangelical views. It began in 1906 as a private group with the title 'Group Brotherhood', becoming a public body in 1923. It was formally terminated in 1967.

ANGLICAN–METHODIST CONVERSATIONS. On the basis of a suggestion made by Abp. G. *Fisher in 1946, that union between the Free Churches and the C of E might be achieved if the former would accept episcopacy, the *Methodist Conference and the *Convocations of Canterbury and York agreed to enter into conversations in 1955. The Final Report of these Conversations, issued in 1963, outlined a plan in two stages. Stage I was to be inaugurated by a Service of Reconciliation which would unite the existing ministries and be followed by the consecration of Methodist bishops. No date was set for the achievement of Stage II (complete integration). A new Commission in 1968 produced a detailed scheme. In 1969 this was accepted by the Methodist Conference but failed to gain the necessary 75 per cent majority in the Convocations; it secured even less support when it was brought before the *General Synod in 1972, and so lapsed.

ANGLICAN ORDINATIONS. Until the subject was removed from discussion in the RC Church by *Leo XIII's bull '*Apostolicae Curae' (1896), there was diversity of opinion in that Church about the validity of Anglican *Orders. The grounds on which their validity was attacked fall into two classes: (1) attacks on the historical continuity of the laying on of hands; and (2) attacks on the *Ordinal introduced under *Edward VI as either defective in *intention or invalidated by the omission of the Tradition of the *Instruments and other rites. Neither ground is now seriously accepted.

ANGLICANISM. Though properly applied to the system of doctrine and practice upheld by Christians in communion with the see of *Canterbury, the word is used in a more restricted sense of that system in so far as it emphasizes its claim to possess a religious outlook distinguishable from that of other Christian communities. It was in the reign of *Elizabeth I that Anglicanism as a doctrinal system came into existence; its golden age was the 17th cent., when the *Caroline divines and others confirmed the rejection of the claims of Rome and refused to adopt the theological system of the Continental Reformers. The historic episcopate was preserved, though many did not regard it as of divine origin. The legitimacy of ecclesiastical development was not denied, but its extent was held to be limited by the appeal to Scripture as containing all things necessary to eternal salvation. Truth was to be sought from the joint testimony of Scripture and ecclesiastical authority, which in its turn was to be based on the traditions of the first four centuries. After the secession of the *Nonjurors (1690), Anglicanism suffered a decline until the rise of the *Oxford Movement, whose leaders once more advanced the claims of the Caroline divines.

ANGLO-CATHOLICISM. The name given to the more advanced section of the '*High Church' movement in the C of E. The word dates from 1838.

ANGLO-SAXON CHURCH. The Church in England from the end of the 6th cent. to the Norman Conquest (1066). In 597 the Roman mission of St. *Augustine landed in Thanet in the south and sees were quickly set up at *Canterbury, London, *Rochester, and *York. In the north, the *Celtic St. *Aidan established himself at *Lindisfarne c. 635. For a time the work of the missions was hindered by disputes over differences in such customs as the date of observing Easter, but after the Synod of *Whitby (664), union between the north and the south was gradually achieved. In 669 *Theodore of Tarsus arrived as Abp. of Canterbury and began his great work of reform and organization. The Danish invasions were a blow to the Church, although the victory of *Alfred secured the nominal acceptance of Christianity by the invaders. In the 10th cent. reforms were initiated by St. *Dunstan, and closer contact with the Continent was established. In the Anglo-Saxon Church monasticism was strong, and most of the evangelization was done by monks. There were also esp. close links between the Church and State. The conversion of a district usually began in the royal palace; bishoprics were conterminous with tribal areas, and it is often difficult to decide whether a particular assembly was primarily ecclesiastical or secular.

ANIMA CHRISTI (Lat., 'Soul of Christ'), the well-known prayer, beginning 'Soul of Christ, sanctify me', used esp. as a private Eucharistic devotion. It appears to date from the early 14th cent.

ANNA COMNENA (b. 1083; d. after 1148). The daughter of the Emp. Alexius I, Comnenus, she conspired to depose her brother and then retired to a convent. Here she composed the *Alexiad*, a panegyric account of her father's reign. It is of interest as an example of Orthodox hostility to the W. Church and to the *Crusades as a menace to the E. Empire.

ANNAS. The Jewish *High Priest from A.D. 6 (or 7) to 15 and father-in-law of *Caiaphas. Acc. to Jn. 18: 13 Christ was brought before Annas before being sent on to Caiaphas.

ANNATES. The first year's revenue of an ecclesiastical benefice, paid to the Papal curia. In England payments were transferred to the Crown in 1534; in 1704 they were converted into '*Queen Anne's Bounty'.

ANNE, St., Mother of the BVM. Her name (not found in the Bible) and the legend of her life occur in the *Protevangelium of James (2nd cent.). Her cult developed during the Middle Ages and was an object of special attack by M. *Luther and other Reformers.

ANNE (1665–1714), Queen of Great Britain and Ireland from 1702. The second daughter of *James II, she was brought up as an Anglican. She created '*Queen Anne's Bounty' (1704). She tried, by exercising her right of nominating bishops, to introduce a High Church and Tory element on the Bench, and she supported the *Occasional Conformity Bill (introduced 1702; passed 1711). The results of her policy did not outlast her reign.

ANNEXED BOOK, The. The actual BCP annexed to the Act of *Uniformity of 1662, which prescribed the use of 'true and perfect copies' of it.

ANNO DOMINI (Lat., 'in the year of the Lord'). The current system of dating by 'A.D.', based on the supposed year of the birth of Christ. It is now commonly held that the actual birth was several years earlier.

ANNUNCIATION OF THE BVM. The feast, observed on 25 Mar. ('Lady Day'), commemorates the announcement of the Incarnation by the angel *Gabriel to the BVM and the conception of Christ in her womb (Lk. 1: 26–38).

ANOINTING. A ceremonial action to separate persons and things from profane use and to obtain for them the infusion of Divine grace. In the OT priests and kings are anointed, and the future deliverer is designated the 'Anointed One' or '*Messiah' (q.v.). See also *Chrism*, *Unction*, and *Coronation Rite in England*.

ANOMOEANS. 4th-cent. exponents of a doctrine akin to *Arianism. Their leaders were *Aetius and *Eunomius (qq.v.).

ANSELM, St. (c. 1033–1109), Abp. of *Canterbury from 1093. He had been Abbot of *Bec. He had various disputes with William II and in 1098 he went to Rome. He first learnt of the papal decrees against lay *investiture in 1099; when the new king, Henry I, recalled him to England in 1100, he insisted on observing the decrees without compromise. In 1103 he again went to Rome and remained in exile until 1107, when the Pope and the King agreed to a compromise behind his back.

As a theologian and philosopher Anselm has a foremost place among the earlier Scholastic thinkers. Unlike his contemporaries, he preferred to defend the faith by intellectual reasoning rather than by arguments based on Scripture and other authorities. The object of his *Monologion* was to establish the being of God solely from the consideration of truth and goodness as intellectual notions. In the *Proslogion* this reasoning was given the more systematic form of the *Ontological Argument. His *Cur Deus Homo* was the most considerable contribution to the theology of the *Atonement in the Middle Ages. It interpreted the doctrine in terms of the satisfaction due to the outraged majesty of God, and repudiated the notion that the devil had rights over fallen man which it was a leading purpose of the Cross to satisfy.

ANSELM OF LAON (d. 1117), theologian. He taught in the cathedral school at Laon. His lectures on the Bible discussed points of interest as they arose; after his death these lectures were reworked and enlarged into systematic *Summae*. The corpus of his work is not yet settled, but he certainly also arranged commentaries on the Psalter, the Pauline Epp., and Jn., which are the foundation of the *Glossa Ordinaria.

ANSELM OF LUCCA (d. 1073), Pope. See *Alexander II*.

ANSELM OF LUCCA, St. (c. 1036–86). Nominated to the see of Lucca in 1071, he accepted *investiture from the Emp. *Henry IV, but repented and resigned. At the insistence of *Gregory VII, he later returned to his see, but his attempts to impose strict discipline led to his expulsion (c. 1080). He wrote a treatise against lay investiture and made a collection of *canons, later incorporated into *Gratian's 'Decretum'.

ANSKAR, St. (801–65), the 'Apostle of the North'. A monk of *Corbie, he went to Westphalia, *Denmark, and *Sweden, where he built the first Christian church. About 832 he became Bp. of Hamburg and c. 848 Abp. of Bremen. After his death Scandinavia relapsed into paganism.

ANSON BY-LAW, The. The law allowing a child to be withdrawn from a primary school during time allotted to religious observance or instruction if the parent so desires and arrangement has been made for the child to attend religious observance and instruction elsewhere. The 1936 Education Act made the principles of the by-law applicable everywhere. It was so called after William Reynell Anson, Parliamentary Secretary to the Board of Education when the 1902 Education Act was passed.

ANTE-CHAPEL. The western end of certain medieval college chapels.

ANTE-COMMUNION. In the C of E the earlier part of the service of Holy Communion down to and including the Prayer for the Church Militant, esp. when recited without the remainder of the service.

ANTELAPSARIANISM. See *Supralapsarianism*.

ANTEPENDIUM. A vesture or *frontal which hangs in front of the altar.

ANTHEM. The Anglicized form of the word *antiphon. In current English usage it is usually applied to sacred vocal music set to Scriptural words. In the C of E the proper place for the anthem is after the third collect at Morning and Evening Prayer.

ANTHONY, St. See *Antony, St*.

ANTHROPOLOGY. In its more exact sense the word designates the study of man as contrasted, e.g. with that of God or angels. It enables the Christian apologist to exhibit the true nature of man and his superior status to the animal creation as against views which represent him as an economic unit or a mass of psychological reflexes. In popular usage 'anthropology' is used of the science which studies the life and environment of primitive man.

ANTHROPOMORPHISM. The attribution to God of human characteristics. The Bible frequently uses anthropomorphic language, usually clearly metaphorically (e.g. 'the

Lord God walking in the garden', Gen. 3: 8). In Christian philosophy, seemingly anthropomorphic conceptions, such as personality and will, are often predicated of God. Without the use of such modes of expression, any developed exposition of the nature and attributes of God would be impossible.

ANTHROPOSOPHY. A system of spiritual development evolved by R. *Steiner (q.v.), including belief in *reincarnation. Though it acknowledges Christ as a central force, its teaching about Him is very different from that of orthodox Christianity.

ANTIBURGHER. A member of the group in the Secession Church in Scotland which in 1747 separated from the '*Burgher' group because it refused to admit the lawfulness of taking the 'Burgess Oath'.

ANTICHRIST. The prince of Christ's enemies. In the NT he is referred to by name only in 1 and 2 Jn. (where he is identified with those who deny the Incarnation), but many see him in the strange beasts of Rev. and in the 'man of sin' in 2 Thess. 2: 3–10. Some have held that there was a Jewish Antichrist legend which was developed by Christians; others have connected Antichrist not with a person but with an evil principle; yet others have seen in Antichrist a reference to some historical person (e.g. *Nero).

ANTICLERICALISM. A liberal movement in politics and religion. Rooted in the religious indifference of 18th-cent. Europe, it first became an active political force through the French Revolution (1789). In general it was opposed to any dogmatic and denominational form of Christianity; it directed its attacks esp. against the RC Church and its civil privileges. Its influence was esp. strong in France, where in 1905 the State ceased to recognize the RC religion or to grant any privileges to its representatives. There were also anticlerical movements in *Spain and *Portugal, and in Italy an anticlerical party went hand in hand with the nationalist movement.

ANTIDIDAGMA, The. The reply issued in 1544 by the cathedral chapter of *Cologne to the plan set out by Abp. *Hermann of Wied to reform Catholic practices.

ANTIDORON. In the E. Church, the remains of the loaves from which the bread for the Eucharist is cut. It is distributed at the end of the Liturgy, in theory only to those who have not received Communion, but in practice to all present. It is regarded as sharing in some measure in the Eucharistic blessing.

ANTILEGOMENA. The designation given by *Eusebius of Caesarea to those Scriptural books whose claim to be considered part of the NT Canon was disputed.

ANTI-MARCIONITE   PROLOGUES, The. Short introductory prologues prefixed to the Gospels of Mk., Lk., and Jn. in some 40 MSS. of the *Vulgate.

ANTIMINSION, also **Antimension**. In the E. Church a silk or linen cloth, containing relics; it was orig. intended for use when there was no consecrated altar, but it is now used like a W. *corporal.

ANTINOMIANISM. A general name for the view that Christians are by grace set free from the need to observe any moral law. Various *Gnostic sects held that, as matter was sharply opposed to spirit, bodily actions were indifferent and therefore licentiousness was admissible. At the Reformation antinomian teaching was renewed, e.g. by the *Anabaptists, as following from the *Lutheran doctrine of *justification by faith.

ANTIOCH. In size and importance Antioch in Syria was the third city of the Roman Empire. A Christian community existed here from early days and it was here that the followers of Christ were first called 'Christians' (Acts 11: 26). Acc. to tradition St. *Peter was the first bishop. By the 4th cent. the see ranked after *Rome and *Alexandria as the third patriarchal see of Christendom. The rise in power of *Constantinople and the erection of *Jerusalem into a Patriarchate reduced the importance of Antioch, which was further diminished by the *Nestorian and *Monophysite schisms. See also *Antiochene Theology*.

ANTIOCH, Council of (341). The Council was held on the occasion of the consecration of *Constantine's 'Golden Church' at Antioch. Four creeds were put forward to replace that of *Nicaea. The 25 (mainly disciplinary) 'Canons of Antioch' are generally thought to be the work of this Council.

ANTIOCHENE THEOLOGY. Perhaps because of their Semitic outlook, the theologians of *Antioch emphasized the oneness of God; they abhorred any suggestion of *tritheism and held the Persons of the Trinity to be distinguished only in their mode of operation. In the *Christological controversies of the 5th cent., against the *Alexandrians, they emphasized the humanity of Christ and inclined to belief in a loose union of the Divine and human natures in Christ. The tradition was discredited after the Council of *Ephesus in 431.

Antiochene exegesis of Scripture was historical and looked not for a hidden meaning in the text but for the sense intended by the writer.

ANTIOCHUS EPIPHANES (d. 163 B.C.), king of Syria from 175 B.C. In 169 B.C. he attacked *Jerusalem and pillaged the *Temple; in 167 B.C. Jewish customs were forbidden, the Temple was defiled, and pagan cults instituted. This led to the *Maccabean revolt. His exploits are recorded in Maccabees.

ANTIPHON (orig. 'something sung alternately by two choirs'). In the W. Church, sentences, usually from Scripture, recited before and after the *Psalms and *Canticles in the Divine *Office. The name is also used of the four Anthems of the BVM, one of which is sung after *Compline. In the E. Church the word is applied to various chants sung antiphonally.

ANTIPHONAL, also **Antiphonary**. Originally the liturgical book in the W. Church containing the parts of the Office and Mass which were sung by the choir antiphonally. In later times the Office and Mass portions were separated and in current usage the word is restricted to the former.

ANTIPOPE. A person set up as Bp. of Rome in opposition to the person holding the see or held to be lawfully elected to it.

ANTITRINITARIANISM. A term used to denote various professedly Christian systems which agree only in rejecting the doctrine of the *Trinity. They have included *Ebionites, upholders of *Subordinationism, *Modal-ists, *Arians, and in modern times *Unitarians.

ANTONELLI, GIACOMO (1806–76), Cardinal Secretary of State. In 1848 he arranged the flight of *Pius IX to Gaeta and after his return to Rome in 1850 became virtually the temporal ruler of the city until 1870. He opposed the convening of the First *Vatican Council, and while it was sitting he advised the Pope to drop the *Infallibility question.

ANTONIANS. Several communities claiming the patronage of, or descent from, St. *Antony of Egypt: (1) the original disciples of St. Antony in the desert; (2) a congregation founded by Gaston de Dauphiné in 1095, known as the 'Hospital Brothers of St. Antony'; (3) an order in the *Armenian Church founded in the 17th cent. to maintain the connection with the RC Church; (4) a congregation founded in Flanders in 1615.

ANTONINUS, St. (1389–1459), Abp. of Florence from 1446. A *Dominican, he governed various convents, everywhere seeking to restore the primitve rule. By his integrity and wisdom he became the counsellor of popes and statesmen. He was also a distinguished theological writer. As an economist he maintained that money invested in business was true capital and that it was therefore not necessarily wrong to receive interest.

ANTONY, St., of Egypt (251?–356), hermit. About 269 he gave away his possessions and c. 285 he retired completely to the desert, where he is said to have fought demons under the guise of wild beasts. About 305 he came out of his solitude to organize his disciples into a community of hermits living under a rule, though with much less common life than the later religious orders. He retired into solitude again c. 310, but he later exercised his influence in support of the Nicene party in the *Arian controversy; in this he was closely associated with St. *Athanasius, who wrote his biography.

ANTONY, St., of Padua (1195–1231), *Franciscan friar. He was an *Augustinian Canon, but, filled with desire for martyrdom, he was allowed to join the Franciscans in 1220/1. He sailed for Morocco but was forced by illness to return to Europe. When suddenly called upon to preach at an ordination, his unexpected eloquence and learning were discovered. He was appointed the first lector in theology in the Franciscan Order and held a series of other offices.

Possibly in his lifetime, and certainly after his death, he was regarded as a worker of miracles. He is chiefly invoked for the return of lost property, possibly because of the incident of the novice who ran away with a Psalter he was using and was forced by an alarming apparition to return it.

APELLES (2nd cent.), founder of a *Gnostic sect. Originally a disciple of *Marcion, he modified his dualism in an attempt to defend a less *Docetic doctrine of the Person of Christ. Christ, he held, came down from the good God, who was not himself the creator of the world, however, and really lived and suffered in a body miraculously formed out of the elements.

APHRAATES (early 4th cent.), the first of the Syriac Church Fathers. He was an ascetic, evidently holding high ecclesiastical office. His *Demonstrations* (inaccurately known as his *Homilies*) were completed between 337 and 345. The first 22 give a survey of Christian faith, the last being an appendix.

APHTHARTODOCETAE. A division of the *Monophysites, founded by *Julian, Bp. of Halicarnassus. They taught that from the moment of the incarnation the earthly body of Christ was in its nature incorruptible, impassible, and immortal, though this fact did not preclude Him from accepting suffering and death as a free act of will.

APIARIUS. A priest in proconsular Africa who was deposed for misconduct. The incident is important in connection with the growth of papal jurisdiction. Apiarius appealed to Pope *Zosimus (417–18), who ordered his reinstatement. A Council of *Carthage in 418 then forbade appeals beyond the sea. The Pope protested and the case dragged on.

APOCALYPSES. See the following entry.

APOCALYPTIC LITERATURE. The word 'apocalypse' means a 'revelation' or 'unveiling', so that apocalyptic books claim to reveal things which are normally hidden or to reveal the future. The Jewish Apocalyptic books belong to the period from c. 200 B.C. to A.D. c. 100; they deal with the end of the present order and with the next world. All pseudonymous, they include the Book of *Daniel and, outside the OT, the Book of *Enoch, the Book of the Secrets of Enoch, the Apocalypses of *Abraham and *Baruch, the Fourth Book of *Ezra, the Assumption of *Moses, *Jubilees, the Ascension of *Isaiah, and the *Testaments of the Twelve Patriarchs. The two most important Christian apocalypses are *Revelation and the (non-canonical) Apocalypse of *Peter.

APOCATASTASIS. The Greek name for the doctrine that ultimately all free moral creatures—angels, men, and devils—will be saved. It was formally condemned at the Council of *Constantinople in 543. The doctrine, which has had modern defenders, is also known as 'universalism'.

APOCRISIARIUS. An ecclesiastical deputy or other official of high rank. (1) The envoys used by the Patriarchs as diplomatic representatives in other patriarchal cities or at imperial courts. (2) Senior court chaplains of the Frankish courts.

APOCRYPHA, The (Gk., 'the hidden [things]'). The Biblical Books received by the early Church as part of the Greek version of the OT, but not included in the Hebrew Bible. Their position in Christian usage has been ambiguous. In the *Vulgate and versions derived from it they are mostly part of the OT; but in the AV, RV, NEB, and other non-RC versions they form a separate section between the OT and NT, though they are sometimes omitted. They comprise (in the order of the AV): 1 and 2 *Esdras, *Tobit, *Judith, the Rest of *Esther, the *Wisdom of Solomon, *Ecclesiasticus, *Baruch with the Epistle of *Jeremy, the *Song of the Three Children, the History of *Susanna, *Bel and the Dragon, the Prayer of *Manasses, and 1 and 2 *Maccabees.

The Church received these writings from Hellenistic Judaism, esp. that of *Alexandria. In the *Septuagint (LXX), which incorporated all except 2 Esdras, they are in no way differentiated from other parts of the OT. They date from the period 300 B.C.–A.D. 100 approximately, and mostly from 200 B.C. to A.D. 70, i.e. before the definite separation of the Church from Judaism. Some of them, being written in Hebrew, might have gained canonical status but did not; others, being written in Greek, were never current among Aramaic-speaking Jews. When the Hebrew *Canon of Scripture was settled (c. A.D. 100), the Hebrew text of the excluded Books ceased to be copied. The Greek, on the other hand, survived because of its use by Christians who at first received all Books of the LXX equally as Scripture.

In the 4th cent. many of the Greek Fathers came to recognize a distinction between those Books of the LXX which were canonical in Hebrew and the rest. St. *Jerome accepted the distinction and introduced the term 'Apocrypha' for the latter class. With few exceptions the W. continued to regard all the LXX Books as equally canonical. In the E. opinion varied, but at the Synod of *Jerusalem in 1672 it was decided that Tob., Judith, Ecclus., and Wisd. were alone to be regarded as canonical. At the Reformation Protestant leaders refused the status of inspired Scripture to those Books of the Vulgate not found in the Hebrew Canon. M. *Luther, however, included most of them as an appendix to his translation of the Bible. The Council of *Trent (1548) confirmed the full canonicity of the Books, except 1 and 2 Esdras and the Prayer of Manasses, a decision repeated at the First *Vatican Council in 1870. In the C of E the *Thirty-Nine Articles say that the Apocryphal Books should be read for 'example of life and instruction of manners', but not used to establish doctrine. Parts of them have been included in successive C of E lectionaries. They are regarded with suspicion by the *Presbyterians and other English Nonconformists, and so frequently omitted from English Bibles, though their value as historical sources has been increasingly recognized in modern times.

APOCRYPHAL NEW TESTAMENT, The.
A modern title for various early Christian books outside the *Canon of the NT, which are similar in general form to the corresponding canonical Scriptures.

Many Apocryphal Gospels exist. In a few places some of them may embody trustworthy oral traditions. Others were intended to support heretical, esp. *Gnostic, views, while a third group aimed at satisfying popular curiosity about the childhood of Christ or His post-Resurrection life.

The most important Acts are those of *Peter, *Paul, *John, *Andrew, and *Thomas, all prob. 2nd cent. Their subject-matter is made up partly of stories parallel to and perhaps inspired by the Acts of the Apostles, partly credible oral tradition, partly evident romance.

There were numerous epistles and other writings such as that of Paul to the *Laodiceans and many *apocalypses besides Revelation.

APODEIPNON.
In the E. Church the late evening liturgical service, which is the counterpart of W. *Compline.

APOLLINARIS, St.
(date unkown), first Bp. of *Ravenna and acc. to St. Peter *Chrysologus a martyr.

APOLLINARIS, SIDONIUS.
See *Sidonius Apollinaris*.

APOLLINARIUS, CLAUDIUS
(2nd cent.), Bp. of Hierapolis and an *Apologist. His writings, all lost, included a 'Defence of the Faith', presented to *Marcus Aurelius, prob. in 172.

APOLLINARIUS and APOLLINARIANISM.
Apollinarius (or Apollinaris) (c. 310–c. 390) became Bp. of Laodicea c. 360. His *Christological teaching was condemned by synods at Rome in 374–80 and by the Council of *Constantinople in 381. He seceded from the Church c. 375. Most of his extensive writings have been lost and those that survive have been preserved under the names of other authors.

The objects of Apollinarianism, the first great Christological heresy, were: (1) to assert the unity of Godhead and manhood in Christ; (2) to teach the full Deity of Christ; and (3) to avoid teaching any moral development in Christ's life. Apollinarius asserted that Christ had a human body and soul, but that in Him the spirit was replaced by the Divine *Logos. The fundamental objection to this doctrine is that if there was no complete manhood in Christ, He could not redeem the whole of human nature, but only its spiritual elements.

APOLLONIUS OF TYANA
(d.c. 98), Neopythagorean philosopher. The virtues of his life and reforming religious tendencies were so exaggerated after his death that anti-Christian writers composed biographies of

him which consciously paralleled the Gospel life of Christ.

APOLLOS. A learned Jew of Alexandria, who was a follower of *John the Baptist before becoming a Christian (Acts 18: 24–6). It has sometimes been supposed that he was the author of the Ep. to the *Hebrews.

APOLOGETICS. The defence of the Christian faith on intellectual grounds. The 2nd cent. *Apologists were concerned to present the case for Christianity to non-Christians, but the task came to include the defence of orthodox teaching against those who dissent from it. The present function of Christian apologists is considered to be that of setting down the rational ground of the faith, without necessarily having any particular antagonist in view. It is not generally claimed that the truth of Christianity is demonstrable by logical or scientific methods, but it is maintained that it is possible to show by these means that its acceptance is in accordance with the demands of reason.

APOLOGIA PRO VITA SUA (1864). J. H. *Newman's 'history of [his] religious opinions' down to his reception into the RC Church in 1845. It was provoked by a gibe of C. *Kingsley in *Macmillan's Magazine* for Jan. 1864.

APOLOGISTS. The name given esp. to the Christian writers who (c. 120–220) first addressed themselves to the task of making a reasoned defence and recommendation of their faith to outsiders. They include *Aristides, *Justin Martyr, *Tatian, *Athenagoras, *Theophilus, *Minucius Felix, and *Tertullian. They had to contend with both pagan philosophy and the general outlook which it influenced and specifically Jewish objections.

APOLYSIS. The concluding blessing in E. rites.

APOLYTIKION. In the E. Church the principal *troparion of the day, celebrating the particular feast or saint commemorated in the calendar.

APOPHTHEGM. An alternative name for '*Paradigm' (q.v.).

APOPHTHEGMATA PATRUM. A collection of sayings of the Egyptian monks, arranged alphabetically acc. to the speakers. It dates from 4th–5th centuries.

APOSTASY. In the early Church, abandonment of Christianity. In the RC Church it is now used of: (1) total defection from the Christian faith; (2) public defection from the RC Church; (3) desertion by a religious who has taken perpetual vows.

APOSTICHA. In the E. Church, brief liturgical hymns or *stichera attached to verses from the Psalter.

APOSTLE. (1) The name given in the Gospels and later to the twelve chief disciples of Christ, viz. Sts. *Peter, *Andrew, *James, *John, *Philip, *Bartholomew, *Thomas, *Matthew, *James (the Less), *Thaddaeus, *Simon, and *Judas Iscariot. After the suicide of Judas his place was taken by *Matthias, and the term was applied to him, as well as in the Acts and Epp. to *Paul and *Barnabas. In modern times it is sometimes used of the leader of the first Christian mission to a country, e.g. St. *Patrick, the 'Apostle of Ireland'. See also *Apostolic Succession*. (2) A name given to the *Epistle read at the Eucharist in the E. Church. (3) An official in the *Catholic Apostolic Church.

APOSTLE OF THE GENTILES, The. A title given to St. *Paul (cf. Gal. 2: 7).

APOSTLES' CREED, The. A statement of faith used in the W. Church. Like other early *Creeds, it falls into three sections dealing with God the Father, Jesus Christ, and the Holy Spirit. Its title is first found in a letter of St. *Ambrose, c. 390, by which time the legend of its joint composition by the Apostles was current. By the early Middle Ages it was everywhere employed at Baptism in the W., and between the 7th and 9th cents. it secured a place in the daily offices. The BCP orders its use at *Mattins and *Evensong on most days of the year.

APOSTLESHIP OF PRAYER, The. A RC pious association founded in 1844 and under the guidance of the *Jesuits.

APOSTOLIC AGE, The. A modern title for the first period in the history of the

Church, falling approximately within the lifetime of the *Apostles.

APOSTOLIC CANONS, The. A series of 85 canons attributed to the Apostles; they form the concluding chapter of the '*Apostolic Constitutions'. They mostly deal with the conduct of the clergy. The first 50 were translated into Latin by *Dionysius Exiguus and so became part of the *canon law of the W. Church.

APOSTOLIC CHURCH ORDER, The. An early Christian document containing regulations on ecclesiastical practice and moral discipline. Its contents are ascribed to various Apostles, but it was prob. composed, in Greek, in Egypt c. 300.

APOSTOLIC CONSTITUTIONS, The. A collection of ecclesiastical laws dating from the latter half of the 4th cent. and almost certainly of Syrian provenance.

APOSTOLIC DELEGATE. A person appointed by the Pope to keep the *Vatican informed of ecclesiastical affairs in the territory assigned to him.

APOSTOLIC FATHERS, The. A title given since the later 17th cent. to those Fathers of the age immediately succeeding the NT period whose works have survived in whole or part. They are *Clement of Rome, *Ignatius, *Hermas, *Polycarp, and *Papias, and the authors of the *Ep. of *Barnabas, the *Ep. to *Diognetus, 2 *Clement, and the *Didache.

APOSTOLIC SEE, The. The see of Rome, so called because of its traditional association with the Apostles St. *Peter and St. *Paul.

APOSTOLIC SUCCESSION. The method whereby the ministry of the Church is held to be derived from the original apostles by a continuous succession of *bishops. The continuity of the succession, emphasized by *Clement of Rome before the end of the 1st cent., has occasionally been disputed; the necessity of it, widely taught in the RC Church, is denied by most Protestants and asserted only with qualifications by some other theologians. Doubts about the continuity of the Apostolic Succession were among the reasons leading to the condemna-

tion of *Anglican Orders (q.v.) by Rome in 1896.

APOSTOLIC TRADITION, The. A liturgical treatise, now generally agreed to be the work of *Hippolytus, which contains a detailed description of the rites and practices which were presumably in use at Rome in the early 3rd cent. It was formerly known as the 'Egyptian Church Order'.

APOSTOLICAE CURAE (1896). The encyclical which condemned *Anglican Orders as invalid.

APOSTOLICI (Lat., 'Apostolics'). The bodies to whom the title has been applied, by themselves or others, include: (1) some *Gnostic communities of the 2nd–4th cents.; (2) an ascetic body which flourished in the 12th cent. around *Cologne and at Périgueux in France; (3) a sect originating at Parma in 1260, which drew its inspiration from *Franciscan teaching on poverty and was condemned in 1286 and 1291; (4) certain *Anabaptist sects.

APOSTOLICITY. One of the four characteristics of the Church set forth in the *Nicene Creed. On a Catholic view the word means identifiable with the Apostles by succession (see *Apostolic Succession*) and continuity of doctrine, to which RCs would add communion with the 'see of Peter'. By Protestants the word is generally understood to mean 'primitive', as contrasted with postapostolic corruptions.

APPARITOR. An officer chosen by an ecclesiastical judge to summon persons to appear before, and to execute the decrees of, his court.

APPEALS. Applications from a lower to a higher judicial authority. Appeals by clergy and laity to authorities higher than their diocesans were based on Roman civil law and regulated by several councils. In England from the time of Henry II successive kings had tried to limit appeals to Rome; they were finally abolished in 1534 by *Henry VIII, who made the Court of *Delegates the final arbiter in ecclesiastical causes.

APPELLANTS. (1) The 31 RC secular priests who in 1599 appealed to Rome for the cancellation of the appointment of G. *Blackwell (q.v.) as *archpriest and superior of the mission. They represented the party which repudiated the use of political means for the conversion of England. The original appeal failed, but, after further appeals in 1601 and 1602, Blackwell was reprimanded. (2) The name assumed by those of *Jansenist sentiments who, after the condemnation by '*Unigenitus' (1713) of 101 of P. *Quesnel's propositions, tried to prevent its acceptance.

APPIAN WAY, The. The road constructed by the censor Appius Claudius Caecus in 312 B.C. from Rome to S. Italy. St. *Paul, travelling on the Appian Way, was met by groups of Christians at Appii Forum and Three Taverns (Acts 28: 15). Owing to the construction of the Via Appia Nuova, for the first few miles out of Rome the old road remains much as it was in ancient times; it is flanked by many Christian monuments and sanctuaries.

APPROPRIATION. The practice of permanently annexing to a monastery the *tithes and other endowments intended for parochial use. See also *Impropriation*.

APRON. A shortened form of *cassock, which is part of the distinctive dress of Anglican bishops, deans, and archdeacons.

APSE. A semicircular or polygonal eastern end to a chancel. It was a universal feature of the primitive *basilican type of church architecture. The altar stood on the chord of the apse, with seats for the bishop and presbyters in the curved space behind.

A.P.U.C. (Association for the Promotion of the Unity of Christendom). A society founded in 1857 to further the cause of reunion, esp. between the C of E and Rome.

AQUARIANS. An early sect or sects which used water instead of wine in the Eucharist.

AQUAVIVA, CLAUDIUS (1543–1615), 5th General of the *Jesuit Order (from 1581). He was faced with many difficulties, including the Spanish schism in the order and demands of the *Inquisition to examine its constitution. He possessed remarkable gifts of statesmanship, and under him the order was consolidated and its missionary

activity developed. He also strengthened its inner life; he ordered the drawing up of the '*Ratio Studiorum' and a comprehensive interpretation of the '*Spiritual Exercises'.

AQUILA, St. See *Priscilla, St.*.

AQUILA, Version of. A Greek version of the OT. It was the work of Aquila, who became a proselyte to Judaism and learnt Hebrew from the Rabbis. His translation, which was prob. finished c. 140, was extremely literal.

AQUILEIA, on the Adriatic coast, became an important city during the late Roman Empire. Acc. to legend it was evangelized by St. *Mark. In 381 its bishop, Valerian, appears as *metropolitan of the Churches in the area and under him and his successor, *Chromatius, Aquileia was a centre of learning. In the 6th cent. its bishops assumed the title of patriarch. The floor of the basilica (rebuilt in the 11th cent.) is covered with early 4th-cent. mosaics.

AQUINAS, St. THOMAS. See *Thomas Aquinas, St.*

ARAMAIC. The Semitic language which was the vernacular in Palestine in the time of Christ and which He almost certainly used. In later OT times it increasingly ousted *Hebrew as the spoken language of Palestine, and a few sections of the OT are written in it. By NT times Aramaic paraphrases of Scripture (*Targums) were issued to satisfy the needs of the people. Many passages in the NT reflect Aramaic modes of thought and occasionally Aramaic words are preserved (e.g. Mk. 5: 41).

ARCHAEOLOGY, Christian. The phrase now commonly denotes the study of Christian monuments, as distinct from documents, for the light they can throw upon Christian antiquity. The main classes of early Christian monuments are *cemeteries, buildings (churches, *baptisteries, and *monasteries), sculpture, mosaics, liturgical implements, and miscellaneous objects such as lamps, medals, and rings. The foundations of Christian archaeology were laid by the study of the Roman *catacombs, which began to be rediscovered in the 16th cent. There are also important Christian monuments at *Ravenna and in N. Africa. The size, character, and development of churches and cemeteries help to illustrate the growth, resources, and even the racial composition of individual communities, while paintings, mosaics, and *sarcophagi throw light on popular beliefs.

ARCHANGEL (Gk., 'chief angel'). In Christian tradition *Michael and *Gabriel are reckoned among the archangels. See also *Angel*.

ARCHBISHOP. The title, applied in the 4th–5th cents. to *patriarchs and holders of other outstanding sees, came to be extended to all *metropolitans having jurisdiction over an ecclesiastical province.

ARCHDEACON. In the Anglican Communion, a cleric having administrative authority delegated to him by the bishop; the territory assigned to him is known as his archdeaconry and gives him a territorial title, e.g. 'Archdeacon of Lindsey'. The duties normally include general disciplinary supervision of the clergy and care over the temporal administration of ecclesiastical property. As the name implies, an archdeacon was originally the chief of the *deacons who assisted diocesan bishops in their work.

ARCHDIOCESE. A diocese of which the holder is *ex-officio* *Archbishop, e.g. *Canterbury, or in the RC Church *Westminster.

ARCHES, Court of. The *Consistory Court of the province of *Canterbury which formerly met in *Bow Church ('S. Maria de Arcubus').

ARCHIMANDRITE. In the E. Church the term originally meant either the head of one religious house or the head of a group of monasteries; today it is used simply as a title of honour for a member of the monastic clergy.

ARCHPRIEST. In early times the title was given to the senior presbyter of a city who performed many of the bishop's liturgical and governmental functions in his absence or during a vacancy; in the countryside it was given to the cleric who presided over the group of parishes which united for the Sunday Eucharist and other functions previously performed by the bishop. In the RC and Orthodox Churches the title is still one of honour. It was given to the superior in charge of the secular priests sent to England between 1598 and 1621. The dispute between the *Appellants (1) and G. *Blackwell (qq.v.) is known as the 'Archpriest Controversy'.

ARCOSOLIUM. A particular kind of tomb found in the walls of the Roman *catacombs. It consisted of two parts, the lower being a *sarcophagus, on which after burial a marble slab was placed horizontally, and the upper being an arch carved out to a depth equal to the width of this slab.

AREOPAGITE, The. A title sometimes applied to *Dionysius (6), the Pseudo-Areopagite.

AREOPAGUS, The ('Mars' Hill'). A spur of land not far from the western end of the Acropolis in Athens. The name was also applied to an oligarchical council which met on the hill. It is not clear whether, when St. *Paul was brought to the Areopagus to explain his teaching (Acts 17: 19), it was before the official court or whether the place was merely chosen as convenient for a meeting.

ARGENTINA, Christianity in. Argentina, originally a Spanish colony, gained its independence in 1816. The state religion has always been RC and the president of the republic must be of that faith.

ARIANISM. The principal heresy which denied the true Divinity of Christ, so called after its author *Arius. It maintained that the Son of God was not eternal but was created by the Father from nothing as an instrument for the creation of the world, and that therefore He was not God by nature but a changeable creature, His dignity as Son of God having been given Him by the Father on account of His foreseen righteousness. Though condemned in *Alexandria (c. 320), this teaching spread and continued to agitate the masses until *Constantine, anxious for peace in the Empire, called a General Council which met at *Nicaea in 325. The Council, largely under the leadership of *Athanasius, defined the Catholic faith in the coeternity and coequality of the Father and the Son; the famous term '*homoousios' was used to express their consubstantiality. Constantine at first supported the Nicene faith, but he soon wavered and recalled *Eusebius of Nicomedia and other bishops who had been exiled. After his death (337) Constantius, the new Emperor of the East, openly embraced Arianism, and various E. Councils accepted more or less Arian formulas. The Arians, however, split into three main groups: the extreme party, the '*Anomoeans', pressed the differences between the Father and the Son; the '*Homoeans' tried to avoid precision by simply affirming that the Son is similar to the Father 'according to the Scriptures'; the '*Semi-Arians' favoured the term 'homoiousios' as expressing both the similarity and the distinction between the first Two Persons of the Trinity. A Homoean formula was accepted by a double Council of E. and W. bishops who met at Seleucia and *Ariminum respectively in 359. This crowning victory of Arianism was the turning-point in its history, since it frightened the Semi-Arians into the ranks of orthodoxy. The death of Constantius in 361 deprived the Arians of their chief supporter. The final victory of orthodoxy came at the Council of *Constantinople in 381. After being driven from the Empire, Arianism retained a hold among the Teutonic tribes, which prevented their assimilation with their Catholic subjects when they overran most of the W. Empire and caused persecutions in Spain and N. Africa. The conversion of the Franks to Catholicism (496) was the prelude to the disappearance of Arianism.

ARIDITY. A term of *ascetic theology, denoting a state devoid of sensible fervour in which the soul finds it impossible, or at least very difficult, to produce the normal acts of prayer.

ARIMINUM AND SELEUCIA, Synods of. Two synods to which the Emp. Constantius summoned the Bishops of W. and E. respectively in 359 to deal with the *Arian dispute. Although the majority at Ariminum (Rimini) were orthodox, under imperial pressure they recanted their original decision and subscribed to an Arianizing Creed. This was also accepted at Seleucia.

ARISTEAS, Letter of. A Jewish pseudepigraphical letter; it contains a legend of how the LXX came to be miraculously written. Its composition has been variously dated between 200 B.C. and A.D.. 33.

ARISTIDES (2nd cent.) of Athens, Christian philosopher and *Apologist. In an 'Apology' presented either to the Emp. Hadrian in 124 or to Antoninus Pius (d. 161), Aristides sought to defend the existence of God, and to show that Christians had a fuller understanding of His nature than the barbarians, Greeks, or Jews, and that they alone live acc. to His precepts.

ARISTION (1st cent.). Acc. to *Papias (as reported by *Eusebius), he was a primary authority, with *John the Presbyter, for the traditions about the Lord.

ARISTO OF PELLA (c. 140), *Apologist. He apparently wrote a (lost) 'Disputation'; in it Jason, a baptized Jew, converted Papiscus, a fellow Jew, by proving the fulfilment of the Messianic prophecies in Christ.

ARISTOBULUS, St. In Rom. 16: 10 St. *Paul sent greetings to the 'household of Aristobulus'. Nothing further is certainly known. Acc. to a Spanish legend he became Bp. of Britonia in Spain. He has sometimes been identified with the Aristobulus who, acc. to the Gk. *menologies, was one of the seventy disciples (Lk. 10: 1), a brother of St. *Barnabas and father-in-law of St. *Peter.

ARISTOTLE (384–322 B.C.), Greek philosopher. He was a member of the group which gathered round *Plato in Athens. He was later tutor to the future Alexander the Great. On his return to Athens, though he did not completely sever his connection with the Academy, he opened a rival school at the Lyceum in 335.

Though he was a disciple of Plato, his philosophical position was very different. Whereas Plato set out from a world of 'ideas', Aristotle asserted that ideas exist only as expressed in the individual object. Thus he held that, so far from there being an idea 'tree' possessing existence in its own right, it is the union of the 'form' tree with 'matter' which makes the real individual tree. This view required a theory of causation to account for the conjunction of form and matter, and Aristotle was thus led to postulate a 'First Cause', though he did not hold this supreme cause to be personal in the Christian sense.

Aristotle's philosophy was regarded with suspicion in the early Church and again when his works were recovered through

Arabic translations and translated into Latin in the 12th cent. This hostility was dissipated when such competent Christian philosophers as *Albertus Magnus and *Thomas Aquinas built up their systems on an avowedly Aristotelian basis, which has been accepted by Latin theology in the W. ever since.

ARIUS (c. 250–c. 336), heresiarch. A priest in *Alexandria, c. 319 he came forward as a champion of subordinationist teaching about the Person of Christ; he was condemned by a Council at Alexandria and excommunicated. The General Council of *Nicaea (325) also condemned him. He spent some years in banishment but, owing to the influence at court of *Eusebius of Nicomedia, he was recalled from exile c. 334. He died suddenly in the streets of Constantinople. See also *Arianism*.

ARK. (1) The Ark which *Noah built to preserve life during the *Flood (q.v.).

(2) The Ark of the Covenant, the most sacred religious symbol of the Hebrew people and believed to represent the Presence of God. It was in the form of a wooden rectangular box, overlaid with gold inside and out. Acc. to the traditional accounts the Israelites carried the Ark from the time of the *Exodus (c. 13th cent. B.C.) into the land of *Canaan. In Solomon's *Temple its home was the 'Holy of Holies', which the *High Priest alone entered once a year. It was apparently captured when *Jerusalem fell in 587–586 B.C. and nothing further is known of its history.

The Christian Fathers interpreted the Ark of Noah as typifying the Church, the Ark of the Covenant as the symbol of the Lord.

ARLES, Synods of. Among the more important were those of: 314, summoned by *Constantine to deal with the *Donatist schism; 353, an *Arianizing Council; 1234, against the *Albigensian heresy; and 1263, which condemned the doctrines of *Joachim of Fiore.

ARMAGH. Archiepiscopal see in N. *Ireland. It was prob. founded by St. *Patrick, but little is known of its early history. Reforms were carried out in the 12th cent., but when Ireland passed under English domination in 1215 the see lost most of its independence. The first Protestant bishop was appointed in 1552. Henceforth there was

both a Protestant and a RC succession. Since the later Middle Ages the claims of primacy of the Abps. of Armagh have been contested by the Abps. of *Dublin, Catholic and Protestant.

ARMAGH, The Book of. An 8th–9th cent. vellum codex in *Trinity College, Dublin. It includes two lives of St. *Patrick, the life of St. *Martin of Tours by *Sulpicius Severus, and a complete non-Vulgate text of the Latin NT.

ARMENIA, Christianity in. The Armenians were converted by *Gregory the Illuminator, who was consecrated bishop in 294. In the early 5th cent. St. *Isaac the Great and St *Mesrob introduced reforms, and the Bible and liturgy were translated from Syriac into Armenian. The Armenians took no part in the *Monophysite troubles and were not represented at the Council of *Chalcedon (451), but about 50 years later, partly for political reasons, they repudiated that Council; the Armenian Church has since been reputed Monophysite. The Armenians have been persecuted by Persians, Arabs, Turks, and Russians. There was a period of independence for the medieval kingdom of Cilicia, or Little Armenia, from the end of the 12th cent. to 1375; during this time the people of Little Armenia were united with the RC Church. The Armenians sent representatives to the Council of *Florence (1438–9), which issued the instruction 'Pro Armenis' on the Sacraments. The decree of union, however, had few practical results. There are thought to be c. 2 million Armenian Christians, incl. c. 100,000 in communion with Rome.

ARMILL. One of the British *Coronation regalia. The word means a bracelet, but in the *Liber Regalis* and elsewhere it has been applied to a garment resembling a *stole and held to signify the quasi-priestly character of the anointed king. At the coronation of Queen Elizabeth II (1953) the use of armills in the form of bracelets was restored.

ARMINIANISM. Jacobus Arminius (Jakob Hermans or Harmens, 1560–1609) was a Dutch Reformed theologian, ordained in 1588. Study of the Epistle to the *Romans led him to doubt the Calvinistic doctrine of *predestination. In 1603 he was appointed professor at *Leyden and he was immediately drawn into controversy with F. *Gomar.

Arminian doctrines, formally set out in the *Remonstrance of 1610, were a theological reaction against the deterministic logic of *Calvinism. The Arminians insisted that the Divine sovereignty was compatible with a real free will in man; that Christ died for all men and not only for the elect; and that both the *Supralapsarian and the *Sublapsarian views of predestination were unbiblical. The Arminians were condemned at the Synod of *Dort (1618–19); many of them were banished and others persecuted. As representatives of a more liberal school of theology than the strict Calvinists, however, they exercised considerable influence on the formation of modern Protestant theology.

ARNAULD, ANTOINE (1612–94), French theologian and philosopher. From 1638 he was in touch with *Saint-Cyran and *Port-Royal, to which he retired in 1641. His book *De la fréquente communion* (1643), with its stress on the need for a thorough preparation for Communion and its emphasis on the right dispositions, did much to propagate *Jansenist principles among a wide public. From 1644 he was the acknowledged leader of the Jansenists. An attack on *Jesuit methods in the confessional led to his being censured by the *Sorbonne in 1656 and solemnly degraded; after the '*Peace of the Church' of 1668, he was restored to his position as Doctor. When the Jansenist controversy began to revive in 1679, he went to Holland, where he continued writing.

ARNAULD, JACQUELINE MARIE ANGÉLIQUE (1591–1661), 'Mère Angélique'. The sister of Antoine *Arnauld, she became Abbess of *Port-Royal in 1602. She shared without protest the relaxed discipline of the house until she was converted by a sermon in 1608. She promptly introduced drastic reforms. In 1625 she moved the community to a larger house in Paris. Though her sister Agnès was elected Abbess in 1630, she continued to exercise great influence. In the following years she came under the influence of *Saint-Cyran, under whom the community became an enthusiastic upholder of *Jansenist principles and practices.

ARNDT, JOHANN (1555–1621), *Lutheran theologian and mystical writer. He is chiefly remembered for his *Vier Bücher vom wahren Christentum* (1606); against the penal theory of the *Atonement, he dwelt on the work of Christ in the heart of man.

ARNOBIUS (d. *c.* 330), Christian Apologist. In his *Adversus Nationes* he defended the consonance of the Christian religion with the best pagan philosophy.

ARNOBIUS JUNIOR (5th cent.), African monk. He attacked St. *Augustine's doctrine of *grace, and wrote allegorizing commentaries on the Psalms, notes on the Gospels, and an anti-*Monophysite treatise. The *Praedestinatus* has sometimes been attributed to him.

ARNOLD OF BRESCIA (d. 1155), reformer. He taught that confession should be made not to a priest but by Christians to one another, that the sinfulness of a priest destroyed the value of the sacraments he administered, and that spiritual persons should not possess worldly goods or exercise secular power. St. *Bernard of Clairvaux secured the condemnation of his doctrines at the Council of *Sens in 1140. In 1145 he went to Rome; he supported the anti-papal party and was excommunicated. After the accession of the Emp. *Frederick Barbarossa, he was captured and executed.

ARNOLD, GOTTFRIED (1666–1714), German Protestant theologian and devotional writer. His main work, the *Unparteiische Kirchen- und Ketzer-Historie* (1699–1700), though less impartial than its title claims, is important as a history of Protestant mysticism and for its use of out-of-the-way documents. After 1701 he applied himself increasingly to pastoral work, and his writings of this period are devotional. He is also well known as a hymn-writer.

ARNOLD, THOMAS (1795–1842), Headmaster of Rugby from 1828 to 1841. He fostered a system of education based on a foundation of religious training, seeking to educate the sons of middle-class parents into a high sense of duty, of public service, and of the importance of personal character. He objected to the *Tractarians on the ground of their *ecclesiasticism.

ARNULF, St. (*c.* 580–before 655), Bp. of Metz. He rose to high position in the court of Austrasia, renouncing an early desire for a solitary life in order to undertake the duties of government. He was consecrated Bp. of Metz *c.* 614. He was eventually allowed to resign his see and retired to a deserted place for meditation and prayer. Before his consecration he was married; he was an ancestor of the Carolingian kings of France.

ARTEMON (also **Artemas**) (3rd cent.), *Adoptionist heretic. He taught that Christ was only a man, though He excelled the Prophets. His doctrine was attacked by the author of the '*Little Labyrinth'.

ARTICLES. See *Forty-Two Articles*; *Irish Aricles*; *Lambeth Articles*; *Organic Articles*; *Six Articles*; *Ten Articles*; *Thirty-Nine Articles*; *Twelve Articles*.

ARTOPHORION. In the E. Church the *tabernacle in which the Bl. Sacrament is reserved.

ARUNDEL, THOMAS (1353–1414), Abp. successively of *York and *Canterbury. He was a prominent politician, several times Chancellor of England. He strenuously opposed the *Lollards, holding a provincial council against them at Oxford in 1408.

ASAPH, St. (*fl.* 570), Welsh saint. Acc. to tradition, when St. *Kentigern returned to Scotland *c.* 570, Asaph succeeded him as head of the monastery of Llanelwy (later called *St. Asaph) and became the first bishop of the see.

ASBURY, FRANCIS (1745–1816). One of the two first *Methodist bishops in America. He was sent to America by J. *Wesley in 1771. When the American Methodists became a separate organization in 1784, he and Thomas Coke became joint superintendents.

ASCENSION OF CHRIST, The. The withdrawal of Christ into Heaven, witnessed by the Apostles. Lk. 24: 50–3 has been held to imply that the Ascension took place on the evening of the Resurrection, but acc. to Acts 1: 3 it occurred 40 days later. It marked the end of the post-Resurrection appearances and the exaltation of Christ to the heavenly life. Its theological implication consists in the fact that thereby Christ's human nature was taken into Heaven.

Ascension Day, kept on the 6th Thursday, i.e. the 40th day, after Easter, is one of the chief feasts in the Christian year.

ASCENSION OF ISAIAH. See *Isaiah, Ascension of.*

ASCENT OF MOUNT CARMEL, The. The earliest of the spiritual treatises of St. *John of the Cross (q.v.).

ASCETICAL THEOLOGY. The theological discipline which deals with the so-called 'ordinary' ways of Christian perfection, as distinct from *Mystical Theology, whose subject is the 'extraordinary' or passive ways of the spiritual life. It is thus the science of Christian perfection in so far as this is accessible to human effort aided by grace. It also treats of the means to be employed and the dangers to be avoided if the end of the Christian life is to be attained.

ASCETICISM. The word denotes a system of practices designed to combat vices and develop virtues by means of self-discipline, such as are found in many religions. In the NT there are repeated exhortations to self-denial. The theoretical foundation of Christian asceticism was developed by *Clement of Alexandria and *Origen. Taking over from the *Stoics the idea of ascetic action as a purification of the soul from its passions, they saw in it a necessary means of loving God more perfectly and for attaining to contemplation. In the 3rd cent. the ascetic ideal as a way of life spread through Christendom, leading to the age of the Desert Fathers and the beginnings of *monasticism in the 4th cent. The monks in both East and West, and later the *Mendicant Orders, became the leading representatives of asceticism. At the end of the Middle Ages there was a reaction against the ascetic ideal, esp. among the Protestant Reformers, whose doctrine of the total depravity of man and of *justification by faith alone undercut the theological foundation of ascetic practices. The ascetic ideal was, however, upheld in the RC Church of the *Counter-Reformation and later. It also played an important part in *Methodism and among the *Tractarians and their successors.

Acc. to its classical Christian exponents asceticism is a necessary means of fighting the concupiscence of the flesh; it is also of value as an imitation of the sacrificial life of Christ and as a means of expiation of one's own sins and those of others. It springs from the love of God and aims at overcoming all the obstacles to this love in the soul.

ASH WEDNESDAY. The first day of *Lent. At one time public penitents were ceremoniously admitted to begin their *penance on this day; when this discipline was dropped, the general penance of the congregation took its place. This was symbolized by the imposition of ashes on the heads of clergy and people, a rite still ordered in the Roman Missal.

ASKE, ROBERT (d. 1537), leader of the '*Pilgrimage of Grace'. In 1536 he put himself at the head of the 'Pilgrimage' when rebellion broke out in Yorkshire. After treating with the royal leaders, in 1537 he returned northward with a safe-conduct from *Henry VIII and a promise of the redress of grievances. After a fresh outbreak of violence Aske was seized, condemned for treason, and hanged in chains.

ASKEW, ANNE (1521–46), Protestant martyr. In 1545 she came under suspicion of heresy because of her beliefs about the Eucharist. She was examined, refused to recant, and was burnt at *Smithfield.

ASPERGES. In the W. Church the ceremony of sprinkling *holy water over the altar and people during the principal Mass on Sundays.

ASPERSION. The method of *baptism whereby the candidate is merely sprinkled with the baptismal water. It is held to be permissible only in exceptional cases.

ASPIRANT. One who aspires to a vocation to the *religious life.

ASSEMANI (Syriac, 'Simon'). The family name of four *Maronite Orientalists: (1) **Joseph Simonius** (1687–1768), who was Prefect of the *Vatican Library and Abp. of Tyre. His chief work, the *Bibliotheca Orientalis* (1719–28), is a collection of *Syriac documents, mainly on the history of the Churches of Syria, Chaldaea, and Egypt. (2) **Stephen Evodius** (1707–82), his nephew. He catalogued various collections of Oriental MSS. (3) **Joseph Aloysius** (1710–82). His relationship is not clear. He edited the *Codex Liturgicus Ecclesiae Universae* (1749–66), a valuable collection of material

on the E. liturgies. (4) **Simon** (1752–1821), grand-nephew of Joseph Simonius. He published works on Arabic subjects.

ASSEMBLIES OF GOD. The name taken by many national groupings of individual *Pentecostal Churches. These organizations, though loosely affiliated, are autonomous; they vary in structure from country to country. The earliest was formed in the U.S.A. in 1914.

ASSEMBLIES OF THE FRENCH CLERGY. The quinquennial meetings of representatives of the Catholic clergy which from the end of the 16th cent. were an established institution in France. They lasted until the Revolution (1789) and exercised considerable influence.

ASSENT, Declaration of. The declaration of assent to the BCP, the *Ordinal, and the *Thirty-Nine Articles imposed on the clergy of the C of E at ordination and on entering certain ecclesiastical offices. It replaced a more detailed subscription required until 1865 and was itself made less rigid in form in 1975.

ASSISI. A city in the Umbrian Hills, famous as the birthplace of St. *Francis. The remains of St. Francis and St. *Clare rest in two of its *basilicas, and the *Portiuncula chapel is c. 2 miles away.

ASSOCIATIONS, Law of. The French law of 1901, acc. to which no new religious congregation could be formed without authorization from the State, and congregations recognized in the past were subject to various restrictions. In 1902 congregations were forbidden to carry on any educational activity. The men's orders went into exile and most of the women's orders became nursing congregations. The final consequence of this legislation was the complete break between Church and State in France in 1905.

ASSUMPTION OF THE BVM, The. The belief that the BVM, 'having completed her earthly life, was in body and soul assumed into heavenly glory' (definition, 1950). The belief was unknown in the early Church; it first appears in certain NT apocrypha dating from the 4th cent. The doctrine was formulated in orthodox circles in the West by *Gregory of Tours (d. 594); it seems to have been widely known by the end of the 7th cent. and it was defended by various of the *Schoolmen. In 1950 *Pius XII defined the doctrine. In the E. Church belief in the corporal assumption is general, though in less precise terms than those of the RC definition.

The date on which the feast of the Assumption is celebrated (15 Aug.) is prob. connected with the dedication of some church to the BVM. In the C of E the feast disappeared from the BCP in 1549, but it is now observed in some places.

ASSUMPTION OF MOSES. See *Moses, Assumption of.*

ASSUMPTIONISTS (Augustinians of the Assumption). A religious congregation founded at Nîmes in 1843 for the active religious life. Its members follow a modification of the *Augustinian rule. Their work includes the care of schools and colleges, the dissemination of literature, and missionary work.

ASSYRIAN CHRISTIANS. A small group of Christians of *Nestorian sympathy, so called because of their supposed descent from the Assyrians of Nineveh. Acc. to tradition they were converted by St. *Thomas, but the earliest certainly known fact is the protection they afforded to Nestorius after his condemnation at the Council of *Ephesus (431). After the Muslim invasions of the Middle East they survived in the mountains of N. Kurdistan. In 1885 the Abp. of Canterbury, E. W. *Benson, sent a mission to assist them in educational and other ways. Driven out of Kurdistan in the 20th cent., they live mainly in Syria, Iraq, Lebanon, and the U.S.A.

ASTERISCUS. A utensil placed over the blessed bread during the Byzantine Liturgy to keep it from contact with the veil that covers it.

ASTERIUS (d. after 341), the 'Sophist', *Arian theologian. He was present at the Council of *Antioch of 341. Fragments of his *Syntagmation* are preserved by St. *Athanasius and *Marcellus of Ancyra, and portions of his commentaries and homilies on the Psalms have recently been recovered.

ASTRUC, JEAN (1684–1766), physician and Pentateuchal critic. In his (anonymous) *Conjectures sur les Mémoires originaux dont il paroît que Moyse s'est servi pour composer le Livre de la Genèse* (1753) he maintained that in its present form the Book of *Genesis was a piecing together of earlier documents.

ASYLUM, Right of. See *Sanctuary.*

ATHANASIAN CREED, The. A profession of faith which has been widely used in W. Christendom. It expounds the doctrines of the *Trinity and *Incarnation, adding a list of the most important events in the Lord's life; it includes *anathemas against those who do not believe its affirmations. The attribution to St. *Athanasius has been generally abandoned, chiefly on the ground that it contains doctrinal expressions which arose only in later controversies. The recitation of the Athanasian Creed is ordered on certain occasions in the Roman *Breviary and in the BCP. Since 1867 there have been various attempts in the C of E to have it removed or truncated, and its use in Anglican churches has become rare.

ATHANASIUS, St. (c. 296–373), Bp. of *Alexandria. He was secretary to *Alexander, Bp. of Alexandria, and accompanied him to the Council of *Nicaea (325), succeeding him as bishop in 328. He incurred the enmity of the powerful *Arianizing party, who secured his exile from Alexandria on a number of occasions between 336 and 366. He then helped to build up the new Nicene party by whose support orthodoxy triumphed over Arianism at the Council of *Constantinople in 381.

In his famous (and prob. early) *De Incarnatione*, he expounds how God the Word, by His union with mankind, restored to fallen man the image of God, and by His death and resurrection met and overcame death. As bishop he was the greatest and most consistent theological opponent of Arianism. Between 339 and 359 he wrote a series of works in defence of the true Divinity of the Son. From c. 361 he worked to reconcile the *Semi-Arians to the Nicene term '*homoousios' ('of one substance'). He was also concerned to uphold the Divinity of the Holy Spirit and the full manhood of Christ against *Macedonian and *Apollinarian tendencies. As the friend of *Pachomius and *Serapion, and the biographer of *Antony, he aided the ascetic movement in Egypt and was the first to introduce knowledge of monasticism to the West.

ATHANASIUS, St. (*c.* 920–1003), the Athonite. He became a monk in Bithynia but migrated to Mount *Athos, where he established the first of its famous monasteries (961). He became Abbot-General of the communities on the Mount, of which 58 existed when he died.

ATHEISM. Disbelief in the existence of God. Until the word '*agnosticism' came into general use in the 19th cent., 'atheism' was at least popularly used to describe the position of those who thought the existence of God an unprovable thesis. Modern nontheists are usually either 'logical positivists', who hold that since assertions about God are not capable of empirical verification they are meaningless, or materialists, whose atheism is often practical rather than speculative. The Dialectical Materialism of Communism is, however, consciously and avowedly atheist.

ATHENAGORAS (2nd cent.), *Apologist. His 'Apology' or 'Supplication', addressed *c.* 177 to *Marcus Aurelius and his son, sought to rebut the current calumnies against the Christians, viz. *atheism, Thyestian banquets, and Oedipean incest. A treatise 'On the Resurrection' is also ascribed to him, though this attribution has been challenged.

ATHENAGORAS (1886–1972), Patr. of *Constantinople from 1948. His attempts to secure closer co-operation between the Churches of the *Orthodox communion bore fruit in the Panorthodox Conferences which met on his initiative in Rhodes in 1961 and the following years. In the field of ecumenical relations his most striking achievements were his meeting with Pope *Paul VI in Jerusalem in 1964 and the revocation of the anathemas between the RC and Orthodox Churches in 1965.

ATHENS. The city, which was important for its schools of philosophy, was visited by St. *Paul, but his preaching seems to have met with little response (Acts 17: 15–18: 1). There was a Christian community in Athens in the 2nd cent. It appears to have been one of the earliest centres of a philosophical interpretation of Christianity, though its schools were closed by *Justinian in 529 for

their support of paganism. See also *Greece, Christianity in.*

ATHOS, Mount. The peninsula off the coast of Greece which terminates in Mount Athos has long been the property of the monasteries of the E. *Orthodox Church. The first settlement was the *Lavra founded by *Athanasius the Athonite in 961. There are now 20 virtually independent monasteries, though matters of common concern are settled by a council. No women or female animals are allowed on the peninsula.

ATONEMENT ('at-one-ment'). In Christian theology, man's reconciliation with God through the sacrificial death of Christ.

The need for such reconciliation is implicit in the OT conception of God's absolute righteousness; its achievement is represented as dependent on an act of God Himself, whether by the appointment of a sacrificial system by which uncleanness might be purged, or by the giving of a new covenant. Christ spoke of giving His life 'a ransom for many' (Mk. 10: 45), and in the earliest Christian teaching His death is proclaimed to be 'for our sins' (1 Cor. 15: 3).

The Fathers posed questions which did not come within the purview of the Biblical writers. For *Origen the death of Christ was the ransom paid to Satan, who had acquired rights over man by the *Fall. Others, notably St. *Athanasius, held that God the Son, by taking our nature upon Him, had effected a change in human nature as such. The general patristic teaching is that Christ is our representative rather than our substitute and that the effect of His suffering, obedience, and resurrection extends to the whole of humanity and beyond. In the 11th–12th cents., with *Anselm's *Cur Deus Homo, the emphasis shifted. The role of Satan receded and its place was taken by the idea of satisfaction due to God for sin. The death of Christ was then seen not as a ransom paid to the devil but as a debt paid to the Father. At the *Reformation M. *Luther rejected the satisfaction theory and taught that Christ, in bearing by voluntary substitution the punishment due to man, was reckoned by God a sinner in man's place. J. *Calvin went further, holding that Christ 'bore in His soul the tortures of a condemned and ruined man'. In reaction against the exaggerations of this 'penal theory' arose the doctrine, defended by the *Socinians, which denied the objective efficacy of the Crucifixion and looked upon the death of Christ primarily as an example to His followers. There has been no official formulation in orthodox Christianity on the mystery of the Atonement.

ATONEMENT, Day of. The annual Jewish festival designed to cleanse the people from sin and to re-establish good relations with God. Much of the ritual ordered in the OT, such as the entry of the *High Priest into the Holy of Holies in the *Temple, has necessarily lapsed, but the day is still widely observed by Jews with fasting and prayer. Its Hebrew name is 'Yom Kippur'.

ATRIUM. The main court in a Roman house. The word is also used of the forecourt attached to early Christian churches, which usually consisted of a colonnaded quadrangle with a fountain in the middle.

ATTERBURY, FRANCIS (1662–1732), Bp. of *Rochester, 1713–23. In his (anonymous) *Letter of a Convocation Man* (1697) and his *Rights and Privileges of an English Convocation* (1700) he was the champion of *Convocation against the Crown and of the inferior clergy against the bishops. In 1723 he was deprived of office and exiled for alleged complicity in a Jacobite plot.

ATTICUS (d. 425), Patr. of *Constantinople. He was a bitter opponent of St. John *Chrysostom, and in 405 he succeeded Arsacius, who had held the see after Chrysostom's expulsion. After Chrysostom's death (407) he made concessions to his supporters and readmitted his name to the *diptychs. He obtained from *Theodosius II a rescript extending the authority of his see over the whole of Illyria and the 'Provincia Orientalis'.

ATTILA (d. 453), King of the Huns from 433. He invaded Gaul in 451 and Italy the next year. At the prayers of *Leo I he desisted from trying to capture Rome. In Christian legend he is known from his savagery as the 'Scourge of God', i.e. a minister of Divine vengeance.

ATTO (*c.* 885–961), Bp. of Vercelli from 924. His writings, which are of remarkable erudition, include a commentary on the Pauline Epp. and a collection of ecclesiastical canons.

ATTRITION. The sorrow for sin which proceeds from the fear of punishment or a sense of the ugliness of sin. It is contrasted with *contrition, which is held to proceed from the love of God.

AUBIGNÉ, J. H. M. d'. See *Merle d'Aubigné, J. H.*

AUBURN DECLARATION, The. A statement of the principal doctrines of the American *Presbyterians of the 'New School' which was accepted at Auburn, New York State, in 1837, and made the theological basis on which the 'New School' was organized as a separate body.

AUCTOREM FIDEI (1794). The papal bull which condemned 85 articles of the Synod of *Pistoia (1786).

AUDIANI. A 4th-cent. rigorist sect, founded by Audius; it separated from the Church on the ground that the clergy were too secularized.

AUDIENCE, Court of. Formerly an ecclesiastical court of the Province of *Canterbury in which the Archbishop exercised his *legatine authority. In the 17th cent. it was merged in the Court of *Arches.

AUDIENCES, Pontifical. Receptions given by the Pope to visitors to Rome and officials having business with the Holy See.

AUDIENTES (Lat., 'hearers'). In the early Church, those who belonged to the first stage of the *catechumenate.

AUDREY, St. See *Etheldreda, St.*

AUFKLÄRUNG (Germ., 'Enlightenment'). A movement of thought which appeared in an esp. clear-cut form in 18th-cent. Germany. It combined opposition to all supernatural religion and belief in the all-sufficiency of human reason with an ardent desire to promote the happiness of man in this life. One of its ideals was religious toleration. See also *Enlightenment*.

AUGSBURG, The Confession of (1530). The *Lutheran confession of faith presented to the Emp. *Charles V at the Diet of Augsburg in 1530. Its language is studiously moderate. The first part epitomizes the essential Lutheran doctrines; the second reviews abuses for which remedy is sought.

The original text of the Confession (the so-called 'Invariata') remains a standard of faith in Lutheran Churches. A revised text issued by P. *Melanchthon in 1540 (the 'Variata') is accepted by the Reformed (Calvinist) Churches in some parts of Germany.

AUGSBURG, The Interim of. The doctrinal formula accepted at the Diet of Augsburg in 1548 as the provisional basis of a religious settlement between Catholics and Protestants; it was intended to last until the Council of *Trent reached a final settlement. The main concessions to the Protestants were clerical marriage and *communion in both kinds.

AUGSBURG, Peace of (1555). The settlement of religious affairs in the German Empire reached between Ferdinand I and the Electors at Augsburg in 1555. It recognized the existence of Catholicism and Lutheranism (but not Calvinism), providing that in each land subjects should follow the religion of their rulers.

AUGUSTINE, St., of Canterbury (d. 604/5), first Abp. of *Canterbury. Sent from Rome by *Gregory I, Augustine landed in Kent in 597; within a few months Christianity was formally adopted by *Ethelbert, King of Kent, whose wife was already a Christian. About 603 Augustine tried, unsuccessfully, to reach an agreement with representatives of the *Celtic Church in Britain on differences in discipline and practice. Prob. in 604 he sent *Justus to preach west of the R. Medway and *Mellitus to work among the East Saxons.

AUGUSTINE, St., of Hippo (354–430), Bp. of Hippo Regius and '*Doctor of the Church'. He was born in N. Africa, of a pagan father and a Christian mother (St. *Monica). At Carthage he abandoned what Christianity he had and took a mistress, to whom he remained faithful for 15 years. In 374 he adopted *Manichaeism, with which he became disillusioned in 383. He migrated first to Rome, where he opened a school of rhetoric, and then to Milan. Here he came under the influence of St. *Ambrose. He became a *Neoplatonist and gradually drew nearer to Christianity, being finally convinced after a glance at Rom. 13: 13 f., in response to a Divine oracle ('Tolle lege'). He was eventually baptized in 387. He returned to Africa in 388 and established a kind of monastery at Tagaste. On a visit to Hippo he was seized by the people and presented to the bishop for ordination. In 395 he was consecrated coadjutor bishop to Valerius and from c. 396 presided as sole bishop of the see.

As bishop, Augustine was called upon to deal with three major heresies, and it was mainly through his struggle with them that his own theology was formulated. Against the Manichaean attempt to solve the problem of evil by posing the existence of an evil agency eternally opposed to the good God, he defended the essential goodness of all creation. God, he maintained, was the sole creator of all things and evil is, properly speaking, the privation of some good that ought to be had. In the case of physical evil this results from the imperfect character of creatures; in the case of moral evil it springs from free will. The *Donatist controversy forced him to carry the doctrines of the Church, the *Sacraments, and sacramental grace to a stage beyond that reached by any of his predecessors. The Church was 'one' through the mutual charity of her members and 'holy' because her purposes, not her members, are holy. She contains within her fold both good men and evil. His teachings also fostered the distinction between 'validity' and 'regularity' in the administration of the Sacraments. His later years were largely taken up with the *Pelagian controversy, which evoked his teaching on the *Fall, *Original Sin, and *Predestination. He held that man was created with certain supernatural gifts which were lost by the Fall of Adam. As a result man suffers from a hereditary moral disease, and is also subject to the inherited legal liability for Adam's sin; from these evils we can be saved only by God's grace. At times Augustine shows himself to be frankly predestinarian, and this side of his teaching exercised a strong influence on J. *Calvin and some of the other Reformers.

As a result of these controversies, much of Augustine's writing was polemical in form. Of his other works the two most celebrated are the *Confessions (q.v.) and the City of God, the latter occasioned by the fall of Rome to *Alaric in 410. Conceived as a reply to the pagans who attributed the fall of the city to the abolition of heathen worship, it dealt with the fundamental contrast between Christianity and the world. His other writings include a philosophical treatise *De Trinitate*, letters, sermons, philosophical dialogues, and the *Retractations* in which, shortly before his death, he reviewed his literary work. His influence on subsequent W. theology has been immense.

AUGUSTINE OF HIPPO, Rule of St. This consists of two parts: a short introductory prologue laying down certain precise monastic observances and a longer and more general consideration of the common life. It was prob. drawn up by one of St. *Augustine's followers, possibly during his life and with his co-operation. It has been adopted by various monastic bodies, incl. the *Augustinian Canons and the *Dominicans.

AUGUSTINIAN CANONS, also known as Austin or Regular Canons. In the middle decades of the 11th cent. various communities of clerics in N. Italy and S. France sought to live a common life of poverty, celibacy, and obedience. Their way of life was approved at *Lateran synods in 1059 and 1063. By the early 12th cent. members of these communities, which had spread throughout W. Europe, came to be known as 'Regular Canons'; they had also generally adopted the Rule of St. *Augustine. A regular canon thus became synonymous with an Augustinian canon, i.e. one who follows the Rule of St. Augustine. Independent Augustinian congregations were also founded, incl. the *Victorines and *Premonstratensians.

AUGUSTINIAN HERMITS or FRIARS. A religious order formed of several Italian congregations of hermits which, in the interests of ecclesiastical efficiency, were banded together under the Rule of St. *Augustine by Pope Alexander IV in 1256, with a constitution modelled on that of the *Dominicans. It was to a congregation of this order that M. *Luther belonged. See also *Recollects*.

AUGUSTINIANS OF THE ASSUMPTION. See *Assumptionists*.

'AUGUSTINUS'. The title of the treatise by C. *Jansen (d. 1638) on grace and human nature, published in 1640. See also *Jansenism*.

AULÉN, GUSTAV (1879–1978), Bp. of Strängnäs, 1933–52. With A. Nygren he was a leader of the *Motivsforschung* school, which seeks to see the essential truth behind a doctrine rather than to stress the form in which it is presented. Many of his books have been translated into English.

AUMBRY. A recess in the wall of a church or sacristy in which in medieval times sacred vessels, books, and occasionally the reserved Sacrament were kept.

AURELIUS, St. (d. *c*. 430), Bp. of Carthage from *c*. 391. He presided over a number of Councils and was held in honour by St. *Augustine.

AUREOLE. In sacred pictures, the background of gold which sometimes surrounds a figure, as distinct from the 'nimbus' (or *halo) which covers only the head.

AURICULAR CONFESSION. Confession of sins to God in the hearing of a priest. See also *Penance*.

AUSONIUS (*c*. 310–*c*. 395), Roman poet. Decimus Magnus Ausonius became tutor to the future Emp. Gratian, who in 379 raised him to the consulship. Some of his poems suggest that he made some profession of Christianity. He wrote to *Paulinus of Nola (in verse), trying to dissuade him from becoming a monk.

AUSTIN. An older English form of '*Augustine'.

AUSTRALIA, Christianity in. A C of E chaplain sailed with the first convict fleet, which reached Australia in 1788. By 1820 RC priests were also employed. *Wesleyan ministry started in 1815 and *Presbyterian in 1823. It is disputed whether the C of E was ever legally established in Australia. For some years it received special grants of land for building churches and schools in New South Wales and Tasmania; after 1836–7 general subsidies were shared between the main denominations. By the 1870s religion was no longer state-aided and in state schools religious teaching was undenominational.

The Methodists and Presbyterians were the first to establish autonomous Australian institutions. The RC Church was predominantly Irish and was closely associated with the Australian Labour Party. The C of E tended to be upper-class and dependent upon England; it became autonomous in 1962. Australian Churches have been chiefly responsible for missionary work in Papua, New Guinea, and parts of Melanesia, and there are Aboriginal mission stations dating from the 1820s.

AUTHORITY. Christianity claims authority because it is based on truths revealed by God; for Christians the revelation given through Christ is final and His teaching has absolute authority.

Catholics hold that this teaching, handed on by the Church through Scripture and *tradition, has authority for the further reason that the Church is divinely guided by the Holy Spirit; RCs hold that one of the organs of this authority is the Pope in his *ex cathedra* statements. Protestants have generally confined this authority to the Bible, guaranteed by its appeal to the individual conscience rather than by the consent of the Church.

AUTHORIZED VERSION OF THE BIBLE. See *Bible, English Versions* (3).

AUTO-DA-FÉ. (Portug., 'act of faith'). The ceremony of the Spanish *Inquisition at which, after a Procession, Mass, and Sermon, sentences were read and executed. Those sentenced to death were handed over to the secular power to be burnt at the stake.

AUTO SACRAMENTAL. Spanish religious plays, somewhat analogous to the English *morality plays. They date from medieval times, but their classical period was the 15th–16th cents., when they were always associated with the feast of *Corpus Christi; in their later development they took the form of allegorical treatments of the mystery of the Eucharist. They were prohibited in 1765.

AUTOCEPHALOUS. The term was used in the early Church of bishops who were independent of both *Metropolitan and *Patriarch, and of those directly dependent on the Patriarch without intermediate reference to the Metropolitan. It is currently used of those national Churches of the E. Orthodox Church which are governed by their own synods.

AUXENTIUS (d. 373/4), Bp. of Milan from 355. He was one of the most prominent supporters of *Arianism in the West. Despite condemnations for heresy at *Ariminum (359), Paris (360), and Rome (372), he remained in possession of his see until his death.

AUXILIARY SAINTS (Lat., *auxilium*, 'assistance'). A group of 14 saints venerated for the supposed efficacy of their prayers on behalf of human necessities.

AVANCINI, NIKOLA (1611–86), *Jesuit ascetic writer and theologian. He wrote extensively, and his *De Vita et Doctrina Jesu Christi ex Quattuor Evangelistis Collecta* (1665), a collection of terse and pithy meditations, was translated into many languages and widely used.

AVE MARIA. The Latin form of 'Hail Mary' (q.v.).

AVE MARIS STELLA. A popular Marian hymn, dating at least from the 9th cent. It has been attributed to various authors, incl. *Paul the Deacon. One Eng. tr. begins 'Hail Thou Star of Ocean'.

AVE VERUM CORPUS. A short anonymous Eucharistic hymn, prob. dating from the 14th cent. A common Eng. tr. begins 'Jesu, Word of God Incarnate'.

AVERROISM. Averroes (Ibn Rushd, 1126–98) came of a good Muslim family at Cordova in Spain and until 1195 he was in favour at the court of the Caliph. His fame rests on his commentaries on *Aristotle. Acc. to Averroes God, the Prime Mover, is completely separated from the world, while the celestial spheres are intelligences emanating from God in a descendent series until they reach man. He also taught the eternity and potentiality of matter and the unity of the human intellect, i.e. that only one intellect exists for the whole race, in which every individual participates, to the exclusion of personal immortality.

The theories of Averroes became known in Catholic Europe c. 1230, but they were not immediately understood. In 1256 Pope Alexander IV instructed *Albert the Great to investigate Averroes's teaching on the unity of the intellect. In Paris *Siger of Brabant expounded Averroist theories which were attacked by St. *Thomas Aquinas, and in 1270 the Bp. of Paris condemned 13 errors arising from Averroist teaching. Averroism ceased to be taught in the University of Paris, though it infiltrated again in the 14th cent. and survived in Italy until the Renaissance.

AVESTA. The Sacred Books of the *Zoroastrians which set forth the theology and religious system of the ancient Persians. The work was put together under Shapur II (310–79), when it reached substantially its present form. The short portion known as the Gathas may go back to Zoroaster himself.

AVICEBRON (*c.* 1020–*c.* 1070). The name commonly given to the Spanish Jewish philosopher Salomon ben Gabirol. His system was in essence *pantheistic, and St. *Thomas Aquinas wrote against him. His chief treatise, the *Fons Vitae*, was an Arabic work in dialogue form, which in a Latin translation became very popular in the Middle Ages.

AVICENNA (980–1037), Arabian philosopher. He held that there was a hierarchy of emanations from the Godhead which mediate between God and man. He distinguished between necessary and contingent being, holding that God was necessary and the universe contingent; but between the two he set the world of ideas, which he held to be necessary, though not of itself but because God had made it so. He exercised great

influence on the early *Schoolmen.

AVIGNON. From 1309 to 1377 Avignon was the residence (see *Babylonian Captivity*) of the Popes, though it did not become papal property until 1348, when Clement VI bought it from the Queen of Naples.

AVITUS, St. (d. *c.* 519), Bp. of Vienne from *c.* 490. Of Roman senatorial family, as bishop he exercised an enduring influence on the ecclesiastical life of Burgundy and won the *Arian King Sigismund to the acceptance of Catholic orthodoxy.

AXUM, also **Aksum.** The ancient religious and political capital of *Ethiopia. Christianity was established here in the 4th cent.

AYLIFFE, JOHN (1676–1732), English jurist. His *Parergon Iuris Canonici Anglicani* (1726), arranged alphabetically, remains a treatise of high authority.

AYTON, JOHN (d. before 1350), or **Acton,** English canonist. He wrote a commentary on the constitutions of the Papal legates Otto and Ottobon which was printed in the 1496 and later editions of W. *Lyndwood's *Provinciale*.

AZYMITES. The name given to the W. Church by the Easterns at the time of the schism of 1054, with reference to their use in the Eucharist of unleavened bread which, on the E. view, invalidated the rite. See also *Bread, Leavened and Unleavened.*

B

BAAL. The word was used esp. of the Semitic deities who were held to produce agricultural and animal fertility. The Hebrew Prophets had constantly to resist attempts to fuse the worship of *Yahweh with that of the local Baalim.

BABEL, Tower of. Acc. to Gen. 11: 1–9, the tower reaching to heaven, the presumptuous construction of which was frustrated by God through confusion of languages among its builders.

BABYLAS, St. (d. *c.* 250), Bp. of *Antioch from *c.* 240. Acc. to John *Chrysostom he refused an emperor (prob. *Philip the Arabian) access to a church on the ground of an unrepented crime. He was imprisoned in the *Decian persecution and died in bonds.

BABYLONIAN CAPTIVITY. The captivity in Babylon, whither the Jews were deported in two batches in 597 and 586 B.C. The expression was used metaphorically of the exile of the Popes at *Avignon from

1309 to 1377.

BACH, JOHANN SEBASTIAN (1685–1750), German composer. He was cantor at the Thomas school at Leipzig from 1723 until his death. His chief religious works belong to this period, notably the two great Passions acc. to St. Matthew and St. John and the Mass in B minor. The music was originally designed for use at Protestant services, but is now performed almost exclusively outside Divine worship. Of his other choral works the 'Magnificat' and 'Christmas Oratorio' are the most famous.

BACON, FRANCIS (1561–1626), philosopher, essayist, and lawyer. He won the favour of *James I and held various appointments, in 1618 becoming Lord Chancellor and Viscount St. Albans. He was disgraced in 1621 and retired into private life. His idea, that by inductions from the simplest facts of experience man can reach to fundamental principles, attracted much attention among his contemporaries. He issued his *Essays* with additions in each new edition (1597, 1612, 1625); that on 'Atheism' first appeared in 1612.

BACON, ROGER (c. 1214–c. 1292), 'Doctor mirabilis', English philosopher. His earliest writings are a series of *quaestiones* on works attributed to *Aristotle; they are among the earliest lectures on these books. He entered the *Franciscan Order c. 1257. In the Franciscan convent at Paris he had the chance to expound his ideas on the defects of theological education to a priest who in 1265 became Pope Clement IV. The Pope bade him dispatch to Rome an account of his doctrines, in the mistaken belief that they were already in writing. Bacon set to work and in 1267 sent the Pope an encyclopaedic work known as the *Opus maius*, in seven parts: causes which have hindered the progress of philosophy among the Latins, the services that philosophy can render to theology, the importance of the study of languages for a proper understanding of the text of the Bible, mathematics, optics, experimental sciences, and moral philosophy. Two shorter works, the *Opus minus* and *Opus tertium*, were partly synopses and partly elaborations of the *Opus maius*. The death of Clement IV in 1268 ended any hope of papal commendation of his ideas. He wrote later works on philosophy, mathematics, and theology. In 1277 he is said to have been condemned by the General of the Franciscan Order for 'suspect novelties' and 'dangerous doctrines' and imprisoned for a time. The background of the condemnation is not known.

BAEUMER, S. See *Bäumer, S.*

BAGOT, RICHARD (1782–1854), successively Bp. of *Oxford and of *Bath and Wells. At Oxford (1829–45) he induced J. H. *Newman to cease publication of the tracts but in 1842 he defended the *Tractarians while denouncing their 'lamentable want of judgement'. The closing months of his life were taken up with a controversy with G. A. *Denison on Eucharistic doctrine.

BAINBRIDGE, CHRISTOPHER (c. 1464–1514), Abp. of *York from 1508. *Henry VIII sent him to Rome as ambassador in 1509. In 1511 *Julius II, having made him a cardinal, entrusted to him a military expedition against Ferrara. He died of poison administered by one of his chaplains. He was a courageous defender of English interests at the Curia.

BAIRD LECTURES. A series of lectures delivered annually at Glasgow on the benefaction of James Baird (1802–76) for the defence of orthodox *Presbyterian teaching. The lecturer must be a minister of the Church of *Scotland.

BAIUS, MICHEL (1513–89), Flemish theologian. Despite an earlier censure by the *Sorbonne, he was one of the representatives of the University of Louvain at the Council of *Trent. A papal bull of 1567 condemned a number of propositions from his writings without mentioning him by name. He later made a formal recantation.

The main principles of 'Baianism' were: (1) that in the primitive state innocence was not a supernatural gift of God to man but the necessary complement of human nature itself; (2) that *original sin is not merely a privation of grace but habitual *concupiscence, transmitted by heredity, and so even in unconscious children is a sin or moral evil of itself; and (3) that the sole work of *redemption is to enable us to recover the gifts of original innocence and live moral lives; this end is achieved by the substitution of charity for concupiscence as the motive for each meritorious act. The grace conferred by redemption is thus not considered to be supernatural.

BAKER, AUGUSTINE (1575–1641), *Benedictine writer. *Sancta Sophia, or Holy Wisdom* (1657) is a posthumous collection of his ascetical writings; it expounds the way of contemplation. He also wrote on the history of the Benedictine Order in England.

BAKER, SIR HENRY WILLIAMS, Bart. (1821–77), hymn-writer. From 1851 he was Vicar of Monkland, near Leominster. His many hymns include 'The King of Love my Shepherd is' and 'Lord, Thy Word abideth'. He was the promoter and compiler of the orginal edition of *Hymns, Ancient and Modern* (1861).

BALDACHINO. A canopy used to cover an altar, also called **Umbraculum** or **Ciborium**. It may be made of wood, stone, or metal, in which case it is supported on pillars, or of silk or velvet, when it is suspended from the ceiling or attached to the wall. The word is also used for the canopy over a bishop's throne, over statues, and of the movable canopy carried in processions, e.g. of the Bl. Sacrament.

BALDWIN (d. 1190), Abp. of *Canterbury. A *Cistercian monk, he became Bp. of *Worcester in 1180. His election to Canterbury in 1184 was contested by the monks of Christ Church, who disliked his austere ideals. He took part in a *Crusade in 1190 and bequeathed his fortune to the liberation of the Holy Land. He was the first Abp. of Canterbury to secure the supremacy of the see over *Wales.

BALE, JOHN (1495–1563), Bp. of Ossory from 1552. Much controversy was aroused in Ireland by his refusal to be consecrated by the Roman rite and his insistence on the use of the BCP. He left Ireland soon after *Mary's accession. His *Illustrium Majoris Britanniae Scriptorum, hoc est, Angliae Cambriae ac Scotiae Summarium* (1548–9) is an indispensable catalogue of British authors and their writings, though often inaccurate and biased.

BALFOUR, ARTHUR JAMES (1848–1930), British statesman and philosopher. His *Defence of Philosophic Doubt* (1879), despite its title, endeavours to show that the ultimate convictions of mankind rest on the non-rational ground of religious faith. His *Foundations of Belief* (1895) attracted wide attention in view of the eminence to which he had risen as a statesman.

BALL, JOHN (d. 1381), priest. During Wat Tyler's insurrection (1381) he was freed by the rebels from the Abp. of *Canterbury's prison at Maidstone. He incited the populace to kill those who opposed social equality and was present at the death of Abp. *Simon of Sudbury. He was executed as a traitor.

BALLERINI, PIETRO (1698–1769), patristic scholar. In 1748 he was sent to Rome to defend the interests of the republic of *Venice. He was commissioned by the Pope to prepare an edition of the works of *Leo the Great to replace that of P. *Quesnel, which was tainted with *Gallicanism. This edition (1753–7), published in conjunction with his brother Girolamo, has remained the standard text. The joint work of the brothers included editions of the works of H. *Noris, St. *Zeno, St. *Antoninus, and *Ratherius.

BALSAMON, THEODORE (c. 1140–after 1195), Greek canonist. His *Scholia* consists of: (1) a commentary on the 'Nomocanon' of *Photius and (2) one of the principal collections of *canon law in the East.

BALTIMORE, Councils of. A series of ecclesiastical councils at Baltimore, Maryland, three plenary (1852–84) and ten provincial (1829–69), by which many details of the administration and discipline of the RC Church in the U.S.A. were settled.

BALUZE, ÉTIENNE (1630–1718), French ecclesiastical historian. His works include an edition of the letters of *Innocent III (1682; incomplete, since he was denied access to the *Vatican archives), *Conciliorum Nova Collectio* (1683), and *Vitae Paparum Avenionensium* (1693: put on the *Index for alleged *Gallicanism).

BAMPTON LECTURES. The will of John Bampton, Canon of Salisbury (d. 1751), created an endowment for eight lectures to be delivered annually in St. Mary's, Oxford. Their subject is the exposition and defence of the Christian faith as expressed in the Creeds, on the authority of Scripture and the

Fathers. Since 1895 they have been given biennially.

BANCROFT, RICHARD (1544–1610), Abp. of *Canterbury. An outspoken opponent of *Puritanism and *Presbyterianism, he became Bp. of London in 1597. He wielded virtually archiepiscopal power because of the age and incapacity of J. *Whitgift, whom he succeeded in 1604. His refusal to compromise was one of the causes of the failure of the *Hampton Court Conference.

BÁÑEZ, DOMINGO (1528–1604), Spanish *Dominican theologian. From 1580 he held the chief professorship at Salamanca. He was an exponent of the traditional Scholastic theology and took part in the Jesuit–Dominican controversy on *grace. He was the director and confessor of St. *Teresa of Ávila.

BANGOR. Of the many places of this name, the best known are: (1) 'Bangor Fawr', Gwynedd, Wales. The see was traditionally founded by St. *Deiniol (d. *c.* 584). The cathedral was burnt in 1402. Bp. Henry Deane (d. 1503) began to rebuild the choir, and the work was completed by Bp. Thomas Skevington (d. 1533). See also *Bangorian Controversy*.
(2) 'Bangor Iscoed', Clwyd, Wales, the site of a large early monastery. Its monks refused to co-operate with St. *Augustine of Canterbury.
(3) Bangor in Co. Down, N. Ireland. St. *Comgall founded an abbey in 555 or 559. It was the original home of St. *Columbanus and St. *Gall.

BANGOR, Use of. Of the pre-Reformation liturgical 'Use of Bangor' mentioned in the preface to the 1549 BCP, nothing can be discovered. It is likely that it preserved ancient *Celtic elements.

BANGORIAN CONTROVERSY, The. The dispute which followed the sermon preached by B. *Hoadly, Bp. of *Bangor, before George I in 1717. The sermon sought to show that the Gospels afford no warrant for any visible Church authority. To save Hoadly from synodical condemnation, the King prorogued *Convocation, which did not meet again, except formally, until 1852.

BANNS OF MARRIAGE. The custom of announcing a forthcoming marriage during Divine Service seems to have been developed in the early Middle Ages to prevent possible *consanguinity. The BCP regards the publication of banns as the normal prelude to marriage; they must be published in church on three Sundays preceding the marriage. See also *Marriage Licences*.

BAPTISM. The *Sacramental rite which admits a candidate to the Christian Church. It has commonly been held that the Lord instituted the Sacrament either at some unspecified date before His Passion or after the Resurrection when He gave the disciples the command to baptize in the three-fold Name (Mt. 28: 19); many modern critics have denied that the Sacrament was instituted by Christ. It is, however, clear that Baptism was practised in the Church from the first, and the two constituent parts of the Sacrament, water and the Trinitarian formula, are both contained in the NT. In the early Church Baptism, which involved total *immersion, was normally conferred by the Bishop and was closely associated with *Confirmation and the *Eucharist. From the 2nd to the 4th cents. it was commonly given only at *Easter and *Pentecost, but other feasts came to be added. In the first four or five centuries it was common to defer Baptism until death was believed to be imminent, because of the responsibilities attached to it, but this practice fell into disuse with the increase of *Infant Baptism and the development of the penitential system.

The theology of Baptism was elucidated by the 3rd-cent. controversy on the validity of Baptism administered by heretics. Largely through the influence of St. *Augustine, it eventually came to be accepted that the validity of the Sacrament depended on the correct form, regardless of the faith or worthiness of the minister. Against the *Pelagians, Augustine also maintained that the chief effect of the Sacrament was the removal of the stain of *Original Sin on the soul which bars even the new-born child from Heaven. He also developed the doctrine of the Baptismal '*character', which marks the soul as the property of the Trinity and remains even in an apostate. Various aspects of the Catholic teaching were rejected by the 16th-cent. Reformers. M. *Luther sought to combine belief in the necessity of Baptism with his doctrine of *justification by faith alone:

Baptism was a promise of Divine grace after which a man's sins are no longer imputed to him. H. *Zwingli denied the necessity of Baptism, seeing in it only a sign admitting man to the Christian community. J. *Calvin taught that it was efficacious only for the elect, since they alone had the faith without which it was worthless. The BCP preserved the traditional Catholic teaching. At the Council of *Trent, the RC Church stressed that Baptism is not merely a sign of grace, but actually contains and confers it on those who put no obstacle in its way.

The forms of the rite used in the RC Church are the most elaborate. In the case of children it includes an undertaking from the parents that the child shall be brought up in the Christian faith, a prayer of *exorcism, blessing of water, renunciation of evil by parents and *godparents and a declaration of faith, Baptism by immersion or *affusion with the Trinitarian formula, and anointing with *chrism. The child's father holds a candle lit from the *Paschal Candle, which is lit for all Baptisms. The Baptism of Adults is not very different, except for the omission of the chrismation; it is followed immediately by confirmation. The C of E rite is similar but simpler. Renunciation of evil is followed by Baptism by immersion or affusion, accompanied by the Trinitarian formula and the signing of the Cross. It may now take place within the Eucharist.

BAPTISM IN THE HOLY SPIRIT. The expression is used by *Pentecostals of an experience attributed to the Holy Spirit, and empowering them for witness. It is generally believed to be distinct from conversion or sacramental *Baptism (known as 'water-baptism') and subsequent to it. The Pentecostals maintain that, as the Holy Spirit fell on the first Apostles, so those summoned to be likewise 'filled' (cf. Acts 2: 4) are 'baptized with the Holy Spirit' (cf. Acts 11: 15 f.), and that the normal outward sign of this 'baptism' is their breaking into tongues (i.e. *glossolalia) (cf. Acts 10: 44–7). Many NT exegetes question the Scriptural basis of the doctrine, but the teaching has been accepted by many 'neo-Pentecostals' in the major denominations.

BAPTISM OF CHRIST, The. Acc. to Mk. 1: 9–11 Christ came to *John the Baptist and, like others, received baptism at his hands. The event is also recorded by Mt. and Lk. and is implied in Jn.

BAPTIST MISSIONARY SOCIETY. The Society was founded in Northamptonshire in 1792. Its first missionary, W. *Carey, went to India, where much of its work is still done. Its other main fields have been Jamaica, China, the Cameroons, and Zaïre.

BAPTISTERY. The building or part of the church in which *Baptism is administered. From the 3rd cent. onwards the baptistery was often a separate building west of the church and polygonal in shape. The spread of *Infant Baptism led to the increasing use of *fonts placed within the church, often at the west end.

BAPTISTS. One of the largest Protestant bodies. They trace their origin in modern times to the action of John *Smyth, a *Separatist exile in Amsterdam who in 1609 reinstituted the Baptism of conscious believers as the basis of fellowship of a gathered Church. The first Baptist Church in England consisted of members of Smyth's Church who had returned to London in 1612 under the leadership of Thomas *Helwys. From this sprang a number of other Churches. They were *Arminian in theology and their polity was of a connectional kind. They became known as '*General Baptists'. In 1633 the adoption of believers' Baptism by a group of *Calvinist London Separatists led to the rise of '*Particular Baptist' Churches in many parts of the country. Many Baptists were associated with the more radical spiritual and political movements of the 17th cent., but after the *Restoration they moved closer in spirit and temper to the *Presbyterians and *Independents and became recognized as one of the *Three Denominations of Protestant Dissenters. John *Bunyan was an outstanding figure among them.

In America the first Church on Baptist principles was established by Roger *Williams at Providence, Rhode Island, in 1639. In the next century the *Great Awakening aroused great missionary zeal among American Baptists; it led to rapid and spectacular growth as the frontier was carried westwards and in some of the Southern States Baptists became the largest religious community. By 1975 there were over 27 million Baptists in N. America, and about two-thirds of the total Negro Church membership is Baptist.

In 1834 a Baptist Church was founded in

Hamburg and from this arose a widespread Baptist movement on the Continent of Europe. It spread from German-speaking to Slav-speaking people. Baptists were severely persecuted under Czarist Russia; they increased in the early years of the Soviet regime but later suffered from the general restriction of religious freedom.

The rigid Calvinism of the 18th-cent. Baptists was later modified and in the 19th cent. most Baptist Churches adopted open communion. Baptists in Britain shared in the *Free Church Council movement and are members of the *World Council of Churches, but they have shown hesitation over schemes for organic reunion because of their concern over believers' Baptism. For this reason Baptist conventions in some parts of the world have not joined the World Council of Churches.

BARABBAS. The robber whom *Pilate released from prison rather than Christ (Mk 15: 6–15).

BARBARA, St. Acc. to tradition, the daughter of a pagan of Nicomedia who, on being converted to the Christian faith, was handed over by her father to the prefect and martyred. Her prayers are sought as a protection against thunderstorms and fire, and she is the patroness of artillerymen and firemen.

BARBAROSSA. See *Frederick I*.

BARCLAY, JOHN (1734–98), founder of the '*Bereans' (q.v.) or 'Barclayites'. While he was assistant to A. Dow, the *Presbyterian minister at Fettercairn in Scotland, Barclay published *Rejoice Evermore* (1766), in which he expounded a doctrine of immediate Divine Revelation. He was censured by the Presbytery and not appointed to succeed Dow on his death in 1772. At Edinburgh in 1773 he constituted a new Church, known as the Berean Assembly, from its zeal for the study of the Bible (cf. Acts 17: 10 f.).

BARCLAY, ROBERT (1648–90), Scottish *Quaker theologian. He followed his father in becoming a Quaker in 1667. His *Apology*, published in Latin in 1676, was issued in an English version in 1678; its impressive defence of the doctrine of the '*Inner Light' against the supremacy of external authorities, incl. the Bible, made it the classic exposition of Quaker principles. Barclay won the

favour of the Duke of York (later *James II), and was able to assist W. *Penn in the foundation of Pennsylvania. In 1683 he was appointed governor of East New Jersey, which was given a constitution on Quaker principles.

BAR-COCHBA. The leader of a Jewish rebellion in Palestine in A.D. 132. He claimed to be, and was accepted as, the Messiah.

BARDESANES (154–222), correctly 'Bar-Daisan', heretic. A native of *Edessa, he was converted to Christianity in 179, later excommunicated, and fled to Armenia *c.* 216. He prob. taught a kind of astrological fatalism. He wrote 'A Dialogue of Destiny' and a large number of Syriac hymns.

BAR HEBRAEUS (1226–86), the usual name of Abû-l-Farag, *Jacobite bishop and philosopher. The son of a Jewish physician, he was converted to Christianity, consecrated bishop in 1246, and in 1264 became *Primate of the East. He transmitted the learning of his predecessors by condensation and reproduction in a large corpus of works, most of them in Syriac, a few in Arabic.

BARLAAM AND JOASAPH, Sts., subjects of a popular medieval legend. Because of a prophecy that he would be converted to Christianity, Joasaph, the son of a heathen Indian king, was shut up in a palace so that he should know nothing of the evils of life. He escaped and was won to the Christian faith by the hermit Barlaam. The story apparently dates from the 8th. cent. It has traditionally been ascribed to *John of Damascus.

BARLOW, WILLIAM (d. 1568), Bp. of *Chichester. In early life he was an *Augustinian canon, but he showed Protestant tendencies as early as 1529. He became Bp. of *St. Davids in 1536 and of *Bath and Wells in 1548. Under Queen *Mary he fled abroad, but he was appointed Bp. of Chichester on her death. His position as chief consecrator of Abp. M. *Parker has given rise to controversy, since there is no surviving record of his own consecration.

BARLOW, WILLIAM (*c.* 1565–1613), Bp. successively of *Rochester (from 1605) and *Lincoln (from 1608). He attended the

*Hampton Court Conference in 1604; his *Summe and Substance of the Conference ... at Hampton Court* (1604), despite contemporary and later criticism, remains the most satisfactory account. He was one of the translators of the AV.

BARMEN DECLARATION, The (1934). The statement drawn up at the first Synod of the *Confessing Church at Barmen in Germany to define the beliefs and mission of the Church in face of the liberal tendencies of the Nazi *German Christians.

BARNABAS, St. A Jewish *Levite who became one of the earliest Christian disciples at *Jerusalem. He introduced St. *Paul to the Apostles after his conversion and went with him on his first 'missionary journey'; later, owing to a dispute over John *Mark, they parted, and Barnabas sailed for *Cyprus. He is the traditional founder of the Cypriot Church and legend asserts that he was martyred at Salamis in A.D. 61.

BARNABAS, Epistle of. An early Christian Epistle ascribed to the Apostle *Barnabas, but prob. written by a Christian of *Alexandria between A.D. 70 and 100. It contains a strong attack on Judaism and claims to find in the OT testimonies for Christianity.

BARNABAS, Gospel of. A writing in Italian, apparently forged not earlier than the 15th cent. by a native of Italy who renounced Christianity for Islam.

BARNABITES. A small religious order founded at Milan in 1530. Officially known as the 'Clerks Regular of St. Paul', their popular name derives from their church of St. Barnabas in Milan.

BARNETT, SAMUEL AUGUSTUS (1844–1913), social reformer. From 1873 to 1894 he was vicar of St. Jude's, Whitechapel, in London, and from 1884 to 1896 first Warden of Toynbee Hall, which he helped to found. Throughout his life he was active in initiating projects directed to the reform of social conditions on Christian principles and in urging Christians to study them.

BARO, PETER (1534–99), French anti-Calvinist divine. Compelled to flee from France, in 1574 he was appointed Lady Margaret Professor of Divinity at Cambridge. Here, despite his earlier personal association with J. *Calvin, he became a critic of the more predestinarian of the Calvinist doctrines. In 1596 he found it expedient to leave Cambridge for London.

BARONIUS, CESARE (1538–1607), ecclesiastical historian. A member of the *Oratory, he was made a cardinal in 1596. His main work, the *Annales Ecclesiastici* (12 vols., 1588–1607), is a history of the Church (to 1198), undertaken as a RC reply to the *Centuriators of Magdeburg. He tried to secure accuracy, but his information was often scanty and in error.

BAROQUE. The ornate style of art and architecture which flourished in Italy in the 17th and 18th cents. and spread throughout the Continent, esp. to France and Spain. With its lofty grandeur and richness of decoration it attempted to infuse new life and religious feeling into the cold correctness of the later Renaissance.

BARRINGTON, SHUTE (1734–1826), Bp. successively of *Llandaff, *Salisbury, and *Durham, he was one of the most influential *prelates of his age. He deprecated any relaxation of the obligation to subscribe to the *Thirty-Nine Articles on the ground that precise articles of faith were indispensable in an Established Church.

BARROW, HENRY (c. 1550–93), also **Barrowe**, English *Congregationalist. In 1586, when visiting J. *Greenwood in prison, he was detained and kept in confinement until his death. He wrote in defence of separatism and congregational independence; in controversy with R. *Browne, he argued that any idea of Church order was corrupt. In 1590 he was charged with circulating seditious books and three years later he was sentenced to be hanged.

BARSUMAS (d. 458), *Monophysite *archimandrite. He was one of the leaders of the Eutychian party at the Synod of *Constantinople of 448, at the *Latrocinium (449), and at the Council of *Chalcedon (451).

BARSUMAS, (c. 420–c. 490), *Nestorian Bp. of Nisibis. He established an influential theological school at Nisibis, and, when the school of *Edessa was closed in 489, he welcomed its exiles.

BARTH, KARL (1886–1968), Swiss Protestant theologian. He wrote his famous 'Commentary on Romans' (*Der Römerbrief*, 1919) while he was pastor of Safenwil (Aargau). The originality, critical power, and actuality of its message gained him a wide hearing. In 1921 he became extraordinary professor at Göttingen and then professor at Münster (1925) and Bonn (1930). With the outbreak of the 'Church Struggle' (1933) he threw in his lot with the '*Confessing Church'. He enjoyed some freedom of speech as a Swiss subject, but on his refusal to take an oath of unconditional allegiance to Hitler, he was deprived of his chair. In 1935 he became professor of theology at Basle, where he remained until he retired.

Barth's primary object was to lead theology away from what he believed to be the fundamentally erroneous outlook of modern religious philosophy and to bring it back to the principles of the Reformation and the prophetic teaching of the Bible. The Christian message, he held, affirmed the Supremacy and Transcendence of God, whose infinite superiority to all human aspirations meant the worthlessness of human reason. Since the *Fall, which brought man wholly under the dominion of sin, his natural capacities, including his reason, had been perverted, so that all 'natural theology', as well as all religion grounded in experience, had become impossible. God's sole revelation is in Jesus Christ and the Word of God is His only means of communication with man.

The systematic exposition of his theology occupied much of Barth's life. The first volume of *Die kirchliche Dogmatik* appeared in 1932, the final section in 1967. His influence was immense; he was certainly the most outstanding Protestant theologian, and perhaps the most notable Christian prophet, of his time.

BARTHOLOMEW, St. One of the twelve Apostles, he is sometimes identified with *Nathaniel. He may have visited *India. He is traditionally said to have been flayed alive at Albanopolis in Armenia.

BARTHOLOMEW, Gospel of St. An apocryphal Gospel whose existence was known to *Jerome and *Bede. It has perhaps been incorporated into the *Gnostic 'Questions of Bartholomew' which treat of Christ's descent into Hell, the summons of the Devil to judgement, and other subjects.

BARTHOLOMEW'S DAY, Massacre of St. The massacre of a large number of *Huguenots which took place on the night of 23-4 Aug. 1572 and the two following days in Paris and other French cities.

BARTHOLOMEW OF THE MARTYRS (1514–90), Portuguese theologian. Bartholomew Fernandez owes his name 'of the martyrs' to the church in which he was baptized. A *Dominican, from 1548 to 1582 he was Bp. of Braga. At the Council of *Trent he took part in drafting the decrees on the reform of the clergy.

BARTHOLOMEW OF PISA (c. 1260–1347), *Dominican theologian, famous chiefly for his alphabetically arranged *Summa de Casibus Conscientiae* (1338).

BARTHOLOMITES. (1) *Armenian.* A community of Armenian monks who fled from their country in 1296 and settled in 1307 at Genoa, where a church dedicated to St. *Bartholomew was built for them. They were suppressed in 1650.

(2) *German.* A congregation of secular priests founded in 1640 to revive the morals and discipline of clergy and laity after the decline due to the *Thirty Years War. They lived in community without vows. Their extinction was brought about by the secularization of the German ecclesiastical states in 1803.

BARTIMAEUS. A blind beggar healed by Christ on His last journey to Jerusalem (Mk. 10: 46–52).

BARTOLOMMEO, FRA (c. 1475–1517), painter. A follower of *Savonarola, in 1498 he entered the *Dominican Order at San Marco in Florence. His works include the fresco of the 'Last Judgement' in Sta Maria Nuova (on which he collaborated with Mariotto Albertinelli) and his 'Descent from the Cross' in the Pitti Palace, both at Florence.

BARTON, ELIZABETH (c. 1506–34), the 'Maid of Kent'. A servant girl, she had trances, claimed to utter prophecies, and became a nun in *Canterbury. Her prophecies then attacked *Henry VIII for his intention to divorce his Queen. After she had confessed that her trances were feigned, she was executed.

BARUCH, Book of. A Book of the *Apocrypha to which is attached the 'Epistle of Jeremy', the two forming, with *Lamentations, appendices to the Book of *Jeremiah. It consists of an introduction professing to be by Baruch, the disciple of Jeremiah, a liturgical confession, a sermon, and a set of canticles. It is generally dated in post-*Maccabean times, possibly after A.D. 70.

BARUCH, II. 'The Syrian Apocalypse'. A *Pharisaic work which professes to have been written by Baruch, *Jeremiah's secretary. It was prob. written after the fall of *Jerusalem in A.D. 70 to encourage the Jews after the destruction of the *Temple. It was composed in Greek, but mostly survives only in Syriac.

BARUCH, III and IV. 'The Greek Apocalypse of Baruch' (traditionally called III Baruch) is an apocryphal work describing the vision of the seven heavens granted to Baruch. It is apparently of Jewish origin but worked over by a Christian hand. It may date from the 2nd cent. 'The Rest of the Words of Baruch' (traditionally called IV Baruch) deals with the end of Jeremiah's life. It is prob. the work of a Jewish Christian and also dates from the 2nd cent. The numbering of III and IV Baruch are sometimes interchanged.

BASEL, Confessions and **Council of.** See *Basle, Confessions* and *Council of*.

BASIL, St., 'the Great' (c. 330–79), one of the *Cappadocian Fathers. He was the brother of St. *Gregory of Nyssa. Having been educated in the best pagan and Christian culture of his day, he settled as a hermit near Neocaesarea in 358; he left his retirement only when called upon by his bishop to defend orthodoxy against the *Arian Emp. Valens. In 370 he became Bp. of Caesarea in Cappadocia. This office involved him in controversies with the extreme Arian party led by *Eunomius, as well as with the *Pneumatomachi, who denied the divinity of the Holy Spirit, and with those who refused to recognize *Meletius as Bp. of *Antioch.

His writings include a large collection of letters, a treatise 'On the Holy Spirit', and three 'Books against Eunomius'. With St. *Gregory of Nazianzus he compiled the '*Philocalia'. He tried to reconcile the *Semiarians to the formula of *Nicaea and to show that their term *Homoiousios* ('like in substance [to the Father]') had the same implications as the Nicene *Homoousios* ('of one substance'). The virtual termination of the Arian controversy after the Council of *Constantinople of 381 is a tribute to his success. He possessed great talent for organization and impressed on E. monasticism the structure and ethos which it has retained ever since. See also the following entries.

BASIL, Liturgy of St. The Liturgy still used in the E. Church on a few specified days in the year. In its general structure it may possibly be the work of St. *Basil the Great, but it has been considerably modified over the centuries. Apart from some of the prayers it agrees closely with the usual Liturgy of St. *Chrysostom.

BASIL, Rule of St. The monastic rule put forward by St. *Basil the Great in 358–64, which is the basis of the usual rule still followed by religious in the E. Church. While strict, it avoided encouraging the more extreme austerities of the hermits of the desert. It owes its present form to a revision by St. *Theodore of Studios (d. 826).

BASIL OF ANCYRA (4th cent.), *Arian bishop. Elected to succeed *Marcellus in the see of Ancyra in 336, he was deposed at the Council of *Sardica in 343, but reinstated by Constantius c. 348. He took part in various Arianizing synods, but his increasing criticism of extreme Arian doctrines led to his removal in 360.

BASIL OF SELEUCIA (d. c. 459), Abp. of Seleucia from c. 440. Having condemned *Eutyches in 448, he acquiesced in his rehabilitation at the *Latrocinium in 449, but recanted and signed the *Tome of Leo in 450.

BASILICA. An early form of church, apparently modelled on a Roman building of the same name. Approached by a narrow porch (*narthex), it consisted of a nave and two (or four) *aisles with pillars supporting horizontal architraves and later arches; above these rose the clerestory, pierced with windows. The east end was completed by an arch and semi-circular *apse. The *altar, raised on a platform, stood out from the wall on the chord of the apse; underneath it and partly below floor level was the 'confessio' or chapel which sometimes contained the body of the patron saint. The title 'basilica' is now given by the Pope to certain privileged churches.

BASILIDES. A theologian of *Gnostic tendencies who taught at *Alexandria in the second quarter of the 2nd cent. His system is difficult to reconstruct, since only fragments of his works survive and conflicting accounts are given. His followers soon formed a separate sect.

BASILIKON DORON. A book addressed to his eldest son Henry (d. 1612) by King *James I of England. Its professed purpose was to guide Henry in his duties when he succeeded to the throne, but its real object was to rebuke ministers of religion who meddled in state affairs. Published openly in 1603, it was immediately popular.

BASLE, Confessions of. The [first] 'Confession of Basle', compiled by O. *Myconius, was made the basis of the reform introduced at Basle in 1534. It represents a compromise between the positions of M. *Luther and H. *Zwingli. The 'First *Helvetic Confession' of 1536 is sometimes known as the 'Second Confession of Basle'.

BASLE, Council of (1431–49). The Council was convened and opened by *Martin V. When the new Pope, *Eugenius IV, dissolved the Council, it disregarded his action and reaffirmed the decrees of the Council of *Constance on the superiority of a *General Council to the Pope. Under political pressure in 1433 the Pope recognized the Council, which continued in its antipapal attitude. In 1437 the *Hussite question was settled against the Papal views by ratification of the 'Compactata', conceding to the Bohemians *Communion in both kinds. In the same year occurred the break with the Orthodox Church over the place of meeting for a council which was intended to unite the E. and W. Churches; Eugenius then transferred the Council to *Ferrara. Those who remained at Basle declared him deposed and elected an antipope, Felix V, in 1439. In 1448 they were driven from Basle and in 1449 submit-

ted.

BASSENDYNE BIBLE, The. The earliest edition of the English Bible to be printed in Scotland. The NT appeared in 1576, the whole Bible in 1579.

BATH AND WELLS. A see in the Province of *Canterbury, founded in 909 as the diocese of *Wells. In 1088 the see was moved to Bath. *Honorius III authorized the title 'Bath and Wells' in 1219, and in 1245 *Innocent IV ordered that elections should be made alternately in Bath and Wells by the two chapters jointly, with enthronement at the place of election. Since the *dissolution of Bath Abbey in 1540 Wells has been the sole cathedral of the diocese; the abbey church at Bath has served as a parish church.

BATIFFOL, PIERRE (1861–1929), French Church historian, for some time associated with the early *Modernists. His work on the *Eucharist in 1905 created such a stir by its unorthodox views that he was forced to resign from his rectorship of the Institut Catholique at Toulouse and in 1911 the book was placed on the *Index. His later years were mainly taken up with the history of the Church and esp. of the growth of papal power up to the time of *Leo I.

BAUER, BRUNO (1809–82), German theologian. He adopted a position even more extreme than that of D. F. *Strauss, attributing the Gospel story to the imagination of a single (2nd-cent.) mind.

BÄUMER, SUITBERT (1845–94), *Benedictine liturgical scholar. His chief work, *Die Geschichte des Breviers* (1895), upheld the liturgical importance of *Gregory I and the widespread influence of *Gregory VII's rite in the papal chapel through its subsequent adoption by the *Franciscans. In his later years he collaborated with E. *Bishop.

BAUR, FERDINAND CHRISTIAN (1792–1860), German Protestant theologian and founder of the *Tübingen School. He developed his characteristic doctrines under the influence of G. W. F. *Hegel's conception of history. In his work on the *Pastoral Epistles (1835) Hegelian principles were first applied to the NT, primitive Christianity being represented as a struggle between divergent views, the synthesis of which was the Catholic Church. He later applied the same principles to the development of Christian doctrines, breaking new ground by treating his subject historically rather than systematically. His monograph on St. *Paul (1845) aroused a storm of controversy; in it he denied the authenticity of all the Pauline Epp. except Gal., 1 and 2 Cor., and Rom. In his work on the canonical Gospels (1847) he assigned the earliest date to Mt., as representing the Judaizing party, and the latest to Jn., as depicting the final reconciliation. This last Gospel he held to be devoid of historical value.

BAVON, St. (d. *c.* 653), patron saint of Ghent and Haarlem.

BAXTER, RICHARD (1615–91). *Puritan divine. He was ordained in 1638 but in 1640 rejected belief in episcopacy in its current English form. In 1641 he became curate to the incumbent of Kidderminster; he laboured here until 1660, largely ignoring denominational distinctions. Early in the Civil War he joined the Parliamentary Army; after leaving it in 1647, he wrote his devotional classic, *The Saints' Everlasting Rest* (1650). He took part in the recall of *Charles II in 1660, but declined to accept the bishopric of *Hereford. At the *Savoy Conference he presented the *Exceptions to the BCP. Between 1662 and 1687 he suffered persecution. He left nearly 200 writings. They breathe a spirit of unaffected piety and reflect his love of moderation. He wrote several hymns, including 'Ye holy angels bright'.

BAY PSALM BOOK, The. The metrical version of the Psalms produced at Cambridge, Mass. (popularly known in the U.S.A. as 'Bay State'), in 1640. It was the first book to be printed in British America.

BAYEUX TAPESTRY, The. An embroidered band of linen, preserved at Bayeux in Normandy, which depicts the Norman invasion of England and the events preceding it. It was prob. made for Bp. *Odo of Bayeux.

BAYLE, PIERRE (1647–1706), sceptical writer. He was a professor at Rotterdam from 1681 to 1693. He held that religion and morality being independent of one another, all private and social virtues may be equally practised by atheists, and he championed universal toleration. His most famous work was his *Dictionnaire historique et critique* (1695–7).

BAYLY, LEWIS (d. 1631). The author of *The Practice of Piety* (3rd edn., 1613; the date of its original publication is not known), a work which enjoyed remarkable popularity, esp. among *Puritans. From 1616 he was Bp. of *Bangor.

B.C.M.S. (Bible Churchmen's Missionary Society). A society formed out of the *C.M.S. when a group broke away from the parent body in 1922 in order to assert its fidelity to the traditional doctrines of the *Evangelical party, and esp. to the belief in the complete inerrancy of Scripture.

BEA, AUGUSTIN (1881–1968), cardinal from 1959. A German *Jesuit, his life was devoted mainly to Biblical scholarship until *John XXIII appointed him President of the newly created Secretariat for Christian Unity in 1960. Bea stressed the importance of the *Baptism of non-RCs and it was largely through his influence that the documents of the Second *Vatican Council described them as 'separated brethren' rather than outside the Church.

BEAD. Originally the word meant a prayer, but later it was transferred to the small spherical bodies used for 'telling beads' (i.e. counting the beads of a *rosary), and hence also applied e.g. to the parts of a necklace. 'To bid a bead' thus means 'to offer a prayer'. See also *Bidding Prayer*.

BEADLE. In the Church of *Scotland an official appointed by the *session to care for the place of worship and to perform other similar functions.

BEARD, CHARLES (1827–88), *Unitarian divine. He edited the *Theological Review* and gave the series of Hibbert Lectures for 1883 on *The Reformation*, in which he stressed the humanistic, rather than the definitely theological, aspects of the Reformers' work.

BEARDS, Clerical. The wearing of beards by clerics has remained the practice of the E. Church from Apostolic times. From the 5th cent. onwards W. clerics became clean-shaven, though in the 15th cent. beards became widely popular again under the influence of secular fashion.

BEATIFIC VISION The. The vision of the Divine Being in heaven which, acc. to Christian theology, is the final destiny of the redeemed. Acc. to some theologians the vision is granted in exceptional circumstances for brief periods in this life.

BEATIFICATION. In the RC Church the act by which the Pope permits the public veneration after his death of some faithful Catholic in a particular church, diocese, country, or religious order, or, very occasionally, throughout the RC Church. See also *Canonization*.

BEATING OF THE BOUNDS. A ceremony common in medieval England and associated with the *Rogationtide procession round the parish. The bounds were solemnly beaten with willow rods, and on occasion boys of the parish were beaten or bumped on the ground. It has been revived in some parishes.

BEATITUDES The. Christ's promises of coming blessings in the *Sermon on the Mount (Mt. 5: 3–11) and the Sermon on the Plain (Lk. 6: 20–2). They describe the qualities of Christian perfection.

BEATON (or **BETHUNE**), DAVID (c. 1494–1546), Cardinal Abp. of St. Andrews. He held high office under James V of Scotland and on his death (1542) made a bid for the regency. He is remembered in Scotland for the trial and condemnation of G. *Wishart, who seems to have been involved in political plotting and designs on Beaton's life. He was assassinated.

BEAUDUIN, LAMBERT (1873–1960), founder of *Chevetogne. In 1906 he entered the *Benedictine Abbey of Mont-César at Louvain. Here he wrote *La Piété de l'Église* (1914), which popularized the aims of the *Liturgical Movement. After *Pius XI had urged Benedictines to pray for Christian unity, Beauduin founded a monastery of Union at Amay-sur-Meuse (see *Chevetogne*). He attended Cardinal *Mercier at the *Malines Conversations and in a report expressed his desire that the Anglican Church should be 'united with Rome, not absorbed'; as a result he had to leave Amay

in 1928 and in 1930 he was condemned by a Roman tribunal. He was able to return to his community, now at Chevetogne, in 1950.

BEAUFORT, HENRY (c. 1375–1447), Cardinal from 1426. The son of John of Gaunt, declared legitimate in 1397, he became Bp. of *Lincoln in 1398 and of *Winchester in 1404. He attended the Council of *Constance, where he was largely responsible for the election of *Martin V. He played a prominent part in English politics, was several times Chancellor, and from 1424 to 1426 he virtually ruled the country. At Winchester he completed the transformation of the nave of the cathedral. He stands out for his financial ability and statesmanship rather than as a Churchman.

BEAUFORT, MARGARET. See *Margaret, Lady*.

BEAULIEU, Abbey of. This *Cistercian abbey in Hampshire was founded by King *John in 1204 for 30 monks from *Cîteaux. From the first it possessed rights of *sanctuary. The Early English refectory is now used as a parish church.

BEC, Abbey of. The *Benedictine abbey of Bec, in Normandy, was founded by Bl. Herluin and consecrated in 1041; it was rebuilt on a larger scale in 1060. Its notable monks included *Lanfranc, *Anselm of Canterbury, and Pope *Alexander II. Bec was taken over by the *Maurists in 1626; it was suppressed in 1790. In 1948 Benedictine life (*Olivetan Congregation) was re-established.

BECKET, St. THOMAS (?1118–70), Abp. of *Canterbury from 1162. He was Chancellor and an intimate friend of Henry II; he accepted the archbishopric reluctantly, knowing a break with the king to be inevitable. He resigned the Chancellorship and adopted an austere mode of life. In 1164 he refused to affix his seal to the Constitutions of *Clarendon (q.v.); he was then subjected to a demand for a large sum of money in settlement of the accounts during his Chancellorship. When he refused to pay, the king required a Council of bishops and barons at Northampton to pass sentence on him, but he escaped to France, appealing to Pope *Alexander III. A reconciliation was effected in 1170. On his return Becket refused to absolve the bishops who had taken part in the coronation of Henry's son unless they swore obedience to the Pope. Henry, in a fit of rage, uttered some words which inspired four knights to go to Canterbury and assassinate Becket in his cathedral. The murder provoked great indignation and miracles were soon recorded at Becket's tomb. His shrine made Canterbury one of the chief centres of pilgrimage in Christendom.

BECON, THOMAS (*c.* 1511–67), Protestant Reformer. He held various offices under *Edward VI; he was expelled under *Mary, and prob. taught at *Marburg University; on the accession of *Elizabeth I he became a canon of *Canterbury Cathedral. His writings were at first moderate in tone and devotional in intent, but after his exile they became coarser and *Zwinglian in standpoint. For the *Book of *Homilies he wrote the one against adultery.

BEDA, The. The college at Rome where English candidates for the RC priesthood who have discovered their vocation late in life, incl. converts from non-Roman ministries who wish to be ordained in the RC Church, are trained.

BEDE (prayer). See *Bead*.

BEDE, St. (*c.* 673–735), Biblical scholar and 'Father of English Church History'. At the age of 7 he was sent to the monastery of *Wearmouth; he transferred to Jarrow, prob. at the time of its foundation (682). His *De Temporibus* was prob. written to make clear to the clergy the principles for calculating the date of *Easter acc. to the Roman usage adopted at the Synod of *Whitby; together with his other works it did much to establish the practice of dating events from the Incarnation. His extensive Biblical commentaries were highly esteemed by his contemporaries and immediate successors. His historical works, for which in modern times he is best known, include the *Historia Abbatum*, which traces the history of his monastery from its foundation to 716, metrical and prose lives of St. *Cuthbert, and the *Historia Ecclesiastica Gentis Anglorum* (completed in 731). This last, a primary authority for early English history, owes its value to his care in collecting information, his meticulous listing of his authorities, and the separation of historical fact from hearsay and tradi-

tion. Less than a century after his death he was honoured with the title of *Venerable.

BEDLAM. Originally the name given to the 'Hospital of St. Mary of Bethlehem' in Bishopsgate, founded in 1247. It is uncertain when insane persons were first admitted, but lunatics are stated to have been there in 1402. By an extension of meaning the word 'Bedlam' is applied to any lunatic asylum or scene of disorder within doors.

BEELZEBUB. The name applied to the 'prince of devils' in the Gospels, where Christ's enemies accuse Him of 'casting out devils by Beelzebub' (Mk. 3: 22–6), i.e. of acting by the power of, or of being an agent of, the evil one, not of God.

BEGUINES, BEGHARDS. The Beguines were members of certain sisterhoods, founded in the Netherlands in the 12th cent. They lived a semi-religious, austere communal life without vows, but they were free to hold private property and to leave the community. The Beghards were their male counterparts; they, however, had a common purse and no private property. They were suspected of heresy and their teaching was condemned at the Council of *Vienne in 1311. Many of the Beghards adopted a reform and were allowed to continue.

BEL. Another form of '*Baal' (q.v.).

BEL AND THE DRAGON. Two stories attached to the Book of *Daniel in some Greek MSS. of the OT and hence included (as a single item) in the *Apocrypha of the English Bible. The former recounts how Daniel convinced the Babylonian king that the provisions which were daily set before the image of Bel were not consumed by the god but removed by the priests; the priests were executed and the image destroyed. The latter describes how Daniel killed the dragon by throwing a bolus into its throat; the people insisted that Daniel be cast into a den of seven lions, from which he was miraculously liberated.

BELGIC CONFESSION, The (1561). The confession of faith of the Reformed Churches drawn up on the basis of the *Gallican Confession. Its adoption in synod at Antwerp in 1566 marked the final acceptance of Calvinist priniciples in the Netherlands.

BELGIUM, Christianity in. Before the Revolution of 1830, when Belgium became independent of *Holland, the RC Church had suffered severe restrictions imposed by the Dutch *Calvinist minority. The Revolution was carried through by the 'Union' of 1828 between the Belgian Liberals, whose principles were based on free religious thought, and the Catholics. The population of Belgium has always been predominantly RC.

BELIAL. A Hebrew word prob. meaning 'worthlessness', 'wickedness', or 'destruction'. It is usually found in combination with a noun, e.g. 'sons of Belial'. It occurs several times in the OT, only once in the NT.

BELL, GEORGE KENNEDY ALLEN (1881–1958), Bp. of *Chichester from 1929 to 1958. He was one of the leaders of the *Life and Work movement. He supported the *Confessing Church in its struggle against the Nazi government. During the Second World War he criticized the indiscriminate bombing of German cities. After the War his international contacts facilitated the first meeting of the *World Council of Churches in 1948. He supported the Church of *South India and was joint chairman of the *Anglican–Methodist Conversations.

BELLARMINE, St. ROBERT (1542–1621), theologian, Roberto Francesco Romolo Bellarmino became a *Jesuit in 1560. He was made a cardinal in 1599 and from 1602 to 1605 he was Abp. of Capua.

He was a vigorous and successful opponent of Protestantism; his chief work, *Disputationes de Controversiis Christianae Fidei* (1586–93), provides a systematic and clear apologia for the RC position. He took part in the production of the revised edition of the *Vulgate in 1592. His view that the Pope had only an indirect and not a direct power in temporal affairs brought him into disgrace with *Sixtus V. He was one of the greatest and most saintly figures of his time.

BELLOC, JOSEPH HILAIRE PIERRE (1870–1953), RC historical writer and critic. He joined G. K. Chesterton and his brother in a series of political broadsides popularly known as 'Chesterbellocs'. He became a well-known figure in journalism, expounding Catholic economic liberalism. His numerous historical writings seldom contributed to serious knowledge.

BELLS. The tradition that *Paulinus of Nola introduced bells into Christian worship (c. 420) rests on slender evidence. They were used in *Scotland and *Ireland from the 6th cent. and came into general use in the Church in the 8th cent. They are used to summon the people to church and on other occasions, e.g. to announce the death of a parishioner or for the ringing of the *angelus.

BELL-TOWER. See *Campanile*.

BEMA. The E. counterpart of the *sanctuary.

BENEDICAMUS DOMINO (Lat., 'Let us bless the Lord'). A formula used in the Roman rite at the conclusion of some *Offices. The response is 'Deo Gratias' ('Thanks be to God').

BENEDICITE (Lat., 'Bless ye [the Lord]'). The canticle or song of praise put into the mouths of Shadrach, Meshach, and Abednego as they stood in the 'fiery furnace' (cf. Dan. 3). It forms part of the '*Song of the Three Children'. It has been used in Christian liturgical worship from early times.

BENEDICT, St. (c. 480–c. 550), of Nursia, 'Patriarch of Western monasticism'. The licentiousness of society at Rome led him to withdraw c. 500 to a cave at *Subiaco to live as a hermit. A community grew up around him and he established twelve monasteries, each with twelve monks under an abbot. Local jealousy prompted him to move, with a small band of monks, to *Monte Cassino c. 525. Here he elaborated plans for the reform of monasticism and composed his Rule (see *Benedict, Rule of*). He does not seem to have been ordained or to have contemplated founding an order.

BENEDICT, Oblates Regular of St. See *Oblates Regular of St. Benedict.*

BENEDICT, Rule of St. The monastic Rule drawn up by St. *Benedict of Nursia c. 540 for his monks, mostly laymen, at *Monte Cassino. Drawing freely on earlier Rules, St. Benedict created a taut, inclusive, and individual directory of the spiritual as well as of the administrative life of a monastery.

BENEDICT OF ANIANE, St. (*c.* 750–821), abbot. In 779 he founded on his own property at Aniane in Languedoc a monastery which became the centre of an extended reform of French monastic houses. His systematization of the *Benedictine Rule received official approval as the 'Capitulare Monasticum' at the Synod of Aachen in 817.

BENEDICT BISCOP, St. (*c.* 628–689/90), *Benedictine monk. Of noble Northumbrian ancestry, he became a monk at *Lérins in 666. Three years later he accompanied Abp. *Theodore to *Canterbury. In 674 he founded the monastery of St. Peter at *Wearmouth and in 682 that of St. Paul at Jarrow. He visited Rome five times and promoted Roman chant and liturgical practice.

BENEDICT JOSEPH LABRE, St. See *Labre, St. Benedict Joseph.*

BENEDICT XII (d. 1342), Pope from 1334. Jacques Fournier was the third of the *Avignon Popes. A *Cistercian monk and abbot, as Pope he inaugurated several ecclesiastical reforms. He fought the rapacity of the clergy, forbade the holding of benefices *in commendam* except by cardinals, and was a zealous reformer of religious orders. In the political field he was less successful. In his constitution 'Benedictus Deus' (1336) he defined the doctrine that the souls of the just who have no faults to expiate enjoy the *Beatific Vision immediately after death.

BENEDICT XIII (d. 1423), Antipope at *Avignon from 1394 to 1417. Pedro de Luna took part in the election of *Urban VI, but later supported the antipope Clement VII. On Clement's death (1394) he was elected antipope, largely because he promised to end the schism, if necessary by abdication. After his enthronement he refused to resign. The Council of *Pisa deposed him in 1409; that of *Constance confirmed his deposition in 1417, and his last adherents then left him.

BENEDICT XIII (1649–1730), Pope from 1724. A *Dominican, he presided over the provincial Lateran Council of 1725 which tried to reform clerical morals. Also in 1725 he confirmed the bull '*Unigenitus', though he suffered members of his own order to preach a doctrine of *grace verging on that of the *Jansenists.

BENEDICT XIV (1675–1758), Pope from 1740. He was an exemplary administrator, conciliatory in his dealings with the secular powers and concerned to strengthen the moral influence of the Papacy. His *De Servorum Dei Beatificatione et Beatorum Canonizatione* (1734–8) remains the classic treatment of the history and procedure of *beatification and *canonization. He also compiled an authoritative work on Diocesan Synods (1748), wrote on the Sacrifice of the Mass (1748), and issued a standard edition of the *Caeremoniale Episcoporum* (1752). He had a real interest in science and learning which is reflected in many of his Bulls.

BENEDICT XV (1854–1922), Pope from 1914. Elected Pope shortly after the outbreak of the 1914–18 War, he protested against inhuman methods of warfare and made strenuous efforts to bring about peace.

BENEDICTINE ORDER. St. *Benedict of Nursia founded no order. His Rule made its way gradually and for almost two centuries it was one among several rules from which an abbot chose what observances he wished. In Gaul and to a lesser extent in England the more severe Rule of St. *Columbanus was gradually superseded, and when in the early 8th cent. St. *Boniface set out to evangelize Germany, he established the Benedictine ideal there and reconstructed continental monasticism on Benedictine lines. Up to this time the Rule of St. Benedict was the only link between the various autonomous abbeys, but the 'Capitulare Monasticum' of St. *Benedict of Aniane, imposed upon the monks and nuns of the Empire in 817, tended to reform the Benedictine life in the direction of greater uniformity. Henceforth successive temporary relaxations of Benedictine discipline were countered by attempts at collective reform, such as that of *Cluny (10th cent.). One result of this tendency was the formation of separate orders, in which the twin principles of austerity and centralization were carried further than the primitive Rule of St. Benedict permitted. These orders included the *Camaldolese, the *Carthusian, and the *Cistercian. Popes and Councils throughout the Middle Ages tried to bring the Benedictines under a centralized constitution. The Benedictines themselves preferred to found local congregations as instruments of reform; the abbeys of such congregations (e.g. the *Maurists) sacrificed some degree of autonomy, but the congregations remained independent of any wider organization. The *Reformation ended monastic life in N. Europe and two centuries later the policy of such rulers as *Joseph II and the French Revolution (1789) resulted in the suppression of nearly all Benedictine foundations; but since 1830 there has been a remarkable revival of the Benedictine life in Europe and America. Apart from the spiritual function of the Rule, the Black Monks have rendered great service to civilization, not only in preparing the social organization of the Middle Ages but also, during the period of chaos after the fall of the Roman Empire, in preserving the ideals and practice of scholarship and in maintaining and restoring the use of good art in liturgical worship. Today Benedictine abbeys are autonomous, but are grouped in Congregations, the whole forming a Confederation.

The Benedictine nuns, established by St. Benedict and his sister *Scholastica, live acc. to the same Rule. In the Middle Ages they were enclosed but in modern times the Benedictine Rule has become the foundation of many communities devoted to charitable and educational work as well as of enclosed orders.

BENEDICTIO MENSAE. A liturgical form of grace at meals developed in monastic circles.

BENEDICTION. See *Blessing*.

BENEDICTION OF THE BLESSED SACRAMENT. An extra-liturgical service formerly popular in the RC Church. In solemn Benediction a large Host is exposed to view in a *monstrance, surrounded by lights and censed; hymns are sung and prayers recited; the ceremony is concluded by blessing the congregation with the Host. In the simple form of Benediction the *ciborium containing the Hosts for Communion is shown at the open door of the *tabernacle and after hymns and prayers the people are blessed with the veiled ciborium.

BENEDICTIONAL. In the W. Church the liturgical book containing certain forms of blessing formerly used by bishops.

BENEDICTUS. The Song of Thanksgiving (Lk. 1: 68–79) uttered by *Zacharias for the birth of *John the Baptist. In the W. Church it is sung liturgically at *Lauds, whence it was taken over for *Mattins in the BCP.

BENEDICTUS QUI VENIT. The Latin form of Mt. 21: 9: 'Blessed is he that cometh in the name of the Lord'. In most ancient liturgies it is sung or said after the *Sanctus.

BENEFICE. A term originally used for a grant of land for life as a reward for service, in *canon law it came to imply an ecclesiastical office which prescribed certain duties or conditions for the due discharge of which it provided certain revenues. Holders of parochial benefices in the C of E are known as either *rectors or *vicars (qq.v).

BENEFIT OF CLERGY. The exemption from trial by a secular court on being charged with felony which was accorded to the clergy in the Middle Ages. The privilege was finally abolished in England in 1827.

BENET, St. An older English form of the name of St. *Benedict.

BENGEL, JOHANNES ALBRECHT (1687–1752), *Lutheran NT scholar. His text and critical apparatus of the NT (1734) mark the beginning of scientific work in this field.

BENNETT, WILLIAM JAMES EARLY (1804–86), Anglican *High Churchman. As priest-in-charge of St. Paul's, Knightsbridge, in London, he built St. Barnabas's, Pimlico (opened 1850); the advanced ceremonial which he introduced provoked mob rioting. In 1867 a public letter to E. B. *Pusey, in which he dealt with the *Real Presence in the Eucharist, led to a series of legal actions. The legitimacy of his Eucharistic treatment was allowed.

BENSON, EDWARD WHITE (1829–96), Abp. of *Canterbury from 1883. He was zealous and active in the Church's interests, but intolerant of opposition and criticism. To deal with the ritual charges brought against E. *King, Bp. of Lincoln, he revived the 'court of the Abp. of Canterbury' (see also *Lincoln Judgement*).

BENSON, RICHARD MEUX (1824–1915), founder of the *Society of St. John the Evangelist. In 1850 he was appointed Vicar of Cowley, near Oxford. He was on the point of going to India in 1859 when Bp. S. *Wilberforce persuaded him to remain and take charge of a suburb developing at the Oxford end of his parish. A sermon preached by J. *Keble inspired him to found the Society of St. John the Evangelist in 1865.

BENTLEY, RICHARD (1662–1742), Master of Trinity College, Cambridge, from 1700. He was an able apologist for Christianity against the *Deists, but it was as a classical scholar that he made his real mark. In 1691 he issued a Latin letter to John Mill as an appendix to Mill's edition of the 'Chronicle' of *John Malalas; this brilliantly restored many passages where the text was corrupt.

BERAKAH. The characteristic Jewish prayer which takes the form of a blessing or thanksgiving to God. It has been suggested that the use of the word 'Eucharist' (which is one of the two Greek translations of the Heb. *berakah*) for the central Christian rite arose from the fact that the Eucharistic prayer was a Christian adaptation of the Jewish berakah which was recited over a cup of wine.

BERDYAEV, NICHOLAS (1874–1948), Russian philosopher and author. From 1922 he lived in Paris. In *Freedom and the Spirit* (written 1927; Eng. tr., 1935) he attempts to adapt Christianity to the requirements of modern intellectuals and proclaims a 'spiritual Christianity' which has no need of doctrinal definitions, bourgeois morality, or set worship.

BEREANS, also known as **Barclayans** and **Barclayites.** A religious sect founded at Edinburgh in 1773 by J. *Barclay and so called from their zeal in studying the Bible (cf. Acts 17: 10 f.). Berean communities were established in London and Bristol as well as in Scotland, but after Barclay's death (1798) they soon melted away, mainly merging with the *Congregationalists.

BERENGAR OF TOURS (*c.* 1010–88), scholastic theologian. His family was connected with St. Martin's, Tours, and by 1030 he was a canon there. He was archdeacon and treasurer of Angers cathedral, but he returned to Tours and from *c.* 1070 he was 'master of the schools'. Some time after 1080 he retired to a hermitage. He was much criticized for his Eucharistic doctrine. His

main surviving work, the *De Sacra Coena*, is a reply to *Lanfranc's criticism. In it Berengar maintains the fact of the Real Presence but denies that any material change in the elements is needed to explain it.

BERGGRAV, EIVIND (1884–1959), Bp. of Oslo from 1937 to 1950. He soon became a leader of the *Ecumenical Movement. After the Nazi occupation of Norway (1940), he organized resistance; he was arrested in 1941 and remained a solitary prisoner in a log cabin until 1945. He assisted in the foundation of the *World Council of Churches.

BERGSON, HENRI (1859–1941), French philosopher. Believing that the way to reality was by intuition, Bergson aimed at a radical criticism of all forms of intellectualism. He held that all intellectualist conceptions of reality rest on spatial patterns which distort the truth and must be abandoned for a new view of time. Reality is evolutionary and progressive, and at the root of moral action lies a 'life force' (*élan vital*). His ideas appealed to many religious thinkers (notably RC *Modernists) who were dissatisfied with the dominating position which traditional theology assigns to the human intellect.

BERKELEY, GEORGE (1685–1753), philosopher. From 1734 he was Bp. of Cloyne. Berkeley held that when we affirm material things to be real, we mean no more than that they are perceived. Material objects continue to exist when they are not perceived by us solely because they are objects of the thought of God. The only things that exist in a primary sense are spirits, and material objects exist simply in the sense that they are perceived by spirits.

BERNADETTE, St. (1844–79), a peasant girl of *Lourdes. At the age of 14 she received 18 Apparitions of the BVM at the Massabielle Rock, near Lourdes. She later joined the Sisters of Notre-Dame at Nevers.

BERNARD, St. (1090–1153), Abbot of *Clairvaux. In 1112 he entered the monastery of *Cîteaux, with thirty other noblemen of Burgundy. Three years later he was sent to establish a new house at Clairvaux, which soon became one of the chief centres of the *Cistercian Order. Before long Bernard was one of the most influential religious forces in Europe. In 1128 he obtained recognition for the Rule of the Order of Knights *Templar, which he is said to have compiled. In the disputed papal election of 1130 he secured the victory of Innocent II; his power became even greater when a former pupil was elected Pope as *Eugenius III in 1145. In his last years he preached the Second *Crusade.

The severely orthodox cast of Bernard's character led him to condemn *Abelard at the Council of *Sens (1140) and to attack *Gilbert de la Porrée. It was his personality rather than the force of his intellect which made him powerful. His writings reveal a clear and penetrating grasp of theological problems, an intimate knowledge of the Bible, and above all a faith inspired by a sublime *mysticism.

BERNARD OF CHARTRES (d. *c.* 1130). He was the chief formative influence on the *Platonist tradition of the school of *Chartres.

BERNARD OF CLUNY (*c.* 1140), also **Bernard of Morval** or **Morlass**. He was a monk of *Cluny during the abbacy of *Peter the Venerable. In a long poem, *De Contemptu Mundi*, he attacks the monastic disorders of his time and stresses the transitoriness of life on earth. It is the source of the hymn 'Jerusalem the Golden'.

BERNARD, JOHN HENRY (1860–1927), successively Abp. of *Dublin (from 1915) and Provost of *Trinity College, Dublin (from 1919). He played a notable part in the Convention on the self-government of Ireland. The most considerable of his scholarly works was his commentary on St. John's Gospel (1928).

BERNARDINES. The title popularly given to the 'Reformed Congregation of St. Bernard', i.e. the Italian branch of the *Feuillants.

BERNARDINO OF SIENA, St. (1380–1444), *Franciscan reformer. He became a Franciscan friar at the age of 22 and in 1438 was elected Vicar General of the Friars of the Strict *Observance in Italy. He was an eloquent preacher, responsible for moral reform in many cities, and at the time of his death perhaps the most influential religious force in Italy. He promoted devotion to the *Name of Jesus.

BERNE, Theses of. Ten theological propositions which were the basis of a convocation of Swiss clergy and laity at Berne in Jan. 1528. They were drawn up in defence of Reformed theology and embodied in a decree which enforced the Reformation in Berne.

BÉRULLE, PIERRE DE (1575–1629), Cardinal from 1627. He established the reformed *Carmelites in France and in 1611 founded the *Oratory, inspired by, but independent of, that founded by St. *Philip Neri. His chief fame rests on his spiritual teaching.

BESSARION, JOHN (1403–72), Cardinal, Greek scholar, and statesman. In 1437 he was made Abp. of Nicaea by the Emp. John VII Palaeologus, whom he accompanied to the Council of Ferrara–*Florence in 1438. He was enthusiastic for the union of the Greek and Latin Churches; when it was repudiated by many of the Greeks he remained in communion with Rome and settled in Italy. He was made a cardinal in 1439, fulfilled important ecclesiastical missions, and was nearly elected Pope. He translated *Aristotle's *Metaphysics* into Latin, wrote various works, and was a patron of scholars.

BETHABARA. Acc. to Jn. 1: 28 (AV) the place where *John the Baptist baptized, and thus presumably the site of Christ's *Baptism. Many important MSS., followed by the RV, read '*Bethany' at this point.

BETHANY. The village of *Martha, *Mary, and *Lazarus, *c.* 2 miles from *Jerusalem, where Christ lodged during the week before His Passion. Its modern name is El 'Azeriyeh, i.e. 'the place of Lazarus'. 'Bethany beyond Jordan' (Jn. 1: 28 RV) is another village.

BETHEL (Heb., 'house of God'). (1) Formerly the chief sanctuary in *Palestine of the *Israelite (i.e. non-Judaean) tribes. (2) The small town near Bielefeld in Westphalia which gives the popular name to the *Bodelschwinghsche Stiftungen*. These consist of homes for epileptics, training centres for deaconesses and male nurses, and a college for Protestant theological students. (3) A name used, esp. by some *Methodists and *Baptists, for a place of religious worship.

BETHESDA. A pool at *Jerusalem (Jn. 5: 2) believed to have possessed healing properties connected with a periodical disturbance of the water. It has been variously identified.

BETHLEHEM. The small town 5 miles S. of *Jerusalem which was the native city of *David and the birthplace of Christ. It contains the 'Church of the Nativity', built by *Constantine in 330 on the supposed site of Christ's birth; despite rebuilding in the 6th cent., much of the original church survives. For the Council of Bethlehem (1672) see *Jerusalem, Synod of*.

BETHLEHEMITES. The name of several orders of religious, none of which survives.

BETHPHAGE. A village near *Bethany. Its exact site is uncertain.

BETHSAIDA. A predominantly Gentile city on the E. bank of the River *Jordan at the point where it enters the Sea of Galilee. It was visited by Christ (Mk. 8: 22). 'Bethsaida of Galilee' (Jn. 12: 21) may have been a different place.

BETHUNE, D. See *Beaton, D.*

BETROTHAL. A free promise of future marriage between two persons. In many countries formal betrothal before witnesses is customary, but in England the Church has ceased to exercise any authority in the matter.

BETTING and GAMBLING. A gamble is a contract whereby the loss or gain of something of value is wholly dependent on an uncertain event. The morality of gambling, considered as a species of recreation, is disputed. Some hold it to be always illicit, but most Christians regard it as permissible, though open to abuse. It must not be about an unlawful matter, the stake must not be excessive, and it must be for some end other than pure avarice, e.g. recreation.

BEUNO, St. (d. *c*. 640), Abbot of Clynnog. He is said to have founded monasteries in Herefordshire, but his chief mission work is believed to have been in N. Wales, where his tomb was long venerated at Clynnog Faur (Gwynedd).

BEURON, Abbey of. The mother house of the 'Beuron Congregation' of *Benedictine monks in Hohenzollern, on the upper Danube. The present abbey and congregation were formed in 1863, though *Augustinian Canons were established at Beuron in the 11th cent. The abbey became famous through its work in the *Liturgical Movement.

BEVERIDGE, WILLIAM (1637–1708), Bp. of *St. Asaph from 1704. In 1672 he became Vicar of St. Peter's, Cornhill, where he had a daily service and Eucharist every Sunday. When T. *Ken was deposed in 1691, Beveridge was offered (but declined) the vacated see of *Bath and Wells.

BEVERLEY MINSTER. The minster, which stands on the site of a Saxon church founded by *John of Beverley (d. 721), is now a parish church. The existing building was constructed after a fire destroyed the earlier church in 1188.

BEYSCHLAG, WILLIBALD (1823–1900), German Evangelical theologian. One of the leading exponents of the '*Vermittlungstheologie', he rejected *Chalcedonian Christology. After 1870 he helped to draw up the new constitution for the Prussian Church; he supported the Prussian Government in the *Kulturkampf; and he was one of the chief agents in founding the *Evangelischer Bund.

BEZA, THEODORE (1519–1605), *Calvinist theologian. De Besze (the original spelling of his name) renounced Catholicism in 1548. He was professor of Greek at Lausanne from 1549 to 1558, when J. *Calvin offered him a professorship at the newly founded academy at Geneva. Beza took part in the Colloquy of *Poissy in 1561. On Calvin's death (1564) he became leader of the Swiss Calvinists. In 1565 he brought out his first edition of the Greek text of the NT; this is the earliest critical text, for which he consulted 17 MSS. He presided over the French National Synod of La Rochelle in 1571. His theological opinions, contained esp. in his *Tractationes Theologicae* (1570–82), are permeated with the Calvinist spirit and rigidly determinist in character. See also *Codex Bezae*.

B.F.B.S. See *British and Foreign Bible*

Society.

BIBLE. The word 'Bible' derives from the Greek word meaning 'books'; as the Biblical Books came to be regarded as a unity, the word came to be used as a single noun.

Jewish Scriptures. The Jews classified their Scriptures into three groups: (1) The Law, which comprised the *Pentateuch (Gen.–Deut.) and was regarded as on a higher level than the rest; (2) The Prophets (Jos., Jgs., 1 and 2 Sam., 1 and 2 Kgs., Is., Jer., Ezek., and the Twelve *Minor Prophets); and (3) The 'Writings', comprising the remaining Books of the English OT, as well as some others, e.g., Tobit, which the Jews later rejected. By the time of Christ Jews recognized the Law and Prophets as Scripture, but the exact compass of the Writings was still undefined. The *Canon of the Jewish Scriptures was prob. settled at about the end of the 1st cent. A.D.

Greek OT. Before the Christian era the Hebrew Scriptures had been translated into Greek, including some which were later rejected from the Canon. The translation in most general use was the *Septuagint (LXX), and it was in this version that Christians first received the Jewish Bible. The Jewish rejection of certain Books c. A.D. 100 was at the time unheeded by the Church; later the Books rejected from the Hebrew Canon came to be known as the '*Apocrypha' (q.v.).

NT. At an early date the Church came to regard some of its own writings, esp. those of Apostolic origin, as of equal authority and inspiration to those she had received from Judaism. The Canon of the NT, based on the four Gospels and the Epistles of St. *Paul, came into existence largely without definition. It was prob. formally fixed at Rome in 382 when the Christian OT (based on the LXX) was also defined.

Authority and Interpretation. The respect shown by Christ and the early Church to the Scriptures of Judaism formed the basis of the Christian attitude to the Bible. If many of the ordinances of Judaism were superseded by the Christian revelation, the OT as a whole retained its authority; its message was completed by the NT, the two together forming a single record of God's revelation. Apart from the challenge of *Marcion, this view was accepted by orthodox and heretics alike. Further, apart from the latitude afforded by *allegorical methods of interpretation, the

Divine inspiration of Scripture was generally held to require belief in the truth of all its assertions on matters not only of history, doctrine, and ethics, but also on cosmology and natural science. In the earlier phases of the modern scientific movement (16th and 17th cents.), this view of inspiration was held by Protestants and Catholics alike. In the 19th cent., however, the critical study of the Bible was seriously undertaken, and at first met with much opposition. It sets out from the belief that an ancient writing must be interpreted in its historical perspective and related to the circumstances of its composition and its meaning and purpose for its author and first readers. As a result the Pentateuch is no longer attributed to the personal authorship of *Moses, and in the NT differences in historical value between the Fourth Gospel and the *Synoptics are recognized. The more important critical conclusions are now widely accepted, though the *Fundamentalists still resist this approach. In the 'post-critical' period attention has shifted to the theology of the Bible and the interrelation of different parts of the OT and NT. See also *Textual Criticism*.

For translations of the Bible into Latin, see *Old Latin* and *Vulgate*; for other ancient versions see *Syrian*, *Ethiopic*, &c. For English versions see following entry; and for translations into other languages see under names of the translators, e.g. M. *Luther.

BIBLE (English Versions). (1) PRE-REFORMATION VERSIONS. There were Anglo-Saxon interlinear glosses of the Gospels and Psalms and translations of portions of the Bible, sometimes abridged. From c. 1250 Middle English metrical versions of certain Books, esp. the Psalms, were made. In the 14th cent. several anonymous translations of NT Books appeared, apparently under the influence of J. *Wycliffe. The so-called 'Wycliffite' Bible exists in two versions: the earlier was prob. the work of *Nicholas of Hereford c. 1390; the later was prob. produced under the leadership of J. *Purvey. The Council of Oxford in 1407 prohibited the making of any fresh translations of the whole or part of the Bible.

(2) THE REFORMATION PERIOD. The first translations made directly from the original languages were the work of W. *Tyndale (q.v.). His NT was printed on the Continent in 1526; it was followed by the *Pentateuch (1529–30), Jonah (1531), and revisions of

the NT. In 1534 Canterbury *Convocation petitioned *Henry VIII that the whole Bible might be translated into English, and in 1535 Miles *Coverdale (q.v.) published a complete Bible dedicated to the King. He based his rendering on Tyndale's version where available; the other OT Books he translated from the German of M. *Luther and others. His Psalter has remained in use in the BCP version of the Psalms. In 1537 '*Matthew's Bible' appeared, with the King's authorization. This consisted of Tyndale's Pentateuch, a version of Josh.–2 Chron. made from the Hebrew, prob. by Tyndale and not previously published, Tyndale's NT of 1535, and the rest in Coverdale's version. Further revisions of the whole Bible followed: the '*Great Bible' of 1539, the '*Geneva Bible' of 1560 (which used verse-divisions), the '*Bishops' Bible' of 1568, and for RCs the *Douai–Reims Bible (qq.v.).

(3) THE AUTHORIZED VERSION. At the *Hampton Court Conference (1604) J. *Rainolds suggested that there should be a new translation of the Bible, and *James I ordered the work. The 54 revisers were instructed to take the Bishops' Bible as their basis, to retain ecclesiastical terms ('Baptism' for 'Washing'), and to exclude marginal notes unless needed to explain Hebrew or Greek words. The result of their work, published in 1611, was a version of great felicity which within a generation displaced previous translations and became the only familiar form of the Bible for generations of English-speaking people. In the U.S.A. it is known as the 'King James Version'.

(4) THE REVISED VERSION AND AMERICAN STANDARD VERSION. The growth of Biblical scholarship as well as changes in English usage since 1611 led to increasing dissatisfaction with the AV in the 19th cent. In 1870 the Convocation of Canterbury took the matter up and a committee of revisers, to which non-Anglican scholars were co-opted, was appointed. They were instructed to introduce as few alterations into the text of the AV as possible consistent with faithfulness and to limit the expression of such alterations to the language of the AV and earlier versions. The NT was published in 1881, the OT in 1885, and the *Apocrypha in 1895. The *American Standard Version*, published in 1901, incorporated into the text of the RV those renderings favoured by the American scholars who had co-operated (by correspon-

dence).

(5) MODERN TRANSLATIONS. In addition to translations of single Books produced in connection with commentaries, there have been a number of private translations of the NT or the whole Bible, aimed increasingly at making the Bible intelligible to the common man. These have included the NT of R. F. Weymouth (1902); the NT (1913) and OT (1924) of J. *Moffatt; the NT (1945) and OT (1948–9) of R. A. *Knox; *The New Testament in Modern English* (1958) of J. B. Phillips; and two versions in non-ecclesiastical English: the *Good News Bible*, Today's English Version, published by the Bible Societies (N.T., 1966; whole Bible, 1976), and *The Living Bible*, paraphrased by K. N. Taylor (1971). The most important Biblical translations, however, have been corporate ventures. The *Revised Standard Version* (NT, 1946; OT, 1952; Apocrypha, 1957) is a revision of the *American Standard Version* undertaken by a committee representing the major Protestant Churches of N. America. The revisers took account of current scholarship and changes in language to produce a more accurate version and one free from archaisms thought to be misleading, unintelligible, or unnecessary, but preserving a dignity suitable for public worship. The RSV is widely used not only in America but in Britain and other English-speaking countries. A Catholic edition is available. The *New English Bible* (NT, 1961; whole Bible, 1970) was made under the direction of a Joint Committee of the non-RC Churches of the British Isles, established in 1947 on the initiative of the Church of *Scotland, to arrange a new translation of the Bible in contemporary English, to be made from the original languages and drawing on the best scholarship and literary judgement. The *Jerusalem Bible* (1966) is an English parallel, made by a group of English-speaking RCs, of *La Bible de Jérusalem*, a French rendering of the original texts by members of the *Dominican École Biblique of Jerusalem and published in France (1948–54). The English text was made with reference to the original languages and is accompanied by revised notes.

BIBLE CHRISTIANS. One of the bodies, also known as Bryanites, which made up the *United Methodist Church in 1907. It was founded in 1815 in N. Devon by William O'Bryan, a local preacher of the *Wesleyan

Methodist Church who had extended his evangelism beyond the limits of his own circuit. The movement spread rapidly and engaged in missionary work abroad.

BIBLE CHURCHMEN'S MISSIONARY SOCIETY. See *B.C.M.S.*

BIBLE SOCIETY, British and Foreign. See *British and Foreign Bible Society.*

BIBLIA PAUPERUM (Lat., 'the Bible of poor men'). Though used from the early Middle Ages to describe various short Biblical summaries for elementary education, the title came to denote specifically a Bible picture-book in which on each page a set group of figures illustrates a NT antitype flanked by two corresponding OT *types, with short explanatory notes.

BIBLIANDER (= Buchmann), THEODOR (*c.* 1504–64), Zwinglian theologian. Succeeding H. *Zwingli in his chair at Zurich, he attacked the *Calvinist doctrine of *Predestination.

BIBLICAL COMMISSION. A committee of cardinals, assisted by assessors, was instituted by *Leo XIII in 1902 for the double purpose of furthering Biblical studies in conformity with the requirements of modern scholarship and of safeguarding the authority of Scripture against the attacks of exaggerated criticism. In 1971 it was reorganized as a part of the Congregation for the *Doctrine of the Faith; it now consists of 20 scholars who advise the Pope and Congregation on Biblical matters.

BIBLIOLATRY. Excessive veneration for the letter of Scripture, found among certain Protestants.

BIDDING PRAYER. The Anglican form of prayer for the Church and State used by preachers before the sermon at University and Assize Sermons and on State occasions. It derives from a group of intercessions, usually in litany form, which in the ancient liturgies occurred after the sermon or Gospel.

BIDDLE, JOHN (1615–62), English *Unitarian. His 'XII Arguments' against the deity of the Holy Spirit was published in 1647; he was saved from sentence of death by his friends among the *Independent Parliamen-

tarians. On the passing of the Act of Oblivion (1652), his adherents began regular Sunday worship. He died in prison.

BIEL, GABRIEL (*c.* 1420–95), scholastic philosopher. He joined the *Brethren of the Common Life and in 1479 became provost of the house at Urach. He took part in the foundation of the University of Tübingen, where he was professor of theology. He was a follower of the *nominalist thought of *William of Ockham. He held that the 'just price' was determined by supply and demand rather than by theological maxims and that the merchant is a useful member of society.

BIGAMY. (1) A 'second marriage' contracted by a person whose 'first' husband or wife is still alive, when the 'first' marriage has not been declared null. (2) Acc. to older usage the term denotes a second marriage after the death of one of the parties of the first marriage. See also *Digamy.*

BILNEY, THOMAS (*c.* 1495–1531), Protestant martyr. He is said to have converted H. *Latimer to the doctrines of the Reformation and to have influenced M. *Parker. In 1531 he was tried for *Lollardy; after recanting and relapsing he was burnt at Norwich.

BILOCATION. The presence of a person in more than one place at the same moment.

BINATION. The celebration of two Masses on the same day by one priest. In the RC Church it is forbidden, except by special dispensation granted by the local bishop if pastoral necessity requires it.

BINDING AND LOOSING. The power given by Christ to St. *Peter (Mt. 16: 19) and later to all the Apostles (Mt. 18: 18). It seems to be a general authority to exercise discipline over the Church, though some have identified it with the power of forgiving or retaining sins (Jn. 20: 23).

BINGHAM, JOSEPH (1668–1723), Anglican divine. His famous work, the *Origines Ecclesiastiae; or the Antiquities of the Christian Church* (10 vols., 1708–22), with its wealth of systematically arranged information on the hierarchy, organization, rules, discipline, and calendar of the early Church, has not been superseded.

BINITARIANISM. The belief that there are only two Persons in the Godhead, involving denial of the deity of the Holy Spirit.

BIRETTA. A hard square cap sometimes worn by clergy in the W. Church.

BIRGITTA. St. See *Bridget, St., of Sweden.*

BIRINUS, St. (d. 649/50), first Bp. of *Dorchester, near Oxford, and Apostle of the West Saxons. He was consecrated in Genoa and landed in Wessex in 634. In 635 he converted and baptized King Cynegils, who gave him Dorchester as his episcopal see.

BISCHOP, S. See *Episcopius.*

BISHOP. The highest order of ministers in the Church. In Catholic Christendom (incl. the Anglican Communion) Bishops are held to be distinguished from other priests chiefly by their power to confer Holy *Orders and to administer *Confirmation. They normally receive consecration at the hands of a *Metropolitan and two other Bishops, and are consecrated to rule a particular *diocese in that Metropolitan's *province. In the RC Church the election of a Bishop is normally performed by the Pope. Elsewhere a Bishop is usually elected by the *Dean and *Chapter of the *cathedral of the diocese or some other ecclesiastical body existing for the purpose; in the C of E the Crown gives the Dean and Chapter leave to elect, and nominates the person to be elected. The candidate must be of mature age (30 years in the C of E), of legitimate birth, have spent a certain period in priest's orders, and be of good character and sound doctrine. The chief duties of a modern bishop consist in administering those Sacraments which he alone is competent to administer and in the general oversight of his diocese. Diocesan bishops may be assisted by other bishops known as *suffragans, auxiliaries, coadjutors, or assistants. In the E. Church bishops, unlike other priests, are required to be celibate. From medieval times English bishops have had a seat in the House of Lords, but since 1878 only 26 English bishops enjoy this privilege. The traditional insignia of Bishops include the throne in the cathedral (*cathedra), *mitre, *pastoral staff, *pectoral cross, and *ring.

The beginnings of the episcopate have long been disputed. It seems that at first the terms 'episcopos' and 'presbyter' were used interchangeably (cf. e.g. Acts 20: 17 and 20: 28). But for *Ignatius (early 2nd cent.) Bishops, Presbyters, and Deacons are quite distinct. By the middle of the 2nd cent. the leading centres of Christianity would appear to have had their own Bishops and until the Reformation Christianity was everywhere organized on an episcopal basis. After the Reformation the title of Bishop was retained in some *Lutheran Churches, but it usually implied no claim to *Apostolic Succession or any of the peculiar powers deriving therefrom. It is also similarly used in the *Methodist Episcopal Churches in America and Africa.

See also *Apostolic Succession* and *Chorepiscopus.*

BISHOP, EDMUND (1846–1917), liturgist. He became a RC in 1867. Weak health prevented him from becoming a monk at *Downside, but he collaborated with A. F. *Gasquet. He made notable contributions to the early history of the *Canon of the Mass and the *Gregorian Sacramentary.

BISHOPS' BIBLE. An English version of the Bible compiled at the direction of Abp. M. *Parker and published in 1568. It was a revision of the *Great Bible. Churchwardens were ordered to obtain a copy for their churches in 1571.

BISHOPS' BOOK, The (1537). Entitled 'The Institution of a Christen Man', it was compiled by a committee of English bishops and divines. It expounded the *Creed, *Sacraments, *Decalogue, *Lord's Prayer, and *Ave Maria, and dealt with various questions disputed between the C of E and the RC Church. A revision publd. by *Henry VIII in 1543 became known as the *King's Book.

BISHOPS' WARS. Two brief campaigns in Scotland in 1639 and 1640. After *Charles I tried to enforce the use of the BCP in Scotland, the Scots rebelled, with the avowed aim of abolishing episcopacy.

BLACK CANONS. A popular name for the *Augustinian Canons.

BLACK FRIARS. A popular name for the *Dominicans, so called from the black mantle which is worn over their white habit.

BLACK LETTER DAYS. The lesser (mainly non-Scriptural) Saints' Days (printed in black), as distinct from the major festivals, which formerly appeared in red letters in the BCP calendar.

BLACK MASS. A popular name for: (1) a *Requiem Mass, so called from the custom of using black vestments; (2) a parody of the Mass celebrated with blasphemous intent.

BLACK MONKS. A name given to the *Benedictine monks, who were so called from their black habits.

BLACK RUBRIC, The. A 19th-cent. name for the 'Declaration on Kneeling' printed at the end of the Holy Communion Service in the BCP. It was inserted at the last moment in the Book of 1552 without Parliamentary authority. When *rubrics came to be printed in red, the fact that the 'Declaration' was not a rubric was indicated by printing it in black.

BLACKWELL, GEORGE (c. 1545–1613), RC *Archpriest. Employed on the English mission since 1576, he supported the policy of those (mainly *Jesuits) who wanted to destroy the government of *Elizabeth I, against the secular clergy who sought a *rapprochement* with the Crown. In 1598 he was made superior of the mission, with the title of Archpriest; 31 seculars (*Appellants) appealed to Rome in 1599; a reply was issued in Blackwell's favour, but after further appeals he was rebuked in 1602. He was imprisoned in 1607 and took the Oath of Allegiance to *James I.

BLAKE, WILLIAM (1757–1827), poet and artist. His works include *Songs of Innocence* (1789); *Songs of Experience* (1794); his poem *Milton* (1804), the proem of which consists of the famous 'Jerusalem', widely used as a hymn; and his allegorical poem *Jerusalem*. His books were mostly engraved by hand and illustrated by coloured drawings. In the *Illustrations for the Book of Job* (1826) the figures, often of elemental strength and beauty, move in the atmosphere of crude black and white contrasts which give Blake's works their characteristic impression of haunting unreality. His art, which spurns reason as well as nature and lives solely in the realm of imagination, was inseparable from his religion, which was itself a religion of art. Opposed to both

dogma and asceticism, it flowed from a sympathy with all living things which Blake identified with the forgiveness of sins proclaimed by the Gospel.

BLASIUS, St. Acc. to a historically worthless legend he was Bp. of Sebaste in Armenia and martyred in the 4th cent. He is said to have saved the life of a child choking over a fish-bone; his intercession is sought for the sick, esp. those with throat trouble.

BLASPHEMY. Speech, thought, or action manifesting contempt of God. It may be directed either immediately against God or mediately against the Church or the saints, and it is by its nature a mortal sin. It was previously also a legal offence but is so in Britain now only if calculated to offend believers or cause a breach of the peace.

BLASTARES, MATTHEW (*fl.* 1335), monk of Thessalonica. He composed an alphabetical handbook on *canon law.

BLEMMYDES, NICEPHORUS (1197–1272), Greek theologian active in attempts to reunite the E. and W. Churches.

BLESSED. The title given to a person who has been *beatified.

BLESSED SACRAMENT. A term used of the Sacrament of the *Eucharist and applied both to the service itself and more esp. to the consecrated elements.

BLESSED VIRGIN, The. See *Mary, The Blessed Virgin*.

BLESSING. The authoritative pronouncement of God's favour. Blessings of people and things are recorded in the OT. In Christian practice blessing finds a frequent place in the liturgy, esp. in the blessing of the elements in consecration. In many places it is now customary to end all services with a blessing, often given at the altar.

BLOMFIELD, CHARLES JAMES (1786–1857), Bp. of London from 1828. During his episcopate over 200 new churches were built and consecrated. His Churchmanship appeared inconsistent. He supported the *Jerusalem Bishopric scheme of 1841, but signed the protest against R. D. *Hampden's appointment to the see of

*Hereford.

BLONDEL, DAVID (1590–1655), French ecclesiastical historian. For most of his life he was a country pastor, though in 1650 he succeeded G. J. *Voss at Amsterdam. His *Pseudo-Isidorus et Turrianus Vapulans* (1628) finally discredited the historicity of the *False Decretals.

BLONDEL, MAURICE (1861–1949), French philosopher. In *L'Action* (1893), his analysis of action led him to conclude that the human will which produces action cannot satisfy itself, because its fundamental desire is never fulfilled by any finite good. From this point of departure he developed an argument for the being of God resting on volition, in the light of which he modified the Scholastic proofs. God imposes Himself on the will as the first principle and the last term; we must therefore 'opt' either for Him or against Him. In his later works Blondel accords a greater place to abstract conceptions and affirms the legitimacy of methodical argumentation, e.g. in the rational proofs of the existence of God. But for him it is the existence of an obscure yet positive affirmation of God that is the very condition that makes the Aristotelian and Thomist proofs possible. For several years he was closely associated with the leaders of the *Modernist Movement.

BLOW, JOHN (1648–1708), composer and organist. His appointments included that of organist of *Westminster Abbey (1669–80). Of his religious works over 100 anthems and 14 services survive.

BLOXAM, JOHN ROUSE (1807–91), ceremonialist. A careful and learned ecclesiologist, he was the real originator of the ceremonial revival in the C of E. As J. H. *Newman's curate at Littlemore, he introduced various ornaments which were copied by F. *Oakeley at the Margaret Chapel in London and thence spread into general use.

BLUMHARDT, JOHANN CHRISTOPH (1805–80), Protestant evangelist. The nephew of Christian Gottlieb Blumhardt, who founded the Protestant 'Basel Mission', in 1838 he became pastor at Möttlingen in Württemberg. His evangelical work attracted attention, largely because of the physical cures which sometimes accompanied it.

From 1852 he worked at Bad Boll, near Göppingen, which became an influential centre of missionary work.

BOANERGES. The surname given by Christ (Mk. 3: 17) to *James and *John, the sons of Zebedee.

BOBBIO. A small town in the Apennines, once the seat of an abbey founded in 612 by St. *Columbanus. Its celebrated collection of early MSS. (now largely in the *Vatican, *Ambrosiana, and Turin) included the 'Bobbio Missal' (in Paris), an important collection of liturgical texts dating from the 8th cent.

BODMER PAPYRI. A collection of unusually important MSS., most on papyrus (see *Papyrology*), acquired by purchase for his library in Geneva by M. Martin Bodmer. They include an almost complete MS. of Jn. (P. 66) of *c.* A.D. 200, over four-fifths of a 3rd-cent. codex of Lk. and Jn. (P. 75), and a copy of *Melito, 'On the Pasch'.

BODY OF CHRIST, The. (1) The human body which Christ took of the BVM and which, acc. to Christian theology, was changed but not abandoned at the Resurrection; (2) the Church; (3) the consecrated Bread at the Eucharist; (4) in its Latin form, ''*Corpus Christi', the feast commemorating the institution of the Eucharist; also used as a designation of churches and colleges dedicated in honour of the Eucharist.

BOEHME, JAKOB (1575–1624), German *Lutheran theosophical writer. He claimed in his writings to describe only what he had learnt by Divine illumination. Most of his works were issued posthumously.

Acc. to Boehme God the Father is the 'Ungrund', the indefinable matter of the universe, neither good nor evil, but containing the germ of either, unconscious and impenetrable. This 'abyss' tends to know itself in the Son, who is light and wisdom, and to expand and express itself in the Holy Ghost. The Godhead has two wills, one good and one evil, which drive Him to create nature. Though evil, being part of God, is necessary, yet man, whose character depends on the constellation of the stars under which his body is formed, can avoid hell by uniting himself to Christ by faith. He will then be a conqueror on earth and will ultimately replace Lucifer, the fallen angel, in the heavenly city. Boehme's writings, which are obscure, had a wide influence.

BOETHIUS, ANICIUS MANLIUS TORQUATUS SEVERINUS (*c.* 480–*c.* 524), statesman and philosopher. He became the friend and adviser of *Theodoric and was consul in 510. He was accused of treason and executed.

His *De Consolatione Philosophiae*, written in prison, describes how the soul attains through philosophy to the knowledge of God. This was widely read in succeeding centuries, and translated into Anglo-Saxon by King *Alfred. Boethius's translations of, and commentaries on, *Aristotle's *De Interpretatione* and *Categories*, and his commentary on *Victorinus Afer's translation of *Porphyry's *Isagoge* were a main source of knowledge of Aristotle in the Middle Ages. It now seems clear that he was a Christian.

BOETTICHER, P. A. See *Lagarde, P. A. de*.

BOGOMILS. A medieval Balkan sect of *Manichaean origin. They taught that the world and the human body were the work of Satan, only the soul being created by God. The ideals of abstinence from marriage, meat, and wine, and renunciation of all possessions, were practised only by the 'Perfect'; the ordinary faithful might sin but were obliged to obey the Perfect and would receive 'spiritual baptism' on their deathbeds. In the 11th cent. the heresy spread to France and Italy as well as Asia Minor. With the Tartar invasions of Hungary, Bogomilism became the national religion. After the Turkish conquests many Bogomils adopted *Islam and practically no trace of the heresy remains.

BOHAIRIC. One of the principal dialects of *Coptic. It originated in the N. part of the Nile delta, but supplanted other dialects throughout Egypt. The Bohairic version of the Scriptures prob. dates from the 6th-7th cents. and is the official version of the *Coptic Church.

BOHEMIAN BRETHREN, later known as '*Moravian Brethren' and 'Unitas Fratrum'. They were a group of *Utraquists who formally separated from that body in 1467; they stood for a simple and unworldly Christianity. Organized as a Church by Lukáš of Prague (d. 1528), the sect spread rapidly. After 1547 repressive measures were taken against them; many migrated to Poland, where they united with the *Calvinists in 1555. Those that remained in Bohemia obtained freedom to practise their cult in 1575; they fixed their principal seat in Moravia, but after the Battle of the White Mountain (1620) they were exiled. In 1721 the remains of the sect accepted an offer by N. L. von *Zinzendorf to settle at *Herrnhut. They laid special emphasis on Church services, organization, and education; their contribution to Czech literature was considerable, esp. through their translation of the Bible (1579–93).

BOHEMOND I (*c.* 1052–1111), Crusader. He led the S. Italian contingent in the First *Crusade. In return for his undertaking to secure the surrender of *Antioch, the other leaders promised him possession of the city, which should have been returned to the Emp. Alexius I; he was invested by the new Latin Patriarch of Jerusalem. He was later defeated by the Byzantines and died in relative obscurity.

BOLLANDISTS. The *Jesuit editors of the '*Acta Sanctorum', so called after John van Bolland (1596–1665), the founder and first editor of the work.

BOLOGNA, N. Italy. In the Middle Ages its university (founded in the 12th cent.) was the chief centre in Europe for the study of *canon and civil law.

BOLOGNA, Concordat of (1516). The agreement between *Leo X and Francis I of France which ended the *Pragmatic Sanction of Bourges. The King was given wide rights to nominate ecclesiastics, who were to be confirmed by the Pope.

BOLSEC, HIERONYMUS HERMES (d. 1584), Reformation theologian. He challenged J. *Calvin's teaching on *Predestination at Geneva in 1551. The Swiss Churches of Basle, Zürich, and Berne, to whom the Genevan Council referred the matter, gave Calvin only moderate support, but Bolsec was nevertheless banished. Calvin deemed the challenge sufficiently grave to reformulate his doctrine on Predestination in the '*Consensus Genevensis'. In his last years Bolsec returned to the RC Church.

BOLSENA, The Miracle of. Acc. to the traditional story, a German priest celebrating Mass in the Umbrian town of Bolsena was disturbed by doubts about the *transubstantiation of the bread and wine; these were resolved when he saw Blood issue from the Elements and bathe the *corporal.

BONAVENTURE, St. (c. 1217–74), *Franciscan theologian, 'Doctor Seraphicus'. Giovanni di Fidanza prob. became a Franciscan in 1243. He taught at *Paris. In 1257 he was elected Minister General and he did much to settle internal dissensions in the order. He was mainly responsible for the election of *Gregory X in 1271 and in 1273 he was made a Cardinal. He took part in the Council of *Lyons in 1274.

As a theologian he had less sympathy with *Aristotelian doctrines than did St. *Thomas Aquinas. In his *Itinerarium Mentis in Deum* he emphasized the folly of all human reason when compared with the mystical illumination which God sheds on the faithful Christian. He had a lasting influence as a spiritual writer.

BONHOEFFER. DIETRICH (1906–45), German *Lutheran pastor. He sided with the *Confessing Church and signed the *Barmen Declaration in 1934. After serving as chaplain to the Lutheran community in London, he returned to Germany in 1935 to become head of a seminary of the Confessing Church at Finkenwalde. He was forbidden by the government to teach and banned from Berlin; in 1937 his seminary was closed. In 1942 he tried to form a link between the Germans opposed to Hitler and the British government. He was arrested in 1943 and hanged in 1945.

His writings have enjoyed wide influence. The best-known, *Widerstand und Ergebung* (1951; Eng. tr. *Letters and Papers from Prison*, 1953), is concerned with the growing secularization of man and the need to speak about God in a secular way.

BONIFACE, St. (680–754), the 'Apostle of Germany'. Wynfrith, as he was originally called, was born at *Crediton. After two earlier missionary journeys, his courage in felling the Oak of Thor at Geismar, near Fritzlar, won him success and he was able to lay the foundations of a settled ecclesiastical organization in Germany. He also reformed the Frankish Church. About 747 he became Abp. of Mainz, but after a few years he resigned to return to Frisia, where he was martyred.

BONIFACE I, St. (d. 422), Pope from 418. He was faced with an antipope during the first months of his pontificate. He did much to restore the authority of the Papacy after the hesitating rule of *Zosimus, e.g. he firmly condemned *Pelagianism.

BONIFACE VIII (c. 1234–1303), Pope from 1294. His pontificate was dominated by his struggle with Philip the Fair of France. The bull '*Clericis laicos' (1296) forbade extraordinary taxation of the clergy without papal consent; Philip then stopped the transport of gold and valuables to Rome, and the Pope had to concede to him the right to decide for himself cases of necessity when he might levy taxes. The struggle broke out again in 1301. In his bull '*Unam Sanctam' (1302) Boniface defended the jurisdiction of the Pope over all creatures; in 1303 Philip tried to bring Boniface to trial. The Pope prepared a bull of excommunication but was taken prisoner at Anagni; though he was released after three days he was broken in health and soon died. Among his achievements was the compilation of the '*Sext' and the foundation of the Roman University, the 'Sapienza', in 1303.

BONIFACE OF SAVOY (d. 1270), Abp. of *Canterbury. He entered the *Carthusian Order as a boy. He was elected Abp. of Canterbury in 1241, but papal confirmation was delayed and he did not reach England until 1244; he was not enthroned until 1249. His metropolitical visitation of his province met with strong resistance. He spent much time abroad.

BONN REUNION CONFERENCES. Two conferences held at Bonn in 1874 and 1875 under the presidency of J. J. I. von *Döllinger to foster reunion between Churches which had retained the faith and order of historic Christianity. Their direction was in the hands of the newly separated *Old Catholics.

BONNER, EDMUND (c. 1500–69), the last Bp. of London to die in communion with the Papacy. Appointed Bp. of *Hereford in 1538 and of London in 1539, he remained uncompromising in defence of traditional doctrines. He was deprived under *Edward VI, restored under *Mary, and under *Elizabeth I refused to take the oath under the Act of *Supremacy of 1559 and died in the Marshalsea prison.

BONOSUS (d. *c.* 400). A Bp. of Naïssus (modern Niš in Yugoslavia) who denied the perpetual virginity of the BVM. His followers, 'Bonosians', survived until the 7th cent.

BOOK ANNEXED, The; **BOOK OF ADVERTISEMENTS**; **OF ARMAGH**; **OF COMMON ORDER**; **OF COMMON PRAYER**; **OF CONCORD**; **OF KELLS**. See *Annexed Book, The*; *Advertisements, Book of*; *Armagh, Book of*; *Common Order, Book of*; *Common Prayer, Book of*; *Concord, Formula and Book of*; *Kells, Book of*.

BOOK OF LIFE. The phrase occurs some 6 times in the NT. The conception of a heavenly register of the elect is based on ideas found in the OT and in *Enoch.

BOOK OF SPORTS. See *Sports, Book of*.

BOOKS OF DISCIPLINE, The. See *Discipline, The Books of*.

BOOTH, WILLIAM (1829–1912), founder and first General of the *Salvation Army. Of partly Jewish origin, he was for some time a *Methodist revivalist preacher. In 1861 he left the Methodists and established a revivalist movement of his own, then called the Christian Mission, which undertook evangelistic, social, and rescue work. From 1880, when the Army spread to the U.S.A., Australia, and Europe, he spent much of his time travelling and addressing meetings.

BORBORIANS. A sect of libertine *Gnostics who flourished from the 2nd to the 5th cents.

BORDEAUX PILGRIM, The. The earliest known pilgrim from the W. to the *Holy Land. He made his journey in A.D. 333–4.

BORGIA, CESARE (1475–1507), Italian prince. The illegitimate son of Pope *Alexander VI, he was made a cardinal before he was 20; he later married the sister of the

King of Navarre. An able soldier, he ruled his subjects with justice and firmness, and on him Machiavelli is said to have based his portrait of the Prince.

BORGIA, St. FRANCIS (1510–72), *Jesuit. He succeeded his father as Duke of Gandia in 1543, but on the death of his wife he joined the Jesuits in 1546. He was the friend and adviser of St. *Ignatius Loyola and St. *Teresa and he soon gained a widespread reputation for piety. In 1565 he became the third General of the order.

BORROMEO, St. CHARLES. See *Charles Borromeo, St*.

BORROW, GEORGE HENRY (1803–81), traveller and author of *The Romany Rye* (1857). He was an agent of the *British and Foreign Bible Society and translated portions of Scripture into various little known languages. *The Bible in Spain* (1843) became popular through its picturesque narrative.

BOSANQUET, BERNARD (1848–1923), Idealist philosopher. With F. H. *Bradley he was the leading exponent of Absolute Idealism in England. His understanding of religion was *pantheistic. He conceived of it only as a stage towards metaphysics and the God of religion as merely the highest of the appearances of the Absolute; the *Incarnation he found meaningless.

BOSCO, St. JOHN (1815–88), founder of the *Salesian Order. A vision at the age of nine aroused in him a keen interest in winning boys to the Christian faith, and in 1859 near Turin he founded the 'Pious Society of St. *Francis de Sales', commonly known as the Salesians. He exercised the minimum of restraint, combined with a careful watch over his pupils' development and personal and religious encouragement.

BOSIO, ANTONIO (*c.* 1576–1629), Italian archaeologist. He was the first to recognize the significance of an accidental discovery of a subterranean burial-place on the Via Salaria in 1578. His *Roma sotterranea* ('1632', really 1634) remained the standard work on the *catacombs until G. B. *de Rossi's researches.

BOSSEY, Switzerland. An Ecumenical Institute of the *World Council of Churches was opened in 1946 at the Château de Bossey, 12 miles from Geneva.

BOSSUET, JACQUES BÉNIGNE (1627–1704), French preacher and from 1681 Bp. of Meaux. His fame as a preacher grew rapidly and in 1669 he delivered the first of his great 'Funeral Orations' (on *Henrietta Maria). He was tutor to the Dauphin (1670–81) and later took a prominent part in French ecclesiastical affairs. In 1682 he was mainly instrumental in securing the support of the French clergy for the moderate *Gallicanism of the Four *Gallican Articles which he drew up. He approved the revocation of the Edict of *Nantes (1685) and directed various works against the Protestants. In his last years the case of Mme *Guyon led him into a bitter controversy with F. *Fénelon, and Bossuet was mainly responsible for Fénelon's condemnation in 1699. His *Méditations sur l'Évangile* (publd. 1731) and his *Élévations sur les mystères* (publd. 1727) are classics of French Catholic devotional literature. By common consent he is among the greatest preachers of all time.

BOTULPH, St. (mid-7th cent.), also **Botolph, Botwulf**. Acc. to the Anglo-Saxon Chronicle, in 654 he founded a monastery at Icanhoe (either Iken in Suffolk or Boston in Lincolnshire).

BOURCHIER, THOMAS (*c.* 1410–86), Abp. of *Canterbury from 1454 and Cardinal from 1467. He was much involved in political affairs. In 1457 he took a leading part in the trial of R. *Pecock, Bp. of Chichester, for heresy.

BOURDALOUE, LOUIS (1632–1704), French preacher. He entered the *Jesuit Order in 1648. His twelve courses of sermons delivered in Lent and Advent before Louis XIV and his court in and after 1670 earned him the reputation of the best preacher of his time.

BOURIGNON, ANTOINETTE (1616–80), Flemish enthusiast. She tried unsuccessfully to found a new ascetic order. After 1662 she became estranged from organized Christianity and thought herself to be the 'woman clothed with the sun' of Rev. 12. The 'Bourignonians', who believed in her pretensions, flourished in Scotland in the early 18th cent.

BOUSSET, WILHELM (1865–1920), German NT scholar. He investigated the connections of later Judaism and early Christianity with the contemporary Hellenistic religions. The growth of the '*Religionsgeschichtliche Schule' owed much to his researches.

BOW CHURCH. The church of St. Mary-le-Bow (S. Maria de Arcubus) in Cheapside, London, so called from the stone arches of the original 11th-cent. church on the site. The present church was built by C. *Wren. It gave its name to the Court of *Arches (q.v.).

BOWING. From early times Christians have bowed 'at the name of Jesus' on the authority of Phil. 2: 10. How far back the custom of bowing at other times, esp. to the altar, can be traced, is disputed.

BOY BISHOP. It was customary in the Middle Ages in some English monasteries, schools, and country parishes to elect on St. *Nicholas's Day (6 Dec.) a boy who should execute until *Holy Innocents' Day (28 Dec.) various functions in church ordinarily performed by a bishop.

BOYLE, ROBERT (1627–91). A leading scientist, he wrote theological treatises vindicating the harmony between the new scientific methods and the Christian faith. He left £50 a year for a series of lectures against unbelievers (the 'Boyle Lectures').

BRABOURNE, THEOPHILUS (1590–*c.* 1661), English *Puritan. In 1628 and 1631 he published pamphlets maintaining that Saturday, not Sunday, should be kept as the Christian Sabbath; for the second of these he was imprisoned for 18 months.

BRADFORD, JOHN (*c.* 1510–55), Protestant martyr. Turning to theology comparatively late in life, he was ordained deacon in 1550 by N. *Ridley, who made him his chaplain. Soon after *Mary's accession he was imprisoned on a charge of sedition; 18 months later he was burnt at *Smithfield.

BRADLAUGH, CHARLES (1833–91), free-thinker. He became an *atheist. He was President of the London Secular Society (1858–90), and from 1860 he conducted the *National Reformer* in defence of freethinking. Prosecution for its alleged sedition, followed by a legal contest as to whether Bradlaugh as an atheist could give evidence (1867-9), led to the passing of the Evidence Amendment Act of 1869. In 1880 he was elected M.P. for Northampton. He was several times excluded from the House of Commons and re-elected; he was finally able to take his seat under the Parliamentary Oaths Act of 1885, which provided for depositions by atheists.

BRADLEY, FRANCIS HERBERT (1846-1924), English exponent of Absolute Idealism. He argued that everywhere in the fields of natural science, ethics, &c. there are patent contradictions and that therefore these realms cannot be conceived of as reality. The only true reality is to be found in an all-inclusive experience, the Absolute, wherein all contradictions, including the gulf between subject and object, are transcended. Theism and personal immortality are rejected.

BRADWARDINE, THOMAS (c. 1290–1349), Abp. of *Canterbury. He taught at Oxford before he became chancellor of *St Paul's Cathedral in 1337. About the same time he became confessor to Edward III. He was consecrated Abp. of Canterbury in 1349, but died later in the year.

Bradwardine sought to build up a theological system on evident propositions, using esp. the *Ontological Argument. Against the prevalent *Pelagian ideas he insisted on the necessity of grace and the 'irresistible' efficacy of the Divine Will, which is the cause of all action, whether necessary or contingent.

BRADY, N. See *Tate, N., and Brady, N.*

BRAGA, Rite of. The form of the Latin rite in use in the cathedral of Braga in N. Portugal. It differs only in details from the traditional Roman rite.

BRAMHALL, JOHN (1594-1663), Abp. of *Armagh from 1661. He went to Ireland as Strafford's chaplain in 1633, becoming Bp. of Derry in 1634. He retired to England in 1642 and to the Continent in 1644. He devoted his exile to defending the English Church against attacks, writing against the *Puritans, against the philosophical materialism and determinism of T. *Hobbes,

and against the RC Church.

BRANCH THEORY OF THE CHURCH. The theory that, though the Church may have fallen into schism within itself and its several parts be out of communion with each other, each may yet be a 'branch' of the Church of Christ, provided that it holds the faith of the undivided Church and maintains the *Apostolic Succession of its bishops.

BRASSES. A form of monument in which the figure of the dead person, engraved on a flat brass panel, was let into a wall or pavement. They were much used between the 13th and 16th cents.

BRAWLING. The offence of creating a disturbance in a church or churchyard.

BRAY, THOMAS (1656 1730), founder of the *S.P.C.K. and *S.P.G. When an appeal for help with the ecclesiastical organization of Maryland, U.S.A., reached H. *Compton, Bp. of London, the Bishop appointed Bray his commissary. In view of the poverty of the clergy, Bray worked out a scheme for the provision of free libraries in the colony; he promoted a similar project at home. Another of his schemes took shape in the foundation of the S.P.C.K. (1698) He sailed for Maryland in 1699, but, finding he could achieve more in Britain, he soon returned. With others, he founded the S.P.G. as a separate society for foreign missions (1701).

BRAY, The Vicar of. The hero of a well-known ballad whose pretended zeal for each new form of established religion from *Charles I to George I assured his tenure of his benefice.

BRAZIL, Christianity in. The conversion of Brazil was effected largely by the *Jesuits, who founded the city of São Paulo in 1554. Brazil became independent of Portugal in 1822 and in the 19th cent. there was a movement against *Ultramontanism. With the establishment of the Republic in 1889, the Church was disestablished. A movement for social reform has been inspired by H. P. *Câmara, RC Abp. of Olinda and Recife. In recent times Protestantism has increased.

BREAD, Leavened and Unleavened. In the Eucharistic rite most of the E. Churches use leavened bread, the W. Church unleavened; the divergence became a cause of dissension. In the C of E either is now permitted.

BREAKSPEAR, N. See *Hadrian IV.*

BREASTPLATE OF ST. PATRICK. An ancient Irish hymn familiar in the translation beginning 'I bind unto myself today The strong Name of the Trinity'. Its ascription to St. *Patrick, though possible, is unlikely.

BREDA, Declaration of. The declaration made by *Charles II at Breda (Holland) in Apr. 1660, immediately before the Restoration. It promised 'liberty to tender consciences' in matters of religion not affecting the peace of the realm.

BREECHES BIBLE, The. A popular name for the *Geneva Bible of 1560 from its rendering of Gen. 3: 7, where the AV has 'aprons'.

BREMOND, HENRI (1865–1933), French spiritual writer. His principal work, *Histoire littéraire du sentiment religieux en France* (1915–32, + index, 1936), is a history of French spirituality, chiefly in the 17th cent., in the form of a series of essays on outstanding religious personalities.

BRENDAN, St. (484–577 or 583), also **Brenainn,** Abbot of Clonfert. The legend of the 'Navigation of St. Brendan' (*c.* 1050) describes his visit to the 'northern and western isles', perhaps the Orkneys and Hebrides. The tradition that he founded the monastery of Cluain Fearta (Clonfert, in Co. Galway, Ireland) may well be true.

BRENT, CHARLES HENRY (1862–1929), Anglican *ecumenical leader. Born and trained in Canada, in 1901 Brent became Protestant Episcopal Bp. of the Philippine Islands, where he combated the opium trade, and in 1918 Bp. of Western New York. After the *Edinburgh Conference of 1910 he induced the General Convention of the *Protestant Episcopal Church to convene a 'World Conference on *Faith and Order'; when the Conference met at *Lausanne in 1927 Brent was its President.

BRENTANO, FRANZ (1838–1917), Austrian philosopher. Ordained to the RC priest-hood in 1864, in 1873 he separated from the Church. Through his lectures at Vienna from 1880 to 1915 he exercised great influence on philosophers of the next generation, esp. in his criticism of Idealism.

BRENZ, JOHANN (1499–1570), reformer of Württemberg. In 1522 he was appointed Preacher at the church of St. Michael in Schwäbisch Hall; he actively supported the Reformation with such success that by the Hall *Kirchenordnung* of 1526 the Reformation in Württemberg was completed. In his *Syngramma Suevicum* (1525) he insisted on the *Real Presence in the Eucharist and thus ensured the acceptance of the *Lutheran teaching over most of Württemberg. In 1553 he became Provost of the Stiftskirche in Stuttgart.

BREST–LITOVSK, Union of. The union concluded in 1596 between the *Ruthenian and RC Churches.

BRETHREN OF THE COMMON LIFE, The. An association founded in the 14th cent. to foster a higher level of Christian life and devotion. The original leader was G. de *Groote (q.v.); he demanded no vows but left his disciples free to continue their ordinary vocations. They founded many schools offering excellent free education, and many of their members engaged in copying MSS. and later in printing. After de Groote's death (1384) a group of them adopted a rule and organized themselves as *Augustinian Canons. The Brethren included I. *Busch, *Thomas à Kempis, and G. *Biel.

BRETHREN OF THE FREE SPIRIT. A name applied by medieval writers to members of various sects who professed to be independent of ecclesiastical authority and to live in the freedom of the Spirit.

BRETHREN OF THE LORD, The. The 'Lord's brethren' referred to in the NT may have been: (1) sons of the BVM and *Joseph, born after Christ; (2) acc. to St. *Jerome, sons of Mary, 'the mother of James and Joses' (Mk. 15: 40), whom he identified with the wife of Clopas and sister of the BVM; (3) sons of Joseph by a former marriage (so the E. Church); or (4) sons of Mary, 'the mother of James and Joses' (not identified with the sister of the BVM), and Clopas, who was perhaps the brother of

Joseph.

BRETSCHNEIDER, KARL GOTTLIEB (1776–1848), German theologian. In his *Probabilia* (1820) he anticipated later NT criticism by questioning the historicity of the Fourth Gospel on the ground of its divergence from the other three. In 1834 he founded the *Corpus Reformatorum*, a series of reprints of the works of the 16th-cent. Reformers.

BRETT, THOMAS (1667–1744), *Nonjuror. On the accession of George I (1714) he resigned his living; he was received as a nonjuror by G. *Hickes, after whose death he was consecrated bishop in 1716. He took part in the abortive negotiations for reunion of his party with the Greek Church and he was involved in the controversy over *Usages. His *Dissertation on the Ancient Liturgies* (1720) is still of some value.

BREVIARY. The liturgical book containing the Psalms, *hymns, lessons, &c. to be used in the Divine *Office of the RC Church.

The primitive Office prob. consisted almost entirely of Psalms and Scriptural readings, to which hymns, *responsories, *canticles, and *collects were added later. By about the 8th cent. the traditional cycle of *Hours was fixed (see *Office, Divine*). Major reforms of the Breviary were undertaken in 1568 and 1911, largely with a view to simplification. The new Breviary of 1971 provides for an *Office of Readings (to be said at any time during the day), *Lauds, a midday Office (which may be *Terce, *Sext, or *None), *Vespers, and *Compline. The Psalter is now spread over a month and most parts of the Bible (except the Gospels, which are included in the Mass lectionary) are read each year.

BRIDE, St. (d. *c.* 523), also **Brigid**, Second Patron Saint of *Ireland. Little can be said with certainty. Acc. to the common view she was born at Faughart, near Dundalk, of parents baptized by St. *Patrick; she took the veil, acc. to one account received episcopal orders, and founded the first nunnery in Ireland at 'Cill-Dara' (the Church of the Oak), now Kildare.

BRIDGES, ROBERT SEYMOUR (1844–1930), poet laureate from 1913. In 1882 he abandoned medicine for literature

and music. *The Testament of Beauty* (1929) is a philosophical poem which seeks to reconcile scientific knowledge with Christian faith. In the *Yattendon Hymnal* (1895–9) he revived many fine 16th- and 17th-cent. melodies; his work was extensively drawn on in the *English Hymnal.

BRIDGET OF SWEDEN, St. (*c.* 1303–73), founder of the *Brigittines. Of wealthy family, she married early and had 8 children. After her husband's death, she founded the Order of Brigittines at Vadstena in Sweden (*c.* 1346). She spent most of the rest of her life at Rome. The revelations which she was held to have received in visions were highly regarded during the Middle Ages.

BRIDGEWATER TREATISES, The. Eight treatises, published between 1833 and 1836, on various aspects of the 'power, wisdom, and goodness of God, as manifested in the Creation'. F. H. *Egerton, 8th Earl of Bridgewater, left £8,000 for the purpose.

BRIGGS, CHARLES AUGUSTUS (1841–1913), OT scholar. He held professorships at the *Union Theological Seminary, New York. An exponent of *Higher Criticism, he was one of the editors of the *International Critical Commentaries* and also of the standard Hebrew *Lexicon*.

BRIGITTINE ORDER (*Ordo Sanctissimi Salvatoris*). The order founded by St. *Bridget of Sweden *c.* 1346. Its members were originally organized in double communities of men and women, using the same chapel, and living in separate parts of the monastery, but this arrangement was given up in the 16th cent.

BRITISH AND FOREIGN BIBLE SOCIETY. One of the largest Bible Societies. A strictly interdenominational body, it was founded in London in 1804 for the printing and distribution of Bibles at home and abroad. It has published translations of the Bible (excluding the *Apocrypha) in many languages.

BRITISH COUNCIL OF CHURCHES. An organization created in 1942 to further common Christian action and to promote the cause of unity among the Christian Churches of Great Britain. It is an 'Associated Council' of the *World Council of Churches. '*Christian Aid' is one of its divisions.

BRITISH ISRAEL THEORY. The theory that the British people is ultimately descended from the Israelite tribes which were taken captive into Assyria in 722–721 B.C. and thereafter disappeared from history.

BROAD CHURCH. A popular term, coined on the analogy of *High Church and *Low Church, for those of the C of E who objected to positive definitions in theology and sought to interpret the Anglican formularies in a broad and liberal sense.

BROAD STOLE. A broad band of material formerly worn like a *stole by the deacon during parts of *High Mass in certain penitential seasons.

BROADCASTING, Religious, in Great Britain. Beginning with hymns and sermons, religious broadcasting has come to include most types of worship. Religious plays, discussions, and talks are also broadcast. Both the B.B.C. and the independent television companies devote several hours a week to religious subjects, including programmes for Jews and other non-Christian groups.

BROMPTON ORATORY. The house and church of the *Oratorians in London. The present church in a somewhat florid Italian style was consecrated in 1884.

BROOKS, PHILLIPS (1835-93), Bp. of Massachusetts in the *Protestant Episcopal Church from 1891. He was the most celebrated American preacher of his day. He wrote the carol 'O little town of Bethlehem'.

BROTHER LAWRENCE of the Resurrection (**Nicolas Herman**) (c. 1605–91), *Carmelite lay brother and mystic. His writings, published after his death as *Maximes spirituelles* (1692) and *Mœurs et entretiens de F. Laurent* (1694), recommend an elevated form of prayer consisting in the simple practice of the presence of God, whether by the imagination or the intellect.

BROTHERS HOSPITALLERS. The order, whose members are mostly laymen, developed out of the work for the sick of St. *John of God (d. 1550). In 1572 *Pius V

approved the order, which adopted the *Augustinian Rule.

BROTHERS. See *Brethren*.

BROWNE, EDWARD HAROLD (1811-1891), Bp. of *Winchester. He became Norrisian Professor of Divinity at Cambridge in 1854, Bp. of *Ely in 1864 and of Winchester in 1873. He was a moderating influence in the conflicts aroused by *Essays and Reviews* (1860) and J. W. *Colenso's work on the *Pentateuch (1862 ff.).

BROWNE, GEORGE (d. 1556), Abp. of *Dublin from 1535. He had been an *Augustinian friar. As Archbishop he took an active part in the suppression of the Irish monasteries and the union of the Irish Church with the C of E under the supremacy of the Crown. Being married, he had to resign his see on *Mary's accession.

BROWNE, ROBERT (c. 1550–1633), *Puritan separatist. A relative of William Cecil, Lord Burleigh, at Cambridge Browne came under the influence of T. *Cartwright and he established independent congregations at *Norwich and elsewhere. He was promptly imprisoned. Having been freed by Cecil, he migrated with his flock to Middelburg in Holland. He fell out with his congregation, fled to Scotland, and then returned to England. He made a formal submission to the C of E, was ordained in 1591, and became rector of Achurch, Northamptonshire. He exercised a powerful influence on the beginnings of *Congregationalism, whose early members were often termed 'Brownists'.

BROWNE, SIR THOMAS (1605–82), physician and author. His fame rests principally on his writings, of which the most celebrated are *Religio Medici* (1642) and *Hydriotaphia, or Urn-Burial* (1658). The former, which expounds his religious outlook, manifests independence of judgement and attempts 'to combine daring scepticism with implicit faith in revelation' (A. H. Bullen).

BROWNISTS. See *Browne, R*.

BRÜGGLERS. A small Swiss sect founded at Brügglen, near Berne, c. 1745, by two brothers, Christian and Hieronymus Kohler, who proclaimed several fantastic doctrines. They were exiled by the Berne government in 1749 and in 1753 Hieronymus was burnt.

BRUNNER, EMIL (1889–1966), Swiss *dialectical theologian. From 1922 to 1953 he taught mainly at Zürich and then until 1956 at Tokyo. He supported K. *Barth in opposing theological liberalism, but he was sharply divided from him by the influence of M. *Buber and by his acceptance of the Catholic doctrine of *analogy, by which a limited knowledge of God may be gained from creation. This, though it did not, like revelation, provide a personal meeting, was a necessary condition of Christian thought. His works include *Der Mittler* (1927; Eng. tr., *The Mediator*, 1934) and *Das Gebot und die Ordnungen* (1932; Eng. tr., *The Divine Imperative*, 1937).

BRUNO, St. (c. 925–65), Abp. of *Cologne from 953. The youngest son of the Emp. Henry I, he took a leading part in furthering the ecclesiastical and temporal policy of his brother, the Emp. Otto I.

BRUNO, St. (c. 1032–1101), founder of the *Carthusian Order. He became head of the cathedral school at *Reims c. 1057. Soon after 1080 he turned to the religious life. After a short time under the direction of St. *Robert of Molesme, he went with six companions into the mountainous district of Grenoble, where he laid the foundations of the Carthusian Order (1084). In 1090 he was summoned to Italy by his former pupil, Pope *Urban II. He refused the archbishopric of Reggio, retired to Calabria, and founded the monastery of La Torre, where he died.

BRUNO, GIORDANO (1548–1600), Italian philosopher. In 1562 he joined the *Dominican Order at Naples, but on being censured for unorthodoxy he fled in 1576. In 1592 he was captured by emissaries of the *Inquisition and was kept in confinement until he was burnt at the stake. He was a fierce opponent of *Aristotelian doctrines and an admirer of N. *Copernicus. His enthusiasm for nature led him to hold an extreme form of *pantheistic immanentism. In the later 19th cent. his name was identified with anticlerical elements in the movement for Italian nationalism.

BRUYS, PIERRE DE. See *Peter de Bruys*.

BRYANITES. See *Bible Christians*.

BRYENNIOS, PHILOTHEOS (1833–1914), the discoverer of the '*Didache'. He became director of the school of the *Phanar at Constantinople in 1867, Metropolitan of Serrae in 1875 and of Nicomedia in 1877. In 1873 he discovered in a library at Constantinople a MS., written in 1056, which included the text of the 'Didache'; he published this for the first time in 1883.

BUBER, MARTIN (1878–1965), Jewish religious thinker. A native of Vienna, he played an active part in the Zionist movement. He was deprived of his professorship at Frankfurt in 1933; in 1938 he became professor at the Hebrew University at Jerusalem.

Buber exercised considerable influence on German Protestant thought as well as on the German Youth Movement, esp. through his small treatise *Ich und Du* (1923; Eng. tr., *I and Thou*, 1937). This contrasts the 'I-It' relationship, which is appropriate between man and things, with the 'I-Thou' relationship, which finds its full expression between man and man and man and God.

BUCER, MARTIN (1491–1551), also **Butzer**, German divine. A former *Dominican, in 1523 he began to preach *Lutheranism in Alsace and was excommunicated. After the death of H. *Zwingli in 1531, he became leader of the *Reformed Churches in Switzerland and S. Germany. He took part in various unsuccessful conferences between Catholics and Protestants. After unavailing opposition to the *Augsburg Interim of 1548, Bucer came to England in 1549 and was made Regius Professor of Divinity at Cambridge. T. *Cranmer is said to have asked his advice on many points, and he influenced parts of the Anglican *Ordinal of 1550.

BUCHMAN, FRANK (1878–1961), founder of the *Oxford Group (q.v.). He served as a *Lutheran minister and undertook social work in America before resigning in a spirit of disillusionment. On a visit to England he attended a *Keswick Convention and experienced conversion. He visited India and the Far East, and in 1920 he went to Cambridge. Some Cambridge undergraduates joined him in visiting Oxford, and out of this visit the Group movement grew.

Buchman visited South Africa as leader of the movement in 1929 and subsequently travelled widely. In 1938 he launched the *Moral Rearmament movement, which stressed international and social morale in place of the individual emphasis of the Group's earlier teaching.

BUCHMANN, T. See *Bibliander, T.*

BÜCHNER, KARL FRIEDRICH CHRISTIAN LUDWIG (1824-99), German philosopher. In *Kraft und Stoff* (1855) he defended a purely materialistic doctrine of the natural world, seeking to reduce everything in the universe, whether mental or physical, to a single non-spiritual source.

BUCKFAST ABBEY, Devon. The first abbey was founded in 1018. Under *Savigny from 1136 to 1147, it was then *Cistercian until its *dissolution in 1539. A private house was built on the site in the 19th cent. and to this the exiled French monks from the abbey of La Pierre qui Vire came in 1882. The present abbey church was consecrated in 1932.

BUGENHAGEN, JOHANN (1485-1558), *Lutheran theologian. As pastor of *Wittenberg, he acted as M. *Luther's confessor. He played a leading part in the organization of Lutheran Church life in N. Germany and *Denmark. The 'Brunswick Church Order' of 1528 was mainly his work. In 1537 he went to Denmark; here he rearranged ecclesiastical affairs on a Protestant basis, himself consecrating seven men as superintendents or 'bishops'. The Danish Church thus lost the *Apostolic Succession.

BUGIA (also **scotula**, **palmatorium**). A portable candlestick with lighted candle sometimes held beside a RC bishop when he reads certain prayers.

BULGAKOV, SERGIUS (1871-1944), Russian theologian. Expelled from Russia during the 1917 Revolution, he was Dean of the Orthodox Theological Academy in Paris from 1923 until his death. He was widely known in W. Europe and America through his participation in the *Ecumenical Movement. Theologically he is best known for his contributions to Sophiology, a body of thought which seeks to solve the problems of the relation between God and the world by the concept of the Divine *Wisdom or *sophia*.

BULGARIA, Christianity in. The official introduction of Christianity into Bulgaria occurred in 864-5, with the baptism of Prince Boris. Missionaries from both E. and W. were at work; *c.* 870 Boris decided in favour of the E. Church. Under Tsar Simeon (893-927) the Bulgarian Church became *autocephalous, but during the Turkish period it became increasingly subject to Constantinople. On attaining political independence in 1870, the Bulgarians created an autocephalous *Exarchate, but were excommunicated by the Patriarch of Constantinople in 1872 for nationalism; the schism continued until 1945. In 1953 the Metropolitan of Sofia assumed the title of *Patriarch and was so recognized by the *Oecumenical Patriarch in 1961.

BULL. A written mandate of the Pope of a more serious and weighty kind than a 'brief'.

BULL, GEORGE (1634-1710), Bp. of *St. Davids from 1705. He was a staunch High Churchman. His *Harmonia Apostolica* (1669-70) was an attack on the more Protestant theories of *justification. His celebrated *Defensio Fidei Nicaenae* (1685) maintained, against D. *Petavius, that the teaching of the pre-Nicene Fathers on the Trinity agreed with that of orthodox theologians of Nicene and post-Nicene times. Bull received the unusual tribute of the formal thanks of the French clergy.

BULLARIUM. A collection of Papal *bulls and other similar documents. Such collections, being the work of private individuals, have no authority beyond that attaching to their component parts.

BULLINGER, JOHANN HEINRICH (1504-75), Swiss reformer. On H. *Zwingli's death (1531), Bullinger succeeded him as chief pastor of Zürich. He joined with J. *Calvin in producing the '*Consensus Tigurinus' (1549), and the Second *Helvetic Confession of 1566 was his work. He enjoyed great prestige in England; after *Pius V's excommunication of *Elizabeth I in 1570, she turned to Bullinger to prepare her reply to the Papal charges.

BULTMANN, RUDOLF (1884-1976), NT

scholar and theologian. He was professor at *Marburg from 1921 to 1951. Bultmann carried the methods of *Form Criticism to the point of radical methodological scepticism in his work on the *Synoptic Gospels. In his *Jesus* (1926; Eng. tr., 1934) he saw the mission of Jesus in His summoning men to a decision to accept His proclamation and to obey His radical command. With his historical scepticism Bultmann combined the insights of *dialectical theology and of the *Lutheran doctrine of *justification by faith alone to make an almost complete hiatus between history and faith, leaving only the bare fact of Christ crucified as necessary for Christian faith. His later work was concerned with *demythologizing the NT message. Holding that not only particular incidents but the whole framework of the *kerygma presupposed an obsolete conception of the universe, he maintained that these mythological elements needed to be reinterpreted so that the *kerygma* might become meaningful to modern man.

BUNSEN, CHRISTIAN CARL JOSIAS VON (1791–1860), German diplomat and amateur theologian. As ambassador to London from 1841 to 1854, he was the chief instrument in the scheme for a joint *Lutheran and Anglican bishopric in *Jerusalem.

BUNTING, JABEZ (1779–1858), Wesleyan *Methodist minister. In 1835 he became president of the first Wesleyan Theological College, established at Hoxton in London. His main work was to transform the Methodist society into a Church, with a sound and consolidated organization, independent of the C of E.

BUNYAN, JOHN (1628–88), author of *The *Pilgrim's Progress*. Few facts about his life are known, other than that he came from poor parents and took part in the Civil War on the Parliamentary side (1644–6). He probably acquired his knowledge and mastery of the English language from reading the Bible. In 1653 he joined an *Independent congregation; he was formally recognized as a preacher in 1657 and soon became well known. After the *Restoration he spent most of the years 1660–72 in Bedford gaol. During and after his imprisonment he wrote extensively. His chief works are his autobiography, *Grace Abounding to the Chief of Sinners* (1666); *The Pilgrim's Progress*

(q.v.); and *The Holy War* (1682). For Bunyan the world was exclusively the scene of a spiritual warfare and nothing mattered save the salvation of the soul.

BURCHARD (*c.* 965–1025), Bp. of Worms in Germany from 1000. Between *c.* 1008 and 1012 he compiled his *Decretum*, a collection of *canon law, which exercised great influence until it was superseded by the collections of the Hildebrandine Reform.

BURCKARD (or **Burchard**), JOHN (d. 1506), Papal Master of Ceremonies from 1483. His principal work was a pioneer collection of rubrics giving detailed instructions for the celebration of Mass. This *Ordo servandus*, publd. in 1502, was later inserted in printed texts of the Missal. His diary is a primary source for the history of the Papacy in the late 15th and early 16th cents.

BURCKHARDT, G. See *Spalatin, G.*

BURDETT-COUTTS, ANGELA GEORGINA (1814–1906), heiress and philanthropist. She inherited her wealth from Thomas Coutts, the banker. She included among her benefactions to the C of E the building and endowment of a number of famous churches and the endowment of the Anglican bishoprics of Cape Town, Adelaide, and British Columbia.

BURGHER. A member of the group in the Scottish Secession Church which in 1747 defended the lawfulness of the religious clause in the civil Burgess Oath and thus separated from the *Antiburghers.

BURIAL ACTS. A series of enactments passed between 1852 and 1900, giving to local government authorities powers to deal with the overcrowding of churchyards and to supervise all burial grounds to secure decency of burial and adequate sanitary precautions.

BURIAL SERVICES. Christian burials were at first occasions of joy; when the spread of nominal Christianity made such joy not always fitting, the service became 'black' and the prayers petitions for speedy purification. By the Middle Ages the burial itself, with committal prayers, was preceded overnight by *Vespers, after which *Mattins and *Lauds (*Dirge) were said in the night, and in the morning a *Requiem Mass. The 1969 RC *Exsequiarum Ordo* provides various alternative forms, in some cases allowing all the funeral rites, including the Mass, to take place in the house of the deceased. In the BCP the Dirge in a modified form (sentences, psalm, and lesson) is ordered, followed by committal prayers at the graveside. Some Anglican revisions recognize *cremation. See also *Dead, Prayers for the*.

BURMA, Christianity in. The first Christian mission to Burma came from the RC Church in 1722. In the 19th cent. the *Baptists opened a mission, followed much later by the *Methodists. The *S.P.G. worked esp. among the English-speaking Burmese. In 1930 the Anglican Church of India, Burma, and Ceylon became legally independent of the C of E, and in 1970 Burma became a separate Province of the Anglican Communion.

BURNET, GILBERT (1643–1715), Bp. of *Salisbury from 1689. A Scot by birth, he settled in England. In 1685 he went abroad after the collapse of the *Exclusion agitation, returning with William of Orange and Mary in 1688. His episcopate was a model of zeal and activity. His writings include his *History of My Own Time* (1723–34).

BURNEY, CHARLES FOX (1868–1925), OT scholar. From 1914 he was Oriel Professor of the Interpretation of Holy Scripture at Oxford. One of the most original scholars of his generation, he emphasized the importance of the Aramaic background of the Gospels.

BURNING BUSH, The. The scene of *Moses' call, where the angel appeared 'in a flame of fire out of the midst of a bush' (Exod. 3: 2–4).

BURROUGH, EDWARD (1634–63), *Quaker. After hearing G. *Fox preaching in 1652, Burrough joined the *Friends and began preaching himself. He was arrested in 1662 and died in prison.

BUSCH, JAN (1399–*c*. 1480), one of the principal *Brethren of the Common Life. He took a prominent part in reforming monasteries in the spirit of the Council of *Basle and for a time worked in co-operation with

*Nicholas of Cusa. He wrote a history of the Brethren's house at *Windesheim.

BUSHNELL, HORACE (1802–76), American *Congregationalist. He was a pioneer of liberal theology in New England. On the ground that language was essentially symbolic, he held that while the doctrine of the Trinity might be true for man in that God was experienced under three different aspects, it did not provide real information as to the inner nature of the Godhead.

BUTLER, ALBAN (1710–73), author of the work commonly known as *The Lives of the Saints* (1756–9). The lives are arranged acc. to the ecclesiastical calendar; their chief purpose was edification, but they remain a monument of wide, if uncritical, research. Butler was a mission priest in England (1746–66), and then President of the English College at St.-Omer.

BUTLER, JOSEPH (1692–1752), Bp. of *Durham. From 1718 to 1726 he was preacher at the *Rolls Chapel (London), where he delivered the sermons which won him his reputation. In 1726 he obtained the rich benefice of Stanhope, Co. Durham, where he prepared his famous *Analogy of Religion* (1736; q.v.). As Clerk of the Closet from 1736 he attended Queen Caroline; in 1738 he was rewarded with the see of Bristol; in 1750 he was translated to Durham.

Butler ranks among the greatest exponents of natural theology and ethics in England since the Reformation. His writings were esp. directed against attacks on the Christian conception of the world and the fundamental grounds of morality. They came to be appreciated only in the 19th cent.

BUTLER, JOSEPHINE ELIZABETH (1828–1906), social reformer. Her main interest was in the reclamation of prostitutes and the suppression of the 'white slave' trade. Her activity was based on a life of prayer, in which she took as her model St. *Catherine of Siena, of whom she published a life in 1878.

BUTLER, WILLIAM JOHN (1818–94), Dean of *Lincoln from 1885. In 1846 he became Vicar of Wantage. Through a long incumbency he trained many curates and in 1848 he founded St. Mary's Sisterhood, which, as the Community of St. Mary the

Virgin (C.S.M.V.), has grown into one of the largest and most active of the Anglican *religious communities.

BUTTERFIELD, WILLIAM (1814–1900), architect. He was a keen Churchman who came under the influence of the *Oxford Movement. He built a number of churches, incl. All Saints', Margaret Street, London, and Keble College, Oxford.

BUTZER, M. See *Bucer, M.*

BYE PLOT, The (1603), also known as the **Priests' Plot**. The lesser of two plots (the 'Main' and 'Bye' plots) against *James I on his accession to the English throne. The perpetrators conspired to kidnap the King in the hope of extorting religious concessions from him, but they were betrayed.

BYRD, WILLIAM (*c.* 1543–1623), English composer. He became organist of *Lincoln Cathedral in 1563; in 1570 he was sworn as a Gentleman of the *Chapel Royal, where he became organist with T. *Tallis. He was a practising RC, but was not thereby prevented from executing his duties. Besides his three superb Masses and two books of *Gradualia*, he set to music the Preces and Responses and Litany of the English liturgy, and composed at least two complete services and a number of anthems, incl. 'Sing Joyfully' and 'Bow Thine Ear'.

BYZANTINE TEXT OF THE NT. The form of the Greek NT which has become standard in the Greek-speaking Church; it is now more generally known as the 'Lucianic Text' (q.v.).

BYZANTIUM. See *Constantinople.*

C

CABASILAS, NICHOLAS (b. *c.* 1322), Byzantine mystical writer. In a set of discourses 'Concerning the Life in Christ' he explained how, through *Baptism, *Confirmation, and the *Eucharist, spiritual union with Christ was to be achieved. He also wrote an 'Interpretation of the Divine Liturgy'.

CABBALA. A system of Jewish *theosophy which, by the use of an esoteric method of interpreting the OT, was believed to reveal to its initiates hidden doctrines. A Christian form of it had a vogue in the 15th and 16th cents.

CABROL, FERNAND (1855–1937), *Benedictine liturgical scholar. He was Prior and then Abbot of Farnborough. He collaborated with H. *Leclercq in editing the *Monumenta ecclesiae liturgica* (1900–13) and the *Dictionnaire d'archéologie chrétienne et de liturgie* (1903–53), besides writing works of his own.

CAECILIAN (d. c. 345), Bp. of Carthage from 311. His importance lies in his part in the opening stages of the *Donatist controversy. The rigorist party at Carthage consecrated a rival bishop, urging that Caecilian's consecration was invalid on the ground that he had received his orders from a '*traditor'.

CAEDMON (d. *c.* 680), the earliest English Christian poet. Acc. to *Bede, Caedmon was a labourer at the monastery of Whitby, who received in a vision the gift of composing verses in praise of God; he then became a monk and turned the Scriptures into verse.

CAEREMONIALE EPISCOPORUM. In the RC Church the liturgical book containing the rites and ceremonies for a bishop. It also contains a certain amount of non-episcopal material, such as instructions for cathedral ceremonies celebrated in the absence of the bishop.

CAEREMONIALE ROMANUM. (1) A Latin service book, compiled *c.* 1275, which contains the rite for investing a newly elected Pope. (2) A treatise, also known as the 'Caeremoniale Capellae Pontificiae', which describes the ceremonial of the Papal curia. It was composed in 1488 by P. Piccolomini, Bp. of Pienza.

CAESAR. The word was virtually a title of the Roman emperors in the 1st–3rd cents. A.D. To the inhabitants of Palestine and the provinces it denoted the imperial throne rather than the person occupying it.

CAESAREA (Palestine). A city on the coast north of Jaffa, it was rebuilt by *Herod the Great and renamed in honour of the Emp. Augustus. It became the capital of Palestine (c. 13 B.C.). In the course of a visit by St. *Peter, the Holy Spirit was here first given to the Gentiles (Acts 10: 44 f.). St. *Paul was imprisoned here for two years (Acts 23: 23, 24: 27), during which he may have written the *Captivity Epistles. The home of *Origen from 231, Caesarea became noted as a seat of learning.

CAESAREA PHILIPPI, now Banias, at the foot of Mount Hermon. The scene of St. *Peter's confession of Christ's *Messiahship.

CAESAREAN TEXT. A form of the Greek text of the Gospels which B. H. *Streeter claimed to identify. From the study of the text of Mk. used by *Origen in his commentary on Jn., the latter part of which is known to have been written at *Caesarea in Palestine, Streeter deduced that it was the text in use at Caesarea in the 3rd cent. More recent study has thrown doubt on the existence of the Caesarean text as a distinct entity.

CAESARIUS, St. (c. 470–542), Abp. of Arles from 502. He took a prominent part in the ecclesiastical administration of S. Gaul and was largely instrumental in securing the condemnation of *Semi-Pelagianism at the Council of *Orange in 529. He was a celebrated preacher. The '*Statuta Ecclesiae Antiqua' has, prob. mistakenly, been attributed to him by many modern scholars.

CAESARIUS OF HEISTERBACH (c. 1180–1240), ecclesiastical writer. In 1199 he entered the *Cistercian monastery at Heisterbach (in the vicinity of Bonn). His 'Dialogus Miraculorum' (c. 1223) is a collection of spiritual anecdotes written for the edification of novices. He also wrote 8 books (not all extant) 'On Miracles' and a life of St. *Elizabeth of Hungary.

CAESAROPAPALISM. The system whereby an absolute monarch has supreme control over the Church within his dominions and exercises it even in matters (e.g. doctrine) normally reserved to ecclesiastical authority. The term is most generally used of the authority exercised by the Byzantine emperors over the E. patriarchates.

CAIAPHAS. The Jewish *High Priest before whom Christ was tried (Mt. 26: 3, &c.).

CAINITES. A *Gnostic sect which, regarding the God of the OT as responsible for the evil in the world, exalted those who withstood him, e.g. Cain.

CAIRD, EDWARD (1835–1908), Scottish philosopher and theologian. A leading representative of the neo-*Hegelian movement in British philosophy, he maintained that the religious principle was a necessary element in consciousness, and that Christianity, in that it overcame the antithesis of the real and the ideal, was the absolute religion.

CAIUS. See *Gaius.*

CAJETAN, St. (1480–1547), founder of the *Theatine Order. A priest in Rome, with Pietro Caraffa (later *Paul IV) and two others in 1524 he founded a congregation known as Theatines for clerics bound by vow and living in common, but engaged in pastoral work.

CAJETAN, THOMAS DE VIO (1469–1534), *Dominican theologian. As General of his order (1508–18), Cardinal (1517), and Bp. of Gaeta (1519), he played an important part in ecclesiastical affairs, urging the cause of reform before the Lateran Council of 1512, reasoning with M. *Luther in 1518, and opposing the projected divorce of *Henry VIII (1530). His commentary on St. *Thomas Aquinas's *Summa Theologica* (1507–22) was the first monument of the 16th-cent. revival of *Thomism.

CALAMY, EDMUND (1) (1600–66), 'the elder', English *Presbyterian. He was one of the authors of the composite work *Smectymnuus.* In the *Westminster Assembly of 1643 he tried to defend Presbyterianism as a middle way between prelacy and congregationalism. He took a moderate line at the

*Savoy Conference but, refusing to conform, was ejected from his preferments in 1662.

CALAMY, EDMUND (2) (1671–1732), historian of *Nonconformity, grandson of the preceding. His writings throw particular light on the ministers and fellows of colleges ejected in 1662.

CALCED (Lat. *calceatus*, 'shod'). A term applied to some branches of certain religious orders to distinguish them from their '*Discalced' brethren. Thus the unreformed *Carmelites, who wear shoes, are called 'calced' as opposed to the Discalced members of the *Teresian reform.

CALDERWOOD, DAVID (1575–1650), Scottish Church historian. He co-operated with A. *Henderson in drawing up the 'Directory of Public *Worship' His main work, *The True History of the Church of Scotland*, was commissioned by the *General Assembly. It is characterized by anti-*Erastian bias, but is a valuable source of information on ecclesiastical history in Scotland in the 16th and 17th cents.

CALDEY ISLAND, off the S. coast of Wales, was the seat of a monastery in the 5th cent. In 1906 an abbey for Anglican *Benedictines was established there. In 1913 most of the community transferred their allegiance to the RC Church; they left Caldey for Prinknash, near Gloucester, in 1928, and the island was taken over by *Trappists from Chimay in Belgium.

CALEFACTORY. The room in a medieval monastery in which a fire or fires were maintained for the use of the monks.

CALENDAR. The calendar in use when Christianity began was that devised by Julius Caesar in 46 B.C. In this the length of the year was not quite exactly calculated. The error was rectified by the *Gregorian calendar of 1582 (q.v.).

Beginning the Christian era with the date of the Incarnation was suggested by *Dionysius Exiguus in the 6th cent. and in due course adopted throughout Christendom. Calculations began from 25 Mar. A.D. 1, the supposed date of the *Annunciation, which was taken as New Year's Day. The Gregorian calendar restored the beginning of the

year to 1 Jan.

For the ecclesiastical calendar, see *Year, Liturgical*.

CALFHILL (or **Calfield**), JAMES (*c.* 1530–70), *Calvinist writer. He held various (mainly academic) positions; in 1570 he was elected Bp. of *Worcester, but died before consecration. In 1565 he published his main work, an *Answer to the 'Treatise of the Cross'* (by John Martiall, 1534–97).

CALIXTINES. The moderate party of the *Hussites of Bohemia and Moravia, also known as *Utraquists (q.v.).

CALIXTUS, GEORG (1586–1656), Protestant theologian. He was professor of theology at Helmstedt from 1614. He tried to build up a theological system (*Syncretism) which would reconcile *Lutherans, *Calvinists, and Catholics on the basis of the Scriptures, the *Apostles' Creed, and the faith of the first five cents.

CALLING. A technical term which came into use in Reformation theology for the Divine act whereby those destined for salvation are persuaded to accept the Gospel.

CALLISTUS I, St. (d. *c.* 222), Bp. of Rome from 217. His pontificate was marked by controversy. He was attacked by *Hippolytus for countenancing *Sabellianism and for his laxity, esp. in re-admitting to Communion those guilty of fornication and adultery, but some of the charges may be discounted.

CALLISTUS II (d. 1124), Pope from 1119. Guido of Burgundy was connected with most of the royal houses of Europe. He was a strong opponent of lay investiture; during his pontificate the long-drawn-out *Investiture Controversy was settled by the Concordat of *Worms (1122). At the *Lateran Council of 1123 he issued a series of decrees on simony, clerical celibacy, and the election of prelates.

CALLISTUS III (1378–1458), Pope from 1455. Originally a supporter of *Benedict XIII, he induced his successor Clement VIII (antipope, 1423–9) to submit to *Martin V. He was thereupon appointed Bp. of Valencia and in 1444 made a cardinal. The main efforts of his papacy were directed to the organization of a crusade against the Turks, but his plans had little success. He annulled the sentence against *Joan of Arc.

CALOVIUS, ABRAHAM (1612–86), German *Lutheran theologian. A man of great learning, he took part in many controversies. As a staunch defender of Lutheran orthodoxy he opposed G. *Calixtus's policy for reuniting the Confessions. He also attacked *Socinianism and *Pietism.

CALOYER. A designation for Greek monks.

CALVARY, Mount. The place of Christ's crucifixion, just outside *Jerusalem. Its Hebrew name is 'Golgotha'. See also *Holy Sepulchre*.

CALVIN, JOHN (1509–64), French reformer and theologian. His break with the RC Church appears to have taken place in 1533 after a religious experience in which he believed he had received a mission to restore the Church to its original purity. He resigned his benefices and in 1535 fled to Basle. He issued the first edition of his *Institutes* in 1536. Later that year he yielded to G. *Farel's request to help organize the Reformation at Geneva. His *Articuli de Regimine Ecclesiae* (1536), containing regulations for admission to the Lord's Supper and requiring a profession of faith from all citizens, were accepted, but his use of the discipline of excommunication and his refusal to conform the usages of the Church of Geneva with those of Berne led to the expulsion of both Farel and Calvin in 1538. Calvin spent the next three years as minister to the French congregation and lecturer at Strasburg. Here he issued a fresh edition of the *Institutes* (1539) and a commentary on Romans (1540), and wrote his famous letter to Card. *Sadoleto, defending Reformation principles. In 1541 he returned to Geneva, where he devoted himself to establishing a theocratic regime on OT lines. This was achieved by a series of 'Ordinances' which placed the government in the hands of pastors, elders, and deacons, assisted by a *consistory court, which was chiefly a tribunal of morals. It wielded the power of excommunication, and new legislation inflicted severe punishments various for purely religious offences. Opposition was overcome by force; the most famous of those executed was M. *Servetus

(1553). By 1555 Calvin was uncontested master of Geneva. He took part in the affairs of other Protestant communities and gave shelter to English Protestant refugees. He also wrote commentaries on the NT, on most books of the OT, and a treatise on Predestination (1552). In 1559 he founded the Academy of Geneva to continue his teaching. See also the following entry.

CALVINISM. The theological system of J. *Calvin, which is generally accepted in most non-Lutheran reformed Churches. It shares with *Lutheranism belief in the Bible as the only rule of faith, the denial of human free will after the *Fall of Adam, and the doctrine of *justification by faith alone. To these Calvin added the doctrines of the inamissibility of grace and the gratuitous *predestination of some to salvation and others to damnation. He differed from M. *Luther also in defending the subjugation of the State to the Church. He attempted a compromise between Luther's belief in the *Real Presence in the Eucharist and H. *Zwingli's view of a mere symbolism, but his language here is ambiguous.

The most influential document of strict Calvinism was the second *Helvetic Confession of 1566, which was accepted in many reformed countries. The *Huguenots were Calvinist, and in 1622 Calvinism became the state religion in *Holland. In England Calvinism had some influence on the *Thirty-Nine Articles and gained a firm footing in the Nonconformist Churches. In *Scotland it found congenial soil. In North America many sects profess it in a more or less modified form. In Germany it replaced Lutheranism in some places. Calvinism suffered setbacks in the 18th and 19th cents., but in modern times it has again come to the fore, esp. through the works of K. *Barth.

CALVINISTIC METHODISM. The Church which was established in *Wales through the revivalist preaching of H. *Harris and others. Their first Association was held in 1743. They had no wish to separate from the C of E, but in the face of persecution they were obliged to seek the protection of the *Toleration Act, and their meeting-houses were registered as Dissenting Chapels. The first ordination of ministers took place in 1811. The Confession of Faith (based on the *Westminster Confession) was drawn up in 1823 and the *Constitutional*

Deed formally completed in 1826. The Church is *Presbyterian in government and mainly Welsh-speaking.

CAMALDOLESE. A religious order founded *c.* 1012 by St. *Romuald at Camaldoli, near Arezzo. Its ideal was the minimum of communal ties, though by 1102 a monastery was founded at Fontebuono on *coenobitic lines, and practices have varied in different congregations.

CÂMARA, HELDER PASSOA (1909–), RC Abp. of Olinda and Recife in *Brazil since 1964. A native of Brazil, he was ordained priest in 1930 and consecrated bishop in 1952. He has played a prominent part in the movement for social reform in the country, and has strongly advocated simplicity in the life of the Church.

CAMBRIDGE CAMDEN SOCIETY. A society founded in 1839 by J. M. *Neale and B. *Webb for the study of ecclesiastical art. Renamed the 'Ecclesiological Society' in 1846, it survived until 1868.

CAMBRIDGE PLATONISTS, a group of influential philosophical divines who flourished at Cambridge between 1633 and 1688. They stood between the *Puritans and the High Anglicans and advocated tolerance and comprehension within the Church, basing their demand on their conception that reason was the arbiter both of natural and of revealed religion. They held that reason could judge the data of revelation by virtue of the indwelling of God in the mind. They included B. *Whichcote, R. *Cudworth, and H. *More.

CAMERARIUS, JOACHIM (1500–74), German classical scholar and reformer. He took part in drawing up the Confession of *Augsburg, wrote the life of P. *Melanchthon, and discussed with Francis I in 1535 and with Maximilian II in 1568 the possibility of reunion between Catholics and Protestants.

CAMERLENGO. The chamberlain of the Papal court who administers the property of the Holy See. One of his duties is to assemble and direct the *conclave. He is always a *cardinal.

CAMERON, JOHN (d. 1446), Bp. of Glasgow from 1428 and Chancellor of Scotland. He supported the king in his attack on the ecclesiastical courts; on refusing a papal summons to Rome in 1433 he was excommunicated. He nevertheless attended the Council of *Basle and in 1436 he obtained the Pope's promise to take steps to reform the Church in Scotland.

CAMERON, JOHN (*c.* 1579–1625), Scottish Protestant theologian. He held academic posts in France and Scotland, but his exalted views on the nature of the secular authority led him into trouble. In his theological works he argued that Christ's action on the will was moral, not physical; he was thus considered by stricter *Calvinists to be inclining to *Pelagianism. His doctrines were accepted by a group of contemporary theologians ('Cameronites').

CAMERON, RICHARD (d. 1680), Scottish *Covenanting leader. He was an eloquent field-preacher in the Covenanting cause. In 1680 he joined in the 'Sanquhar Declaration', which disowned allegiance to *Charles II and attacked Covenanters who accepted the royal indulgence then offered. He died in a skirmish with royal troops.

CAMERONIANS. A term applied to extreme *Covenanters, such as the followers of R. *Cameron, and esp. to the *Reformed Presbyterian Church.

CAMILLUS OF LELLIS, St. (1550–1614), founder of the 'Ministers of the Sick'. Having been reduced to poverty through gambling, he was employed by the *Capuchins at Manfredonia and in 1575 he began to embrace a penitential life. He became a nurse at the hospital of S. Giacomo in Rome, was ordained priest in 1584, and about the same time established a congregation, whose members take a fourth vow to devote themselves to the material and spiritual care of the sick, esp. the plague-stricken. They are also known as 'Camillians' or '*Agonizants'.

CAMISARDS. A group of fanatical French Protestants, who rose in revolt in the Cévennes district in 1702 after rigorous steps were taken by Louis XIV to suppress their religion.

CAMPANELLA, TOMMASO (1568–

1639), Italian *Dominican philosopher. He incurred the hostility of his ecclesiastical superiors and was suspected by the civil authorities of complicity in anti-Spanish plots; he spent much of his life in prison. Anticipating R. *Descartes, Campanella held that individual consciousness was the fundamental fact of experience, and that the existence of God could be deduced from the idea of God in human consciousness.

CAMPANILE. In general any bell-tower or bell-steeple; the name is applied esp. to the detached bell-towers which originated in Italy.

CAMPBELL, ALEXANDER (1788–1866), founder of the 'Campbellites' or '*Disciples of Christ'. The son of a *Presbyterian minister, he emigrated from Scotland to the U.S.A. in 1809. Having become convinced of the necessity for baptism by *immersion, he joined the *Baptists, but differences of belief over credal statements brought separation from that body and in 1827 he founded an independent congregation known as the Disciples of Christ (q.v.).

CAMPBELL, JOHN McLEOD (1800–72), Scottish theologian. In 1831 he was found guilty of heresy by the *General Assembly and deprived of his cure. The thesis of his principal work was that the spiritual context of the sufferings of Christ, rather than their penal character, made atonement for sin.

CAMPEGGIO, LORENZO (1472–1539), Abp. of *Bologna from 1523. He was sent to England in 1518 to try to gain *Henry VIII's support for a crusade against the Turks, and in 1524 Henry made him Bp. of *Salisbury. After work in Germany he returned to England in 1528 in the matter of Henry's projected divorce. He was instructed with T. *Wolsey to settle the question of fact, though the Pope had secretly pledged him to refer the matter to Rome before passing judgement. Failing to satisfy the king, Campeggio left England in 1529.

CAMPION, St. EDMUND (1540–81), *Jesuit. He became a Junior Fellow of St. John's College, Oxford, in 1557 and was ordained deacon in the C of E in 1569. In 1571 he went to *Douai and was received into the RC Church. He became a Jesuit in 1573 and in 1580 he joined R. *Parsons in

the first Jesuit mission to England. He was arrested in 1581, charged with conspiracy, and executed. He was among the *Forty Martyrs canonized in 1970.

CAMP MEETING. A revivalist meeting held out of doors and lasting for several days.

CANAAN. The land, later known as Palestine, which the Israelites conquered and occupied in the later part of the second millennium B.C., or possibly rather earlier.

CANADA, Christianity in. The early 17th-cent. settlements were inspired by two objects: the pursuit of the fur trade and the conversion of the Indians. The *Recollects undertook the first missionary efforts, but leadership soon passed to the *Jesuits. After the British conquest of 1759 immigrants from the American colonies and Britain introduced a variety of denominations, and frontier revivalists contributed a strong evangelical tradition. The C of E was at first established but the numerical preponderance of other groups led to its loss of special status. The United Church of Canada was formed in 1925 by the union of *Methodists, *Congregationalists, and most *Presbyterians. The main denominations are now RC, United, and Anglican.

CANDLE. The widespread use of candles as ornaments of the *altar appears to have developed from processional lights which in earlier times were stood beside or on the altar. Votive candles are lit before statues in church as personal offerings. See also *Altar Lights* and *Paschal Candle*.

CANDLEMAS. The feast, now observed on 2 Feb., commemorating the purification of the BVM and the presentation of Christ in the Temple 40 days after His birth (Lk. 2: 22–39). It was kept locally at *Jerusalem from *c.* 350. In 542 *Justinian ordered its observance at *Constantinople; it spread throughout the E. Church and somewhat later in the W. A procession with lighted candles is a distinctive feature of the RC rite of the day.

CANGE, C. D. DU. See *Ducange, C. D.*

CANISIUS, St. PETER (1521–97), *Jesuit. He founded a Jesuit colony at *Cologne and attacked the Protestant views of Abp. *Hermann of Wied. From 1549 he worked in Bavaria, Vienna, and Prague. He compiled a number of popular catechisms. In 1556 he became Provincial of Upper Germany and to him more than any other was due the success of the *Counter-Reformation in S. Germany.

CANO, MELCHIOR (1509-60), Spanish *Dominican theologian. He took part in the debates on the *Eucharist and on *Penance at the Council of *Trent and later became involved in Spanish politics. He defended the unusual thesis that the consent of the parties is merely the *matter of the sacrament of *matrimony, the *form being the sacerdotal blessing.

CANON. The Greek word originally meant a rod or bar; it came to be used of the rules of an art or trade or to signify a list or catalogue. In Christian language it denotes the list of books regarded as Scripture (*Canon of Scripture); the central part of the Mass (*Canon of the Mass); and the rules concerning the life and discipline of the Church (*Canon Law).

CANON (ecclesiastical title). Though first applied to all clergy on the official staff of a diocese, the word came to be limited to those secular clergy belonging to a cathedral or collegiate church. 'Residentiary canons' form the permanent salaried staff of a cathedral and are responsible for the maintenance of its services, fabric, &c. A 'non-residentiary canon' is one who holds an unsalaried post, which may entail certain privileges and responsibilities. See also *Minor Canon* and *Prebend* and *Prebendary*.

CANON (hymnological). In the E. Church stanzas of poetry began to be inserted between the verses of the Biblical *Canticles sung during the second part of *Orthros. In most places the text of the Canticles (except the *Magnificat) then disappeared, leaving only the sets of odes which are known as the canon.

CANON EPISCOPALIS. In the Latin rite the bishop's liturgical book containing the *Ordinary of the Mass with the form of episcopal blessing and other prayers and forms used by bishops.

CANON LAW. The body of ecclesiastical rules or laws concerning matters of faith, morals, and discipline. Its beginnings may be traced to the practice of convening Councils to settle matters of uncertainty or dispute and their issue of *ad hoc* pronouncements (known as 'canons') on matters of doctrine and discipline. The degree of authority of such pronouncements varied; those of the Council of *Nicaea (325) came to possess a primacy in E. and W. The decrees of influential bishops were another source of ecclesiastical legislation, and special authority attached to the letters of Popes (*Decretals). An important stage in the development of Canon Law was reached when *Gratian issued his *Decretum* (c. 1140). Though in essence this was a private collection, such authority was accorded to it that it was supplemented by a series of later collections to form the *Corpus Iuris Canonici* (q.v.), which enjoyed authority until it was overhauled and codified in the *Codex Iuris Canonici* issued in 1917.

In addition to laws regarded as universally binding, there have been others of local authority, such as the Synodical Constitutions of the Province of *Canterbury. See also *Canons, The*.

CANON OF THE MASS. The consecratory prayer of the Mass used practically throughout the RC Church until 1968. A nearly related form is quoted by St. *Ambrose (d. 397), and by the time of Pope *Gregory I (590-604) it was virtually fixed. Beginning with the words '*Te igitur', it is a succession of short prayers, including the Words of *Institution. The want of any clear sequence of thought and the existence of two lists of saints have suggested that the text was dislocated at an early stage in its history. Alternative forms of *Eucharistic Prayers (q.v.) were introduced in 1968.

CANON OF SCRIPTURE. The term '*canon' gradually acquired a technical meaning for the Books which were officially received as Scripture. Acc. to Jewish tradition the Hebrew Canon (of the OT) was closed by the 'Great Synagogue' in the 5th cent. B.C., after the return from Exile; modern scholars are agreed that it was formed gradually at a later period and was prob. closed towards the end of the 1st cent. A.D. The Jews of the *Diaspora also regarded as equally inspired certain other Books, which came to be known as the

*Apocrypha (q.v.). The kernel of the NT Canon, the four Gospels and 13 Pauline letters, came to be accepted *c*.A.D. 130 and were placed on the same footing with the OT between 170 and 220. Other NT writings were received later, while some other works, such as the Epistle of *Barnabas, were admitted by individual Churches, though rejected by the majority. St. *Athanasius in his *Festal Letter* for 367 is the earliest exact witness to the present NT Canon. A Council prob. held at Rome in 382 under *Damasus gave a complete list of the canonical Books of the OT and NT which is identical with that given at the Council of *Trent.

CANONESS. A member of certain religious communities of women founded in the *Carolingian period; they were bound by less severe restrictions than contemporary nuns. After the 11th cent. some orders of '*canons regular' had counterparts for women, known as 'canonesses regular'.

CANONIZATION. In the RC Church the definitive sentence by which the Pope declares a particular dead person to have already entered into heavenly glory and ordains for the new 'saint' a public cult throughout the Church. In the Orthodox Church canonizations are usually made by a synod of bishops within a particular *autocephalous Church.

In the early Church bishops controlled the cult of saints within their own dioceses, but the veneration of some saints spread beyond local limits and the resulting problems brought papal intervention. The first historically attested canonization is that of *Ulrich of Augsburg in 993. About 1170 *Alexander III asserted that no one should be venerated as a saint without the authority of the Roman Church; the assertion was included in the *Decretals of *Gregory IX and became part of W. Canon Law. Papal authority is now given only after a long legal process.

CANONS, Apostolic. See *Apostolic Canons.*

CANONS, The. The main body of canonical legislation in the C of E after the Reformation was until recently the Book of Canons passed by the *Convocation of Canterbury in 1604 and that of York in 1606. The subjects covered included the conduct of Divine service and the administration of the Sacraments, the duties and behaviour of clerics, the care of churches, and ecclesiastical courts. Apart from the section of Canon 113 dealing with the *seal of confession (which remained unrepealed), the 17th–cent. canons have now been superseded by a new set, promulgated in two parts, in 1964 and 1969. They cover much the same ground.

CANONS REGULAR. A body of canons living under rule which originated in the 11th cent. In the 12th cent. they largely adopted the Rule of St. *Augustine and have come to be known as *Augustinian Canons (q.v.).

CANOPY, Processional. An awning carried over the Bl. Sacrament in processions, and also over certain ecclesiastical dignitaries, in the RC Church.

CANOSSA, N. Italy, the scene of the public humiliation and submission of *Henry IV to *Gregory VII. The Emperor is said to have stood for three days in the snow outside the Pope's lodgings before absolution from excommunication was granted.

CANTATA. A form of musical composition usually consisting of a series of recitatives and arias for solo voices concluding with a chorale, sung in parts by a choir. Those of J. S. *Bach and G. F. *Handel are among the best known. In the 18th cent. cantatas were used instead of the *gradual in the Lutheran Ante-Communion service.

CANTATE DOMINO (Lat., 'O sing unto the Lord'), Ps. 98, from its opening words. It is provided as an alternative to the *Magnificat at Evensong in the BCP.

CANTERBURY. In 597 St. *Augustine arrived in Canterbury and established his first church there. He had been instructed to organize England in two provinces, with archbishops at London and *York, but from the first the place of London was taken by Canterbury. The struggle for precedence between the archiepiscopal sees of Canterbury and York ended in the 14th cent., with the victory of the former, whose archbishop is 'Primate of All England'. See also *Anglican Communion.*

Acc. to *Bede an already existing Roman basilica was converted by St. Augustine as the Cathedral Church of Christ. Destroyed by fire in 1067, the church was rebuilt in Norman style by *Lanfranc, extended under *Anselm, and consecrated in 1130. After a fire in 1174 the choir was rebuilt in Transitional style; under Abp. *Sudbury the nave was pulled down and rebuilt in Perpendicular style. The chief glory of the cathedral in the Middle Ages was the shrine of St. Thomas *Becket, dedicated in 1220.

About 598 a monastery, dedicated to St. Peter and St. Paul, was established east of the city to accommodate the bodies of future bishops and kings. In 978 St. *Dunstan rededicated the conventual church in honour of Sts. Peter and Paul and St. Augustine, and the monastery came to be known as St. Augustine's. A building on the site was opened as a college for missionaries in 1848; it has since been used for various other purposes.

CANTERBURY CAP. A soft cloth cap sometimes worn by English clerical dignitaries and others.

CANTICLE. A song or prayer (normally other than one of the Psalms) derived from the Bible, which is used in the liturgical worship of the Church. In the E. and W. Churches the NT Canticles, the *Magnificat and *Nunc Dimittis (and in the W. also the *Benedictus), are used in the Office every day. The OT Canticles prescribed for use in the E. Church are usually omitted; in the W. they vary from day to day.

CANTICLE OF THE SUN, The. A hymn of St. *Francis in praise of the Divine revelation in nature.

CANTICLES, Book of. See *Solomon, Song of.*

CANTILUPE, St. THOMAS DE (c. 1218–82), also **St. Thomas of Hereford,** Bp. of *Hereford from 1275. He was Chancellor of Oxford University in 1261 and again in 1273, and for a short time Chancellor of England in 1265. As bishop he combated simoniacal practices and nepotism. His later years were filled with disputes with J. *Peckham over jurisdiction; these led to his excommunication in 1282. The fame of his sanctity and the miracles at his tomb nevertheless led to his canonization in 1320.

CANTILUPE, WALTER DE (d. 1266), Bp. of *Worcester and uncle of Thomas de *Cantilupe. He was consecrated by *Gregory IX in 1237. His support of the barons against Henry III is said to have been the only hindrance to his canonization.

CANTOR. A singer who pre-intones and leads in the liturgical music of the choir office and in liturgical processions.

CANTORIS (Lat., '[the seat] of the cantor'). As the traditional place of the *cantor is on the north side of the choir, the term is used to indicate those who in antiphonal singing sit on that side.

CAPERNAUM. A town of uncertain site, near the Sea of Galilee, which became the headquarters of Christ.

CAPITAL PUNISHMENT. The infliction of death by judicial sentence of the State. St. *Paul appears to recognize its legitimacy (Rom. 13: 1–5), and no religious body as such holds it to be immoral except the Society of *Friends. Individual Christians have sometimes held that it contravenes the 6th commandment.

CAPITILAVIUM (Lat., 'washing of the head'), an early medieval name for *Palm Sunday.

CAPITO, WOLFGANG (1478–1541), Protestant reformer. His real name was Köpfel. In the early stages of the Reformation, Capito was its leading figure in Strasburg, and he later assisted in compiling the *Tetrapolitan Confession. He favoured gentle methods and toleration.

CAPITULAR MASS. The public Mass said or sung in RC cathedrals and collegiate churches, attended by the whole chapter.

CAPITULARY. (1) A collection of civil statutes; (2) a compilation of previously enacted laws made by bishops for the guidance of clergy and laity in the diocese; (3) in Biblical MSS. a brief summary of the contents, put at the head of each Book.

CAPPA MAGNA. In the RC Church a cloak with a long train and large hood, the use of which is reserved to cardinals, bishops, and certain other dignitaries.

CAPPADOCIAN FATHERS, The. St. *Basil the Great, St. *Gregory of Nazianzus, and St. *Gregory of Nyssa (qq.v.).

CAPREOLUS, JOHN (c. 1380–1444), *Thomist philosopher and theologian. A *Dominican, he lectured at *Paris and Toulouse. His main work (*Defensiones*, 1409–33) was a defence of the teaching of St. *Thomas Aquinas against numerous attacks; it did much to revive the authority of Thomism.

CAPTIVITY EPISTLES, The. The four epistles—Phil., Col, Eph., and Philem.—believed to have been written by St. *Paul in captivity. See artt. on individual epistles.

CAPUCHINS. An offshoot of the *Franciscan Order, founded by Matteo di Bassi of Urbino (d. 1552), an *Observant Friar, who wished to return to the primitive simplicity of the order. Its members wear a pointed cowl (*capuche*). The Rule, drawn up in 1529, re-emphasized the Franciscan ideals of poverty and austerity. The Capuchins long remained the strictest of the Franciscan families.

CARBONARI (Ital., 'charcoal-burners'). A secret political society of the early 19th cent. They aimed at advancing liberal ideas in politics and religion; they rejected all forms of Divine revelation and regarded *natural religion as a sufficient basis for virtue. They flourished chiefly in Italy and France.

CARDINAL. The title, at first applied to any priest permanently attached to a church, came to be restricted to the clergy of Rome, i.e. the parish priests, the bishops of the *suburbicarian dioceses, and the 7 (later 14) district deacons. These gradually formed a college and became (when assembled in *consistory) the Pope's immediate counsellors. They assumed the government of the RC Church during a vacancy of the Holy See, and since 1179 the right of electing a Pope has been exclusively theirs.

The three ranks of cardinals originated at different times. The cardinal-priests were the parish clergy of the various Roman churches. Cardinal-deacons had care of the poor of the seven districts of Rome. Cardinal-bishops were created about the 8th cent., when the increase in papal business necessitated invoking the help of neighbouring bishops to act from time to time as the Pope's representative. Cardinals are nominated by the Pope. Their main functions are administrative. Unless excused or bishops of foreign dioceses, they reside in Rome and act as heads of curial offices and *Roman congregations and preside over ecclesiastical commissions.

CARDINAL VIRTUES. The virtues of prudence, temperance, fortitude, and justice. By Christian writers they are contrasted with the *theological virtues.

CAREY, WILLIAM (1761–1834), Baptist missionary. Baptized as an Anglican, he became convinced of Baptist teaching (1783). Largely through his inspiration the *Baptist Missionary Society was founded in 1792, and in 1793 he sailed for *India. He worked on a translation of the NT into Bengali (published 1801), and when Fort William College was opened in Calcutta, he was appointed professor of Sanskrit, Bengali, and Marathi. He translated the whole Bible into Bengali (1809) and the whole or part into 24 other languages or dialects.

CARLILE, WILSON (1847–1942), founder of the *Church Army. After a successful business career, he was ordained in 1880. In 1882 he founded the Church Army, and combined his work as its honorary Chief Secretary with various parochial appointments.

CARLISLE. The see was erected in 1133, when Henry I turned the Earldom of Carlisle into a bishopric. The church, which had been served by Regular Canons since c. 1102 (*Augustinians after 1122), became the new cathedral. It was badly ravaged in the 17th cent. Its chief glory is the E. window.

CARLSTADT (c. 1480–1541), German reformer, so named from his birthplace. From 1505 he taught at *Wittenberg. A visit to Rome in 1515 led to a spiritual crisis and he became an exponent of the doctrine of the powerlessness of the human will. He disputed with J. *Eck, taking a 'Protestant' position, and from 1519 he was recognized as the most extreme of the Reformers. In 1521 he celebrated the first Protestant Communion Service, with neither *vestments nor *canon, the laity being communicated in both kinds. He came into conflict with M.

*Luther, renounced his professorship in 1524, and spent most of the rest of his life in Switzerland.

CARMEL, Mount. A high ridge in N. Palestine. It was the scene of a contest between *Elijah and the prophets of *Baal (1 Kgs. 18). A church was built there c. A.D. 500, and a monastery founded by Greek monks. It was later the home of the *Carmelite Order.

CARMELITE ORDER. The 'Order of Our Lady of Mount *Carmel' was founded in Palestine by St. Berthold c. 1154. The primitive rule laid down in 1209 was one of extreme asceticism. After the failure of the *Crusades, the order was reorganized in Europe under the generalship of St. *Simon Stock. An order of Carmelite Sisters was founded in 1452. During the 16th cent. discipline relaxed until St. *Teresa of Avila restored in many houses the 'Primitive Rule', with some additions to foster the contemplative life. St. *John of the Cross did the same for the friars. The so-called 'Teresian Reform' was adopted in most houses, whose members were called '*Discalced', in contrast to the '*Calced' Carmelites who continued to follow the 'Mitigated Rule'. The order has produced great mystics.

CARNIVAL. The name given in RC countries to the period of feasting immediately before *Lent.

CAROL. A song of joy, originally accompanying a dance; now applied esp. to traditional songs of a religious character. Modern English practice has tended to confine the singing of carols to Christmastide and to break down the distinction between hymns and carols.

CAROLINE BOOKS, The. A treatise compiled c. 790-2, which purports to be the work of *Charlemagne. It attacks the *Iconoclastic Council of 754 (for prohibiting images altogether) and *Nicaea II of 787 (for allowing excessive reverence to be paid to them). It was long attributed to *Alcuin but is prob. the work of *Theodulf of Orleans.

CAROLINE DIVINES, The. Anglican divines of the 17th cent., esp. when considered as exponents of High Church principles.

CAROLINGIAN SCHOOLS. During the reign of *Charlemagne (768-814) there was a lasting intellectual Renaissance. Responsibility for this revival rests largely with Charlemagne himself and his advisers *Alcuin and *Theodulf of Orleans. In 787 Charlemagne issued a *capitulary ordering that in all monasteries and bishops' houses there should be study and 'let those who can, teach'. Later capitularies demanded the establishment of schools. A Palace School was attended by members of the court, children of the nobility, and other laity. Most schools of the period, however, were connected with cathedrals and monasteries. The Carolingian schools were not outstanding for originality of thought, but they restored Latin to the position of a literary language, and their scholars were largely responsible for the formation of a more accurate orthography. They also copied and preserved texts of the classics, both Christian and pagan.

CARPENTER, JOSEPH ESTLIN (1844-1927, English *Unitarian. The grandson of Lant *Carpenter, from 1906 to 1915 he was principal of Manchester College, Oxford. He was one of the chief figures in modern Unitarianism.

CARPENTER, LANT (1780-1840), *Unitarian minister. He sought to foster a more liberal spirit in English Unitarianism. In 1825, when three older societies amalgamated into the British and Foreign Unitarian Association, he was instrumental in expunging from the constitution of the new body a preamble branding Trinitarianism as idolatrous.

CARPOCRATES (2nd cent.), *Gnostic teacher, prob. a native of *Alexandria. His disciples, the 'Carpocratians', who survived until the 4th cent., preached a licentious ethic, the transmigration of souls, and the doctrine that Jesus was born by natural generation.

CARROLL, JOHN (1735-1815), first bishop of the RC hierarchy in the U.S.A. A native of Maryland, he was trained at *St.-Omer and became a *Jesuit in 1753. When the Jesuits were suppressed in 1773, he returned to America. Partly through the influence of Benjamin Franklin, in 1784 *Pius VI appointed Carroll Superior of the Missions, a step which made the Church of the U.S.A. independent of the *Vicars Apostolic in England. In 1789 Carroll was appointed Bp. of Baltimore; in 1808 he was made an archbishop, his diocese being divided into four sees.

CARSTARES, WILLIAM (1649–1715), statesman and *Presbyterian divine. Though almost certainly involved in plots against *Charles II in 1683–4, he escaped severe punishment. He was the chief adviser of William of Orange on Scottish matters. He was four times *Moderator of the Church of *Scotland. He also took a prominent part in bringing about the Act of Union in 1707.

CARTA CARITATIS. The 'Charter of Love', so called in opposition to the obligatory charters of the *Cluniac Order, was the document outlining the constitution of the *Cistercian Order. It was presented to Pope *Callistus II in 1119. The final form dates from *c.* 1155; the nucleus is prob. the work of *Stephen Harding.

CARTER, THOMAS THELLUSSON (1808–1901), sub-*Tractarian divine. He became rector of Clewer, near Windsor, in 1844. Here in 1849 he founded a House of Mercy for the rescue of fallen women and in 1852 a sisterhood, the Community of St. John the Baptist, to look after it.

CARTESIANISM. The philosophical principles embodied in the teaching of R. *Descartes.

CARTHAGE, Councils of. Early ecclesiastical Councils held at Carthage include: (1) Those under *Cyprian in 251, 252, 254, 255, and 256. The earlier ones were concerned with the reconciliation of those who had lapsed in the *Decian persecution, the later with the dispute over the rebaptism of heretics. (2) The long series under *Aurelius from 393 to 424. The most celebrated was that of 419, when the claims of Rome to exercise jurisdiction over Africa were contested (see *Apiarius*).

CARTHUSIAN ORDER. This strictly contemplative order was founded by St. *Bruno in 1084 at the *Grande Chartreuse (hence its name). The monks were vowed to silence; each lived in his own cell, working and devoting several hours daily to mental prayer, and meeting for the *Office, conven-

tual Mass, and for meals only on feast days. In 1127 Guigues de Châtel, Prior of the Grande Chartreuse, compiled as their Rule the 'Consuetudines Carthusiae', which received papal approval in 1133. Subsequent elaborations have done little to modify the austerity which characterized the order from the beginning. At the end of the 18th cent. the Carthusians suffered badly in the French Revolution, and in 1901 they were again driven from the Grande Chartreuse, to which they returned in 1940. The order includes a few houses of nuns.

CARTOUCHE. A type of memorial tablet widely introduced into English churches in the 17th and 18th cents.

CARTWRIGHT, THOMAS (1535–1603), *Puritan divine. He held high office at Cambridge, but was deprived because of his criticism of the constitution of the C of E. His sympathies with the *Admonition to Parliament* involved him in further controversy and he fled to the Continent until 1585. On *James I's accession he drew up the *Millenary Petition (1603), but he died before the *Hampton Court Conference, at which it had been intended that he should be the leading *Presbyterian spokesman.

CASAUBON, ISAAC (1559–1614), classical scholar. He was successively professor at Geneva and Montpellier and sub-librarian to *Henry IV at Paris. On Henry's death (1610) he decided to settle in England, where he received a prebendal stall at *Canterbury and a pension from *James I. Besides his classical works, which included an edition of *Suetonius, in 1614 he issued a severe criticism of C. *Baronius's annals.

CASEL, ODO (1886–1948), liturgist. In 1902 he became a *Benedictine monk at *Maria Laach. He was concerned to expound the theological aspects of the liturgy and saw in the Eucharist a re-enactment of the mysteries of Christ by His Church (*Mysterienlehre*). His teaching is summarized in English in *The Mystery of Christian Worship* (1962).

CASHEL, Synod of (1171/2). A synod held under Henry II after his invasion of Ireland. It completed the task of conforming the usages of the *Celtic Church with those of the rest of W. Christendom.

CASSANDER, GEORG (1513–66), Catholic theologian. He tried to mediate between Catholics and Protestants. In his chief work he sought to show that abuses were no sufficient reason for leaving the RC Church, but when it was submitted to the Colloquy of *Poissy (1561) it gave offence to both sides. In 1564 the Emp. Ferdinand I invoked his aid in the official attempt at re-union, but Cassander's endeavour to put a Catholic interpretation on the official Protestant formularies again met with disapproval from both sides.

CASSIAN, JOHN (c. 360–435), monk. As a young man he joined a monastery at *Bethlehem, but he left soon afterwards to study monasticism in Egypt. About 415 he founded two monasteries near Marseilles. His *Institutes* sets out the ordinary rules for the monastic life and discusses the chief hindrances to a monk's perfection; it was taken as the basis of many W Rules. The *Conferences* recount his conversations with the leaders of E. monasticism. He was apparently the founder of *Semi-Pelagianism (q.v.).

CASSINESE CONGREGATION. A *Benedictine Congregation which originated in a reform instituted by Ludovico Barba at Padua in 1409. The aim of the reformers was to overcome the evils of appointing abbots 'in *commendam', and the congregation was characterized by the over-all authority of the General Chapter and the centralized system of appointing abbots on a temporary basis. It took its present title after the accession of *Monte Cassino in 1504. The 'Cassinese Congregation of the Primitive Observance' was a 19th-cent. offshoot.

CASSINO. See *Monte Cassino*.

CASSIODORUS, SENATOR, FLAVIUS MAGNUS AURELIUS (c. 485–c. 580), Roman scholar and monk. He held a number of high offices. He founded two monasteries on *Benedictine lines at Vivarium, where he became a monk when he retired from public life in 540. His classic *Institutiones Divinarum et Saecularium Litterarum* advocates the union of sacred and profane studies in Christian education. His *Historia Ecclesiastica Tripartita*, a compilation from *Socrates, *Sozomen, and *Theodoret, was designed to continue and supplement *Rufi-

nus's adaptation of *Eusebius's Church History; despite many errors, it was much used throughout the Middle Ages.

CASSOCK. The long garment, now usually black, worn by the clergy. It originated in the ankle-length dress which was retained by the clergy when in the 6th cent. shorter garments became normal for secular use. In the W. cassocks of bishops are purple, those of cardinals red, and the Pope's white.

CASTEL GANDOLFO. A small town c. 18 miles SE. of Rome, which since the 17th cent. has been the site of the Pope's summer residence.

CASTELLIO, SEBASTIAN (1515–63), *Calvinist theologian and humanist. He was converted to Protestantism by J. *Calvin, but theological differences led to their separation in 1544. In 1551 Castellio published a Latin translation of the Bible. It aroused much opposition, esp. on account of its annotations, with their unecclesiastical attitude to religious truth and their demand for toleration.

CASUISTRY. The art or science of bringing general moral principles to bear on particular cases. The introduction of universal private *penance was the natural cause of the rise of formal casuistry in the Church, and by the 7th cent. '*Penitential Books' were common. From the 16th cent. various systems of casuistry, such as *Probabilism, *Probabiliorism, and *Equiprobabilism, developed in the RC Church.

CASWALL, EDWARD (1814–78), hymnwriter. He was *Perpetual Curate of Stratford-sub-Castle in Wiltshire from 1840 to 1847; in 1847 he became a RC and in 1850 joined the *Oratorians. His many popular translations of Latin hymns include 'Jesu, the very thought of thee'.

CATACOMBS. Subterranean early Christian burial-places, of which the most extensive are at Rome. Since Roman law regarded all burial-places as sacrosanct, Christians could use the catacombs in eras of persecution, and their violation was rare. The law required that they be built outside the walls of the city, and they are found along the great roads out of the capital, esp. to the NE. and S. They consist of labyrinths of galleries and connecting chambers. The bodies were placed in niches (*loculi*) hewn in the side walls, each of which could hold two or three bodies and which were closed by stone slabs or large tiles. The chief services in the catacombs were the Eucharistic celebrations on the anniversaries of the *martyrs. In the 5th cent. fear of barbarian invasions caused burials in the catacombs to cease, and their existence was forgotten until an accidental discovery in 1578 renewed interest in them.

CATAFALQUE. An erection resembling a bier, formerly used at *Requiem Masses to represent the body in its absence. The term is now also used in a general sense of the coffin and its appurtenances.

CATECHESIS. Instruction given to Christian *catechumens preparing for *Baptism, esp. in the primitive Church. The word is also used of books containing such instruction.

CATECHETICAL SCHOOL OF ALEXANDRIA, The. From the later 2nd cent. a theological school existed at *Alexandria, which addressed itself to the propagation of the Christian faith among the cultured classes. It rose to its greatest prominence under *Clement (*c.* 190–*c.* 202) and *Origen (*c.* 202–31). It attracted Christians from distant parts.

CATECHISM. A popular manual of Christian doctrine. Originally the term was applied to the oral instruction given to children and adults before *Baptism; the name passed to the book containing such instruction. In the Middle Ages prescriptions for catechizing the faithful were frequently issued, and books were produced containing explanations of the *Lord's Prayer and *Creed, lists of mortal sins, &c. J. *Gerson's *ABC des simples gens* became popular in the 15th cent. The *Reformation brought a flood of new catechisms. M. *Luther's *Kleiner Katechismus* (1529) is still the standard book of the *Lutheran Churches. The *Heidelberg Catechism (1563) occupies a similar position in the *Calvinist communion. The RC Church also produced a number of catechisms, of which the most famous is St. Peter *Canisius's *Summa Doctrinae Christianae* (1554). RCs in England until recently commonly used *A Catechism of Christian Doctrine* (1898), popularly known as the 'Penny Catechism', which is based on the work of R. *Challoner.

The so-called 'Roman Catechism' (1566) is not a catechism in the ordinary sense, but a doctrinal exposition for the use of RC priests. See also *Geneva Catechism*, *Westminster Catechism*, and the following entry.

CATECHISM, The Prayer Book. The 'Instruction' in the BCP, in the form of questions and answers, to be learned by candidates for *Confirmation. It deals with *Baptism, the *Apostles' Creed, the Ten *Commandments, the *Lord's Prayer, and the *Eucharist. Though its authorship is uncertain, it was prob. largely the work of A. *Nowell. The Revised Catechism, authorized in 1962, widened the scope of the Prayer Book Catechism and modernized its language.

CATECHIST. (1) In the early Church a teacher of *catechumens or a lecturer in a catechetical school. (2) In modern usage occasionally a person appointed to give instruction in Christianity, e.g. to children. (3) In the mission field a native teacher.

CATECHUMENS. In the early Church those undergoing training and instruction preparatory to *Baptism. Those who had reached the stage of awaiting Baptism at the coming *Easter formed a separate group. There was an elaborate ritual of preparation in the preceding *Lent, with the candidates finally being admitted at the *Paschal Vigil.

In the RC Church a restored catechumenate became a normal prelude to all adult Baptisms in 1972. Various ceremonies mark the different stages.

CATECHUMENS, Mass of the. The first part of the Eucharist, so named because in the early Church it was the part of the service which *catechumens, who were dismissed before the *Anaphora, were allowed to attend.

CATEGORICAL IMPERATIVE, The. In the ethical theory of I. *Kant, the absolute moral law, given in reason, and therefore unconditionally binding upon every rational being.

CATENA (Lat., 'chain'). A word applied to the Biblical commentaries dating from the 5th cent. onwards, in which the successive verses of the Scriptural text were elucidated by 'chains' of passages derived from previous commentators.

CATESBY, ROBERT (1573-1605), English *recusant and conspirator. He was the original mover of the *Gunpowder Plot, with which he persevered even after he knew it had been betrayed.

CATHARI (Gk., 'pure'). The name was applied to several sects in Patristic times, but it is used mainly of a medieval sect which came to be so known in Germany in the 12th cent. It was later applied to this sect in Italy, whereas in S. France its adherents were commonly called '*Albigenses'. Their doctrines were akin to those of the *Bogomils of Bulgaria, but it is not clear whether W. dualism was an importation from the Balkans or a separate development. See also *Albigenses*.

CATHARINUS, AMBROSIUS (c. 1484-1553), theologian. Lancelot Politi became a *Dominican in 1517, taking the name of Ambrosius Catharinus in honour of two saints of his order. His superiors soon employed him as a controversialist against *Lutheranism. In his (later) writings on *predestination he seems to have distinguished between two kinds of men—those predestined by God in a special way, such as the BVM, who received such strong graces that they could not resist them, and the majority of men who receive 'sufficient grace', which they may accept or reject, though this only in accordance with Divine decrees. He took a prominent part in the Council of *Trent. He was made Bp. of Minori in 1546 and Abp. of Conza in 1552.

CATHEDRA. The bishop's chair or throne in his cathedral. The phrase 'ex cathedra' (i.e. 'from the throne') is used esp. of the pronouncements uttered by the Pope with the full weight of his office; such pronouncements are held by RCs to be *infallible.

CATHEDRAL. The church which contains the throne or *cathedra of the bishop of the diocese. It is usually large and of some splendour. It was originally served by the bishop and his household, but responsibility for the cathedral was gradually delegated to a separate body of clergy, which developed into an ecclesiastical corporation or *chapter.

In medieval England, some chapters were secular, some monastic. With the *dissolution of the monasteries, the religious foundations came to an end. On the eight cathedrals previously served by religious, new constitutions were imposed by the king; they have hence become known as 'New Foundations', in contrast with the other nine which, retaining their medieval statutes, are known as 'Old Foundations'. In addition five further 'New Foundations' survived out of the six bishoprics which *Henry VIII created. In each case an earlier (usually monastic) church was constituted the cathedral. The creation of new English dioceses in modern times has brought a corresponding growth of cathedrals. In most cases an existing church has been used, but in some (e.g. *Coventry) new buildings have been erected. In the RC Church the restoration of the hierarchy in England in 1850 was followed by the foundation of cathedrals, e.g. at *Westminster.

English cathedrals are normally governed by a body of residentiary *canons presided over by a *dean (in recent foundations a *provost). There is generally also a body of non-residentiary honorary canons. The cathedral staff also includes *minor canons, responsible for rendering the priest's part of the musical services, and a choir consisting of an organist, choirmen (sometimes called 'lay clerks'), and choristers. In the older cathedrals there has been a tradition of high musical performance.

CATHEDRAL SCHOOLS. Schools established in medieval times or later for the education of the choir-boys of cathedral churches. Most of them also admit other, fee-paying pupils.

CATHEDRALS, Friends of the. Voluntary organizations designed to support the work and fabric of English cathedrals. The earliest was the Friends of *Canterbury Cathedral, founded in 1927.

CATHERINE, St., of Alexandria. Acc. to tradition she was a virgin martyred in the 4th cent. Legend represents her as of noble family and great learning, who was tied to a wheel, tortured, and beheaded. Her body was said to have been discovered c. 800 on Mount *Sinai, whither, acc. to her *Acts, it was transported by angels after her death. Her symbol is a spiked wheel; she is the patroness of young men, wheelwrights, attorneys, and scholars.

CATHERINE, St., of Genoa (1447–1510), mystic. Caterinetta Fieschi was married at the age of 16; she was suddenly converted 10 years later. She subsequently underwent a number of remarkable mental experiences. Her spiritual doctrine is contained in the *Vita e dottrina* (1551), though perhaps she did not put this account of her visions into their present form.

CATHERINE, St., dei Ricci (1522–90), Italian visionary. She entered the *Dominican Order in 1535. She is chiefly remarkable for an ecstasy into which she was rapt for 28 hours a week over a number of years.

CATHERINE, St., of Siena (1347 [?1333]–1380), mystic. Caterina Benincasa became a *Dominican *tertiary at the age of 16. In 1376 she went to *Avignon to plead with *Gregory XI on behalf of Florence and to persuade him to return to Rome. In Siena, she gathered around her a group of supporters who were attracted by her spirituality, her gifts of infused, ecstatic prayer, her devotion to the *Precious Blood, and her apostolic powers, esp. in reconciling sinners. Many of her letters survive, as well as her *Dialogo*, a spiritual work of some importance.

CATHERINE, St., of Sweden (1331–81). The daughter of St. *Bridget, in 1374 she succeeded her as head of the *Brigittine order. She spent most of the rest of her life in Italy.

CATHERINE DE' MEDICI (1519–89), Queen-Consort of France from 1547 and Queen-Mother from 1559. In the wars of religion she at first favoured toleration for political reasons; between 1567 and 1570 she took violent measures against the Protestants; after an interval of mildness she tried to re-establish her position by the murder of G. *Coligny and the Massacre of St. *Bartholomew's Day (1572).

CATHOLIC. The word, meaning 'general' or 'universal', has come to have various uses in Christian terminology: (1) Of the universal Church as distinct from local Christian communities. (2) In the sense of 'orthodox', as distinct from 'heretical' or 'schismatical'. (3) Of the undivided Church before the schism of the E. and W. in 1054. Thereafter the W. Church referred to itself as 'catholic', the E. preferring to describe itself as 'orthodox'. (4) Since the *Reformation RCs have come to use it exclusively of themselves. Anglicans and *Old Catholics have also adopted it to cover besides themselves and the RC Church also the E. Orthodox Church in the belief that these communions together represent the undivided Church of earlier ages. (5) In general it is employed of those Christians who claim to possess a historical and continuous tradition of faith and practice, as opposed to Protestants who tend to find their ultimate standards in the Bible as interpreted on the principles of the 16th-cent. Reformation.

CATHOLIC ACTION. Organized religious activity, esp. of a social, educational, or quasi-political kind, on the part of the RC laity. In 1922 *Pius XI encouraged the creation of flexible organizations under the direction of the clergy.

CATHOLIC APOSTOLIC CHURCH. A religious body partly inspired by the teaching of E. *Irving; its members are also known as Irvingites. It developed out of the revivalist circles which gathered round H. *Drummond. They believed in the imminence of the Second Coming of Christ, in preparation for which they resolved to re-establish the primitive offices of Apostles, prophets, &c. The first 'Apostle' was appointed by Drummond in 1832; the full college of 12 held their first 'council' in London in 1835. Their influence in Britain declined after the death of the last 'Apostle' in 1901. They survive in the U.S.A. and Germany.

CATHOLIC ASSOCIATION, The. An association founded in 1823 by D. *O'Connell for the defence of RC interests in Ireland. Its influence largely contributed to the passing of the *Catholic Relief Act of 1829.

CATHOLIC EMANCIPATION. See *Catholic Relief Acts*.

CATHOLIC EPISTLES. A title used properly of the NT Epp. of Jas., 1 and 2 Pet., 1 Jn., and Jude, because they are 'general' and not addressed to specific individuals or Churches. It is usual, however, to include also 2 and 3 Jn. among them.

CATHOLIC MAJESTY, His. A traditional title of the kings of *Spain.

CATHOLIC RELIEF [or EMANCIPATION] ACTS. A series of Acts freeing RCs from civil disabilities. By that of 1778 RCs in Ireland were allowed to own land; in 1791 RC worship and schools were tolerated. By the 'Roman Catholic Relief Act' of 1829 almost all disabilities were removed and RCs were admitted to most public offices.

CATHOLIC TRUTH SOCIETY. A RC society founded in 1884 for the printing of cheap literature of a devotional, educational, or controversial nature.

CATHOLIC UNIVERSITY OF AMERICA. The university was founded at Washington, D.C., in 1889, for the education of clergy and laity under RC direction.

CATHOLICOS. A title now restricted to the *Patriarchs of the *Nestorian and *Armenian Churches.

CATON, WILLIAM (1636 65), an early *Quaker, who became an itinerant preacher and tried to implant his doctrines in France and Holland. His *Journal* is still read among Friends.

CAUSSAUDE, JEAN PIERRE DE (1675–1751), French ascetic writer. Becoming a *Jesuit in 1693, he travelled widely and was much appreciated as a preacher. His influence did much to rehabilitate mysticism at a time when it was still suffering from the condemnation of *Quietism.

CAUTEL. A rubrical direction for the correct administration of the Sacraments.

CAXTON, WILLIAM (c. 1422–91), the first English printer. After some years in commerce, he entered the service of Margaret, Duchess of Burgundy, for whom he made several English translations. Tiring of copying these by hand, he learnt the new art of printing at *Cologne (1471–2) and introduced it at Bruges. In 1476 he set up his own press at the Almonry, Westminster. Much of his printing was of religious works.

C.C.C.S. (Commonwealth [originally Colonial] and Continental Church Society). A society founded in 1838 to enable *Evangel-icals in the C of E to take an active part in the work of Church extension in the British Colonies

CECILIA, St. (2nd or 3rd cent.), Roman martyr. Acc. to her (apocryphal) acts, she converted her husband and brother, who were both martyred before her, and, after dying for the Christian faith, she was buried in the *catacomb of St. Callistus. When her relics were discovered in the catacomb of Praetextatus by Paschal I (817–24), they were moved to the church which bears her name in Trastevere in Rome; here her body is said to have been found uncorrupted when the church was repaired in 1599. She is the patroness of Church music. Feast day, 22 Nov.

CEDD, St. (d. 664), Bp. of the East Saxons. The brother of St. *Chad, he was brought up at *Lindisfarne. He was sent to evangelize Essex and consecrated bishop in 654. He founded the abbey of Lastingham, N. Yorks., of which he became first abbot. At the Synod of *Whitby (664) he accepted the Roman Easter.

CEDRON (or **Kidron**). The valley or gorge on the E. of *Jerusalem, between the city and the Mount of *Olives. It was crossed by Christ on the night before His Passion (Jn. 18: 1).

CELEBRET (Lat , 'let him celebrate'). In the RC Church a certificate authorizing its possessor to say Mass.

CELESTINE I, St. (d. 432), Pope from 422. His support for *Apiarius led a Council at *Carthage, c. 424, to protest against what the Africans regarded as an infringement of their rights. He sent *Germanus of Auxerre to Britain to combat *Pelagianism. At a Roman Synod in 430 he formally condemned *Nestorius.

CELESTINE III (c. 1106–98), Pope from 1191. He defended *Abelard at the Council of *Sens (1140) and later urged Thomas *Becket to adopt a less intransigent attitude. Elected Pope in his 85th year, his reign was marked by indecision. He crowned Henry VI Emperor and was pacified by his feigned promises of a *crusade. He approved the orders of Knights *Templar, the *Hospitallers, and the newly formed *Teutonic Order.

CELESTINE V, St. (*c.* 1215–96), Pope from July to Dec. 1294. He became a *Benedictine, but retired to Monte Morrone in the Abruzzi, where the many disciples who gathered round him became the nucleus of the *Celestine Order. Elected Pope when he was nearly 80, he was naïve and ignorant of procedure and became a tool of Charles II of Naples; he abdicated. He is sometimes known as St. Peter Celestine from his baptismal name of Peter.

CELESTINE ORDER. A branch of the *Benedictine Order founded by Pope *Celestine V in 1250. Its discipline was severe. The last house closed in 1785.

CELESTIUS (5th cent.), heretic. A native of Britain, he was practising as an advocate in Rome when he met *Pelagius. They became convinced that the contemporary low morality could be reformed only by stressing the responsibility of men for their actions; they emphasized man's freedom of will, leaving no room for *grace. Celestius denied that Adam's sin was transmitted to his descendants (*original sin). He migrated to Africa *c.* 410, was condemned by a Council at *Carthage, and went to *Ephesus. See also *Pelagianism.*

CELIBACY OF THE CLERGY. In the E. Church the legal position has always been that priests and deacons may marry before ordination but not after, and that bishops must be celibate. In the W. Church a legal position was gradually reached by which all the higher clergy were required to be celibate. The earliest canonical statement is can. 33 of the Council of *Elvira (*c.* 306); throughout the Middle Ages there were repeated enactments to enforce celibacy on those in Holy Orders. This position is retained in the RC Church, though since the Second *Vatican Council some older married men have been made *deacons. In the C of E the obligation to celibacy of the clergy was abolished in 1549.

CELL. (1) The private room of a *religious of either sex. It usually contains only bare necessities. (2) A monastic house dependent on its mother house. (3) In modern times the word has come into use for small groups of Christians who have pledged themselves to intensive work for the propagation of the Christian faith in their secular surroundings.

CELLA (also **cella coemeterialis**). A small chapel erected in cemeteries in early Christian times.

CELLARER. One of the officials in a medieval monastic community. He was responsible for seeing that there was sufficient food and drink to hand, and in practice he was usually in charge of nearly all the monastery's dealings with outside tradesmen.

CELSUS (2nd cent), pagan philosopher. His 'True Discourse' (*c.* 178) is the earliest literary attack on Christianity.of which details have survived; most of it is preserved in *Origen's reply. Celsus praised the *Logos doctrine and the Christian moral code, but he objected to the exclusive claims of the Church and appealed to Christians to abandon their religious and political intolerance. He found the doctrines of the Incarnation and Crucifixion repugnant.

CELTIC CHURCH, The. The Church that existed in the British Isles before the arrival of St. *Augustine in 597. It was founded in the 2nd or 3rd cent. by missions from Rome or Gaul and sent bishops to the Council of *Arles (314). In spite of the withdrawal of the Romans, the Celtic Church kept in close touch with the Church on the Continent until the Saxon invasions of the 5th cent. submerged Celtic culture in most of England. The Celtic Christian communities which survived in Cornwall, *Wales, *Scotland, and *Ireland found it hard to accept the Roman Christianity of St. Augustine, but after the Synod of *Whitby (664) they gradually conformed to Roman usages.

CEMETERY. A place set apart for the burial of the dead. The Greek from which the word is derived means a 'sleeping-place', and seems to have been used exclusively of Christian burial-grounds.

CENACULUM, The. The 'upper room' in *Jerusalem in which the *Last Supper was celebrated and the Holy Spirit descended at *Pentecost. Acc. to *Epiphanius a church existed on the site from the time of Hadrian (117–38). A large basilica was erected later; it fell into Muslim hands in the 16th cent.

CENOBITES. See *Coenobites.*

CENSER. Another name for a *thurible.

CENSURES, Ecclesiastical. Penalties imposed upon an offender against the law of the Church for the good of his soul and the well-being of the community. They include deposition from Holy *Orders, public *penance, and *excommunication.

CENTRE PARTY. The party founded by the Prussian Catholics in 1870–1 to counteract the anti-Catholic policy of the Conservatives and esp. of the National Liberals. It was the most effective opponent of Bismarck in the '*Kulturkampf'. It was suppressed by Hitler with other German parties in 1933.

CENTURIATORS OF MAGDEBURG, The. The authors of the *Historia Ecclesiae Christi* (1559–74), a history of the Church divided by 'centuries'. This depicted the pure Christianity of the NT as coming progressively under the power of the 'Papal Antichrist' until liberated by M. *Luther.

CERDO (2nd cent.), Syrian *Gnostic who taught at Rome *c.* 140. He held that the Creator God of the OT was to be distinguished from the Father of Jesus Christ.

CERE CLOTH (Lat. *cera*, 'wax'). Acc. to W. usage, a cloth impregnated with wax which is laid on the surface of the altar to prevent the linen cloths above from being soiled, e.g. by the oils used in consecrating the *mensa.

CEREMONIAL. In ecclesiastical usage, the performance of Divine worship with prescribed and formal actions.

CERINTHUS (*fl. c.* 100), *Gnostic. He is said to have taught that the world was created not by the supreme God, but either by a *Demiurge (a less exalted being) or by angels. Jesus, he held, began His earthly life as a mere man, though at His Baptism 'the Christ', a higher Divine power, descended upon Him, to depart before the crucifixion. *Irenaeus asserts that St. *John wrote his Gospel to refute Cerinthus.

CERULARIUS. See *Michael Cerularius*.

CESARINI, JULIAN (1398–1444), Cardinal from 1426. In 1431 he was made president of the Council of *Basle, where he at first tried to persuade *Eugenius IV to adopt a more conciliatory attitude. After the transfer of the Council to *Florence he took a prominent part in the negotiations for union between the Greek and Roman Churches. He persuaded the king of Hungary to renew war against the Turks; the Christians were totally defeated at Varni, Cesarini being killed in the fight.

CHABURAH (cf. Heb. חָבֵר, 'friend'). In Jewish practice a group of friends formed for religious purposes. They often shared a common weekly meal, usually on the eves of sabbaths or holy days. It has been argued that Christ and His disciples formed such a chaburah and that the *Last Supper was a chaburah meal.

CHAD, St. (d. 672), Bp. of *Lichfield and brother of St. *Cedd. He was irregularly made Bp. of *York during St. *Wilfrid's absence in France, but on Wilfrid's return he accepted the ruling of Abp. *Theodore and retired to Lastingham in N. Yorks. In 669 he was sent to be Bp. of the Mercians and fixed his see at Lichfield.

CHALCEDON, Council of (451). The Fourth *Oecumenical Council. It was convoked by the Emp. *Marcian to deal with the heresy of *Eutyches, whom the Council condemned. It then drew up a statement of faith, the so-called Definition of *Chalcedon. Though nearly all the bishops present were Easterns, the W. Church accepted its dogmatic decisions.

CHALCEDON, The Definition of. The statement of faith made by the Council of *Chalcedon (451). It reaffirmed the *Christological definitions of *Nicaea and *Constantinople and formally repudiated the errors of *Nestorius and *Eutyches. It expressly excluded the views of those who imply that the Humanity of Christ is separable from His Divine Person and of those who confuse the Divine and Human natures in one. It affirmed the existence of One Person in Two Natures, which are united unconfusedly, unchangeably, indivisibly, and inseparably. By the end of the 7th cent. the Definition had been generally accepted in E. and W., except among the small *Monophysite bodies.

CHALDEAN CHRISTIANS. The descendants of the ancient *Nestorian Churches now in communion with Rome. When in the 13th cent. the Nestorians of Turkey and Persia came into contact with RC missionaries, negotiations for reunion began; in 1830 a small Chaldean body was eventually established with a *Uniat Patriarch of Babylon. For the group in Malabar, see *Malabar Christians*.

CHALDEE. An alternative, but misleading, name for *Aramaic.

CHALICE. In ecclesiastical usage the cup used to contain the wine consecrated in the Eucharist. The earliest chalices were commonly made of glass; by the 4th cent. the precious metals were general. In the Middle Ages chalices came to have stems which were gradually elongated.

CHALICE VEIL. A square of material, normally corresponding in colour to the Eucharistic vestments, used in the W. to cover the *chalice and *paten during the parts of the Mass when they are not in use, i.e. until the *offertory and after the *ablutions.

CHALLONER, RICHARD (1691–1781), author of *The *Garden of the Soul* and other devotional works. Of *Presbyterian parents, he became a RC while still a boy. He was a student and then a professor at *Douai. In 1741 he was consecrated at Hammersmith Bishop (*in partibus*) of Debra and coadjutor to the *Vicar Apostolic, whom he succeeded in 1758.

CHALMERS, JAMES (1841–1901), Scottish *Congregationalist missionary. After ordination, in 1866 he sailed for Rarotonga in the New Hebrides. There he did much to make the Church indigenous before he sailed for New Guinea in 1877. He slowly won the confidence of the people and was able to facilitate the establishment of British rule in the north of the country in 1888. He was brutally killed off the coast of Papua.

CHALMERS, THOMAS (1780–1847), theologian and philanthropist. His chief importance lies in his leadership of the movement for the choice of ministers in the Established Church of *Scotland by the people and the schism which followed its failure in 1843. In that year he left the Estab-

lished Church with a considerable band of followers and founded the *Free Church of Scotland. See also *Disruption*.

CHAMBERS, ROBERT (1802–71), Scottish publisher and author. He joined his brother in the publishing firm of W. & R. Chambers, and was part or sole author of various encyclopaedic works. His *Vestiges of the Natural History of Creation* (1844) was a popular handbook defending an evolutionary theory of man's origin which helped to prepare the public for *Darwinism.

CHANCEL. Originally the part of the church immediately about the altar, now called the 'sanctuary'. When further space was reserved for clergy and choir westward from the sanctuary, the word was applied to this area as well and hence now normally designates the whole area in the main body of the church east of the nave and transepts.

CHANCELLOR, Diocesan. In the C of E he is a professional lawyer who represents the Bishop in the administration of the temporal affairs of the diocese. He is the usual president of the *Consistory Court. His chief function is normally the hearing of applications for and granting of *faculties &c. He is also responsible for hearing complaints against clerics under the *Ecclesiastical Jurisdiction Measure of 1963, when these do not involve matters of doctrine, ritual, or ceremonial.

In the RC Church the Diocesan Chancellor, who is always a priest, is responsible for the diocesan archives. He is sometimes in addition the confidential secretary of the Bishop.

In England the title of chancellor is also held by one of the four dignitaries of *cathedrals of the 'Old Foundation'. He is responsible for the cathedral school and library.

CHANCERY, Papal. The name attached in the late 12th cent. to the Pope's secretariat. In the 14th cent. the Chancery exercised quasi-judicial powers, but from the 15th cent. its influence diminished.

CHANNEL ISLANDS, Christianity in the. Christianity was apparently introduced about the 5th–6th cent. After the separation of England and Normandy in 1204, the islands were annexed politically to England.

For most of the period before the Reformation they were ecclesiastically part of the diocese of Coutances in Normandy; since 1586 they have been attached to *Winchester. In the 16th cent. *Huguenot refugees induced the islanders to adopt *Presbyterianism, but Anglicanism was imposed in the reign of *James I.

CHANNING, WILLIAM ELLERY (1780–1842), American *Unitarian. He became pastor of a Congregational Church in Boston in 1803. In the schism between liberal and conservative *Congregationalists in the U.S.A., Channing espoused the liberal or Unitarian cause. From c. 1820 he was reckoned a Unitarian.

CHANTAL, St. JANE. See *Jane Frances de Chantal, St.*

CHANTRY. A term applied to the office or benefice maintained to say Mass for the souls of the founder and his friends, and also to any little chapel in which such Masses were said. The chapel usually took the form either of an altar within the parent church or of a building constructed as a 'chantry chapel'. In the 14th and 15th cents. chantries became numerous. The chantry priest often acted also as schoolmaster, curate, or chaplain. The suppression of the chantries following the Act of 1547 involved a great loss to education in England.

CHAPEL. The word is used of a variety of sacred buildings which are less than churches. They include: (1) Chapels of private institutions, e.g. schools or hospitals. (2) RC and dissenting places of worship, in distinction from English parish churches. (3) Part of a large church with a separate altar, e.g. a '*Lady Chapel'. (4) A *Proprietary Chapel. See also *Chantry, Oratory,* and the two following entries.

CHAPEL OF EASE. A chapel subordinate to the parish church, founded for the ease of those living at some distance. Many acquired parochial status.

CHAPEL ROYAL. A private chapel attached to a royal court. In England these chapels are not subject to the jurisdiction of the bishop of the diocese in which they are situated but are under that of the sovereign, which is exercised by the 'Dean of the Chapels Royal'. Several of them have a distinguished tradition of choral music.

CHAPLAIN. Ordinarily a cleric who performs non-parochial duties. Chaplains are often appointed to monarchs, bishops, and other high ecclesiastical dignitaries; to serve in institutions such as schools, prisons, and embassies abroad; and in the armed forces of most Christian countries.

CHAPLET. The name given to the three parts into which the devotion of the *Rosary is divided. It consists of five *decades and forms a complete devotion in itself.

CHAPMAN, JOHN (1856–1933), NT and Patristic scholar. He became Abbot of *Downside in 1929. His *Spiritual Letters* (1935) are much valued.

CHAPTER. (1) A section of a monastic rule, such as was daily read publicly in religious houses; (2) the assembly of the members of a religious house to hear this reading and for other purposes, and then the members in their corporate capacity; (3) the members of any corporate body responsible for an ecclesiastical institution, esp. the *canons of a *cathedral.

CHAPTER, Little. A short lesson of a verse or two of Scripture included in most *Breviary Offices.

CHAPTER HOUSE. A building used for meetings of a cathedral or monastic chapter.

CHARACTER. In Catholic Sacramental theology the indelible quality which *Baptism, *Confirmation, and *Ordination are held to imprint upon the soul.

CHARDON, LOUIS (c. 1596–1651), French *Dominican. In *La Croix de Jésus* (1647) he built his doctrine of the mystical life on the action of sanctifying *grace in the soul and the presence in it of the Three Divine Persons; he also emphasized the salutary effects of spiritual desolation.

CHARGE. An address delivered by a bishop, archdeacon, or other ecclesiastical person at a *visitation of the clergy under his jurisdiction. Charges are also delivered to ordinands by bishops (and in the *Presbyterian Church by ministers) immediately before *ordination.

martyrdom.

CHARISMATA (Gk., 'gifts of grace'). The blessings, spiritual and temporal, bestowed on any Christian for the fulfilment of his vocation. In a narrower sense the word is used of supernatural graces, such as are listed in 1 Cor. 12.

CHARISMATIC RENEWAL MOVEMENT. See *Pentecostalism*.

CHARITY. The usual AV translation of the Gk. word *agape*, elsewhere usually rendered love (q.v.).

CHARLEMAGNE (*c.* 742–814), 'Charles the Great', the first Emperor (from 800) of the *Holy Roman Empire. The son of *Pepin III, he became sole ruler of the Franks in 771. He extended his kingdom in all directions. First he subdued Lombardy, at the request of *Hadrian I; then he conducted campaigns against the Saxons and against the Muslims in Spain. At home he created a strong central administration and encouraged learning and ecclesiastical reform. He had real theological interests and employed *Alcuin to write against the *Adoptianist heresy of *Felix of Urgel. It was through the king, acting through mixed ecclesiastico-civil councils, that the restoration of the hierarchy and Church discipline, the unity of the liturgy, and the definition of doctrine were achieved. The culmination of his reign was his coronation by *Leo III as first Holy Roman Emperor on Christmas Day 800. See also *Carolingian Schools*.

CHARLES I (1600–49), King of Great Britain and Ireland from 1625. He favoured the party in the Church which sought to return to a theological position nearer to traditional Catholicism. He promoted High Churchmen, appointing W. *Laud Abp. of *Canterbury in 1633, and later shared in his unpopularity. In Scotland his attempt to impose the BCP was met in 1638 by the inauguration of the *National Covenant, which pledged Scotland to *Presbyterianism. The Civil War, which broke out in England in 1642, was only in part caused by the ecclesiastical situation, but the defeat of Charles in 1645–6 meant the disestablishment of the C of E and the establishment of Presbyterianism. He refused to compromise over episcopacy, and his execution has been seen as

CHARLES II (1630–85), King of Great Britain and Ireland (in exile) from 1649; restored in 1660. He promised religious toleration in the Declaration of *Breda, and after the Restoration he tried to give effect to it in the *Declarations of Indulgence of 1662 and 1672. The sentiment of the country was, however, exclusively Anglican and led to the passing of the Act of *Uniformity (1662), the *Conventicle Act (1664), the *Five Mile Act (1665), and the *Test Act (1673).

CHARLES V (1500–58), Emperor. When he was elected in 1519 he held Spain and the Spanish Empire, the Netherlands, Naples, and the county of Burgundy. The most urgent problem confronting him was the rise of *Lutheranism. The Diet of *Worms (1521) banned M. *Luther, but Charles's other difficulties prevented him from taking consistent action. At the Diet of *Augsburg (1555) the Protestant princes forced upon him the principle of '*cuius regio, eius religio'. He abdicated in 1556.

CHARLES BORROMEO, St. (1538–84), Abp. of Milan and cardinal from 1560. He was one of the leaders of the *Counter-Reformation. He took part in the last group of sessions of the Council of *Trent. He initiated reform in his diocese; he patronized the *Jesuits, established seminaries for the education of the clergy, and founded a confraternity for instructing children. His influence was extensive.

CHARLES MARTEL (*c.* 690–741), Frankish ruler. He was Mayor of the Palace of the Merovingian kings. His victory over the Saracens at Poitiers in 732 was of decisive importance for the future of Christendom. In his later years he penetrated into Germany and Frisia, where he protected St. *Boniface and other missionaries.

CHARLES, ROBERT HENRY (1855–1931), Biblical scholar. He was Professor of Biblical Greek at *Dublin from 1898 to 1906 and from 1913 Canon of *Westminster. In matters of Jewish eschatology and apocalyptic he was the greatest authority of his day.

CHARRON, PIERRE (1541–1603), French preacher and philosopher. His main work,

De la Sagesse (1601), reflected pagan rather than Christian thought; it opened the way for the secularization of morals, for *Deism, and for free thought.

CHARTER OF LOVE. See *Carta Caritatis.*

CHARTERHOUSE. The English name for a *Carthusian house. The English public school commonly so called was founded on the site of such a house in London.

CHARTRES. Since the 4th cent., with intervals, this French town has been the seat of a bishop. The magnificent cathedral, begun in the 11th cent., was dedicated in 1260. In the early Middle Ages Chartres was famous for its school.

CHARTREUSE, La Grande. See *Grande Chartreuse, La.*

CHASUBLE. The outermost garment worn by bishops and priests when celebrating the Eucharist, and rarely at other times. It derived from the outdoor cloak worn by both sexes in the later Greco-Roman world.

CHATEAUBRIAND, FRANÇOIS RENÉ, VICOMTE DE (1768–1848), French romantic writer. He had a distinguished career as a politician. His *Génie du christianisme* (1802) is a brilliant rhetorical defence of Catholic Christianity. He sought to lift Christianity from the discredit into which the destructive work of 18th-cent. rationalist philosophers had brought it by transferring the debate from the plane of reason to that of feeling.

CHAUCER, GEOFFREY (1343/4–1400), English poet. He fought in France, was captured, ransomed by the king, and entered his service. The *Canterbury Tales* were apparently begun *c.* 1387 and remained unfinished at the time of his death. Despite attempts to depict him as agnostic and anticlerical, it seems that Chaucer was not hostile to the Church. He strove to depict 14th-cent. life as he saw it.

CHELTENHAM LIST, See *Mommsen Catalogue.*

CHEMNITZ, MARTIN (1522–86), *Lutheran theologian. He spent most of his life in Brunswick. He defended M. *Luther's doctrine of the *Real Presence of Christ in the Eucharist, though he deprecated further elaboration as to the mode of the Presence. He was a leading influence in consolidating Lutheran doctrine and practice in the generation after Luther's death.

CHERUBICON, also 'The Cherubic Hymn'. In the E. Church a hymn sung during the *Greater Entrance.

CHERUBIM. The second of the nine orders of *angels.

CHESTER. The city was perhaps the seat of the bishops of Mercia, but for most of the Middle Ages it was not a bishopric. The see was refounded in 1541 by *Henry VIII, who made the church of the dissolved abbey of St. *Werburgh the cathedral, with a new dedication to Christ and the BVM.

CHESTER BEATTY PAPYRI. A group of papyrus codices, now in Dublin, most of which were acquired in 1931 by A. Chester Beatty (d. 1968). They include a number of substantial Biblical texts which provide valuable evidence for the Greek Bible, since they are a century or more older than the earliest vellum MSS.

CHEVETOGNE. The *Benedictine community which has been at Chevetogne in Belgium since 1939 was founded in 1925 at Amay-sur-Meuse by L. *Beauduin in response to *Pius XI's request that Benedictines should pray for unity. The community seeks to restore closer relations between the RC and other Churches; it is divided into two groups, the Latin and the Eastern, the one following the W. rite, the other the E. (Greek and Slavonic).

CHICHELE, HENRY (?1362–1443), Abp. of *Canterbury from 1414. He was among the English delegates to the Council of *Pisa in 1409, and in 1414 he was among those appointed to assist the Duke of Bedford in administering the realm. He was reprimanded by *Martin V for failing to secure the repeal of the Statutes of *Provisors and *Praemunire, and his legatine powers were suspended. He founded All Souls College at Oxford (1438).

CHICHESTER. The see, which was

founded at Selsey by St. *Wilfrid during his exile from York, was transferred to Chichester in accordance with the decree of the Council of London of 1075. The cathedral was built in the 12th–13th cents.

CHILDREN'S CRUSADE (1212). A march of children who gathered from France and W. Germany after the diversion of the Fourth *Crusade (1202–4), with the intention of 'recapturing *Jerusalem'. Few ever seem to have got as far as embarking.

CHILE, Christianity in. The Spanish invasion of Chile, begun in 1535, was followed by great missionary activity. The complete conversion of the country was achieved some 150 years later. In 1810–28 political separation from *Spain was secured, but the RC Church continued to be 'protected' and subsidized; other religions are tolerated.

CHILIASM. Another name *Millenarianism.

CHILLINGWORTH, WILLIAM (1602–1644), Anglican divine. He became a RC and went to *Douai in 1630. The next year he returned to England, and in 1634 again declared himself a Protestant. His *Religion of Protestants a Safe Way to Salvation* (1638) defended the rights of reason and free inquiry in doctrinal matters, and denied that any Church was infallible.

CHIMERE. A silk or satin gown, without sleeves, worn by Anglican bishops and by doctors of divinity.

CHINA, Christianity in. Acc. to legend St. *Thomas the Apostle preached in China. The *Sigan-Fu stone shows that *Nestorian missionaries reached China in the 7th cent.; Nestorian Christianity survived until the 14th cent. The first W. mission was that of John of Monte Corvino (c. 1294); this was ended by the advent of the Ming dynasty in 1368. The famous mission of the *Jesuits began in 1582. They succeeded in building up a Chinese Christian community, but their method of *accommodation gave rise to controversy, and the subsequent assertion of papal authority in the 18th cent. antagonized the Emperor. Persecution and imperial decrees banning Christianity followed.

The 19th-cent. missionary movement was faced with the isolationist policy of the Manchu dynasty. The first Protestant missionary, Robert *Morrison, who arrived in Canton in 1807, was able to remain only because he was employed as a translator by the East India Company. In the period 1839–65 the Western powers by military action secured for themselves rights of residence and jurisdiction. Missionaries then came from all the main denominations in Europe and America; they founded churches, schools, and hospitals throughout the country. When the Communists came to power in 1949 Christian institutions were taken over by the State, many churches were closed, and the activities of missionaries were curtailed; most were withdrawn by 1952. The organization among Chinese Christians of the 'Three-Self Patriotic Movement' (self-supporting, self-governing, and self-propagating) was encouraged and a limited religious liberty was tolerated, but the cultural revolution of 1966 has been followed by further persecution.

CHINA INLAND MISSION (C.I.M.). An interdenominational mission to the interior of *China founded by J. H. *Taylor in 1865. Since 1951 the sphere of its work has been extended to other parts of Asia. In 1965 it was renamed the 'Overseas Missionary Fellowship'.

CHOIR (architectural). The part of a church containing the seats of the clergy. In the Roman *basilicas these seats were set round the *apse behind the altar; the choir is now usually included in the *chancel, at its W. end.

CHOIR (musical). A body of singers assisting at Divine Service. As early as the 4th cent. such bodies existed, made up of clerics in *minor orders and boys, and by the time of *Gregory I (d. 604) the *Schola Cantorum seems to have been established. In the Middle Ages the choirs of cathedrals and monasteries were almost the only places where music was taught. About the 15th cent. harmonized music began to supplement the *plainsong of the Church and lay singers augmented Church choirs.

CHOIR SISTERS. Nuns who are under obligation to attend all choir *offices, as contrasted with *lay sisters, who, though living under rule, attend only certain services.

CHOREPISCOPUS. In the early Church a bishop of a country district in full episcopal orders. He had restricted powers and was wholly subject to the authority of the diocesan. In the E. there were many in the 4th cent., esp. in Asia Minor, but their functions were progressively restricted and by the 13th cent. they had disappeared. In the W. they are first mentioned in 439, were numerous in missionary districts of Germany in the 8th cent., but disappeared in the 12th.

CHRISM. A mixture of olive oil and balsam used in the ritual of the Greek and Latin Churches. It may be consecrated only by a bishop; in the E. by the *Patriarchs alone. Acc. to present Latin usage, chrism is consecrated on *Maundy Thursday, since 1955 at a special Mass of the Chrism. It is used in the Sacraments of *Baptism, *Confirmation, and Holy *Orders, as well as in the dedication of churches and altars.

CHRISMATORY. A small vessel for keeping the three kinds of holy oil, viz. oil of the catechumens, oil of the sick, and *chrism.

CHRIST (Gk., lit. 'Anointed One'). The word is a Gk. translation of the Heb. *Messiah. Originally a title, it soon came to be used by the followers of the risen Jesus as a proper name for their Lord, so that they themselves came to be known as *Christians. See also *Jesus Christ* and *Christology*.

CHRIST, Disciples of. See *Disciples of Christ*.

CHRIST THE KING, Feast of. The feast instituted in the RC Church in 1925 to celebrate the all-embracing authority of Christ. Since 1970 it has been kept on the last Sunday before the beginning of Advent.

CHRIST CHURCH, OXFORD. A college in the University of *Oxford, founded by T. *Wolsey on the site of the monastery of St. *Frideswide as 'Cardinal College'. In 1546 it was reconstituted by *Henry VIII. At the same time the new episcopal see was moved to the church of St. Frideswide, which thus became both a cathedral and a college chapel.

CHRISTADELPHIANS. A sect founded in America in 1848 by John Thomas. They hold that the core of the Gospel is belief in the return of Jesus Christ in power to set up a visible theocracy beginning at Jerusalem, and that assurance of this is necessary to salvation. They reject the doctrine of the *Trinity.

CHRISTIAN. The name was originally applied to the followers of Christ by outsiders, acc. to Acts 11: 26 being first used at *Antioch *c.* 40–4. Acc. to *Tacitus it was current among the people at Rome at the time of the *Neronian persecution (A.D. 64) and it was always the official Roman designation of members of the Church; thus in times of persecution it was often the confession or denial of this name that was crucial. It was later adopted by the Church as a designation to distinguish itself from other religions.

In modern times the name Christian has been claimed by every form of belief stemming from historical Christianity, and has tended, in nominally Christian countries, to lose any credal significance and imply only what is ethically praiseworthy.

CHRISTIAN AID. A division of the *British Council of Churches which originated in the work of the Ecumenical Refugee Commission set up in 1944. It provides assistance for the poorer nations and for refugees and the victims of disaster throughout the world, working with members of the Churches in the areas concerned. A special Christian Aid week to raise funds in Britain has been held annually since 1957.

'CHRISTIAN BELIEVING' (1976). A Report of the Doctrine Commission of the C of E on 'The Nature of the Christian Faith and its Expression in Holy Scripture and Creeds'. It consists of a joint report subscribed by all members of the Commission, with two appendices on slightly technical matters, and eight essays by individual members.

CHRISTIAN MAJESTY, His Most. A title of the kings of France.

CHRISTIAN SCIENCE. The tenets of a religious body. It was founded by Mrs. Mary Baker Eddy (1821–1910), who set out her principles in *Science and Health* (1875). The system is based on the theory that mind is the only reality and matter an illusion; suffering and death are the effects of false thinking, which consists in a mistaken belief in the existence of matter; health is to be restored by opposing right thinking to the illusions of the patient. In 1879 the first 'Church of Christ Scientist' was opened in Boston, Mass. Christian Science spread, esp. in English-speaking countries and Germany.

CHRISTIAN SOCIALISM. A 19th-cent. movement for social reform, initiated by members of the C of E. It aimed at reform of individuals and society by the application of Christian principles in all social relations. Its best-known leaders were J. M. F. *Ludlow, F. D. *Maurice, C. *Kingsley, and Thomas Hughes. They organized evening classes, which developed into the 'Working Men's College' established in 1854, and in 1850 they opened a co-operative workshop for tailoring and other crafts. The failure of the movement was largely due to the unresponsiveness of the workers themselves.

CHRISTIAN YEAR, The. The collection of poems for the Sundays and holy days of the year, published by J. *Keble in 1827.

CHRISTINA (1626–89), Queen of Sweden. The only surviving child of *Gustavus Adolphus, she succeeded to the Swedish throne in 1632. Assuming government in 1644, she made it her first aim to end the *Thirty Years War, and she was partly responsible for the Treaty of *Westphalia (1648). She promoted education at home and patronized foreign scholars. She abdicated in 1654. In 1655 she became a RC and settled at Rome. She made a famous collection of MSS., now incorporated in the *Vatican Library ('Reginenses').

CHRISTKATHOLIKEN. The official name of the *Old Catholics of Switzerland.

CHRISTMAS. The commemoration of Christ's nativity. The time of year when He was born is unkown. The earliest mention of its being celebrated on 25 Dec. is in the *Philocalian Calendar, which represents Roman practice in 336. The date was prob. chosen to oppose the pagan feast of the *Natalis Solis Invicti* by a celebration of the birth of the 'Sun of Righteousness'; its observance in the W. spread from Rome. In the E. the closely related feast of the *Epiphany has tended to be more important.

The day is celebrated in the W. rite by three Masses, of the night (normally at midnight), of the dawn, and of the day.

CHRISTOCENTRIC. (1) Of systems of theology which maintain that God has never revealed Himself to man except in the Incarnate Christ; they preclude the possibility of *natural religion. (2) More generally, of any set of religious beliefs which is focused on the Person of Christ.

CHRISTOLOGY. The study of the Person of Christ, and in particular of the union in Him of the Divine and human natures. The Gospels indicate that the historical Christ claimed to be both God and man, and from the Acts and Epistles it is clear that the earliest Christians regarded Him as such. It was only when one-sided distortions of the truth came into being that the *Apologists of the 2nd cent. began elaborating the philosophical implications of the *Incarnation.

The main Christological heresies have either failed to maintain the unity and distinctness of the Person of the Son or denied the reality either of His Divinity or of His humanity. *Arius denied that the Son is truly God; he also denied that there are two natures in Christ, asserting instead that the nature of the Son took the place of the human soul in Christ. *Apollinarius was concerned to maintain Christ's Godhead; he held that the Divine nature took the place of His human spirit, thus reducing His humanity to the animal elements present in human nature. *Theodore of Mopsuestia and *Nestorius were so concerned to preserve the reality of Christ's human experience that they separated the Divinity and humanity in Him almost to the point of making Him into two Persons. *Eutyches taught that, though in Christ there were two natures 'before the Incarnation', there was only one 'after the Incarnation'. These heresies were in turn condemned by the Councils of *Nicaea (325), *Constantinople (381), *Ephesus (431), and *Chalcedon (451). The Chalcedonian Definition of 'one ... Christ ... in two natures, without confusion, without change, without division, without separation', was eventually almost universally accepted, though the next two centuries saw the wide prevalence of *Monophysitism and *Monothelism, condemned respectively in 553 and 680 at the 2nd and 3rd Councils of *Constantinople. See also *Incarnation*.

CHRISTOPHER, St. (Gk., 'one who carried Christ'). Acc. to tradition he was martyred in Asia Minor in the 3rd cent. A legend represents him as a giant who earned his living by carrying travellers across a river; one passenger was a small child who caused him to bow beneath his burden as the child was Christ and His weight that of the world. He is the patron of wayfarers; recently he has been adopted esp. by motorists.

CHRISTOPHERSON, JOHN (d. 1558), Bp. of *Chichester from 1557. He was among the first to introduce Greek studies in Cambridge. He was chaplain and confessor to Queen *Mary. After *Elizabeth I's accession he preached a violent sermon against the Reformation, was imprisoned, and died soon afterwards.

CHRODEGANG, St. (d. 766), Bp. of Metz from 742. He was a leading ecclesiastical reformer. In 748 he founded the abbey of *Gorze and he caused the canons of his cathedral to live a community life, drawing up for them the 'rule' that bears his name (c. 755). This allowed them to hold private property. He also introduced the Roman chant and liturgy into his diocese.

CHROMATIUS, St. (d. 407), Bp. of *Aquileia from c. 388. He was a learned scholar and tried to mediate between *Jerome and *Rufinus. Some of his sermons have long been known; others have been identified in modern times.

CHRONICLES, Books of. These OT Books record the history of Israel and Judah from the Creation to the return from Exile under Cyrus (536 B.C.). In the Heb. Canon they are a single Book; the division goes back to the *Septuagint, where they are called '*Paralipomenon', i.e. 'that which is left over' sc. from Sam. and Kgs. The term 'Chronicles' was introduced by *Jerome, whence it passed into English versions. The work appears to have been written in the latter half of the 4th cent. B.C.

CHRONICON EDESSENUM (Edessene Chronicle). A Syriac chronicle extending from 133 B.C. to A.D. 540, the date of its compilation, but with few entries before the 3rd cent. A.D. Its main interest lies in the history of *Edessa.

CHRONICON PASCHALE. A Byzantine chronicle, compiled in the early 7th cent., so named because it was based on the Easter reckoning. It extended from the creation of *Adam to A.D. 629, but not all of it has survived.

CHRONOGRAPHER OF A.D. 354, The. The name given by T. Mommsen to the compiler of an almanac drawn up for the use of Christians at Rome in the 4th cent. The document includes a list of the dates of death of the Bps. of Rome from 255 to 352, a primitive Roman *martyrology, and a list of Roman Bishops from St. *Peter to Pope *Liberius (the *Liberian Catalogue).

CHRONOLOGY, Biblical. (1) *Old Testament.* It is difficult to date the events recorded, partly because of the paucity of allusions to events known from outside sources, and partly because the times given for the duration of events in the Hebrew text are not always consistent, and there are frequent divergences in the *Septuagint. From the 9th cent. B.C. onwards dates of events narrated can be roughly discovered by comparing them with Assyrian and Persian chronologies.

(2) *New Testament.* Complications are caused by the different methods by which the years of monarchs were reckoned and by the intricacies of the Jewish calendar. Acc. to Mt. 2: 1 Jesus was born 'in the days of *Herod the king' (d. c. 4 B.C.), but acc. to Lk. 2: 2 during 'the first enrolment made when Quirinus was governor of Syria' (prob. A.D. 6–9). There are similar discrepancies about other events in His life, but all are agreed that he 'suffered under Pontius *Pilate', who was procurator of Judaea from A.D. 26 to 36. The date of St. *Paul's conversion is also disputed. The outline of the events recorded is unaffected by these uncertainties.

CHRYSIPPUS (c. 405–79), 'of Jerusalem', ecclesiastical writer. He became guardian of the Holy Cross at the Church of the *Holy Sepulchre. His few surviving works include four panegyrics.

CHRYSOGONUS, St. Acc. to legend he was arrested in Rome during *Diocletian's persecution and slain at *Aquileia. His cultus at Rome dates from the 5th cent. at latest and his name was included in the traditional

*Canon of the Mass.

CHRYSOLOGUS, St. PETER (*c.* 400–450), Bp. of *Ravenna. He preached his first sermon as Bishop in the presence of the Empress *Galla Placidia, and received her support for his ambitious building projects. In a letter to *Eutyches (449) he asserted the necessity for adherence to the Roman see in matters of faith. A large collection of sermons attributed to him survives.

CHRYSOM. The 'chrism-robe' put on a child at Baptism, as a symbol of the cleansing of its sin. It may originally have been a cloth put over the head to prevent the *chrism from being rubbed off. In the C of E it disappeared in 1552, but it survives in the RC Church.

CHRYSOSTOM, St. JOHN (*c.* 347–407), Bp. of *Constantinople and '*Doctor of the Church'. He studied at *Antioch and then became a hermit. Made deacon in 381 and priest in 386, he was specially charged with the task of preaching (the name 'Chrysostom' means 'golden-mouthed'), and during the years 386–98 he delivered at Antioch the series of Homilies on Gen. and various NT Books which establish his title as the greatest Christian expositor. These works combine a great facility for seeing the spiritual meaning of an author with an equal ability for immediate practical application. He was, however, opposed to the *allegorical exegesis of Scripture and insisted that it must be interpreted literally. In 398 he was made Patr. of Constantinople. He incurred the hostility of the Empress Eudoxia and of *Theophilus, Patr. of Alexandria, his disappointed rival. At the Synod of the *Oak (403) he was condemned and banished. Though recalled by the Court, his plain speaking antagonized the Empress and on a technicality he was exiled first to near Antioch and then to Pontus, where he died.

CHRYSOSTOM, Liturgy of St. The liturgy in general use in the E. Orthodox Church except on a few days in the year. In its present form it is much later than the time of St. *Chrysostom; it prob. owed its influence to being the liturgy of the imperial capital.

CHRYSOSTOM, The Prayer of St. The prayer in the BCP was drawn by T.

*Cranmer from the Liturgy of St. *Chrysostom. Its authorship is unknown.

CHURCH. The term denotes both a church building and the Christian community, local or universal. The NT as a whole teaches that the Church as an organic society was established by Christ as the New Israel and endowed by Him with the Holy Spirit at Pentecost; it is not merely a voluntary association of individual disciples. In the following period the Divine constitution and corporate nature of the Church were stressed, and its essence came to be epitomized in the four traditional *notes of the Church, viz. unity, holiness, catholicity, and apostolicity. Its membership, its orders of ministers, and its unity are constituted by participation in visible Sacraments, viz. those of *Baptism and *Confirmation, Holy *Orders, and the *Eucharist respectively. In addition to the visible Church on earth there exists the invisible Church of the faithful departed.

The *Reformation led to a reformulation of the idea of the Church. It sought to proclaim its being in terms of the Word of God rather than in Sacramental relationships. Among Protestants, two doctrines gained wide acceptance: (1) that the Church is a visible body and in the Divine intention one throughout the world, but that in view of the errors and corruptions which have arisen it is justified within a particular nation in reforming itself, even if this involves a breach of visible unity; (2) that the true Church is an invisible body of this saved whose precise membership is known only to God. Most holders of this view maintained that it was desirable that the Church should possess an outward organization, membership of which should correspond as far as possible with that of the invisible Church. Some Protestants held that visible unity should be secured in each nation by an 'established religion' determined by the ruler; others regarded unity of organization between Christian communities as unnecessary.

In modern times both among Catholics and Protestants there has been a renewed interest in the theology of the Church, which is recognized as a fundamental fact in the Christian Revelation. There has also been an increased recognition of the Church's transcendence over and separateness from the world.

CHURCH, RICHARD WILLIAM

(1815–90), Dean of *St. Paul's from 1871. In 1845 as Junior Proctor in Oxford he shared in the dramatic vetoing of the condemnation of *Tract 90 in the University convocation. *The Oxford Movement, Twelve Years, 1833-1845* (posthumously publd., 1891) is a masterpiece of judicious and balanced interpretation.

CHURCH ARMY. A voluntary Anglican organization of lay workers, founded in 1882, on the model of the *Salvation Army, for evangelistic purposes, by Wilson *Carlile. Since 1889 its activities have included social and moral welfare work among the poor.

CHURCH ASSEMBLY. This body, officially the National Assembly of the Church of England, was established by the *Convocations in 1919; in 1970 it was superseded by the General *Synod. It consisted of a House of Bishops; a House of Clergy; and a House of Laity elected by representative electors of the Diocesan Conferences. Its most important function was to prepare ecclesiastical measures for transmission to Parliament under powers provided by the *Enabling Act of 1919.

CHURCH ASSOCIATION, The. A society founded in 1865 by several Evangelical Churchmen to maintain the Protestant ideals of faith and worship in the C of E. In 1950 it became (with the National Church League) the Church Society.

CHURCH COMMISSIONERS for England. The body formed by the fusion of the *Ecclesiastical Commissioners and *Queen Anne's Bounty in 1948 to manage the estates and revenues of the C of E. It consists of the Abps. and Bps. of England, three lay 'Church Estates Commissioners', and a number of other clergy and lay persons.

CHURCH CONGRESSES. A series of unofficial gatherings of Anglican Churchmen held between 1861 and 1938.

CHURCH HOUSE, WESTMINSTER. The building, completed in 1940, in which the *Convocation of Canterbury and the General *Synod of the C of E generally meet and the headquarters of many Anglican organizations.

CHURCH HYMNARY, The. The authorized hymnal of the Church of *Scotland and several other *Presbyterian Churches. It was issued in 1898 and revised in 1927 and 1973.

CHURCH MEETING. The regular assembly of all members of a *Congregational or *Baptist Church for the purposes of Church administration, the admission of members, the election of officers, and the exercise of discipline.

CHURCH MISSIONARY SOCIETY. See *C.M.S.*

CHURCH MISSIONS TO JEWS. An Anglican society founded in 1809 as the 'London Society for Promoting Christianity amongst the Jews'; in 1962 its title was changed to the 'Church's Ministry among the Jews'.

CHURCH OF ENGLAND. The presence of British bishops at the Council of *Arles (314) is evidence of the existence of an organized Church. The *Celtic Church (q.v.) was later confined to the W. parts of Britain. In 597 St. *Augustine arrived in Kent. The differences between the Celtic and Roman missions sprang from fundamental divergences in temper, though they found expression mainly over minor points; the Roman usages were gradually accepted after the Synod of *Whitby (664). Unification and organization of the *Anglo-Saxon Church (q.v.) was achieved under *Theodore of Tarsus, who summoned national ecclesiastical councils, divided dioceses, and encouraged learning. After a period of decline, reforms were initiated by St. *Dunstan and contacts with the Continent began to be reestablished. The Norman Conquest by *William I ensured that the English Church entered the main stream of European religion at a time when the Hildebrandine reform movement was exercising a powerful influence. *Lanfranc, assisted by a body of foreign bishops and abbots, led the way to a revival of religious life in England. The Norman age also saw the removal of episcopal sees from remote villages to cities, the beginning of an outburst of building activity, and the reorganization of ecclesiastical administration. Most important of all, the royal separation of the ecclesiastical and civil courts opened the way for the entrance of the

Roman *canon law, the chief agent of papal control in the W. Church. There were a number of disputes between the Church and State, notably about *investiture and the limits of the royal power, but by the 13th cent. papal power in England had become very great. Soon, however, with the accentuation of national self-consciousness on the one hand, and the papal scandals of the *Babylonian captivity and the *Great Schism on the other, the exactions and policy of the Roman see became the subject of increasing criticism in England; there was, for instance, legislation to curtail the papal practice of diverting the income of English benefices for the support of foreign ecclesiastics.

When in the 16th cent. the Tudor monarchs deemed it expedient to measure their strength against the Papacy, many elements in the nation were ready to support them. Criticism of ecclesiastical wealth had been prominent for some time and the merchants cast hungry eyes at monastic property. Evidence of religious dissatisfaction was represented among the learned by the Renaissance revolt against Scholasticism and among the unlettered by vague strivings for a more personal and spiritual religion. The occasion of the Reformation was the famous 'divorce' of *Henry VIII. The *Convocations acknowledged the King to be the Supreme Head on earth of the Church of England, and a series of laws severed the financial, judicial, and administrative bonds between England and Rome. The monasteries were dissolved. Under *Edward VI, Abp. T. *Cranmer produced the First and Second Books of *Common Prayer in 1549 and 1552. The advance to Protestantism was reversed under *Mary. Upon the accession of *Elizabeth I the papal obedience was again renounced, the Crown assumed the title of 'Supreme Governor', the second BCP with some changes became the service-book of the C of E, and the *Thirty-Nine Articles its doctrinal formulary. The Elizabethan attempt to achieve a comprehensive national settlement was challenged by both the Popish *Recusants and the *Puritans. The majority of the latter body remained within the Church, but the controversy drove the bishops into close dependence on the Crown, which worked through the Court of *High Commission to enforce uniformity. Episcopacy and Anglicanism were among the issues in the Civil War, and the victory of Parliament led first to a *Presbyterian reform and then to *Independency. With the Restoration of *Charles II, the C of E again became the established Church and repressive measures were taken against dissenters. *James II's attack on the C of E was largely responsible for his downfall.

After the Revolution of 1688, the C of E, weakened by the secession of the *Nonjurors, settled to a period of quiescence. A limited toleration was granted to dissenters, theological disputes became unpopular, and the alliance of Church and State was a mutually defensive pact against all subversive forces. The *Methodist revival was the parent both of a new Christian body and of the Anglican *Evangelical revival. *Latitudinarianism dominated the intellectual atmosphere until well into the 19th cent., which witnessed the foundation of new parishes and bishoprics and much administrative reform. The *Oxford Movement emphasized the Catholic and apostolic character of the established Church, but ceremonial novelties led to litigation and dispute. Some readjustment in the relations between the Church and State was effected by the *Enabling Act of 1919, which gave to the *Church Assembly the power to prepare legislation for consideration by Parliament; in 1927 and 1928 Parliament rejected a revised BCP. In recent years the Church has achieved a considerable measure of control of its services, first by the Prayer Book (*Alternative and Other Services) Measure of 1965 and then by the *Church of English (Worship and Doctrine) Measure of 1974.

CHURCH OF ENGLAND (WORSHIP AND DOCTRINE) MEASURE, 1974. This Measure, which repealed the Prayer Book (*Alternative and Other Services) Measure of 1965, allows the General *Synod to regulate the forms of service used in the C of E, provided that those contained in the BCP remain available. It also allows the Synod to determine the forms of *assent and subscription to doctrine required of the clergy and other officers.

CHURCH OF THE BRETHREN. See *Tunkers*.

CHURCH PASTORAL AID SOCIETY. See *C.P.A.S.*

CHURCH SISTERS. In the Church of *Scotland women specially set apart to help in parochial work. They have now been merged in an order of *Deaconesses.

CHURCH SOCIETY. See *Church Association.*

CHURCH TIMES, The. A weekly religious newspaper, founded to propagate *Anglo-Catholic principles. It dates from 1863.

CHURCH UNION, The. An Anglican association formed in 1934 by the amalgamation of the *English Church Union and the *Anglo-Catholic Congress.

CHURCH UNITY OCTAVE. An *octave of prayer observed since 1908 from 18 to 25 Jan. by a group of Anglican High Churchmen and others for the visible reunion of the Church.

CHURCHES OF CHRIST. See *Disciples of Christ.*

CHURCHING OF WOMEN, The. The form of thanksgiving which Christian women make after childbirth. In the RC Church it has been replaced by a blessing at the end of the *baptismal service.

CHURCHMEN'S UNION. See *Modern Churchmen's Union.*

CHURCHWARDENS. In the C of E two churchwardens are chosen annually by the incumbent and parishioners. They represent the laity and are responsible for the movable property in the church. In the past they had also the duty of presenting offenders against ecclesiastical law.

CHURCHYARD. Properly the ground in which the church stands. The word is often used as though it were equivalent to '*cemetery'.

CIBORIUM. (1) A chalice-shaped vessel, with a lid, used to contain the Sacramental Bread of the Eucharist. (2) A canopy over the altar or *baldachino.

CIMABUE (*c.* 1240–*c.* 1302), the usual name of 'Cenni di Pepo', Florentine painter. Among the works attributed to him are the 'Madonna and Child with Angels' in the National Gallery, London, and the paintings

in the church of St. Francis at *Assisi. The mosaics in the Cathedral at Pisa were executed in the last years of his life.

CIRCUMCELLIONS. Fanatical bands of peasants who flourished in N. Africa in the 4th cent. and became linked with the *Donatists.

CIRCUMCISION. Though circumcision had long been in use as a religious rite among the Jews, it was abandoned at an early date by the Church. In St. *Paul's Epistles 'the circumcision' is often used substantively of the Jewish people.

CIRCUMCISION, Feast of the. The feast traditionally kept on 1 Jan., the 8th day after *Christmas, in commemoration of Christ's circumcision. The observance dates from the mid-6th cent. Since 1960 the RC Church has devoted 1 Jan. to other observances.

CIRCUMINCESSION, also Circuminsession. In Christian theology the technical term for the interpenetration of the Three Persons of the Trinity.

CISTERCIAN ORDER. The order was founded at *Cîteaux in 1098 by *Robert of Molesme and others who wanted a form of *Benedictinism stricter and more primitive than any then existing. After some precarious years St. *Bernard arrived as a novice in 1112; in the following decades the order spread rapidly.

The Cistercian life was to be one of secluded communal intercession and adoration. Its churches were to be plain, and manual work was given its primitive prominent position. The constitution was laid down in the *Carta Caritatis. Each house regulated its own affairs in accordance with the ordinances of the annual General Chapter at Cîteaux, at which it was represented, but it was 'visited' annually by the abbot of its founding abbey.

In the 17th cent. Cîteaux lost control of foreign houses with the formation of national congregations. The same period saw the rise of a movement for reform known as the Strict Observance, based on the literal observance of the rule and jettisoning the deviations which had become customary (the Common Observance). At the end of the 18th cent. the Revolution practically obliterated the Common Observance in France, but it survived in the Austro-Hungarian lands and is strong in the U.S.A. After the Revolution the monks of *La Trappe were the first to return to France; they acquired a supremacy among the followers of the Strict Observance, who are now known as *Trappists.

CITATION. A summons to appear before a court of justice, esp. an ecclesiastical court.

CÎTEAUX. The mother house of the *Cistercian Order (q.v.), in Burgundy. The house and property, lost to the Order in 1791, were restored in 1898. It then adopted the Strict Observance and its Abbot, who resides in Rome, is the General of the Cistercians of the Strict Observance (or *Trappists).

CIVIL CONSTITUTION OF THE CLERGY, The (1790). The legislative measures passed during the French Revolution which imposed upon the Church of France a schismatic organization. The Constitution was designed to secure the independence of the Church from the Papacy, except in doctrinal matters. The Pope was deprived of all actual power in France, and the salaries of the clergy were regulated by the State. Most of the bishops and clergy refused to take the Constitutional Oath imposed in Nov. 1790 and were deprived of their offices. See also *Constitutional Church*.

CLAIRVAUX. The fourth house of the *Cistercian Order, founded by St. *Bernard in 1115. It rapidly rose to fame. The buildings were taken over by the State in 1790, during the French Revolution.

CLANDESTINITY. The celebration of marriages without the cognizance of proper authority. Attempts to deal with the abuse, which was widespread in the Middle Ages, were made by both Catholics and Protestants in the 16th century. The Reformers generally held that marriages without parental consent were null and void; RC theologians that clandestine marriages were valid but irregular. In the C of E publicity is secured by the requirements relating to *banns, *marriage licences, and witnesses, these last also being required by civil law.

CLAPHAM SECT. An informal group of wealthy Anglican *Evangelicals, so named because the majority of its members lived near Clapham and worshipped in its parish church. They included J. *Venn, Z. *Macaulay, and W. *Wilberforce. They supported the campaign against the *slave-trade, the extension of missionary enterprise, the formation of the *British and Foreign Bible Society, and the extension of *Sunday Schools.

CLAPTON SECT. A loosely defined group of Anglican High Churchmen at the beginning of the 19th cent., so called because the home of its most prominent member was at Clapton (and with allusion to the *Clapham Sect). They were also known as the 'Hackney Phalanx' after the rector of Hackney.

CLARE, St. (1194–1253), foundress of the '*Poor Clares'. About 1212 she gave up her possessions and joined St. *Francis at the *Portiuncula. At first he placed her in a *Benedictine house, but soon, when other women wanted to live on Franciscan lines, he set up a separate community, with St. Clare as abbess (1215); she occupied this position for the rest of her life.

CLARENDON, The Constitutions of. Sixteen enactments put forward by Henry II of England to regulate the relations between the ecclesiastical and lay jurisdiction and other matters. They were presented at the Council of Clarendon (1164) for the assent of Thomas *Becket, Abp. of Canterbury, who refused to affix his seal. A long dispute followed.

CLARKE, SAMUEL (1675–1729), Anglican divine. In 1704 and 1705 he delivered two sets of *Boyle Lectures in defence of rational theology against the empiricism of J. *Locke. Though a critic of the *Deists, he sympathized with some aspects of their teaching. His *Scripture-Doctrine of the Trinity* (1712), which had *Unitarian leanings, aroused criticism in Convocation, though no formal retractation was imposed.

CLARKSON, THOMAS (1760–1846), anti-slave-trade agitator. In 1787, with some leading *Quakers and with W. *Wilberforce, he formed a group which pressed in the House of Commons for the abolition of the slave-trade in the British Empire. Their vigorous efforts were rewarded by the Act of 1807, ending the traffic, and by the emancipation of the slaves in 1833.

CLASS MEETING. A meeting, usually weekly, of small sections of each *Methodist congregation, at which contributions to Church funds are paid, and inquiry is made into the conduct and spiritual progress of individual members.

CLAUDEL, PAUL LOUIS CHARLES (1868-1955), French RC author and diplomat. His chief claim to fame rests on his plays, which revivified the French theatre; their central theme was the consecration of the world to God in Christ.

CLAUDIANUS MAMERTUS (*c*. 425–*c*. 474), Christian philosopher. After practising as a rhetorician he became a monk. In *De Statu Animae* (467–72) he defended the doctrine that the soul was immaterial against *Faustus of Riez, who held that the soul, as a created substance, was of corporeal and extended character.

CLAUDIUS (d. *c*. 830–40), Bp. of Turin from *c*. 817. He had little regard for the authority of the Roman see. He made a series of attacks on image-worship, relics, the adoration of the Cross, and every visible sign of Christ's life, as well as on pilgrimages and the intercession of saints. He was also famous for his Biblical commentaries.

CLAUDIUS APOLLINARIUS. See *Apollinarius, Claudius*.

CLAUSURA. (1) The practice of separating a part of a religious house to the exclusion of those of the opposite sex to the community, and sometimes even to lay persons of the same sex; and (2) the portion so enclosed.

CLAYTON, JOHN (1709–73), one of the first *Methodists. At Oxford he was a member of the '*Holy Club' founded by the *Wesleys. In 1740 he became chaplain, and in 1760 a Fellow, of the Manchester Collegiate Church.

CLEMENT OF ALEXANDRIA, St. See after Pope *Clement XIV*.

CLEMENT OF ROME, St. (*fl. c*. 96), Bp. of *Rome. He was prob. the third bishop after St. *Peter. Besides the spurious '*Clementine Literature' (q.v.), two 'Epist-

les to the Corinthians' have been ascribed to him. The former (I Clement) is genuine. It was written *c*. 96 in the name of the Roman Church to deal with fierce strife in the Church at *Corinth, where certain presbyters had been deposed; it insisted that the deposed presbyters must be reinstated and legitimate superiors obeyed. It affords valuable evidence on the state of the ministry at the time. The so-called 'Second Epistle of Clement' is really a homily, assigned on stylistic grounds to a separate author. It is the earliest surviving Christian sermon; it deals with the character of the Christian life and the duty of repentance. Acc. to later tradition, Clement was banished to the Crimea and forced to work in the mines; he was bound to an anchor and thrown into the Black Sea.

CLEMENT V (1264–1314), Pope from 1305. Bertrand de Got came of an influential French family. His policy was largely subservient to French influence, which increased when he fixed the papal residence at *Avignon in 1309. He acquiesced in Philip the Fair's attack on the *Templars, suppressing the order at the Council of *Vienne (1311); though the Pope assigned the Templars' property to the *Hospitallers, Philip managed to get most of their possessions. Clement did much to further scholarship, founding the universities of Orleans and Perugia, and he added the '*Clementines' to the canon law.

CLEMENT VI (1291–1352), Pope from 1342. He was elected Pope at *Avignon, the sovereignty of which he purchased in 1348. His French sympathies prevented him from making a lasting peace between France and England, and he continued his predecessors' struggle against Louis of Bavaria. After Louis's death in 1347 he received the submission of the schismatic Franciscans who had supported him. His attempts to meet expenses by reserving to himself an increasing number of appointments to bishoprics and benefices caused hostility, esp. in England, where Edward III replied in 1351 with the First Statute of *Provisors.

CLEMENT VII (1478–1534), Pope from 1523. Though personally blameless in character, his lack of courage caused his pontificate to be marked by shifty diplomacy and intrigue. He tried to steer a middle course between the conflicting aims of Francis I of France and the Emp. *Charles V, and he irresolutely procrastinated over the divorce of *Henry VIII.

CLEMENT VIII (c. 1536–1605), Pope from 1592. It was his policy to secure the representation of all the conflicting influences in the *curia. He supported the League against *Henry of Navarre, but at the same time negotiated with Henry, who became a RC in 1595. He issued new editions of the *Vulgate, *Missal, and *Breviary.

CLEMENT XI (1649–1721), Pope from 1700. In the political sphere he met with little success, and in the Treaty of Utrecht (1713) his rights in Sardinia and elsewhere were ignored. His condemnation of *Jansenism in '*Vineam Domini Sabaoth' (1705) was followed by the condemnation of P. *Quesnel's work in 1708 and by '*Unigenitus' (1713). In the dispute between the *Dominicans and the *Jesuits over the Chinese Rites, he supported the *Holy Office which censured the opinion of the Jesuits. In 1708 he made the feast of the *Immaculate Conception of the BVM one of obligation throughout the Church.

CLEMENT XIII (1693–1769), Pope from 1758. The main preoccupation of his pontificate was the storm over the *Jesuits. When the Parlement of Paris demanded drastic changes in their constitution in 1761, Clement refused. Nearly all French Jesuits had to go into exile in 1764; the Pope replied by issuing a bull praising the work of the Jesuits (1765). The demand of the ambassadors of Spain, Naples, and France in 1769 for the destruction of the order is thought to have hastened Clement's death.

CLEMENT XIV (1705–74), Pope from 1769. He was elected after a stormy conclave, the Bourbon courts having decided to recognize only a Pope ready to suppress the *Jesuits; whether he made any promise is uncertain. His chief aim was to preserve peace with the Catholic powers in order to secure their support against the growing irreligion. He suppressed the Jesuit Order in 1773. The former papal possessions of *Avignon and Benevento were restored, but in France a royal commission continued suppressing religious houses without papal approval, and in Portugal the secular authori-

ties interfered in ecclesiastical affairs and education.

CLEMENT OF ALEXANDRIA, St. (c. 150–c. 215), theologian. He succeeded *Pantaenus as head of the *Catechetical School at Alexandria in 190. In 202 he was forced by persecution to flee. His main works are the *Protrepticus*, the *Paedagogus*, and the *Stromateis*. He agreed with the *Gnostics in holding 'gnosis' or religious knowledge to be the chief element in Christian perfection, but for him the only true 'gnosis' was that which presupposed the faith of the Church. Christ, the *Logos, was both the source of human reason and the interpreter of God to mankind. He became man in order to give a supreme revelation, and that through Him men might partake of immortality. *Clement VIII excised Clement of Alexandria's name from the *martyrology on the grounds of the unorthodoxy of some of his writings.

CLEMENT OF ROME, St. See before Pope *Clement V*.

CLEMENTINE LITERATURE. A number of apocryphal works circulated in the early Church under the name of St. *Clement of Rome, but by convention the term 'Clementines' is restricted to three of them.
   (1) The CLEMENTINE HOMILIES is a religious and philosophical romance which Clement is supposed to have sent from Rome to *James, the Lord's brother, preceded by two letters from St. *Peter and Clement addressed to James. They describe Clement's travels in the East, where he met Peter and witnessed his conflict with *Simon Magus.
   (2) The CLEMENTINE RECOGNITIONS resemble the 'Homilies' and the narrative goes over much of the same ground, with some added details. The original Greek, which can be dated between 211 and 231, is lost; they survive in a Latin translation by *Rufinus and in Syriac.
   (3) Two Greek EPITOMES of the above. They are evidently later and introduce an account of Clement's martyrdom.

CLEMENTINES. In canon law the collection of *Decretals issued by *Clement V in 1314. It contains the Decretals of *Boniface VIII, Benedict XI, and Clement himself. It was the last item officially embodied in the

'*Corpus Iuris Canonici'.

CLEOPAS. One of the two disciples to whom the risen Christ appeared on the road to *Emmaus.

CLERGY, BENEFIT OF. See *Benefit of Clergy*.

CLERICAL DISABILITIES ACT, 1870. The Act which allows a cleric of the C of E after resigning his preferments to execute a Deed of Relinquishment and thereby regain such civil rights as he lost through being a clergyman.

CLERICAL STATE, ADMISSION TO THE. In the RC Church the rite by which candidates for Holy *Orders are admitted to the clerical state and *incardinated into a diocese. It is completely separate from the conferring of Orders; it replaced the former rite of *tonsure in 1972.

CLERICAL SUBSCRIPTION ACT, 1865. The Act changing the form of declaration made by Anglican clergy on ordination and on accepting preferment. Acknowledgement of the Royal Supremacy was no longer required, and only a general assent to the *Thirty-Nine Articles was demanded. In 1975 the form of assent was made even less rigid.

CLERICIS LAICOS. The bull issued by *Boniface VIII in 1296 forbidding any cleric to pay ecclesiastical revenues to laymen without papal approval, and any layman to receive such payments.

CLERK, Parish. See *Parish Clerk*.

CLERK IN HOLY ORDERS. A designation, chiefly legal and formal, for a bishop, priest, or deacon in the C of E.

CLERK OF THE CLOSET. In the C of E, the cleric who presides over the Royal College of Chaplains. When a vacancy occurs among the chaplains he is asked to suggest possible names to the Sovereign; he also presents bishops to the Sovereign when they do homage after consecration.

CLERKS REGULAR. A term applied to certain bodies of RC clergy, bound under religious vows, who live in community and engage in active pastoral work. Such Regular Clerks originated in the 16th cent. through the efforts of various bands of clerics to perfect their work by the stimulus of ordered discipline. They include the '*Theatines' (founded 1524), the *Barnabites (1532), and the *Jesuits (1534).

CLERMONT, The Council of (1095). Summoned by *Urban II to plan the First *Crusade, it was attended by over 200 bishops. It confirmed the '*Truce of God' and made other regulations for the conduct of the crusades. It also issued 32 canons on a wide variety of subjects.

CLETUS, St. See *Anacletus, St.*

CLIFFORD, JOHN (1836–1923), British *Baptist minister. He became President of the Baptist Union in 1888 and from 1905 to 1911 he was President of the World Baptist Alliance. He led the movement for 'passive resistance' to A. J. *Balfour's Education Act of 1902, which he held to be injurious to Nonconformist interests.

CLIMACUS, St. JOHN. See *John Climacus, St.*

CLITHEROW, St. MARGARET (c. 1556–1586), the 'martyr of York'. She became a RC at the age of 18. In 1586 she was arrested and charged with harbouring priests. To save her children from having to witness against her, she refused to plead, and was crushed to death. She was among the *Forty Martyrs of England and Wales canonized in 1970.

CLOISTER. An enclosed space which normally forms the central part of a monastery or other religious building. The term is also used in general for a religious house and for the religious life.

CLOSE, FRANCIS (1797–1882), Dean of *Carlisle from 1856 to 1881. He was previously, from 1826, incumbent of Cheltenham. Here his sermons made him the best-known *Evangelical preacher, and he exercised great influence on public life.

CLOTILDE, St. (474–545), Frankish queen. In 492 or 493 she married *Clovis (q.v.), whom she at once tried to convert to Christianity. After his death in 511 she retired to the abbey of St. *Martin at Tours.

CLOUD OF UNKNOWING, The. An anonymous English mystical treatise of the 14th cent. The author insists on the impossibility of knowing God by human reason. The 'cloud of unknowing' which lies between God and man is pierced not by the intellect but only by a 'sharp dart of love'; contemplative prayer therefore takes place in the affective and not the intellectual part of the soul and thus necessarily contains an element of ignorance.

CLOVESHO, Councils of. A series of synods representing both the Church and State of all England south of the Humber in the 8th and 9th cents. The site of Clovesho is unknown.

CLOVIS (*c*. 466–511), King of the Salian Franks from 481. The decisive event in his career was his conversion to Catholic Christianity and his baptism in 496. This step provided him with an excuse to attack the *Arian King of the Visigoths, Alaric II, and brought him the aid of the Catholic bishops and Roman officials in governing the country.

CLUNY, Order of. The monastery of Cluny, in Burgundy, was founded in 909. The high standard of monastic observance from an early stage led to the adoption of its customs by other houses, old and new. The objects of the reform included a return to the strict *Benedictine Rule, esp. as expounded by St. *Benedict of Aniane, cultivation of personal spiritual life, stress on the choir office (which tended to grow to excessive length) and the splendour and solemnity of worship generally, with a corresponding reduction in manual labour. It seems clear that the Cluniac houses were not welded into a system until the time of *Odilo (abbot, 994–1048); by the mid-12th cent. the order was highly centralized. Esp. in the 11th and 12th cents. Cluny exercised great influence on the life of the Church and largely inspired the reforms associated with *Gregory VII. Its influence declined in the later Middle Ages. The monastery survived until 1790.

C.M.S. The Church Missionary Society, founded in 1799, was the first effective organ of the C of E for missions to the heathen. Its theology has always been *Evangelical.

COADJUTOR BISHOP. A bishop appointed to assist a diocesan bishop, often with the right of succession to the see at the next vacancy. The practice of appointing coadjutor bishops is common in the RC Church and in the *Protestant Episcopal Church of America.

COAT OF CHRIST. See *Holy Coat*.

COCCEIUS, JOHANNES (1603–69), Johann Koch, dogmatic theologian. A German by birth, he taught at Franeker in Holland and at *Leyden. He sought to expound dogmatic theology on a purely Biblical basis. He interpreted the relation between God and man in terms of a personal covenant; his system thus became known as *Föderaltheologie*.

COCHLAEUS, JOHANNES (1479–1552), RC controversialist. He had a strong sympathy with the *Platonist and humanist revival of the Renaissance. He engaged in writing against M. *Luther, but the bitter tone of his polemic won little favour.

CO-CONSECRATOR. A bishop who assists the chief consecrator in the laying on of hands at the making of a bishop.

C.O.C.U. See *Consultation on Church Union*.

CODEX ALEXANDRINUS ('A'). The early 5th-cent. MS. of the Greek Bible which Cyril *Lucar offered to *James I; it is now in the British Library. It also contains the two (so-called) Epistles of *Clement.

CODEX AMIATINUS. The oldest extant MS. of the Latin *Vulgate. It was written at *Wearmouth or Jarrow between *c*. 690 and 700. From the 9th or 10th cent. the MS. was in the monastery of Monte Amiata, hence its name; after the suppression of the monastery in 1782 it passed to the Laurentian Library in Florence.

CODEX BEZAE ('D'). This (prob. 5th-cent.) Graeco-Latin MS. of the Gospels and Acts, with a fragment of the Latin of 3 Jn., was presented in 1581 to the University of Cambridge by T. *Beza. It is the chief representative of the *Western text.

CODEX EPHRAEMI ('C'). A 5th-cent. Greek MS. of the Bible now at Paris. In the 12th cent. it was converted into a *palimpsest by a covering of some of the writings of St. *Ephraem Syrus.

CODEX IURIS CANONICI ('CIC'). The code of *canon law in force in the RC Church since 1918.

CODEX SINAITICUS ('ℵ'). The MS. of the Greek Bible, discovered by C. *Tischendorf in the monastery of St. Catherine on Mount *Sinai. He arranged for its purchase by the Tsar of Russia; in 1933 the Soviet Government sold it to the Trustees of the British Museum. The MS. also contains the 'Epistle of *Barnabas' and part of the 'Shepherd' of *Hermas. Most scholars believe that it was written in Egypt; its date is prob. later 4th cent. The NT text is closely allied to that of the *Codex Vaticanus, together with which it is the chief witness to the *Neutral text.

CODEX VATICANUS ('B'). The 4th-cent. MS. of the Greek Bible, now in the *Vatican Library, where it has been since at least 1481. In the NT all after Heb. 9: 14 has been lost. Most scholars incline to think that the MS. was written at *Alexandria. The NT readings, together with those of the *Codex Sinaiticus, are the chief witness to the *Neutral text.

COENACULUM. See *Cenaculum*.

COENOBITE. A religious in vows who lives in a community (as opposed to a *hermit). The term is also used in a technical sense of *anchorites who occupy separate dwellings and observe a rule of silence, but live otherwise as a community of *monks in a common enclosure.

COFFIN, CHARLES (1676–1749), hymn-writer. In 1718 he became rector of the University of Paris. He published a collection of Latin hymns in 1727; several of them are well known in English versions, e.g. 'On Jordan's banks the Baptist's cry'.

COGITO ERGO SUM (Lat., 'I think, therefore I am'). The primary datum of truth accepted by R. *Descartes, on the ground that, however much a man doubted, he could never think away himself as the doubting subject.

COLENSO, JOHN WILLIAM (1814–83), Bp. of Natal from 1853. Storms of protest were aroused by his commentary on Romans (1861), with its denial of eternal punishment, and by his papers on the *Pentateuch and *Joshua, which challenged the traditional authorship and the accuracy of these Books; and in 1863 he was declared deposed by his Metropolitan, Robert *Gray. Colenso appealed to the *Judicial Committee of the Privy Council, which ruled in his favour (1865) on the ground that the Letters Patent appointing him preceded those appointing Gray. Hence, though solemnly excommunicated by Gray, who consecrated another bishop, Colenso maintained his position and obtained the cathedral and endowment of the see. The schism in Natal was formally ended only in 1911.

COLET, JOHN (1466?–1519), Dean of *St. Paul's from 1504. He learnt Greek in Italy. On his return he constantly inveighed against ecclesiastical abuses and, though he never challenged the doctrines of the Church, he was often accused of heresy. He spent part of a large fortune in re-founding St. Paul's School.

COLETTINES. A branch of the *Poor Clares founded by St. Colette (1381–1447), a native of *Corbie in Picardy who was canonized in 1807.

COLIGNY, GASPARD DE (1519–72), *Huguenot. He was converted to *Calvinism in 1560 and in 1569 he became the recognized leader of the Huguenot cause. His influence at court led the French to aid the Netherlands in their revolt. *Catherine de' Medici tried to have him assassinated, and when the attempt failed, provoked the Massacre of St. *Bartholomew's Day, in which he was killed.

COLLATION. (1) The light meal allowed on days of fasting in addition to the main meal; (2) the lives of the *Fathers, esp. as arranged for reading in monasteries; and (3) *institution to an ecclesiastical benefice when the *ordinary is himself the patron (i.e. when presentation and institution are one and the same act).

COLLECT. The short form of prayer constructed (with variations in detail) from (1) an invocation, (2) a petition, and (3) a pleading of Christ's name or an ascription of glory to God. The prayers later known as *Secrets and *Post-Communions are structurally indistinguishable, but the term 'collect' in the Eucharistic rite is normally confined to the prayer (or prayers) which immediately precedes the lections. Such prayers were familiar by the 5th cent. They secured a place in the daily *Offices as well as in the Eucharist. The collects in the BCP mostly derive from medieval sources, but some were T. *Cranmer's original compositions.

COLLEGIALISM. The thesis that the Church and State are purely voluntary associations (*collegia*) in which supreme authority rests with the body of the members, and that the civil magistrate has no other relations with the Church than those which he has with other voluntary associations in his territory.

COLLEGIALITY. A word used in a theological context to signify that the bishops constitute a body, of which each is a part, and not a mere collection of individuals.

COLLEGIANTS. An obscure offshoot of the *Remonstrants, founded in *Holland c. 1619, and so called because they termed their communities 'colleges'.

COLLEGIATE CHURCH. A church which is endowed for a body of canons and/or prebendaries (the 'chapter'), but is not, like a *cathedral, a bishop's see.

COLLIER, JEREMY (1650–1726), English *Nonjuror. In 1696 he was outlawed for giving absolution on the scaffold to two attempted assassins of William III, but he returned to London in 1697. In 1713 he was consecrated 'bishop of the Nonjurors' and he joined in their attempt at reunion with the Orthodox Church. He was largely responsible for the production of the Nonjurors' Communion Office of 1718.

COLLINS, ANTHONY (1676–1729), English *Deist. His main work, *A Discourse of Freethinking* (1713) argued that free inquiry was the only means of attaining to the truth and was commanded by Scripture. It was designed as a defence of Deism and contained bitter attacks on the ministers of all denominations; it provoked replies by many Churchmen.

COLLOQUY OF MARBURG. See *Marburg, Colloquy of.*

COLLUTHUS (4th cent.), schismatic priest of *Alexandria. During the episcopate of *Alexander (312–28) he assumed the power of conferring orders, though only a presbyter. In 324 he was deposed.

COLLYRIDIANS. A 4th-cent. sect, which apparently originated in Thrace and consisted mainly of women, who offered an idolatrous cult to the BVM.

COLMAN, St. (d. 676), leader of the *Celtic party in Northumbria. He became Bp. of *Lindisfarne in 661. At the Synod of *Whitby (664) he pleaded for the retention of such customs as the Celtic time for keeping Easter and the Celtic *tonsure and appealed to the authority of St. *Columba. He afterwards left Lindisfarne for a monastery in Ireland.

COLOGNE. The see was founded in or before the reign of *Constantine (d. 337). In the 11th–12th cents. the Abps. of Cologne became important secular princes and in 1356 were recognized as imperial electors. The cathedral dates from the 13th–15th and the 19th cents., and contains the shrine of the *Magi.

COLOMBINI, Bl. GIOVANNI (*c.* 1300–1367), founder of the *Gesuati (q.v.). He came of an old patrician family in Siena. After reading the life of St. *Mary of Egypt, he devoted himself to the service of the poor and sick, later persuading his wife to accept separation. When his example was followed by other young nobles, the city authorities exiled him; he was recalled when an epidemic broke out.

COLONIAL AND CONTINENTAL CHURCH SOCIETY. See *C.C.C.S.*

COLONNA FAMILY. A distinguished Roman family which played a considerable part in Papal and European politics, esp. between the 12th and 18th cents. They were vassals of the Pope, but their political leanings in the Middle Ages were mostly pro-Imperial. A member of the family was elected Pope as *Martin V.

COLOSSEUM, The. The name by which

the 'Flavian Amphitheatre' at Rome has been known since about the 8th cent. Completed c. A.D. 80, it has long been venerated as the scene of many early martyrdoms, though the truth of this tradition has been questioned.

COLOSSIANS, Epistle to the. This short NT epistle was written by St. *Paul when he was in prison, prob. at *Rome, possibly at *Ephesus. The Church at Colossae, in the western part of modern Turkey, had been founded not by St. Paul but by Epaphras. The primary purpose of the epistle was to recall its readers to faith in Christ as their all-sufficient Redeemer and Lord.

COLOURS, Liturgical. A sequence of colours at different seasons of the ecclesiastical year for vestments and other liturgical objects is first found in the use of the *Augustinian Canons at Jerusalem in the early 12th cent. The standard sequence in the W. Church (white, red, green, purple, and black) was established much later. There are no definite rules about colours in the E. Church.

COLUMBA, St. (c. 521–97), abbot and missionary. Of noble Irish family, he founded several churches and monasteries in his own country. About 563 he established himself, with twelve companions, on *Iona. From here he evangelized the mainland of Scotland and Northumbria and established monasteries in neighbouring islands.

COLUMBANUS, St. (c. 543–615), abbot and missionary. A native of Ireland, c. 590 he went to Gaul, where he set up monasteries at Annegray and *Luxeuil. He aroused opposition by his introduction of the usages of the *Celtic Church. His monks, expelled from Burgundy in 610 for their outspoken rebukes of the royal court, eventually settled at *Bobbio in N. Italy, where their house became a centre of learning. Both the 'Monastic Rule' and the 'Penitential' attributed to him have been shown to be substantially his work.

COMENIUS, JOHANNES AMOS (1592–1670), educationalist. He belonged to the *Bohemian Brethren (Moravian) and was minister at Fulneck and later at Lissa in Poland. He founded a school at Sáros-Patak in Hungary. After the destruction of Lissa in 1656, he found refuge in Holland.

His educational ideas were influenced by his personal religious experience. Hoping for a Utopian Church which would unite all religions in Christian love, he regarded education as the means to its fulfilment; the development of character on Christian lines, rather than learning, was to be the ultimate aim. The methods he advocated were in advance of his time.

COMES (Lat. *Liber Comitis*, *Liber Comicus*), a book containing the passages to be read at Mass as Epistles, or as Gospels, or as both. Originally it was merely a list of the opening words of the readings, but later the name came to be applied to books with their complete text.

COMFORTABLE WORDS, The. Four short passages from the NT which the BCP instructs the celebrant to read at the Holy Communion after the Absolution of the people.

COMFORTER, The. A title of the Holy Spirit.

COMGALL, St. (c. 516–c. 601), first abbot of *Bangor (in Ireland). He is said to have served in the army. Returning to Ulster, he was ordained and became a zealous propagator of monasticism, Bangor being his most famous foundation (555 or 559).

COMMANDERY. Among the *Hospitallers an estate or manor in the charge of a member of the order.

COMMANDMENTS, The Ten. Precepts divinely revealed to *Moses on Mt. *Sinai and engraved on two tables of stone. The text is preserved in two closely similar versions (Exod. 20: 1–17 and Deut. 5: 6–21). Many older critical scholars held them to date from the Mosaic age; J. *Wellhausen and others argued that they legislated not for wandering nomads but for a settled agricultural community and dated them in the 7th cent. B.C. More recently there has been a reaction and few serious critics would deny the possibility that their basis may go back to Moses himself.

The Ten Commandments have played a substantial part in the teaching of the Church. They were esp. prominent in the development of the penitential systems of the

9th cent. and in the popular teaching of the 16th-cent. Reformers. In the 1552 BCP their recitation was introduced into the Communion Office, but in modern practice they are usually replaced by the *Kyrie Eleison or by the Lord's two Great Commandments (Mt. 22: 36–40), practices sanctioned in the *Alternative Services rites.

COMMANDMENTS (or Precepts) OF THE CHURCH. Certain moral and ecclesiastical precepts imposed by the RC Church on all its members. Their number has varied. At present there are four, viz. to hear Mass on Sundays and *Feasts of Obligation, to observe the days of penance (see *Fasts*), to go to confession once a year, and to receive Holy Communion during the *Easter season.

COMMEMORATION. Acc. to traditional W. liturgical practice, when two feasts fall on the same day, until recently that of the lesser rank was 'commemorated' by including some of its prayers after the corresponding prayers of the feast being observed.

COMMENDAM. An individual (who could be a layman) was said to hold an ecclesiastical benefice *in commendam* when its revenues were granted to him temporarily during a vacancy. Gradually the term came to be restricted to benefices which a bishop or other dignitary held more or less permanently along with his see.

COMMENDATIO MORIENTIUM (Lat., 'Commendation of the Dying'). The prayers prescribed in the W. Church to be said at the bedside of a dying person. It was formerly called 'Commendatio Animae'.

COMMINATION SERVICE. The service drawn up by the compilers of the BCP for use on *Ash Wednesday and other days appointed by the *ordinary. It consists of an exhortation (in the course of which the Curses against various classes of evil-doers are recited), Ps. 51, suffrages, and prayers.

COMMODIAN, Christian Latin poet. He is generally held to have flourished in Africa in the mid-3rd cent., but some have dated him later. He was a convert from heathenism. Two of his poems have survived.

COMMON LIFE, Brethren of the. See *Brethren of the Common Life*.

COMMON OF THE SAINTS. Those parts of the *Missal and *Breviary containing the offices of such saints as do not have a complete individual office (a '*proper') of their own.

COMMON ORDER, Book of. (1) The directory of worship drawn up by J. *Knox in 1556 for the English Protestant congregation in Geneva. It was appointed for use in *Scotland by the *General Assembly in 1562; it was replaced by the *Westminster Assembly's 'Directory of Public *Worship' in 1645.
(2) The service book authorized by the General Assembly for use in the Church of Scotland. The present book was issued in 1940. It draws extensively on earlier authorized books.

COMMON PRAYER, Book of. The official service book of the C of E containing the daily offices of *Morning and *Evening Prayer, the forms for the administration of the *Sacraments and other rites, the *Psalter, and (since 1552) the *Ordinal. The book was compiled because of the desire of T. *Cranmer and others to simplify and condense the Latin service books of the medieval Church and to produce in English a simple, convenient, and comprehensive volume as an authoritative guide for priest and people.
The First BCP was issued in 1549 and its use ordered by the first Act of *Uniformity. In doctrine and ritual it was a compromise between the old and new schools and pleased neither. Revision in the light of Protestant criticism led to the issue of the Second BCP in 1552. After the reign of *Mary, this was reissued, with a few alterations, as the Elizabethan BCP of 1559, to which the *Ornaments Rubric was attached. After the *Restoration, the 1662 Act of Uniformity authorized a BCP revised by *Convocation. The most important change was the introduction of the AV for the Epistles and Gospels. This 1662 Book remained almost unchanged until modern times.
In 1904, in the face of persistent ritual controversies, a Royal Commission on *Ecclesiastical Discipline was appointed, and in 1906 it recommended that 'Letters of Business' be issued to the Convocations with a view to Prayer Book revision. The Convocations decided to retain the 1662 Book and incorporate all changes in a new book,

whose use should be wholly permissive. The new Book rearranged the Eucharistic Canon and permitted *Reservation. It was passed by the Convocations and *Church Assembly but rejected by the House of Commons in 1927 and again, after some amendments, in 1928. In 1955 the Abps. of Canterbury and York appointed a Liturgical Commission to prepare a revision of the BCP. The Prayer Book (Alternative and Other Services) Measure of 1965 authorized experimentation. (See *Alternative Services*.)

Outside England the BCP underwent numerous revisions. The Scottish (Episcopalian) BCP of 1764 influenced the American BCP of 1789. Elsewhere the English 1662 Book was used until the Church of *Ireland, freed by disestablishment from the Act of Uniformity, in 1877 produced its own BCP, a conservative revision in a Protestant direction. In the 20th cent. revisions, parallel to the English revision of 1928, appeared in most countries. After the Second World War experimental revision of individual services was common; it was sometimes followed by the issue of a single book.

COMMONWEALTH AND CONTINENTAL CHURCH SOCIETY. See *C.C.C.S*.

COMMUNICANTES. A section of the traditional Roman *Canon of the Mass, so named from its opening word; it comes shortly before the Words of *Institution.

COMMUNICATIO IDIOMATUM (Lat., 'interchange of the properties'). The doctrine that, while the human and Divine natures in Christ were separate, the attributes of the one may be predicated of the other in view of their union in the one Person of the Saviour.

COMMUNION, Frequency of. On a possible interpretation of Acts 2: 46 the apostolic community communicated daily; from other passages in the NT and 2nd-cent. writers it seems that the members of the local Churches all communicated at the Sunday Eucharist. Later, though attendance at the liturgy was general, Communion became very infrequent. The Fourth *Lateran Council (1215) ordered Communion at least once a year. Nearly all post-medieval revivals, Catholic and Protestant, have sought to increase frequency of Communion. In the RC Church it was advocated most notably by *Pius X. At present weekly Communion is

common among the devout laity of the RC Church and the C of E; daily Communion is not unknown. In the E. Church and among most Protestant non-episcopal bodies until recently it was unusual for Communion to be made more often than once a month.

COMMUNION, The Order of the (1548). A form for administering Communion, drawn up in English, and originally interpolated into the Latin Mass between the Communion of the priest and that of the people. Its essential parts were an exhortation, a brief address to the intending communicants, the General Confession and Absolution, the *Comfortable Words, the Prayer of *Humble Access, the Words of Administration (for both kinds), and the Blessing. Its contents passed into the BCP.

COMMUNION ANTHEM or ANTIPHON. In the Roman Mass the short passage said or sung during the administration of the Communion.

COMMUNION IN BOTH KINDS. The custom of receiving Communion under the two species of bread and wine was general until about the 12th cent., though there were a few exceptions. By the 13th cent. in the W. the chalice was restricted to the celebrant. The legitimacy of the practice was denied by the *Hussites. The 16th-cent. Reformers also insisted that Communion in both kinds alone had Scriptural warrant, and the practice was adopted in all Protestant Churches, including the C of E. In the RC Church the Council of *Trent ruled that there was no Divine precept to communicate in both kinds and that the existing practice was justified by the doctrine of *concomitance. Since the Second *Vatican Council, however, provisions have been made for general reception in both kinds on an increasing number of occasions.

COMMUNION OF SAINTS. Part of the 9th article of the *Apostles' Creed. It is usually interpreted as the spiritual union existing between each Christian and Christ, and so between every Christian whether in *Heaven, *Purgatory, or on earth.

COMMUNION PLATE. In the RC Church the plate of silver or metal gilt held under the chin of the communicant as he receives the Sacrament. The term is also used collectively of the vessels used in the celebration of the Eucharist, which are often plated with gold.

COMMUNION SUNDAY. A Sunday on which the Holy Communion is celebrated.

COMMUNION TABLE. The table at which the Holy Communion is celebrated. In the C of E the term is used esp. by *Low Churchmen, High Churchmen preferring the word '*altar' as better expressive of the Eucharistic sacrifice which they believe is offered on it.

COMMUNION TOKENS. Metal tokens stamped with such devices as texts or chalices which served as certificates of fitness for admission to the Communion. They were used mainly in the Church of *Scotland, where their place has been largely taken by printed cards on which the names of the communicants are written.

COMMUNION UNDER BOTH SPECIES. See *Communion in Both Kinds*.

COMMUNITY OF THE RESURRECTION. This Anglican community was founded at Oxford in 1892 by C. *Gore. It moved to Mirfield, West Yorks., in 1898. The Community conducts a college for the training of ordinands and engages in pastoral and educational work in S. Africa and Rhodesia.

COMNENA, ANNA. See *Anna Comnena*.

COMPARATIVE RELIGION. The branch of study which investigates by scientific and historical methods the religions of the world and their mutual relations. It developed in the later 19th cent. Its successful pursuit as a science rests on the universality of religion and the frequent recurrence of certain patterns of religious experience in widely separated ethnological and social groups. It is not concerned with questions of ultimate validity. It has posed problems for Christian faith by its recognition that much that was thought to be exclusive to the Christian tradition is held in common with other world religions; on the other hand it has brought out the distinctiveness of some elements in the Christian religion, including, it is held, its conceptions of God and of human personality.

COMPETENTES (Lat., 'those qualified'). In the early Church *catechumens admitted to the final stage of preparation for *Baptism.

COMPLINE. The last of the canonical day hours (see *Office*) in the W. Church, said before retiring for the night. Basically it consists of an evening hymn, Psalms, and the *Nunc Dimittis. The essential parts of it were incorporated into the *Evensong of the BCP.

COMPLUTENSIAN POLYGLOT. The first *polyglot edition of the whole Bible, begun in 1502 at the expense of Card. F. *Ximenes, who assembled a group of scholars at Alcalá (Lat. 'Complutum'), where the Bible was finely printed in 6 vols., 1514–17.

COMPOSTELA. A city in NW. Spain, properly 'Santiago [i.e. 'St. James'] de Compostela', traditionally supposed to be the burial-place of St. *James the Apostle, and a centre of pilgrimage.

COMPRECATION. The intercessions which the saints are believed to make on behalf of the rest of the Church. The word is also loosely used of requests to God for the intercession of saints.

COMPTON, HENRY (1632–1713), Bp. of London from 1675. He was tutor to the princesses Mary and Anne, but his anti-papal attitude brought him into disfavour with *James II, and he was restrained from the exercise of his spiritual functions on the ground of his failure to suspend J. *Sharp for his anti-Roman sermons. He officiated at the coronation of William III and supported the project for comprehension and the *Toleration Act.

COMTE, AUGUSTE (1798–1857), founder of French *Positivism and of the 'Religion of Humanity'. The foundation of his system is the law of the three stages—the theological, the metaphysical, and the 'positive'. In the first two stages of development the human mind seeks a cause or essence to explain phenomena, but in the third or positive phase explanation is discovered in a law. Comte advocated the organization of mankind in one vast system in which altruism was to conquer egoism. Conceiving this to be possible only on a religious basis, he constructed a new kind of religion, with humanity in the place of God, and an elaborate cultus, mainly borrowed from Catholicism.

CONCELEBRATION. The joint celebration of the Eucharist by a number of priests reciting the central parts of the *Canon together. It was prob. common in the early Church. In the RC Church the practice was restored in 1963.

CONCEPTION OF THE BVM. See *Immaculate Conception of the BVM*.

'CONCERNING THE SERVICE OF THE CHURCH'. The present title of the preface of the original (1549) edition of the BCP.

CONCILIAR THEORY. The doctrine that supreme authority in the Church lies with a *General Council. From the 13th cent. the increasing claims of Papal authority had led to speculation about the theoretical possibility of deposing a heretical Pope; the outbreak of the *Great Schism in 1378 raised the question of authority in an acute form. At the Council of *Constance the claims of the conciliarists figured prominently, but the very success of the Council in ending the schism weakened their position. After the 15th cent. support for the Conciliar Theory waned.

CONCLAVE. The closed apartment in which the college of *cardinals is confined during the process of electing a new Pope. The word 'conclave' is also loosely applied to the meeting itself.

CONCOMITANCE. The doctrine that in the Eucharist the Body and Blood of Christ are present in each of the consecrated species. See also *Communion in Both Kinds*.

CONCORD, The Formula (1577), and Book (1580) of. The 'Formula of Concord', the last of the classical *Lutheran formulas of faith, was drawn up by a number of theologians. Its language is precise. After much discussion, the Formula, together with the three Creeds (*Apostles', *Nicene, and *Athanasian), the *Augsburg Confession and P. *Melanchthon's 'Apology' for it (1530), the *Schmalkaldic Articles (1537), M. *Luther's two *Catechisms, and three earlier drafts of the Formula, was published at Dresden in 1580 as the 'Book of Con-

cord'. It encountered much opposition outside Germany.

CONCORD OF WITTENBERG. See *Wittenberg, Concord of*.

CONCORDANCE. A book of reference indicating and usually quoting in full all the passages of Scripture in which a given word is found. The most famous (and still the standard) English concordance is that compiled in 1737 by A. *Cruden.

CONCORDAT. An agreement between the civil and ecclesiastical authorities on some matter of concern to both parties.

CONCORDAT OF 1801. The agreement concluded between *Pius VII and Napoleon, then First Consul, which led to the formal restitution of the RC Church in France.

CONCORDIA REGULARIS. See *Regularis Concordia*.

CONCUPISCENCE. In moral theology the inordinate desire for temporal ends which has its seat in the senses. Catholic theology in general holds concupiscence to be the result of *Original Sin, rather than a part of it, and regards it as *materia exercendae virtutis* (material for the exercise of virtue), since it provides reason and will with opportunities to resist the disordered movements of the senses. Protestant theology looks upon concupiscence itself as sin and its existence as an offence against God.

CONCURRENCE. The falling on consecutive days of ecclesiastical feasts or other days to be observed, so that the Second *Vespers or *Evensong of the first coincides with the First Vespers or Evensong of the second. In the W. Church there are various liturgical regulations governing the procedure to be adopted, depending on the rank of the feasts concerned.

CONCURSUS DIVINUS (Lat., 'Divine concourse'). A technical term for the co-operation of the *grace of God with the actions of finite creatures. Details about its operation are disputed by theologians of various schools.

CONDIGNITY. In the Scholastic theology of *grace, those actions which man performs as a Christian in conscious reliance on the Holy Spirit are held to merit the grace of God 'by condignity' (*gratia de condigno*), i.e. as from a Debtor.

CONDITIONAL IMMORTALITY (also **Annihilationism**). The theory that immortality is not a necessary attribute of the soul but conditional on its behaviour during its life in the body. The idea found favour in the 19th cent. as a means of accounting for the fate of the impenitently wicked without accepting either the orthodox doctrine of eternal punishment or the theory of *universalism.

CONDREN, CHARLES DE (1588–1641), French theologian and mystic. He entered the *Oratory in 1617, and in 1629 succeeded P. de *Bérulle as Superior-General. He was famous as a director of souls, and his teaching has survived largely through his letters. The focal points of his doctrine were a strong theocentrism and an intense devotion to the mysteries of the Incarnate Christ.

CONFESSING (or CONFESSIONAL) CHURCH. The group of German Evangelical Christians most actively opposed to the '*German Christians' sponsored by the Nazis. It grew out of the 'Pastors' Emergency League' founded in 1933 under the leadership of M. *Niemöller. In 1934 it began to establish its own canonical authorites in areas where the offical administration was 'German Christian'; it also issued the *Barmen Declaration. The outbreak of war in 1939 made open resistance impossible. At the end of the war in 1945 leaders of the Confessing Church made a 'Declaration of Guilt' to a delegation of the provisional *World Council of Churches, which later gave considerable help to the Confessing Church. After the establishment of the *Evangelical Church in Germany the influence of the Confessing Church declined.

CONFESSIO AUGUSTANA, CONFESSIO HELVETICA, CONFESSIO SCOTICA. See *Augsburg*, *Helvetic*, and *Scottish Confession*.

CONFESSION. (1) The tomb of a *martyr or '*confessor'; the structure or shrine built around such a tomb; or the church in which a martyr is buried. (2) The profession of faith by a martyr or confessor, and so in general a declaration of religious belief; the term is used esp. of the Protestant professions of the 16th cent. From this sense derives its use for a communion or religious body. (3) An acknowledgement of sin, made either in general terms by a congregation in the course of liturgical worship or by an individual penitent in private or *auricular confession. See also *Absolution* and *Penance*.

CONFESSION, Seal of. See *Seal of Confession*.

'CONFESSIONS OF ST. AUGUSTINE, The'. The title is to be taken in the Biblical sense of 'confessing', i.e. 'praising' God, the work, written *c*. 400, being St. Augustine's thanksgiving for his conversion. Its purpose is to demonstrate the work of God's grace in his soul. Books 1–9 are autobiographical; 10 deals with the faculty of memory; 11 offers a theory of time; and 12 and 13 contain an allegorical exposition of the first verses of *Genesis.

CONFESSOR. (1) In the early Church one who suffered for confessing his or her faith, but only to an extent which did not involve martyrdom. Later the word was applied to holy men and ultimately to those pronounced such by the Pope. (2) A priest who hears (esp. private) confessions.

CONFIRMATION. In Sacramental theology, the rite whereby the grace of the Holy Spirit is conveyed in a fuller measure to those who have already received it in some degree at *Baptism.

Some theologians have found instances of Confirmation in the NT, but in the early evidence it is hard to discern the precise relationship between the various elements of washing with water, anointing with oil, and the laying on of hands which were all associated with initiation into the fullness of the Christian life. By the 3rd cent. there is evidence of Confirmation (though not by this name) as a rite clearly distinct from Baptism, and by the 4th cent. it was generally separate. As the numbers seeking admission to the Church made it impossible for the Bishop to baptize them all himself, the functions of the parish priest (immersion) and the bishop (anointing), originally closely associated, became separated. In the E. Church the primitive custom of conferring Confirmation at the same time as Baptism was retained. This was achieved by confining the Bishop's part to the consecration of the oil used for the anointing. The oil was conveyed to the parish priest, who performed the actual rite of Confirmation as occasion required. In the W. the Bishop retained his position as the regular minister of the rite, and Confirmation was deferred until an opportunity arose of presenting the candidates to the Bishop in person.

Since the later Middle Ages the normal practice in the RC Church has been to confirm as soon as convenient after the 7th birthday, but since 1971 the possibility of a later age has been envisaged. The candidates renew their Baptismal promises, and the Bishop, extending his hands over them, prays that they may receive the Holy Spirit and traces the sign of the Cross with *chrism on the forehead of each. In some cases priests may confirm on their own with chrism blessed by the bishop.

At the Reformation the C of E continued the medieval practice, though the use of oil ceased in 1549 and the sign of the Cross in 1552. The *Alternative Service of 1967 introduced a shorter formula of administration than that provided in the BCP. According to the BCP none is to be admitted to Communion until he is confirmed or 'ready and desirous to be confirmed'. A course of instruction usually precedes Confirmation, which is administered at various ages. The rite is also in use among *Lutherans and some other Protestant bodies.

CONFITEOR (Lat., 'I confess'). A form of confession of sins (so named from its first word) which is commonly used in the RC Church, e.g. at *Mass and *Compline.

CONGAR, YVES (1904–   ), French *Dominican theologian. One of the leading RC supporters of the *Ecumenical Movement, Congar has written a number of books on the nature of the Church, some very controversial; he also had some part in planning the *Amsterdam Assembly of 1948. His ecumenical activities and his association with the worker–priest movement in France incurred the distrust of the ecclesiastical authorities, and in 1954 he ceased to teach regularly in Paris. In 1962 Pope *John XXIII nominated him to the theological commission of the Second *Vatican Council, and he helped draft various Council documents. He is now a member of the RC International

Theological Commission.

CONGÉ D'ÉLIRE (Fr., 'permission to elect', sc. a bishop). In 1215 King *John agreed that bishops in England should be elected by the dean and chapter of the cathedral, but royal permission, the congé d'élire, was to be secured first and the election confirmed by the Royal Assent. Since the Reformation the congé d'élire has been accompanied by a 'letter missive' requiring the dean and chapter to elect the person named therein by the Sovereign.

CONGREGATION OF THE LORD, The (also **The Congregation of Christ** or simply **The Congregation**). The title assumed by the Scottish Reformers who supported J. *Knox.

CONGREGATIONAL COUNCIL FOR WORLD MISSION. The Council, formed in 1966, by which the *Congregational Churches in the British Isles, South Africa, Australia and New Zealand discharged the responsibility for missionary work which they took over from the *L.M.S. and the Commonwealth Missionary Society. In 1977 its membership was enlarged and it became the Council for World Mission.

CONGREGATIONALISM. The form of Church polity which rests on the independence and autonomy of each local Church. The system is held to represent the primitive form of Church order. Modern Congregationalism, however, dates from the Reformation. As early as 1550 bodies of men and women began meeting together to preach the Word of God and administer the Sacraments as separatists from the national Church. The numbers of such bodies increased under *Elizabeth I. The movement was driven underground by persecution, but reappeared in Holland and spread to America. In England the Independents (as they were called) formed the backbone of O. *Cromwell's army, and they defended their position at the *Westminster Assembly and restated their principles in the *Savoy Declaration of 1658. The 1662 Act of *Uniformity made Nonconformists of Independents and Presbyterians alike, though the *Toleration Act (1689) gave them the right to exist. Attempts to fuse these two types of Church at this time were unsuccessful, mainly because of theological differences.

The independence of the Congregational

Churches did not involve them in complete isolation. They recognized the bond of common faith and order and in time came to form County Associations for mutual intercourse and support. In 1832 these Associations combined in the Congregational Union of England and Wales. In 1972 the majority of Congregational Churches of England and Wales united with the Presbyterian Church of England to form the *United Reformed Church.

CONGREGATIONS, Religious. Religious societies in simple vows, in contradistinction to those in solemn vows or orders in the strict sense. The congregations in the RC Church are a modern development, among the earliest being the *English Ladies (approved in 1703). The individual houses are governed by a superior responsible to a *Provincial; the provinces are under the authority of the Superior-General, who is elected by the *General Chapter.

The term 'congregation' is also applied to groups of monastic houses which have arisen since the close of the Middle Ages, to facilitate discipline and reform (e.g. the *Cassinese Congregation). In these, individual monasteries retain their independence.

CONGREGATIONS, Roman. See *Roman Congregations*.

CONGRUISM. The doctrine that God confers *grace for the performance of good works (*gratia de congruo*) in accordance with such human circumstances as He sees will be most favourable to its use.

CONNOLLY, RICHARD HUGH (1873–1948), English *Benedictine *Patristic scholar. His main work was in the field of early Syrian Christianity. He also established the *Hippolytean authorship of the *Apostolic Tradition* and made a strong case for the *Ambrosian authorship of the *De Sacramentis*.

CONRAD OF GELNHAUSEN (*c*. 1320–90), theologian. He was one of the earliest advocates of the *Conciliar theory. In his *Epistola Concordiae* (1380) he urged that the circumstances of the *Great Schism provided a sufficient reason for summoning a General Council without Papal convocation.

CONRAD OF MARBURG (*c*. 1180–1233), *Inquisitor. He was charged with reforming missions in Germany and won the confidence of the Landgrave Ludwig IV of Thuringia; in 1225 he became the director and confessor of his wife, St. *Elizabeth. In 1231 he was appointed the first Papal Inquisitor in Germany, with absolute power over heretics. He exercised his authority ruthlessly and was murdered.

CONSALVI, ERCOLE (1757–1824), Italian statesman. He entered the papal service early and in 1800 was created cardinal and made Secretary of State. He was chiefly responsible for the negotiation of the *Concordat of 1801. He represented the Pope at the Congress of Vienna (1815) and secured the restoration of the Papal States.

CONSANGUINITY, blood-relationship. Within certain degrees it renders marriage not only unlawful but null and void. See also *Kindred and Affinity, Table of.*

CONSCIENCE. The word now denotes the capacity for judging the rightness of actions, whether in general or in particular. Christians are agreed that it is among the higher faculties of man, to whom it is unique. There has, however, been much debate as to how far it is affected by the *Fall, and over the reality and limits of the authority of conscience. The *Schoolmen generally maintained that, though conscience may err, it should always be followed; if the resulting actions are faulty, their imperfection may be excused by *invincible ignorance. The followers of S. Freud regarded feelings of guilt as simply an unhealthy product of faulty relationships in early life. Other thinkers have held that the inexorable claims of conscience point man to a Being higher than himself. Most Christian moralists have declined to equate the utterances of conscience with Divine Law.

CONSECRATION. In Christian vocabulary the term is used: (1) Of the *Eucharist: the act whereby the bread and wine become the Body and Blood of Christ. (2) Of *Bishops: the conferment by bishops of the *character which is inherent in their office upon others. (3) Of *altars and churches: the solemn setting apart of these things exclusively for the service of God. See *Dedication of Churches.*

CONSECRATION, The Prayer of. The central prayer in the Eucharistic rite in the BCP.

CONSENSUS GENEVENSIS. J. *Calvin's elaborate reformulation of his teaching on *Predestination to combat that of H. H. *Bolsec. He presented it to the City Council of Geneva in 1552.

CONSENSUS TIGURINUS (Lat., 'the Zürich agreement'). The formula of faith agreed upon in 1549 by the representatives of the Protestants of French and German Switzerland. They were primarily concerned to set forth a doctrine of the Eucharist which conformed with *Calvinist principles and was free of the objections which the *Zwinglians felt to *Consubstantiation.

CONSIGNATORIUM. The room or building in which the bishop used to confirm the newly baptized by 'signing' them with the *chrism. Some fine examples have been found in N. Africa.

CONSISTORY. In the RC Church the Consistory is the assembly of *cardinals convoked by and meeting in the presence of the Pope. Various ceremonial functions take place at public consistories. Private consistories are the ordinary court at which important papal business is conducted.

The Consistory Court in the C of E is the Bishop's court for the administration of ecclesiastical law within his diocese. In many *Presbyterian Churches it is the name given to the court corresponding to the *Kirk Session in Scotland.

CONSTANCE, Council of (1414–17). The Council was convoked by *John XXIII at the instigation of the Emp. Sigismund. Its purpose was to end the *Great Schism, reform the Church, and combat heresy.

In 1414 there were three Popes: Gregory XII in the line of *Urban VI; *Benedict XIII, the successor of *Clement VI of Avignon; and John XXIII, who was in the line inaugurated at the Council of *Pisa. John offered to resign if his rivals would do the same. He then left Constance in disguise on 20 Mar. 1415. The Council, before summoning John to return, passed the decree 'Haec sancta'; this declared that the Council held its power direct from Christ. John was brought back and deposed on 29 May 1415. Gregory abdi-

cated on 4 July, though only after his representative had reconvoked the Council, which was then joined by his cardinals. After various political manœuvres further delegates arrived, and on 26 July 1417 Benedict was deposed. By a special procedure, Oddo *Colonna was elected Pope on 11 Nov. 1417; he took the name of *Martin V.

Reform of the Church presented difficulties, and many of the aspirations of the individual nations were settled by *concordats. In its attempts to combat heresy the Council condemned over 200 propositions of J. *Wycliffe; John *Huss, who came to Constance under a safe-conduct from the Emperor, was condemned as a heretic and burnt. *Jerome of Prague suffered the same fate.

The Council is usually reckoned as the 16th General Council, but opinions differ as to whether its oecumenicity dates from the beginning, from Gregory's reconvocation, or from Martin's election. Its importance lay in its ending of the schism and in its crystallizing and diffusing of ideas about authority in general and especially about authority in the Church which were to have far-reaching effects.

CONSTANCE MISSAL. See *Missale Speciale*.

CONSTANTINE THE GREAT (d. 337), Roman Emperor. The son of the Emp. Constantius Chlorus and St. *Helena, he was proclaimed Emperor at *York in 306, and became senior ruler of the Empire after the battle of the *Milvian Bridge (312). Here he adopted the *Labarum* standard as the champion of Christianity, and soon afterwards toleration and imperial favour were given to the Church.

Constantine's policy was to unite the Church to the secular State by the closest possible ties. In 313 the *Donatists appealed to him to settle their controversy with the Church in Africa; in 316 he heard the case and gave judgement against the Donatists. A similar appeal from the contending parties led him to summon the Council of *Nicaea (325) to settle the *Arian dispute about the Person of Christ. At this he presided.

After his victory at Chrysopolis (324) had made him sole Emperor, Constantine fixed his capital at Byzantium (rebuilt and inaugurated as '*Constantinople' in 330). This move left the Bishop of Rome the most prominent figure in the West. It is hard to say when Constantine decided to embrace Christianity. He was not baptized until just before his death, but deferment of Baptism was then common. In 321 he ordered that *Sunday should be a public holiday. He also liberally endowed Christian church building, esp. in Palestine. Legend has added much to history, including among its embellishments the '*Donation of Constantine'. In the E. he is venerated as a saint.

CONSTANTINOPLE. In 330 *Constantine inaugurated Constantinople as his capital on the site of the Greek city of Byzantium. The capital of the E. Empire, it fell to the Turks in 1453.

Byzantium had a Christian community at least from the 2nd cent. In 381 its Bishop was given honorary pre-eminence after the Bp. of Rome. Constantinople was challenged by *Alexandria for supremacy in the East, but by the 6th cent. the Patr. of Constantinople was recognized as the *Oecumenical Patriarch in the East. Gradual estrangement from Rome developed, leading to the final breach between the Catholic West and Orthodox East, usually assigned to the year 1054.

CONSTANTINOPLE, First Council of (381). It came to be regarded as the Second *Oecumenical Council, even though no W. bishops were present. The work of the Council of *Nicaea on the doctrine of Christ was ratified, and the humanity of Christ was safeguarded by condemning *Apollinarianism. The so-called Niceno-Constantinopolitan Creed (see *Nicene Creed*), traditionally ascribed to this Council, was prob. not drawn up by it.

CONSTANTINOPLE, Second Council of (553). The Fifth *Oecumenical Council, convoked by the Emp. *Justinian to settle the controversy over the *Three Chapters (q.v.). The Council, attended mainly by E. bishops, condemned the Three Chapters and anathematized their authors. Meanwhile Pope *Vigilius, who refused to attend the Council, drew up the so-called 'Constitutum'; this condemned 60 propositions of *Theodore of Mopsuestia but refused to anathematize his person. Pressed by the Emperor, Vigilius finally agreed to accept the Council and annulled his former decisions in favour of the Three Chapters.

CONSTANTINOPLE, Third Council of (680–1). The Sixth *Oecumenical Council, convoked to deal with the *Monothelite controversy in the E. Church. The Council, attended by delegates of Pope *Agatho, condemned the Monothelitic formulas and their adherents, and proclaimed the existence of two wills in Christ, Divine and human, to be the orthodox faith.

CONSTANTINOPOLITAN CREED. See *Nicene Creed*.

CONSTITUTIONAL CHURCH, The. The schismatic Church established in France during the Revolution by the *Civil Constitution of the Clergy (1790). It was organized in 1791, under the protection of the National Assembly, while beside it the 'legitimate Church', whose priests refused to take the Constitutional Oath, continued to exist. When Napoleon concluded the *Concordat of 1801, *Pius VII was able to secure its abolition by the secular power.

CONSUBSTANTIAL. Of one and the same substance. The word is used esp. of the eternal relationship which subsists between the Three Persons of the Trinity.

CONSUBSTANTIATION. In the doctrine of the Eucharist, the belief that after the consecration the substances of both the Body and Blood of Christ and of the bread and wine co-exist in union with each other.

CONSUETUDINARY. See *Customary*.

CONSULTATION ON CHURCH UNION, The. An *ecumenical organ set up in 1962 in response to a proposal by Dr. C. E. Blake of the United *Presbyterian Church in the U.S.A. The other original members were the *Protestant Episcopal Church, the *Methodist Church, and the *United Church of Christ; it was later joined by other Protestant denominations. In 1970 it produced a Plan of Union. The Presbyterians withdrew in 1972 and the Plan of Union was set aside the following year.

CONTAKION. In the E. Church a hymn composed in a series of strophes and intended for liturgical use.

CONTARINI, GASPARO (1483–1542), cardinal. An adherent of the New Learning, he became famous as a theologian. Though only a layman, he was made a cardinal in 1535. In 1536 he was put on a commission which was to prepare the way for the Council (of *Trent) and at the Conference of *Ratisbon (1541) he took an active part in this last attempt to secure union with the *Lutherans.

CONTEMPLATION. As used by modern religious writers the term denotes non-discursive mental prayer, as distinguished from *meditation.

CONTEMPLATIVE LIFE, The. Though a measure of contemplation is demanded of all Christians, the term 'Contemplative Life' is normally confined to certain religious living under vows. The life is normally very austere and much time is devoted to prayer, both vocal and mental.

CONTRACEPTION. See Humanae Vitae.

CONTRA-REMONSTRANTIE. The counter-declaration in which in 1611 the more rigid *Calvinists stated their objections to the *Arminian '*Remonstrance'. It included a statement of belief in the unconditional *predestination of some souls to damnation.

CONTRITION. A form of interior repentance or sorrow for sin. Moral theologians hold that it must have its grounds in the love of God, and hence distinguish it from *attrition, an imperfect sorrow for sin, inspired by such lower motives as the fear of punishment.

CONVENT. In ecclesiastical usage either the building in which a body of religious live together, or the religious community itself. Historically the term has been applied to the domicile of religious of either sex, but it now tends to be restricted to houses of nuns.

CONVENTICLE ACT (1664). The Act which declared illegal all meetings of more than five persons (in addition to the household) for worship other than that prescribed in the BCP.

CONVENTUAL MASS. The public Mass sung (or occasionally said) in religious communities in which the choir *office is recited. It is attended by the whole community.

CONVENTUALS. The branch of the *Franciscan Order which favoured the accumulation and common holding of property and followed a mitigated rule.

CONVERSI. A name widely used of *lay brothers in monasteries.

CONVERSION OF ST. PAUL, Feast of the. The feast, kept on 25 Jan., is peculiar to the W.; it is of *Gallican origin.

CONVOCATIONS OF CANTERBURY AND YORK. The two ancient provincial assemblies of the clergy of the C of E, dating from *Anglo-Saxon times. They originally consisted only of prelates, but in 1225 Stephen *Langton also summoned *Proctors for the cathedral and monastic chapters. From the end of the 13th cent. they were composed of Bishops, Abbots (until the Reformation), Deans, Archdeacons, and representatives of the clergy of each diocese and cathedral chapter. At first the Bishops and lower clergy sat together, but since the 15th cent. they have sat as two separate Houses.

Until 1664 these assemblies were the means by which the clergy taxed themselves. Legislation was normally by *Canon. The '*Submission of the Clergy' (q.v.), which *Henry VIII extorted from the Convocations, greatly restricted their powers. After 1664 they ceased to be licensed for business. In the course of the *Bangorian Controversy they were prorogued by Royal Writ. Their meetings were then purely formal until the Convocation of Canterbury in 1852, and that of York in 1861, began discussing business again. Joint sittings of the two Convocations were initiated at the beginning of the 20th cent. By the *Synodical Government Measure of 1969 nearly all the functions of the Convocations were transferred to the General Synod, though provision was made for them each to meet separately.

CONVULSIONARIES. Enthusiasts of the party of *Jansenist *Appellants against the bull '*Unigenitus' (1713), who exhibited supposedly miraculous phenomena, akin to those of epilepsy.

CONYBEARE, FREDERICK CORNWALLIS (1856–1924), English scholar. His works included editions of early documents of the *Armenian Church. His discovery of a MS. in which the concluding verses of Mk.

were attributed to *Aristion attracted attention.

CONYBEARE, WILLIAM JOHN (1815–57), joint author with J. S. *Howson of *The Life and Epistles of St. Paul* (1852). This work embodied the results of extensive study, but its treatment kept in mind the needs and interests of the general reader.

COOPER, THOMAS (*c*. 1520–94), also **Cowper**, Bp. successively of *Lincoln and of *Winchester. Of Protestant sympathy, he was not ordained until shortly after *Mary's death (1558). He was a man of great learning. He answered an attack on J. *Jewel's *Apology* and wrote against the *Marprelate tracts.

COORNHEERT, DIRCK VOLCKERTS-ZOON (1522–90), Dutch theologian. An advocate of liberalism against the strongly *Calvinist doctrines current in Holland, he also urged the necessity of interior piety, rejected the idea of a visible Church, and maintained the supremacy of a faith inspired by the Bible and the Apostles' Creed. The *Arminians and the *Pietists owed something to his thought.

COPE. A semicircular cloak worn at liturgical functions in the W. Church when the *chasuble is not used. The 1604 *Canons ordered the use of a cope by the celebrant at the Holy Communion in cathedrals and collegiate churches. Its use in the C of E was widely revived in the 19th cent.

COPERNICUS, NICOLAS (1473–1543), the father of modern astronomy. He was a canon of Frauenburg from 1497. Rejecting the generally accepted Ptolemaic system of the universe, he found the centre of the solar system not in the earth but in the sun. A brief outline of this theory, the *Commentariolus* (1531), received papal approbation. The full treatise *De revolutionibus orbium coelestium* was not published until 1543. The *Galileo affair led to its being placed on the *Index in 1616.

COPTIC (language). Coptic was the language usually spoken by the native populace of Egypt from about the middle of the 3rd to the 10th cent A.D. and is still that of the liturgy of the *Coptic Church. In essence it is the language of ancient Egypt, into which

a large number of Greek words have been incorporated, and it is written in an alphabet akin to that of the Greeks. The NT was translated into all four Coptic dialects.

COPTIC CHURCH. Acc. to tradition the Church in Egypt was founded by St. *Mark; *Alexandria was one of the chief sees in the early Church. The Egyptian Church suffered severely in the persecution under *Diocletian. In the 4th cent. *monasticism was founded in Egypt by St. *Antony and others. After the condemnation of *Dioscorus, Patr. of Alexandria, at the Council of *Chalcedon (451), the Egyptian Church became formally *Monophysite and increasingly isolated from the rest of Christendom. The Orthodox (*Melchite) body established in Alexandria received little support from the local population, but bitter disputes persisted. In Upper Egypt, however, there was a rapid development of monasticism. In the 7th cent. the Copts were conquered by the Arabs, whose rule has lasted to the present day. The number of the Copts has declined. Outside Egypt there are Coptic dioceses at *Jerusalem, in the Sudan, and in S. Africa, while the *Ethiopian Church is an autonomous daughter of the Egyptian Church. There is also a small *Uniat Coptic Church dating from 1741, when Athanasius, the Coptic Bishop of Jerusalem, joined the RC Church.

CORBIE. The celebrated monastery, east of Amiens, was founded from *Luxeuil *c*. 660. It possessed a very fine library.

CORDELIERS. A name sometimes given in France to the *Franciscan *Observantines from the knotted cord which they wore round the waist. It was also assumed by a political party during the French Revolution.

CORINTH. In NT times Corinth (in modern Greece) was the capital of the Roman province of Achaia and was a commercially important city. The Church there was established by St. *Paul *c*. 50. It included prominent Jewish converts but appears to have consisted mainly of Gentiles, who, on the whole, belonged to the poorer classes.

CORINTHIANS, Epistles to the. These two NT Epistles of St. *Paul were written in *Ephesus *c*. 52–5. 1 Corinthians, occasioned by news which St. Paul had received from the Church at *Corinth, deals with a variety of subjects. The sections on the *Eucharist (10: 16 ff., 11: 20 ff.), on Love (13), and on the Resurrection (15) are among the most important in the NT. In 2 Corinthians the main topic is St. Paul's position in relation to the Church at Corinth; the Church had apparently failed in a matter of morality, and his own status as an apostle had been challenged. The tone of chapters 10–13 is different from that of the rest and it is widely held that they are part of a different Epistle, sent on an earlier occasion than chapters 1–9, or that the two groups of chapters were addressed to different groups within the Corinthian Church.

CORINTHIANS, Third Epistle to the. An apocryphal letter written in reply to an equally apocryphal letter from the Church of Corinth. The two prob. formed part of the 'Acts of *Paul' (c. 170). The author's purpose was anti-*Gnostic.

CORNELIUS (d. 253), Bp. of Rome from 251. Elected after the papacy had been vacant for 14 months, he was faced with opposition from the *Novatianist schismatics, who objected to his relatively lenient policy towards those who had lapsed during the persecutions. He died in exile, traditionally a martyr.

CORNELIUS A LAPIDE (1567–1637), Cornelis Cornelissen van den Steen, Flemish Biblical exegete. He became a *Jesuit in 1592. In 1616 he was called to Rome and there he completed his commentaries covering all the Canonical Books except Job and Psalms. His works owed their enduring popularity to their clarity, deep spirituality, and allegorical and mystical exegesis, buttressed by wide erudition.

CORONATION OF OUR LADY, The. The final triumph of the BVM in heaven, wherein she is crowned by her Divine Son. It is the subject of the last *Glorious Mystery of the *Rosary.

CORONATION RITE IN ENGLAND. The rite falls into three parts: (1) the promises made by the sovereign and his acclamation by the people; (2) the consecration and anointing of the sovereign; (3) the vesting, coronation, and enthronement, followed by the homage and the sovereign's Communion.

The rite in use in the 9th cent. (and possibly earlier) was based on that used for the coronation of Popes. This was displaced in 973 by a rite prob. consciously adapted from the rite used in imperial coronations. In 1603 it was translated into English and the Eucharist in general conformed to that in the BCP.

CORPORAL. In W. liturgical usage a square piece of linen on which the bread and wine are placed and consecrated in the Eucharist.

CORPORAL WORKS OF MERCY. These are traditionally seven: (1) feeding the hungry; (2) giving drink to the thirsty; (3) clothing the naked; (4) harbouring strangers; (5) visiting the sick; (6) ministering to prisoners; (7) burying the dead. See also *Spiritual Works of Mercy.*

CORPORATION ACT (1661). The Act requiring members of municipal corporations to take an oath abjuring rebellion against the king, declaring the *Solemn League and Covenant null and unlawful, and affirming that they had received Communion acc. to the rites of the C of E in the year preceding their election.

CORPUS CATHOLICORUM. An organization formed by the RC states in the *Holy Roman Empire to maintain RC interests against the *Corpus Evangelicorum. It first met in 1524.

CORPUS CHRISTI, Feast of. The feast commemorating the institution and gift of the *Eucharist, observed in the W. Church on the Thursday after *Trinity Sunday. The institution of the feast was largely due to the influence of St. *Juliana (d. 1258). Its observance was ordered by Pope Urban IV in 1264 and became universal in the W. in the 14th cent. The services of the day have traditionally been attributed to St. *Thomas Aquinas, but this ascription is doubted.

CORPUS EVANGELICORUM. A body of delegates from the Evangelical states in the *Holy Roman Empire whose aim was to defend Protestant interests in the Imperial Diet. Its organization developed gradually but did not crystallize until the Diet of Ratisbon (1653).

CORPUS IURIS CANONICI. The chief collection of *canon law in the W. Church before the promulgation of the *Codex Iuris Canonici in 1917. It was composed of the 'Decretum' of *Gratian, a private collection of canons of councils and decrees of Popes; 5 books of *Decretals, collected by *Raymond of Peñafort at the command of *Gregory IX, who added his authority to that already possessed by the component parts; the '*Sext', a sixth book added to the Decretals by *Boniface VIII; the '*Clementines', compiled by *Clement V and promulgated after his death by *John XXII; the '*Extravagantes' of John XXII; and the 'Extravagantes Communes,' the decrees of various Popes between 1261 and 1471.

CORRECTORY. In the Middle Ages, a book containing a set of variant readings for 'correcting' the corrupted text of the Latin *Vulgate Bible.

CORRODY. Originally the right possessed by some benefactors of religious houses or their nominees to board and lodging within them. The term came to be applied to pensions and other allowances made by the monastery to those who had served its needs or had secured a corrody by payment.

COSIN, JOHN (1594–1672), Bp. of *Durham. His famous *Collection of Private Devotions* (1627) was compiled for the use of Queen *Henrietta Maria's English maids of honour. He was deprived of his benefices by the Long Parliament and in 1642 went to Paris. He became Bp. of Durham at the Restoration (1660). He favoured elaborate ritual, and some of his suggestions were incorporated in the 1662 BCP; his translation of the '*Veni Creator' was included in the *Ordinal. He used all his legal powers to make both Puritans and RCs conform to the C of E in his diocese.

COSMAS AND DAMIAN, Sts., the patron saints of physicians. Nothing precise is known of their lives. Acc. to later tradition, the twin brothers practised their profession without claiming any reward from their patients. Both are supposed to have suffered martyrdom.

COSMAS INDICOPLEUSTES (i.e. 'Cosmas, the Indian navigator', 6th cent.). He was a merchant of *Alexandria, who became a monk. His 'Christian Topography' (*c.* 547) attacked the Ptolemaic system of astronomy; its chief value lies in its geographical information, esp. on Sri Lanka, and its witness to the spread of Christianity.

COSMAS MELODUS, St. (b. *c.* 700), author of Gk. liturgical hymns. He was adopted by the father of St. *John of Damascus; *c.*732 he entered the *Lavra of St. Sabas at Jerusalem; and in 743 he became Bp. of Maïuma nr. Gaza. His most famous works are his '*canons', odes in honour of the great Christian feasts, of which 14 are incorporated in the liturgical books of the E. Church.

COSMOCRATOR (Gk., 'Lord of the World'). The word, taken from pagan religious vocabulary, came to be used as a technical term for Satan, e.g. by the *Gnostics and *Marcion.

COSMOLOGICAL ARGUMENT. The argument which defends the existence of God from the existence of the world. It contends that no satisfactory explanation of the data of experience can be given without assuming the existence of a self-sufficient primary cause responsible for the world of phenomena.

COSMOLOGY. The part of *metaphysics which deals with the world, considered as a totality of phenomena in time and space.

COTTA. A shortened form of the *surplice, until recently widely used in the RC Church.

COUNCIL. A formal meeting of bishops and representatives of several Churches convened for the purpose of regulating doctrine or discipline. General or *Oecumenical Councils are assemblies of bishops of the whole Church, and their decrees are held to possess the highest authority.

COUNCIL FOR WORLD MISSION. See *Congregational Council for World Mission.*

COUNSELS OF PERFECTION, The. Traditionally they are: poverty, or renunciation of personal property; chastity, or abstention from sexual relations; and obedience, or submission of the will to a superior. They form the basis of the specifically religious life.

COUNTER-REFORMATION. The revival of the RC Church in Europe, usually considered as extending from the middle of the 16th cent. to the period of the *Thirty Years' War (1618–48). Though stimulated by Protestant opposition, reform movements within the RC Church had begun almost simultaneously with the *Lutheran schism. The new religious orders of the 1520s (*Capuchins, *Theatines, *Barnabites) should perhaps be regarded as the first organic signs of the Counter-Reformation. These preceded the foundation of the *Jesuit Order, but this body soon became the spearhead of the movement both within Europe and as a missionary force in America and the East. The definitions of doctrine and various internal reforms accomplished in the last session of the Council of *Trent (1562–3) sealed the triumph of the Papacy both over those Catholics who wished for conciliation with the Protestants and over those French and Spanish bishops who had opposed Papal claims. Within Europe the greatest triumph of the movement was the reconquest to the Roman obedience of S. Germany and Poland.

COUNTESS OF HUNTINGDON'S CONNEXION. See *Huntingdon, Selina*.

COURAYER, PIERRE FRANÇOIS LE (1681–1776), French theologian. He corresponded with W. *Wake about the episcopal succession in the C of E and in 1723 he published a treatise defending the validity of *Anglican Ordinations. He was excommunicated in 1728 and spent the rest of his life in England.

COURT OF DELEGATES. See *Delegates*.

COURT OF ECCLESIASTICAL CAUSES RESERVED. A court in the C of E established by the *Ecclesiastical Jurisdiction Measure of 1963. It has original jurisdiction over offences involving matters of doctrine, ritual, or ceremonial and it hears appeals from the *Consistory Courts in faculty cases involving these matters.

COURT OF FACULTIES, OF HIGH COMMISSION. See *Faculties, Court of*; *High Commission, Court of*.

COURTENAY, WILLIAM (*c.* 1342–96), Abp. of *Canterbury from 1381. The great-grandson of King Edward I, he rose rapidly to high position. He was a vigorous opponent of J. *Wycliffe; he presided over the Blackfriars Council of 1382, which condemned Wycliffe's doctrines.

COUSTANT, PIERRE (1654–1721), *Maurist scholar. He edited the works of St. *Hilary (1693). He was entrusted with the task of editing a complete collection of Papal letters from St. *Clement of Rome to *Innocent III; after over 20 years' work the first volume, covering the period A.D. 67–440, appeared in 1721.

COUTURIER, PAUL IRÉNÉE (1881–1953), French priest and worker for Christian unity. He spent most of his life in Lyons. In the 1920s he came into touch with Russian refugees, and, while staying at Amay-sur-Meuse (see *Chevetogne*) in 1932, his interest in the *ecumenical movement was aroused. He introduced a Triduum or three-day period of prayer for Christian unity at Lyons in 1933, followed in 1934 by an octave of prayer from 18 to 25 Jan. He engaged in a vast correspondence in connection with his ecumenical work, produced and distributed innumerable tracts on prayer for unity, and was in close touch with the leaders of the *World Council of Churches.

COVEL, JOHN (1638–1722), Master of Christ's College, Cambridge, from 1688. In 1669 he was appointed chaplain to the British Embassy at *Constantinople, and there he amassed material for his future work. His *Account of the Present Greek Church* (1722) was one of the few books giving information on the Greek Church before the 19th cent.

COVENANT. A bond entered into voluntarily by two parties by which each pledges himself to do something for the other. The idea of a covenant between the God of Israel and His people is fundamental to the religion of the OT. The original bond was perhaps simply the payment of sacrificial dues by Israel in return for the help of *Yahweh in war, but the Prophets stressed that a perfect relationship between God and man must be based on inward righteousness of the heart. In the life and death of Christ is the perfect covenant between God and man, wherein man, instead of offering his own imperfect righteousness in exchange for the mercies of God, receives a supernatural gift of Divine grace whereby his righteousness may be made perfect.

COVENANT, The National. See *National Covenant*.

COVENANTERS. Bodies of *Presbyterians in Scotland who bound themselves by oath to maintain their religion. Various small covenants were signed between 1556 and 1562, leading up to the *King's Confession of 1581. *Charles I's attempt to introduce the Scottish Prayer Book of 1637 prompted the *National Covenant of 1638. After the outbreak of the Civil War the English Parliament made an alliance with the Scots in terms of the *Solemn League and Covenant (1643; q.v.). The persecution of Presbyterians in Scotland between 1661 and 1688 gave rise to further Covenants.

COVENTRY. A *Benedictine house was founded at Coventry in 1043 and in 1095 Coventry became the seat of a bishopric. Though the title of Bp. of Coventry and *Lichfield remained until 1836, it was only in the 12th cent. that Coventry was a genuine see town. The diocese was reconstituted in 1918. The collegiate church of St. Michael (completed in 1433) became the cathedral. It was largely destroyed in an air raid in 1940. A new cathedral, completely modern in design, was consecrated in 1962.

COVERDALE, MILES (1488–1568), translator of the Bible. As an *Augustinian friar at Cambridge, he became an enthusiast for reform and was forced to reside abroad. In 1535 he produced on the Continent the first complete English Bible; in 1539, with R. *Grafton, he issued the '*Great Bible'. In 1551 he became Bp. of *Exeter. Under *Elizabeth I he was one of the *Puritan leaders.

COWL. A garment with a hood worn by monks.

COWLEY FATHERS. A colloquial name for the priests of the *Society of St. John the Evangelist, founded in the neighbourhood of Cowley, near Oxford.

COWPER, T. See *Cooper, T.*

COWPER, WILLIAM (1731–1800), poet and hymn-writer. He was called to the Bar in 1754, but fear of a competitive examination provoked a suicidal mania in 1763 and he was sent to a private lunatic asylum. In 1767 he moved to Olney, Bucks. Here he worked as a lay assistant to the incumbent, John *Newton, at whose request he began writing hymns. He suffered several later attacks of insanity. He contributed his finest hymns to the 'Olney Collection', published in conjunction with J. Newton in 1779. They include 'God moves in a mysterious way' and 'Hark, my soul! it is the Lord'.

COWPER TEMPLE CLAUSE. The section in the 1870 Education Act which provides that in elementary schools under public control no religious teaching 'which is distinctive of any particular denomination shall be taught'.

COX, RICHARD (*c.* 1500–81), Bp. of *Ely (1559–80). He sat on the commission which drew up the *King's Book (1543), and he helped to compile the 'Order of *Communion' of 1548 and the BCP of 1549 and 1552. At Oxford he introduced *Peter Martyr and other foreign divines into the university. As bishop he refused to minister in *Elizabeth I's chapel on account of its crucifix and lights.

C.P.A.S. (Church Pastoral Aid Society). A society founded in 1836 to assist the home mission of the C of E by making grants for the stipends of curates and lay workers.

CRAKANTHORPE, RICHARD (1567–1624), Anglican divine. He interested himself in the Romanist controversy; his principal work, *Defensio Ecclesiae Anglicanae* (1625; posthumous) was an answer to M. A. *de Dominis's defence of his recantation.

CRANACH, LUCAS (1472–1553), 'the Elder', German painter. In his youth he was celebrated as a painter of altar-pieces and all his life of portraits. He espoused the *Lutheran cause.

CRANMER, THOMAS (1489–1556), Abp. of *Canterbury. He was a Fellow of Jesus College, Cambridge. When it seemed likely in 1529 that the royal divorce proceedings against Catherine of Aragon would break down, Cranmer's suggestion that the Universities of Europe might be consulted gratified *Henry VIII, and in 1532 Cranmer was made Abp. of Canterbury. In 1533 he annulled Catherine's marriage with Henry and three years later pronounced a similar judgement on the King's marriage with Anne Boleyn. He also married him to and divorced him from Anne of Cleves. He was partly responsible for the *Ten Articles and for the dissemination of the Bible in the vernacular. After Henry's death (1547) Cranmer was one of the most influential counsellors of *Edward VI, and his ideas developed in an increasingly Protestant direction. He was largely responsible for the abolition of the old Church ceremonies, for the destruction of images, for the BCP of 1549 and that of 1552, as well as for the *Forty-Two Articles. On the accession of *Mary (1553) he was accused of treason, tried and sentenced, but the Queen spared his life. He was, however, imprisoned, tried for heresy, and degraded. He made several recantations but renounced them and was burnt at the stake.

CRASHAW, RICHARD (c. 1613–49), religious poet. The son of a *Puritan divine, he came under High Church influence, and in 1644 he was expelled from a fellowship at Peterhouse, Cambridge, on refusing to subscribe to the *National Covenant. He went to France and became a RC. His poetry is filled with a devotion nourished on the Song of Songs and the mysticism of St. *Teresa.

CREATION. In theology, the doctrine that the Universe was brought into being out of nothing by the free act of God, hence termed the Creator. This teaching is characteristic of the Hebrew-Christian tradition. Though increased scientific knowledge affects views on the order, dating, and character of the events recorded in the OT, it does not touch the fundamental notion of creation.

CREATIONISM. The doctrine that God creates de nihilo a fresh soul for each human individual at its conception or birth. It came to be generally accepted in the Middle Ages. It is opposed to Traducianism (q.v.).

CREDENCE. A small side table, also known as a 'credence table', placed near the altar to hold the bread, wine, and water to be used at the Eucharist, and other accessories of the service.

CREDITON. The birthplace of St. *Boniface, in 909 Crediton became the see of a new bishopric covering Devon and Corn-

wall. Cornwall was detached before 931 but re-united in 1027. In 1050 the see was moved to *Exeter. Since 1897 Crediton has provided the title of a *suffragan bishop.

CREDO UT INTELLIGAM (Lat., 'I believe so that I may understand'). A formula in which St. *Anselm summarized his conception of the relation between faith and knowledge.

CREED. A concise, formal, and authorized statement of important points of Christian doctrine. The classical examples are the *Apostles' Creed and the *Nicene Creed. Candidates for baptism originally accepted short formulas of belief; these gradually became crystallized into creeds. After the Council of Nicaea (325) credal professions of faith came to be used as standards of orthodoxy. The practice of reciting the (Nicene) Creed at the Eucharist arose as a local custom in the E. in the 5th cent.; it was not adopted at Rome until 1014.

CREED, The Apostles'; The Nicene. See Apostles' Creed; Nicene Creed.

CREED OF PIUS IV. The formula, also known as the **Professio fidei Tridentinae**, published by *Pius IV in 1564. It contains a summary of the doctrines promulgated at the Council of *Trent. It was imposed on holders of ecclesiastical office in the RC Church until 1967, when it was replaced by a shorter and less explicit formula.

CREED OF ST. ATHANASIUS. See Athanasian Creed.

CREEPING TO THE CROSS. See Veneration of the Cross.

CREIGHTON, MANDELL (1843–1901), historian and bishop. He was a professor at Cambridge (1884–91), Bp. of *Peterborough (1891–7), and then of London. His History of the Papacy (1882–94) is a clear, dispassionate, and erudite work. His episcopate was marked by statesmanship and tact, esp. in dealing with the conflicts between Ritualists and *Kensitites.

CREMATION. Disposal of the dead by reducing the body to ashes. Belief in the *resurrection of the body made cremation repugnant to the early Christians, and *burial was generally adopted. Cremation was revived in the 19th cent., largely in free-thinking circles. It was permitted in the RC Church in 1963; in the C of E its legitimacy was recognized in the 1969 *Canons.

CRIB. In the W. Church by popular custom a representation of the crib (or manger) in which Christ was laid at His birth, with a model of the Holy Child, is placed in church on Christmas Eve. St. *Francis of Assisi is thought to have made the first model of the crib at Greccio in 1223.

CRISIS, Theology of. Another name for the *Dialectical Theology of K. *Barth and his disciples, based on various associations of the Greek word κρίσις.

CRISPIN and **CRISPINIAN, Sts.** (c. 285), martyrs. Acc. to a purely legendary account, the two brothers fled from Rome during the *Diocletianic persecution and set up at Soissons as shoemakers, taking only such money as was freely offered them.

CRITICAL APPARATUS. In printed texts, a list of MS. readings differing from those in the accepted text. It is commonly printed at the foot of the page. See also *Textual Criticism*.

'CRITIQUE OF PURE REASON', The. The English title of the treatise in which I. *Kant first set out the principles of his 'Critical Philosophy'. The first edition of 1781 was followed by a much-altered second edition in 1787.

CRITOPULOS, METROPHANES. See *Metrophanes Critopulos*.

CROCE, BENEDETTO (1866–1952), Italian philosopher. His philosophy is a form of 'Creative Idealism' which concentrates on the forms taken by the life of the Spirit. Of these forms Croce recognized four: 'Intuition' (art), 'Concept' (science, philosophy, and history), 'Individuality' (economics), and 'Universality' (ethics). Religion he held to be a sub-form of Intuition, and Theology an illicit application of Concept, and both only transitory manifestations of the Spirit.

CROMWELL, OLIVER (1599–1658), Lord Protector. Having been elected M.P. for Cambridge in 1640, he strongly sup-ported the religious and political views of the *Puritan party, which he combined with the fervent spirituality of the *Independents. When the Civil War broke out (1642), it appeared to him, as to *Charles I, as a religious struggle. He built up a magnificently trained army, which defeated the royal forces. He urged the need to execute the King and was among those who signed Charles I's death warrant. He then ruthlessly put down rebellion in *Ireland and defeated the Scots. In 1653 he dismissed the Long Parliament and was installed as 'Lord Protector'. He ruled England by a series of constitutional experiments; to some extent he remodelled the C of E on Puritan lines, establishing a committee of *Triers to eject unfit clergy. Even before his death there were signs of dissatisfaction. He regarded himself as the instrument of Divine providence, but his character has been variously assessed.

CROMWELL, THOMAS (c. 1485–1540), created Earl of Essex in 1540. He took some part in suppressing a number of small monasteries to provide endowments for T. *Wolsey's colleges; after Wolsey's disgrace (1529), he entered the King's service. He became a strong advocate of Protestantism. In 1535 he was made Vicar General. He arranged for the visitation and *dissolution of the monasteries between 1536 and 1539, and he acted as the chief intermediary between *Henry VIII and the Reformation Parliament. He issued the *Injunctions of 1536 and 1538, the latter ordering a Bible to be set up in every church. He arranged the marriage of Henry VIII and Anne of Cleves, which was mainly responsible for his fall. He was sentenced for treason and beheaded.

CROSIER. The staff carried by bishops and sometimes also by abbots and abbesses. The form resembling a shepherd's crook, familiar in the W., is due to late symbolism.

CROSS, Devotion to the. See *Exaltation*, *Invention*, and *Veneration of the Cross*.

CROWLAND ABBEY. This monastery in the fens was founded in 716 in honour of St. *Guthlac, who had lived as a hermit on the site. It was rebuilt after a fire in 1091. At the *Dissolution (1539), part of the church became the parish church.

CROWN OF THORNS. One of the instruments of Christ's Passion. Its supposed preservation is first mentioned in the 5th cent. The relic is said to have come into the possession of *Louis IX of France, who built the *Sainte-Chapelle to house it. Acc. to other traditions it was broken up into smaller relics.

CROZIER. See *Crosier.*

CRUCIFIX. A model of the cross, bearing an image of the crucified Lord. Crucifixes are widely used as objects of devotion in the W. In the E. their place is taken by crosses with a flat likeness, i.e. a form of *ikon.

CRUCIFIXION. Infliction of death by nailing or binding to a cross. It was much used by the Romans as the extreme punishment for slaves, though it might also be inflicted upon any person who could not prove Roman citizenship. *Constantine abolished crucifixion as a legal punishment. The Crucifixion of Christ between two thieves is recorded by all four Evangelists.

CRUDEN, ALEXANDER (1701–70), compiler of the 'Biblical Concordance'. His life was marked by eccentricities bordering on insanity. In 1732 he established a bookshop in London. He began to compile his *Concordance of the OT and NT in 1736 and in Nov. 1737 he presented a copy to Queen Caroline. In later life he set himself to reform the morals of the country.

CRUETS. Vessels of glass or precious metal in which the wine and water for the Eucharist are brought to the altar.

CRUSADES. The primary use of the term is to describe the series of expeditions from W. Europe to the E. Mediterranean, beginning in 1095, which were designed to recover the Holy Land from Islam and then to retain it in Christian hands, and later to counteract the expanding power of the Ottoman Empire. Many factors, ideological and social, were involved. Crusaders were granted *indulgences and the status of *martyr in the event of death.

The history of the Crusades may be divided into three periods.

(a) 1095–1204. The *First Crusade* was solemnly proclaimed by *Urban II at the Council of *Clermont (1095), with the double object of relieving the pressure of the Seljuk Turks on the E. Empire and of securing free access for pilgrims to *Jerusalem. A series of expeditions set out. *Antioch was captured in 1098 and Jerusalem in 1099. *Godfrey of Bouillon was appointed Defender of the Holy Sepulchre; on his death in 1100 his brother Baldwin was crowned King of Jerusalem During the next 20 years a series of Latin states was established in Syria and Palestine. These proved difficult to defend. The *Second Crusade* of 1147, provoked by the fall of *Edessa (1144), was preached by St. *Bernard of Clairvaux; it was led by Louis VII of France and the Emp. Conrad III. It did not ease the situation and in 1187 Saladin captured Jerusalem. The *Third Crusade* of 1189–92, in which the Emp. *Frederick I, Richard I of England, and Philip II of France all took part, failed to recover Jerusalem. In 1202 the *Fourth Crusade* set out, but it was diverted to *Constantinople, where a Latin Empire was established from 1204 to 1261.

(b) 1204–91. Attempts to defend the remaining W. possessions in Syria continued. Jerusalem was recovered by negotiation by *Frederick II and was in Latin hands from 1229 to 1244. The two largest crusades were directed against Egypt, but both failed. In 1291 the last remaining possession on the mainland fell.

(c) 1291–1464. The expansion of Ottoman power in the E. provoked a series of intermittent attempts to organize joint action. The largest of these expeditions was that of 1396, defeated by the Turks at Nicopolis. In 1464 *Pius II died after failing to secure European co-operation for a further Crusade.

During the whole period there were many other expeditions planned or approved by the Papacy, for which the same spiritual benefits were promised. They included expeditions against non-Christians (such as the Muslims in Spain), against heretics (e.g. the *Albigensians), and against the political opponents of the Papacy. In the 19th and 20th cents. the terms 'Crusade' and 'Crusader' have been used for a variety of Christian movements, often designed for evangelism.

See also *Children's Crusade*; *Hospitallers*; *Templars*.

CRUTCHED FRIARS (Fratres Cruciferi). A general name given to several religious congregations, mostly of *canons regular, whose history is obscure. They derive their name from their habit of carrying a cross in their hands or having one sewn on the front of their habit. The oldest body of crutched friars prob. dates from Crusading times.

CRYPT. A cellar or vault beneath a church, often used as a chapel or burying-place.

CRYPTO-CALVINISM. The doctrine of the Reformer, P. *Melanchthon (1497–1560), also known as '*Synergism'. Melanchthon advocated a policy of conciliation towards both RCs and Calvinists; he was attacked by the strict *Lutherans as a secret ('crypto') Calvinist.

CUDWORTH, RALPH (1617–88), *Cambridge Platonist. From 1654 he was Master of Christ's College, Cambridge. In *The True Intellectual System of the Universe* (1678) he argued that the only real source of knowledge was the Christian religion. Religious truth was embodied in three great principles: the reality of the supreme Divine intelligence and the spiritual world which that intelligence has created, the eternal reality of moral ideas, and the reality of moral freedom and responsibility. In this way he tried to assert the need for a revealed religion against the atheism of his day.

CUIUS REGIO, EIUS RELIGIO (Lat., 'In a [prince's] country, the [prince's] religion'). The formula adopted at the Peace of *Augsburg (1555), by which the princes of the Empire were permitted to settle whether the religion of their lands should be RC or Lutheran.

CULDEES. A name given to certain early Irish and Scottish monks. They appear to have been in origin *anchorites who gradually banded together. By the 11th cent. they were indistinguishable from secular canons; they were gradually superseded by *canons regular.

CULLMANN, OSCAR (1902–   ), NT scholar and theologian. From 1948 he has been professor simultaneously at Basle and Paris. He has been esp. concerned to develop a theory of *Heilsgeschichte*. Acc. to Cullmann what is distinctive in the NT is its view of time and history. Throughout human history there has been a narrow stream of sacred

history. This sacred history, whose central point is Jesus Christ, provides the clue to the understanding of general history, which is seen to be linear in form and to run from creation to consummation. He has also written on *Christology and on St. *Peter.

CUM OCCASIONE. The constitution of *Innocent X in 1653 condemning 5 propositions which embodied the dogmatic substance of *Jansenism.

CUMBERLAND, RICHARD (1632–1718), Bp. of *Peterborough from 1691 and moral philosopher. In *De legibus naturae* (1672) he maintained that the laws of nature were ethical and immutable, and that their root principle was that of 'Universal Benevolence'. He was the real founder of English *Utilitarianism.

CUNEIFORM. The characters of wedge-shaped components in which ancient Accadian, Persian, and other inscriptions were written.

CURATE. Properly, a clergyman who has the charge ('cure') of a parish, i.e. in England a *rector or *vicar. Such a clergyman is also known as the 'incumbent'. He is chosen by the 'patron' and admitted to the cure of souls by the bishop (see *Advowson*). In general speech, however, the word is now used to denote an assistant or unbeneficed clergyman, appointed, e.g., to assist the incumbent in the performance of his duties. Assistant curates are nominated by the incumbent or the bishop, and licensed by the bishop. See also *Perpetual Curate*.

CUR DEUS HOMO (Lat., 'Why [did] God [become] man?'). The title of St. *Anselm's treatise on the *Atonement.

CURÉ D'ARS. The, Jean-Baptiste Marie Vianney (1786–1859). Ordained in 1815, from 1818 he was parish priest at Ars. At first from neighbouring villages and then from far afield all sorts of people sought his counsel and he was forced to spend long hours in the confessional.

CURETON, WILLIAM (1808–64), *Syriac scholar. At the British Museum he catalogued the MSS. brought back by H. *Tattam. His discoveries included the Syriac text of three of St. *Ignatius's Epistles, the

'Curetonian' *Old Syriac text of the Gospels, and the 'Festal Letters' of St. *Athanasius.

CURIA. The Papal court and its functionaries, esp. those through whom the government of the RC Church is administered. The term is also used in the RC Church of the court of diocesan officials who act on behalf of an individual diocesan bishop.

CURSIVE SCRIPT. The formal bookhand, properly called 'Greek minuscule', which used small rounded ('lower-case') letters, joined together for speed of writing.

CURSOR MUNDI. An early English poem on the history of the world, prob. dating from the late 13th cent. The first six books extend from the Creation to the latter part of the life of Christ and the Apostles, and the seventh deals with the Last Judgement.

CUSANUS, NICOLAUS. See *Nicholas of Cusa*.

CUSTOMARY (also known as a **Consuetudinary** or **Liber Ordinarius**). The book containing (1) the rites and ceremonies for the services, and/or (2) the rules and customs of discipline, of a particular monastery, cathedral, or religious order.

CUTHBERT, St. (d. 687), Bp. of *Lindisfarne. He became a monk at Melrose in 651. In 664 he moved with his abbot to Lindisfarne, where they both accepted Roman usages. In 676 he withdrew as a hermit to Farne. He became Bp. of Lindisfarne in 685; his short episcopate was marked by missionary zeal. His body reached its final resting-place at *Durham in 999.

CYNEWULF (early 9th cent.), Anglo-Saxon poet. Four religious poems are certainly his work. The second part of *Christ*, the only part by Cynewulf, celebrates the mystery of the Ascension; *Juliana* is the account of the martyrdom of the saint; *Elene* tells the story of the finding of the True Cross by St. *Helena; and *The Fates of the Apostles* is a fragment incorporating legends about the Apostles after their dispersal. Of the author nothing is known.

CYPRIAN, St. (d. 258), Bp. of Carthage, N. Africa. Thascius Caecilianus Cyprianus was a pagan rhetorician converted to Christianity *c.* 246. Within two years he was elected Bp. of Carthage. When the *Decian persecution began (249) he was forced to flee; he returned in 251. He was opposed to the easy reconciliation of Christians who had lapsed or secured * *libelli pacis*; two councils (251 and 252) decided that they should be reconciled only after suitable penance and delay. Meanwhile the schism of *Novatian, arising out of the question of the lapsed, gave rise to the controversy over Rebaptism. Cyprian demanded the rebaptism of schismatics on the ground that no one outside the Church could administer her Sacraments. The Church at Rome held that both schismatics and heretics could validly administer baptism. The ensuing violent correspondence between Cyprian and *Stephen was significant for later controversy on papal claims. Persecution cut short the dispute. Cyprian was martyred in 258.

Cyprian's writings enjoyed great popularity. Some are of theological importance, esp. those dealing with the Church, the ministry, and the Sacraments. His *De Catholicae Ecclesiae Unitate*, on the nature of true unity in the Church in its relation to the episcopate, is held in special esteem.

CYPRIAN, St. (*c.* 300), a converted magician of *Antioch. Acc. to a worthless legend he was converted while using his magic arts to ensnare a Christian virgin, Justina. He became a bishop and, with Justina, was beheaded in the *Diocletianic persecution.

CYPRIAN, St. (d. 549), Bp. of Toulon. He was the principal author of the life of *Caesarius of Arles. At the Council of *Orange (529) he took part in combating *Semi-pelagianism.

CYPRUS, Christianity in. Cyprus was evangelized by St. *Paul and St. *Barnabas (Acts 13). There were three bishops from Cyprus at the Council of *Nicaea (325), and that of *Ephesus in 431 recognized the claims of the Cypriot bishops to independence of the Patriarchates. The Cypriots came under Arab rule but were set free in the 10th cent., and at this time the great monasteries were built. The *Crusaders introduced a Latin hierarchy in 1196. The Latin Church was extinguished when the Turks took the island in 1571, but the Greeks were eventually allowed to reconstitute their Church.

CYRIL, St. (*c.* 315–86), Bp. of *Jerusalem from *c.* 349. In 357 *Acacius, the *Arian Bp. of *Caesarea, had Cyril banished on the ground of his opposition to Arianism, but the Council of *Seleucia recalled him in 359. Two further banishments followed. Meanwhile Cyril's beliefs about the Godhead of Christ had become suspect in the opposite quarter because he disliked as man-made the term *Homoousios. The Council of *Antioch in 379 sent St. *Gregory of Nyssa to investigate; he reported that the faith of the Church of Jerusalem was sound.

The 24 'Catecheses', delivered *c.* 350 as instructions in Lent and Eastertide to the catechumens who were baptized on *Holy Saturday, are Cyril's chief surviving work.

CYRIL, St. (d. 444), Patr. of *Alexandria from 412. The most important of the many conflicts in which he engaged arose out of the support given by *Nestorius, Patr. of *Constantinople, to a chaplain who objected to the application of the word *Theotokos ('God-bearer') to the BVM on the ground that she was the mother of only the humanity of Christ. Cyril defended the contested word in his Paschal letter for 429. He then persuaded Pope *Celestine I to summon a Council at Rome in 430 and condemn Nestorius. With the sentence, which Cyril was charged to deliver, he sent a covering letter with 12 anathemas. At the Council of *Ephesus (431) he had Nestorius deposed before the Antiochene bishops arrived. The Antiochenes held a separate Council and deposed Cyril, but in 433 he reached agreement with the moderate Antiochenes.

The most brilliant representative of the *Alexandrian theological tradition, Cyril put into systematic form the classical Greek doctrines of the Trinity and of the Person of Christ. His writings are marked by precision in exposition, accuracy in thought, and skill in reasoning, though they lack elegance. They include letters, exegetical works, treatises on dogmatic theology, and sermons.

CYRIL, St. (826–69), and **METHODIUS, St.** (*c.* 815–85), the 'Apostles of the Slavs'. The two brothers were sent from *Constantinople as missionaries to what is now Moravia. Cyril (who was called 'Constantine' before he became a monk) invented the *Glagolitic alphabet, adopted Slavonic in the liturgy, and circulated a Slavonic Bible. He died in Rome. Methodius was then consecrated bishop. He met with resistance from the German bishops, and Pope John VIII deemed it expedient to withdraw permission to use Slavonic as a liturgical language.

CYRIL LUCAR. See *Lucar, Cyril.*

CYRIL OF SCYTHOPOLIS (6th cent.), Greek monk and hagiographer. He went to *Jerusalem in 543. He belonged to the community founded by St. *Euthymius; after this was brought to an end by the *Origenist controversy (555), he entered the monastery of St. Sabas. He was the author of the lives of seven Palestinian abbots; they are remarkable for their accurate detail.

CYRILLIC. The alphabet used by the Slavonic people in the E. Church. It was named after St. *Cyril, one of the 'Apostles of the Slavs', though *Glagolitic, not Cyrillic, is the alphabet he invented.

CZECHOSLOVAK HUSSITE CHURCH, The. Its origins go back to an association of Catholic priests, called 'Jednota' (or Union), formed in 1890. They sought to introduce the Czech language into the liturgy and abolish clerical celibacy. When their demands, submitted to Rome in 1919, were refused, they set up an independent religious body in 1920. It was constituted on *Presbyterian lines. It prob. never included more than *c.* 5 per cent of the population.

D

'D'. In *Pentateuchal criticism the source most characteristically represented by the Book of Deut. Its composition is assigned to the early 7th cent. B.C. See *Deuteronomy, Book of.*

D'ACHÉRY, JEAN LUC (1609–85), *Maurist scholar. He edited various ancient authors, whose MSS. he recovered from oblivion. His works include an edition of *Lanfranc and 13 vols. of *Spicilegium* (1655–77). He trained J. *Mabillon.

DAILLÉ, JEAN (1594–1670), French Reformed theologian and controversialist. From 1626 until his death he was pastor at Charenton, where the Reformed Church of Paris held its services. He rejected the authority of the Fathers, claiming that all Christian doctrines are either stated in Scripture or deducible from it.

D'AILLY, PIERRE (1350–1420), theologian. He taught at *Paris and in 1397 he became Bp. of Cambrai. His main concern was to find a means of ending the *Great Schism. To this end he broke with *Benedict XIII in 1408 and in 1409 attended the Council of *Pisa, where he supported the newly elected *Alexander V. Alexander's successor, *John XXIII, made him a cardinal in 1412. In 1414 he took part in the Council of *Constance, where he upheld the *Conciliar Theory, without, however, entirely approving the 'Decrees of Constance'. In 1416 he published his influential *Tractatus super Reformatione Ecclesiae*.

In his doctrinal teaching D'Ailly usually accepted the views of *William of Occam. He held that the existence of God was not a rationally demonstrable truth, and that sin was not inherently evil but sinful only because God wills it to be so. He maintained that bishops and priests received their jurisdiction directly from Christ and not mediately through the Pope, and that neither Pope nor Council was infallible. His views were developed by the Reformers and influenced *Gallicanism.

DALE, ROBERT WILLIAM (1829–95), *Congregationalist. He took a leading part in the municipal affairs of Birmingham, where he ministered. He was president of the International Congregational Council in 1891. In *The Atonement* (1875) he maintained a penal doctrine, but sought to emphasize its ethical rather than its forensic aspects.

D'ALEMBERT, JEAN LE ROND (1717–83), French mathematician, philosopher, and *Encyclopaedist. He showed remarkable mathematical talent and in 1743 he published a treatise in which he developed the mechanical principle henceforward known as 'D'Alembert's Principle'. He was drawn into religious disputes by his collaboration in D. *Diderot's *Encyclopédie*, to which he contributed the *Discours préliminaire*, as well as many articles.

DALMAN, GUSTAF HERMAN (1855–1941), Biblical scholar. He held academic posts in Germany and Palestine. He researched into the language, ideas, and customs of 1st-cent. Judaism, and he established that Christ ordinarily spoke in Aramaic, not Greek.

DALMATIC. The over-tunic worn in the W. Church at Mass by *deacons, and on certain occasions also by bishops. It is ornamented with two coloured strips running from front to back over the shoulders.

DAMASCUS. The ancient capital of Syria. Mentioned as early as the 16th cent. B.C., it lost much of its importance after its fall in 732 B.C. to the Assyrian king. It was on the road from *Jerusalem to Damascus that St. *Paul was converted to the Christian faith. A Christian community has existed there continuously from Apostolic times.

DAMASCUS FRAGMENTS. See *Dead Sea Scrolls*.

DAMASUS, St. (c. 304–84), Pope from 366. On the death of *Liberius a fierce conflict broke out between the supporters of Damasus and those of his rival Ursinus, each being elected in a different basilica. The Emp. Valentinian I intervened on behalf of Damasus and banished Ursinus. Damasus was active, by synods and with the help of the imperial power, in suppressing heresy. He also made provision for the proper housing of papal archives and adorned the tombs of the martyrs. At a Council prob. held in Rome in 382 he promulgated a Canon of Scriptural Books and he commissioned his secretary, St. *Jerome, to revise the Biblical text (see *Vulgate*). See also *Fides Damasi* and *Tome of Damasus*.

DAMIAN, St. See *Cosmas and Damian, Sts.*

DAMIAN, St. PETER. See *Peter Damian, St.*

DAMIEN, Father (1840–89), leper missionary. Joseph de Veuster became a member of the Picpus Society (Fathers of the Sacred Heart of Jesus and Mary) in 1859, taking in religion the name 'Damien'. He went to the Sandwich Islands in 1863 and in 1873 was sent, at his own request, to a settlement of lepers at Molokai. He ministered singlehanded to the spiritual and physical needs of 600 lepers. He died of the disease.

DAMNATION. In general, 'condemnation', but esp. to eternal loss (*damnum*) in hell.

DANCE OF DEATH, The. An allegorical subject in European art, in which the figure of Death, often represented as a skeleton, is shown meeting various characters and leading them all in a dance to the grave.

DANIEL, Book of. This OT Book consists of: (a) a narrative section (1-6) describing the experiences of Daniel and his three companions under Nebuchadnezzar and Belshazzar, kings of Babylon, and Darius the Mede; and (b) a series of visions (7-12) which reveal the future destinies of the Jewish people. The traditional belief that the Book was written in the 6th cent. B.C. by Daniel, one of the Jewish exiles in Babylon, is now almost universally regarded as untenable. The consensus of modern critical opinion is that it dates from 168 to 165 B.C.

See also *Song of the Three Children*; *Susanna, Book of*; *Bel and the Dragon*.

DANIEL, St. (d. 493), *Stylite. A disciple of St. *Simeon Stylites, at the age of 47 he took up his position on a pillar four miles from *Constantinople. He lived on it for 33 years, descending only once to rebuke the Emp. Basiliscus.

DANTE ALIGHIERI (1265–1321), poet and philosopher. Dante was born in Florence. He first met his Beatrice in 1274; after her death in 1290, he promised her a poem 'such as had been written for no lady before', a promise fulfilled in the *Divina Commedia*. He then studied philosophy, entered politics, and was banished from Florence in 1301. He became a supporter of the Emp. Henry VII, for whom he wrote the *De Monarchia*; this argued the need for a universal monarchy to achieve the temporal happiness of mankind and the independence of the Empire from the Pope and the Church. Henry's death in 1313 shattered Dante's prospects. The last years of his life were devoted to completing the *Divina Commedia* (q.v.).

DARBOY, GEORGES (1813–71), Abp. of *Paris from 1863. His *Gallican sympathies and claims to episcopal independence brought him into conflict with Rome; before and during the First *Vatican Council he opposed the definition of Papal *Infallibility, though he eventually subscribed to it. When the Commune gained control of Paris in 1871, he was seized and shot.

DARBY, JOHN NELSON (1800–82), *Plymouth Brother. He was ordained in the C of E but resigned in 1827 and joined a sect called the 'Brethren', then newly founded by A. N. Groves; this rejected all Church order and outward forms. A quarrel within this body led to a local schism at Plymouth in 1845 and at Bristol in 1847; Darby became the leader of the stricter Brethren, who were organized as a separate body ('Darbyites').

D'ARCY, MARTIN CYRIL (1888–1976), *Jesuit philosopher. From 1933 to 1945 he was Master of Campion Hall, Oxford, and from 1945 to 1950 Provincial of the English Province. He expounded Catholic principles and philosophy to a public with less narrowly theological interests.

DARK AGES, The. A term in current use for the period in W. Europe extending from the decay of classical culture (c. the 5th cent.) to the beginning of medieval culture (c. the 11th cent.).

DARWINISM. The form of the theory of evolution put forward by Charles Darwin, esp. in *The Origin of Species* (1859) and *The Descent of Man* (1871). Darwin held that species of living beings evolve by natural selection, the fittest for their biological purpose alone surviving.

D'AUBIGNÉ, J. H. MERLE. See *Merle d'Aubigné, J. H.*

DAVENPORT, CHRISTOPHER (1598–1680), English RC theologian. He became a *Franciscan in 1617. He was chaplain to Queens *Henrietta Maria and Catherine of Braganza. He tried to show that the *Thirty-

Nine Articles could be interpreted in conformity with Catholic tradition.

DAVENPORT, JOHN (1597–1670), *Puritan divine. In 1633 he resigned his living in London and became co-pastor of the English church in Amsterdam. He sailed for Boston in 1637 and in 1638 founded the colony of New Haven; here Church membership was obligatory for electors and civil officers. In 1662 he became involved in a controversy over Baptism, connected with the *Half-Way Covenant.

DAVID (prob. d. *c*. 970 B.C.), first king of the Judaean dynasty. His reign is recounted in 1 Sam. 16–1 Kgs. 2 and in the idealized description of 1 Chron. 2 f. and 10–29. He first appears when he is anointed by *Samuel to the future kingship. After his victory over Goliath, the Philistine giant, he was promoted by Saul and married his daughter. He subsequently provoked Saul's jealousy and fled. On Saul's death he set himself up at Hebron as king of the Judaean tribes and later was accepted also by the Israelites. He made *Jerusalem his capital and reigned there for 33 years. He restored the *Ark to the city, planned the building of the *Temple, and broke the ascendancy of the Philistines. He is traditionally regarded as the author of the *Psalms, but it is unlikely that more than a fraction of the Psalter is his work.

In Hebrew tradition the name of David occupied a central place. His house and dominion were to stand for ever. But his dynasty lost the allegiance of the northern tribes (Israel) on the death of *Solomon and fell to the Babylonians in 586 B.C. The prophets then looked for the re-establishment of the sovereignty of 'David' (i.e. of the house of David) as part of the deliverance of the nation to be achieved by a future prince of the house. In the NT the Evangelists assume the Davidic descent of the *Messiah, and it is as 'Son of David' that the Lord is welcomed to Jerusalem before His Passion. The Fathers regarded David as the *type of Christ.

DAVID, St. (d. *c*. 601), patron saint of *Wales. Acc. to legend he came of noble family, founded 12 monasteries, and settled at Mynyw or Menevia (later called *St. Davids), where he established an abbey with a life of extreme asceticism. One of the few historically established facts is that he attended the Synod of Brefi (the modern Llanddewi Brefi) *c*. 560.

DAVID OF AUGSBURG (*c*. 1200–72), preacher and mystic. A native of Augsburg, he entered the *Francisan Order at Regensburg; in 1243 he was transferred to the newly founded convent at Augsburg. His Latin works have frequently been ascribed to St. *Bernard and to St. *Bonaventure. He was the first author to publish spiritual treatises in German. His teaching was practical and his works continued in use in the later Middle Ages, esp. in the Netherlands.

DAVID OF DINANT (*fl*. 1200), naturalist and philosopher. He prob. came from Dinant in Belgium, but practically nothing is known of his life. A provincial Council of Sens in 1210 ordered that his writings be burnt. The surviving portions of his work show knowledge of the original text of *Aristotle; they also set out some startling doctrines. He held that all distinctions in real being are to be explained by a primal possible being, which he identified with the Divine Being. All things, material, intellectual, and spiritual, have one and the same essence, viz. God. The circulation of his views led to the condemnation of the study of Aristotle's *Metaphysics* and his works on natural philosophy in *Paris.

DAVIDSON, RANDALL THOMAS (1848–1930), Abp. of *Canterbury from 1903 until his resignation in 1928. As confidential adviser to Queen Victoria and then as Primate he exercised great influence in the Church and nation. As Archbishop he had to deal with the disestablishment of the Church in *Wales, the controversy following the *Kikuyu conference, the *Enabling Act, the *Malines Conversations, and revision of the BCP.

DAY HOURS. Traditionally the services of the *Breviary other than *Mattins, viz. *Lauds, *Prime, *Terce, *Sext, *None, *Vespers, and *Compline. For the arrangement of offices in the 1971 Breviary, see *Breviary*.

DAY OF ATONEMENT. See *Atonement, Day of*.

DAY'S PSALTER. A popular name for the

metrical edition of the Psalms by T. *Stern-hold and J. Hopkins printed by John Day from 1562 onwards.

DEACON. The rank in the Christian ministry next below the presbyter (priest) and bishop. The institution of the diaconate is traditionally seen in the ordination of the *Seven (Deacons) for the service of the poor and distribution of alms recorded in Acts 6: 1–6, though the word is not used here. Where it occurs in the NT in a technical sense (e.g. Phil. 1: 1) it is used of ministers who serve under presbyter-bishops. In Patristic times the office was normally held for life. The deacons' functions varied somewhat from place to place, but their responsibility for collecting and distributing alms gave them considerable importance, and the *archdeacon, the chief deacon in a given place, became the bishop's principal assistant. During the Middle Ages their influence declined. In most W. episcopal Churches (including the C of E) the diaconate is now a stage in preparation for the priesthood. The Second *Vatican Council, however, envisaged the possibility of restoring a permanent diaconate in the RC Church and allowed bishops in some cases to ordain older married men as deacons. The E. Church has retained a permanent diaconate. Deacons normally assist at the liturgy but are debarred from celebrating the Eucharist or giving absolution.

In many Protestant Churches the name is applied to holders of an office in the ministry. In the *Lutheran Church the word denotes an assistant parochial minister, even though in full Lutheran orders. In *Presbyterianism there are two classes of deacons, those who administer alms and those who care for the poor and sick; the deacons' court is responsible for the proper distribution of Church goods.

DEACONESS. In the early Church a woman officially charged with certain functions. The deaconess devoted herself to the care of the sick and poor of her sex and assisted in the baptism of women when, for reasons of propriety, many of the ceremonies could not be performed by a deacon. When adult baptisms became rare the office declined in importance. Two 6th-cent. councils abrogated it, but in some places deaconesses survived until the 11th cent.

In the 19th cent. the office was revived in a modified form. The first Protestant community of deaconesses was that established at *Kaiserswerth in 1836. The first deaconess in the C of E was dedicated to her work in 1861. *Methodists and the Church of *Scotland followed in 1888.

DEAD, Prayers for the. The practice of praying for the dead depends on the belief that those members of the Church who have died but not yet arrived at the *beatific vision can be helped by the prayers of those who are still alive. There is ample evidence of the practice in the inscriptions of the *catacombs, in the early liturgies, and in the writings of the Fathers. Prayer is not offered for the saints, because they are believed to be already in possession of beatitude; nor, it is held, can the damned be benefited by our prayers, though who they are is known to God alone. The Reformers after a time denounced prayer for the dead, partly on the ground that it was not ordered in the Bible (2 Macc. 12: 40–5 was dismissed, since the *Apocrypha no longer ranked as Scripture), and partly through their rejection of the doctrine of *purgatory. In the C of E express prayers for the dead disappeared from the BCP in 1552, but they have been widely used since the mid-19th cent.

DEAD SEA, The. The inland sea to the SE. of Palestine into which the R. *Jordan flows.

DEAD SEA SCROLLS. A popular name for the remains of a once considerable collection of Hebrew and Aramaic MSS., discovered in caves in the neighbourhood of Qumran, at the NW. end of the *Dead Sea, in 1947 and the years following. Nearly all Books of the canonical OT are represented, besides other works, some not previously known. They include: (1) a series of OT commentaries which interpret the Biblical text as prophecy fulfilled in the commentators' own times; (2) a collection of 'Psalms of Thanksgiving', similar to the Biblical Psalms; (3) a strange, possibly apocalyptic, work, to which the name 'The War of the Sons of Light against the Sons of Darkness' has been given; (4) a handbook variously called 'The Manual of Discipline' or 'The Sectarian Document', containing the rules governing the life of the religious community to which the compiler belonged; and (5) the so-called 'Damascus Fragments' or 'Zadokite Documents', similar in character to the

Manual, and otherwise known from an earlier discovery in the *geniza of the synagogue at Cairo in 1896.

The Scrolls belonged to the library of a Jewish community centred at Qumran about the beginning of the Christian era. It is generally agreed that they are to be dated within the limits 20 B.C. and A.D. 70. They are important for our knowledge of the history of the OT text and for their evidence of Jewish life and thought at the time.

DEADLY SINS. See *Seven Deadly Sins*.

DE ALEATORIBUS (or Adversus Aleatores). A short homily denouncing dice-playing and all games of chance. Its authorship is much disputed. It was at one time believed to be the work of *Cyprian (d. 258).

DEAN. The title of various officials. (1) The dean of a *cathedral controls its services and, with the *chapter, supervises its fabric and property. (2) The heads of the *collegiate churches of *Westminster and other *peculiars which are governed by deans and chapters. (3) In the RC Church the Dean (the head) of the *Sacred College is a *Cardinal Bishop elected by the *suburbicarian cardinals from among their number. (4) The *Lutheran superintendent and the *Calvinist overseer are sometimes styled dean. See also *Rural Dean* and the following entry.

DEAN OF THE ARCHES. The lay judge in the Court of *Arches.

DEARMER, PERCY (1867–1936), writer on religious music and ceremonial. He tried to popularize the adaptation of medieval English ceremonial to the Prayer Book rite, setting out his ideas in *The Parson's Handbook* (1899) and putting them into practice as Vicar of St. Mary's, Primrose Hill (1901–15). From 1916 to 1936 he was professor of ecclesiastical art at *King's College, London. He was co-editor of the *English Hymnal* (1906) and *Songs of Praise* (1925).

'DEATH OF GOD' THEOLOGY. See *God* (last paragraph).

DE AUXILIIS. The 'Congregatio de Auxiliis' was appointed by *Clement VIII in 1597 to deal with the contemporary controversy

on *grace. Both Clement and *Paul V declined to ratify its condemnation of the work of L. de *Molina.

DECADE. A division of the *Rosary, so called because it consists of ten *Hail Marys, which are preceded by the *Lord's Prayer and followed by the *Gloria Patri.

DECALOGUE, The. An alternative name for the Ten *Commandments (q.v.).

DECANI (Lat., '[the place] of the dean'). As the dean's stall is on the south side of the cathedral, the term is used to indicate those who in antiphonal singing sit on that side of the choir.

DE CANTILUPE, St. THOMAS and WALTER. See *Cantilupe, St. Thomas de* and *Walter de*.

DECAPOLIS. A region consisting of ten allied cities E. of the *Jordan in N. Palestine.

DE CAUSSADE, J. P. See *Caussade, J. P. de*.

DECEASED WIFE'S SISTER'S MARRIAGE ACT (1907). The Act allows the marriage of a widower with his wife's sister. Its provisions, and those of the corresponding Deceased Brother's Widow's Marriage Act (1921), were in conflict with the ecclesiastical law of the C of E until the *Canons were amended in 1946.

DECIUS (d. 251), Roman Emperor from 249. He undertook the first systematic persecution of Christians, beginning with the execution of *Fabian, Bp. of Rome, in 250. All citizens were required to furnish proof of having offered sacrifice to the Emperor. The defections raised in an acute form the question whether penance was possible for the *lapsed. See also *Libellatici*.

DECLARATION AGAINST TRANSUBSTANTIATION. Under the *Test Act of 1673 the declaration was imposed on all persons holding civil or military office.

DECLARATION OF ASSENT. See *Assent, Declaration of*.

DECLARATION OF THE SOVEREIGN,

also known as the 'Royal Declaration'. The oath repudiating the RC faith which Parliament imposed on William and Mary when they came to the throne. It has been taken by all subsequent British sovereigns, though its form was simplified in 1910.

DECLARATIONS OF INDULGENCE, The. Four proclamations issued by *Charles II and *James II on religious *toleration. The Worcester House Declaration of 1660 granted a temporary indulgence in ceremonial matters. Of the Declarations of Indulgence properly so called, the first, in 1662, announced Charles II's intention of placing before Parliament a bill allowing him more power to suspend the operation of the penal laws against dissenters from the C of E. The other three, in 1672, 1687, and 1688, suspended the operation of these laws by virtue of the royal prerogative. See also *James II*.

DECLARATORY ACTS. In the (Presbyterian) Church of *Scotland, two Acts relieving ministers from their obligation to subscribe to every item of the subordinate standards of faith, esp. of the *Westminster Confession. That of the *United Presbyterian Church was passed in 1879; that of the *Free Church of Scotland in 1892.

DECOLLATION OF ST. JOHN THE BAPTIST, The. The feast celebrated on 29 Aug. in commemoration of the martyrdom of St. *John the Baptist as related in Mt. 14: 3–12 and Mk. 6: 14–30.

DE CONDREN, C. See *Condren, C. de*.

DECRETALS. Papal letters, strictly those in response to a question. They have the force of law within the Pope's jurisdiction. The first decretal was that sent in 385 by *Siricius to Himerius, Bp. of Tarragona. The earliest influential collection was made by *Dionysius Exiguus (*c.* 520). See also *False Decretals*.

DECRETUM GELASIANUM. An early Latin document which contains, among other things, a list of Books of the Bible. In the MSS. it is most frequently attributed to Pope *Gelasius (492–6); it prob. dates from the 6th cent.

DEDICATION, The Jewish Feast of the. The feast instituted by *Judas Maccabaeus in 165 B.C. to commemorate the purification of

the *Temple after its defilement by *Antiochus Epiphanes. The lighting of lamps was a feature of the feast, which was sometimes known as the 'Feast of the Lights'.

DEDICATION OF CHURCHES. The earliest recorded instance of the dedication of a Christian church is that of the cathedral at Tyre in 314. For the solemn consecration of permanent churches, an elaborate ritual developed, consisting of six main parts, followed by the Eucharist. Acc. to the 1977 RC Ordo the dedication takes place within the framework of the Mass and includes anointing the altar and walls of the church with *chrism. For temporary churches a simpler ceremony of blessing is used.

The Feast of the Dedication is the annual celebration of the day of the dedication of the church. A feast of the dedication of the Church of the *Holy Sepulchre is described by *Etheria. In 1536 the English *Convocations ordered that the Feast of Dedication should be kept on the first Sunday in October; this practice is commonly followed in the C of E when the date of consecration is not known.

DE DOMINIS, MARCO ANTONIO (1566–1624), Abp. of Spalato from 1602 to 1616. Political and personal difficulties led him to resign his see. He was welcomed in England by *James I and made Dean of *Windsor in 1617. In his *De Republica Ecclesiastica* he attacked the monarchical government of Rome and defended national Churches. He left England in 1622, was reconciled with Rome, and then wrote against the C of E.

DEFENDER OF THE FAITH. A title conferred on *Henry VIII by *Leo X in 1521 in recognition of his treatise defending the doctrine of the *seven sacraments. In 1544 Parliament recognized the style as an official title of the English monarch; it has been borne by all subsequent sovereigns.

DEFENDER OF THE MATRIMONIAL TIE. A person whose duty is to uphold the marriage tie when cases of disputed validity or nullity are heard in RC ecclesiastical courts. The office dates from 1741.

DEFENSOR (late 7th cent.), monk of Ligugé, near Poitiers. He compiled the *Liber Scintillarum*, an ascetic work which had a wide circulation in the Middle Ages; it was attributed to *Bede and others.

DE FIDE. In Catholic theology, a proposition is said to be *de fide* (or *de fide catholica*) if it has been expressly declared and defined by the Church to be true.

DE FOUCAULD, CHARLES EUGÈNE (1858–1916), French explorer and hermit. After some time in the French army, he explored Morocco. In 1890 he entered a *Trappist monastery, but, desiring greater solitude and austerity, he left the order in 1897. He was ordained priest in 1901; soon afterwards he went to Algeria, where he lived as a hermit, first at Beni Abbès and then in the remote Hoggar Mountains and at Tamanrasset. He was assassinated.

He composed rules for communities of 'Little Brothers' and 'Little Sisters', but no companions joined him. In 1933 René Voillaume and four other priests settled on the edge of the Sahara and adopted a monastic way of life based on his first rule. Since 1945 small communities have been established in most parts of the world. While maintaining a contemplative element in their lives, the 'Little Brothers of Jesus' seek to conform to the economic and social milieu in which they live; they mostly earn their living in factories, farms, &c., exercising their influence by sharing the life of those around them. With similar aims, the Little Sisters of the Sacred Heart were founded near Montpellier in 1933, the Little Sisters of Jesus at Touggourt in the Sahara in 1939, to be followed by the Little Brothers and Little Sisters of the Gospel in 1958 and 1965 respectively.

DE GROOT, H. See *Grotius, H.*

DE HAERETICO COMBURENDO (1401). An English statute under which those found guilty of heresy in an ecclesiastical court were to be burnt by the secular authority. It was intended to repress *Lollardy.

DE HAURANNE, DUVERGIER. See *Saint-Cyran, Abbé de.*

DEINIOL, St. (d. *c.* 584), Welsh saint. He was prob. the founder of the monastery of *Bangor Iscoed and is alleged to have been consecrated first Bp. of Bangor by St. *Dubricius in 516. St. Deiniol's Library, Hawarden, is a residential library, founded by W.

E. *Gladstone in 1896.

DEISM. A system of natural religion which was developed in England in the late 17th and 18th cents. The classic exposition is J. *Toland's *Christianity not Mysterious* (1696). At first there were various classes of Deists, from those who held that God was the Creator, with no further interest in the world, to those who accepted all the truths of natural religion, including belief in a world to come, but rejected revelation. Gradually all belief in Divine Providence and in rewards and punishments was abandoned, and the chief mark of later Deism was belief in a Creator God whose further intervention in His creation was rejected as derogatory to His omnipotence and unchangeableness. Never widely accepted in England, Deism exercised great influence in France and Germany.

DEISSMANN, ADOLF (1866–1937), German Protestant theologian. He did distinguished pioneer work in Biblical philology, making full use of material from the recently discovered *papyri.

DE LAGARDE, P. A. See *Lagarde, P. A. de.*

DE LA TAILLE, MAURICE (1872–1933), French *Jesuit theologian. His main work, *Mysterium Fidei* (1921), is an original and comprehensive study of the Mass. He argues that there is only one real immolation, that on Calvary, to which the *Last Supper looks forward and the Mass looks back.

DELEGATES, Court of. In England the court set up in 1534 to deal with appeals from the Archbishops' courts, which had hitherto gone to Rome. It was abolished in 1832, and in 1833 its place was taken by the *Judicial Committee of the Privy Council.

DELEHAYE, HIPPOLYTE (1859–1941), *Bollandist. He was a major contributor to the *Acta Sanctorum* and joint editor of several volumes. He catalogued scattered hagiographical MSS. (*Bibliotheca Hagiographica Graeca*, 1895), as well as those of the Bibliothèque Nationale in Paris and the *Vatican. His books were all based on wide erudition, but some were directed to a nonspecialist public.

DE LISLE, AMBROSE LISLE MARCH PHILLIPPS (1809–78), English writer. He became a RC in 1824. He was active in furthering reunion between the C of E and Rome; in 1857 he took part in founding the 'Association for Promoting the Union of Christendom' (*A.P.U.C.), withdrawing, however, when it was condemned by Rome in 1864.

DELITZSCH, FRANZ JULIUS (1813–1890), German OT scholar and orientalist. Of pietist *Lutheran background and Jewish descent, he sought to further the conversion of Jews. He established at Leipzig an Institutum Judaicum (1886; later Institutum Delitzschianum and translated the NT into Hebrew (1877). He also published a long series of commentaries on the OT and wrote extensively on Rabbinic subjects.

DELITZSCH, FRIEDRICH (1850–1922), Assyriologist, son of F. J. *Delitzsch. His most celebrated book was his *Babel und Bibel* (1902–3; Eng. tr., 1903), which claimed that several OT narratives were of Babylonian origin and that Judaism was essentially dependent on Babylonian culture.

DELLA ROBBIA, LUCA (1399–1482) and ANDREA (1431–1528), Florentine artists. Luca's work includes the bronze sacristy door of the cathedral at Florence. This is divided into panels representing the BVM, St. *John the Baptist, and other saints. That of his nephew Andrea includes the Madonna adoring the Child, now in the National Museum at Florence.

DE LUGO, J. See *Lugo, J. de.*

DE MAISTRE, JOSEPH (1753–1821), French *Ultramontane writer. He was influenced by 18th-cent. rationalism, but after the 1789 Revolution he became a reactionary. In his main work, *Du pape* (1819), he argued that the only true basis of society lay in authority, which took the double form of spiritual authority vested in the Papacy and temporal authority in human kings. His ideas contributed to the overthrow of *Gallicanism.

DE MARCA, P. See *Marca, P. de.*

DEMETRIUS, St. (d. 231/2), Bp. of *Alexandria from 189. He appointed

*Origen head of the Catechetical School c. 203. Later, when Origen preached in Palestine while still a layman, Demetrius recalled him and censured his conduct. In 231 he banished him for having been ordained priest irregularly at *Caesarea and soon afterwards deprived him of the priesthood.

DEMIURGE. The English form of a Gk. word meaning 'craftsman', used of the Divine Being by *Plato in his account of the formation of the visible world, and so by Christian writers of God as the Creator of all things. The *Gnostics used the word disparagingly of the inferior deity to whom they ascribed the origin of the material universe, distinguishing him from the supreme God.

DEMYTHOLOGIZATION. A term used by R. *Bultmann for a method of interpreting the Bible in the categories of modern man by eliminating the mythological forms (e.g. belief in a three-storied universe) which were taken for granted by the Biblical writers.

DENIFLE, HEINRICH SEUSE (1844–1905), *Dominican Church historian. In 1880 he was called to Rome as associate to the General of the Order. His writings include his monumental *Chartularium Universitatis Parisiensis* (in conjunction with A. Chatelain, 1889–97), works on the 14th-cent. mystics, Meister *Eckhart, J. *Tauler, and H. *Suso, and an unfinished work on M. *Luther.

DENIS. See *Dionysius.*

DENISON, GEORGE ANTHONY (1805–96), Archdeacon of Taunton from 1851. Between 1854 and 1858 he was unsuccessfully prosecuted in the civil courts for teaching the doctrine of the *Real Presence in the *Eucharist.

DENMARK, Christianity in. Christianity gained a firm footing in the 9th cent., when the Danish chief, Harold, was baptized on a visit to the Frankish king *Louis the Pious, and on his return brought with him St. *Anskar. In the 11th cent. Christianity became generally accepted. The Reformation in Denmark took place between 1520 and 1540. A *Lutheran Creed was adopted in 1530 and in 1537 J. *Bugenhagen set up a

Lutheran episcopacy and introduced a new liturgy. A revival of orthodox Lutheranism in the 19th cent. was largely due to N. F. S. *Grundtvig. By laws of 1849 and 1852, which granted complete religious liberty, the Evangelical Lutheran Church was disestablished, though it continues to receive State support.

DENNEY, JAMES (1856–1917), Scottish *Free Church theologian. He held high office in the *United Free Church and took a leading part in the movement for reunion with the Established Church of *Scotland. Doctrinally he moved from a liberal to an evangelical position.

DE NOAILLES, LOUIS ANTOINE (1651–1729), Abp. of *Paris from 1695. He was made a cardinal in 1700 and head of the *Sorbonne in 1710. He was a devoted pastor and an ardent reformer. His commendation (1695) of P. *Quesnel's *Réflexions morales* and his disapproval of *Probabilism led to his being suspected of *Jansenism, and for some time he opposed the bull '*Unigenitus' (1713).

DE NOBILI, ROBERT (1577–1656), *Jesuit missionary. He was sent to *India in 1604. He adopted the way of life of the Indians whom he sought to convert; his methods aroused opposition, but it is estimated that his converts numbered some 100,000.

DENYS. See *Dionysius*.

DEO GRATIAS (Lat., 'Thanks be to God'). A liturgical formula in constant use in the services of the W. Church. During the *Donatist controversy it was a mark of orthodoxy as contrasted with the 'Deo laudes' used by the schismatics.

DEOSCULATORIUM. Another name for the *Pax Brede.

DEPRECATIO GELASII (Lat., 'Intercession of Gelasius'). A Latin litany for the Church universal. The ascription to Pope *Gelasius (492–6) is now generally accepted. He appears to have introduced it into the Roman Mass at the place where the *Kyrie became established.

DE PROFUNDIS (Lat., 'Out of the deep').

Ps. 130, so called from its opening words. It is traditionally used in the W. on behalf of the dead.

DE RANCÉ, A. J. Le B. See *Rancé, A. J. Le B. de*.

DER BALYZEH FRAGMENTS. A few incomplete pages of a Greek *papyrus codex discovered at Der Balyzeh in Upper Egypt in 1907. They contain liturgical prayers and a (*c.* 6th-cent.) Creed. The prayers, which have been variously dated, show the existence of an *Epiclesis before the Words of *Institution.

DE' RICCI, S. See *Ricci, S. de'*.

DE ROSSI, GIOVANNI BATTISTA (1822–94), archaeologist. He devoted his life to the study and excavation of the Roman *catacombs. He published a number of important books, mostly on the archaeology of Rome.

DE SACRAMENTIS. A short liturgical treatise, almost certainly the work of St. *Ambrose (d. 397). Addressed to the newly baptized, it treats of *Baptism, *Confirmation, and the *Eucharist. It is the earliest witness to the Roman *Canon of the Mass in substantially its traditional form.

DESCARTES, RENÉ (1596–1650), French philosopher and scientist. In 1629 he settled in Holland, where he wrote his main works. His significance as a philosopher lies chiefly in his originality of method. He based philosophical reasoning upon the principles and methods of mathematics, thereby refusing (as he believed) to make any initial metaphysical assumptions. The beginning of his philosophy was his own self-consciousness — 'Cogito, ergo sum'. He then turned to the ideas of his own mind. The first 'clear and distinct idea' which a thinking ego finds outside itself is the idea of God, and this idea is unaccountable except on the assumption that God exists; the truth of our other ideas is guaranteed in turn by God's existence and goodness (implied in the conception of a perfect being).

DESCENT OF CHRIST INTO HELL, The. Most Christians believe that this article in the Creed refers to the Lord's visit after His death to the realm of existence in which the souls of pre-Christian people waited for the message of the Gospel. It first occurs in 4th-cent. *Arian formularies, from which it spread in the W. and found its way into the *Apostles' Creed.

DESERT FATHERS. See *Monasticism*.

DETERMINISM. A name, popularized esp. by J. S. Mill, for systems of philosophy which hold that the entire universe, including all human activity, is subject to a rigid law of cause and effect, leaving no room for the exercise of free will.

DEUSDEDIT, St. (before consecration known as **Frithonas**) (d. 664), Abp. of *Canterbury from 655. He was the first Anglo-Saxon to hold this position.

DEUTEROCANONICAL BOOKS, The. Another name for the *Apocrypha (q.v.).

DEUTERO-ISAIAH. The name commonly given to the unknown author of the later chapters of Is. Older critics, believing Is. 40–66 to be a unity, applied the term to the author of all these chapters. It is now commonly restricted to the author of chs. 40–55, which date from 549–538 B.C. See also *Trito-Isaiah*.

DEUTERONOMIC HISTORY, The. A name given by M. *Noth and others to the Books Deut.–2 Kgs., all of which appear to have been compiled on the same editorial principle, i.e. originally independent units of material have been assembled together and set in a framework by an editor or editors who believed that obedience to the Divine commands led to success and disobedience to disaster.

DEUTERONOMY, Book of. The last Book of the *Pentateuch. It contains *Moses' final utterances, consisting essentially of seven mainly legislative and hortatory addresses (including the Ten *Commandments); it ends with an account of his death.

The distinctive style and diction of Deut. mark it off from the rest of the Pentateuchal Books. Acc. to the traditional view it was written by Moses, but most modern critics assign it in its present form to a much later date, mostly to the 7th cent. B.C.; it certainly embodies earlier tradition.

DEUTSCHE CHRISTEN. See *German-Christians*.

DEUTSCHE THEOLOGIE. The vernacular title of *Theologia Germanica* (q.v.).

DEUTSCHER ORDEN. See *Teutonic Order*.

DE VEUSTER, J. See *Damien, Father*.

DEVIL. In theological terminology the chief of the fallen angels. In the narrative of the *Fall (Gen. 3) the serpent which seduces *Eve is traditionally considered an embodiment of the devil, and in the Book of Job Satan acts as a tempter and tormentor. In the NT the devil tempts the Lord at the beginning of His ministry (see *Temptation of Christ*), and Christ shows his powerlessness against those who resist him. Satan also wanted the disciples, esp. St. *Peter (Lk. 22: 31–2). At the Last Judgement he and those who belong to him will depart into eternal fire (Mt. 25: 41). An account of the angels' fall is given in Rev. 12: 7–9.

Most of the Fathers held that the fall of the angels was caused by their envy of men, though others attributed it to pride. In the Middle Ages there was much speculation on the subject. The *Dominicans held that the initial sin of the devil consisted in a desire for a natural beatitude obtained by his own power, and that the fall of the other angels was caused by their assent to this sin. The *Franciscans taught that the devils committed various sins before becoming obstinate in evil, that Lucifer, their chief, desired equality with God, and that his sin consisted in inordinate love of his own excellence. Since the 16th cent. the traditional teaching has been accepted by most Christians, but there has been a reaction against speculative elaboration.

DEVIL'S ADVOCATE, The. See *Promotor Fidei*.

DEVOTIO MODERNA (Lat., 'Modern Devotion'). A revival of spiritual life which originated in Holland at the end of the 14th cent. It stressed the inner life of the individual and encouraged methodical meditation. Among the common people it made its way through associations of secular priests and lay people, called '*Brethren of the Common Life'; among the religious the *Windesheim Canons were its chief representatives.

DEVOUT LIFE, Introduction to the (1609). The celebrated treatise on the spiritual life by St. *Francis de Sales. It was addressed in the first instance to those living in the secular atmosphere of the French royal court, but its teaching is of general application.

DE WETTE, WILHELM MARTIN LEBERECHT (1780–1849), German theologian. His radical rationalism led to his being deprived of his professorship at Berlin; from 1822 he was professor at Basle. In his later years he became more conservative, but his doubts about the Biblical miracles and his reduction of the stories of the Birth, Resurrection, and Ascension of Christ to myths caused offence.

D'HULST, MAURICE (1841–96), French scholar and priest. He played a major part in founding the Catholic University of *Paris and in 1890 he became rector of the newly constituted *Institut Catholique. At first he associated with many who later became *Modernists.

DIACONICON. The area to the south of the sanctuary in a Byzantine church, so called because the *deacons have charge of it. The sacred vessels, vestments, and service-books are kept here.

DIADOCHUS (5th cent.), Bp. of Photike after 451. He wrote (in Greek) 100 'Capita Gnostica' on the means of attaining spiritual perfection; they enjoyed great popularity. Various other works have been attributed to him with less certainty.

DIALECTICAL THEOLOGY. A name applied to the theological principles of K. *Barth and his school, on the ground that it finds the truth in a dialectic apprehension of God. Rejecting the liberal tradition in modern theology, Barth sought to return to the basic tenets of the Reformers, esp. J. *Calvin; his teaching spread rapidly, esp. on the Continent of Europe.

DIAMPER, Synod of (1599). A synod of *Malabar Christians some 12 miles south of Calcutta which brought into being the Malabar *Uniat Church. *Nestorianism was renounced and complete submission to Rome imposed, though the Syriac liturgy was retained.

DIASPORA, Jewish. The Dispersion of the Jews began with the Assyrian and Babylonian deportations (722 and 597 B.C.). Later it spread throughout the Roman Empire. The Jews of the Dispersion remained in close touch with their home country, paying the *Temple taxes and keeping their religion and the restrictions of the Law. The Jewish synagogues in Asia Minor and Greece were the first scenes of Christian preaching.

DIATESSARON. The edition of the four Gospels in a continuous narrative, compiled by *Tatian c. 150–60. It circulated widely in Syriac-speaking countries, where it became the standard text until it gave way to the four separate Gospels in the 5th cent. Its original language was prob. Syriac or Greek.

DIBELIUS, MARTIN (1883–1947), German NT scholar. He was a pioneer in the method of *Form Criticism. He laid great emphasis on preaching as a medium of transmission of the Lord's words; he was generally more conservative in his attitude to the Gospel traditions than most Form Critics. He supported the *Ecumenical Movement and was a leader of the *Faith and Order Commission.

DIBELIUS, OTTO (1880–1967), Bp. of Berlin. The cousin of M. *Dibelius, he was put under restraint during much of the Nazi period because of his support of the *Confessing Church. In 1945 he became Bp. of Berlin and in 1949 Presiding Bishop of the *Evangelical Church in Germany.

DIDACHE (the Gk. word for 'teaching'). The elements in primitive Christian apologetic of an instructional kind, as contrasted with *kerygma or 'preaching'.

DIDACHE, The. A short Christian manual on morals and Church practice. The ecclesiastical organization described is undeveloped. Baptism is to be by *immersion if possible, and two Eucharistic prayers, of an unusual and primitive kind, are given. It is the earliest of a series of 'Church Orders', but the author, date, and place of origin are unknown. Many have assigned it to the first cent., though English-speaking scholars have tended to put it later.

DIDASCALIA APOSTOLORUM, an early 'Church Order', professedly 'the Catholic Teaching of the Twelve Apostles'. It is addressed to readers in various states of life and deals with miscellaneous subjects, such as penance, liturgical worship, and behaviour during persecution, but the arrangement is disorderly. It is esp. directed against Christians who regard the Jewish ceremonial law as still binding. It seems to have been composed in N. Syria in the 3rd cent. Written in Greek, it survives entire only in a Syriac version.

DIDEROT, DENIS (1713–84), French *encyclopaedist. A request from a bookseller for a translation of Chambers's *Cyclopaedia* suggested to Diderot the idea of a new encyclopaedia; the work occupied most of his life. The first volume appeared in 1751; its advocacy of toleration and democracy was resented by the Church and the work was formally suppressed in 1759. It continued to be issued clandestinely and was completed in 1780. Among the articles which Diderot wrote were those on Christianity, Faith, Liberty, and Providence.

DIDYMUS. An alternative name for the Apostle St. *Thomas.

DIDYMUS THE BLIND (*c.* 313–98), theologian. Blind from infancy, he was head of the *Catechetical School at *Alexandria. His writings 'On the Holy Spirit', 'On the Trinity', 'Against the Manichaeans', and fragments of exegesis have long been known. The discovery in 1941 of a group of papyrus codices near Toura, south of Cairo, revealed further Biblical commentaries. In Trinitarian theology Didymus was a staunch *Nicene, but he was condemned as an *Origenist at the Council of *Constantinople in 553.

DIES IRAE (Lat., 'Day of Wrath'), the opening words and hence the name of the *sequence in the Mass for the Dead in the W. Church. Its author was almost certainly a 13th-cent. *Franciscan. Since 1969 its use has been optional.

DIETRICH OF NIEHEIM (or of 'Niem') (*c.* 1340–1418), papal notary. He took a prominent part in the efforts to end the *Great Schism. At the Council of *Constance he renounced *John XXIII and both

there and in his writings upheld the *Conciliar Theory. His historical works, though one-sided, are a valuable source for contemporary events.

DIGAMY. In the early Church, those who married again after the death of their first spouse were regarded with disfavour. The Council of *Nicaea (325) insisted that they should not be excluded from Christian fellowship. The E. Church has always been more severe in the matter than the W., and even now the nuptial blessing is not given in the same form as for a first marriage.

DIGGERS. See *Fossors*.

DIGGERS (17th cent.), a section of the *Levellers. Believing that Christian principles required a communistic mode of life and the cultivation of crown property and common land, they began digging up waste land in 1649. The movement soon collapsed.

DIKIRION, TRIKIRION. Candles held in candlesticks with two or three branches respectively, used by E. bishops when giving the blessing.

DILLMANN, CHRISTIAN FRIEDRICH AUGUST (1823–94), German Biblical scholar and orientalist. To him more than anyone else is due the revival of Ethiopic studies in the 19th cent. He produced an Ethiopic grammar and lexicon and editions of Ethiopic texts.

DILTHEY, WILHELM (1833–1911), German philosopher. He was the virtual creator of the philosophy of history in its modern form. He stressed the fundamental differences between the methods of the 'Human Sciences', employed in the study of culture, art, religion, &c., and those adopted in the Natural Sciences. He was, however, critical of the possibility of a systematic sociology, holding that the spiritual life was too complicated to be comprehended in formulas. His own studies in religion were esp. directed to it as an element in human culture.

DIOCESE. In ecclesiastical usage, the territorial unit of administration in the Church. In the W. it is governed by a *bishop, with the assistance of the inferior clergy, and is usually divided into *parishes. Dioceses are commonly associated to form a province, over which one of the diocesan bishops presides, with varying powers of intervention in the affairs of other dioceses. In the E. Church the word denotes the area controlled by a *patriarch.

DIOCLETIAN. VALERIUS DIOCLE-TIANUS (245–313), Roman Emperor 284–305. He was proclaimed Emperor by the Army. He created an absolute monarchy, centring all power in himself as a semi-Divine ruler. In 286 he associated Maximian in government as co-Augustus, taking the Eastern Empire himself and giving Maximian the West. He further divided the Empire by the creation of two 'Caesars' in 293. In 305 he abdicated, compelling Maximian to take a like step.

For most of his reign Christians seem to have enjoyed tranquillity. In 303 the Great *Persecution broke out. Edicts inflicted imprisonment, torture, and sometimes death, first on the clergy and then on the laity. There were many martyrs. The collapse of the persecution was due to *Constantine's victory at the *Milvian Bridge in 312.

DIOCLETIANIC ERA. The reckoning of time from the year of *Diocletian's accession (A.D. 284). It is also known as the 'Era of the Martyrs'.

DIODORE (d. *c*. 390), Bp. of Tarsus from 378. He had combated *Arianism in *Antioch and opposed *Julian the Apostate. In 381 he was named by *Theodosius I one of the bishops communion with whom was a test of orthodoxy. He followed the *Antiochene tradition in theology, insisting on literal and historical exegesis and, against *Apollinarius, on the complete humanity of Christ. Only fragments of his writings survive.

DIOGNETUS, The Epistle to. A letter in Greek written by an unknown Christian to an otherwise unknown inquirer. It prob. dates from the 2nd or 3rd cent. The author explains why paganism and Judaism cannot be tolerated, describes Christians as the soul of the world, and insists that Christianity is the unique revelation of God.

DIONYSIUS (1) THE AREOPAGITE. His conversion by St. *Paul at *Athens is recorded in Acts 17: 34. Confusion was caused by attempts to identify with him Dionysius (3) and (6) below.

DIONYSIUS (2) (*c*. 170), Bp. of *Corinth. Several of his letters are preserved by *Eusebius.

DIONYSIUS (3) St., of Paris (*c*. 250), also St. Denys, patron saint of France. Acc. to *Gregory of Tours (6th cent.), he was sent to convert Gaul and, after becoming Bp. of Paris, was martyred. In 626 his remains were translated to *St.-Denis. In a 9th-cent Life he was identified with Dionysius (1) the Areopagite and consequently believed to be the author of the Pseudo-Dionysian writings (6).

DIONYSIUS (4) The Great (d. *c*. 264), Bp. of *Alexandria from 247. He fled from the city during the *Decian persecution and was banished in that of Valerian (257). He took part in various important controversies. He decided to readmit to the Church those who had lapsed under persecution and, with Pope *Stephen, not to rebaptize heretics and schismatics. He attacked *Sabellianism but was accused of tritheism by Dionysius (5) of Rome.

DIONYSIUS (5) (d. 268), Bp. of Rome from 259. Little is known of him apart from his controversy on *Subordinationism with Dionysius (4) of Alexandria.

DIONYSIUS (6), the Pseudo-Areopagite (*c*. 500), mystical theologian. The name given to the author of a body of writings in Greek to which the *Monophysites appealed in 533, attributing them to Dionysius (1) of Athens. The author is now believed to have written *c*. 500, prob. in Syria. His extant writings are: the 'Celestial Hierarchy', the 'Ecclesiastical Hierarchy', the 'Divine Names', and 'Mystical Theology'.

The Pseudo-Dionysian writings aim at achieving a synthesis between Christian dogma and *Neoplatonist thought. Their leading idea is the intimate union between God and the soul, and the progressive deification of man. This is to be obtained by a process of 'unknowing', in which the soul leaves behind the perceptions of the senses as well as the reasoning of the intellect. The soul will then enter an obscurity in which it will be increasingly illuminated by the 'Ray of Divine Darkness' and brought ultimately to the knowledge of the ineffable Being that transcends affirmation and negation alike. There are three stages in the spiritual life by which this goal is reached: the purgative, the illuminative, and the unitive ways, a division which has become the groundwork of subsequent treatises on the mystical life. The supposed apostolic authority of the writings, added to their intrinsic merit, gave them a profound influence on medieval theology in both the E. and W., where they were known through the translations of John Scotus *Erigena.

DIONYSIUS (7) EXIGUUS, a Scythian monk who lived in Rome c. 500–50. When called upon to construct a new *Easter cycle, he abandoned the era of *Diocletian, and (wrongly) accepting 753 A.U.C. as the year of the Incarnation, introduced the system still in use. His corpus of *canon law was the first collection to gain wide influence.

DIONYSIUS (8) THE CARTHUSIAN (Denys van Leeuwen, Denys Ryckel) (1402–71), theologian and mystic. Besides commentaries on the Bible, the works of *Boethius, *Peter Lombard, *John Climacus, and *Dionysius (6), the Pseudo-Areopagite, he wrote on moral theology and ecclesiastical discipline. He was not an original thinker, but his works were popular.

DIOSCORUS (d. 454), Patr. of *Alexandria from 444. He supported *Eutyches and in 449 presided over the '*Latrocinium' at Ephesus, deposing *Flavian, Bp. of Constantinople. After the reversal of theological policy on the death of the Emp. *Theodosius in 450, Dioscorus was deposed and excommunicated at the Council of *Chalcedon (451) and banished by the civil authorities.

DIPPEL, JOHANN KONRAD (1673–1734), German *Pietist. The works written after he became a Pietist emphasized the alleged contrast between Christianity and the Church, between right living and right doctrine, and maintained that the development of Christianity from *Constantine onwards had been one of decline from the ideals of primitive times. The *Lutheran ecclesiastical authorities forbade him to issue further theological publications. He then turned to chemistry, inventing Prussian Blue, and alchemy.

DIPTYCHS. The lists of names of living and departed Christians for whom prayer is made in the Greek and Latin Eucharistic Liturgies. In early times the diptychs were recited publicly, and the inclusion or exclusion of a name was held to be a sign of communion or excommunication.

DIRECTORY OF CHURCH GOVERNMENT, The (1644). An English translation of a Book of Discipline compiled in Latin by W. *Travers c. 1586. It circulated in manuscript among the Elizabethan *Puritans and was issued in 1644 in the interests of the projected introduction of *Presbyterianism in England.

DIRGE. A traditional name for the Office of the Dead. It derives from the former antiphon, 'Dirige Domine Deus ...' (Ps. 5: 8). It was originally confined to the morning Office but came to include the *Vespers sung on the previous evening.

DIRIMENT IMPEDIMENT. In *canon law, a fact or circumstance relating to a person that makes him or her incapable of contracting a valid marriage. Such impediments include an already existing marriage, holy orders, *affinity, and *consanguinity; those not of Divine law may be dispensed by the ecclesiastical authorities.

DISCALCED (lit. 'unshod'). The term is applied to certain religious orders and congregations whose members wear sandals rather than shoes, e.g. the Discalced *Carmelites and *Passionists.

DISCIPLES, The. See *Apostle.*

DISCIPLES OF CHRIST. The religious body which originated in the U.S.A. in 1811 through the work of Alexander *Campbell (q.v.) as a group within *Presbyterianism and was organized as a separate religious body in 1827. They are variously known as 'Campbellites', 'Disciples of Christ', and 'Churches of Christ'. The Churches are congregationally organized, the Bible is the only basis of faith, and all credal formulas are rejected.

DISCIPLINA ARCANI (Lat., 'Discipline of the Secret'). The practice ascribed to the early Church of concealing certain theological doctrines and religious usages from *catechumens and pagans. It was prob.

adopted partly through the reticence necessary in an age of persecution, and partly through the natural human instinct to withdraw the most intimate and sacred elements of faith from outsiders; it was reflected in the custom of not admitting catechumens to the central part of the Eucharist.

DISCIPLINE. The word has several religious connotations: (1) the totality of ecclesiastical laws and customs relating to the religious and moral life of the Church; (2) a system of mortification, e.g. that involved in the religious life; (3) a scourge of knotted cords used as an instrument of penance; and (4) as a technical term the word is applied to the *Calvinist polity, which was built up on rigid principles. It is the duty of consistories, formed by elders and pastors, to fix penalties for neglect of religious duties, culminating in excommunication.

DISCIPLINE, Books of. The 'First Book of Discipline' (1560) was drawn up by J. *Knox and others as a plan for the ordering and maintenance of the new Scottish Church. Parts of it were obnoxious to the nobility and it remained a dead-letter.

The so-called 'Second Book of Discipline' (1578), chiefly the work of A. *Melville, was prepared as a manifesto of the stricter *Presbyterians against efforts to restore a modified episcopacy.

DISCUS. In the E. Church the plate on which the bread of the Eucharist is offered and consecrated.

DISMAS. The traditional name of the Good Thief (Lk. 23: 39-43) crucified with Christ.

DISPENSATIONS. Licences granted by ecclesiastical authority to do some otherwise canonically illegal act, or for the remittance of a penalty for so doing. By the end of the Middle Ages the dispensing power had become virtually a Papal prerogative, but in 1965 RC diocesan bishops were given ordinary power to dispense from the general law of the Church in particular cases, except in matters specially reserved for the Pope. Objects of dispensation include matters relating to *vows, *marriage, and *divorce. In England the dispensing power was transferred in a restricted form to the Abps. of *Canterbury in 1534; it has seldom been used.

DISPERSION, The. See *Diaspora*.

DISRUPTION, The (1843). The split in the Established Church of *Scotland when the *Free Church of Scotland was formed by the secession of 474 (out of 1203) ministers. The dispute centred in the demand of the laity for a voice in matters of patronage. See also *Ten Years' Conflict*.

DISSENTERS. In a religious context, those who separate themselves from the communion of the Established Church.

DISSENTERS' MARRIAGE ACT (1836). The Act allowed marriage to be solemnized in any registered place of religious worship or in a registrar's office.

DISSOLUTION OF THE MONASTERIES, The. Though there was some criticism of the monasteries in the later Middle Ages, it was in order to replenish his treasure and to facilitate the establishment of the royal supremacy that *Henry VIII abolished the whole system. The Act for the Dissolution of the Smaller Monasteries (1536) ordered the suppression of all religious houses with an annual value of less than £200; some 250 were involved. The Act for the Dissolution of the Greater Monasteries (1539) completed the process by vesting in the Crown all monasteries that had been or should be surrendered; the last house surrendered in 1540. Apart from the friars, the religious were pensioned. The bulk of the proceeds passed from the Crown to the Tudor nobility and gentry, though part was used to found six new dioceses.

DIURNAL. The service-book containing the '*Day Hours'.

DIVES (Lat., 'rich'). A word which has become a convenient, almost a proper, name for the unnamed rich man in the parable, Lk. 16: 19-31.

DIVINA COMMEDIA, La. The name commonly given to *Dante's poem describing his vision of the three realms of the world to come, *Inferno*, *Purgatorio*, and *Paradiso*. In his vision Dante travels from a dark forest on this side of the world down through Hell to Satan at the centre of the Earth and up the seven terraces of the mount of Purgatory, an island in the Antipodes opposite Jerusalem, to its summit, the Earthly Paradise, where *Adam and *Eve were created. So far *Virgil has been his guide, but now he meets Beatrice, who conducts him through the nine planetary and stellar spheres to the Empyrean, where St. *Bernard of Clairvaux takes her place. St. Bernard presents Dante to the BVM, at whose intercession the poet is granted a glimpse of the *Beatific Vision. The date, purpose, and detailed interpretation of the poem are widely disputed.

DIVINE PRAISES, The. A series of praises, beginning 'Blessed be God', commonly said in the vernacular after *Benediction of the Bl. Sacrament before the Host is replaced in the Tabernacle. The nucleus is thought to have been compiled *c*. 1779 by Louis Felici, S.J., to be used in reparation for blasphemy and profanity.

DIVINE RIGHT OF KINGS. The doctrine that a monarch in the hereditary line of succession has a divine and indefeasible right to his kingship and authority, and that for a subject to rebel against him is the worst of political crimes, and even a sin against God. The origin of the doctrine is linked with the contest between the medieval Emperors and the Papacy. In England it was strongly upheld under the Stuarts, but *James II's attack on the C of E eroded much of its support.

DIVINE SERVICE. Strictly the term would seem to denote the offices of *Mattins and *Evensong and not to include Holy Communion, but it is often used loosely for any form of religious service.

DIVINE WORSHIP, Congregation for. See *Rites, Congregation of Sacred*.

DIVINO AFFLATU (1911). The constitution of *Pius X which introduced reforms in the Divine Office and rules for celebrating Mass.

DIVORCE. The word is used both of a dissolution of the marriage bond and of legal separation. Since W. *canon law insists on the indissolubility of marriage, divorce in the first sense is not permitted in the RC Church and is contrary to the canons and formularies of the C of E. Popes have, however, claimed to dissolve unconsummated marriages. In the second sense W. canon law permits divorce for grave causes, esp. adultery. In the E. Church divorce is allowed on a number of grounds.

DIX, GREGORY (1901–52), Anglican Benedictine monk. He entered *Nashdom Abbey in 1926. In his later years he became one of the best-known figures in the C of E, owing his influence to his brilliance, unconventionality, and good humour as a controversialist. His most considerable work, *The Shape of the Liturgy* (1945), did much to revive and popularize liturgical studies in the C of E.

DOCETISM. In the early Church a tendency, rather than a formulated doctrine, which considered the humanity and sufferings of the earthly Christ as apparent rather than real. In some forms it held that Christ miraculously escaped the ignominy of death, e.g. by *Judas Iscariot or *Simon of Cyrene exchanging places with Him just before the Crucifixion.

DOCTORS, Scholastic. In later medieval times the outstanding Scholastic teachers and others were often given distinguishing epithets, e.g. *Doctor angelicus* (St. *Thomas Aquinas), *Doctor seraphicus* (St. *Bonaventure).

DOCTORS' COMMONS. An association of ecclesiastical lawyers founded in London in 1511. It served as a college of advocates for those practising in the ecclesiastical courts, and the judges in the Archbishops' courts were selected from its members. It was dissolved in 1857.

DOCTORS OF THE CHURCH. A title regularly given since the Middle Ages to certain Christian theologians of outstanding merit and acknowledged saintliness. Sts. *Gregory the Great, *Ambrose, *Augustine, and *Jerome were originally held to be the 'four doctors' *par excellence*; the list has been increased to over 30.

'DOCTRINE IN THE CHURCH OF ENGLAND' (1938). The Report of the Commission on Doctrine set up in 1922 by the Abps. of *Canterbury and *York. The first part deals with the doctrines of God and Redemption, the second with the Church and Sacraments. The third part, on *Eschatology, was added because of confusions arising from the current tendency to interpret literally the apocalyptic symbolism of the NT.

DOCTRINE OF THE FAITH, Congregation of the. See *Holy Office*.

DODD, CHARLES HAROLD (1884–1973), NT scholar. He held professorships at Manchester and Cambridge. His theory that Christ regarded the *Kingdom of God as having already arrived with His ministry ('realized eschatology') was widely discussed. He later argued that the traditions underlying St. *John's Gospel were of greater historical value than was generally allowed. From 1950 he was General Director of the NEB (see *Bible, English Versions*, 5); he played a major part in translating the NT.

DODDRIDGE, PHILIP (1702–51), Nonconformist divine and hymn-writer. In 1723 he became Minister at Kibworth, Leicestershire, and later he took charge of an Independent congregation at Northampton. In 1730 he was 'ordained a presbyter' by 8 ministers, of whom 5 were *Presbyterians. He laboured to obliterate party lines and unite the Nonconformists. His many hymns were largely modelled on those of I. *Watts; they include 'Hark the glad sound! the Saviour comes' and 'O God of Bethel, by Whose hand'.

DODWELL, HENRY (1641–1711), 'the elder', theologian. He defended the *Nonjuring bishops and in 1691 he was deprived of his office in Oxford for refusing to take the Oath of Allegiance. His many writings were learned, but cumbrous and often eccentric in judgement. His son, Henry Dodwell 'the younger' (d. 1784), was a *Deist.

DOGMA. In Christianity the term signifies a religious truth established by Divine Revelation and defined by the Church.

DOLD, ALBAN (1882–1960), *Benedictine scholar. He was professed at *Beuron in 1903. He devoted himself to the study of liturgical *palimpsests; he elaborated new techniques and developed a photographic process for reading difficult texts by fluorescence.

DOLLING, ROBERT WILLIAM RADCLYFFE, **'Father Dolling'** (1851–1902), *Anglo-Catholic missioner. In 1885 he was put in charge of St. Agatha's, Landport, the Winchester College Mission. Here he fought successfully against the evils of slum life. In 1896 opposition to his ceremonial by R. T. *Davidson, then Bp. of Winchester, led to his resignation. He became Vicar of St. Saviour's, Poplar.

DÖLLINGER, JOHANN JOSEPH IGNAZ VON (1799–1890), Bavarian Church historian. From 1826 until 1873 he was professor of Church history at Munich. At first he held strongly *Ultramontane views, but he gradually became distrustful of Roman influence. The *Letters of *Janus* (in conjunction with others, 1869) and *Letters of *Quirinus* (1869–70) revealed him as a formidable critic of the First *Vatican Council and of the doctrine of papal *infallibility. After refusing to accept the conciliar decisions, he was excommunicated in 1871. In his later years he largely identified himself with the *Old Catholic Churches and worked for reunion (see *Bonn Reunion Conferences*).

D.O.M., i.e. **Deo Optimo Maximo** (Lat., 'to God, the Best and Greatest'). Originally a pagan formula addressed to Jupiter, it came to be used with a Christian application over the doors of churches and on sepulchral monuments.

DOM (abbreviation of *Dominus*, 'Master'). A title given to professed monks of the *Benedictine and some other religious orders.

DOME OF THE ROCK, The. The Muslim shrine in *Jerusalem, built in the area of the Jewish *Temple. It dates from c. 800. The rock from which it takes its name is believed in *Islam to be that from which Muhammad ascended to heaven, and by Jews to be that on which *Abraham prepared to sacrifice *Isaac. The shrine is also known as the 'Mosque of Omar'.

DOMINE QUO VADIS? (Lat., 'Lord, whither goest thou?'). See *Quo Vadis?*

DOMINIC, St. (1170–1221), founder of the *Dominican Order. A Spaniard by birth, in 1199 he became a canon of Osma and was soon head of the community of *Augustinian canons. In 1203 he went with his bishop on a preaching tour against the *Albigensians in Languedoc. His efforts to win back the heretics during the *Crusade launched against them by *Innocent III met with little success. When the castle of Casseneuil was put at his disposal in 1214, his plan to found a special order for the conversion of the Albigensians took definite shape. Several volunteers joined him; they were approved by the Pope on condition that they followed one of the established rules. In 1216 Dominic went to Rome, where he obtained formal sanction from *Honorius III. His subsequent years were spent in establishing friaries and organizing the order.

DOMINICAN ORDER (Ordo Praedicatorum, O.P.). The Dominicans are also known as **Friars Preachers** or, in England, as ***Black Friars**. The order took definite shape under the direction of St. *Dominic (q.v.) at two General Chapters at Bologna in 1220 and 1221. At his suggestion it was decided that, like the *Franciscans, they should practise not only individual but corporate poverty and live by begging. The order spread rapidly. In the 14th and 15th cents. it was agitated by controversies, and there was much relaxation of discipline. In 1475 Pope *Sixtus IV revoked the law of corporate poverty and allowed the order to hold property.

The Dominicans are specifically devoted to preaching and study. There is a carefully organized teaching system culminating in the 'Studia Generalia', usually located in connection with a university. In the Middle Ages they supplied many leaders of European thought; the adaptation of *Aristotle to Christian philosophy was largely the work of Dominicans, esp. St. *Albertus Magnus and St. *Thomas Aquinas. The Popes also used them for preaching crusades and for staffing the *Inquisition. They followed the Portuguese and Spanish explorers as missionaries in both the E. and W. hemispheres. With the rise of the new orders in the *Counter-Reformation period they fell somewhat into the background.

The Dominicans have a Second Order of enclosed contemplative nuns; the majority of the Sisters of the Third Order live an active life without strict enclosure. There are also Dominican *Tertiaries.

DOMINIS, M. A. DE. See *De Dominis, M. A.*

DOMINUS AC REDEMPTOR (1773).

The brief of *Clement XIV which suppressed the *Jesuit Order.

DOMINUS VOBISCUM. A Latin liturgical salutation, meaning 'The Lord be with you', to which the response is *Et cum spiritu tuo*, 'And with your spirit'. Both are ancient.

DOMITIAN, TITUS FLAVIUS (A.D. 51–96), Roman Emperor from A.D. 81. He assumed despotic power and demanded that public worship be given him as *Dominus et Deus*. At the end of his reign *persecution of the Christians and Jews broke out.

DOMITILLA, FLAVIA (c. A.D. 100). A Roman matron of the Imperial family who became a Christian. Her husband, a cousin of *Domitian, was put to death and she was banished to the island of Pandateria, prob. in both cases for professing Christianity.

DONATION OF CONSTANTINE. A document fabricated in the 8th–9th cent. to strengthen the power of the Church and esp. of the see of Rome. In it the Emp. *Constantine purported to confer on Pope *Sylvester I (314–35) primacy over *Antioch, *Constantinople, *Alexandria, and *Jerusalem, and dominion over all Italy; the Pope was also made supreme judge of the clergy and was offered the Imperial crown (which he refused). Its authenticity was challenged and its falsity demonstrated in the 15th cent.

DONATISM. The Donatists were a schismatic body in the African Church. They refused to accept *Caecilian, Bp. of Carthage, on the ground that his consecrator had been a *traditor* in the *Diocletianic Persecution. The Numidian bishops consecrated Majorinus as a rival to Caecilian; he was succeeded by Donatus, from whom the schism is named. A commission under *Miltiades, Bp. of Rome, investigated the dispute in 313 and decided against the Donatists. The State employed coercion 316–21, and again early in the 5th cent. The schism nevertheless continued until the African Church was destroyed by the Arabs in the 7th–8th cent. The Donatists drew on African regional feeling, Numidian jealousy of Carthage, and economic unrest. Theologically they were rigorists and maintained that they alone formed the Church.

DONNE, JOHN (1571/2–1631), *metaphysical poet. In 1598 he became secretary to the Lord Keeper, Sir Thomas Egerton, but he was dismissed in 1602 because of his secret marriage to his master's niece. He then lived in poverty and dependence on the charity of friends. After repeated failure to find secular employment, he was ordained in 1615. In 1621 he became Dean of *St. Paul's.

Donne's secular poetry was mainly written in his youth; his religious poetry belongs mostly to his troubled middle years. He wrote both the famous 'Hymn to God the Father' and his *Devotions upon Emergent Occasions* (1624) during a serious illness in 1623. His sermons are masterpieces of the old formal style of preaching, but his great strength is as a moral theologian, preaching as a sinner who has found mercy to other sinners.

DOORKEEPER. The doorkeepers constituted the lowest of the *Minor Orders in the W. Church. They are mentioned in a letter of 251. Their functions were similar to those of a modern verger. In the RC Church the office was abolished in 1972.

DORCHESTER, Oxfordshire. In 635 St. *Oswald, King of Northumbria, and Cynegils, King of the West Saxons, concurred in establishing it as a see, with St *Birinus as bishop. About 1072–3 the see was transferred to *Lincoln. The abbey of *Augustinian canons, founded in 1140, was suppressed in 1536. The abbey church is now the parish church. In 1939 the bishopric was re-created, suffragan to *Oxford.

DORDRECHT, Synod of. See *Dort*.

DORMITION OF THE BVM, The. In the E. Church, the Feast of the Falling Asleep (*dormitio*) of the BVM, corresponding to the *Assumption in the W. It is observed on 15 August.

DORNER, ISAAK AUGUST (1809–84), German *Lutheran theologian. In theology he tried to interpret the *Kantian and post-Kantian systems in terms of the traditional Lutheran faith. The best-known of his writings was on the history of the doctrine of the Person of Christ.

DOROTHEUS, St. (6th cent.), ascetical writer. About 540 he founded a monastery near Gaza, of which he became *archimandrite. For its members he wrote a series of 'Instructions' on the ascetic life, though not all the 24 items in the standard edition are his work. He gave a high place to humility, even putting it before love.

DOROTHY, St., virgin and martyr, prob. in the persecution of *Diocletian (d. 313). Acc. to her legendary *Acta,* she was mocked on her way to execution by a young lawyer, Theophilus, who asked her to send him the fruits of the garden to which she was going; later an angel appeared with a basket of apples and roses, which she sent to Theophilus; he became a Christian and a martyr.

DORSAL, also **Dossal.** A piece of cloth which is sometimes hung at the back of an altar in place of a *reredos.

DORT, Synod of (1618–19). The assembly of the Dutch Reformed Church convened at Dort (Dordrecht) by the States-General to deal with the *Arminian controversy. It passed five articles asserting unconditional election, a limited atonement, the total depravity of man, the irresistibility of grace, and the final perseverance of the saints. It also confirmed the *Belgic Confession and the *Heidelberg Catechism. As a result some 200 Arminian clergy were deprived, and H. *Grotius was sentenced to perpetual imprisonment.

DORTER. A dormitory, esp. in a monastery.

DOSITHEUS (2nd cent.), Judaeo-*Gnostic. He came from Samaria and, acc. to *Origen, claimed to be the Messiah foretold in Deut. 18: 18. A small body of followers survived to the 10th cent. A short work entitled 'A Revelation by Dositheus' was discovered at *Nag Hammadi; it is not known whether it claims to be the work of this Dositheus or some otherwise unknown namesake.

DOSITHEUS (1641–1707), Patr. of *Jerusalem from 1669. He convened the 1672 Synod of Jerusalem (q.v.) and he was the main author of its decrees and confession. His patriarchate was marked by the inauguration of various monastic and financial reforms and by his vigorous defence of the Greeks against the Latins, e.g. in the dispute with the *Franciscans over their rights to the Holy Places. He also tried to extend the influence of Hellenism in Russia.

DOSTOIEVSKY, FEODOR MICHAELOVITCH (1821–81), Russian novelist. In his life-time he was known chiefly as a journalist; his more enduring works were the novels in which he penetrated the recesses of the human mind. They include (in Russian) *Crime and Punishment* (1865–6), *The Idiot* (1869), and *The Brothers Karamazov* (1880). The centre of his religious experience is the consciousness of salvation as the free gift of God to the weak and miserable and the refusal to admit any co-operation between God and man. The result is a complete absence from religion of reason and will, and the moral effort that flows from them. The characters in his novels live entirely by their emotions, of which the foremost is boundless and irrational compassion.

DOUAI, in Flanders, was the seat of several colleges set up for the benefit of RCs in exile under *Elizabeth I. That founded by W. *Allen in 1568 became an important seminary for the training of mission priests to work in England; its members were responsible for the *Douai–Reims Bible. The *Benedictine community of St. Gregory, begun at Douai in 1607, is now at *Downside Abbey, Somerset.

DOUAI–REIMS BIBLE. The English version of the Bible used by RCs until modern times. It was the work of members of the English College at *Douai. The NT was published in 1582 at Reims, whither the college had temporarily migrated; the OT was published at Douai in 1609. The translation was made from the *Vulgate and is very literal. Modern editions are based on the revision of R. *Challoner in 1749–50.

DOUBLE FEASTS. The name formerly given in the Roman *Missal and *Breviary to the more important feasts.

DOUBLE MONASTERY. A religious house for both men and women. The two sexes lived in separate but contiguous establishments, worshipped in distinct parts of a common church, and were united by a common superior. Such monasteries are first found in the E. in the last years of the Roman Empire. In the W. they were numerous in the Dark Ages but mostly disappeared in the 9th and 10th cents.

DOUBLE PROCESSION OF THE HOLY SPIRIT. The doctrine of the W. Church that the Holy Spirit proceeds from the Father and the Son. Against it E. theologians have urged that there must be a single Fount of Divinity in the Godhead; they hold that the Holy Spirit proceeds from the Father 'through the Son'. The question did not become a matter of controversy until the time of *Photius (864); it was one of the chief points of difficulty at the Council of *Florence. See also *Filioque*.

DOUKHOBORS. A Russian sect of uncertain origin. It seems to have arisen among the peasants in the district of Kharkov *c.* 1740. The Doukhobors came repeatedly into conflict with the Russian government, and most of them migrated to Cyprus or Canada. They believe in one God manifested in the human soul as memory (Father), reason (Son), and will (Holy Spirit); Jesus Christ is not God but a man possessing Divine reason in the highest degree; and the human soul is eternal and suffers *metempsychosis.

DOVE. The dove is used as a Christian symbol for peace and reconciliation, for the Holy Spirit, for the Church, and for the individual soul regenerated by baptism; it also denotes theological knowledge and certain Christian virtues. The 'Eucharistic Dove' is a hollow receptacle in the shape of a dove designed to contain the Blessed Sacrament.

DOWNSIDE ABBEY, near Bath. The *Benedictine community traces its origin to a small settlement of English monks at *Douai in 1607; this had a school for the education of English RC boys. Expelled from Douai in the French Revolution, the monks came to England; in 1814 they settled at Downside. The abbey is now a centre of RC life, with a scholarly tradition and a large school.

DOWSING, WILLIAM (?1596–?1679), *Puritan iconoclast. He was zealous in carrying out the 1643 order of Parliament for the destruction of ornaments in churches, working in Cambridgeshire and Suffolk.

DOXOLOGY. An ascription of glory to the

Persons of the Trinity. Besides the *Gloria in Excelsis* (the Greater Doxology) and the *Gloria Patri* (the Lesser Doxology), there are metrical forms appended to some hymns.

DRAGONNADES (1683–6). Persecutions of the *Huguenots, so named from the mounted troops ('dragoons') quartered on them with a view to forcing them to accept Catholicism.

DRAMA. In the first centuries of the Christian era, drama existed only in the form of *spectacula*, which were intimately connected with paganism and so necessarily incurred the hostility of the Church. These traditional pagan shows ended with the destruction of the Roman Empire. In the 10th cent. a new development is instanced by the edifying 'comedies' written by the Saxon nun *Hrosvit and by *Ethelwold's reference to the 'praiseworthy custom' of celebrating the death and resurrection of Christ by a representation, with mime and dialogue, performed in church during or after the liturgical rites. This liturgical drama developed into the *Mystery (or Miracle) Plays (q.v.). There was also a great development of secular drama in all parts of Christendom. Since most of the plays were at least ostensibly edifying, and the players were organized in ostensibly pious confraternities, the medieval Church had little reason to object. From the 16th cent. drama generally lost its ecclesiastical connection. The more puritanical of the Reformers tended to repudiate the stage altogether, but most Christians have acquiesced in the establishment of the drama as a normal part of social life. The traditional religious plays have survived in some places, e.g. *Oberammergau, and in modern times there has been a revival of religious drama in England, e.g. with such plays as T. S. *Eliot's *Murder in the Cathedral* (1935).

DREXELIUS, i.e. **Jeremias Drexel** (1581–1638), *Jesuit spiritual writer. His devotional works circulated among both Protestants and Catholics.

DRIVER, SAMUEL ROLLES (1846–1914), OT and Hebrew scholar. From 1883 he was Regius Professor of Hebrew in Oxford. His wide and exact knowledge of the OT, combined with sound judgement, caution, and strong Christian faith, did much to foster the spread of the critical view of the OT in Britain.

DROSTE-VISCHERING, CLEMENS AUGUST VON (1773–1845), Abp. of *Cologne. Of noble family, he was elected Abp. in 1835 at the suggestion of the Prussian government, who hoped thereby to reconcile the nobility to their policy. He came into conflict with the government, first for refusing to approve *Hermesianism and then over *mixed marriages; under pretext of treasonable activities he was imprisoned in 1837. J. J. von *Gorres took up his cause in his tract *Athanasius* (1838). He was freed in 1839 and retired to Münster.

DRUMMOND, HENRY (1786–1860), politician and *Irvingite leader. From 1826 he took a prominent part in founding the *Catholic Apostolic Church, which he helped to finance. In 1834 he was ordained 'angel for Scotland'.

DRUMMOND, HENRY (1851–97), revivalist. He assisted D. L. *Moody and I. D. Sankey on missions and later conducted missions to several British universities. He was known as a geologist and explorer in N. America and Africa.

DRUMMOND, JAMES (1835–1918), *Unitarian divine. From 1885 to 1906 he was principal of Manchester New College, first in London and from 1889 at Oxford. He valued Unitarianism for its encouragement of theological freedom rather than for its dogmatic negations. He held that the Resurrection and nature miracles of the Gospels were not *a priori* impossible, though the evidence for affirming them was insufficient.

DRY MASS. An abbreviated form of Mass, common in the late Middle Ages. It was not properly a Mass at all, since the *Offertory, *Canon, and Communion were omitted. It was used, for instance, when a priest wished to say a second Mass on a particular day or if a priest who had not broken his fast was not available.

DUALISM. (1) A metaphysical system which holds that good and evil are the product of separate and equally ultimate first causes. (2) The view that in the Incarnate Christ there were not merely two natures but two persons, a human and a Divine.

DUBLIN. Settled by Norse invaders in 841, Dublin became a bishopric in the 11th cent. (traditionally in 1038) and an archbishopric in 1152. The English invasion of *Ireland took place during the archiepiscopate of St. Laurence O'Toole (1162–80); all subsequent Abps. until the *Reformation were Englishmen nominated by the Crown. Under *Elizabeth I the (Protestant) Church of Ireland was finally established, and in 1591 *Trinity College was founded to support the settlement. The majority of the population, however, remained RC; Dublin was frequently governed by *vicars-general, but normal diocesan life was resumed under Thomas Troy (Abp. 1786–1823). Under him *Maynooth College was founded, the pro-cathedral begun in 1815, and many schools and religious houses established.

DUBLIN REVIEW, The. An influential RC quarterly, of which the first issue appeared in 1836. In its early years N. P. S. *Wiseman and D. *O'Connell were largely responsible for its success. In 1969 it was incorporated into *The Month*.

DUBOURG, ANNE (*c.* 1520–59), French Protestant martyr. He became *conseiller clerc* to the Parlement of Paris in 1557. At Easter 1559 he made his communion with the *Huguenots and subsequently defended them in the Parlement. He was burnt in Paris.

DUBRICIUS, St. (6th cent.), reputed Bp. of *Llandaff. He seems to have established monastic settlements in S. Wales, but generally the traditions about him do not merit credence. He is said to have consecrated St. *Samson of Dol and St. *Deiniol.

DU CANGE, CHARLES DUFRESNE (1610–88), French historian and philologist. His *Glossarium ad scriptores mediae et infimae latinitatis* (1678) remains the main complete dictionary of Late Latin. It was followed in 1688 by a similar work on Late Greek.

DUCHESNE, LOUIS (1843–1922), French Church historian. From 1895 he was director of the French school at Rome. He was eminent esp. in the field of Christian archaeology and the history of the early Church, though his sharp critical sense and negative attitude to traditional legends aroused opposition.

DUFF, ALEXANDER (1806–78), Scottish *Presbyterian missionary. The first missionary of the Established Church of *Scotland in *India, he reached Calcutta in 1830. He opened a school, which developed into the centre of W. education in India, and he was later concerned with the foundation of the University of Calcutta.

DUGDALE, WILLIAM (1605–86), author of the *Monasticon Anglicanum* (q.v.). This work was based on the documents collected by Roger Dodsworth, whom Dugdale met in 1638. Soon afterwards, in view of the dreaded civil war, he was commissioned by Sir Christopher Hatton to make exact drafts and records of monuments in the principal churches of England. He wrote other antiquarian works.

DUHM, BERNHARD (1847–1928), OT scholar. From 1888 he was a professor at Basle. His main work was on the Prophets. In his commentary on *Isaiah (1892) he separated Is. 56–66 from 40–55 (*Deutero-Isaiah) as a later composition (*Trito-Isaiah) and he argued that the *Servant Songs were not the work of Deutero-Isaiah.

DUKHOBORS. See *Doukhobors*.

DULIA. The reverence which, acc. to Orthodox and RC theologians, may be paid to the saints; it is contrasted with *latria, which is reserved for God alone.

DU MOULIN, PIERRE (1568–1658), French Reformed theologian. He took a prominent part in religious controversy, upholding a mediating position which irritated Catholics and Calvinists alike.

DUNKERS. See *Tunkers*.

DUNS SCOTUS, JOHANNES (*c.* 1265–1308), *Franciscan philosopher. He was prob. born near Roxburgh. He lectured at Cambridge, *Oxford, and *Paris, moving to *Cologne in 1307. His chief work is his commentary on the *Sentences* of *Peter Lombard.

His teaching combines with the *Aristotelianism prevalent in his time some elements from the older *Augustinianism. The root difference between him and St. *Thomas Aquinas is that in the Thomist system knowledge and reason hold the first place, whereas Duns Scotus gives the primacy to love and will. Thus he holds that the natural law depends wholly on the will of God and not, as Aquinas teaches, on His mind, and that it is therefore not absolutely immutable; also that the beatitude of the souls in heaven does not formally consist in the intellectual vision, but in the act of love for God. He also held a conception of *form and *matter which differed from that of Aquinas. He was the first great theologian to defend the *Immaculate Conception. The Scotist system was accepted by the Franciscans as their doctrinal basis and exercised a profound influence in the Middle Ages. The word 'dunce', used by humanists and the Reformers to ridicule the subtleties of the Schools, is a curious testimony to its popularity.

DUNSTAN, St. (c. 909–88), Abp. of *Canterbury. He was a monk, and from c. 940 abbot, of *Glastonbury. He reformed the monastery and imposed the full observance of the *Benedictine Rule. A year after Edgar became King of Wessex, Dunstan was made Abp. of Canterbury (960); together they planned and carried through a reform of Church and State. The restoration of monastic life, which seems to have been almost extinct in England, was almost wholly Dunstan's work. See also *Regularis Concordia*.

DUPANLOUP, FÉLIX ANTOINE PHILIBERT (1802–78), Bp. of Orleans from 1849. He became one of the foremost Catholic educationalists in France and he was active in securing for the Church the right, conceded in 1850, to conduct voluntary schools. At the *Vatican Council in 1870 he advised the minority to abstain from voting and to withdraw, but he accepted the decision of the Council when promulgated.

DUPERRON, JACQUES DAVY (1556–1618), French cardinal. He became a RC in 1577 or 1578. He was a friend of Henry III and after his death (1589) supported *Henry IV, whose conversion he brought about in 1593; in 1595 he obtained the King's absolution from heresy. In 1600 he defeated P. *Du Plessis-Mornay in public debate. He was created a cardinal in 1604 and Abp. of Sens in 1606. From 1610 he was involved in the conflicts between *Gallicans and *Ultramontanes in France.

DUPIN, LOUIS ELLIES (1657–1719), theologian of *Gallican sympathies. His vast *Nouvelle Bibliothèque des auteurs ecclésiastiques* (1689–1719) aroused opposition, but was not put on the *Index until 1757. His other works include what is still the standard edition of J. *Gerson. He entered into relations with Abp. W. *Wake in an unsuccessful attempt to achieve union between the Anglican and RC Churches.

DU PLESSIS-MORNAY, PHILIPPE (1549–1623), *Huguenot leader. In 1589 he became governor of Saumur, where he founded a Protestant university. *Henry IV's conversion (1593) came as a blow to him, but he continued to work for the toleration of the Huguenots and in 1598 secured the Edict of *Nantes. In 1598 he issued a treatise on the Eucharist; J. D. *Duperron charged him with misquotations and in a public disputation Du Plessis-Mornay was defeated. With the renewal of persecution in 1621 he retired to his own castle.

DUPLEX QUERELA. In the C of E the form of action open to a cleric whom the bishop refuses to institute to a benefice to which he has been presented.

DUPLICATION. An alternative name for *Bination*.

DUPPA, BRIAN (1588–1662), Bp. successively of *Chichester (from 1638), *Salisbury (1641), and *Winchester (1660). From 1645 to 1660 he was one of the leaders of the persecuted Church; he did his utmost to keep the extruded clergy together during the Commonwealth and he held private *ordinations when opportunity offered.

DURA EUROPOS, an ancient city on the R. Euphrates. A Seleucid fortress, then a Parthian caravan city, it was occupied by the Romans from c. A.D. 165; it was abandoned c. 256. Excavations have revealed an early well-preserved Jewish *synagogue (A.D. 245) and the earliest known Christian church. This was constructed from two rooms of a private house and prob. dates from the 240s.

DURANDUS OF SAINT-POURÇAIN (c. 1275–1334), *Dominican philosopher. He taught at *Paris; in 1313 he was summoned to be Lector at the Papal court of

*Avignon; later he became a bishop. He was
one of the earliest exponents of what came to
be called *Nominalism, which he developed
in avowed opposition to the teaching of St.
*Thomas Aquinas. Rejecting the current
doctrine on intelligible and sensible species,
he held that the only real entities were individuals and that the search for a principle of
individuation was meaningless. In theology
he stood for a sharp contrast between faith
and reason.

DURANDUS OF TROARN (*c.* 1010–88),
Abbot of Troarn from 1059. In one of the
earliest medieval treatments of Eucharistic
doctrine he attacked *Berengar of Tours,
upheld the conversion of the elements into
the Body and Blood of Christ, but emphasized the spiritual nature of the change.

DURANDUS, WILLIAM (*c.* 1230–96),
Bp. of Mende from 1285. He was one of the
principal medieval canonists; he drafted the
decrees of the second Council of *Lyons
(1274) and wrote on canon law. His best-
known work, his *Rationale divinorum offi-
ciorum*, is a compendium of liturgical knowledge with mystical interpretation. His *Pontifical was taken as a model for content and
arrangement.

DÜRER, ALBRECHT (1471–1528), German painter and engraver. His religious
paintings included some famous altar-pieces.
He is also known for his woodcuts, which
were used as illustrations to the Bible, and
for his copperplate work. Although he never
renounced the Catholic faith, he was sympathetic towards the Reformation.

DURHAM. At the end of the 10th cent. the
see of *Lindisfarne was moved to Durham,
and a cathedral was begun as a shrine for the
relics of St. *Cuthbert. Bp. Carilef began
building the present cathedral in 1093 and he
replaced the secular clergy by a *Benedictine
community, which lasted until the *dissolution in 1540. The Galilee chapel, projecting
from the W. end, was built at the end of the
Norman period; the Chapel of Nine Altars,
with its rose window and elaborate carving,

is Early English. The medieval bishops held
wide jurisdiction, ranking as Counts Palatine; this dignity attached to the see until the
time of W. van *Mildert (Bp. 1826–36).
Durham shares with London and *Winchester a rank inferior only to *Canterbury and
*York, and the bishop is entitled to sit in the
House of Lords as soon as he takes possession of his see. The university was founded
in 1832.

DURHAM BOOK, The. A copy of the
BCP printed in 1619 with MS. notes by J.
*Cosin and W. *Sancroft designed as a first
draft for the revision of 1662. It is preserved
in *Durham.

DURIE, JOHN (1596–1680), Scottish
divine. In Prussia he devised plans for the
reunion of the non-RC Churches, esp. the
*Lutherans and *Calvinists. In 1634 he was
ordained priest in the C of E. He continued
to travel in the cause of religious unity. At
first a royalist, in 1645 he returned to London to take part in drawing up the *Westminster Confession and Catechisms.

DUVERGIER DE HAURANNE. See
Saint-Cyran, Abbé de.

DYKES, JOHN BACCHUS (1823–76),
writer of hymn-tunes. In 1862 he became
vicar of St. Oswald's, Durham; here his
High Church sympathies led to a long and
unhappy conflict with the bishop. His hymn-
tunes became popular. They include those to
'Jesu, Lover of my soul' and 'The King of
Love my Shepherd is'.

DYOPHYSITES. A title used by the
*Monophysites for the Catholics in reference
to the orthodox belief that in the Person of
Christ the two separate natures of God and
man coexist.

DYOTHELETES. Those who, as against
the *Monothelites, hold the orthodox doctrine that in the Person of Christ there are
two separate wills, the one human and the
other Divine.

E

'E'. The name given since the work of J. *Wellhausen to the Elohistic source held to be embodied in the *Pentateuch. It is distinguished from '*J' by its use of *'elohim* ('God') where 'J' uses the Divine name Yahweh. It is later than 'J'.

EADMER (c. 1060–c. 1128), English historian and theologian. He was a member of the household of St. *Anselm. His writings include lives of St. Anselm and other English saints (incl. *Wilfrid and *Dunstan), a history of England covering the period from c. 1066 to c. 1122, and a treatise defending the doctrine of the *Immaculate Conception of the BVM, formerly attributed to St. Anselm.

EARLE, JOHN (c. 1601–65), Bp. of *Salisbury from 1663. He gained literary fame by his *Microcosmography* (1628), a pleasant collection of character studies. In 1643 he became Chancellor of Salisbury Cathedral. Deprived by the *Puritans, he accompanied *Charles II in his exile and received rapid promotion at the Restoration. He was tolerant towards Nonconformists.

EARTHQUAKE SYNOD, The (1382). A synod held at Blackfriars, London, under Abp. W. *Courtenay, during which the city was shaken by an earthquake. It condemned as heretical 24 theses from the writings of J. *Wycliffe.

EASTER. The Feast of the Resurrection of Christ, the greatest and oldest feast of the Christian Church. In the ancient Church the *catechumens, after watching all Saturday night, were baptized early on Easter Day and received Holy Communion. In the E. Church the original vigil was kept unaltered, but in the W. the ceremonies were put back to the Saturday; between 1951 and 1955 the RC Church restored them to the night of Saturday–Sunday (see *Paschal Vigil Service*).

The date of Easter is determined by the Paschal Full Moon, its extreme limits being 21 March and 25 April. For disputes on the computation of Easter see *Paschal Controversies*.

EASTER LITANY. The principal confession of faith of the *Bohemian Brethren. It is based on the *Apostles' Creed, with considerable expansions. It dates from 1749.

EASTERN ORTHODOX CHURCH. See *Orthodox Church*.

EASTERTIDE. See *Paschaltide*.

EASTWARD POSITION. The practice of the celebrant of the Eucharist standing on the W. side of the altar and facing E., which was introduced at Rome in the 8th or 9th cent., had probably been customary in other places much earlier. In the C of E the authority for its use depends on the interpretation of three rubrics in the BCP, which was disputed in the 19th cent.; in 1890 Abp. E. W. *Benson pronounced in favour of its legitimacy. See also *North End* and *Westward Position*.

EBEDJESUS (Abdh-isho bar Berikha) (d. 1318), Metropolitan of *Armenia. He was the last important *Nestorian theological writer. His surviving works, in Syriac, include his *Margaritha* (The Pearl), a theological work, a collection of ecclesiastical *canons, and his *Paradisus-Eden*, a series of 50 poems.

EBERLIN, JOHANN (1470–1533), Reformation controversial writer. He was born in Bavaria and became a *Franciscan. He supported M. *Luther almost from the outset. In some of his early writings he sought to foster radical social changes, but he later adopted a more moderate line.

EBIONITES. An ascetic sect of Jewish Christians which flourished, esp. on the E. of the R. *Jordan, in the early years of the Christian era. Their main tenets seem to have been: (1) a 'reduced' doctrine of the Person of Christ, to the effect, e.g., that Jesus was the human son of Joseph and Mary and that the Holy Spirit in the form of a dove lighted on Him at His Baptism, and (2) over-emphasis on the binding character of the Mosaic Law. They are said to have rejected the Pauline Epistles and to have used only one Gospel.

EBIONITES, Gospel according to the. The name given by modern scholars to the *apocryphal Gospel supposed to have been used by the *Ebionites. This may have been the work commonly known as the 'Gospel according to the *Hebrews' (q.v.).

'ECCE HOMO' (Lat., 'Behold the Man!'). The title of a controversial Life of Christ published by Sir John *Seeley in 1865. It depicted the Lord as a moral reformer.

ECCHELLENSIS. See *Abraham Ecchellensis*.

ECCLESIASTES, Book of. The main theme of this OT Book is the worthlessness and vanity of human life. Though it is traditionally ascribed to *Solomon, he is no longer seriously held to be its author. Considerations of subject-matter and linguistic style make it clear that the Book is the product of a late age in OT history and it is known that it was one of the latest Books to be admitted to the Hebrew *canon.

ECCLESIASTICAL COMMISSION-ERS. The body which from 1835 to 1948 managed the estates and revenues of the C of E. In 1948 it was united with *Queen Anne's Bounty to form the *Church Commissioners for England.

ECCLESIASTICAL COURTS COMMISSIONS. (1) The Parliamentary Commission set up in 1830 recommended the replacement of the Court of *Delegates by the Privy Council as the final court of appeal in ecclesiastical matters. As a result the *Judicial Committee of the Privy Council was formed in 1833. (2) Another Commission was appointed in 1881, with the immediate object of finding a better way to deal with the ritual controversies. In 1883 it recommended a radical revision of the courts. No legislation followed.

ECCLESIASTICAL DISCIPLINE, The Royal Commission on. A Commission appointed in 1904 to inquire into 'breaches or neglect of the Law relating to the conduct of Divine Service' in the C of E. In 1906 it

reported that the law was too narrow and that the machinery for discipline had broken down. One of its recommendations initiated the Prayer Book Revision which was defeated in Parliament in 1927 and 1928 (see *Common Prayer, Book of*).

ECCLESIASTICAL JURISDICTION MEASURE, 1963. A Measure designed to simplify ecclesiastical law and jurisdiction in the C of E. It established the *Court of Ecclesiastical Causes Reserved, which hears cases involving doctrine, ritual, or ceremonial; appeal lies to a Royal Commission consisting of three Lords of Appeal and two Bishops. Other cases against clerics are dealt with in the first instance by the *Consistory Courts. The censures which may be imposed under the Measure are deprivation, *inhibition, suspension, monition, and a new penalty of rebuke.

ECCLESIASTICAL TEXT OF THE NT. A name occasionally given to the *Byzantine text.

ECCLESIASTICAL TITLES ACT (1851). The Act forbidding the assumption by RCs of territorial titles within the U.K. Introduced as a counter-measure to the restoration of the RC hierarchy in 1850, it was a dead-letter; it was repealed in 1871.

ECCLESIASTICISM. (1) Over-attention to the external details of ecclesiastical practice and administration; (2) the point of view which is guided solely by the interests of the Church as an organization.

ECCLESIASTICUS. A Book of the *Apocrypha. It was written or compiled in Hebrew by Jesus (i.e. Joshua) the son of Sirach of Jerusalem; the translator's prologue also states that the translation into Greek was made by the author's grandson in Egypt after 132 B.C. (The first prologue printed in the AV is spurious.) The historical catalogue of famous men (44–50) and other internal evidence confirm a date about two generations before 132 B.C. for the original.

ECCLESIOLOGY. (1) The science of the building and decoration of churches; (2) the theology of the Church.

ECK, JOHANN (1486–1543), **Johann Maier 'of Eck'** (from his birthplace, Egg an der Günz), German theologian. He came under Humanist influence and his early writings are almost anti-Scholastic in their theology. Until the controversy over *indulgences broke out, he was on good terms with M. *Luther, but in the public debate at Leipzig in 1519 he opposed *Carlstadt and Luther, and he was largely responsible for securing the latter's excommunication. For the rest of his life he took a prominent part in organizing Catholic opposition to German Protestantism.

ECKHART (c. 1260–1327), 'Meister Eckhart', German *Dominican mystic. He became famous as a preacher at *Cologne. Accused of heretical teaching, he was tried before the court of the Abp. of Cologne in 1326, but appealed to the Pope and died during the proceedings. In 1329 *John XXII condemned 28 propositions as heretical or dangerous. This censure seriously affected the circulation of his works, many of which are lost. He has been acclaimed the forerunner of a variety of movements, largely through misunderstanding.

ECLECTICISM. Any system of theology or philosophy which selects elements from different schools or traditions and combines them.

ECPHONESIS. In the E. Church the concluding words, uttered in an audible voice, of a prayer, the rest of which has been said silently.

ECSTASY, a preter- or supernatural state. The ecstasies described in the OT usually consisted of a sudden temporary seizure of a prophet by the Divine power which spoke through his mouth or showed him the future in visions. Ecstasy in the Christian sense is one of the normal stages in the mystic life. Its main characteristic is alienation of the senses, caused by the violence of the Divine action on the soul; the body becomes immovable, and sight, hearing, etc., cease to function. In contrast to the pathological 'case', the mystic remembers what has taken place during the ecstasy.

ECTENE. In the E. Church a prayer consisting of short petitions said by the deacon to which choir or congregation respond with *Kyrie Eleison.

ECTHESIS, The (Gk. ἔκθεσις, 'a statement of faith'). The formula issued in 638 by the Emp. *Heraclius forbidding the mention of 'energies', whether one or two, in the Person of Christ and asserting that the two Natures were united in one Will. See *Monothelitism.

ECUMENICAL COUNCILS. See *Oecumenical Councils.*

ECUMENICAL MOVEMENT. The movement in the Church towards the visible union of all believers in Christ. Aspirations for unity can be traced from NT times. The modern ecumenical movement may be dated from the *Edinburgh Conference of 1910, though this owed much to earlier developments. It led to the establishment of the International Missionary Council; its impetus was behind the creation in 1925 of the Universal Christian Conference on *Life and Work and of the first World Conference on *Faith and Order which met in *Lausanne in 1927. These two bodies were fused in the *World Council of Churches (q.v.).

The initiative for the movements between 1910 and 1927 came mainly from within W. Protestantism. By 1937 the E. *Orthodox and the so-called 'younger Churches' of Asia and Africa were taking an important part. Until the early 1960s RC participation was expressed only through interested individuals. A changed atmosphere was reflected in the Second *Vatican Council Decree on Ecumenism (1964), which referred to members of other communions as 'separated brethren' rather than as outside the Church. Regional and national Councils of Churches have been formed in most parts of the world and now include RC representatives. There have also been unions of non-RC Churches on a regional basis, such as that of *South India. See also *Reunion.*

EDEN, The Garden of. The original home of *Adam and *Eve (Gen. 2: 8–3: 24).

EDESSA. The present city (now Urfa) was founded in 304 B.C. It was the centre of an independent kingdom from c. 132 B.C. to A.D. 214, and then a Roman colony. From an early date it was the centre of Syriac-speaking Christianity. It was the home of the *Nestorian 'Persian School' until that was closed in 489, and it has remained a centre of *Monophysitism. It was the capital of a small crusader principality. See also *Abgar, Legend of*, and *Chronicon Edessenum*.

EDICTS OF MILAN and **NANTES**. See *Milan, Edict of; Nantes, Edict of.*

EDINBURGH CONFERENCE (1910). The World Missionary Conference was convened as a consultative gathering to study missionary endeavour in the light of the circumstances of the day; it was significant for its presentation of the ideal of world-evangelization and as a forerunner of the *Ecumenical Movement (q.v.).

EDINBURGH CONFERENCE (1937). The second World Conference on *Faith and Order. Its subjects were Grace, the Word of God, the Communion of Saints, the Ministry and Sacraments, and the Church's unity in life and worship. Considerable differences, as well as agreements, were apparent. The Conference approved the proposal of a *World Council of Churches (q.v.).

EDMUND, St., of Abingdon (also wrongly **Edmund Rich**) (*c.* 1180–1240), Abp. of *Canterbury from 1233. He tried, boldly but ineffectually, to check royal mismanagement and Papal exactions. In his earlier years he taught the new logic at *Oxford; his association with the University is commemorated in St. Edmund Hall. He wrote a devotional treatise, *Speculum ecclesie*, which had a wide circulation.

EDMUND CAMPION, St. See *Campion, St. Edmund.*

EDMUND THE MARTYR, St. (*c.* 840–69), King of East Anglia by 865. In 869 his kingdom was invaded and he was captured by the Danes. He was offered his life if he would share his kingdom with the Danish leader, but as a Christian he refused to associate himself thus with a pagan. He was made the target of the Danes' archery practice and finally beheaded. His cult started almost immediately; in the 10th cent. his body was translated to Bury St. Edmunds, which became a place of pilgrimage.

EDWARD, St. (*c.* 963–78), king and martyr. With the support of Abp. *Dunstan, he succeeded his father, Edgar the Peaceful, as King of England in 975. Three years later

he was stabbed to death. In 1001 he was officially styled a martyr.

EDWARD THE CONFESSOR, St. (1003–66), King of England from 1042. Though outwardly peaceful, his reign was marked by struggles between the advisers he brought from Normandy and Earl Godwin and his Saxon supporters. At his death the disputed succession plunged the nation into hostilities. Edward himself was mainly occupied with religious matters, esp. the building of *Westminster Abbey.

EDWARD VI (1537–53), King of England from 1547. He was the son of *Henry VIII and Jane Seymour. Having delegated his royal authority to the Privy Council, he was of little account personally. His reign, however, was outstanding ecclesiastically because of the numerous alterations forced on the C of E in a *Calvinist direction. It was marked by the issue of the *Injunctions of 1547, recognition of clerical marriage (1548), the Acts of *Uniformity of 1549 and 1552 imposing the First and then the Second BCP, and a new *Ordinal (1550).

EDWARDS, JONATHAN (1703–58), American *Calvinist philosopher. He was minister of the *Congregational church at Northampton, Mass., until his wish to exclude all 'unconverted' from the Communion led to his removal in 1749. His most famous work was on *Freedom of the Will* (1754). He rejected freedom as popularly understood, maintaining that self-determination was 'unphilosophical, self-contradictory and absurd' and that the essence of virtue and vice lay 'not in their cause but in their nature'. It was his desire to defend the extreme Calvinist position on 'election' that inspired his metaphysical account of freedom. A 'New England Party' of philosophical Calvinists carried on his teaching. See also *Great Awakening*.

EDWIN (*c.* 585–633), Northumbrian king from 617. In 625 he married Ethelburga, daughter of King *Ethelbert, a Christian who came to Northumbria with St. *Paulinus as her chaplain. In 627 Edwin was baptized. He appointed Paulinus Bp. of *York and set about building a stone church there. He was defeated and killed at the battle of Heathfield (633).

EFFETA. See *Ephphatha*.

EFFICACIOUS GRACE. In the RC theology of *grace, grace to which free consent is given by the will, so that it always produces its effect. It has been disputed whether the efficacy of such grace depends on the character of the grace or on the fact that it is given under circumstances which God foresees to be congruous with the disposition of the recipient.

EGBERT (d. 766), Abp. of *York. He became Bp. of York *c*. 732, and, on the advice of *Bede, applied for the *pallium in 735. He founded the cathedral school and carried out many reforms. His name is associated with a collection of canons (in its present form not earlier than the 11th cent.), a treatise on Church discipline and a 'Poenitentiale', both added to in later times, and a 'Pontificale', which is an important liturgical source.

EGBERT, St. (d. 729), Northumbrian hermit. A monk of *Lindisfarne, he went to *Ireland and was influential in organizing the evangelization of Germany; he arranged the mission of St. *Willibrord and others. From 716 he lived on *Iona.

EGEDE, HANS (1686–1758), the 'Apostle of the Eskimos'. He went as a *Lutheran missionary from Norway to Greenland in 1721. In 1736 he returned to Copenhagen, where he founded a seminary for missionaries to Greenland.

EGERIA. See *Etheria*.

EGERTON, FRANCIS HENRY (1756–1829), 8th Earl of Bridgewater. He bequeathed to the President of the Royal Society £8,000, which financed the *Bridgewater Treatises, and to the British Museum his MSS. and money to augment his collection, which became known as the 'Egerton MSS.'. See also the following entry.

EGERTON PAPYRUS. Two imperfect leaves and a scrap of papyrus in the British Library ('Egerton Papyrus 2') containing passages from a Greek writing akin to, but distinct from, the canonical Gospels. It dates from not later than *c*.A.D. 150 and is thus (with the possible exception of the *Rylands St. John) the oldest known specimen of Christian writing.

EGINHARD (*c*. 770–840), also **Einhard**, Frankish historian. He was a trusted friend of *Charlemagne, whose successor gave him the estates to which he retired *c*. 830. His 'Life of Charlemagne' presents a fresh and accurate picture of the Emperor's character and rule.

EGYPT, Christianity in. See *Coptic Church*.

EGYPTIAN CHURCH ORDER, The. An early name for the '*Apostolic Tradition' (q.v.) of St. *Hippolytus.

EGYPTIANS, Gospel according to the. An apocryphal Gospel, written from an ascetic standpoint, prob. in Egypt in the early 2nd cent. Only a few quotations from it survive.

EHRLE, FRANZ (1845–1934), German *Jesuit. From 1895 to 1914 he was prefect of the *Vatican library, which he reorganized on modern lines, attaching to it a reference library and a department for the restoration of MSS. He was made a cardinal in 1922. With H. S. *Denifle, he was the founder of the scientific study of the history of *Scholasticism.

EICHHORN, JOHANN GOTTFRIED (1752–1827), German Biblical scholar and orientalist. He was among the earliest critics to divide Gen. between the 'Jehovist' and 'Elohist' sources and to distinguish the priestly law in Exod.–Lev.–Num. from the popular code in Deut.

EIGHTEEN BENEDICTIONS The. A group of prayers, now 19, largely made up of Biblical phrases, which are recited on weekdays at each of the three services in the Jewish synagogue. They date mainly from pre-Christian times.

EIKON BASILIKE, 'The Portraiture of His Sacred Majesty in His Solitude and Sufferings'. A royalist publication issued just before the death of *Charles I and purporting to be his work.

EILETON. In the E. Church, a silk cloth spread on the altar during the Liturgy. It is the counterpart of the W. *corporal.

EINHARD. See *Eginhard*.

EINSIEDELN. *Benedictine abbey and place of pilgrimage in Switzerland. Previously the dwelling-place of St. *Meinrad, the abbey was founded in 937. The library has a valuable collection of MSS.

ELDER. A Church officer in the *Presbyterian Church. There are two kinds: (1) 'Teaching elders', whose function is pastoral; (2) 'Ruling elders', laymen set apart by ordination who assist the pastor in the administration and government of the Church. When the word is used without specification, the latter class is commonly meant. For the office in the early Church, see *Presbyter*.

ELECTION. In the vocabulary of theology, an act of the Divine Will exercising itself on creatures, among whom it chooses some in preference to others. In the OT the Divine election bore esp. on Israel, the 'Chosen People'; in the NT the place of the Old Israel was taken by members of the new Christian community. In the teaching of the Fathers and Schoolmen the term plays an important part in connection with *Predestination. It came to be a matter of dispute, esp. among the *Calvinists, whether God's election was wholly without relation to faith and works.

ELEPHANTINE PAPYRI, The. A collection of *Aramaic documents of the 5th cent. B.C. found in 1904–8 on the site of an ancient Jewish military colony at Elephantine in the far south of Upper Egypt.

ELEVATION, The. At the Eucharist, the lifting of the sacred elements in turn by the celebrant immediately after each species has been consecrated. The practice of elevating the Host apparently originated in the 13th cent.; the elevation of the chalice was added later.

ELGAR, EDWARD (1857–1934), musician. He rose to fame as a composer of choral-orchestral music and in 1929 became Master of the King's Music. His religious works include a setting of J. H. *Newman's 'Dream of *Gerontius'.

EL GRECO (1541–1614), properly Domenico Theotocopuli, religious painter. From 1577 he lived at Toledo. His works are marked by a quality of mysticism as well as by personal idiosyncrasies. Formal modelling is abandoned as human forms and facial expressions are exaggerated and even distorted to produce an emotional rather than a literal likeness.

ELIAS. See *Elijah*.

ELIAS OF CORTONA (*c.* 1180–1253), *Franciscan. He was one of the earliest companions of St. *Francis, and was mainly responsible for the erection of a basilica for his relics at *Assisi. In 1232 he became third General of the Franciscan Order; his government was marked by repeated crises and despotic behaviour, and he was deposed by *Gregory IX in 1239. He then supported *Frederick II.

ELIGIUS, St. (*c.* 590–660), patron saint of metalworkers. Through his skill in working in precious metals, he rose to high office in the courts of the Frankish kings. He was consecrated Bp. of Noyon in 641 and evangelized Flanders.

ELIJAH (Gk. form, 'Elias') (9th cent. B.C.), Hebrew prophet. Acc. to Kgs. he maintained the ascendancy of the worship of Yahweh in the face of Canaanite and Phoenician cults, upheld the claims of moral righteousness and social justice, and was translated into heaven. His return was held to be a necessary prelude to the deliverance and restoration of Israel.

ELIOT, THOMAS STEARNS (1888–1965), poet and critic. An American by birth, he worked for a time in a bank in London. From 1923 to 1939 he edited *The Criterion*. He joined the board of Faber, the publisher, in 1925.

Brought up in the *Unitarian tradition, Eliot passed through a period of agnosticism. He later adopted an *Anglo-Catholic position, apparent in *Ash Wednesday* (1930). He employed a complicated poetic technique characterized by an extreme form of compression by means of allusion, the juxtaposition of contrasting ideas, and the indirect communication of meaning by suggestion.

ELIPANDUS (*c.* 718–802), Abp. of Toledo. He was the originator and chief exponent of the *Adoptianist heresy in Spain. His doctrines were condemned as heretical at various synods from 792 onwards, but he retained his see until his death.

ELIZABETH, St. The mother of *John the Baptist and 'cousin' (Lk. 1: 36) of the BVM. Acc. to a few MSS. of the NT it was she who spoke the words known as the *Magnificat.

ELIZABETH, St., of Hungary (1207–31). The daughter of the King of Hungary, in 1221 she married Ludwig IV, Landgrave of Thuringia. After his death (1227) she was driven from court on the ground that her charities were exhausting the State finances. She settled at Marburg; under the direction of *Conrad of Marburg she gave up her children and led a life of great austerity.

ELIZABETH I (1533–1603), Queen of England from 1558. She was the daughter of *Henry VIII and Anne Boleyn, placed in the succession after *Edward VI and *Mary by Act of Parliament. On her accession one of the main difficulties was the religious question. The Queen, who was regarded as illegitimate by Catholics, aimed at a compromise, and in the country changes were made slowly, the old and the new rites often being celebrated side by side. The Second BCP of Edward VI (1552) was reissued (1559) with some changes to make it less offensive to RCs. The *Thirty-Nine Articles and M. *Parker's 'Advertisements' (1566) were more *Calvinist than the Queen would have wished, but the government was being forced to rely increasingly on the Protestant party for support. *Paul V's excommunication of Elizabeth in 1570 was followed by more severe measures against RCs. In 1587, under the threat of Spanish invasion, the Queen ordered the execution of *Mary Stuart, fearing that she might become a rallying centre for disaffected RCs. The defeat of the Armada (1588) removed the Spanish peril. In the latter part of her reign she opposed all the attempts of the *Puritans to change the C of E.

ELKESAITES. A Jewish Christian sect which arose c. A.D. 100 in the country E. of the R. *Jordan. They insisted on the strict observance of the rites and teaching of the Mosaic Law, rejected sacrifices and certain Biblical Books, and held a *Docetic view of the Person of Christ.

ELLERTON, JOHN (1826–93), English divine. He is esp. remembered for his many hymns, both original compositions and translations. They include "The day Thou gavest, Lord, is ended'.

ELLICOTT,   CHARLES   JOHN (1819–1905), English divine. He held high academic posts before becoming Bp. of *Gloucester and Bristol in 1863. He sat on many commissions, being chairman of the British New Testament Revision Company, 1870–81.

ELMO, St. The popular name for St. Peter González (c. 1190–1246), the patron saint of seamen. A *Dominican, he accompanied Ferdinand III on an expedition against the Moors and then devoted the rest of his life to work among the seafarers of the Spanish coast.

ELOHIM. A Heb. word meaning 'gods'. In the OT it is generally used of the God of Israel, esp. frequently in what is commonly reckoned the second oldest Pentateuchal source (the supposed author of which is therefore referred to by critics as 'the Elohist').

ÉLOI, St. The French form of St. *Eligius.

ELVIRA, Council of. A Spanish Council held in c. 306. It imposed severe penalties for apostasy and adultery, and required continence of all clergy.

ELY. In 673 St. *Etheldreda founded a *double monastery for monks and nuns. It was destroyed by the Danes in 870, but restored, for monks only, in 970. The see of Ely was formed in 1109; the prior and monks became the *cathedral chapter. At the *Dissolution the prior became dean and eight canonries were founded (1541). The cathedral is famous for its Galilee Porch (1198–1215) and its central octagon (1322–8), the roof of which (known as the 'Lantern') is the only Gothic dome in the world.

EMBER DAYS. Four groups each of three days, viz. the Wednesday, Friday, and Saturday after St. *Lucy (13 Dec.), the first Sunday in *Lent, *Whitsunday, and *Holy Cross Day (14 Sept.) respectively, which have been observed as days of fasting and abstinence in the W. Church. Originally connected with the crops, they came to be associated with *ordinations.

EMBOLISM. In the Roman Mass, the prayer after the *Canon, beginning 'Deliver us', inserted between the Lord's Prayer and the Prayer for Peace.

EMBURY, PHILIP (1728–75), the first *Methodist preacher in America. A native of Ireland, he was converted by J. *Wesley. In 1768 he built the first Methodist church in America, in New York, but in 1770 he moved to Camden, where he founded a Methodist society.

EMERSON, RALPH WALDO (1803–82), American essayist, philosopher, and poet. He was a *Unitarian minister at Boston from 1829 to 1832. His philosophy was founded on a combination of rationalism and mysticism. It appears that he believed fundamentally in 'Transcendentalism', viz. the doctrine that 'the highest revelation is that God is in every man'. It follows that man contains all that is needful in himself and that even redemption is to be sought within the soul. He enjoyed wide influence.

EMINENCE. A title of honour given to *cardinals in the RC Church.

EMMANUEL. See *Immanuel.*

EMMAUS. The village in which the Lord made a Resurrection appearance to two of the disciples (Lk. 24: 13–35). Its site is disputed.

EMMERICK, ANNA KATHARINA (1774–1824), ecstatic. She entered an *Augustinian convent in Westphalia in 1802; when this was closed in 1812 she took refuge in a private house, where she had a serious illness. She received the *Stigmata of the Passion. Her 'Meditations on the Passion' and other visions were taken down and published after her death.

EMMONS, NATHANIEL (1745–1840), American *Congregationalist divine. He developed a system of 'consistent *Calvinism'; though avowedly opposed to all forms of *Arminianism, *Universalism, and *Unitarianism, he nevertheless asserted that man's part in regeneration is active, not passive.

EMS, Congress of. A conference attended by representatives of the Abps. of Mainz, Trier, *Cologne, and Salzburg in 1786. It issued the 'Punctation of Ems', which sought to limit Papal intervention in Germany. The project failed to secure the support of the German bishops.

EMSER, HIERONYMUS (1478–1527), RC writer. He engaged in controversy with M. *Luther from 1519 until his death. In 1527 he published a counter-edition to Luther's 'December Bible' of 1522, which it was made to resemble, with introduction and notes added. Emser's Bible went through many editions.

ENABLING ACT, The. The common name for 'The Church of England Assembly (Powers) Act', 1919. Its chief effect was to confer upon the *Church Assembly the power to prepare ecclesiastical measures and present them to Parliament, which could accept or reject (but not amend) them.

ENARXIS. In the Byzantine liturgy, the section between the *Proskomide and the *Lesser Entrance. It consists of three Diaconal Litanies, with antiphons sung by the choir.

ENCOLPION. An oval medallion worn by bishops in the E. Church. It is suspended from the neck by a chain.

ENCLOSURE. See *Clausura.*

ENCRATITES. A title applied to several groups of early Christians who carried their ascetic practice and doctrines to extremes which were in many cases considered heretical.

ENCYCLICAL. A circular letter sent to all the Churches in a given area. In early times the word might be applied to letters sent out by any bishop, but in modern RC usage it is confined to those of the Pope.

ENCYCLOPAEDISTS. The contributors to the *Encyclopédie* published under the editorship of D. *Diderot between 1751 and 1780. Many of them were supporters of an exclusively natural religion.

ENERGUMEN. In ancient Christian literature the term was used of demoniacs and others possessed of abnormal mental and physical states, esp. insanity.

ENGLAND, Church of. See *Church of England* (for history); *Anglicanism* (for theological outlook).

ENGLISH CHURCH MUSIC, School of. See *Royal School of Church Music.*

ENGLISH CHURCH UNION. A society founded in 1859 as the 'Church of England Protection Society' and renamed in 1860. Its object was to defend, and further the spread of, High Church principles in the C of E. In 1934 it was united with the *Anglo-Catholic Congress to form the '*Church Union'.

ENGLISH COLLEGE, The. The seminary at Rome for English candidates for the RC priesthood. It was founded in 1362 as a hospice for English pilgrims. In 1579 it became a seminary, whose students took an oath to go to England when it seemed good to their superiors. It was closed during the French occupation of Rome in 1798, but restored in 1818.

ENGLISH HYMNAL, The. An Anglican hymnbook, published in 1906, which to some extent reflects the *Anglo-Catholic sympathies of those responsible for its production. The editorial committee in charge of the words included P. *Dearmer and T. A. *Lacey; the musical editor was R. Vaughan *Williams.

ENGLISH LADIES. A popular name for the 'Institute of the Blessed Virgin Mary', an active body of religious founded in 1609 at St.-Omer by Mary *Ward. It was designed as an order for women similar to the *Jesuit Order for men.

ENHYPOSTASIA. The doctrine that in the Incarnate Christ the personal humanity of Christ was not lost but included within the *hypostasis of the Godhead, and that thereby He included within Himself all the attributes of perfect humanity.

ENLIGHTENMENT, The. Though the term originated as a translation of the German *Aufklärung*, it is now applied more generally to the movement of ideas which characterized much of 18th-cent. Europe. Its adherents distrusted all authority and tradition in matters of intellectual inquiry, and believed that truth could be obtained only through reason, observation, and experiment. They sought to diffuse knowledge as much as to create it and where possible to further tolerance, justice, and the moral and material welfare of mankind. The movement, however, embraced a vast spectrum of views and aims, and many of its leaders came into conflict with the Church, esp. in Catholic countries.

ENNODIUS, St., MAGNUS FELIX (*c.* 473–521), Christian rhetorician and from *c.* 514 Bp. of Pavia. In the dispute about the succession to Pope Anastasius II (d. 498) he defended *Symmachus, and he was twice sent by *Hormisdas on missions to *Constantinople. His numerous writings prob. represent the last serious attempt to combine a fundamentally pagan culture with the profession of the Christian creed.

ENOCH, OT patriarch. Many legends became attached to his name. See also the following entry.

ENOCH, Books of. 1 Enoch, or 'Ethiopic Enoch', so called because it survives complete only in Ethiopic, is one of the more important Jewish *pseudepigrapha. It embodies a series of revelations, of which *Enoch is the professed recipient, on such matters as the origin of evil, angels, and the nature of *Gehenna and *Paradise. It is clearly a composite work. The passages on 'the *Son of Man' in the 'Parables' or 'Similitudes' (chs. 37–71) have been widely held to have influenced the NT writings, but it is now argued that the section is a later (Christianized) insertion into the Book.

2 Enoch, or 'Slavonic Enoch', or 'The Book of the Secrets of Enoch', which survives only in Slavonic, has points of contact with 1 Enoch. About its origin, date, authorship, and original language opinions have differed widely.

3 Enoch is a Jewish work dating from well within the Christian era.

ENTHRONIZATION. The rite by which an Archbishop, Bishop, or Sovereign is put into possession of his throne. It is usually performed by ceremonially leading him to it and seating him thereon; in the case of the

Sovereign it forms part of the *Coronation rite. Bishops seem originally to have been enthroned in silence by the consecrating Bishop immediately after consecration. In the 12th cent., when bishops were commonly consecrated outside their cathedrals, enthronization became a separate rite, and in the 13th cent. it came to be understood as the formal assumption of the see. At the same time *Metropolitans began to delegate the task of enthroning bishops to their *archdeacons.

ENTHUSIASM. The original meaning of the word, 'being possessed by a god', was current in the 17th cent. It later took on the sense of fancied inspiration, and in the 18th cent. was widely used for extravagance in religious devotion.

ENTRANCE, Greater; Lesser. See *Greater Entrance*; *Lesser Entrance*.

ENURCHUS, St. (4th cent.), Bp. of Orleans. Little is known of him. His feast (7 Sept.) was included in the calendar of the BCP to mark Queen *Elizabeth I's birthday.

EPAPHRODITUS. A fellow-worker of St. *Paul mentioned in Philippians.

EPARCHY. In the E. Church, the name for an ecclesiastical province. Its ecclesiastical head is the 'eparch', often called the 'metropolitan', who has a veto on the election of bishops in his eparchy.

EPHESIANS, Epistle to the. This NT Epistle was apparently written when its author was in prison, but considerations of style have led some scholars to question whether it is the work of St. *Paul. Since the words 'in Ephesus' in 1: 1 are missing in some MSS., it has been suggested that it was a circular letter in which the appropriate place-name was inserted in the copies sent to different Churches. There are close literary parallels with Col., and it has sometimes been held that Eph. is a working-up of Col. into a more systematic doctrinal treatise, or even an exposition of Pauline teaching designed as an introduction to the first collection of his letters.

EPHESUS. In NT times Ephesus was the capital of the Proconsular Province of Asia and an important commercial centre. It was famous for the temple dedicated to Artemis, or 'Diana' as the Romans called her. It was the scene of important labours of St. *Paul and traditionally the home of the aged St. *John the Apostle. It was one of the *Seven Churches addressed in Rev. (2: 1–7). See also the preceding and following entries and *Seven Sleepers of Ephesus.*

EPHESUS, Council of (431). The third *Oecumenical Council, summoned by *Theodosius II in the hope of settling the *Nestorian controversy. *Cyril of Alexandria opened the Council without waiting for the Syrian bishops, headed by *John of Antioch, or for the Papal legates. Nestorius was deposed, his doctrines condemned, and the Creed of *Nicaea reaffirmed. In 433 an agreement was reached between John and Cyril.

EPHESUS, Robber Council of 499. See *Latrocinium.*

EPHOD. A Jewish ecclesiastical vestment of linen and beaten gold. It was apparently worn only by the *High Priest, though a similar garment of linen only was worn by others (e.g. Samuel and *David).

EPHOR. In the E. Church, a lay guardian or protector in whose charge monastic property was often vested from the 10th cent. onwards.

EPHPHATHA. A ceremony in the RC Baptismal rite in which the celebrant, pronouncing the words 'Ephphatha, that is, Be opened' (Mk. 7: 34), touches the ears and mouth of the candidate.

EPHRAEM SYRUS, St. (c. 306–73), Syrian Biblical exegete and ecclesiastical writer. He was ordained deacon, perhaps by St. *James of Nisibis. After the cession of Nisibis to Persia in 363 he settled at *Edessa, where most of his extant works were written. His voluminous exegetical, dogmatic, controversial, and ascetical writings are mainly in verse. They include cycles of hymns on the great feasts of the Church and on the Last Things and refutations of heretics. He wrote exclusively in Syriac, but his works were translated into Armenian and Greek at an early date.

EPICLESIS. Although the term originally

meant 'invocation' and subsequently 'prayer' in general, it is commonly used in Christian writing only for the petition for the consecration of the bread and wine in the Eucharist, and it is usually restricted to the form of the petition which asks the Father to send the Holy Spirit upon the bread and wine and make them into the Body and Blood of Christ.

The history and significance of the epiclesis are controversial. A prayer asking for the descent of the Holy Spirit seems to have become universal in E. liturgies by the 4th cent. In the traditional Roman *Canon of the Mass there is no specific mention of the Holy Spirit. The three new RC *Eucharistic prayers ask for the operation of the Spirit both before and after the consecration, and the compilers of many other modern W. rites have included an epiclesis.

EPICTETUS (c. 50–c. 130), *Stoic philosopher. A slave in the household of *Nero, he was freed and taught at Rome until c. 90, when he settled at Nicopolis in Epirus. His discourses were taken down by a disciple and issued in two treatises. The influence of Christian ideals on Epictetus and vice versa has often been discussed, but the resemblances hardly go beyond similarity of moral temper.

EPICUREANISM. The system of philosophical ethics founded by the Greek thinker Epicurus (342–270 B.C.). Epicurus held that the senses, as the source of all our ideas, provided the sole criterion of truth, and he sought the goal of human conduct in pleasure.

EPIGONATION. In the E. Church, a lozenge-shaped stiffened vestment used by certain ecclesiastical dignitaries.

EPIMANIKIA. Cuffs worn over the ends of the sleeves of the *sticharion by bishops, priests, and deacons in the E. Church.

EPIPHANIUS, St. (c. 315–403), Bp. of Salamis and *Metropolitan of *Cyprus from 367. He was an ardent upholder of the faith of *Nicaea, took part in the *Apollinarian and *Melitian controversies and, after meeting St. *Jerome in 382, joined with him in his attack on *Origenism. The most important of his writings was his 'Panarion' or 'Refutation of all the Heresies', in which he described and attacked every heresy known to him.

EPIPHANY (from Greek for 'manifestation'). A feast of the Church kept on 6 Jan. It originated in the E., where it has been celebrated in honour of the Lord's Baptism since the 3rd cent., one of its main features being the solemn blessing of the Baptismal water. It was introduced into the W. Church in the 4th cent. Here it became chiefly associated with the manifestation of Christ to the Gentiles in the persons of the *Magi.

EPISCOPACY. The system of Church government by *Bishops.

EPISCOPAL CHURCH, Protestant. See *Protestant Episcopal Church*.

EPISCOPALIAN. Properly a member of any Church ruled by Bishops, but used esp. of the *Anglican Communion.

EPISCOPI VAGANTES (Lat., 'wandering bishops'). The name given to persons who have been consecrated bishop in an irregular or clandestine manner or who, having been regularly consecrated, have been excommunicated by the Church that consecrated them and are in communion with no recognized see. A man is also included in this group when the number in communion with him is so small that the sect appears to exist for his sake.

EPISCOPIUS. The assumed name of Simon Bischop (1583–1643), who systematized the typical tenets of *Arminianism. He was among those condemned and expelled by the Synod of *Dort (1619). He remonstrated against the current Calvinist view of *predestination, stressed the responsibility of man, not God, for sin, and taught a reduced view of the divinity of Christ and a *subordinationist doctrine of the Trinity.

EPISTLE. It was long customary for two passages of Scripture to be read or sung at the Eucharist; the former came to be known as the 'Epistle', doubtless because it was usually taken from one of the NT Epistles. In 1969 the RC Church restored the earlier practice of including lessons from the OT and a reading from the non-Gospel part of the NT is no longer always obligatory on weekdays. Similar arrangements are now permitted in the C of E.

EPISTLE OF THE APOSTLES, The. See *Testament of Our Lord in Galilee*.

EPISTOLAE OBSCURORUM VIRORUM. A famous pamphlet in the dispute between J. *Reuchlin and the *Dominicans of Cologne. It appeared in two parts (1515 and 1517). It is a bitter satire on the methods of later Scholasticism, on the religious practices of the age, and on many ecclesiastical institutions and doctrines.

EPITAPHION. In the E. Church, a veil embroidered with the scene of Christ's burial. It is carried in procession on *Good Friday and *Holy Saturday and remains on the altar during Eastertide.

EPITRACHELION. The form of the *stole worn by priests in the E. Church.

EQUIPROBABILISM. The moral system defended by St. *Alphonsus Liguori. It holds that the stricter course should be followed if the question concerns the cessation of the law, while the laxer course may be pursued if the question is whether the law ever existed.

ERA OF THE MARTYRS. See *Diocletianic Era*.

ERASMUS, DESIDERIUS (prob. 1469–1536), humanist. He reluctantly became an *Augustinian canon in 1486, but later left his monastery with the agreement of his superiors. He studied at Paris, visited Oxford, Louvain, and Italy, and was the first teacher of Greek at Cambridge. In 1521 he settled at Basle, in the house of the printer J. *Froben, refusing all offers of official position. When the Reformation was introduced at Basle in 1529, he fled to Freiburg.

Erasmus's *Praise of Folly* (1509) is a bitter satire on monasticism and the corruptions of the Church. In 1516 his celebrated Greek NT appeared, with his own translation into classical Latin. He entered the Reformation controversy in 1524, writing against M. *Luther on free will. Next to his Greek NT, his most important work was prob. his attempt to print reliable texts of the Fathers, though in some cases his own share in the editions perhaps did not go much beyond writing the prefaces. He was the most

renowned scholar of his age. Though he paved the way for the Reformation by his satires, he remained loyal to the Church as the safeguard of stability. In later life he was held suspect by both parties and after his death his writings were forbidden by *Paul IV in 1558.

ERASTIANISM. The ascendancy of the State over the Church in ecclesiastical matters, so named from the Swiss theologian Thomas Erastus (1524–83). Acc. to Erastus, in a State which professes but one religion the civil authorities have the right and duty to exercise jurisdiction in both civil and ecclesiastical matters. With the growth of the modern secular State the doctrine came to be modified and is now generally understood of the claim of the representatives of the State, whether professing any religion or none, to legislate on religious matters concerning the Established Church.

ERCONWALD (d. *c*. 693), Bp. of London from 675. Of princely family, he founded religious houses at Barking and Chertsey. He was a pious and able prelate.

ERIGENA, JOHN SCOTUS (*c*. 810–*c*. 877), philosopher. An Irishman, he became head of the palace school at Laon. He took a notable part in the controversy on *predestination centring on *Gottschalk, and in that on the *Eucharist initiated by *Paschasius Radbertus.

His philosophy is an attempt to reconcile the *Neoplatonist idea of emanation with the Christian idea of creation. In his *Periphyseon* or *De Divisione Naturae*, Erigena argues that Nature should be divided into four categories: first, Nature which is not created, but creates, i.e. God; secondly, Nature which is created and which creates, i.e. the world of primordial causes or Platonic ideas; thirdly, Nature which is created and which does not create, i.e. things perceived through the senses; and lastly, Nature which neither creates nor is created, i.e. God, to whom all things must in the end return. Thus the world was held to begin and end with God. Erigena also translated into Latin the works of *Dionysius the Pseudo-Areopagite.

ERRINGTON, GEORGE (1804–86), English RC prelate. In 1855 he was appointed coadjutor to N. P. S. *Wiseman and titular Abp. of Trebizond, with the right of succession to *Westminster. His relations with Wiseman became strained because of his coolness towards converts from the *Oxford Movement; he rejected *Pius IX's proposal that he should resign and in 1862 his connections with Westminster were severed by the Pope. He took part in the *Vatican Council of 1869–70 and was one of the signatories of the Anti-Infallibility Petition.

ERSKINE, EBENEZER (1680–1754), founder of the Scottish Secession Church. He was Moderator of the Synod of Stirling and Perth when he became involved in a dispute about the rights of the laity in Church patronage; he formed an 'associate presbytery' in 1733. After he had issued a 'judicial testimony' against the Established Church he was deposed from his charge and founded the Secession Church in 1740.

ERSKINE, THOMAS (1788–1870), Scottish religious thinker. He held liberal views, finding the meaning of Christianity mainly in its conformity with man's spiritual and ethical needs. In 1831 he championed J. McL. *Campbell after his deposition by the General Assembly for teaching the universal atonement.

ESCHATOLOGY. The part of systematic theology which deals with the final destiny both of the individual soul and of mankind in general. In the OT eschatological teaching is bound up with the Messianic hope; in the NT it is the subject of many of the Lord's Parables. When the eschatological predictions were not fulfilled in the literal sense expected by the first Christians, attempts were made either to interpret the Biblical teaching along allegorical lines or to translate it into individual, as opposed to cosmic, terms. In the 19th cent. J. *Weiss again emphasized the centrality of the eschatological element in the teaching of Christ, and eschatological considerations have been a dominant factor in the teaching of K. *Barth and the school of *Dialectical theology, which sees the life of each Christian and of the Church as a series of 'decisions' invested with an eschatological character. More recently attempts have been made to show that Christ regarded the *Kingdom of God as having already arrived with His ministry ('realized eschatology') or at least as having

been inaugurated by it.

ESDRAS, Books of. 'Esdras' is the Greek and Latin form of *Ezra. The *Septuagint contains Esdras A, a Greek Book based on parts of 2 Chron., Ez., and Neh., with an additional story not in the Hebrew, and Esdras B, a straight rendering of the Hebrew of Ez.–Neh. (treated as one Book). In the current form of the *Vulgate I and II Esdras are St. *Jerome's rendering of Ez. and Neh., treated as separate Books; III Esdras is the *Old Latin version of Esdras A, and IV Esdras is another Book not extant in Greek. In 1546 III and IV Esdras were rejected from the RC *Canon and in subsequent editions of the Vulgate they appear as an appendix after the NT. In the *Geneva Bible (1560) and subsequent English versions I and II Esdras of the Vulgate are entitled 'Ezra' (q.v.) and 'Nehemiah', while III and IV Esdras are the '1' and '2' Esdras of the *Apocrypha.

1 ESDRAS (i.e. Esdras A of the LXX, III Esdras of the Vulgate, or The Greek Ezra) is mainly composed of matter taken from the Hebrew canonical Books It is generally dated between c. 200 and 50 B.C.

2 ESDRAS (IV Esdras of the Vulgate or The Ezra Apocalypse) is composite, viz.: (a) 1–2, an introductory section partly based on the NT; (b) 3–14, the 'Ezra-Apocalypse' proper, in which the writer relates his visions and discourses with an angel; this section is dated after A.D. 70 and not later than the reign of Hadrian (117–38); (c) 15–16, an appendix, in some MSS. reckoned as 'V Esdras'.

ESPEN, Z. B. VAN See Van Espen, Z. B.

ESPOUSALS OF THE BVM. A feast observed in parts of the RC Church on 23 Jan.

ESSAYS AND REVIEWS (1860). A collection of essays by seven Anglican authors who believed in the necessity of free inquiry in religious matters. The liberalism of the book was denounced by S. *Wilberforce; it was condemned by a meeting of bishops in 1861 and synodically condemned in 1864.

ESSAYS CATHOLIC AND CRITICAL (1926). An influential volume of 15 essays by a group of *Anglo-Catholic scholars on leading themes of Christian belief, with special reference to the issues raised by recent

Biblical studies and philosophy.

ESSENES. A Jewish ascetic sect. They seem to have originated in the 2nd cent. B.C. and to have come to an end in the 2nd cent. A.D. Their manner of life was highly organized and communistic. Many scholars have identified the Essenes with the community of the *Dead Sea Scrolls (q.v.).

ESTHER, Book of. This relates how Esther, a Jewess, obtained a position of influence as the consort of Xerxes I, King of Persia (here called 'Ahasuerus'), and used it to save her fellow-countrymen. In its present form it seems to be a popular romance. It was prob. included in the *canon of the OT because it described the institution of *Purim.

ESTIENNE, H. and R. See *Stephanus*.

ESTIUS (1542–1613), Latinized name of Willem Hessels van Est, exegete and hagiographer. His history of the *Gorcum martyrs (1603) was an important piece in the process of their beatification. His main work, a commentary on the Pauline and Catholic Epistles (1614–16), is valuable for its careful exegesis of the literal sense and its judicious choice of patristic material.

ETERNAL CITY, The. A designation of Rome used by classical and Christian authors.

ETERNAL LIFE. In Christianity, not only a life of endless duration but the fullness of life of which the believer becomes possessed here and now through participation in God's eternal being.

ETHELBERT, St. (d. 616), King of Kent from c. 560. He married Bertha, daughter of Charibert, the Frankish king; prob. under her influence, he welcomed St. *Augustine and the Roman mission in 597, was himself converted, and then supported the cause of Christianity in his realm.

ETHELBERT, St. (d. c. 793), King of the East Angles and martyr. He was buried at *Hereford, where the cathedral is placed under his patronage, jointly with that of the BVM.

ETHELBURGA, St. (d. c. 676), abbess.

The sister of St. *Erconwald, she was the first abbess of his *double monastery at Barking.

ETHELDREDA, St. (d. 679), also **Audrey**, founder of *Ely. The daughter of a Christian king of the East Angles, she was married twice. She became a nun c. 672. In 673 she founded the *double monastery at Ely, of which she was abbess until her death.

ETHELHARD (d. 805), Abp. of *Canterbury. He was elected in 791 but not consecrated until 793. The opposition of the Kentish people to a Mercian archbishop broke into open revolt in 796. After a visit to Rome, Ethelbert obtained the abolition of the archiepiscopal status of *Lichfield; the supremacy of Canterbury over the Mercian sees was acknowledged at the Council of *Clovesho in 803.

ETHELWOLD, St. (c. 908–84), Bp. of *Winchester from 963. He was one of the leaders of the reform movement in the English Church and did much to revive English monasticism. The *Regularis Concordia is partly, perhaps mainly, his work.

ETHERIA, Pilgrimage of. The account of a journey by a (prob.) Spanish abbess or nun to Egypt, the *Holy Land, *Edessa, Asia Minor, and *Constantinople at the end of the 4th cent. In the first part she records her identification of places with the sites of Biblical events; in the second the descriptions are mainly of liturgical matters, esp. the services of *Jerusalem and the neighbourhood. The document is also known as the 'Peregrinatio Silviae'.

ETHICAL MOVEMENT. In 1876 the 'Society for Ethical Culture' was founded in the U.S.A. by Felix Adler, to unite those who hold that morality is the fundamental element in religion. A corresponding movement begun in Britain in 1887 attracted less support.

ETHIOPIAN (or Abyssinian) CHURCH. Christianity was introduced into Ethiopia in the 4th cent. by St. *Frumentius and Edesius of Tyre, who were apparently originally taken there as prisoners. There was a further Byzantine mission, prob. from Syria, in the late 5th and early 6th cent. After a brief period of prosperity, the Abyssinian Church

declined with the spread of *Islam. When
c. 640 the patriarchate of *Alexandria was
transferred to Cairo, the Abyssinian Church
became dependent on it and its *Monophysite patriarch. A period of renewed vitality
began in the 13th cent., and there were
repeated attempts to restore communion with
Rome. The Act of Union accepted by the
Abyssinian delegates to the Council of
*Florence in 1442 came to nothing. In 1621
the Emp. Susenyos became a Catholic, but
with his abdication in 1632 this union came
to an end and the *Jesuits were banished.
Missionaries continued to be sent from
Rome, but were frequently martyred. When
in 1936 the country was again opened to the
W. by the Italian conquest, the Monophysite
Patriarch was confirmed in his office, though
compelled to break with the *Coptic Church
in Egypt. Since 1950 the Ethiopian Church
has been virtually *autocephalous. See also
Ethiopic Versions of the Bible.

ETHIOPIC BOOK OF ENOCH. See
Enoch, Books of.

ETHIOPIC VERSIONS OF THE BIBLE.
The Bible was translated into Ethiopic
(Ge'ez) prob. from the Greek, in the
4th–5th cent. The Ethiopic OT contains, in
addition to the *Septuagintal Books,
*Jubilees, Ethiopic *Enoch, IV *Esdras, the
Rest of the Words of *Baruch, and other
items.

EUCHARIST. (1) *Name.* The title
'Eucharist' (meaning 'thanksgiving') for the
central act of Christian worship is explained
either because at its institution Christ 'gave
thanks' or because the service is the supreme
act of Christian thanksgiving. Other names
are the 'Holy Communion', the '*Lord's
Supper', and the '*Mass'.
    (2) *Origin.* The institution of the
Eucharist is recorded by St. *Paul in 1 Cor.
11: 23–5 and in the three *Synoptic Gospels. From Acts it is clear that from a very
early date it was a regular part of Christian
worship.
    (3) *Doctrine.* That the Eucharist con-
veyed to the believer the Body and Blood of
Christ was universally accepted from the
first. The Eucharistic elements were themselves referred to as the Body and Blood.
During the Patristic period some theologians
wrote as if they believed that the bread and
wine persisted after the consecration, others

as if they held that they were no longer there;
there was no attempt at precise definition. In
the 9th cent. *Paschasius Radbertus raised
doubts about the identity of Christ's
Eucharistic Body with His Body in Heaven,
and in the 11th cent. much stir was provoked
by the teaching of *Berengar, who denied
that any material change in the elements was
needed to explain the Eucharistic Presence.
Some more precise definition was felt to be
desirable and at the Fourth *Lateran Council
(1215) the *Transubstantiation of the elements was affirmed.
    At the Reformation there was much con-
troversy on the subject. M. *Luther
defended a doctrine of *Consubstantiation,
according to which both the bread and the
wine and the Body and Blood of Christ co-
existed. H. *Zwingli affirmed that the
Lord's Supper was a memorial rite and that
there was no change in the elements. J. *Calvin and his followers held an intermediate
position. They denied that any change in the
elements took place, but maintained that the
faithful received the power or virtue of the
Body and Blood of Christ, a doctrine which
became known as *Virtualism. The ambiguous wording of the BCP has permitted the
coexistence of a variety of doctrines in the C
of E. The Council of *Trent reaffirmed the
doctrine of transubstantiation, but since the
Second *Vatican Council some RC theologians have explored the notions of 'transig-
nification' and 'transfinalization' to express
the mode of the Eucharistic presence.
    It was also widely held from the first that
the Eucharist was in some sense a sacrifice,
though here again definition was gradual.
Among the Reformation theologians there
was a tendency to deny the sacrifice or to
explain it in an unreal sense. The Council of
Trent affirmed that the Sacrifice of the Mass
was propitiatory, that it availed for the living
and the dead, and that it did not detract from
the sufficiency of the Sacrifice of *Calvary.
In modern times there has been considerable
discussion about the nature of the Eucharistic
sacrifice.

EUCHARISTIC CONGRESSES. Interna-
tional congresses organized by the RC
Church for promoting devotion to the Bl.
Sacrament.

EUCHARISTIC FAST. By this is commonly understood complete abstinence from
food and drink for a period preceding the

reception of Communion. The traditional period of the fast in the W. was from the previous midnight. The observance was almost universal in the Middle Ages. It was taken over by the Reformers, but gradually died out among Protestants, though it was encouraged in the C of E by the *Tractarians. In the RC Church there has been a tendency to relax and curtail the discipline; in 1964 the period of the fast was reduced to one hour before receiving Communion. In the E. Church a strict fast is observed from the time of rising.

EUCHARISTIC PRAYERS (RC). From at least the 6th cent. the *Canon of the Mass was the only consecratory prayer used in the Roman rite. In 1968, however, the Congregation of Sacred *Rites provided three other forms of Eucharistic Prayer, each of which may be used as an alternative to the Canon at the option of the celebrant. Further variations have since been authorized.

EUCHARISTIC VESTMENTS. In the W. the traditional vestments of the celebrant of the Eucharist are the *amice, *alb, *girdle, *maniple, *stole, and *chasuble. They derive from the secular clothing of Roman citizens in the 2nd cent. In the E. Church the vestments are fundamentally the same, though different in shape. In the C of E they fell into disuse after the Reformation; their revival in the 19th cent. aroused controversy, but they are clearly permitted by the 1969 *Canons. See also *Cope*, and entries on separate vestments.

EUCHELAION. In the Greek Church the regular term for the Sacrament of *Unction.

EUCHERIUS, St. (d. *c.* 449), Bp. of Lyons from *c.* 434. Although married, he became a monk at *Lérins. As Bishop he presided, with *Hilary of Arles, over the Synod of *Orange in 441. He wrote exegetical and ascetical works.

EUCHITES. Another name for the *Messalians.

EUCHOLOGION. In the E. Church the liturgical book containing the text and rubrics of the three Eucharistic rites in current use, the invariable parts of the Divine Office, and the prayers required for the administration of the *Sacraments and *Sacramentals.

EUDES, St. JOHN (1601–80), French missioner. He joined the *Oratory in 1623; after spending ten years conducting missions, he withdrew in 1643 and founded at Caen the 'Congregation of Jesus and Mary', an association of priests whose object was to run seminaries. He fostered devotion to the *Sacred Heart of Jesus and sought to give it a theological foundation; he also encouraged devotion to the *Sacred Heart of Mary.

EUDISTS. The common name for members of the 'Congregation of Jesus and Mary', founded by St. John *Eudes. They are now engaged mainly in secondary education.

EUDOXIUS (300–70), *Anomoean leader. Appointed Bp. of Germanicia by the *Arians, he took part in many of the Arian councils of the 4th cent. He became Bp. of *Constantinople in 360.

EUGENIUS III (d. 1153), *Cistercian, Pope from 1145. He was much influenced by St. *Bernard, under whom he had entered *Clairvaux in 1135. In 1147 he commissioned him to preach the Second *Crusade. In 1148 he held synods at *Reims, which dealt with the heresy of *Gilbert de la Porrée, and at Cremona, where he excommunicated *Arnold of Brescia.

EUGENIUS IV (1383–1447), Pope from 1431. One of his first acts was to dismiss the Council of *Basle, though when it refused to dissolve he recognized it as canonical in 1433. Relations deteriorated and an antipope, Felix V, was elected in 1439. Meanwhile Eugenius had called a council at Ferrara (1438); after its transference to *Florence he concluded a short-lived union of the Greek and Roman Churches. See *Florence, Council of*.

EUGIPPIUS (*c.* 455–535), Abbot of Lucullanum, near Naples. About 511 he wrote the life of St. *Severinus of Noricum. He also made a collection of extracts from the writings of St. *Augustine which was widely read in the Middle Ages.

EULOGIA. In early times the word meant a 'blessing' or 'something blessed'. It was applied to the blessed bread distributed to *catechumens and others after the Mass was ended. See also *Pain Bénit*.

EUNAN, St. See *Adamnan, St.*

EUNOMIUS (d. 394), *Arian Bp. of Cyzicus. A pupil of *Aetius, he became Bp. of Cyzicus, prob. in 360, but he resigned a few months later. He died in exile at Dakora.

His main work, an Apology, was written c. 360. It was answered by *Basil of Caesarea. *Gregory of Nyssa's *Contra Eunomium* was a reply to Eunomius's rejoinder. Eunomius taught a single supreme Substance, whose simplicity is opposed to all distinction; he denied that the generation of the Son took place within the Divine Nature, but regarded Him as being immediately produced by the Father, from whom He received the creative power which caused Him to resemble the Father. Eunomius's chief importance lies in the reaction of the *Cappadocian Fathers, whose doctrines of God and human knowledge of God largely took shape as a critique of his teaching.

EUPHEMIA, St. (perhaps 4th cent.), virgin and martyr. She was venerated in the E., esp. as patroness of the church where the Council met at *Chalcedon in 451.

EUSEBIAN CANONS, The. The system of tables devised by *Eusebius of Caesarea to enable the reader of the Gospels to turn up the passages in the other Gospels parallel to the one before him.

EUSEBIUS (c. 260–c. 340), Bp. of *Caesarea from c. 315, the 'Father of Church History'. During the *Arian controversy he was the leader of the moderate party. At the Council of *Nicaea (325), where his orthodoxy seems to have been on trial, he ultimately accepted the *Nicene Creed; his fear of *Sabellianism, however, prevented him from giving *Athanasius his full support.

Eusebius's 'Ecclesiastical History' is the principal source for the history of Christianity from the Apostolic Age to his own day. It contains an immense range of material on the E. Church, largely in the form of extracts taken over bodily from earlier writers. His other works include 'the Martyrs of Palestine', an account of the *Diocletianic persecution; a 'Chronicle' or summary of universal history with a table of dates; a 'Life of *Constantine', which,

though panegyric, contains valuable historical matter; and a pair of treatises, the 'Preparation for the Gospel' and the 'Demonstration of the Gospel'. The former of these shows why Christians accept the Hebrew and reject the Greek tradition; the latter attempts to prove Christianity from the OT.

EUSEBIUS (mid-5th cent.), Bp. of Dorylaeum (in modern Turkey) by 448, when he attacked the heresy of *Eutyches at the 'Home Synod' in Constantinople. He was deposed by the *Latrocinium (449), but took a prominent part in the Council of *Chalcedon (451).

EUSEBIUS (d. c. 359), Bp. of Emesa (the modern Homs) in Syria. He was a Biblical exegete and writer on doctrinal subjects, of *Semi-Arian sympathies. Having declined the see of *Alexandria when *Athanasius was deposed in 339, he became Bp. of Emesa soon afterwards. Until recently only fragments of his work were known; 17 homilies have now been ascribed to him with some probability.

EUSEBIUS (d. c. 342), Bp. of Nicomedia. He was the leader of the *Arian party in the first half of the 4th cent. His ascendancy over the Emp. *Constantine, whom he baptized in his last illness, and over Constantius (d. 361) enabled him to organize the forces of the State and of the Church against *Athanasius and his supporters.

EUSEBIUS, St. (d. 380), Bp. of Samosata from 361. He was strongly opposed to *Arianism. In 374 he was exiled for his orthodoxy but he was recalled four years later.

EUSEBIUS, St. (d. 371), Bp. of Vercelli from 340. He was a strong supporter of orthodoxy in the *Arian controversy. He lived with his clergy under rule and hence has sometimes been regarded by the *canons regular as one of their founders. Three letters have survived; various works which have come down under the names of other authors have been attributed to him in modern times.

EUSTACE, St., also Eustachius, patron of hunters and of the city of Madrid. His existence is doubtful. He is said to have been a Roman general, converted by a vision of a stag with a crucifix between its antlers, and later roasted to death in a brazen bull.

EUSTATHIUS, St., Bp. of *Antioch from *c.* 324 to 330. At the Council of *Nicaea (325) he was given a place of honour. His uncompromising orthodoxy brought him into conflict with *Eusebius of Caesarea; he was deposed at a Council at Antioch in 330 and banished to Thrace. Of his writings only *De Engastrimutho* (against *Origen) survives.

EUSTATHIUS (*c.* 300–*c.* 377), Bp. of Sebaste in Pontus from *c.* 357. He was a pupil of *Arius and throughout his life vacillated in his attitude to the *Nicene cause. His main interests were in the *monastic movement, in the organization of which he took a prominent part.

EUSTOCHIUM, St. JULIA (370–*c.* 419), Roman virgin. With her mother, St. *Paula, she came under the influence of St. *Jerome. A letter which he addressed to her on virginity created such a stir that they left Rome (385). They settled at *Bethlehem, where they built four monasteries.

EUTHALIUS. The reputed author of a collection of editorial material found in many MSS. of the Greek NT. Attached to the Euthalian prologue to the Pauline Epistles is a 'Martyrium Pauli', apparently dated either 458 or 396, but this may not be by the same author. Virtually nothing is known of Euthalius except that he is described as a deacon.

EUTHANASIA. Since 1869 the word has come to denote the termination of life on humanitarian grounds. It is opposed by moral theologians as a breach of the Sixth Commandment and as a denial of the Christian attitude to suffering. On the other hand there is no obligation to use extraordinary efforts to prolong life, and it is commonly held that drugs may legitimately be used to relieve pain even when the indirect result is to shorten life.

EUTHYMIUS, St. (377–473), monk. A native of Armenia, he came to *Jerusalem in 405 and established a *lavra at Khan-el-Ahmar *c.* 426. He was loyal to the decisions of the Council of *Chalcedon and he exercised a formative influence upon Palestinian monasticism.

EUTHYMIUS ZIGABENUS (early 12th cent.), Byzantine theologian. A monk at *Constantinople, he wrote his *Panoplia Dogmatica*, describing all heresies, at the Imperial command. The section (27) on the *Bogomils is the principal source on the subject. He also wrote extensive Biblical commentaries.

EUTYCHES (*c.* 378–454), heresiarch. He was *archimandrite of a monastery at *Constantinople. His opposition to *Nestorius in 448 led to his being accused of the opposite heresy of confounding the natures in Christ; he was deposed by *Flavian, Abp. of Constantinople, acquitted at the *Latrocinium (449), and deposed and exiled at the Council of *Chalcedon (451). He denied that the manhood of Christ was consubstantial with ours, a view which went far to rendering our redemption through Him impossible. He also maintained that there were 'two natures before, but only one after, the Union' in the Incarnate Christ, and was thus the real founder of *Monophysitism.

EVAGRIUS PONTICUS (346–99), spiritual writer. He was a noted preacher at *Constantinople. In 382 he set out for the *Nitrian desert, where he spent the rest of his life. He was the first monk to write extensively, and he occupies a central place in the history of Christian spirituality.

EVAGRIUS, 'SCHOLASTICUS' (*c.* 536–600), Church historian. His History, extending from 431 to 594, uses good sources.

EVANGELIARY. (1) A book containing the text of the four Gospels. (2) The liturgical book containing the portions of the Gospel to be read at the Eucharist, arranged according to their place in the ecclesiastical year.

EVANGELICAL ALLIANCE. An interdenominational body formed in London in 1846 to 'associate and concentrate the strength of an enlightened *Protestantism against the encroachments of *Popery and *Puseyism, and to promote the interests of Scriptural Christianity'. Its influence declined in the 20th cent. In 1951, at a joint meeting of the American National Association of Evangelicals and the British Evangelical Alliance, the World Evangelical Fellowship was founded on similar principles.

EVANGELICAL ASSOCIATION, The. See the following entry.

EVANGELICAL CHURCH, The. A small American Protestant sect, also known as the **Albright Brethren** after Jacob Albright (1759–1808). Albright broke away from the *Methodist Episcopal Church and created for his followers an independent organization, known from 1816 as the Evangelical Association. Internal controversies led to a schism; this was healed in 1922 and the reunited body called itself the Evangelical Church. It joined with the United Brethren in Christ to form the Evangelical United Brethren Church in 1946.

EVANGELICAL CHURCH IN GERMANY, The (*Die Evangelische Kirche in Deutschland*). A federation of 27 autonomous Protestant territorial Churches in E. and W. Germany, formed in 1945. It includes both *Lutheran and *Reformed Churches. In 1969 the 8 East German Churches were compelled to form a separate League and to sever their formal connection with their sister Churches in W. Germany.

EVANGELICALISM. (1) In a wider sense the term 'Evangelical' has been applied since the Reformation to the Protestant Churches because of their claim to base their teaching pre-eminently on the Gospel. (2) In Germany and Switzerland 'Evangelical' was long used esp. of the *Lutheran group of Protestant Churches as contrasted with the *Calvinist (Reformed) Churches. (3) In the C of E the term is currently applied to the school which lays special stress on personal conversion and salvation by faith in the atoning death of Christ. The group originated in the 18th cent. to bring reality into religion when a low tone pervaded English life, and it had several points of contact with the *Methodist revival. In the 19th cent. it took a leading part in missionary work and social reform. See also *Liberal Evangelicalism*.

EVANGELICAL UNION, The. A religious denomination formed in Scotland in 1843 by James *Morison (q.v.). The Union was an association of independent Churches over whom it exercised no jurisdiction; in 1897 most of the Churches in the Union joined the *Congregational Union of Scotland.

EVANGELISCHE BUND, Der (Germ., 'The Evangelical League'). An alliance of German Protestants founded in 1866–7 by W. *Beyschlag and others for the defence of Protestant interests against the growing power of Catholicism.

EVANGELISCHE KIRCHE IN DEUTSCHLAND, Die. See *Evangelical Church in Germany*.

EVANGELIST. (1) In the NT the word is thrice used of a travelling missionary. Prob. no specific office is designated. (2) In a more technical sense, the author of one of the four canonical *Gospels.

EVANGELIUM VERITATIS (Lat., 'The Gospel of Truth'). A treatise included among the Coptic texts found at *Nag Hammadi. It expounds the mission of Jesus as 'the Word' or 'the Name' of the Father, alludes briefly to His teaching ministry, and comments on His death and its significance. It includes some unusual features, such as the attribution of evil to Error, personified as a female figure. Some scholars have identified it with a work of this title referred to by *Irenaeus as having been produced by the disciples of *Valentinus.

EVANSON, EDWARD (1731–1805), divine. He developed views with *Unitarian affinities; though prosecution failed on a technical point, he resigned his living in the C of E. He published the earliest formal attack on the traditional authorship of St. *John's Gospel.

EVANSTON, Illinois. The Second Assembly of the *World Council of Churches met at Evanston in 1954.

EVE. The first woman, the wife of *Adam. In the Genesis story (ch. 2f.), she is tempted to eat the forbidden fruit of the tree of knowledge; she and Adam disobey, '*fall', and are driven out from *Eden; and Eve is punished with the pain of childbirth.

EVELYN, JOHN (1620–1706), Anglican diarist. After travelling widely, he settled in 1652 at Sayes Court, near Deptford. Under the Commonwealth he befriended many of the dispossessed clergy. He enjoyed royal favour under *Charles II and *James II and held various appointments. He played a prominent part in Church affairs, esp. in the rebuilding of *St. Paul's Cathedral. His *Diary* is an important document for social history.

EVENING COMMUNION. There are possible references to evening celebrations of the Eucharist in the NT, but it seems that an early hour of the day soon became the usual time. After the Reformation some Protestant Churches celebrated the Lord's Supper in the morning and evening indifferently. In the RC Church rules about the *Eucharistic fast were relaxed during the Second World War and evening Masses were permitted in military establishments; they are now common in both parish and monastic churches. In the C of E celebrations of the Eucharist in the evening were a mark of *Low Churchmanship from the middle of the 19th to the middle of the 20th cent.

EVENSONG. The common name for the C of E service of Evening Prayer. The office in the BCP consists basically of Psalms, an OT lesson, the *Magnificat, a NT lesson, the *Nunc Dimittis, the *Apostles' Creed, and prayers. In substance it is a conflation of *Vespers and *Compline. The *Alternative Services introduced various changes, mainly in the direction of curtailment and the provision of alternatives.

EVURTIUS, St. The correct form of the name of St. *Enurchus.

EWALD, HEINRICH GEORG AUGUST (1803–75), German OT theologian and Orientalist. His 'Hebrew Grammar' (1827) was a landmark in the history of OT philology, while his History of Israel exercised wide influence on British scholarship, restraining the negative tendencies of much OT criticism of his day.

EXALTATION OF THE CROSS, The. The feast kept in honour of the Cross of Christ, observed on 14 Sept., and also known as 'Holy Cross Day'. In the W. Church it now commemorates the exposition of the supposed true Cross at Jerusalem in 629 after its recovery from the Persians.

EXAMINING CHAPLAINS. In the C of E the duty of examining candidates for holy orders properly belongs to the *archdeacons, but other ministers are also appointed for this purpose.

EXARCH. The title of: (1) certain civil governors in the later Roman Empire; (2) certain bishops lower in rank than *patriarchs but having rights over the *metropolitans in one civil diocese.

EXCARDINATION. In W. canon law the liberation of a cleric from his present *ordinary with a view to fresh enlistment (*incardination) under a new superior.

EX CATHEDRA. See *Cathedra*.

EXCEPTIONS, The. The list of objections made by the *Puritans at the *Savoy Conference (1661) to the existing BCP (of 1604) with a view to its revision.

EXCLUSION, Right of. The right formerly claimed by the heads of certain Catholic states to name a particular candidate whom they desired to exclude from being elected Pope. It was annulled in 1904.

EXCLUSION CONTROVERSY. After T. *Oates's announcement of the *Popish Plot, the Whigs tried to exclude James, Duke of York (later *James II), from the succession to the throne. A bill failed to pass beyond the Commons in 1679 and another was rejected by the Lords in 1680.

EXCOMMUNICATION. An ecclesiastical censure which excludes those subject to it from the communion of the faithful and imposes certain other deprivations and disabilities. It does not profess to extend to the union of the soul with God.

In the RC Church an excommunicate person ('excommunicatus toleratus') may not lawfully administer or receive the Sacraments; one pronounced 'excommunicatus vitandus' by the Holy See is also deprived of any office or dignity, any ecclesiastical action he may perform is rendered invalid, and the faithful are warned against social intercourse with him. In the C of E the 1969 *Canons envisage excommunication, but its use is very rare.

EXEGESIS. The act of explaining a text, in theology usually a sacred text. The purpose may be either to describe the author's meaning or to apply that meaning to a contemporary situation.

Biblical exegesis has been practised from early times by both Jews and Christians. Christian writers insisted that the meaning must be elucidated in conformity with apostolic tradition. A chiefly *allegorical mode of interpretation was fostered by the *Alexandrian school, while that of *Antioch cultivated the explanation of the literal sense of the Bible. The *Schoolmen favoured the fourfold method of literal, allegorical, moral, and anagogical (or mystical) exegesis. At the Reformation many Protestant theologians rejected the authority of the Church's tradition as a criterion of exegesis, substituting the interior witness of the Holy Spirit. It was among Protestants that literary and historical criticism first came to be practised; it emerged in Germany in the 18th cent. From the beginning of the 19th cent. much attention was given to the origin, nature, and history of individual Biblical documents and to the reconstruction of Biblical history, including the life of Jesus. With notable exceptions among the *Modernists, RC exegesis has until recently largely ignored or reacted against critical Biblical scholarship, though a new openness and independence is now apparent. See also *Hermeneutics*.

EXEMPLARISM. The view of the *Atonement which holds that the value of the death of Christ for us lies purely in the moral example which it sets us of complete love and self-surrender, thus moving our imagination and will to repentance and holiness.

EXEMPTION. In an ecclesiastical sense, freedom from control by one's normal superior (usually the Bishop of the diocese) and hence in general immediate subjection either to the superior of one's religious house or order, or to the Pope.

EXEQUATUR (Lat., 'he may perform'). The right, also known as the 'Regium Placet', claimed by certain governments to prevent ecclesiastical enactments of the Roman see from taking automatic effect in their territories.

EXETER. When the diocese of *Sherborne was divided in 909, a see for Devon and Cornwall was established at *Crediton; in 1050 it was transferred to Exeter. Since the foundation of the diocese of *Truro that of Exeter has been almost conterminous with the county of Devon.

A monastery was founded at Exeter by Aethelstan in 932, and refounded by Canute in 1019. This was destroyed to make way for a Norman cathedral, of which only the towers remain. The present cathedral is mainly Decorated in style. Notable are the *misericords, a clock made at *Glastonbury in 1285, the Bishop's throne, and the West front.

EXETER HALL. A building in the Strand, London, used until 1907 for religious and philanthropic assemblies, esp. by those of Evangelical sympathies. 'Exeter Hall' came to be used allusively for a certain type of *Evangelicalism.

EXILE, The. The phrase is used absolutely of the captivity of the Jews in Babylon from 586 to 538 B.C.

EXISTENTIALISM. Certain types of philosophical thinking which share a practical concern for the individually existing person and his freedom. The contemporary movement goes back to S. *Kierkegaard, F. W. *Nietzsche, and E. Husserl, whose *Phenomenology provided a systematic method of describing the universal elements in human consciousness. The main body of Existentialist thinking seems to derive from the discovery of Kierkegaard by philosophers in Germany in the early 20th cent., esp. by theologians in opposition to Liberal Protestantism, and from the shattering of cultural values in Europe after the First World War. Leading writers have included M. *Heidegger, J. P. Sartre, G. Marcel, and K. *Jaspers.

The question of a Christian Existentialism has been prominent in Protestant theological debate. Opponents have claimed that Existentialism reduces theology to anthropology, dissolves the historical foundations of Christianity, and treats salvation as only a self-generated decision in favour of authentic existence. Supporters have held that an Existentialist standpoint is implicit in the NT, and that to acknowledge the salvation event as part of history only serves to confirm the radical nature of faith, locating salvation not in external events but in an encounter between God and our personal existence.

Existentialism was condemned by the encyclical '*Humani Generis' (1950), but it has continued to influence some RC theologians.

EXODUS, Book of. This OT Book records the events attending the 'Exodus' (i.e. the release of the Israelites under *Moses from their Egyptian bondage) and the giving of the Law on Mount *Sinai. Its authorship has traditionally been ascribed to Moses, but modern critics believe it to be a composite work of a later age, its strata prob. having been written between the 9th and 5th cents. B.C. The date of the Exodus is also debated; the extreme limits seem to be 1580 B.C. and 1215 B.C., most scholars favouring the 13th cent. B.C. The deliverance was throughout Jewish history regarded as the outstanding instance of God's favour to His chosen people; Christian writers have used the imagery of the *Passover with reference to the sacrifice of Christ on Calvary and of the *Eucharist.

EXOMOLOGESIS. In the early Church the word was applied to the whole process of confession, satisfaction, and forgiveness by which a penitent sinner was reconciled to the Church.

EX OPERE OPERATO. A term used by theologians to express the essentially objective mode of operation of the Sacraments, and its independence of the subjective attitudes of either the minister or the recipient.

EXORCISM. The practice of expelling evil spirits by means of prayer and set formulas was common among Jews and pagans. From NT times the Church, after Christ's example, has exorcized persons possessed of an evil spirit. Exorcism has also been applied to *catechumens; it is included in the 1972 RC Order for Adult Initiation and in the 1969 Order for the Baptism of Infants, though in the latter case it may be omitted. Such exorcisms, as well as the lesser exorcisms used in the blessing of water, &c., do not presuppose a state of possession, but are prayers asking for the restraint of evil.

EXORCIST. The second of the traditional *Minor Orders. The power of exorcizing evil spirits, however, was never confined to members of a particular order. The duties of the exorcist came to include the imposition of hands on '*energumens' and the exorcizing of *catechumens. In the RC Church the office was finally suppressed in 1972.

EXOUCONTIANS. The extreme party of

the *Arians, also known as '*Anomoeans'.

EXPECTANT, The Church. The body of Christians waiting between earth and heaven, in what is traditionally called *Purgatory.

EXPIATION. The atoning or making up for an offence committed against God or one's neighbour. Christianity claims that the only sufficient expiation of human sin is the offering made by Christ of His earthly life and death, and that the merits of this offering are infinite. See also *Atonement*.

EXPIATION, Day of. An alternative name for the Day of *Atonement.

EXPOSITION OF THE BLESSED SACRAMENT. The exhibition of the consecrated Eucharistic *Host for the purpose of devotion. The form of service which accompanies Exposition is similar to that of *Benediction.

EXSURGE, DOMINE. The bull issued by *Leo X in 1520 excommunicating M. *Luther. After an unsuccessful appeal for a *General Council, Luther broke with the Papacy by publicly burning the bull.

EXTRA-LITURGICAL SERVICES. Services for which no fixed form is provided in the authorized liturgical formularies.

EXTRAVAGANTES. The term, at one time applied to certain officially recognized Papal *decretals which were not included in the 'Decretum' of *Gratian ('extra decretum vagantes'), is now used almost exclusively of the two concluding sections of the *Corpus Iuris Canonici (q.v.).

EXTREME UNCTION. See Unction.

EXULTET. In the W. liturgy the 'Paschal Proclamation' sung by the deacon at the blessing of the *Paschal Candle on *Holy Saturday, and so named from its opening word.

EYCK, H. and J. VAN. See Van Eyck, H and J.

EZEKIEL, Book of. Ezekiel was the last of the 'Greater' OT Prophets, the successor of *Isaiah and *Jeremiah. The Book prophesies the destruction of *Jerusalem, doom for various foreign nations, and the redemption and reconstitution of the Jewish people. The author writes as one overawed by the majesty and holiness of God.

The traditional view is that the Book was written in Babylon, whither Ezekiel had been deported in 597 B.C. Some scholars hold that only a small part of the Book goes back to Ezekiel himself; others that Ezekiel was never in Babylon at all; yet others that the Book is a *pseudepigraphon to be dated in the 3rd cent. B.C.

EZNIK (5th cent.), Bp. of Bagrevand in *Armenia. He wrote a *Confutation of the Sects* and took part in translating the Armenian version of the Bible.

EZRA. Jewish priest and scribe. His activities are recorded in the Books of *Ezra and Nehemiah and of 1 *Esdras. He took strict measures to secure the racial purity of the Jews and he promulgated a code of law. The chronology is obscure, but it appears that his arrival in Jerusalem is to be dated in 397 B.C. If so, he belonged to a later generation than *Nehemiah.

EZRA and NEHEMIAH, Books of. These OT Books continue the history of the Hebrew people begun in *Chronicles, and are evidently the work of the same compiler. Ez. records the return of the exiles from Babylon and their attempts to rebuild the *Temple at *Jerusalem and *Ezra's mission and work. Neh. records *Nehemiah's plans for the restoration of Jerusalem and his arrangements for the occupation of the city and other reforms. See also *Esdras, Books of*.

F

FABER, FREDERICK WILLIAM (1814–63), *Oratorian. Brought up a *Calvinist, he came under the influence of J. H. *Newman at Oxford and was ordained in the C of E. In 1845 he became a RC. With other converts he formed a small community, which in 1848 joined the Oratory of St. *Philip Neri; the next year Faber became head of the London house. He wrote many hymns and devotional books.

FABER, JACOBUS (c. 1455–1536), also known as **Lefèvre d'Étaples** or **Stapulensis**, French humanist. Two critical essays on St. *Mary Magdalene led to his condemnation by the *Sorbonne in 1521. His attitude to the *Reformation was similar to that of D. *Erasmus. He published the first printed text of the (Lat.) *Ignatian Epistles (1498) and a French translation of the *Vulgate (NT, 1523; OT, 1528).

FABER, JOHANN (1478–1541), Bp. of Vienna from 1530. His friendship with D. *Erasmus led him at first to sympathize with P. *Melanchthon and H. *Zwingli in their desire for reform, but as the doctrinal cleavage became clear he withdrew his support and defended Catholic orthodoxy.

FABIAN, St. (d. 250), Bp. of Rome from 236. When the *Decian persecution broke out in 250 he was the first to suffer martyrdom.

FABIOLA, St. (d. 399), Roman matron. She divorced her husband, remarried, but after the death of her second husband did public penance. In 395 she went to *Bethlehem and put herself under the direction of St. *Jerome. Returning to Rome, she continued in charitable work.

FABRI, FELIX (1442–1520). A learned *Dominican who has left a vivid record of a pilgrimage to *Jerusalem in 1483.

FABRICIUS, JOHANNES ALBERT (1668–1736), *Lutheran scholar. His *Bibliotheca Graeca* (1705–28), covering the period from Homer to 1453, and a corresponding survey of Latin writing, laid the foundations for subsequent histories of literature. He did important work on the *Apocrypha and in 1716–18 he produced the first edition of the works of *Hippolytus.

FACULTIES, Court of. The court established in 1534 when the granting of *dispensations, licences, and *faculties in the provinces of *Canterbury and *York was transferred from the Pope to the Abp. of Canterbury.

FACULTY. A dispensation or licence from an ecclesiastical superior permitting someone to perform an action or occupy a position which without it he could not lawfully do or hold. In 1534 the 'Court of *Faculties' was created to restrain people from suing for dispensations from Rome. Since in every diocese the consecrated lands and buildings and their contents are in the ultimate guardianship of the Bishop, faculties are needed for additions or alterations to churches or churchyards; in such cases they are normally issued by the Bishop's *Chancellor or the *Archdeacon.

FACUNDUS (6th cent.), Bp. of Hermiane in Africa. In the *Monophysite controversy he was one of the chief supporters of the *Three Chapters. He went to *Constantinople and there in 547–8 he completed a treatise upholding the orthodoxy of *Ibas, *Theodore of Mopsuestia (with some reservations), and *Theodoret. After his return to Africa he wrote two further works.

FAIRBAIRN, ANDREW MARTIN (1838–1912), *Congregationalist. He was principal of Mansfield College, Oxford, from 1886 to 1909. He visited Germany and became a warm advocate of theological liberalism. He occupied a unique position among Congregational divines of his generation.

FAITH. The term is used in two distinct senses.
(1) The body of truth ('the Christian faith') to be found in the *Creeds, the definitions of Councils, &c., and esp. in the Bible. This complex of doctrine is held to embody or to follow from the teaching of Christ and to be wilfully rejected by man only at the peril of his salvation.
(2) To this objective faith is opposed 'subjective' faith. This is the human response to Divine truth. Faith in this sense is a supernatural, not a natural, act, and is dependent on God's action on the soul. It demands an act of the will and is thus more than intellectual. This voluntaristic moment in the act of faith accounts for the moral quality which it is held to possess and the

conviction that wilful unbelief, as a misdirection of the will, merits the censure of God. As a supernatural act, faith is a higher faculty than reason. In the Middle Ages a distinction was drawn between those truths accessible to the human intellect by the light of natural reason, e.g. the existence of God, and those which could be appropriated only by faith, e.g. belief in the *Trinity. At the Reformation the part of faith in the Christian religion received a new emphasis. M. *Luther's teaching on *justification by 'faith alone' stressed the voluntaristic side of faith, in so far as faith was allowed to be a human act at all. The chief moment in it was trust, a supremely personal trust in the atoning work of Christ.

FAITH, Defender of the and **Promoter of the.** See *Defender of the Faith* and *Promotor Fidei.*

FAITH, St. (d. c. 287), virgin and martyr. Acc. to late legend she suffered for the faith at Agen in Aquitaine. Her relics were brought c. 855 to the abbey of Conques, which became a famous place of pilgrimage.

FAITH AND ORDER. A branch of the *Ecumenical Movement by which Conferences were organized at *Lausanne in 1927 and at *Edinburgh in 1937. It was absorbed into the *World Council of Churches.

FAITHFUL, Mass of the. The part of the *Eucharist from the *Offertory to the end, so called because in early times only the baptized (the faithful) remained for the central part of the service.

FALDA. A white vestment worn only by the Pope.

FALDSTOOL. In the RC Church a folding stool used in the sanctuary by bishops and other prelates when they do not occupy the throne.

FALK, PAUL LUDWIG ADALBERT (1827–1900), German Liberal politician. From 1872 to 1879 he was Minister of Public Worship and Education, appointed with explicit instructions to defend the State against the Church in the *Kulturkampf. His *May Laws failed because of opposition from orthodox Protestants as well as RCs.

FALL, The. The first act of disobedience of *Adam and *Eve whereby man lost his primal innocence. Acc. to Gen. 2 f., Eve, tempted by a serpent, ate the forbidden fruit of the 'tree of the knowledge of good and evil' and induced Adam to do likewise. The punishment was expulsion from the Garden of *Eden, the imposition of toilsome work on Adam and the pains of childbirth on Eve, and the decree of perpetual enmity between the serpent and man. The Biblical narrative teaches that sin arose by human choice and that all human life has thereby been radically changed for the worse, so that its actual state is different from that prepared for it by the Creator. There has been much debate about the ultimate origin of the evil manifested in Adam and Eve's sin and about the nature and extent of the consequences for mankind.

Until modern times the common Christian belief regarded the Fall of Adam and Eve as a historical event. The serpent was identified with the *Devil, a spiritual being who must have been created good and himself previously fallen, and hence the original Fall was inferred to be that of Satan rather than of Adam and Eve. Since all subsequent humanity was believed to have descended from Adam and Eve, the consequences of the Fall were held to affect all mankind by inheritance. Though in modern times the concept of the Fall has often been held to be inconsistent with the facts of man's development known to science, orthodox theologians still see in the story of Gen. 2 f. a fundamental truth about man in his relation to God, even if the truth is now held to be there conveyed in legendary form. See also *Original Sin*.

FALSE DECRETALS, The. A collection of documents, attributed to St. *Isidore of Seville (d. 636), but really compiled in France c. 850. It contains: (1) letters of ante-Nicene Popes, all forgeries; (2) a collection of canons of councils, mostly genuine; and (3) a collection of letters of Popes from *Sylvester I (d. 335) to *Gregory II (d. 731), of which 35 are spurious. They were drawn up to defend the rights of diocesan bishops against their metropolitans and to claim early authority for Papal supremacy.

FAMILISTS. Members of a sect called the 'Family of Love', founded by H. *Nicholas. They propagated a vague philanthropism of pantheistic hue and *antinomian tendencies. The sect disappeared at the end of the 17th cent., amalgamating with the *Quakers and others.

FAN, Liturgical. From at least the 4th cent. fans were sometimes used at the Eucharist to keep insects away from the oblations. Their surviving use in some E. Churches is now purely symbolic.

FANON. The word has been applied to various accessories of religious worship, but it is now confined to the collar-shaped garment worn by the Pope over his *amice when celebrating a solemn pontifical Mass.

FAREL, GUILLAUME (1489–1565), Reformer. He introduced the Reformation at Neuchâtel in 1530, and in 1535, with P. *Viret, he led a triumphant struggle which established the Reformation at Geneva. The next year he persuaded J. *Calvin to stay in Geneva and declared him called to be a preacher and teacher of theology.

FARMERY, another form of 'infirmary', esp. of a monastery.

FARRAR, FREDERIC WILLIAM (1831–1903), Dean of *Canterbury from 1895. A 'Broad Church Evangelical', he had great influence on the religious feeling and culture of the Victorian middle class, esp. through his *Life of Christ* (1874) and *Life and Works of St. Paul* (1879).

FAST. See *Fasts and Fasting*.

FASTIDIUS (early 5th cent.), British *Pelagian writer. *Gennadius calls him a bishop and attributes to him two works, *De vita christiana* and *De viduitate servanda*; their identity is disputed.

FASTS and FASTING. Fasting, as a penitential discipline, is designed to strengthen the spiritual life by weakening the attractions of sensible pleasures. It was practised in Judaism and recommended by Christ both by His example and His teaching. In the early Church regular weekly fast days were established, notably *Friday and for some time also *Wednesday or *Saturday. The fast of *Lent came to extend to 40 days before *Easter. The E. Church added three further periods of fasting.

In early times fasting meant complete

abstinence from food during the whole or part of the fast day. In the E. it is still observed with strictness. In modern RC practice fasting generally means one chief meal with a light '*collation' in the morning and evening, and also demands abstention from flesh meat; days of *abstinence have been distinguished from fast days since 1781. The only two fast days remaining in the RC Church are *Ash Wednesday and *Good Friday. In the C of E days of fasting are mentioned in the 1969 *Canons, but no specific instructions are given for the mode of their observance.

FATHER. Originally the title of Bishops, the word was later applied to confessors, called in medieval England 'ghostly fathers'. In England all RC priests, whether secular or religious, are now called 'Father'; this usage is also found among Anglo-Catholics.

FATHERS, Apostolic; White. See *Apostolic Fathers*; *White Fathers*.

FATHERS OF THE CHURCH. From the late 4th cent. the title has been used of a more or less clearly defined group of ecclesiastical writers of the past whose authority carried special weight; they were held to be characterized by orthodoxy of doctrine, holiness of life, the approval of the Church, and antiquity. The *patristic period is commonly regarded as closing with St. *Isidore of Seville in the W. and St. *John of Damascus in the East.

FATIMA. A small town in Portugal, famous as a place of pilgrimage. In 1917 three illiterate children saw visions of a woman, who declared herself to be 'Our Lady of the Rosary', told them to recite the *Rosary daily, and asked for a chapel to be built in her honour.

FAULHABER, MICHAEL VON (1869–1952), German cardinal. He became Abp. of Munich in 1917 and was created cardinal in 1921. In his earlier years he made some important contributions to patristic studies; later he was the leader of the right-wing Catholics and an outspoken critic of the Nazis.

FAUSTINUS and **JOVITA, Sts.** (2nd cent.), martyrs of Brescia. Acc. to legend they were brothers of noble birth, taken pri-

soner under Trajan, tortured, and transported to Milan, Rome, and Naples, making converts on the way.

FAUSTUS OF MILEVIS (4th cent.), *Manichaean propagandist. He won fame at Rome, but when he visited Carthage in 383, *Augustine, himself then a Manichee, found him a fraud.

FAUSTUS OF RIEZ, St. (*c.* 408–*c.* 490), *Semi-Pelagian teacher. A monk of *Lérins, he became Bp. of Riez *c.* 459. He wrote his *De Gratia* in response to a request from the Abp. of Arles that he should refute the *predestinarian doctrines of a certain Lucidus; he insisted on the necessity of human co-operation with Divine grace, and on the initial free will of men, even when in sin, for the acceptance of that grace.

FAWKES, GUY (1570–1606), the most famous member of the *Gunpowder Plot conspiracy. He was given the task of firing the gunpowder, but he was arrested while keeping watch.

FAYÛM GOSPEL FRAGMENT. A 3rd-cent. papyrus fragment, discovered in 1882, which contains an imperfect prediction of St. *Peter's denial, akin to Mk. 14: 27–30.

FEASTS, Ecclesiastical. These come under three main headings: (1) *Sundays*, the weekly commemoration of the Resurrection. (2) *Movable Feasts*. The most important are *Easter, the annual commemoration of the Resurrection, and *Whitsunday (q.v.). Certain other feasts vary with the date of Easter. (3) *Immovable Feasts*. The earliest were prob. the anniversaries of *martyrs, to which other saints' days were added later. By the 4th cent. various fixed feasts of the Lord, esp. *Christmas and the *Epiphany, became generally observed. See also *Year, Liturgical*.

FEASTS OF OBLIGATION. In the RC Church feasts of outstanding importance which the laity as well as the clergy are obliged to observe by hearing Mass and abstaining from *servile work.

FEATHERS TAVERN PETITION (1772). A petition to Parliament signed at the Feathers Tavern, Strand, London, by *c.* 200 liberal Christians for the abolition of subscription to the *Thirty-Nine Articles and its replacement by a simple declaration of belief in the Bible.

FEBRONIANISM. The movement in the RC Church in 18th-cent. Germany against the claims of the Papacy, esp. in the temporal sphere. In 1763 J. N. von *Hontheim, who had been asked by the three Archbishop-Electors to investigate their grievances, published his findings under the penname 'Justinus Febronius'. The Archbishop-Electors tried to assert their claims at Bad *Ems in 1786.

FELICITY, St. (2nd cent.), Roman martyr. Acc. to her *acta*, she was martyred with her seven sons. She may be the Felicity named in the traditional *Canon of the Mass.

FELICITY, St. (d. 203), African martyr. She was one of the companions of St. *Perpetua.

FELIX, St. (d. c. 648), Bp. of Dunwich. After converting the E. Anglian prince Sigeberht, then in exile, to Christianity, he successfully preached the Gospel to the heathen in E. Anglia.

FELIX (d. 818), Bp. of Urgel in Spain and one of the leaders of the *Adoptianist heresy. He was charged as a heretic at the Council of Ratisbon (792) and recanted. He later became convinced of his heresy again and was unmoved by the criticism of his doctrine written by *Alcuin. He was formerly accused at the Councils of *Frankfurt (794) and Aachen (798); at the latter he again recanted.

FELL, JOHN (1625–86), Bp. of *Oxford from 1676. Under the Commonwealth he maintained C of E services in a private house, and in 1660 he became Dean of *Christ Church. He largely brought about the re-imposition of Anglican orthodoxy on the University. He produced a valuable edition of the works of St. *Cyprian (1682).

FÉNELON, FRANÇOIS DE SALIGNAC DE LA MOTHE (1651–1715), Abp. of Cambrai from 1695. He was superior of a house for recent converts, undertook a mission to the *Huguenots in Saintonge, and in 1689 he was appointed tutor to Louis XIV's grandson. He became acquainted with Mme *Guyon in 1688; he was attracted by her doctrine of pure love, though it is not clear how far he shared her *Quietist views. In 1696 he signed the Articles of *Issy condemning Quietism, but in 1697 he published his *Explication des maximes des saints*; this provided a reasoned defence of mystical spirituality. It was attacked by J. B. *Bossuet and a bitter controversy followed. When 23 propositions from the work were condemned by the Holy See (1699), Fénelon submitted. His letters of spiritual counsel are much valued.

FERDINAND II (1578–1637), Holy Roman Emperor from 1619. He tried to exterminate Protestantism in the Habsburg estates by a rigid application of the principle of '*cuius regio, eius religio'. His 'Edict of Restitution' (1629) ordered Protestants to restore all ecclesiastical property appropriated since 1552; the Protestants rebelled and under *Gustavus Adolphus nearly overthrew the Emperor. See also *Thirty Years War*.

FERDINAND V (1452–1516), King of Aragon. In 1469 he married his cousin *Isabella, the heiress of Castile, thereby uniting the two kingdoms when he succeeded his father in 1479. From his expulsion of the Moors from Granada in 1492 and his zeal for the *Inquisition he earned the title of 'the Catholic'.

FERETORY. Another name for a *shrine in which a saint's relics were deposited and venerated.

FERIA. While in classical Latin the word means 'feast day' or 'holiday', in ecclesiastical usage it is applied to such days other than Sundays on which no feast falls.

FERMENTUM. In Rome (5th cent.), the fragments of the Bread of the Eucharist sent on Sundays from the Papal Mass to presbyters in the parish churches to typify the unity of the faithful in Christ.

FERRANDUS (Fulgentius Ferrandus), deacon at Carthage from 520 to 547. His 'Breviatio canonum' is an epitome of canons of early Councils. He also wrote the life of St. *Fulgentius.

FERRAR, NICHOLAS (1592–1637),

founder of *Little Gidding. He was elected a Fellow of Clare Hall, Cambridge, travelled widely, was Deputy Treasurer of the Virginia Company, and entered Parliament. In 1625 he settled at Little Gidding, where other members of his family joined him to establish a kind of community life in accordance with the principles of the C of E. He was made deacon in 1626. Under his direction the household of c. 30 persons lived a life of prayer and work under a strict rule.

FERRAR MSS. A group of NT MSS., the common origin of the first four of which was established by W. H. Ferrar in 1868.

FERRARA–FLORENCE, Council of. See *Florence, Council of*.

FESTIVALS. See *Feasts*.

FESTUM (Lat., 'feast'). The name given in current RC liturgical documents to festivals of intermediate importance.

FESTUM OVORUM (Lat., 'feast of eggs'). The Saturday before the beginning of *Lent, which marked a stage towards the Lenten fast. Though no longer of ecclesiastical significance, it is noted in some calendars.

FEUARDENT, FRANÇOIS (1539–1610), French *Franciscan patristic scholar and controversialist. He wrote against *Calvinism and edited the works of *Ildefonsus of Toledo (1576), *Irenaeus (1576), Michael *Psellus (1577), *Ephraem Syrus (1579), and *Arnobius (1596).

FEUERBACH, LUDWIG ANDREAS (1804–72), German philosopher. He sought to recast the teaching of G. W. F. *Hegel in a positivistic sense openly hostile to Christianity. Rejecting all belief in transcendence, he held that theology and philosophy were properly concerned only with the nature of man.

FEUILLANTS. The reformed *Cistercians of Le Feuillant (near Toulouse) founded in 1577 by Abbot J. de la Barrière, who established in the house a new rule stricter than the original. The order became independent in 1589 but came to an end during the Napoleonic wars.

FICHTE, JOHANN GOTTLIEB (1762–1814), Idealist philosopher. He was appointed professor of philosophy at Jena in 1794 but was dismissed for atheism in 1799. From 1809 he was a professor at Berlin.

Fichte claimed that his philosophical doctrines were implicit in those of I. *Kant. Acc. to him the objects of our knowledge are the products of the consciousness of the ego as regards both their matter and their form. This ego, however, is not the individual 'I' but the Absolute Ego, which can be known only by philosophical intuition. It develops in three phases. In the first it posits itself, in the second it posits a non-ego against itself, and in the last it posits itself as limited by the non-ego. Acc. to Fichte God is the Absolute Ego, 'the living operative moral order'; but He is not to be conceived as personal. True religion consists in 'joyously doing right'. When society has reached a condition in which morality is the norm, the Church will be unnecessary.

FICINO, MARSILIO (1433–99), Italian humanist and philosopher. He enjoyed the patronage of Cosimo de' Medici, who wanted to found a Platonic Academy; Ficino became its head. He studied Greek and embarked on a fresh translation of *Plato which remained the standard Latin text for a hundred years. He defended Greek philosophy and expounded his synthesis of Christianity and Greek mysticism in *De Religione Christiana* (1477). His main philosophical work, *Theologia Platonica de Immortalitate Animorum* (1487), was largely based on Plato's *Phaedo*. He also translated into Latin the works of *Plotinus, *Porphyry, and *Dionysius the Pseudo-Areopagite.

FIDEI DEFENSOR. See *Defender of the Faith*.

FIDEISM. A term applied to a variety of doctrines which hold in common belief in the incapacity of the intellect to attain to knowledge of divine matters and correspondingly put an excessive emphasis on faith.

FIDES DAMASI (Lat., 'Faith of Damasus'). An important credal formula which was formerly attributed to St. *Damasus or St. *Jerome, but is now generally believed to have originated in Gaul towards the end of the 5th cent.

FIDES HIERONYMI. An early form of the *Apostles' Creed, prob. late 4th cent. and perhaps the work of St. *Jerome.

FIELD, FREDERICK (1801–85), Anglican divine. In 1870 he became a member of the OT Revision Company. He was one of the most learned and accurate patristic scholars of the 19th cent. He published important editions of St. *Chrysostom's Homilies on Mt. (1839) and on the Pauline Epp. (1849–62) and of *Origen's *Hexapla* (1875).

FIELD, JOHN (1545–88), *Puritan. Ordained priest, uncanonically early, in 1566, he soon became a leading member of an extreme Puritan group in London and was debarred from preaching for 8 years (1571–9). In 1572 he wrote the bitter 'View of Popish Abuses yet remaining in the English Church' which appeared with *The *Admonition to the Parliament*; Field and T. Wilcox were imprisoned for a year. Field was an adept propagandist and organizer, though he failed in his attempt to impose a *Presbyterian uniformity on English Puritans.

FIELD, RICHARD (1561–1616), Dean of *Gloucester from 1609. He took part in the *Hampton Court Conference of 1604. His main work, *Of the Church* (1606–10), argued that the counterpart of the modern RC Church was to be found in early times in the *Donatists, with their claim to exclusiveness and purity.

FIFTH MONARCHY MEN. A fanatical sect of the mid-17th cent. in England whose members aimed at bringing in the 'Fifth Monarchy' (Dan. 2: 44) which should succeed the empires of Assyria, Persia, Greece, and Rome. After unsuccessful risings in 1657 and 1661, their leaders were beheaded and the sect died out.

FIGGIS, JOHN NEVILLE (1866–1919), historian and theologian. In 1907 he joined the *Community of the Resurrection. He wrote a number of works on political theory; he was a resolute opponent of the idea of absolute sovereignty and he was among the first Christian thinkers alive to the dangers to religion and human freedom in the modern omnicompetent State.

FILASTER. See *Philaster*.

FILIOQUE (Lat., 'And the Son'). The dogmatic formula expressing the *Double Procession of the Holy Spirit added by the W. Church to the *Nicene Creed immediately after the words 'the Holy Ghost ... who proceedeth from the Father'. It is first met with as an interpolation at the Third Council of *Toledo (589). From *c.* 800, when the Creed began to be generally chanted in the Eucharist throughout the Frankish Empire, the words became widely familiar. It has been one of the chief grounds of attack of the E. Church on the W. See also *Double Procession*.

FINAN, St. (d. 661). The successor of St. *Aidan as Bp. of *Lindisfarne. He had been a monk of *Iona and he upheld the Celtic ecclesiastical traditions against attempts to introduce Roman customs.

FINDING OF THE CROSS. See *Invention of the Cross*.

FINLAND, Christianity in. The origins of Christianity in Finland are obscure. It is clear that by the 12th cent. Finland had received Christianity from *Sweden and *Russia, and in 1220 an independent Church organization was established. *Lutheranism was introduced in 1523; Michael Agricola's translation of the NT (1548) virtually created the Finnish written language. In 1809 Finland came under Russian rule, and the Greek Orthodox Church of Finland increased in numbers and influence. The National Church of Finland is a Lutheran body, in which episcopal succession was maintained until 1884; it was then lost when all three sees became vacant simultaneously, but it has gradually been recovered with the help of the Church of Sweden.

FINNIAN, St. (*c.* 495–579), patron of Ulster. A pupil of St. *Colman, he made a pilgrimage to Rome and, having brought back a copy of the *Vulgate NT and Pentateuch, established a monastery at Moville.

FIORETTI, The. See *Little Flowers of St. Francis, The*.

FIRMICUS MATERNUS, JULIUS (d. after 360), a rhetorician converted to Christianity in adult life. His chief work, *De errore profanarum religionum*, is an appeal to the Emps. Constantius and Constans to destroy the pagan idols by force.

FIRMILLIAN, St. (d. 268), Bp. of Caesarea in Cappadocia from *c.* 230. He supported St. *Cyprian against Pope *Stephen I in holding that baptism could be validly performed only within the Church and that heretics must therefore be 'rebaptized'. In 264 he was president of the first of the synods of Antioch held to consider the case of *Paul of Samosata.

FIRST FRIDAYS. The special observance of the first Friday in each month in the RC Church is based on the promise which Christ is supposed to have made to St. *Margaret Mary Alacoque that unusual graces would be given to all who received Holy Communion on the first Friday of nine consecutive months.

FISH. In Christian art and literature the fish is a symbol of Christ, also sometimes of the newly baptized and of the Eucharist. In modern times some C of E associations willing to help those in need have adopted the symbol of a fish.

From early times fish has taken the place of meat on days of fasting and abstinence. See *Fasts*.

FISHER, GEOFFREY FRANCIS (1887–1972), Abp. of *Canterbury from 1945 to 1961. As Bp. of London (1939–45) he showed great administrative skill in dealing with the pastoral reorganization necessitated by war damage and as Chairman of the Churches' Main War Damage Committee. In 1946 he preached an influential sermon on *reunion at Cambridge; he presided over the *Lambeth Conferences of 1948 and 1958; and in 1960, when he travelled to meet the Orthodox Patriarch of Jerusalem, the Oecumenical Patriarch of Constantinople, and Pope *John XXIII, he was the first Abp. of Canterbury to visit the Vatican since 1397.

FISHER, St. JOHN (1469–1535), Bp. of *Rochester from 1504. As soon as *Henry VIII contemplated divorce, Fisher, who was the Queen's confessor, protested. In 1531 he secured the insertion into the Act acknowledging Henry as head of the English Church of the words 'as far as the Law of God allows it'. After his refusal to take the oath demanded by the Act of Succession he was confined to the Tower; he gave his opinion on the royal supremacy in confidence but was tried and condemned to death as a traitor. The fact that the Pope made Fisher a cardinal in 1535 increased the fury of the king, who had him beheaded.

FISHER THE JESUIT (1569–1641), i.e. **John Fisher,** RC controversialist. His real name was Percy. Converted to the RC faith as a young man, he joined the *Jesuits in 1594. On the English mission he made many converts, incl. W. *Chillingworth. His Anglican opponents included *James I and W. *Laud.

FISTULA. A tube, usually of gold or silver, through which the laity occasionally received communion from the chalice in the Middle Ages.

FITZRALPH, RICHARD (*c.* 1295–1360), Abp. of *Armagh from 1347. In 1350, on a visit to *Avignon, he presented the complaints of the secular priests against the privileges of the Mendicant Orders. In his treatise *De Pauperie Salvatoris* he dealt with the question of evangelical poverty and the connection between the state of grace on the one hand and dominion, possession, and use on the other; it later influenced J. *Wycliffe.

FIVE MILE ACT, The (1665). This prohibited those clergymen who refused to conform to the 1662 Act of *Uniformity from preaching, teaching, or coming within five miles of a city, town, or parish where they had previously officiated, unless they took an oath not to try to alter the government of Church or State.

FLACIUS, MATTHIAS (1520–75), also known from his birthplace as **Illyricus**, *Lutheran theologian. He was appointed professor of Hebrew at *Wittenberg in 1544, but he became an anti-humanist and as a strong dogmatist he opposed the *Augsburg Interim and the *Adiaphorists; he had to leave Wittenberg. In 1557 he became professor of NT at Jena, but had to leave here also. He was a theologian of great erudition and the leading spirit among the *Centuriators of Magdeburg. See also *Missa Illyrica*.

FLAGELLANTS. Bands of men who scourged themselves in public processions, often to the accompaniment of psalms, in penance for the sins of the world. Such organized exhibitions of penance date from the 13th cent. They began in Italy and in the 14th cent. appeared all over Europe.

FLAVIAN, St. (d. 449), Patr. of *Constantinople from 446. In 448 at a synod in Constantinople he excommunicated *Eutyches for heretical teaching about the Person of Christ. The maltreatment which Flavian subsequently suffered at the *Latrocinium is said to have caused his death.

FLÉCHIER, ESPRIT (1632–1710), French preacher. In Paris his sermons soon made him famous; he was at his best in his funeral panegyrics. In 1687 he became Bp. of Nîmes; his conciliatory disposition did much to quiet the passions aroused by the revocation of the Edict of *Nantes (1685) and to win over many of the *Huguenots.

FLEMING, RICHARD (d 1431), Bp. of *Lincoln from 1420. As Junior Proctor at Oxford in 1407, Fleming had *Wycliffite sympathies. He represented the English nation at the Councils of Pavia and Siena in 1423, and impressed *Martin V. In 1427 he founded Lincoln College, Oxford, primarily to train opponents of Wycliffite teaching (which he had since forsworn).

FLETCHER, JOHN WILLIAM (1729–1785), Vicar of Madeley in Shropshire from 1760. A Swiss by birth and education, he settled in England c. 1750 and soon afterwards joined the *Methodist Movement in the C of E. From 1768 to 1771 he exercised a general supervision over the Countess of *Huntingdon's college at Trevecca for the training of ministers. He was a man of great sanctity.

FLEURY. The place owed its celebrity to the (real or supposed) transference hither in the 7th cent. of the remains of Sts. *Benedict and *Scholastica from *Monte Cassino and the monastery erected to house them. It is also known as Saint-Benoît-sur-Loire. Brought under the control of *Cluny c. 930, it became an important centre of study and played a large part in the monastic revival of the 10th cent. The abbey was suppressed in 1790. In 1944 monks returned to Fleury and a new abbey has been built.

FLEURY, CLAUDE (1640–1723), ecclesiastical historian. After Louis XIV's death (1715) he was chosen as confessor to the young Louis XV as one who was 'neither Jansenist nor *Molinist nor *Ultramontane, but Catholic'. He is chiefly remembered for his *Histoire ecclésiastique* (20 vols., 1691–1720), the first large-scale history of the Church, which is held in repute for its learning and judgement.

FLOOD, The. The 'flood of waters' which, acc. to Gen. 6: 5–9: 17, God brought upon the earth to destroy all flesh because of the wickedness of the human race, only *Noah and his family, with specimens of animal life, being preserved in the *Ark to repeople the earth. Parallel flood stories are found in Mesopotamian sources.

FLORENCE, Council of (1438–45). The Council met successively at Ferrara (1438–9), Florence (1439–43), and Rome (1443–5). Its chief object was reunion with the Greek Church, which sought support from the W. against the Turks. The main points of controversy were the *Double Procession of the Holy Spirit, the use of unleavened *bread in the Eucharist, the doctrine of *purgatory, and the primacy of the Pope. The *Filioque clause presented particular difficulty, but its legitimacy was eventually accepted by the Greeks. The Decree of Union was signed on 5 July 1439 and promulgated the following day. After the Greeks had left, the Council continued in session. All members of the Council of *Basle were declared heretics and excommunicated and the superiority of the Pope over Councils was affirmed. Union was established with the *Armenians in 1439, with the *Copts in 1442, and with various other E. Churches.

The union with the Greeks was challenged by popular resentment in Constantinople. The city was captured by the Turks in 1453 and the union ceased. That with Armenia lasted until 1475. Exact information about the other unions is lacking. The importance of the Council lies in its definition of doctrine and in the principle it established for Church union—unity of faith with diversity of rite.

FLORENTIUS RADEWYNS (1350–1400), one of the earliest members of the *Brethren of the Common Life. On G. *Groote's death in 1384 he became head of the community which he had founded at Deventer in Holland. Under his influence the monastery at *Windesheim was founded in 1387.

FLORILEGIA. Collections of selected passages from the writings of previous authors. Special interest attaches to the Greek *patristic florilegia. Besides those composed of excerpts from commentaries on the Bible (known as *catenae), a number of dogmatic florilegia, compiled from the 5th cent. onwards, have survived. They were often drawn up to establish the orthodoxy or heterodoxy of individual theologians, and many were incorporated in the *acta* of councils. They sometimes incorporate passages from works of which the bulk has been lost. Latin florilegia were also common; they included collections of dogmatic, moral, and ascetical extracts.

FLOROVSKY, GEORGE (1893–1979), Russian theologian. He left Russia in 1920 and in 1926 became a professor at the Orthodox Theological Academy in Paris. Moving to the U.S.A. in 1948, he held professorial chairs at Harvard and Princeton. He wrote (mainly in Russian) on the Greek Fathers and published a study of Russian religious thought. He was active in the *Ecumenical Movement.

FLORUS (*c.* 790–*c.* 860), Deacon of Lyons and a canon of the cathedral church. He wrote on canon law, liturgy, and theology. When *Amalarius tried to make changes in the liturgy, Florus attacked him in a series of works. In the controversy on *predestination, he defended *Gottschalk.

FLUE, NIKOLAUS VON. See *Nicholas of Flüe*.

FOLDED CHASUBLE. A form of the *chasuble, pinned up in front, formerly worn in the W. Church by the *deacon and *subdeacon at High Mass in penitential seasons.

FOLIOT, GILBERT (d.1187), Bp. of London. A monk of *Cluny, he became Abbot of *Gloucester (1139) and Bp. of *Hereford (1148). He supported Matilda, acted as confidential adviser to *Theobald, Abp. of *Canterbury, and opposed the election of *Becket as archbishop. When translated to London in 1163, he objected to taking the customary vow of canonical obedience to Canterbury on the ground that he had already done so when he became Bp. of Hereford. He supported the king against the primate and acted as one of Henry's envoys to the Pope. In defiance of the rights of Canterbury, he joined with the Abp. of *York in crowning Henry's son. Though in no way responsible, he was popularly associated with Becket's murder.

FONT. Receptacle for baptismal water, normally made of stone. Originally, usually a large basin below ground level in which the candidate stood while water was poured over him, fonts became smaller and higher when *affusion became the prevalent form of baptism.

FONTEVRAULT, Order of. A 'double order' of monks and nuns, living under the rule of one abbess, though in separate convents. The abbey of Fontevrault in France was founded in 1100 by Robert d'Arbrissel and given a constitution *c.* 1115. It disappeared in the French Revolution but was revived as an order for women only in 1806.

FOOLS, Feast of. A mock religious festival widely celebrated in the Middle Ages on or about 1 Jan., esp. in France. It was an occasion of buffoonery and extravagance; it disappeared in the 16th cent.

FOOT-WASHING. See *Pedilavium*.

FORBES, ALEXANDER PENROSE (1817–75), Bp. of Brechin from 1848, the 'Scottish Pusey'. He laboured to further *Tractarian principles in Scotland; his defence of the doctrine of the *Real Presence in his primary charge, delivered in 1857, led to his censure by the college of bishops.

FORBES, GEORGE HAY (1821–75), Patristic scholar. Brother of the preceding, despite severe paralysis of the legs, he was ordained priest in 1849. He started an episcopal mission at Burntisland, where he built a church and set up his own printing press. Here he issued a number of patristic and liturgical works, all marked by meticulous accuracy.

FORM. The concept of form played an important part in Greek philosophy. In *Aristotle it was the unchanging element in an object, considered apart from the changing manifestations of the things of sense-experience. In Scholastic philosophy it was the intrinsic determining principle of things, that is the 'nature' of things by which they are what they are. In the theology of the Sacraments the form is held to consist of the words which give significance to the sacramental use to which the matter is being put; thus in Baptism the matter of the Sacrament is water, whereas the form consists of the Trinitarian formula.

FORMAL SIN. A sinful act which is both wrong in itself and known by the person committing it to be wrong.

FORM CRITICISM. As applied esp. to the Bible, the attempt to discover the origin and trace the history of particular passages by analysis of their structural forms. It entails three distinct processes: (1) the analysis of the material into their separate units, the form of which is held to have been generally fixed in the process of transmission from mouth to mouth; (2) the recovery of the earlier history of these forms; and (3) the ascertainment of the historical setting which determined the various forms.

The method was developed in connection with the OT but its most notable use has been upon the oral traditions behind the *Synoptic Gospels. The main classes of form which emerge are: (1) *Paradigms (i.e. models for preachers) or *Apophthegms. These are short stories culminating in a saying of Jesus; (2) Miracle Stories; (3) Sayings; and (4) Historical Narratives and Legends (i.e. narrative material).

FORMGESCHICHTE. The German for *Form Criticism.

FORMOSUS (c. 816-96), Pope from 891. He acted constructively towards the E. Church, proposing a compromise solution to the question of *Photius's ordinations. After his death the party opposed to him in Imperial politics charged him with usurping the Holy See; in 897 a synod declared him deposed, but this decision was reversed by later Popes.

FORMULA MISSAE ET COMMUNIONIS. The reformed Communion Service put out by M. *Luther in 1523. The Latin language was retained, but the central part of

the rite was drastically altered to exclude any suggestion of the doctrine of the Eucharistic sacrifice.

FORMULA OF CONCORD. See *Concord, Formula of*.

FORSYTH, PETER TAYLOR (1848-1921), *Congregationalist divine. He became principal of Hackney College, Hampstead, in 1901. In early life he was a liberal in theology, but he later modified his attitude because of a deep sense of the need for *Atonement through the Cross.

FORTESCUE, ADRIAN (1874-1923), writer. In 1907 he became the RC parish priest at Letchworth, where he built a church which he made a centre of liturgical life. He wrote on a variety of subjects, esp. on the liturgy and the E. Churches. *The Ceremonies of the Roman Rite* (1918) was until recently a widely used directory of ceremonial practice.

FORTUNATUS, VENANTIUS. See *Venantius Fortunatus*.

FORTY HOURS' DEVOTION. A modern RC devotion in which the Bl. Sacrament is exposed (see *Exposition*) for a period of c. 40 hours, and the faithful pray before it by turns throughout this time. In its present form the devotion began in Italy in the 16th cent.

FORTY MARTYRS OF ENGLAND AND WALES. Forty English and Welsh RCs put to death by the State between 1535 and 1680. In 1960 the promoters of the causes of those who had been executed in this period decided to concentrate on a select number, termed the Forty Martyrs. The faithful were encouraged to ask favours in the name of the whole group, and the Roman authorities agreed to accept proof of two resulting miracles for the whole group instead of each member of it. The Forty Martyrs were canonized in 1970.

FORTY MARTYRS OF SEBASTE. See *Sebaste, Forty Martyrs of*.

FORTY-TWO ARTICLES. The collection of Anglican doctrinal formulas issued in 1553. The RC faith was restored under *Mary (1553-8) and subscription to these articles was never enforced.

FORTY-TWO-LINE BIBLE. See *Mazarin Bible*.

FORUM (Lat., 'place of public assembly', hence 'judicial tribunal'). In *moral theology the term is applied to the exercise by the Church of her judicial power. A distinction is made between the 'internal forum', where, esp. in the Sacrament of *Penance, judgement is given on matters which relate to the spiritual good of the individual, and the 'external forum', e.g. the ecclesiastical courts, where the public good of the Church is in question.

FOSDICK, HARRY EMERSON (1878–1969), American divine. From 1926 to 1946 he was minister of the *Baptist Riverside Church, New York. He wrote many books from the evangelical liberal point of view.

FOSSORS, grave-diggers. In early Christian times they were regarded as inferior clergy, and in the late 4th and early 5th cents. they formed powerful corporations controlling the management of the *catacombs.

FOUCAULD, C. E. DE. See *De Foucauld, C. E.*

'FOUNDATIONS'. A theological symposium, published in 1912. It professed to be a 'statement of Christian belief in terms of modern thought', and consisted of nine essays, with an introduction by B. H. *Streeter. It created much controversy.

FOUNTAINS ABBEY. A *Cistercian abbey near Ripon, founded from *York in 1132. It was one of the richest Cistercian houses at the time of the *Dissolution. Extensive ruins of the church and cloister survive.

FOUR CROWNED MARTYRS. See *Quattro Coronati*.

FOUR GALLICAN ARTICLES. See *Gallican Articles*.

FOX, GEORGE (1624–91), founder of the Society of *Friends. The son of a Leicestershire weaver, Fox won moral victory in 1646 after long interior struggles. He gave up

attending church and in 1647 began to preach, teaching that truth is to be found in the inner voice of God speaking to the soul. He was often in prison, but he attracted followers ('Friends of the Truth') whom he formed into a stable organization. His *Journal* was published in 1694.

FOXE, JOHN (1516–87), martyrologist. On *Mary's accession, Foxe fled to the Continent. He wrote a history of Christian persecutions, first issued in Latin at Strasburg in 1554. An expanded English version appeared in 1563 as the *Acts and Monuments of matters happening in the Church*, commonly known as 'Foxe's Book of Martyrs'. Its main object was to extol the heroism of the Protestant martyrs of Mary's reign.

FOXE, RICHARD (? 1448–1528), Bp. of *Winchester from 1501. His ecclesiastical appointments were intended mainly to provide him with financial means while he engaged in diplomatic work; from 1511 he was gradually superseded by T. *Wolsey. He founded Corpus Christi College, Oxford, in 1515–16.

FRA ANGELICO, FRA BARTOLOMMEO. See *Angelico (Fra)*, *Bartolommeo (Fra)*.

FRACTION. The formal breaking of the bread which in all Eucharistic liturgies takes place before the Communion. It goes back to Christ's action at the original institution and was a sufficiently striking element in the primitive rite to make the 'breaking of bread' a regular name for the Eucharist. The precise manner and moment of the Fraction varies in different liturgies.

FRANCE, Christianity in. It is uncertain when Christianity first reached Roman Gaul, but in 177 there was a Christian community at Lyons, which suffered persecution. The Synod of the W. Church at *Arles in 314 marks the importance of Christian Gaul at this time. The Christianization of the rural districts was, however, incomplete when the country was overrun first by the Visigoths, who were *Arians, and then by the Franks, who were pagans, but whose king, *Clovis, was baptized as a Catholic in 496. In 751 the Pope consented to the formal assumption of the throne by the Carolingian house and in

800 *Leo III crowned *Charlemagne *Holy Roman Emperor. After the division of the Empire in 843, Hugh Capet emerged as leader and, with ecclesiastical support, he was enthroned in 987. Under the new dynasty the influence of the Church upon the affairs of State was great. Several of the reforming Popes were Frenchmen and the new religious orders had their beginnings in the congregation of *Cluny. Under the influence of St. *Bernard France played a leading part in the early *Crusades. The university of *Paris made France the centre of the *Scholastic Movement. Philip the Fair (reigned 1285-1314), however, claimed to override Papal power, and there were serious disputes between him and *Boniface VIII, followed by the removal of the Papal court to *Avignon. In the 15th cent. the *Conciliar Movement was strongly supported in France. The growing power of France was diverted from troubling the Papacy by the concessions of *Leo X in the Concordat of *Bologna (1516), which admitted the right of the king to nominate to benefices in France; by thus surrendering Church temporalities the Pope removed any financial advantage for the king in supporting the *Reformation.

The *Calvinists were the main Protestant group in France. Despite persecution from 1547 they became a significant political faction, and war ensued. In the adoption of the RC faith by *Henry IV in 1593 the Catholic majority secured its final triumph. The wide toleration granted in the Edict of *Nantes (1598) was revoked in 1685. See *Huguenots.*

Louis XIV (reigned 1643-1715) had absolutist conceptions of his own power and in his attempt to remove the French Church from the immediate control of Rome he induced the French clergy to publish the *Gallican Articles of 1682. The 17th and early 18th cent. also saw the *Quietist and *Jansenist controversies, as well as the increase in influence of the *Jesuits and the foundation of various other missionary societies in France. Later France shared in the moral decadence and religious unbelief of the 18th cent. The Revolution brought the *Civil Constitution of the Clergy (1790), but most of the clergy refused to take the oath to this constitution and the *Concordat of 1801 virtually restored the power of the RC Church. The tyranny of Napoleon in ecclesiastical affairs produced popular reaction against *Gallicanism and the temper of the

country was ready for the growth of *Ultramontanism. Towards the end of the 19th cent., however, various acts were passed which weakened the influence of the Church, the most significant being the 1882 Education Act which secularized primary education. In the early 20th cent. most religious orders were expelled from France and in 1905 the entire severance of Church and State took place. The State grant to the Church ceased and with it all recognition of the Church as an institution. At the same time radical thinking in ecclesiastical circles was going on, esp. among the *Modernists. During the First World War the French clergy fought alongside the laity, and the estrangement of many of the French laity from the Church was reduced. A large part of the French people remain alienated from the Church, but there is still much devotion and there has been an increasing measure of understanding.

FRANCES OF ROME, St. (1384-1440), foundress of the *Oblates Regular of St. Benedict. Though anxious to enter the religious life, she married and was an exemplary wife and mother. In 1425 she founded a society of pious women, not under strict vows, to help the poor; after her husband's death (1436) she entered the community and became its superior.

FRANCIS OF ASSISI, St. (1181/2-1226), founder of the *Franciscan Order. The son of a rich merchant, he was taken prisoner in a border dispute in 1202. After his release he became dissatisfied with his worldly life; on a pilgrimage to Rome he changed clothes with a beggar and himself spent a day begging. When he returned to Assisi, after being disowned by his father, he devoted himself to repairing a ruined church. In 1208, hearing read in church the Lord's words bidding His disciples leave all (Mt. 10: 7-19), Francis understood them as a personal call and set out to save souls. He soon gathered a band of followers. He drew up for himself and his associates a simple rule of life ('Regula Primitiva'), based on sayings from the Gospels, and on a visit to Rome in 1209-10 he secured the approval of it by *Innocent III. In 1212 his ideals were accepted by St. *Clare, who founded a similar society for women. In 1219 he went on a preaching tour in Eastern Europe and Egypt; during this absence direction of the Franciscan Order passed into other hands and he never sought to resume the leadership. In 1221 he founded the *Tertiaries, i.e. a body of those who wished to adopt his ideals as far as was compatible with a normal mode of life. He received the gift of the *Stigmata in 1224. His generosity, his simple faith, his passionate devotion to God and man, his love of nature, and his deep humility have made him one of the most cherished saints in modern times. See also *Franciscan Order*, *Canticle of the Sun*, and *Little Flowers of St. Francis*.

FRANCIS BORGIA, St. See *Borgia, St. Francis*.

FRANCIS OF PAOLA, St. (1416–1507), founder of the Order of *Minims and patron of seafarers. Of poor family, he spent a year with the *Franciscans. In 1431 he began to live as a hermit in a cave near the Tyrrhenian Sea. He was joined by two companions in 1435 and later by others, a church and a house being built in 1453.

FRANCIS OF SALES, St. (1567–1622), Bp. of Geneva from 1602, and one of the leaders of the *Counter-Reformation. He gave up brilliant secular prospects in response to an overmastering vocation to holy orders. He met St. *Jane Frances de Chantal in 1603; through their combined labours the *Visitandines were founded in 1610. His most famous writings, the *Introduction to the *Devout Life* (1609) and the *Treatise on the Love of God* (1616), were adapted from instructions given to individuals.

FRANCIS OF VITORIA. See *Vitoria, Francisco de*.

FRANCIS XAVIER, St. (1506–52), 'Apostle of the Indies' and 'of Japan'. Of aristocratic Spanish-Basque family, he was one of the original *Jesuits, in 1534 vowing to follow Christ in poverty and chastity and to evangelize the heathen. In 1542 he reached Goa, which he made his headquarters. He went on to Travancore, Malacca, the Molucca Islands, and Sri Lanka. In 1549 he landed in Japan. He returned to Goa in 1552 and died on the way to China. His work is remarkable for the extent of his journeys and the large number of his converts.

FRANCISCAN ORDER. The Order of Friars Minor was founded by St. *Francis of Assisi in 1209 when he gave his followers their first rule, now lost. This rule was recast in 1221 and brought into its final form in 1223, when *Honorius III confirmed it by Bull. Its distinguishing feature is insistence on complete poverty not only for individual friars but corporately for the order. With the spread of the order two factions developed: the '*Spirituals' (q.v.), who insisted on a literal interpretation of the rule, and the majority who preferred a more moderate view. In 1317–18 the question was decided against the stricter party by two Bulls of *John XXII which allowed the order corporate ownership of property. Many of the Spirituals fled, and laxity increased in the 14th cent. A return to poverty was brought about by the '*Observants' (q.v.), who gained ecclesiastical recognition at the Council of *Constance in 1415; in 1517 they were separated from the '*Conventuals' and declared the true Order of St. Francis. Another reform led to the establishment of the *Capuchins, whose rule was drawn up in 1529. In the 17th and 18th cents. reform parties sprang up again. Of these the chief were the 'Reformati', the *Recollects, and the *Discalced, who lived according to their own statutes though remaining under the same General. At the end of the 19th cent. the order gained new vigour by the reunion of its different branches, confirmed in 1897.

To the Franciscan friars is attached their organization of *Tertiaries living in the world. Their Second Order of contemplative nuns are the *Poor Clares (q.v.); their Third Order communities of women are devoted to charity and have no strict enclosure.

In the C of E a group inspired by Franciscan ideals settled at Cerne Abbas in Dorset in 1921, ministering in the first place to the unemployed. In 1931 they took vows and were constituted a religious community. There are also small Anglican communities for women.

FRANCK, SEBASTIAN (c. 1499–c. 1542), German humanist. About 1525 he became a *Lutheran. He later advocated complete freedom of thought and defended an undogmatic form of Christianity for which he was attacked by Catholics and Reformers alike.

FRANCKE, AUGUST HERMANN (1663–1727), German *Pietist and educationalist. He was attracted to Pietism under the influence of P.J. *Spener. He was appointed a professor at Halle in 1692. In 1696 he founded his 'Paedagogium' and orphanage, both of which grew rapidly.

FRANKFURT, Councils of. The best-known of the many councils held at Frankfurt on Main was that called by *Charlemagne in 794 to condemn the *Adoptianist heresy.

FRANZELIN,   JOHANN   BAPTIST (1816–86), Austrian *Jesuit. He took a prominent part in the preparations for the *Vatican Council of 1869–70, and he was made a cardinal in 1876. He was a man of great learning and wrote a number of dogmatic treatises.

FRASER,   ALEXANDER   CAMPBELL (1819–1914), Idealist philosopher. He was ordained in the *Free Church of Scotland in 1844 and in 1856 became a professor at Edinburgh. His main philosophical interest was the study of G. *Berkeley, whose works he edited.

FRATER. The hall of a monastery or friary used for meals or refreshment.

FRATICELLI. A name originally applied to all members of the *Mendicant Orders, but since the condemnation of the followers of Angelo Clareno by Pope *John XXII in 1317, esp. to the *Spiritual Franciscans.

FREDERICK I (Barbarossa) (c. 1122–90), Holy Roman Emperor from 1155. In Italy Frederick pursued an aggressive policy towards the Lombard communes, while his plans for the south threatened the temporal lordship of the Papacy. There was tension with *Hadrian IV; when at the Papal election of 1159 two Popes emerged, Frederick in 1160 recognized the minority candidate, Victor IV, against *Alexander III. After his defeat at Legnano in 1176 he was faced with the need to make concessions either to the Lombard League or to Alexander III; he preferred to submit to the Pope. His long absence in Italy had weakened his position in Germany, where Henry the Lion rebelled. After Henry's overthrow in 1181, Frederick became an awe-inspiring figure. In 1189 he set off on a *Crusade, but was drowned in Cilicia.

FREDERICK   II (1194–1250),   Holy Roman Emperor and King of Sicily. The son of the Emp. Henry VI (d. 1197), he grew up in Palermo. When his guardian, *Innocent III, needed his help against the Guelph Emp. Otto IV, Frederick was able to regain his lost family position north of the Alps. At his coronation in 1215 he took the cross of a *crusader, but kept postponing his departure. Excommunicated by *Gregory IX, he set out in 1228. He regained *Jerusalem by agreement with the Sultan. Back in Italy he extracted absolution from the Pope in 1230. He crushed a rebellion in Germany and soon afterwards opened an offensive against the Lombard communes; the inevitable breach with the papacy followed.

FREDERICK III (1463–1525), Elector of Saxony from 1486, surnamed 'the Wise'. In 1502 he founded the university of *Wittenberg and later invited M. *Luther and P. *Melanchthon to teach there. When Luther was cited to Rome in 1518, Frederick secured his trial on German soil, and after the Diet of *Worms (1521) he procured for him a hiding-place at the *Wartburg. How far he accepted Lutheran ideas is disputed.

FREDERICK III (1516–76), Elector Palatine of the Rhine from 1559, surnamed 'the Pious'. Through his wife he became well disposed to the *Calvinists. He tried to foster unity between Calvinists and *Lutherans in his dominions, but meeting with little success in 1563 he came out openly on the Calvinist side and caused the *Heidelberg Catechism to be drawn up and imposed on Catholics and Lutherans alike.

FREE CHURCH FEDERAL COUNCIL. In 1896 a *National Council of the Evangelical Free Churches was formed, with local councils affiliated to it. In 1919, under the leadership of J. H. *Shakespeare, the Federal Council of the Evangelical Free Churches was organized, with membership on an officially approved representative basis. The two bodies united in 1940 to form the Free Church Federal Council; this provides machinery for joint representation and action by the Free Churches and for the possible development of federal relations between them.

FREE CHURCH OF ENGLAND. A small Protestant body which originated in a dispute in 1843 between H. *Phillpotts, Bp. of Exeter, and one of his clergy, James Shore. In 1927 it united with the Reformed Episcopal Church, a similar group which had separated from the American *Protestant Episcopal Church in 1873.

FREE CHURCH OF SCOTLAND. The religious body formed at the *Disruption (1843) by the separation of nearly one third of the ministers and members of the Church of *Scotland. In 1900 it joined with the *United Presbyterian Church to form the *United Free Church.

FREE CHURCHES; FREE FROM ROME MOVEMENT; FREE SPIRIT, Brethren of the. See *Nonconformity*; *Los von Rom*; and *Brethren of the Free Spirit*.

FREEMASONRY. In the 12th cent. the English masons established a religious fraternity to guard the secrets of their craft. The brotherhood was abolished in 1547, but later reorganized for social and educational purposes; it ceased to have any connection with stoneworkers. In France, Italy, and other Latin countries the Masonic Lodges were hostile to the Church, whereas in England, Germany, and the Germanic countries they professed an undoctrinal Christianity. Freemasonry has been repeatedly condemned by the RC Church.

FREER LOGION, The. A saying attributed to Christ in a passage added to the text of Mk. 16: 14 in the 5th cent. Greek codex 'W', now in the Freer Museum, Washington.

FREEWILL OFFERINGS. In the Hebrew sacrificial system one of the three forms of peace-offering (Lev. 7: 11–16), so named because it went beyond what legal demands required. In modern times the term has been applied to a method of Church finance.

FREQUENCY OF COMMUNION. See *Communion, Frequency of*.

FRERE, WALTER HOWARD (1863–1938), Bp. of *Truro from 1923 to 1935. A High Churchman, in 1892 he joined the *Community of the Resurrection. He was an authority on liturgical matters.

FRIAR. The distinctive title of a member of one of the *Mendicant Orders founded in the Middle Ages.

FRIDAY. Friday is widely kept as a weekly commemoration of Christ's Passion, being traditionally observed by *abstinence from meat, or other forms of penitence or charity. See also *First Fridays* and *Good Friday*.

FRIDESWIDE, St. (d. *c*. 735), patron saint of the city and university of *Oxford. Acc. to late sources, she was the daughter of a Mercian prince; after taking a vow of virginity she fled to Oxford to avoid marriage and founded a nunnery, of which she became abbess. A monastery bearing her name existed in Oxford before the Conquest; the church of this monastery is now the chapel of *Christ Church and the cathedral of the diocese.

FRIEDRICH. See also *Frederick*.

FRIEDRICH, JOHANNES (1836–1917), German Church historian. He attended the First *Vatican Council, opposed the definition of Papal *Infallibility and, refusing to accept the decrees of the Council, he was excommunicated in 1871. He was at first a leading member of the *Old Catholic communion, but later withdrew.

FRIENDS, Religious Society of (i.e. 'Friends of Truth'), a body of Christians also called Quakers. Its founder, G. *Fox, emphasized the immediacy of Christ's teaching and held that to this consecrated buildings and ordained ministers were irrelevant. By 1655 Quakers had spread throughout Britain and Ireland and to the Continent of Europe, and in 1682 W. *Penn founded Pennsylvania on a Quaker basis. Their refusal to take oaths, pay tithes, or show deference to social superiors led to persecution until the passing of the *Toleration Act of 1689.

Between 1667 and 1671 a series of Meetings for Church Affairs was established. The 'Monthly Meeting' (in Britain covering several congregations) is responsible for membership, pastoral care, and discipline. There are also county 'Quarterly Meetings' and a 'Yearly Meeting' in London for the whole country. Other 'Yearly Meetings' are linked through the 'Friends World Committee for Consultation' (established in 1937).

The tenets of the Friends were set out by

R. *Barclay. Their central doctrine is the *Inner Light; its possession consists chiefly in the sense of the Divine and direct working of Christ in the soul, by which man is freed from sin, united to Christ, and enabled to perform good works. From the paramount importance given to the Inner Light derives the rejection of the Sacraments, the ministry, and all set forms of worship. The Quakers' devotion to social and educational work (and esp. in the 20th cent. to international relief) has earned them wide respect.

FRIENDS OF CATHEDRALS; FRIENDS OF GOD. See *Cathedrals, Friends of*; *Gottesfreunde*.

FRITH, JOHN (c. 1503–33), Protestant martyr. In 1525 T. *Wolsey made him a junior canon of 'Cardinal College' (*Christ Church), Oxford. He was imprisoned for heresy in 1528 but escaped to Marburg, where he assisted W. *Tyndale. On his return in 1532 he was arrested and condemned to death for denying that *purgatory and *transubstantiation were necessary dogmas.

FROBEN, JOHN (c. 1460–1527), printer and scholar. In 1491 he started a press at Basle. He worked in conjunction with J. Amerbach and from c.1513 with D. *Erasmus, for whom he printed the first edition of the Greek NT (1516) and several of the Fathers.

FROISSART, JEAN (c. 1335–c. 1405), French chronicler. From 1373 to 1382 he was parish priest at Les Estinnes, near Thuin, and from 1383 canon at Chimay. His 'Chroniques' relate the history of the more considerable European countries between 1325 and 1400, most of it being based on eye-witness accounts.

FRONTAL. The panel of embroidered cloth, or in some cases wood or metal, ornamented with carving or enamel, placed in front of the altar. It is usually changeable, its colour agreeing with the liturgical colour of the season or day.

FROUDE, RICHARD HURRELL (1803–36), *Tractarian. A Fellow of Oriel College, Oxford, he collaborated with J. H. *Newman and J. *Keble in the early stages of the *Oxford Movement. His *Remains* (posthumously published, 1838–9), which were largely extracts from private diaries, created a storm by their strictures on the Reformers and their disclosure of his own spiritual and ascetic practices.

FRUCTUOSUS, St. (d. 259), Bp. of Tarragona. With two deacons he was arrested under Valerian and burnt at the stake.

FRUMENTIUS, St. (c. 300–c. 380), 'Apostle of the Abyssinians'. He was captured by the *Ethiopians on his way back from 'India' and later assisted in governing the country. He took the opportunity to engage in missionary work and was consecrated bishop by St. *Athanasius c. 340.

FRY, ELIZABETH (1780–1845), *Quaker prison reformer. The daughter of John Gurney, in 1800 she married Joseph Fry, a London merchant and a strict Quaker; she became a 'minister' in 1811. In 1813 her interest was aroused in the state of the prisons and she devoted herself to the welfare of female prisoners in Newgate. She campaigned for the separation of the sexes, classification of criminals, female supervision of women, and the provision of secular and religious instruction. She gave evidence to a committee of the House of Commons and travelled in Europe, fostering prison reform.

FULBERT. St. (c. 960–1028), Bp. of *Chartres from 1007. In 990 he became chancellor of the cathedral school at Chartres, which under him became one of the most vigorous in Europe. His writings include many hymns, the best-known being the Latin original of 'Ye choirs of new Jerusalem'.

FULDA. The *Benedictine abbey of Fulda in Hesse was founded in 744 by a disciple of St. *Boniface, whose tomb made it a place of pilgrimage. Under *Rabanus Maurus (abbot, 822–42) it was one of the foremost centres of Christian culture. The abbey was finally secularized in 1802.

FULGENTIUS, St. (468–533, or perhaps c. 462–527), Bp. of Ruspe in N. Africa from c. 507 (or 502). He suffered constant persecution from the *Arian king, Thrasamund. Soon after he became bishop he was banished to Sardinia. He returned to Africa c. 515 (or 510) for a debate with the Arian clergy, was banished again two years later, and finally returned in 523.

FULGENTIUS FERRANDUS. See *Ferrandus.*

FULKE, WILLIAM (1538–89), *Puritan theologian. As a Fellow of St. John's College, Cambridge, he became involved in the *Vestiarian controversy; he was for a time expelled. In 1578 he became Master of Pembroke Hall. His attack on the *Reims version of the NT led to its becoming widely known in England.

FULLER, ANDREW (1754–1815), *Baptist divine. *The Gospel worthy of all Acceptance* [c. 1785] was directed against the extreme form of *Calvinism which allowed 'nothing spiritually good to be the duty of the unregenerate'. In 1792 Fuller became the first secretary of the *Baptist Missionary Society.

FULLER, THOMAS (1608–61), Anglican historian. He held various benefices and

managed to escape deprivation under O. *Cromwell. His witty and popular style won him a wide reputation. His best-known works are his *Church History of Britain* (1655) and his *Worthies of England* (1662).

FUNDAMENTALISM. A movement in various Protestant bodies. Apparently in reaction against the evolutionary theories and Biblical criticism of the 19th cent., series of Biblical Conferences of Conservative Protestants were held in various parts of America; that of Niagara in 1895 issued a statement containing what came to be known as the 'five points of fundamentalism', viz. the verbal inerrancy of Scripture, the divinity of Jesus Christ, the *Virgin Birth, a substitutionary theory of the *Atonement, and the physical resurrection and bodily return of Christ. In the first half of the 20th cent. nearly all Protestant Churches in the U.S.A. were divided into Fundamentalist and Modernist groups. In a wider sense the term is applied to all profession of strict adherence to (esp. Protestant) orthodoxy in the matter of Biblical inspiration.

FUNERAL SERVICES. See *Burial Services.*

G

GABBATHA. Acc. to Jn. 19: 13 the place in *Jerusalem where *Pilate sat in judgement on Christ. Opinion about its location is divided.

GABIROL, S. BEN. See *Avicebron.*

GABRIEL. One of the seven *archangels. He figures in Dan., foretells the birth of *John the Baptist, and announces the conception of the Lord to the BVM.

GABRIEL SEVERUS (1541–1616), theologian. He was consecrated Metropolitan of Philadelphia, now Ala-Shehr, in Asia Minor, in 1577. As the see was in Turkish hands he acted as bishop to the Greek Christians in Venice. His best-known work is a defence of the Greek practice of venerating the Eucharistic elements at the *Greater Entrance.

GAIRDNER, WILLIAM HENRY TEMPLE (1873–1928), missionary. He went to Cairo as a *C.M.S. missionary in 1898. He studied Arabic and Islamics and threw himself into the reorganization of the Arabic Anglican Church. He was a pioneer teacher of colloquial Arabic.

GAIUS, also **CAIUS** (early 3rd cent.), Roman presbyter. He held Jn. and Rev. to be the work of *Cerinthus. His reference to the 'trophies of the apostles' is one of the key texts in discussions about the excavations under *St. Peter's, Rome.

GALATIANS, Epistle to the. St. *Paul wrote this letter to his Galatian converts on receiving news of a counter-mission requiring them to keep all the commandments of the Jewish Law and thereby (as he thought) imperilling the whole value of their faith in Christ. The Epistle may have been addressed to Christians in the country of Galatia in the interior of Asia Minor, which had been peopled by Gauls in the 3rd cent. B.C. (the traditional 'North Galatian' view); alternatively 'Galatia' may refer to the Roman province of Galatia, which covered a wider area (the 'South Galatian' view). Exponents of the latter theory date the Epistle in A.D. 50 or a little earlier, making it the earliest of the NT letters; those of the former view put it c. A.D. 57–8.

GALE, THOMAS (c. 1635–1702), antiquary. From 1697 he was Dean of *York. He edited the *Historiae Anglicanae Scriptores Quinque* (1687) and *Historiae Britannicae Scriptores* (1691), the latter containing the texts of *Gildas, Nennius, and Eddi. Both are valuable sources for the history of medieval England.

GALERIUS (d. 311), Roman Emperor from 305. In 293 he became *Diocletian's co-regent in the E.; he persuaded him to issue the edicts inaugurating the Great Persecution (303). Only under the threat of an alliance between *Constantine and Maxentius did he issue his 'Edict of Toleration' in 311.

GALGANI, St. GEMMA (1878–1903), Italian *stigmatic. Ill-health prevented her from becoming a *Passionist nun. She enjoyed frequent ecstasies, and received the stigmata and marks of scourging intermittently between 1899 and 1901.

GALILEE. (1) Originally the term was applied only to part of the tribe of Naphtali, but in NT times it denoted all the district of N. Palestine from the Mediterranean to the *Jordan. It was the scene of almost all the Lord's earlier life and of a great part of His ministry.
(2) In medieval cathedrals an outer porch or chapel.

GALILEI, GALILEO (1564–1642), popularly 'Galileo', Italian astronomer and mathematician. He invented the hydraulic balance and discovered the law of dynamics, but the success of his methods, based on empirical observation rather than deduction from abstract principles, earned him the hostility of the *Aristotelians. His discovery of

the four satellites of Jupiter (1610) by the aid of his newly invented telescope revolutionized the study of astronomy. It also led him to assert his belief in the *Copernican theory of the solar system and thus brought him into conflict with the *Holy Office; in 1633 he was summoned to Rome and forced to recant under threat of torture.

GALL, St. (c. 550–645), missionary. He accompanied St. *Columbanus from the (Irish) *Bangor to *Luxeuil but separated from him in 612 and remained in the part of Swabia which is now Switzerland, living mainly as a hermit. The *Benedictine monastery of St. Gallen dates from about a hundred years later. From the end of the 9th cent. its '*scriptorium' and collection of MSS. were famous.

GALLA PLACIDIA (c. 390–450), Roman Empress. The daughter of *Theodosius I, on the accession of her son as Valentinian III (425), she acted as regent. She supported Pope *Leo III in the *Eutychian controversy.

'GALLIA CHRISTIANA'. A documentary account of the bishoprics, bishops, abbeys, and abbots of France. It derives from a work of this title published in 1626 and since revised and continued.

GALLICAN ARTICLES, The Four. The rights and privileges claimed by an assembly of the French clergy in 1682. They denied that the Pope had dominion over things temporal and affirmed that kings are not subject to the Church in civil matters; they reaffirmed the authority of a General Council over the Pope; insisted that the ancient liberties of the French Church were inviolable; and asserted that the judgement of the Pope was not irreformable.

GALLICAN CHANT. The early chant in use in S. France and some other places such as *Reims and *Paris. It was superseded by the *Gregorian chant in Carolingian times.

GALLICAN CONFESSION. The *Confession de foi* or *Confessio Gallicana*, adopted by the First National Synod of Protestants at Paris in 1559. It was written in French and contained 35 articles; in substance it was an epitome of J. *Calvin's central doctrines.

GALLICAN PSALTER. St. *Jerome's

version of the Latin Psalter made c. 392 on the basis of the *Hexaplaric Greek text of the LXX. It became popular in Gaul (hence the name 'Gallican'), and came to be used in public worship throughout the W. Church.

GALLICAN RITE. The term is used with three meanings: (1) for the liturgical forms used in Gaul before the adoption of the Roman rite under *Charlemagne; (2) loosely, for all non-Roman rites in the early W. Church; and (3) for the 'neo-Gallican' liturgies of the 17th and 18th cents.

It is not known why the rites of N. Italy, Gaul, Spain, and the *Celtic Church in early times differed from that of Rome; various suggestions have been made. In the case of the rite in Gaul perhaps the least unsatisfactory view is that it was indigenous and developed with the introduction of prayers varying according to the Church calendar. The composition of Masses came to be a literary activity in Gaul and Spain. In the Mass used in Gaul the order of the various items differed somewhat from that of the Roman rite; the *Canon, apart from the Words of *Institution, varied with the season, and there was a form of *epiclesis. In Baptism there was an additional rite of *pedilavium. Ordinations seem to have included a public ceremony for the *Minor Orders which was taken over by Rome.

GALLICANISM. The collective name for the body of doctrine which asserted the more or less complete freedom of the RC Church, esp. in France, from the ecclesiastical authority of the Papacy. In the 14th and 15th cents. the main question at issue was the claim of the French Church to a privileged position in relation to the Papacy. In the Concordat of *Bologna (1516) the Pope conceded the right of the French king to nominate to bishoprics and other high ecclesiastical offices. In 1663 the *Sorbonne published a declaration, in substance reaffirmed by an Assembly of the French clergy in 1682 in the formula known as the Four *Gallican Articles (q.v.). Gallican principles were preached in the 18th cent. by the opponents of the Bull '*Unigenitus', and codified and proclaimed at the Synod of *Pistoia (1786). The definition of Papal *Infallibility at the First *Vatican Council (1869–70) made Gallicanism incompatible with Roman Catholicism.

GALLIO, LUCIUS JUNIUS. The brother of *Seneca. He was the Proconsul of Achaia before whom St. *Paul was accused at *Corinth (Acts 18: 12).

GAMALIEL. The Jewish rabbi who was the teacher of St. *Paul in his pre-Christian days. His tolerant views were exemplified in his attitude to St. *Peter and his companions (Acts 5: 34–40).

GAMBLING. See *Betting and Gambling*.

GANDOLPHY, PETER (1779–1821), *Jesuit preacher. He made many converts at the Spanish Chapel in London. In 1812 he issued *A Liturgy*, modelled on the Anglican BCP; he was accused of heresy and, though vindicated, retired to his family home.

GANGRA, Council of. The Council held at Gangra in Paphlagonia c. 345 passed 20 canons directed against false asceticism. To these was added an epilogue, often called 'canon 21', explaining the true nature of asceticism.

GANSFORT, WESSEL HARMENUS. See *Wessel*.

GARDEN OF EDEN; GARDEN OF GETHSEMANE. See *Eden, Garden of*; *Gethsemane, Garden of*.

'GARDEN OF THE SOUL, The'. The 'Manual of Spiritual Exercises and Instructions for Christians who, living in the world, aspire to Devotion', compiled by R. *Challoner and first published in 1740. It had a wide influence.

GARDINER, STEPHEN (c. 1490–1555), Bp. of *Winchester from 1531. He was employed in negotiations with Rome for annulling *Henry VIII's marriage to Catherine of Aragon, and in 1533 he was an assessor in the court which declared the marriage null and void. For a time he accepted the royal supremacy but he opposed the Protestant influence of T. *Cromwell. He was imprisoned under *Edward VI but restored by *Mary and became Lord High Chancellor.

GARNET or **GARNETT,** HENRY (1555–1606), English *Jesuit. He was sent on the English Mission in 1586 and became

Superior of it in 1587. He was arrested and executed, some months after the *Gunpowder Plot, for not having revealed his knowledge of it.

GASCOIGNE, THOMAS (1403–58), English scholar. He declined nearly all ecclesiastical preferment and devoted his life to scholarly pursuits at *Oxford. Though hostile to *Wycliffite influences, he denounced ecclesiastical abuses. His main work was a theological dictionary.

GASQUET, FRANCIS AIDAN (1846–1929), cardinal from 1914. He was elected Prior of *Downside in 1878. In 1896 he went to Rome, where he was a member of the Commission on *Anglican Ordinations. In 1919 he became Librarian of the *Vatican. He was a fertile writer whose works increased knowledge of English medieval monasticism.

GAUDEN, JOHN (1605–62), Bp. successively of *Exeter (1660) and *Worcester (1662). In the early days of the Civil War his sympathies were with Parliament. Later he changed his views but retained his living under the Commonwealth. He published controversial works against the *Puritans and was prob. the author of the *Eikon Basilike (q.v.).

GAUDENTIUS, St. (4th–5th cent.), Bp. of Brescia from before 397. In 404–5 he went to *Constantinople to plead on behalf of St. John *Chrysostom, without avail.

GAUME, JEAN JOSEPH (1802–79), theological writer. He was Vicar-General of *Reims and then of Montauban. He came to notice by advocating the replacement of pagan classics by patristic texts in Christian schools. His *Manuel des confesseurs* (1837) was adapted for the use of Anglican confessors by E. B. *Pusey (1877).

GAUNILO, Count. The 11th-cent. *Benedictine monk who, in the guise of the 'fool', criticized the validity of the *Ontological Argument for the existence of God used by *Anselm in his *Proslogion*. Anselm replied.

GAVANTI, BARTOLOMMEO (1569–1638), *Barnabite liturgist. He took part in the reform of the *Breviary and *Missal under Popes *Clement VIII and *Urban VIII.

GEDDES, JENNY. Acc. to tradition, the vegetable-seller who in 1637 threw her stool at the head of the Bp. of Edinburgh in St. Giles' Cathedral when the Scottish Prayer Book was used for the first time.

GEHENNA. A valley to the S. and SW. of *Jerusalem. From early times this was a place of human sacrifice and in later Jewish thought it was regarded as a Divinely appointed place of punishment for apostates and other great sinners. Hence in NT times the word is used for the final place of torment for the wicked after the Last Judgement.

GEILER VON KAISERSBERG, JOHANN (1445–1510), 'the German *Savonarola', preacher. He held teaching posts at Freiburg and Basle, but his reforming interests led him to abandon academic work. From 1478 he held a special office of cathedral preacher created for him at Strasburg. Although he demanded reform, he never seems to have contemplated leaving the Church.

GEISSHÄUSSLER, O. See *Myconius*.

GELASIAN DECREE, The. See *Decretum Gelasianum*.

GELASIAN SACRAMENTARY, The. The term is applied both to a particular MS. (Vat. Reg. Lat. 316) and to the class of sacramentaries to which it belongs. The Vatican MS. dates from the mid-8th cent. The ascription of the text to Pope *Gelasius (492–6) is mistaken.

GELASIUS, St. (d. 496), Pope from 492. He upheld the primacy of the Roman see against *Constantinople during the *Acacian Schism. To rebut the *Manichaean abhorrence of wine, he insisted on the Eucharist being received in both kinds. He also laid down that Ordinations should be at the *Ember seasons. He wrote a treatise on Two Natures in Christ. Although the *Gelasian Sacramentary and the *Decretum Gelasianum have been wrongly attributed to him, some of his work may be traced in the *Leonine Sacramentary.

GELASIUS (d. 395), Bp. of *Caesarea in

Palestine from *c*. 367. As a convinced *Nicene, he was ousted from his see for a time in the reign of Valens. He wrote a continuation of the 'Ecclesiastical History' of *Eusebius, a treatise against the *Anomoeans, and an 'Expositio Symboli'.

GELASIUS OF CYZICUS (*fl*. 475), ecclesiastical historian. He wrote a 'Syntagma', or collection of the *Acta* of the Council of *Nicaea (325), to refute the *Monophysite claim that their faith was identical with that of the Nicene Fathers.

GELLERT, CHRISTIAN FÜRCHTEGOTT (1715–69), German poet. He wrote many hymns which became popular with Lutherans and RCs. They include 'Jesus lives! thy terrors now'.

GEMATRIA. A method of interpretation employed by the Rabbis to extract hidden meanings from words. It depended on the fact that every Hebrew letter possessed a numerical value and it was thus possible by counting the value of the letters in a Hebrew word to assign it a numerical value. The method was occasionally used by early Christians. In Rev. 13: 18 the *number of the beast is given as 666, which is the numerical equivalent of the Hebrew words for 'Nero Caesar'.

GEMISTUS PLETHON, GEORGIUS (*c*. 1355–*c*. 1450), Renaissance scholar. He was an admirer of *Plato. In 1438–9, when he attended the Council of *Florence as one of the E. spokesmen, he was welcomed by some of the Italian humanists and did much to overthrow the previous dominance of *Aristotle in the West. His 'Laws' was modelled on the work of Plato.

GEMMA GALGANI, St. See *Galgani, St. Gemma*.

GENEALOGIES OF CHRIST, The. The Gospels of Mt. and Lk. contain (somewhat differing) genealogies of Christ; they are intended to emphasize that He belonged to the House of *David.

GENERAL. The usual name for the head of a religious order or congregation. It is commonly combined with a noun. Thus the *Franciscans and *Capuchins have a 'Minister General', the *Dominicans a 'Master

General', and the *Jesuits, *Redemptorists, and others a 'Superior General'.

GENERAL ASSEMBLY. The highest court of a Church in *Presbyterianism.

GENERAL BAPTISTS. As contrasted with the *Particular Baptists, those *Baptists whose theology was *Arminian and whose polity allied with that of the *Presbyterians. To this group belonged the earliest English Baptists, led by T. *Helwys. After many General Baptist Churches had moved towards *Unitarianism, a New Connection was formed in 1770. This group united with the Particular Baptists in 1891.

GENERAL CHAPTER. A canonical meeting of the heads and representatives of a religious order or congregation, esp. to elect new superiors and deal with business concerning the whole order.

GENERAL CONFESSION. (1) In the BCP the Confession at the beginning of *Mattins and *Evensong said by the whole congregation. (2) A private confession where the penitent (exceptionally) resolves to confess all his past sins and not only those since his last confession.

GENERAL COUNCILS. See *Oecumenical Councils*.

GENERAL JUDGEMENT, The, also the **Last Judgement.** In contrast with the so-called *Particular Judgement on souls immediately after death, in Christian theology the General Judgement after the Resurrection of the Dead is held to be the occasion of God's final sentence on humanity as a whole, as well as His verdict on each individual.

GENERAL SUPERINTENDENT. Formerly the highest ecclesiastical office in many German Protestant Churches. In modern times the title has often been replaced by that of Präses in W. Germany, and in E. Germany a Bishop of Berlin has been set up over the General Superintendents.

GENERAL THANKSGIVING, The. In the BCP the first of the thanksgivings 'to be used before the two final prayers of the Litany or of Morning and Evening Prayer', so named to distinguish it from the particular thanksgivings ('for rain', &c.) which follow.

GENERAL THEOLOGICAL SEMI-NARY, New York City. The largest training centre for clergy of the *Protestant Episcopal Church, founded in 1817.

GENESIS, Book of. The opening Book of the OT. It contains the story of the creation of the universe and the early history of man. It has traditionally been held to be the work of *Moses, but nearly all modern Biblical critics agree that it is a composite structure made up of material from sources which can also be traced in other Books of the *Pentateuch. It contains the Biblical basis for much Christian doctrine, e.g. of the *Creation and *Fall.

GENEVA BIBLE. The English translation of the Bible first published at Geneva in 1560, and widely used for 50 years. It had marginal notes written from a *Calvinist standpoint. See also *Bible, English Versions*.

GENEVA GOWN. The black preaching-gown worn by the early *Reformed ministers, loose-fitting and with full sleeves. It is still worn by *Presbyterians and other *Calvinists.

GENEVAN ACADEMY. This was founded in 1559 by J. *Calvin with the support of the City Council, primarily for the education of theologians. The scope of its studies gradually widened; in 1872 it was transformed into the modern university.

GENEVAN CATECHISM, The. Two formulas of J. *Calvin: (1) *Catechismus Genevensis Prior*, a compendium of doctrine issued in 1537 and imposed on the inhabitants of Geneva; (2) *Catechismus Genevensis*, a catechism in the form of question and answer, issued in French in 1542 and in Latin in 1545. This became one of the basic documents of the Genevan ecclesiastical State.

GENEVIÈVE, St. (*c.* 422–*c.* 500), chief patroness of *Paris. Acc. to her Life, she consecrated herself at the age of 7, took the veil at 15, and led a life of mortification. Her intercession is said to have diverted the Huns under *Attila from Paris in 451.

GENIZA. The chamber attached to a *synagogue used to house MS. books unfit for use in worship, e.g. worn-out copies of Scripture, and heretical works. Valuable fragments of Biblical and other MSS. were discovered in 1896–8 in a geniza at Cairo.

GENNADIUS I (d. 471), Patr. of *Constantinople from 458. In his earlier years he opposed the *Christological teaching of St. *Cyril of Alexandria. He wrote many Biblical commentaries as well as dogmatic works.

GENNADIUS II. See *George Scholarius*.

GENNADIUS OF MARSEILLES (*fl.* 470), presbyter and ecclesiastical historian. His *De Viris Illustribus* is a continuation of *Jerome's book of the same name; its bibliographical information is invaluable. The *Statuta Ecclesiae Antiqua* is sometimes attributed to him.

GENNESARET. A district on the W. shore of the Sea of *Galilee.

GENTILE, GIOVANNI (1875–1944), Italian philosopher. An early Fascist, as Minister of Education (1922–4) he carried out pedagogic reforms and reintroduced the teaching of Catholicism in State schools. He developed his Idealist philosophy in conjunction with B. *Croce. Reality, which was fundamentally historical, was the idea as realized in the human mind. God was the 'transcendent pure thinking'; religion was a complete intuition of life, and the Catholic form of it was esp. suited to the needs of the Italian people.

GENTILES. A Biblical term usually denoting non-Jews.

GENUFLECTENTES (Lat., 'those who kneel'). In the early Church a class of penitents who were permitted to be present at the first part of the liturgy, kneeling at the W. end of the nave.

GENUFLEXION. A momentary kneeling on the right knee, with the body erect, used in the W. Church as a ceremonial reverence when passing before the Bl. Sacrament and on certain other occasions.

GEOFFREY OF MONMOUTH (*c.* 1100–54), Bp. of *St. Asaph from 1152 and chronicler. He was prob. a *Benedictine monk. He died before entering his diocese. His *Historia Britonum* purports to be a translation of an old Celtic book brought to England by William the Archdeacon. Its historical value is slight, but it acquired a great reputation and wide influence.

GEORGE, St., patron saint of England and martyr. Little is known of him, though his historical existence is now generally accepted. It is not improbable that he suffered martyrdom at or near Lydda before the time of *Constantine (d. 337). His cult did not become popular before the 6th cent.; the slaying of the dragon was not attributed to him until the late 12th cent. His rank as patron of England (in place of *Edward the Confessor) prob. dates from the reign of Edward III, who founded the Order of the Garter under St. George's patronage (*c*. 1347).

GEORGE (*c*. 640–724), 'Bishop of the Arabians'. He became bishop of the Arabian nomads in Mesopotamia in 686. His writings are one of the main sources for the history of *Syriac Christianity and literature.

GEORGE OF CAPPADOCIA (4th cent.), extreme *Arian bishop. He was intruded into the see of *Alexandria in 357 and held it until he was murdered in 361. Some elements of his martyrdom passed into the legends about St. *George.

GEORGE HAMARTOLOS (9th cent.), 'George the Sinner', also 'George the Monk', Byzantine historian. He wrote a 'Chronicon Syntomon', extending from the Creation to A.D. 842; it is an important source for the period immediately before *Photius. It was continued by other writers.

GEORGE OF LAODICEA (4th cent.), *Semi-Arian bishop. A supporter of the *Arian party which followed *Eusebius of Nicomedia, *c*. 335 he was appointed Bp. of Laodicea in Syria. Doctrinally he was less extreme than Eusebius, and he became one of the chief exponents of the *Homoiousian theology.

GEORGE SCHOLARIUS (*c*. 1405–*c*. 1472), Patr. of *Constantinople. At the Council of *Florence he supported the scheme for reunion, but later he opposed all such projects. He became a monk *c*. 1450,

taking the name of 'Gennadius'. After the capture of Constantinople, in 1454 the Sultan made him Patriarch as 'Gennadius II'. He was a prolific writer and translated the works of St. *Thomas Aquinas into Greek.

GEORGE SYNCELLUS (*fl. c.* 800), Byzantine historian. He was the *Syncellus of *Tarasius, Patr. of *Constantinople. He wrote an important 'Chronicle', extending from the Creation to the time of *Diocletian, continued after his death to A.D. 813.

GEORGIA, Church of. The preaching of a Christian slave-woman from Cappadocia led to the conversion of the royal house *c*. 330 and so to the adoption of Christianity as the religion of the country. In 1811 the Georgian Church was absorbed by that of *Russia, but since 1917 it has theoretically been *autocephalous again.

GERALD DE BARRI. See *Giraldus Cambrensis*.

GERHARD, JOHANN (1582–1637), German *Lutheran theologian. In his *Loci communes theologici* (1610–22) he issued a systematized and detailed exposition of Lutheran theology which was long a standard work.

GERHARD OF ZUTPHEN (1367–98) (Gerhard Zerbolt), member of the *Brethren of the Common Life. He became a priest and librarian of the house at Deventer. One of his writings influenced the '*Spiritual Exercises' of *Ignatius of Loyola.

GERHARDT, PAUL (*c*. 1607–76), German *Lutheran hymn-writer. He held important pastoral offices. Though in his theology he was an uncompromising Lutheran, he was susceptible to the influence of Catholic mysticism, and one of his hymns, 'O sacred head, sore wounded', is based on the 'Salve caput cruentatum' attributed to St. *Bernard. Many of his hymns are widely known.

GERHOH OF REICHERSBERG (1093–1169), one of the main agents of the Gregorian reform (see *Gregory VII*) in Germany. When the plans for reform which he submitted at the First *Lateran Council (1123) were rejected, he joined the *Augustinian Canons at Rottenbuch in 1124, and introduced a reform of the rule. In 1132 he became Provost of the Canons Regular of St. Augustine at Reichersberg. His treatise *De Investigatione Antichristi* advocates a clearer definition of the spheres of Papal and Imperial power. He also wrote a commentary on the Psalms.

GERMAIN, St. See *Germanus, St.*

GERMAN BAPTISTS. See *Tunkers.*

GERMAN-CHRISTIANS   (Deutsche Christen). The Protestants who, during the Hitler regime, tried to bring about a synthesis between Nazism and Christianity. Their most prominent member, L. *Müller, was elected *Reichsbischof in 1933, but his extreme measures alienated the embryonic *Confessing Church. The German-Christians nevertheless dominated more than half the German *Landeskirchen* during the Second World War.

GERMANUS, St. (*c.* 378–448 [or 445]), Bp. of Auxerre from 418. In 429 he came to Britain to combat *Pelagianism and silenced the heretics at Verulamium. In 447 (or possibly 444–5) he revisited Britain, where he led the British troops to victory over the Picts and Saxons.

GERMANUS, St. (*c.* 496–576), Bp. of *Paris from 555. A monk before he became bishop, he tried to check the licence of the Frankish kings and to stop perpetual civil wars. The church of *St.-Germain-des-Prés stands on the site of his tomb.

Two letters, almost certainly wrongly attributed to him, have played an important part in the history of the *Gallican rite. They were prob. written in S. France, *c.* 700.

GERMANUS, St. (*c.* 634–*c.*733), Patr. of *Constantinople. He was one of the promoters of the *Quinisext Council (692) and became Abp. of Cyzicus, prob. soon afterwards. He was elected Patriarch in 715. He anathematized the *Monothelites. When the Emp. *Leo III issued his first edict against the veneration of icons (see *Iconoclastic Controversy*), Germanus resisted; in 730 he was forced to resign. He wrote a treatise *De haeresibus et synodis*, dogmatic letters, and homilies fostering the cult of the BVM.

GERONTIUS, The Dream of. A poem by J. H. *Newman, first issued in 1865. It is a

vision of a just soul leaving the body at death and its subsequent intercourse with the angels.

GERSON, JEAN LE CHARLIER DE (1363–1429), French Churchman and spiritual writer. He studied at *Paris, becoming a doctor of theology and in 1395 Chancellor. He worked for the reform of the Church from within and the ending of the *Great Schism; the return of France to the obedience of *Benedict XIII was largely due to his work. In 1415 he went to the Council of *Constance. He asserted the superiority of a General Council over the Pope and demanded that doctors of theology should have a voice in it together with the bishops. He also took part in drawing up the Four Articles of Constance. His denunciation of the propositions advanced by Jean Petit in favour of tyrannicide earned him the hatred of the Duke of Burgundy; he was unable to return to France until after the Duke's death (1419).

Gerson developed the *Conciliar theory, but without rejecting the primacy of the Pope. In moral theology he accepted the extreme *Nominalist doctrine, acc. to which nothing is sinful in itself, but the sinfulness or goodness of an action depends solely on the will of God. His mystical teaching had marked *Augustinian tendencies; he consciously opposed the spiritual teaching of the 'antiqui' to the dry intellectualist activities of the Nominalist 'moderni', who threatened to convert theology into mere dialectics. The chief of his many treatises devoted to the spiritual life is *The Mountain of Contemplation* (1397). Both his Conciliar views and his mystical teaching were immensely influential. The attribution to him of the '*Imitation of Christ' has generally been abandoned.

GERTRUDE, St. (1) (629–59), abbess. The daughter of Pepin the Elder, she became first abbess of the convent founded by her mother at Nivelles in Belgium. She resigned *c.*656 to give herself to devotion.

(2) (1256–*c.* 1302), German mystic. Entrusted as a child to the nuns of Helfta in Thuringia, at 25 she experienced a conversion and then led a life of contemplation. Her *Legatus Divinae Pietatis* (of which only the second book was written by her, the other four being based on notes) is one of the finest literary products of Christian mysticism. She was an early exponent of devotion to the

*Sacred Heart and is the patroness of the W. Indies.

GERVASIUS and PROTASIUS, Sts., protomartyrs of Milan. Nothing certain is known of them. In 386 St. *Ambrose, obeying a 'presentiment', dug in search of relics; two skeletons were recognized as the remains of these martyrs and transferred to a new church, where miraculous healings are said to have taken place.

GESENIUS, HEINRICH FRIEDRICH WILHELM (1786–1842), German orientalist and Biblical scholar. His *Hebräisches und chaldäisches Handwörterbuch* (1810–12) formed the basis of the Hebrew Lexicon (1906) of C. A. *Briggs, S. R. *Driver, and F. Brown.

GESS, WOLFGANG FRIEDRICH (1819–91), German theologian. He was among the earliest defenders of a *kenotic doctrine of the Incarnation.

GESUATI (or, officially, **Clerici apostolici S. Hieronymi**). A congregation of laymen founded *c.* 1360 by Bl. John *Colombini. They secured papal approbation in 1367 on condition that they established proper monasteries. The congregation was dissolved in 1668.

GETHSEMANE, The Garden of. The garden, just outside *Jerusalem, to which the Lord retired after the Last Supper and which was the scene of His agony and betrayal.

GEULINCX, ARNOLD (1624–69), Belgian philosopher. He was deprived of his professorship at Louvain in 1658; he then went to *Leyden and became a *Calvinist.
   Geulincx developed the theory known as *Occasionalism. He denied that finite things had efficient causality and held that God is the sole cause of all movement and thought. Man can achieve nothing of himself. God, however, is wholly inaccessible to man, and to lead the moral life man must turn to the Divine in himself, i.e. the human reason by which he participates in the Divine nature.

GHÉON, HENRI, pseudonym of Henri Léon Vangeon (1875–1944), French Catholic writer. He tried to build up a Christian theatre, producing his own plays and working with a company of young RCs

which he founded in 1924. Many of his works dealt with the lives of saints and other sacred themes; their deliberate naïvety of tone sought to reproduce the atmosphere of medieval hagiography. His biographies appealed to a wide public.

GHETTO. In former times the street or quarter of a city in which the Jewish population customarily lived. The earliest ghettos date from the 11th cent.; they became common in the Middle Ages. In modern times the word is loosely used of any close settlement of a minority group.

GIBBON, EDWARD (1737–94), historian of the later Roman Empire. He became a RC in 1753 but returned to Protestantism in 1754. He travelled widely on the Continent of Europe, conceiving the plan of the *Decline and Fall of the Roman Empire* in Rome in 1764. It appeared between 1776 and 1788. It is unchallenged as a history on a grand scale, but its hostile attitude to the Church aroused controversy.

GIBERTI, GIAN MATTEO (1495–1543), Bp. of *Verona from 1524. He was one of the leading advocates in Italy of ecclesiastical reform who prepared the way for the Council of *Trent. He also produced some good editions of patristic writings.

GIBSON, EDMUND (1669–1748), Bp. of London. One of the fruits of his part in the current controversy between the two Houses of *Convocation was his *Synodus Anglicana: or the Constitution and Proceedings of an Anglican Convocation* (1702), a standard manual. His *Codex Iuris Ecclesiastici Anglicani* (1713) is still the most complete collection of English ecclesiastical statutes. A High Church Whig, he became Bp. of *Lincoln in 1716 and of London in 1723. Here he promoted the religious welfare of the American colonies, then under his jurisdiction.

GICHTEL, JOHANN GEORG (1638–1710), German sectarian. He lived mainly in Amsterdam. He made the first complete edition of the works of J. *Boehme (1682), and founded a small sect which condemned marriage and Church services.

GIFFORD LECTURES. A series of lectures delivered in the Scottish universities under the foundation of Adam Gifford, Lord

Gifford (1820–87), for promoting and diffusing the knowledge of God and the foundation of ethics. The first course was delivered in 1888.

GILBERT DE LA PORRÉE (c. 1080–1154), *Scholastic theologian. He taught at Poitiers, *Chartres, and *Paris. In 1142 he became Bp. of Poitiers. He wrote commentaries on the Psalter and Pauline Epistles, but he is chiefly remembered for that on the theological *opuscula* of *Boethius. The language used in this work on how to reconcile the statements 'God is one' and 'God is three' aroused opposition, and Gilbert was summoned to appear before the Council of Reims in 1148. There was no formal condemnation. His followers were known as the Porretani.

GILBERT OF SEMPRINGHAM, St. (c. 1083–1189), founder of the Gilbertine Order. As parish priest at Sempringham in Lincolnshire, he encouraged 7 women to adopt a rule of life founded on a *Cistercian model and received their profession. Lay brothers and sisters were soon associated with them, and their numbers grew. The Cistercians having declined to govern communities of women, Gilbert entrusted their direction to *Canons Regular following the *Augustinian Rule; the communities then took the form of *double monasteries.

GILDAS, St. (c. 500–c. 570), monk and first British historian. The facts of his life are uncertain. Acc. to an 11th-cent. life he was a pupil of St. *Illtyd in Wales, spent some time in *Ireland, made a pilgrimage to Rome c. 520, and founded a religious house at Ruys in Brittany on the way back. His *De Excidio et Conquestu Britanniae* is the only history of the Celts; it covers the period from the coming of the Romans to Gildas's own time, but its historical value is limited.

GILES, St. (? 8th cent.), patron of cripples, beggars, and blacksmiths. Acc. to a 10th-cent. life, he was an Athenian who became a hermit near the mouth of the Rhône; here he lived on herbs and the milk of a hind. Flavius Wamba, king of the Visigoths, hunted the hind to Giles's abode and was so impressed by his holiness that he built him a monastery. The town of St.-Gilles, which grew up near his grave, became a place of pilgrimage.

GILES OF ROME (c. 1243/7–1316), medieval philosopher. Born in Rome, he became an *Augustinian hermit at *Paris. He was made Abp. of Bourges in 1295. He was a fertile author whose writings include commentaries on works of *Aristotle and *Peter Lombard; treatises against the *Averroists, on *Angels, and on *Original Sin. The most popular, his *De Regimine Principum*, was written c. 1285 for his pupil, the future King Philip the Fair. His treatise *De Summi Pontificis Potestate* was the foundation of *Boniface VIII's bull '*Unam Sanctam'.

GILGAMESH, The Epic of. A long Babylonian poem, dating in part at least from c. 1198 B.C. It depicts the hero, Gilgamesh, a historical figure, as a demi-god, ruling tyrannically. Its account of the *Flood has close parallels with the Biblical narrative of Gen. 6–9.

GILL, ERIC (1882–1940), sculptor, letterist, and wood-engraver. He joined the RC Church in 1913 and became a *Dominican tertiary. As a stone carver he excelled in producing inscriptions and small objects such as crucifixes and holy-water stoups. The *Stations of the Cross in *Westminster Cathedral are his work. He was also a pacifist and a writer.

GILPIN, BERNARD (1517–83), 'Apostle of the North'. A great-nephew of C. *Tunstall, he disapproved of the doctrinal changes under *Henry VIII, but found the persecutions under *Mary hateful. He was offered, but declined, high preferment under *Elizabeth I, and he accepted the new order reluctantly. He made long and successful missionary journeys in the North of England, collecting a large following.

GILSON, ÉTIENNE (1884–1978), *Thomist philosopher. He held professorships in France and, after his retirement in 1951, at the Pontifical Institute of Mediaeval Studies in Toronto. His earliest work was on R. *Descartes, but most of his life was devoted to the study of medieval philosophy; he wrote on different aspects of this and on key figures. In his later years he wrote on art.

GIOBERTI, VINCENZO (1801–52), Italian politician and philosopher. He was banished in 1834, taught in Brussels, and returning to Italy in 1847, he became a member of the Cabinet of Victor Emmanuel II in 1849. His philosophical ideas were basically *Ontologistic. He held that there was an exact correspondence between the orders of being and knowing and that the human mind directly perceived the absolute necessary Being, God, the creative cause of all existence and the source of human knowledge. Some of his works were put on the *Index.

GIOVANNI   CAPISTRANO,   St. (1386–1456), friar. He became governor of Perugia in 1412. Taken prisoner in war, he had a vision of St. *Francis; on his release he joined the *Franciscans in 1416. He took part in the General Chapter which met at Assisi in 1430 to secure union of the *Conventuals and the *Observants, and on several occasions he was Vicar-General of the order. In 1451 he was sent to Austria to help combat the *Hussites. In Hungary, with Hunyady, he raised an army which defeated the Turks.

GIRALDUS CAMBRENSIS (c. 1147–1223), **Gerald de Barri,** historian. From 1175 to 1203 he was Archdeacon of Brecon. He was twice elected Bp. of *St. Davids, but failed to obtain consecration. His historical works are amusing and vivid, but the facts are sometimes exaggerated.

GIRDLE. As an article of liturgical attire, a usual accompaniment of the *alb, and hence one of the six *Eucharistic vestments.

GLABRIO, MANIUS ACILIUS, consul in A.D. 91. Ordered by *Domitian to fight with wild beasts in the amphitheatre, he was then banished and finally executed c. 96. It is prob. that he was a Christian.

GLADSTONE,   WILLIAM   EWART (1809–98), British statesman. Brought up as an *Evangelical, he became a High Churchman. In 1854 he supported G. A. *Denison, who was prosecuted for teaching the *Real Presence. In 1867 he became leader of the Liberal Party. He fought the next general election on the issue of the disestablishment of the Church of *Ireland, which he carried through as Prime Minister in 1869. In 1874 he opposed Abp. A. C. *Tait's *Public Worship Bill in the interests of the liberty of the C of E, and in the same year he published several bitter attacks on the RC Church, esp.

on the decrees of the *Vatican Council. He was responsible for the foundation of many sees in the growing British Empire. He defended the doctrine of *Conditional Immortality in *Studies Subsidiary to the Works of Bishop Butler* (1896).

GLAGOLITIC. The ancient Slavonic alphabet devised by St. *Cyril in the 9th cent.

GLANVILL, JOSEPH (1636–80), religious writer. In 1666 he became rector of the Abbey Church, Bath. One of the original members of the Royal Society, he tried to show that evidence derived from physical phenomena supported religious belief.

GLASITES (also **Sandemanians**), a small sect named after John Glas and his son-in-law Robert Sandeman. Glas, who was minister of Tealing, near Dundee, came to doubt the Scriptural basis for the *Presbyterian civil polity and to hold that a national Church was unscriptural; he was deposed in 1730. His followers organized communities on a *Congregational basis. Leadership gradually passed to Sandeman, who adopted a number of unusual rites and practices.

GLASTONBURY ABBEY, Somerset. Originally a *Celtic foundation, under St. *Dunstan Glastonbury became one of the main educational and religious centres of England. *William of Malmesbury wrote a history of the abbey c. 1135; a 13th-cent. revision of this work records the legends associating Glastonbury with *Joseph of Arimathaea, King Arthur, and St. *Patrick. The abbey was suppressed in 1539. The 'Glastonbury Thorn' was a Levantine hawthorn, around which several legends collected; it was cut down under O. *Cromwell, but descendants of it remain.

GLEBE. In English and Scottish ecclesiastical law the land devoted to the maintenance of the incumbent of the parish. The term now excludes the parsonage house and the land on which it stands.

GLORIA IN EXCELSIS. The initial words in Latin, and hence the common designation, of the hymn 'Glory be to God on high', &c. Its date and authorship are unknown. In the 4th cent. it formed part of morning prayers.

In the W. it is now used in the Eucharist.

GLORIA PATRI. The first words of the Lesser *Doxology ('Glory be to the Father', &c.), an ascription of praise to the Trinity. Its use at the end of Psalms dates from the 4th cent., and it is found quite early in metrical form at the end of hymns in the *Offices.

GLORIOUS MYSTERIES, The Five. The third *chaplet of the *Rosary, consisting of: (1) the *Resurrection; (2) the *Ascension; (3) the Descent of the Holy Spirit; (4) the *Assumption of the BVM; and (5) the *Coronation of the BVM.

GLOSSA ORDINARIA. The standard medieval commentary on the Bible. It was drawn up largely from extracts from the Fathers, and was arranged in the form of marginal and linear glosses. It was begun in the school of *Anselm of Laon, who was responsible for the Gloss on the Pss., Pauline Epp., and Jn. The whole Bible was covered by about the middle of the 12th cent.

GLOSSOLALIA. The faculty of speaking with 'tongues'. It was a common phenomenon in NT times (cf. Acts 2: 4 and 1 Cor. 14: 1 ff.) and is constantly met with in religious revivals. It plays a prominent part in modern *Pentecostalism.

GLOUCESTER. A religious house was founded in 681 and converted into a college of secular priests in 823. It was refounded as a *Benedictine monastery by *Wulfstan, Abp. of York, in 1022. The present (cathedral) church was begun under Serlo (abbot, 1072–1104). It is notable for the Perpendicular panelling superimposed on the Norman pillars in the choir, and for the cloisters, with their early fan tracery (before 1377). The monastery was suppressed in 1540. The diocese was founded in 1541, with the abbey church as the cathedral.

GLOVES, Liturgical. In the W. Church liturgical gloves may be worn by the Pope and certain other dignitaries during a *Pontifical Mass; their use ceased to be obligatory in 1968.

GNOSTICISM. A complex religious movement which in its Christian form came into prominence in the 2nd cent. With its origins in trends of thought current in pagan circles, Christian Gnosticism appeared first as a school of thought within the Church; by the end of the 2nd cent. the Gnostics had mostly formed separate sects. Different forms were developed by particular teachers, such as *Valentinus, *Basilides, and *Marcion, but some features are common to the movement as a whole. A central importance was attached to 'gnosis', the supposedly revealed knowledge of God and of the origin and destiny of mankind, by means of which the spiritual element in man could receive redemption. The source of this special 'gnosis' was held to be either the Apostles, from whom it was derived by a secret tradition, or a direct revelation given to the founder of the sect. Gnostic teaching distinguished between the *Demiurge or 'creator god' and the supreme, remote, and unknowable Divine Being. From the latter the Demiurge was derived by a series of emanations or 'aeons'. It was he who was the immediate source of creation and ruled the world, which was therefore imperfect and antagonistic to what was truly spiritual. But into the constitution of some men there had entered a seed or spark of Divine spiritual substance, and through 'gnosis' and the rites associated with it this spiritual element might be rescued from its evil material environment. The function of Christ was to come as the emissary of the supreme God, bringing 'gnosis'. As a Divine Being He neither assumed a properly human body nor died, but either temporarily inhabited a human being, Jesus, or assumed a phantasmal human appearance.

Until recently the anti-Gnostic writers were the main source of information. In 1945–6 a collection of *Coptic texts was found at *Nag Hammadi in Upper Egypt. It comprised over 40 treatises, all but two previously unknown. They vary widely in date and style; some are thought to date from the 2nd cent. or earlier, though the actual copies are not earlier than the 4th cent. Most of the items are superficially Christian and display Gnostic tendencies in varying degree. They include the so-called 'Gospel of Truth' (see *Evangelium Veritatis*) and the 'Gospel of *Thomas'.

GOAR, JACQUES (1601–54), *Dominican liturgist. The most important of his works is the celebrated Εὐχολόγιον sive *Rituale Graecorum* (Paris, 1647; ed. 2, Venice, 1730). It contains the rites of the Greek Liturgy,

Offices, Sacramentaries, &c., with Latin translations and notes; it is the basis of all subsequent research in the field.

GOD. The word is used both as a common noun, e.g. in polytheism, where a number of supposed existences claim belief, worship, and service, and as a proper name, e.g. in monotheism, where there can be only one such existence. Christianity affirms that God is a *Trinity, consisting of 'three persons in one substance', the Father being the Source of all existence, the Son the Eternal Object of the Father's love and the Mediator of that love in creation and redemption, and the Holy Spirit the Bond of Union between Father and Son.

In the OT revelation to *Moses, God made Himself known in the Divine name '*Yahweh' as the unique God who tolerates no rival. The Prophets developed the different aspects of God acc. to their character and mission. With *Jonah the idea of God as the saviour of the Gentiles as well as of the Jews made its first appearance. This universality is reflected in some of the Psalms. In popular Jewish teaching, however, He remained pre-eminently the God of a single nation, whose chief function was to fulfil the earthly hope of temporal blessedness. In the events recorded in the NT a new revelation was given. This was made through Jesus Christ, the Incarnate Son, who revealed God as the Father of all men, whose infinite goodness had no need to manifest itself in material recompenses.

In the Patristic age the development of the doctrine of God was determined by the data of Scripture, controversies with pagans, Jews, and heretics, and by the Greek philosophy which was the foundation of the education of most of the Fathers. Their wide speculations were gathered into a synthesis in the works of St. *Augustine, who gives several proofs for the existence of God, e.g. from contingency, from the order and beauty of the world, and from the moral argument of conscience. In his theology the three ways of conceiving God—by affirmation, negation, and eminence—are combined. Thus, while His goodness (way of affirmation) is asserted, He may also be called 'not good', i.e. not good in the way a man is called good (way of negation), and 'super-good', i.e. above all human ideas of goodness (way of eminence). These last two methods of conceiving the Divine Being were esp. favoured

by the Greek theologian *Dionysius the Pseudo-Areopagite.

One of the concerns of the Schoolmen was to investigate the Divine Nature by the method of rational proof, without direct appeal to revelation. St. *Anselm was the author of the *Ontological Argument for His being. St. *Thomas Aquinas rejected this but elaborated his own five-fold proof for the existence of God (*Quinque Viae), which became the basis of Tridentine Catholic theology. The shattering personal experiences of the Reformers were reflected in their intensely personal conception of God. Subsequent theology has veered between emphasis on His transcendence and His *immanence, with attacks on speculative metaphysics of any kind dating from the 18th cent.

The reaffirmation of the Divine transcendence which characterized the first half of the 20th cent., and in Protestant theology was associated with the name of K. *Barth, has been followed in recent times by various radical lines of speculation. These have included the ideas of the so-called 'death of God' theologians, who ranged from those who maintained that God literally died on the Cross and has been dead ever since, to those for whom the death of God was primarily a cultural phenomenon, and '*process theology', acc. to which God is Himself in process of development through His intercourse with a changing world.

'GOD SAVE THE KING (QUEEN)'. The British National anthem. The phrase 'God save the King' occurs in the English Bible at various places and it is likely that the anthem arose from a series of common loyal phrases being gradually combined. There is some evidence that the words were put into substantially their present form for use in the RC chapel of *James II. The tune also seems to be a 17th-cent. recasting of earlier phrases.

GODCHILDREN. See *Godparents*.

GODFREY OF BOUILLON (c. 1060–1100), one of the leaders of the First *Crusade. He took a prominent part in the capture of *Jerusalem in 1099 and became its ruler under the title of 'Advocate [i.e. protector] of the Holy Sepulchre'. In later legend he appears as the type of the ideal Christian knight.

GODPARENTS, also **Sponsors**. Witnesses to a Christian *baptism who assume responsibilities for the Christian upbringing of the newly baptized. In the case of infant baptism they also make the promises of renunciation, faith, and obedience in the child's name.

GOERRES, J. J. VON. See *Görres, J. J. von.*

GOG and **MAGOG**. In Rev. 20: 8 they are two powers under the domination of Satan, and in later literature they are conventional figures for those opposed to the people of God. The wooden statues of Gog and Magog at the Guildhall, London (destroyed in 1940), represented two giants of medieval legend.

GOGARTEN, FRIEDRICH (1887–1967), Protestant theologian. From 1935 to 1953 he was a professor at Göttingen. He formulated an interpretation of culture and civilization in the spirit of K. *Barth's *Dialectical Theology, from a *Lutheran point of view. Real historical happenings take place only in the obedience of faith when the Ego accepts the unconditional claims of a concrete 'Thou'.

GOLDEN CALF. An object of worship set up (1) by the Israelites in the wilderness (Exod. 32) and (2) by King Jeroboam I (1 Kgs. 12: 28)

GOLDEN LEGEND, The. A popular manual, consisting mainly of lives of the saints and short treatises on the Christian festivals, drawn up by *Jacob of Voragine between 1255 and 1266. Its chapters are disposed acc. to the Christian year.

GOLDEN NUMBER, The. The number of any year in the Metonic cycle (devised in 432 B.C. by the Athenian astronomer Meton); it is used in computing the date of *Easter.

GOLDEN ROSE. An ornament of gold and gems in the form of a rose which is blessed by the Pope on the Fourth Sunday in Lent and may afterwards be presented as a mark of favour to an individual or community.

GOLDEN RULE. A (modern) name for the precept 'All things whatsoever ye would that men should do to you, do ye even so to them' (Mt. 7: 12).

GOLDEN SEQUENCE, The. The *Sequence for *Whitsunday, '*Veni, Sancte Spiritus'.

GOLGOTHA. The Hebrew form of Calvary (q.v.).

GOMAR, FRANCIS (1563–1641), Dutch *Calvinist. In 1594 he was appointed professor of theology at *Leyden. Here he became an upholder of rigid Calvinist principles and engaged in a prolonged controversy with J. *Arminius. At the Synod of *Dort (1618–19) he was among the chief opponents of Arminianism.

GONZALES, St. PETER. See *Elmo, St.*

GOOD FRIDAY. The Friday before *Easter, kept as the anniversary of the Crucifixion. It is a day of fast, abstinence, and penance.

The present RC rite consists of: lessons and prayers; the *Veneration of the Cross, with the chanting of the *Reproaches and *Trisagion; and a General Communion of the people with Hosts reserved on *Maundy Thursday (see *Mass of the *Presanctified*). The C of E provides for a normal celebration of the Eucharist, but this now rarely happens; an *antecommunion is more common. Of the extra-liturgical services the best known is the *Three Hours' Service.

GOOD SAMARITAN, The. The *Samaritan of the Parable in Lk. 10: 30–7 who tended the traveller who had fallen among thieves.

GOOD SHEPHERD, The. A title of Christ based esp. on His discourse in Jn. 10: 7–18 and on the Parable of the Good Shepherd (Lk. 15: 3–7).

GORCUM MARTYRS, The. A group of 19 RC priests put to death by the *Calvinists after the capture of Gorcum (S. Holland) by the *Gueux in 1572. They were canonized in 1867.

GORDON RIOTS (also **No Popery Riots**). The riots which broke out in London in 1780 when a mob, headed by Lord George Gordon, marched to Parliament with a petition for the repeal of the *Catholic Relief Act of 1778.

GORDON'S CALVARY. A site outside the Damascus Gate in the north wall of *Jerusalem held by some archaeologists to be the place of Christ's Crucifixion. The name derives from General C. G. Gordon, one of its advocates.

GORE, CHARLES (1853–1932), Bp. of Oxford, 1911–19. He was the first principal of Pusey House, Oxford (1884–93). His independent mind and strength of character brought a new strand into the *Anglo-Catholic Movement. He defended the Catholic doctrine of episcopacy in *The Ministry of the Christian Church* (1888), and he edited *Lux Mundi* (1889). He was also concerned in the foundation of the *Community of the Resurrection. In 1902 he became Bp. of *Worcester, and in 1905 the first Bp. of Birmingham. Here he was highly successful. He was less happy after his translation to Oxford.

GORGONIA, St. (d. c. 370), sister of St. *Gregory Nazianzen. An incident in her life has sometimes (but prob. wrongly) been taken as an early instance of devotion to the Reserved Sacrament.

GORHAM CASE. In 1847 the Rev. G. C. Gorham was presented to the vicarage of Brampford Speke. The Bp. of *Exeter, H. *Phillpotts, found him unsound on the doctrine of baptismal regeneration and refused to institute him. Gorham appealed to the *Judicial Committee of the Privy Council, which, attributing to him a view which he did not hold, declared it to be not contrary to the doctrine of the C of E. The decision aroused much controversy.

GÖRRES, JOHANN JOSEPH VON (1776–1848), German Catholic writer. After various adventures, he was offered a professorship at Munich in 1827; here he became the centre of a circle of RC scholars including J. J. I. von *Döllinger and J. A. *Möhler. When in 1837 the Abp. of *Cologne, C. A. von *Droste-Vischering, was deposed and imprisoned, Görres took up his cause in his tract *Athanasius* (1837), which brought all Catholic Germany to the defence of the Church. His writings contributed to the spread of Catholic ideas in modern Germany.

GORTON, SAMUEL (c. 1592–1677),

founder of the 'Gortonites'. A London clothier, c. 1636 he sailed for Boston, Mass., in the hope of enjoying complete religious liberty, but there he encountered difficulties with the civil authorities. He came to hold many unorthodox doctrines, e.g. he denied that of the *Trinity and professed belief in *conditional immortality. His followers survived as a sect until the 18th cent.

GORZE, *Benedictine monastery near Metz, founded in 748 by St. *Chrodegang. After difficulties in the 9th cent., it was revived and built up by Albero I, Bp. of Metz (919–62), and became one of the chief centres of monastic reform. One of the salient features of the reform associated with Gorze was that the abbots put themselves at the disposal of patrons, both lay and episcopal, who invited them to take charge of and reform monasteries in their domain. Such houses did not form a network of institutions, and their association found expression chiefly in the bonds of confraternity and mutual prayer.

GOSCELIN (d. after 1107), English hagiographer. A *Benedictine monk at St.-Omer, in 1058 he entered the service of Herman, then Bp. of Ramsbury (later Bp. of *Salisbury). For a time he was also a chaplain of the nuns at Wilton. He fell into disfavour with Herman's successor and seems to have stayed in a succession of religious houses, writing the lives of local saints. From c. 1090 he was at St. Augustine's, *Canterbury.

GOSPEL. (1) The central content of the Christian revelation, the glad tidings of redemption. (2) The title of the books in which the Christian Gospel was set forth. The unique authority of the four Gospels of Mt., Mk., Lk., and Jn. was established by the mid-2nd cent. The so-called '*Apocryphal Gospels', which mostly arose in heretical circles, are inferior works of later date, devoid of historical value.

GOSPEL (in the Liturgy). In the Eucharistic rite the lection from the Gospel proper to each Mass. It always occupies the last place (i.e. after the *Epistle and other lections, if any) as the position of honour. Traditionally it is the privilege of the *deacon to read it.

GOSPEL OF TRUTH. See *Evangelium*

Veritatis.

GOSPELLER. The person who sings or reads the Gospel in the Eucharist.

GOTHER, JOHN (d. 1704), RC controversialist. Of *Presbyterian family, he became a RC at an early age. In 1668 he entered the English College at Lisbon. He was sent to England in 1682. In 1685 he published the first part of *A Papist Misrepresented and Represented*, the second and third parts following in 1687. It evoked many replies.

GOTHIC VERSION. Acc. to *Philostorgius, *Socrates, and *Sozomen, the Greek Bible was translated into the Gothic language by *Ulphilas (d. 383). Of the NT only 2 Cor. and considerable portions of the Gospels and other Pauline Epistles survive; of the OT only three short fragments of Ezra and Neh. exist.

GOTHIC VESTMENTS. A style of Eucharistic vestments introduced in the mid-19th cent. and supposed to represent the medieval pattern.

GOTTESFREUNDE (Germ., 'friends of God'). A group of 14th-cent. mystics in the Rhineland and Switzerland. They stressed the transforming personal union of their souls with God. For the most part they remained within the Church. The *Theologia Germanica* came from their circle.

GOTTHARD, St. (d. 1038), Bp. of Hildesheim from 1022. He became a monk at Nieder-Altaich in 990; he was later commissioned by the Emp. Henry I to reform monasteries in Upper Germany. The St. Gotthard Pass in the Alps is said to take its name from a former chapel dedicated to him on the summit.

GOTTSCHALK (c. 804–c. 869), heterodox theologian. Entered as an *oblate at *Fulda, he later sought to leave the monastic life. He elaborated an extreme doctrine of *predestination, acc. to which the chosen are predestined to blessedness but others to eternal fire, though he denied that the latter were predestined to sin. He was ordained by a *chorepiscopus and propagated his views in Italy and the Balkans. In 848 he returned to Germany and at the Synod of Mainz his teaching was condemned. He was sent to

*Hincmar, Abp. of Reims, and at the Synod of *Quiercy in 849 he was again condemned, deprived of his orders, and sentenced to imprisonment. He replied to a pastoral letter of Hincmar with the statement of his views known as the 'Confessio prolixior'. He also took part in the Eucharistic controversy raised by *Paschasius Radbertus.

GRABMANN, MARTIN (1875–1949), historian of medieval philosophy and theology. In 1918 he became professor of theology at Munich. Inspired by H. S. *Denifle and F. *Ehrle, he was the first to give a clear account of the development and ramifications of *Scholastic thought, and to seek in the works of *Thomas Aquinas the evolution and changes of thought rather than the outline of a fixed system.

GRACE. In Christian theology, the supernatural assistance of God bestowed upon a rational being with a view to his sanctification. While the need for this aid is generally admitted, the manner of it has been the subject of much discussion.

The theology of grace first emerged clearly in the controversy between St. *Augustine and *Pelagius. St. Augustine regarded man, since the *Fall, as totally evil and deserving of damnation; by himself fallen man could only sin, and grace was necessary for the performance of all good actions. Pelagius, on the other hand, held that man was free to choose the good and able to take the initial steps to salvation by his own efforts; grace was given that the commands of God might be more easily fulfilled. Though the logical inference of Augustine's teaching was *predestination to damnation as well as to salvation, he himself sought to safeguard man's free will by various distinctions such as that between prevenient grace (i.e. grace antecedent to conversion) and subsequent grace, in which the Divine energy co-operates with man after his conversion. *Semi-Pelagianism was an attempt to mediate between the positions of Augustine and Pelagius. The Second Council of *Orange (529) attempted to settle the question on an Augustinian basis, with modifications; prevenient grace was held to be rendered necessary by the Fall, but emphasis was laid on human co-operation after conversion, and predestination to damnation was anathematized. The debate on the relationship of grace and freewill continued in various forms throughout the Middle Ages. The Reformers returned to a more rigid Augustinianism. J. *Calvin taught absolute predestination and added the doctrine of the indefectibility of grace. This teaching was challenged by J. Arminius and his followers (see *Arminianism*). In the post-Reformation RC Church there have been two main controversies, that associated with the teaching of L. de *Molina and the *Jansenist controversy.

The exact relationship between the giving of grace and the reception of the Sacraments has given rise to similar problems.

GRACE AT MEALS. The custom of giving thanks before and after food is not exclusively Christian. Various fixed forms are recited audibly in religious houses, colleges, and schools.

GRACE, Pilgrimage of. See *Pilgrimage of Grace*.

GRADINE. A ledge above and behind the altar upon which the cross, candlesticks, and other ornaments are sometimes placed.

GRADUAL. In the W. Church the set of *antiphons, usually from the Psalms, sung immediately after the first Scriptural lesson in the Eucharist. Since 1969 a Psalm has often taken its place.

GRADUAL PSALMS. A group of Psalms, Pss. 120–34, each of which bears in Hebrew a title rendered by St. *Jerome 'canticum graduum' (AV 'A Song of Degrees'; RV 'A Song of Ascents'). Various explanations have been offered.

GRAFFITI (Ital.). The name given to ancient inscriptions which are roughly scratched and not properly carved. Christian graffiti are numerous, esp. in the *catacombs of Rome.

GRAFTON, RICHARD (d. *c*. 1572), printer. An enthusiastic supporter of the Reformation, *c*. 1536 he arranged with E. *Whitchurch for the printing at Antwerp of *Matthew's Bible (1537). He was then responsible for the printing of the *Great Bible at Paris; when this was suspended by the *Sorbonne, he escaped to England. He also printed the 1549 and 1552 BCP.

GRAHAM, 'BILLY' (William Franklin Graham) (1918–   ), American evangelist. He entered the Southern *Baptist ministry, took a leading part in the 'Youth for Christ' movement in 1943, and began his first great evangelistic campaign at Los Angeles in 1949. He first visited Britain in 1954.

GRAIL, The Holy. In medieval romances, a vessel possessing spiritual powers and affording, under certain conditions, mystical benefits to its beholders. It is sometimes identified with the cup used by Christ at the *Last Supper. The whole legend, however, remained within the field of secular literature and was never recognized by ecclesiastical authority.

GRANDE CHARTREUSE, La. The mother house of the *Carthusian Order, some 15 miles north of Grenoble. A primitive monastery was built by St. *Bruno in 1084; the present house was begun in 1676.

GRANDMONT, Order of. A French religious order, founded by St. Stephen of Muret (d. 1124), with its mother house at Grandmont in Normandy. The discipline was originally severe, but became relaxed. In 1643 a Strict Observance branch was founded. The order came to an end in the French Revolution.

GRATIAN (d. not later than 1159), canon lawyer. Practically nothing is known of his life. His *Concordantia Discordantium Canonum*, known as his *Decretum*, is a collection of patristic texts, conciliar decrees, and papal pronouncements, presented within the framework of a treatise designed to resolve the contradictions in his sources. It was used as an authority in the practice of the papal *curia and formed part of the *Corpus Iuris Canonici*.

GRATRY, AUGUSTE JOSEPH ALPHONSE (1805–72), French Catholic apologist. He was concerned with the revival of Church life in France and took a prominent part in the restoration of the *Oratory. His many books, which had a wide circulation, sought to present the Christian faith to educated opinion.

GRAVAMEN (Med. Lat., a 'grievance'). A memorandum sent from the Lower to the Upper House of *Convocation with a view to securing a remedy.

GRAVE-DIGGERS. See *Fossors*.

GRAY, ROBERT (1809–72), Bp. of Cape Town from 1847 and Metropolitan of Africa from 1853. In 1861 he suspended from cure of souls Mr. Long, a clergyman who contended that the Letters Patent appointing Gray gave him no authority to summon him to synods; the decision of the *Judicial Committee of the Privy Council in Long's favour was of constitutional importance because it ended the legal contention that the C of E as a body established by law extended to all the dominions of the Crown. In 1863 J. W. *Colenso, Bp. of Natal, was presented to Gray on a charge of heresy; his sentence was reversed by the Judicial Committee of the Privy Council who held that Gray's Letters Patent gave him no authority over Colenso, who had been appointed earlier.

GREAT AWAKENING, The. A widespread religious revival in the U.S.A. Beginning among the Dutch Reformed Churches c. 1726, it spread to the *Presbyterians and *Congregationalists and reached its zenith in New England in the 1740s. It was closely associated with the preaching of J. *Edwards and G. *Whitefield. A similar revival in the later 18th and early 19th cents. is sometimes known as the 'Second Great Awakening'.

GREAT BIBLE, The. The edition of the English Bible which T. *Cromwell in 1538 ordered to be set up in every parish church. It was not issued until 1539. It was the work of M. *Coverdale.

GREAT SCHISM. The term is used in two senses:

(1) The breach between East and West, traditionally dated 1054, when Cardinal *Humbert excommunicated *Michael Cerularius and the latter excommunicated the Western legates. Negotiations continued over a long period. The formal repudiation of the Union of *Florence by the Synod of Constantinople in 1484 marks the final breach.

(2) The period 1378–1417, during which W. Christendom was divided by the creation of antipopes. The Council of *Constance ended the schism with the election of *Martin V.

GREATER ANTIPHONS. See *O-Antiphons*.

GREATER ENTRANCE. In the E. Church, the solemn procession before the *Offertory at which the Eucharistic bread and wine are carried from the *prothesis to the *altar.

GREECE, Christianity in. Christianity was preached in Greece in the 1st cent., principally by St. *Paul. During the Frankish occupation from 1204 onwards, though the Church was subject to a RC archbishop, it retained its E. character and its hold on the people. When the Turks became masters of Greece in 1503, they favoured the Greek clergy. In the War of Independence it was Abp. Germanus of Patras who raised the standard of revolt in 1821. The Greek Church is in communion with *Constantinople, though it repudiated hierarchical connection with it in 1833.

GREEK (Biblical and Patristic). The basis of the Greek of the *Septuagint and the NT is the Hellenistic Greek (known as the *Koine* or 'Common' dialect) which spread over the Near East as a result of the conquests of Alexander the Great (d. 323 B.C.). This was a simplified form of Attic Greek, with some contributions from other dialects. There are, however, differences between writers. In the LXX, the *Pentateuch and Is. are in good Hellenistic Greek; the other Prophets, Pss., Chron., and most of Sam. and Kgs. are nearer to the vernacular. On the other hand, some of the later books (Dan., 1 Esd., Est., Job, Prov., Wisd.) are more literary in style. In the NT, *Luke is the most literary writer, then St. *Paul and the author of Heb. At the other end of the scale, Rev. is in an uneducated vernacular Greek, frequently ungrammatical.

For the first three cents. Christian writers remained generally free from the influence of pagan literature. When Christianity became the religion of the Empire, Christians shared the education of the Greek world. A deliberate cultivation of Attic models and a conscious elaboration of style coloured Patristic Greek, esp. the works of John *Chrysostom and *Gregory of Nazianzus. The language was also progressively affected by modifications in the meanings of words necessitated by the requirements of Christian theology and philosophy.

GREEN, THOMAS HILL (1836–82), philosopher. He sought to re-think and propagate in England the idealistic doctrines of I. *Kant and G. W. F. *Hegel. He held that the analysis of consciousness showed that reality was an organic whole and not a mere aggregate; that the evidence of art, morality, and religion all pointed to the spiritual nature of reality; that God, the eternal consciousness, was realized in each individual person; and that, since personality alone gave meaning to the evolutionary process, the permanence and immortality of the individual were assured.

GREEN THURSDAY. A name, used esp. in Germany, for *Maundy Thursday.

GREENWOOD, JOHN (d. 1593), a leader of the early *Separatists. He either found or created the 'Ancient Church' in a house in St. Paul's churchyard, London. He was imprisoned in 1586. With H. *Barrow, he wrote many pamphlets. Both were hanged.

GREGORIAN CALENDAR. The calendar as reformed in 1582 by *Gregory XIII and now in general use. The calendar devised by Julius Caesar (46 B.C.) did not correspond exactly to the period taken by the earth to go round the sun, and an error of 10 days had accumulated. Protestant countries were reluctant to introduce the Gregorian calendar, and it was not adopted in England until 1752.

GREGORIAN CHANT. See *Plainsong*.

GREGORIAN SACRAMENTARY, The. The name given to a family of Sacramentaries traditionally ascribed to *Gregory I (590–604). The most important of these is the book sent by *Hadrian I to *Charlemagne. This was defective, as it made no provision for parts of the year. The deficiencies were made good from *Gelasian service-books current in Gaul. From a fusion of these two sources, 'Gregorian' and 'Gelasian', the later Roman Missal is derived. The ascription to Gregory I of the book sent by Hadrian cannot be taken literally, as it contained a Mass for his feast, but it has been shown to include material composed by him.

GREGORIAN WATER. Acc. to W. usage, solemnly blessed water formerly used in the consecration of churches and altars. It is so named from the formula used in blessing it being attributed to Pope *Gregory I.

GREGORIANA. The *Jesuit university at Rome. It was founded in 1551 as the 'Collegium Romanum' by St. *Ignatius Loyola and in 1582–4 provided by Pope *Gregory XIII with adequate buildings and resources and constituted a university.

GREGOROVIUS, FERDINAND (1821–1891), German historian. He spent over 20 years in Italy, where he wrote his *Geschichte der Stadt Rom im Mittelalter* (1859–72; Eng. tr., *History of Rome in the Middle Ages*, 1894–1900), covering the period from 400 to 1534. It was a monumental work, brilliantly written, though subjective in judgement.

GREGORY I, St. (*c*. 540–604) (**Gregory the Great**), Pope from 590, the last of the traditional Latin '*Doctors of the Church'. He was Prefect of Rome in 573. He then devoted his wealth to the relief of the poor, founded seven monasteries, and entered one of them. He was later one of the seven deacons of Rome and then 'apocrisiarius' at the Imperial Court at *Constantinople. When he became Pope, Italy was in a bad way. He made a separate peace with the Lombards in 592–3, setting aside the authority of the Emperor's representative. He appointed governors to Italian cities and established the temporal power of the Papacy. He refused to recognize the title of '*Oecumenical Patriarch' adopted by the Patr. of Constantinople. One of the achievements of his pontificate was the conversion of England, for which he selected St. *Augustine (later of Canterbury) with monks from his own monastery.

Gregory was a fertile author. His *Liber Regulae Pastoralis* sets out directions for the pastoral life of a bishop. The 'Dialogues' relate the lives and miracles of St. *Benedict and other early Latin saints. He also wrote a commentary on Job and Homilies on the Gospels. He developed the doctrine of *Purgatory and popularized the mystical teaching of *Dionysius the Pseudo-Areopagite. He promoted monasticism, made important changes in the liturgy, fostered the development of liturgical music, and gave the Roman '*schola cantorum' its definite form.

GREGORY II, St. (669–731), Pope from 715. He was confronted with danger from the Saracens, against whom he had the walls of Rome repaired, and by the paganism of the German tribes. To them in 719 he sent St. *Boniface, aided by British monks and nuns. In the *Iconoclastic controversy he rebuked the Emp. *Leo III in 727, without, however, countenancing the planned revolt of Italy.

GREGORY VII, St. (c. 1021–85), Pope from 1073. Hildebrand was educated at a monastery in Rome, became chaplain to Gregory VI, and exercised great influence after the accession of *Leo IX (1049). As Pope he worked for the reform and moral revival of the Church. He issued decrees against *simony and the incontinence of the clergy in 1074. In 1075 he forbade lay *investiture. This measure was violently opposed, esp. in Germany, France, and England. The Emp. *Henry IV, threatened with excommunication and deposition, summoned synods which declared the Pope deposed. Gregory excommunicated and deposed Henry and freed his subjects from their allegiance. The Emperor was forced to submit at *Canossa in 1077, did penance, and was absolved from his censures. The German princes nevertheless elected Rudolf of Swabia, whom Gregory did not recognize until 1080, when Henry was again excommunicated. Henry then set up an antipope and besieged Rome. Gregory was freed by Norman troops, but died at Salerno.

GREGORY IX (c. 1148–1241), Pope from 1227. He excommunicated *Frederick II for his delay in fulfilling his promise to go on a *crusade, and when he sailed unreconciled proclaimed an *interdict over his land and wherever he went. In 1230 he agreed to a treaty with the Emperor, but in 1239 he excommunicated him again and died while Frederick was besieging Rome.

A friend of St. *Francis of Assisi, he became Protector of the *Franciscan Order in 1220. In 1230 he commissioned *Raymond of Peñafort to collect the papal decretals (publd. 1234) and in 1232 he entrusted the *Inquisition to the *Dominicans.

GREGORY X (1210–76), Pope from 1271. He recognized Rudolf of Hapsburg as Emperor, inducing Alfonso of Castile to resign his claims to the German throne. At the Council of *Lyons (1274–5) the Greek Emp. Michael Paleologus made his submission to the Pope, though the reunion was shortlived. One of the most important innovations of his pontificate was the introduction of the *Conclave at the election of the Pope by a Constitution of 1274.

GREGORY XI (1329–78), Pope from 1370. Elected Pope at *Avignon, he was persuaded to return to Italy by St. *Catherine of Siena. He entered Rome in 1377 but was unable to end the disturbances. He condemned the teaching of J. *Wycliffe (1377). His death was followed by the *Great Schism.

GREGORY XIII (1502—85), Pope from 1572. His main endeavour was to reform the life of the Church and to restore the Catholic faith, and he carried into effect the decrees of the Council of *Trent wherever possible. He erected numerous seminaries, mainly under the direction of the *Jesuits; he approved the Congregation of the *Oratory (1575) and the Discalced *Carmelites (1580), and he fostered missions in the Far East. He also instituted the *Gregorian Calendar.

GREGORY XVI (1765–1846), Pope from 1831. Soon after his election revolution broke out in the Papal states and was quelled only by the intervention of Austria. The troubles continued, and for most of his pontificate Gregory's relations with foreign powers remained strained. He condemned liberalism in the person of F. R. de *Lamennais (1834) and its application to theology in the German scholar G. *Hermes (1835). He did much for the foreign missions, erecting new bishoprics and vicariates.

GREGORY, St. (late 6th cent.), Bp. of Agrimentum in Sicily. He was consecrated bishop in Rome and appears to have been the victim of a plot against his character. He had either died or been deposed by 594. A commentary on Ecclesiastes was formerly attributed to him.

GREGORY DIALOGUS, St. A title sometimes given to Pope *Gregory I.

GREGORY OF ELVIRA, St. (d. after 392), Bp. of Elvira, near Granada. An intransigent opponent of *Arianism, he supported the refusal of *Lucifer of Cagliari to pardon those who had arianized at the Council of *Ariminum (359), and after Lucifer's death he became the leader of the Luciferians. Controversy continues over the extent of his writings.

GREGORY THE ILLUMINATOR, St.

(*c.* 240–332), the 'Apostle of *Armenia'. Apparently brought up as a Christian while in exile in Cappadocia, after his return to Armenia, *c.* 280 he converted the king, Tiridates, to the Christian faith. He was consecrated bishop (*Catholicos), and the episcopate remained for some generations in his family.

GREGORY OF NAZIANZUS, St.

(329–89), '*Cappadocian Father'. The son of the Bp. of Nazianzus in Cappadocia, he studied at Athens. He then adopted the monastic life. About 372 he was consecrated Bp. of Sasima, a village in Cappadocia, and assisted his father as suffragan. In 379 he was summoned to *Constantinople, where his preaching helped to restore the *Nicene faith. In 381 he was appointed Bp. of Constantinople, but he retired before the end of the year. His writings include his 'Five Theological Orations', which contain an elaborate treatment of the doctrine of the Holy Spirit; the '*Philocalia', selections from the writings of *Origen which he compiled with St. *Basil; letters against *Apollinarianism; and poems.

GREGORY OF NYSSA, St.

(*c.* 330–*c.* 395), '*Cappadocian Father'. The brother of St. *Basil, he entered a monastery. He was consecrated Bp. of Nyssa in Cappadocia *c.* 371, deposed by the *Arians in 376, but regained his see in 378. At the Council of *Constantinople in 381 he championed the *Nicene cause.

He was a thinker and theologian of great originality and knowledge. His chief theological works are polemical treatises against *Eunomius, *Apollinarius, and the *Tritheistic teaching of a certain Abladius. In his famous 'Catechetical Orations' he expounded the doctrines of the Trinity, Incarnation, and Redemption, and the Sacraments of Baptism and the Eucharist. His exegetical works deal esp. with the mystical sense of Scripture. He also wrote treatises on virginity and Christian perfection, and a Life of his sister, St. *Macrina. In his account of the *Atonement he uses, perhaps for the first

time, the simile of the fish-hook by which the Devil was baited.

GREGORY   PALAMAS,   St,

(*c.* 1296–1359), Greek theologian and exponent of *Hesychasm. He was a monk of Mt. *Athos. In 1337 he became involved in controversy with Barlaam, a monk from Calabria, who stated the doctrine of God's unknowability in an extreme form. When criticized by Gregory, he attacked the contemplative practices of the Hesychasts, and in answer Gregory wrote his 'Triads in defence of the Holy Hesychasts'. He argued that the physical exercises used by the Hesychasts in prayer, as well as their claim to see the Divine Light with their bodily eyes, could be defended in virtue of the Biblical notion of man as a single whole, body and soul together. In 1347 he was consecrated Abp. of *Thessalonica.

GREGORY OF RIMINI (d. 1358), philo-

sopher. An *Augustinian hermit, he taught at *Paris. His philosophical doctrines carried further the *nominalist teaching of *William of Occam. In theology he was thoroughly Augustinian. He was elected General of his order in 1357.

GREGORY   THAUMATURGUS,   St.

(*c.* 213–*c.* 270), Church Father. He was converted to Christianity by *Origen. About 238 he returned to Neocaesarea in Pontus, his native city, and soon afterwards became its bishop. In 264–5 he took part in the first Synod of Antioch against *Paul of Samosata; he also fought against *Sabellianism and *Tritheism. The wealth of legends and miracles attributed to him, and to which he owes his surname of Thaumaturgus or wonder-worker, testify to the strength of his character. Only a few of the writings attributed to him are genuine; they include his *Ecthesis* or Creed and the so-called 'Canonical Letter', which contains information on the penitential discipline of the early Church.

GREGORY OF TOURS, St. (*c.* 540–94),

Bp. of Tours from 573 and historian of the Franks. His *Historia Francorum*, which he began writing *c.* 576, covers the period from the Creation up to 591, from 575 in detail. His position enabled him to obtain original documents, and his work is of prime importance for the history of France. His hagiographical *Miraculorum Libri* are of less value.

GREMIAL. Acc. to W. usage, a cloth spread by the bishop upon his lap when seated during parts of the Mass to prevent his hands from soiling the vestments.

GREY FRIARS. Friars of the *Franciscan Order, so named from the colour of their habits (now brown).

GREY NUNS. A name given to Sisters of Charity in various countries. The best known are those founded by Madame d'Youville (Ven. Marie-Marguerite Dufrost de Lajemmerais) at Montreal in 1737 as a small community of ladies who devoted themselves to the care of the sick.

GRIESBACH, JOHANN JAKOB (1745–1812), NT scholar. From 1775 he was professor of the New Testament at Jena. In 1775–7 he published an edition of the Greek NT in which, for the first time in Germany, the '*Textus Receptus' was abandoned, and thereby laid the foundations of all subsequent work.

GRIGNION DE MONTFORT, St. LOUIS MARIE (1673–1716), priest. In 1704 he began to realize his true vocation, the giving of missions in W. France. His *Traité de la vraie dévotion à la Sainte Vierge* (recovered in 1842) has exercised a powerful influence on RC devotion.

GRIMSHAW, WILLIAM (1708–63), perpetual curate of Haworth, W. Yorks., from 1742. He invited to his pulpit *Methodists and *Evangelicals and himself engaged in itinerant preaching. His evident sincerity won for him a measure of support from his diocesan.

GRINDAL, EDMUND (?1519–83), Abp of *Canterbury. He was chaplain to *Edward VI, went into exile under *Mary, became Bp. of London in 1559, Abp. of *York in 1570, and Abp. of Canterbury in 1575. He was one of the revisers of the BCP in 1559. He had considerable *Puritan sympathies.

GROCYN, WILLIAM (?1449–1519), Renaissance scholar. He studied Greek and Latin in Italy from *c.* 1489 to 1491; on his return to Oxford he was recognized as the foremost English scholar and teacher of his time. In his religious attitude he was generally conservative.

GROOTE, GEERT DE (1340–84), mystic and founder of the '*Brethren of the Common Life'. In 1374 he was converted from luxury to a simple life. His outspoken criticism of current abuses led to his licence as a preacher being withdrawn in 1383, but his appeal against the sentence was never answered. He gathered round him a few friends who lived a quasi-monastic life at Deventer and became the nucleus of the Brethren of the Common Life.

GROPPER, JOHANN (1503–59), theologian. Called upon by *Hermann, Abp. of *Cologne, to combat the teaching of the Reformers, he drew up an *Enchiridion* expounding the *Creed, *Sacraments, &c.; it was well received at the time as a possible basis for reconciliation. When Hermann became a Protestant, Gropper secured his deposition and the restoration of Catholicism in Cologne.

GROSSTESTE, ROBERT (*c.* 1175–1253), Bp. of *Lincoln from 1235. At *Oxford he was the most famous master of his time; he taught at the *Franciscan house from 1224 to 1235. As bishop he deposed many abbots and priors who failed adequately to staff the parish churches in their care. In 1245 he attended the Council of *Lyons and in 1250 he visited Rome, where he made a famous speech directed against the custom of appointing Italians to English livings.

His interests covered a wide range of learned studies, including scientific subjects. He translated into Latin and commented on works of *Aristotle and *Dionysius the Pseudo-Areopagite, and he wrote various philosophico-theological treatises. He built up a system of metaphysics around the Augustinian doctrine of light, which he held to be a subtle corporeal substance and the first form to be created in prime matter, from which all else develops according to immanent laws. He also taught that God was the exemplary cause of all things and that His existence could be immediately known but could also be proved from the argument of motion; he upheld the primacy of will over intellect.

GROTIUS, HUGO (1583–1645), Huig de

Groot, Dutch jurist and theologian, the 'Father of International Law'. He was an *Arminian, of peaceable disposition. In 1618 he was sentenced to life imprisonment, but he escaped to Paris.

His main religious work, the *De Veritate Religionis Christianae* (1622), was designed as a practical handbook for missionaries. It sought to uphold the evidence of natural theology and to establish the superiority of Christianity to other creeds. The famous *De Jure Belli ac Pacis* (1625) severed law from theology, fixing the principle of justice in the unalterable Law of Nature, which has its source in man as a social being.

GROTTAFERRATA. The site of a Greek Orthodox monastery near Rome, founded in 1004. In 1881 *Leo XIII re-established a purely Byzantine rite.

GROU, JEAN NICOLAS (1731–1803), French *Jesuit. He published works on *Plato, but he is best known for his spiritual writings.

GROUP MOVEMENT. See *Oxford Group*.

GRUNDTVIG, NIKOLAI FREDRIK SEVERIN (1783–1872), Danish religious leader. From 1839 he was preacher at the Vartov Hospital in Copenhagen; in 1861 he was given the title and rank of 'Bishop'. In 1824 he started a reforming movement in Danish Lutheranism ('Grundtvigianism'), attacking the rationalism and State domination of religion. He was also active in founding the Folk High Schools which have proved a strong Christian influence in Denmark.

GRÜNEWALD, MATTHIAS (*c.* 1475–1528), German painter. Little is known of his life. The most famous work attributed to him is the altar-piece of Isenheim, near Colmar, now in the Colmar Museum.

GUALBERT, St. JOHN. See *John Gualbert, St*.

GUARANTEES, The Law of. The law passed in 1871 to regulate relations between the first government of the new kingdom of Italy and the Papacy.

GUARDIA NOBILE; GUARDIA

PALATINA D'ONORE. See *Noble Guard*; *Palatine Guard*.

GUARDIAN. The superior of a *Franciscan friary.

GUARDIAN, The. A weekly Anglican religious newspaper, founded in 1846 to uphold *Tractarian principles and to show their relevance to secular thought. It ceased publication in 1951.

GUARDIAN ANGELS. The belief that God assigns to every man an angel to guard him in body and soul was common to the pagan and Jewish world, though it is not clearly formulated in the OT. At least in the case of children, it was confirmed by Christ (Mt. 18: 10). Though generally accepted by the Fathers, it was first clearly defined by *Honorius of Autun (d. 1151); he held that each soul was entrusted to an angel at the moment it was introduced into the body.

GUDULE, St. (d. ? 712), Patroness of Brussels. Little is certainly known. Since 1047 the main church in Brussels has been dedicated to her; it contains her remains.

GUÉRANGER, PROSPER LOUIS PASCAL (1805–75), *Benedictine monk. With a view to re-establishing the Benedictine Order in France, he bought the priory of *Solesmes in 1832, opened it in 1833, and in 1837 became its first abbot. He was keenly interested in liturgical matters. Some of his books circulated widely.

GUEST, EDMUND (1518–77), Bp. of *Salisbury from 1571. His *Treatise against the Privy Mass* (1548) repudiated the Eucharistic Sacrifice and adoration of the consecrated elements, and in 1549 he spoke against *Transubstantiation. Under *Mary he remained in hiding. On *Elizabeth I's accession he became domestic chaplain to M. *Parker and in 1560 Bp. of *Rochester.

GUEUX (Fr., 'ragamuffins'). Orig. those who petitioned Margaret of Parma against the *Inquisition in 1566; then other Protestant bodies who opposed the Spaniards in the Low Countries.

GUNKEL, HERMANN (1862–1932), Protestant theologian. He held academic posts in Germany. He was a leading member of the *Religionsgeschichtliche Schule and a pioneer of *Form Criticism. He worked out the method in his commentary on Genesis (1901) and then extended it to the Psalms. He concluded that Hebrew religious poetry had a long history and that its forms had taken shape in oral tradition at a comparatively early date and become fully developed before the Exile.

GUNNING, PETER (1614–84), Bp. of *Ely from 1674. He ministered to Anglican congregations during the Commonwealth, and at the Restoration he received rapid promotion. He took a leading part in the *Savoy Conference. He may have written the draft of the prayer for 'All Sorts and Conditions of Men' in the BCP.

GUNPOWDER PLOT, The (1605). The attempt to blow up the Houses of Parliament and destroy the King, Lords, and Commons together, in the hope that the RCs would then be able to seize the government. The plot was revealed and the leading conspirators executed.

GÜNTHER, ANTON (1783–1863), religious philosopher. He spent most of his life in Vienna. He held that human reason could prove scientifically the mysteries of the Trinity and Incarnation, and that there was no cleavage between natural and supernatural truth. He also held that the dogmas of the Church were liable to revision in the light of fuller knowledge.

GUSTAV-ADOLF-VEREIN. A German Protestant society to aid weaker sister Churches in Catholic areas. It was founded in 1832 to commemorate the bicentenary of *Gustavus Adolphus's death, but it did not become important until the court preacher Karl Zimmermann amalgamated it with a similar society of his own in 1842.

GUSTAVUS II ADOLPHUS (1594–1632), King of *Sweden from 1611. He made peace with Denmark in 1613 and with Russia in 1617, and began a war against the Catholic Vasas of Poland in 1621. After repeated defeats he concluded a six-year truce in 1629. In 1630 his fear of the increasing Imperial power in the Baltic led him to intervene in the *Thirty Years War. He obtained help from France, but was at first opposed by the German Protestant princes, most of whom joined him after his victory at Breitenfeld (1631). He penetrated deep into W. and S. Germany. He was killed in battle at Lützen.

GUTENBERG, JOHANN (c. 1396–1468), inventor of printing. He was a native of Mainz. By c. 1449 he seems to have possessed movable metal type cast in separate letters and had invented a type-casting machine. He printed the 42–line (*Mazarin) Bible, the first full-length book ever printed.

GUTHLAC, St. (? 673–714), hermit. Of royal blood, he was a monk at Repton. He later migrated to an island in the fens, where he lived a life of severe asceticism. The Guthlac Roll (now in the British Library) consists of drawings depicting his life. See also *Crowland Abbey*.

GUTHRIE, JAMES (c. 1612–61), Scottish *Presbyterian divine. He excommunicated General J. Middleton as an enemy of the *National Covenant and made him do public penance in 1650. In 1654 the English Privy Council appointed Guthrie one of the *Triers. After the Restoration he was arraigned for treason and hanged.

GUTHRIE, THOMAS (1803–73), Scottish divine. At the *Disruption (1843) he supported the Free Church; he had much success in collecting funds for manses for the disestablished ministers. From 1847 he was engaged in establishing 'Ragged Schools', where the poor could be given a sound education on a Protestant basis.

GUYARD, MARIE (1599–1672), Ven. Marie de l'Incarnation. Though drawn to the religious life, she married in 1617 and had a son. In 1631 she entered the *Ursuline convent at Tours. She was among those who accepted an invitation to form a convent at Quebec in 1639; she became its first superior. She was the recipient of visions from childhood.

GUYON, Madame (1648–1717), French *Quietist author. After her husband's death (1676) she came under the influence of the Quietist works of M. de *Molinos, and in 1681 she began touring France with a *Barnabite friar. They were arrested in 1687. Mme Guyon was released through the efforts of Mme de Maintenon and soon became prominent in royal circles. From 1688 she corresponded with F. *Fénelon (q.v.). After J. B. *Bossuet had sent her a doctrinal letter in 1694, she demanded a commission to clear her; the resulting Conference of *Issy (1695)

condemned her. She taught complete indifference, even to eternal salvation, and that in contemplation all distinct ideas should be repulsed.

H

HABAKKUK, Book of. *Minor Prophet. Habakkuk complains of oppression and lawlessness; God answers that punishment is imminent in the invasion by the Chaldeans. Ch. 3 describes a vision of God coming to deliver His people.

The Book has been variously dated; the later 7th cent. B.C. seems most likely. Most critics agree that ch. 3 is an independent addition. The Book's central message, that 'the just shall live by his faith' (2: 4), has played an important part in Christian thought.

HABIT (religious dress). The distinctive outward sign of the religious life. A habit is worn by members of the old orders (monks, friars, and nuns); it normally consists of a tunic, belt or girdle, scapular, hood for men and veil for women, and a mantle. In recent years drastic changes have been made in some orders.

HADES. The place of waiting of departed spirits before judgement, visited by Christ after the Crucifixion. See also *Descent of Christ into Hell*.

HADRIAN I (d. 795), Pope from 772. By persuading *Charlemagne to conquer Lombardy (774) and depose its king, Hadrian freed the Papacy from a long-standing menace. He also enlisted Charlemagne's help in suppressing *Adoptianism and supported his efforts to achieve unity in liturgy and canon law.

HADRIAN IV (*c.* 1100–59), Nicholas Breakspear, Pope from 1154. He is the only Englishman who has held the Papacy. He secured the execution of *Arnold of Brescia and exacted full homage from *Frederick I (Barbarossa) before consenting to crown him. His claim that the Emperor held his crown as a *beneficium* from the Pope preci-

pitated a quarrel which became acute under *Alexander III. He is said to have granted the overlordship of *Ireland to Henry II of England, but the facts are disputed.

HADRIAN VI (1459–1523), Pope from 1522. He was tutor to the future *Charles V and from 1516 the virtual ruler of Spain. As Pope his main aims were to reform the *curia, reconcile the European princes, check the spread of Protestantism, and deliver Europe from the menace of the Turks. His efforts at reform were frustrated and Rhodes fell in Oct. 1522.

HADRIAN THE AFRICAN, St. (d. 709), monk. Having declined Pope *Vitalian's offer of the see of *Canterbury, he was instrumental in securing the appointment for *Theodore of Tarsus. He set off for England with him in 668 and became the abbot of the monastery of Sts. Peter and Paul in Canterbury.

HADRIANUM. The name given by modern scholars to the mass-book sent by *Hadrian I to *Charlemagne. See *Gregorian Sacramentary*.

HAGENAU, Conference of. The gathering convened by *Charles V in 1540 to discuss the points in dispute between the Catholics and Protestants in Germany. It broke up without positive result.

HAGGADAH (Heb., 'narrative'). Those parts of the traditional Jewish interpretation of Scripture which are of a non-prescriptive kind, i.e. parables, legends, narrative, folklore, &c.

HAGGAI, Book of. *Minor Prophet. The Book, dated in the second year of Darius, i.e. 520–519 B.C., consists of four discourses concerned to promote the rebuilding of the *Temple. The fourth, promising Zerubbabel victory over his enemies, has frequently been regarded as a reference to the *Messiah.

HAGIOGRAPHA (Gk., 'sacred writings'). A title applied to the third division of the OT canonical Scriptures, i.e. all Books not belonging to the 'Law' or the 'Prophets'. The Books comprised are Pss., Prov., Job, Ruth, Lam., Song of Songs, Eccles., Esther, Dan., 1 and 2 Chron., Ezra, and Neh.

HAGIOGRAPHY. The writing of the lives of the saints. It involves a study and comparison of the sources, the assessment of their historical importance, and relating them to contemporary secular history. The critical examination of sources, which dates from the 17th cent., has been esp. fostered by the *Bollandists.

HAGIOLOGY. The literature dealing with the lives and legends of the saints and their cultus.

HAGIOS O THEOS. See *Agios O Theos*.

HAGIOSCOPE, also 'squint'. An opening in the chancel walls of some churches to permit worshippers to see the *Elevation at Mass.

HAIL MARY. A form of prayer to the BVM, based on the greetings of *Gabriel (Lk. 1: 28) and *Elizabeth (Lk. 1: 42). It is widely used in the RC Church.

HAIR-SHIRT. A shirt made of cloth woven from hair, worn as a means of discipline.

HALACHA (Heb., 'that by which one walks'). In the Jewish schools, the body of legal decisions not directly enacted in the Mosaic law. It forms the bulk of the *Talmud, the non-Halachic remainder being known as the *Haggadah.

HALES, ALEXANDER OF. See *Alexander of Hales*.

HALES, JOHN (1584–1656), Anglican divine. He prob. had a large share in H. *Savile's edition of *Chrysostom (1610–13). He became a Fellow of Eton in 1613 and in 1639 chaplain to Abp. W. *Laud and canon of *Windsor. He was dis-

possessed of his canonry in 1642 and of his Fellowship in 1649.

HALF-WAY COVENANT, The. A doctrine current in 17th- and 18th-cent. American *Congregationalism which was held to express the relationship to God of those (esp. baptized) members of the community who were devoid of personal religious faith.

HALIFAX, CHARLES LINDLEY WOOD (1839–1934), Second Viscount Halifax. He was associated with the foundation of *S.S.J.E. in 1865, and as President of the *English Church Union (1868–1919 and 1927–34) he was involved in most of the ecclesiastical controversies of his time. Friendship with E. F. Portal led him to promote reunion between the C of E and the RC Church; with Portal he was responsible for initiating conversations in 1894–6. After the *Lambeth Appeal of 1920, he reopened the matter with Cardinal D. J. *Mercier, with whom he arranged the *Malines Conversations (q.v.).

HALL, JOSEPH (1574–1656), Bp. of *Norwich. He attended the Synod of *Dort as one of *James I's representatives. In 1627 he became Bp. of *Exeter, but was held suspect by W. *Laud. When the bishops were attacked in Parliament in 1640, Hall defended his order. He was translated to Norwich in 1641, but his income was impounded by Parliament and he lived in poverty.

HALL, ROBERT (1764–1831), *Baptist. He became an influential preacher in Bristol (1785–90 and 1826–31), Cambridge (1791–1806), and Leicester (1807–25).

HALLEL (Heb., 'praise'). A name given by the Jews to Pss. 113–18. They were used at the chief Jewish festivals and may have been the hymn sung by Christ and His Apostles at the *Last Supper (Mt. 26: 30).

HALLELUJAH. See *Alleluia*.

HALLER, BERCHTOLD (1492–1536), Reformer. A canon of Berne, he ceased to say Mass in 1525. He took part in the Conferences at Baden (1526) and *Berne (1528), and collaborated in composing a Protestant liturgy and the reformatory edict of 1528. He became the acknowledged religious leader of

Berne.

HALO (or **NIMBUS**). A circle or disc of light round the head or, more rarely, the whole body. In Christian art its use was originally restricted to Christ, but from the 5th cent. it was extended to the BVM, angels, and saints, and later to other important persons. In modern RC practice a halo is permitted only for persons canonized or beatified or whose cult has been otherwise approved.

HAMANN, JOHANN GEORG (1730–88), religious thinker. He was one of the fathers of the 'Storm and Stress' movement in German literature. He insisted on the importance of inner experience in matters of religion, proclaimed the rights of individual personality, and attacked the rationalism of the *Enlightenment. In *Golgatha und Scheblimini!* (1784) he upheld Christianity as the historical revelation of the Triune God, of Atonement, and of Redemption. He regarded himself as the rejuvenator of *Lutheranism.

HAMARTOLOS, GEORGE. See *George Hamartolos*.

HAMILTON, JOHN (1511–71), Abp. of St. Andrews and Primate of Scotland from 1546. He held synods to reform the morals of the clergy and the religious education of the laity; the chief result was the compilation of a catechism in the vernacular known by his name (1552). In 1560 he protested against the acceptance by Parliament of J. *Knox's confession of faith. He was imprisoned in 1563, but released at the intervention of Queen *Mary, whom he supported faithfully. After her flight he was pronounced a traitor and hanged.

HAMILTON, PATRICK (c. 1504–28), Scottish Protestant proto-martyr. He was attracted to M. *Luther's writings and visited *Wittenberg and *Marburg. On his return to Scotland he converted A. *Alesius, who had been deputed to convince him of his errors. He was charged with heresy and burnt.

HAMILTON, WALTER KERR (1808–69), Bp. of *Salisbury from 1854 and the first *Tractarian to become a diocesan bishop in England. He did much to stimulate spiritual life in his diocese. In 1861–4 he prosecuted R. *Williams (a contributor to *Essays and Reviews*), who was beneficed in his diocese.

HAMMOND, HENRY (1605–60), Anglican divine. As rector of Penshurst in Kent he had daily services in church and a monthly Eucharist. In 1645 he became Chaplain in Ordinary to *Charles I, whom he attended until his imprisonment in Dec. 1647. Hammond was then deprived of his canonry in Oxford and for a time confined. He devoted himself to relieving the deprived clergy and raising funds to train future ordinands. He commented on the books of the NT and helped B. *Walton in the compilation of his *Polyglot*.

HAMPDEN, RENN DICKSON (1793–1868), Bp. of *Hereford from 1848. In his *Bampton lectures on *Scholastic Philosophy* in 1832 he expounded a view of Christianity in which its dogmatic elements were much reduced. The *Tractarians tried unsuccessfully to prevent his becoming Regius Professor of Divinity at Oxford in 1836; strong opposition was aroused by his appointment as bishop.

HAMPTON COURT CONFERENCE (1604). The conference between the English bishops and the *Puritan leaders to consider the Puritan demands for reform set out in the *Millenary Petition. The only concessions made were slight changes in the BCP.

HANDEL, GEORGE FRIDERIC (1685–1759), musical composer. He was born in Germany, spent some years in Italy, and from 1710 lived mainly in England. Of his religious compositions, the most famous are the *oratorios. The best-known, the 'Messiah' (1741), was first performed in 1742.

HANDS, Imposition of. A manner of blessing used in the OT (e.g. Gen. 48) and followed by Christ, who used it in working miracles, and by the Church. The Apostles and the primitive Church appear to have used it in *Confirmation and *Ordination, and it has certainly traditionally been used by the Church in these rites. Acc. to the Latin rite it is also used in *Unction.

HANNINGTON, JAMES (1847–85), missionary. He landed in Zanzibar in 1882 but was forced by sickness to return to England in 1883. He was consecrated the first Bp. of Eastern Equatorial Africa in June 1884 and was back in Mombasa in Jan. 1885. In Oct. he was murdered.

HARDENBERG, ALBERT (*c.* 1510–74), Reformer. He entered the monastery of Aduard *c.* 1527. He later came into contact with J. *Laski and other Reformers, whom he openly joined in 1542. He went to *Cologne to help Abp. *Hermann of Wied, took part in the Diets of Speyer (1544) and Worms (1545), and in 1547 was appointed cathedral preacher at Bremen; he was expelled from this post in 1561 for his denial of the *Lutheran doctrine on the Lord's Supper. From 1567 he was preacher at Emden.

HARDING, St. STEPHEN. See *Stephen Harding, St.*

HARDOUIN, JEAN (1646–1729), scholar. He was a *Jesuit and spent most of his life in Paris. He published excellent editions of classical texts, but he is chiefly remembered for his edition of the texts of the ecclesiastical councils from NT times onwards.

HARDWICKE, Act of Lord (1754). This Act made *clandestine marriages, previously regulated by canon law, subject to statute. Marriages were normally required to be celebrated in the parish church of one of the parties, after *banns.

HARE, JULIUS CHARLES (1795–1855), a *Broad Churchman. He travelled widely in Germany and came under the influence of German theologians and men of letters; he introduced many German ideas into English theology. In 1840 he became Archdeacon of Lewes.

HARKLEAN VERSION. A revision of the *Philoxenian Syriac version of the NT made by Thomas of Harkel in 616.

HARLESS, GOTTLIEB CHRISTOPH ADOLPH VON (1806–79), theologian. He held high academic positions and was one of the most influential representatives of *Lutheran orthodoxy in his generation. In 1852 he became president of the supreme consistory of Bavaria, where he reorganized the State Church.

HARMONY SOCIETY. A communist sect, founded by J. G. Rapp (1757–1847). The community settled in the U.S.A.; it had almost died out by the mid-19th cent.

HARMS, CLAUS (1778–1855), *Lutheran theologian. He became provost of St. Nicolai at Kiel in 1835. He is remembered chiefly for his defence of Lutheran theology at a time when its distinctive elements were threatened by the movement for uniting the Protestant confessions in Prussia.

HARNACK, ADOLF (1851–1930), German Church historian and theologian. From 1889 to 1921 he was a professor at Berlin. He was prob. the most outstanding Patristic scholar of his generation, dealing esp. with the pre-Nicene period. He aroused conservative opposition by his critical attitude to traditional Christian dogma and by his emphasis on the moral aspects of Christianity to the exclusion of the doctrinal. He also published notable studies on the *Synoptic problem.

HARRIS, HOWELL (1714–73), founder of Welsh *Calvinistic Methodism. After a conversion experience in 1735, he became an ardent mission preacher. Being refused ordination in the C of E, he separated. Soon after 1751 he established a religious community at Trevecca in S. Wales; he gained the support of Selina, Countess of *Huntingdon.

HARRIS, JAMES RENDEL (1852–1941), English Biblical scholar and orientalist. In 1889 he discovered at the St. Catherine's monastery on Mt. *Sinai the Syriac text of the 'Apology' of *Aristides (publd. 1891); and in 1910 he issued the Syriac text of the 'Odes of *Solomon'.

HARRISON, FREDERIC (1831–1923), English *Positivist. In his earlier years he was a member of the C of E, but he came under the influence of A. *Comte and embraced Positivism in 1870. He became the recognized leader in England of that school of thought.

HARROWING OF HELL, The. The medieval English term for the defeat of the powers of evil at the *Descent of Christ into Hell after His death.

HARTMANN, EDUARD VON (1842–1906), German philosopher. He saw in the

'Unconscious' an all-pervasive monistic principle which was at once will and presentation and also the ground of evolutionary development. Christianity, which was only a stage along the way to the religion of Absolute Spirit, was dead and its gravedigger was modern Protestantism.

HARVEST THANKSGIVING. In Britain an unofficial religious festival of thanksgiving for the fruits of the earth, usually observed on a Sunday in Sept. or Oct., after the ingathering of the harvest. An annual festival had become common by the mid-19th cent., and a parochial thanksgiving replaced the traditional Harvest Home.

HASMONAEANS. The family name of the *Maccabees.

HASTINGS, JAMES (1852–1922), *Presbyterian divine. He is famous as the editor of the *Dictionary of the Bible* (1898–1904), the *Encyclopaedia of Religion and Ethics* (1908–26), and other religious encyclopaedic works.

HAT, Cardinal's. See *Red Hat*.

HATFIELD, Council of (680). This Council of the English Church, which met under Abp. *Theodore at Hatfield (or ? Heathfield), repudiated *Monothelitism, accepted the decrees of the first five General Councils, and affirmed its belief in the *Double Procession of the Holy Spirit.

HAURANNE, J. D. DE. See *Saint-Cyran*.

HAWKINS, EDWARD (1789–1882), Provost of Oriel College, Oxford, from 1828. He influenced J. H . *Newman. Though a High Churchman, he was involved in a bitter struggle with the *Tractarians.

HAYMO OF FAVERSHAM (d. 1244), *Franciscan. Born at Faversham in Kent, he entered the Franciscan Order in 1224. He took a leading part in the deposition of *Elias and was elected General of the Order in 1240. His works include an order for private and conventual Mass on ferias and notes for a ceremonial.

HEADLAM, ARTHUR CAYLEY (1862–1947), Bp. of *Gloucester from 1923 to 1945. He previously held high academic

offices. A central Churchman who disliked all ecclesiastical parties (*Anglo-Catholics, *Evangelicals, and *Modernists), he was one of the most influential English prelates in the inter-war period.

HEARNE, THOMAS (1678–1735), English antiquary. He collated MSS. and held appointments in the Bodleian Library, Oxford, but, refusing to take the oath to George I in 1716, he was deprived of his posts and denied access to libraries. Though at times uncritical, his accuracy in transcribing authorities makes his works valuable for reference.

HEARSE. (1) A triangular frame or stand, holding 15 candles, formerly used at *Tenebrae. (2) Various funeral furnishings, now esp. the car bearing the coffin.

HEART. In the Bible the heart usually designates the whole personality, though, in contrast to modern secular usage, the emphasis is on the activities of reason and will rather than on the emotions. In Christian spirituality the heart is regarded as the organ for the love of God. See also *Sacred Heart*.

HEAVEN. In Christian theology the dwelling-place of God and the angels, and ultimately of all the redeemed, wherein they receive their eternal reward. In the Bible it is conceived as above the sky.

It is the distinctive Christian hope and belief that all faithful disciples (and not merely exceptional human beings) will, through Christ's victory, eventually reign with Him in glory. This may be thought of as attained in the *Kingdom of God at the end of history, but it is also believed that even before the general resurrection some at least of the redeemed are with Christ, i.e. in heaven. Acc. to traditional Catholic theology, such souls (except the BVM) await reunion with their bodies until the general *resurrection of the dead.

HEBDOMADARIAN. In cathedral churches and monasteries the priest who presides at the Eucharist and Divine Office, normally for a week at a time.

HEBER, REGINALD (1783–1826), Bp. of Calcutta from 1823. A former *Bampton lecturer, he laboured for the spread of Christianity in his diocese and beyond. His hymns include 'Holy, holy, holy, Lord God Almighty' and 'From Greenland's icy mountains'.

HEBREW (people). The inhabitants of Palestine, who entered the land with the *Patriarchs and *Moses. They generally spoke of themselves as 'Israelites'; the term 'Hebrew' was largely used of them by other people.

HEBREW (tongue). The Semitic language in which practically all the OT was written. In the NT 'Hebrew' may denote either classical Hebrew or the colloquial *Aramaic dialect of Palestine.

Apart from brief texts, the only surviving literature is the OT itself. The vocabulary is small, the style is simple and direct. The earliest Hebrew was written in a form of ancient Phoenician script, running from right to left, which was also the ancestor of the Greek alphabet and of our own. During the Babylonian captivity (586–538 B.C.) this gave way to an Aramaizing form of the same script, from which the so-called 'Assyrian' or 'square' script was developed. This alphabet consisted of 22 signs for consonants. The absence of vowels was remedied first by using certain of the existing consonants to represent both vowels and consonants, and later by the development of a system of strokes and dots known as *vowel points.

HEBREWS, Epistle to the. Traditionally ascribed to St. *Paul, this Ep., unlike most others in the NT, does not contain the name of the writer or of those addressed; the traditional title is prob. an inference from its contents. The Ep. asserts the finality of the Christian dispensation and its superiority to the Old Covenant. Its theological teaching, notably on the Person of Christ, reaches a level unsurpassed in the NT.

From an early date it was received at *Alexandria as Pauline, whether considered as a translation from Paul's Hebrew, or his in substance but written by someone else. In the W. it was known to *Clement of Rome, but not quoted as Pauline or certainly canonical until the 4th–5th cent. Modern scholars consider that internal evidence marks it as non-Pauline, while its style shows that it is unlikely to be a translation. Attempts to identify its author are conjectural. Both its author and its intended readers were familiar with Jewish worship, but it is disputed whether it was addressed to converts from Judaism or to Gentiles. A date before A.D. 70 has been supported by several scholars; others argue for a date under *Domitian.

HEBREWS, Gospel according to the. An *apocryphal Gospel, acc. to St. *Jerome used by the *Nazarenes, and hence also known as the 'Gospel of the Nazarenes'. Jerome reports that it was composed in *Aramaic speech written in Hebrew letters and that some regarded it as the original version of St. *Matthew's Gospel. It contains certain sayings of Christ not recorded in the canonical Gospels. There is wide divergency of views but a tendency to believe that in some places it is based on independent traditions of historical value.

HECKER, ISAAC THOMAS (1819–88), founder of the *Paulists. He became a RC in 1844, entered the novitiate of the *Redemptorists in Belgium in 1845, and returned to his native New York in 1851. Difficulties having arisen with his Redemptorist superiors, in 1857 he was dispensed from his vows and founded a new congregation for missionary work in the U.S.A. which was known as the 'Paulists'. It has been suggested that *Leo XIII's condemnation of *Americanism in 1899 had Hecker in mind.

HEDONISM. The ethical doctrine which maintains that the proper end of all moral action is pleasure.

HEFELE, KARL JOSEPH (1809–93), Church historian. From 1869 he was Bp. of Rottenburg. He had an important part in the preparations for the First *Vatican Council, drawing up the procedure. He opposed the definition of Papal *Infallibility. His main work was his history of the ecclesiastical councils (completed by J. *Hergenrother, 1855–90).

HEGEL, GEORG WILHELM FRIEDRICH (1770–1831), German Idealist philosopher. In 1818 he succeeded J. G. *Fichte as professor of philosophy in Berlin. His system grew out of the Critical Idealism of I. *Kant. It was a logic not of mere being, but of becoming, and the logical idea fell under the three heads of being, essence, and notion. Development followed through a dialectical process in which a *thesis* was succeeded by an *antithesis*; through the ensuing conflict the two were brought together again at a higher level as a *synthesis*. In this way he expounded an essentially evolutionary view of the universe and brought within the purview of his system not only the natural sciences but also such disciplines as history, law, and religion. Truth lay not in individual truths or in individual disciplines, but in the whole. His influence has been immense.

HEGESIPPUS, St. (2nd cent.), Church historian. He wrote five Books of 'Memoirs' against the *Gnostics. It appears that he drew up a 'succession list' of the early bishops of Rome; it has been argued that the list in *Epiphanius (*Haer.*, 27.6) is a reproduction of this; if so, it is the earliest witness to the names of the first Roman bishops.

HEGUMENOS. A title in the E. for the ruler of a monastery.

HEIDEGGER, MARTIN (1889–1976), German *existentialist. He was a professor at Freiburg from 1929 to 1951. He elaborated a metaphysic of the human person. In *Sein und Zeit* (1927; Eng. tr., *Being and Time*, 1962) he uncovers man's temporal being in order to focus on Being in its unity and totality. Man's personal existence (*Dasein*; lit. 'there-ness') is a unique transcendent possibility, which is rooted in immediate temporal relationships. Authentic existence, facing nothingness, is lived out only in the full acceptance of death. In his later works it seems that Being is intuitively grasped rather than philosophically explored.

HEIDELBERG CATECHISM. The Protestant confession of faith compiled in 1562 by Z. Ursinus and K. Olevian, two Heidelberg theologians, and others, at the instance of the Elector *Frederick III, and accepted in 1563 as the standard of doctrine in the Palatinate.

HEILER, FRIEDRICH (1892–1967), German religious writer. As a RC he studied Catholic theology, but in 1919 he joined the *Lutheran Church at *Upsala. He became the organizer of a German High Church movement and founded an Evangelical order of Franciscan *Tertiaries. His principal work, *Das Gebet* (1918), is a comprehensive historical analysis of prayer.

HEIM, KARL (1874–1958), *Lutheran theologian. In 1920 he became a professor at *Tübingen. He was a leading opponent of the (pagan) German Faith Movement. In theology he stressed the contrast of faith and reason and emphasized the transcendence of faith.

HEIRIC OF AUXERRE (841–876/7), teacher and hagiographer. He entered the monastery of St. *Germanus at Auxerre as an oblate when he was about 7. After studying elsewhere he taught at Auxerre until his death. His chief work is a metrical life of Germanus. He is a link between the *Carolingian schools and the later Middle Ages.

HEIRMOS. The opening stanza in each ode of the *canon.

HELENA, St.(*c*. 255–*c*. 330), also **Helen**, mother of the Emp. *Constantine. Abandoned by her husband, she was accorded a position of honour on Constantine's accession. She zealously supported the Christian cause. In 326 she visited the Holy Land, where she founded basilicas on the Mount of *Olives and at *Bethlehem. Acc. to later tradition she discovered the Cross on which Christ was crucified.

HELIAND. An Old Saxon Biblical poem of the 9th cent. It is based on *Tatian's harmony of the Gospels and written in alliterative verse. Acc. to the Latin 'Praefatio', it was written at the order of *Louis the Pious for the benefit of his recently converted Saxon subjects.

HELL. The word is used in English translations of the Bible to represent both the Hebrew '*Sheol', the place of the departed, and the Greek '*Gehenna', the place of punishment for the wicked after death. In Christian theology it normally signifies the place or state to which unrepentant sinners are held to pass, by God's final judgement, after this life. Acc. to traditional Scholastic theology, souls in hell experience both the *poena damni*, i.e. exclusion from God's presence and loss of contact with Him, and a certain *poena sensus*, denoted in the Bible by fire and usually interpreted as an external agent tormenting them. Modern theology stresses that hell is but the logical consequence of ultimate rejection of the will of God which (since God cannot take away free will) necessarily separates the soul from God, and hence from all possibility of happiness. See also *Descent of Christ into Hell*.

HELVETIC CONFESSIONS, The. Two Reformation Confessions of Faith. The First Helvetic Confession (also known as the 'Second Confession of *Basle') was compiled at Basle in 1536 by J. H. *Bullinger and others as a uniform confession of faith for the whole of Switzerland. The Second Helvetic Confession was the work of J. H. Bullinger, issued in 1566 in response to a request from the Elector-Palatine *Frederick III, who had announced his adhesion to *Calvinism. It soon won acceptance not only among the Swiss Protestant Churches but among other 'Reformed' (i.e. Calvinists) outside Switzerland.

HELVIDIUS (4th cent.). A Latin theologian who was attacked by St. *Jerome for his denial of the perpetual virginity of the BVM.

HELWYS, THOMAS (*c.* 1550–*c.* 1616), English *Baptist. Having migrated to Holland with J. *Smyth in 1608, he became convinced that 'Infant Baptism' was invalid, and he joined Smyth's separatist community, the first Baptist Church to come into existence. In 1612 he returned to London, where he founded the first Baptist congregation in England.

HEMEROBAPTISTS. A Jewish sect for which daily ablution was an essential part of religion. They are mentioned by various of the Fathers.

HEMMERLIN, FELIX, also 'Hemerli' (*c.* 1388–*c.* 1460), reformer. In 1421 he became provost of St. Ursus at Solothurn, where he revised the statutes of his collegiate clergy. He also advocated reforms of all kinds and attacked the *Mendicant Orders and the *Lollards. In his later years he was involved in politics and lost his ecclesiastical offices.

HENDERSON, ALEXANDER (*c.* 1583–1646), Scottish Covenanting leader. He was mainly responsible for drafting the *National Covenant of 1638, and during the *Bishops' Wars of 1639–40 he was the recognized leader of the Scottish *Presbyterians. He prepared the drafts of the *Solemn League and Covenant (1643) and of the Directory for

*Public Worship (1644).

HENOTHEISM. A primitive form of faith which recognizes the existence of several gods, but regards one particular god as the deity of the family or tribe; makes him the centre of its worship; and for practical purposes neglects the existence of other gods. Modern scholars commonly hold that the early Hebrew faith took this form.

HENOTICON. The theological formula put forward in 482 to secure union between the *Monophysites and the Orthodox, and sponsored by the Emp. *Zeno. It was widely accepted in the E. but never countenanced at Rome.

HENRICIANS. A medieval heretical sect which arose in the 12th cent. under the inspiration of *Henry of Lausanne.

HENRIETTA MARIA (1609–69), Queen. She married *Charles I in 1625, on condition that the penal laws against RCs were suspended and the Queen be allowed free exercise of her religion. She was unpopular in England.

HENRY II, St. (972–1024), German King and Holy Roman Emperor from 1002. In 1006 he created and endowed the see of Bamberg. He frequently interfered in the affairs of the Church, but he commonly had the political support of Rome. In his later years he supported the *Cluniac reform. Legend saw in him a monarch of outstanding piety; he was canonized in 1146.

HENRY IV (1050–1106), German King and Holy Roman Emperor. He succeeded to the throne in 1056. His reign was troubled by rebellious Saxon princes on the one hand and the reforms of *Gregory VII (q.v.) on the other. Threatened with excommunication and deposition, Henry declared Gregory deposed; his subjects were then released from their allegiance and the Saxons rose; Henry submitted to the Pope at *Canossa in 1077. In 1080 he was again excommunicated; he set up an anti-Pope who crowned him Emperor in 1084.

HENRY IV (1553–1610), King of France. Brought up a Protestant, he became King of Navarre in 1572. He took part in the wars of religion on the Protestant side. In 1589 he inherited the crown of France; despite military victory, he was not recognized as king until he became a RC in 1593. In 1598 he issued the Edict of *Nantes, granting freedom of worship to Protestants in certain places.

HENRY VI (1421–71), King of England from 1422. Throughout his reign difficulties in France increased and the situation in England was unsettled. The birth of a son in 1453 excluded Richard, Duke of York, from the succession, but the King was seized by an attack of mental derangement and Richard governed. After his recovery civil war broke out. Henry was taken prisoner, confined in the Tower, and eventually murdered. He was a deeply religious man. He founded Eton College and King's College, Cambridge.

HENRY VIII (1491–1547), King of England from 1509. From an early date he opposed the Reforming Movement and his *Assertio Septem Sacramentorum* (1521) won him the title of '*Defender of the Faith'. In 1527 he began taking steps to dissolve his marriage with Catherine of Aragon, the widow of his brother, which had taken place by papal dispensation in 1509. The only surviving child was *Mary, and Henry was worried over the succession; he had also conceived a passion for Anne Boleyn. Proceedings in England before T. *Wolsey and L. *Campeggio were terminated in 1529 when *Clement VII revoked the case to Rome. Henry then turned to the repudiation of papal authority. He associated his people with him by summoning Parliament to pass Acts which would transfer the headship of the Church in England to him. In 1531 the clergy were accused of breaches of *praemunire; they secured pardon by payment of a fine and *Convocation's recognition of the Royal Supremacy. In 1532 Convocation accepted the *Submission of the Clergy. After the death of Abp. T. *Warham, T. *Cranmer was appointed his successor, the Pope having been persuaded to grant the necessary bulls. In 1533 Cranmer pronounced Henry's marriage to Catherine invalid and a few days later pronounced him married to Anne Boleyn. Clement excommunicated Henry and declared his divorce and remarriage null. The following year (1534) Parliament passed the series of Acts which severed financial, judicial, and administrative links with Rome. The *dissolution

of the monasteries (1536 and 1539) won support from the beneficiaries, though the *Pilgrimage of Grace demonstrated that there was serious opposition. For a time Henry showed a measure of toleration of Protestantism, countenancing the *Ten Articles (1536), but the *Six Articles (1539) reaffirmed Catholic doctrine, and it was not until after his death that doctrinal Protestantism became the official policy.

HENRY BEAUFORT. See *Beaufort, Henry*.

HENRY OF BLOIS (d. 1171), Bp. of *Winchester from 1129. He was a grandson of *William the Conqueror. On the death of William of Corbeil (1136) he hoped for the see of *Canterbury, but *Theobald was appointed in 1138. In the following year Pope Innocent II gave Henry a legatine commission, which made him in some ways Theobald's superior. Henry then sought the elevation of Winchester into an archiepiscopal see. In the *Becket controversy he tried to mediate between the king and the archbishop. He was a great builder and founded the Hospital of St. Cross at Winchester.

HENRY OF GHENT (d. 1293), theologian. He was one of the chief representatives among the secular clergy of Augustinianism, which he defended at *Paris. In his *Quodlibeta* and (unfinished) *Summa theologica* he opposed both St. *Thomas Aquinas and *Siger of Brabant in his attempt to combine the old Augustinianism with the new *Aristotelian teaching.

HENRY OF LAUSANNE (d. after 1145), sectarian. An itinerant preacher, he was expelled from the diocese of Le Mans on account of his heretical teaching and continued his activities in S. France. Acc. to St. *Bernard he denied the objective efficacy of the Sacraments and made it dependent on the worthy character of the priest.

HENRY SUSO (c. 1295–1366), German mystic. He entered a *Dominican house at the age of 13; after 15 years of moderate piety he experienced a conversion. He studied under J. *Eckhart at *Cologne. Despite difficulties with his order, he preached widely and was valued as a spiritual director in many women's convents. His principal work, *Das Büchlein der ewigen Weisheit* ('The Little Book of Eternal Wisdom') is a practical meditation book, with little theoretical discussion; it is one of the classics of German mysticism.

HENSON, HERBERT HENSLEY (1863–1947), Bp. of *Hereford (1918–20) and then of *Durham (1920–39). He defended latitudinarian views in a series of publications, and his nomination to the see of Hereford aroused protest on account of his doctrinal position, esp. his attitude to the *Virgin Birth and *miracles; a crisis was averted when Abp. R. T. *Davidson and Henson issued a joint statement in which Henson appeared to retract his earlier views. Until Parliament rejected the revised Prayer Book (1927–8), he was a strong advocate of the Establishment; he then sought freedom for the Church from State control.

HEORTOLOGY. The study of the origin, history, and meaning of the festivals and seasons of the ecclesiastical *year.

HEPTATEUCH. A name sometimes used for the first seven books of the OT on account of their supposed unity.

HERACLEON (*fl. c.* 145–80), *Gnostic teacher. He wrote a commentary on St. *John's Gospel and may be the author of the 'Tractate on the Three Natures' found at *Nag Hammadi.

HERACLIUS (575–641), Byzantine Emperor from 610/11. In 629 he brought back to *Golgotha the Cross which the Persians had removed in 614. In an attempt to secure doctrinal unity he issued the '*Ecthesis' (q.v.) in 638.

HERBERT, EDWARD (1583–1648), first Lord Herbert of Cherbury; philosopher and poet. He held that the essence of religion lay in five innate ideas: that there is a God; that He ought to be worshipped; that virtue is the chief element in this worship; that repentance for sin is a duty; and that there is another life of rewards and punishments. He was a forerunner of the *Deists.

HERBERT, GEORGE (1593–1633), poet and divine. A brother of the preceding, he seemed marked out for the career of a courtier. The death of *James I and the influence

of N. *Ferrar led him to study divinity. In 1630 he was ordained priest and accepted the rectory of Fugglestone with Bemerton, near *Salisbury.

His most famous prose work, *A Priest to the Temple; or the Country Parson* (1652), outlines a sober and well-balanced ideal of the English clergyman. His collection of poems, entitled *The Temple*, was entrusted to Ferrar on his deathbed and published in 1633. Those in current use as hymns include 'The God of love my Shepherd is' and 'Let all the world in every corner sing'.

HERDER, JOHANN GOTTFRIED (1744–1803), German critic. In 1776 he became *Generalsuperintendent and court preacher at Weimar, where he spent the rest of his life. His interests were wide, but his main contribution to the ideas of his time was in the philosophy of history.

HEREFORD. The see was founded in 676 by Putta, Bp. of *Rochester, who had fled from the heathen invaders of his diocese. St. *Ethelbert, king of the East Angles, was buried in the cathedral and, with the BVM, designated its joint patron. The main part of the present cathedral dates from 1079–1110. In 1786 the west end collapsed, carrying part of the nave with it; the later restoration was poorly done.

HEREFORD, NICHOLAS. See *Nicholas of Hereford*.

HERESIARCH. The originator of a heresy or the founder of a heretical sect.

HERESY. The formal denial or doubt of any defined doctrine of the Catholic faith. From early days the Church claimed teaching authority and consequently condemned heresy. The need to rebut heresy has sometimes stimulated the formulation of orthodox Christian doctrine.

The RC Church regards 'formal heresy', that is the wilful adherence to an error in matters of faith by a baptized person, as a grave sin involving excommunication; 'material heresy', the holding of heretical doctrines 'in good faith', involves neither crime nor sin.

HERGENRÖTHER, JOSEPH (1824–90), ecclesiastical historian. He represented the more conservative element in German

Catholicism. He defended the definition of Papal *Infallibility at the First *Vatican Council and wrote against J. J . I. von *Döllinger. His Church History (1876–80) was long a standard work.

HERIMANNUS CONTRACTUS (1013–1054), **Hermann the Lame**, poet and chronicler. A monk of *Reichenau, he wrote on a wide range of subjects. His works include many hymns and antiphons, but the attribution to him of the '*Salve Regina' and the 'Alma Redemptoris Mater' rests on insufficient evidence.

HERITOR. In Scotland heritors were the owners of heritable property in a parish to whom descended the obligation to pay the *teinds or tithes to the minister and to keep the parish church and manse in repair. An Act of Parliament in 1925 provided for the termination of their rights and duties.

HERMAN, EMMA (1874–1923), writer. The wife of a *Presbyterian minister, she spent part of her life in Constantinople and Sydney. Later she joined the C of E. Her chief works were *The Meaning and Value of Mysticism* (1915) and *Creative Prayer* (1921).

HERMANN OF REICHENAU. See *Herimannus Contractus*.

HERMANN OF WIED (1477–1552), reformer. He became Abp.-Elector of *Cologne in 1515. In his earlier years he was hostile to the Protestant movement, but c. 1539 he set out to create a parallel movement within the Catholic Church. His increasing adhesion to the Protestant cause led to his excommunication and deposition in 1546. His proposals for reform influenced the compilers of the BCP.

HERMAS (2nd cent.), author of 'The Shepherd', accounted one of the '*Apostolic Fathers'. A Christian slave, he was freed, married, became a rich merchant, and then lost his property.
'The Shepherd' is divided into three parts, viz. 5 'Visions', in which a matron appears to Hermas representing the Church; 12 'Mandates', in which Hermas gives his teaching on Christian behaviour and virtues; and 10 'Similitudes', in which Christian principles are represented under a series of images. The work inculcates the need for penance and the possibility of the forgiveness of post-Baptismal sin.
Though Hermas says that he was a contemporary of St. *Clement of Rome, the *Muratorian Canon attributes his work to a brother of *Pius I, and many scholars thus date it between 140 and 155. In the E. Church it was widely regarded as Scripture in the 2nd and 3rd cents.

HERMENEUTICS. The science of the methods of *exegesis. Whereas exegesis is usually the act of explaining a text, hermeneutics is the science or art by which exegetical procedures are devised. In theology hermeneutical theory arises out of awareness of the ambiguity of a sacred text and the consequent analysis of the art of understanding. In some modern theological usage 'hermeneutics', as a preliminary to exegesis, is distinguished from 'hermeneutic', the wider study of how Biblical faith may be conveyed in the language of fundamentally different civilizations.

HERMESIANISM. The system of philosophical and theological doctrines taught by Georg Hermes (1775–1831), professor of theology at Münster. Holding that our only certain knowledge was of ideas actually present in the mind, he taught that the criterion of objective truth must be found in our subjective beliefs. He held that, starting from this principle, the existence of God could be proved by theoretical reason, and that the possibility of supernatural revelation could then be demonstrated.

HERMETIC BOOKS. A collection of Greek and Latin religious and philosophical writings ascribed to Hermes Trismegistus, a later name for the Egyptian God Thoth, who was believed to be the father and protector of all knowledge. They prob. date from the mid-1st to the late-3rd cent. A.D.

HERMIAS (date uncertain), Christian philosopher. He is known only as the author of a small treatise, the 'Irrisio' or 'Mockery of the Heathen Philosophers'. Modern scholars have assigned to him various dates between the 2nd and 6th cents.

HERMIT. One who from religious motives has retired into a solitary life. Christian hermits began to abound in Egypt and the surrounding regions towards the end of the 3rd cent. In the W. they died out after the *Counter-Reformation; in the E. they survive.

HEROD FAMILY. *Herod the Great* was appointed king of the Jews by the Romans in 40 B.C. and ruled from 37 to 4 B.C. Christ was born during his reign. On his death his territory was divided between his sons: *Archelaus*, as ethnarch of Judaea, Idumaea, and Samaria, who was deposed in A.D. 6; *Antipas*, as tetrarch of *Galilee and Peraea, the 'Herod the tetrarch' of the Gospels (4 B.C.–A.D. 39) who beheaded *John the Baptist; and *Philip*, as tetrarch of the remaining territory (4 B.C.–A.D. 34). *Agrippa I*, the son of Herod the Great's second son, Aristobulus, succeeded to all these territories; he ruled until A.D. 44 and is the 'Herod' of Acts. His son, *Agrippa II*, is the 'King Agrippa' before whom St. *Paul appeared.

HERODIANS. A party mentioned in the Gospels as hostile to Christ. They were presumably partisans of the *Herod family.

HERRING, THOMAS (1693–1757), Abp. successively of *York (1743) and *Canterbury (1747). His chief claim to fame is his York Visitation Returns for 1743, which are an important document for the religious history of his time.

HERRMANN, WILHELM (1846–1922), theologian. In 1879 he became professor of systematic theology at *Marburg. Though he regarded the Gospels as in some sense the record of a historical personality, he insisted that the Church should teach only those facts about Christ which will act upon man, e.g. His moral teaching as distinguished from His Virgin Birth and Resurrection.

HERRNHUT. A village some 40 miles east of Dresden, built and settled in 1722 by a group of *Moravian Brethren on a site presented by N. L. von *Zinzendorf.

HERTFORD, Council of (673). A Council of bishops held under *Theodore, Abp. of Canterbury, to promote the reorganization of the English Church. It issued 10 canons, concerned esp. with the rights and duties of clerics and monks.

HERVETUS, GENTIAN (1499–1584),

French theologian, translator, and controversialist. He translated various Greek Fathers into Latin in the service of Card. R. *Pole and Card. M. Cervini (later Pope Marcellus II), and he attended the Council of *Trent. In 1561 he joined a group of theologians formed by Card. Charles of Lorraine for fighting Protestantism and published a number of controversial pamphlets.

HERZOG, JOHANN JAKOB (1805–82), Reformed theologian. Professor successively at Lausanne, Halle, and Erlangen, he edited the *Realencyklopädie für protestantische Theologie und Kirche* (1853–68), a standard work of reference.

HESYCHASM. In the E. Church, the tradition of inner, mystical prayer, associated esp. with the monks of Mt. *Athos. The Hesychasts attached special importance to unceasing recitation of the *Jesus Prayer. They recommended a particular bodily posture, with breathing controlled to keep time with the recitation of the prayer. Their immediate aim was to secure what they termed 'the union of the mind with the heart', so that their prayer became 'prayer of the heart'. This leads, in those chosen by God, to the vision of the Divine Light, which, it was believed, can be seen with the material eyes of the body.

HESYCHIUS (*fl. c.* 300), Biblical textual critic. Acc. to *Jerome, he revised the text of the LXX in the light of the Hebrew.

HESYCHIUS OF ALEXANDRIA (prob. 5th cent.), lexicographer. His lexicon is an important authority for the Greek dialects and the vocabulary of some of the Fathers.

HESYCHIUS OF JERUSALEM, St. (d. after 451), Greek exegete. In early life he was a monk. He is said to have commented on the whole Bible. Surviving portions of his commentaries prob. include most of that on the Pss., formerly attributed to *Athanasius.

HEXAEMERON. The account of the creation of the universe in six days in Gen. 1; also patristic commentaries on this narrative.

HEXAPLA. The elaborate edition of the OT produced by *Origen, in which the Hebrew text, the Hebrew text transliterated into Greek characters, and the four Greek versions of *Aquila, *Symmachus, the *Septuagint (in a revised text with critical signs), and *Theodotion were arranged in parallel columns. For some sections of the OT, up to three further Greek versions were added, making nine columns in all.

HEXATEUCH. The name given by J. *Wellhausen and others to the first six books of the Hebrew Bible in the belief that they were compiled from a single set of literary sources.

HEXHAM in Northumberland. An abbey was founded there by St. *Wilfrid in 674. In 678 a new see of Bernicia was established at Hexham; it survived until 821, when it was united with *Lindisfarne. Since the *Dissolution in 1536 the abbey church has been used as the parish church.

HEYLYN, PETER (1600–62), Anglican controversialist. His championship of *High Church views attracted the notice of W. *Laud. When J. *Williams, Bp. of Lincoln, declined to institute him as rector of Hemingford, *Charles I made him a prebendary of *Westminster (1631), and other preferment followed. In 1633 he was called upon to help W. Noy prepare the case against W. *Prynne; he wrote a *History of the Sabbath* (1636) against the Puritans at the King's command. Under the Commonwealth his controversial writings led to trouble.

HIBBERT, ROBERT (1770–1849), founder of the Hibbert Trust. He employed a *Unitarian minister for the benefit of the slaves on his estate in Jamaica. In 1847 he founded the Hibbert Trust 'for the spread of Christianity in its most simple and intelligible form' and the 'unfettered exercise of the right of private judgement in matters of religion'; its aims are anti-Trinitarian.

HICKES, GEORGE (1642–1715), *Nonjuring bishop. He became Dean of *Worcester in 1683, but in 1689 he refused to take the oaths to William and Mary and in 1690 he was deprived of his deanery. In 1694 he was consecrated titular Bp. of Thetford by the Nonjurors, and after the death of W. Lloyd (1709) was their acknowledged leader. In order to continue the Nonjuring succession, he consecrated three bishops in 1713.

HICKS, ELIAS (1748–1830), American

*Quaker. He opposed the creation of any credal basis for Quakerism, notably in his *Doctrinal Epistle* (1824). A schism ensued at Philadelphia and elsewhere between his followers (the 'Liberal Branch' or 'Hicksites') and the orthodox; it had repercussions in England.

HICKS, GEORGE DAWES (1862–1941), English philosopher. In his *Hibbert Lectures on *The Philosophical Bases of Theism* (1937) he defended the traditional Christian position, arguing that besides the strictly intellectual grounds of theistic belief there was a legitimate place for the argument from religious experience.

HICKSITES. See *Hicks, E.*

HIERARCHY. The word has been used for the ordered body of the Christian clergy since Patristic times. The threefold hierarchical order of bishops, priests, and deacons has been retained in the C of E in common with the RC and E. Churches.

HIEROME, HIERONYMUS. Forms of Jerome (q.v.).

HIERONYMIAN MARTYROLOGY. A *martyrology composed in Italy in the mid-5th cent. It is so named from a statement in the apocryphal correspondence preceding the text that its compilation was the work of St. *Jerome.

HIERUSALEM. A Latinized form of *Jerusalem.

HIGH ALTAR. The main altar of a church, traditionally standing in the centre of the east end.

HIGH CHURCHMEN. The group in the C of E which stresses her historical continuity with Catholic Christianity, and hence upholds a 'high' conception of the episcopate and of the nature of the Sacraments. The existence of such a school goes back to the Elizabethan age; it flourished under the Stuarts, and came into prominence again with the *Oxford Movement.

HIGH COMMISSION, Court of. From 1549 ecclesiastical commissions to check heresy and enforce the forms of public worship were often appointed in England. The term 'High Commission' began to appear c. 1570 and was normally employed after 1580, a development corresponding with the elevation of an *ad hoc* commission into a permanent court. It was increasingly occupied with suits between parties, and it became the normal court of appeal from the ancient ecclesiastical courts in doctrinal and disciplinary cases. It was abolished in 1641.

HIGH MASS (Missa solemnis). In the W. for centuries the normal, though not the most usual, form of the Mass. Its essential feature was the presence of the *deacon and *subdeacon assisting the celebrant. Since the Second *Vatican Council the term has disappeared from RC official documents.

'HIGH PLACES', The. In the OT the local sanctuaries other than *Jerusalem at which God was worshipped with sacrifice in early times. The cultus acquired heathen associations and was denounced by the Prophets; the 'high places' were destroyed in 621 B.C.

HIGH PRAYERS. A title for the service in certain Oxford college chapels on great festivals.

HIGH PRIEST. In the OT the head of the *Levitical priesthood whose institution is described in Exod. 28. His chief function was the superintendence of the Temple worship, and it was his special prerogative to offer the Liturgy on the Day of *Atonement. In post-exilic times he was the head of the Jewish State as well as the chief religious functionary.

HIGHER CRITICISM. The critical study of the literary methods and sources used by the authors of (esp.) Biblical Books, in distinction from *Textual ('Lower') Criticism, which is concerned solely with recovering the text of the Books as it left their authors' hands.

HILARION, St. (c. 291–371), the founder of the *anchoritic life in Palestine. He was converted to Christianity at *Alexandria, and under the influence of St. *Antony retired to the Egyptian desert as a hermit. In 306 he returned to Palestine, where he lived a life of extreme asceticism near Gaza.

HILARY OF ARLES, St. (403–49), leader of the *Semi-Pelagian party. A monk of *Lérins, he became Abp. of Arles in 428/429. He presided over several councils. In 444, by deposing a bishop, he appears to have exceeded his rights and Pope *Leo I deprived Arles of its metropolitical jurisdiction.

HILARY OF POITIERS, St. (c. 315–67), the '*Athanasius of the West'. A convert from *Neoplatonism, he was elected Bp. of Poitiers c. 353. He became involved in the *Arian controversy and was exiled for four years. In 359 he defended the cause of orthodoxy at the Council of *Seleucia. He was the most respected Latin theologian of his age. His main works were a treatise *De Trinitate* (against the Arians); *De Synodis*, valuable for the history of the period; and the so-called *Opus Historicum*.

HILDA, St. (614–80), Abbess of Whitby. Descended from the Northumbrian royal line, in 657 she founded a monastery for men and women at 'Streanaeshalch', later named Whitby by the Danes, which grew in fame and influence. At the Synod of *Whitby (664) she sided with St. *Colman in his defence of the *Celtic customs.

HILDEBERT OF LAVARDIN (1056–1133), poet and canonist. Elected Bp. of Le Mans in 1096, he continued the building of his cathedral (consecrated in 1120), expelled *Henry of Lausanne from his diocese, and prob. took part in the First *Lateran Council of 1123. In 1125 he became Abp. of Tours. He is famous chiefly for his literary works, which were regarded as a model of elegant style in the Middle Ages. Not all those attributed to him are genuine.

HILDEBRAND. See *Gregory VII*.

HILDEGARD, St. (1098–1179), Abbess of Rupertsberg, the 'Sibyl of the Rhine'. Born of noble family and subject to supernatural religious experiences from childhood, c. 1116 she joined the *Benedictine community at Diessenberg, becoming abbess in 1136. Between 1141 and 1151 she dictated her *Scivias* (prob. an abbreviation for 'Sciens vias'); these contain 26 visions, with denunciations of the world and enigmatic prophecies of disaster. Some time between 1147 and 1152 she moved her community to Rupertsberg, near Bingen. She seems to have exerted a wide influence.

HILLEL, School of. The followers of Hillel, a rabbinical teacher of the time of Christ. In opposition to the school of *Shammai, they upheld a liberal and lenient interpretation of the Law.

HILTON, WALTER (d. 1396), English mystic. He incepted in *canon law, prob. at Cambridge, and after a period as a hermit became an *Augustinian canon at Thurgarton Priory, Notts. His most famous work in English, the *Scala Perfectionis*, describes the reformation of the defaced image of God in the soul in two stages: the first 'in faith', the second 'in faith and feeling', separated by a mystical 'dark night' in which the soul is detached from earthly things and directed to the things of the spirit. Hilton also wrote in Latin.

HINCMAR (*c.* 806–82), Abp. of *Reims from 845. He opposed Lothair, King of Lorraine, when he wished to divorce his wife, and he strove to defend his metropolitan rights both against his own bishops and against the Pope. After Lothair's death (869) he secured the succession of Charles the Bald.

Though not a speculative theologian, Hincmar took a prominent part in the controversy with *Gottschalk on *predestination. He himself wróte against Gottschalk and he called upon John Scotus *Erigena for help. Another dispute with Gottschalk and *Ratramnus arose when Hincmar changed the words 'Trina Deitas' in one of the Vespers hymns to 'Summa Deitas', because he suspected the former phrase of *tritheism.

HINNOM, Valley of. The literal meaning of *Gehenna (q.v.).

HINSLEY, ARTHUR (1865–1943), Abp. of *Westminster from 1935 and cardinal from 1937. He founded the '*Sword of the Spirit' in 1940 and became widely known through his vigorous spiritual and national leadership of English RCs in the early part of the Second World War.

HIPPO, Council of (393). A council of the Catholic (i.e. non-*Donatist) Church in Latin Africa. A *breviarium* of its canons passed into general canon law.

HIPPOLYTUS, St. (*c.* 170–*c.* 236), theologian. He was a presbyter at Rome, apparently of some importance. He took an active part in attacking the doctrines of *Sabellius. He seems to have set himself up as anti-Pope under *Callistus (217–22). In the persecution of the Emp. Maximin, Hippolytus and Pope Pontianus (230–5) were both exiled to Sardinia. The bodies of both were brought back to Rome in 236.

A list of his writings as well as his Easter tables were discovered on a statue, prob. made in his lifetime and found in Rome in 1551. His chief work is his 'Refutation of all the Heresies', published in 1851 under the title 'Philosophumena'. His other writings include Biblical commentaries as well as the important treatise on the '*Apostolic Tradition' (q.v.). The '*Little Labyrinth' is also sometimes ascribed to him.

The most interesting element in his teaching is his *Logos doctrine. He distinguished two states of the Word, the one immanent and eternal, the other exterior and temporal. He opposed the mitigation of the penitential system brought about by the influx of pagan converts.

HIPPOLYTUS, Canons of St. A collection of canons, prob. compiled *c.* A.D. 500. They were attributed to St. *Hippolytus and hence received disproportionate attention.

HISPANA CANONS. A collection of canons and decretals apparently compiled in Spain in the 6th–7th cent. It has sometimes been (wrongly) ascribed to St. *Isidore of Seville.

HOADLY, BENJAMIN (1676–1761), Bp. successively of *Bangor (1716), *Hereford (1721), *Salisbury (1723), and *Winchester (1734). He won the leadership of the *Low Church divines favoured by the Whigs through his controversy with F. *Atterbury and O. Blackall, Bp. of *Exeter, on passive obedience and non-resistance. His sermon in 1717 on 'The Nature of the Kingdom or Church of Christ' provoked the *Bangorian Controversy.

HOBBES, THOMAS (1588–1679), English philosopher. He displeased both Royalists and Parliamentarians by holding that, although sovereignty is ultimately derived from the people, it is transferred to the monarch by implicit contract, so that while the power of the sovereign is absolute, it is not of *Divine Right. From 1640 to 1651 he was in exile. On his return to England he published the *Leviathan* (1651), a philosophical exposition of political absolutism. His teaching cut at the root of ethics, as it left no room for any genuine distinction between good and evil.

HOCKTIDE. The second Monday and Tuesday after *Easter.

HODGE, CHARLES (1797–1878), *Presbyterian theologian. He taught at Princeton nearly all his life. Though not an original thinker, he had a great influence and following.

HODY, HUMPHREY (1659–1707), Anglican divine. He showed that the 'Letter of *Aristeas' was a forgery and worked on the text of the LXX.

HOFBAUER, St. CLEMENT MARY (1751–1820), the 'Apostle of Vienna'. The son of a grazier and butcher, he joined the *Redemptorists in 1784. Unable to found a house in Vienna because of the anti-religious *Josephinist legislation, he went to Warsaw. When he was driven from Warsaw by Napoleon in 1808, he returned to Vienna. Here his influence extended from the highest to the lowest, powerfully counteracting the effects of Josephinism and the *Enlightenment.

HÖFFDING, HARALD (1843–1931), Danish philosopher. While he upheld a spiritual interpretation of the universe, he denied that there were sufficient theoretical grounds for applying the notions 'cause' or 'personality' to the Absolute or for affirming (or denying) belief in personal immortality. He described his position as 'critical monism'.

HOFFMANN, MELCHIOR (*c.* 1500–*c.* 1543), German *Anabaptist. He joined the *Lutherans and became a lay-preacher in 1523. He became increasingly imbued with eschatological ideas and finally joined the Anabaptists at Strasburg. He preached in various places between 1530 and 1533, returning to Strasburg to await the Last Day. He was imprisoned for life. The 'Melchiorites' survived him as a distinct party among the Anabaptists.

HOFFMEISTER, JOHANNES (*c.* 1509–1547), *Augustinian hermit. His life was devoted to the defence of his order against *Lutheran teaching and to the inner reform of the Church by preaching and writing. In 1546 he became Vicar-General of the Augustinian houses in Germany.

HOFMANN, JOHANN CHRISTIAN KONRAD VON (1810–77), German *Lutheran theologian. From 1845 he was professor of theology at Erlangen. He aimed at being an uncompromising exponent of Lutheran doctrine. His disciples became known as the 'Erlangen School'.

HOHENHEIM, T. B. VON. See *Paracelsus.*

HOLCOT, ROBERT (d. 1349), *Scholastic theologian. He entered the *Dominican Order, and studied and taught at *Oxford. By 1343 he had been transferred to Northampton, where he is said to have died nursing the sick during the plague. His commentary on the *Sentences* circulated widely. At a time when it was no longer possible to maintain that rational proof could be found for the existence of God, Holcot taught that God communicates sufficient knowledge of Himself for salvation. In his Biblical commentaries the main emphasis is on the application of the text for preaching.

HOLIDAYS OF OBLIGATION. See *Feasts of Obligation.*

HOLINESS, The Code of, also 'Law of Holiness'. The collection of Mosaic legislation in Lev. 17–26, so named by A. Klostermann in 1877, and designated 'H'. Acc. to most scholars, it is a product of the Exile in *Babylon. It prob. left its compiler's hand *c.* 550 B.C. and was incorporated in *P some 75–100 years later.

HOLINESS, His. A title of Patriarchs in the E. Church and of the Pope in the W.

HOLINESS CHURCHES. A number of American Churches who hold in common belief in a single experience of justification freeing their adherents from all taint of sin; this experience is regarded as completely independent of sacramental *Baptism. The movement originated within *Methodism in the 19th cent. and has its roots in J. *Wesley's teaching on *perfection. It has certain affinities with *Pentecostalism. The largest of the Holiness Churches is the Church of the Nazarene, which emerged as a distinct denomination in 1908.

HOLLAND, Christianity in. The conversion of the area which now comprises Holland was mainly the work of St. *Willibrord, Bp. of Utrecht from 695 to 739. In the 16th cent. *Calvinism formed a rallying creed for the revolt against Spain. There was a conflict between the orthodox and liberal parties in the early 17th cent., but after the Synod of *Dort (1618-9), strict Calvinism was the official creed.

From 1580 to 1853 the RC Church in Holland was governed by *Vicars Apostolic or Papal Legates. In 1697 accusations of *Jansenism were made against the RCs in Holland; after the condemnation in 1702 of Petrus Codde, the Vicar General, a schism developed, Codde's followers being known as the '*Old Catholics'. In modern Holland RCs form a vigorous body, comprising c. 38 per cent of the population. In recent years Dutch RCs have been noted for their advanced thinking.

HOLOCAUST. A sacrifice completely consumed by fire, and thus a perfect sacrifice.

HOLSTE, LUCAS (1596–1661), *Vatican Librarian. Converted to RC-ism in 1625–6, he received Queen *Christina of Sweden's public abjuration of Protestantism at Innsbruck in 1655. He was a scholar of enormous erudition.

HOLTZMANN, HEINRICH JULIUS (1832–1910), German Protestant theologian and Biblical critic. He was a moderate liberal in his beliefs. He defended the *Marcan hypothesis and later argued for a psychological development in the Lord's self-consciousness.

HOLY ALLIANCE, The. The declaration signed in 1815 by the sovereigns of Russia, Austria, and Prussia, and later by others, declaring that henceforth the relations of the Powers would be based on 'the sublime truths which the Holy Religion of our Saviour teaches'.

HOLY CITY, The. *Jerusalem.

HOLY CLUB, The. The nickname given to the group of '*Methodists' which Charles and John *Wesley formed at Oxford in 1729 for the deepening of personal religion.

HOLY COAT, The. Both the cathedral at Trier and the parish church at Argenteuil claim possession of Christ's 'coat without seam' (Jn. 19: 23). Both traditions date from the 12th cent.

HOLY CROSS DAY. The name given in the BCP calendar to 14 Sept., also known as the '*Exaltation of the Holy Cross'.

HOLY DAYS OF OBLIGATION. See *Feasts of Obligation*.

HOLY DOOR, The. The door in the façade of *St. Peter's, Rome, nearest to the *Vatican Palace. Normally sealed with brickwork, it is opened during the *Holy Year for the passage of those wishing to gain the *Indulgence of the Holy Year.

HOLY FAMILY, The. The Infant Jesus, His Mother (the BVM), and His foster-father (St. *Joseph). The cult of the Holy Family became popular in the RC Church in the 17th cent.

HOLY FATHER, The Most. A title of the Pope.

HOLY GHOST, The. An alternative title for the *Holy Spirit.

HOLY INNOCENTS. The children of *Bethlehem, 'from two years old and under', massacred by order of *Herod in an attempt to destroy the Infant Jesus (Mt. 2: 16–18). The event is commemorated on 28 Dec.

HOLY ISLAND; HOLY LANCE. See *Lindisfarne*; *Lance, the Holy*.

HOLY LAND, The. Palestine.

HOLY MOUNTAIN, The. Mount *Athos.

HOLY NAME OF JESUS. See *Name of Jesus*.

HOLY OFFICE, The. The *Roman Congregation established in 1542 as the final court of appeal in trials of heresy. In 1965 it became the 'Congregation of the Doctrine of the Faith' and was charged with the positive function of promoting as well as safeguarding sound doctrine.

HOLY OILS. See *Chrism* and *Unction*.

HOLY ORDERS. The higher grades of the Christian ministry, viz. those of *Bishop, *Priest, and *Deacon.

HOLY PLACES, The. The places in Palestine to which pilgrimage is made on account of their traditional association with Biblical events.

HOLY ROMAN EMPIRE. The Empire set up in the W. following the coronation of *Charlemagne as Emperor in Rome by Pope *Leo III in 800. The title of Emperor temporarily disappeared in 924, but it was revived in 962 when Otto I of Germany was crowned Emperor by *John XII; it was held by his successors of the Saxon, Salian, and Hohenstaufen dynasties, and later by the Habsburg dynasty until 1806, though *Charles V was the last Emperor to be crowned as such. The style 'Holy Empire' was used from 1157; 'Holy Roman Empire' from 1254.

HOLY SATURDAY. The day before *Easter Sunday. It commemorates the resting of Christ's body in the tomb. See *Paschal Vigil Service*.

HOLY SEE, The. The term normally denotes the Papacy.

HOLY SEPULCHRE, The. The rock cave in *Jerusalem where, acc. to early tradition, Christ was buried and rose from the dead. The first church on the site was dedicated *c.* 335; it was destroyed in 614. Later churches were built in 626, *c.* 1050, *c.* 1130 (taking in the neighbouring Holy Places, incl. the site of *Calvary), in 1310, and in 1810. The present church has several chapels and shrines in which different Christian bodies have rights; their liturgies take place simultaneously on Sunday mornings, and each celebrates its *Holy Week rites acc. to its own calendar.

HOLY SHROUD, The. A relic preserved at Turin and venerated as the winding-sheet in which Christ's body was wrapped for burial (Mt. 27: 59 &c.).

HOLY SPIRIT. In Christian theology, the Third Person of the *Trinity, distinct from, but consubstantial, coequal, and coeternal with, the Father and the Son, and in the fullest sense God.

In the OT the Spirit of God is seen as operative at the Creation, as inspiring deeds of valour, and later as conveying wisdom and religious knowledge. It was through the overshadowing of the Spirit that the BVM conceived the Saviour. The Spirit descended on Christ at His Baptism and was an operative power throughout His ministry. But acc. to Jn., His full mission then still lay in the future. The descent of the Holy Spirit in His fullness on the Church took place at *Pentecost; it was marked by the gift of tongues. The early Church is represented in Acts as possessed by belief in the Spirit's operation. The gift of the Spirit was so far entrusted to the Apostles that it was conveyed to others through the imposition of their *hands.

Though implicit in the NT, the doctrine of the Spirit was not fully elaborated for some centuries. From 360 it became a matter of controversy. The *Pneumatomachi, while maintaining the Divinity of the Son, denied that of the Spirit. At the Council of *Constantinople in 381 this heresy was finally repudiated and the full doctrine of the Spirit received authoritative acceptance in the Church. See also *Double Procession* and *Filioque*.

HOLY SYNOD. From 1721 to 1917 the supreme organ of government in the *Russian Church. It was a committee of bishops and clergy, orig. established by Peter the Great.

HOLY WATER. Water which has been blessed for certain specific religious purposes. It is used for blessings, dedications, exorcisms, and for ceremonial cleansing on entering a church, as well as the *Asperges. A small quantity of *salt is sometimes added to the water.

HOLY WEEK. The week preceding *Easter, observed as a period of devotion to the Passion of Christ. For the ceremonies proper to each day, see *Palm Sunday, Maundy Thursday, Good Friday*, and *Paschal Vigil Service*.

HOLY YEAR. A year during which the Pope grants a special *Indulgence, the so-called Jubilee, to all who visit Rome on cer-

tain conditions. It was instituted in 1300 by
*Boniface VIII, who meant it to be cele-
brated every 100 years; the interval was
settled at 25 years in 1470. One of the main
ceremonies is the opening of the *Holy Door
by the Pope before the First Vespers of
Christmas and its walling-up a year later. A
Holy Year was last celebrated in 1975.

HOMBERG, Synod of. A synod convoked
by *Philip, Landgraf of Hesse, in 1526 to
establish a constitution on Protestant principles for the Church in his domains. It
appointed a committee to draw up a Church
Order for Hesse; the document which it
issued, however, insisted on the independence of each congregation and was never
promulgated.

HOMILIARY. A collection of homilies
arranged acc. to the ecclesiastical calendar
for reading at the Office of *Mattins.

HOMILIES, The Books of. The plan of
issuing prescribed homilies for the use of
disaffected and unlearned clergy was agreed
in Convocation in 1542. *Henry VIII,
however, refused to authorize the collection
of 12 homilies produced in 1543; it was
issued under the authority of *Edward VI's
Council in 1547. A 'Second Book' with 21
further homilies was issued under *Elizabeth
I, in its final form in 1571. The Homilies
retain a measure of authority in view of the
references to them in the *Thirty-Nine
Articles.

HOMILIES, Clementine. See *Clementine
Literature*.

HOMOEANS. The *Arian party which
came into existence c. 355 under the leadership of *Acacius, Bp. of Caesarea. They
sought to confine discussion of the Person of
Christ to the assertion that He was like (Gk.
ὅμοιος, 'like') the Father.

HOMOOUSION (Gk., 'of one substance').
The term used in the *Nicene Creed to
express the relations of the Father and the
Son within the Godhead and originally
designed to exclude *Arianism. Some theologians preferred the term 'Homoiousion'
('of like substance'), which was held to
leave more room for distinctions within the
Godhead.

'HONEST TO GOD'. The title of a book,
first publd. in 1963, by J. A. T. Robinson,
then Bp. of Woolwich, in which many of the
traditional concepts about the transcendence
of God were criticized.

HONORATUS, St. (c. 350–429), Abp. of
Arles from 426. Of a consular family, he
was converted to Christianity. He settled at
*Lérins, where he founded the monastery
(c. 410). His writings are lost.

HONORIUS I (d. 638), Pope from 625. His
action in the *Monothelite controversy was
one of the arguments against Papal *Infallibility. About 634 *Sergius, Patr. of Constantinople, wrote to him about the question of
'one energy' in Christ. This formula, while
confessing the two natures, attributed only
one mode of activity, viz. that of the Divine
Word, to the Incarnate Christ. It had been
found useful in reconciling the *Monophysites, but was strenuously opposed by
*Sophronius of Jerusalem. Honorius sent
Sergius a favourable reply, in which he used
the unfortunate expression 'one will'. This
formula was utilized in the '*Ecthesis', and
Honorius himself was anathematized at the
Third Council of *Constantinople in 681.

HONORIUS III (d. 1227), Pope from
1216. He crowned *Frederick II in 1220 and
he took a prominent part in the political
affairs of Europe. He approved the *Dominican, *Franciscan, and *Carmelite Orders.
His writings include a *Liber Censuum
Romanae Ecclesiae* (1192), which provides
a valuable record of the secular relations of
the Papacy.

HONORIUS 'OF AUTUN' (early 12th
cent.), popular theologian. The view that
'Augustodunensis', used by Honorius of
himself, refers to Autun, has been abandoned, but no agreed alternative has been
found. He prob. lived for a time in England,
later in S. Germany as a monk, perhaps a
recluse. He was a prolific writer. Wide and
lasting popularity were enjoyed by his *Eluci-
darium*, one of the earliest surveys of Christian doctrine, and by his *Imago mundi*, a
compendium of cosmology and geography.
He was a popularizer rather than an original
thinker.

HONTHEIM, JOHANN NIKOLAUS VON
(1701–90), founder of *Febronianism. In

1742 he began an investigation, on behalf of the German Archbishop-Electors, of the historical position of the Papacy; in 1763, under the pseudonym 'Justinus Febronius', he published his conclusions, *De statu ecclesiae et legitima potestate Romani Pontificis*. Because of its *Gallican tendencies the book was placed on the *Index in 1764. In 1778 Hontheim made a formal retractation.

HOOK, WALTER FARQUHAR (1798–1875), Dean of *Chichester from 1859. As Vicar of Leeds (1837–59) he was involved in controversy with E. B. *Pusey. He wrote many theological and historical works.

HOOKER, RICHARD (*c.* 1554–1600), Anglican divine and apologist *par excellence* of the Elizabethan settlement. Though the work was designed to justify episcopacy, Hooker embodied a broadly conceived philosophical theology in his *Treatise on the Laws of Ecclesiastical Polity* (Books I–V, 1594–7; Books VII–VIII, 1648–62; Book VI is spurious). His opposition to the *Puritans, who held that whatever was not commanded in Scripture was unlawful, led him to elaborate a whole theory of law, based on the 'absolute' fundamental of natural law. This natural law is the expression of God's supreme reason, and everything, including the Bible, must be interpreted in the light of it. But the permanence of law does not preclude development of detail. The Church is an organic, not a static, institution, and methods of Church government and administration will change according to circumstance. Hence the C of E, though reformed, possesses continuity with the medieval Church.

HOOPER, JOHN (d. 1555), Protestant martyr. In 1550 he was nominated to the see of *Gloucester; he accepted only when the reference to angels and saints had been omitted from the Oath of Supremacy and after prolonged hesitation about the lawfulness of episcopal vestments. In 1552 he became Bp. of *Worcester. On *Mary's accession he was imprisoned, and in 1555 he was tried for heresy and burnt. He was one of the chief exponents of Continental Protestantism and influenced the *Puritans through his writings.

HOPE. One of the three *theological virtues. In its widest sense it may be defined as the desire and search for a future good, difficult but not impossible of attainment. As a Christian virtue its primary end, its motive, and its author is God Himself.

HOPKINS, GERARD MANLEY (1844–1889), poet. He became a RC in 1866, joined the *Jesuits in 1868, and from 1884 he was professor of Greek at the Royal University, *Dublin. He was unknown as a poet in his life-time, and the preservation of his MSS. is due to R. *Bridges, who edited them in 1918. His works, of which the most ambitious is *The Wreck of the Deutschland*, are marked by intensity of feeling, freedom in rhythm, and individual use of words.

HORMISDAS, St. (d. 523), Pope from 514. His chief importance lies in his healing of the *Acacian Schism. In 519 he secured the signature of John, Patr. of *Constantinople, and *c.* 250 E. bishops to a dogmatic formula in which the *Chalcedonian Definition and Leo's *Tome were accepted, Acacius and other heretics condemned, and the authority of the Roman see emphasized.

HORNE, GEORGE (1730–92), Bp. of *Norwich from 1790. Though an adherent of *High Church principles, he was in sympathy with the spiritual earnestness of the *Methodists and refused to forbid J. *Wesley to preach in his diocese.

HOROLOGION. In the E. Church the liturgical book containing the recurrent portions of the ecclesiastical *office throughout the year.

HORSLEY, SAMUEL (1733–1806), Bp. successively of *St. Davids (1788), *Rochester (1793), and *St. Asaph (1802). He is famous chiefly for his controversy with J. *Priestley over the doctrines of the Trinity and Christ's Divinity; he defended the traditional view that the pre-Nicene Church was unanimous in its theology of the Lord's consubstantiality with the Father.

HORT, FENTON JOHN ANTHONY (1828–92), NT scholar. From 1878 he held professorships at Cambridge. He worked, in conjunction with B. F. *Westcott, on the Greek text of the NT almost continuously from 1852 until its publication in 1881. The work is remarkable for its accuracy and the sobriety of its judgements. From 1882 to 1890 he was engaged in work on the RV of Wisdom and 2 Macc. He also made important contributions in the field of Patristics.

HOSANNA. The Greek form of the Hebrew petition 'Save, we beseech Thee'. It was used by the multitudes when they greeted the Lord on His triumphal entry into Jerusalem on *Palm Sunday, and was introduced into the Christian liturgy at an early date.

HOSEA, Book of. *Minor Prophet. Hosea interprets his experiences with his unfaithful wife as a parable of what has taken place between God and Israel (1–3) and then (4–14) develops the theme of Israel's unfaithfulness despite the enduring love of God. He is the first Biblical writer to use the family tie as an illustration of the relationship between God and man. He prophesied before 721 B.C.

HOSIUS or **OSSIUS** (c. 257–357), Bp. of Cordova from c. 296. He seems to have been *Constantine's ecclesiastical adviser from 313 to 325. In the early stages of the *Arian struggle he was sent to *Alexandria to investigate and it was apparently as a result of his report that the Emperor summoned the Council of *Nicaea (325). He may have presided at this Council and he certainly presided at that of *Sardica in 343. His support for St. *Athanasius led to his banishment in 355.

HOSIUS, STANISLAUS (1504–79), Polish cardinal. In 1551 he was made Bp. of Ermland, where one of his main tasks was to combat Protestantism. In his chief work, the *Confessio Catholicae Fidei Christiana* (1552–3), he tried to prove that Catholicism and Christianity were identical. In 1560 *Pius IV appointed him nuncio to Ferdinand I, and in this capacity he prepared the reopening of the Council of *Trent. In 1561 he was created cardinal and appointed papal legate at Trent, where he played a leading part in the doctrinal discussions.

HOSKYNS, Sir EDWYN CLEMENT (1884–1937), Anglican divine. From 1919 he was Dean of Chapel of Corpus Christi College, Cambridge. In his contribution to *Essays Catholic and Critical* (1926) he argued that the so-called 'historical Jesus' of Liberal Protestantism was unhistorical and

that the teaching behind the Synoptic Gospels was more complex than supposed by liberal NT critics. Besides writing on the NT, he translated K. *Barth's *Commentary on Romans* (1933).

HOSMER, FREDERICK LUCIAN (1840–1929), American hymn-writer. He was ordained to the *Unitarian ministry in 1869. His hymns, which had a wide appeal among the adherents of the emancipated liberal theology of the late 19th cent., include 'Thy Kingdom come, On bended knee'.

HOSPITALLERS, also **Knights Hospitaller**; from 1310 also **Knights of Rhodes** and from 1530 **Knights of Malta**. Their full title, 'Knights of the Order of the Hospital of St. John of Jerusalem', derives from the dedication of their headquarters at *Jerusalem at the end of the 11th cent. to St. *John the Baptist.

The origins of the order are uncertain. Its first historical personage is Master Gerard, under whom, after the successes of the *Crusaders in 1099, the order obtained papal sanction. In the 12th cent. it added the care of the sick to its original duties of providing hospitality for pilgrims and Crusaders, and it established an armed guard for the defence of pilgrims. Its members were divided into 'military brothers' and 'brothers infirmarians'; to the latter were added 'brothers chaplains', responsible for worship and spiritual needs. The knights shared in the successes and defeats of the Crusaders. After the fall of Acre (1291) they escaped to Cyprus and later conquered Rhodes (1309). Here their character became predominantly military; their wealth increased after the suppression of the Knights *Templar (1312). They received the sovereignty of Malta from *Charles V in 1530. They took part in the battle of *Lepanto in 1571, but declined in the 17th and 18th cents.

In England their property was sequestered in 1540. In 1831 the Grand Priory was revived on a mainly Anglican basis and constituted an order of chivalry in 1888. It was responsible for the foundation of the St. John Ambulance Association in 1878 and the St. John Ambulance Brigade in 1888.

HOSPITALS. Christian hospitals were founded from the 4th cent. onwards and became numerous in the Middle Ages, when they were commonly associated with monastic orders. The majority of medieval hospitals in England were almshouses for the aged.

HOST. A sacrificial victim, and so the consecrated Bread in the *Eucharist, regarded as the Sacrifice of the Body of Christ.

HOURS, Canonical. The times of daily prayer laid down in the *Breviary, and esp. the services appointed to be recited at these times. See also *Office, Divine*.

HOUSEL. A medieval English name for the Eucharist. The 'houselling cloth' was the (late medieval) long white linen cloth spread before, or held by, communicants at the time of receiving the Sacrament.

HOWARD, JOHN (c. 1726–90), prison reformer. A man of *Evangelical piety, in 1773 he became High Sheriff of Bedford, where what he saw of the afflictions of both tried and untried prisoners in the county gaol inspired him to work for reform. He secured official salaries for gaolers; he travelled widely visiting prisons, and wrote on the *State of the Prisons* (1777). The Howard League for Penal Reform, a small influential voluntary body, was founded in his memory in 1866.

HOWE, JOHN (1630–1705), *Puritan divine. In 1652 he was ordained by the rector of Winwick, whom he regarded as a 'primitive bishop'. He became domestic chaplain to O. *Cromwell. He was among those ejected in 1662. In 1676 he became co pastor of the *Presbyterian congregation at Haberdashers' Hall. His standpoint inclined to *latitudinarianism, and he tried to unite the Presbyterians and *Congregationalists.

HOWLEY, WILLIAM (1766–1848), Abp. of *Canterbury from 1828. He was the last of the 'Prince-Archbishops', the revenues of his see coming under the control of the *Ecclesiastical Commissioners on his death.

HOWSON, JOHN SAUL (1816–85), Dean of *Chester from 1867. His *Life and Epistles of St. Paul* (1852; in conjunction with W. J. *Conybeare) was an impressive work of scholarship for its time; it was learned but not beyond the general reader.

HROSVIT (10th cent.), poet. She was a nun of the *Benedictine abbey of Gandersheim in Saxony. She wrote 8 poems on saints, 6 plays, and an unfinished panegyric on the Ottos. Her plays were designed to oppose to Terence's representations of the frailty of women the chastity of Christian virgins and penitents.

HUBER, SAMUEL (c. 1547–1624), Protestant controversialist. He was banished from Switzerland in 1588 after asserting the universality of Christ's atonement. He later signed the Formula of *Concord and held office in the *Lutheran Church in Germany.

HUBERT, St. (d. 727), 'Apostle of the Ardennes'. He succeeded St. *Lambert as Bp. of Tongeren (or Maestricht) c. 705 and transferred the see to Liège. The story that he was converted after meeting a stag with a crucifix between its horns is of late date.

HUBERT WALTER (d. 1205), Abp. of *Canterbury from 1193. In 1190 he accompanied Richard I on the Third *Crusade and on his return raised the ransom for the King's release. In 1194 he was appointed justiciar of England and in the King's absence ruled England for the next four years. He incurred unpopularity because of heavy taxation and other causes, resigned the justiciarship in 1198, but resumed it the following year.

HÜBMAIER, BALTHASAR (?1485–1528), German *Anabaptist. In 1521 he became parish priest at Waldshut; here he allied himself with H. *Zwingli and in 1523 introduced the Reformation. By 1525, however, he had abandoned Zwinglian doctrines for those of the Anabaptists. He soon became entangled in the *Peasants' War and may have been the author of the *Twelve Articles. He was burnt at Vienna.

HUCUSQUE. The opening word of the preface to the supplement to the *Sacramentary sent by *Hadrian I to *Charlemagne and often used to designate the supplement itself. This sets out to remedy the deficiencies of the Sacramentary; it contains Sunday Masses, those of the *Common of Saints, and other items. See also *Gregorian Sacramentary*.

HUET, PIERRE DANIEL (1630–1721), French scholar. He produced an edition of

*Origen and with Anne Lefèvre edited the 'Delphin Classics' in some 60 volumes for the Dauphin. In 1689 he became Bp. of Avranches. His valuable MSS. passed eventually into the Bibliothèque Nationale.

HÜGEL, F. VON. See *Von Hügel, F.*

HUGH, St. (1024–1109), Abbot of *Cluny from 1049. *Leo IX took Hugh into his confidence and as adviser to nine Popes Hugh exercised a dominating influence on ecclesiastical and political affairs. He took part in securing the condemnation of *Berengar of Tours (1050); assisted Nicholas II in the decree on Papal elections (1059); encouraged *Gregory VII's efforts for reform; and took a leading part in the organization of the First *Crusade. His monastery reached a position never surpassed and in 1068 he settled the usages for the whole Cluniac order.

HUGH, St. (1052-1132), Bp. of Grenoble from 1080. He welcomed St. *Bruno and his monks to his diocese, granting them the *Grande Chartreuse (1084).

HUGH, St. (*c.* 1140–1200), Bp. of *Lincoln from 1186. He became a *Carthusian at the *Grande Chartreuse in 1160; in 1175 King Henry II secured his services as prior of Witham, the first Carthusian house in England. As bishop he administered his diocese well and showed a courageous independence of the king. He was revered for his holiness and his tomb became a place of pilgrimage.

HUGH OF ST.-VICTOR (d. 1142), theologian. Little is known of his life except that *c.* 1115 he entered St.-Victor, an Augustinian house of canons in Paris (see *Victorines*). He wrote on grammar, geometry, and philosophy; the *Didascalion*, which is a guide to the study of the *artes* and of theology; Biblical commentaries; a commentary on Ps.-*Dionysius' *Celestial Hierarchy*; a treatise on the Sacraments; and works on spirituality. In all these fields he made a distinctive contribution, with no parade of learning or claims to originality.

HUGHES, HUGH PRICE (1847–1902), *Methodist divine. In 1885 he started the *Methodist Times*, a weekly which became a leading organ of Nonconformist opinion. He worked to secure co-operation between Non-

conformist bodies and in 1896 became first President of the *National Council of the Evangelical Free Churches.

HUGUENOTS, the *Calvinist French Protestants. The name, prob. a nickname based on a medieval romance about a King Hugo, was applied to the French Protestants *c.* 1560. The movement has been traced back to the publication of a commentary on St. *Paul's Epistles by J. *Faber (1512), which upheld the doctrine of *justification by faith alone, but its real originator was J. *Calvin, who dedicated his *Institutes* (1536) to Francis I. At the Synod of Paris (1559) the French Protestant Church formally organized itself on a Calvinist basis. The movement was resisted by the family of the Guises, but was consolidated by the Colloquy of *Poissy (1561). From 1562 to 1594 there was almost continuous civil war with the Catholic majority. Full freedom of worship was granted by the Edict of *Nantes (1598), but the Huguenots continued to be a disruptive element in the State until their fortress of La Rochelle was reduced in 1628. After the Revocation of the Edict of Nantes in 1685 many Huguenots were forced to apostatize or flee from France. Only in 1802 was the legal standing of the Huguenot Church established, and their numbers increased in the 19th cent.

HULST, M. D'. See *D'Hulst, M.*

HUMANAE VITAE (1968). The encyclical of *Paul VI condemning *abortion and all forms of birth control except the 'rhythm method'.

HUMANI GENERIS (1950). The encyclical of *Pius XII condemning various intellectual movements and tendencies in the RC Church, including *Existentialism.

HUMBERT OF SILVA CANDIDA (d. 1061), ecclesiastical reformer and statesman. A monk of Moyenmoutier (in the Vosges Mountains), he was created Cardinal-Bishop of Silva Candida in 1050 and was put in charge of the mission to *Constantinople at the time of the schism (1054). He wrote a treatise against *simony.

HUMBLE ACCESS, The Prayer of. The prayer in the Order of Holy Communion in the 1662 BCP which immediately precedes the Prayer of Consecration. It was composed for the 'Order of *Communion' of 1548 and originally stood between the Communion of the priest and that of the people.

HUME, DAVID (1711–76), Scottish philosopher and historian. He reduced reason to a product of experience. All perceptions of the human mind are either impressions of experience or ideas, i.e. faded copies of these impressions. But whereas the relations between ideas can be known with certainty, the facts of reality cannot be established beyond an appearance of probability. Causality is not a concept of logic, but a result of habit and association, impressed on our imagination, and the human soul itself is but a sum of perceptions connected by association. Hence there is no such science as metaphysics; and belief in the existence of God and of the physical world, though a practical necessity, cannot be proved by reason. Our moral life is dominated by the passions, which determine our will and actions. By reducing all cognition to single perceptions and by ruling out any purely intellectual faculty for recording and sifting them, Hume destroyed all real knowledge and taught pure scepticism.

HUME, GEORGE BASIL (1923–   ), English cardinal. He became a *Benedictine monk at *Ampleforth, where he had been at school. He was Abbot of Ampleforth from 1963 to 1976, when he became Abp. of *Westminster. He was made a cardinal later the same year.

HUMERAL VEIL. In the W. Church, a silk shawl laid round the shoulders serving to cover the hands. At *High Mass the *subdeacon used to hold the *paten with it. It is still worn by the celebrant in processions of the Bl. Sacrament and at *Benediction.

HUMILIATI. An order of penitents, founded in the 12th cent., which followed the *Benedictine Rule. It was suppressed in 1571.

HUMILITY. A moral virtue, defined by St. *Thomas Aquinas as 'keeping oneself within one's bounds, not reaching out to things above one'. It was enjoined and practised by Christ and is considered essential to the spiritual life.

HUNDRED CHAPTERS, Council of the. See *Russia, Christianity in*.

HUNGARY, Christianity in. The preaching of Christianity in the 4th cent. left no permanent impression; in the 9th and 10th cents. Christianity spread in both its E. and W. forms, the W. Church prevailing. A formal constitution for the Church was laid down in 1001 by King (St.) *Stephen, who established episcopal sees, and State control of the Church has always been strong. Since the 16th cent. there has been a Protestant minority in the eastern part of the country, mainly *Calvinist.

HUNT, WILLIAM HOLMAN (1827–1910), Pre-Raphaelite painter. He formed a connection with D. G. *Rossetti and in 1848 they founded the Pre-Raphaelite Brotherhood. The most famous of his paintings, *The Light of the World*, represents the Lord knocking at the door of the soul. The original, painted in 1854, is in Keble College, Oxford; his repainting of the same subject (1904) is in *St. Paul's Cathedral.

HUNTING. Though hunting has generally been held lawful for the laity, it was early forbidden to the clergy. It is, however, disputed whether all hunting is forbidden, or only 'noisy' hunting, the 'quiet' kind being permitted in moderation.

HUNTINGDON, SELINA, COUNTESS OF (1707–91), Selina Hastings, foundress of the body of *Calvinistic Methodists known as 'the Countess of Huntingdon's Connexion'. She joined the *Wesleys' Methodist society in 1739. She supported Methodist ministers by constituting them her *chaplains, but her contention that she could, as a peeress, appoint to the rank of chaplain as many priests of the C of E as she wished, and employ them publicly, was disallowed by the consistory court of London in 1779. She then registered her chapels as dissenting places of worship under the *Toleration Act; she formed them into an association in 1790.

HUPFELD, HERMANN (1796–1866), German OT scholar. He distinguished for the first time between the two sources *P and *E, both of which in Gen. use the same word *Elohim as the Divine Name.

HUSS, JOHN (*c*. 1372–1415), Bohemian reformer. He was a well-known preacher at the 'Bethlehem Chapel' in Prague. When the writings of J. *Wycliffe became known in Bohemia, Huss was attracted by his political doctrine and was sympathetic to his teaching on *predestination and the Church of the elect. At first he was encouraged by Abp. Sbinko of Prague, but soon his violent sermons on the morals of the clergy provoked hostility and he was forbidden to preach. In the course of the dispute between rival candidates for the Papacy, the king gave control of the University of Prague to the Czech 'nation' (1409) and Huss became Rector. Abp. Sbinko soon transferred his allegiance to *Alexander V, who rewarded him with a Bull (1410) ordering the destruction of Wycliffite books and, to curb Huss's influence, the cessation of preaching in private chapels; in 1411 *John XXIII excommunicated Huss. Opinion moved against Huss and the King removed him from Prague; he took refuge with the Czech nobility and devoted himself to writing his main work, *De Ecclesia* (1413), part of which was taken directly from Wycliffe. Having appealed from the decision of the papal curia to a General Council, he went to the Council of *Constance with a safe-conduct from the Emp. Sigismund. He was imprisoned and burnt, and became a national hero.

HUTTEN, ULRICH VON (1488–1523), German humanist and controversialist. He left the monastery of *Fulda in 1505, visited various universities, and engaged in military service. About 1515 he became a contributor to the *Epistolae Obscurorum Virorum*. From 1519 he devoted his life to the propagation of M. *Luther's reformation, in which he saw the deliverance of Germany from the power of Rome. He wrote a series of treatises in German and Latin for this purpose. At the end of his life H. *Zwingli gave him refuge.

HUTTERITES. See *Anabaptists*.

HUTTON, RICHARD HOLT (1826–97), religious writer. He trained for the *Unitarian ministry but became a member of the C of E. In 1861 he was offered the joint-editorship and proprietorship of the *Spectator*, which he used as a pulpit from which to challenge, on Christian principles, the regnant agnosticism of J. S. Mill and T. H.

*Huxley. He was one of the original members of the *Metaphysical Society.

HUXLEY, THOMAS HENRY (1825–95), English biologist. He defended the view that man descended from the lower animal world in his *Zoological Evidences as to Man's Place in Nature* (1863), and in a lecture on 'The Physical Basis of Life' in 1868 he expounded *agnosticism. Man, he argued, cannot know the nature of either spirit or matter; metaphysics is impossible; and man's primary duty in life is the relief of misery and ignorance. He discussed *miracles in his study of D. *Hume (1879); he did not reject miracles, 'because nobody can presume to say what the order of nature must be', but he explicitly abandoned the theological concept of a Personal God. His attacks on Christian orthodoxy became more persistent in later life.

HY. See *Iona*.

HYACINTH, St. (1185–1257), 'Apostle of the North', known to the Poles as St. Iaccho. Having received the habit from St. *Dominic at Rome in 1220, he set out with other Dominicans for Poland and engaged in missionary work there and in the adjacent countries. His activities are reputed to have extended from *Sweden and *Norway to the Black Sea.

HYDROPARASTATAE. An alternative name for the *Aquarians.

HYLOZOISM. The doctrine that all matter is endowed with life.

HYMNARY. The medieval liturgical book of the W. rite which contained the metrical hymns of the Divine *Office arranged acc. to the liturgical year.

HYMNS. Sacred poetry set to music has always formed part of Christian worship, whether to express doctrine or the devotion of individuals. At first OT texts, esp. the Psalms, were used, but at an early date distinctively Christian compositions, e.g. the *Magnificat and *Benedictus, appeared, and what seem to be quotations from early hymns are found in various places in the NT. The use of hymns is mentioned by several of the early Fathers, and the '*Phos Hilaron' is among those dating from pre-Nicene times;

hymns became more generally used, however, from the 4th cent. From this time they were employed not only to celebrate the Christian mysteries, but also to promote and refute heresy, e.g. in the *Arian controversy. Although from the 5th cent. some Christians held that no words other than those of Scripture should be allowed in the liturgy, *troparia (single-stanza hymns) are found in E. service books of the period; they were later joined together to form *contakia and *canons.

Latin hymns appear later than Greek, the real impetus coming from St. *Ambrose. Though only three hymns can certainly be ascribed to him, he laid down the lines of development of Latin hymnody as simple, devotional, and direct, and it was through his influence that hymns became a recognized and integral part of the public worship of the W. Church. Although hymns were not admitted into the Roman *Office until the 13th cent., their development came to be towards an ordered sequence for use at different times and seasons, designed to express not the feelings of individual worshippers but the meaning of the feast or Office. The *Counter-Reformation led to the remodelling of a number of the old *Breviary hymns and the composition of new ones in a more classical diction and metre.

Vernacular hymns were written all through the Middle Ages, but they were not admitted to the liturgy and were largely the work of those outside the main religious stream. With the *Reformation the situation changed. *Lutheranism had a wealth of new hymns written in German by M. *Luther himself and later by P. *Gerhardt. *Calvinism would tolerate nothing but the words of Scripture in its services; hence the Psalms were put into *metrical versions (q.v.). In the C of E hymns virtually disappeared from the service-books, mainly it seems because T. *Cranmer's literary powers lay in other directions.

Modern hymn-writing and hymn-singing were mainly the creation of the 18th cent. A prominent part was taken by I. *Watts, whose hymns were written to express the spiritual experience of the singer. They were followed by the works of John and Charles *Wesley. The practice of singing hymns was encouraged by the *Methodists and spread among the *Evangelical party in the C of E. In America the Negro Spirituals were a powerful factor in the Second *Great Awakening of 1795–1805. By the early 19th cent. prejudice against the use of hymns in the C of E was dying and the time was ripe for a hymnbook which could be integrated into the BCP scheme of worship. R. *Heber intended his collection (1827) to fulfil this purpose. It was never widely used, but it helped to break down the hostility to hymns outside Evangelical circles. A further influence in fostering the use of hymns came from the *Oxford Movement. The publication of various collections followed, of which the most widely used were prob. *Hymns, Ancient and Modern* (1861) and *The *English Hymnal* (1906). Among RCs a demand for popular hymns in the 19th cent. was met by such writers as F. W. *Faber. Since the introduction of the vernacular liturgy after the Second *Vatican Council, hymns have been widely used at Mass. All other English-speaking Churches, except the *Quakers, have assigned an important place to hymns as being an integral part of Christian worship, rather than an adjunct to it.

'HYMNS, ANCIENT AND MODERN' (1861). A hymnal, edited by H.W. *Baker, which drew freely on ancient and modern sources and incorporated many of the traditional *office hymns (often in translations by J. M. *Neale). The music assisted its popularity. A revised edition was issued in 1950.

HYPAPANTE. The name used in the E. Church for the feast of *Candlemas.

HYPATIA (c. 375–415), philosopher. She was the glory of the *Neoplatonist School of *Alexandria. On the suspicion that she had set the pagan prefect of Alexandria against the Christians, she was attacked by a Christian mob and killed.

HYPERDULIA. The special veneration paid to the BVM on account of her eminent dignity as Mother of God.

HYPOCRISY. The hiding of interior wickedness under the appearance of virtue. The Lord denounced it in the case of the *Pharisees as the vice of those who do good deeds only to be seen of men and not for the glory of God.

HYPOSTASIS. The Greek word (lit. 'substance') had various meanings. In *Christological contexts from the mid-4th cent. it was used as equivalent to 'person'; this usage led to confusion among W. theologians until the terminology was clarified at the Council of *Constantinople in 381.

HYPOSTATIC UNION. The substantial union of the Divine and human natures in the One Person ('Hypostasis') of Jesus Christ.

The doctrine was formally accepted by the Church in the Definition of *Chalcedon (451).

HYPSISTARIANS. A 4th-cent. sect whose members refused to worship God as 'Father', but revered Him as the 'All Ruler and Highest'.

I

IAMBLICHUS (c. 250–c. 330), the chief *Neoplatonist of the Syrian school. He held an elaborate theory of mediation between the spiritual and physical worlds, radically modifying the doctrine of *Plotinus by duplicating the Plotinian One and distinguishing between its transcendental and creative aspects. This distinction lies at the basis of the negative and affirmative theologies which have differentiated E. and W. theology (see *God*).

IBAS, Bp. of *Edessa from 435 to 449 and from 451 to 457. In the contemporary *Christological controversies he took a mediating position. He was deposed by the *Latrocinium and restored at the Council of *Chalcedon, but his only surviving work, a letter to Bp. Mari of Hardascir of 433, was condemned by *Justinian. See also *Three Chapters*.

ICELAND, Christianity in. Christianity reached Iceland from *Norway c. 980. At the *Reformation Iceland followed *Denmark, to whose rule she had been subject since c. 1380, in adopting *Lutheranism.

I.C.F. See *Industrial Christian Fellowship*.

ICHABOD, the son of Phineas and grandson of the priest Eli. The name means 'The glory has departed' (I Sam. 4: 21); hence its use as an exclamation.

ICHTHUS. The Greek for *fish. It is made up of the initial letters of the Greek for 'Jesus Christ, Son of God, Saviour' ('Ιησοῦς Χριστός, Θεοῦ Υἱὸς Σωτήρ).

ICON. Icons are flat pictures, usually painted in egg tempera on wood, but also

wrought in mosaic, ivory, and other materials, to represent Christ, the BVM, or another saint, which are venerated in the Greek Church. As it is believed that through them the saints exercise their beneficent powers, they preside at all important events of human life and are held to be powerful channels of grace. See also the following entry.

ICONOCLASTIC CONTROVERSY. The controversy on the veneration of *icons which agitated the Greek Church from c. 725 to 842. In 726 the Emp. *Leo III published a decree declaring all images idols and ordering their destruction. Disturbances and persecution followed. In 753 the Synod of Hieria, called by the Emp. Constantine V, alleged that by representing only the humanity of Christ, the icon-worshippers either divided His unity as the *Nestorians or confounded the two natures as the *Monophysites, and declared that the icons of the BVM and the saints were idols and ordered their destruction. Persecution increased. It abated under Leo IV (775–80), and after his death the Empress Irene, regent for her son, reversed the policy of her predecessors. The Seventh General Council, which met at *Nicaea in 787, undid the work of the Synod of Hieria, defined the degree of veneration to be paid to icons, and decreed their restoration throughout the country.

The outbreak of the 'Second Iconoclastic Controversy' took place in 814 under Leo V the Armenian, who removed icons from churches and public buildings; the Patr. *Nicephorus was deposed (815), and St. *Theodore of Studios was sent into exile. Persecution ended only with the death of the Emp. Theophilus in 842. His widow, Theodora, caused Methodius to be elected patriarch in 843 and on the first Sunday in Lent a feast was celebrated in honour of the icons; it has since been kept in the E. Church as the 'Feast of *Orthodoxy'.

ICONOGRAPHY, Christian. The earliest Christian art was mainly symbolic: Christ was represented by a *fish or a young shepherd, while a ship stood for the Church. From the 6th cent., however, there are examples of Christ depicted with a beard and in eastern dress, and the Crucifixion began to be portrayed with pathos. There was a reaction in the E., and Byzantine churches often exhibit a planned system of stylized and didactic decoration, sometimes covering the whole interior. In the W. art was didactic, but the artist was freer and his subject-matter more comprehensive. By the 15th cent. religious art had become frankly realistic and picturesque. Since the Renaissance no dominant tradition has been discernible.

ICONOSTASIS. The screen which, in Byzantine churches, separates the sanctuary from the nave. It is pierced by doors leading to the altar, the *Diaconicon, and the *Prothesis.

IDIORRHYTHMIC. A term applied to certain monasteries on Mount *Athos, which allow considerable freedom to their monks, incl. the right to possess personal property.

IDIOT, The. The pseudonym of a popular medieval spiritual writer. He is generally identified as Raymundus Jordanus, a French *Augustinian Canon who flourished c. 1381.

IGNATIUS, St. (c. 35–c.107), Bp. of *Antioch. Nothing is known of his life except that he was taken from Antioch to Rome under a guard of soldiers. He was received at Smyrna by St. *Polycarp, and from there he wrote to the Churches of *Ephesus, Magnesia, and Tralles letters of encouragement, and to the Church of Rome begging them not to deprive him of martyrdom by intervening with the authorities. At Troas he wrote to the Churches of *Philadelphia and Smyrna and to Polycarp. The *Colosseum is the traditional place of his martyrdom.

A Latin version of eleven letters was published by J. *Faber in 1498. The genuineness of this collection was long disputed. On the basis of quotations, J. *Ussher in 1644 demonstrated that the text was interpolated. Though there was further controversy in the 19th cent., J. B. *Lightfoot's defence of the seven letters (1885) has won general acceptance.

Ignatius insists on the reality of both the Divinity and the Humanity of Christ, whose life is continued in the *Eucharist. The best safeguard of the unity of the Christian faith is the *bishop, without whose authority neither the Eucharist nor marriage may be celebrated.

IGNATIUS LOYOLA, St. (1491/5–1556), founder of the *Jesuits. Of noble birth, he embarked on a military career, but was wounded in 1521. He then decided to become a soldier of Christ. He hung up his sword at *Montserrat and spent a year (1522–3) at Manresa, where he prob. wrote most of the *Spiritual Exercises. He studied in Spain and at Paris. In 1534 he and his six companions made a vow of poverty, chastity, and of a pilgrimage to Jerusalem if possible, to be followed by a life devoted to apostolic labours. In 1537 they went to Italy. The pilgrimage being prevented, they offered their services to the Pope. In 1540 the Society of Jesus was solemnly sanctioned and Ignatius became its first *general. He drew up the constitutions of the Society between 1547 and 1550.

IGNATIUS, Father. The Rev. Joseph Leycester Lyne (1837–1908), mission preacher. His chief aim was to revive the *Benedictine Order in the Anglican Church, and in 1869 he acquired a site for his monastery at Capel-y-ffin, near Llanthony. He remained a deacon from 1860 until 1898, when he was ordained priest by J. R. *Vilatte.

IGNORANCE, Invincible. See *Invincible Ignorance*.

IHS. A monogram from the name of Jesus, formed by abbreviating the corresponding Greek word which in *uncials is written ΙΗΣΟΥΣ.

ILDEFONSUS, St. (c. 607–67), Abp. of Toledo from 657. He is said to have written many works, but only four survive. One is a defence of the privileges of the BVM, directed against the Spanish Jews; one is on *Baptism and another on the spiritual life of the soul after Baptism; the fourth, *De Viris Illustribus*, is an important source for the history of the Spanish Church in the 7th cent.

ILLINGWORTH, JOHN RICHARDSON (1848–1915), Anglican divine. His rectory at Longworth, Oxon., was the centre of the *Lux Mundi* group; he contributed two essays to the volume.

ILLTYD, St. (450–535), Welsh saint. He was apparently a native of Brittany, came to Britain *c.* 470, was converted to Christianity in 476, and founded a monastery (prob. Llantwit Major, perhaps *Caldey), which was a centre of missionary activity in Wales.

ILLUMINATI. A name applied to several bodies of religious enthusiasts, incl. (1) the *Alumbrados; (2) the *Rosicrucians; and (3) a masonic sect founded in Bavaria in 1778 by Adam Weishaupt. Repudiating the claims of all existing religious bodies, they professed themselves to be those in whom alone the 'illuminating' grace of Christ resided.

ILLUMINATIVE WAY. The intermediate stage of the mystic way between the *purgative and *unitive ways.

ILLYRICUS. See *Flacius, Matthias*.

IMAGES. The use of any representation of men, animals, or plants was forbidden in the Mosaic Law (Exod. 20: 4) because of the danger of idolatry, but when the theological significance of the *Incarnation was grasped, it seemed to many Christians that there was no obstacle to the use of images in the service of religion. The earliest Christian pictures were the paintings in the *catacombs. After the period of the persecutions sacred images came to play an increasing part in the cultus, esp. in the E. Despite the *Iconoclastic Controversy, *icons, which remain the only form of representation legitimate in the Greek Church, have remained an important element in Orthodox religion. In the W. the veneration of images, which included statues, made slower progress. It was given a doctrinal basis by St. *Thomas Aquinas, who developed the E. justification that honour paid to the image passes to its prototype. At the *Reformation the use of images was opposed by most of the Reformers, esp. the followers of H. *Zwingli and J. *Calvin, who were followed by the *Puritans.

IMAGO DEI (Lat., the 'image of God'), in which man was created (Gen. 1: 26 f.). Acc. to Catholic theologians this image was obscured, but not lost, in the *Fall; it is contrasted with the *similitudo Dei* ('likeness to God'), which was destroyed by *original sin but is restored by *Baptism. In what the *imago* consists is disputed. Protestant theologians have emphasized the vitiating effect of the Fall on the *imago Dei*, and sometimes held man to be utterly corrupt.

'IMITATION OF CHRIST', The. A manual of spiritual devotion designed to instruct the Christian how to seek perfection by following Christ as his model. It was put into circulation in 1418 and has traditionally been attributed to *Thomas à Kempis; attempts since the 17th cent. to assign it to other writers have failed to win general assent.

IMMACULATE CONCEPTION OF THE BVM. The dogma that 'from the first moment of her conception the Blessed Virgin Mary was ... kept free from all stain of original sin' was defined by *Pius IX in 1854. The doctrine was a matter of dispute throughout the Middle Ages, but was generally accepted by RCs from the 16th cent. The feast, first approved in 1476, is kept on 8 Dec.

IMMACULATE HEART OF MARY. See *Sacred Heart of Mary*.

IMMANENCE, Divine. The omnipresence of God in His universe. The doctrine is a necessary constituent of the Christian conception of God.

IMMANUEL, or EMMANUEL (Heb., 'With us [is] God'). The word occurs in Is. 7: 14 and 8: 8, but it is not clear to whom it refers. In Mt. 1: 23 the prophecy is interpreted with reference to the birth of Christ.

IMMERSION. A method of *baptism, whereby part of the candidate's body is submerged in the baptismal water which is poured over the remainder. It is still found in the E. Church and is permitted in the RC Church.

IMMOLATION. An act of sacrificial offering. The word has occupied an important place in modern Eucharistic theology.

IMMORTALITY. Though not a specifically Christian doctrine the hope of immortality is an integral element in Christian belief. In pre-Christian times Greek philosophers had inferred the existence of the soul before birth and its survival after death, and had regarded the body as a prison-house from which death brought the release of the soul into a fuller existence. Early Hebrew thought about the next world was shadowy, but in later pre-Christian Judaism a greater sense of the reality of the future life developed. The essential shape which the doctrine assumed in Christianity arose from the fact of Christ's *Resurrection. No longer was the highest destiny of man seen as the survival of an immortal soul, but as a life of union with the Risen Christ which would reach completion only with the reunion of body and soul. See also *Resurrection of the Dead* and *Conditional Immortality*.

IMPANATION. A term applied to certain doctrines of the Eucharist. It was used in the 11th cent. in connection with the followers of *Berengar and was later applied to various views which were designed to safeguard a belief in the *Real Presence while denying the destruction of the natural elements.

IMPASSIBILITY OF GOD, The. Orthodox theology has commonly held that God is not subject to action from without, changing emotions from within, or feelings of pain or pleasure caused by another being. In Christianity there is, however, tension between the idea of the immutability, perfection, and all-sufficiency of God, which would seem to exclude all passion, and the central conviction that God in His essence is love, and that His nature is revealed in the Incarnate Christ, not least in His Passion.

IMPEDIMENT. In *canon law, an obstacle standing in the way of a properly constituted marriage. In RC canon law an impedient impediment prohibits a marriage but does not invalidate it if it is contracted despite the impediment; a *diriment impediment invalidates it.

IMPOSITION OF HANDS. See *Hands, Imposition of*.

IMPRECATORY PSALMS, The. Psalms which in whole or part invoke the Divine vengeance (e.g. Ps. 58).

IMPRIMATUR (Lat., 'let it be printed'). The certification that a book has been passed for publication by the appropriate authority. In England various licensing laws in force from 1586 to 1695 required an Imprimatur from a civil or ecclesiastical authority for the printing or importation of books. In the RC Church certification by a 'censor', normally appointed by the diocesan bishop, is required before writings on theological or moral subjects are published.

IMPROPERIA. The Latin name of the *Reproaches.

IMPROPRIATION. The assignment or annexation of an ecclesiastical benefice to a lay proprietor or corporation. When at the *Dissolution many benefices appropriated to monasteries passed into the hands of '*lay rectors', it became necessary for such rectors to appoint '*perpetual curates' to execute the spiritual duties of impropriated benefices.

IMPUTATION. In theology the ascription to a person, by deliberate substitution, of the righteousness or guilt of another. The *Lutheran doctrine of *Justification by Faith asserts that a man is formally justified by the imputation of the obedience and righteousness of Christ, without becoming possessed of any personal righteousness of his own. By a legal fiction God is thus held to regard the sinner's misdeeds as covered by the imputation of the sanctity of Christ. It is opposed to the traditional Catholic doctrine, acc. to which the merits of Christ are not imputed but imparted to man, producing a real change from the state of sin to a state of grace.

IN COENA DOMINI (Lat., 'On the Lord's Supper'). A series of excommunications of specified offenders against faith and morals which were regularly issued in the form of a Papal Bull. Its publication came to be confined to *Maundy Thursday (hence its name); the practice was abrogated in 1869.

IN COMMENDAM. See *Commendam*.

INCARDINATION. In W. canon law, the permanent enlistment of a cleric under the jurisdiction of a new *ordinary.

INCARNATION, The. The Christian doctrine of the Incarnation affirms that the eternal Son of God took human flesh from His human mother and that the historical Christ is at once fully God and fully man. It asserts an abiding union in Christ's Person of Godhead and Manhood and assigns the beginnings of this union to a definite and known date in human history.

The doctrine took shape under the influence of the controversies of the 4th–5th cents. (see *Christology*); it was formally defined at the Council of *Chalcedon in 451. The Chalcedonian Definition, however, only determined the limits of orthodoxy and within these limits discussion continued. In the Middle Ages a much disputed (but never settled) point was whether the Incarnation would have occurred but for the *Fall. In modern times the application of historical methods to the study of the Gospels has raised the question of the limits of Christ's knowledge and its bearing on belief in His Divinity.

INCENSE. Incense is used in many religious rites, the smoke being considered symbolic of prayer. There is no clear evidence of its Christian use before c. A.D. 500. In the W. incense was long used only at solemn sung services, but since 1969 it has been permitted at any Eucharistic service. In the E. it is used more frequently than in the W. The legality of its use in the C of E has been disputed.

INCUBATION. The practice of sleeping in churches or their precincts in expectation of visions, revelations, and healing from disease. Of pagan origin, the custom came to be associated with particular churches.

INCUMBENT. In the C of E the holder of a parochial charge, i.e. a *rector, *vicar, or (until 1968) a *perpetual curate.

INCUNABULA. Early printed books, esp. those printed before 1501.

INDEPENDENTS. Another name for the *Congregationalists, as upholders of the independence or autonomy of each congregation.

INDEX LIBRORUM PROHIBITORUM

(Lat., 'List of prohibited books'), in short 'the Index', the official list of books issued by the RC Church which its members are normally forbidden to read or possess. The first Index was issued by the Congregation of the Inquisition or *Holy Office in 1557. In 1571 *Pius V established a 'Congregation of the Index' to be in charge of this list and revise it as needed; in 1917 its duties passed back to the Holy Office. The Index itself was abolished in 1966.

INDIA, Christianity in. The Church has certainly existed in India since the 4th cent. The tradition that St. *Thomas the Apostle preached there can be regarded as no more than a possibility. For the history of the Thomas Christians, see *Malabar Christians*.

W. Christianity was brought to India by the Portuguese in 1498. Attempts to evangelize the inhabitants of the country as a whole date from the arrival of the *Jesuits in 1542. In 1637 the *Propaganda in Rome consecrated a Brahman as *Vicar Apostolic for the non-Portuguese regions of India. Though the policy of choosing Indians for the post lapsed, Vicars Apostolic were appointed in increasing numbers. In 1886 *Leo XIII created a regular hierarchy for India.

From 1660 the English and later the Dutch were in India. The greater part of their Church work consisted in the spiritual care of their own people through chaplains. Protestant missionary work began seriously in 1706, when King Frederick IV of Denmark founded a mission to work in his territory of Tranquebar in S. India. As the work spread beyond the limits of the Danish possession, the *S.P.C.K. took over support of the missionaries. In 1793 the first English missionary, W. *Carey, landed in Bengal. Since the East India Company opposed missionary activity, Carey established his mission in the Danish territory of Serampore. At the revision of the East India Company's charter in 1813, *Evangelical opinion secured the insertion of provision for a bishopric of Calcutta and freedom for missionary enterprise. The *C.M.S. sent missionaries, and Anglican clergy went to India in large numbers. By the end of the 19th cent. there were also numerous missionaries from the U.S.A. and the Continent of Europe. At the same time a native Indian ministry was formed through the ordination of those trained in their own language and with no knowledge of English; the first such

·ordination took place in 1850. In 1930 the Anglican Church in India, which had hitherto been a part of the C of E, acquired independence as the Church of India, Burma, and Ceylon (Pakistan was added to the title in 1947). Other denominations established independent Churches in the following period.

Co-operation among the non-RC Churches in India dates from 1855. A series of conferences led to the formation in 1908 of the South India United Church (*Presbyterian and *Congregational), the first trans-confessional union of modern times. Similar movements eventually led to the formation of the Churches of *South India (1947), of *North India (1970), and of *Pakistan (1970). The number of Christians in India is not more than 3 per cent of the population, less than 1 per cent in Pakistan.

INDICOPLEUSTES. See *Cosmas Indicopleustes*.

INDUCTION. The final stage in the appointment of a new *incumbent. After the priest has been *instituted by the Bishop, he is inducted to his *benefice, usually by the *Archdeacon, who places his hand on the key of the church door and causes him to toll the bell. The legal effect is to give him possession of the temporalities and control of the parish.

INDULGENCE, Declarations of. See *Declarations of Indulgence*.

INDULGENCES. The remission by the Church of the temporal penalty due to forgiven sin, in virtue of the merits of Christ and the saints. The practice of granting indulgences presupposes that sin must have a penalty either on earth or in *purgatory, even after the sinner has been reconciled to God by *penance and absolution; that the merits of Christ and the saints are available to the Church in virtue of the Communion of Saints; and that the Church has the right to administer the benefit of these merits.

In the early Church the intercession of confessors and those awaiting martyrdom was allowed by the ecclesiastical authorities to shorten the canonical discipline of those under penance, and from this beginning the idea developed that the merits of Christ and the saints made up deficiencies in penances. There is no certain evidence for general indulgences before the 11th cent., but from the 12th cent. indulgences became common. *Plenary indulgences were offered to those who took part in the *Crusades, and in the later Middle Ages their growth led to considerable abuses. In 1967 *Paul VI revised the practical application of the traditional doctrine; the number of plenary indulgences was reduced and the system simplified.

INDULT. A faculty granted by the *Apostolic See to deviate from the common law of the Church.

INDUSTRIAL CHRISTIAN FELLOWSHIP (I.C.F.). An Anglican organization which seeks to present the Christian faith to the world of industry both by missions to industrial workers and by relating the theory and practice of Christianity to modern industry. It was founded in 1918 by the fusion of two earlier bodies.

INEFFABILIS DEUS. The constitution issued in 1854 defining the dogma of the *Immaculate Conception.

INFALLIBILITY. Inability to err in teaching revealed truth. While many Christians maintain that the Church is infallible, on the basis of such texts as Jn. 16: 13, various beliefs have been held as to the seat where such infallibility rests. At the First *Vatican Council (1870) the RC Church declared that the Pope was infallible when he defined that a doctrine concerning faith or morals was part of the deposit of divine revelation.

INFANCY GOSPELS, The. The apocryphal stories about the birth and childhood of Christ which were put into circulation in early Christian times.

INFANT BAPTISM. Although from the first *Baptism was the universal means of entry into the Christian community, the NT contains no specific authority for its administration to infants. Since at least the 3rd cent., however, children born to Christian parents have been baptized in infancy. In the 16th cent. the practice ('paedobaptism') was rejected by the *Anabaptists, and since the 17th cent. also by the *Baptists.

Various passages in the NT, such as those which mention the Baptism of whole households, suggest that children may have been baptized as well as adults, but there is no clear evidence. Indications of infant Baptism become more positive in the post-Apostolic period, and *Origen refers to it as an established custom. In the 4th cent. Baptism was sometimes deferred because of the prevalent belief in the impossibility or great difficulty of the remission of post-baptismal sin, but the practice of infant Baptism soon became almost universal.

In the E. Church infant Baptism is followed at once by the administration of *chrism and Holy Communion. In the W. these are deferred until the age of conscious participation (see *Confirmation*). Acc. to Catholic theology the Baptism of infants conveys the essential gift of regeneration. Those who reject it do so on the grounds that it lacks NT warrant and that as a mere ceremony (not a *sacrament) it can convey no benefit to its unconscious recipient. In modern times there has also been some reconsideration of the traditional view on the ground that many who bring their children to be baptized are themselves only nominally Christian, and the 1969 RC Order for the Baptism of Infants acknowledges that in some cases Baptism should be deferred.

INFIDEL. A person who has a positive disbelief in every form of the Christian faith.

INFIRMARIAN. In a religious house, the person in charge of the sick-quarters.

INFRALAPSARIANS. See *Sublapsarianism*.

INGE, WILLIAM RALPH (1860–1954), Dean of *St. Paul's from 1911 to 1934. His sympathies with *Platonic spirituality found expression in a series of theological and devotional writings. His grasp of the tastes and prejudices of the English mind, his provocative and epigrammatical manner of writing, and his pure English style made him one of the best-known Churchmen of his generation.

INHIBITION. An episcopal order suspending from the performance of his office an *incumbent whose conduct makes such action advisable.

INITIATION. See *Baptism*.

INJUNCTIONS, Royal. Tudor proclamations on ecclesiastical affairs. *Henry VIII's

Injunctions of 1536 required the clergy to observe the anti-papal laws, abandon various practices, and teach the people in English. Those of 1538 ordered, among other things, the setting up of the *Great Bible in all churches. *Edward VI's Injunctions (1547) required regular sermons against the Pope's authority and in favour of the royal supremacy. Those issued by *Mary in 1554 required married priests to be removed or divorced, and clerics 'ordained after the new sort' to have 'that thing which wanted in them before' supplied. *Elizabeth I in 1559 substantially re-enacted the Injunctions of 1547, with their extreme anti-Romanism toned down; she also added others on how services should be conducted and other matters.

INNER LIGHT. The principle of Christian certitude, consisting of inward knowledge or experience of salvation, upheld by the Society of *Friends.

INNERE MISSION. The term covers all voluntary religious, charitable, and social work organized within the Protestant Churches in Germany, apart from parish work. The central organization of the mission dates from 1848; in 1957 it was united with the *Hilfswerk*, an organ of the *Evangelical Church in Germany established in 1945 to relieve distress and make contact with those alienated from the Church.

INNOCENT I (d. 417), Pope from 402. He made more substantial claims for the Papacy than any of his predecessors, exercising authority in the E. as well as in the W. Through his instrumentality in 404 the Emp. Honorius issued his decree against the *Donatists.

INNOCENT III (1160–1216), Pope from 1198. In making the right of the Papacy to interfere in secular affairs depend upon its duty to control the moral conduct of rulers and upon the theory of papal feudal overlordship, Innocent was enabled by the circumstances of the age and his own personality to make theory and practice coincide to an extent unparalleled before or since. The Emp. Henry VI having died in 1197, Innocent pressed claims to examine as well as to crown the person elected as Emperor; he then supported rival candidates in turn; *Frederick II was elected on condition that he did homage to the Pope for Sicily. In France Innocent compelled Philip Augustus to be reconciled to his Queen. The quarrel over the appointment of S. *Langton to the see of *Canterbury led to the submission of King *John of England, who recognized Innocent as his feudal overlord. Elsewhere also the Pope extended his influence. He patronized the new orders of friars, the *Franciscans and the *Dominicans. The *Lateran Council of 1215 was the culminating event of his reign. His pontificate marked the climax of the medieval Papacy.

INNOCENT IV (d. 1254), Pope from 1243. He tried, without success, to compose the papal dispute with *Frederick II and at the Council of *Lyons in 1245 declared him deposed. He supported Henry III against the barons in England. He also allowed the use of torture by the *Inquisition.

INNOCENT X (1574–1655), Pope from 1644. Elected in spite of opposition from the French court, he supported the protest of his legate against the Peace of *Westphalia (1648), and he condemned five propositions from the *Augustinus of C. O. *Jansen in the bull '*Cum occasione' (1653).

INNOCENT XI, Bl. (1611–89), Pope from 1676. He struggled against the absolutism of Louis XIV in Church affairs, disapproving of the revocation in 1685 of the Edict of *Nantes; he also opposed *Gallicanism. He similarly disapproved of *James II's measures to restore RCism in England. He condemned 65 *laxist propositions in 1679 and 68 *Quietist propositions in 1687.

INNOCENTS, Holy. See *Holy Innocents.*

INOPPORTUNISTS. Those who at the *Vatican Council of 1869–70 opposed the definition of Papal *Infallibility on the ground that the moment for its promulgation was 'not opportune'.

INQUISITION, The. 'Inquisition' denotes the juridical persecution of heresy by special ecclesiastical courts. The Inquisition properly so called came into being in 1232 when *Frederick II issued an edict entrusting the hunting-out of heretics to State officials. *Gregory IX claimed the office for the Church and appointed Papal inquisitors. They were largely chosen from the *Domini-

cans and *Franciscans. If those accused of heresy refused to confess, they were tried before an inquisitor, assisted by a jury of clerics and laymen. Penalties in grave cases were confiscation of goods, imprisonment, and surrender to the secular arm, which meant death at the stake. In 1542 *Paul III established the *Holy Office as the final court of appeal in trials for heresy.

The so-called Spanish Inquisition was established with papal approval by *Ferdinand V and *Isabella in 1479. It was originally intended to deal with those converted from Judaism and Islam, but later served also against Protestantism. It was finally suppressed in 1820.

INSCRIPTIONS, Early Christian. If the well-known SATOR word-square (a cryptogram of doubtful interpretation found throughout the ancient world) is Christian, the examples of it found at Pompeii (destroyed in 79) are the earliest extant Christian inscriptions. 3rd-cent. inscriptions are fairly common in the Roman *catacombs and from the 4th cent. they are very common in Rome, N. Africa, Syria, and Asia Minor.

In contrast to pagan inscriptions, Christian inscriptions give little personal detail. They are valuable *en masse* as evidence of the texture of the community and the expansion of the Church, and bear witness to the beliefs of rank-and-file Christians of the period.

INSTALLATION. The formal induction of a canon or prebendary to a seat or stall in a cathedral or collegiate church.

INSTANTIUS (late 4th cent.), a Spanish bishop who supported *Priscillian. He is perhaps the author of 11 treatises ascribed to Priscillian.

INSTITUTES, The. The abbreviated English title of J. *Calvin's *Christianae Religionis Institutio*. The first edition was published in Latin in 1536; the final edition in 1559 (in Latin) and 1560 (in French). The treatise soon became the textbook of Reformed theology. Its central doctrines are the absolute sovereignty of God, the basis of all Christian faith in the Word of God revealed in Scripture, and the inability of man to find pardon or salvation apart from the working of the free grace of God.

INSTITUTION. The admission by a bishop of a new *incumbent into the spiritual care of a *parish.

INSTITUTION, The Words of. The words 'This is My Body' and 'This is My Blood' used by Christ in instituting the *Eucharist. In the W. it has been commonly held that these words in the liturgy effect the consecration of the elements.

INSTITUTS CATHOLIQUES. The five 'free' Catholic institutions for higher studies founded in the late 19th cent. at *Paris, Angers, Lille, Lyons, and Toulouse.

INSTRUMENTS, Tradition of the. The solemn delivery to those being ordained of the instruments characteristic of their ministry. In the RC Church deacons receive the Gospel book and priests the *paten with bread and the *chalice; the ceremony was formerly sometimes held to form the essential '*matter' of the sacrament of *ordination. The Anglican *Ordinal directs that a NT be delivered to deacons and a Bible to priests.

INSUFFLATION. The action of blowing or breathing upon a person or thing to symbolize the influence of the Holy Spirit. The RC Church still has a special rite of insufflation in connection with the consecration of *chrism.

INTENTION. (1) In moral theology, an act of free will directed to the attainment of an end. Such intention may be 'actual' if one wills with conscious attention; 'virtual' if one continues to will in virtue of a previous decision, though at the time not consciously aware of it; or 'habitual' if all voluntary action has ceased but without the original decision being revoked. The intention influences the morality of an action. (2) In the administration of the Sacraments, the purpose of doing what the Church does. Such intention on the part of the minister is essential. It was esp. on the ground of defect of intention that *Leo XIII condemned *Anglican Ordinations in 1896. (3) The special object, material or spiritual, for which a prayer of *intercession is made. (4) In *Scholastic theories of knowledge the term was sometimes used of the objects of knowledge in so far as they are present to the knowing consciousness.

INTERCESSION. Petitionary prayer on behalf of others.

INTERDICT. An ecclesiastical punishment in the RC Church excluding the faithful from participation in spiritual things, but without loss of the Communion of the Church. Interdicts are of various kinds. The 'personal' interdict is attached only to particular persons; the 'local' forbids sacred action in particular places; the 'general' refers to a whole district or its population. The chief effect of an interdict is the cessation of the administration of the Sacraments, though certain exceptions are permitted.

INTERIM OF AUGSBURG. See *Augsburg Interim*.

INTERIM RITE. The Order of Holy Communion in the C of E proposed in 1931 by Bp. A. Chandler after the rejection of the proposed BCP of 1927–8. It was widely hoped that it might be episcopally approved for use until a formal revision was authorized: hence the title 'Interim Rite'. The *Alternative Services, Holy Communion (Series I), authorized a use closely akin to it.

INTERNATIONAL BIBLE STUDENTS' ASSOCIATION. See *Jehovah's Witnesses*.

INTERSTICES. The space of time which, by *canon law, must elapse between the conferment of different *orders in the Christian ministry upon the same person.

INTHRONIZATION. See *Enthronization*.

INTINCTION. In liturgical usage, the practice of dipping the Eucharistic bread into consecrated or unconsecrated wine before Communion. It became a regular method of Communion with the two consecrated species in both the E. and W.; it had disappeared in the W. by c. 1200. In the Anglican Church it is sometimes used as a method of giving Communion to the sick. In the RC Church it was authorized in 1965 as one of three ways of receiving Communion in both kinds.

INTROIT. In the W. Church, the opening act of worship in the Mass. Originally it consisted of a whole Psalm, sung with *antiphon and *Gloria Patri; later only a part of the

Psalm was sung and in the RC Church some other chant may now be substituted. In the C of E, the *Alternative Services now provide for the use of a Psalm or hymn as the ministers enter the church.

INVENTION OF THE CROSS, The. Acc. to legend the three crosses of Christ and the two robbers were found (Lat. *inventae*) by St. *Helena, that of Christ being identified by a miracle. Veneration of the Cross, part of which was preserved in the church of the *Holy Sepulchre at Jerusalem, is described by *Etheria. The commemoration of the finding of the Cross, formerly observed on 3 May, was suppressed in the RC Church in 1960.

INVESTITURE CONTROVERSY. The dispute over the claim of the Emperor and other lay rulers to invest an Abbot- or Bishop-elect with the ring and staff and to receive homage from him before his consecration. The custom, which was linked with lay patronage, was condemned by Pope Nicholas II in 1059; in 1075 all lay investiture was forbidden by *Gregory VII, and this prohibition was frequently repeated. After acute controversy, compromises were reached in England in 1105 and in France in 1107, and a final settlement with the Empire was achieved in the Concordat of *Worms (1122). Generally the lay ruler ceased to invest with ring and staff but continued to bestow the temporalities and to receive homage either before or after the consecration.

INVINCIBLE IGNORANCE. A term in *moral theology denoting ignorance of a kind which cannot be removed by serious moral effort. It excuses from sin because, being involuntary, it can involve no intention to break the law of God.

INVITATORY. In the *Breviary, the Psalm *Venite (AV Ps. 95; Vulg. Ps. 94) with its corresponding *antiphon, which stand at the beginning of the first *Office of the day. The antiphon (itself sometimes termed the Invitatory) varies with the season.

INVOCATION OF THE SAINTS. See *Saints, Devotion to the.*

I.O.D.G. See *U.I.O.D.G.*

IONA (or HY). An island of the Inner Hebrides. In 563 St. *Columba landed on Iona and founded a monastery which became a centre of *Celtic Christianity and from which missionaries were sent to *Scotland and N. England. It survived until the Reformation.

The Iona Community was founded in 1938 by the Rev. George MacLeod to express the theology of the Incarnation in social terms, using the restoration of the conventual buildings of the abbey (completed in 1966) as the symbol of its purpose. Its members live in community on Iona for three months in the year in preparation for work in Scottish industrial areas and in the mission field.

IOTA. The Greek letter ι, the smallest letter of that alphabet.

IRELAND, Christianity in. Christianity was prob. introduced in the 4th cent., but the early history is obscure. *Celestine I (422–32) sent *Palladius as first Bishop to the 'Irish believing in Christ'; he was followed by St. *Patrick later in the 5th cent. After the break-up of the Roman civilization, Ireland, isolated from the rest of Christendom, developed a peculiar Church life of her own. Bishops were subordinated to the heads of land-owning communities, and no parochial system developed. The monasteries were centres of learning and missionary activity. Gradually under influences from S. Wales the communities were brought into closer alignment with contemporary practice elsewhere, but it was not until a generation after the Synod of *Whitby (664) that the differences between the *Celtic and Roman disciplines were settled. In the 12th cent. fixed sees were established and the English conquest of 1172 completed the ecclesiastical process.

The *Reformation was less thorough in Ireland than elsewhere. Under *Elizabeth I the Church was officially reformed on the same lines as in England and by the enactments of the Irish Parliament of 1560 made dependent on the State. But in many places the old service-books continued in use and there was practically no persecution of those who did not conform. In the 17th cent. the plantation of English and Scots settlers provided a stronghold of militant Protestantism in Ulster. In 1615 the *Irish Articles were promulgated. The RC rebellion of 1641 led

O. *Cromwell to set up a Protestant economic ascendancy a few years later. At the beginning of the 18th cent. a stricter penal code brought further unpopularity to the Church of Ireland, which seems to have suffered a general spiritual decline. Disestablishment, provided by the Act of 1869, came into force in 1871.

After the Reformation Catholicism retained its hold on the masses. The maintenance of contact with Rome and of Catholic life was facilitated by the *Franciscans and the *Jesuits, who came to Ireland at an early date. The repressive penal measures in the early 18th cent. were largely due to the Vatican's continued recognition of *James II's son; they excluded RCs from public office and led to their further economic decline. Tension eased gradually and towards the end of the century freedom of worship and education were granted by various *Catholic Relief Acts; emancipation was achieved in 1829. A period of rapid expansion and reorganization followed, with church building on a vast scale. Since the creation of the Irish Free State in 1922, the RC Church in the Republic has had strong government support. The vitality of Irish Catholicism in daily life is unsurpassed. In the Republic over 90 per cent of the population is RC. In Northern Ireland just over one third is RC; under a third is *Presbyterian, and about a quarter Anglican.

IRENAEUS, St. (*c.* 130–*c.* 200), Bp. of Lyons from *c.* 178. He is generally supposed to have been a native of Smyrna, and he wrote in Greek; he is the first great Catholic theologian. His *Adversus Omnes Haereses* is a detailed attack on *Gnosticism, esp. the system of *Valentinus, and the *millenarianism popular in *Montanist circles; the text survives entire in Latin. In modern times a second work, *The Demonstration of the Apostolic Preaching*, has been found in an Armenian translation. Irenaeus opposed Gnosticism, not by setting up a rival Christian Gnosis, but by emphasizing the traditional elements in the Church. He also developed a doctrine of 'recapitulation', or summary, of human evolution in the humanity of the Incarnate Christ, thereby giving a positive value of its own to the Lord's full manhood.

IRISH ARTICLES. The 104 articles of faith adopted by the Church of *Ireland in 1615 at its first Convocation. They were more *Calvinistic than the *Thirty-Nine Articles (of the C of E), which were accepted in Ireland in 1635.

IRON CROWN of Lombardy. A crown made for Theodelinda, widow of Authoris, King of Lombardy, and presented in 594 to the Duke of Turin, from whom it passed to the recent royal house of Italy. The inner circlet of iron is said to have been made from a nail of the true Cross.

IRVING, EDWARD (1792–1834), Scottish minister associated with the origin of the '*Catholic Apostolic Church' (q.v.). In 1822 he was appointed minister of the Caledonian chapel in Hatton Garden, London. He turned to *millenarian ideas and came into contact with the circle of H. *Drummond. In 1830 he was excommunicated by the London Presbytery for a tract declaring Christ's human nature sinful; he rejected the decision, but in 1832 he was finally removed from his church and his followers constituted themselves the 'Catholic Apostolic Church'.

ISAAC, OT patriarch. The Divinely promised son of *Abraham and Sarah. To try Abraham's faith God asked Isaac in sacrifice, but, satisfied with the obedience of father and son, accepted a ram instead (Gen. 22). In the NT Isaac appears as a type of Christ and of the Church, and his sacrifice is connected with that of Christ. The latter theme was elaborated by the Fathers.

ISAAC THE GREAT, St. (*c.* 350–440), *Catholicos of the *Armenian Church from 390. By gaining from *Constantinople recognition of the metropolitical rights of the Armenian Church, he ended its dependence on Caesarea in Cappadocia. He fostered a national Armenian literature, with St. *Mesrob translating much of the Bible.

ISAAC OF NINEVEH (d. *c.* 700), also 'Isaac Syrus', *Nestorian Bp. of Nineveh. After a brief episcopate he retired to the monastery of Rabban Shapur. He wrote extensively in Syriac, mostly on ascetic subjects.

ISABELLA OF CASTILE (1451–1504), Queen of Spain. The daughter of John II, King of Castile and León, in 1469 she married *Ferdinand, heir to the Aragonese throne, and in 1474 she ascended the Castilian throne. The reign of the 'Catholic Sovereigns', as she and Ferdinand were called, laid the foundations of Spanish power.

ISAIAH, Hebrew prophet. He was influential at the court of the kings of Judah, esp. over foreign affairs. Called to the prophetic office *c.* 740 B.C., he continued his work until the Assyrian invasion of Judah in 701 B.C. Acc. to tradition he was martyred. He asserted the supremacy of Yahweh, the God of Israel, emphasized His moral demands, and stressed the Divine holiness. See also the following entries.

ISAIAH, Ascension of. An apocryphal work well known in the early Church. The first part (chs. 1–5) describes the circumstances of Isaiah's martyrdom; the second (chs. 6–11) his ascent in ecstasy through the heavens and the revelations made to him there. The work as a whole cannot be later than A.D. 350.

ISAIAH, Book of. Traditionally the whole of this OT Book has been ascribed to *Isaiah, but only parts of the earlier chapters have any claim to be his. The Book falls into three sections.
(1) Chs. 1–35. The parts most prob. by Isaiah are the greater part of chs. 1–12, 16–22, and 28–32. These mainly concern the political situation in Judah under Syrian pressure in 740–700 B.C. There is no compelling reason to question Isaiah's authorship of the Messianic passages in 9: 2–7 and 11: 1–9, which have long been referred by Christian authors to Christ.
(2) Chs. 36–9. A section mainly taken from 2 Kings.
(3) Chs. 40–66. These chapters appear to be later than the two previous sections. Modern scholars ascribe chs. 40–55 to '*Deutero-Isaiah' and chs. 56–66 to '*Trito-Isaiah'. The theme is Israel's redemption and her mission to the world. See also *Servant Songs*.

ISCARIOT. See *Judas Iscariot*.

ISHO'DAD OF MERV (9th cent.), *Nestorian Bp. of Hedatta on the R. Tigris. He wrote commentaries in Syriac on the whole of the OT and NT.

ISIDORE, St. (d. *c.* 450), of Pelusium, abbot and exegete. He intervened with *Cyril of Alexandria on behalf of the memory of *Chrysostom, whose exegesis he chiefly followed, and he opposed *Nestorius and *Eutyches.

ISIDORE, St. (*c.* 560–636), Abp. of Seville from *c.* 600. He founded schools and convents and worked for the conversion of the Jews. He presided over the Fourth Council of *Toledo (633), the canons of which reflect his organizing ability. He was famous for his learning, sanctity, and almsgiving.

His works were a storehouse of information freely used by medieval authors. The most important of them, the *Etymologiae*, is an encyclopaedia of the knowledge of his time, covering secular as well as religious subjects; the name derives from the (often fanciful) etymological explanations of the words signifying the different subjects. See also *False Decretals*.

ISIDORE MERCATOR. The pseudonym adopted by the author of the *False Decretals, doubtless to suggest a connection (if not identity) with St. *Isidore, Abp. of Seville.

ISLAM, the religion founded by Muhammad (or Mohammed) (*c.* 570–629), the adherent of which is called a Muslim. The central dogma is the absolute unity of God (Allah). At several points of history God has sent prophets, one of whom was Jesus. In Muslim belief Jesus, though born of a Virgin and being 'a spirit from God and His Word', is nevertheless created and not begotten, and his crucifixion was only apparent. The last of the prophets is Muhammed.

ISRAEL. The Hebrew people, so called because of its descent from the Patriarch Israel (*Jacob). In their history of the period of the Monarchy the Biblical writers normally applied the word (esp. in contrast to 'Judah') to the Ten Northern Tribes, i.e. those who attached themselves to Jeroboam after *Solomon's death. In the NT the Church is regarded as the new Israel.

ISSY, Articles of. The 34 articles drawn up at Issy, near Paris, in 1695 by the ecclesiastical commission charged with examining Mme *Guyon's works. Signed by J. B. *Bossuet, F. *Fénelon, and Mme Guyon herself, they were directed against various

*Quietist tenets.

ISTANBUL. The Turkish name for *Constantinople.

ITALA, The. A name sometimes given to the *Old Latin (pre-*Vulgate) version of the Bible.

ITALO-GREEKS. The Greek communities descended from (1) Greek settlers in Sicily and S. Italy in Byzantine times; (2) later Greek colonies established in Italian seaports; and (3) Greek and Albanian refugees from the Muslim invasion. Their status is *uniat.

ITE, MISSA EST. The traditional concluding formula of the Roman Mass. In English it is rendered 'The Mass is ended, go in peace'. Since 1970 two alternative forms of dismissal have been provided.

ITINERARIUM. A brief office formerly included in the *Breviary and prescribed for recitation by clerics about to set out on a journey.

IVES, St. (? 7th cent.). Traditionally a British bishop of Persian origin who preached Christianity in Cambridgeshire. The town of St. Ives in Cornwall is named after a different saint.

IVO, St. (c. 1040–1115), Bp. of *Chartres from 1090. He was the most learned canonist of his age, and his three treatises, the *Collectio Tripartita*, the *Decretum*, and the *Panormia*, exercised a determining influence on the development of canon law.

IZNIK. The modern name of *Nicaea, now only a village in Turkey.

J

'J'. The name given to the Jahvistic (Yahwistic) source held to be embodied in the *Pentateuch. It is distinguished from the later sources '*D' and '*P' by its simple narrative style and relatively primitive ideas, and from '*E' (and also from 'P') by its use of the Divine name Yahweh from the first, even before it was revealed to Moses in Exod. 3: 14 f.

JABNEH. See *Jamnia*.

JACOB, Hebrew patriarch. The son of *Isaac, he deprived his brother Esau of his birthright by an elaborate ruse and fled to Haran in Mesopotamia. On his way back to Canaan he wrestled with a mysterious Divine stranger and received the name of '*Israel'. The twelve tribes of Israel took their names from those of his sons.

JACOB BARADAEUS (c. 500–78), reputed founder of the *Jacobites. About 528 he went to *Constantinople to plead the cause of *Monophysitism and remained there until he was consecrated Bp. of *Edessa c. 542. He wandered for the rest of his life from Egypt to the Euphrates, preaching and founding independent Monophysite Churches.

JACOB OF EDESSA (c. 640–708), *Monophysite Syrian scholar. In 684 he became Bp. of *Edessa, but he withdrew from his see after less than five years. He knew Greek and Hebrew, and revised the *Peshitta text of the OT on the basis of the *Hexapla. His writings include a continuation of *Eusebius's 'Chronicle' to A.D. 692, many *scholia on the Bible, and translations of some of the works of *Severus of Antioch.

JACOB OF NISIBIS, St. (early 4th cent.), Bp. of Nisibis. He was always a prominent figure in Syriac Church tradition, and in later times he acquired a reputation for learning, ability, and holiness, but apart from his presence at the Council of *Nicaea (325), little is certainly known. He seems to have been a champion of orthodoxy against *Arius.

JACOB OF SARUG (or SERUGH) (c. 451–521), Syriac ecclesiastical writer. He became Bp. of Batnae in NW. Syria in 519. His chief writing was a series of metrical homilies, mainly on Biblical themes, which earned him the title 'The Flute of the Holy Ghost'. His doctrinal position is disputed; he was prob. an adherent of the *Monophysite cause.

JACOB OF VORAGINE (c. 1230–c. 1298), author of the '*Golden Legend' (q.v.). He became a *Dominican in 1244 and was made Abp. of Genoa in 1292. He also wrote a history of Genoa to 1296, sermons, and a defence of the Dominicans. A cult developed after his death.

JACOBINS. A name given originally to the *Dominicans in France from their Paris house in the ruc St.-Jacques. In 1789 the house was acquired by the revolutionary political club which thence assumed the name.

JACOBITES. The body of Syrian *Monophysites who rejected the teaching of the Council of *Chalcedon (451) on the Person of Christ. They took their name from *Jacob Baradaeus, through whose labours they became the national Church of Syria, though the title 'Jacobites' is not found until 787. See also Syrian Catholics and Syrian Orthodox.

JACOBUS. See Jacob and James.

JACOPONE DA TODI (Jacopo Benedetti) (c. 1230–1306), *Franciscan poet. He became a Franciscan *lay-brother c. 1278. In 1294 he and some others were given permission by *Celestine V to live in a separate community, observing the rule of the order in its original strictness. This decision was reversed in 1298 and Jacopone as one of the *Spirituals was imprisoned until 1303. He wrote exquisite and deeply devotional poems (Laude) in Latin and the Umbrian dialect, prob. including the *Stabat Mater.

JAHWEH. An alternative form of *Yahweh.

JAIRUS. A Galilaean 'ruler of the synagogue' whose daughter Christ restored to life (Mk. 5: 21–43).

JAMES. The normal English form of the Latin Jacobus, which represents one form of the Hebrew name transliterated into English as Jacob. In English versions of the Bible the form 'Jacob' is retained in the OT and those passages of the NT which refer to the OT patriarch.

JAMES, St., 'the Lord's brother' (Mk. 6: 3 and parallels). The natural interpretation of the NT evidence implies that he was the son of the BVM and St. *Joseph, but see Brethren of the Lord. From an early date he was, with St. *Peter, a leader of the Church at *Jerusalem, and after Peter had left Jerusalem, James appears as the chief authority. Acc. to *Clement of Alexandria he was chosen 'bishop of Jerusalem'; *Hegesippus says that he was put to death in A.D. 62. He was held in high repute among Jewish Christians. See also James, Apocalypses of; James, Apocryphal Epistle of; James, Book of; James, Epistle of; and James, Liturgy of St.

JAMES, St., 'the Great', Apostle. The elder brother of St. *John, he belonged to the privileged group of disciples who were present at the *Transfiguration and the Agony in *Gethsemane. Because of their zeal James and John were named 'Boanerges', i.e. 'sons of thunder', by the Lord (Mk. 3: 17). James was beheaded in A.D. 44 (Acts 12: 2). The tradition that he preached in Spain is now almost universally abandoned.

JAMES, St., 'the Less'. The title derives from the description of 'James the less' in Mk. 15: 40, but it is commonly applied to James, the son of Alphaeus (Mk. 3:18 &c.), one of the Twelve Apostles, who is thus identified with the James of Mk. 15: 40. The epithet is prob. attached to the Apostle to distinguish him from St. James 'the Great' (of the previous entry).

JAMES, Apocalypses of. Two short *Gnostic works found at *Nag Hammadi. They embody dialogues between Christ and *James, the Lord's brother.

JAMES, Apocryphal Epistle of. A *Gnostic work discovered at *Nag Hammadi. It purports to record Christ's last discourse before His Ascension, delivered to *Peter and *James, the Lord's brother, who is ostensibly the writer.

JAMES, Book of. An apocryphal *Infancy Gospel, professedly by *James, the Lord's brother, and apparently dating from the middle of the 2nd cent. It consists mainly of a highly embellished version of the events connected with Christ's birth related in Lk. 1 f. It is also known as the 'Protevangelium'.

JAMES, Epistle of. This NT Book, in the form of an Ep. of 'James, a servant of God and of the Lord Jesus Christ, to the twelve tribes of the Diaspora', stands first among the *Catholic Epistles. It is written in a clear forceful style, using good Greek, and is almost entirely moral in content. The traditional view that the author was *James, the Lord's brother, has to meet formidable objections, none of which is conclusive. In any case, it seems likely that the Ep. was composed before A.D. 95, certainly not later than 150.

JAMES, Liturgy of St. This ancient liturgy, extant in a Greek and Syriac form, is traditionally ascribed to St. *James, the Lord's brother. It cannot be later than the middle of the 5th cent. It is still on occasion used in the Orthodox Church.

JAMES I (1566–1625), King of England and VI of Scotland. He became King of Scotland in 1567 on the abdication of his mother, *Mary, Queen of Scots, and he succeeded to the English throne on *Elizabeth I's death (1603) by virtue of his mother's descent from Henry VII. On his way to London he was presented by the *Puritans with the *Millenary Petition. At first he adopted a mediating position at the *Hampton Court Conference, but, confusing the English Puritans with the Scottish *Presbyterians, he decided to support episcopacy. He authorized a new translation of the *Bible (the 'Authorized Version' of 1611). In 1610 he persuaded the Assembly of the Scottish Church to agree to the introduction of episcopacy and eventually got the Articles of *Perth accepted. In 1618 he issued the Book of *Sports, approving lawful games on Sunday. Throughout his reign he quarrelled with his Parliaments over foreign policy.

JAMES II (1633–1701), King of England, 1685–8. He became a RC c. 1670, and there were various attempts to exclude him from the succession. At the beginning of his reign he supported the position of the C of E, but he increasingly sought to improve the position of his co-religionists, e.g. by dispensing them from the provisions of the *Test Act and by issuing *Declarations of Indulgence in 1687 and 1688. The refusal of W. *Sancroft and six other bishops to publish the second of these Declarations from the pulpit led to the Trial of the *Seven Bishops. William, Prince of Orange, landed in England and James fled to France.

JAMES BARADAEUS. See *Jacob Baradaeus.*

JAMES THE DEACON (7th cent.), companion of St. *Paulinus, Bp. of *York. He remained in the North of England when Paulinus returned to Kent in 633, and on the restoration of Christianity in Northumbria he took an active part in preaching the Gospel.

JAMES OF EDESSA, JAMES OF NISIBIS, JAMES OF SARUG, JAMES OF VORAGINE. See *Jacob of Edessa,* &c.

JAMES, WILLIAM (1842–1910), American *Pragmatist philosopher. A professor at Harvard, he held that we have a 'right to believe in' the existence of God (because it makes us 'better off'), but no certainty of the validity of that belief. *The Varieties of Religious Experience* (1902) made a scientific analysis of conversion.

JAMNIA or JABNEH, a city c. 13 miles S. of Joppa. After the fall of *Jerusalem (A.D. 70), an assembly of Jewish religious teachers was established here. The status of certain Biblical Books whose canonicity was still open to question in the 1st cent. A.D. was apparently one of the subjects of discussion, but there is no evidence to substantiate the suggestion that a particular synod of Jamnia, held c. 100, settled the limits of the OT *canon.

JANE FRANCES DE CHANTAL, St. (1572–1641), foundress of the Order of the *Visitation. After the death of her husband in 1601, her friendship with St. *Francis de Sales led to the establishment at Annecy in 1610 of the Congregation of the Visitation for young girls and widows unable to endure the severe ascetic life of the ordinary religious houses but eager to enter religion. She spent the rest of her life in the cloister.

JANNES AND JAMBRES. Two reputed Egyptian magicians who imitated the miracles performed by *Moses (Exod. 7 ff.).

JANSEN, CORNELIUS OTTO (1585–1638), author of the *Augustinus* (q.v.). In 1617 he became director of a newly founded college at Louvain, and the following year he began writing the *Augustinus*, after reading St. *Augustine's works many times. In 1636 he was consecrated Bp. of Ypres. See also the following entry.

JANSENISM. Technically Jansenism is summed up in five propositions taken from the *Augustinus* (1640) of C. O. *Jansen and condemned as heretical by *Innocent X. The sense of these propositions is that without a special *grace from God, the performance of His commands is impossible to man, and that the operation of grace is irresistible; hence man is the victim of either a natural or a supernatural determinism, limited only by not being coercive. This theological pessimism was expressed in the general harshness and moral rigorism of the movement.

The first generation of Jansenists were disciples of *Saint-Cyran, Jansen's friend and collaborator; they included the convent of *Port-Royal. After Saint-Cyran's death in 1643, Antoine *Arnauld became the leader. In 1653 Innocent X condemned five propositions as summarizing the Jansenist position. The Jansenists sought to evade the condemnation by admitting that the propositions condemned were heretical, but declaring them to be unrepresentative of Jansen's doctrine; this distinction was disallowed by *Alexander VII (1656). In 1668 the Jansenists were persuaded into a qualified submission, but the movement continued to gain sympathizers. P. *Quesnel's reassertion of Jansenist tenets was condemned in the Bull '*Unigenitus' (1713), which was followed by persecution of Jansenists in France. In *Holland, however, Jansenism was tolerated and a schism developed with the consecration of an *Old Catholic Bishop of Utrecht in 1724. They also remained strong in Tuscany.

JANUARIUS, St., Bp. of Benevento, patron saint of Naples. He prob. died in the *Diocletianic persecution. The alleged 'liquefaction' of his blood, preserved in a glass phial, is believed to take place on about 18 occasions each year.

JANUS. The pseudonym over which J. J. I. von *Döllinger and others in 1869 published a series of letters attacking the *Syllabus Errorum.

JAPAN, Christianity in. St. *Francis Xavier brought Christianity to Japan in 1549. Despite intermittent persecution from 1596 onwards, the exclusion of foreigners, and the proscription of Christianity until 1859, thousands of Christians in small communities kept the faith alive. The Franco-Japanese treaty of 1859 was followed by the arrival of fresh RC missionaries, Anglican missionaries from America, and *Presbyterians. In 1861 a mission came from the Russian *Orthodox Church under Fr. (later Abp.) Nicolai Kassatkin, who founded a community whose numbers were exceeded only by the RCs. The various Anglican missions in 1887 joined to form the 'Nippon Sei Ko Kwai' (Holy Catholic Church of Japan); this was reconstituted after the Second World War under an entirely Japanese episcopate.

JARROW. See *Wearmouth and Jarrow*.

JASPERS, KARL (1883–1969), German philosopher. He developed a Christian *Existentialism in an attempt to interpret the crisis in post-1918 Germany in secular philosophy and culture. He put religion and philosophy in contrast, and stressed the limits of science, notably in its ability to reach the self. This self is the ground of all existence and esp. characterized by the need for self-communication. Jaspers repudiated the exclusive claims of Christ, though in his last works he seems to have accorded Him a special position.

JASSY, Synod of (1642). A synod of the E. Church which met at Jassy (in modern *Rumania). It condemned the *Calvinist teachings of Cyril *Lucar and ratified (a somewhat emended text of) Peter *Mogila's *Orthodox Confession*.

JEAN-BAPTISTE MARIE VIANNEY, St. See *Curé d'Ars, The*.

JEANNE D'ARC, St. See *Joan of Arc, St*.

JEANNE FRANÇOISE FRÉMYOT DE CHANTAL. See *Jane Frances de Chantal, St*.

JEHOSHAPHAT, The Valley of. On the basis of Joel 3: 2 and 12, the traditional scene of the Lord's Coming Judgement. Since the 4th cent. A.D. the name has been used of the valley separating *Jerusalem from the Mount of *Olives.

JEHOVAH. A form of the Hebrew Divine Name. See *Tetragrammaton*.

JEHOVAH'S WITNESSES. A sect of American origin, founded by C. T. *Russell (q.v.) under the name 'International Bible Students' and also known as the 'Watch Tower Bible and Tract Society'. Russell believed in the near end of the world for all save his own adherents, the 'elect of Jehovah', who would be the sole members of the Messianic Kingdom.

JEREMIAH (7th cent. B.C.), prophet of Judah. He proclaimed the coming destruction of *Jerusalem and the *Temple, counselled submission to the Babylonians, and suffered during the siege of Jerusalem. After the destruction of the city (586) he was left free to live in Judah, but the Jews forced him to flee with them to Egypt. Acc. to tradition he was stoned to death. His sufferings have been interpreted as figures of the life of Christ, and the Church has used the Books of *Jeremiah and *Lamentations (ascribed to Jeremiah) in her Offices for *Passiontide.

JEREMIAH, Book of. Jewish tradition ascribes this OT Book to *Jeremiah, but most critics attribute a great part of it to editors, esp. Jeremiah's amanuensis Baruch, and date the promises of restitution and the giving of a New Covenant (chs. 30–1) to an author living after the return of the exiles to *Jerusalem (537 B.C.). There are striking differences between the *Septuagint and the *Massoretic texts.

The Prophet extols both the transcendence and the justice of God, who condemns His people because they have abandoned righteousness. His sense of Divine justice causes Jeremiah's astonishment at seeing the wicked prosper, and here for the first time in the OT is raised the problem of the good fortune of sinners and the sufferings of the just. The most striking feature of the Book is the New Covenant (31: 31–4) which God will make with His people and in which the Gentiles too will participate (16: 19–21).

JEREMIAH, Lamentations of. See *Lamentations of Jeremiah*.

JEREMY, Epistle of. A short item in the OT *Apocrypha. In it *Jeremiah declaims to the exiles in Babylon against the folly of idol-worship. It was prob. written in Greek, in the 2nd cent. B.C. In the *Vulgate and some English Bibles it appears as the conclusion of *Baruch (ch. 6).

JERICHO. A town in Palestine, north-east of *Jerusalem.

JEROME, St. (c. 342–420), Biblical scholar. Born near *Aquileia, he spent 4–5 years as a hermit in the Syrian desert, where he learnt Hebrew. Back in Rome from 382 to 385, he was secretary to Pope *Damasus and successfully preached asceticism. In 386 he settled at *Bethlehem.

Jerome's greatest achievement was his translation of most of the Bible into Latin (see *Vulgate*). He also wrote many Biblical commentaries. He advocated that the Church should accept the Hebrew *Canon of Scripture, excluding the Books which came to be called the *Apocrypha. He translated and continued *Eusebius's 'Chronicle', compiled a bibliography of ecclesiastical writers (*De Viris Illustribus*), and translated into Latin works by *Origen and *Didymus. His passionate nature led him into many controversies.

JEROME EMILIANI, St. (1481–1537), founder of the *Somaschi. Ordained priest in 1518, he devoted his life to work among the poor and afflicted, founding orphanages, hospitals, and houses for fallen women. In 1532 he founded a society to foster this work, with its mother house at Somasca.

JEROME OF PRAGUE (c. 1370–1416), Bohemian Reformer and friend of J. *Huss. He studied at *Oxford, whence he brought back writings of J. *Wycliffe. On his return to Prague in 1407 he took an active part in the religious controversies and became a leader of the nationalist university students. In 1415 he followed Huss to *Constance. Under pressure after Huss's death he read a document anathematizing the teaching of Wycliffe and Huss and accepting the authority of the Pope and Council. The sincerity of this recantation was suspect and his trial resumed in 1416. He took back his abjuration and was burnt at the stake.

JERUSALEM, the capital of Judah, the site

of its religious sanctuary (the *Temple), and as such the 'Holy City'. Archaeological evidence indicates that part of the site was inhabited as early as c. 3000 B.C. About 1000 B.C. the Jebusite stronghold known as 'Zion' was captured by *David, who made Jerusalem the capital of the United Monarchy. *Solomon built the Temple and enlarged the city. In 597 B.C. and again in 586 it was captured and devastated by Nebuchadnezzar, and all except the lower classes were deported. After the Exile Jerusalem was not rebuilt until the end of the 6th cent. B.C., with the building of the Second Temple. The Jews were then an ecclesiastically governed State under the suzerainty first of Persia and then of the Seleucids. The *Maccabaean wars of the 2nd cent. B.C. were followed by the revival of Jewish national glory under a short dynasty of priest-kings. After Pompey's conquest in 64 B.C. the country was ruled by Rome. The Jews rebelled in A.D. 66; Jerusalem was besieged, and when it fell in 70 the city was destroyed. It was refounded as a Gentile city under the name of *Aelia Capitolina by the Emp. Hadrian (A.D. 135).

The Christian history of the city begins with the short ministry of the Lord, culminating in His Crucifixion and Resurrection. The Apostles lived and taught in Jerusalem for some time after *Pentecost and met in Jerusalem for the first Christian Council (Acts 15; c. A.D. 49). It was not, however, until the visit of St. *Helena (c. A.D. 326) and the beginning of the fashion of venerating holy places that Jerusalem became important as a Christian centre. The see, previously suffragan to *Caesarea, was granted patriarchal dignity at the Council of *Chalcedon (451), but it never attained the prestige of the other patriarchates. The Christian centre of the city is the Church of the *Holy Sepulchre. The traditional sites of *Calvary and the Holy Sepulchre lie outside the walls of the town of *Herod the Great but are within the present Old City.

JERUSALEM, Anglican Bishopric in. In 1841 a bishopric was set up in *Jerusalem by the joint efforts of England and Prussia to serve Anglicans and Protestants in the Middle East. The bishop was to be nominated by England and Prussia alternately. The scheme collapsed in 1886; since then the see has been maintained by Anglicans alone.

JERUSALEM, Synod of (1672). A synod of the E. Church held in the Basilica of the Nativity at *Bethlehem (hence also known as the 'Synod of Bethlehem'). It sought to repudiate the movement fostered by Cyril *Lucar towards accommodation with *Calvinism and, along with the Synod of *Jassy (1642), marked the closest approximation of E. Orthodoxy to *Tridentine Catholicism.

JESSE WINDOW. A window whose design is based on the descent of Jesus from the royal line of *David, usually in the form of a tree springing from Jesse (David's father) and ending in Jesus or the Virgin and Child, with the intermediary descendants placed on scrolls of foliage branching out of each other.

JESU, DULCIS MEMORIA. The late 12th cent. poem familiar through translations of sections of it in the English hymns 'Jesu, the very thought of Thee' and 'Jesu! the very thought is sweet'. It has traditionally been ascribed to St. *Bernard of Clairvaux, but is prob. the work of an English *Cistercian. It is sometimes known as the 'Rosy Sequence'.

JESUITS. The Society of Jesus, founded by St. *Ignatius Loyola in 1534, was approved by *Paul III in 1540. Its aims were twofold: to foster reform within the Church, esp. in the face of problems posed by the *Reformation, and to undertake missionary work among the heathen, esp. in the recently discovered parts of the world. The constitution laid down that the services of the order should be at the disposal of the Pope. Members of the order wear no distinctive *habit and are exempt from any obligation to say the *Office in choir. Superiors hold office for limited periods. Supreme authority is vested in a General Congregation representative of members; for routine administration authority is concentrated in the *General, who is elected for life.

The Jesuits undertook a variety of tasks arising from the Reformation crisis, but their work soon came to consist mainly in teaching, conducting catechisms, and giving the '*Spiritual Exercises', as well as in administering the Sacraments. Ignatius himself established missions in *India, Malaya, Zaïre, *Brazil, *Japan, *Ethiopia, and *China. By the beginning of the 17th cent. the Society seemed secure both in Europe and in the mission field. In the later 17th cent., however, the Jesuits encountered serious opposition within the RC Church. They were attacked by the *Jansenists for their casuistry and came under fire on the question of *accommodation in the Chinese Rites controversy. A combination of their opponents brought about their expulsion from France in 1764; in 1759 they were banished from *Portugal and in 1767 5,000 Jesuits were deported from Spain and its Empire. In 1773 *Clement XIV suppressed the Society. The suppression did not mean that the Society was extinguished. In Austria and Germany Jesuits were allowed to teach, and they were protected by Frederick II of Prussia and the Emp. Catherine of Russia. They also survived in England. In 1814 the Society was formally restored by *Pius VII. They now operate in most non-Communist countries.

JESUS. The Greek form of the Hebrew Joshua. By Divine command the name was given to the Infant Christ.

JESUS CHRIST. Jesus was born before the death of *Herod the Great (4 B.C.), but prob. not more than three or four years earlier. His mother *Mary and her husband (St. *Joseph) were pious Jews. See also *Virgin Birth*.

Jesus began His public ministry after His *Baptism by *John the Baptist, which was followed by the *Temptation; the account of this expresses (perhaps in a generalized form) His initial and persistent choice of the way of self-abnegation and dependence on the Father's will. The main scene of His activity was *Galilee and the neighbouring districts of N. Palestine.

The central and unifying theme of Jesus's preaching was the imminent approach of the *Kingdom of God. By this phrase Jewish teachers had meant the visible manifestation of the sovereign power of God; in Jesus's teaching the kingdom 'comes', 'is given', 'received', or 'entered'; it is not a creation of human activity but an eruption of Divine judging and saving power. Sometimes He speaks of the coming of the Kingdom as in the future, when the present order of things will come to an end; sometimes it is implied that the Kingdom has already arrived or begun to arrive. It appears that He envisaged the arrival of the Kingdom as an extended series of events in which His own coming and teaching were the decisive beginning.

Linked with the message of the Kingdom is Jesus's teaching on the Fatherhood of God. God is Father, Judge, and King. Man may enter into sonship with God through faith in His providential power, through repentance and forgiveness, and through obedience to His commandments.

Jesus's mission was confined almost entirely to the Jewish people. He accepted Israel's privileged position. But his interpretation of the precepts of the Law was at once more free and more exacting than any known to Judaism: ceremonial observance was not rejected but placed in subordination to fundamental principles of charity, sincerity, and humility. The Jewish leaders detected in His teaching the assumption of an authority which was as Divine as that of the Mosaic Law itself. His pronouncement of the forgiveness of the sins of individuals and the implication that He spoke not merely as a prophet, but as *Messiah, presented the Jewish Establishment with an inescapable challenge.

Jesus selected an intimate band of twelve disciples (see *Apostles*) and to them alone He spoke explicitly of His claims and authority. On the night before the Crucifixion He interpreted His death to His disciples at the *Last Supper. He took bread and having blessed it gave it to them to eat, describing it as His body given for them; He took a cup of wine and, having similarly blessed it, gave it to them to drink, calling it the covenant of His blood. The people of Israel having decided to reject Him, Jesus founded a new people or Church, of whom the nucleus was to be the Twelve, to be the heirs of the blessings of the Kingdom.

The Jewish authorities, after a preliminary investigation, presented Jesus to the Roman governor, Pontius *Pilate, as worthy of death, and He suffered crucifixion as a claimant to Messianic dignity. For the date of His death the years A.D. 29, 30, or 33 have been suggested. On the third day (i.e. the next day but one) after the Crucifixion, the tomb in which the body of Jesus had been laid was found empty and, during a short period that followed, Jesus presented himself alive in a glorified but recognizable form to individual disciples and to groups of them. The disciples were convinced that God had raised Him from death. See also *Resurrection of Christ*.

The first Jewish disciples accepted Jesus as the promised Messiah, but it soon became clear that their ideas about Him would not fit into the traditional Messianic conceptions inherited from Judaism. The early Church saw that He was more than an inspired prophet and gradually it became clear that He was divine. For the development of the doctrine of His person, see *Christology*.

JESUS MOVEMENT (or **Jesus Revolution**). A popular term for the amorphous movement of relatively spontaneous groupings, normally fervent, evangelical, and *fundamentalist, which emerged in the 'hippie' culture of the late 1960s, beginning in California. The 'Jesus people', who combined a 'hippie' life-style with ethical rigorism and often with *millenarian expectations, widely distrusted organized Christianity; many adopted *pentecostal practices and teaching. The 'Children of God', a sect which emerged from the movement, has adherents in Europe as well as the U.S.A.

JESUS, Name of. See *Name of Jesus*.

JESUS PRAYER, The. The prayer 'Lord Jesus Christ, Son of God, have mercy upon me', which is widely used in the *Orthodox Church. It is first found in a work of the 6th–7th cent.

JESUS, Sayings of. See *Sayings of Jesus*.

JEU, Books of. Two *Gnostic treatises ascribed to *Enoch.

JEUNESSE OUVRIÈRE CHRÉTIENNE. See *Jocists*.

JEW, The Wandering. See *Wandering Jew, The*.

JEWEL, JOHN (1522–71), Bp. of *Salisbury from 1560. His celebrated defence of the C of E, the *Apologia Ecclesiae Anglicanae* (1562), argued that a general Reformation had been necessary, that reform by such a body as the Council of *Trent was impossible, and that local Churches had the right to legislate through provincial synods. Its publication was followed by bitter controversy.

JEWISH PEOPLE. See *Judaism*.

JEWS, Missions to the. Mutual hostility between Judaism and Christianity developed early and, despite some protests, persecution

rather than efforts to secure genuine conversion followed. The impulse to create missionary societies came in the 19th cent. from Christian Jews. Thus J. S. C. F. Frey (1771–1851) was responsible for the foundation in 1809 of the 'London Society for Promoting Christianity among the Jews', which was later known as '*Church Missions to Jews'. Various other similar societies were founded in the course of the 19th cent.

JIMÉNEZ DE CISNEROS, F. See *Ximénez de Cisneros, F.*

JOACHIM, St. The husband of St. *Anne and father of the BVM. He is first mentioned in the 'Book of *James' (2nd cent.).

JOACHIM OF FIORE (c. 1132–1202), or of 'Flora', mystic. He entered the *Cistercian Order and was elected Abbot of Corazzo in 1177. He soon resigned and founded a monastery of his own at Fiore in Calabria; it received papal sanction in 1196.

The central doctrine of his chief works is a Trinitarian conception of history, which is viewed in three great periods. The first, characterized by the 'Ordo conjugatorum', is the age of the Father in which mankind lived under the Law until the end of the OT dispensation; the second, characterized by the 'Ordo clericorum', is that of the Son which is lived under grace and covers the NT dispensation; the third, belonging to the 'Ordo monachorum' or 'contemplantium', is the age of the Spirit which will be lived in the liberty of the 'Spiritualis Intellectus' proceeding from the OT and the NT and will be inaugurated c. 1260. This last age would see the rise of new religious orders destined to convert the whole world and to usher in the 'Ecclesia Spiritualis'. His ideas had far-reaching influence.

JOAN, Pope. The legend that a woman, disguised as a man, was elected Pope c. 1100 and died after giving birth to a child, first appeared in the 13th cent. It is without foundation.

JOAN OF ARC, St. (1412–31), the 'Maid of Orleans'. The daughter of a peasant, in 1425 she experienced the first of the supernatural visitations, which she described as voices accompanied by a blaze of light. In 1429 she convinced the French king (Charles VII) of her mission to save France, led an expedition which relieved Orleans, and then persuaded Charles to proceed to *Reims for his coronation. She was taken prisoner in 1430, sold to the English, and charged with witchcraft and heresy. After trial by an ecclesiastical court, she was burnt. A revision of her trial in 1456 declared her innocent; she was canonized in 1920.

JOASAPH, St. See *Josaphat, St.*

JOB, Book of. The main subject of this OT Book is the problem of innocent suffering. Job rejects the traditional view that suffering is the result of sin, since he has no doubt of his own innocence. No final solution to the problem is offered, apart from emphasis on the omnipotence of God. A consensus of scholarly opinion dates the Book *c.* 400 B.C.

JOCISTS. The association of factory workers in the RC Church known as the **Jeunesse Ouvrière Chrétienne (J.O.C.)**. It seeks to bring Christian moral principles to bear in industry and to keep the young of the working class within the Church. It grew up after the 1914–18 war in Belgium and spread to France.

JOEL, Book of. *Minor Prophet. The first section of the Book (1: 1–2: 17) tells of a plague of locusts, and against this background depicts the approaching Day of the Lord with its call to repentance; the rest of the Book foretells the future outpouring of the Spirit on all flesh, the final salvation of Judah, and the destruction of foreign nations.

JOHANNINE COMMA (also known as the 'Three Witnesses'). An interpolation in the text of 1 Jn. 5: 7 f., viz. the words in italic in the following passage of the AV: 'For there are three that bear record *in heaven, the Father, the Word, and the Holy Ghost, and these Three are One. And there are three that bear witness in earth,* the Spirit, and the Water, and the Blood, and these three agree in one'. They are not part of the original Epistle and are omitted in scholarly modern translations.

JOHN, St., Apostle. Acc. to tradition, the author of the Fourth Gospel, of *Revelation, and of three of the *Catholic Epistles. Together with his brother St. *James and St. *Peter, he belonged to the inner group of dis-

ciples who were present at the raising of Jairus's daughter, the *Transfiguration, and the Agony in *Gethsemane. In Acts he is several times mentioned with St. Peter, and he was present at the Apostles' Council in *Jerusalem (Gal. 2: 9).

In the Fourth Gospel John is never mentioned by name, but tradition identifies him with the disciple 'whom Jesus loved', who reclined on His bosom at the Last Supper, to whom He entrusted His Mother at the foot of the Cross, who ran with Peter to the tomb on the morning of the Resurrection, and who recognized the Lord at the Sea of Tiberias. The identification has been contested in modern times. It is defended on the ground that the consistent omission in the Fourth Gospel of so important a disciple is inexplicable except on the assumption that he is referred to under some other designation.

Acc. to tradition St. John settled at *Ephesus, was exiled to *Patmos, where he wrote Rev., and returned to Ephesus and here wrote the Gospel and Epistles in old age. See also the following entries.

JOHN, Acts of. A Greek apocryphal treatise describing events in the life of the Apostle St. *John. A fragment, discovered in 1886, contains an account of Christ's passion in *Docetic language, and a hymn known in modern times as the 'Hymn of Jesus'.

JOHN, Epistles of. Three NT Epistles which tradition ascribes to St. *John, the Apostle and author of the Fourth Gospel. Modern scholars who defend the authorship of the Gospel commonly also admit that of the First Epistle; among those who reject the Apostolic origin of the Gospel, opinion is divided. The Second and Third Epistles were not generally admitted as authentic in antiquity, and many modern critics assign them to a different author from that of the First Epistle.

The First Epistle, which is the longest, opposes false doctrines on the Person of Christ. The Second insists on the necessity of professing right doctrine and avoiding communion with the teachers of error, and the Third on hospitality.

JOHN, Gospel of St. The Fourth Gospel, which in both content and outlook differs from the three preceding 'Synoptics', raises a series of problems generally known as the 'Johannine Question'. Acc. to tradition going back to the second half of the 2nd cent., it was written by St. *John the Apostle. The Apostolic origin of the Book, however, is contested by a large body of modern scholars whose positions vary from a complete rejection both of its authenticity and its historicity to the admission of Apostolic inspiration and some historical value. The unity of the Book is also disputed. Where unity is admitted its attribution to 'John the Presbyter' (perhaps a different John from the Apostle, mentioned by *Papias; see art. *John the Presbyter*) is favoured. Conservative scholars, however, claim that the Apostolic authorship is supported not only by tradition but also by internal evidence, such as the author's claim to have been an eye-witness (1: 14).

The Fourth Gospel differs from the Synoptics in shifting the Lord's activities from *Galilee to *Jerusalem and extending His ministry from one year to three. It also gives a different date for the Last Supper and Crucifixion (13 and 15 Nisan rather than 14 and 15). Its whole tenor is also different. The Lord's teaching is given not in parables and pithy sayings but in long discourses; His Divinity is emphasized; and important events such as the institution of the Eucharist are not described. These differences have been explained on the ground that the author presupposed knowledge of the Synoptics in his readers and that his concern was not with the popular teaching of Christ but with the higher doctrines reserved for His disciples.

The principal purpose of the Gospel is to strengthen the reader's faith in Jesus as the Christ and the Son of God (20: 31). Its main theme is the progressive manifestation of the Divine Word, the Light in the darkness. At first the Light is received by men with joy, then men take sides for and against the Lord. In chs. 13–17 He is surrounded by a small group of followers to whom He reveals the secret of His Person. In chs. 18–19 the powers of darkness seem to conquer, but the concluding chs. (20–1) show the final triumph of the Risen Christ. The whole Gospel teaches a high *Christological doctrine. It is not a simple account of the Lord's miracles and popular teaching, but a deeply meditated representation of His Person and doctrine by a contemplative conscious of inspiration by the Holy Spirit.

JOHN XII (d. 964), Pope from 955. The son of the ruler of Rome, he became Pope when he was 18. His addiction to pleasure and vice caused grave scandal. He invited Otto I of Germany to help him against the rulers of N. Italy and in 962 he crowned Otto Emperor. In exchange Otto granted the 'Privilegium Ottonis', by which the Carolingian donations were enlarged but which also confirmed the rights of the Emperor in papal elections. John regretted his action and turned to Berengar II, Otto's enemy. In 963 Otto held a synod in Rome which deposed John and elected a successor; in 964 John returned to Rome and cancelled the actions of the synod. He died while Otto was on his way back.

JOHN XXII (1249–1334), Pope from 1316. He resided at *Avignon. He became involved in the difficulties threatening to split the *Franciscan Order; in 1317 he dissolved the party of the *Spirituals, whose doctrines he denounced as heretical. Soon afterwards he condemned the thesis that the poverty of Christ and the Apostles was absolute, and several of the Franciscans fled to Louis of Bavaria, who supported them. In 1324 the Pope declared Louis a heretic, and a violent literary feud ensued. Louis seized Rome and in 1328 established an antipope, who submitted, however, in 1330. John was also involved in a dispute over the *Beatific Vision, which he denied could be enjoyed by the souls of the blessed before the Last Judgement. The authorship of the '*Anima Christi' has sometimes been assigned to him.

JOHN XXIII (d. 1419), *Antipope to *Benedict XIII and Gregory XII from 1410 to 1415. He was crowned Pope in 1410, but the validity of his election has been contested as being simoniacal. Of the three Popes then existing he had most supporters. In 1413 he convoked a General Council to end the W. schism; it met at *Constance. He soon fled from Constance to deprive the Council of authority. He was brought back by force and deposed in 1415.

JOHN XXIII (1881–1963), Pope from 1958. Angelo Giuseppe Roncalli was born of humble parents. He became titular Abp. of Areopolis and Vicar Apostolic in Bulgaria in 1925. In 1934 he was appointed Apostolic Delegate in Turkey and Greece, and in 1944 he was sent as Papal Nuncio to Paris, where the leaders of the French Resistance Movement were accusing many of the French bishops of having collaborated with the German army of occupation. He was made a *cardinal in 1953 and later in the year Patriarch of Venice.

As Pope one of his first actions was to increase the number of cardinals dramatically. In 1959 he proposed to the cardinals three undertakings: a diocesan synod for Rome, an oecumenical council for the Church, and a revision of canon law. The synod was held in 1960 and dealt with local problems. The Second *Vatican Council (q.v.) was the most important event in his pontificate. He attributed the idea of convening it to the Holy Spirit, and he gave to the Council the task of renewing the religious life of the Church. He opened and closed the first session, once intervening to encourage those in favour of change. During his pontificate the Secretariat for Promoting Christian Unity was established in 1960, the RC Church was for the first time represented at an assembly of the *World Council of Churches (1961), and non-RC observers were invited to the Vatican Council.

JOHN (1167–1216), King of England from 1199. He lost most of his possessions in France. On the death of Abp. *Hubert in 1205, he became involved in a quarrel with the chapter of *Canterbury. When *Innocent III appointed Stephen *Langton archbishop (1207), John refused to recognize him; in 1208 England was placed under an *interdict, and in 1209 John was excommunicated. Unsure of his barons, threatened with deposition by the Pope and invasion from France, John submitted in 1213, placing England and Ireland under the suzerainty of the Papacy. In 1215 the barons obtained the grant of Magna Carta.

JOHN OF ANTIOCH (d. 441), Bp. of *Antioch from 429 and leader of the moderate Easterns in the *Nestorian controversy. When *Cyril of Alexandria, not waiting for John, condemned Nestorius at the Council of *Ephesus (431), John held a counter-council which condemned Cyril and vindicated Nestorius. In 433 he was reconciled with Cyril.

JOHN OF APAMEA (*fl.* early 6th cent.), Syriac spiritual writer, also known as 'John the Solitary'. His writings include a 'Dialogue on the Soul'.

JOHN OF ÁVILA, St. (1500–69), Spanish mystic. He sold his property and in 1527 prepared for missionary work in Mexico. In 1528 he was persuaded to divert his efforts to reviving the faith in Andalusia, where he preached for nine years before returning to Seville. He was a highly effective preacher and the trusted counsellor of St. *Teresa of Ávila. His writings include a treatise on Christian perfection (*Audi Filia*).

JOHN THE BAPTIST, St., the 'Forerunner of Christ'. He was the son of *Zachariah and *Elizabeth, and his birth was foretold by an angel (Lk. 1: 13–20). He appeared *c.* A.D. 27 on the banks of the *Jordan, demanding repentance and baptism from his hearers. Christ Himself was among those baptized by him. John's denunciation of *Herod Antipas for his marriage led to his imprisonment and death (Mt. 14: 1–12). His continued influence is attested in Acts (18: 25), and outside the NT he is mentioned by *Josephus. The early importance of his cult is testified by his place in the traditional *Canon of the Mass.

JOHN BAPTIST DE LA SALLE, St. (1651–1719), founder of the Institute of the Brothers of Christian Schools. A canon of *Reims from 1667, he was ordained in 1678 and in 1679 assisted in the opening of two free schools in Reims. He soon became interested in fostering religious principles in the teachers, a group of whom lived in his house. In 1683 he resigned his canonry and devoted himself to training his community. Schools were opened in various places and in 1693 he drew up the first rule. He was also a pioneer in educational practice.

JOHN BAPTIST MARY VIANNEY, St. See *Curé d'Ars, The.*

JOHN OF BEVERLEY, St. (d. 721), Bp. of *York. A monk of Whitby, he was consecrated Bp. of *Hexham *c.* 687. In 705 he was translated to York, then being claimed by *Wilfrid. Before his death he retired to the abbey which he had founded at *Beverley. A cultus developed in England.

JOHN BOSCO; JOHN CAPISTRAN; JOHN CAPREOLUS; JOHN CHRYSOSTOM. See *Bosco, St. John*; *Giovanni Capistrano*; *Capreolus, J.*; and *Chrysostom, St. John.*

JOHN CLIMACUS, St. (*c.* 570–649), ascetic and spiritual writer. He was a monk and later Abbot of *Sinai. His 'Ladder of Paradise' treats of monastic virtues and vices and the nature of complete dispassionateness, which is upheld as the ideal of Christian perfection.

JOHN OF THE CROSS, St. (1542–91), Spanish mystic, '*Doctor of the Church', and joint founder of the Discalced *Carmelites. He became a Carmelite in 1563. He was dissatisfied with the prevalent laxity of the order and with St. *Teresa's aid he brought her Reform to include friars. After the anti-Reformist General Chapter of the Calced Carmelites (i.e. of the Mitigated Observance) in 1575, he was seized and imprisoned in 1577. He escaped after nine months, and the separation of the Calced and Discalced Carmelites was effected in 1579–80. John became Prior of Granada in 1582 and of Segovia in 1588. He incurred the hostility of the Vicar General of the Discalced Carmelites, was banished to Andalusia in 1591, and died after a severe illness.

His extensive treatises on the mystical life consist of commentaries on his own poems, the *Spiritual Canticle*, the *Ascent of Mount Carmel*, and the *Living Flame of Love*. His commentaries on the first two deal with the purgation of the soul by the 'night of the senses', when, becoming detached from all sensible devotion, the soul maintains itself in pure faith. This is followed, usually after a period of rest, by a second purgation, the 'night of the spirit', when the soul is further spiritualized by the Divine action, normally accompanied by intense suffering, to fit it for the transforming union described in the *Living Flame* and its commentary. The works of St. Teresa and of St. John of the Cross on the progress of the soul are regarded as possessing a unique authority.

JOHN OF DAMASCUS, St. (*c.* 675–*c.* 749), Greek theologian. Born of a rich Christian family in *Damascus, he succeeded his father as the chief representative of the Christians to the Caliph. He was compelled for his faith to abandon this office *c.* 716 and withdrew to a monastery near *Jerusalem. He was a strong defender of *Images in the *Iconoclastic Controversy, writing three discourses on the subject.

His most important work, the *Fount of Wisdom*, is divided into three parts dealing with philosophy, heresies, and the Orthodox faith ('De Fide Orthodoxa'). This last is a comprehensive presentation of the teaching of the Greek Fathers on the main Christian doctrines, esp. on the Trinity, Creation, and the Incarnation. His other great work, the *Sacra Parallela*, preserved only in fragments, is a vast compilation of Scriptural and Patristic texts on the Christian moral and ascetical life. He also wrote a commentary on the Pauline Epistles, homilies, and poems; some of these have found their way into modern English hymn-books, e.g. 'Come, ye faithful, raise the strain'. The 'Life of *Barlaam and Joasaph' (q.v.) is apparently also his work. He exercised great influence on later theology.

JOHN OF EPHESUS (*c.* 507–86), *Monophysite historian. In 542 he was sent to convert the pagans in the region of *Ephesus, of which he was consecrated bishop by *Jacob Baradaeus. His *Ecclesiastical History*, of which only the third part survives complete, covers the period 571–85.

JOHN EUDES, St. See *Eudes, St. John*.

JOHN THE FASTER, St. (d. 595), John IV, Patriarch of *Constantinople from 582. In 588 he assumed the challenging title of 'Oecumenical Patriarch'; despite protests from Popes Pelagius II and *Gregory I, John bequeathed the title to his successors. The manual for confessors attributed to him is not earlier than the 9th cent.

JOHN FISHER, St. See *Fisher, St. John*.

JOHN OF GOD, St. (1495–1550), founder of the 'Order of Charity for the Service of the Sick' or '*Brothers Hospitallers'. After serving as a soldier, in middle age he changed his mode of life and sought to spread the faith by hawking tracts and pamphlets in Spain. In 1538 he was converted to a life of great sanctity by St. *John of Ávila, who directed his energies to the care of the sick.

JOHN GUALBERT, St. (*c.* 990–1073), founder of the *Vallumbrosan Order. He entered a *Benedictine monastery near Florence, left this for *Camaldoli, and eventually settled at the place later known as Vallombrosa. Here he collected a body of monks who lived under a modified form of the *Benedictine Rule, austere in its demands and adapted to the conditions of a semi-hermit life.

JOHN, KING OF ENGLAND. See after *John XXIII, Pope*.

JOHN LATERAN, Church of St. See *Lateran Basilica*.

JOHN MALALAS (later 6th cent.), i.e. 'John Rhetor' or 'Scholasticus', Byzantine historian. He is prob. to be identified with *John Scholasticus (d. 577, q.v.). His *Chronicle*, mainly from a *Monophysite standpoint, extended to 574, but survives only to 563.

JOHN MARK, St. See *Mark, St.*

JOHN OF MATHA, St. (d. 1213), founder of the *Trinitarian Order. He was a native of Provence, founded his order for the redemption of captives, and died at Rome.

JOHN MOSCHUS. See *Moschus, John*.

JOHN OF NEPOMUK, St. (*c.* 1340–93), Bohemian martyr. As vicar-general of the archdiocese of Prague, he resisted the attempts of King Wenceslas IV to suppress an abbey. By the king's order he was drowned in the Moldau, but his recovered body became the centre of a cult.

JOHN OF PARMA, Bl. (1209–89), *Franciscan. Elected Minister General in 1247, he tried to restore the original asceticism and discipline of the order. His austerity and his leanings towards the teaching of *Joachim of Fiore made him enemies, and he was accused of heresy at Rome. He resigned his office in 1257. On the examination of his doctrine he narrowly escaped condemnation; he retired to the hermitage of Greccio.

JOHN AND PAUL, Sts. Two Roman martyrs of the 4th cent. of whom virtually nothing is known. Their names figure in the traditional *Canon of the Roman Mass.

JOHN PECKHAM. See *Peckham, John*.

JOHN XII, XXII, XXIII, Popes. See after *John, Gospel of St.*

JOHN THE PRESBYTER. The term 'the presbyter' or 'elder' is applied to himself by the author of 2 and 3 Jn., and *Papias refers to a 'John the Presbyter'. Some scholars think that Papias's evidence suggests the existence at *Ephesus of a second John besides St. *John the Apostle. Of those who hold this view some attribute to the Presbyter the Fourth Gospel and the Johannine Epistles; others 2 and 3 Jn. and possibly Rev. The traditional view that 'the presbyter' was a local designation at Ephesus for the Apostle still has supporters.

JOHN OF RAGUSA (d. *c.* 1443), *Dominican theologian. John Stojković was a native of Ragusa (Dubrovnik in Yugoslavia) who became a Dominican at an early age. In 1431 *Martin V sent him to the Council of *Basle as Papal theologian, and in 1435 and 1437 he acted as legate to the Council of Constantinople in order to gain the Greeks for union with Rome. In Constantinople he assembled an important collection of Greek MSS., which he bequeathed to the Dominican house at Basle.

JOHN OF RUYSBROECK. See *Ruysbroeck, Jan van*.

JOHN OF ST. THOMAS (1589–1644), Spanish *Dominican theologian, so named because of his devotion to St. *Thomas Aquinas. As against the modified Thomism of F. de *Suarez and G. *Vázquez, John's system claimed to follow exactly the principles of Aquinas in that it paid heed not only to his conclusions, but also to the arguments by which he reached them.

JOHN OF SALISBURY (*c.* 1115–80), humanist. He was attached to the household of *Theobald, Abp. of *Canterbury, and on his death entered the service of his successor, Thomas *Becket. In 1176 he became Bp. of *Chartres.

His chief writings are the *Policraticus*, a survey of courtly life with a discussion of political problems, and the *Metalogicon*, a defence of the study of grammar, rhetoric, and logic. His *Historia Pontificalis*, covering the years 1148–51, deals chiefly with the affairs of the Papal court. His letters are an important source for the history of the contest between Becket and Henry II.

JOHN SCHOLASTICUS (d. 577), John III, Patr. of *Constantinople from 565. His collection of canons ('Synagoge') is one of the primary sources for E. canon law. He is probably to be identified with *John Malalas (q.v.).

JOHN THE SCOT. See *Erigena.*

JOHN OF WESEL (John Rucherat or **Ruchrat)** (*c.* 1400–81), ecclesiastical reformer. He became cathedral preacher at Worms in 1463. Charged with preaching *Hussite doctrines on the Church and Sacraments, he was deposed from his office in 1477 and tried before the *Inquisition in 1479. After recanting he was imprisoned for life. His writings include a 'Commentary on the Sentences', a treatise against *Indulgences, and a work on the *Immaculate Conception.

JOHNSON, SAMUEL (1709–84), author and lexicographer. He was a strong *High Churchman, whose religious beliefs and practices were of a standard rare in the 18th-cent. C of E. He wrote a number of works besides his *Dictionary of the English Language* (1755).

The American hymn-writer Samuel Johnson (1822–82) is not to be confused with the lexicographer.

JOINVILLE, JEAN DE (*c.* 1224–1319), French historian. Seneschal of Champagne from 1233, Joinville accompanied *Louis IX to Egypt and Palestine on the Sixth *Crusade in 1248 and with him was taken prisoner. He was one of the witnesses for Louis's canonization and he wrote a famous life of the king.

JONAH, Book of. *Minor Prophet. The Book relates the Divine call to Jonah to go to Nineveh and preach repentance, his attempt to escape by sea, his being thrown overboard and swallowed by a fish, his deliverance after three days, and the success of his mission. The psalm in ch. 2 is generally held to be independent of the rest of the Book, which is assigned by critics to the post-Exilic period. The 'sign of Jonah' (Mt. 12: 39 &c.) is interpreted as a prophecy of Christ's resurrection.

JONAS, JUSTUS (1493–1555), originally 'Jodocus Koch', German Reformer. As rector of Erfurt University, he introduced Greek and Hebrew into the curriculum. In 1521 he accompanied M. *Luther to Worms and subsequently took a leading part in the Protestant cause. He translated the German works of Luther and P. *Melanchthon into Latin and the Latin works into German.

JONES, GRIFFITH (1683–1761), founder of the Welsh circulating schools. He was rector of Llanddowror from 1716. In 1730 he began to found his 'circulating schools' for adults and children, with travelling teachers who instructed their pupils in reading the Welsh Bible.

JONES, INIGO (1573–1652), English architect. He held royal appointments under *James I and *Charles I and served on a commission for the restoration of old *St. Paul's. His best-known ecclesiastical works are Lincoln's Inn chapel and St. Paul's, Covent Garden.

JONES, RUFUS MATTHEW (1863–1948), American *Quaker. His many works include *Studies in Mystical Religion* (1909).

JONES, WILLIAM, 'of Nayland' (1726–1800), Anglican divine. He became Rector of Pluckley, Kent, in 1765 and in 1777 perpetual curate of Nayland, Suffolk, whence his traditional epithet. He tried to keep alive the High Church traditions of the *Nonjurors. In *The Catholic Doctrine of the Trinity* (1756) he sought to prove from Scriptural texts that the Trinitarian dogma is contained in the Bible.

JORDAN, River. Formed from the waters of four streams which converge, the Jordan flows through the 'Sea of Galilee' and eventually enters the *Dead Sea. By their passage of the Jordan the Hebrews first entered the Promised Land (Jos. 3: 16); *John the Baptist preached on its banks, and Christ was among those baptized in its waters (Mt. 3: 13). The Jordan became an emblem of the achievement of purity (esp. in baptism) and of the last hindrance to man's final blessedness.

JOSAPHAT, St., also 'Joasaph'. In medieval legend, the son of an Indian king converted to Christianity by Barlaam. See *Barlaam and Joasaph, Sts.*

JOSAPHAT, St. (1580/84–1623). John Kunsevich was Abp. of Polotsk from 1618 and a supporter of the Union of *Brest-Litovsk. In 1867 he was the first saint of the

E. Church to be formally canonized in the RC Church.

JOSEPH, St., husband of the BVM. Both Mt. and Lk. state that Mary was 'betrothed' to him at the time of the Lord's birth, but both emphasize her virginity. He was a pious Jew of Davidic descent and, acc. to Mt. 13: 55, a carpenter. Christ grew up in his household at Nazareth for at least twelve years (Lk. 2: 42 and 51). Acc. to the 'Book of *James' he is said to have been old at the time of his marriage to Mary, and as a pattern of holiness he is the subject of various legends. The veneration of him originated in the E. and developed comparatively late in the W. Church. In the RC Church he is now commemorated in the Feast of St. Joseph the Worker on 1 May.

JOSEPH OF ARIMATHAEA, St. The 'counsellor' who after the Crucifixion requested from *Pilate the body of Christ and gave it burial. The story that he came to England with the Holy Grail and built the first church in the country at *Glastonbury is not found before the 13th cent.

JOSEPH CALASANCTIUS, St. (1556–1648), founder of the *Piarists. Of aristocratic Spanish family, he was ordained priest in 1583. In 1592 he went to Rome. Here he interested himself especially in the education of homeless and neglected children, and under his influence the first free school was opened in 1597. To give permanence to his work he established the Piarist Order (q.v.).

JOSEPH OF CUPERTINO, St. (1603–63), *Franciscan. The son of a poor carpenter, he found employment as a stableboy at the Franciscan convent of La Grotella, near Cupertino. He became a choir religious in 1625 and was ordained priest in 1628. His subsequent life is said to have been a series of miracles and ecstasies.

JOSEPH THE HYMNOGRAPHER, St. (c. 810–86), Greek hymn-writer. He left *Constantinople for Rome during the *Iconoclastic Controversy, but was captured by pirates and spent some years in slavery. He eventually escaped and established a monastery at Constantinople. He is said to have composed 1,000 *canons.

JOSEPH OF VOLOKOLAMSK, St. (1439/40–1515), Russian monastic reformer. After some years of monastic life, he instituted a strict reform and founded the monastery of Volokolamsk, nr. Moscow. Unike *Nil Sorsky, he welcomed gifts, and he created a large community with a rigorous life of obedience, work, and lengthy liturgical services.

JOSEPHINISM. The principles which actuated the ecclesiastical reforms of Joseph II, Holy Roman Emperor from 1765 to 1790. They included religious toleration, the right of the State to regulate ecclesiastical affairs, and the restriction of the powers of the Papacy within spiritual limits, as laid down by *Febronius. They found expression in the Toleration Edict of 1781.

JOSEPHUS, FLAVIUS (c. 37–c. 100), Jewish historian. He was a native of Palestine and a *Pharisee. In 66 he took a leading part in the Jewish War. After being taken prisoner, he won Vespasian's favour by prophesying that he would become emperor, and during the siege of *Jerusalem he acted as interpreter to Titus. He returned with Titus to Rome, received Roman citizenship and a pension, and devoted himself to literary work. His *Jewish War* opens with a summary of events from the time of *Antiochus Epiphanes to the outbreak of the war; the latter part is largely an eye-witness account. His *Antiquities of the Jews* traces the history of the Jews from the Creation to the beginning of the Jewish War. The reference to Christ (XVIII.iii.3) in its present form is prob. an early Christian interpolation.

JOSHUA, Book of. This OT Book traces the history of the Israelites from the death of *Moses to that of his successor, Joshua, and gives an account of the entry into and conquest of Palestine, its partition among the twelve tribes, and Joshua's last speeches. Though some of its sources may go back to the 9th cent. B.C. or earlier, the Book prob. did not reach its present form until the 6th cent. or later.

JOVIAN (c. 332–64), Roman Emperor from June 363 to Feb. 364. After the death of the Emp. *Julian, Jovian was chosen Emperor by the troops and forced to conclude a humiliating peace with Persia. In theological disputes he supported orthodoxy and received *Athanasius.

JOVINIAN (d. c. 405), an unorthodox monk condemned by synods at Rome and Milan. He denied that virginity as such was a higher state than marriage and that abstinence was better than thankful eating.

JOWETT, BENJAMIN (1817–93), Master of Balliol College, Oxford, from 1870. He was a keen liberal in theology. His essay on 'The Interpretation of Scripture' in *Essays and Reviews* (1860) was one of the most debated items in the volume; his orthodoxy was henceforth gravely suspect and he ceased to write on theological subjects. His most important work was his translation of *Plato (1871).

JOYFUL MYSTERIES, The Five. The first chaplet of the *Rosary (q.v.), consisting of (1) the *Annunciation, (2) the *Visitation, (3) the Nativity of Christ, (4) the *Presentation of Christ in the Temple, and (5) the Finding of the Child Jesus in the Temple.

JUBE. The rood loft dividing the nave of a church from the choir.

JUBILATE (Lat., 'O be joyful'). The first word of Ps. 100, to which it gives its name. At Morning Prayer it is provided as an alternative to the *Benedictus in the BCP and to the *Venite in the *Alternative Services, Series II Revised and Series III.

JUBILEE, Year of. (1) Acc. to the Jewish law (Lev. 25) a year occurring every 50 years, when Jewish slaves regained their freedom and land reverted to its former owners. (2) In the RC Church a '*Holy Year' (q.v.).

JUBILEES, Book of. An apocryphal Jewish work, also called 'The Little Genesis'. It reinterprets the contents of Gen. 1–Exod. 12 and purports to have been delivered by God to *Moses on Mt. *Sinai. Its aim appears to be to show that the Law, with its prescriptions about fasts, the Sabbath, &c., dates from patriarchal times. The most probable date for its composition is c. 140–100 B.C.

JUDAEA. The region reoccupied by the Jews in 537 B.C. after the *Babylonian Captivity. In Christ's time it usually designated the southern part of Palestine.

JUDAH, Tribe of. The most powerful of the twelve tribes of Israel. After the reign of *Solomon, Judah with Benjamin formed a separate kingdom.

JUDAISM. The faith and practice of the Jewish people. The word 'Jew' and 'Judaism' are ultimately derived from the name of *Judah, the Southern Kingdom in Palestine which came to an end with the Babylonian Exile (586 B.C.). The changed circumstances of the Exile were the historical background of the rise of Judaism, though in a wider sense it may be said to go back to the Patriarchs and their election centuries earlier. See also Israel.

The Jewish community in general may be characterized: (a) geographically, by their concentration in the Near East, Europe, and esp. since the 19th cent. in America; (b) statistically, by an expansion into several millions at the beginning of the Christian era, a reduction to c. 1 million by the end of the Middle Ages, and an increase to c 13 millions in 1970; (c) linguistically, by the constantly revived use of *Hebrew and *Aramaic in addition to modern languages; (d) juridically, by the Ten *Commandments, the division into revealed and rational laws, traditional methods of interpretation, and the development of large law-codes; (e) theologically, by *Monotheism, belief in a central revelation, the Covenant and election of Israel, and future Messianism; (f) socially, by groups and schism. Besides the *Samaritan schism the chief early groupings were the *Sadducees, *Pharisees, *Essenes, and *Karaites. (g) Liturgically Judaism is characterized by emphasis on the *Sabbath and by the close association of religious and national elements in festivals. Jewish influences on Christian worship include the use of Scripture readings in worship and the obvious festival correspondences Sabbath/Sunday; Passover/Easter, &c.

The history of the Jews falls into three (overlapping) periods: (a) The Oriental (down to the 12th cent. A.D.). This includes the migration of the Hebrews and the Patriarchs (2nd millennium B.C.), the *Exodus from Egypt and the conquest of Canaan, the Babylonian Exile (586–538) and the Persian support for the restored community in Judaea (ending in 332 B.C.); the conquest by Alexander the Great, the rise of the *Hasmonaean and *Herodian kingdoms, dependence upon Rome, and the Roman destruction of the *Temple and *Jerusalem (A.D. 70); the rise of the academy at *Jamnia and the Palestinian patriarchate and the growing independence of the Jews of the *Diaspora. (b) The European period (139 B.C.–A.D. 1492) was marked by the rise of new centres of Jewish life in Spain, France, and Germany, and emigration towards Eastern Europe. (c) The landmarks of the Universal period (1492 onwards) are the death of Uriel da Costa (1640), the French Revolution (1789), the age of emancipation extending to the 'minority clauses' of the Treaty of Versailles (1919), the extermination of 6 million Jews by the Nazis (1935–45), and the establishment of the State of Israel (1948). The period is marked by gradual secularization and participation in European and American life and letters, as well as by the growth of political Zionism.

JUDAIZERS. In the early Church a section of Jewish Christians who regarded the OT Levitical laws as still binding on all Christians.

JUDAS ISCARIOT. The Apostle who betrayed Christ to the Jewish authorities. He later committed suicide.

JUDAS MACCABAEUS (d. 161 B.C.), leader of the Jews in the revolt against the Syrians. He won a series of victories in 166–164 and in 163 gained full religious liberty from *Antiochus IV, Epiphanes. He negotiated with Rome for help against the Syrians, but before the results of his mission were known he was killed in battle.

JUDE, St., *Apostle. He is generally identified, at least in the W., with the author of the NT Epistle of *Jude. The apocryphal 'Passion of *Simon and Jude' describes the preaching and martyrdom of the two Apostles in Persia, and in the W. Church they are commemorated together. In the RC Church St. Jude is much invoked in cases of special difficulty.

JUDE, Epistle of. One of the *Catholic Epistles of the NT. It purports to have been written by 'Jude … brother of James', who is commonly identified with the Apostle *Jude. The aim of the Epistle is to combat the spread of dangerous doctrine. Its composi-

tion is usually assigned to the close of the Apostolic Age.

JUDGES, Book of. This OT Book traces the history of the Israelites from Joshua's death to the beginning of the monarchy, describing incidents connected with the conquest of Palestine, and woven round the names of several leaders ('judges') who ruled the country before the time of Saul. Though it professes to be a sequel to the Book of *Joshua, it covers the same material, prob. giving a more accurate picture.

JUDGEMENT, General (Particular). See *General (Particular) Judgement*.

JUDICIAL COMMITTEE OF THE PRIVY COUNCIL. A Court of Appeal constituted by an Act of 1833 to regularize the extensive ecclesiastical jurisdiction of the King in Council. Under the *Ecclesiastical Jurisdiction Measure (1963) it ceased to have any jurisdiction in cases of discipline.

JUDITH, Book of. This Book of the *Apocrypha relates how, when Nebuchadnezzar sent his general Holofernes to punish the Jews, Judith made her way to the camp of Holofernes, captivated him by her charms, and then cut off his head. The head was publicly displayed, the Israelites encouraged to advance, and the Assyrians fled in panic. The Book is wholly unhistorical and prob. dates from the *Maccabean period.

JUDSON, ADONIRAM (1788–1850), American missionary in Burma. He came to England to confer with the *L.M.S., and was ordained a *Congregationalist minister in 1812. On reaching Serampore he became a *Baptist and was then refused permission to continue working in the territories of the East India Company. In 1813 he went to Rangoon, where he began to translate the Bible into Burmese. He met with success working among the Karens.

JULIAN THE APOSTATE (332–63), 'Flavius Claudius Julianus', Roman Emperor from 361. A nephew of *Constantine, he was won to *Neoplatonism and initiated into the Eleusinian mysteries. In 355 he was presented to the army as Caesar and in 360 proclaimed Emperor by the troops. After the Emp. Constantius II's death (361), Julian embarked on ambitious reforms. His policy with regard to the Church was to degrade Christianity and promote paganism by every means short of open persecution. His strict discipline and anti-Christian policy were unpopular; he was struck by an arrow and died. He was an extensive writer. Most of his treatise *Adversus Christianos* can be recovered from *Cyril of Alexandria's refutation.

JULIAN (*c.* 386–454), Bp. of Eclanum in Apulia from *c.* 416. When he refused to sign *Zosimus's condemnation of *Pelagianism in 417, he was deprived of his see and banished. Considerable portions of his *Ad Turbantium* and *Ad Florum* are preserved in St. *Augustine's replies; they are a powerful indictment of Augustine's doctrine of the total depravity of man. Some exegetical works have also been attributed to Julian.

JULIAN (d. after 518), Bp. of Halicarnassus. He was a *Monophysite who, on being deposed from his see *c.* 518, took refuge in *Alexandria, where he became the leader of the party known to their opponents as '*Aphthartodocetae'.

JULIAN OF NORWICH (*c.* 1342–after 1413), English mystic. Little is known of her life except that she prob. lived as an *anchoress, outside the walls of St. Julian's church, *Norwich. She received a series of visions on 8 May 1373 and the following day. Her book, *The Sixteen Revelations of Divine Love*, was written 20 years later. In Divine Love lies the clue to all the problems of existence, particularly that of evil, which, lacking the Divine reality, is but an aberration of the human will that serves to reveal more clearly the merciful love of God.

JULIANA OF LIÈGE, St. (1192–1258), champion of the Feast of *Corpus Christi. Professed in an *Augustinian convent near Liège, she experienced visions and tried to bring about the establishment of a feast of Corpus Christi. In 1230 she became Superior, but was soon forced to leave the convent and took refuge in Liège. Here she secured the interest of James Pantaléon, then Archdeacon of Liège, who after her death as Pope Urban IV instituted the feast (in 1264).

JULIUS I, St. (d. 352), Pope from 337. In the *Arian struggle he was a strong supporter

of orthodoxy, sheltering *Marcellus of Ancyra and *Athanasius. In 342–3 he convoked the Council of *Sardica, which consolidated the W. against Arianism and pronounced Athanasius the rightful occupant of his see.

JULIUS II (1443–1513), Pope from 1503. The main achievement of his pontificate was the restoration and enlargement of the temporal power of the papacy. He conducted various campaigns in Italy, defeating *Venice with the aid of France. In 1511 he founded the Holy League against France. Louis XII called a Council at Pisa to depose the Pope; the Pope called the Fifth *Lateran Council and won the Emp. Maximilian to his side.

Julius II was a patron of Renaissance art. His *indulgence for the rebuilding of *St. Peter's was later the occasion of M. *Luther's 95 theses.

JULIUS III (1487–1555), Pope from 1550. In 1545 he opened the Council of *Trent as its first president and papal legate and played a part in its transference to Bologna in 1547. As Pope in 1551 he commanded the Council to resume its sessions, but had to suspend it the following year. He did much for the *Jesuit Order.

JULIUS   AFRICANUS,   SEXTUS (*c.* 160–*c.* 240), Christian writer. He was prob. a native of *Jerusalem and lived for some years at *Emmaus. He went on an embassy to Rome and enjoyed close relations with the royal house of *Edessa. His chief work was a 'History of the World' to A.D. 217, of which fragments are preserved in other writers. He held that the world would last for 6000 years from the Creation and that the Birth of Christ took place in the year 5500.

JUMIÈGES, *Benedictine abbey 17 miles W. of Rouen. Founded by St. *Philibert in 654, it became one of the cultural centres of N. Europe. In the 17th cent. it was linked to the *Maurist reform. Benedictine life ended in 1790.

JUMPERS. A nickname for the Welsh *Calvinistic Methodists.

JUNG CODEX, The. One of the MSS. discovered at *Nag Hammadi. It was acquired by the Jung Institute for Analytical Psychology at Zürich.

JURIEU, PIERRE (1637–1713), French *Calvinist. In 1674 he became professor of Hebrew at the Protestant academy of Sedan and was soon involved in controversies with J. B. *Bossuet and A. *Arnauld. When the academy was closed in 1681, he accepted a professorship at Rotterdam. From 1689 to 1702 he was employed by the Admiralty in London as an agent against the French. In his numerous writings he sought to defend the claims of strict Calvinism, confining membership of the true Church within narrow limits.

JUS DEVOLUTUM. In the Church of *Scotland, the right devolving on a *presbytery to elect a minister to a vacant charge when the congregation after nine months has failed to make an appointment.

JUSTIFICATION. The English word derives from the Latin 'justum facere', meaning 'to make just', but it is also commonly used to translate a Greek phrase which may mean not 'to make just' but 'to pronounce just'. Esp. in Protestant theology it is used to designate the act whereby God, in virtue of the Sacrifice of Christ, acquits a man of the punishment due to his sins and in His mercy treats him as though he were righteous. M. *Luther held that such justification was granted to men in response to the disposition of faith alone and that it brought with it the imputation to the sinner of the merits of Christ.

JUSTIN MARTYR, St. (c. 100–c. 165), Christian *Apologist. Born of pagan parents, Justin embraced Christianity c. 130. He taught for a time at *Ephesus; later he opened a Christian school in Rome. He and some of his disciples were denounced as Christians c. 165 and on refusing to sacrifice they were scourged and beheaded.

Though of no great philosophical or literary skill, Justin was the first Christian thinker to seek to reconcile the claims of faith and reason. His 'First Apology' (c. 155) was addressed to the Emp. Antoninus Pius and his adopted sons. It defends Christianity as the only truly rational creed and contains an account of contemporary Baptismal ceremonies and Eucharistic belief and practice. The 'Second Apology',

addressed to the Roman Senate, is concerned to rebut specific charges against Christians. In his 'Dialogue with Trypho the Jew' Justin develops the identity of the *Logos with the God of the OT and the vocation of the Gentiles to take the place of Israel.

JUSTINA, St. See *Cyprian, St., of Antioch.*

JUSTINIAN I (483–565), Roman Emperor from 527. He reconquered N. Africa and Italy; he built many *basilicas; and he issued a new legal Code (see next entry). As the champion of orthodoxy he persecuted the *Montanists and closed the philosophical schools at *Athens in 529. His efforts to reconcile the *Monophysites issued in the *Three Chapters controversy.

JUSTINIAN, The Code of. This revision of the *Theodosian Code was issued by *Justinian in 529. It was supplemented by further constitutions known as 'Novellae' and by the 'Digest' and 'Institutes of Justinian'; together they constituted the *Corpus Iuris Civilis*, which became the authoritative statement of Roman law. It strongly influenced the development of W. *canon law.

JUSTUS, St. (d. c. 627), Abp. of *Canterbury from 624. He was sent to England in 601 in *Gregory I's second band of missionaries and made first Bp. of *Rochester in 604. As Abp. he consecrated St. *Paulinus for mission work in Northumbria.

JUVENAL (d. 458), Bp. of *Jerusalem from c. 422. His main ambition seems to have been to make Jerusalem into a '*Patriarchal see'. He sided with *Cyril of Alexandria against *Nestorius at the Council of *Ephesus in 431, but he failed to gain Cyril's support for his claims. In the *Eutychian controversy he supported *Dioscorus at the *Latrocinium in 449 but at the Council of *Chalcedon (451) he voted for his condemnation. The Council recognized Jerusalem as a Patriarchal see with jurisdiction over Palestine.

JUVENCUS, CAIUS VETTIUS AQUILINUS (4th cent.), poet. He was a Spanish presbyter of noble birth. About 330 he wrote a harmony of the Gospels in some 3,200 Latin hexameters.

JUXON, WILLIAM (1582–1663), Abp. of *Canterbury from 1660. He succeeded W. *Laud as Bp. of London in 1633. Though known to be a *High Churchman, he was widely trusted. He attended *Charles I at his execution; he was deprived of his bishopric but otherwise unmolested under the Commonwealth. He survived only three years as archbishop.

K

KAFTAN, JULIUS WILHELM MARTIN (1848-1926), German Protestant theologian. Believing that St. *Paul's system of theology was the outcome of reflection on his vision on the Damascus road, Kaftan held that the *Atonement must be understood by mystical and ethical categories, and that there was no place in the doctrine of Christ's work for notions of satisfaction or of the reconciliation of God with man (as contrasted with that of man with God).

KAGAWA, TOYOHIKO (1888–1960), Japanese social reformer. Of a wealthy Buddhist family, after his conversion to Christianity he studied at the *Presbyterian seminary at Kobe (1905–8) and at Princeton. He returned to Japan in 1917 and devoted himself to the improvement of social conditions. Many of his writings have been translated into English.

KÄHLER, MARTIN (1835–1912), *Lutheran theologian. In 1867 he became professor of systematic theology at Halle. He is remembered chiefly for a collection of essays, *Der sogenannte historische Jesus* (1892; abridged Eng. tr., 1964), in which he attacked the 19th-cent. attempts to reconstruct the Jesus of history.

KAISERSWERTH. The band of Protestant *deaconesses in this Rhineland town was founded in 1836 to meet the need of the reformed Churches for an organization of women devoted to nursing and education. The house trains deaconesses who devote themselves to the care of the sick and poor, teaching, or parish work.

KAMELAVCHION. The black cylindrical hat worn by monks and clergy in the E. Church.

KANT, IMMANUEL (1724–1804), German philosopher. He spent his whole life in Prussia; from 1770 he was Professor of Logic at Königsberg. He expounded his 'Critical Philosophy' for the first time in his *Critique of Pure Reason* (*Der Kritik der reinen Vernunft*, 1781); he applied the same principles to other problems in later works.

It seems that Kant's main object was to discover a definitive rationale for the admitted validity of mathematics and natural science. He argued that it was the understanding (*Verstand*) which prescribed to nature her laws. The validity of the causal law ('every event has a cause') rests not on some constraining principle in the external world of nature, but in the fact that consciousness is so constituted that it cannot but so interpret the empirical data which it receives. Knowledge is thus the result of a synthesis between an intellectual act and what is presented to the mind from without In holding that all knowledge required an ingredient derived from nature, Kant cut at the root of traditional metaphysics, with its claim to provide knowledge of subjects which transcend nature. The traditional proofs of the existence of God were also invalidated. But while insisting that Natural Theology was an illusion, Kant believed that the stern voice of conscience in man assures him of truths which reason is impotent to establish. The sense of duty assures us of freedom. Correlative with belief in freedom is belief in immortality and a Divine Being, since the maladjustments of virtue and happiness in this world require a righteous God who will vindicate the claims of Justice, and another world for His operation. Kant defined religion as the recognition of our duties as Divine commands; there is no place, he held, for mystical experience, no need for a personal redeemer, and no place (as in traditional Christianity) for the historical as such. His thought had immense influence.

KARAITES. A Jewish sect which bases its teaching solely on Scripture, rejecting Rabbinical tradition.

KARLSTADT. See *Carlstadt*.

KATAVASIA. In the E. Church the concluding stanza of an ode of the *canon.

KATHISMA. The Byzantine Psalter is divided into twenty sections; the term 'kathisma' is used to designate both these sections and the brief liturgical hymn sung at the end of each of them during *Orthros.

KEBLE, JOHN (1792–1866), *Tractarian leader. The son of John Keble, vicar of Coln St. Aldwyn, he resigned his post as tutor at Oriel College, Oxford, in 1823 to assist his father in the cure of his parish. Here he wrote the poems which he published in 1827 as *The *Christian Year*. In 1831 he was elected Professor of Poetry at Oxford. He became increasingly conscious of the dangers threatening the C of E from the reforming and liberal movements, and on 14 July 1833 he preached before the University an assize sermon on *National Apostasy*. He took a leading part in the *Oxford Movement, contributing several of the *Tracts for the Times*. He co-operated closely with E. B. *Pusey in keeping the High Church Movement steadily attached to the C of E. From 1836 he was vicar of Hursley, nr. Winchester. Keble College, Oxford, was founded in his memory.

KEIM, KARL THEODOR (1825–78), Protestant scholar. He held academic posts at *Tübingen, Zürich, and Giessen. His chief work, *Die Geschichte Jesu von Nazareth* (1867–72), is a somewhat rationalistic presentation of the life of Christ. It rejects the supernatural elements in the Gospel, including the Resurrection, but is less radical than the *Tübingen School.

KEITH, GEORGE (c. 1639–1716), 'Christian Quaker'. Trained for the *Presbyterian ministry, he became a *Quaker in 1662 and migrated to America in 1688. He became suspect among his fellow Quakers for denying the 'sufficiency of the light within' and was interdicted from preaching. He gathered round himself followers whom he called 'Christian Quakers'. He returned to England in 1694, conformed to the C or E, and, after

ordination, was one of the first missionaries sent by the *S.P.G. to America.

KELLS, The Book of. A finely ornamented MS. of the Gospels, written at Kells in Co. Meath, c. 800.

KEMPE, JOHN (c. 1380–1454), Abp. successively of *York (from 1425) and *Canterbury (from 1452), and *Cardinal from 1439. He was a politician rather than a Churchman.

KEMPE, MARGERY (c. 1373–after 1433), author of the *Book of Margery Kempe*. About 1393 she married John Kempe, a burgess of Lynn, by whom she had 14 children. She received several visions after a period of madness, and she and her husband went on a pilgrimage to *Canterbury. Her denunciation of all pleasure aroused opposition and accusations of *Lollardy. She publicly rebuked Abp. *Arundel for the behaviour of his followers. She visited the Holy Land in 1413, *Compostela in 1417, and Norway and Danzig in 1433. Her *Book* describes her travels and mystical experiences.

KEMPIS, THOMAS À. See *Thomas à Kempis*.

KEN, THOMAS (1637–1711), *Nonjuror. In 1683 he refused the use of his house to Nell Gwyn, the royal mistress; *Charles II respected his boldness and in 1684 appointed him Bp. of *Bath and Wells. Though Ken was one of the *Seven Bishops who refused to read the *Declaration of Indulgence in 1688, he declined to take the oath to William and Mary and was deposed from his see. He spent the rest of his life in retirement, but opposed the consecration of further Nonjuring bishops. He lived an ascetic life. He wrote the hymns 'Awake, my soul, and with the sun' and 'Glory to Thee, my God, this night'.

KENNETT, WHITE (1660–1728), Bp. of *Peterborough from 1718. He was an active supporter of the Revolution of 1689, a leading *Low Churchman, and in the *Bangorian Controversy he opposed the proceedings against B. *Hoadly. He was a keen antiquarian.

KENOTIC THEORIES. Certain theories concerned to explain the condescension involved in the Incarnation. The title comes from the Gk. verb (κενόω) in Phil. 2: 7, translated in the RV '*emptied* himself'. Some 19th-cent. *Lutheran theologians held that the Divine Son abandoned His attributes of deity in order to become man; others have held that within the sphere of the Incarnation the deity so restrained its activity as to allow the existence in the Lord of a limited and genuinely human consciousness. Traditional orthodoxy has generally admitted a self-emptying of the Lord's deity only in the sense that, while remaining unimpaired, it accepted union with a physically limited humanity.

KENSIT, JOHN (1853–1902), Protestant propagandist. He started the City Protestant bookshop in Paternoster Row in London in 1885 and in 1890 he became secretary of the newly founded 'Protestant Truth Society'. From 1898 he organized resistance to the growth of 'ritualism' in the dioceses of London and Liverpool, causing friction and disturbance wherever he went.

KENT, Maid of. See *Barton, Elizabeth.*

KENTIGERN, St. (d. 603), also known as **St. Mungo,** missionary. Apparently the grandson of a British prince in S. Scotland, he became a missionary to the Britons of Strathclyde and was consecrated their bishop. After being driven out by persecution he preached in Cumbria, Wales, and finally in the district around Glasgow.

KEPLER, JOHANN (1571–1630), German astronomer. In 1613 at the Diet of Ratisbon he defended the *Gregorian calendar against the attacks of his fellow Protestants. His fame is chiefly due to his discovery of the three laws of planetary motion.

KERYGMA (the Gk. word for 'preaching'). The element of proclamation in Christian apologetic, as contrasted with '*didache' or its instructional aspects.

KESWICK CONVENTION. An annual gathering of *Evangelical Christians which began in 1875.

KETTELER, WILHELM EMMANUEL (1811–77), Bp. of Mainz from 1850. He made it his chief aim to free the RC Church in Germany from State control. At the *Vati-

can Council of 1869–70 he opposed the dogma of *Infallibility on the ground that its promulgation was 'inopportune'.

KETTLEWELL, JOHN (1653–95), devotional writer and *Nonjuror. During the revolution of 1689 he preached against rebellion under any pretext and in 1690 he was deprived of his living. His *Practical Believer* (1687) was widely read.

KEVIN, St. (d. 618), the founder and abbot of Glendalough, in Co. Wicklow, which was the parent of several other monasteries and later one of the chief centres of pilgrimage in Ireland.

KHOMIAKOFF, ALEXIS STEPANO-VICH (1804–60), Russian philosophical theologian. Over against the RC ('unity without freedom') and the Protestant ('freedom without unity') conceptions of the Church, Khomiakoff saw in the Orthodox Church an organic society of which Christ was the Head and the Holy Spirit the Soul and whose essence was 'freedom in the spirit at one with itself'. Of this Church the essential quality was inward holiness, and those who partook of it could be saved even though not in external communion with it. Khomiakoff was under ecclesiastical suspicion in his lifetime, but his conception of the Church has influenced Orthodox ecclesiology, Greek as well as Russian.

KIDDUSH. The Jewish ceremony of the sanctification of the *Sabbath or other holy day. It takes place at the evening meal on the eve of the day in question, when the head of the household says the 'Kiddush' or 'Blessing' of the day over a cup of wine and water. It has been argued that Christ's blessing of the cup at the *Last Supper was the Kiddush of the *Passover.

KIDRON. See *Cedron.*

KIERKEGAARD, SØREN AABY (1813–55), Danish philosopher. Of wealthy *Lutheran family, he spent almost all his life in Copenhagen. To the prevailing *Hegelian philosophy, he opposed his own '*existential' dialectics, pointing out what was involved in the position of man 'existing before God'. His oft-repeated statement, 'truth is subjectivity', links truth with the existing subject instead of with its object, and so, in the last resort, makes its communication to other subjects impossible. He drew the theological consequences from this position by denying the possibility of an objective system of doctrinal truths. His religious works have aroused less interest than his philosophical writings. His total influence on contemporary thought is considerable.

KIKUYU. A village in Kenya where a missionary conference of Anglicans, Presbyterians, and other Protestants was held in 1913. A federation of constituent Churches was proposed, with the recognition of common membership between the Churches in the federation, carrying with it the right of receiving Communion in any of them.

KILHAM, ALEXANDER (1762–98), *Methodist. He advocated complete separation from the Established Church, was expelled by the Methodist Conference in 1796, and in 1798 founded the '*Methodist New Connexion'.

KILIAN, St. (d. c. 689), 'Apostle of Franconia'. A native of *Ireland, he was prob. already a bishop when he went as a missionary to the Franks and established his headquarters at Würzburg. He made many conversions before he was put to death.

KILWARDBY, ROBERT (d. 1279), Abp. of *Canterbury from 1273 to 1278, when he was made a *Cardinal and translated to Porto in Italy. He had been a Master of Arts at *Paris, entered the *Dominican Order, and studied theology at *Oxford. In 1277 he visited Oxford and in conjunction with the Masters of the University condemned 30 propositions; the condemnation was directed mainly against certain views maintained by St. *Thomas Aquinas on the unity of form.

KINDRED AND AFFINITY, Table of. The table, published by Abp. M. *Parker in 1563 and customarily printed at the end of the BCP, is based on the degrees of intermarriage prohibited in Lev. 18. It was intended to set out the marriages forbidden by Divine Law and therefore incapable. of being allowed by dispensation. The list was amended slightly in 1946 and again in 1969, when adopted children were added.

KING, EDWARD (1829–1910), Bp. of *Lincoln from 1885. He was a *Tractarian

High Churchman, of great holiness of life. In 1888 a 'ritual prosecution' was brought against him by the *Church Association. See *Lincoln Judgement.*

KING, MARTIN LUTHER (1929–68), Negro *Baptist minister and champion of civil rights in the U.S.A. As pastor of a church in Montgomery, Alabama, he organized a successful boycott of buses by Negroes in 1955. In 1960 he resigned from his pastorship to devote himself to the civil rights movement. He organized demonstrations but adhered to the principles of non-violence. He was awarded a Nobel Peace Prize in 1964. In 1968 he was assassinated.

KING, WILLIAM (1650–1729), Abp. of *Dublin from 1703. He energetically promoted the spiritual and temporal welfare of the Church of *Ireland; he was passed over for the primacy because of his Whig sympathies. His *De Origine Mali* (1702; Eng. tr., 1731) seeks to reconcile the existence of evil with the conception of an omnipotent and beneficent God.

KING JAMES VERSION. A title used, esp. in America, for the English translation of the Bible commonly known in England as the Authorized Version (1611) (see *Bible, English Versions,* 3).

KING'S BOOK, The. The name commonly given to *A Necessary Doctrine and Erudition for any Christian Man,* put forth by *Henry VIII in 1543. It was based on the *Bishops' Book of 1537, but for the most part its theology was a reaction in a Catholic direction.

KING'S BOOKS, The. See *Valor Ecclesiasticus.*

KING'S COLLEGE, LONDON. The College, incorporated in 1829, was designed as an Anglican counterpart to the undenominational University College, London, which was established by charter in 1827. It is now part of the University of London.

KING'S CONFESSION, The. The Protestant statement of belief drawn up by John Craig in 1581 when it was feared that Popery might be revived in Scotland. It was signed by King *James (VI of Scotland); hence its common designation. It formed the basis of the *National Covenant of 1638.

KING'S EVIL, Touching for the. The tradition that there existed some virtue in the royal touch for healing the 'King's evil', or scrofula, can be traced back to the 11th cent. In England various healings by *Edward the Confessor are recorded. Queen *Anne was the last sovereign to perform the ceremony.

KINGDOM OF GOD, The. The roots of the Christian conception of the Kingdom of God lie in Hebrew thought. In Hebrew thought God was eternally king in heaven, but His kingdom was not always visibly effective on earth, though it would be so at the 'Day of the Lord'. In the time of Christ the Kingdom of God would normally have been understood in an *eschatological sense.

In the NT the theme of the Kingdom of God (or the Kingdom of Heaven) becomes central. But Christ profoundly modified the idea. In contrast to the many who thought mainly of the visible rewards to be given to the righteous by an immediate intervention of God, the Lord stressed the ethical and religious qualities demanded of those who were to enjoy ('enter' or 'receive') the Kingdom. On some other points His teaching is less explicit. He seems to some extent to have accepted the current expectation of a future earthly manifestation of the Kingdom, i.e. that it would 'come' in a sense in which it was not present when He spoke of it. The Church has linked this future full manifestation of the Kingdom with belief in Christ's *Second Coming, *Eternal Life, and the Resurrection of the body. Elsewhere the Kingdom of God is declared to be actually present at the time He was speaking and its coming is represented as a present, but hidden, reality. 'The kingdom of God is within you' or 'in the midst of you' (Lk. 17: 21).

The conception of the Kingdom of God as a present reality, including spiritually all those who are God's true subjects, suggested a relationship between the Kingdom and the Church. St. *Augustine identified the Kingdom with the body of the elect who were predestined to salvation, and in places he tended to speak as if the identification applied to the visible hierarchical Church; he was followed, with less reserve, by medieval thinkers.

KINGS, Books of. The two Books of Kings were originally a single Book, which was divided by the Greek translators, who also grouped them with the Books of *Samuel and called all four the 'Books of the Reigns'. This method of designation (1–4 Reg.) came to be printed in the headlines of the Clementine edition of the *Vulgate; hence 1 and 2 Kings of the AV are called 3 and 4 Kings in the *Douai version.

The narrative covers the reign of *Solomon and the building of the *Temple, the history of the two separate kingdoms after the division on Solomon's death to the fall of the kingdom of Israel to Assyria in 721 B.C.; thereafter it is concerned solely with Judah, ending with the fall of *Jerusalem in 586 B.C. Events of religious significance are described in detail, whereas those of the highest political importance are passed over cursorily.

KINGSHIP OF CHRIST, Feast of the. See *Christ the King, Feast of.*

**KINGSLEY, CHARLES (1819–75), social reformer and novelist. In 1844 he became vicar of Eversley, Hants, where he spent most of the rest of his life. He was a leading spirit in the *Christian Socialist Movement, but he looked to educational and sanitary reform rather than political change for improvement. He was averse to all forms of asceticism. An ill-conceived jibe at J. H. *Newman in 1863 led to the publication of the latter's *Apologia.* His own works include *Westward Ho!* (1855), *The Heroes* (1856), and *The Water-Babies* (1863).

KIRK. The Scottish equivalent of 'Church'.

**KIRK, KENNETH ESCOTT (1886–1954), Bp. of Oxford from 1937. He was widely recognized as the foremost Anglican writer on moral theology in his day.

KIRK-SESSION, also known as the **Session.** The lowest court in the Church of *Scotland and other *Presbyterian Churches.

KISS OF PEACE, also **PAX.** The mutual greeting of the faithful in the Eucharistic Liturgy, as a sign of their love and union. It is first mentioned by St. *Justin Martyr and is prob. a usage of the Apostolic period. Originally an actual kiss, the form of the Peace has been modified in all rites. In recent years hand-shaking has become common in the W.

KLOPSTOCK, FRIEDRICH GOTTLIEB (1724–1803), German poet. He spent part of his life in Denmark, where King Frederick V gave him a pension to enable him to complete *Der Messias*. This poem, of nearly twenty thousand lines, is concerned with the Passion and forty days after the Resurrection. It not only describes events on earth, but introduces hosts of angels and devils, even the Trinity itself appearing, and gives to every event and action its deeper significance. From a literary point of view the work is important as the first modern German epic.

KLOSTERNEUBURG, a monastery of *canons regular of St. *Augustine, nr. Vienna, founded not later than 1108. It possesses great art treasures and a valuable library. In modern times it has become noted for its support of the *Liturgical Movement.

KNEELING, Declaration on. See *Black Rubric*.

KNIGHTS HOSPITALLER; KNIGHTS OF MALTA; and **KNIGHTS OF RHODES.** See *Hospitallers*.

KNIGHTS TEMPLAR. See *Templars*.

KNOX, EDMUND ARBUTHNOTT (1847–1937), Bp. of Manchester from 1903 to 1921. He was one of the most prominent *Evangelicals of his generation. He attacked the liberal school of Biblical critics and opposed the revised BCP (rejected in 1927 and 1928).

KNOX, JOHN (*c*. 1513–72), Scottish Reformer. In 1551 he was made chaplain to *Edward VI and as such assisted in the revision of the Second BCP. On *Mary's accession he fled to the Continent and in 1556 he accepted a call to the English church at Geneva. He returned to *Scotland in 1559 and became the leader of the Reforming party. He drew up the *Scottish Confession (q.v.) and brought into being a commission which abolished the authority of the Pope in Scotland and forbade the celebration of, and attendance at, Mass. The *First Book of *Discipline* (1560) and the *Book of *Common Order* (q.v., 1556–64) were largely his work. After *Mary Stuart's return to Scotland in 1561 he came into repeated conflict with the Queen. His principal work is the *History of the Reformation of Religion within the Realm of Scotland* (publd. in full, 1644).

KNOX, RONALD ARBUTHNOTT (1888–1957), Catholic apologist and translator of the Bible. The son of E. A. *Knox, he became a RC in 1917. He was chaplain to the RC undergraduates at Oxford from 1926 to 1939, when he resigned to devote himself to translating the Bible. His version was based on the Latin *Vulgate and sought to put the Bible into timeless English. The NT appeared in 1945, the OT in 1949; the whole Bible in one volume in 1955. It was authorized for public use in RC churches.

KOCH, J. See *Cocceius, J.*

KOHLER, CHRISTIAN and HIERONYMUS. See *Brügglers*.

KOLYVA. In the E. Church a cake blessed during memorial services for the departed and distributed to those present.

KOMVOSCHINION. In the E. Church, a knotted cord, roughly corresponding to the W. *rosary.

KONTAKION. See *Contakion*.

KORAN. The sacred book of *Islam, which Muhammad claimed had been revealed to him as the Word of God, through the mediation of the archangel *Gabriel.

KORNTHAL, NW. of Stuttgart, *Pietist settlement. It was founded in 1819 as a centre of Pietist life in opposition to the increasing rationalism of the *Lutheran State Church. The lives of its members are minutely regulated; educational institutes and missionary work have been their main achievements. They number *c.* 1200.

KRAUS, FRANZ XAVIER (1840–1901), ecclesiastical historian. From 1878 he was professor of Church history at Freiburg. His political theories, which upheld the rights of the State against interference from the Church, led the government to support his candidature for the episcopate, but no appointment was made. The most considerable of his many works was his *Geschichte der christlichen Kunst* (1896–1908).

KRÜDENER, BARBARA JULIANA FREIFRAU VON (1764–1824), *Pietist. She influenced the Czar Alexander I and gained his support for the idea of the *Holy Alliance.

KULTURKAMPF. The repressive political movement in Germany in the 1870s against the RC Church. In 1871 Bismarck suppressed the Catholic department of the Prussian Ministry of Public Worship and in 1872 appointed P. L. A. *Falk Minister of Public Worship; under his aegis the famous *May Laws (1873) were passed. In view of the strong opposition aroused, Bismarck gradually became convinced that a *concordat would serve the German Empire better. At the end of the 1870s the previous policy was reversed and peace was made with the new Pope, *Leo XIII.

KÜNG, HANS (1928–   ), Swiss RC theologian. In 1960 Küng became professor of fundamental theology in the Catholic faculty of theology at *Tübingen. The most prominent of the younger RC progressive theologians, he attended the Second *Vatican Council. His works include *Rechtfertigung: Die Lehre Karl Barths und eine katholische Besinnung* (1957; Eng. tr., *Justification: the Doctrine of Karl Barth and a Catholic Reflection*, 1964); *Die Kirche* (1967; Eng. tr., *The Church*, 1967), *Unfehlbar?* (1970; Eng. tr., *Infallible?*, 1971), a trenchant criticism of modern Papal claims and the Papacy's use of authority, which precipitated wide controversy, and *Christ sein* (1974; Eng. tr., *On being a Christian*, 1977).

KUYPER, ABRAHAM (1837–1920), Dutch *Calvinist theologian and politician. He was a professor of the Calvinist university which he founded at Amsterdam; in 1886 he established the strictly Calvinistic Reformed Church Community. In his Stone Lectures delivered in Princeton and published under the title *Calvinism* (Amsterdam and New York, 1899; London 1932), he presented Calvinism as a religious belief opposed to *Liberal Protestantism and also discussed its bearing on social and political life. He was Minister of the Interior from 1901 to 1905.

KYRIALE. The Latin liturgical book containing the musical chant for the *Ordinary of the Mass, so called from its opening part, the *Kyrie.

KYRIE ELEISON (Gk. for 'Lord, have mercy'). A prayer for Divine mercy used in liturgical worship. In the E. the words formed the response of the people to petitions made by the *deacon in the 4th cent.; in the W. towards the end of the 5th cent. a *litany containing this response was inserted in the Mass. In a letter of 598 *Gregory I mentions that at Rome the 'Kyrie eleison' is supplemented by a similar prayer 'Christe eleison' ('Christ, have mercy'), and the whole seems to have been placed at that time in what became its traditional position at the beginning of the Mass. In the C of E the Kyrie was replaced in the 1552 BCP by the Ten *Commandments, but its use was revived in the 19th cent. and is permitted in the *Alternative Services, Communion Rites.

L

LABADISTS. A small Protestant sect named after Jean de Labadie (1610–74), its founder. They held *Pietist views and were organized on a communistic basis; they survived de Labadie's death by some fifty years.

LABARUM. The military standard adopted by the Emp. *Constantine after his vision before the Battle of the *Milvian Bridge. It incorporated a Christian monogram, viz. the Greek letters X and P (the first two letters of ΧΡΙΣΤΟΣ, 'Christ') intersecting.

LABERTHONNIÈRE, LUCIEN (1860–1932), RC *Modernist theologian. He developed a pragmatic view of religious truth, called moral dogmatism, which he expounded in *Essais de philosophie religieuse* (1903) and *Le Réalisme chrétien et l'idéalisme grec* (1904); both were put on the *Index.

LABRE, St. BENEDICT JOSEPH (1748–83), pilgrim and mendicant saint. Born near Boulogne, he was rejected by the *Trappists, *Carthusians, and *Cistercians as unsuitable for community life and found his vocation in solitude and pilgrimage. He visited most of the leading sanctuaries in Europe.

LACEY, THOMAS ALEXANDER (1853–1931), canon of *Worcester from 1918. He was an apologist for the *Anglo-Catholic position. He was also devoted to the cause of reunion, and when a Papal commission was examining the validity of *Anglican ordinations in 1896, Lacey supplied much of the material from the Anglican side.

LACHMANN, KARL (1793–1851), German philologist and textual critic. He was the first scholar to produce an edition of the Greek NT based entirely on the earliest known evidence, disregarding the *textus receptus*. He also put the *Marcan hypothesis on a sound footing.

LACORDAIRE, HENRI DOMINIQUE (1802–61), French *Dominican. In 1835–6 he gave his first series of Conferences or sermons at *Notre-Dame in Paris; they drew a vast concourse, largely from the intelligentsia. His political liberalism and *Ultramontane theology aroused distrust, however, and he retired to Rome. In 1839 he entered the Dominican Order and in 1843 established at Nancy the first Dominican house in France since the suppression of the order in 1790. In 1850 he became Provincial of the newly founded French province.

LACTANTIUS (*c.* 240–*c.* 320), Christian apologist. Lucius Caecilius Firmianus Lactantius, on his conversion to Christianity (*c.* 300), was deprived of his post as teacher of rhetoric at Nicomedia. Later he was tutor to *Constantine's son Crispus. His *Divinae Institutiones* seeks to commend Christianity to men of letters and for the first time to set out in Latin a systematic account of the Christian attitude to life. The *De Mortibus Persecutorum* describes the deaths of the persecutors of the Church.

LACTICINIA. Milk and foods made from milk, which (as well as meat and eggs) were forbidden on fast days in the early Church.

LADISLAUS, St. (1040–95), King of *Hungary from 1077. In the *Investiture Controversy between the Emperor and the Pope, he took the side of *Gregory VII and Victor III, but when *Urban II claimed suzerainty over part of the country he refused to recognize him as temporal lord. He laboured to spread the Christian faith, esp. in Croatia and Dalmatia.

LADY, Our. A common designation among Catholics for the Blessed Virgin *Mary (BVM).

LADY CHAPEL. A chapel dedicated to the BVM ('Our *Lady') when it forms part of a larger church.

LADY DAY. The feast of the *Annunciation of the BVM, 25 Mar.

LAETENTUR COELI. The opening words of : (1) the Greek Formulary of Union sent in 433 by *Cyril, Patr. of Alexandria, to *John, Bp. of Antioch, embodying the terms of reunion agreed by both parties, after John had been giving qualified support to *Nestorius; and (2) the bull issued by *Eugenius IV in 1439 decreeing the union settled at the Council of *Florence between the Orthodox E. Church and the W.

LAGARDE, PAUL ANTON DE (1827–91), Protestant theologian and critic. He changed his name from Bötticher to de Lagarde in 1845; in 1869 he became a professor at Göttingen. He produced works on a wide range of subjects, including editions of the Syriac text of the *Didascalia (1854), the 'Hebrew Psalter' (see *Psalters, Western*), and part of the *Lucianic recension of the *Septuagint.

LAGRANGE, MARIE JOSEPH (1855–1938), *Dominican Biblical scholar. In 1890 he founded at *Jerusalem the 'École Pratique d'Études Bibliques' and in 1892 the *Revue Biblique*. He supported *Leo XIII's efforts to encourage the critical study of the Bible in the RC Church; his own position perhaps approached as near to that of the *Higher Critics as was compatible with Catholic orthodoxy.

LAINEZ. J. See *Laynez, J.*

LAITY. Members of the Church who do not belong to the clergy.

LAKE, KIRSOPP (1872–1946), Biblical and patristic scholar. He held professorships at Leiden and later at Harvard. In his earlier years he was a provocative NT critic, challenging the sufficiency of the evidence for the empty tomb and holding that the course of early Christianity was much influenced by the mystery religions. He was a devoted student of the palaeography of Greek MSS.

LAMB. The use of a lamb as a symbol of Christ is based on such passages as Jn. 1: 29 and Rev. 5: 12. It dates from an early period. See also *Agnus Dei* and *Paschal Lamb*.

LAMBERT, St. (*c*. 636–*c*. 700), martyr. He was Bp. of Maestricht from *c*. 670, though in exile for political reasons from *c*. 675 to 682. It seems clear that he suffered a violent death, but the circumstances are differently recorded.

LAMBERT (or LAMPBERT) OF HERSFELD (*c*. 1024–after 1077), chronicler. He became a *Benedictine at Hersfeld in 1058. His *Annals*, which begin with the creation of the world, are very detailed from 1072 to 1077; they used to be regarded as the chief source for the struggle between *Henry IV and *Gregory VII, but their accuracy is now less widely accepted.

LAMBERT, FRANCIS (1486–1530), Reformer. A notable *Franciscan, he established relations with H. *Zwingli in 1522 and left his order. He was called to Hesse by the Landgraf *Philip in 1526. He took part in the *Homberg Synod, was charged with the preparation of a Protestant 'Church Order' for Hesse, and became professor of exegesis at *Marburg University in 1527.

LAMBETH. For over 700 years Lambeth has been the London residence of the Abps. of *Canterbury. Abp. *Baldwin (1185–90) acquired the manor and manor-house of Lambeth, though it was not described as 'Lambeth Palace' until *c*. 1658. The Library, founded in 1610, has some 2,500 MSS., including the Registers of the Archbishops from 1279 to 1928.

LAMBETH APPEAL. See *Lambeth Conferences*.

LAMBETH ARTICLES. Nine extreme *Calvinistic propositions compiled at *Lambeth in 1595 by a committee which met under Abp. J. *Whitgift. They were never formally authorized.

LAMBETH CONFERENCES. Assemblies of the bishops of the Anglican Communion held about once every ten years under the presidency of the Abp. of *Canterbury, usually in *Lambeth Palace. The first Conference was held in 1867, in response to the desire of the Anglican Church in *Canada. The original idea of a Council authorized to define doctrine had been abandoned, and the resolutions of Lambeth Conferences, though significant expressions of the opinions of the Anglican episcopate, are not binding. The Conference of 1920 issued an important 'Appeal to all Christian People' for Reunion, which was sent to the leaders of Christian communities throughout the world.

LAMBETH DEGREES. Degrees in Divinity, Arts, Law, Medicine, and Music which the Abp. of *Canterbury may confer in virtue of 25 Hen. VIII, c. 21, which gave him many of the rights which he had previously enjoyed as '*Legatus natus' of the Pope.

LAMBETH OPINIONS, The. In 1899 the Abps. of *Canterbury and *York, in response to questions raised by some English bishops, gave their opinion at *Lambeth Palace that the liturgical use of *incense and the carrying of lights in procession were 'neither enjoined nor permitted' in the C of E. Further opinions in 1900 denied the legality of *Reservation.

LAMBETH QUADRILATERAL. Four Articles approved by the *Lambeth Conference of 1888 as stating the essentials for a reunited Church. They deal with the Bible, the *Apostles' and *Nicene Creeds, *Baptism and the *Eucharist, and the episcopate.

LAMENNAIS, FÉLICITÉ ROBERT DE (1782–1854), French religious and political writer. Reluctantly, he was ordained in 1816. In 1818 he published the first volume of his *Essai sur l'indifférence en matière de religion*. In this he developed the principle of authority, which he equated with the 'raison générale' or 'sens commun', and maintained that the individual is dependent on the community for his knowledge of the truth.

Later volumes (1820–3) equated Catholic Christianity with the religion of all mankind, denied the supernatural, and proclaimed subjects freed from their loyalty to temporal sovereigns when rulers refused to conform their conduct to Christian ideals. To combat the evils of the time he desired a theocracy, with the Pope as supreme leader of kings and peoples. The work was approved by Leo XII, who possibly contemplated making Lamennais a cardinal. In later writings Lamennais prophesied a revolution and called for the union of all freedom-loving men; believing that the Pope would put himself at the head of a crusade for freedom, he went to Rome in 1832 to defend his ideas before *Gregory XVI, but they were condemned in the encyclical '*Mirari vos' (1832). His famous reply, *Paroles d'un croyant* (1834), which admitted the authority of the Church in matters of faith but denied it in the sphere of politics, was condemned in June 1834. Lamennais left the Church and all attempts to reconcile him failed. He was a forerunner of *Modernism.

LAMENTABILI (1907). The decree of the *Holy Office condemning 65 propositions believed to be derived from the teaching of contemporary *Modernists.

LAMENTATIONS OF JEREMIAH. This OT Book deals with the desolation of Judah after the destruction of *Jerusalem in 586 B.C. Its traditional ascription to *Jeremiah is generally rejected by modern scholars; they date its composition later. Christians commonly interpret the Book in reference to Christ's Passion.

LAMMAS DAY. 1 August. In the past it was customary to consecrate bread made from the first-ripe corn at Mass on this day, prob. in thanksgiving for the harvest.

LAMPBERT OF HERSFELD. See *Lambert of Hersfeld*.

LAMPS. There is no early evidence of the ceremonial use of lamps in Christian worship. The burning of lamps before the altar, and esp. of a white lamp before the reserved Sacrament, came into use in the W. in the 13th cent., but was not obligatory before the 16th cent. See also *Candles*.

LANCE (liturgical). In Byzantine rites, a small knife used to cut the Eucharistic bread at the *Proskomide.

LANCE, The Holy. A relic, believed to be the lance used to pierce the Lord's body (Jn. 19: 34). The first record of its existence dates from the 6th cent. When the Persians captured *Jerusalem in 615, the lance fell into their hands, but its point was saved and brought to *Constantinople. In 1241 this was given to St. *Louis; it was preserved in the *Sainte-Chapelle, but disappeared at the French Revolution. What is claimed to be another part of the lance was sent by the Turks to the Pope in 1492 and is kept in *St. Peter's.

LANFRANC (c. 1010–89), early Scholastic theologian and Abp. of *Canterbury. In 1042 he entered the abbey of *Bec, becoming prior c. 1045. Under him the school became one of the most celebrated of the time. His theological importance rests mainly on his *De Corpore et Sanguine Domini*, the first widely known criticism of the Eucharistic teaching of *Berengar of Tours; in this work Lanfranc employed the tools of logic and approached the doctrine of *transubstantiation.

In 1070 he became Abp. of Canterbury. He preserved peace with *William I and William II. In his dispute with Abp. Thomas of *York, who refused to recognize the supremacy of Canterbury, he obtained victory in 1072. His policy of replacing Saxon bishops and abbots by Normans brought the English Church into closer contact with the Continent and the reform movement of *Gregory VII. He did not, however, carry out the Gregorian programme in its entirety, having no sympathy with the Pope's dislike of lay *investiture. He rebuilt the cathedral at Canterbury.

LANG, COSMO GORDON (1864–1945), Abp. of York from 1908 to 1928 and of *Canterbury from 1928 to 1942. He played an important part in connection with the abdication of King Edward VIII in 1936.

LANGTON, STEPHEN (d. 1228), Abp. of *Canterbury. He became one of the chief theologians at *Paris. In 1206 *Innocent III created him a cardinal and in 1207 nominated and consecrated him Abp. of Canterbury, though owing to King *John's opposition he did not land in England until 1213.

He sympathized with the barons and his name heads the list of counsellors mentioned in Magna Carta, though in later life he supported the regency. He established the claims of the Abp. of Canterbury to be the Pope's '*legatus natus', and he promulgated canons for the English Church. He is credited with the division of the Books of the Bible into chapters which, with small modifications, is still in use.

LAODICEA. A Hellenistic city in the Roman province of Asia. It was the seat of an early Christian community mentioned in Col. 4: 16 and Rev. 3: 14 ff., and a bishopric of some importance for several centuries.

LAODICEA, Canons of. A set of 60 4th-cent. canons which were embodied in the early collections of ecclesiastical law. Nothing definite is known about the 'Council of Laodicea', though mention of the *Photinians in can. 7 points to a date not before c. 345, and prob. the Council took place at least 20 years later.

LAODICEANS, The Epistle to the. A Latin apocryphal Epistle of St. *Paul, doubtless produced to meet the demand suggested by Col. 4: 16. The first clear mention of it occurs in St. *Augustine.

LAPCLOTH. See *Gremial*.

LAPIDE, CORNELIUS A. See *Cornelius a Lapide*.

LAPSI (Lat., 'the fallen'). Those who in varying degrees denied the Christian faith under persecution. At first apostasy was held to be an unforgivable sin, but after the *Decian persecution of 250–1, the Church decided to readmit such persons after penance and probation. This decision led to the *Novatianist schism.

LARDNER, NATHANIEL (1684–1768), Nonconformist apologist. His work on *The Credibility of the Gospel History* (14 vols., 1727–57) sought to reconcile the discrepancies in the Biblical narratives; it is a mine of information for scholars.

LA SALETTE. A village in the Alps where in 1846 a peasant boy and girl saw a vision of the BVM who gave 'to all her people' a promise of Divine Mercy after repentance,

and also a special secret which was later sent to *Pius IX. Pilgrimages quickly followed and in 1852 the first stone of the present church was laid on the scene of the vision.

LAS CASAS, BARTOLOMÉ DE (1474–1566), Spanish missionary, the 'Apostle of the Indies'. He went with the Spanish governor to Hispaniola (Haiti) in 1502, and was ordained priest in 1510. He then devoted himself to the interests of the Indians by opposing, both in America and at the court of Spain, the cruel methods of exploitation used by the settlers. He joined the *Dominicans in 1523 and from 1543 to 1551 he was Bp. of Chiapa in Mexico. His reports of the abuses of the settlers, notably in his *Destrucción de las Indias* (1552), may go beyond the limits of truth.

LASKI or À LASCO, JOHN (1499–1560), Protestant Reformer. A nephew of Jan Laski, Abp. of Gniezno, he held various ecclesiastical appointments. In 1538 he avowed his belief in the Reformed faith, his sympathies being with the extreme *Calvinists. He spent some time in England and is held to have influenced the BCP of 1552.

LAST GOSPEL. A second reading from the Gospels (usually Jn. 1: 1–14) which until 1964 took place at the end of Mass in the W. rite.

LAST JUDGEMENT. See *General Judgement*.

LAST SUPPER. The final meal of Christ with His disciples on the night before the Crucifixion. It was followed by the washing of the Apostles' feet (see *Pedilavium*) and the institution of the *Eucharist. Traditionally it has been held that the meal was the *Passover, in agreement with the *Synoptics, though the Gospel of St. *John has a somewhat different chronology.

LAST THINGS. See *Eschatology*.

LATERAN BASILICA, The. The *basilica, dedicated to St. *John the Baptist (with whom St. *John the Apostle is now associated), stands on the site of a palace which belonged to the family of the Laterani. The palace, given to the Church by *Constantine, was the official residence of the Popes from the 4th cent. until they went to *Avignon

(1309). It was mostly destroyed by fire in 1308. The present church was built under a succession of Popes beginning with *Urban V. It is the cathedral church of Rome.

LATERAN COUNCILS. A series of councils held at the Lateran Palace in Rome from the 7th to the 18th cent.; five of them rank as *oecumenical. The First (1123) ratified the Concordat of *Worms ending the *Investiture Contest; the Second (1139) ended the schism after the election of Innocent II and condemned the followers of *Arnold of Brescia; the Third (1179) regulated Papal elections; the Fourth (1215) defined Eucharistic doctrine (using for the first time the word '*transubstantiate') and prescribed annual confession; the Fifth (1512–17) invalidated the decrees of the anti-papal Council of Pisa convoked by Louis XII of France.

LATERAN TREATY, The (1929). This treaty between the Italian government and the Holy See settled the position of Rome as the capital of Italy and established the *Vatican City as a sovereign state.

LATIMER, HUGH (c. 1485–1555), Reformer. In 1522 he was licensed by the University of Cambridge to preach anywhere in England, but his extreme Protestant teaching led to his censure by *Convocation in 1532. When *Henry VIII formally broke with the Papacy in 1534, Latimer became one of his chief advisers, and in 1535 he was appointed Bp. of *Worcester. He supported the King in the *Dissolution of the Monasteries. In 1539, in accordance with his Protestant beliefs, he opposed the Act of the *Six Articles and resigned his see. Under *Edward VI he returned to favour but on *Mary's accession he was confined in the Tower and in 1555 burnt at the stake.

LATITUDINARIANISM. A term applied opprobriously in the 17th cent. to the outlook of Anglican divines who continued within the C of E but attached relatively little importance to matters of dogmatic truth, ecclesiastical organization, and liturgical practice.

LA TRAPPE, Notre-Dame de. The abbey near Soligny (Orne) often known as la Grande Trappe, which gave its name to the *Trappist reform instituted here by A. de

*Rancé in the 17th cent. The abbey was founded as a *Benedictine house in 1122 and became *Cistercian in 1148. The community was expelled in the Revolution of 1790 but returned in 1817.

LATRIA. The fullness of Divine worship which may be paid to God alone.

LATROCINIUM (i.e. 'Robber Council'). The Council held at *Ephesus in 449. Summoned by *Theodosius II, the Council was dominated by *Monophysites. It acquitted *Eutyches of heresy and reinstated him. Its decisions were reversed at *Chalcedon in 451.

LATTER-DAY SAINTS. See *Mormons*.

LAUD, WILLIAM (1573–1645), Abp. of *Canterbury from 1633. He had earlier been President of St. John's College, Oxford, and Bp. successively of *St. Davids (1621), *Bath and Wells (1626), and London (1628). From an early date he opposed the prevailing *Calvinist theology and sought to restore something of the pre-Reformation liturgical practice of the C of E. His work on the *High Commission and his attempts to impose liturgical uniformity aroused bitter hostility among the *Puritans. In 1637 he tried to enforce a new liturgy in *Scotland. In 1640 he introduced into *Convocation new *canons proclaiming the *Divine Right of Kings and compelling whole classes of people to swear never to consent to alter the government of the Church; this formula, known as the 'etcetera oath', had to be suspended at the order of the king. Soon afterwards Laud was impeached by the Long Parliament. He was imprisoned in 1641, tried in 1644, and executed in 1645.

LAUDA SION. The opening words and hence the name of the *sequence (now optional) composed for the feast of *Corpus Christi by St. *Thomas Aquinas (c. 1264). The familiar Eng. tr., 'Laud, O Sion, thy Salvation', is the work of several authors.

LAUDS. The traditional morning prayer of the W. Church, and one of the oldest parts of the Divine *Office. Until 1911 it always included Pss. 148–50, in which the word *laudate* (Lat., 'praise ye') recurs; hence its name. In the BCP parts of Lauds and *Mattins were combined to form Morning Prayer.

LAURA. See *Lavra*.

LAURENCE, St. (d. 258), deacon and martyr of Rome. Acc. to tradition, on being asked to deliver up the riches of the Church, he assembled the poor and presented them to the Prefect of Rome, saying, 'These are the treasure of the Church'; he was punished by being roasted to death on a gridiron. The story is widely rejected by modern scholars.

'LAUSANNE'. The first Conference of the *Ecumenical Movement of '*Faith and Order' held at Lausanne in 1927. It aimed at promoting doctrinal unity among different branches of Christianity.

LAVABO (Lat., 'I will wash'). The washing of the celebrant's fingers after the offering of the oblations in the Eucharist.

LAVRA (Greek for a street or alley). In the early Church a colony of *anchorites who, while living in separate huts, were subject to a single abbot. The oldest lavras were founded in Palestine in the early 4th cent. In more recent times the term has been applied to important *coenobitic communities.

LAW, Canon and **Natural.** See *Canon Law; Natural Law*.

LAW, WILLIAM (1686–1761), *Nonjuror and spiritual writer. He refused to take the Oath of Allegiance on George I's accession and was deprived of his Cambridge Fellowship. He was tutor to the father of E. *Gibbon. From 1740 he lived at Kings Cliffe, Northamptonshire.

The most famous of his many works is *A Serious Call to a Devout and Holy Life* (1728), a forceful exhortation to embrace the Christian life in its moral and ascetical fullness; it insists esp. on the virtues practised in everyday life, temperance, humility, and self-denial. The simplicity of its teaching and its vigorous style soon established the book as a classic.

LAWRENCE, Brother. See *Brother Lawrence*.

LAXISM. A system of *moral theology which relaxes the obligations of natural and positive law where there is any degree of probability, however slight, in favour of a course of action. Its formulation in the 17th cent. is connected with the appearance of *Probabilism (q.v.). Laxist propositions were condemned by *Innocent XI in 1679.

LAY BROTHER, LAY SISTER. A member of a religious order who is not bound to the recitation of the Divine *Office and is occupied in manual work. The institution originated in the 11th cent. Lay Brothers and Sisters assist at Mass daily and recite a short office.

LAY READER. In the C of E, a lay person licensed to conduct religious services. In its present form the office dates from 1866. Readers are formally admitted to their office by the Bishop, from whom they may receive a licence for a particular parish or for the diocese generally. Since 1969 women have been eligible for the office.

LAY RECTOR. In the C of E, a layman receiving the rectorial *tithes of a benefice. He has a legal duty to repair the chancel of the church.

LAYING ON OF HANDS. See *Hands, Imposition of*.

LAYMEN. See *Laity*.

LAYNEZ, JAMES (1512–65), second *General of the *Jesuits. He helped St. *Ignatius Loyola in founding the order, took a prominent part in the Council of *Trent (where he represented the more irreconcilable elements), and on Ignatius's death (1556) he succeeded him first as 'General Vicar' and from 1558 as General.

LAZARISTS. The name popularly given to the 'Congregation of the Mission', a congregation of secular priests living under religious vows, founded by St. *Vincent de Paul in 1625. The name comes from the priory of St.-Lazare, which was Vincent's headquarters in Paris.

LAZARUS. (1) The brother of Martha and Mary, and friend of Christ, who raised him from the dead (Jn. 11: 1–44). Acc. to E. tradition he became a bishop in Cyprus; acc. to later W. tradition he was Bp. of Marseilles.

(2) The name of the beggar in Christ's parable of *Dives and Lazarus (Lk. 16: 19–31).

LEANDER, St. (c. 550–600/601), Bp. of Seville from c. 584. He took a prominent part in furthering Catholic orthodoxy in Spain against the *Arianism of the Visigoths, and in 589 he presided over the Synod of *Toledo.

LEAVENED BREAD. See *Bread, Leavened and Unleavened.*

LEBBAEUS. An alternative name for *Thaddaeus.

LECLERC, JEAN (1657–1736), *Arminian theologian and Biblical scholar. In 1684 he was appointed professor of philosophy at the *Remonstrant College at Amsterdam. A champion of freedom of thought and an enemy of dogmatism, he defended the unlimited rights of reason in the domain of faith. He attacked the *Mosaic authorship of the *Pentateuch and held advanced critical views on the inspiration of Scripture, which he denied altogether in parts of the OT.

LECLERCQ, HENRI (1869–1945), *Benedictine scholar. A Belgian by birth, from 1914 he lived in London. He was a prolific and voluminous editor and writer, esp. concerned with the history of Latin Christianity; much of his writing suffers from inaccuracy. The latter part of the *Dictionnaire d'archéologie chrétienne et de liturgie* (ed. by F. *Cabrol and himself, 1903–53) was almost entirely Leclercq's work.

LECTERN. A bookstand to support liturgical books, often taking the form of an eagle or pelican with outstretched wings.

LECTIONARY. A book containing the extracts from Scripture to be read in public worship. The apportionment of particular extracts for particular days began in the 4th cent. Originally the beginnings and endings of the passages to be read were noted in the margins of church Bibles, but later the extracts were collected in separate books. Those for Mass used to be incorporated in the *Missal, but in 1969 a separate lectionary was issued in the RC Church. The lessons used at *Mattins and *Evensong in the C of E are regulated by a lectionary ('Table of Lessons') which is amended from time to time by the General *Synod.

LECTOR, also 'Reader'. In the E. and RC Churches, one of the *Minor Orders. In early times the main function of the lector was to read the OT Prophecies, the *Epistle, and in some places the *Gospel. In the RC Church the office was constituted the lower of the remaining 'Ministeria' in 1972 and allotted various duties.

LECTURERS. Stipendiary ministers (often deacons) appointed during the century after 1559 by town corporations, parishes, and occasionally by individual laymen, to provide regular frequent preaching. Lectureships were essentially a *Puritan device to secure preachers of whom Puritans approved.

LEDGER, St. See *Leodegar.*

LEE, FREDERICK GEORGE (1832–1902), Vicar of All Saints', Lambeth, from 1867 to 1899. He promoted reunion between the C of E and the RC Church, helping to found the *A.P.U.C. in 1857. He appears to have been secretly consecrated Bp. by a prelate in communion with the see of Rome c. 1877 and took the title of Bp. of *Dorchester (see *Episcopi Vagantes*). He became a RC in 1901.

LEEN, EDWARD (1885–1944), popular Irish spiritual writer. A member of the Congregation of the Holy Ghost, he held various posts in Ireland. His works include *Progress through Mental Prayer* (1935).

LEFÈVRE D'ÉTAPLES, J. See *Faber, J.*.

LEGATE, Papal. A personal representative of the *Holy See, entrusted with its authority. *Legati a latere*, most commonly called 'Papal Legates', are persons deputed for important missions of a temporary character. *Legati missi*, or *nuncios, have functions corresponding to those of ambassadors of secular states. *Legati nati* are holders of certain offices which convey legatine status *ex officio*.

LEGER, St. See *Leodegar, St.*.

LEIBNIZ, GOTTFRIED WILHELM (1646–1716), philosopher. From 1673 he was in the service of the family of the Duke of Brunswick-Lüneburg, his chief official duty being to assemble material on the house of Brunswick. His main philosophical works date from the latter part of his life. Acc. to the *Monadologie* (publd. 1720), the universe consists of an infinite number of 'monads', i.e. simple substances, and nothing else. These monads, ever active and each different, form a continuously ascending series from the lowest, which is next to nothing, to the highest, which is God. Though Leibniz sometimes described God as the highest of the monads, he could not avoid the difficulties of reconciling the inclusion of God in the monadic series with the Christian view of the Divine transcendence, and in some places he speaks as though God were outside the series and the cause of the monads' existence.

LEIGHTON, ROBERT (1611–84), Abp. of Glasgow from 1670 to 1674. He laboured hard to restore Church unity in Scotland, but failed in his efforts to accommodate the *Presbyterian and *Episcopalian systems.

LEIPZIG, Disputation of (1519). The disputation was provoked by J. *Eck's challenge of *Carlstadt. With the arrival of M. *Luther it turned to the question of the doctrinal authority of the Church. Luther stated that Councils not only may err, but actually have done so. The issues were clarified on both sides.

LEIPZIG INTERIM (1548). A more Protestant formula, put forward by Maurice, Elector of Saxony, which was adopted in parts of Germany where the Interim of *Augsburg (q.v.) was not accepted.

LE NEVE, JOHN (1679–1741), English antiquary. His *Fasti Ecclesiae Anglicanae* (1716), which records the succession of dignitaries in English and Welsh cathedrals, is a standard treatise on matters of ecclesiastical chronology.

LENT. The fast of forty days before *Easter. In the first three cents. the period of fasting before Easter did not normally exceed two or three days. The first mention of a period of forty days, prob. of Lent, dates from A.D. 325, though until a much later date the period was differently reckoned in different Churches.

During the early centuries the observance of the fast was rigid: only one meal a day was allowed and flesh-meat and fish were forbidden. In the W. the fast was gradually relaxed. In the RC Church by the Apostolic Constitution *Paenitemini* (1966) the obligation to fast was restricted to the first day of Lent and *Good Friday.

In the W. Church the penitential character of Lent is reflected in various features of the liturgy, and there is a proper Mass for each day. The period is also observed as a time of penance by abstention from festivities, by almsgiving, and by devoting more time than usual to religious exercises.

LEO I, St. (d. 461), 'Leo the Great', Pope from 440. His pontificate is remarkable for the extent to which he advanced and consolidated the influence of the Roman see. He tried to strengthen the Church by energetic central government and he pressed his claims to jurisdiction in Africa, Spain, and Gaul. He was drawn into E. affairs by the *Eutychian controversy, and his support was coveted by all parties. At the Council of *Chalcedon (451) his legates spoke first, and his *Tome was accepted as a standard of *Christological orthodoxy. He persuaded the Huns to withdraw beyond the Danube (452) and secured concessions when the Vandals took Rome (455). 143 genuine letters and 96 sermons survive.

LEO III, St. (d. 816), Pope from 795. After being attacked in Rome in 799, Leo fled to *Charlemagne, who provided him with an escort. When Charlemagne came to Rome, the Pope crowned him *Holy Roman Emperor (800). He took severe measures against the *Adoptianist heresy at Charlemagne's instigation. He intervened in the differences between the Abps. of *Canterbury and the Anglo-Saxon kings, and in the E. he encouraged the monks in their opposition to the Emp. Constantine VI.

LEO IV, St. (d. 855), Pope from 847. He sought to repair the damage done by the Saracens in 846, putting a wall round the part of Rome on the right bank of the Tiber (henceforth the '*Leonine City'). In 850 he crowned Louis, son of Lothair, as co-emperor; he is said to have 'hallowed' *Alfred as future king of England in 853. The *Asperges is ascribed to him.

LEO IX, St. (1002–54), Pope from 1048. He was a keen supporter of the *Cluniac monastic reform, and after his election he at once began to reform the Church. At the

Easter Synod of 1049 *celibacy was enforced on all the clergy, and soon afterwards various Councils promulgated decrees against *simony and other abuses. At a synod in Rome in 1050 *Berengar of Tours was condemned for his *Eucharistic doctrine.

LEO X (1475–1521), Pope from 1513. Giovanni de' Medici was the second son of Lorenzo 'the Magnificent'. The high hopes placed on him when he was elected Pope were soon disappointed. He squandered the fortune left by *Julius II, and his concern for the independence of the Papal states led him to pursue a shifting political course. He failed to understand what was involved in the revolt of M. *Luther, whom he excommunicated in 1520.

LEO XIII (1810–1903), Pope from 1878. Vincenzo Gioacchino Pecci became Bp. of Perugia in 1846 and a cardinal in 1853. As Pope he restored good relations with Germany after the *Kulturkampf, procuring the gradual abolition of the *May Laws in 1886 and 1887. In 1892 he established an Apostolic Delegation in Washington, and he renewed contacts with *Russia and *Japan. The improvement of relations with Britain found expression in King Edward VII's visit to the Vatican in 1903. Relations with Italy, however, remained strained, and those between the Church and State in *France deteriorated.

His pontificate was important for the lead which he gave on the political and social issues of the time. In some notable encyclicals he developed the Christian doctrine of the State on the basis of St. *Thomas Aquinas. His most important pronouncement on social questions was '*Rerum Novarum' (q.v.) in 1891. He established the *Biblical Commission in 1902 and gave a measure of encouragement to the new methods of Biblical criticism. He encouraged Anglican aspirations for union and appointed a commission to investigate *Anglican Ordinations, which he rejected as invalid in 1896. He also promoted the spiritual life of the Church.

LEO III (c. 675–741), Byzantine Emperor from 717, 'the Isaurian'. After defeating the Saracens in 718, he effected administrative reforms and issued a new code of law. Between 726 and 729 he issued a number of edicts against image worship, thus initiating the *Iconoclastic Controversy.

LEO VI (866–912), known as **Leo the Philosopher**, Byzantine Emperor from 886. He banished the Patr. of *Constantinople, *Photius, to a monastery. In the disputes that followed his own fourth marriage he appealed from the new Patriarch to the Pope, who recognized the validity of the marriage.

LEODEGAR, St., Ledger, or **Leger** (c. 616–79), Bp. of Autun from 663. He imposed the Rule of St. *Benedict on all religious houses in his diocese and prob. ordered the clergy to adopt the *Athanasian Creed as a safeguard against the *Monothelite heresy. After the death of Clotaire III in 670 he became involved in the struggles of the claimants to the throne and was beheaded.

LEONARD, St. (6th cent.), hermit. Acc. to an 11th-cent. life, he was a Frankish nobleman of the court of King *Clovis, whom St. *Remigius converted to Christianity. He lived in a cell near Limoges and later founded a monastery.

LEONARDO DA VINCI (1452–1519), Italian painter and scholar. From 1483 to 1499 he lived at Milan; during this period he executed some of his best-known works, incl. the *Last Supper*. This depicted not the institution of the Eucharist but the moment of the announcement of the betrayal. When the French invaded Milan (1499), Leonardo left and began a nomadic life mainly devoted to scientific and scholarly work.

LEONINE CITY. The part of Rome on the right bank of the Tiber, fortified with a wall by Pope *Leo IV in 848–52.

LEONINE PRAYERS. In the RC rite, the prayers which until 1964 were recited in the vernacular by priest and people at the end of Mass. Their fullest form (three *Hail Mary*s, the *Salve Regina*, a collect, and an invocation of St. *Michael) went back to *Leo XIII.

LEONINE SACRAMENTARY. The earliest surviving book of Mass prayers according to the Roman rite. It exists in a single 7th-cent. MS. preserved at *Verona. Its attribution to Pope *Leo I is arbitrary. It is not a *sacramentary in the proper sense, but a private collection of *libelli. It possesses no *Ordinary or *Canon of the Mass and contains only the variable parts of the liturgy.

LEONTIUS OF BYZANTIUM (6th cent.), anti-*Monophysite theologian. He is prob. to be distinguished from the Scythian monk of the same name who took part in the *Theopaschite controversy, but practically nothing is known of his life. A staunch upholder of *Chalcedonian Christology, he introduced the notion of *Enhypostasia (q.v.). His main theological work was *Libri III contra Nestorianos et Eutychianos*.

LEPANTO, Battle of (1571). The naval · battle in which the 'Christian League' (mainly Venice and Spain) decisively defeated the Turks, who were threatening W. Christendom.

LEPORIUS (early 5th cent.), monk. He taught that Christ's moral experiences were similar to ours, and held other doctrines akin to *Pelagianism and early *Nestorianism. He publicly confessed his error at Carthage.

LÉRINS. The ancient name of two islands off Cannes in the Mediterranean, on the smaller of which (now 'St. Honorat') a celebrated monastery was founded by St. *Honoratus c. 410.

LESLIE, CHARLES (1650–1722), *Nonjuring divine. His voluminous writings are learned and ranked highly as controversial productions in his day. The most celebrated was an attack on the *Deist philosophy

LESLIE, JOHN (1527–96), Bp. of Ross from 1566. In 1569 he became *Mary Queen of Scots' ambassador to *Elizabeth I, but in 1571 he was imprisoned for assisting Mary in her projected marriage to the Duke of Norfolk. He was set free in 1573 on condition that he left Britain; on the Continent he continued to further plans in the RC interest. The later part of his *De Origine, Moribus, et Rebus Gestis Scotorum* (Rome, 1578) is an important authority for contemporary events.

LESSER ENTRANCE, The. In the E. Church, the procession at the Liturgy with the *Gospel Book.

LESSING, GOTTHOLD EPHRAIM

(1729–81), a leading figure of the *Aufklärung*. He followed a literary career. His interest in theological problems was stimulated by the fragments of H. S. *Reimarus which he edited (1774–8). He saw the essence of religion in a purely humanitarian morality independent of all historical revelation; he embodied his views in the principal figure of his play *Nathan der Weise* (1779). His theoretical writings on the subject laid the foundations of the Protestant Liberalism that was to hold sway in Germany all through the 19th cent. He also made some original studies on the Gospels.

LESSIUS, LEONHARD (1554–1623), *Jesuit theologian. He took a prominent part in the controversies on the nature of *grace, defending a position akin to that of L. de *Molina; in 1587 the Louvain Theological Faculty condemned 34 theses from his works. He also wrote on moral theology.

LETTERS OF BUSINESS. The documents formerly issued by the Crown to the English *Convocations permitting them to prepare *canons on a prescribed subject.

LETTERS DIMISSORY. In the C of E the licence which the Bishop of a diocese where a candidate for Holy Orders has his title issues to the Bishop of another diocese to perform the ministerial act of Ordination when the former Bishop finds it inconvenient or impossible to ordain the candidate.

LETTERS OF ORDERS. A certificate issued to those who have been ordained, bearing the seal and signature of the officiating Bishop.

LETTERS TESTIMONIAL. The certificate of 'good life and conversation' which until 1977 a candidate for ordination in the C of E was required to present to the ordaining Bishop.

LEVELLERS. A 17th-cent. English political and religious party. They were opposed to kingship and advocated freedom in religion and a wide extension of the suffrage. The name first occurs in 1647. Their main support was in the Army. They had disappeared by 1660.

LEVI, SON OF ALPHAEUS. The taxgatherer called by Christ to be one of His disciples (Mk. 2: 14). He is identified with St. *Matthew.

LEVIATHAN. An animal referred to at various places in the OT. The name was transferred mythologically to the Devil. T. *Hobbes gave his treatise on 'the matter, form, and power of a Commonwealth' this title.

LEVIRATE MARRIAGE. The marriage of a man with his brother's widow.

LEVITES. Acc. to the Biblical accounts, one of the twelve tribes, descended from Levi, one of *Jacob's sons, and specifically set aside as ministers of the sanctuary. In the *Deuteronomic legislation, the term 'priest' and 'Levite' are interchangeable. After the Exile the Levites were allotted only the inferior duties in the *Temple.

LEVITICUS, Book of. This OT Book is the third in the *Pentateuch. It consists almost wholly of legislation. Chapters 17–26 form a well-defined unity known as the 'Code of *Holiness' (q.v.). The rest of the Book cannot be earlier than the 6th cent. B.C.

LEYDEN. To mark its heroic defence against the Spanish (1574), William of Orange in 1575 gave the city a university with a special college for the study of the Reformed religion. It was at first a stronghold of *Calvinist orthodoxy, but in the 17th cent. it became the scene of various theological controversies.

LIBELLATICI. The name given to those who during the *Decian persecution (249–51) procured certificates by purchase from the civil authorities stating that they had sacrificed to pagan idols, when in fact no such sacrifice had been made.

LIBELLI MISSARUM. Booklets containing the formularies for one or more Masses for a given period for use of a particular church. They did not include the *Canon, which was fixed, the readings from Scripture, or the parts which were sung. They formed the link between the period of free composition and the organization of fixed formularies in a *Sacramentary.

LIBER CENSUUM. The official register of the Roman Church, which recorded the dues (*census*) payable by various institutions, esp. monasteries, churches, cities, and kingdoms, to the Holy See. It was compiled in the late 12th cent.

LIBER COMICUS. See *Comes*.

LIBER DE CAUSIS. A treatise, consisting largely of extracts from Proclus's 'Elements of Theology', which was put together in Arabic by an unknown Muslim philosopher c. 850. Translated into Latin between 1167 and 1187, for about a century it circulated as a work of *Aristotle and deeply influenced medieval philosophy.

LIBER PONTIFICALIS. A collection of early Papal biographies. Those of the earliest Popes are short, but from the 4th cent. onwards they tend to increase in size. The earliest form of the work appears to date from the time of Boniface II (530–2); subsequent redactions carry the history to the death of *Martin V (1431) and even later.

LIBER REGALIS. The Book containing the English *Coronation service introduced for the crowning of Edward II in 1308. It was translated into English for *James I (1603) and remained in use until it was discarded by *James II in 1685.

LIBERAL ARTS, The Seven. See *Seven Liberal Arts*.

LIBERAL EVANGELICALISM. The outlook of those within the C of E who, while maintaining their spiritual kinship with the *Evangelical Revival, have been concerned to re-state old truths in terms felt to be more consonant with modern thought.

LIBERALISM. A general tendency to favour freedom and progress, with various shades of meaning in a theological context. The 'Liberal Catholics', who formed a distinguished group in the RC Church in the 19th cent., were mainly orthodox theologically, though they favoured political democracy and ecclesiastical reform. 'Liberal Protestantism', on the other hand, developed into an anti-dogmatic and humanitarian reconstruction of the Christian faith which seemed to gain ground in nearly all Protestant Churches. The word 'liberalism' is also sometimes used of a belief in secular humanism which is inconsistent with Biblical and dogmatic orthodoxy.

LIBERIAN CATALOGUE. An early list of Popes down to *Liberius (352–66). It is one of the items in a collection of documents made by the '*Chronographer of 354' (q.v.).

LIBERIUS, Pope from 352 to 366. Ordered by the *Arian Emp. Constantius to assent to the condemnation of St. *Athanasius, Liberius refused and was banished from Rome in 355. In 357 he submitted and in 358 he was allowed to reoccupy his see, having signed an Arian formulary; its precise nature is disputed.

LICENCES, Marriage. See *Marriage Licences.*

LICHFIELD. The seat of a Mercian diocese under St. *Chad, it was for a brief period (787–803) an archiepiscopal see. The present cathedral dates mainly from the 13th cent.

LICH-GATE. See *Lych Gate.*

LIDDELL, HENRY GEORGE (1811–98), lexicographer. He was Dean of *Christ Church, Oxford, from 1855 to 1891. The Greek Lexicon, on which he collaborated with R. *Scott, appeared in a modest form in 1843. It has been constantly revised and extended.

LIDDON, HENRY PARRY (1829–90), Canon of *St. Paul's from 1870 and from 1870 to 1882 also Dean Ireland professor of exegesis at Oxford. From the sixties he exercised great influence at Oxford in face of post-*Tractarian liberalism, and throughout his life he used his influence to extend Catholic principles. He was interested in the *Old Catholics and attended the *Bonn Reunion Conferences. He had an intense admiration for E. B. *Pusey, whose life he wrote (posthumously publd., 1893–7).

LIETZMANN, HANS (1875–1942), Church historian. He succeeded A *Harnack at Berlin in 1924. He worked on the Greek patristic *catenae, made a fresh and important attempt to distinguish the genuine and spurious works of *Apollinaris of Laodicea (1904), produced an edition of the *Gregorian Sacramentary (1921), and wrote a manual of Church history (1932–44; Eng.

tr., 1937–51).

'LIFE AND WORK'. The branch of the *Ecumenical Movement concerned with the relation of Christian faith to society, politics, and economics. It held conferences at *Stockholm (1925) and *Oxford (1937).

LIGHT OF THE WORLD, The. A title of Christ derived from Jn. 8: 12. It is the subject of Holman *Hunt's famous picture.

LIGHTFOOT, JOHN (1602–75), Biblical and Rabbinic scholar. He was an influential member of the *Westminster Assembly, in which he opposed the extreme *Presbyterians. He assisted B. *Walton with the *Polyglot Bible of 1657. His own *Horae Hebraicae et Talmudicae* (1658–78) was designed to show the bearing of Jewish studies on the interpretation of the NT, it is not entirely superseded.

LIGHTFOOT, JOSEPH BARBER (1828–89), Bp of *Durham from 1879. He held high academic posts at Cambridge and from 1870 to 1880 he was a member of the Company of Revisers of the NT. His critical work on the NT and the Fathers has stood the test of time. It was marked by wide Patristic and classical erudition, lucid presentation, freedom from technicalities, and avoidance of sectional controversy. It included commentaries on St. Paul's Epistles, an edition of *Clement of Rome (1869), and his famous *Ignatius* (1885), which finally disposed of W. *Cureton's suggestion that only the three Epistles in the Syriac recension were genuine.

LIGHTFOOT, ROBERT HENRY (1883–1953), NT scholar. He taught at Oxford most of his life. His work was marked by accuracy and caution, deference to German *form-criticism, and scepticism about the historicity of the Synoptic narratives.

LIGHTS, Feast of. See *Dedication (Jewish Feast of the).*

LIGUORI, St. ALPHONSUS. See *Alphonsus Liguori, St.*

LIGUGÉ, Defensor of. See *Defensor.*

LIMBO. In Latin theology the abode of

souls excluded from the full blessedness of the *beatific vision, but not condemned to any other punishment.

LINACRE, THOMAS (*c.* 1460–1524), humanist and founder of the Royal College of Physicians. He studied in Italy, and on his return to Oxford was recognized as one of the foremost humanist scholars in the country. He was among the first to encourage the study of Greek in England.

LINCOLN. A see was established here by Bp. Remigius (d. 1092), who transferred it from *Dorchester, Oxon. It became the largest diocese in England, extending from the Thames to the Humber. The cathedral was begun in 1086 and largely completed by 1300.

LINCOLN JUDGEMENT, The. The judgement given in 1890 by E. W. *Benson, Abp. of *Canterbury, upon complaints against Edward *King, Bp. of *Lincoln, for consecrating the Eucharist in the *eastward position, mixing water and wine in the *Chalice, and four other matters. The judgement upheld the bishop in the main.

LINDISFARNE, the 'Holy Island'. After St. *Aidan's arrival in 635, Lindisfarne became a missionary centre and an episcopal see, and the monastic school had some distinguished pupils. The monastery was pillaged by the Danes, but monastic life continued from 1082 until the *Dissolution. Eardulf, the last of the 16 bishops, moved his see to Chester-le-Street in 875; it was transferred to *Durham in 995.

The 'Lindisfarne Gospels' (in the British Library) was written and decorated *c.* 696–8.

LINDSEY, THEOPHILUS (1723–1808), *Unitarian. He held various livings in the C of E. He became doubtful about the doctrine of the *Trinity and, stimulated in his unorthodoxy by friendship with J. *Priestley, he joined in the '*Feathers Tavern' petition to Parliament (1772). After its failure he became a Unitarian and from 1774 he conducted services in London.

LINGARD, JOHN (1771–1851), English historian. Of an old RC family, he was ordained priest in 1795. From 1811 he spent most of his life in a small country mission.

The success of his *History of England* [to 1688] (1819–30) was due to its objectivity, its extensive use of contemporary documents, and the new light in which it viewed such controversial periods as the Reformation. There is some evidence that he was created cardinal *in petto* in 1826.

LINUS, St. Acc. to all the early episcopal lists, Linus was Bp. of Rome after the Apostles *Peter and *Paul. Nothing further is certainly known.

LION. In representations of the story of Daniel in the lions' den (Dan. 6) the lion is conceived as a 'type' of God's redemption of His chosen people. The lion is also a symbol of St. *Mark.

LIPPI, Fra FILIPPO (*c.* 1406–69), Italian painter. He became a *Carmelite in 1420 but was later released from his vows. His works include the *Coronation of the Blessed Virgin* (1441), the *Vision St. Bernard* (1447), and frescoes of *St. John the Baptist* and *St. Stephen* (1452–64).

LIPSIUS, RICHARD ADELBERT (1830–1892), German Protestant theologian. His works on the *apocryphal acts did much to unravel the problems connected with this type of literature, and in 1891, with M. Bonnet, he edited what became the standard text.

LISLE, A. L. M. P. DE. See *De Lisle, A. L. M. P.*

LISMORE, The Book of. A collection of lives of Irish saints, written in medieval Irish, found at Lismore castle in 1814.

LITANY. A form of prayer consisting of a series of petitions or biddings sung or said by a deacon, priest, or cantors, to which the people make a fixed response. The litany apparently originated at *Antioch in the 4th cent.; it spread to *Constantinople and later to the W. Pope *Gelasius I (492–6) introduced into the Mass a litanic intercession, of which the *Kyrie is the sole surviving relic.

LITANY, The (BCP). The form of 'general supplication' appointed to be said or sung after *Morning Prayer in the C of E on Sundays, Wednesdays, and Fridays. It is also included, with additional petitions, in the rites of *Ordination.

LITANY DESK. In the C of E, a low movable desk at which the minister kneels to recite the Litany.

LITANY OF LORETO, The. A litany in honour of the BVM, consisting of a series of invocations to our Lady under various honorific titles such as 'Mother of Divine grace', each followed by the request: 'Pray for us'. Its name derives from *Loreto, though it prob. did not originate there.

LITANY OF THE SAINTS, The. A litany used in the RC Church. It consists of invocations for mercy and deliverance addressed to the Persons of the Trinity and for intercession to the BVM and a list of prophets, patriarchs, angels, saints, confessors, and virgins, individually and in classes. Early forms of such a litany are found in the E. from the end of the 3rd cent. and in the W. from the late 5th cent. The list of saints was revised in 1969.

LITERATE. In the C of E a cleric who has been admitted to Holy Orders without a university degree.

LITERARY CRITICISM. See *Higher Criticism*.

LITTLE BROTHERS OF JESUS. See *De Foucauld, C. E.*

LITTLE ENTRANCE. See *Lesser Entrance*.

LITTLE FLOWER OF JESUS, The. A popular designation for St. *Teresa of Lisieux.

LITTLE FLOWERS OF ST. FRANCIS (the 'Fioretti'). A classic collection of legends about St. *Francis of Assisi (d. 1226) and his companions. It is apparently an anonymous Tuscan translation of part of the Latin 'Acts of the Blessed Francis and his Companions', which was written c. 1325, with some other material. The translation dates from c. 1375.

LITTLE GIDDING. A manor in Cambridgeshire where the Ferrar family lived under a religious rule from 1625 until they were raided by O. *Cromwell's soldiers in 1646. The household, some forty persons in all, consisted of Nicholas *Ferrar, his mother, and the families of his brother and sister. They followed a systematic round of devotion and work, reciting the whole Psalter each day, and engaging in charitable work for the neighbourhood.

LITTLE LABYRINTH, The. A lost 3rd-cent. treatise directed against the *Adoptionist heretics *Theodotus and *Artemon. It was perhaps the work of St. *Hippolytus.

LITTLE OFFICE OF OUR LADY. A brief office in honour of the BVM, modelled on the Divine *Office. First known in the 10th cent., its use spread from the religious orders to the secular clergy, who are, however, no longer bound to recite it. It is the ordinary form of vocal prayer for a number of new congregations of women. In 1953 a revision was approved; this introduced greater variety.

LITTLE OFFICES. Originally these were very short offices, modelled on the *Little Office of Our Lady, and intended for devotional use. In modern times the term has come commonly to denote more elaborate forms of prayer, based on the Divine *Office, and intended for corporate as well as individual use. They are mainly in the vernacular.

LITTLE SISTERS. See *De Foucauld, C. E.*

LITURGICAL COLOURS. See *Colours, Liturgical*.

LITURGICAL MOVEMENT. A movement whose object is to restore the active participation of the laity in the official worship of the Church. In the RC Church it was fostered by certain *Benedictine abbeys in the 19th cent.; it received an impetus from *Pius X's directions relating to Church music (1903) and his promotion of frequent Communion. At about the time of the Second World War in France and slightly later in Germany the movement spread beyond the monastic centres into the parishes. The attempt to restore the scrupulous observance of the liturgy in the form in which it had developed was joined by pressure for the reform of the rite itself, in order to bring it more into line with earlier liturgical practice and with the pastoral and evangelistic needs of the day. These aspirations lay behind the development of the 'dialogue Mass', in which the people joined in the responses, and the custom of reading a vernacular version of the liturgy in the body of the church while the priest celebrated in Latin. *Pius XII began a reform of the liturgical rites with the revision of the *Holy Week liturgy in 1951 and 1955. The Second *Vatican Council encouraged the participation of the laity in the liturgy and legislated for the use of the vernacular; a new Missal followed in 1970.

In the C of E the Ritualist Movement, inaugurated by the *Tractarians to give a central place to sacramental worship, developed in the early 20th cent. More recently there have been changes in the pattern of Sunday worship, with a tendency to replace the various morning services with one 'Parish Communion'; ceremonial designed to stress the corporate aspects of the liturgy has also been introduced in many places. The same influences which have been felt in the RC Church have also played some part in the liturgical revisions authorized by the Prayer Book (*Alternative and other Services) Measure (1965). In other Churches there have been comparable developments and a similar reaction against individualism.

LITURGIOLOGY. The scientific study of liturgies and related subjects.

LITURGY. The word is used in two senses: (1) of all the prescribed services of the Church, as contrasted with private devotion; and (2) esp. in the E. Church, as a title for the *Eucharist. In derived senses it is also used both of the written texts which order services and of the study of these.

LIUDHARD, St. (d. c. 602), chaplain to Queen Bertha, who brought him from Gaul to England under the terms of her marriage to *Ethelbert, King of Kent.

LIUTPRAND (c. 922–c. 972), Bp. of Cremona from 961. He was chancellor to Berengar of Italy, but later attached himself to the Emp. Otto I, who sent him on a number of missions. His writings are the chief authority for the Italian history of the period.

LIVERPOOL CATHEDRALS. (1) *The Anglican Cathedral* was designed by G. G. *Scott in the Romantic Gothic style on a vast scale. The foundation stone was laid in 1904

and work was completed in 1978.

(2) *The RC Cathedral.* A large Gothic-revival building was designed by A. W. *Pugin in 1853, but only the Lady Chapel was built. In 1930 Sir Edwin Lutyens designed a massive domed building on a new site; only the crypt was built. A circular and completely modern building, designed by Sir Frederick Gibberd, was consecrated in 1967.

LIVINGSTONE, DAVID (1813–73), African missionary and explorer. He went to Africa under the auspices of the *L.M.S. and worked as a missionary for some years in the Bechuana country. Reports of his explorations aroused wide interest in England. Returning to Africa in 1858, he discovered the lakes of Shirwa and Nyasa, explored the basin of the Upper Nile, and discovered Lake Bangweulu. He gave pioneer help to the *U.M.C.A.

LLANDAFF. Cathedral city in *Wales, 2 miles north of the centre of Cardiff. A monastery appears to have been founded here by St. *Teilo (d. c. 560), who became its first abbot and bishop. After the change from the monastic to the diocesan episcopate, the diocese became suffragan to *Canterbury in 1107. The cathedral was begun in 1120. It was badly damaged by an air raid in 1941, and when it was restored in 1957 an impressive figure of 'Christ in Majesty' by Sir Jacob Epstein was placed high at the east end of the nave.

L.M.S. The London Missionary Society was founded in 1795 by a body of *Congregationalists, *Anglicans, *Presbyterians, and *Wesleyans who combined to promote Christian missions to the heathen. It was one of its principles that no form of denominationalism should be preached by its members, but that decisions about Church government should be left to those whom they should convert. The Society came to be almost exclusively supported by Congregationalists, and in 1966 its work became the responsibility of the *Congregational Council for World Mission.

LOCKE, JOHN (1632–1704), philosopher. He was secretary to Lord Shaftesbury; on his fall in 1683 Locke fled to Holland. He returned to England soon after the accession of William and Mary.

Locke was the foremost defender of free

inquiry and toleration in the later 17th cent. In the *Letters concerning Toleration* (1689, 1690, and 1692) he pleaded for religious toleration for all except atheists and RCs, whom he excluded as a danger to the State. His ideal was a national Church with an all-embracing creed that made ample allowance for individual opinion, on the ground that human understanding was too limited for one man to impose his beliefs on another. His famous *Essay Concerning Human Understanding* (1690) attacks the *Platonist conception of 'innate ideas'. The human mind is a *tabula rasa* and all ideas come from experience, i.e. sensation or reflection, knowledge through reason being, acc. to him, a 'natural revelation'. Pure reality cannot be grasped by the human mind; consequently there is no sure basis for metaphysics. The spirituality of the soul, though not certain, is at least probable; the existence of God, on the other hand, can be discovered with certainty by reason, and His law gives men their rule of conduct. In *The Reasonableness of Christianity* (1695) Locke maintains that the only secure basis of Christianity is its reasonableness. The work aroused much opposition.

LOCULUS. (1) The commonest type of tomb in the *catacombs, in the form of a horizontal rectangular niche. (2) The hole which contains the relics in a fixed altar.

LOGIA (Gk., 'sayings'). In NT criticism the term is applied to a supposed collection of the sayings of Christ which circulated in the early Church; this collection is sometimes equated with the lost document '*Q'. The term is also used of the '*Sayings of Jesus' found at *Oxyrhynchus.

LOGOS (Gk., 'Word' or 'Reason'), used in Christian theology with reference to the Second Person of the Trinity. The term was known both in pagan and Jewish antiquity. In the OT God's word was not only the medium of His communication with men; what God said had creative power, and by the time of the Prophets the Word of the Lord was regarded as having an almost independent existence. In Hellenistic Judaism the concept of the Logos as an independent *hypostasis was further developed.

In the NT the term in its technical sense is confined to the Johannine writings. In the Prologue to St. John's Gospel the Logos is described as God from eternity, the Creative Word, who became incarnate in the man Jesus Christ of Nazareth. Though it is clear that the author was influenced by the same background as *Philo, his identification of the Logos with the Messiah was new. In Patristic theology the Johannine teaching about the Logos was taken up by St. *Ignatius and developed by the *Apologists of the 2nd cent., who saw in it a means of making the Christian teaching compatible with Hellenistic philosophy.

LOISY, ALFRED FIRMIN (1857–1940), French *Modernist Biblical scholar. He applied historico-critical methods to the study of the Bible. In 1902 he published *L'Évangile et l'Église*. As against A. *Harnack, who sought to base Christianity on the teaching of the historical Jesus apart from later dogmatic accretions, Loisy maintained that its essence was to be sought in the faith of the developed Church as expanded under the guidance of the Spirit. The book was condemned by the Abp. of Paris. In 1903, when Loisy published not only an account of the controversy but also *Le Quatrième Évangile*, *Pius X placed both books on the *Index. Loisy made a formal act of submission and retired to the country. The final breach with the Church came after the Papal acts of 1907 condemning modernism. Loisy published *Simples Réflexions sur le décret du Saint-Office* Lamentabili (1908) and the second volume of *Les Évangiles synoptiques* (2 vols, 1907–8); two months later he was excommunicated.

From 1909 to 1930 Loisy was a professor at the Collège de France. He was a prolific writer, but after his break with the Church his work on the NT was generally regarded as erratic and recklessly conjectural. It appears, however, that he was a mystic, with a pastoral sense.

LOLLARDY. A 'Lollard' was originally a follower of J. *Wycliffe; later the term was applied somewhat vaguely to anyone seriously critical of the Church. The Lollards, following Wycliffe, based their teaching on personal faith, Divine election, and above all the Bible. They commonly attacked clerical *celibacy, *transubstantiation, *indulgences, and *pilgrimages, and they held that the validity of priestly acts was determined by the priest's moral character.

The movement went through several

phases. For about 20 years it enjoyed some academic support, though in 1382 Abp. W. *Courtenay's condemnation of Wycliffe's teaching deprived Lollardy of a base at Oxford. In the early 15th cent. rigorous persecution caused most of the early leaders to recant. After Sir John *Oldcastle's rising of 1414, and another attempted rising of 1431, the movement went underground. Though it never won over the governing classes in strength, it seems to have contributed to the English Reformation by providing areas and minds receptive to *Lutheranism, and some have traced its continued influence in the congregational dissent of the 17th cent.

LOMBARD, PETER. See *Peter Lombard*.

LONDON. See *St. Paul's Cathedral*, *Westminster Abbey*, and *Westminster Cathedral*.

LONDON MISSIONARY SOCIETY. See *L.M.S.*

LONGINUS, St. The name traditionally given to the soldier who pierced the side of Christ with a spear. It is also sometimes attributed to the centurion who, standing by the Cross, confessed Christ the Son of God, and the two persons are often confused.

LONGLAND, JOHN (1473–1547), Bp of *Lincoln from 1521. As *Henry VIII's confessor, he took a prominent part in furthering the divorce proceedings against Catherine of Aragon.

LONGLEY, CHARLES THOMAS (1794–1868), Abp. of *Canterbury from 1862. He proceeded as far as he could against J. W. *Colenso without provoking a conflict with the law, and he convened the first *Lambeth Conference (1867).

LOPEZ, GREGORY (1611–91), the first native Chinese bishop. Of pagan parentage, he embraced Christianity when he grew up. In 1651 he became a *Dominican, and in 1656 he was ordained the first Chinese priest. He twice declined offers of bishoprics, but in 1685 he was consecrated at Canton. There was no further native RC bishop in China until 1918.

LORD OF HOSTS. This Divine title occurs in the OT 282 times. Through its translation in some places in the LXX, and thence into Latin as *Deus omnipotens*, it is the direct ancestor of the English 'Almighty God'.

LORD'S DAY, The. A Christian appellation of *Sunday.

LORD'S PRAYER, The. The prayer beginning 'Our Father', taught by the Lord to the Apostles. In the NT it is given in slightly different forms in Mt. 6: 9–13 and in Lk. 11: 2–4. The form in Mt. is that universally used by Christians. A concluding doxology was prob. added in early times and was taken over into some Gospel MSS.

The prayer is usually divided into the address and seven petitions, the first three asking for the glorification of God, the latter four being requests for the chief physical and spiritual needs of man. As a prayer given to the Church by Christ, it has always been regarded as uniquely sacred. It has regularly had a place in the Eucharist and the Divine *Office, and has frequently been expounded.

LORD'S SUPPER, The. A title for the *Eucharist, now used esp. by Protestants.

LORETO, near Ancona in Italy, is the site of the Holy House, alleged to have been inhabited by the BVM at the time of the *Annunciation and miraculously transported to Loreto by angels in 1295. See also *Litany of Loreto*.

LORIC OF ST. PATRICK. See *Breastplate of St. Patrick*.

LORSCH. A *Benedictine Abbey near Worms. Founded in 764 by monks from *Gorze, it became one of the largest and best-endowed abbeys in Germany. In the 10th cent. it was a centre of the Gorze reform movement.

LOSSKY, VLADIMIR (1903–58), Russian lay theologian. Expelled from Russia in 1922, he spent the rest of his life in France. He became a leading exponent of Orthodox thought to the W. world and a vigorous opponent of the sophiological doctrines of S. *Bulgakov.

LOS VON ROM (Germ., 'free from Rome'). An anti-Roman Movement begun in Austria in 1897 and fostered by the Pan-German party, who aimed at the incorporation of an Austria, freed from the Pope, into

Germany under the protection of the Protestant Hohenzollern Emperors. Though most of those who left the RC Church became nominally Protestant, the Movement was essentially anti-Christian.

LOTZE, HERMANN (1817–81), logician and metaphysician. He was professor of philosophy at Göttingen from 1842 to 1881. He was insistent that philosophy must be rooted in the natural sciences. He had a firm faith in *theism, and, believing in the validity of moral judgements, he became an early exponent of 'value philosophy'.

LOU, TSENG-TSIANG (1871–1949), Chinese statesman and *Benedictine monk. The son of a Protestant catechist, he held various high government offices. He became a RC in 1911. In 1927, after the death of his wife, he entered the abbey of St.-André near Bruges. His intention of returning to the E. to establish a Benedictine Congregation in China was frustrated by ill-health. He saw Christianity as the fulfilment of Confucianism.

LOUIS OF GRANADA. See *Luis of Granada*.

LOUIS I (778–840) **(the Pious or le Débonnaire).** He was the third son of *Charlemagne (d. 814), who appointed him joint emperor in 813. Though politically weak and indecisive, Louis had undoubted religious interests and was a patron of learning.

LOUIS IX, St. (1214–70). King of France from 1226. Having resolved in 1244 to go on a *crusade, he sailed in 1248 and captured the Egyptian port of Damietta in 1249. In 1250, however, the Crusaders were routed and Louis taken prisoner. He returned to France in 1254, imposed peace on Flanders, and signed treaties with Aragon and England. He embarked on a further crusade in 1270, but died of dysentery at Tunis.

A man of austere and prayerful life, Louis embodied the highest ideals of medieval kingship. He built the *Sainte-Chapelle in Paris for the *Crown of Thorns which he acquired from the Emp. Baldwin II in 1239.

LOURDES, a place of pilgrimage in France. In 1858 14-year-old *Bernadette Soubirous had visions here of the BVM, who told her that she was the Immaculate Conception. A spring appeared; miraculous healings were soon reported to have taken place; and the faithful began to flock to Lourdes. Vast churches have been built and a medical bureau established to investigate the character of the cures.

LOVE. In Christian theology, the principle of God's action and man's response. In the NT the Christian conception of love is denoted by the special word ἀγάπη (see *Agape*), which is rendered in some English translations as *charity.

In the OT the loving character of God was recognized, notably by *Hosea, but it was only in the NT that the doctrine that love constitutes the essential nature of God was developed. As the bond between the Father and the Son, it is especially associated with the Holy Spirit. In 1 Cor. 13: 1–8 the manifestations of love are described; it concerns the will rather than the emotions.

LOVE, CHRISTOPHER (1618–51), *Puritan minister. About 1641 he was imprisoned for his criticism of the BCP; soon after the outbreak of the Civil War he became an army chaplain and was ordained. His zeal for *Presbyterianism incurred the hostility of the *Independents and in 1651 he was accused of conspiring with *Charles II and was executed.

LOW CHURCHMEN. The group in the C of E which gives a relatively unimportant or 'low' place to the claims of the episcopate, priesthood, and sacraments, and approximates in its beliefs to those of Protestant Nonconformists.

LOW MASS. In the W. Church, the simplified form of Mass which until recently was the form of Mass in most frequent use. In a Low Mass the celebrating priest had no ministers to assist him except a single server, and no part of the service was sung. The term no longer occurs in the RC *Ordo Missae*, which requires that all Masses celebrated with the people should be community Masses with singing if possible.

LOW SUNDAY. The first Sunday after *Easter.

LOWDER, CHARLES FUGE (1820–80). *Anglo-Catholic priest. In 1856 he joined the staff of St. George's in the East, where he took a leading part in the first regular mission work in East London. The advanced ceremonial led to riots, but the work expanded and Lowder built the church of St. Peter's, London Docks, of which he became vicar.

LOYOLA, St. IGNATIUS. See *Ignatius Loyola, St*.

LUBBERTUS, SIBRANDUS (1556/7–1625), Dutch *Calvinist theologian. In 1585 he became professor of dogmatics at Franeker. Before long he was one of the foremost upholders of orthodox Calvinism in Holland against the rising *Arminianism. He took a prominent part in the Hague Conference of 1607 and in the Synod of *Dort (1618).

LUCAR, CYRIL (1572–1638), Patr. of *Constantinople from 1620. The Synod of *Brest–Litovsk in 1596 had turned him against the RC Church, and he became increasingly friendly towards the *Calvinists and the C of E. He presented the *Codex Alexandrinus to *Charles I in 1628. In 1629 a *Confessio Fidei*, with his signature, was published at Geneva; this reinterprets traditional Orthodox faith in Calvinist terms. He was put to death on a charge of inciting the Cossacks against the Turkish government. His teaching was condemned by various later synods.

LUCIAN OF ANTIOCH, St. (d. 312), theologian and martyr. A presbyter of *Antioch, he founded an influential school of which both *Arius and *Eusebius of Nicomedia were members; his *subordinationist teaching seems to have been the immediate source of the Arian heresy. He revised the Greek text of the Bible (see *Lucianic Text*).

LUCIAN OF SAMOSATA (c. 115–c. 200), pagan satirist. In his account of the life of Peregrinus, a historical person who was converted to Christianity and later apostatized, Lucian depicts the Christians as kindly but credulous. The *Philopatris*, which purports to be his work, is much later.

LUCIANIC TEXT. The text of the Greek Bible, as revised by *Lucian of Antioch, soon became the standard text in Syria, Asia Minor, and *Constantinople, and its NT lies behind the '*Textus Receptus' and AV.

LUCIFER (Lat., 'light-bearer'). In Is. 14: 12 (Vulg. and AV) the epithet is applied to the king of Babylon. Taking this verse in conjunction with Lk. 10: 18, St. *Jerome and other Fathers used the name as a synonym for the Devil.

LUCIFER (d. 370/71), Bp. of Cagliari. A fiercely anti-Arian theologian, at the first session of the Council of Milan (354) he opposed the proposal to condemn *Athanasius; his altercations with the Emp. Constantius led to his banishment. After the accession of *Julian, he made his way to *Antioch, where he resisted all attempts to conciliate repentant Arians. By consecrating Paulinus bishop, he created a schism.

LUCINA. Several pious women of this name figure in the early traditions of the Roman Church. One of them is said to have removed the bodies of St. *Peter and St. *Paul from their resting-place in the *catacombs and laid that of St. Paul in her own property on the *Ostian Way.

LUCIUS. In legend, the first Christian king of Britain. Acc. to an early form of the story, Lucius asked Pope Eleutherus (174–89) for Christian teachers to be sent to Britain, and he, together with many of his subjects, received Baptism at their hands. The story was later much embellished.

LUCY, St. Acc. to tradition she was a native of Syracuse who proclaimed her Christian faith by distributing her goods to the poor at the height of the *Diocletianic persecution. She was denounced to the authorities by the man to whom she was betrothed, and martyred in 303.

LUDLOW, JOHN MALCOLM FORBES (1821–1911), founder of *Christian Socialism. Called to the bar in 1843, he wrote to F. D. *Maurice from Paris after the Revolution of 1848, insisting that 'the new socialism must be Christianized'. He was largely responsible for promoting the Industrial and Provident Societies Act of 1852, and he cooperated with Maurice in founding the Working Men's College. His influence did much to prevent in England the antagonism between the Church and Socialism which exists in most other countries.

LUDOLF, HIOB (1624–1704), German orientalist. He persuaded an Abyssinian to teach him *Ethiopic, which was still spoken in parts of Abyssinia, and then did much to make Ethiopic sources and history known in Europe. In one of his works the *Apostolic Tradition* of *Hippolytus was first made accessible to W. scholars.

LUDOLF OF SAXONY (d. 1378), also 'Ludolf the *Carthusian', spiritual writer. His chief works are a 'Commentary on the Psalms' and his celebrated 'Vita Christi'. The latter is not a biography but a meditation on the life of Christ, with doctrinal, spiritual, and moral instructions as well as prayers. It became very popular.

LUGO, JOHN DE (1583–1660), Spanish *Jesuit. In Rome he achieved fame as a theologian and was made a cardinal in 1643. He held that God gives light sufficient for salvation to every soul. In his Eucharistic teaching he emphasized the element of destruction as the distinctive characteristic of sacrificial worship, maintaining that in the act of Consecration Christ's human nature was in some sense 'destroyed' by being changed into a lower state, of which the primary object was to be consumed as food.

LUIS OF GRANADA (1504–88), Spanish spiritual writer. Luis Sarriá, who was born at Granada, was professed as a *Dominican in 1525. In 1555 he was invited by the Cardinal Infante Henry to go to Portugal, where he spent most of the rest of his life. His fame rests on his books of spiritual guidance, esp. the *Libro de la oración y meditación* ('Book on Prayer and Meditation', 1554) and the *Guía de pecadores* ('Guide for Sinners', 1556–7). He sought to give spiritual guidance for laymen as well as religious. He attributed great importance to the interior life, to mental as distinct from vocal prayer, and saw outward ceremonies as comparatively unimportant.

LUKE, St., Evangelist. Acc. to tradition he was the author of the Third Gospel and of *Acts. He was a physician (Col. 4: 14), and it has been inferred from Col. 4: 11 that he was a Gentile. He accompanied St. *Paul on parts of his second and third missionary journeys (Acts 16: 10–17 and 20: 5–21: 18) and went with him to Rome. Acc. to a tradition recorded in the *Anti-Marcionite Prologues,

he wrote his Gospel in Greece and died at the age of 84.

LUKE, Gospel of St. The third of the *Synoptic Gospels. From the 2nd cent. its authorship has been attributed to St. *Luke, and this attribution is generally accepted. Some scholars date it before A.D. 64; others assign it to a date between A.D. 70 and 100.

The author sets out his method and purpose in a brief prologue (1: 1–4), claiming to have collected his material from eyewitnesses. Acc. to most modern critics the Gospel is composed of two main sources, *Mark and the so-called '*Q'; the material peculiar to Lk. is commonly assigned to a third source called L.

The Gospel is written in idiomatic Greek. Its outstanding characteristic is its insistence on the life, death, and teaching of Christ as a message of universal salvation addressed to all men, not only the Jews. Passages peculiar to Lk. stress the Lord's kindness and human understanding and His care for outcasts, and there are a remarkable number of references to women not found in the other Gospels. Luke assigns a more prominent place to prayer in his picture of Christ than do the other Evangelists, and he stresses the activity of the Holy Spirit both in the events of the Lord's life and in the life of the Christian community.

LULL, RAYMOND (c. 1233–c. 1315), also **Llull**, missionary and philosopher. He was born in Majorca, then recently recovered from *Islamic rule, and educated as a knight. At the age of 30 he had a vision of Christ crucified; thenceforth he devoted himself to the conversion of Islam. For nine years he remained in Majorca studying Arabic and Christian thought; during this time he wrote his 'Book of Contemplation'. In a vision on Mt. Randa (c. 1274) the form in which he was to set out his ideas was revealed to him; he worked this out in his 'Art of Finding Truth'. From 1287 he travelled widely, seeking support for his plans to convert Islam. His one practical success was the decree of the Council of *Vienne (1311-2) establishing *studia* of oriental languages in five universities.

In his writings Lull elaborated an approach by which he sought the conversion of Islam and of the Jews by rational argument, without recourse to the authority of Scripture. He tried to relate 'all forms of knowledge ... to the manifestations of God's "Dignities" [i.e. Divine Attributes] in the universe, taking for its point of departure the monotheistic vision common to Judaism, Islam, and Christianity, and their acceptance of a broadly Neoplatonic exemplarist world-picture, and arguing ... analogically up and down "the ladder of being" ' (R. D. F. Pring-Mill). He made extensive use of diagrams.

LULLUS, St. (d. 786), Bp. of Mainz. An Anglo-Saxon, he went to Germany, where he became associated with St. *Boniface and was promised succession to the see of Mainz. After Boniface's death (754), however, a long dispute ensued between Lullus and the Abbot of *Fulda, and Lullus did not receive the *pallium until *c.* 781. He was learned and influential.

LUNA. P. DE. See *Benedict XIII, Antipope.*

LUND. Apart from one brief break, Lund was the seat of an archbishop from 1104 to 1536. The university dates from 1668. In the 19th cent. the theological faculty stood for a conservative and 'High Church' tradition in contrast to the liberalizing theology of *Upsala. In 1952 the *Faith and Order Commission of the *World Council of Churches held a conference at Lund.

LUPUS, St. (*c.* 383–479), Bp. of Troyes. After seven years of marriage, he and his wife agreed to separate and devote themselves to religion. Lupus became a monk at *Lérins in 426. In 427 he became Bp. of Troyes and held the see for some 50 years.

LUPUS, SERVATUS (*c.* 805–62), Abbot of Ferrières from 840. He took part in various synods and his letters are a primary historical source. His chief theological work, the *Liber de Tribus Quaestionibus* (*c.* 850), which arose out of the controversy provoked by *Gottschalk, defended *predestination to Hell as well as to eternal life, though his position was less rigid than that of Gottschalk.

LUTHER, MARTIN (1483–1546), founder of the German *Reformation. In 1505 Luther entered a monastery of the *Augustinian hermits; he was ordained priest in 1507, and in 1508 he was sent as lecturer to the recently founded university of *Wittenberg. He became anxious about his own salvation, and the fact that the routine of the religious life failed to bring him confidence led him to give up certain of his regular religious duties. The so-called 'Turmerlebnis' ('Tower Experience'), usually dated between 1512 and 1515, took the form of a sudden revelation which convinced him that faith alone justifies without works. He found support for this doctrine in St. *Augustine's anti-*Pelagian works, and from 1516 he gradually came to deny the necessity of the mediatorial function of the Church and the priesthood. When in 1517 J. *Tetzel preached on the *indulgence granted by *Leo X for contributions to the renovation of *St. Peter's, Rome, the crisis came. Luther drew up 95 theses against indulgences and fixed them to the door of the Schlosskirche at Wittenberg. News of his action spread rapidly. The ecclesiastical authorities at first hoped to settle the dispute by means of monastic discipline, but at the chapter of the order in 1518 Luther won over many of his brethren and the rift widened. He was summoned before Card. *Cajetan but, refusing to recant, he fled to Wittenberg under the protection of *Frederick III of Saxony. In a disputation with J. *Eck in 1519 he denied the primacy of the Pope. The breach with the Church was completed in 1520 by his publication of three works. The first of these invited the German princes to take the reform of the Church into their own hands; the second attacked the denial to the laity of *Communion in both kinds and the doctrines of *Transubstantiation and the Sacrifice of the Mass; the third proclaimed that by faith Christians were freed from the obligation to perform good works. The bull '*Exsurge, Domine' (1520) censured 41 of Luther's theses as heretical and in 1521 he was excommunicated. He was summoned before the Diet of *Worms, refused to recant, and was put under the ban of the Empire. He spent the next eight months at the *Wartburg. Here he began to translate the Bible into German. His ideas continued to spread rapidly, and many traditional practices were abandoned. The destruction of altars &c. went to such lengths that in 1522 he returned to Wittenberg to restore order, with the help of the secular authorities. He abolished various Catholic practices, including private Masses, Confession, and fasts; in 1524 he finally discarded his religious habit and in

1525 he married.

Although Luther's advice to the German princes to wage war against the peasants who had risen in revolt (see *Peasants' Revolt*) lost him some popular support, his teaching continued to gain ground. His noble hymns also won many to his innovations. His work was facilitated by the decision of the Diet of *Speyer (1526), which established the right of the princes to organize national Churches. The movement also spread to countries outside Germany. But differences between the Reformers became serious. At the Colloquy of *Marburg (1529) a deep cleavage between Luther and H. *Zwingli on the *Eucharist revealed itself. In 1530 Luther approved of the comparatively conciliatory *Augsburg Confession drawn up by P. *Melanchthon, but he discountenanced all further attempts to restore union with the RC Church. His last years were darkened by increasing dissensions among his adherents, which could be subdued only by placing the cause of doctrinal unity in the hands of the secular authorities. See also the following entry.

LUTHERANISM. The teaching of M. *Luther found early systematic expression in his own *Catechisms* (1529) and other formularies which were combined in the *Book of Concord* (1580). Scripture is affirmed to be the sole rule of faith, to which the creeds and other traditional statements of belief are subordinated. The principal Lutheran tenet is *justification by faith alone.

These doctrines were elaborated in a scholastic mould in the later 16th and early 17th cents. The *Pietism of the 17th cent. was a reaction against this intellectualism; it stressed the need for personal sanctification. In the 18th cent. Rationalism led to a depreciation of all supernatural elements in Christianity. In 1817 Frederick William III of Prussia tried to unite the Lutheran and *Reformed Churches in his kingdom; the formation of the 'Altlutheraner' (1830) and an increasing doctrinal imprecision on the part of the State Church were the results. This development was fostered by a growing interest in Biblical criticism, which threatened to remove the Lutheran foundations. In the 20th cent. there has been a revival of Lutheran orthodoxy, while the persecution of Christianity by the Third Reich produced a renewal of the Christian spirit. After the end of the Second World War (1945) attempts were made to unite the Lutheran Churches in Germany in a 'United Evangelical Lutheran Church of Germany', inside the looser framework of the '*Evangelical Church in Germany', which embraces Lutherans, *Calvinists, and others.

Apart from Germany, where two-thirds of the population had accepted Lutheranism by the end of the 16th cent., Lutheranism became the official religion of the Scandinavian countries. From all these lands Lutherans migrated to the *United States of America and *Canada. The earliest group arrived in the 17th cent., but the various waves of immigrants led to a proliferation of Lutheran Churches in the U.S.A. There have been a number of mergers between these bodies, which are now comprised mainly in the American Lutheran Church (which came into being in 1960) and the Lutheran Church in America (1962).

In Europe Lutheranism is usually organized in State Churches. There is one order of clergy, normally examined and financed by the government. Worship varies in different countries, but its chief feature is the sermon, set in the framework of a vernacular liturgy.

LUX MUNDI (1889). A collection of essays by a group of Anglicans, ed. by C. *Gore. Its acceptance of modern critical views of the OT gave offence to some of the older school of *High Churchmen.

LUXEUIL. The abbey, established *c.* 590 by St. *Columbanus, soon became the most important in France. Destroyed in 732, it was re-established under *Charlemagne and survived until 1790.

LXX. An abbreviation in common use for the *Septuagint.

LYCH-GATE. The roofed gateway to a churchyard beneath which the coffin is set down to await the arrival of the officiating minister.

LYING. A lie is a statement not in accordance with the mind of the speaker, made with the intention of deceiving. Both in the OT and even more strongly in the NT the practice of lying is denounced. Theologians have argued whether a lie may ever be lawful, e.g. to save an innocent person's life. Many would admit that conflicts of duty may arise where a lie is the lesser evil, but such cases are exceptional.

LYNDHURST, Act of Lord (1835). This Act made all future marriages within the *prohibited degrees *ipso facto* null and void, and not (as had been the previous rule) voidable only by an explicit pronouncement of the ecclesiastical courts.

LYNDWOOD, WILLIAM (*c.* 1375–1446), canonist and from 1442 Bp. of *St. Davids. He was closely associated with H. *Chichele in the proceedings against the *Lollards. His *Provinciale* (completed 1430) is a digest of the synodical constitutions of the province of *Canterbury from 1222 to 1416, with glosses; it remains a standard authority on English ecclesiastical law.

LYNE, J. L. See *Ignatius, Father.*

LYONS, Council of (1245). This Council was convoked by *Innocent IV and attended by bishops mostly from France, Italy, and Spain. Its main achievement was the formal deposition of the Emp. *Frederick II. The objections of Frederick's representative, that the accused had not been cited to the Council and that it was irregular for the Pope to be both plaintiff and judge, were overruled.

LYONS, Council of (1274). This Council was convoked by *Gregory X. Its main achievement was to bring about union with the Greek Church. The desire of the Greeks for union arose chiefly out of their fear of Charles of Anjou, who sought to become Latin Emp. of Constantinople, and the legates of the Greek Emperor, Michael VIII Paleologus, were ready to submit to Rome. The union ended in 1289.

LYRA. See *Nicholas of Lyra.*

M

MAASSEN, FRIEDRICH (1823–1900), historian of early *canon law. The studies embodied in his *Geschichte der Quellen und der Literatur des canonischen Rechts* (vol.I, 1870 [all published]) form the basis of the work of later scholars.

MABILLON, JEAN (1632–1707), *Benedictine scholar. He was prob. the most erudite and discerning of all the *Maurists. He produced some 20 folio works, including editions of St. *Bernard and of various important liturgical documents.

MACARIUS, St., of Alexandria (4th cent.), Egyptian hermit, often confused with St. *Macarius of Egypt. A monastic rule has been ascribed to him, prob. erroneously.

MACARIUS, St., of Egypt (*c.* 300–*c.* 390), 'Macarius the Great'. A native of Egypt, when he was about 30 he founded a colony of monks in the desert of Scetis (Wadi-el-Natrun); it became one of the main centres of Egyptian monasticism.

Fifty Homilies and various other works have traditionally been ascribed to Macarius. It seems probable that these were written in Syria rather than Egypt, but debate continues about their authorship and theological background.

MACARIUS, St. (d. *c.* 334), Bp. of *Jerusalem from *c.* 313. A supporter of orthodoxy against *Arianism, he was present at the Council of *Nicaea (325). Soon afterwards he was commissioned by *Constantine to build the Church of the *Holy Sepulchre in Jerusalem.

MACARIUS MAGNES (4th–5th cent.), Christian apologist. His *Apocriticus* attacked the objections which a learned and clever *Neoplatonist (perhaps *Porphyry) had raised against the Christian faith.

MACARIUS OF MOSCOW (1816–82), Metropolitan of Moscow from 1879. Michael Bulgakov took the name of Macarius when he became a monk. He held academic posts until he was appointed Bp. of Tambov in 1857. His two main works on Orthodox theology reflect the official position of the Russian Church. He also wrote a comprehensive history of the Russian Church [to 1667] (12 vols., 1857–82).

MACAULAY, ZACHARY (1768–1838), Anglican *Evangelical philanthropist and father of Thomas Babington Macaulay, the historian. Working in Jamaica, he was disgusted at the conditions of the slaves. He returned to England and made the cause of the abolition of the slave-trade and of *slavery his main concern. He was a member of the '*Clapham Sect'

MACCABEES. The celebrated Jewish family who did much to free Judaea from the Syrian yoke. The revolt began in 168 B.C. at Modin, where Mattathias, an aged priest, killed an apostate Jew who was about to offer a pagan sacrifice. The struggle was carried on by his five sons, three of whom, *Judas, Jonathan, and Simon, led the Jews in their struggle.

MACCABEES, Books of. Four Books are found in some MSS. of the *Septuagint; the first two are included in the *Canon of Scripture in the Greek and Latin Churches and in the *Apocrypha of the English Bible.

1 Macc. is a history of the Jews from the accession of *Antiochus Epiphanes (175 B.C.) to the death of Simon Maccabaeus in 135 B.C. It describes the desecration of the *Temple and the resistance of Mattathias and his sons. It is a primary source for the period. 2 Macc. covers the history of the Maccabaean wars from 176 to 161 B.C., ending with *Judas Maccabaeus's victory over Nicanor and the latter's death. It is an epitome of a larger work and of little historical value.

3 Macc. describes the attempt of Ptolemy IV to enter the Sanctuary of the Temple (217 B.C.), his frustration, and his attempt to take vengeance on the Jews of Egypt. It is prob. thus named on the analogy of the events described with those of the Maccabaean period. 4 Macc. is a philosophical treatise on the supremacy of devout reason over the passions, illustrated by examples from the history of the Maccabees.

The Books contain important teaching on *immortality (2 Macc. 7: 9 and 23 and 4 Macc.) and on prayers for the *dead (2 Macc. 12: 43–5).

MACCABEES, Feast of the Holy. A feast formerly kept in the W. Church to commemorate the seven brothers whose deaths are described in 2 Macc. 7.

MACEDONIUS (d. *c.* 362), Bp. of *Constantinople from *c.* 342. He supported the *Semi-Arian cause and defended his position at the Council of *Seleucia in 359. In 360 he was deposed by the Arian Council of Constantinople. From the 5th cent. he has been regarded as the founder of the '*Pneumatomachi', but it is doubtful how far this association is correct.

MACHUTUS or **Malo, St.** (d. *c.* 640), Breton saint. Acc. to tradition, he was trained in the monastic life by St. *Brendan, settled at Aleth, opposite the present town of St.-Malo, and led an ascetic life.

MACKAY, ALEXANDER MURDOCH (1849–90), *C.M.S. missionary. He reached Uganda in 1878. His printing of parts of Scripture in Swahili interested King Mtesa, and he was allowed to carry on missionary work. He soon met with opposition from both RCs and Muslims, and in 1887 he was expelled. He reduced the vernacular of Uganda to writing and translated the Bible into it.

MACKINTOSH, HUGH ROSS (1870–1936), Scottish theologian. He had marked sympathy with the Liberal Movement in German Protestant theology and sought to make German teaching known in Britain. In 1932 he was elected *Moderator of the General Assembly of the Church of Scotland.

MACKONOCHIE, ALEXANDER HERIOT (1825–87), *Anglo-Catholic leader. By 1862, when he was put in charge of the newly built church of St. Alban's, Holborn, he was recognized as an advanced 'ritualist', and from 1867 he was constantly prosecuted by the *Church Association for his ceremonial practices (e.g. *mixed chalice and *altar lights).

MACLAREN, ALEXANDER (1826–1910), *Baptist preacher and expositor. He was President of the Baptist Union (1875 and 1901), and he presided over the first Congress of the Baptist World Alliance in 1905.

MACLEOD, NORMAN (1812–72), Scottish divine. In 1869 he was elected *Moderator of the General Assembly of the Church of Scotland. He was a favourite of Queen Victoria and one of the most prominent and respected parochial ministers of Scotland in the 19th cent.

MACRINA, St. (*c.* 327–79), sister of St. *Basil the Great and of St. *Gregory of Nyssa. She is known as 'Macrina the Younger' to distinguish her from 'Macrina the Elder', her paternal grandmother. She influenced her brothers and established a flourishing religious community on the family estate in Pontus.

MADAURAN MARTYRS, The (2nd cent.), first reputed Christian martyrs in Africa. The four martyrs are supposed to have suffered at Madaura in 180. The earliest evidence comes from the 4th cent.

MADEBA MAP. A map of Palestine and the Near East in coloured mosaics, uncovered in 1896 in the church of Madeba to the E. of the *Dead Sea. It almost certainly dates from the 6th cent.

MADONNA (Ital., 'My Lady'). A designation of the BVM, used esp. with reference to statues and pictures of her.

MADRIGAL. Originally a type of poetry and then a polyphonic song without musical accompaniment. In the 16th cent. madrigals were adapted to devotional purposes, esp. in Italy.

MAFFEI, FRANCESCO SCIPIO (1675–1755), historian. His main work centred on his native city of *Verona, though he also wrote on other subjects. In 1712 he rediscovered the ancient manuscripts in the Chapter Library of Verona.

MAGDALENE, St. MARY. See *Mary Magdalene, St.*

MAGDALENES. In reference to St. *Mary Magdalene, the word has often been applied to reformed prostitutes. In the Middle Ages it was widely adopted as a title by religious communities consisting of penitent women to whom others of blameless life attached themselves.

MAGI (Gk. for 'sages' or 'wise men'). The Magi were the first Gentiles to believe in Christ (Mt. 2: 1–12). Guided by a star, they came from the E. to *Bethlehem with gifts of gold, frankincense, and myrrh for the Christ

Child. The idea that they were kings appears first in Christian tradition in *Tertullian; *Origen is the first to give their number as three. What are claimed as their relics are enshrined in *Cologne Cathedral. See also *Epiphany.*

MAGNIFICAT. The song of praise (so called from the opening word of the Latin text) which the BVM sang when her cousin *Elizabeth greeted her as the mother of the Lord (Lk. 1: 39–55). From an early date it has been the canticle of *Vespers in the W. Church; it is included in Evensong in the BCP. In the Greek Church it forms part of the Morning Office. Some scholars argue that Luke originally attributed it to Elizabeth and not to the BVM.

MAGNUS, St. (1) Martyr. The supposed existence of a saint of this name occurring in the Roman *martyology for 19 Aug. seems to have been due to a blunder. (2) (d. *c.* 750), Apostle of the Allgäu, Bavaria. Very little is known of his life. (3) (d. 1116), son of Earl Erlin, ruler of the Orkneys. He led a life of prayer and penance, and was killed by his cousin.

MAHOMETANISM. See *Islam.*

MAI, ANGELO (1782–1854), *Cardinal from 1838. He was successively custodian of the *Ambrosiana at Milan and prefect of the *Vatican library. He was renowned esp. as a reader of *palimpsests. He published collections of classical and theological texts.

MAID OF KENT; MAID OF ORLEANS. See *Barton, E.,* and *Joan of Arc, St.*

MAIER, J. See *Eck, J.*

MAIMONIDES, MOSES (1135–1204), Jewish philosopher, known to Jewish writers as 'Rambam'. A native of Cordova, he finally settled at Fostat (Cairo). He wrote a commentary on the *Mishnah and an extensive *Talmudic code ('Mishneh Torah'). His principal treatise, the 'Guide for the Perplexed' (written in Arabic), sought to reconcile the data of the Jewish revelation with the findings of human reason proposed by *Aristotle. His work had great influence on Christian thought in the Middle Ages.

MAISTRE, J. DE. See *De Maistre, J.*

MAJOR ORDERS. The higher grades of the Christian ministry, in contradistinction from the *Minor Orders (q.v.). The Major Orders are now usually reckoned as those of *bishops, *priests, and *deacons. In the past the *subdiaconate was sometimes accounted a Major Order, the other two then being the diaconate and priesthood (including the episcopate).

MAJORISTIC CONTROVERSY. The controversy aroused among German Protestants in 1551 by the teaching of Georg Major (or Maier) to the effect that the performance of good works was necessary for a Christian's salvation. This teaching was held to be opposed to the Lutheran doctrine of *justification by faith alone.

MAJUSCULE SCRIPT. See *Uncial Script*.

MALABAR CHRISTIANS. A group of Christians in SW. *India, also known as 'Thomas Christians'. They claim that their Church was founded by St. *Thomas the Apostle, but the earliest certain evidence of their existence dates from the 6th cent. They prob. came originally from E. Syria. At the Synod of *Diamper in 1599 they renounced *Nestorius and united with the RC Church. Though there was a breach with the W. in 1653, about two-thirds of them returned to communion with Rome in 1662. The rest joined the *Jacobites; they have their own *Catholicos, but recognize the *Syrian Orthodox Patriarch of Damascus as supreme head of the Church. At the end of the 19th cent. a reforming group constituted themselves the 'Mar Thoma' Church; this has links with the Church of *South India. Another section sought reunion with Rome, and in 1930 the *Malankarese Church came into being.

MALACHI, Book of. *Minor Prophet. The author emphasizes the love of God for His people and announces that a day of judgement will surely come. The language and thought of the Book are of the age following the Exile (i.e. after 538 B.C.). The prophecy about the messenger who shall prepare the way of the Lord (3: 1) is applied to *John the Baptist (Mk. 1: 2), while the reference to the 'pure offering' in 1: 11 is taken in Christian tradition as a prophecy of the *Eucharist.

MALACHY, St. (1094–1148), Abp. of *Armagh. A supporter of Roman practices, he was nominated to the see in 1129, but for some time he was unable to get possession of it. He was a friend of St. *Bernard, his future biographer, and he introduced the *Cistercian Order into Ireland.

MALACHY, Prophecies of. The so-called Prophecies of Malachy have no connection with St. *Malachy apart from their erroneous attribution to him. Contained in a document apparently composed in 1590, they purport to give a motto for every Pope from Celestine II (1143–4) to 'Peter II' at the end of the world.

MALALAS, JOHN. See *John Malalas*.

MALANKARESE CHURCH. The group of *Malabar Christians (q.v.) who entered into communion with Rome in 1930.

MALCHION (3rd cent.), *Antiochene presbyter. He was chosen to interrogate *Paul of Samosata at the Council of Antioch (c. 270).

MALDONADO, JUAN (1533–83), Spanish theologian and exegete. After becoming a *Jesuit in 1562, he taught in Paris. In 1574 the *Sorbonne attacked his teaching as heretical; though vindicated in 1576, he withdrew from Paris. His commentaries on the Gospels (publd. 1596–7) are held in high repute.

MALEBRANCHE, NICOLAS (1638–1715), French philosopher. He became an *Oratorian in 1660. His most important works are *Recherche de la vérité* (1674) and *Traité de la nature et de la grâce* (1680). He denied that any action of matter upon mind was possible, and explained sensation as the effect of a new creative act in the mental order to correspond with things in the physical creation.

MALINES CONVERSATIONS. The meetings of a group of Anglican and RC theologians held at Malines in Belgium between 1921 and 1925 under the presidency of Card. D. J. *Mercier. The initiative came from Lord *Halifax. It was agreed that the Pope should be given primacy of honour; that the Body and Blood of Christ are taken in the Eucharist; that the Sacrifice of the

Eucharist is a true sacrifice, but after a mystical manner; and that Episcopacy is by Divine law. The Conversations issued in no tangible result.

MALMESBURY, formerly the seat of a *Benedictine abbey. A school was founded here by Maildulf, an Irish or Scottish monk, c. 635, and developed into a monastery under his pupil St. *Aldhelm. It became one of the chief English religious houses; it was dissolved in 1539.

MALO, St. See *Machutus, St.*

MALTA, Knights of. See *Hospitallers.*

MALTESE CROSS. A black cross of eight points on a white ground, so named because it was adopted by the Knights of Malta, i.e. the *Hospitallers.

MALVERN CONFERENCE. The Anglican Conference which met at Malvern in 1941, under the presidency of Abp. W. *Temple, to consider in the light of the Christian faith the crisis confronting civilization. Its 'findings' were esp. concerned with the relation of the Church to economic life.

MAMERTINE PRISON. A building in Rome, consisting of two cells in which, acc. to tradition, St. *Peter was imprisoned and converted his gaolers.

MAMERTUS, St. (d. c. 475), Abp. of Vienne in Gaul from c. 461. About 470 he introduced the 'litanies' on the days immediately before *Ascension Day as an act of intercession against earthquakes and other perils, a practice which led later to the institution of the *Rogation Days.

MAN, Isle of. See *Sodor and Man.*

MANASSES, Prayer of. This short book in the OT *Apocrypha consists of a penitential prayer put into the mouth of Manasseh, King of Judah. It was used in the early Church. Its date is uncertain, but it is attested by the early 3rd cent. A.D. It appears in modern printed editions of the *Vulgate in the appendix.

MANDAEANS. A *Gnostic sect which originated as a small community E. of the *Jordan in the 1st or 2nd cent. A.D., and still sur-

vives S. of Baghdad. They hold that man's soul, unwillingly imprisoned in the body and persecuted by demons, will be freed by the redeemer, the personified 'Knowledge of Life'. These notions may be of Christian origin and refer to Jesus Christ, though the sect has been hostile to Christianity since Byzantine times.

MANDE, HENDRIK (c. 1360–1431), one of the *Brethren of the Common Life. At a date after 1390 he entered the monastery at *Windesheim, where he wrote twelve mystical treatises.

MANDYAS. A form of cloak worn by monks and bishops in the E. Church.

MANES (or **MANI**) and **MANICHAEISM.** There are contradictions among the sources, but it appears that Manes (c. 216–76) was born near Seleucia-Ctesiphon, the capital of the Persian Empire, and began teaching in 240. Opposition from the *Zoroastrians drove him into exile in India. He returned in 242, was at first supported and then attacked by Sapor I, and was finally put to death by being flayed alive.

Manes' system was a radical offshoot of the *Gnostic traditions of Persia. It was based on a supposed primeval conflict between light and darkness. It taught that the object of the practice of religion was to release the particles of light which Satan had stolen from the world of Light and imprisoned in man's brain, and that Jesus, Buddha, the Prophets, and Manes had been sent to help in this task. To achieve this release, severe asceticism, including vegetarianism, was practised. Within the sect there was hierarchy of grades professing different standards of austerity: the 'Elect' were supported by the 'Hearers' in their determined missionary endeavours and in an otherworldly state of perfection.

The sect spread rapidly. It appears to have been established in Egypt before the end of the 3rd cent. and at Rome early in the 4th. In the later 4th cent. Manichaeans were numerous in Africa and for a time included St. *Augustine among their adherents. It is disputed how far Manichaeism influenced the *Albigensians, *Bogomils, and *Paulicians, but it is clear that it survived in Chinese Turkestan to the 10th cent.

MANIPLE. A long thin strip of silk formerly worn over the left arm by ministers at Mass. Its origin was apparently a handkerchief.

MANNA. The food miraculously provided for the *Israelites on their journey from Egypt to the *Holy Land (Exod. 16). It is frequently regarded as a *type of the Christian *Eucharist.

MANNING, HENRY EDWARD (1809–1892), Abp. of *Westminster. He was ordained in the C of E and in 1841 became Archdeacon of *Chichester. Beginning as an *Evangelical, he gradually swung round to the *Tractarian side and was regarded as a leader of the *Oxford Movement. The *Gorham Judgement destroyed his faith in Anglicanism and in 1851 he became a RC. In 1865 he succeeded N. P. S. *Wiseman as Abp. of Westminster. At the First *Vatican Council he supported the definition of Papal *Infallibility. In 1875 he was made a *cardinal. He was prominent in social work and mediated in the London Dock Strike of 1889.

MANSE. The dwelling-house, esp. in *Scotland, of a minister.

MANSEL, HENRY LONGUEVILLE (1820–71), Dean of *St. Paul's from 1868. In his *Bampton Lectures of 1858 on *The Limits of Religious Thought*, he argued that the human intellect acquired its knowledge of the nature of God from supernatural revelation alone. His contentions provoked much criticism.

MANSI, GIOVANNI DOMENICO (1692–1769), canonist and, from 1765, Abp. of Lucca. His only considerable original work was his *Tractatus de Casibus et Censuris Reservatis* (1724), but he also issued a vast series of publications in which his own part did not go beyond annotations: the most celebrated was his edition of the Councils.

MANT, RICHARD (1776–1848), Bp. of Down and Connor from 1823 (with Dromore from 1842). Besides theological works, he wrote some well-known hymns, incl. 'Bright the vision that delighted'.

MANTEGNA, ANDREA (1431–1506), Italian painter. His frescoes representing the *Martyrdom of St. James and St. Christopher*

(1448–57) in the Church of the Eremitani at Padua (almost completely destroyed in 1944) established his reputation. He is famous for his altar-pieces. The celebrated *Dead Christ*, in the Brera of Milan, was one of his last works.

MANTELLETTA. A short mantle open in front and reaching to the knees worn by certain dignitaries in the RC Church.

MANTELLONE. A purple mantle of silk or wool until 1969 worn by certain lesser prelates of the Papal court.

MANTUM. A red mantle of the Pope which from the 11th to the 14th cent. played an important part in Papal elections, since investiture with it expressed the transference to the Pope of his right to govern the Church.

MANUAL ACTS, The. The rubrics of the 1662 BCP require the celebrant at the Holy Communion to take the *paten into his hands, to break the bread, lay his hand upon it, and to perform corresponding acts at the consecration of the wine. In the *Ridsdale case (1875–7) the *Judicial Committee of the Privy Council held that the celebrant must not intentionally stand so as to prevent the congregation from seeing the manual acts.

MANUALE (Lat., 'a book of handy size'). In the Middle Ages the usual name for the book containing the forms prescribed for a priest to administer the Sacraments.

MANUSCRIPTS OF THE BIBLE. Writing in the ancient world was usually either on papyrus (made from the stems of the papyrus plant which flourished in the marshes of the Nile; see *Papyrology*) or on specially prepared skins of animals ('parchment' or 'vellum'). For lengthy items, incl. most Books of the Bible, a number of sheets would be joined together to form either a roll or a 'codex' (in which the sheets were first folded in quires and then sewn together as in a modern book).

The earliest part of the OT about the writing of which we have definite information is the Book of *Jeremiah; this is said to have been written on a roll (Jer. 36: 2). It seems that the roll was the normal form of book used by Jews at the time (cf. Ezek. 2: 9) and it continued so until well into Christian times. The evidence of the *Dead Sea Scrolls shows that both parchment and papyrus were used, but that parchment was preferred, esp. for Biblical Books; esp. noteworthy is the celebrated Isaiah roll (DS IsaᴬA), which is almost complete and dates from the 1st or 2nd cent. B.C. The Jews later adopted the codex for private use, but for reading in synagogue they have remained faithful to the parchment roll to the present day.

The first Greek translations of the OT Books are likely to have been written on papyrus, since they seem to have been made in Egypt. The only certain survivals from the pre-Christian era are fragments of two papyrus rolls, both containing parts of Deut. and both dated 2nd–1st. cent. B.C. The many Christian Biblical fragments datable in the 2nd and 3rd cents. A.D., whether OT or NT Books, are all from codices. During the 4th cent. there was a tendency for parchment to replace papyrus, at least for MSS. written for public reading in church. Such MSS. might contain the whole Bible or only part of it; their text is arranged in columns (2, 3, or even 4 to a page); and they were written in the formal *uncial script, roughly equivalent to our capitals. About the 9th cent. a new style of script was introduced (known as 'minuscule'; see Cursive Script); the use of this script made it possible to accommodate the whole of the NT in one convenient volume. Some 6,000–7,000 Greek manuscripts of different parts of the Bible are accessible today.

The oldest known Latin Biblical MS. is the 4th-cent. Codex Vercellensis, a sumptuous volume written with silver ink on purple parchment, containing an almost complete *Old Latin text of the Gospels. The most ancient complete Bible is the *Codex Amiatinus, written in Northumbria at the end of the 7th cent. As in the E., minuscule types of script were developed, and in the 13th cent. the use of very thin parchment and small writing made it possible to accommodate the whole Bible within single conveniently sized volumes which were termed 'pocket Bibles'. The extant Latin MSS. are even more numerous than their Greek counterparts.

There are also Biblical MSS. in *Syriac (many dating from the 5th cent.), *Coptic (dating from as early as the 4th cent.), and various other languages. The 'bilingual' MSS. are of three kinds: the secondary text is written immediately above the primary text, or the two texts are copied in parallel

columns on the same page, or they are arranged to face each other on opposite pages.

For the use of Biblical MSS. in preparing a text, see *Textual Criticism*.

MARAN, PRUDENTIUS (1683–1762), *Maurist scholar. He co-operated with A. A. Touttée in his edition of St. *Cyril of Jerusalem (1720). He was later driven from *St.-Germain-des-Prés for supposed leanings towards *Jansenism. His masterpiece was his edition of St. *Justin Martyr and the other *Apologists (1742).

MARANATHA. An Aramaic word, meaning either 'The Lord has come' or more probably 'O Lord, come'.

MARBECK, J. See *Merbecke, J.*

MARBURG, Colloquy of (1529). A meeting of M. *Luther and P. *Melanchthon with H. *Zwingli, J. *Oecolampadius, and M. *Bucer. Agreement between the Saxon and Swiss Reformers was reached on 14 out of the 15 'Marburg Articles', but the conference failed because Zwingli refused to accept the Lutheran doctrine on the *Eucharist contained in the remaining article.

MARBURG, University of. Founded by *Philip, Landgraf of Hesse, in 1527, it was the first Protestant university established in Europe. Its theological faculty has been famous, esp. since the middle of the 19th cent.

MARCA, PIERRE DE (1594–1662), French canonist. His *Dissertationes de Concordia Sacerdotii et Imperii* (1641) was a defence of *Gallicanist doctrines; it was put on the *Index. In 1662 Marca became Abp. of *Paris.

MARCAN HYPOTHESIS. The theory that St. Mark's is the earliest of the four Gospels and that in its presentation of the life of Christ the facts are set down with a minimum of disarrangement, interpretation, and embellishment.

MARCELLA, St. (325–410), Christian ascetic. Her palace on the Aventine Hill at Rome was a centre of Christian influence. She suffered when the Goths captured the city in 410.

MARCELLINA, St. (*c.* 330–*c.* 398), the sister of St. *Ambrose.

MARCELLUS (d. *c.* 374), Bp. of Ancyra and a supporter of the *Homoousion at the Council of *Nicaea. He was deposed from his see in 336, restored on the death of *Constantine (337), and again expelled *c.* 339. He taught that in the Unity of the Godhead the Son and the Spirit emerged as independent entities only for the purposes of Creation and Redemption; when the redemptive work is achieved they will be resumed into the Divine Unity. The clause in the *Nicene Creed, 'whose kingdom shall have no end', was inserted to combat his teaching.

MARCIAN (396–457), E. Emperor from 450. He repressed *Monophysitism and attended the sixth session of the Council of *Chalcedon.

MARCIANA. The famous library at *Venice, named after St. *Mark, the patron saint of the city.

MARCION (d. *c.* 160), heretic. A native of Sinope in Pontus, he made his way to Rome *c.* 140, and attached himself to the local Church; he was excommunicated in 144. He organized his followers in compact communities throughout most of the Empire.
Marcion's central thesis was that the Christian Gospel was wholly a Gospel of Love to the exclusion of Law. He consequently rejected the OT, holding that the Creator God depicted therein had nothing in common with the God of Love revealed by Jesus. This contrast of law and grace, he held, was fully understood only by St. *Paul, the Apostles and Evangelists being largely blinded to the truth by remnants of Jewish influence. Hence for Marcion the only Canonical Scriptures were ten of the Epistles of St. Paul (he either rejected or did not know the *Pastorals) and an edited form of St. *Luke's Gospel. His *Christology was *Docetic.

MARCIONITE PROLOGUES, The. A set of short introductory prologues to each of the Pauline Epistles which are found in many MSS. of the *Vulgate. They originated in *Marcionite circles.

MARCOSIANS, the followers of the *Gnostic Marcus, a disciple of *Valentinus.

They flourished in the Rhône valley in the mid-2nd cent.

MARCUS AURELIUS (121–80), Roman Emperor from 161. He had a high moral view of life, in essentials a tempered form of *Stoicism. He came into conflict with the Church, and a number of 'Apologies' were addressed to him by Christian writers. He set down his own ideals of conduct in his 'Thoughts' or 'Meditations', a work of sincerity but without philosophical originality.

MAREDSOUS. The seat of a Belgian *Benedictine abbey, founded in 1872. It is a noted centre of scholarship.

MARGARET, St., of Antioch (in Pisidia), also known as St. Marina. She is supposed to have been a martyr of the *Diocletianic persecution, but nothing about her is certainly known. She is invoked esp. by women in childbirth.

MARGARET, 'The Lady' (1443–1509), Margaret Beaufort, Countess of Richmond and Derby. The mother of King Henry VII, she used her position for religious and educational interests. With the encouragement of J. *Fisher, she founded readerships at Oxford and Cambridge and also founded Christ's College, Cambridge. Her other foundation, St. John's College, Cambridge, was completed after her death.

MARGARET CLITHEROW, St. See *Clitherow, St. Margaret.*

MARGARET MARY ALACOQUE, St. (1647–90), chief founder of the devotion to the *Sacred Heart (q.v.). In 1671 she entered the *Visitandine Convent at Paray-le-Monial in central France. Between 1673 and 1675 she received several revelations of the Sacred Heart: the chief features of the devotion were to be Holy Communion on the *First Friday of each month, the Holy Hour on Thursdays, and the Feast of the Sacred Heart. Her visions at first were treated as delusions but opposition eventually ceased.

MARGARET OF SCOTLAND, St. (*c.* 1045–93), wife of Malcolm III of Scotland, whom she married in 1070. At her instigation many abuses were reformed, and synods were held to regulate the Lenten fast and Easter Communion. She had great personal piety.

MARHEINEKE, PHILIPP KONRAD (1780–1846), Protestant theologian. From 1811 he was a professor at Berlin. An admirer of the philosophy of G. W. F. *Hegel, he sought to invoke its support for the Christian faith. The Protestant and Catholic Confessions were to be united in a higher Hegelian synthesis.

MARIA LAACH. A *Benedictine abbey c. 15 miles from Coblenz, founded in 1093. Monastic life was terminated in 1802. The buildings were recovered for ecclesiastical purposes by the *Jesuits in 1863; in 1892 they reverted to the Benedictines. The monks fostered the *Liturgical Movement.

MARIANA, JUAN (1536–1623/4), Spanish *Jesuit. His book *De Rege et Regis Institutione* (1559), justifying *tyrannicide, encouraged the belief that the Jesuits were responsible for the assassination of *Henry IV of France and the *Gunpowder Plot. He also wrote on the history of Spain.

MARIANISTS. The 'Society of Mary', of Bordeaux. This congregation of RC priests and laymen was founded in 1817 by William Joseph Chaminade to combat religious indifference. Its members devote themselves mainly to educational work.

MARIAVITES. A Polish sect, founded in 1906 by J. Kowalski, a priest of Warsaw, and Felicia Kozlowska, a *Tertiary sister, on their excommunication from the RC Church. In 1909 Kowalski was consecrated bishop by the *Old Catholic Bp. of Utrecht, but after a few years of prosperity the sect declined and in 1924 the Old Catholics severed communion with them.

MARIOLATRY. The erroneous ascription of Divine honours to the BVM. The word is sometimes used abusively by Protestants of what they consider the excessive devotion to the BVM in the RC Church.

MARIOLOGY. The systematic study of the person of the BVM and her place in the economy of the *Incarnation.

MARISTS. The 'Society of Mary' founded at Lyons in 1824 by the Ven. Jean Claude Marie Colin. The congregation comprises priests and lay brothers whose main activities are educational and missionary work. The W. Pacific was allotted to them as their special mission field in 1836.

MARITAIN, JACQUES (1882–1973), French *Thomist philosopher. He became a RC in 1906 and held professorial chairs at Paris, Toronto, and Princeton. In 1970 he became a *Little Brother. In numerous writings he sought to apply the classical doctrines of Thomism in turn to metaphysics and theoretical philosophy, moral, social, and political philosophy, the philosophy of education, history, and culture, as well as to art and poetry. He also wrote on the relations of philosophy to religious experience and mysticism.

MARIUS MERCATOR (early 5th cent.), Latin Christian writer, prob. of African birth. He wrote against both the *Nestorians and the *Pelagians, and his works are one of the main sources of our knowledge of Nestorius's doctrines.

MARK, St., Evangelist. John Mark, a cousin of St. *Barnabas, set out with Barnabas and St. *Paul on their first missionary journey, but turned back. He later accompanied Barnabas to *Cyprus, and he was in Rome with St. *Peter and Paul. It was prob. in Italy, if not in Rome, that he wrote the Gospel. Acc. to *Eusebius he afterwards went to *Alexandria; later tradition also associates him with *Venice.

MARK, Gospel of St. This Gospel was known in the 1st cent. and, acc. to the view most widely held, was used by both Matthew and Luke. *Papias states that it was written by St. *Mark, who drew his information from St. *Peter. Later tradition has accepted both these statements, and internal evidence does not contradict them.

The Gospel is written in 'koine *Greek', that is the popular language that was the *lingua franca* of the E. Mediterranean; it is the least polished of the Gospels. It is arranged as a continuous narrative, opening with the preaching of St. *John the Baptist. A turning-point occurs at 8: 27 ff., with the confession of Peter that Jesus is the *Messiah. From this point the burden of the Lord's teaching is that as Messiah He must suffer, die, and rise from the dead. The account of the Resurrection is brief; the Gospel ends abruptly at 16: 8. 16: 9–20 is one of two early supplements.

MARK, Liturgy of St. The traditional Greek Eucharistic Liturgy of the Church of *Alexandria. Modified versions in Coptic and Ethiopic are used by the Coptic *Monophysites and the *Abyssinians.

MARK THE HERMIT (*fl. c.* 431), ascetical writer. Little is known of his life; he was a hermit possibly in Palestine or Egypt. His writings are mainly practical. His attack on human merit commended him to older Protestant theologians.

MARKS OF THE CHURCH. See *Notes of the Church*.

MARMION, COLUMBA (1858–1923), Abbot of *Maredsous from 1909. An Irishman by birth, he was an unusually gifted spiritual writer and director. His main works originated in series of spiritual addresses.

MARNIX, PHILIPP VAN (1540–98), Baron de Sainte-Aldegonde, Dutch *Calvinist theologian and statesman. Between 1562 and 1569 he won fame by his Protestant and nationalistic writings; *c.* 1566–7 he took up arms as an anti-Spanish leader and formed a close friendship with William the Silent. He worked on a Dutch version of the Bible.

MARONITES. A *Uniat community of Syrian origin, the greater part of whom live in Lebanon. They claim to trace their origin to St. Maro, a friend of St. *Chrysostom (d. 407), but it seems clear that their existence as a separate body arose out of their adoption of *Monothelite doctrines and their subsequent excommunication at the Council of *Constantinople in 680. Since 1182 they have been in formal communion with the RC Church.

MAROT, CLÉMENT (*c.* 1497–1544), French hymn-writer. He openly avowed his adhesion to Protestantism in 1527, but was reconciled to Catholicism in 1536. His French metrical version of selected Psalms (1538) was none the less welcomed by the French Protestants.

MARPRELATE TRACTS, The. A series of violent and often scurrilous *Puritan tracts attacking *Episcopacy, issued under the pseudonym of Martin Marprelate in 1588 and 1589.

MARRIAGE. See *Matrimony*.

MARRIAGE LICENCES. Licences to dispense with the need for *banns have been granted by bishops since the 14th cent. They are now normally granted by *surrogates, appointed by the diocesan chancellor. Before a licence is granted one of the parties has to swear that he knows of no impediment to the marriage and that one of the parties has for the past 15 days resided in the parish or chapelry in which the marriage is to be solemnized or that the church or chapel is the usual place of worship of one of the parties. Special licences to marry at any time and in any church, chapel, or other convenient place may be granted by the Abp. of *Canterbury.

MARRIOTT, CHARLES (1811–58), English divine. After J. H. *Newman seceded to the RC Church, Marriott was one of the leaders of the *Tractarian Movement in Oxford.

MARROW CONTROVERSY, The. A controversy in the Church of *Scotland arising out of the condemnation by the *General Assembly in 1720 of a book called *The Marrow of Modern Divinity*, which was held to favour *Antinomianism.

MARSH, HERBERT (1757–1839), Bp. of *Peterborough from 1819. In Germany he became conversant with the prevalent critical methods, esp. as applied to the Gospels, and on his return he was among the first to popularize German critical methods in England. He became the foremost English bishop of his age.

MARSIGLIO OF PADUA (*c.* 1275–1342), scholar. He studied at Padua and then went to Paris. He completed his main work, the *Defensor Pacis*, in 1324. When its authorship became known in 1326, he fled to the excommunicated Emp. Louis of Bavaria.

Acc. to the *Defensor Pacis*, the State is the unifying power of society; it derives its authority from the people, who retain the right to censure and depose the Ruler. The Church, on the other hand, has no inherent jurisdiction, spiritual or temporal; all her rights are given her by the State, which may withdraw them at will. Her hierarchy is of human, not Divine, institution; St. *Peter was never given the primacy, and the chief authority in ecclesiastical matters is the General Council, which should be composed of priests and laymen. These ideas ran counter to the medieval concept of society, and Marsiglio has been claimed as a forerunner of the *Reformation, and even of totalitarianism.

MARTÈNE, EDMOND (1654–1739), *Maurist liturgist. His main work is the *De antiquis ecclesiae ritibus* (1700–2), a large collection of liturgical texts, with disquisitions on their historical significance.

MARTENSEN, HANS LASSEN (1808–84), Danish Protestant theologian. From 1854 he was Bp. of Seeland. His chief purpose was to set forth a harmonious view of all the departments of human life with Christ at its centre, and his principal work, *Den Christelige Dogmatik* (1849; Eng. tr., 1866), rests on the principle of the harmony between faith and knowledge, in the light of which he interpreted the *Lutheran system of doctrine. He was involved in many controversies.

MAR THOMA CHURCH. See *Malabar Christians*.

MARTHA, St. The sister of *Mary and *Lazarus. From the incident related in Lk. 10: 38–42, she is commonly regarded as typifying the 'active' Christian life as contrasted with Mary, who typifies the 'contemplative'.

MARTIN, St. (316/35–397), Bp. of Tours and a patron saint of France. Of pagan family, he became a *catechumen. He served in the Roman army until, after he had given half his cloak to a beggar, a vision of Christ impelled him to baptism and the religious life. In 360 he joined *Hilary at Poitiers and founded the monastery of Ligugé, the first in Gaul. Becoming Bp. of Tours *c.* 372, he introduced a rudimentary parochial system. His protest against the execution of *Priscillian *c.* 386 raised important issues in the relations between Church and State.

MARTIN, St. (*c.* 520–80), Abp. of Braga. He furthered the conversion of the remaining *Arians in Portugal to Catholicism, and he opposed the Spanish custom of using only one immersion at *Baptism. He wrote several moral treatises and compiled a collection of canons.

MARTIN I, St. (d. 655), Pope from 649. He was a vigorous opponent of the *Monothelites. He refused to sign the *Typos of the Emp. Constans II and was eventually arrested, taken to Constantinople, and banished to the Crimea; he died soon afterwards. He is the last Pope who is venerated as a martyr.

MARTIN IV (*c.* 1210–85), Pope from 1281. He was elected through the influence of Charles of Anjou, on whom he remained dependent throughout his pontificate. With a view to assisting the planned attack on the Greek Empire, in 1281 he excommunicated the Emp. Michael Palaeologus, thus endangering the union of the Latin and Greek Churches achieved at the Council of *Lyons in 1274.

MARTIN V (1368–1431), Pope. Oddo (Otto) *Colonna was unanimously elected Pope at the Council of *Constance in 1417. His reign marked the end of the *Great Schism, the antipope Clement VIII submitting in 1429. He greatly strengthened the papal power by dissolving the Council of Constance in 1418 and that of Pavia and Siena in 1424, and in other ways.

MARTIN, GREGORY (d. 1582), Bible translator. He was a tutor in the household of the Duke of Norfolk; when the Duke was imprisoned he fled to *Douai in 1570. Here he devoted himself to translating the *Vulgate into English.

MARTINEAU, JAMES (1805–1900), *Unitarian divine. In 1869 he became Principal of Manchester New College, but he continued his pastoral activities. He was a staunch upholder of the theist position against the negations of physical science, and he elaborated the 'Design argument' with the modifications made necessary by the Darwinian theory of evolution. He also did much for the organization of Unitarians in England and Ireland.

MARTYN, HENRY (1781–1812), Anglican missionary. He became a chaplain of the East India Company at Calcutta in 1805.

Besides doing missionary work among the natives, he translated the NT into Hindustani and Persian, the Psalms into Persian, and the BCP into Hindustani.

MARTYR. The English word 'martyr' is a transliteration of a Gk. one meaning 'witness'. It was used of the Apostles as witnesses of Christ's life and resurrection (e.g. Acts 1: 8), but with the spread of persecution the term came to be reserved for those who had undergone hardship for the faith, and finally it was restricted to those who had suffered death. Martyrs were venerated as powerful intercessors, their relics were sought after, and their lives were often embellished by legend.

MARTYR, PETER. See *Peter Martyr*.

MARTYRIUM. A church built over the tomb or relics of a martyr or, occasionally, a church built just in honour of a martyr.

MARTYROLOGY. An official register of Christian martyrs. The earliest are calendars, merely naming the martyr and place of martyrdom under the day of the festival. The later 'historical' martyrologies (e.g. that of *Usuard) add stories from sources of varying value. The '*Roman Martyrology' is a revision of Usuard's.

MARTYRS, Acts of the; Era of the. See *Acts of the Martyrs* and *Diocletianic Era*.

MARUCCHI, ORAZIO (1852–1931), Italian archaeologist. The *catacombs of Rome were the chief object of his research.

MARY, The Blessed Virgin, the Mother of Christ. In the NT the BVM figures prominently in the birth stories of Mt. (1–2) and esp. Lk. (1–2). (See also *Virgin Birth*.) Though mentioned several times during Christ's public ministry, she remains mainly in the background; acc. to Jn. (19: 25) she reappears at the foot of the Cross. In the Upper Room at Jerusalem she witnessed the growth of the early Church (Acts 1: 14).

Mary is rarely mentioned in the earliest patristic writings. Her perpetual virginity was first asserted in the apocryphal Book of *James; it was accepted from the 5th cent. onwards. The development of Marian doctrine received great impetus at the Council of *Ephesus (431), which upheld the title

'*Theotokos'. In the 6th cent. the doctrine of the corporeal *Assumption of the BVM was formulated in orthodox circles and the Feast became widely observed. Belief in the Assumption seems to have spread without arousing opposition in the pre-Reformation period; it was defined for RCs in 1950. The doctrine of the *Immaculate Conception, on the other hand, was a matter of dispute in the Middle Ages; it was defined for RCs in 1854. In modern times there have been efforts to secure a papal definition of Mary as 'Mediatrix of All Graces' and 'Co-Redemptress', but the chapter on Mary added to the Constitution on the Church at the Second *Vatican Council was marked by restraint.

The Marian doctrine of the *Orthodox Church is similar to that of RCs. The Reformers stressed the humility of Mary and attacked her glorification by the RC Church; among all Protestant bodies there was a reaction against excessive devotion to her. In the C of E since the *Oxford Movement some theologians have accorded an important place to the BVM, and German Protestant theologians have been tending to restore an element of Marian doctrine.

Belief in the efficacy of Mary's intercession and hence direct prayer to her is prob. very old. It is attested in a papyrus dating from the late 3rd–early 4th cent. Liturgical devotions in the W. came to include the *Little Office of Our Lady as well as the Saturday Mass and Office. Popular piety found expression in the *Hail Mary, *Rosary, *Angelus, and pilgrimages, esp. to *Lourdes and *Fatima. The major feasts of the BVM are the *Nativity (8 Sept.), *Annunciation (25 Mar.), *Purification (2 Feb.), *Visitation (2 July; in the RC Church now 31 May), and Assumption (15 Aug.).

MARY, Gospel of. An early apocryphal *Gnostic Gospel. In it the BVM describes a vision in which the progress of the Gnostic through the seven planetary spheres is explained.

MARY, Gospel of the Birth of. A medieval apocryphal book describing the birth of the BVM, her life in the *Temple from the age of 3 to 12, her betrothal, the *Annunciation, and the *Virgin Birth of Christ.

MARY OF EGYPT, St. (5th cent.), penitent. After a career of infamy at *Alexandria, she is said to have been converted on the threshold of the *Holy Sepulchre at Jerusalem, fled into the desert E. of Palestine, and lived there in isolation for 47 years.

MARY OF THE INCARNATION, Bl. and Ven. See *Acarie, Mme*, and *Guyard, M.*

MARY MAGDALENE, St.
A follower of Christ out of whom He is said to have cast 'seven devils' (Lk. 8: 2). She stood by His Cross (Mk. 15: 40); with two other women she discovered the empty tomb (Mk. 16: 1 ff. &c.); and she was granted an appearance of the Risen Lord early the same day (Mt. 28: 9; Jn. 20: 11 ff.). From early times she has been identified with the 'woman who was a sinner' who anointed Christ's feet (Lk. 7: 37) and with Mary the sister of *Martha, who also anointed Him (Jn. 12: 3), but the Gospels give no warrant for either identification.

MARY MAGDALENE DE' PAZZI, St.
(1566–1607), *Carmelite mystic. In the early years after her profession she was severely tried by spiritual desolation and physical suffering, but from 1590 her life became a series of *ecstasies. During these she often gave spiritual counsels which were taken down and published after her death.

MARY MAJOR, Church of St. See *Santa Maria Maggiore, Rome.*

MARY, Queen of Scots (1542–87). Mary
Stuart was crowned Queen in 1543. She went to France for her education and in 1558 she married the Dauphin. After his death she returned to Scotland in 1561. John Knox and his followers had introduced the *Reformation and Mary had a series of stormy interviews with him. In 1565 she married Lord Darnley, by whom she became the mother of the future *James I (VI of Scotland). In 1567 Darnley was assassinated by the Earl of Bothwell; how far Mary was implicated is disputed. Her marriage with Bothwell was followed by a rising of the Protestant lords. She was imprisoned and later in 1567 she abdicated. The following year she escaped and fled to England. *Elizabeth I feared for the security of her own throne and kept Mary in close captivity. When an unguarded letter implicated Mary in the Babington Plot, she was executed.

MARY TUDOR (1516–58), Queen of
England from 1553. The daughter of *Henry VIII and Catherine of Aragon, she was excluded from the succession on the birth of *Elizabeth, but in 1544 she was given second place after *Edward VI. When she became Queen she at first showed leniency to her Protestant subjects, though proscribing their religion, but after the rising of 1554 she resolved to rule more sternly. Her marriage with *Philip II of Spain was much disliked. In 1555 R. *Pole reconciled England to the Papacy. Soon afterwards the trials for heresy began: T. *Cranmer, H. *Latimer, N. *Ridley, J. *Hooper, and others were burnt as heretics. The persecution of Protestants and Mary's inability to have children lost her the affection of the people.

MARYS IN THE NT. Besides (1) the
Blessed Virgin *Mary and (2) St. *Mary Magdalene, there are: (3) 'The wife of Cleopas' (Jn. 19: 25), who stood by the Cross. Some have identified her with '[Christ's] mother's sister', who is mentioned immediately before. (4) 'The mother of James and Joses' (Mk. 15: 40), who stood by the Cross and was a witness to the Empty Tomb (Mk. 16: 1). She may be the same as (3). (5) Mary of Bethany, the sister of *Martha and *Lazarus (Jn. 11: 1 ff.), who sat at Christ's feet when He visited their village (Lk. 10: 38 ff.). She has, unjustifiably, been identified with Mary Magdalene (q.v.). (6) 'The mother of John *Mark' (Acts 12: 12).

MASS (Lat. *missa*). A title for the
*Eucharist, now used esp. by RCs. It apparently derives from the Latin *mittere*, 'to send' or 'dismiss', and was applied to the service from which the people were dismissed, esp. the Eucharist.

MASS, Music for the. The parts of the service sung by the choir or congregation may be divided into chants for (1) the *Ordinary of the Mass (the *Kyrie, *Gloria in excelsis, *Creed, *Sanctus and *Benedictus, *Agnus Dei, and *Ite Missa est) in which the words are always the same; and (2) the *Propers, which vary according to the occasion. These have traditionally comprised the *Introit, *Gradual, *Offertory and *Communion Anthem, and sometimes a *Sequence.

The oldest chant for the Ordinary is little more than an inflective recitative corresponding to that used in the parts of the Mass sung by the celebrant. With the growth of polyphony from the 11th cent. onwards, compositions for two or more voices began to appear. In the early 15th cent. the *Sanctus* and *Agnus* occur with a common musical arrangement, to be followed by *Gloria-Credo* pairs; later in the 15th cent. a complete series (or 'Mass-cycle') became common. In the earliest examples the *Gregorian chant forms a substratum of the composition, occurring as a *canto fermo* for one of the voices. The full development of polyphony in the 16th cent. led to very elaborate settings, such as those of G. P. *Palestrina and W. *Byrd. In the 18th cent. orchestral settings became popular on the Continent and brought the introduction of music ostensibly designed for the Mass into the concert hall. Against the increasing elaboration of music divorced from the words of the liturgical texts the proponents of the *Liturgical Movement encouraged the revival of *plainchant. In recent times emphasis has been laid on music in which the congregation can take part.

MASS OF THE CATECHUMENS; MASS OF THE FAITHFUL. See *Catechumens, Mass of the*; *Faithful, Mass of the*.

'MASS CANDIDA'. See *Utica, The Martyrs of*

MASSILLON, JEAN-BAPTISTE (1663–1742), French *Oratorian. He was one of the foremost preachers of a great generation, much respected even by the leaders of the *Enlightenment. He often preached before Louis XIV. In 1717 he was nominated Bp. of Clermont; he gave devoted service to his diocese.

MASSORETES. Jewish grammarians who worked on the Hebrew text of the OT between about the 6th and 10th cents. A.D. They strove to preserve a Biblical text free from accretion, alteration, or corruption by providing marginal notes and commentaries. They also introduced *vowel points and accents to show how the words should be pronounced at a time when Hebrew was ceasing to be a spoken language. The text which derives from their work is known as the 'Massoretic text'.

MASTER OF THE SENTENCES, The. A title of *Peter Lombard.

MATER ET MAGISTRA (1961). The encyclical letter of *John XXIII 'On Recent Developments of the Social Question in the Light of Christian Teaching', marking the 70th anniversary of *Rerum Novarum.

MATERIAL SIN. An action which, though in itself ('materially') contrary to Divine Law, is not culpable, because the agent acted either in ignorance or under external constraint.

MATHEW, ARNOLD HARRIS (1853–1919), *Old Catholic bishop. In 1908 he received episcopal consecration from the Dutch Old Catholic Church as their Abp. in Great Britain, but he was repudiated in 1910 on the ground that his consecration had been obtained under a misconception of the extent of his following in England. He left irregular episcopal successions of *Episcopi Vagantes.

MATHURINS. Another name for the *Trinitarian Order (q.v.).

MATINS. See *Mattins*.

MATRIMONY. The Christian conception of marriage differs from earlier practice and from modern secular usage most notably in the equality which it gives to the woman and the indissolubility which it ascribes to the marriage bond. Christ abrogated the Mosaic tolerance of *divorce and condemned remarriage (e.g. Mk. 10: 2–12). (The 'Matthaean exception' (Mt. 19: 9) conflicts with the other Gospels and the rest of the NT and is prob. best understood as an early gloss to render the Christian doctrine easier.) In Eph. 5: 22–33 St. *Paul compares the union of marriage with the relation between Christ and His Church. While he assigns the governance of the household to the husband, he emphasizes the duty of love to the wife, who is an equal partner (1 Cor. 7: 3 f.). In 1 Cor. 7: 15 he states the '*Pauline Privilege' (q.v.).

The preface to the Marriage service in the BCP aptly summarizes the ends of marriage as the procreation of children, the avoidance of sin, and mutual society. The first of these, traditionally understood as the prime end, has led some Christian moralists to repudiate all methods of family limitation. The reluctance of the compilers of the BCP to entitle marriage a *sacrament arose from hesitation about recognizing as such a rite not manifestly productive of grace.

It was only in the 11th cent. that the claim of the Church to exclusive jurisdiction in matrimonial cases was conceded. In England the first breach with canon law was made by Lord *Hardwicke's Marriage Act of 1753. Further Acts of 1836 and 1857 established civil marriage and abolished the jurisdiction of the ecclesiastical courts. Subsequent legislation, culminating in the Divorce Reform Act of 1969, has introduced a sharp cleavage between secular legislation in England and Christian doctrine. In the RC Church suits of *nullity are allowed on various grounds, and in the Orthodox Church divorce has been tolerated since Byzantine times.

The principle that any Christian man or woman may marry has been limited by rules governing *affinity (q.v.), and the minimum age in England is now 16 for both parties. A certain publicity is required. In the case of church marriages this is normally achieved by the publication of the *banns, though *marriage licences (q.v.) may grant dispensations. On practices concerning clerical marriage, see *Celibacy of the Clergy*.

MATTER. In medieval philosophy, the stuff underlying all material existence before it is determined and actualized by *form (q.v.). The *Schoolmen sought to apply this *Aristotelian concept to Sacramental theology.

MATTHEW, St., Apostle and Evangelist. He is described in Mt. 10: 3 as a *publican. The call of Matthew by Christ is recorded in Mt. 9: 9 (in the parallel passages in Mk. and Lk. the name of the person called is given as 'Levi'). Acc. to *Papias he made a collection of Christ's sayings in Hebrew, and he is traditionally held to be the author of the First Gospel (see the following entry).

MATTHEW, Gospel acc. to St. This Gospel stands first in the NT *Canon. Since the 2nd cent. it has been ascribed to St. *Matthew the Apostle. Modern scholars, however, commonly hold that Mt. drew extensively on Mk., which is expanded with the aid of '*Q'. If this is so, the early tradition that Mt. was written in 'Hebrew' (*Aramaic was prob. meant) is untenable, and it is unlikely that an Apostle, who was an eyewitness of the events, would have taken as his chief source the work of *Mark, whose material was second-hand. Mt. is perhaps to be dated *c.* A.D. 80, but the evidence is so indirect that it is consistent with any date between *c.* A.D. 65 and 100.

The characteristic features of the Gospel include the fullness with which it records the Lord's teaching, its interest in the relation of the Gospel to Jewish Law, the special commission given to St. *Peter (16: 17–20), and the record of the post-Resurrection appearances in Galilee (28). It is the most suitable of the *Synoptic Gospels for public reading.

MATTHEW OF AQUASPARTA (*c.* 1240–1302), *Franciscan theologian. In 1287 he became General of his order and in 1288 a *cardinal. His writings include sermons and Biblical commentaries, a commentary on the *Sentences, *quodlibets* and *quaestiones disputatae*. He was a disciple of St. *Bonaventure and in many ways looked forward to *Duns Scotus.

MATTHEW PARIS (*c.* 1199–1259), chronicler. He entered the *Benedictine monastery of *St. Albans in 1217. His *Chronica Majora*, a history of the world from the Creation to 1259, is a valuable source for contemporary events. It contains trenchant criticism of ecclesiastical abuses.

MATTHEW'S BIBLE. An edition of the English Bible issued in 1537. 'Thomas Matthew', the name of its supposed editor, was an alias for John *Rogers (q.v.).

MATTHIAS, St., Apostle. Acc. to the tradition preserved in Acts 1: 15–26, he was chosen by lot to fill the vacancy in the Twelve left by the treachery of *Judas Iscariot. He is not mentioned elsewhere in the Bible.

MATTHIAS, Gospel of St. A lost apocryphal Gospel mentioned by some of the early Fathers.

MATTINS. (1) In the W. the traditional *Breviary Office for the night, which was replaced in the 1971 Breviary by the *Office of Readings. Its principal components were a hymn, Psalms, Lessons, the *Te Deum, and a collect.

(2) The designation in common use for the service of 'Morning Prayer' in the C of E. The Office in the BCP was based on the

medieval Mattins with supplements from *Prime. Its structure is similar to that of *Evensong. The various *Alternative Services provide for a number of modifications.

MATTINS OF BRUGES. The massacre of the French lodged in Bruges by the Flemish inhabitants at daybreak on 18 May 1302.

MAUNDY THURSDAY. The Thursday before *Easter, so called from the *mandatum novum* ('new commandment') given on this day (Jn. 13: 34). The special commemoration of the Lord's Institution of the *Eucharist on this day is attested by the 4th cent. Two other traditional liturgical rites are the Blessing of the Holy Oils and the Reconciliation of Penitents, though the latter has long been obsolete. In the RC Church since 1955 the Maundy Thursday Mass has normally been celebrated in the evening. It is marked by a number of special features; these include the ceremony of foot-washing (see *Pedilavium*), and all present are expected to receive Communion from Hosts consecrated at the Mass. In cathedral churches the Holy Oils are blessed at a special *Chrism Mass in the morning. The royal 'Maundy Ceremony' in England is an abbreviated survival of the *Pedilavium*.

MAUR, St. (6th cent.), disciple of St. *Benedict of Nursia. Nothing is certainly known about his life. He is said to have made his way to France in 543 and founded the abbey of Glanfeuil (afterwards St.-Maur-sur-Loire).

MAURICE, St., leader of the Theban Legion. Acc. to a 5th-cent. source, a legion from the *Thebaid was wholly composed of Christians; when they refused to sacrifice they were massacred during the *Diocletianic persecution. In its present form the story is unhistorical.

MAURICE, FREDERICK DENISON (1805–72), Anglican divine. In 1846 he became professor of theology at the newly created Theological School of *King's College, London. He was deeply moved by the political events of 1848 and became interested in the application of Christian principles to social reform; acquaintance with J. M. F. *Ludlow led to the formation of the *Christian Socialists (q.v.). Maurice's's orthodoxy was constantly under suspi-

cion and he was dismissed from King's College when his *Theological Essays* (1853) provoked a crisis; in one of these he attacked the popular view of the endlessness of future punishment and maintained that in the NT '*Eternity' had nothing to do with time. In 1866 he became Knightsbridge Professor of Moral Philosophy at Cambridge.

MAURISTS. The *Benedictine monks of the congregation of St. *Maur. The congregation was founded in 1621 to represent in France the reform initiated in the Abbey of Saint-Vanne (Lorraine) in 1600. From 1672 the Maurists devoted themselves to historical and literary work; many of their productions are monuments of scholarship. The congregation was dissolved in 1818.

MAXIMILIAN, St. (d. 295), martyr. It is recorded that he was executed at Theveste in Numidia because he refused to serve in the Roman army.

MAXIMUS, St. (d. 408/23). Nothing is known of his life, except that he was Bp. of Turin and that he died between 408 and 423. Over 100 of his sermons survive; they throw light on the history of the liturgy and the survival of paganism in N. Italy.

MAXIMUS, St., 'Confessor' (c. 580–662), Greek theologian and ascetical writer. He was Imperial Secretary under the Emp. *Heraclius. Having become a monk c. 614, he fled to Africa in the face of Persian invasion (626). From c. 640 he was a determined opponent of *Monothelitism, and he had a share in its condemnation at the Lateran Council of 649. He was taken to *Constantinople in 653 and, refusing adherence to the '*Typos' of Constans II, he was banished to Thrace. He was further questioned in 661; a prob. true tradition states that his tongue and right hand were cut off.

Maximus was a prolific writer. His teaching centred on the Incarnation. Man caused evil to come into the world by his desire for pleasure, which destroyed the dominion of reason over the senses; hence Christ had to redeem the race by pain to restore the equilibrium. Through the Incarnate Word man is not only freed from ignorance but given the power to practise virtue. The goal of human life, obtained through abnegation, is union with God by charity.

MAXIMUS THE CYNIC (4th cent.). At *Constantinople he ingratiated himself with *Gregory of Nazianzus; when Gregory was ill one night in 380, Maximus was consecrated to the see. The Council of *Constantinople in 381 declared that Maximus 'neither is nor was a bishop'. For a short time he was supported in the W. He professed to combine belief in the Cynic philosophy with profession of the Nicene faith.

MAX MÜLLER, FRIEDRICH (1823–1900), comparative philologist and religious writer. A German by birth, he went to Oxford in 1848; he soon came to hold senior office. In 1875 he undertook the editing of *The Sacred Books of the East*, a series of translations of E. religious classics in 51 volumes. He also wrote on the comparative study of religion. His writings appealed to the religious liberals of his time.

MAY LAWS. The legislation associated with Bismarck's *Kulturkampf*. The laws, passed in May 1873, were directed against the RC Church in Germany; they were based on the theory of the absolute supremacy of the State.

MAYNE, St. CUTHBERT (1543–77), the first RC seminary priest executed in England. At Oxford he came under the influence of E. *Campion and became a RC. He went to the English College at *Douai. In 1576 he was sent on the English Mission and became chaplain to a landowner in Cornwall. He was discovered and sentenced to death in 1577 for denying the Queen's spiritual supremacy, saying Mass, possessing a printed copy of a bull for a jubilee, and wearing an *Agnus Dei. He was among the *Forty Martyrs of England and Wales canonized in 1970.

MAYNOOTH COLLEGE. The 'Royal Catholic College' at Maynooth, *c.* 15 miles from Dublin, was established by the Irish Parliament in 1795 for the education of the RC clergy of Ireland.

MAZARIN, JULES (1602–61), statesman and from 1641 *cardinal. He was in the service of *Urban VIII before he formally entered that of Louis XIII in 1640. In 1642 he succeeded A. J. *Richelieu as chief minister; he practically ruled France until his death. He enlarged her territory at the Peace

of *Westphalia (1648), but he could not prevent the country's economic disintegration or the civil wars of the Fronde (1648–53). He pursued a policy of reconciliation towards the *Huguenots. He continued the war with Spain and eventually secured the victorious Treaty of the Pyrenees (1659).

MAZARIN BIBLE, The. A Latin Bible so called from a copy in the library of Card. *Mazarin which first attracted the attention of scholars. It is also known as the 'Gutenberg Bible', after J. *Gutenberg, its printer, and as the '42-line Bible', from the number of lines in each column. It is the earliest full-length book ever printed, prob. in 1453–5; it was certainly complete by 1456.

MAZZOLINI, S. See *Prierias, S.*

MECHITARISTS. A community of *Uniat Armenian monks founded at *Constantinople by Mechitar of Sebaste in 1701. They were driven out by the Turks in 1703 and eventually in 1717 settled on the island of San Lazzaro, *Venice. They have issued important Armenian works from their printing-houses.

MECHTHILD, St. (*c.* 1210–*c.* 1280), of Magdeburg, mystic and spiritual writer. Of noble Saxon family, she became a *Beguine at Magdeburg. She wrote down her visions under the title *Das fliessende Licht der Gottheit* ('The Flowing Light of the Godhead'), adding a further volume after she entered the *Cistercian convent at Helfta in 1270.

MEDE, JOSEPH (1586–1638), also 'Mead', English Biblical scholar. His best-known work, *Clavis Apocalyptica* (1627), interprets Rev. on the principle that its visions form an organic and related whole in chronological order; the Day of Judgement is a period of a thousand years of peace for the Church on earth.

MEDINA, BARTOLOMEO (1527–80), Spanish *Dominican theologian. He has been called the 'Father of *Probabilism' (q.v.). In his commentary on St. *Thomas Aquinas's *Summa Theologica*, he defends the view that where there are two opinions, both of which are probable, though in an unequal degree, the less probable may be followed.

MEDITATION. As used by the exponents of Christian spirituality, the term denotes mental prayer in its discursive form. Its method is the devout reflection on a chosen (often Biblical) theme with a view to deepening spiritual insight and stimulating the will and affections.

MEINRAD, St. (d. 861), Patron of *Einsiedeln. A monk at *Reichenau, in middle life he felt a call for greater austerity and settled at the spot where Einsiedeln ('hermitage') now stands. He was put to death by two ruffians to whom he had given hospitality.

MELANCHTHON, PHILIPP (1497–1560), Protestant Reformer. His real name was 'Schwarzerd'. As professor of Greek at *Wittenberg (from 1518) he came under the influence of M. *Luther, whose teaching he helped to cast into a more rational and systematic form. In 1519 he took part in the Disputation of *Leipzig and a controversy with *Carlstadt followed. In 1521 he found himself leader of the Reformation Movement when Luther was confined in the *Wartburg. The original edition of his *Loci Communes* (1521) was the first ordered presentation of Reformation doctrine. In the following years he was engaged in translating and commenting on the Bible. He was the leading figure at the Diet of Augsburg (1530) and was mainly responsible for the *Augsburg Confession; great hopes were placed on his conciliatory spirit as a basis for restoring peace. In 1537 he signed the *Schmalkaldic Articles with the reservation that he would accept the Papacy in a modified form. In his later years he was largely concerned with organizing the Church of Saxony on a semi-episcopal basis and in various controversies.

MELANIA, St. (1) St. Melania the Elder (c. 342–c. 410) was a wealthy aristocratic Roman matron. On the death of her husband she adopted the ascetic life, left Rome in 372, and founded a double monastery with *Rufinus on the Mount of *Olives. (2) Her grand-daughter, St. Melania the Younger (c. 383–438), with her husband joined St. *Jerome at Bethlehem; she founded another monastery on the Mount of Olives.

MELCHIORITES. See *Hoffmann, Melchior.*

MELCHITES (or **MELKITES**). Those Christians of Syria and Egypt who, refusing *Monophysitism and accepting the Definition of *Chalcedon (451), remained in communion with the see of *Constantinople. Today the term is applied to the Christians of the Byzantine rite (whether Orthodox or *Uniat) belonging to the Patriarchates of *Antioch, *Jerusalem, and *Alexandria.

MELCHIZEDEK. Acc. to Gen. 14: 18, the 'King of Salem' and 'Priest of the Most High God' who offered *Abraham bread and wine as he returned from his defeat of the four kings. The author of Heb. (6: 20, 7: 1 f.) regarded his priesthood as prefiguring that of Christ; another Christian tradition has seen in his offering a *type of the *Eucharist.

MELITIAN SCHISMS. (1) Melitius, Bp. of Lycopolis in Egypt, regarded as too lax the terms laid down c. 306 by *Peter, Bp. of Alexandria, for the return of those who had lapsed under persecution. He caused disturbances and was excommunicated by Peter. After a further period of persecution Melitius founded a schismatic Church with clergy of his own ordination. A small body of Melitians seems to have survived until the 8th cent. (2) See the next entry.

MELITIUS, St. (d. 381), Bp. of *Antioch from 360. In the course of the *Arian controversy he was exiled several times, being finally restored in 378. He presided over the Council of *Constantinople in 381. The schism at Antioch arose when the supporters of *Eustathius (Bp. of Antioch c. 324–30) secured the consecration of one Paulinus in 362.

MELITO, St. (d. c. 190), Bp. of Sardis. Very little is known about his life. He was a prolific writer, but only fragments of his works were known until 1940, when a work preserved on *papyrus was published. The main theme of the *Peri Pascha* ('On the Pasch') is the new *Pasch inaugurated by Christ. In it there is much polemic against the Jews and an anti-*Gnostic insistence on the true humanity of Christ.

MELLITUS, St. (d. 624), Abp. of *Canterbury. Sent to England by *Gregory I in 601, he was consecrated missionary bishop for the East Saxons in 604. He succeeded Laurentius as third Abp. of Canterbury in 619.

MELVILLE, ANDREW (1545–1622), Scottish *Presbyterian theologian. He held senior positions in the universities of Glasgow and St. Andrews; his educational reforms were of importance. He also took an active part in abolishing what was left of episcopacy in Scotland, and in 1575 he was entrusted with drawing up the Second Book of *Discipline (q.v.). As *Moderator of the General Assembly in 1582, he prosecuted R. Montgomery, one of the '*tulchan bishops'. On this and other occasions he incurred the displeasure of *James I.

MEMLING or **MEMLINC, HANS** (c. 1440–94), painter. He was a citizen of Bruges. His paintings, which are notable for their colour and harmony, include the Donne Triptych in the National Gallery, London, as well as Madonnas and other altar-pieces.

MEMORARE. A widely used intercessory prayer addressed to the BVM. It has commonly been ascribed to St. *Bernard of Clairvaux, but its real author is unknown. The most popular English version begins 'Remember, O most loving Virgin Mary'.

MEMORIA. The name given in current RC liturgical documents to the least important of the three categories of *feast.

MEMORIALE RITUUM. An obsolete liturgical book containing the services for the last three days of *Holy Week in the shortened form previously used in smaller RC parish churches.

MENAION. In the E. Church, the name given to each of the twelve liturgical books (one for each month) which contain the variable parts of the Divine *Office for the immovable feasts.

MENAS, St. (c. 3rd–4th cent.), Egyptian martyr. He was prob. born and martyred in Egypt, but his story was apparently fused with that of a soldier executed in Phrygia under *Diocletian, possibly another Menas, possibly St. Gordian. His reputed birthplace, SW. of Lake Mareotis, became a pilgrimage centre, associated with miraculous cures by water.

MENAS, St. (d. 552), Patr. of *Constantinople from 536. At the beginning of the *Three Chapters' Controversy (543) he subscribed to the Imperial edict. He was excommunicated by Pope *Vigilius in 547 and 551, but in neither case did the sentence last long.

MENDICANT FRIARS. Members of those orders which are forbidden to hold property in common; they work or beg for their living and are not bound to one convent. In the Middle Ages their work was carried out mainly in towns; their privileges, esp. exemption from episcopal jurisdiction and extensive faculties for preaching and hearing confessions, aroused great hostility.

MENNONITES, the followers of Menno Simons (1496–1561), a parish priest in Dutch Friesland who renounced his connection with the RC Church in 1536 and joined the *Anabaptists. He preached believers' baptism, a connectional type of Church organization with emphasis on the responsibilities and rights of the local congregation, rejection of Christian participation in the magistracy, and non-resistance. In the 17th and 18th cents. the Mennonites became numerous and influential in Holland.

MENOLOGION. In the E. Church, a liturgical book containing the lives of the saints, arranged by months throughout the ecclesiastical year (beginning with Sept.).

MENSA (Lat., 'table'). In early Christian times the word was applied esp. to the large tablets of stone set over or near a grave, and apparently used for receiving food for meals in memory of the deceased. The term is now in common use to designate the flat stone (or other material) which forms the top of an *altar

MENTAL PRAYER. See *Meditation*.

MENTAL RESERVATION. The conflict which may arise between the duty of telling the truth and that of keeping a secret has led to the development of the doctrine of mental reservation. RC moral theologians distinguish between 'strict' and 'wide' mental reservation. In the former a qualification is added mentally which alters the statement pronounced, so that the hearer is necessarily deceived; it is justifiable when the person putting the question has no right to the truth or where a professional secret is involved. In the 'wide mental reservation' words are used which are susceptible of more than one interpretation, without the speaker's giving an indication of the sense in which he uses them.

MERBECKE or **MARBECK**, JOHN (d. *c.* 1585), English divine and musician. Appointed organist at St. George's Chapel, *Windsor, in 1541, he was condemned to the stake for heresy in 1544 because he had written the first *concordance to the English Bible. He was, however, pardoned. In 1550 he produced his *Book of Common Prayer Noted*, in which the plainchant is adapted to *Edward VI's first (1549) liturgy.

MERCATI, GIOVANNI (1866–1957), Prefect of the *Vatican Library from 1919 and cardinal from 1936. He wrote innumerable studies on matters of patristic and palaeographical interest.

MERCATOR, MARIUS See *Marius Mercator*.

MERCEDARIANS. A religious order of men founded *c.* 1220 by St. *Peter Nolasco (hence also known as 'Nolascans') with the objects of tending the sick and rescuing Christians who had been taken prisoner by the Moors; members were pledged to offer themselves as hostages if needed for the redemption of Christian captives.

MERCERSBURG THEOLOGY. A school of thought which sought to oppose the emotionalism of the mid-19th cent. by bringing American Protestant theology into line with Continental European trends, restoring the faith of the early Reformers, and stressing the importance of doctrine. It originated in the work of J. W. *Nevin at Mercersburg in Pennsylvania.

MERCIER, DÉSIRÉ JOSEPH (1851– 1926), Belgian philosopher and prelate. As a professor at Louvain, he was an ardent supporter of the *Thomist revival. In 1906 he was made Abp. of Malines and in 1907 created a cardinal. In his Lenten Pastoral for 1908 he denounced G. *Tyrrell. He was the leading spirit on the RC side in the *Malines Conversations, which were cut short by his death.

MERCY, Works of. See *Corporal Works of Mercy, Spiritual Works of Mercy*.

MERCY-SEAT. In the Jewish *Temple, the covering of solid gold laid on the '*Ark of the Covenant' which was conceived to be God's resting-place.

MERIT. In theology 'merit' · designates man's right to be rewarded for a work done for God. The conception has its foundations in the Bible; in both the OT and the NT rewards are promised to the just for their good works. The theology of merit was elaborated by the *Schoolmen, who distinguished between *condign merit, which confers a claim to a reward due in justice for services rendered, and *congruous merit, which may claim the reward only on grounds of fitness. The traditional doctrine was repudiated by the Reformers, esp. M. *Luther, who taught the sinfulness of all human works, whether done before or after *justification.

MERLE D'AUBIGNÉ, JEAN HENRI (1794–1872), Swiss historian of the Reformation. In 1831 he became professor of Church history at Geneva, where he wrote his *Histoire de la Réformation du XVIe siècle* (1835–53).

MERRY DEL VAL, RAFAEL (1865–1930), Cardinal. Singled out by *Leo XIII for papal service, he was secretary of the commission which pronounced against *Anglican Ordinations (1896). In 1903 he was made a cardinal and Secretary of State by *Pius X, with whose intransigent policy he became identified. He had a strong pastoral sense.

MERSCH, EMIL (1890–1940), *Jesuit theologian. He sought to construct a theological synthesis in terms of the 'Mystical Body of Christ'. He traced the historical development of the Church understood in these terms and expounded the doctrine from a systematic standpoint.

MERSENNE, MARIN (1588–1648), French philosopher, scientist, and theologian. His place in the history of modern philosophy rests on the links which he forged by friendship and correspondence with many of the leading French philosophers and scientists of his day. He did much to prevent the new scientific movement from developing in an anti-religious direction.

MESONYKTIKON. The Midnight Office in the E. Church.

MESROB, St. (*c*. 345–440), historian and Patr. of *Armenia. Over a long period he was *coadjutor-bishop to the Patr. Sahak, whom he succeeded in 440. He tried to eliminate all traces of Syriac institutions from Armenian life. He composed for the Armenians an alphabet which was adopted in 406, and translated the NT and Proverbs in the Armenian Bible issued *c*. 410.

MESSALIANS, also known as **Euchites,** a sect apparently originating in Mesopotamia in the 4th cent. They held that in consequence of *Adam's sin everyone had a demon substantially united with his soul, and that this demon, which was not expelled by baptism, was liberated only by concentrated and ceaseless prayer, the aim of which was to eliminate all passion and desire.

MESSIAH (Heb. for 'anointed'). The word denotes a person invested by God with special powers and functions. It was rendered in Greek by χριστός, from which '*Christ' derives.

In the OT the term could be applied to anyone set apart for a special function, such as the priest in Lev. 4: 3, but it was used more particularly of the king, who was conceived as anointed by Divine command; as 'the Lord's anointed' his person was sacrosanct (1 Sam. 24: 6). Later the whole *Davidic dynasty was regarded as specially chosen by God. The continued expectation of a deliverer who should be descended from the house of David is reflected in the NT (e.g. Mt. 2: 4–6). Acc. to the Synoptic Gospels the Lord was proclaimed as the Christ or Messiah by angels at His birth (Lk. 2: 11). In His public ministry His messiahship was declared at first only by demoniacs (Lk. 4: 41) and suspected by *John the Baptist (Mk. 11: 3). St. *Peter's confession of Him as the Christ at Caesarea Philippi (Mk. 8: 29; Mt. 16: 16) seems to mark a turning-point; on this occasion the Lord did not disclaim the title and acc. to Mt. 16: 17 He acknowledged it openly, though He still charged His disciples not to tell anyone that He was the Christ. At His trial He answered the question 'Art thou the Christ?' in the affirmative (Mk. 14: 61 f.), and after His resurrection He explicitly taught His own identity with the Messiah of the OT expectation (Lk. 24: 26 f.). Acc. to St. *John's Gospel He acknowledged it much earlier (Jn. 4: 26). See also *Christology.*

METAPHRAST, The. A traditional name for *Simeon Metaphrastes.

METAPHYSICAL POETS. A group of 17th-cent. poets, incl. R. *Crashaw, J. *Donne, G. *Herbert, T. *Traherne, and H. *Vaughan.

METAPHYSICAL SOCIETY, The. A society founded in 1869 by Sir James Knowles to foster constructive debate between the leading exponents of science and religion. The last meeting of the Society was held in 1880.

METAPHYSICS. The name given by the Greek editors of *Aristotle to his 'First Philosophy', and by analogy to treatises on cognate subjects; it originally merely indicated the position of the books on the subject in the Aristotelian *corpus*: after (*meta*) the *Physics.* The scope of metaphysical inquiry has been variously understood; it is esp. concerned with the ultimate realities which are beyond empirical verification.

METEMPSYCHOSIS. The doctrine that souls migrate from one body to another until complete purification has been reached. It is found in various religions, but it is fundamentally at variance with the Christian doctrine of the resurrection of the body.

METHODIST CHURCHES. In 1784 J. *Wesley (q.v.) made provision for the continuance as a corporate body of the 'Yearly Conference of the People called Methodists' by nominating under deed poll 100 persons whom he declared to be its members and laying down the method by which their successors were to be appointed. When he died in 1791 the future relations of Methodism with the C of E were a matter of dispute, but the 'Plan of Pacification' adopted by the Conference of 1795 led to the administration of Baptism and Holy Communion in Methodist chapels and the declaration that the admission of a preacher to 'full connexion with the Conference' conferred ministerial rights. Ordination by the imposition of hands of ministers was adopted again in 1836.

The secession of the *Methodist New Connexion in 1797 was small. In the first half of the 19th cent. there were further secessions of the bodies who became the *Primitive Methodist Church, the *Bible Christians, and the Wesleyan Methodist Association and the Wesleyan Reformers who joined together in 1857 as the *United Methodist Free Churches. In 1907 the Methodist New Connexion, the Bible Christians, and the United Methodist Free Churches came together to form the *United Methodist Church; in 1932 this united with the original or 'Wesleyan' Methodist Church and the Primitive Methodist Church to form the Methodist Church in Great Britain as it now exists.

The organization of the Methodist Church is virtually presbyterian, the supreme authority being the Conference, which consists of equal numbers of ministers and laymen. According to a system peculiar to Methodism, 'All members [of the Methodist Church] shall have their names entered on a Class Book, shall be placed under the pastoral care of a Class Leader, and shall receive a Quarterly Ticket of Membership'. The weekly *class meeting for 'fellowship in Christian experience' has been a valuable institution.

In 1784 Wesley 'set apart' T. Coke and others for N. America. With the growth of the U.S.A. Methodist numbers increased rapidly. After the Civil War there were two main Methodist Churches, one in the North and one in the South; they were reunited in 1939. In 1968 the Methodist Church of the United States was joined by the Evangelical Brethren to form the United Methodist Church. There are also a number of other Methodist bodies in America. American Methodism is largely 'episcopal' in possessing superintendents who are called bishops, though claiming no Episcopal Orders in the Catholic sense. There are Methodist Churches in most parts of the world, many under separate Conferences. Those in *Canada, *South India, and Zambia have entered their respective United Churches. Methodist members number over 20 million, of whom some 10 million are in the U.S.A.

METHODIST NEW CONNEXION. The group of Methodists who in 1797 seceded from the Wesleyan *Methodist Church and in the union of 1907 were incorporated in the *United Methodist Church. The secession was led by A. *Kilham; the differences with the Wesleyan Methodists were solely over

matters of Church government.

METHODIUS AND CYRIL, Sts. See *Cyril and Methodius, Sts.*

METHODIUS OF OLYMPUS, St. (d. *c.* 311), bishop in Lycia. Little is known of his life. He was apparently put to death in the *Diocletianic Persecution.

He wrote extensively, but only a small part of his work survives. The 'Symposium, or Banquet of the Ten Virgins' extols virginity. In a treatise on the Resurrection he took issue with *Origen and upheld the identity of the resurrection body with that worn in this life.

METHUSELAH. The eighth in the list of antediluvian patriarchs in Gen. 5 and the longest-lived (969 years; Gen. 5: 27).

METRICAL PSALTERS. At the Reformation metrical psalmody was introduced in the French and Swiss Reformed Churches as a more Biblical form of musical worship than the German *Lutheran hymns. In England metrical versions of the Psalms first appeared under *Edward VI. The most widely used was that of N. *Tate and N. Brady (1696). In Scotland the use of the metrical psalter became a persistent and characteristic feature of national worship.

METROPHANES CRITOPOULOS (1589–1639), Patr. of *Alexandria from 1636. A Greek monk of Mt. *Athos, he was sent by Cyril *Lucar to study theology in England. In 1638 he signed the anathemas pronounced against Lucar for Calvinism.

METROPOLITAN. The title of a bishop exercising provincial, and not merely diocesan, powers. His duties include the summoning and presidency of provincial synods, the visitation of dioceses, the care of vacant sees, some share in the appointment and consecration of his *suffragan bishops, and some disciplinary powers over them. Metropolitans commonly have the titles of *archbishop and *primate.

MEXICO, Christianity in. The pre-Spanish Aztec empire of Mexico appears to have had vague traditions of Biblical and Christian ideas, but their source cannot be traced. Within five years of the first Spanish invasion (1519) *Franciscan and other RC missionaries arrived. Conversions were numerous, if not entirely voluntary, and much paganism remained under an outward profession of Christianity. The independence of Mexico in 1821 was followed by the separation of the Church and State in the 1857 constitution. In the present cent. repressive measures against the Church have been enacted; though they remain on the statute books, they are not nowadays always enforced.

MICAH, Book of. *Minor Prophet. The author after whom this OT Book is named appears to have lived in the 8th cent. B.C. The first three chapters are generally accepted as his work; they foretell the destruction of *Samaria and of *Jerusalem. Most critics regard the rest of the Book as later. Chs. 4–5 predict the regeneration of the people and the advent of a *Messiah; chs. 6–7 are mainly occupied with a dispute between Yahweh and His people. Mic. 6: 3–5 forms the model of the *Reproaches of the Good Friday liturgy in the W. Church.

MICHAEL THE ARCHANGEL, St. In Dan. (10: 13 ff. and 12: 1) he is represented as the helper of the Chosen People; in Jude (v. 9) disputing with the devil over the body of *Moses; and in Rev. (12: 7–9) fighting the dragon. In the Church he was early regarded as the helper of Christian armies against the heathen and as a protector of individual Christians against the devil, esp. at the hour of death. His feast, 'Michaelmas Day' (29 Sept.), is connected with many popular usages.

MICHAEL CERULARIUS (d. 1058), Patr. of *Constantinople from 1043. The beginning of the schism between the E. and W. Churches is conventionally dated in his period of office. The attempted mediation between the E. Emperor and the delegation led by Card. *Humbert of Silva Candida failed; the Latins excommunicated the Easterns; Cerularius anathematized the Latins (1054).

MICHAEL THE SYRIAN (1126–99), *Jacobite Patr. of Antioch from 1166. His chronicle, covering the period from the Creation to 1194/5, preserves many Syriac sources now lost and affords evidence for the Jacobite Church and for the *Crusades.

MICHAELIS, JOHANN DAVID (1717–91), German Protestant theologian. His linguistic studies on *Hebrew and *Aramaic, and esp. his treatment of the legislation of the *Pentateuch as a human achievement, had a far-reaching influence on the development of Biblical criticism.

MICHELANGELO (1475–1564), Italian Renaissance artist. In 1496 Michelangiolo Buonarroti went to Rome, where he carved a *Pietà* (finished in 1501), in which Christian austerity and classic beauty are admirably harmonized. Between 1508 and 1512 he painted the celebrated frescoes in the *Sistine Chapel. He also painted the *Last Judgement* on the altar wall (1534–41). He remained in papal employment and was entrusted with the direction of the building of *St. Peter's.

MICROLOGUS. An 11th-cent. Roman Mass-book, which provides evidence for the development of the W. liturgy. It was prob. the work of Bernold, monk of Schaffhausen (c. 1054–1100).

MIDDLE AGES, The. The era preceding the Renaissance, now usually taken to date from c. 1100, and extending to the end of the 15th cent.

MIDDLETON, THOMAS FANSHAWE (1769–1822), first Bp. of Calcutta from 1814. His episcopate witnessed a great advance in Church life, including the foundation of the Bishop's College at Calcutta in 1820.

MIDRASH (Heb., 'investigation'). A Jewish term referring to exegesis, esp. of Scripture. It acquired a technical meaning with reference to the way in which exegetical material was attached to the text of Scripture (as opposed to *Mishnah, which refers to the repetition of exegetical material apart from the text of Scripture). The earliest collections of Midrashim come from the 2nd cent A.D., although much of their content is older.

MIGETIUS (8th cent.), Spanish heretic. He appears to have taught the curious doctrine that God was revealed successively in *David (as Father), in Jesus (as Son), and in St. *Paul (as Holy Ghost).

MIGNE, JACQUES PAUL (1800–75), editor and publisher of theological literature. He published a vast collection of religious texts and dictionaries, notably the *Patrologia Latina*, a corpus of Latin ecclesiastical writers up to *Innocent III (221 vols., 1844–64), and the *Patrologia Graeca*, of Greek writers to 1439 (162 vols., 1857–66); these collections remain a standard means of citation.

MILAN, Edict of. In 313 the Emps. *Constantine and Licinius met at Milan and agreed to recognize the legal personality of the Christian Churches and to tolerate all religions equally. This policy marked the end of persecution. The so-called 'Edict of Milan' (it is not an edict and it was not issued at Milan) is found in divergent forms in *Lactantius and *Eusebius.

MILANESE RITE. See *Ambrosian Rite*.

MILDRED, St. (*c*. 700), Abbess of Minster-in-Thanet. She was apparently the daughter of St. Ermenburga, foundress and abbess of the nunnery at Minster. She entered her mother's convent, later succeeding her as abbess. In the 11th cent. there were disputes about her relics.

MILÍČ, JAN (d. 1374), pre-*Hussite reformer. After holding office in the Imperial chancery, he abandoned his temporal interests before the end of 1363. At Prague and elsewhere he preached vigorously against the vices of the clergy. In 1367 he was imprisoned by the *Inquisition at Rome.

MILITANT, The Church. The body of Christians still on earth, as distinct from those in *Purgatory and those in *Heaven.

MILL, WILLIAM HODGE (1792–1853), English orientalist. From 1820 to 1838 he was the first principal of Bishop's College, Calcutta. Here he assisted with the publication of works in the Indian vernaculars for spreading the Christian faith. Later, as Regius Professor of Hebrew, he furthered the interests of *Tractarian principles in Cambridge.

MILLENARIANISM. Belief in a future 'millennium', i.e. a 1,000-year period of blessedness. The main source of the concept within Christianity is Rev. 20. Some of its adherents hold that it will follow the Second Coming of Christ, whether it is spent by the saints in heaven or on earth; others that it will precede the Advent and prepare the way for it.

In the early Church Millenarianism was found mainly among the *Gnostics and *Montanists, though it was also accepted by some of the early Fathers. At the Reformation the *Anabaptists and the *Bohemian and *Moravian Brethren were Millenarianists, and the 17th-cent. *Independents in England seem to have held similar views. In the 19th cent. new advocates of apocalyptic and millenarian ideas arose in the U.S.A. and in Britain, among them the *Plymouth Brethren and the *Adventists. The main Christian bodies have treated Millenarianism with reserve.

MILLENARY PETITION. The petition presented in 1603 by the *Puritans to *James I on his way from Scotland to London, in which they prayed to be relieved from their 'common burden of human rites and ceremonies'. It was the immediate occasion of the *Hampton Court Conference (q.v.).

MILMAN, HENRY HART (1791–1868), Dean of *St Paul's from 1849. His *History of the Jews* (1829) aroused criticism by the freedom with which it handled the OT narrative; it treated the Jews as an oriental tribe and attached little weight to the miraculous. His well-known *History of Latin Christianity* (1855), despite many blemishes, fostered intelligent study of medieval life and institutions.

MILTIADES (2nd cent.), Christian *Apologist. Acc. to *Tertullian and *Eusebius, he wrote against the pagans and the Jews, as well as against the *Montanists and *Valentinians, but all his works are lost.

MILTIADES, St. (d. 314), Pope from 310 or 311. His pontificate is remarkable for *Constantine's victory over Maxentius and the issue of the 'Edict of *Milan'. Miltiades held a Council which condemned *Donatism.

MILTITZ, CARL VON (*c*. 1480–1529), Papal nuncio. After Card. T. de V. *Cajetan's failure to silence M. *Luther, Miltiz was deputed to negotiate with him. At a first meeting at Altenburg in 1519, Luther agreed to refrain from further action pending reference of the matter to the German bishops, but he made no offer of recantation. Two further meetings with Luther were fruitless.

MILTON, JOHN (1608–74), poet and controversialist. He early won a high reputation for his scholarship and literary gifts: his *Ode on the Morning of Christ's Nativity* dates from 1629. In 1641 he joined the *Presbyterians, but his *Doctrine and Discipline of Divorce* (1643), pleading for the solubility of marriage, caused a breach. Its publication without a licence from the censor led the case to be submitted to Parliament and drew from Milton his celebrated *Areopagitica* (1644) in defence of the freedom of the press. From this time his religious views tended towards the *Independents, and from 1649 he supported the new government. He wrote in support of the execution of *Charles I. In 1651 he went blind. In his later years he turned again to poetry. In his greatest work, *Paradise Lost* (q.v., publd. 1667), he undertook to 'justify the ways of God to men' and to show the cause of evil and injustice in the world. In 1671 appeared both its sequel, *Paradise Regained*, which deals with the Temptation of Christ, and *Samson Agonistes*, describing the last hours of Samson 'before the prison in Gaza'; here the blind hero partly represented Milton himself.

MILVIAN BRIDGE, Battle of the (312). The battle in which *Constantine defeated Maxentius. It was decisive for the history of Christianity, for it enabled Constantine to establish himself with Licinius as joint Emperor and thus prepared the way for the 'Edict of *Milan'.

MINIMS (Ordo Fratrum Minimorum). The order of friars founded by St. *Francis of Paola in 1435. As the name indicates, they meant particularly to cultivate humility. They practise extreme abstinence. The order spread rapidly, reached its greatest expansion in the 16th cent., but suffered severely between 1791 and 1870.

MINISTER (Lat., 'servant'). A person officially charged to perform spiritual functions in the Church. Among non-episcopal bodies it is used as a general designation for any clergyman. In the liturgical formularies of the C of E it usually means the conductor of a service, who may or may not be a priest.

MINOR CANON. A cleric attached to a *cathedral or *collegiate church to assist in rendering the daily service. He is not a member of the *chapter.

MINOR ORDERS. The inferior ranks of the ministry, below the *Major Orders of *bishops, *priests, and *deacons, to which the W. Church added *subdeacons. In the RC Church until 1972 there were four minor orders, viz. *doorkeepers, *lectors, *exorcists, and *acolytes. In 1972 the minor orders, now called 'ministeria', were reduced to two, lectors and acolytes alone surviving; to them were assigned the former duties of the subdeacon. The rite by which minor orders are conferred consists chiefly of a commission to exercise their office and the handing over of the *instruments. The minor orders surviving in the E. Church are those of lector, cantor, and subdeacon.

MINOR PROPHETS. In the OT the authors of the twelve shorter prophetic Books, as contrasted with the three Major Prophets—*Isaiah, *Jeremiah, and *Ezekiel. They are *Hosea, *Joel, *Amos, *Obadiah, *Jonah, *Micah, *Nahum, *Habakkuk, *Zephaniah, *Haggai, *Zechariah, and *Malachi.

MINORITES. An older name for the *Franciscan 'Friars Minor'.

MINSTER. A name applied in England to certain cathedrals (e.g. *York) and other large churches (e.g. *Beverley). It originally meant a monastic establishment or its church, whether strictly a monastery (e.g. the abbey at *Westminster) or a house of secular canons. In *Anglo-Saxon England 'old minsters', staffed by groups of clergy living in community, were the centres of vast parishes, within which new churches, each served by a single priest, served smaller centres.

MINUCIUS FELIX (2nd or 3rd cent.), author of the *Octavius*. This is a defence of Christianity in the form of a conversation between Octavius, a Christian, and Caecilius, a pagan, who is converted by the argument.

MINUSCULE SCRIPT. See *Cursive Script*.

MIRACLE. A miracle, acc. to the traditional view, is a sensible fact produced by a special intervention of God, transcending the normal order of things, usually termed the Law of Nature. The possibility of miracles began to be questioned with the rise of modern science in the 17th and 18th cents., with its growing tendency to regard the world as a closed system. The miracles of Scripture and history were then regarded as facts within the sphere of natural explanation, misrepresented by credulous contemporaries. On the other hand, it is argued that if God is held to be the supreme First Cause responsible for, and not subject to, the Laws of Nature, it is likely that He should, from time to time, act directly without the intervention of secondary causes.

Whereas Protestant orthodoxy normally confines itself to belief in the miracles recorded in the Bible, Catholics claim that miracles have occurred throughout the Church's history; the reputed cures at *Lourdes are among the best-known.

MIRACLE PLAY. See *Mystery Play.*

MIRARI VOS (1832). *Gregory XVI's encyclical condemning the social and political doctrines of F. R de *Lamennais and his circle.

MIRFIELD. See *Community of the Resurrection.*

MIRK, J. See *Myrc, J.*

MISERERE. A common designation of Ps. 51 (Vulg. 50) derived from the initial word of the Latin version.

MISERICORD. The projection on the underside of a hinged seat of a choir-stall, commonly said to have been designed to provide support for those incapable of standing for long periods during Divine worship.

MISHNAH (Heb., 'instruction'). A method and form of Jewish Scriptural exegesis, in which the exegetical material was collected on its own (as opposed to *Midrash, in which it was attached to the Biblical text). Various collections of mishnaic material were made, culminating in the authoritative Mishnah, attributed to Rabbi Judah ha-Nasi (c. 135– c. 220). With the *Talmud the Mishnah has exercised an influence on Judaism second only to that of Scripture.

MISRULE, Lord of, also known as the **Abbot** (or **Master**) **of Misrule.** In medieval times, a person selected to preside over the Christmas revels and games.

MISSA CANTATA (Lat., 'Sung Mass'). In the W. Church the form of Mass in which the celebrant and congregation sang the liturgical parts of the rite set to music for *High Mass, but without deacon or subdeacon. The term is now obsolete.

MISSA CATECHUMENORUM; MISSA FIDELIUM. See *Catechumens, Mass of the*; *Faithful, Mass of the.*

MISSA ILLYRICA. A mass *ordo* published by M. *Flacius 'Illyricus' at Strasburg in 1557. It was apparently composed at Minden for the use of Bp. Sigebert (c. 1030).

MISSAL. The book containing the words and ceremonial directions for the celebration of Mass. Missals began to appear in the 10th cent., combining in one book what had previously been contained in several (the *Antiphonary, *Evangeliary, etc.); their development was fostered by the practice of saying private Masses. The 1970 *Missale Romanum*, however, omits the Biblical readings which were issued in a separate *lectionary.

MISSALE SPECIALE. A smaller version of the *Missal, containing selections drawn up for special needs. The best-known is that which came to be called the *Missale Speciale Constantiense* (of Constance). This was at one time thought to be the earliest book ever printed, but in 1967 it was shown to date from 1473.

MISSIONS. The propagation of the Christian faith among non-Christian people was one of the main tasks of the Church from the first. Apart from the labours of St. *Paul and the legendary missionary journeys attributed to the Apostles, unknown missionaries soon carried the Gospel to the limits of the Roman world. In the E. *Nestorian missionaries penetrated as far as *China. In the W. St. *Patrick's work in *Ireland (5th cent.) was followed by intensive missionary enterprise embracing *Scotland, Gaul, and England, where St. *Aidan's work in the N. was supplemented in the S. by the Roman mission of St. *Augustine. In the 8th cent. missionaries from England played a prominent part in evangelizing the pagan parts of Europe, esp. Scandinavia. The conquests of *Charlemagne (d. 814) were accompanied by the forcible baptism of the conquered. In Slavonic lands there were missions from *Constantinople as well as Rome. During the Middle Ages efforts were made to convert the remaining heathen tribes of Europe, missions to the Muslims were initiated (though largely overshadowed by the *Crusades), and work was carried on among the Tartars and Chinese.

The *Counter-Reformation brought a renewal of missionary endeavour in the RC Church. New gains were sought to counteract the losses in Europe, and the *Dominicans, *Franciscans, *Augustinians, and the newly founded *Jesuits did heroic work in the Americas and in *India, *Japan, and China. In 1622 Gregory XV formed the Congregation of the *Propaganda, which subsequently had the supervision of all missionary work. After a temporary halt to expansion in the 18th cent., RC missions experienced a powerful renewal in the early 19th cent. Prominence was given to charitable and educational work, and women religious played an important part. It is estimated that during the 19th cent. 8 million pagans in missionary areas accepted Catholicism.

In the Reformed Churches there was little activity at first. The *S.P.C.K. and *S.P.G. were founded in 1698 and 1701 respectively, but the main missionary work was still carried on by the *Moravians. The *Evangelical Revival gave a new impetus to evangelization on a world-wide scale. The *Methodist Missionary Society dates from 1786, the *Baptist Missionary Society from 1792, the London Missionary Society (*L.M.S.) from 1795, the Church Missionary Society (*C.M.S.) from 1799, and the *British and Foreign Bible Society from 1804. Similar organizations were being founded in America and in other parts of Europe. This phenomenal expansion of work saw the rise of other societies with specialized spheres of work, such as the *Universities' Mission to Central Africa (1859). A distinctive feature in the modern missionary effort is the inter-denominational society, such as the *China Inland Mission (1865). During the last 100 years there has been considerable co-operation among the missions of the non-RC Churches. The World Missionary Conference at *Edinburgh in 1910 aimed at world evangelization on an ecumenical basis, and the International Missionary Council (founded in 1921) joined with the *World Council of Churches to become its Division of World Mission and Evangelism in 1961.

In the present century the nature of missionary work has largely changed. The paternalism of the past is no longer possible, and medicine and education have increasingly become the responsibility of the State. In both RC and non-RC Churches native ministries are taking over responsibility, and the establishment of indigenous Churches is encouraged.

MIT BRENNENDER SORGE (Germ., 'with burning anxiety'). The encyclical condemning Nazism which *Pius XI ordered to be read in all RC churches in Germany on Palm Sunday 1937.

MITHRAISM. The cult of Mithras, a Persian and Indian sun-god. It was made an Imperial cult at Rome by the Emp. Commodus (180–92). All creatures were supposed to have sprung from the bull which Mithras overcame and sacrificed before he ascended into heaven, where he guaranteed a blessed immortality to those who had been initiated into his mysteries. There were striking resemblances between these and Christian *Baptism and the *Eucharist.

MITRE. The liturgical head-dress and part of the insignia of a bishop. In the E. Church it takes the form of a crown, decorated with medallions in enamel or embroidery. In the W. Church it is shield-shaped, usually of embroidered satin and often jewelled; two fringed lappets hang down at the back.

MIXED CHALICE. The practice of mixing water with wine for drinking was general in the ancient world. The Church appears to have carried on in the Eucharist what was prob. the practice of the Lord at the *Last Supper. The first BCP of 1549 directed the continuance of this usage, but the direction disappeared in 1552. Its revival in the C of E in the 19th cent. became a matter of dispute between the *Anglo-Catholics and their opponents.

MIXED MARRIAGE. A marriage between Christians of different religious allegiance. A marriage is so described esp. when one of the parties is a RC.

MOABITE STONE (*c.* 850 B.C.). An inscription in Moabite (virtually a Hebrew dialect), discovered near the Dead Sea in 1868, and commemorating the successes of Mesha, King of Moab, against Israel. The text has points of contact with the Bible.

MOBERLEY, ROBERT CAMPBELL (1845–1903), Anglican theologian. His main works were *Ministerial Priesthood* (1897) and *Atonement and Personality* (1901), the latter perhaps the most original and profound study of the *Atonement in modern Anglican theology.

MODALISM. In the early Church a form of unorthodox teaching on the *Trinity which denied the permanence of the three Persons and maintained that the distinctions in the Godhead were only transitory. It was a form of *Monarchianism (q.v.).

MODERATES. In the Church of *Scotland, the party in the ascendant in the second half of the 18th cent. They held a more moderate conception of doctrine and discipline than their opponents (the 'Evangelicals').

MODERATOR. In *Presbyterian Church courts the Moderator is the presbyter appointed *primus inter pares* to constitute the court and to preside over its proceedings. The Moderator of the *General Assembly of the Church of Scotland serves as the Church's representative and in court precedence in Scotland he comes before the peers.

MODERN CHURCHMEN'S UNION. An Anglican society, founded in 1898 as the 'Churchmen's Union' (until 1928), for the advancement of liberal religious thought. It seeks to uphold the comprehensiveness of the C of E and to maintain the legitimacy of doctrinal restatement in accordance with the requirements of modern science.

MODERN DEVOTION. See *Devotio Moderna*.

MODERNISM. A movement within the RC Church which aimed at bringing the tradition of Catholic belief into closer relation with the modern outlook in philosophy, the historical and other sciences, and social ideas. It arose spontaneously in several countries in the late 19th cent.; it was esp. strong in France.

The main tenets of the movement were: (1) whole-hearted adoption of the critical view of the Bible, by then generally accepted outside the RC Church; (2) an inclination to reject the 'intellectualism' of Scholastic theology and to subordinate doctrine to practice; and (3) a teleological attitude to history, finding the meaning of the historic process in its issue rather than in its origins. Since the Church's growth took place under the guidance of the Spirit, the essence of the Gospel will lie in its full expansion rather than in its primitive kernel. This belief was sometimes reflected in extreme scepticism about Christian origins.

Leaders of the movement included A. *Loisy, M. *Blondel, L. *Laberthonnière, F. *von Hügel, and G. *Tyrrell. *Leo XIII tolerated the movement; *Pius X condemned it in 1907.

In the wider sense the term 'Modernist' has been used of radical critics of traditional theology in non-RC Churches, esp. of the thought associated with the '*Modern Churchmen's Union'.

MOFFAT, ROBERT (1795–1883), pioneer missionary in *South Africa. Operating under the auspices of the *L.M.S., he converted the Hottentot chief known as Africaner, and by reconciling him to the British Government gained official support. He worked first among the Bechuanas and later among the Matabele. In 1840 he persuaded D. *Livingstone, his future son-in-law, to go to Africa. He translated the Bible into Sechwana.

MOFFATT, JAMES (1870–1944), NT scholar. A minister of the *Free Church of Scotland, from 1927 to 1939 he taught at the *Union Theological Seminary, New York. He was well known as a writer in many fields. His translation of the Bible is written in colloquial English; the NT appeared in 1913, the OT in 1924, and the whole was revised in 1935.

MOGILA, PETER (1597–1646), Orthodox theologian and from 1632 Metropolitan of Kiev. The most important of his writings was his 'Confession'. A comprehensive survey of the faith of the Orthodox Church, it was approved by the Synod of *Jassy (1642) and remains a primary witness to Orthodox doctrine.

MOHAMMEDANISM. See *Islam*.

MÖHLER, JOHANN ADAM (1796–1838), RC historian and theologian. He held professorships at *Tübingen and Munich. Though his *Symbolik* (1832; Eng. tr., 1843) caused offence to more conservative RCs, his work contributed to the theological revival in the Church. He was a considerable apologist.

MOLINA, LUIS DE (1535–1600), Spanish *Jesuit and author of the *Concordia liberi arbitrii cum gratiae donis* (1588).

The term 'Molinism' is used to describe doctrines of *grace of the kind elaborated in Molina's *Concordia*; their central tenet is that the efficacy of grace has its ultimate foundation, not within the substance of the Divine gift of grace itself, but in the Divinely foreknown fact of free human co-operation with this gift.

MOLINAEUS, PETRUS. The Latinized form of P. *Du Moulin (q.v.).

MOLINOS, MIGUEL DE (*c.* 1640–97), Spanish *Quietist. At Rome he became one of the most celebrated confessors and spiritual directors. In his 'Spiritual Guide' (*Guida spirituale*, 1675) he recommended the prayer of acquired contemplation and an excessive indifference of the soul. In the account of the spiritual life contained in his letters of direction he found the state of perfection in perpetual union with and complete transformation into God, to which all external observances, mortifications, and even resistance to temptation, were a hindrance. After disturbances among the nuns whom he directed, he was imprisoned in 1685; in 1687 his teaching was condemned.

MOMMSEN CATALOGUE, The, also known as the **Cheltenham List.** A list of Biblical Books, dating from 359, which was discovered in 1885 by T. Mommsen in a 10th-cent. *Phillipps MS. at Cheltenham. It has several notable features.

MONARCHIANISM. A 2nd- and 3rd-cent. theological movement. Its adherents, in their attempt to safeguard the Unity ('Monarchy') of the Godhead, failed to do justice to the independent subsistence of the Son. There were two groups. The 'Adoptionist' Monarchians held that Jesus was God only in the sense that a power or influence from the Father rested upon His human person. The '*Modalist' Monarchians held that in the Godhead the only differentiation was a succession of modes or operations; they were also called '*Patripassians', as it followed from their doctrine that the Father suffered as the Son.

MONARCHIAN PROLOGUES, The. The short introductory narrative passages prefixed in many MSS. of the *Vulgate to each of the Gospels. They were formerly held to be of 2nd–3rd-cent. date and from *Monarchian sources: hence the name. Most recent critics have put them in the 4th cent. or later.

MONASTERY. The house of a religious community.

MONASTIC BREVIARY. The *Breviary traditionally used by monks and nuns following the Rule of St. *Benedict. Among its notable features is the omission of the *Nunc Dimittis at *Compline. After the Second *Vatican Council the former uniformity among *Benedictines was replaced, first by a period of experimentation, and then by the 4 alternative forms of the *Office provided in the *Thesaurus Liturgiae Monasticae Horarum* (1977).

MONASTICISM. Christian monasticism owes its origin to the desire to lead a life of perfection in greater security than is normally possible in the world. The chief aim of the monk is personal sanctification in fulfilling his three *vows of poverty, chastity, and obedience. His day is spent in the two activities of prayer and work, centred on the Divine *Office. The scope of the work, at first restricted to manual labour, came to extend to copying MSS., teaching, art, and scholarly research; the monks were a powerful civilizing influence in Europe.

From the middle of the 3rd cent. there were Christian *hermits in the deserts of Egypt; a very rudimentary form of community life was introduced among the desert fathers by St. *Antony. Monasticism spread to the W. in the 4th cent. The first monks in Gaul and Italy followed E. models, esp. the rules of St. *Pachomius and St. *Basil. St. *Benedict's Rule was the first detailed piece of monastic legislation adapted to European needs. It superseded all other rules and from the 8th to the 12th cent. *Benedictine monasticism was the only form of religious life known in the W. From then onwards there was a proliferation of monastic, canonical, and *mendicant orders. In the 16th cent. monasticism disappeared in the Reformed Churches, but it continued to flourish in RC countries until the French Revolution and Napoleonic conquests, when it came near to extinction. A revival took place in the mid-19th cent. in most countries of Europe and was carried to N. America and elsewhere.

Monasticism also flourished in the Byzantine Empire. In the E. there were two main forms: those of the *coenobium and the small group of individuals (*lavra, skete), living respectively a community and an idiorrhythmic (individual) life. Monasticism spread with Christianity to the Slav countries, reaching Kiev c. 1050 and Moscow, with St. *Sergius, in 1354. As in the W., large and wealthy monasteries attracted the attention of governments, and a general secularization took place in *Russia in 1764. A revival in the 19th cent. continued until the virtual elimination of Russian monasticism in 1917. A special place in Orthodox monasticism is held by Mt. *Athos.

See also under the various religious orders and *Religious Orders in Anglicanism*.

MONASTICON ANGLICANUM. A vast collection of monastic charters and other sources relating to English monasteries and collegiate churches in the Middle Ages, publd. by Sir William *Dugdale (1655–73).

MONE, FRANZ JOSEPH (1796–1871), German historian and liturgical scholar. His *Lateinische und griechische Messen* (1850) contains the text of some early Masses which are notable for the absence of all reference to the cycle of liturgical feasts; they are commonly known as the 'Mone Masses'.

MONICA, St. (c. 331–87), mother of St. *Augustine of Hippo. Widowed at the age of 40, Monica became apprehensive at Augustine's waywardness and prayed earnestly for his conversion. She pursued him from Africa to Italy and from Rome to Milan, where she came under the influence of St. *Ambrose and witnessed her son's conversion.

MONISM. The philosophy which seeks to explain all that is in terms of a single reality. It is incompatible with the Christian belief in a radical distinction between the various grades of being.

MONK. The word is popularly used of a member of any religious community of men living under *vows of poverty, chastity, and obedience, but it is properly applied only to those bodies in which community life is an integral element. See also *Monasticism*.

MONOGENES, The. A Greek hymn, so called from its opening word, which forms part of the Byzantine Liturgy.

MONOLATRY. Restriction of worship to one god, when other gods may be held to exist. Some OT scholars have held it to be a necessary stage in the transition from polytheism to *monotheism, and that it marked Israel's condition from the time of the *Sinai Covenant (Exod. 24) to that of the Prophets.

MONOPHYSITISM. The doctrine that in the Person of the Incarnate Christ there was but a single, and that a Divine, Nature, as against the orthodox teaching of a double Nature, Divine and human, after the Incarnation. Its adherents came into being as a distinct body immediately after the Council of *Chalcedon (451), which formally defined the Dyophysite doctrine. Variant forms soon developed. An extreme type was held by the followers of *Julian of Halicarnassus; a more moderate party was led by *Severus of Antioch. Despite attempts to reconcile the Monophysites to the Catholics, the break became final in the 6th cent., when Monophysitism consolidated itself in three great Churches: among the *Copts and *Abyssinians, the Syrian *Jacobites, and the *Armenians.

MONOTHEISM. Belief in one personal and transcendent God. Acc. to traditional Christian teaching it was the original religion of man, lost by most men as a consequence of the *Fall. In the 19th cent. it was frequently maintained that the religious beliefs of man had progressed from animism by way of polytheism to monotheism, but this theory is now less widely held.

MONOTHELITISM. A 7th-cent. heresy confessing only one will in Christ. Under the auspices of the Emp. *Heraclius a formula seemingly acceptable to both *Monophysites and Chalcedonians was produced in 624; it asserted two natures in Christ but only one mode of activity or 'energy'. When *Sergius, Patr. of Constantinople, wrote to *Honorius c. 634, the Pope in his reply used the unfortunate expression 'one will' in Christ, which henceforth replaced the 'one energy'. The '*Ecthesis', issued by Heraclius in 638, forbade the mention of one or two energies and admitted only one will. It was accepted by two Councils at Constantinople but rejected by successive Popes. The controversy was finally settled in 681 when the Third Council of *Constantinople proclaimed the existence of two wills in Christ, Divine and human, to be the orthodox faith.

MONSIGNOR, usually abbreviated Mgr. In the RC Church an ecclesiastical title attached to an office or distinction ordinarily bestowed by the Pope.

MONSTRANCE. The vessel used for exposing the Eucharistic Host for veneration. In its modern form it consists of a frame of gold or silver rays in the centre of which is a receptacle with a glass window through which the Host may be seen.

MONTAIGNE, MICHEL DE (1533–92), French essayist. In his first group of *Essais* (1580) he propounded a scarcely Christianized form of Neo-Stoic philosophy; in the third book (1588) he inclined towards an *Epicurean, or even a Cyrenaic, attitude to life, with reservations. The good life, he held, consisted in a due development of the whole of human nature, including its nobler aspects. He impressed his immediate posterity by his presentation of ancient philosophy as a self-sufficient ethical system, independent of religious principles and sanctions.

MONTALAMBERT, CHARLES RENÉ FORBES (1810–70), French RC historian. He associated himself with the movement sponsored by F. R de *Lamennais and H. *Lacordaire, but when *Gregory XVI condemned *liberalism in 1832, he submitted and ceased to propagate his views for some time. His historical works were polished in style, but uncritical. The best-known is his *Moines d'occident* (1860–7; Eng. tr., 1896).

MONTANISM. A 2nd-cent. apocalyptic movement; its adherents expected a speedy outpouring of the Holy Spirit on the Church, and saw the first manifestations of this in their own leaders. Montanus began preaching in Phrygia in 156/7 or in 172. Associated with him were two women, Prisca and Maximilla.

The ascetic traits which developed were esp. prominent in an offshoot of the movement in Roman Africa, which won the allegiance of *Tertullian. It disallowed second marriages, condemned the existing regulations on fasting as too lax, and forbade flight in persecution.

MONTE CASSINO. The principal monastery of the *Benedictine Order, founded by St. *Benedict c. 529, when he migrated from *Subiaco. The house reached the peak of its prosperity in the 11th cent., when the Norman church was consecrated (1071) and the fame of the *scriptorium established. The buildings were almost totally destroyed in 1944, but they have been restored.

MONTES PIETATIS. In the later Middle Ages, charitable institutions for lending money in cases of necessity. From the mid-15th cent. the Italian *Franciscans established a number of successful *montes*, which charged a low contribution towards expenses. They were opposed by the *Dominicans on the ground that they offended the canonical prohibition of *usury, but they were approved by *Leo X in 1515.

MONTESQUIEU, CHARLES LOUIS JOSEPH DE SECONDAT, **Baron de la Brède et de** (1689–1755), French historian and philosopher. His *Lettres persanes* (publd. anonymously, 1721), a successful satire on European society, attacked Louis XIV's government and the Catholic Church. His most important work, the *Esprit des lois* (1748), defends the English principle of the division of power as the safeguard of liberty and the way to an ideal form of government. Here he regards Christianity as a powerful moral force in society which, though directly occupied only with the next life, makes for order and happiness in this.

MONTFAUCON, BERNARD DE (1655–1741), one of the foremost *Maurist scholars. He produced splendid editions of

St. *Athanasius (1698), of the '*Hexapla' of *Origen (1713), and of St. *Chrysostom (1718–38).

MONTH'S MIND. The *Requiem Mass celebrated on the 30th day after death or burial.

MONTINI, GIOVANNI BATTISTA. See *Paul VI*.

MONT-ST-MICHEL. On a rocky island off the north coast of France an oratory is said to have been established by St. Aubert, Bp. of Avranches (8th cent.), in obedience to the commands of an apparition of St. *Michael. In 966 a *Benedictine monastery was founded, to which a fortress was added later.

MONTSERRAT. This mountain, near Barcelona, is surrounded by legends which locate there the castle of the Holy *Grail. The *Benedictine monastery, whose church enshrines the famous image of 'Our Lady of Montserrat', was founded at the beginning of the 11th cent. St. *Ignatius Loyola hung up his sword there after his conversion. It is still a popular place of pilgrimage.

MOODY, DWIGHT LYMAN (1837–99), American evangelist. Becoming a *Congregationalist in 1856, Moody undertook evangelistic work in connection with his Sunday School at Chicago. In 1870 he was joined by Ira David Sankey (1840–1908), who regularly accompanied his preaching with singing and organ-playing. They toured both America and Britain. The 'Sankey and Moody Hymn Book' (1873) incorporated many of the songs used by Sankey and other revivalists who found the hymns in use in England unsuited to their type of appeal.

MORAL PHILOSOPHY. The branch of philosophy which examines the goodness of human actions apart from any considerations derived from supernatural revelation.

MORAL REARMAMENT. The watchword of a campaign for moral and spiritual regeneration on the principle of the *Oxford Group, launched by F. N. D. *Buchman in 1938.

MORAL THEOLOGY. The study of Christian character and conduct. As tradi-

tionally conceived, it treats of God as the one object and reward of human endeavour, and of the means by which He may be obtained; thus it sets out the basic rules of human conduct and traits of character which are both obligatory in themselves and conducive to a healthy spiritual life.

The content of moral theology derives partly from the Bible and partly from Christian tradition. The foundations of a system of moral theology were laid down by St. *Augustine, who established charity as the fundamental principle of Christian morality, from which all other virtues flow. The real founder of moral theology in the modern sense, however, is St. *Thomas Aquinas. Building on *Aristotle and Augustine, he devoted the whole of the second part of his *Summa Theologica* to the subject, which he linked with the whole organism of natural and supernatural virtues and to the gifts of the Holy Spirit.

In the RC Church since the Council of *Trent there have been controversies over the different systems of morality, esp. *Probabilism, and numerous special manuals and treatises on moral theology have been produced, notably by members of the *Dominican and *Jesuit Orders. This development was fostered by the increased frequency of sacramental confession and the accompanying attempts to apply the findings of moral theology to individual cases. The most famous moral theologian of modern times is St. *Alphonsus Liguori, whose *Theologia Moralis* (1753–5) finally established the milder Probabilist and *Equiprobabilist method of resolving doubtful cases against the harsher *Probabiliorism, then largely followed in France and Italy.

In general Protestant Churches have tended to eschew attempts to produce detailed systems of duties binding on all Christians and to confine themselves to general presentations of Christian duties. Traditional treatments of moral theology have in recent years been criticized on a number of grounds and attempts are being made to think constructively about the dilemmas presented by modern secular society.

MORALITY PLAY, or **MORALITY.** A form of drama, popular in the 15th and 16th cents., in which a moral truth or lesson was inculcated by the chief characters personifying various abstract qualities. It was a development from the earlier *Mystery Plays. 'Everyman' is the best known.

MORAVIAN BRETHREN. The name in common use for the Protestant Church which is the direct continuation of the *Bohemian Brethren (q.v.) after their 'renewal' under Count N. L. von *Zinzendorf in 1722. There was a strong *Pietist element in the community, which had close links with the *Lutheran Church. From an early date they were active missionaries; in 1732 two brethren went to the Negroes in the *West Indies and in 1733 a mission was begun in Greenland. Over half their number are now in N. America.

MORE, HANNAH (1745–1833), religious writer and philanthropist. She established schools at Cheddar and in the neighbouring villages at a time when popular education was almost unprecedented; religious teaching was combined with training in spinning. She also established friendly societies and other organizations for the relief and education of adults. Between 1793 and 1799 she wrote many tracts designed to combat the influence of the French Revolution (collected as *Cheap Repository Tracts*).

MORE, HENRY (1614–87), '*Cambridge Platonist'. In various discursive works he defended theism and immortality. He emphasized the instinctive reasonableness of Divine truth and affirmed the existence of a higher principle than reason, which he termed the 'Divine Sagacity'. He held that it was possible to apprehend this higher truth only through the cultivation of a righteous disposition and a free intellect.

MORE, St. THOMAS (1478–1535), Lord Chancellor of England. His house in Chelsea was a centre of intellectual life, frequented by D. *Erasmus, J. *Colet, and W. *Grocyn. His most famous work, the *Utopia* (1516), describes an ideal community living according to the natural law and practising a natural religion, with side-thrusts at contemporary abuses.

From the time of *Henry VIII's accession, More held a series of offices, succeeding T. *Wolsey as Lord Chancellor in 1529. The turning-point in his career came when he opposed the King over his divorce. He resigned the Chancellorship in 1532. When he refused to take the oath on the Act of Suc-

cession in 1534 he was confined to the Tower. After 15 months he was accused of treason on the ground of having opposed the Act of *Supremacy and was beheaded.

MORIN, JEAN (1591–1659), French *Oratorian theologian. A Biblical and patristic scholar, he advised *Urban VIII on the subject of *orders. He came to reject the idea that the Tradition of the *Instruments constituted the *matter of Ordination.

MORISON, JAMES (1816–93), founder of the '*Evangelical Union'. As minister of the *United Secession Church at Kilmarnock, he preached that Christ made atonement for all, and published his beliefs in a short tract. He was expelled from the United Secession Church in 1841; in 1843 he founded the 'Evangelical Union'.

MORITZ, St. An alternative form of St. Maurice (q.v.).

MORLEY, GEORGE (1597–1684), Bp. of *Winchester from 1662. He was ejected from his living as a royalist in 1648. He became Bp. of *Worcester in 1660 and took a prominent part in the *Savoy Conference. At Winchester he rebuilt Wolvesey Palace.

MORMONS. The popular name for the 'Church of Jesus Christ of Latter-Day Saints'. This was founded at Manchester, New York, in 1830 by Joseph Smith (1805–44), who claimed to have discovered through a revelation the 'Book of Mormon'; this is accepted as Scripture along with the Bible. Their headquarters was moved to Salt Lake City, Utah, in 1847. Their practice of polygamy brought them into conflict with the Federal Government until 1890, when the President of the Mormons advised his followers to conform to the law.

The characteristic teaching of the Mormons has a strong *Adventist element. They hold that after His resurrection Christ ministered briefly in America and that Zion will be built in the western hemisphere.

MORNING PRAYER. See *Mattins*.

MORONE, GIOVANNI (1509–80), cardinal. He became nuncio to Germany in 1536 and he was present at the Diets of *Hagenau (1540), *Ratisbon (1541), and Speyer (1542). He showed some sympathy with the

Reformers' grievances and tried to establish less embittered relations. In 1542 he was nominated as one of three to preside over the forthcoming Council of *Trent. In 1557 *Paul IV imprisoned him for supposed heresy. He was cleared of all the charges under *Pius IV, who employed him during the last sessions of the Council.

MORRIS, WILLIAM (1834-96), English artist and author. His interest in the Middle Ages was stimulated by contact with the *Oxford Movement. He aimed at the reintegration of life and art, the unity of which he held had been broken by the specialization and mechanization of post-medieval times. Believing that sound social life was a prerequisite of healthy art, in 1884 he became the leader of the Socialist League. His earlier romances were modelled on G. *Chaucer; the later ones deal with either the remote past or the distant future. In 1890 he founded the famous Kelmscott Press.

MORRISON, ROBERT (1782-1834), first Protestant missionary in *China. Working under the *L.M.S., Morrison was sent to Canton in 1807. With great difficulty he secured lessons in Chinese, which could not then be taught to foreigners. He published a Chinese grammar, a dictionary, and a translation of the Bible, based partly on an old *Jesuit version.

MORTAL SIN. A deliberate act of turning away from God as man's last end by seeking his satisfaction in a creature. A sin, to be mortal, must be committed with a clear knowledge of its guilt and full consent of the will, and must concern a 'grave matter'. It is held to involve loss of sanctifying grace and eternal damnation, unless repented and forgiven.

MORTIFICATION. An ecclesiastical term used to describe the action of 'killing' or 'deadening' of the flesh and its lusts through ascetic practices, e.g. the infliction of bodily discomfort or fasting.

MORTMAIN. Land held by an ecclesiastical or other corporation that cannot be alienated. Statutes of Mortmain to limit the Church's power to acquire property were repeatedly enacted in the Middle Ages. The present law in England is regulated by the Mortmain and Charitable Uses Act of 1888

and its subsequent amendments.

MOSCHUS, JOHN (c. 550-619), spiritual writer. About 575 he retired to a monastery near Jerusalem; later he travelled widely, visiting or settling at various monastic centres. His *Pratum Spirituale* contains a large collection of anecdotes on the monastic life; it became extremely popular.

MOSES, the Founder and Lawgiver of Israel. Acc. to the *Pentateuchal narrative, Moses was born in Egypt and owed his life to being hidden in a basket and rescued by Pharaoh's daughter. Later he received a Divine command to rescue the Hebrews from their bondage and he eventually led the people out of Egypt. During the journey across the desert they often rebelled against him, but by his intercession they were given *manna for food as well as the Ten *Commandments. He was granted a sight of the Promised Land and died in Moab.

Acc. to the traditonal view, Moses wrote the entire Pentateuch. Nearly all modern scholars see interwoven in these Books a number of independent documents of different dates and varying degrees of historicity. The majority agree that some such commanding figure as Moses is presupposed by the unity of the Israelite tribes and that the Hebrew people would hardly have sought their beginnings in bondage unless such had been the case.

Moses figures prominently in Christian tradition. At the *Transfiguration scene he appears as the Representative of the Law. He was the subject of various legends.

MOSES, The Assumption of. A composite Jewish work of the 1st cent. A.D., much of which has been lost. It contained a speech of *Moses prophesying the history of the Israelites and prob. also an account of Moses' death and taking up into heaven.

MOSES BAR KEPHA (c. 815-903), *Jacobite Bp. of Mosul from c. 863. He is said to have written commentaries on most Books of the Bible; parts of those on Gen., the Gospels, and the Pauline Epistles survive.

MOSES OF CHORENE (prob. 8th cent.), *Armenian Christian scholar. His 'History of Armenia', though less reliable than formerly supposed, is a work of the first importance, which incorporates many literary remains of the pre-Christian period.

MOSHEIM, JOHANN LORENZ VON (1694–1755), German ecclesiastical historian and divine. His work was marked by a hitherto unprecedented objectivity and penetration, and he may be considered the first modern ecclesiastical historian.

MOSLEMS. See *Islam*.

MOSQUE OF OMAR. See *Dome of the Rock*.

MOTET. A form of polyphonal chant. Prob. of secular origin, it came into liturgical worship in the 13th cent., either following or replacing the *Offertory at Mass. The composition of motets reached its height at the end of the 16th cent., with the work of Orlando di Lasso, G. P. *Palestrina, and others.

MOTHER OF GOD. See *Theotokos*.

MOTHERING SUNDAY. The Fourth Sunday in Lent. The name has been referred to: (1) the custom in some parts of England of visiting one's mother on this day; (2) the practice of visiting the cathedral or mother church on this day; or (3) the words in the traditional *epistle for the day, 'Jerusalem ... which is the mother of us all' (Gal. 4: 26).

MOTHERS' UNION, The. An organization of women in the C of E which aims at upholding 'the sanctity of marriage' and developing in mothers a sense of responsibility in the training of their children. It was founded in 1876, originally as a parochial organization, by Mary Elizabeth Sumner. It spread rapidly, was incorporated in 1910, and granted a royal charter in 1926. It now operates in 190 dioceses of the Anglican Communion.

MOTT, JOHN RALEIGH (1865–1955), American *Methodist. He became known for his zealous propaganda on behalf of missions, and he was chairman of the committee which called the first International Conference at *Edinburgh in 1910. His interest in the *Ecumenical Movement dated from this time. He took a prominent part in the '*Faith and Order' and '*Life and Work' Conferences, and also in the formation of the

*World Council of Churches.

MOTU PROPRIO (Lat., 'on his own impulse'). A letter written by the Pope on his own initiative and bearing his personal signature. It may be addressed to the Church at large, to some part of it, or to particular persons.

MOULE, HANDLEY CARR GLYN (1841–1920), Bp. of *Durham from 1901. On the establishment of Ridley Hall, Cambridge, as a theological college on *Evangelical principles, Moule became its first principal in 1881. He was a leading influence for Evangelicalism at Cambridge and later at Durham.

MOULTON, WILLIAM FIDDIAN (1835–98), Biblical scholar. He was an authority on NT Greek, and in 1870 he became secretary of one of the NT committees occupied on the RV.

His son, James Hope Moulton (1863–1917), brought to bear on NT Greek the new evidence from non-literary *papyri.

MOUNT CARMEL; MOUNT OF OLIVES. See *Carmel, Mount; Olives, Mount of*.

MOVABLE FEASTS. Annual ecclesiastical feasts which do not fall on a fixed day in the secular calendar, but vary acc. to certain rules. Thus *Easter Day is the first Sunday after the full moon between 21 Mar. and 18 Apr.

MOWINCKEL, SIGMUND OLAF PLYTT (1884–1965), Norwegian OT scholar. Of his many contributions to OT study, the most noteworthy relate to the Psalms. Mowinckel held that the Psalms which celebrate Yahweh's kingship are parts of the liturgies of a pre-exilic festival in which the enthronement of Yahweh was annually celebrated, and that its themes provided the pattern of the later eschatological hope. He also wrote on the *Messianic hope, *Ezra-Nehemiah, and the *Hexateuch.

MOZARABIC CHANT. The earliest records of the music of the *Mozarabic rite cannot now be read, but it appears to have been not very different in style from the *Gregorian, though perhaps more florid.

MOZARABIC RITE. The conventional name for the liturgical forms which were in use in the Iberian Peninsula from the earliest times until the 11th cent. Its replacement by the Roman rite was a result of the Christian reconquest of *Spain. There was resistance to its abolition in Toledo, and here it was allowed to remain in use in six parishes. Its preservation in modern times is due to F. *Ximénes de Cisneros, who caused a *missal and *breviary to be printed (1500 and 1502).

The Mozarabic rite has affinites with the *Gallican, from which some scholars hold it to be derived. There are also some elements, such as the Procession of the Oblations, which appear to have been introduced direct from Byzantium. The Mass is characterized by the use of formulas which vary from day to day. There are three lessons: the Prophecy (usually from the OT) as well as the *Epistle and *Gospel. The dismissal of the Catechumens and penitents before the Mass proper was retained. The *fraction of the Host was made into seven or nine pieces, representing the mysteries of the life of Christ. In the *Offices a distinction between the secular and monastic Offices survived. The secular Office consisted of *Vespers and *Mattins; the monastic Office, in its developed form, appears to have had twelve Offices.

MOZLEY, JAMES BOWLING (1813–78), post-*Tractarian theologian. After the secession of J. H. *Newman in 1845, Mozley was for a time one of the foremost representatives of the *Oxford Movement. His Bampton Lectures on *Miracles* (1865) were acclaimed a masterly contribution to what was then a pressing issue.

MOZETTA. A short cape-like garment to which a small hood is attached. It is worn by Popes, cardinals, and other dignitaries.

MUGGLETONIANS. A small sect founded c. 1651 by Ludowicke Muggleton and his cousin. They denied the doctrine of the Trinity, and held that during the period of the Incarnation the government of heaven was left to Elijah. The last known member of the sect died in 1979.

MÜLLER, F. M. See *Max Müller, F.*

MÜLLER, GEORGE (1805–98), philan-thropist and preacher. Moving to Teignmouth in 1830, he associated himself with the *Plymouth Brethren. He became a local preacher, abolished pew rents, refused a salary, and supported himself with offerings from his followers. Two years later he moved to Bristol. Here he devoted himself to the care of orphan children, again relying on voluntary offerings which flowed in as a result of his writing. At the age of 70 he set out on a preaching tour lasting 17 years.

MÜLLER, JULIUS (1801–78), German Protestant theologian. In his principal work, *Die christliche Lehre von der Sünde* (1839–44), he tried to interpret the fact of sin on the assumption of an extra-temporal fall occasioned by a free and intelligent act of decision on the part of each individual.

MÜLLER, LUDWIG (1883–1946), *Reichsbischof. In 1933 Hitler made him his confidential adviser in Church affairs, and under strong Nazi pressure he was elected Bp. of Prussia and Reichsbischof. Resistance from the embryonic *Confessing Church led to his virtual supersession in 1935 by the appointment of H. Kerrl as Minister for Church Affairs, though Müller remained nominally in office.

MUNGO, St. See *Kentigern, St.*

MUNIFICENTISSIMUS DEUS (1950). The Apostolic Constitution defining the doctrine of the *Assumption of the BVM.

MÜNSTER, SEBASTIAN (1489–1552), Hebrew scholar. He produced the first German edition of the Hebrew Bible (1534–5; with a literal Latin version and notes). M. *Coverdale made extensive use of it for the OT of the *Great Bible (1539).

MÜNZER, THOMAS (c. 1490–1525), German *Anabaptist. He became a Protestant preacher at *Zwickau in 1520, but was expelled on account of the subversive nature of his preaching. At Allstedt he organized the first services in German. He then attacked M. *Luther, the Scriptural principle, and *Infant Baptism, and preached revolt. He tried to link his movement with the *Peasants' Revolt, placed himself at the head of the rebels, was captured and executed.

MURATORI, LODOVICO ANTONIO (1672–1750), Italian historian and theological scholar. From 1700 he was archivist and librarian to the Duke of Modena. He published a vast corpus of medieval sources of Italian history, *Rerum Italicarum Scriptores* (25 vols., 1723–51), and an important collection of liturgical documents under the title *Liturgia Romana Vetus* (1748). See also the next entry.

MURATORIAN CANON. The oldest extant list of NT writings, discovered by L. A. *Muratori in an 8th-cent. *Ambrosiana MS. It is generally held to date from the later 2nd cent. It mentions all the NT Books except Heb., Jas., and 1 and 2 Pet.

MURILLO, BARTHOLOMÉ ESTEBÁN (1617–82), Spanish painter. He is esp. known as the painter of the 'Immaculate Conception', which he executed more than 20 times.

MYCONIUS, FRIEDRICH (1490–1546), Reformer. He was drawn to the teaching of M. *Luther and left the *Franciscan Order in 1524. In the same year Duke Johann appointed him preacher at Gotha. Here he married, reformed the schools, and exercised a powerful moral influence. In correspondence with Luther and P. *Melanchthon, he played a leading part in the Reform Movement.

MYCONIUS, OSWALD (1488–1552), originally Geisshäusler, Swiss Reformer and humanist. He collaborated with H. *Zwingli in the propagation of the Reformation at Zürich, and in 1532 he succeeded J. *Oecolampadius at Basle. The undogmatic temper manifested in his desire to reach a compromise with the *Lutheran theologians on the matter of *Consubstantiation aroused distrust among the stricter Zwinglians.

MYRC, JOHN, also spelled 'Mirc' (*fl. c.* 1400), religious writer. He was prior of the *canons regular of Lilleshall in Shropshire. His surviving writings are his *Liber Festialis*, a collection of sermons for the main festivals of the Christian year; a *Manuale Sacerdotum*; and *Instructions for Parish Priests*, written in English verse.

MYSTERIES OF THE ROSARY. The fifteen subjects of meditation connected with the *decades of the *Rosary. They are divided into three groups known as the *Joyful, *Sorrowful, and *Glorious Mysteries (qq.v.).

MYSTERY (or MIRACLE) PLAYS. The religious dramas ('mysteries') of the Middle Ages are commonly held to have developed from the dramatic parts of the Liturgy, though they may have been composed by individual writers from Biblical and other sources. The most important and impressive were the Passion Plays, but *Corpus Christi processions offered occasions for elaborate representation of Gospel stories. The plays were usually performed out of doors, on temporary or fixed stages. See also *Drama*.

MYSTICAL THEOLOGY. In Catholic theology, the science of the spiritual life, in so far as this is dependent on the operation of Divine grace. It is commonly contrasted with *Ascetical Theology (q.v.).

MYSTICISM. An immediate knowledge of God attained in this life through personal religious experience. It is primarily a state of prayer, and as such admits of various degrees from short and rare Divine 'touches' to the practically permanent union with God in the so-called 'mystic marriage'. It issues in an increase of humility, charity, and love of suffering. Christian mysticism emphasizes two elements often absent in other religions. In contrast to all pan-cosmic conceptions of the underlying Reality as an impersonal Unity, it recognizes that the Reality to which it penetrates transcends the soul and the cosmos. And in place of all notions of absorption of the soul into the Divine, it posits that the union is one of love and will in which the distinction between Creator and creature is permanently retained. Psychophysical phenomena, such as trances, visions, and ecstasies, have been frequent concomitants of mystical experience, but they are not held to be essential to it, and are sometimes considered a hindrance to its proper realization. Though Christian thinkers have differed widely in their attitude to mysticism, a measure of it is encountered in the Christian life at its more serious levels in all periods.

N

NAASSENES.. A *Gnostic sect similar to, if not identical with, the *Ophites (q.v.).

NAG HAMMADI PAPYRI. A collection of 13 papyrus codices found in 1945 at Nag Hammadi (Chenoboskion) near the Nile. They contain 49 Gnostic treatises, all written in *Coptic, and constitute the most important single contribution to our knowledge of *Gnosticism (q.v.).

NAG'S HEAD STORY, The. A tale fabricated in the 17th cent. to discredit the validity of M. *Parker's episcopal consecration. It alleged that at the Nag's Head Tavern in Cheapside J. *Scory constituted Parker and others bishops by placing a Bible on the neck of each of them in turn with the words 'Take thou authority to preach the Word of God sincerely'.

NAHUM, Book of. '*Minor Prophet'. It predicts the fall of Nineveh (612 B.C.), which is regarded as so imminent that the Book is usually dated shortly before this event. The Psalm of the opening verses (1: 2–9 or 1: 2–2: 2) may come from an independent source.

NAME OF JESUS. Because of the close relation between name and person, the name of Jesus is used in the NT as a synonym for Christ, denoting His character and authority. The disciples perform miracles and exorcisms 'in the name of Jesus', i.e. by His power (Mk. 9: 38 ff., Acts 4: 30), and baptize in it (Acts 2: 38). Devotion to the Holy Name was popularized by the *Franciscans in the 15th cent. A feast was officially granted to them in 1530 and prescribed for the whole RC Church in 1721; it was suppressed in 1969. It had been assigned to various dates in Jan. In the Anglican Communion it is sometimes observed on 7 Aug., the date assigned to it in the calendar of the BCP.

NANTES, Edict of (1598). The edict signed by *Henry IV at Nantes, which ended the French wars of religion. The *Huguenots were granted free exercise of their religion and a state subsidy for the support of their troops and pastors. It was revoked in 1685.

NARSAI (d. *c.* 503), also **Narses**, *Nestorian theologian. He became head of the famous school of *Edessa, but *c.* 471 he fled to Nisibis, where the bishop, *Barsumas, asked him to found a school. He was one of the formative theologians of the Nestorian Church. A large number of metrical homilies and some hymns survive.

NARTHEX. In a Byzantine church, the antechamber of the nave, from which it is separated by columns, rails, or a wall. *Catechumens, candidates for baptism, and penitents occupied the narthex.

NASHDOM, Bucks., Anglican *Benedictine abbey. After the submission to Rome of most of the Anglican community on *Caldey Island in 1913, the remaining Anglicans went to Pershore. In 1926 the community moved to Nashdom, a house designed by Sir Edwin Lutyens at Burnham, Bucks.

NASH PAPYRUS, The. The oldest surviving MS. of any portion of the Hebrew OT, now at Cambridge. It contains the Ten Commandments, followed by a brief introductory passage and the *Shema. It is perhaps to be dated as early as the 2nd cent. B.C.

NASOREAN. See *Nazarene.*

NATALIS, ALEXANDER (1639–1724), French *Dominican. His main work, *Selecta Historiae Ecclesiasticae Capita* (1676–86), was put on the *Index because of its treatment of the conflict of the Empire and the Papacy.

NATALITIA (Lat., 'birthday'). In the early Church the word was used of the death-days of Christians, esp. of martyrs, in the sense of their birthdays into eternal life.

NATHANAEL. A disciple of Jesus. His call

is related in Jn. 1: 43–51. He is commonly identified with St. *Bartholomew.

NATIONAL ANTHEM, The. See *God save the King*.

NATIONAL APOSTASY, Sermon on. A sermon with this title preached by J. *Keble in 1833 is commonly regarded as the beginning of the *Oxford Movement.

NATIONAL ASSEMBLY OF THE CHURCH OF ENGLAND. See *Church Assembly*.

NATIONAL COUNCIL OF THE EVANGELICAL FREE CHURCHES. An association of the Free Churches, founded in 1896 for mutual consultation, co-operation, and witness. In 1940 it was merged in the *Free Church Federal Council.

NATIONAL COVENANT, The (1638). The Covenant of Scottish *Presbyterians inaugurated at Edinburgh as an answer to the attempt to impose on the Scottish Church the 1637 BCP.

NATIONAL SOCIETY, The. The popular name of the Society founded in 1811 as 'The National Society for the Education of the Poor in the Principles of the Established Church'. It was one of the main agents promoting popular education before 1870. Under the 1944 Education Act its schools became either 'Aided' or 'Controlled' by the Local Authorities, with greater or less scope for distinctive Church teaching. Some of its activities have been taken over by the Departmental Councils of the C of E Council for Education (set up in 1948).

NATIVITY OF OUR LORD, Feast of the. See *Christmas*.

NATIVITY OF ST. JOHN THE BAPTIST. A feast observed on 24 June, at least since the 4th cent., to commemorate the miraculous birth of the Baptist recorded in Lk. 1.

NATIVITY OF THE BLESSED VIRGIN. This feast, which is observed on 8 Sept., is attested in the E. in the 8th cent. It was not generally observed in the W. until the 11th cent. The choice of date is unexplained.

NATURAL LAW. An expression used with a variety of meanings, but in a theological context the law implanted in nature by the Creator, which rational creatures can discern by the light of reason. Modern philosophers have largely abandoned the theory.

NATURAL THEOLOGY. The body of knowledge about God which may be obtained by human reason alone without the aid of *revelation. Reformation theologians generally rejected the competence of fallen human reason to engage in Natural Theology. See also *Philosophy of Religion*.

NAUMBURG CONVENTION (1561). A meeting of princes and representatives of the German Protestant leaders held at Naumburg with a view to securing doctrinal unity. The *Lutherans and *Calvinists were unable to agree.

NAVE. The part of a church, between the main front and the chancel and choir, which is assigned to the laity.

NAYLER, JAMES (*c.* 1618–60), *Quaker. He retired from the Parliamentary army in 1651 and in the same year he was convinced by G. *Fox of the Quaker doctrine of the *Inner Light. He was second only to Fox in the leadership of the movement. About 1656 he came under the influence of a group of *Ranters, led by Martha Simmonds, who tried to worship him as Christ. He was accredited with raising a woman from the dead, quarrelled with Fox, and entered Bristol in the manner that the Lord entered Jerusalem. He was imprisoned until 1659.

NAZARENE (or Nasorean). (1) In the NT Christ is called 'Jesus the Nazarene'; this is usually understood as meaning 'from *Nazareth'. (2) The 'Nazarenes' was a Jewish term for the Christians. (3) 'Nazarenes' occurs as a name used by 4th-cent. writers of a group of Christians of Jewish race in Syria, who continued to obey much of the Jewish Law. They used the 'Gospel acc. to the *Hebrews' (which has hence sometimes been termed the 'Gospel of the Nazarenes'). (4) The *Mandeans are sometimes called 'Nasoreans'.

NAZARENE, Church of the. See *Holiness Churches*.

NAZARETH. The village in *Galilee where Christ was brought up and where He lived until the beginning of His ministry.

NAZARITES (more correctly 'Nazirites'). A body of Israelites specially consecrated to the service of God who were under vows to abstain from consuming wine, to let their hair grow, and to avoid defilement by contact with a dead body (Num. 6).

NAZARIUS, St. A martyr whose body St. *Ambrose discovered in a garden outside Milan c. 395 and translated to a church in the city.

NEAL, DANIEL (1678–1743), historian. Pastor of the *Independent congregation in Aldersgate Street, London, he was recognized as one of the best preachers of his day. His *History of the Puritans, 1517–1688* (1732–8), is a valuable compilation, with a strong *Puritan bias.

NEALE, JOHN MASON (1818–66), *High Church Anglican divine. In 1855 he founded the Sisterhood of St. Margaret in E. Grinstead. This community, devoted to education and the care of the sick, became one of the main *religious orders in the C of E. His ritualistic practices led to his *inhibition from 1847 to 1863.
Neale excelled as a hymn-writer. His own compositions include 'O happy band of pilgrims' and 'Art thou weary', and his translations from Lat. and Gk. hymns 'Jerusalem the golden' and 'Christian, dost thou see them?'. *Hymns, Ancient and Modern* owes much to his inspiration.

NEANDER, JOACHIM (1650–80), German hymn-writer. He became an ardent adherent of the *Pietistic Movement. His hymns reflect his love of nature as well as his deep faith. Those translated into English include 'Praise to the Lord, the Almighty'.

NEANDER, JOHANN AUGUST WILHELM (1789–1850), ecclesiastical historian. David Mendel was a Jew by birth, who was converted and took the name of Neander. His General Church History (1826–52) was somewhat uncritical but exercised great influence.

NECTARIUS, St. (d. 397), Bp. of *Constantinople. Though unbaptized, he was selected by *Theodosius I in 381 to succeed St. *Gregory Nazianzen in the imperial see. He presided over the final stages of the *Oecumenical Council then in session.

NECTARIUS (1605–c. 1680), Patr. of *Jerusalem, 1661–9. He was an opponent of all W. theology. In 1662 he expressed approval of the 'Confession' of P. *Mogila and in 1672 he took a prominent part in the Synod of *Jerusalem.

NEHEMIAH, Jewish leader of the postexilic period. The cup-bearer of the Persian king Artaxerxes, he obtained leave to visit Palestine. He arrived in *Jerusalem in 444 B.C. and supervised the rebuilding of the city walls. In 432 B.C. he made a second journey to Jerusalem; he then introduced important moral and religious reforms. For the Book of Nehemiah, see *Ezra and Nehemiah, Books of*.

NEMESIUS OF EMESSA (*fl. c.* 390), Christian philosopher and Bp. of Emessa in Syria. His treatise 'On Human Nature' is an attempt to construct on a mainly Platonic basis a doctrine of the soul agreeable with the Christian revelation.

NEOCAESAREA, Council of. A Cappadocian Council of uncertain date (prob. early 4th cent., before 325). Its 15 canons, mainly on disciplinary and marriage questions, became a constituent part of the canon law of E. and W.

NEOPHYTE (Gk., lit. 'newly planted'). The word was generally used in the early Church of those recently baptized.

NEOPLATONISM. The philosophical system of *Plotinus (c. 205–70) and his successors, who included *Porphyry, *Iamblichus and Proclus (410–85). The Neoplatonists sought to provide a sound intellectual basis for a religious and moral life. In the ultimate One which lies beyond all experience, the dualism of Thought and Reality was to be overcome. This One can be known by man only by the method of abstraction. He must gradually divest his experience of all that is specifically human, so that in the end, when all attributes have been removed, only God is left. The Neoplatonists were not, however, entirely negative, and they held that the Absolute could be reached by mystical experience. Pure Neoplatonism was essentially inimical to Christianity, but Neoplatonist influences made themselves felt on Christian theology, esp. through their diffusive impact on the whole later Roman world. See also *Platonism*.

NEOSTADIENSIUM ADMONITIO (1581). The reply made by the members of the 'Reformed' (*Calvinist) Church at Heidelberg to the *Lutheran 'Formula of *Concord' (1580). It sets out the distinctive tenets of Calvinism.

NEOT, St. (*c.* 9th cent.). Acc. to untrustworthy legends he was a monk of *Glastonbury who in search of solitude retired to the place now known as St. Neot in Cornwall; after his death his relics seem to have found their way to St. Neots, Cambs.

NEPOMUK, JOHN OF. See *John of Nepomuk*.

NEPOTISM. The bestowal of office or patronage on one's relations. It was a frequent charge against certain 16th-cent. Popes.

NEREUS and **ACHILLEUS, Sts.** (perhaps 1st cent.), Roman martyrs. Acc. to their legendary 'Acta', they were transported with St. *Domitilla to the island of Terracina, where Nereus and Achilleus were beheaded and Domitilla burnt.

NERI, St. PHILIP. See *Philip Neri, St.*

NERO, CLAUDIUS (37–68), Roman Emperor from 54. The first 8 years of his reign under the guidance of *Seneca saw an enlightened administration and an extension of Roman power. Later his relations with the administrative classes were embittered and his personal behaviour alienated popular opinion. During the Jewish rebellion in Palestine the army turned against him and he committed suicide.

In 64, when Nero wanted a scapegoat for the fire at Rome, he picked on the Christians. Later tradition makes him the formal author of the technique of all Christian persecutions. But he was the Caesar to whose jurisdiction St. *Paul appealed, though he prob. did not hear the case himself. Both St. *Peter and St. Paul were prob. executed at Rome in his reign.

NERSES, St. (d. *c.* 373), sixth *Catholicos of the *Armenian Church. A direct descendant of *Gregory the Illuminator, when he became Catholicos (perhaps *c.* 363), he undertook the reform of the Armenian Church. He censured the new king for his immorality and was poisoned by him.

NESTLE, EBERHARD (1851–1913), German Biblical scholar. His edition of the Greek NT, first issued in 1898, came to be widely used; it has been frequently and drastically revised.

NESTORIANISM. The doctrine that there were two separate Persons in the Incarnate Christ, the one Divine and the other human, as opposed to the orthodox teaching that the Incarnate Christ was a single Person, at once God and man.

Nestorius, from whom the heresy takes its name, was a monk at *Antioch, whom *Theodosius II invited to fill the see of *Constantinople in 428. When his chaplain Anastasius preached against the use of the term '*Theotokos', Nestorius supported him. A violent controversy developed around the propriety of the term. At a Council in Rome in 430 Pope *Celestine condemned Nestorius's teaching, and *Cyril of Alexandria was commissioned to pronounce sentence of deposition if he did not submit. The Emperor called a General Council which met at *Ephesus in 431 and deposed Nestorius (see *Ephesus, Council of*). In 436 he was banished to Upper Egypt, where he died some years later (date unknown).

Nestorius's chief writings were letters and sermons which have mostly survived only in fragments. He also wrote a treatise known as the 'Bazaar of Heracleides'. This was written when the theological climate had changed; in it Nestorius claimed that his own beliefs were identical with those then being sustained by the orthodox (against the *Eutychians). What he taught and how far it was heretical is disputed.

After the Council of Ephesus the E. bishops who refused to accept the Formula of 433 gradually constituted themselves a separate Nestorian Church. It had its centre in Persia, with the Patriarchal see at Seleucia-Ctesiphon on the Tigris. A school of Nestorian theology developed at *Edessa, but the school at Nisibis, founded by *Barsumas, gradually supplanted Edessa as the main seat of Nestorian culture. From the early 6th cent. the Nestorian Church was active in missionary work and established Christian settlements in Arabia, *India (see *Malabar Christians*), and *China The Arab conquest of Persia was completed by 651, but under the Caliphate the Christians met with reasonably good treatment, and *c.* 755 the Patriarchal see was transferred to Baghdad. After the conversion of the Mongol dynasty to Islam in 1295, the Nestorian Church suffered drastic losses. A remnant fled to Kurdistan, where their descendants survived until modern times under the name of *Assyrian Christians (q.v.).

NESTORIAN STONE, The. See *Sigan-Fu Stone, The.*

NE TEMERE (1907). A decree of the Sacred Congregation of the Council on marriage. It lays down that to be valid a marriage in which either or both parties are RCs must be celebrated before the parish priest or the *ordinary or a priest delegated by one of them. In 1970 *Paul VI allowed some relaxation in cases of *mixed marriage.

NETHERLANDS, The. See *Holland.*

NETTER, THOMAS (*c.* 1377–1430), English *Carmelite theologian. He was confessor to Henry V and spiritual adviser to *Henry VI. His main work, *Doctrinale antiquitatum fidei ecclesiae catholicae*, was designed to refute the doctrines of J. *Wycliffe and the *Hussites. The *Fasciculi Zizaniorum* (a collection of anti-Wycliffite documents) is traditionally ascribed to Netter, but prob. only the latter part is his work.

NEUMANN, THERESE (1898–1962), of Konnersreuth in Bavaria, stigmatized visionary. During Lent 1926 she began to have visions of the Passion and received the *stigmata. She was reputed to have taken no nourishment after 1927, except Holy Communion daily. She was credited with various supernatural faculties. The RC ecclesiastical authorities have made no pronouncement on the case.

NEUME. In plainsong, a prolonged group of notes sung to a single syllable, or the sign used to indicate the melody.

NEUTRAL TEXT, The. The type of text of the Greek NT represented by the two MSS.,

*Codex Vaticanus and *Codex Sinaiticus, and so designated by F. J. A. *Hort because it was supposed to be less subject to corrupting influences of editorial revision than any other.

NEVIN, JOHN WILLIAMSON (1803–86), American theologian. He had abandoned *Presbyterianism for a more liberal theology before he became professor of theology in the 'German Reformed' Theological Seminary at Mercersburg, Pa., in 1840. He attacked the prevailing methods of revivalist preaching in *The Anxious Bench* (1843). In 1844 P. *Schaff joined him, and the theological doctrines for which they stood became known as the '*Mercersburg Theology'. In *The Mystical Presence* (1846) Nevin defended a more sacramental conception of Christianity than is ordinarily held by Protestants

NEW ENGLISH BIBLE. See *Bible (English Versions).*

NEW (JERUSALEM) CHURCH. See *Swedenborg, E.*

NEW ROME. A name for *Constantinople, apparently given to the city by *Constantine himself.

NEW TESTAMENT. The Canonical Books belonging exclusively to the Church, as contrasted with those styled *Old Testament, which the Church shares with *Judaism. The NT contains the four Gospels, Acts, the Pauline and 'Catholic' Epistles, and Rev. See also *Canon of Scripture.*

NEW YEAR'S DAY. Christians avoided the 'Saturnalia' which marked the beginning of the Roman New Year (1 Jan.). Later they reckoned the beginning of the year on different days in different countries; in England the year began with the Feast of the *Annunciation (25 Mar.). With the introduction of the *Gregorian Calendar, 1 Jan. came to be accepted. In the E. *Orthodox Church New Year's Day (here 1 Sept.) is solemnized in many hymns, but in the W. Church it has traditionally had no liturgical significance apart from the fact that it coincided with the Feast of the *Circumcision. In England an informal 'watch-night' service is common, esp. in the *Methodist Church.

NEW ZEALAND, Christianity in.
Europeans first made permanent settlements in New Zealand in 1805, and the first missionaries arrived in 1814. Missionary work, in the usual sense, has long ceased, as most Maoris accepted Christianity. In the population as a whole, Anglicans form the largest denomination; there are also many Scottish *Presbyterians; the RC Church and *Methodists form large minorities.

NEWMAN, JOHN HENRY (1801–90), Cardinal. Brought up under *Evangelical influence, he became a Fellow of Oriel College, Oxford, and in 1828 Vicar of St. Mary's. He was intimately associated with the *Oxford Movement, and the leading spirit in it. He wrote 24 of the *Tracts for the Times. Directed 'against Popery and Dissent', they defended his thesis of the 'Via media', i.e. the belief that the C of E held an intermediate position, represented by the patristic tradition, as against modern Romanism on the one hand and modern Protestantism on the other. In *Tract 90* (1841) he advocated an interpretation of the *Thirty-Nine Articles in a sense generally congruous with the decrees of the Council of *Trent; the tract was condemned by the Hebdomadal Board of the University and the Bp. of Oxford imposed silence on its author. Meanwhile from 1839 Newman had begun to have doubts about the claims of the C of E. From 1842 he lived at Littlemore, where he set up a semi-monastic establishment. He resigned from St. Mary's in 1843; in 1845 he became a RC. He issued his *Essay on the Development of Christian Doctrine* (1845) in defence of his change of allegiance.

In 1864 a controversy with C. *Kingsley resulted in Newman's *Apologia pro vita sua*, which won him much sympathy. The following year he wrote *The Dream of *Gerontius* (q.v.). Much of his ripest thought is contained in *A Grammar of Assent* (1870). This is remarkable for its differentiation between real and notional assent, its analysis of the function of conscience in our knowledge of God and of the role of the 'illative sense', i.e. the faculty of judging from given facts by processes outside the limits of strict logic, in reaching religious certitude. He was made a cardinal in 1879. His greatness has been increasingly recognized in modern times.

NEWTON, ISAAC (1642–1727), English mathematician and natural philosopher. He formulated the law of gravitation, discovered the differential calculus, and correctly analysed white light. His religious convictions found expression in his *Philosophiae Naturalis Principia Mathematica* (1687); for him belief in God rested chiefly on the order of the universe. Though a conforming Churchman, he denied the doctrine of the *Trinity on the ground that such a belief was inaccessible to reason.

NEWTON, JOHN (1725–1807), *Evangelical divine. On being offered the curacy of Olney, Bucks., he was ordained in 1764. Here he collaborated with W. *Cowper in the production of the *Olney Hymns* (1779). From 1780 he was rector of St. Mary Woolnoth, London. His hymns include 'Glorious things of Thee are spoken' and 'How sweet the Name of Jesus sounds'.

NICAEA, First Council of (325). The first *Oecumenical Council, summoned by the Emp. *Constantine, mainly to deal with the *Arian controversy. After an Arian creed submitted by *Eusebius of Nicomedia had been rejected, *Eusebius of Caesarea laid before the Council the baptismal creed of his own Palestinian community, and this, supplemented by the word '*Homoousios', was accepted. The Creed promulgated by the Council, however, was not this, but another, prob. a revision of the baptismal creed of *Jerusalem. With four anti-Arian anathemas attached, it was subscribed by all the bishops present, except two who were deposed and banished. In the Arian struggle at the Council it seems that *Athanasius was the leading champion of orthodoxy. The Council also reached decisions on the *Melitian schism in Egypt and the *Paschal Controversy, and issued 20 canons. The traditional number of bishops present (318) is prob. only a symbolic figure; between 220 and 250 is more likely.

NICAEA, Second Council of (787). The 7th *Oecumenical Council, convoked by the Empress Irene to end the *Iconoclastic Controversy. The Council declared its adherence to the doctrine on the veneration of images expounded in a letter from Pope *Hadrian I, adding that images are honoured with a relative love (not the adoration due to God alone), the honour given to the image passing on to its prototype.

NICENE CREED, The. Two Creeds are so

named:

(1) The Creed issued in 325 by the Council of *Nicaea (q.v.), known to scholars as N. It was drawn up to defend the orthodox faith against *Arianism and includes the word '*Homoousios'. Appended to it are four anti-Arian anathemas which came to be regarded as an integral part of the text.

(2) The longer formula which is called the 'Nicene Creed' in the *Thirty-Nine Articles and is in regular use in the Eucharist, in both E. and W. It is also known as the 'Niceno-Constantinopolitan Creed' and is referred to as C. From the time of the Council of *Chalcedon (451) it has been regarded as the Creed of the Council of *Constantinople of 381, but this is doubtful. Like N, it prob. derives ultimately from the baptismal creed of Jerusalem.

NICEPHORUS, St. (c. 758–829), Patr. of *Constantinople. He retired from court life to a monastery, but was recalled and made Patriarch in 806. In return for the Imperial favour, the Emp. Nicephorus demanded the reinstatement of a priest who had been deposed for blessing the adulterous marriage of the Emp. Constantine VI; after some hesitation the Patriarch gave way. When the Emp. Leo V (813–20) resumed an *iconoclastic policy, Nicephorus resisted; he was exiled in 815 and retired to his former monastery. Besides writing in the image controversy, he compiled a Byzantine history from 602 to 770.

NICEPHORUS CALLISTUS (c. 1256–c. 1335), 'Xanthopoulos', Byzantine historian. His main work, a 'Church History', covers the period from the birth of Christ to the death of the Emp. Phocas (610). It preserves material on some of the early controversies and heresies. In 1555 it was translated into Latin and furnished material for the defence of images and relics.

NICETA, St. (d. c. 414), Bp. of Remesiana (Bela Palanka in Yugoslavia) from c. 370. His *Explanatio Symboli* is a primary witness for the history of the *Apostles' Creed, containing the oldest attestation for the words 'communio sanctorum'. He also wrote against the *Arians and *Pneumatomachoi, and works of liturgical interest. Some scholars attribute to him the authorship of the *Te Deum.

NICETAS ACOMINATOS (d. after 1210), Byzantine scholar. He rose rapidly in the Imperial service at *Constantinople. His writings include a 'Treasury of Orthodoxy', directed against contemporary heresies and the main source for the Councils held between 1156 and 1166, and a History of the period 1180–1206, which is esp. valuable for its account of the capture of Constantinople by the Latins in 1204.

NICHOLAS, St., Bp. of Myra. Practically nothing about him is certain. Acc. to tradition he was imprisoned in the *Diocletianic persecution and was present at the first Council of Nicaea; the latter supposition is improbable. He is regarded as the patron saint of sailors and of Russia; also of children, bringing them gifts on 6 Dec. (whence 'Santa Claus', a corruption of 'Saint Nicholas'). His symbol is sometimes 3 bags of gold, the dowry he is supposed to have given to save 3 girls from degradation.

NICHOLAS I, St. (d. 867), Pope from 858. His pontificate witnessed a protracted struggle with the E. Church. He refused to sanction the Emperor's deposition of Ignatius and appointment of *Photius to the see of Constantinople, and in 863 he pronounced Ignatius restored. He also tried to win over the newly converted *Bulgars to Rome. In 867 Photius declared the Pope deposed, but was himself deprived of office later in the year. In the W. Nicholas took a firm stand in the divorce case of Lothair II of Lorraine; he asserted the supremacy of the see of Rome over Abp. John of *Ravenna, and he forced *Hincmar of Reims to accept the right of the Papacy to intervene in disputes.

NICHOLAS V (1397–1455), Pope from 1447. By his conciliatory spirit and diplomatic skill he obtained recognition of the Papal rights in the matter of benefices and bishoprics in the Concordat of Vienna in 1448, and in 1449 he ended the schism by receiving the submission of the antipope Felix V and that of the Council of *Basle before its dissolution. He made a serious attempt to reform abuses. He was of blameless personal life and anxious to reconcile religion with the new learning.

NICHOLAS OF BASLE (d. c. 1395), heretic. He was a *Beghard, who taught that all who submitted to his direction were sinless and need not obey any authority. For many years he evaded the *Inquisition, but he was eventually burnt at the stake in Vienna.

NICHOLAS CABASILAS. See *Cabasilas, N.*

NICHOLAS OF CUSA (1401–64), German philosopher. At the Council of *Basle he worked for the reconciliation of the *Hussites and in 1433 he procured the acceptance of the *Calixtines by the Council. He originally favoured the *Conciliar Movement, but he became estranged from its supporters and from 1437 devoted himself wholly to the cause of the Pope. *Nicholas V made him a cardinal and in 1450 appointed him Bp. of Brixen (in the Tyrol) and papal legate for the German-speaking countries. He worked zealously for reform until a conflict with Duke Sigismund forced him to leave his diocese. He spent his last years in Rome.

In intellectual outlook Nicholas was a forerunner of the Renaissance. His main work, *De Docta Ignorantia*, was a defence of his two celebrated principles, 'docta ignorantia' and 'coincidentia oppositorum'. 'Docta ignorantia' was the highest stage of intellectual apprehension accessible to the human intellect, since Truth, which is absolute, one, and infinitely simple, is unknowable to man. Knowledge by contrast is relative, multiple, complex, and at best only approximate. The road to Truth therefore leads beyond reason and the principle of contradiction; it is only by intuition that we can discover God, the 'coincidentia oppositorum', wherein all contradictions meet. God is at once infinitely great and infinitely small, the centre and circumference of the world, everywhere and nowhere, neither One nor Three, but Triune.

NICHOLAS OF FLÜE, St. (1417–87), 'Brother Klaus', Swiss ascetic. In 1467 he obtained the consent of his wife to leave her and their 10 children, to lead the life of a hermit in the Ranft valley in Switzerland. He is said to have lived there for 19 years with no food save the Eucharist. In 1481 a dispute of the Swiss confederates at Stans was settled by his counsel. He is the patron saint of Switzerland.

NICHOLAS OF HEREFORD (d. *c.* 1420), *Lollard writer. At Oxford he

became a supporter of J. *Wycliffe and by 1382 he was preaching Wycliffite doctrines. For this he was condemned and twice imprisoned. He seems to have recanted *c.* 1391 and in 1394 he became a canon of *Hereford. He prob. took part with J. *Purvey in the translation of the Bible into English.

NICHOLAS OF LYRA (*c.* 1270–1340), *Franciscan scholar. He was the best-equipped Biblical scholar of the Middle Ages; he knew Hebrew and was familiar with the commentaries of Jewish expositors. His *Postillae perpetuae in universam S. Scripturam* was very popular. He is supposed, perhaps wrongly, to have influenced M. *Luther.

NICHOLAS OF ORESME. See *Oresme, N.*

NICHOLAS OF TOLENTINO, St. (*c.* 1245–1306), *Augustinian friar. His life was pious, but uneventful. Fragments of his body, interred at Tolentino, are reputed to bleed shortly before great calamities.

NICHOLAS, HENRY (*c.* 1502–*c.* 1580), or **Hendrik Niclaes**, founder of the *Familists (q.v.). In 1539 or 1540 he believed that he had Divine communications commanding him to found a new sect, the 'Family of Love'. He spent the next 20 years at Emden, where he wrote a number of books, but in 1560 the authorities took steps against his sectarian activities and he spent his last years as a fugitive in Holland and Germany. His teaching was a kind of mystic pantheism.

NICODEMUS. The Jew who came to Jesus by night and evoked the discourse on Christian rebirth narrated in Jn. 3: 1–15. He later helped *Joseph of Arimathaea to give Him burial (Jn. 19: 39).

NICODEMUS OF THE HOLY MOUNTAIN, St. (*c.* 1749–1809), Greek monk of Mount *Athos and spiritual writer. His main publications were the *Philocalia (q.v.) and a commentary on E. canon law entitled the *Pidalion* or 'Rudder' (1800). He urged the need for frequent Communion. He also published Greek editions of RC writers, incl. the *Spiritual Exercises* of St. *Ignatius Loyola.

NICOLAITANS. Sectaries mentioned in the NT at Rev. 2: 6 and 2: 14 f., where they appear as the advocates of a return to paganism. It is possible that the name is allegorical and no such sect existed, though a *Gnostic sect of the name is mentioned by some of the early Fathers. In the Middle Ages the term was sometimes applied to married priests by the upholders of clerical *celibacy.

NICOLE, PIERRE (1625–95), French theologian and controversialist. He formed a close friendship with A. *Arnauld, in collaboration with whom many of his works were written. His writings on the *Jansenist controversy were more moderate in tone than most on the subject. He also wrote against *Calvinism and *Quietism. In his *Essais de morale* (1671–8) he showed originality of outlook in his application of Christian teaching to everyday life.

NICOLÒ DE' TUDESCHI. See *Panormitanus*.

NICOMEDES, St., early Christian martyr. It appears that he was buried in a *catacomb on the Via Nomentana near the wall of Rome. Nothing is known of the circumstances or date of his death.

NIEBUHR, HELMUT RICHARD (1894–1962), American theologian. The brother of Reinhold *Niebuhr, he taught at Yale from 1938 until his death. He was esp. concerned with the correlations between religious beliefs and social groupings in the United States.

NIEBUHR, REINHOLD (1892–1971), American theologian. From 1928 to 1960 he was Professor of Applied Christianity at the *Union Theological Seminary, New York. He sought to return to the categories of the Biblical revelation and was critical of both liberal theology and metaphysics. He reinstated the doctrine of *original sin and tried to expound a 'vital prophetic Christianity'. His 'Christian realism' exercised an influential critique on American social and political institutions.

NIEHEIM, DIETRICH OF. See *Dietrich of Nieheim*.

NIEMÖLLER, MARTIN (1892–1984), German *Lutheran pastor. His anti-Nazi activities in 1937 led to his arrest and confinement in a concentration camp. Offered release on certain conditions, he refused, and he became the symbolic figure of Protestant opposition to National Socialism. After the Second World War he took a leading part in the 'Declaration of Guilt' at Stuttgart. He held various offices but his influence in Germany declined.

NIETZSCHE, FRIEDRICH WILHELM (1844–1900), German philosopher. He was a professor at Basle from 1869 to 1879, when he resigned because of ill-health. In 1889 he lost his reason.

Nietzsche was a prophet rather than a systematic thinker. He held that life is the will to power; but power, not as exercised collectively by the masses, but the power of the great individual, the superman. To make this superman possible, the present values derived from Christianity must be abolished, since the weak and disinherited 'herd', by proclaiming humility, pity, &c., as virtues, have put themselves into power to the detriment of the strong.

NIGHT OFFICE. An alternative name for *Mattins.

NIHILIANISM. The doctrine that Christ, in His human nature, was nothing, His essential Being being contained in the Godhead alone. It was condemned in 1170 and 1177.

NIKON (1605–81), Patr. of Moscow from 1652 to 1658. He sought to revise the Russian liturgy by bringing the prescriptions of the service-books into conformity with Greek usage and to eradicate corruptions. He had such details settled as the use of the threefold *Alleluia. In 1658 he fell from Imperial favour and resigned. He tried to regain his position, but at the Council of Moscow in 1667 he was deposed and banished, though his liturgical reforms were sanctioned.

NIL SORSKY, St. (1433–1508), Russian monk and mystic. On a visit to Mount *Athos he found his vocation in the contemplative life of *Hesychasm. Returning to Russia, he introduced a new form of the ascetic monastic life, that of the small group (*skit*) guided by a spiritual father (* *staretz*), for which he wrote a directory.

NILUS THE ASCETIC, St. (d. *c.* 430), also (erroneously) called 'Nilus of Sinai'.

Acc. to the traditional account, he was a high officer in the *Constantinopolitan court, who became a monk on Mt. *Sinai. It appears, however, that he was a native of Ancyra, that he studied at Constantinople, and that he then founded and became superior of a monastery near Ancyra. From here he conducted a large and influential correspondence. His writings deal mainly with ascetic and moral subjects. His idea of the spiritual life was a 'Christian philosophy' based on a 'moderated poverty'.

NIMBUS. See *Halo*.

NINE FRIDAYS. See *First Fridays*.

NINEVEH, Fast of. A two-week pre-*Lenten fast kept by the *Nestorians, *Jacobites, *Copts, and *Armenians.

NINIAN, St. (*c*. 360–*c*. 432), Scottish missionary. He went as a youth to Rome, where he was consecrated bishop in 394. On his return to Scotland he founded at Whithorn in Wigtownshire a church known as 'Candida Casa' (White House), prob. from the colour of its stone. From here Ninian and his monks went out to convert the neighbouring Britons and Picts.

NISAN. The opening month of the Jewish year, roughly corresponding to April. The *Passover lamb was slain on the 14th day of Nisan.

NITRIAN DESERT. The region in Libya W. of the Nile delta, celebrated as a centre of early Christian monasticism.

NITZSCH, KARL IMMANUEL (1787–1868), German *Lutheran theologian. As an opponent of contemporary unbelieving rationalism, he rejected a purely speculative interpretation of Christianity and emphasized the immediacy of religious feeling which, he held, produces the foundations of religious knowledge.

NOAH (or 'Noe'). Acc. to the story in Gen. 6–9, Noah and his family alone were saved in an *ark of gopher-wood, when the rest of mankind was destroyed in the *Flood.

NOAILLES, L. A. DE; **NOBILI,** R. DE. See *De Noailles, L. A.*; *De Nobili, R.*

NOBIS QUOQUE PECCATORIBUS (Lat., 'To us sinners, also'). The opening words of one of the sections of the traditional Roman *Canon of the Mass.

NOBLE GUARD. The bodyguard of 77 men of noble rank who formerly attended the Pope at public functions. They were instituted in 1801 and disbanded in 1970.

NOCTURN. A division of the traditional night office (*Mattins) of the *Breviary.

NOETICS. An early 19th-cent. group of dons at Oriel College, Oxford. They criticized traditional religious orthodoxy and sought to increase the comprehensiveness of the C of E.

NOETUS (*c*. 200), heretic. He was prob. the first to teach *Patripassian doctrines, viz. that it was God the Father who in the Incarnation was born, suffered, and died; he also rejected the *Logos doctrine and accused his opponents of ditheism. He was condemned at Smyrna *c*. 200.

NOLASCANS. See *Mercedarians*.

NOMINALISM. The theory of knowledge which denies reality to universal concepts. The form evolved by *Roscellinus and P. *Abelard in the 12th cent. was directed against the *Realists who held that *universals (q.v.) had a separate existence apart from the individuals in which they were embodied. Abelard described universals as names ('nomina') as opposed to things ('res'), though he does not seem to have denied that the resemblances among individual things justified the use of universals for establishing knowledge.

A different form of Nominalism appeared in the 14th cent.; it is associated with *William of Occam. He asserted that the universal is not found at all in reality, but only in the human mind; universals are only a way of knowing individual things. In its application to theology Nominalism denies the plurality of God's attributes and simplifies His being to such a degree that the reality of the Three Persons, which depends on formal distinctions and relations, can be accepted only on the authority of faith. It paved the way for the disintegration of *Scholasticism.

NOMOCANON. In the E. Church, a collection of ecclesiastical canons and Imperial laws, arranged acc. to subject-matter.

NONCONFORMIST CHAPELS ACT, 1844. This lays down that where no particular religious doctrine or mode of worship is provided by the Trust Deeds, the usage of the congregation for the past 25 years is to be taken as conclusive evidence of what may properly be done in such meeting-houses.

NONCONFORMITY. Refusal to conform to the doctrines, polity, or discipline of the Established Church. The word is now applied generally to all dissenters from the C of E., esp. those of Protestant sympathy.

NONE. The last of the *Breviary Little Hours. For its structure see *Terce*.

NONJURORS, The. Members of the C of E who after 1688 scrupled to take the Oaths of Allegiance and Supremacy to William and Mary on the ground that by doing so they would break their earlier oaths to *James II and his successors. They numbered 9 bishops (incl. Abp. W *Sancroft and T. *Ken) and c. 400 priests, who were deprived of their livings, as well as prominent laymen. Since the bishops were deprived by Act of Parliament, with no canonical sentence, the Nonjuring clergy regarded them as their lawful bishops and many of the conforming clergy refused to accept their sees. To perpetuate the succession two further bishops were secretly consecrated in 1694. By the end of the 18th cent. most of the Nonjurors had been absorbed back into the Established Church.

NONNUS OF PANOPOLIS (*c.* 400). The probable author of two Greek poems. The surviving part of one of them, a 'Paraphrase on the Fourth Gospel', throws some light on the Biblical text.

NORBERT, St. (*c.* 1080–1134), founder of the *Premonstratensians. He underwent a conversion in 1115. He became famous as an itinerant preacher in N. France and in 1120 he founded the Order of the Premonstratensians in the valley of Prémontré. He was appointed Abp. of Magdeburg in 1126; his zeal for reform made him many enemies. Accompanying the Emp. Lothair II to Rome in 1132–3, he supported Innocent II against Anacletus and prevented the outbreak of fresh quarrels over *Investiture.

NORIS, HENRI (1631–1704), theologian. He was Custodian of the *Vatican Library and from 1695 a cardinal. His *Historia Pelagiana* (1673), a history of the *Pelagian controversy, followed by a defence of the *Augustinian doctrine of grace, aroused much opposition.

'NORTH END', The. The position sometimes adopted at the Communion table by the celebrant of the Eucharist in the C of E. It is now confined to pronounced *Evangelicals, who claim that it rules out any ascription to the celebrant of a priestly or mediatorial function.

NORTH INDIA, Church of. The Church inaugurated in 1970 by the union of six Christian bodies, incl. *Anglicans, *Congregationalists and *Presbyterians, some *Methodists, *Baptists, and *Disciples of Christ.

NORWAY, Christianity in. Attemps were made to introduce Christianity to Norway in the 9th and 10th cents., but without permanent success. The country was finally converted under St. *Olave (d. 1030), largely at the point of the sword.

The Reformation was largely imposed by the Danes, who conquered Norway in 1537. *Lutheranism became the State religion, and no other was recognized until 1845. Since then both RCism and Protestant dissent have spread.

NORWICH, The conversion of East Anglia dates from the 7th cent. In 673 *Theodore, Abp. of Canterbury, divided the diocese between the North Folk and the South Folk, making Elmham a new diocese for Norfolk. In 1094 the see was transferred to Norwich by Herbert of Losinga (Bp. 1091–1119), who founded the Cathedral of the Holy and Undivided Trinity and constituted it a monastic church under the *Benedictine Rule. The cathedral is mainly a Norman building with a 15th-cent. spire and fine 15th- and 16th- cent. vaulted roofs.

NOTARIES. Specially appointed persons who confirm and attest the truth of deeds or writings in order to render them authentic. In the Middle Ages their appointment lay with the Pope or his delegates. Nowadays the

English notary, who is an ecclesiastical officer, is nominated by the judge of the provincial courts of *Canterbury and *York.

NOTES OF THE CHURCH. The four characteristic marks of the Church, first enumerated in the so-called *Nicene Creed, i.e. one, holy, catholic, and apostolic. At the time of the *Reformation RC theologians began to utilize them to discern the true Church among the rival Christian communions. The *Tractarians employed them to demonstrate the Catholicity of the C of E.

NOTH, MARTIN (1902–68), German OT scholar. His earlier work was concerned with the social and political structure of early Israel. He also engaged in *traditio-historical criticism. Of special importance was his contention that Jos., Jgs., 1 and 2 Sam., and 1 and 2 Kgs. form a '*Deuteronomic History', to which the bulk of Deut. is a preamble rather than the concluding section of the *Pentateuch.

NOTKER. Two monks of St. *Gall, both masters of the monastic school:

(1) **Notker Balbulus** (c. 840–912), 'the Stammerer'. He is famous for his literary work, esp. the compilation of *sequences and his introduction of them into the liturgy. He is also the prob. author of the *Gesta Caroli Magni*, a collection of stories about *Charlemagne, by a 'monk of St. Gall'.

(2) **Notker Labeo** (c. 950–1022), 'Notker the German'. To make Latin literature more accessible to his pupils he took the unprecedented step of translating many classical and other writings into German, at a time when Old High German was still undeveloped.

NOTKER (c. 940–1008), Bp. of Liège from 972. He owed his position to the Emp. Otto I and throughout his life he defended German interests in Italy and Lorraine. He attracted some celebrated scholars to Liège.

NOTRE-DAME, PARIS. The cathedral church of Paris. Built in the early French Gothic style, it was begun in 1163 and consecrated in 1182. The west front was added in 1200–20.

NOVATIANISM. A rigorist schism in the W. Church. Novatian was a Roman presbyter and author of a treatise on the doctrine of the *Trinity. Apparently because he was disappointed by the election of *Cornelius as Pope (251), he joined the rigorist party which deprecated concessions to those who had compromised in the *Decian persecution, and he was consecrated rival Bp. of Rome. He suffered martyrdom in 257–8. The Novatianists, though doctrinally orthodox, were excommunicated. They survived into the 5th cent.

NOVELLO, VINCENT (1781–1861), Church musician. He was organist of the Portuguese embassy chapel in London and of the RC Church in Moorfields. He is esp. remembered for his editions of sacred music and for his rehabilitation of such works as the Masses of J. Haydn and W. A. Mozart and the music of G. P. da *Palestrina in England.

NOVENA. In the W. Church, a period of nine days' private or public devotion, by which it is hoped to obtain some special grace.

NOVICE. A probationary member of a religious community. A novice is under the authority of the superior, and wears the dress and follows the rule of the community. A novice may be dismissed or may leave at any time without incurring ecclesiastical penalties.

NOWELL, ALEXANDER (c. 1507–1602), Dean of *St. Paul's from 1560. He wrote three 'Catechisms'—the 'Large', the 'Middle', and the 'Small'. The last-named, published in 1572, so closely resembles the *Catechism of the 1549 BCP that it has been argued that Nowell wrote that as well.

NULLITY. In *canon law the absence of legal validity from an act or contract, owing to the omission of an integral requirement. Thus a pretended marriage is invalidated at the outset by the existence of an *impediment, e.g. the relation of the parties to one another within the *prohibited degrees, or the intention of one or both of them to form a union which was not indissoluble. In England the civil law regards as of no effect marriages which were null from the beginning in canon law. Marriages may also be made legally void by a civil decree of nullity which may be granted on one of four specific grounds, viz. wilful refusal to consummate the marriage, insanity, venereal disease in a communicable form, and pregnancy by some other person.

NUMBER OF THE BEAST, The. The number 666 (or, acc. to some MSS., 616) in Rev. 13: 18. As in both Greek and Hebrew each letter of the alphabet represented a figure as well as a letter, every name could be represented by a number corresponding to the sum of its letters. Many explanations have been given of the cryptogram. The most prob. is that '*Nero Caesar' is intended.

NUMBERS, Book of. The bulk of this OT Book narrates the experiences of the Israelites under *Moses during their wanderings in the desert. Its English title is explained by its two records of a census (1–4 and 26).

NUMINOUS. A word coined by R. *Otto to denote the elements of a non-rational and amoral kind in what is experienced in religion as the 'holy'. The Numinous is held to include feelings of awe and self-abasement as well as an element of religious fascination.

NUN. A member of a religious order or congregation of women living under vows of poverty, chastity, and obedience.

NUN OF KENT; NUNS' RULE. See *Barton, E.*, and *Ancren Riwle*.

NUNC DIMITTIS. The Song of *Simeon (Lk. 2: 29–32), so named from its initial words in the *Vulgate version. In the E. it is said at *Vespers; in the Roman and many other W. *Breviaries its use is ordered at *Compline, whence it passed into the *Evensong of the BCP.

NUNCIO. A permanent diplomatic representative of the *Holy See accredited to a civil government and often of ambassadorial status.

NUPTIAL MASS. The wedding Mass which includes the celebration of the marriage and contains the nuptial blessing. Since 1966 a Nuptial Mass has been permitted at *mixed marriages, though the non-RC partner may not receive Communion.

NUREMBERG DECLARATION, The (1870). The statement of belief issued by a group of 14 German Catholic professors and teachers which met at Nuremberg in protest against the decrees of the first *Vatican Council on the papal claims. The declaration was later signed by others. The signatories formed the nucleus of the *Old Catholic Movement (q.v.).

O

OAK, Synod of the (403). A synod held by Imperial command in a suburb of Chalcedon called 'The Oak'. It condemned St. John *Chrysostom on a number of fabricated charges.

OAKELEY, FREDERICK (1802–80), *Tractarian divine. From 1839 to 1845 he was in charge of the Margaret Chapel, London, on the site of the present All Saints', Margaret Street; the chapel became a centre of Tractarian worship in London. He became a RC in 1845; from 1852 he was a canon in the diocese of Westminster.

O-ANTIPHONS (also known as the *Greater Antiphons*). The *Antiphons, each

beginning 'O ...', which are sung before and after the *Magnificat at *Vespers, acc. to the Roman use, on the seven days preceding Christmas Eve.

OATES, TITUS (1649–1705), conspirator. He spread stories of alleged RC intrigues to assassinate *Charles II and place his brother *James on the throne. The panic lasted from 1678 to 1681, and many people were executed on his false testimony.

OATH. Several Christian bodies, e.g. the *Baptists and *Quakers, interpret Mt. 5: 33–7 as forbidding all oaths, but the general Christian teaching is that an oath, though not desirable, is admissible for reasons of serious necessity. It must be concerned only with what one knows to be true, its object must be morally good, and in order to be valid it must be taken with the intention to swear. See also *Allegiance, Oath of*.

OBADIAH, Book of. *Minor Prophet and the shortest Book in the OT. It foretells the punishment of the Edomites in the coming Day of the Lord. Most modern scholars divide it into a number of sections which are variously dated from the 9th to the 5th cent. B.C.

OBEDIENCE. The moral virtue which inclines a man to carry out the will of his lawful superior. While absolute obedience is due to God alone, obedience to men is limited by the bounds of authority and by the claims of conscience. Obedience is the subject of one of the three *vows taken by *religious.

OBEDIENTIARY. An almost obsolete name of the permanent officials in a monastery, appointed by a superior.

OBERAMMERGAU, in Upper Bavaria. To express gratitude for the cessation of a plague in 1633, the villagers vowed to enact the Passion and Death of the Lord at ten-year intervals. The play, normally enacted in the decimal years, lasts some six hours and is repeated many times throughout the summer.

OBERLIN, JEAN FRÉDÉRIC (1740–1825), *Lutheran pastor, educationalist, and philanthropist. He was pastor of Waldersbach in the Vosges from 1767 until he died. He initiated schemes of road-building, introduced savings banks, promoted new agricultural techniques, and established schools. He was a pioneer in kindergarten work based on child psychology.

OBLATE. In the early Middle Ages the term was applied esp. to children dedicated to a monastery by their parents and placed there to be brought up. Later it was widely used of laity who lived at a monastery or in close connection with it, but who did not take full religious vows. It has been adopted in the title of some religious communities in the RC Church.

OBLATES REGULAR OF ST. BENE-

DICT. A society of ladies living under a modified form of the *Benedictine Rule. They have no strict vows, retain their property, and make revocable promises of obedience to the Mother President. They were founded by St. *Frances of Rome in 1425.

OBLATIONS. In Christian usage the term is applied to both the bread and wine offered for consecration in the Eucharist, and also to any other kind of gift presented by the faithful at Mass for the use of the clergy, the sick, the poor, &c.

OBLIGATION, Feasts of. See *Feasts of Obligation*.

O'BRYAN, W. See *Bible Christians*.

OBSCURANTISM. Active opposition, esp. from supposedly religious motives, to intellectual enlightenment.

OBSERVANTINES, also 'Observants'. Those members of the *Franciscan Order who claimed to 'observe' the primitive Rule of St. *Francis as confirmed in 1223. The movement, which started in Italy in 1368, drew its inspiration largely from the *Spiritual Franciscans. In 1517 the Observantines were separated from the *Conventuals and declared the true Order of St. Francis. They later divided into several branches, but in 1897 they were all incorporated into the one Order of Friars Minor.

OCCAM, WILLIAM OF. See *William of Occam*.

OCCASIONAL CONFORMITY ACT, The (1711). The Act laid down that civil or military officers who had been obliged to receive Communion in the C of E in order to qualify for Government posts, and were subsequently discovered at a *Nonconformist conventicle, should be fined and cease to hold office. It was repealed in 1719.

OCCASIONAL OFFICES. In the BCP those offices which are used only as occasion demands, e.g. *Baptism and the *Visitation of the Sick.

OCCASIONAL PRAYERS. In the BCP a collection of 11 prayers prescribed for use upon 'several [i.e. appropriate] occasions' before the final prayers of the *Litany and Morning and Evening Prayer.

OCCASIONALISM. The philosophical theory of the relation of mind to matter which denies that finite beings have efficient causality and postulates that God always intervenes to bring about a change in matter when a change occurs in the mind, and vice versa.

OCCURRENCE. The falling of two feasts (or other commemorations) on the same day in the ecclesiastical year, e.g. the coincidence of Christmas Day with a Sunday. The feast of the higher rank is kept.

OCHINO, BERNARDINO (1487–1564), Protestant Reformer. He was an *Observantine Franciscan and then a *Capuchin, in each case holding high office. He became a *Lutheran in 1541. In 1547 T. *Cranmer invited him to England. Here he wrote against the Papacy and against the Calvinist doctrine of *Predestination. On *Mary's accession he returned to Switzerland. In 1555 he became a pastor at Zürich, but he was later expelled from office, being unsound on the doctrine of the Trinity and on monogamy.

OCKHAM. See *William of Occam*.

'O COME, ALL YE FAITHFUL'. See *Adeste Fideles*.

O'CONNELL, DANIEL (1775–1847), Irish politician. He began publicly denouncing the Union on behalf of Irish RCs in 1800. In 1823 he founded the *Catholic Association with the object of securing emancipation for RCs by legal means. In 1828 he was returned as M.P. for Clare. After the passing of the *Catholic Relief Act of 1829 he worked for the repeal of the Union. He held 'monster meetings' and in 1843 he was arrested on a charge of creating disaffection. Though he was freed from imprisonment on appeal, his policy henceforth lacked firmness. His influence on Irish history was profound.

OCTATEUCH. The first 8 Books of the OT.

OCTAVE. In Christian liturgical use, the eighth day after a feast, reckoning inclu-

sively, and so always falling on the same day of the week as the feast itself. The term is also used of the whole period of eight days, during which the observance of certain major feasts came to be continued. In the RC Church only Christmas and Easter are now so observed.

OCTOECHOS. A liturgical book in the E. Church which contains the variable parts of the services from the first Sunday after *Whitsun till the tenth Sunday before *Easter.

ODES OF SOLOMON. See *Solomon, Odes of.*

ODILIA, St. (d. c. 720), patroness of Alsace. She is said to have been born blind and later miraculously recovered her sight. Having been granted by her father the castle at Hohenburg (now the Odilienberg) in the Vosges Mountains, she founded a large nunnery which she ruled as Abbess; it became a centre of pilgrimage.

ODILO, St. (c. 962–1049), Abbot of *Cluny from 994. Under him the order was extended and also strengthened by centralization. He was highly esteemed by Popes and Emperors, and the '*Truce of God' for S. France and Italy was largely his work. He introduced the commemoration of *All Souls' Day (2 Nov.), which soon spread from Cluny to the whole W. Church.

ODIUM THEOLOGICUM (Lat., 'theological hatred'). A proverbial expression for the ill-feeling to which theological controversy often gives rise.

ODO, St. (879–942), second Abbot of *Cluny. In 909 he entered the monastery of Baume, where he was soon in charge of the monastic school. He succeeded St. Berno as Abbot of Cluny in 927. He was largely instrumental in raising the monastery to the high position which it held in the next centuries. During his abbacy the monastic church was completed and the influence of Cluny over other monasteries greatly extended.

ODO, St. (d. 959), Abp. of *Canterbury from 942. He is said to have been the son of a Dane and originally a pagan. He was active in restoring the cathedral buildings and raising the morals and discipline of his clergy.

ODO (*c.* 1030–97), Bp. of Bayeux from 1049/50. A half-brother of *William the Conqueror, he was present at the Battle of Hastings and prob. commissioned the *Bayeux Tapestry. In 1067 he was made Earl of Kent, but he fell into disgrace in 1082. After the failure of his rebellion under William II, he left England. He set out on the First *Crusade in 1096, but died at Palermo. Though much engaged in temporal affairs, he had a good reputation as a bishop.

OECOLAMPADIUS, JOHN (1482–1531), German Reformer. He was cathedral preacher at Basle. After some hesitation he threw in his lot with the Reformers in 1522. His influence led to the adoption of Reformation principles in Basle, and he secured their acceptance in the canton of Berne. At the Colloquy of *Marburg (1529) he defended *Zwinglian doctrine on the Eucharist.

OECUMENICAL COUNCILS. Assemblies of bishops and other ecclesiastical representatives of the whole world whose decisions on doctrine, discipline, &c., are considered binding on all Christians. Acc. to RC canon law, an Oecumenical Council must be convened by the Pope, and its decrees have binding force only if sanctioned and promulgated by the Holy See; they are then infallible.

Seven councils are held both in E. and W. to be oecumenical, viz. those of *Nicaea I (325), *Constantinople I (381), *Ephesus (431), *Chalcedon (451), *Constantinople II (553), *Constantinople III (680–1), and *Nicaea II (787). The RC Church reckons 14 further councils as possessing oecumenical authority.

OECUMENICAL PATRIARCH, The. The style borne by the Abps. or Patrs. of *Constantinople since the 6th cent.

OECUMENIUS (6th cent.), author of the oldest extant Gk. commentary on Rev., to whom tradition has assigned the designations 'Rhetor' and 'Philosopher'. The commentary, which is vigorous, modest, but uneven, accepts Rev. as a divinely inspired canonical Book.

OENGUS, St. (8th–9th cent.), Irish saint, commonly, but perhaps erroneously, called the *Culdee. Of royal birth, he was educated at the monastic school at Clonenagh, lived as a hermit, and is said to have communed with angels. He later joined the fraternity of Tallaght, near Dublin. He collaborated on the Martyrology of Tallaght, which is prob. the oldest of the Irish martyrologies. His own Félire, or Festology of saints, was begun at Clonenagh and finished at Tallaght early in the 9th cent.

OFFA (d. 796), King of the Mercians from 757. He gradually secured dominion, either directly or as overlord, of the whole of England south of the Humber. He supported the Church, was a generous benefactor of monasteries, and is the reputed founder of the abbeys of *St. Albans and *Bath.

OFFERTORY. In the Eucharist: (1) The worshippers' offering of bread and wine (and water) to be consecrated. (2) The short anthem formerly sung in the Roman rite at the time of the act of offering.

OFFICE, Divine. In the W. Church, the daily public prayer which priests, religious, and some clerics are bound to recite. The traditional monastic office of the seven 'Day Hours' (viz. *Lauds, *Prime, *Terce, *Sext, *None, *Vespers, and *Compline) and the Night Office (*Mattins) began to develop in the Roman basilicas of the later 5th cent. Their arrangement in detail was fixed by St. *Benedict. Recitation gradually became obligatory not only for monks but for all clergy. All eight hours consisted of Psalms, hymns, lessons, antiphons, versicles and responses, and prayers. At the Reformation their place was taken in the C of E by the two Offices of Morning and Evening Prayer (Mattins and *Evensong). In the 1971 RC Breviary the Offices were radically rearranged. See *Breviary.*

OFFICE, Holy. See *Holy Office.*

OFFICE HYMNS. *Hymns appear as a fixed part of the Monastic Office in the Rule of St. *Benedict, though they were not generally used in the Roman liturgy until the 13th cent. The 1971 *Breviary places a hymn before the Psalms in each Office, provides two sets of hymns, and allows conferences of bishops to introduce others.

OFFICE OF READINGS. The Office in the 1971 *Breviary which replaced *Mattins. It may be said at any time of day. The main elements are a hymn, Psalms, and two Lessons or Readings, of which only the first is from the Bible.

OFFICIAL PRINCIPAL, also 'Official'. In ecclesiastical law, the person to whom a bishop formerly entrusted the exercise of his coercive jurisdiction, and hence nowadays the judge in an ecclesiastical court.

OIKONOMOS, CONSTANTINE (1780–1857), Greek scholar and theologian. He wrote an elaborate work on the *Septuagint, which, though setting out from wrong premisses, contains valuable investigations. He opposed W. influences.

OILS, Holy. See *Chrism* and *Unction*.

OLAVE, St. (995–1030), patron saint of *Norway. Olaf Haraldssön was converted to Christianity in England. He became king of Norway in 1016 and sought to impose Christianity, but the harshness of his methods provoked resistance and in 1029 he fled to Russia. He was killed in battle.

OLD BELIEVERS. The section of the *Russian Church which refused to accept the liturgical reforms of the Patr. *Nikon. They were excommunicated in 1667 and persecuted. They split into two sections: the one, called 'Popovtsy', sought means of establishing their own priesthood; the other, the 'Bezpopovtsy', denied its necessity. In 1846 a deposed bishop joined the Popovtsy and established a hierarchy.

OLD CATHOLICS. A group of small national Churches, consisting of Christians who have separated from the RC Church.

(1) The Church of Utrecht, with 3 bishops, separated from Rome in 1724 (see *Holland, Christianity in*).

(2) The German, Austrian, and Swiss Old Catholic Churches. This group of Churches was created from those who refused to accept the dogmas of the *infallibility and universal ordinary jurisdiction of the Pope as defined by the *Vatican Council of 1870, and seceded from the RC Church soon afterwards. They received their episcopal succession from the Church of Utrecht.

(3) Small groups of Slav origin. National Church movements among the Poles in the U.S.A. (1897) and the Croats (1924) resulted in the establishment of separate Churches.

The doctrinal basis of the Old Catholic Churches is the 'Declaration of *Utrecht', agreed upon in 1889.

OLD LATIN VERSIONS, The. The Latin versions of the Scriptures in use in the Church before they were superseded by the *Vulgate. The existence of Latin translations of the Bible in S. Gaul and N. Africa is attested before the end of the 2nd cent. The MSS. of the Old Latin differ among themselves and it was largely the desire to remedy the inconvenience arising from such differences that led St. *Jerome to undertake the Vulgate.

OLD ROMAN CREED, The. An earlier and shorter form of the *Apostles' Creed, which at least from the end of the 2nd cent. was the official Baptismal creed of the Church of Rome.

OLD SYRIAC VERSIONS, The. The Syriac translations of the NT which circulated before the construction of the *Peshitta version in the 5th cent. Only two MSS. are known, both of the Gospels, but the existence of a Syriac text of Acts is attested by a commentary on it.

OLD TESTAMENT. The collection of Canonical Books which the Church shares with *Judaism. Like the NT, the OT Books are regarded as inspired in the Church, which from the time of *Marcion has defended them against attack. See also *Bible*.

OLDCASTLE, Sir JOHN (*c.* 1378?–1417), *Lollard leader. In 1413 he was accused of heresy before *Convocation and upheld Lollard opinions. He was given 40 days to repent, escaped from the Tower of London, and put himself at the head of a conspiracy for a Lollard rebellion, which, however, collapsed. When captured he was executed.

OLDHAM, JOSEPH HOULDSWORTH (1874–1969), missionary statesman and leader of the *Ecumenical Movement. He was secretary of the World Missionary Conference in *Edinburgh in 1910 and of its Continuation Committee. Called upon by missionaries to pursue with the Government the question of indentured labour in E. Africa, he became involved in the debate on the political future of colonial territories. In 1934 he became Chairman of the Research Commission of the Universal Christian Council for '*Life and Work'; he thus had a leading part in the *Oxford Conference of 1937 and that at Utrecht in 1938 which set up the provisional committee of the *World Council of Churches.

OLIER, JEAN-JACQUES (1608–57), founder of the Society and seminary of *Saint-Sulpice (q.v.). Having lost his sight, he was cured and converted to a life of godliness during a pilgrimage to *Loreto. Ordained priest in 1633, he established a seminary at Vaugirard in 1641. In 1642 he took charge of the parish of Saint-Sulpice in Paris, which was then in a depraved condition. He transferred his seminary there and built up a society of secular priests, hoping to Christianize the *Sorbonne and reform the neighbourhood. His spiritual writings are in the tradition of St. *Vincent de Paul and St. John *Eudes.

OLIVER PLUNKET, St. See *Plunket, St. Oliver*.

OLIVES, Mount of. The highest point in the range of hills E. of *Jerusalem. It appears that Christ often went there. The traditional site of the *Ascension was marked by a church known as the 'Imbomon' before 378. Another 4th-cent. church, the 'Eleona', was built over the grotto where Christ was believed to have discoursed on the Last Things (Mk. 13).

OLIVETAN (c. 1506–38), Protestant Reformer. His real name was Pierre Robert. He preached Reformation doctrines to the *Waldenses in Piedmont, and for the purposes of his mission he translated the Bible into French (publd. 1535).

OLIVETANS ('The Order of Our Lady of Mount Olivet'). A strict branch of the *Benedictine Order founded in 1319 by Giovanni Tolomei at Monte Oliveto, nr. Siena. They joined the Benedictine Confederation in 1960. They have 24 houses, incl. the Abbey of *Bec.

OLIVI, PETRUS JOANNIS (c. 1248–98),

*Spiritual Franciscan. As leader of the rigorists in the *Franciscan Order, he was accused of heresy in the General Chapter of Strasburg in 1282 and 34 propositions from his works were censured in 1283. At the General Chapter of Montpellier (1287), however, he established his orthodoxy, which was confirmed at Paris in 1292. After his death the Spiritual Franciscans accorded him exaggerated veneration and at the Council of *Vienne (1311) certain propositions believed to be his were repudiated.

OLLÉ-LAPRUNE, LÉON (1839–98), French philosopher. He stressed the limits of a purely intellectual approach to the issues of philosophy and emphasized the part played by the will and heart in cognition.

OMAN, JOHN WOOD (1860–1939), *Presbyterian theologian. From 1907 to 1935 he taught in Cambridge. Holding the uniqueness and independence of the religious consciousness as an immediate, self-authenticating awareness of the Supernatural, he nevertheless insisted that it should not be isolated from other spheres of experience. In *The Natural and the Supernatural* (1931) he set out a philosophic justification of his position.

OMBRELLINO. In the W. Church, a small umbrella-like canopy carried over the Bl. Sacrament when it is moved informally from one place to another.

OMOPHORION. A long scarf used by E. bishops at the Liturgy. It is worn round the shoulders and falling loose towards the ground.

ONEIDA COMMUNITY, The. A Christian communist society established at Oneida, N.Y., in 1848, and also known as the Perfectionists. It became prosperous and in 1881 was formed into a joint-stock company.

ONESIMUS. The Phrygian slave on whose behalf St. *Paul wrote his Epistle to *Philemon.

ONTOLOGICAL ARGUMENT, The. The *a priori* argument for the Being of God on the ground that the existence of the idea of God necessarily involves the objective existence of God. It was first elaborated by

St. *Anselm.

ONTOLOGISM. A philosophical system favoured by certain Catholic philosophers in the 19th cent. The ontologists asserted that God Himself is the guarantee of the validity of human ideas; that all human knowledge, itself a mode of truth, implies an immediate intuition of uncreated Truth; and that the idea of being, which is the first and simplest idea of all, is an immediate perception of absolute Being.

OPHITES and **NAASSENES.** *Gnostic sects who attached special importance to the serpent. In some cases the serpent was worshipped, in others regarded as a hostile power.

OPTATUS, St. (*fl.* 370), Bp. of Milevis in N. Africa. Nothing is known of him save his treatise 'Against Parmenian the Donatist'. His arguments against *Donatism formed the starting-point of St. *Augustine's refutation. An appendix ('dossier') of important historical documents has received much attention from modern scholars.

OPTION. The right formerly possessed by an archbishop, when about to consecrate a bishop, of choosing within the latter's see a benefice to which he would act as patron at the next vacancy. The word is also used of the right of members of certain monastic chapters to receive at choice a particular benefice or title.

OPUS DEI (Lat., 'the work of God'). A *Benedictine designation for the Divine *Office.

Opus Dei is also the name of a RC organization devoted to fostering the application of Christian principles to daily living in all walks of life. It was founded in Madrid in 1928. It maintains a number of educational establishments.

OPUS OPERATUM. See *Ex opere operato.*

ORACLES, Sibylline. See *Sibylline Oracles.*

ORANGE, Councils of. Two synods were held at Orange in S. France in 441 and 529. The 25 dogmatic *capitula* of the latter upheld many of St. *Augustine's doctrines on the nature of *grace as against the *Semi-Pelagianism being advocated by *Faustus of Riez.

ORANGISM. The movement defending the cause of Protestantism in *Ireland, maintained by the Orange Association (founded 1795).

ORARION. In the E. Church, the deacon's stole.

ORATORIANS. (1) The Oratory of St. *Philip Neri is a congregation of secular priests living in community without vows, approved in 1575. The name prob. derives from the oratory of S. Girolamo, Rome, where they held their 'Exercises'. The chief task of the Oratorians is to lead men to God by prayer, preaching, and the Sacraments. They lay stress on attractive services, esp. on good music; the modern '*oratorio' grew out of the *laudi spirituali* sung in their devotional exercises. They were introduced into England by J. H. *Newman in 1848.

(2) The French Oratory was founded in 1611 by P. de *Bérulle. Though formed on the Italian model, it differs mainly in that it is a centralized organization. One of its chief activities is the training of priests in seminaries, run on the lines laid down by the Council of *Trent.

ORATORIO. The musical setting of a religious libretto for chorus, orchestra (or other accompaniment), and soloists, without (in modern practice) the use of dramatic action, scenery, or costume. Oratorio apparently derives from the dramatic services of St. *Philip Neri (d. 1595) at the *Oratory in Rome. Celebrated oratorios include G. F. *Handel's *Messiah* (1742), F. Mendelssohn's *Elijah* (1846), and Benjamin Britten's *War Requiem* (1962).

ORATORY. The term, used in antiquity of both churches and private chapels, has come to be restricted to places of worship other than the parish church. RC canon law distinguishes between public, semi-public, and private oratories, and defines what may be done in each. The position of oratories in the C of E is governed by the *Private Chapels Act (1871).

'The Oratory' is used absolutely for the *Oratorians (q.v.) or 'Congregation of the Oratory' and for churches belonging to it, e.g. *Brompton Oratory.

ORDEALS. A method of judicial trial among Teutonic peoples in which the innocence of the accused person was determined by the results of some physical test to which he was submitted. The result was regarded as the immediate judgement of God. The tests included that of the hot iron in which the accused carried a ball of hot iron for nine steps; if the wound festered the man was held guilty. In England the Ordeal began to be disused after the Norman Conquest and quickly disappeared after the Fourth *Lateran Council (1215) forbade the clergy to take part.

ORDERICUS VITALIS (1075–?1142), Anglo-Norman historian. In 1085 he entered the *Benedictine house of St.-*Évroul(t) in Normandy. He wrote an Ecclesiastical History, beginning with the birth of Christ. The latter part is a prime source for the political and ecclesiastical history and the customs of his time.

ORDERS, Anglican. See *Anglican Ordinations*.

ORDERS AND ORDINATION. The ministry of the Church traces its origins to the Lord's commissioning of the Twelve (Mt. 10: 1–5 &c.) and of the Seventy (Lk. 10: 1) to the work of the kingdom. References to Ordination in the early Church may be found at a number of places in the NT, including the appointment of the Seven (Acts 6: 1–6) and the commissioning of *Barnabas and Saul (Acts 13: 1–3), in both instances by prayer and the laying-on of hands.

In the early days there seems to have been a broad distinction between the 'missionary' ('itinerant' or 'apostolic') ministry of apostles and *prophets (q.v.), and the 'local' or 'settled' ministry of *bishops, *presbyters, and *deacons; the latter was the nucleus of the traditional three-fold ministry. By the middle of the 3rd cent. other Orders had appeared, and from the end of the Middle Ages it was the prevalent view that there were seven Orders, a distinction being made between the three *Major Orders of bishop, *priest, and deacon (or bishop and priest reckoned as one Order, deacon, and *subdeacon), and the *Minor Orders of *acolytes, *exorcists, *lectors, and *doorkeepers. Acc. to Catholic theology the gift of

Order is a Sacrament, and it is held to impart an indelible *character. In the Middle Ages Orders lower than the diaconate were commonly regarded as included within the Sacrament of Orders, but RC theologians now reject this view on the ground that they are of ecclesiastical (not Divine) institution.

It is traditionally held that only a baptized and confirmed male person may be validly ordained. He must be of good moral character and convinced that he has a Divine call ('vocation') to the office. He must be of due age (see *Age, Canonical*) and generally needs a '*title' to the cure of souls. Traditional theology also holds that the Sacrament of Orders can validly be conferred only by a duly consecrated bishop.

Ordination has always taken place in the context of the Eucharist. The rite, which long remained simple in the E., had become elaborate in the W. by the end of the Middle Ages. In the RC Church new and much simplified rites of Ordination were introduced in 1968. The Bishop now lays hands on each candidate for the diaconate in silence and then says the Ordination prayer over them all. After each candidate has been vested in *dalmatic and *stole, the Bishop gives him a book of the Gospels with a charge to proclaim and live by it. In the case of candidates for the priesthood the Bishop is joined by other clergy in the laying-on of hands, and a different formula is used in the Ordination prayer; it no longer contains any mention of the power to forgive sins. The Bishop anoints the hands of each candidate with *chrism and delivers to him the paten and chalice with bread and wine offered by the people. In the ordering of bishops, the co-consecrators join with the consecrating Bishop in saying that part of the consecratory prayer held to be necessary for validity; while this prayer is being said, the book of the Gospels is held over the head of the candidate. The consecrating Bishop then anoints his head, delivers the Gospels to him, puts a *ring on his finger and a *mitre on his head, and gives him a pastoral staff or *crosier. For rites in the C of E, see *Ordinal*.

In the W. the *Ember seasons were the customary times for the ordination of priests and deacons. In recent years the feast of St. *Peter has tended to replace *Trinity Sunday.

ORDINAL. (1) In the Middle Ages, a manual to acquaint the priest with the Office to be recited in acc. with variations in the ecclesiastical year.

(2) In the C of E, 'The Form and Manner of Making, Ordaining, and Consecrating of Bishops, Priests, and Deacons'. There have been four English Ordinals, in 1550, 1552, 1559, and 1662, the first being based on the *Sarum Pontifical. None of them has any provision for *Minor Orders. In the Consecration of Bishops the medieval custom of anointing, putting on of gloves, and the delivery of the *ring and *mitre were omitted. In the Ordering of Priests the tradition of the *Instruments was dropped in 1552, but all the Ordinals include in the formula accompanying the laying-on of hands the words 'Receive the Holy Ghost' and 'Whose sins thou dost forgive, they are forgiven; whose sins thou does retain, they are retained'.

ORDINARY. In canon law, an ecclesiastic in the exercise of the jurisdiction permanently and irremovably annexed to his office. In the RC Church the term is closely defined; its meaning in the BCP is not precisely determined, though it usually refers to the Bishop.

ORDINARY OF THE MASS, The (Lat. *Ordo Missae*). Until recently the term was widely used to describe the invariable or almost invariable parts of the Mass, as distinguished from the parts which varied with the ecclesiastical calendar. The 1970 *Missale Romanum*, however, applies the term 'Ordo Missae' to the whole service.

ORDINATION. See *Orders and Ordination*.

ORDINES ROMANI. Ancient collections of ceremonial directions for the performance of the various parts of the Roman rite. They date from between the 8th and 10th cents. and are of importance for the history of liturgy.

ORESME, NICOLAS (c. 1320–82), French medieval philosopher. From 1377 he was Bp. of Lisieux. His book *De l'origine, nature et mutation des monnaies* greatly influenced the development of medieval economic ideas. In the field of natural science his *De coelo et mundo* carried further Buridan's theory of the earth's rotation.

ORGANIC ARTICLES, The (1802). The provisions of Napoleon regulating public worship and the relations of Church and State in France. They were not repealed until 1905.

ORGANS. The use of an organ is recorded at *Malmesbury in the 8th cent.; by the 13th cent. they were common in larger parish churches and by the end of the Middle Ages almost universal. The *Puritans objected to them. In 1644 legislation for the destruction of organs and their cases was carried through, and consequently few pre-Commonwealth organs exist. They were reinstated after the Restoration (1660). In the 18th cent. barrel organs, with a limited selection of tunes, were introduced. From c. 1887 the modern type of 'positive' (or stationary) organ evolved to give much the same effect as a larger instrument at lower cost. Since c. 1930 pipeless or electronic organs have been used in some churches.

ORIENTATION. The construction of a church so that its longer axis runs east to west. Though orientation is derived historically from a pagan habit of praying towards the sunrise, Christians have seen in its adoption symbolic reference to Christ as the Rising Sun.

ORIGEN (c. 185–254), Biblical critic, theologian, and spiritual writer. He was brought up as a Christian and appointed by *Demetrius, Bp. of *Alexandria, to succeed *Clement as head of the *Catechetical School. When trouble broke out in 215, he went to Palestine; his preaching here as a layman was regarded as a breach of Alexandrian ecclesiastical discipline and he was recalled. In 230 he went to Palestine again and was ordained priest by the bishops who had invited him to preach on his previous visit. In consequence Demetrius deprived him of his chair, deposed him from the priesthood, and exiled him. He found refuge at *Caesarea (231), where he established a school which became famous. In 250, in the *Decian persecution, he was imprisoned and tortured.

Origen was a prolific writer, but many of his works have perished and most of the others survive only in translation. His main work on Biblical criticism was his famous '*Hexapla' (q.v.). His chief theological work is the *De Principiis*, which covers a wide range of doctrinal topics; it survives in the Latin translation of *Rufinus and the more faithful but fragmentary version of St. *Jerome. His two ascetical works, 'Exhortation to Martyrdom' and 'On Prayer', were much read in antiquity. He also wrote an apologetic work against *Celsus (q.v.).

As a Biblical scholar, Origen recognized a triple sense—literal, moral, and allegorical—of which he favoured the last. The point of departure of his doctrinal teaching was faith in the unity of God. This unity in its fullest sense is understood of God the Father, and for Origen the Son is divine only in a lesser sense than the Father. His philosophical speculations led him into audacious thought, though it is not always clear that he held as certain the propositions he expressed. He affirmed that creation was eternal. He maintained that all spirits were created equal, but through the exercise of their free will they developed in hierarchical order and some fell into sin and so became demons or souls, imprisoned in bodies. Death does not finally decide the fate of the soul, which may turn into a demon or an angel. This ascent and descent goes on until the final *Apocatastasis (q.v.), when all creatures, even the devil, will be saved.

ORIGENISM. The group of theories enunciated by, or attributed to, *Origen. Among his earliest opponents was *Methodius of Olympus, who rejected his teaching on the pre-existence of souls and his denial of the identity between the mortal and resurrection bodies. The 4th-cent. controversy was concerned mainly with the Trinitarian teaching of the *De Principiis*. St. *Epiphanius's attack was taken up by St. *Jerome. In 398 *Rufinus issued his Latin translation, which was designed to vindicate Origen's orthodoxy, but in 400 a Council at *Alexandria condemned Origenism, and Pope Anastasius I and the Bps. of Palestine and Syria adhered to the condemnation.

The controversy flared up again in Palestine in the 6th cent. The opponents of Origenism secured the support of the Emp. *Justinian, who issued an edict giving a list of Origenistic errors and their refutation. The Origenist monks at Jerusalem then split into two parties. The Second Council of *Constantinople (553) finally condemned Origen's teaching.

ORIGINAL RIGHTEOUSNESS. Acc. to Catholic theology, God's gratuitous impartation to man of perfect rectitude in his original condition before the *Fall. The state of Original Righteousness in which man was created is held to have included freedom from concupiscence, bodily immortality, and happiness.

ORIGINAL SIN. In Christian theology, the state of sin in which man has been captive since the *Fall (q.v.). The Scriptural foundation of the doctrine is the Pauline teaching that 'through one man [i.e. Adam] sin entered into the world', so that 'by the trespass of the one the many died' (cf. Rom. 5: 12–21). The doctrine was accepted by almost all the Greek Fathers, but precise formulation of how Adam's guilt was transmitted and the nature of the consequences for man was left to the West. Here *Tertullian, St. *Cyprian, and St. *Ambrose taught the solidarity of the whole race with Adam not only in the consequences of the sin but in the sin itself, which is transmitted through natural generation. Beyond this two schools of thought developed. St. *Augustine and his followers maintained that Adam's guilt was transmitted to his descendants by concupiscence, making of humanity a *massa damnata* and much enfeebling, though not destroying, the freedom of the will. St. *Thomas Aquinas, however, distinguished, in the state of Adam before the Fall, 'pure nature' from the supernatural gifts which perfected it. Hence Original Sin consists in the loss of those supernatural privileges which had directed man to his supernatural end and enabled him to keep his inferior powers in submission to reason, a rectitude not natural to a being composed of body and soul such as man. This conception entails a more optimistic view of man than that of Augustine and his successors, in that it leaves to the reason, will, and passions of man their natural powers. Acc. to Aquinas, Original Sin is transmitted not as the personal fault of Adam but as a state of human nature, yet constituting a fault inasmuch as all men are regarded as one great organism of which Adam was the first mover. The instrument of transmission is generation, regardless of the accompanying concupiscence.

The Thomist synthesis was not everywhere immediately accepted, but the leading Schoolmen now defined Original Sin as lack of *Original Righteousness and tended to eliminate the element of concupiscence. In his later development of the Thomist position, D. *Soto identified Original Sin with the absence of sanctifying grace; this view was widely accepted among RCs. The Augustinian view was revived by the *Reformers and also by the *Jansenists. From the 18th cent. the influence of rationalism and natural science tended to attenuate the dogma of Original Sin, but it has been strongly reaffirmed by modern RC orthodox theologians and, in its Protestant version, esp. by K. *Barth and his school.

ORNAMENTS RUBRIC, The. The common name for the ruling in the 1559 BCP that the ornaments of the Church and the ministers should be those in use 'by the authority of Parliament in the second year of the reign of King *Edward VI'. Its meaning has been disputed since the 16th cent.

OROSIUS (5th cent.), Paulus Orosius, historian. Migrating to Africa in 414, he was sent by St. *Augustine to Palestine to enlist the support of St. *Jerome in the fight against *Pelagianism. His *Historia adversus Paganos* attacked the pagan complaint that Rome's troubles were due to her abandonment of her gods; only after A.D. 378 is it of historical value.

ORSISIUS, St. (d. c. 380), ascetic and abbot of Tabenne (an island in the Nile). He was a disciple and friend of *Pachomius. He wrote a 'Doctrina de Institutione Monachorum' (prob. in Coptic), which survives in Latin translation.

ORTHODOX CHURCH, The, also termed the 'Eastern', 'Greek', or 'Greco-Russian Church'. A family of Churches, mostly in E. Europe; each Church is independent in its internal administration, but all share the same faith and are in communion with each other, acknowledging the honorary primacy of the Patr. of *Constantinople (or *Oecumenical Patriarch).

The Orthodox Church developed historically from the Church of the Byzantine Empire. It first became limited on its E. side by the *Monophysite and *Nestorian schisms of the 5th–6th cents. From the 9th cent. onwards there was increasing tension between Rome and Constantinople, leading to the final breach which is conventionally dated in 1054; it was in fact a gradual process. The main doctrinal points at issue were

the Papal claims and the *Filioque. The schemes of Union proposed at the Councils of Lyons (1274) and *Florence (1438–9) were never effective. Bounded on the E. and W., the Orthodox Church expanded to the North. A missionary advance was inaugurated in the 9th cent. by Sts. *Cyril and Methodius. *Bulgaria, *Serbia, and subsequently *Russia were converted to the Christian faith largely through the efforts of Byzantine missionaries. Since the fall of Constantinople to the Turks (1453), the Church of Russia has been the largest and most influential member of the Orthodox communion.

The faith of the Orthodox Church is based primarily on the dogmatic definitions of the seven *Oecumenical Councils. Certain local Councils have also exercised a decisive influence on Orthodox doctrine, esp. those of Constantinople of 1341 and 1351, which endorsed the teaching of *Hesychasm concerning the divine light, and the Councils of *Jassy (1642) and *Jerusalem (1672), which clarified Orthodox teaching on the Eucharist and the nature of the Church. The Orthodox Church acknowledges the *seven sacraments, or 'mysteries' as they are termed, though no rigid distinction is drawn between them and other sacramental actions such as burial of the dead. Baptism is by *immersion, and children are taken to Communion from infancy. In principle services are in the language of the people, but in many places an archaic form is used. The veneration of *icons plays an important part in Orthodox worship, both private and public. Monasteries have been influential throughout Orthodox history; since the 10th cent. the chief monastic centre has been Mount *Athos. Bishops are drawn from the monastic clergy; parish priests are generally married.

ORTHODOXY. As a religious system, right belief as contrasted with heresy. The word is used esp. in connection with those Churches of the E. in communion with *Constantinople (see previous entry).

ORTHODOXY, Feast of. A feast established in 843 to celebrate the downfall of the *Iconoclastic party and the restoration of images. It is now observed in the E. Church on the first Sunday of Lent to commemorate the triumph of right faith over all heresies.

ORTHROS. The morning *office in the E. Church.

ORTLIEB OF STRASBURG (*c*. 1200), founder of an ascetic sect ('Ortlibarii') whose teaching was condemned by *Innocent III. They maintained the eternity of the world and unorthodox doctrines on the Trinity and Incarnation.

O SALUTARIS HOSTIA (Lat., 'O Saving Victim'). The last two verses of St. *Thomas Aquinas's hymn 'Verbum supernum prodiens'. In the RC Church it is often sung during *Benediction.

O SAPIENTIA (Lat., 'O Wisdom'). The initial apostrophe of the first of the *O-Antiphons, incl. in English calendars against 16 Dec.

OSCULATORIUM. An alternative name for the *Pax Brede.

OSIANDER, ANDREAS (1498–1552), theologian. He joined the *Lutherans in 1522 and took part in the *Marburg Colloquy of 1529. In his *De Justificatione* (1550) he opposed M. *Luther's doctrine of *justification by faith, maintaining that justification was not a mere imputation of Christ's merits, but a substantial transference of His righteousness to the believer.

OSMUND, St. (d. 1099), Bp. of *Salisbury from 1078. He built the cathedral at *Sarum and drew up the constitution of its cathedral chapter, which became the model of many other foundations. He is credited with instituting the Sarum liturgical use, but the definitive formation of this is much later.

OSSERVATORE ROMANO. An Italian daily newspaper, founded in 1861 and owned by the *Vatican.

OSSIUS. Prob. the correct spelling of the Bp. of Cordova commonly known as *Hosius (q.v.).

OSTENSORY. A receptacle for showing objects of religious devotion to the people. The word is now commonly restricted to the *monstrance.

OSTIAN WAY, The. The ancient road which led from Rome to the seaport of Ostia.

OSTIARIUS. Latin for *doorkeeper (q.v.).

OSWALD, St. (*c*. 605–42), King of Northumbria. Forced to flee to Scotland after his father's death in 616, he was converted to Christianity by the monks of *Iona. He returned in 634 and, after erecting a wooden cross on the battlefield, defeated the British king, Caedwallon, at Heavenfield, near Hexham. He began to establish Christianity in his kingdom, giving full support to St. *Aidan. He was killed in battle against the pagan Penda of Mercia and is honoured as a martyr.

OSWALD, St. (d. 992), Abp. of *York. He was consecrated Bp. of *Worcester by St. *Dunstan in 962 and retained this see after he became Abp. of York in 972. He took an active part in the reform of abuses and established many monasteries. He also took pains to improve the theological knowledge of his clergy.

OSWIN, St. (d. 651), Anglo-Saxon king. The southern part of Northumbria came under his rule on the death of his kinsman, St. *Oswald, in 642. He was a devout Christian and a friend of St. *Aidan.

OTTO, St. (1062/3–1139), the 'Apostle of Pomerania'. He was nominated Bp. of Bamberg in 1102 and consecrated in 1106. He took part in the foundation of over 20 monasteries and in completing his cathedral. He tried to maintain a neutral attitude in the *Investiture controversy, though his sympathies were with the Pope. He went to Pomerania in 1124, after the Pomeranians had promised to accept Christianity as a condition of peace. He converted many of the important towns and most of the nobles.

OTTO OF FREISING (*c*. 1114/15–58), historian. The uncle of *Frederick Barbarossa, he became Bp. of Freising in 1138. His *Chronicon seu historia de duabus civitatibus* modified St. *Augustine's conception of the two cities, seeing their union in the Church as the continuation of the Roman Empire. His *Gesta Friderici* describes the first part of Frederick I's reign, largely on the basis of original documents.

OTTO, RUDOLF (1869–1937), Protestant theologian. The central theme of *Das Heilige* (1917; Eng. tr., *The Idea of the*

Holy, 1923) was insistence on the part played by the *numinous in the religious consciousness.

OUEN, St. (*c.* 610–84), Abp. of Rouen from 641. He encouraged scholarship, founded monasteries, and fought *simony and other abuses.

OUR FATHER. See *Lord's Prayer*.

OVERALL, JOHN (1560–1619), Bp. of *Coventry and Lichfield (1614–8) and then of *Norwich. The section on the Sacraments added to the BCP *Catechism in 1604 was drawn up by Overall on the basis of A.' *Nowell's 'Small Catechism' of 1572. He also took part in the translation of the AV Bible.

OVERBECK, FRANZ (1837–1905), Protestant theologian. Holding that the Christian Gospel was wholly eschatological and world-negating, Overbeck came to reject historic Christianity and expounded a 'secular Church history', in which the course of ecclesiastical history was understood as a radical departure from the original revelation in Scripture. He exercised considerable influence on modern *Dialectical Theology.

OVERSEAS MISSIONARY FELLOW-SHIP. See *China Inland Mission*.

OWEN, JOHN (1616–83), *Puritan divine and statesman. His preaching won the ear of O. *Cromwell, who in 1651 made him Dean of *Christ Church, Oxford. He was one of Cromwell's *Triers and a member of the *Savoy Conference. After the *Restoration he preached and wrote in London.

OXFORD. The ecclesiastical history of Oxford appears to begin with St. *Frideswide (d. 735), around whose shrine the town grew up. In 1542 *Henry VIII created the see of Oxford, with the suppressed Oseney Abbey as the cathedral church; in 1546 he transferred the seat of the bishopric to *Christ Church.

The origins of the university are also obscure. It was prob. in origin a secular foundation, dating from the second half of the 12th cent. and modelled on that of *Paris. By *c.* 1230 Oxford was a famous university. The Friars came between 1220 and 1270. The colleges developed out of the boarding-houses under religious or secular

control. In 1571 the university was incorporated by Act of Parliament and from then until 1871 subscription to the *Thirty-Nine Articles was required of all its members.

OXFORD CONFERENCE (1937). The second Conference of the 'Life and Work' branch of the *Ecumenical Movement was held at Oxford under the title of 'Church, Community, and State'. It was agreed to take steps to fuse the 'Life and Work' Movement with that of '*Faith and Order'. See also *World Council of Churches*.

'OXFORD GROUP', The. In 1920 F. N. D. *Buchman (q.v.) visited Cambridge and then Oxford; his preaching impressed undergraduates and in Oxford he received support from some senior members of the University. In 1929 he went to South Africa with a group of followers; here the movement first became known as 'the Oxford Group'. Despite opposition, it was incorporated under this name in 1939. It spread in the early 1930s, esp. among the professional and upper classes in England. It has no regular ministry or meeting-houses of a denominational kind; it works through personal contact, publications, and meetings and conferences (or 'house parties'). See also *Moral Rearmament*.

OXFORD MOVEMENT, The. A movement in the C of E which aimed at restoring *High Church principles. In the early 19th cent. various factors caused misgivings among Churchmen, incl. the decline of Church life and the spread of 'Liberalism' in theology. The plan to suppress ten Irish bishoprics in 1833 evoked from J. *Keble a sermon in the university church at Oxford which is regarded as the beginning of the movement.

Its chief object was the defence of the C of E as a Divine institution, of the doctrine of the *Apostolic Succession, and of the BCP as a rule of faith. The *Tracts for the Times were designed for this purpose. The leaders of the movement were Keble, J. H. *Newman, and E. B. *Pusey. It soon gained influential support, but it was also attacked by the liberals within the University and by the Bishops. Within the movement there gradually arose a party which tended towards submission to Rome. After the censure by the Convocation of Oxford in 1845 of a book by W. G. *Ward, and again after the *Gorham case in 1850, there were a number of conversions to the RC Church. But the majority remained in the C of E, and, despite the hostility of the press and of the Government, the movement spread. Its influence was exercised in the sphere of worship and ceremonial, in the social sphere (the slum settlements were among its notable achievements), and in the restoration of the *religious life in the C of E.

OXYRHYNCHUS PAPYRI. The collection of thousands of fragments of papyri found from 1897 onwards at Oxyrhynchus, c. 10 miles W. of the Nile. It includes some substantial fragments of Greek and Latin literary texts and of Christian literature. Among the most famous are the MSS. of '*Sayings of Jesus'.

OZANAM, ANTOINE FRÉDÉRIC (1813–53), French scholar. In 1833 he founded the 'Society of St. *Vincent de Paul', an association of laymen for personal service among the poor. He became a professor at the *Sorbonne, and he edited some early *Franciscan poetry (1852), of importance for the history of medieval spirituality. Together with H. D. *Lacordaire he founded the Ère nouvelle in 1848 as a mouthpiece for their ideas on Catholic socialism.

P

'P'. The 'priestly source' held to be embodied in the *Pentateuch. It is marked by a preponderance of ritual and ceremonial enactments over narrative and the avoidance of anthropomorphic or primitive ideas of God. In its final redaction it is the latest element in the Pentateuch.

PACELLI, E. See Pius XII.

PACEM IN TERRIS (1963). An encyclical letter of *John XXIII on international peace.

PACHOMIUS, St. (c. 290–346), the founder of *coenobitic monasticism. He apparently served as an army conscript; after his discharge in 313, he was converted and baptized. Having been for a time a disciple of the hermit Palaemon, c. 320 he founded a monastery at Tabennisi in the *Thebaid, to which his fame attracted large numbers. Other foundations followed. His 'Rule' survives complete only in Latin translation.

PACIAN, St. (4th cent.), Bp. of Barcelona. He defended the Catholic doctrine of the forgiveness of sins against the *Novatianists. He is remembered esp. for the epigrammatic passage in one of his letters: 'My name is Christian; my surname is Catholic'.

PACIFISM. See War, Christian Attitude to.

PADRE. A popular designation of a chaplain in the armed forces, also used of all clergymen.

PAEDOBAPTISM. See Infant Baptism.

PAENITEMENI (1966). An Apostolic Constitution which revised the rules of penitential observance in the RC Church. It reduced the number of days of *fasting and empowered episcopal conferences to substitute for the traditional *abstinence on penitential days some other form of penance, esp. works of charity and piety.

PAGET, FRANCIS (1851–1911), Bp. of *Oxford from 1901. He supported the reinterpretation of *Tractarian principles by the *Lux Mundi group. His Spirit of Discipline (1891) contains a notable essay on '*Accidie'.

PAGNINUS, SANTES (d. 1536), *Dominican scholar. He was the first modern scholar to translate the whole Bible from the original languages. His Latin version, publd. in 1528, was extensively used by M. *Coverdale in preparing the *Great Bible (1539).

PAIN BÉNIT. The blessed bread often, until recently, distributed to the people after Mass in French and Canadian churches.

PAINE, THOMAS (1737–1809), political

reformer. Born in Norfolk, he went to America in 1774. In 1791 he published the first part of his famous *Rights of Man* in reply to E. Burke's *Reflections on the Revolution in France*. After the publication of the second part (1792) he had to flee to France to escape arrest. *The Age of Reason* (1794-5) ridiculed the beliefs and institutions of Christianity as full of superstition and bad faith.

PAKISTAN, Church of. The Church inaugurated in 1970 by the union of *Anglicans, *Methodists, *Presbyterians, and *Lutherans in Pakistan.

PALAMAS. See *Gregory Palamas*.

PALATINE GUARD. A corps of militia in the Papal service. It was created in 1850 out of two existing bodies; it was disbanded in 1970.

PALESTRINA, GIOVANNI PIERLUIGI DA (*c.* 1525–94), Italian composer. He held a series of appointments in the major churches of Rome, being choirmaster of *St. Peter's from 1571 until his death. Under the influence of St. *Philip Neri, he devoted himself to the interests of the Church. His best-known works include *Improperia, his *Missa Papae Marcelli*, the Mass *Assumpta est Maria*, and *motets to words from the Song of Songs. His music is deeply religious. The austere polyphony of his work became an important factor in the subsequent development of sacred music.

PALEY, WILLIAM (1743–1805), Anglican divine. His *Horae Paulinae* (1790), written to prove the historicity of the NT by a comparison of the accounts of St. *Paul in the Epistles and Acts, was his only original work. His famous *View of the Evidences of Christianity* (1794), though its arguments added little that was new, became popular from its effective presentation of the facts and its clear style.

PALIMPSEST. A vellum or papyrus MS. from which the original writing has been obliterated and the surface then used for some other (usually quite different) writing. A famous example is the *Codex Ephraemi: the remaining parts of a 5th-cent. Greek NT were covered in the 12th cent. with writings of St. *Ephraem Syrus.

PALL. In ecclesiastical usage: (1) the small linen cloth with which the *chalice is covered at the Eucharist, in its modern form stiffened with a piece of cardboard; and (2) a cloth spread over the coffin at a funeral.

PALLADIUS (*c.* 365–425), historian of early monasticism. He spent several years with the monks of Egypt, and was a pupil of *Evagrius Ponticus. In 400 he became Bp. of Helenopolis in Bithynia. His 'Lausiac History', though at times credulous, is the most valuable single writing that survives for the history of early monasticism. He was also prob. the author of a 'Dialogue' on the life of St. *Chrysostom.

PALLADIUS, St. (5th cent.), Irish missionary. Acc. to *Prosper of Aquitaine, he persuaded *Celestine I (422–32) to send St. *Germanus, Bp. of Auxerre, to stamp out the *Pelagian heresy in Britain, and was himself consecrated by the same Pope, who sent him to the Irish as their first bishop. He worked in Wicklow.

PALLIUM. The circular band of white material with two hanging strips and marked with six dark purple crosses which is worn on the shoulders by the Pope and granted by him to archbishops (and occasionally also to other bishops) of the RC Church. It is made from the wool of lambs blessed on St. *Agnes's Day in the church of Sta Agnese fuori le mura, Rome, while the *Agnus Dei is being sung, and before despatch it rests for a night on the tomb of St. *Peter in the Vatican. It is held to symbolize the 'plenitude of the pontifical office' It went out of use in the C of E at the Reformation, but still appears in some armorial bearings.

PALLOTTINI FATHERS, The. A society of RC priests founded in 1835 by Bl. Vincent Pallotti; since 1854 they have been known as the 'Pious Society of Missions' (P.S.M.: *Pia Societas Missionum*). One of their main interests is the reunion of Oriental Christians with the RC Church.

PALM SUNDAY. The Sunday before *Easter. The distinctive ceremonies of the day are the blessing of palms and the procession, representing the Lord's triumphal entry into *Jerusalem.

An elaborate rite for blessing the palms developed in the early Middle Ages, similar in structure to the Mass. In the C of E the ceremony was abolished in 1549. In the RC Church it was simplified in 1955. Before the Mass there is now a general blessing of the palms held by the people, the Gospel account of Christ's entry into Jerusalem is read, and clergy and people process singing the traditional 'Gloria, laus' ('All glory, laud and honour', by *Theodulph of Orleans) or some other chant.

PALMER, WILLIAM (1811–79), Fellow of Magdalen College, Oxford, from 1832. In 1840 and 1842 he visited Russia to explore the possibilities of intercommunion between the Anglican and Orthodox Churches, and he did much to foster interest in the E. Churches in Britain. He became a RC in 1855.

PAMMACHIUS, St. (c. 340–410), Roman Christian and friend of St. *Jerome. After the death of his wife, he took the monastic habit and spent his possessions on works of piety, including the famous hospital for pilgrims at Portus and the church of SS. Giovanni e Paolo in Rome.

PAMPHILUS, St. (c. 240–309), disciple of *Origen. He was educated at *Alexandria and directed a theological school at *Caesarea in Palestine, where he was martyred. While imprisoned in the persecution of Maximinus Daza he wrote an 'Apology' for Origen, to which *Eusebius of Caesarea added a sixth book.

PANAGIA (Gk., 'all holy'). A favourite title of the BVM in the E. Church. The word is also used of: (1) an oval medallion depicting the BVM worn suspended on a chain by Orthodox bishops; and (2) bread which is solemnly blessed honour of the BVM.

PANCRAS, St. (d. 304), martyr. There is no reliable information about him. Acc. to tradition he was a member of the Roman Church who at the age of 14 was martyred in the *Diocletianic persecution. St. Pancras railway station in London is named after the dedication of the church of the parish in which it is situated.

PANGE LINGUA. The title of two famous Latin hymns, viz. the *Passiontide hymn by *Venantius Fortunatus (*Pange lingua gloriosi proelium certaminis*; 'Sing, my tongue, the glorious battle') and the *Corpus Christi hymn by St. *Thomas Aquinas (*Pange lingua gloriosi corporis mysterium*; 'Of the glorious Body telling'). On the latter see also *Tantum ergo*.

PANNYCHIS. In the E. Church the liturgical preparation for a feast, lasting through the night. It is the counterpart of the W. *vigil.

PANORMITANUS (1386–1445), canonist. Nicolò de' Tudeschi became Abp. of Palermo (hence Panormitanus) in 1435. He was sent to the Council of *Basle by Alfonso of Aragon, who was a contender for the throne of Naples against a nominee of *Eugenius IV: he consequently usually supported the antipope and held that the Pope was inferior to a *General Council. His main writings were on *canon law.

PANPSYCHISM. The 19th-cent. doctrine that everything in the universe is endowed with a measure of consciousness. It has found little favour with Christian theologians.

PANTAENUS, St. (d. c. 190). The first known head of the *Catechetical School at Alexandria. He seems to have taught at Alexandria from c. 180 until his death.

PANTALEON, St. (d. c. 305), martyr. Nothing is certainly known of him. Acc. to one form of the legends, he was a physician to the Emp. Galerius at Nicomedia, apostatized, was reconverted, and martyred when *Diocletian gave orders to purge the court of Christians.

PANTHEISM. The belief or theory that God and the universe are identical. The word appears to have been coined by J. *Toland in 1705, but pantheistic systems go back to early times. Mysticism, with its passionate search for God in nature and its desire for union with the Divine, has often verged on pantheism.

PAPA ANGELICUS (or **Pastor Angelicus**). A belief arose in 13th-cent. Italy that a Pope would arise who would revive Apostolic simplicity and zeal in the Church and inaugurate a new age. In St. *Malachy's prophecy the 106th Pope, i.e. *Pius XII, is so designated.

'PAPAL AGGRESSION'. The name popularly given to the action of *Pius IX in 1850 making England and Wales an ecclesiastical province of the RC Church with an archbishop and 12 *suffragans all with territorial titles. The wording of the papal brief was provocative and a storm of indignation was aroused.

PAPAL LEGATE; PAPAL STATES. See *Legate, Papal; States of the Church.*

PAPEBROCH, DANIEL (1628–1714) (or van Papenbroeck), *Bollandist. He became J. Bollandus's assistant in 1659, and his name appears on 18 volumes of the *Acta Sanctorum.*

PAPHNUTIUS, St. (d. *c.* 360), Bp. of the Upper Thebaid. He was an Egyptian monk who suffered badly in the persecution of Maximinus Daza (305–13). He is said to have dissuaded the Council of *Nicaea from ordering all clergy to put away their wives.

PAPIAS (*c.* 60–130), Bp. of Hierapolis in Asia Minor. His writing survives only in quotations in *Irenaeus and *Eusebius. In the fragments on the origin of the first two Gospels he states that St. *Mark, having become the interpreter of St. *Peter, set down accurately, though not in order, everything that he remembered of the words and actions of the Lord; and that St. *Matthew composed 'the oracles' in Hebrew, and everyone translated them as best he could.

PAPYROLOGY. The science of dealing with MSS. on papyrus. Papyrus is a writing material made out of the fibres of the stems of a water plant which formerly grew plentifully in the Nile. It was used in ancient Egypt and became the chief writing material in the Greco-Roman world from about the 5th cent. B.C. to the 4th cent. A.D., when it gradually gave way to vellum. Papyrus MSS. have survived in few areas apart from Egypt, where they were first found in 1778. See also *Manuscripts of the Bible.*

PARABLES. The similitudes drawn from nature or from human affairs, esp. those suggesting or containing a short narrative, which Christ used to convey a spiritual meaning. In each parable there is one main point of comparison, and apart from this the details may, or may not, have a particular meaning. There are 30–40 distinct parables in the *Synoptic Gospels; there are none in Jn.

PARABOLANI. An association of men, orginally at *Alexandria, but later also at *Constantinople, devoted to nursing the sick. They are mentioned in 5th- and 6th-cent. laws, from which it appears that they were clerics under episcopal jurisdiction, exempt from public duties.

PARACELSUS. The name used by Theophrastus Bombastus von Hohenheim (1493–1541), Swiss physician. He made important advances in therapeutics and chemistry. He also elaborated a mystical theosophy on a *Neoplatonic basis; he held that, just as we know nature only to the extent that we are ourselves nature, so we know God only in so far as we are God.

PARACLETE. A Johannine epithet of the Holy Spirit, traditionally translated 'Comforter'.

PARADIGM. The name given by M. *Dibelius and other *Form-critics to passages in the Gospels which contain narratives woven round a particular saying of Christ in order to drive its teaching home.

PARADISE. The word is prob. of Persian origin, denoting an enclosed park or pleasure-ground. It is used in the LXX of Gen. 2 and 3 as the Greek rendering of the 'garden' planted by God in *Eden. In later Jewish literature it came to signify a state of blessedness, whether material or spiritual. In Lk. 23: 43 it has been variously interpreted as referring either to the intermediate state of the just before the Resurrection (*Limbo) or as a synonym of the heaven of the blessed; it is used in the second sense in 2 Cor. 12: 4 and Rev. 2: 7.

'PARADISE LOST'. The magnificent epic of J. *Milton describing the *Fall of man and its consequences.

PARAGRAPH BIBLES. In 1755 a NT arranged in paragraphs (as opposed to the usual AV arrangement in verses), with a revised text, was issued by J. *Wesley. An edition of the whole AV text in paragraphs was published in England by the *Religious Tract Society in 1838. It is the arrangement adopted in the RV and most other modern translations.

PARALIPOMENON. The name by which the two Books of *Chronicles are sometimes known to RCs.

PARALLELISM. A characteristic of Hebrew poetry. There are three main kinds: synonymous parallelism, consisting in the simple repetition of the same thought in slightly different words; antithetical parallelism, produced by contrasting the first member with the second (e.g. 'A merry heart doeth good like a medicine: But a broken spirit drieth the bones', Prov. 17: 22); and synthetic parallelism, in which the first member is developed or completed by a similar thought in the second or third (e.g. 'The kings of the earth stand up: And the rulers take counsel together: Against the Lord and against His Anointed', Ps. 2: 2).

PARAPHRASES OF ERASMUS, The. The Commentary on the Gospels written by D. *Erasmus which *Edward VI's *Injunctions of 1547 ordered should be placed in every parish church.

PARCLOSE. A screen or set of railings for enclosing a *chantry altar for *requiems and one or more seats for members of the family of the deceased. At the Reformation these enclosures developed into the 'family pew'.

PARDON. (1) Another name for an *indulgence (q.v.). The 'pardoners', who hawked the right to share in an indulgence, were denounced by G. *Chaucer, W. Langland, and J. *Wycliffe. (2) In Brittany, the feast of the patron saint of a church at which an indulgence may be granted. It is often accompanied by a village fair.

PARIS. The city was a centre of Christianity at an early date. Acc. to St. *Gregory of Tours, St. *Denis, its first bishop, was one of those sent out by Pope *Fabian c. 250. Under Hugh Capet (987–96) Paris became the capital of France. The beginnings of the University date from the 12th cent.; it received its statutes from *Innocent III in 1215. The early 13th cent. saw the foundation of colleges, which originally provided lodging and food for poor students; the most famous was the *Sorbonne. In the 13th cent. Paris was the chief centre of *Scholasticism,

including among its teachers St. *Albert the Great, St. *Thomas Aquinas, and *Siger of Brabant. It continued to play an important part in the time of the *Great Schism and of the Reform Councils, when some of its most learned men favoured the *Conciliar party. At the end of the 14th cent. decadence set in. Paris became an archdiocese in 1622. During the 17th cent. it witnessed a religious regeneration brought about by the activities of St. *Francis de Sales, St. *Vincent de Paul, P. de *Bérulle, and P. *Olier, who counteracted *Jansenism and *Gallicanism, which numbered many adherents in the capital. In the Revolution of 1789 the old university was abolished; a new one was established in 1806 by the combination of the faculties of arts, medicine, and law, but without theology, which, since 1875, has been represented by the *Institut Catholique.

PARIS, MATTHEW. See *Matthew Paris.*

PARISH. In England, an area under the spiritual care of a C of E clergyman (the *incumbent), to whose religious ministrations all the inhabitants are entitled. The incumbent is nominated by the patron of the benefice and can be removed only in exceptional cases. The roots of the parochial system, incl. its forms of patronage, are prob. to be sought in the relations between Teutonic landlords and pagan priests in pre-Christian times, when the owner of land was bound to provide facilities for worship for his dependants. Since the Third *Lateran Council of 1179, however, the bishop has had the right of *institution.

From an early date the English parish was a unit of civil administration, but with the abolition of Church Rates in 1868 the civil importance of the parish declined. Since 1968 the establishment of parishes has been virtually controlled by diocesan Pastoral Committees and the *Church Commissioners.

PARISH CLERK. A church official (usually a layman), who assists the priest, chiefly by making the responses of the congregation in the services, and also in the general care of the church. The office is an ancient one.

PARKER, JOSEPH (1830–1902), *Congregationalist divine. In 1869 he accepted a call to the Poultry Street Chapel in London, where his preaching attracted a large congregation. By 1874 he had completed the City Temple on Holborn Viaduct; he ministered there until he died.

PARKER, MATTHEW (1504–75), Abp. of *Canterbury from 1559. Appointed by *Elizabeth I, he was consecrated by four bishops who had held sees in *Edward VI's reign. He sought to preserve the settlement of 1559 from further change and to retain as far as possible the links with the past. He took part in the issue of the *Thirty-Nine Articles and of the '*Bishops' Bible', and in 1566 published his '*Advertisements', which commanded, among other things, the use of the *surplice. He had to face opposition from the *Puritans.

PARKER, THEODORE (1810–60), American *Unitarian preacher. In his *Discourse of Matters Pertaining to Religion* (1842) he argued that the permanent essence of Christianity was the influence of Jesus and that belief in miracles was unnecessary.

PAROCHIAL CHURCH COUNCIL. A council set up in every parish of the C of E by the Church of England Assembly (Powers) Act of 1919, to give the laity a share in parochial administration.

PAROISSIEN. The name for various prayer-books in the vernacular designed for the use of the laity which have been published in France since the 17th cent. They usually contain a considerable amount of liturgical matter as well as private devotional exercises.

PAROUSIA (Gk. for 'presence' or 'arrival'). The word is used esp. to denote the future return of Christ in glory (the 'Second Coming') to judge the living and the dead, and to terminate the present world order. Primitive Christianity believed this event to be imminent, and this belief has often been revived, but the prevailing Christian tradition has opposed speculation on the time and manner of the Coming.

PARSON. Properly, the holder of an ecclesiastical benefice who has full possession of its rights, i.e. a *rector. This use was general until the 17th cent. The current use for any (esp. C of E) clergymen has superseded the original sense.

PARSONS, ROBERT (1546–1610), also **Persons,** *Jesuit. He left Oxford, became a RC at Louvain, and in 1575 he joined the Jesuits. Chosen with St. Edmund *Campion to lead the mission to England in 1580, he was soon (1581) forced to flight. He became a trusted counsellor of Popes and other rulers (esp. *Philip II of Spain). Though he was a skilled controversialist, the most influential of his writings was a spiritual treatise, *The Christian Directory* (1582).

PARTICULAR BAPTISTS. The group of *Baptists whose theology was essentially *Calvinist. Their first community in England was established in 1633. In 1891 the *General Baptists (q.v.) of the New Connexion joined the Baptist Union which had been formed among the Particular Baptists.

PARTICULAR JUDGEMENT. In Catholic theology, the judgement on each individual soul immediately on its separation from the body. It is thus prior to and quite distinct from the *General Judgement (q.v.) on the Last Day.

PARVIS. Originally the court in front of a cathedral or other large church, the word came also to be used of the portico of a church porch. It is sometimes erroneously applied to the room over such a porch.

PASCAL, BLAISE (1623–6?), French theologian, mathematician, and savant. Having been brought up to regard matters of faith as beyond reason, Pascal came into contact with the *Jansenists in 1646 (his 'first conversion'). He entered into direct communication with *Port-Royal, but was not yet ready to accept all its demands. His 'definitive conversion' took place in 1654.

The condemnation of A. *Arnauld by the *Sorbonne in 1655 prompted Pascal's *Lettres écrites à un provincial* (commonly known as his 'Lettres provinciales', 1656–7). This attack on the *Jesuit theories of grace (*Molinism) and moral theology (*Probabilism) was intended to expose the moral character of their casuistry and to oppose to it the rigorist morality of the Jansenists. The *Pensées* were designed as a vindication of the truth of Christianity against the indifference of the *libertins* whom, though inaccessible to philosophical reasoning, Pascal hoped to convince by the presentation of facts and fulfilment of prophecy and by an appeal to the heart. A selection of the material which he left unfinished was published in 1670; the rest were stuck into an album regardless of sequence, and the whole has been frequently re-edited.

PASCH. A name used for both the Jewish *Passover and the Christian festival of *Easter.

PASCHAL II (d. 1118), Pope from 1099. Though he did not settle the *Investiture Controversy with the Empire, compromises had been reached with England and France by 1107. He supported the rebellion of the future Emp. Henry V against *Henry IV, but when Henry V practised investiture Paschal opposed him and renounced the concessions extorted from him when Henry had taken him prisoner in 1111. The support which he gave to *Bohemond I's attack on the Eastern Emp. Alexius in 1107-8 caused bitter resentment.

PASCHAL BAYLON, St. (1540–92), *Franciscan lay brother. He was born on the border of Castile and Aragon; in obedience to a vision he entered the neighbouring convent of the Franciscans of the Alcantarine reform where he practised extreme mortification. He was esp. devoted to the cult of the Bl. Sacrament.

PASCHAL CANDLE. In the *Paschal Vigil Service the Paschal Candle is lit from the New Fire and carried through the darkened church by the deacon, who solemnly stops three times before he reaches the altar, in each case singing 'Lumen Christi' ('Light of Christ'). Other candles are lit from the Paschal Candle. At the sanctuary the *Exultet is sung. The Paschal Candle is lit at liturgical functions in Eastertide and in the RC Church at all Baptisms.

PASCHAL CHRONICLE. See *Chronicon Paschale*.

PASCHAL CONTROVERSIES. Disputes on how to settle the date of *Easter. (1) Whether Easter should be observed on a fixed day of the lunar month (14 Nisan) or on the following Sunday. See *Quartodecimanism.* (2) Divergences in the different methods of determining the 'Paschal Moon' used by the *Antiochenes (who accepted the Jewish reckoning) and the *Alexandrians,

who used an independent reckoning; the first Council of *Nicaea (325) decided in favour of the latter. (3) Differences between the Roman and Alexandrian methods of computation through the use of divergent 'paschal cycles' in the 5th and 6th cents. The *Anatolian cycle used at Alexandria was formally adopted in the W. by *Dionysius Exiguus (525). (4) The *Celtic Churches had their own method of computing Easter; this was a matter of dispute after the arrival of St. *Augustine's mission. The Roman practice was accepted at the Synod of *Whitby (664).

PASCHAL LAMB. The lamb sacrificed and eaten at the Jewish *Passover. By analogy Christ is regarded as a 'Paschal Lamb'.

PASCHALTIDE, the period in the ecclesiastical year immediately after *Easter. It extends from Easter Sunday to *Pentecost in the RC Church, and to the Saturday before *Trinity Sunday in the C of E.

PASCHAL VIGIL SERVICE. The main celebration of *Easter, observed during the night of *Holy Saturday/Easter Sunday. There seems at first to have been a single celebration of the Passion and Resurrection of Christ, and this was closely associated with *Baptism. From the 4th cent., with the separate observance of *Good Friday, the emphasis of the Paschal Vigil Service came to centre on the Resurrection. In the W. Church it was put back to the Saturday morning, but in 1951 in the RC Church it was restored to the late evening.

Acc. to the current RC rite, the *Paschal Candle (q.v.), lit from the New Fire blessed outside the church, is carried through a darkened church, and other candles are lit from it. The *Exultet is sung. Up to nine Bible readings follow, and then a sermon. After a procession to the *font, the Baptismal Water is blessed. Baptism is administered to any candidates (and *confirmation also if a bishop or priest with a faculty to confirm is present). The congregation then renew their Baptismal vows. The service continues with the remaining part of the Easter Eucharist.

PASCHASINUS (c. 440), Bp. of Lilybaeum (now Marsala) in Sicily. He corresponded with *Leo I about the *Paschal Controversy and was one of the Papal legates at the Council of *Chalcedon (451).

PASCHASIUS RADBERTUS, St. (c. 790–865), theologian. He was a monk, and from 843/4 to 849 abbot, of the *Benedictine monastery of *Corbie. He wrote commentaries on Lam. and Mt.; the latter was the main source of the *Glossa ordinaria. He is known chiefly from his treatise *De Corpore et Sanguine Domini*. In maintaining the Presence of Christ in the Eucharist, Radbertus specified it further as the flesh born of Mary, which had suffered on the Cross and risen again, and which is miraculously multiplied by the omnipotence of God at each consecration. His teaching was attacked by *Ratramnus and *Rabanus Maurus.

PASSION, The. The term is used absolutely of the Lord's redemptive suffering during the last days of His earthly life, esp. of the Crucifixion.

PASSION PLAYS. See *Mystery Plays*; also *Oberammergau*.

PASSION SUNDAY. The fifth Sunday in *Lent. See also *Passiontide*.

PASSIONAL. (1) A book containing the lections from the Lives or Acts of the Saints read at *Mattins on their festivals. (2) A book containing the narratives of the Lord's Passion from the four Gospels. (3) The particular book (King Aethelstan's Book) on which the English kings from Henry I to Edward III took the Coronation Oath. It contained the Gospel of John complete, followed by the Passions of Matthew, Mark, and Luke.

PASSIONISTS. The popular name for the members of the 'Congregation of Discalced Clerks of the Most Holy Cross and Passion of our Lord Jesus Christ', founded by St. *Paul of the Cross. He drew up its rule in 1720 and erected the first house in 1737. The Passionists take a fourth vow to foster the memory of Christ's Passion in the souls of the faithful.

PASSIONS. See *Acts of the Martyrs*.

PASSIONTIDE. Traditionally the last two weeks of *Lent. It was customary to veil in purple all crucifixes, pictures, and images, and to omit the *Gloria Patri during this period. In the RC Church the title of

*Passion Sunday and any particular observance of the week following it were dropped in 1969.

PASSOVER. The Jewish festival celebrated each spring in connection with the *Exodus. Acc. to the account of its institution in Exod. 12, a lamb is to be slain in each household and its blood sprinkled on the lintel and door-posts of the house in memory of the fact that when the first-born in Egypt were slain, the Lord 'passed over' the houses which were so marked. Later the lambs were sacrificed in the *Temple. In the time of Christ it was the chief Jewish festival of the year, celebrated on the night of 14/15 Nisan.

Whether the *Last Supper was a Passover Meal (as the chronology of the *Synoptic Gospels would suggest) or not (as Jn.), it is clear that the Eucharist was instituted at Passover time, and Christians have seen in the death of Christ the fulfilment of the sacrifice foreshadowed by the Passover.

PASTOPHORION. In the E. Church, the sacristy adjacent to the *apse, used for the *reservation of the Sacrament.

PASTOR AETERNUS (1870), The Dogmatic Constitution of the First *Vatican Council defining the primacy and infallibility of the Pope.

PASTOR OF HERMAS. See *Shepherd of Hermas*.

PASTOR, LUDWIG (1854–1928), historian of the Popes. His *Geschichte der Päpste seit dem Ausgang des Mittelalters* (1886–1933), which has been translated into many languages, aims at giving a balanced picture of the history of Catholicism in modern times.

PASTORAL EPISTLES, The. A designation for the Epistles to *Timothy and Titus (q.v.).

PASTORAL LETTERS. Official letters of a bishop to all members of his diocese. They are distinguished from 'encyclical letters' addressed by the bishop only to his clergy.

PASTORAL STAFF. Another name for the *crosier.

PASTORALIA. The branch of theology

concerned with the principles regulating the life and conduct of the parish priest.

PATARENES. The name first appears in the 1050s at Milan as the designation of an extreme reforming movement enjoying considerable support at Rome; it is supposed to derive from that of the rag-pickers' quarter in Milan. Matters came to a head in 1071 when the Emp. *Henry IV invested a new Abp. of Milan; the Pateranes demanded a free canonical election, propagated their movement elsewhere in Lombardy, and became *Gregory VII's allies against Henry. The movement persisted at Milan until the early 12th cent. In the 1170s the name reappeared as a general label for heretics.

PATEN. The dish, now usually of silver or gold, on which the bread is placed at the celebration of the Eucharist.

PATER NOSTER. The opening words of the Latin version of the *Lord's Prayer (q.v.).

PATMOS. A small island in the Aegean on which St. *John saw the Apocalypse (Rev. 1: 9). Acc. to tradition he was exiled to Patmos under *Domitian (81–96) and returned to *Ephesus under Nerva (96–8). In 1088 St. Christodulus founded a monastery on the island; it rapidly grew in importance and still survives.

PATON, JOHN GIBSON (1824–1907), missionary to the New Hebrides. A member of the rigid '*Reformed Presbyterian Church of Scotland', Paton worked on the island of Tana and later on that of Aneityum. His autobiogrphy (1889) did much to stimulate interest in the Pacific.

PATRIARCH (Biblical). Literally the father or ruler of a family or tribe, the term is applied most frequently to *Abraham, *Isaac, *Jacob, and the twelve sons of Jacob.

PATRIARCH (Ecclesiastical). A title dating from the 6th cent. for the bishops of the five chief sees of Christendom: *Rome, *Alexandria, *Antioch, *Constantinople, and *Jerusalem, whose jurisdiction extended over the adjoining territories. In modern times the title has been given to the heads of certain *autocephalous Churches of the E.

(e.g. *Russia and *Bulgaria).

PATRIARCHS, The Testaments of the Twelve. See *Testaments of the Twelve Patriarchs, The*.

PATRICK, St. (prob. *c.* 390–*c.* 460), 'Apostle of the Irish'. Patrick was born in Britain and brought up as a Christian. At the age of 16 he was captured by Irish pirates and spent six years as a herdsman in Co. Mayo. He turned earnestly to God and received a Divine message that he was to escape. He made his way to a port, persuaded some sailors to give him passage to Britain, and joined his family, a changed man. He underwent training for the Christian ministry, prob. in Britain not Gaul. He was sent from Britain as 'bishop in Ireland' (his own phrase); he spent the rest of his life there, evangelizing, conciliating local chieftains, ordaining clergy, and constituting monks and nuns. He prob. set up his episcopal see at *Armagh. One of his letters has survived. He also wrote a moving account of his spiritual pilgrimage, called his *Confession*. It is unlikely that the '*Breastplate' or any of the collections of canons attributed to St. Patrick are his. See also *St. Patrick's Purgatory*.

PATRICK, SIMON (1625–1707), Bp. successively of *Chichester (1688) and *Ely (1691). In 1648 he was ordained a *Presbyterian minister, but the study of H. *Hammond and H. *Thorndike determined him to seek episcopal ordination. He was a prominent *Latitudinarian. In 1687 he resisted reading the *Declaration of Indulgence, and in 1688 he took the Oath of Allegiance to William and Mary. He supported the *S.P.C.K., which he helped to found, and the *S.P.G. He wrote extensively.

PATRIMONY OF ST. PETER, The. The estates belonging to the Church of Rome. Once an edict of *Constantine in 321 had enabled the Church to hold permanent property, the patrimony came to include vast estates in Italy and lands in other countries. As the further patrimonies were conquered, Popes concentrated on defending the region round Rome. In 753 *Stephen II appealed for protection to *Pepin, King of the Franks. By the Donations of 754 and 756 Pepin gave the Papacy territory in the exarchate of *Ravenna, the Duchy of Rome, and elsewhere, and, renouncing the Byzantine authority, founded the Papal States independent of any temporal power. See also *States of the Church*.

PATRIPASSIANISM. A form of *Monarchianism (q.v.) which arose in the 3rd cent. Its adherents held that God the Father suffered as the Son.

PATRISTICS. The branch of theological study which deals with the writings of the Fathers. The title 'Father' is sometimes given to important Christian writers of all ages up to the 13th cent., but in its stricter usage it belongs to those teachers who wrote between the end of the 1st cent. (when the NT was almost, if not quite, completed) and the close of the 8th cent., and this is the period commonly termed the 'Patristic Age'.

PATROLOGY. A systematically arranged manual on the *patristic literature.

PATRON. See *Parish* and *Advowson*.

PATRON SAINT. A saint who has been chosen as the special intercessor or advocate in heaven of a particular place, person, or organization. The custom of having patron saints for churches arose from the practice of building churches over the tombs of martyrs.

PATTESON, JOHN COLERIDGE (1827–1871), missionary. In 1855, under the influence of G. A. *Selwyn, he set out for the *South Seas to found the Melanesian Mission. He toured the islands in the *Southern Cross* and in 1861 he was consecrated first Bp. of Melanesia. He was murdered in 1871.

PAUL, St. (d. *c.* A.D. 65), the 'Apostle of the Gentiles'. Born at *Tarsus in the early years of the Christian era, the future St. Paul, originally 'Saul', was the son of a Jew, possessed of Roman citizenship. He was brought up a *Pharisee and studied at *Jerusalem under *Gamaliel. Within a few years of the Crucifixion, he came into contact with the new 'Way' of the followers of Jesus, and, meeting it with intense opposition, he assisted at the martyrdom of St. *Stephen. His conversion occurred on the road to *Damascus. He saw a great light and heard the words 'Saul, Saul, why persecutest thou me?', and, in reply to his question 'Who art thou, Lord?', received the answer, 'I am Jesus, whom thou persecutest'. In Damascus he received Baptism and the imposition of hands from Ananias, and then departed for Arabia.

Some years later St. *Barnabas fetched him from Tarsus to help in the conversion of *Antioch. About A.D. 44 they both went to Jerusalem to take food to the Christian community. Soon after their return, the 'prophets and teachers' of the Church at Antioch sent them out on the so-called First Missionary Journey. They set sail for *Cyprus. Here Barnabas, hitherto the leader, ceded his place to Paul (the change of name from Saul at Acts 13: 9 may indicate the reversal of roles). From Cyprus they went to Asia Minor. At Antioch in Pisidia Paul preached first to the Jews, and when they opposed him, turned to the Gentiles, among whom he made converts. The Apostles returned overland to Antioch (*c.* A.D. 49).

The growth of Gentile Christianity raised problems for the Church. Paul found himself opposed by Jewish Christians who held that without *circumcision Gentiles could not be saved. He and Barnabas went to Jerusalem, where it was decided that the Jewish Law should not be imposed on Gentile Christians and Paul's mission was recognized by the Jerusalem Church (Acts 15).

Having separated from Barnabas, Paul set out on his Second Missionary Journey with Silas. He revisited the Churches in the interior of Asia Minor and prob. evangelized the *Galatians. Prevented, as he believed, by Divine intervention, from going on to Bithynia, he crossed over to Macedonia, thus extending the sphere of his ministry to Europe. He visited Philippi, Thessalonica, and Beroea, where he made many Gentile converts, and *Athens, where he had little success. At *Corinth he founded a flourishing Church, wrote to the *Thessalonians, and after 18 months returned to Antioch. His stay in Corinth can be dated to A.D. 51 or 52.

On his Third Missionary Journey he stayed two years at *Ephesus. The communities of the hinterland (Colossae, *Philadelphia, Hierapolis, *Laodicea) prob. owe their origin to Paul's sojourn at Ephesus. Here he wrote 1 *Corinthians. Driven out by the silversmiths, he spent three years in Achaia, prob. at Corinth (A.D. 57), where it is likely that he wrote the Epistle to the *Romans. He sailed for Jerusalem with contributions to relieve the poverty of the mother Church.

At Jerusalem he had a hostile reception.

Accused of teaching transgression of the Law, he was beaten by the mob and only rescued by Roman soldiers. Information of a plot against Paul's life caused the captain to send him to the governor at *Caesarea. His trial was deferred for two years and Paul appealed to Caesar. On the voyage to Rome he was shipwrecked. In Rome he was kept in mitigated custody. Acc. to many scholars he wrote one or more of the *Captivity Epistles (Phil., Col., Philem., and Eph.) while awaiting his trial; others argue that some or all of them were written during an earlier imprisonment at Ephesus or at Caesarea. Acts ends with the statement that he remained in captivity in Rome for two years. Several of the *Fathers accept the tradition that he visited *Spain. If the *Pastoral Epistles are genuine, they were presumably written after his return. He is said to have been martyred at Rome during the *Neronian persecution.

St. Paul is the most powerful human personality in the history of the Church. His epistles laid the foundations on which later Christian theology was built. To the Judaizers' rigid conception of the *Mosaic Law he opposed the freedom of the Gospel as the only efficacious means of salvation. Sinful humanity is redeemed and justified by Divine grace through faith in Jesus Christ, who by His Life, Death, and Resurrection abrogated the Old Law and ushered in the new era of the Spirit. Christ is not only the *Messiah in whom the OT promises were fulfilled but the eternal, pre-existent Son of God. He is identified with the Church as His Mystical Body, whose members share in His life through Baptism and the Eucharist, until His return in glory.

PAUL, Acts of. An apocryphal book written in Greek and put into circulation in the 2nd cent. It was designed to glorify St. *Paul's achievements and is romantic in character. A number of treatises which circulated independently are now known to be parts of this work, among them the 'Martyrdom of Paul', the 'Acts of *Paul and Thecla', and the 'Third Epistle of Paul to the *Corinthians' (qq.v.).

PAUL, Apocalypse of. An apocryphal apocalypse, written in Greek and dating from the 4th cent., which describes what St. *Paul saw when he was taken up into the 'third heaven' (2 Cor. 12: 2). It became very popular.

PAUL, Clerks Regular of St. See *Barnabites.

PAUL, Martyrdom of. An apocryphal account of the death of St. *Paul. It forms the concluding section of the 'Acts of *Paul'.

PAUL AND THECLA, Acts of. An apocryphal work which is part of the 'Acts of *Paul'. It describes how St. *Paul preached the benefits of chastity at Iconium and won St. Thecla from Thamyris, to whom she was betrothed. Paul was charged before the civil authorities and beaten, while Thecla was condemned to death but miraculously saved. It concludes with the record of Thecla's death at Seleucia.

PAUL III (1468–1549), Pope from 1534. In his personal life Alessandro Farnese was a typical Renaissance Pope, but he promoted the inner reform of the Church. He created as *cardinals men of virtue and scholarship, established commissions to draw up plans for reform, and favoured the new religious orders, esp. the *Jesuits, whom he approved in 1540. He restored the *Inquisition and fought hard against the opposition to the General Council which finally opened at *Trent in 1545. He was less successful in his political efforts to check the spread of Protestantism.

PAUL IV (1476–1559), the first of the *Counter-Reformation Popes (from 1555). Giovanni Pietro Caraffa was Bp. of Chieti (Theate) from 1504 to 1524. He resigned his bishopric to found, in conjunction with St. *Cajetan, the *Theatine Order, which is named after him. As Pope his opposition to anything savouring of Protestantism was so violent that its effect was to consolidate the Protestant forces.

PAUL V (1552–1621), Pope from 1605. When the Senate of *Venice refused to repeal the laws of 1604–5 restricting the erection of religious buildings and the donation or sale of secular property to the Church, the Pope excommunicated the Senate and put the city under an *interdict. In 1606 and again in 1607 he condemned the Oath of Allegiance required by *James I in England. He made futile attempts to re-establish the RC Church in *Russia and he saw the beginning of the *Thirty Years War in Germany. He was a skilful canonist and tried to enforce the decrees of the Council of *Trent.

PAUL VI (1897–1978), Pope from 1963. Giovanni Battista Montini was the son of a wealthy landowner. He took up office in the Papal Secretariat of State in 1924; after L. Maglione's death in 1944 he discharged his business directly under the Pope. In 1954 he became Abp. of Milan. *John XXIII made him a *cardinal and continually brought him forward at the Second *Vatican Council; when John XXIII died, he was elected Pope.

Paul VI convened the Second, Third, and Fourth Sessions of the Vatican Council. On the day before it closed he took part in a historic gesture of friendship with the E. *Orthodox Church: a joint declaration of the Pope and Patr. *Athenagoras expressing their regret for the events of 1054 was read, and the Pope exchanged embraces with the Patriarch's envoy. (For the decrees of the Council, see *Vatican Council, the Second.)

At the close of the Council the Pope proclaimed an extraordinary *Holy Year, in order that the faithful might be familiarized with the teaching of the Council and that the life of the Church might be renewed. He also established a number of Post-Conciliar Commissions to put into effect the wishes of the Council, and he confirmed the permanent Secretariats for the Promotion of Christian Unity, for Non-Christian Religions, and for Non-Believers. The reforms which came into being through the working of the Post-Conciliar Commissions have included a re-ordering of the RC liturgy, which may now be in the vernacular. The Pope's own encyclicals have often appeared more conservative in tone; the best-known is *Humanae Vitae (1968), which dealt with birth control. In the early years of his pontificate he undertook a number of notable journeys abroad.

PAUL OF CONSTANTINOPLE, St. (d. 350). He became Bp. of Constantinople in 336, but was soon displaced by the Semi-Arian *Macedonius. He twice regained his see but was again exiled and finally strangled. He was a zealous upholder of orthodoxy.

PAUL OF THE CROSS, St. (1694-1775), founder of the *Passionists. Paul Francis Danei was the eldest son of a noble but impoverished family. In 1720 a vision inspired him to found a religious order in honour of the Passion of our Lord; the first house was opened in 1737. He was a celebrated preacher and famous as a miracle-worker and spiritual director.

PAUL THE DEACON (c. 720–c. 800), chronicler. Of Lombard descent, he received an exceptionally good education. After the conquest of Lombardy by *Charlemagne in 774, he was banished to *Monte Cassino and became a monk. His most important work, the *Historia Gentis Langobardorum*, covers the period from 568 to 744; based largely on documents no longer extant, it is the main source for the Lombardy history of the time, being especially valuable for Franco-Lombard relations and for its vivid picture of life in that age.

PAUL OF SAMOSATA (3rd cent.), heretical Bp. of *Antioch from c. 260. His teaching on the Person of Christ was condemned at two, or possibly three, Synods of Antioch, and in 268 he was deposed from his see. He taught a form of Dynamic *Monarchianism, in which the Godhead was a closely knit Trinity of Father, Wisdom, and Word, and until creation formed a single *hypostasis. From the Incarnation, he held, the Word rested upon the human Jesus as one person upon another, and the Incarnate Christ differed only in degree from the Prophets. In the course of the controversy the famous '*Homoousios' first came into dispute. His followers, the Paulianists, long survived his death.

PAUL THE SILENTIARY. See *Paulus Silentiarius*.

PAUL OF THEBES, St. (d. c. 340), traditionally the first Christian *hermit. He fled to the desert in the *Decian persecution (249–51). St. *Antony is said to have visited him when he was 113 years old, and later to have buried him.

PAULA, St. (347–404), Roman matron. In 385 she and her daughter, St. *Eustochium, followed St. *Jerome to *Jerusalem; in 386 she settled at *Bethlehem, founding communities for monks and nuns.

PAULICIANS. Members of a sect in the Byzantine Empire. Their founder seems to have been Constantine of Mananali, who established a community at Kibossa in Armenia, and was stoned c. 684. They were severely persecuted in the 9th cent.; many accepted *Islam, and some later amalgamated with the *Bogomils. They professed a *dualist doctrine, denied the reality of Christ's body and of the Redemption, and considered His teaching to be Christ's most important work. Like *Marcion, they repudiated the OT and held St. *Luke's Gospel and the Pauline Epistles in particular esteem.

PAULINE PRIVILEGE. The privilege conceded by St. *Paul (1 Cor. 7: 15) to the partner of a heathen marriage to contract a new marriage on becoming a Christian if the non-Christian partner wished to separate or put serious obstacles in the way of the convert's faith and practice.

PAULINUS, St. (c. 726–802), Bp. of *Aquileia. He was a learned scholar whom *Charlemagne summoned to the Frankish court in 776 and appointed Patr. of Aquileia in 787. He took a prominent part in the suppression of *Adoptianism, and he was a poet of no mean order.

PAULINUS, St. (353/4–431), Bp. of Nola. After a short public career, he was baptized by the Bp. of Bordeaux in 390, and, in agreement with his wife, he retired from the world and began to distribute his wealth. He settled at Nola and in 409 he was made bishop. His widespread correspondence kept him in touch with several famous Christians of the time; many of his letters have survived. His poetic works rank him with *Prudentius as the foremost Christian Latin poet of the patristic period.

PAULINUS, St. (d. 644), Bp. of *York. He was sent to England by *Gregory I in 601. When in 625 *Edwin, King of Northumbria, married Ethelburga of Kent, Paulinus was consecrated bishop and went with her to York. As a result of his preaching, Edwin and his chiefs accepted Christianity at the assembly of Goodmanham (627). When Edwin was defeated in 633, Paulinus returned with Ethelburga to Kent and became Bp. of *Rochester.

PAULISTS. The popular name for members of 'The Missionary Society of St. Paul the Apostle in the State of New York', founded by I. T. *Hecker in 1858 to further the work and interests of the RC Church in the U.S.A.

PAULUS SILENTIARIUS (6th cent.; a *silentiarius* was an usher who maintained silence in the Imperial palace), Christian poet. His chief work was a hymn to mark the consecration of *Santa Sophia at Constantinople in 562; it gives a full description of the church.

PAX. See *Kiss of Peace* and following entry.

PAX BREDE (also **Pax** or **Osculatorium**). A small plate of ivory, metal, or wood, with a representation of some religious subject on the face and a projecting handle on the back, formerly used for conveying the *Kiss of Peace. It was kissed by the celebrant and then by others who received it in turn.

PEACE OF THE CHURCH, The. The term is applied to: (1) the new situation in the Church when persecution ended with the 'Edict of *Milan' (313); and (2) the temporary cessation of the *Jansenist conflict in 1668.

PEACOCK, R. See *Pecock, R.*

PEAKE, ARTHUR SAMUEL (1865–1929), Biblical scholar. The son of a *Primitive Methodist minister, he was the first Rylands Professor of Biblical Criticism and Exegesis at Manchester University from 1904. He was an accurate, balanced, and cautious scholar. He is chiefly remembered for his editorship of a *Commentary on the Bible* in one volume (1919). The so-called new edition of *Peake's Commentary*, ed. M. Black and H. H. Rowley (1962), is a completely new work.

PEARSON, JOHN (1613–86), Bp. of *Chester from 1673. He was perhaps the most erudite and profound divine of a learned and theological age. His classic *Exposition of the Creed* (1659) originated in a series of lectures at St. Clement's, Eastcheap. He also defended the authenticity of the Epistles of St. *Ignatius against the attacks of J. *Daillé; his conclusions have been strengthened by the work of later scholars.

PEARSON, JOHN LOUGHBOROUGH (1817–97), architect. His work was mainly geometrical-gothic and ecclesiastical; the best-known example is *Truro cathedral.

PEASANTS' REVOLT, The. The insurrection of the German peasants in 1524–6. Economic distress was reinforced by the doctrines of some of the Reformers, esp. T. *Münzer, which incited the peasants to seek greater freedom by violent means. They were supported by some townspeople, knights, and apostate priests dissatisfied with the existing order. The *Twelve Articles (1525) demanded the abolition of certain taxes and of serfdom, and freedom to elect their own pastors; religious privileges were soon added to their demands. M. *Luther at first tried to mediate between landlords and peasants, but he was alienated by the brutality of the rebels and in 1525 issued a pamphlet advocating their extermination. The movement was ruthlessly stamped out.

PECKHAM, JOHN (c. 1225–92), Abp. of *Canterbury. He was born at Patcham (formerly Pecham) in Sussex, studied at *Paris and then at *Oxford, where he joined the *Franciscans c. 1250. He lectured at Paris, Oxford, and Rome, before he was appointed Abp. of Canterbury in 1279. He immediately inaugurated a vigorous policy of reform, which brought him into conflict with some of his *suffragans.

In theology he upheld the Franciscan tradition; he opposed the teaching of St. *Thomas Aquinas on the unity of form in man, going so far as to insist on its condemnation as heretical (1286). He wrote on theological subjects; he produced a standard treatise on optics; and he was a gifted poet.

PECOCK, REGINALD (c. 1393–1461), Bp. successively of *St. Asaph (from 1444) and *Chichester (from 1450). He was accused of heresy in 1457 and, though he recanted, he was deprived of his bishopric.

His best-known work, *The Repressor*, was written to combat the *Lollards; it emphasizes the 'law of kind', 'written in mennis soulis with the finger of God', to which the Scriptures are subordinate and supplementary.

PECTORAL CROSS. A cross of precious metal worn on the breast, suspended by a chain which goes round the neck. In the C of E its use is almost exclusively confined to bishops; in the RC Church and esp. in the E.

it is more widely worn.

PECULIAR. A place exempt from the jurisdiction of the bishop of the diocese in which it is situated. The Royal Peculiars are churches connected with a royal castle or palace (e.g. St. George's Chapel, *Windsor, and *Westminster Abbey), which are exempt from any jurisdiction except that of the Sovereign. Most of the rights and privileges of the other types of Peculiar (e.g. Monastic and Cathedral Peculiars) have now been removed.

PECULIAR PEOPLE, The, also 'Plumstead Peculiars'. A small sect of faith-healers, founded in London in 1838.

PEDILAVIUM. The ceremony of foot-washing performed in the liturgy on *Maundy Thursday in memory of Christ's action before the *Last Supper (Jn. 13). When the Maundy Thursday Mass came to be celebrated in the morning, the Pedilavium remained in the evening as a separate service, confined to cathedral and abbey churches. *Pius XII's Holy Week Ordinal placed it in the restored evening Mass immediately after the Gospel and recommended its observance in all churches. Twelve men are led into the sanctuary, where the celebrant washes and dries the feet of each in turn.

PEEL PARISH. In the C of E the term is used for a *parish set up under the New Parishes Act, 1843, passed when Sir Robert Peel was Prime Minister, or one of the subsequent Acts on the subject.

PÉGUY, CHARLES PIERRE (1873–1914), French writer. He gave up his studies at the *Sorbonne to manage a bookshop in Paris. At first an ardent socialist and Dreyfusard, he later became a mystical nationalist with strong sympathy for medieval Catholicism. He remained estranged from his Catholic contemporaries by his anti-clericalism, and he was distrusted by republicans and socialists alike because of his pessimism on the future of the secular order. His works none the less exercised a deep influence on later French RC writers.

PELAGIA, St. (d. c. 311), virgin and martyr. She was a 15-year-old girl of *Antioch who, when her house was surrounded by soldiers, threw herself out of a window into the sea to preserve her chastity. To the name of this historical person a legend became attached of a 4th-cent. actress of Antioch who was suddenly converted and lived as an austere recluse in a grotto of the Mount of *Olives. The story of a third Pelagia, a virgin martyr of *Tarsus, seems to be a combination of the former two. This Pelagia is supposed to have been burned to death for refusing to become the mistress of the Emperor.

PELAGIANISM. Theologically, Pelagianism is the heresy that man can take the initial steps towards salvation by his own efforts, apart from Divine *Grace. Historically, it was an ascetic movement composed of disparate elements united under the name of the British theologian Pelagius, who taught in Rome in the late 4th and early 5th cents. His contribution was to supply a theology vindicating Christian asceticism against the charge of *Manichaeism by emphasizing man's freedom to choose good by virtue of his God-given nature. The denial of the transmission of *Original Sin seems to have been introduced into Pelagianism by Rufinus the Syrian, who influenced Pelagius's supporter *Celestius.

In 409 or 410, when Rome was menaced by the Goths, Pelagius and Celestius left Italy for Africa, whence Pelagius soon moved to Palestine. Celestius was accused of denying the transmission of Adam's sin to his descendants and was condemned by a Council of *Carthage in 411. Soon afterwards St. *Augustine began to preach and write against Pelagian doctrines. In 415 Pelagius was accused of heresy by *Orosius. He cleared himself at a diocesan synod at *Jerusalem and at a provincial synod at Diospolis (Lydda), but the African bishops condemned Pelagius and Celestius at two Councils in 416 and persuaded *Innocent I to excommunicate them. Pope *Zosimus reopened the case but in 418 he confirmed his predecessor's judgement.

Pelagius himself then disappears from history and his subsequent fate is unknown. Pelagianism was defended by *Julian of Eclanum, who conducted a literary debate of great bitterness with Augustine. Celestius and his followers were again condemned at the Council of *Ephesus in 431, but Pelagian influences continued for some time in Britain, and also in Gaul, where the situation was complicated by the movement known as *Semi-Pelagianism (q.v.).

PELICAN. The image of the pelican, wounding herself with her beak to feed her young with her blood, has been widely used to typify Christ's redeeming work, esp. as mediated through the Eucharist.

PENANCE. Little is known of the early history of the Sacrament. By the 3rd cent. a developed system of public Penance had emerged. After the sinner had asked the Bishop for Penance, he was enrolled in the order of *penitents, excluded from Communion, and committed to a course of prayer, fasting, and almsgiving; after a period whose length was determined by the gravity of the sin, the sinner was reconciled and rejoined the congregation. Penance could then be undergone only once in a lifetime and entailed life-long continence.

A new and different system was developed under the influence of *Celtic and *Anglo-Saxon monk-missionaries. Confession of the details of sin, which had prob. never been public, was secret. Absolution, which was at first witheld until the completion of the Penance, was gradually pushed back until it was granted on confession and before the Penance began. From this developed the 'private Penance' of today, with its confession, absolution, and light formal penance. The Fourth *Lateran Council (1215) required every Christian to confess his sins in Penance at least once a year. The 1974 RC rite of Penance provides in exceptional cases for the granting of absolution without individual confession of sins in the presence of a priest.

It was apparently the doctrine of the early Church that sin must be atoned for in part by the punishment of the sinner. Owing to the grave inconvenience occasioned by long and arduous Penances, the idea of commutation grew up. Prob. from the idea of commutation the later practice of *Indulgences developed.

PENINGTON, ISAAC, the 'Younger' (1616–79), or **Pennington**, *Quaker. He was the eldest son of Sir Isaac Penington, who was Lord Mayor of London (1642–4). In 1657 he heard George *Fox; he and his wife joined the Quakers, who had hitherto had no one of his station in their ranks. In 1660 he was imprisoned and his property confiscated.

PENITENTIAL BOOKS. A set of books containing directions to confessors, including lists of sins with appropriate *penances. They were of *Celtic origin; the best-known was that ascribed to Abp. *Theodore (668–90).

PENITENTIAL PSALMS. See *Seven Penitential Psalms.*

PENITENTIARY. In the RC Church a Penitentiary is a cleric charged with oversight of the administration of the Sacrament of *Penance in a particular area.

PENITENTS. In the ancient system of public *penance (q.v.), penitents were separated from the rest of the congregation by wearing special dress and worshipping apart in the church. Even after restoration to Communion, certain disabilities remained for life.

PENN, WILLIAM (1644–1718), *Quaker. He attached himself to the Quakers as a result of a sermon which he heard in 1665. His writing in defence of his newly-won faith led to his imprisonment in the Tower. During his confinement he wrote *No Cross, No Crown* (1669), a classic of Quaker practice. He became interested in founding a colony in America which would assure liberty of conscience for Quakers and others, and in 1682 he obtained by letters patent grants of East New Jersey and Pennsylvania. He drew up a constitution for the colony which permitted all forms of worship compatible with monotheism and religious liberty, and sailed for America. Having returned to England in 1684, he expressed the Quakers' thanks to *James II for the *Declaration of Indulgence of 1687. In 1692 he was deprived of the Governorship of Pennsylvania.

PENNINGTON, I. See *Penington, I.*

PENRY, JOHN (1559–93), Brownist. He came into conflict with the bishops on account of his *Puritan ideas. When the *Marprelate Tracts appeared, Penry was suspected of their authorship and fled to Scotland. On his return in 1592 he became an adherent of the Separatist Church of R. *Browne. He was hanged on an ill-founded charge of treason.

PENTATEUCH. A title in use among Biblical scholars for the five 'Books of *Moses', *Genesis, *Exodus, *Leviticus, *Numbers, and *Deuteronomy. Most critics hold that these Books were compiled from previously written documents dating from the 9th to the 5th cent. B.C. See also entries '*J*', '*E*', '*P*', '*D*', and *Moses.*

PENTECOST. The Greek name for the Jewish Feast of Weeks, which falls on the 50th day after *Passover. As the Holy Spirit descended on the Apostles on this day (Acts 2: 1), the name was applied to the Christian feast celebrating this event, popularly called *Whitsunday (q.v.).

PENTECOSTALISM. A modern religious movement, now represented not only by specifically Pentecostal Churches but also within the main Christian denominations (where, esp. in the RC Church, it is better known as 'Charismatic Renewal'). Its adherents share a common belief in the possibility of receiving the same experience and gifts as did the first Christians 'on the day of Pentecost' (Acts 2: 1–4). They emphasize the corporate element in worship (often marked by great spontaneity) and lay special stress on the practice of the gifts listed in 1 Cor. 12 and 14 and in Acts (e.g. 'speaking in tongues' or *glossolalia, prophecy, healing, and exorcism).

God is generally held to convey the 'power' to practise these gifts in an experience known as '*baptism in the Holy Spirit', usually regarded as distinct both from conversion and sacramental (or water) *Baptism, and the movement, which had its immediate origin in the American *Holiness Churches, came to be distinguished by the claim (first made in 1900) that this 'Spirit-baptism' is normally signified by the recipient's breaking into 'tongues'. In the RC Charismatic Renewal movement 'Spirit-baptism' tends to be reinterpreted in an attempt to reconcile it with RC sacramental doctrine.

The specifically Pentecostal Churches include the groupings known as *Assemblies of God; one of the U.S A.'s largest 'Black Churches', the Church of God in Christ; and in Britain the Elim Churches, the Apostolic Church, and the New Testament Church of God, which flourishes esp. among immigrants from the *West Indies. Pentecostalism is expanding in the Third World, most notably in Indonesia, among the *African Independent Churches, and above all in

Latin America. It is still essentially a popular lay movement, but (at least in N. America and NW. Europe) it is no longer solely a religion of the poor.

PENTECOSTARION. In the E. Church, the liturgical book which contains the variable prayers and lections for use between *Easter and the Sunday after *Pentecost.

PEPIN III (714–68), Frankish king. The son of *Charles Martel, he succeeded to his father's office of Mayor of the Palace of the Frankish Kingdom. With the assent of Pope *Zacharias, he was elected king by the nobles in 751 in place of the nominal Merovingian, Childeric III, and anointed by St. *Boniface. In 754 the ceremony was repeated by *Stephen (II) III, for whom Pepin promised to win back the exarchate of *Ravenna and the rights and territories of the Roman republic. His 'Donation' of 756 (no longer extant) laid the foundations of the *States of the Church. He was succeeded by his son *Charlemagne. See also *Patrimony of St. Peter*.

PERCIVAL, JOHN (1843–1918), Bp. of *Hereford from 1895. In his latter years he sought to further the cause of reunion between the C of E and Nonconformists; he aroused much opposition by inviting Nonconformists to receive Communion in Hereford Cathedral.

PERCY, J. See *Fisher the Jesuit*.

PEREGRINATIO ETHERIAE (or **Silviae**). See *Etheria, Pilgrimage of*.

PERFECTION. The primary meaning of the term is completeness and in an absolute sense it may be attributed only to God. In the NT, however, perfection is frequently enjoined on the Christian; acc. to Mt. 5: 48 the perfection required of man is related to that of God ('Be ye therefore perfect, even as your Father which is in heaven is perfect'). With the development of monastic life in the 4th cent. a twofold standard of perfection came to be widely accepted; 'Religious Perfection', involving the practice of the so-called '*Counsels of Perfection', was distinguished from 'Christian Perfection' made possible by Baptism.

The idea of perfection has played a central part among the *Methodists. They regard entrance on the way of perfection as an instantaneous experience, which takes place some time after conversion, and convinces those who receive it that sin is rooted out in them.

PERFECTIONISTS. See *Oneida Community*.

PERGAMON. The town, *c*. 50 miles north of Smyrna, was a centre of culture in the 2nd cent. B.C. To this period belongs the invention of parchment ('pergamena carta') as a substitute for papyrus.

One of the '*Seven Churches' addressed in Rev. (2: 12–17), Pergamon is called the 'place where Satan's throne is'. As it was the first city in Asia to receive permission to worship the living ruler, in 29 B.C., the reference is presumably to Emperor-worship. The modern town is known as Bergama.

PERICOPE. A passage from Scripture, esp. one appointed to be read in the Church services. See also *Lectionary*.

PERICOPE ADULTERAE, i.e. Jn. 7: 53–8: 11. These verses, which narrate the Lord's compassionate dealing with the woman taken in the act of adultery, are not part of the original text of Jn. There is, however, no sufficient reason for doubting the historicity of the incident recorded. The passage may belong to Lk.

PERIPATETIC. A philosopher of the school of *Aristotle, so called in reference to Aristotle's practice of moving about while teaching.

PERKINS, WILLIAM (1558–1602), *Puritan theologian. He became prominent in the university at Cambridge as a vigorous anti-Roman theologian and supporter of Puritan principles. His writings were held in high repute throughout 17th cent. by theologians of *Calvinist sympathies.

PERPETUA, St. (d. 203), African martyr. When in 202 the Emp. Septimius Severus forbade conversions to Christianity, Perpetua and other African *catechumens were imprisoned and, after their baptism, condemned to execution in the arena at Carthage. The 'Passion of St. Perpetua' is a contemporary document, possibly edited by *Tertullian.

PERPETUAL CURATE. In the C of E the technical name given before the passing of the Pastoral Measure, 1968, to a cleric who ministered in a parish or district to which he had been nominated by the *Impropriator and licensed by the Bishop. When, after the *dissolution of the monasteries, the parishes which had been appropriated by them passed to *lay rectors, these lay rectors were obliged to nominate a priest to the Bishop for his licence to serve the cure. Curates thus licensed became perpetual. The ministers of new parishes and districts established by various 19th-cent. Acts of Parliament were also Perpetual Curates.

PERRONE, GIOVANNI (1794–1876), Italian *Jesuit. His *Praelectiones Theologicae* (1835–42) was one of the most widely used books on Catholic dogmatics in the 19th cent.

PER SALTUM (Lat., 'by a leap'). A term used of the conferring of a particular rank of *Orders on a candidate who has not previously received the lower grades, e.g. the ordination to the priesthood of a man who is not already a deacon. Such ordinations are valid but gravely irregular.

PERSECUTION. See *Toleration*.

PERSECUTIONS, Early Christian. Since the Roman government respected national religions, Christianity at first sheltered under Jewish privileges, but as the distinction became clear and Gentile Christians refused Emperor-worship, their loyalty was open to suspicion. They also evoked dislike by their aloofness from society, while misunderstandings among non-Christians about the *Agape and *Eucharist aroused scandal. Persecution by the State began almost accidentally and remained intermittent; until 250 its extent was determined more by local feeling than by Imperial policy.

*Nero used Christians as scapegoats for the fire of Rome in A.D. 64. His victims were condemned for arson and not for a particular creed, but a precedent was set for treating Christians generally as criminals and condemning them 'for the Name' [i.e. of Christ] by summary magisterial jurisdiction. In 95 *Domitian executed Flavius Clemens and *Glabrio and banished *Domitilla for 'atheism'; they may have been Christians. Trajan's correspondence with *Pliny in 112 reveals Christian trials in Bithynia. *Marcus Aurelius disliked Christians and sanctioned severe persecution at Lyons in 177. Septimius Severus forbade fresh conversions (*Perpetua), but was not an active persecutor.

The situation changed under *Decius. His order (250) that all his subjects should sacrifice to the State gods under pain of death was a systematic attack on Christianity. Many were punished and many apostatized. After a period of toleration, in 303 *Diocletian ordered that all churches should be destroyed and all Bibles burnt. In 304 he sanctioned bloodshed. After his abdication in 305 persecution continued, but varied in intensity. *Constantine and Licinius proclaimed complete religious liberty in 313. Though Licinius (322–3) and *Julian (361–3) launched new attacks, substantial toleration had been assured.

PERSEVERANCE. In addition to its general meaning, the word is used technically in connection with the doctrine of *predestination, to mean steady continuance, after conversion, in the faith and life proper to the attainment of eternal salvation.

PERSON OF CHRIST. See *Christology* and *Incarnation*.

PERSONS. R. See *Parsons, R.*

PERTH, Articles of. Five articles on such subjects as kneeling at Communion which were forced on the Church in *Scotland by *James I at Perth in 1618. In 1621 they were carried through the Scottish Parliament.

PERUGINO, PIETRO VANNUCCI (c. 1446–1523), Italian painter. In 1482 he painted the *Delivery of the Keys to St. Peter* in the *Sistine Chapel. The devotional warmth of his style created great demand for his religious pictures. His greatest work is the fresco of the *Crucifixion* in Sta Maria Maddalena dei Pazzi at Florence.

PESHITTA, The. The official text of the Bible in Syriac-speaking Christian lands from the early 5th cent. The NT may have been the work of *Rabbula, Bp. of Edessa 412–35, but was prob. begun earlier. It lacks Rev., 2 Pet., 2 and 3 Jn., and Jude. The origins of the OT are obscure, but in part it seems to be the work of Jews.

PETAVIUS, DIONYSIUS (1583–1652), Denis Pétau, *Jesuit historian and theologian. From 1618 he lived in Paris. His *Opus de Doctrina Temporum* (1627) was a fundamental contribution on ancient chronology. He also issued notable editions of the works of *Synesius (1612) and St. *Epiphanius (1622). As a dogmatic theologian he was one of the first to accept the idea of doctrinal development (here he influenced J. H. *Newman) and to concede the inadequacy of much patristic teaching judged by later standards.

PETER, St., Prince of the *Apostles. Acc. to Jn. (1: 35–42) he was brought to Christ by his brother *Andrew and given the name 'Cephas', the Aramaic equivalent of the Greek Peter (πέτρα, 'rock'); acc. to Mt. (4: 18–20) and Mk. (1: 16–18) they were called together. In all the lists of the Twelve [Apostles] Peter is named first. He is present on all three occasions when only a small 'inner group' is admitted, and he usually takes the lead as the mouthpiece of the Apostles. After his confession at *Caesarea Philippi that Jesus is the Christ, the Son of the living God, he receives the answer: 'Thou art Peter, and on this rock I will build my church', together with the promise of the power of binding and loosing (Mt. 16: 18 f.). (The precise interpretation of this passage has been the subject of much controversy.) His pre-eminence is again affirmed by the Lord at the *Last Supper (Lk. 22: 31 f.), but his boast that he will never leave Him is answered by Christ's prediction that before the end of the night he will deny Him thrice. Having followed the Lord to the court of the High Priest he is accused of being one of His followers; he three times denies that he knows Him, remembers His prediction, and repents bitterly (Mt. 26: 69–75). He goes to the Lord's sepulchre as soon as the women report that it is empty (Lk. 24: 12) and he is later favoured with a special appearance of the risen Christ (Lk. 24: 34). After the Ascension he immediately takes the lead of the Apostles and throughout the first half of Acts he appears as their head. He opens the Church to the Gentiles by admitting Cornelius (Acts 10: 1–11: 18) and his authority is evident at the Apostles' Council at Jerusalem (Acts 15: 7–11).

Of the later years of his apostolate outside Palestine, little is known. The tradition connecting him with Rome, however, is early and unrivalled. The later tradition attributing to him an episcopate of 25 years in Rome is much less well supported. His death is placed in the reign of *Nero (54–68), prob. in the persecution of 64. There are historical grounds for believing that his tomb in *St. Peter's, Rome, is authentic. The statement of *Papias that his memoirs lie behind the Gospel of St. *Mark (q.v.) is accepted by many scholars. For the Epistles, see *Peter, Epistles of*.

PETER, Acts of. An apocryphal book, written in Greek c. 150–200. The 'Martyrdom of Peter', which forms part of it, records the '*Quo Vadis?' incident and the crucifixion of St. *Peter head downwards.

PETER, Apocalypse of. This apocryphal apocalypse, dating from the early 2nd cent., describes how the Lord granted to the Apostles a vision of their brethren in the next world and of their rewards. Both *Clement of Alexandria and the *Muratorian Fragment account it Scripture.

PETER, Epistles of. Two NT Epistles are ascribed to St. *Peter.

The First Epistle was written to Christian communities in Asia Minor to encourage them under persecution. If the ascription to St. Peter is correct, it must have been written before his death, i.e. prob. c. 65. Its Petrine authorship has been questioned on the grounds that its literary style is not that of a Galilean fisherman; that passages in it reflect Pauline teaching; and that persecution of the Church in Asia Minor at so early a date is otherwise unattested. These objections, however, are not conclusive and critical opinion is still in the balance.

The main message of the Second Epistle is a warning against false and ungodly teachers. Though it professes to be written by St. Peter, there are various indications that it is of later date, and it was received into the *Canon with considerable hesitation. It is prob. to be dated c. 150.

PETER, Gospel of. An apocryphal Gospel of which the only surviving section was found at Akhmîm in Egypt in 1886–7. It seems to have been a largely legendary work, prob. written in Syria in the mid-2nd cent.

PETER, Liturgy of St. A Mass combining elements from the Byzantine and Roman rites which was prob. drawn up for the use of the Greek communities in Italy, but may have been put together only as a literary experiment.

PETER, Martyrdom of., and Patrimony of St. See *Peter, Acts of,* and *Patrimony of St. Peter.*

PETER, Preaching of. A Greek treatise purporting to be the work of St. *Peter, but prob. dating from the 2nd cent. Apparently intended for missionary propaganda, it emphasized the superiority of Christian monotheism to the beliefs of Greeks and Jews. Only fragments survive.

PETER OF ALCÁNTARA, St. (1499–1562), founder of the Spanish *Discalced Franciscans. He joined the *Observant Franciscans in 1515 and held high office. He realized his exalted ideals of austerity in a little convent at el Pedroso del Acfm, founded *c.* 1557, on which his congregation, the 'Alcantarines', were subsequently modelled. He was much sought after as a spiritual director, and was revered by St. *Teresa of Ávila. The relationship of his small *Tratado de la oración y meditación* (prob. *c.* 1556) to *Luis of Granada's *Libro de la oración y meditación* is disputed.

PETER OF ALEXANDRIA, St. (d. prob. 311), Bp. of *Alexandria from 300. He survived the persecution of *Diocletian and drew up rules for the readmission to the Church of those who had lapsed. When persecution began again in 306, he went into hiding and *Melitius claimed authority over Alexandria. Peter was beheaded in the persecution of Maximin.

PETER DE BRUYS (d. *c.* 1140), heretic. He rejected infant baptism, the Mass, church buildings, prayers for the dead, the veneration of the Cross, as well as large parts of the Bible and the authority of the Church. He was thrown into the flames at St.-Gilles, near Nîmes, by the people.

PETER OF CANDIA; PETER CANISIUS, St. See *Alexander V*; *Canisius, St. Peter.*

PETER THE CHANTER (d. 1197), theo-

logian. He was one of the most influential masters at *Paris in the late 12th cent. He concentrated on practical questions of ethics, and by his discussion of concrete cases for the guidance of confessors he contributed to the doctrine of circumstances to be observed in the administration of *penance.

PETER CELESTINE, St.; PETER CHRYSOLOGUS, St. See *Celestine V*; *Chrysologus, St. Peter.*

PETER CLAVIER, St. (1581–1654), 'Apostle of the Negroes'. A native of Catalonia, he landed in what is now Colombia in 1610 and at once began ministering to the slaves who were brought over in terrible conditions from W. Africa. Ordained priest in 1615, he is said to have baptized over 300,000 Negroes.

PETER COMESTOR (d. *c.* 1179), Biblical scholar. He was dean of the cathedral at Troyes, Chancellor of the University of *Paris, and in 1169 he joined the *Victorines. His *Historia Scholastica,* a continuous history from the Creation to the end of the period covered by Acts, uses the works of the Fathers and pagan authorities to fill the gaps in the Biblical narrative; it became the standard work on Biblical history in the Middle Ages.

PETER DAMIAN, St. (1007–72), reformer and '*Doctor of the Church'. Born of poor parents at *Ravenna, in 1035 he entered the *Benedictine hermitage of Fonte Avella and *c.* 1043 he was chosen prior. He was made Cardinal Bishop of Ostia in 1057, and as such took a prominent part in the work of ecclesiastical reform. Both in his preaching and in his numerous writings he enjoined strict discipline and denounced immorality and simony. He also treated of doctrinal matters, defending the validity of sacraments administered by simoniacal priests at a time when the teaching of the Church on this point was still in flux.

PETER THE FULLER (d. 488), *Monophysite. Acc. to an uncertain tradition, he was a monk at the convent of the *Acoemetae at *Constantinople, where he practised as a fuller. After his expulsion, with the backing of the Emp. *Zeno, he became Patr. of *Antioch in 470. *Gennadius, Patr. of Constantinople, obtained a decree of exile against him, but in 482 he assented to Zeno's '*Henoticon' and regained his see. He is remembered for his addition to the *Trisagion of the Monophysite clause 'who was crucified for us'.

PETER GONZÁLES, St. See *Elmo, St.*

PETER THE HERMIT (1050?–1115). He was one of the most eloquent preachers of the First *Crusade and in 1096 he led a party of country folk as far as Civitot, where most of them were killed by the Turks. He then joined the main army under *Godfrey of Bouillon and entered *Jerusalem. On his return to Europe he became prior of an *Augustinian monastery. After his death he became the hero of many legends.

PETER LOMBARD (*c.* 1100–60), the 'Master of the Sentences'. About 1134 he went to *Paris, where he taught at the Cathedral School. In 1148 he opposed *Gilbert de la Porrée at the Council of Reims, and in 1159 he was appointed Bp. of Paris. His 'Sentences', prob. written 1155–8, are divided into four books on (1) the Trinity, (2) the Creation and Sin, (3) the Incarnation and the Virtues, and (4) the Sacraments and the Four Last Things. Though the orthodoxy of the work was challenged, after 1215 it became the standard textbook of Catholic theology, to be superseded only by St. *Thomas Aquinas's *Summa.*

PETER MARTYR, St. (*c.* 1200–52), *Inquisitor. Born at *Verona (hence known also as **Veronensis**) of parents of the *Cathari sect, he was received into the *Dominican Order by St. *Dominic himself in 1221. In 1251 he was appointed Inquisitor for N. Italy. He gained a reputation as a preacher and miracle-worker and reconciled large numbers of Cathari. He was attacked by assassins, one of whom clove his head with an axe.

PETER MARTYR (1500–62), an Anglicized form of 'Pietro Martire Vermigli', Reformer. Named after St. *Peter Martyr (see previous entry), he joined the *Augustinians and in 1533 became prior of a house in Naples. He was much impressed by reading works of M. *Bucer and H. *Zwingli; sympathy with the Reformers led to accusations of error, and in 1542 he was forced to flee from Italy. In 1547 he came to England

at T. *Cranmer's invitation and became Regius Professor of Divinity at Oxford. He took part in a disputation on the Eucharist in 1549, was consulted over the BCP of 1552, and was one of the commissioners for the reform of canon law. On *Mary's accession he was imprisoned, but he was soon allowed to go to Strasburg.

PETER MOGILA. See *Mogila, Peter.*

PETER MONGO (d. 490), *Monophysite Patr. of *Alexandria. In 477 he was elected successor to *Timothy Aelurus. The Emp. *Zeno forced him to abandon his see temporarily, but he was restored on accepting the '*Henoticon'. His attempts at compromise maintained peaceful relations with Constantinople during the patriarchate of Acacius (d. 489).

PETER NOLASCO, St. (*c.* 1189–*c.* 1256), *Mercedarian. The facts of his life are contested. He is usually regarded as the joint founder, with St. *Raymond of Peñafort, of the Order of Mercedarians (q.v.). He redeemed 400 captives on a journey to Valencia and Granada, and twice went to Africa as ransomer.

PETER'S PENCE, also 'Rome-Scot'. An ecclesiastical tax formerly paid in England to the Pope. It was abolished in 1534.

PETER OF TARANTAISE, St. (d. 1175), from 1142 Abp. of Tarantaise (Moutiers, in Savoy). He had been a *Cistercian monk, and he thoroughly reformed his diocese. He stood high in the confidence of Popes and was commissioned to reconcile Prince Henry (later Henry II) of England and Louis VII of France.

PETER THE VENERABLE (*c.* 1092–1156), Abbot of *Cluny from 1122. Against opposition he carried through important reforms, esp. in the financial and educational spheres. His interest in the pursuit of studies at Cluny brought him into conflict with St. *Bernard, who wanted to see the monastic life confined to prayer and manual work. In 1130 Peter supported Innocent II against the antipope Anacletus II, himself a Cluniac monk, and in 1140 he gave shelter to *Abelard. He had the *Koran translated into Latin and wrote against *Islam. His other works include treatises against *Peter de Bruys and against the Jews, sermons, and some poems. Among his contemporaries he was venerated for his moderation and gentleness, but in the eyes of posterity he has been eclipsed by St Bernard.

PETER OF VERONA, St. See *Peter Martyr, St.*

PETERBOROUGH. At a Saxon village on the site a monastery was established *c.* 655. After the church had been destroyed by the Danes, it was rebuilt *c.* 970 by *Ethelwold, Bp. of Winchester, who dedicated it to St. *Peter; hence the village came to be called 'Peterborough'. This church having been burnt in 1116, the foundations of a new one were laid the following year; it was completed in 1237, and in 1541 it became the cathedral of the newly constituted diocese.

PETITE ÉGLISE. The body of French Catholics who refused to recognize the *Concordat of 1801 and separated themselves from the communion of the Pope. Their last priest died in 1847 and by 1900 the schism had practically ceased to exist.

PETRARCH, FRANCESCO (1304–74), Italian poet and humanist. In 1326 he received *minor orders. His poems on Laura (collected in the *Canzoniere*) and his epic *Africa* on Scipio Africanus won him the poet's crown in 1341. In 1347 he joined the short-lived republican movement of Cola di *Rienzo. In the following years he was employed on various political embassies. His religious nature, which was often in conflict with the sensuousness of the fame-loving poet and the passion of the scholar for pagan culture, found expression in several Latin treatises. His last great poetical work, the *Trionfi*, celebrates in allegorical form the triumph of the Divine over all things and the ultimate redemption of man from the dominion of the senses.

PETRI, OLAUS (1493–1552), Swedish Reformer. He studied at *Wittenberg and returned to Sweden imbued with strict *Lutheran views. Gaining the favour of Gustavus Vasa, by whom he was later made chancellor (1531), he became the leading exponent of doctrinal change in Sweden.

PETROBRUSIANS. The followers of *Peter de Bruys (q.v.).

PETROCK, St. (6th cent.), also 'Pedrog', Cornish saint. He is said to have been the son of a Welsh chieftain who, after studying in Ireland, made his way to Cornwall and founded monasteries at Padstow and Bodmin.

PETRONIUS, St. (5th cent.), Bp. of *Bologna from *c.* 432. He appears to have made a pilgrimage to Palestine in early life and when he became bishop to have erected a church at Bologna modelled on the *Constantinian buildings in *Jerusalem. Various writings have been attributed to him, mostly incorrectly.

PEW. At first the customary postures for worship were standing and kneeling, and no seats were provided for the congregation. Later, as a concession to the infirm, stone seats were attached to the walls of naves. By the end of the 13th cent. many English churches seem to have been equipped with fixed wooden benches, known as pews. They were sometimes elaborately carved at the ends and back.

PFAFF FRAGMENTS OF IRENAEUS. Four fragments published in 1713 by C. M. Pfaff, who claimed that he had found them in the Turin library and attributed them to *Irenaeus. A. *Harnack showed them to be a fabrication of Pfaff himself.

PFLUG, JULIUS VON (1499–1564), Bp. of Naumburg. His humanistic sympathies made him eager for peace with the Protestants, and to this end he took part in several conferences. He was ready to tolerate a married clergy and Communion in both kinds. The 'Interim of *Augsburg' (1548; q.v.) was largely Pflug's work.

PHANAR, The. The official residence and court of the *Oecumenical Patriarch at *Constantinople.

PHARISEES (Heb. for 'separated ones'). A Jewish religious party mentioned by *Josephus and in the NT. Unlike the *Sadducees, who tried to apply the *Mosaic Law precisely as it was given, the Pharisees allowed some interpretation of it to make it more applicable to different situations, and they regarded these oral interpretations as of the same level of importance as the Law itself. In the Gospels they appear as the chief opponents of Christ, who in turn denounced their purely external observance of the Law, their multitude of formalistic precepts, and their self-righteousness. They seem to have been less hostile than the Sadducees to the nascent Church, with whom they shared belief in the resurrection. After the fall of *Jerusalem (A.D. 70) they disappear from history.

PHELONION. The E. form of the *chasuble.

PHENOMENOLOGY, literally 'the science of phenomena'. In modern times the term has been used mainly of the philosophical doctrines of Edmund Husserl (1859–1938) and his school. Acc. to Husserl, phenomenology is a descriptive science concerned with the discovery and analysis of essences and essential meanings. It was the most influential movement in German philosophy in the period 1910–33; it fell into disrepute under the Nazis but has since enjoyed renewed favour. See also *Existentialism*.

PHILADELPHIA. A city in the Roman province of Asia. It was the seat of one of the '*Seven Churches' addressed in Rev., where it is commended for its faithfulness (3: 7–13).

PHILADELPHIANS. A 17th-cent. sect. John Pordage (1607–81), rector of Bradfield, Berks., gathered round him a group of followers who shared his enthusiasm for J. *Boehme; the group was organized in 1670 as the Philadelphian Society for the Advancement of Piety and Divine Philosophy. They professed a kind of nature pantheism, imbued with esoteric and pseudo-mystical teaching, and held that their souls were immediately illuminated by the Holy Spirit.

PHILARET, THEODORE NIKITICH ROMANOV (*c.* 1553–1633), Patr. of Moscow from 1619 and founder of the Romanov dynasty. His son Michael was elected Tsar in 1613, but Philaret, who had been imprisoned by the Poles in 1610, was not freed until 1619; he then virtually ruled Russia. He was a zealous reformer and encouraged the study of theology.

PHILARET DROZDOV (1782–1867), Russian theologian and Metropolitan of Moscow from 1826. He was an exemplary bishop and exercised a profound influence in Church and State. The best-known of his writings is a Christian Catechism, publd. in 1823.

PHILASTER, St. (d. *c.* 397), more correctly 'Filaster', Bp. of Brescia. About 385 he wrote a treatise designed to refute 28 Jewish and 128 Christian heresies. The work suffers from clumsy arrangement and lack of proportion, but it seems to have filled a need in the W., and it was used by St. *Augustine.

PHILEAS, St. (d. *c.* 307), Bp. of Thmuis in Lower Egypt. He was imprisoned, tried before the prefect, and executed at *Alexandria. A letter to his flock from his dungeon (in *Eusebius) and the *acta* of his trial survive.

PHILEMON. The recipient of St. *Paul's brief epistle of that name. He was a Christian of Colossae or the neighbourhood, whose slave, *Onesimus, had run away and had met Paul. Paul sent Onesimus back to his master with this letter, which is a plea for his forgiveness.

PHILIBERT, St. (d. 684), founder and abbot of *Jumièges. He was abbot of Rebais, near Meaux, but the refractory character of his monks led him to retire to Neustria, where he founded the abbey of Jumièges on land given him by Clovis II. In 674 his reproof of the Mayor of the Palace led to his expulsion. He founded another monastery on the island of Her (now Noirmoutier).

PHILIPS IN THE NT. (1) PHILIP THE APOSTLE. Acc. to Jn. (6: 7) at the feeding of the 5,000 he observed that 200 pennyworth of bread would not provide even a scanty meal; when some Greeks wished to see Jesus, they approached Philip, who was from *Bethsaida of Galilee (Jn. 12: 20 f.), and he later asked the Lord, 'Show us the Father' (Jn. 14: 8). His subsequent career is obscure; acc. to some traditions he was crucified.

(2) PHILIP THE EVANGELIST was one of the Seven '*Deacons' whose appointment is recorded in Acts 6. He preached in Samaria, baptized an Ethiopian eunuch (Acts 8), and later entertained St. *Paul at Caesarea (Acts 21: 8).

(3) PHILIP THE TETRARCH. One of the

sons of *Herod the Great, he was ruler from 4 B.C to A.D. 34 of the 'region of Ituraea and Trachonitis' (Lk. 3: 1).

PHILIP, Gospel of. One of the *Gnostic treatises found at *Nag Hammadi. It is a series of reflections on the quest for salvation; it contains no narrative and only a few incidents or sayings attributed to Christ.

PHILIP THE ARABIAN, Roman Emperor 244–9. *Eusebius records that he was a Christian and gives an edifying story of his submission to a bishop. He was prob. commended by Christian writers simply because they detested his rival *Decius.

PHILIP II (1527–98), King of Spain from 1556. His marriage in 1554 to *Mary Tudor (d. 1558) gave him brief influence in England. His chief objective was the defence of Catholicism. In Spain he suppressed *Lutheranism, largely through the *Inquisition, but in the Low Countries he lost the northern provinces in his efforts to uproot *Calvinism. His attempts to regain England for Catholicism in *Elizabeth I's reign culminated in the defeat of the Armada (1588) and the decline of Spanish sea power.

PHILIP (1504–67), Landgraf of Hesse. The most able of the German princes who supported M. *Luther, he introduced the Reformation in Hesse, and in 1527 he founded the University of *Marburg as a school for Protestant theologians. Though he failed to bring about an understanding between Luther and H. *Zwingli, he was more successful in uniting the Protestant princes: in 1531 the *Schmalkaldic League was established. His position was impaired by a bigamous marriage in 1540, and he made peace with the Emperor.

PHILIP NERI, St. (1515–95), the 'Apostle of Rome'. Going to Rome in 1533, he devoted himself to works of charity and spent nights in prayer in the *catacombs; in 1544 he experienced an ecstasy which is believed miraculously to have enlarged his heart. After ordination, he went in 1551 to live in a community of priests at San Girolamo, where his confessional soon became the centre of his apostolate. He also held spiritual conferences, out of which developed the Congregation of the Oratory (see *Oratorians*). He was noted for his gentleness

and gaiety.

PHILIP SIDETES (5th cent.), historian. A native of Side, in Pamphylia, he went to *Constantinople, where he went an unsuccessful candidate for the patriarchate. His 'Christian History' seems to have covered the period from the Creation to A.D. 430; only fragments remain, including the assertion that *Papias had stated that St. *John and his brother *James had been martyred by the Jews.

PHILIPPIANS, Epistle to the. This NT letter is addressed by St. *Paul to the Christian community at Philippi in Macedonia, the first of the Churches which he had founded in Europe. Its authenticity is solidly attested in antiquity and almost unanimously accepted by modern scholars. It was prob. written during the later part of Paul's captivity in Rome.

After thanking the Philippians for their assistance, Paul tells them of the success of his preaching in captivity and exhorts them to charity, self-discipline, and humility. He warns them against Judaizers and ends with a doxology and salutations. Despite its personal character, the Epistle contains a Christological passage (2: 5–11) of great doctrinal importance.

PHILIPPISTS. The followers of the *Lutheran theologian Philip *Melanchthon.

PHILIP'S LENT, St. In the E. Church the period from 15 Nov. to 24 Dec., the counterpart of *Advent in the W. Church.

PHILLIMORE, ROBERT JOSEPH (1810–85), English judge. He was *Dean of Arches from 1867 to 1875. In 1868 he gave judgement in the case against A. H. *Mackonochie, declaring the legality of *altar lights and of kneeling during the prayer of consecration. His *Ecclesiastical Law of the Church of England* (1873) was a standard work.

PHILLIPPS MANUSCRIPTS, The. A famous collection of MSS. assembled at Cheltenham by the antiquary Sir Thomas Phillipps (1792–1872). The MSS. are gradually being sold; many are now in Berlin. They included the *Mommsen Catalogue.

PHILLPOTTS, HENRY (1778–1869), Bp.

of *Exeter from 1830. An old-fashioned High Churchman, he was in sympathy with the *Oxford Movement. His refusal to institute G. C. *Gorham to the living of Brampford Speke, on the grounds of his denial of baptismal regeneration, gave rise to a famous ecclesiastical lawsuit.

PHILO (*c*. 20 B.C.–*c*. A.D. 50), Jewish thinker and exegete. A member of a prosperous priestly family in *Alexandria, Philo was the foremost figure among the Hellenistic Jews and a fertile author. In religious outlook he was essentially an eclectic; he reproduced a variety of doctrines without welding them into a harmonious whole. His most influential achievement was his development of the *allegorical interpretation of Scripture which enabled him to discover much of Greek philosophy in the OT. Of special interest for Christian theology is the central place which he accorded in his system to the *Logos, who was at once the creative power which orders the world and the intermediary through whom men know God. As a spiritual teacher Philo stands in the tradition of the philosophical mystics.

PHILOCALIA. (1) The *Philocalia* of *Origen is an anthology from his writings compiled by St. *Basil the Great and St. *Gregory Nazianzus in 358–9. (2) The *Philocalia* of Sts. Macarius Notaras and *Nicodemus of the Holy Mountain (1782) is a collection of ascetical and mystical writings dating from the 4th to the 15th cent., dealing with the teaching of *Hesychasm.

PHILOCALIAN CALENDAR, The. An alternative name for the '*Liberian Catalogue'.

PHILOMENA, St. In 1802 a *loculus* was found in one of the *catacombs, closed with three tiles on which were painted the letters LUMENA/PAX TE/CUM FI, which, when rearranged, read 'Pax tecum Filumena'. The bones found in the tomb were taken to be those of a martyred Christian virgin, who was for a time widely venerated.

PHILOPATRIS. A Greek dialogue attacking Christianity. It purports to be the work of *Lucian of Samosata, but prob. dates from the 10th cent.

PHILOSOPHY OF RELIGION. The idea of the philosophy of religion as a distinct discipline was the creation of the *Enlightenment. Its aim is the philosophical investigation of the group of phenomena covered by the terms 'religion' and 'religious experience'. It studies the essence, content, origin, and, to some extent, the value of religion as a factor in human life, and examines the claims of religion to be true. The '*natural theology' of earlier writers could be considered as philosophy of religion in its broadest sense, but whereas natural theology was regarded as a prelude to revealed theology, the philosophy of religion takes no cognizance of this distinction.

PHILOSTORGIUS (*c*. 368–*c*. 439), *Arian historian. His 'History of the Church' (from *c*. 300 to 430) survives only in fragments and in an epitome by *Photius. It is inaccurate and biased, but what survives is of value through its use of excellent sources and for its description of some of the chief Arian personalities.

PHILOXENIAN VERSION OF THE NT. The Syriac version of the NT made from the Greek in 508 for *Philoxenus by Polycarp, a *chorepiscopus. It was drastically revised in 616 by Thomas Harkel and for the most part the original text has been lost.

PHILOXENUS (*c*. 440–523), Bp. of Mabbug (Hierapolis in Syria) from 485. Along with his contemporary *Severus, he was one of the leading thinkers and writers of the nascent *Monophysite Church. See also the preceding entry.

PHILPOT, JOHN (1516–55), Reformation divine. At an unkown date under *Edward VI (1547–53) he became Archdeacon of *Winchester. An attack on *Transubstantiation in the first Convocation of *Mary's reign (1553) was followed by imprisonment. He was burnt at *Smithfield.

PHOCAS, St. A bishop of Sinope in Pontus of this name was martyred by suffocation in a bath in 117. He is frequently confused with 'St. Phocas the Gardener', who is said to have been martyred in the *Diocletianic Persecution, and with St. Phocas of Antioch. When the various traditions had been fused, the cult of St. Phocas became popular, esp. among seafaring people.

PHOCYLIDES, Pseudo-. The name given to the author of 230 hexameters inserted into the work of Phocylides of Miletus (6th cent. B.C.). The author may have been a Christian; the work could have been written at any time up to *c.* A.D. 150.

PHOEBADIUS, St. (d. *c.* 395), Bp. of Agen in S. France. He opposed *Arianism and attacked the *Sirmian formula of 357 in his *Liber contra Arianos*. In 359 he signed the formula of *Ariminum but denounced the Council when he realized its import.

PHOENIX. A gorgeously arrayed mythical bird, which was the subject of numerous legends in antiquity. Acc. to one of these, after living for five or six hundred years it burnt itself to ashes and then came back to life with renewed youth. From early times Christian writers regarded it as an image of the Resurrection.

PHOS HILARON. In the E. Church, the hymn sung at 'Hesperinos' (the counterpart of the W. *Vespers). It is widely known in the English translation of J. *Keble ('Hail! gladdening Light').

PHOTINUS (4th cent.), heretic. He became Bp. of Sirmium *c.* 344, but was deposed and exiled in 351. None of his writings has survived and his doctrine is variously described by his detractors; it was clearly a form of *Sabellianism.

PHOTIUS (*c.* 810–*c.* 895), Patr. of *Constantinople. When the Emp. Michael III deposed the Patr. Ignatius in 858, Photius was appointed his successor. On Ignatius's refusal to abdicate, Michael and Photius sent an embassy to Pope *Nicholas I. Although Nicholas's delegates took part in the Synod at Constantinople in 861 which deposed Ignatius, at a Synod in Rome in 863 Nicholas annulled the proceedings and declared Ignatius Patriarch and Photius deposed. In 867 Photius in an encyclical denounced the presence of Latin missionaries in *Bulgaria and gave an exposition of his objections to the *Filioque clause in the Creed. Also in 867 a Council at Constantinople pronounced sentence of deposition against the Pope. With the accession of the Emp. Basil (867), the situation changed. Ignatius was reinstated, and Photius was restored only after his death (877). At a Council

in Constantinople in 879–80 the Papal legates seem to have approved Photius, but he was deposed when *Leo VI became Emperor in 886. He died at the convent of Armeniaki towards the end of the 9th cent.

Though the Photian schism was only one of many similar episodes in the history of the relations of the Greek and Latin Churches, it accentuated the conflict between the Roman claim to be the centre of unity for Christendom and the Greek conception of five patriarchates of almost equal status. He was also the first theologian to accuse Rome of innovating in the matter of the Filioque. His main work, the *Bibliotheca* or *Myriobiblion*, is a description of several hundred books, often with exhaustive analyses and copious extracts; many of the works mentioned in it are now lost.

PHYLACTERY. A small leather case containing vellum strips inscribed with four passages from the OT. From pre-Christian times orthodox Jews have worn them on the forehead and arm during morning prayer on most days of the year to remind them of their obligation to keep the Law.

'PIA DESIDERIA'. P. J. *Spener's book which aimed at fostering a religious revival in German Protestantism and thus created the *Pietist Movement. It was written in German and published in 1675.

PIARISTS. An order of Clerks Regular for the education of the young, so called from the last word of their Latin designation. They were founded in 1597 by St. *Joseph Calasanctius, who in that year opened the first free elementary boys' school in Europe to educate the children at large on the streets of Rome. Its teachers were recognized as a congregation in 1617 and made an order in 1621.

PICA. See *Pie*.

PICO DELLA MIRANDOLA, GIOVANNI (1463–94), Italian nobleman, scholar, and mystical writer. Besides being a good classical scholar, he knew Hebrew, Aramaic, and Arabic; and he was the first to seek in the *Cabbala a clue to the Christian mysteries.

PIE, or PICA. The name given in England in the 15th cent. to the book of directions for saying the services. In the BCP ('Concerning the Services of the Church') it is censured for 'the number and hardness of its rules'.

PIETÀ. A representation of the BVM lamenting over the dead body of Christ, which she holds on her knees.

PIETISM. A movement in the German *Lutheran Church, started by P. J. *Spener to infuse new life into the official Protestantism of the time. He put forward proposals for restoring religion in his *Pia Desideria* (1675), instituted devotional circles for prayer and Bible reading, and proclaimed the universal priesthood of all the faithful, without, however, intending to separate from the Church. The movement quickly won support, but a clash with the orthodox became inevitable when A. H. *Francke (d. 1727) attacked the Leipzig theologians, demanding that lectures be turned into devotional meetings and condemning wholesale philosophy, doctrine, and homiletics. The university at Halle, founded in 1694, was for some time the centre of the movement, which lasted to the 20th cent.

PIGHI, ALBERT (*c.* 1490–1542), Dutch theologian. Called to Rome in 1523, he wrote on the main issues of the time. His principal work, *Hierarchiae Ecclesiasticae Assertio* (1538), is an elaborate defence of *tradition as a source of Christian truth coordinate with Scripture.

PILATE, PONTIUS. The governor ('procurator') of Judaea from A.D. 26 to 36 under whom Christ was crucified.

PILATE, Acts of. An apocryphal work giving an account of the trial, death, and resurrection of Christ. In some MSS. an independent treatise on the *Descent of Christ into Hades is attached to it; and the two together are sometimes known as the 'Gospel of *Nicodemus'. The first part, the 'Acts' proper, is prob. not earlier than the 4th cent. The second part purports to have been written by the sons of *Simeon. The work forms the basis of the medieval play-cycle on the *Harrowing of Hell and of the legends of St. *Joseph of Arimathaea and the Holy *Grail.

PILGRIM FATHERS, The. The English founders of the colony of Plymouth, Mass., who sailed from Holland and England in the *Mayflower* in 1620. The title is comparatively modern.

PILGRIMAGES. Journeys to holy places undertaken from motives of devotion in order to obtain supernatural help or as acts of penance or thanksgiving. The practice of visiting the places connected with Christ's life on earth received a strong impetus from the visit of the Empress *Helena to *Jerusalem (326). Almost on a footing with pilgrimages to Palestine were those to Rome to visit the tombs of the Apostles *Peter and *Paul. From the 8th cent. the practice of imposing a pilgrimage in place of a public *penance added to the number of pilgrims, who, in the Middle Ages, were organized on a grand scale. In modern times *Lourdes has acquired unrivalled fame as a place of pilgrimage.

PILGRIMAGE OF GRACE, The. A series of risings in N. England in 1536–7. The religious element varied. Mixed grievances culminated in insurrection because of widespread hatred of T. *Cromwell and of government innovations in ecclesiastical matters (esp. the *dissolution of the lesser monasteries, and the attacks on the Sacraments and saints' days in the *Ten Articles). Over 200 rebels were hanged, incl. R. *Aske, the leader of the Yorkshire rebellion.

PILGRIM'S PROGRESS, The. The first part of J. *Bunyan's masterpiece was prob. written during his second imprisonment at Bedford gaol in 1676; it was published in 1678. The second part did not appear until 1684. The persons and incidents encountered by Christian in his journey from the 'City of Destruction' to the 'Heavenly City'—'Mr Worldly-Wiseman', 'Greatheart', the 'Slough of Despond', and the 'House Beautiful'—have become part of the language of religion in England.

PILKINGTON, JAMES (*c.* 1520–76), Bp. of *Durham from 1560. He returned from the Continent on *Mary's death in 1558, took a prominent part in the revision of the BCP, and upheld the tenets of the Reformation in Cambridge. At Durham his support for the Protestant cause provoked hostility.

PILLAR SAINTS. See *Stylites*.

PIONIUS, St. (d. 250), martyr. He was

executed at Smyrna during the *Decian persecution; the *Acta* describing his death are reliable documents. He was responsible for the preservation of the *Martyrium Polycarpi*.

PIRCKHEIMER, WILLIBALD (1470–1530), German humanist. In 1497 he became a town councillor at Nuremberg, where his house was a centre of learning. At the beginning of the Reformation he favoured M. *Luther, whose chief opponent, J. *Eck, he attacked in *Eccius Dedolatus*. But he regretted Luther's break with the Church, and in 1521 he asked to be absolved from the ban of excommunication which he had incurred as a follower of the Reformer.

PIRMINIUS, St. (d. 753), perhaps 'Priminius', first abbot of *Reichenau. With the protection of *Charles Martel, he founded Reichenau (724) and other monasteries among the Alamanni in Baden and in Alsace. His *Scarapsus* (or *Dicta Pirminii*) is of interest as the earliest document containing the *Apostles' Creed in its present form.

PISA, Council of. The Council was convoked by the cardinals in 1409 to end the *Great Schism which had divided W. Christendom since 1378. It deposed both Popes *Benedict XIII and Gregory XII and elected a third, who took the name *Alexander V. Its authority has been much discussed. Though it did not end the Schism, it paved the way for the solution found at the Council of *Constance (1417).

PISCINA (Lat., 'basin'). A niche in a wall, usually on the S. side of the altar, for the *ablutions of the priest's hands and of the *chalice and *paten at Mass. It is usually furnished with a shelf for the cruets and a drain connected with the earth to receive the water used for these ceremonies.

PISGAH. The mountain or mountain range E. of the R. *Jordan where *Moses was granted a sight of the Holy Land and the promise made that his descendants would possess it (Deut. 34: 1–4)

PISTIS SOPHIA. A 3rd-cent. work of Egyptian origin which purports to record instructions given by Christ to certain disciples at the end of a 12-year sojourn on earth after the Resurrection. With fantastic imagery it relates the salvation of the personified 'Pistis Sophia' (i.e. 'Faith-Wisdom') from a demon named 'Self-Will'.

PISTOIA, Synod of (1786). The Synod met under the presidency of Scipio de' *Ricci, Bp. of Pistoia-Prato. It passed a number of *Gallican measures, and also decreed alterations in religious practice, e.g. the end of the use of Latin in Church services. *Pius VI's bull '*Auctorem Fidei' (1794) condemned 85 of the Pistoian articles.

PITOU, PIERRE (1539–96), theologian. Brought up as a *Calvinist, he became a RC in 1573. In his treatise *Les Libertés de l'Église gallicane* (1594) the leading principles of *Gallicanism were formulated for the first time.

PITRA, JEAN BAPTISTE FRANÇOIS (1812–89), *Benedictine scholar. Professed at *Solesmes in 1843, he travelled widely in search of MSS., and in 1869 he was appointed Librarian of the *Vatican. His publications include *Spicilegium Solesmense* (1852–8) and *Analecta Sacra* (1876–91), both containing unpublished patristic texts.

PIUS I, St. (d. c. 154), Bp. of Rome from c. 140. Acc. to the *Muratorian Canon, he was the brother of *Hermas. Nothing certain is known of his pontificate.

PIUS II (1405–64), Pope from 1458. Aeneas Sylvius or Enea Silvio de' Piccolomini was a leading humanist. At the Council of *Basle he supported the antipope Felix V against *Eugenius IV, and he advocated the *Conciliar Theory in his *Libellus Dialogorum de Concilii Auctoritate* (1440). In 1445 he was reconciled to Eugenius; he reformed his moral life and was ordained in 1446. From the fall of *Constantinople in 1453 he worked for a *Crusade, and as Pope he subordinated all other interests to the war against the Turks. In his bull 'Execrabilis' (1460) he condemned the practice of appealing to a General Council.

PIUS IV (1499–1565), Pope from 1559. His greatest achievement was prob. the reassembling and successful conclusion of the Council of *Trent (1562–3), whose decrees he began to execute. He published a new *Index in 1564, imposed the 'Professio Fidei Tridentina' on all holders of ecclesiastical office, and reformed the *Sacred College.

PIUS V, St. (1504–72), Pope from 1566. He entered the *Dominican Order at the age of 14, and as Pope he continued to observe the ascetical practices of the religious life. He compelled bishops and clergy to accept the recommendations of the Council of *Trent and he reformed the *Breviary (1568) and *Missal (1570). In his struggle against the spread of the Reformation he made successful use of the *Inquisition in Spain and Italy, but his excommunication of Queen *Elizabeth I in 1570 only aggravated the position of RCs in England. The Turks were defeated by the combined Papal, Spanish, and Venetian fleets at the Battle of *Lepanto in 1571.

PIUS VI (1717–99), Pope from 1775. In his reign Papal prestige was at a low ebb. *Febronian ideas were put into effect by Joseph II (see *Josephinism*), and a visit of the Pope to Vienna in 1782 was without result. In 1786 similar doctrines were adopted at the Synod of *Pistoia; 85 of the Pistoian articles were condemned by Pius in 1794. In 1791 he condemned the *Civil Constitution of the Clergy as schismatical and heretical and suspended all priests and prelates who had taken the civil oath; France then annexed the Papal territories of *Avignon and the Venaissin. Napoleon subsequently occupied the States of the Church; the occupation was ended only by the surrender of territory and valuables. Pius died a prisoner at Valence.

PIUS VII (1740–1823), Pope from 1800. By the *Concordat of 1801 Catholicism was restored in France, but the success of the arrangement was vitiated by the *Organic Articles, against which the Pope protested in vain. In 1808 a French army entered Rome. Pius became a prisoner, and in 1809 the States of the Church were incorporated into the French Empire. Under pressure Pius made extensive concessions to Napoleon at Fontainebleau in 1813, but he revoked them two months later. After Napoleon's fall he returned to Rome in 1814 and in the same year he re-established the *Jesuit Order. The Congress of Vienna (1815) restored the States of the Church, and new concordats were concluded with various countries in the following years.

PIUS IX (1792–1878), Pope from 1846. His temporal power gradually decreased until, after the seizure of Rome by Victor Emman-

uel in 1870, the Papacy was virtually deprived of all temporal sovereignty by the Law of *Guarantees (1871). There were, however, spiritual and ecclesiastical achievements. New dioceses and missionary centres were created and the hierarchy was restored in England (1850) and Holland (1853). Catholic devotion was stimulated by the definition of the doctrine of the *Immaculate Conception of the BVM in 1854. The most important event of his reign was the definition of Papal Infallibility by the First *Vatican Council of 1869–70.

PIUS X, St. (1835–1914), Pope from 1903. From the beginning it was clear that he wished to be a religious rather than a political Pope. When the French Government effected the separation of Church and State in 1905, Pius secured the independence of the Church in France from State interference at the price of material ruin (1906). In 1907 he condemned *Modernism. He undertook various reforms, including the codification of *canon law (promulgated by *Benedict XV in 1917), *Breviary revision, and the restoration of *plainsong to its traditional place in the liturgy. His recommendation of daily Communion in 1905 laid the foundation of the modern *Liturgical Movement.

PIUS XI (1857–1939), Pope from 1922. Achille Ambrogio Damiano Ratti made 'the restoration of all things in Christ' the chief object of his pontificate. To this end he directed his great encyclicals, of which the best-known is '*Quadragesimo Anno' (1931) on social problems. The most important political event of his reign was the *Lateran Treaty of 1929 (q.v.). His last years were overshadowed by the development of events in Europe.

PIUS XII (1876–1958) Pope from 1939. Eugenio Pacelli entered the Papal Secretariat of State in 1901; in 1920 he became Nuncio in Berlin, and in 1930 Papal Secretary of State. He was elected Pope 6 months before the outbreak of the Second World War. His alleged 'silence' in the face of Nazi atrocities has been the subject of criticism; his experience in dealing with the German Government had prob. convinced him that a public stand would provoke worse persecution. Throughout the War (1939–45) he laboured to relieve distress, esp. among prisoners.

His encyclical 'Mediator Dei' (1947) expressed sympathy with the desire to use the vernacular in the liturgy and gave conditional support to the *Liturgical Movement. In 1951 he restored the *Paschal Vigil Service and in the following years he reordered the entire *Holy Week liturgy. In 1953 he standardized the relaxations in the *Eucharistic Fast which had been introduced during the War and in 1957 he permitted further relaxations which made possible the widespread introduction of *Evening Masses. Other events of his pontificate include the definition of the doctrine of the *Assumption of the BVM (1950).

PLACEBO (Lat., 'I will please'). A traditional title for the *Vespers of the Dead, so called from the word with which it used to open.

PLACET. See *Exequatur*.

PLAINSONG. The traditional music of the Latin rite, generally known as Gregorian chant, after St. *Gregory the Great (d. 604), though his exact share, if any, in its codification is disputed.

Plainsong differs from modern music in that it is monodic; it is purely vocal and needs no instrumental accompaniment, though this has often been used; its scales or modes run from D, E, F, and G, the only accidental being a flattened B; and it is printed in square notes on a staff of 4 lines, after 14th-cent. models.

By 1600 or earlier the chant and its execution had reached a low level of decadence. In the second half of the 19th cent. serious work on the restoration of the authentic texts was initiated; it was largely carried out by the Benedictines of *Solesmes. Many transcriptions to English words have been made.

PLANETA. An alternative name for the *chasuble.

PLANTIN, CHRISTOPHER (*c.* 1520–89), printer. Brought up in France, in 1548 he settled in Antwerp, where he soon built up the largest printing and publishing business in Europe. His most celebrated production was the Antwerp *Polyglot Bible (1569–72). He and his successors printed a large number of editions of the *Missal, *Breviary, and other liturgical books, in virtue of a monopoly granted to him within the

dominions of the king of Spain.

PLATINA, BARTOLOMEO (1421–81), Italian humanist. While *Vatican librarian, he compiled his 'Lives of the Popes' (1479). The juxtaposition of a reference to Halley's comet and mention of the prayers and curses of *Callistus III against the Turks gave rise to the fable that the Pope had excommunicated the comet.

PLATO (427–347 B.C.), Greek philosopher. He was a pupil of Socrates. After his master's execution (399), he left Athens. Some time after 388 he returned and established a school on the outskirts of the city near the grove sacred to Academus (hence the 'Academy'). Apart from a brief interlude instructing a youthful tyrant of Syracuse, he seems to have spent the last 40 years of his life at the Academy.

With the exception of a small collection of Letters, Plato's writings are in the form of Dialogues. Socrates is often the main speaker, with various critics or pupils, after whom the different Dialogues are named, taking part in the discussion. It is uncertain how far the speeches represent the real or supposed teaching of the interlocutors, and how far they voice Plato's own beliefs.

In the earlier Dialogues the main emphasis is ethical. They insist that the cultivation of mind and will, 'goodness of soul', is the chief business of life; that this is attained by a rational insight into the nature of goodness, truth, and beauty; that morality and the claims of the enlightened conscience are to be respected in political life; and that the rational moral personality is created by the 'recollection' of what the soul knows of these values. Since the soul naturally aims at what it believes to be good, wrongdoing is the pursuit of a falsely conceived good.

These doctrines are based on a metaphysic which is developed esp. in the later Dialogues. This contrasts the world of sense and everyday experience with the true or higher world of 'Ideas' (or 'Forms'). These 'Forms' are 'present to' individual entities, and by grasping the eternal Forms and participating in them the soul attains its true well-being and is lifted above the flux of 'becoming'. The secret of human destiny is to be found in the soul's search for the good which it sees but does not possess.

Plato's main discussions of theology in the narrower sense are in the *Timaeus* and

Book X of the *Laws*. The *Timaeus* describes how the *Demiurge, who is assumed to be identical with God, brings the world into being, how He makes it as an image of an eternal archetype, and how He enables it to share in His perfection by putting into it mind or soul. The *Laws*, Book X, embodies the earliest known exposition of *natural theology, viz. a form of the *cosmological argument based on the belief that all motions ultimately require at their head a 'perfectly good soul'. It remains obscure how Plato related the highest of the Forms (the 'Form of the Good') to God as the Supreme Soul.

PLATONISM. *Plato's doctrines had a wide following in the Hellenistic age and made an impact on later Judaism. In the 3rd cent. A.D. a recasting of Plato's system by *Plotinus (*Neoplatonism) was developed by *Porphyry in conscious opposition to Christianity.

The beginnings of an interweaving of Platonism with Christian thought go back to *Clement of Alexandria and *Origen. More important for Christian theology was the influence of Platonic doctrines on St. *Augustine, whose authority in the Middle Ages did much to secure for many Platonic notions a permanent place in Latin Christianity. Henceforth the Platonic Forms were regularly interpreted as the creative thoughts of God. The Renaissance led to a revival of interest in Plato himself, and Platonic influences have continued to play an important part in Christian philosophy, esp. in England.

PLAYS, Passion. See *Mystery Plays*; also *Oberammergau*.

PLENARY INDULGENCE. In modern RC theology an *Indulgence (q.v.) which is held to remit the whole of the temporal punishment due to an individual's sins. As its efficacy depends on the perfection of the soul's disposition (of which no one can be certain), there is always an element of doubt whether a soul has profited to the full by a particular plenary indulgence. The earliest known example of the issue of a plenary indulgence was the promise of *Urban II that all *penances incurred by *Crusaders who confessed their sins should be remitted.

PLETHON, G. GEMISTUS. See *Gemistus Plethon, G.*

PLINY'S LETTER ON THE CHRISTIANS. The letter (*c.* 112) in which the younger Pliny, as governor of Bithynia, asked the Emp. Trajan whether Christians should be punished 'for the name' or only for specific crimes. Trajan refused to allow toleration, but told Pliny not to initiate prosecutions or to act on anonymous accusations. The letter throws valuable light on contemporary Christian practices.

PLOTINUS (*c.* 205–70), *Neoplatonist philosopher and mystic. In 244 he established a school at Rome. His writings were published after his death by *Porphyry.

The main concern of Plotinus's thought is with the relations between unity and multiplicity. At the summit of the hierarchy of beings is the One or the Good, the first principle. Beneath it is the intelligible world of Ideas, and on a still lower plane there is the World Soul, the third member of the Plotinian Triad. The World Soul has created all material things and orders the universe; from it individual souls separate by a mysterious process. They have a capacity for the spiritual life, and by contemplation they can attain union with God. To achieve this end the soul has to prepare itself by purity of heart and ascetic practices, turning away from all sensible things. In Plotinus's system union is attained by the unaided effort of the soul, whereas in Christian teaching it is the work of Divine grace; Plotinus nevertheless seems to have exercised much indirect influence on Christian thought.

PLUMSTEAD PECULIARS. See *Peculiar People*.

PLUNKET, St. OLIVER (1629–81), RC Abp. of *Armagh from 1669. During the persecutions that began in 1673 he remained in Ireland and in the fury engendered by the *Titus Oates Plot he was arrested (1679), tried in London, and executed for treason.

PLURALITIES ACT (1838). The first of a series of Acts forbidding clergymen of the C of E simultaneously to hold more than one benefice with cure of souls except in the case of livings of limited value close to each other. The Acts were virtually abrogated by the Pastoral Reorganization Measure, 1949.

PLUVIAL. An almost obsolete name for the *cope.

PLYMOUTH BRETHREN. A Christian religious body so named because its first centre in England was established by J. N. *Darby at Plymouth in 1830, Their teaching combines elements from *Calvinism and *Pietism, and emphasis has often been laid on an expected *Millennium. They renounce many secular occupations, allowing only those compatible with NT standards (e.g. medicine). Controversies on the human nature of Christ and subsequently on Church government led to a division in 1849 between the 'Open Brethren' and the 'Exclusive Brethren'; within these groups there are several subdivisions.

PNEUMATOMACHI. Heretics who denied the full Godhead of the Holy Spirit. The sect, condemned by Pope *Damasus in 374, reached its full development c. 380. It was anathematized at the Council of *Constantinople in 381 and disappeared after 383, when its members became victims of the *Theodosian anti-heresy laws.

POIMANDRES. The first treatise in the corpus of *Hermetic writings (q.v.). It describes a vision seen under the guidance of Poimandres, a semi-divine being, and treats of the creation of the universe and man, the union of spirit with matter after the Fall, and the method of redemption by knowledge. There are some parallels with the NT.

POIRET, PIERRE (1646–1719), French Protestant mystic. From 1676 until her death in 1680 he was the companion of Antoinette *Bourignon. His *Bibliotheca mysticorum* (1708) contains out-of-the-way information on minor writers on mystical subjects.

POISSY, Colloquy of. A conference held in 1561 at Poissy (near Paris) between the French bishops and the Protestant ministers led by T. *Beza. It prepared the way for the edict of 1562 which gave official recognition and a measure of freedom to French Protestants.

POLAND, Christianity in. Poland received Christianity in the 10th cent., prob. from Moravia. In 966 Prince Mieczysław I was baptized and in 1000 Gniezno became a metropolitan see. In the 15th cent. some of the nobility supported the *Hussites, and in the 16th cent. the Reformation made headway, esp. among the nobility, who chafed under the dual control of King and Church. After a religious war mutual toleration of RCs and Protestants was secured in 1573. In 1595 the *Ruthenian Church renounced communion with *Constantinople and submitted to the Pope. The RC Church suffered after the division of Poland in 1772–3; its influence revived when Poland became independent in 1919, though the Orthodox retained their hold in the east. The establishment of a Communist-controlled government in 1945 led to severe difficulties, esp. for the RCs.

POLE, REGINALD (1500–58), Abp. of *Canterbury. Of the blood royal by his mother, Pole declined *Henry VIII's offer of the see of *York or *Winchester in 1530, and wrote a book censuring the King's conduct. *Paul III made him a cardinal in 1536 and in 1538 sent him on a fruitless mission to persuade Spain and France to break with England. He was one of three legates appointed to preside over the Council of *Trent. On *Edward VI's death in 1553, Pole was appointed legate in England. He formally absolved Parliament from schism and presided over a synod of both *Convocations. In 1556 he was ordained priest and consecrated Abp. of Canterbury two days later. He died 12 hours after Queen *Mary.

POLITIQUES. A French political party which advocated religious toleration, esp. after the Massacre of St. *Bartholomew's Day (1572).

POLYCARP, St. (traditionally c. 69–c. 155, but possibly slightly later), Bp. of Smyrna. He seems to have been the leading Christian figure in the Roman province of Asia in the middle of the 2nd cent. A letter addressed to him by St. *Ignatius has survived, as well as his own 'Ep. to Philippians', which is important for its testimony to the NT. He visited Rome towards the end of his life. Soon after his return to Smyrna he was arrested; proclaiming that he had served Christ for 86 years, he refused to recant his faith and was burnt to death. The *Martyrium Polycarpi* gives an account of his trial and martyrdom.

POLYCHRONIUS (d. c. 430), Bp. of Apamaea in Syria. A Biblical exegete of the *Antiochene school, he wrote commentaries on Job, Daniel, and Ezekiel.

POLYCRATES (2nd cent.), Bp. of *Ephesus. He was a leading *Quartodeciman who opposed Pope *Victor in his attempts to secure that *Easter should be uniformly celebrated on a Sunday. In consequence, Victor withdrew from communion with Polycrates.

POLYGLOT BIBLES. A 'Polyglot Bible' is a single Bible containing the text in several languages. Such Bibles were issued esp. in the 16th and 17th cents. The most celebrated is the '*Complutensian Polyglot' (1522), which in parallel columns printed the OT in Hebrew, Latin, and Greek, and the NT in Greek and Latin.

POMPONAZZI, PIETRO (1464–1525), Italian Renaissance philosopher. He held that it was possible to demonstrate by natural reason the mortality of the human soul, and that the only sense in which one could legitimately speak of the immateriality and immortality of the soul was in reference to its capacity for reflective knowledge and conceiving universal concepts. He argued that these doctrines need cause no offence to Christians, since they were merely the deductions of human reason and were transcended by the supernatural revelation made to the Church.

POMPONIA GRAECINA (1st cent.), wife of Aulus Plautius, the conqueror of Britain, and prob. an early convert to Christianity.

PONTIFEX MAXIMUS (Lat., 'Supreme Pontiff'). Originally a pagan title for the chief priest at Rome, from the 15th cent. it became a regular title of honour for the Pope.

PONTIFICAL. The liturgical book in the W. Church containing the prayers and ceremonies for rites used by a bishop, e.g. *Confirmation and Holy *Orders; it does not, however, contain the Pontifical Mass. A pontifical prob. put together at Mainz in the 10th cent. gained acceptance throughout Europe and was received at Rome; the books based on this gave place in the 14th cent. to a clearly arranged private compilation made c. 1293–5 by William *Durandus, Bp. of Mende. His work was the basis of the authoritative edition issued by *Clement VIII in 1596. The revised rites envisaged at the Second *Vatican Council have been appearing since 1961.

PONTIFICALS. The insignia of the episcopal order which are or may be worn by prelates when celebrating Pontifical Mass. They include *sandals, *gloves, *dalmatic, *ring, and *pectoral cross, as well as the *crosier and *mitre.

PONTIUS, St. (d. c. 260), biographer of St. *Cyprian. He was Cyprian's deacon at Carthage.

PONTIUS PILATE. See *Pilate, Pontius*.

POOR CLARES, the 'Second Order' of St. *Francis, founded by him and St. *Clare between 1212 and 1214. It received its first rule in 1219; a fourth rule, sanctioned by Pope Urban IV in 1263, was accepted by most convents, the nuns following it being known as 'Urbanists'. In the 15th cent. St. Colette restored the principle of strict poverty in her houses, and since then the Urbanists and *Colettines have remained the chief branches of the order. Most Poor Clare convents are strictly contemplative; they are regarded as the most austere women's order in the RC Church.

POOR MEN OF LYONS. The name under which the *Waldensians (q.v.) were condemned in 1184.

POORE, RICHARD (d. 1237), Bp. of *Salisbury from 1217 to 1228. In 1219 he removed his see from Old *Sarum to its present site and in 1220 he began building the present cathedral. He drew up the Salisbury Constitutions and prob. gave the 'Use of Salisbury' (q.v.) its final form. The diocesan statutes which he drew up were widely influential in other dioceses. In 1228 he was translated to *Durham.

POPE, The. The title, meaning 'father', is now restricted to the Bp. of Rome. In early times it was used in the W. of any Bishop.

POPE, WILLIAM BURT (1822–1903), *Wesleyan theologian. He was tutor at Didsbury College, Manchester, and in 1877 he presided over the Wesleyan Conference at Bristol. His *Compendium of Christian Theology* (1875) contains a sympathetic defence of the Methodist doctrine of Christian *perfection.

POPERY. A hostile designation for the doctrines and practices of the RC Church.

POPERY, The Declaration Against. The denunciation of *transubstantiation, the Mass, and the Invocation of Saints imposed on Members of Parliament in Britain from 1677 to 1778.

POPISH PLOT, The. The supposed plot to murder *Charles II which T. *Oates (q.v.) claimed that he had discovered in 1678.

POPPY HEADS. In ecclesiology, the ornamental finials at the tops of bench-ends, in form somewhat resembling a fleur-de-lis. They became common in the 15th cent.

PORPHYRY (*c.* 232–*c.* 303), *Neoplatonist philosopher. It is possible that he was at one time a Christian. He was convinced of Neoplatonist principles by *Plotinus, whom he met in Rome in 262.

His work 'Against the Christians' was condemned to be burnt in 448, and survives only in fragments in works written mainly to refute it. He seems to have observed a certain restraint in his remarks about Christ, whom he admired as a teacher, but he considered the apparent failure of His life proof that He was not divine. He launched bitter invective against the Apostles and leaders of the Church. His numerous philosophical works are important for their clear exposition, development, and preservation of much that was obscurely put in Plotinus and others.

PORRECTIO INSTRUMENTORUM. An alternative Latin name for the Tradition of the *Instruments (q.v.)

PORTA SANTA. The Italian for *Holy Door.

PORTER. See *Doorkeeper*.

PORTEUS, BEILBY (1731–1808), Bp. of London from 1787. He was of American descent. He identified himself with the practical ideals of the rising *Evangelical school, and he promoted mission work among Negro slaves in America. He was also a keen *Sabbatarian.

PORTIUNCULA. The village about 2 miles from *Assisi where St. *Francis received his vocation in 1208 and which he made his headquarters. The cell in which he died is surrounded by an imposing church, largely rebuilt after an earthquake in 1832.

PORT-ROYAL, Convent of, *Jansenist centre. A convent of *Cistercian nuns was founded in 1204 at Port-Royal, a marshy site SW. of Paris (hence 'Port-Royal-des-Champs'). In 1602 (Jacqueline Marie) Angélique *Arnauld was appointed abbess; converted to a new view of her responsibilities in 1608, she undertook far-reaching reforms. By 1625 the community was so large that they had to move to a new house in Paris ('Port-Royal-de-Paris'), and in 1627 they formed an autonomous Ordre du St. Sacrement. In 1635 S. Zamet, Bp. of Langres, handed over the direction of Port-Royal to *Saint-Cyran, Jansen's associate; after his death in 1643 his influence was maintained by Antoine *Arnauld, the spokesman of Jansenism. From 1637 some of Saint-Cyran's converts came to live near the community as 'Solitaires', and by 1648 their labours had rendered Port-Royal-des-Champs habitable enough to receive some of the nuns. For a time the two houses existed with a single conventual organization, increasingly openly associated with Jansenism. In 1669 they were separated, Port-Royal-de-Paris being given over to the nuns who had signed the anti-Jansenist formulary before 1668, while the Jansenist minority were established in Port-Royal-des-Champs. In 1705 *Clement XI condemned those who used mental reservations in signing the formulary; the nuns refused to accept this new definition and were finally dispersed in 1709.

PORTUGAL, Christianity in. The independent history of Portugal begins in the 12th cent., when the country became free of Castile and a self-governing vassal of the Papacy. There was subsequently a nationalist anti-Papal movement, but in the *Great Schism anti-Spanish feeling kept the Portuguese bishops on the side of *Urban VI and his successors. In the 15th cent. Portuguese conquests in Africa, *India, and America were accompanied by missionary work which secured mass conversions. The Reformation had no influence in Portugal. The 19th cent. saw the conflict of the Church with political and religious liberalism. The RC Church was disestablished in Portugal in 1911, but under a concordat signed in 1940 it was recognized as a lawful body with various privileges.

POSITIVE THEOLOGY. The branch of theology which treats of matters of historic and particular fact, custom, or enactment, as opposed to '*natural theology', which deals with religious principles and laws of universal validity.

POSITIVISM. In its original and narrower sense, the system of the French thinker Auguste *Comte, which confined intellectual inquiry to observable ('positive') facts and their relations, and eschewed all consideration of ultimate issues, including those of philosophy and theology. The term has come to be used in a wider sense for any form of philosophical outlook which rejects metaphysics, esp. when the physical sciences are regarded as offering the norm of knowledge. Such an outlook was developed by the 'Vienna Circle', formed in 1922, which gave the name 'Logical Positivism' to its doctrines. This has had a lasting effect on 20th-cent. philosophy and indirectly on theology by its demand for verifiability as a criterion of any statement's being meaningful.

POSSIDIUS, St. (*c*. 370–*c*. 440), biographer of St. *Augustine. He became Bp. of Calama in Numidia in 397. Besides a list of Augustine's works, he left a short but valuable sketch of his life.

POSTCOMMUNION. In the Roman Mass the prayer which follows after the Communion.

POSTIL. The word, which in the Middle Ages was used of a gloss on a Scriptural text, came to be applied esp. to a homily on the Gospel or Epistle for the day or to a book of such homilies.

POSTLAPSARIANISM. See *Sublapsarianism*.

POSTULANT. One who is undergoing a preliminary stage of testing as a candidate for a religious order before admission to the *novitiate.

POTAMIUS (d. *c*. 360), the earliest known Bp. of Lisbon. He originally professed and defended the orthodox *Nicene position, but from 355 he aligned himself with the *Arian-

izing policy of the Emp. Constantius II.

POTHINUS, St. (*c*. 87–177), first Bp. of Lyons. He was prob. a native of Asia Minor and a disciple of St. *Polycarp. He was among those martyred in 177.

POTTER, JOHN (*c*. 1674–1747), Abp. of *Canterbury from 1737. As Bp. of *Oxford, he ordained J. *Wesley. His works include a fine edition of *Clement of Alexandria (1715).

POWERS. Acc. to medieval angelology, the sixth order of angels in the celestial hierarchy. The word is also used more generally of any celestial being who exercises control or influence over other parts of creation.

PRAEDESTINATUS. A treatise, prob. composed at Rome during the papacy of Sixtus III (432–40), and directed against the extremer forms of *Predestination then being taught under the influence of certain passages in the writings of St. *Augustine.

PRAEMUNIRE. The title of statutes (first passed in 1353, 1365, and 1393), which were designed to protect rights claimed by the English Crown against encroachment by the Papacy. The name can denote the statutes, the offence, the writ, and the punishment. The statutes were repealed in 1967.

PRAEPOSITANUS OF CREMONA (*c*. 1140–*c*. 1210), theologian and liturgist. He was chancellor of *Paris university in 1206. His *Summa de Officiis* explains the symbolism of the *Offices; it was a source for William *Durandus, Bp. of Mende. His theological writing was untouched by the new problems raised by the introduction of *Aristotle in the W.; it had influence in his time.

PRAGMATIC SANCTION. The term was originally used in later Roman law for an arrangement defining the limits of the sovereign power of a prince, esp. in the matter of the royal succession. The Pragmatic Sanction of Bourges, issued by the French clergy in 1438, was a statement of *Gallicanist principles; it disallowed Papal nominations to vacant benefices. It was superseded by the Concordat of *Bologna (1516).

PRAGMATISM. A system of belief based

on the principle that every truth has practical consequences and that these are a test of its truthfulness. Pragmatism justifies and explains religions according as they satisfy psychological criteria and generate suitable values.

PRASSEDE, St. See *Praxedes, St.*

PRAXEAS (*fl. c.* 200), heretic, against whom *Tertullian wrote a treatise. He is said to have turned the Pope (*Victor or *Zephyrinus) against the *Montanists and proclaimed himself leader of the '*Patripassian Monarchians', i.e. those who held that God the Father suffered. He recanted.

PRAXEDES, St. (1st–2nd cent.), also **Prassede**, martyr at Rome. Acc. to her (spurious) *acta*, she was a Roman virgin who sheltered Christians during the persecution under *Marcus Aurelius. She was buried in the catacomb of St. *Priscilla.

PRAYER. Christian prayer rests on two foundations which give it its special character: belief in the transcendent and personal nature of the God who is revealed in the Bible as Lord of History and Creator of the World, and the acceptance of the intimate relation of God and man disclosed by the atoning work of the Incarnate Christ. It follows that petition, invocation, and adoration, which also belong to other world religions, are practised in Christian spirituality under the two dominant ideas of submission to the Divine will and recognition of the direct relationship of every creature to God. Adoration, thanksgiving, penitence, and petition are acts directed to God 'through Jesus Christ our Lord' or made 'in the Spirit' (Jude 20). The basis of the Christian approach to God is the fruit of '*justification' by Christ. The congruity of humanity with deity, revealed by the Incarnation, supplies a new basis for man's search for God in prayer which leads to the vision of God and union with and likeness to Him.

A distinction is drawn between vocal and mental prayer, and the former is divided into common and individual prayer. Common prayer may be further divided into liturgical prayer (*Eucharist, Divine *Office) and informal gatherings for prayer and praise. In the NT prayer is an art to be learnt; hence the pattern given in the *Lord's Prayer. It is also a weapon in the cosmic spiritual battle of

good and evil (Mk. 9. 29).

Mental prayer, described by *John of Damascus as 'the ascent of the mind to God', includes the direction of the affections as well as of thought. The 'ordinary ways' of mental prayer include discursive meditation, affective prayer, and contemplation (with the prayer of loving regard and prayer of simplicity), while its 'extraordinary ways' comprise mystical and supernatural experiences (see *Mysticism*).

PRAYER BOOK, The. See *Common Prayer, Book of*.

PRAYER OF MANASSES. See *Manasses, Prayer of*.

PRAYERS FOR THE DEAD. See *Dead, Prayers for the*.

PREACHERS, Order of. See *Dominican Order*.

PREBENDARY. The title of the holder of a (now honorary) *cathedral benefice. In the Middle Ages the endowment of most non-monastic cathedrals was divided into separate portions, known as 'prebends', each designed for the support of a single member of the *chapter, and their holders became known as 'prebendaries'. In some English cathedrals the ancient territorial titles of the prebends have been retained, though no income is now attached to them.

PRECENTOR. In *cathedrals, the cleric responsible for the direction of the choral services. In those of the 'Old Foundation' he is a member of the chapter; in 'New Foundations' he is a *minor canon or chaplain.

PRECEPT. In moral theology, a matter of obligation, as contrasted with a 'counsel', which is only a matter of persuasion. For Precepts of the Church, see *Commandments of the Church*.

PRECEPTORY. Among the Knights *Templar a community established on one of their provincial estates.

PRECES FERIALES (Lat., 'ferial prayers'). A short series of prayers consisting of *Kyrie Eleison, the *Lord's Prayer, and versicles and responses, which used to be said on *ferial (non-festal) days in the Offices of the *Breviary. In the BCP they are represented by the prayers between the Creed and Collects at *Mattins and *Evensong.

PRECES PRIVATAE. The short title of a Latin manual of prayers issued by *Elizabeth I in 1564. It has no connection with the 'Preces Privatae' of L. *Andrewes (q.v.).

PRECIOUS BLOOD, Devotion to the. The Blood of Christ, shed during the Passion, has been honoured and regarded as of redeeming virtue since the Apostolic Age, esp. in connection with the Eucharist. Various churches have claimed to possess particles of it, which have been greatly venerated. Feasts of the Precious Blood were celebrated by various orders in the 19th cent., and in 1849 the Feast was extended to the whole RC Church. It was observed on various dates in July: 1 July from 1914 until it was suppressed in 1969.

PRECISIAN. A name used of the *Puritans in the 16th and 17th cents.

PREDELLA. (1) The platform on the uppermost of the steps to an altar, on which the priest formerly stood when celebrating Mass; (2) the lowest piece of a *reredos.

PREDESTINARIANISM. The doctrine acc. to which human free will and co-operation are eliminated from the process of salvation by a thorough-going application of the principle of *Predestination.

PREDESTINATION. The Divine decree acc. to which certain persons are infallibly guided to eternal salvation. It is presupposed in the Gospels, e.g. Mt. 20: 23, where Christ tells the Apostles that sitting on His right and left is reserved 'for them for whom it hath been prepared of my Father'. The most explicit teaching in the NT is in Rom. 8: 28–30, where St. *Paul traces the process of salvation of those 'that are called according to His purpose' from foreknowledge and predestination to vocation, justification, and glorification.

St. *Augustine developed this teaching in the *Pelagian controversy. For him the mystery of Predestination consists in the inaccessibility to the human mind of the reasons for the Divine choice, which, nevertheless, is made in perfect justice. It contains the gift of final perseverance and depends not on

human acceptance, but on the eternal decree of God; it is therefore infallible, without, however, acc. to Augustine, violating free will. Basing himself on Augustine's wrings, *Gottschalk seems to have taught a double predestination of some to eternal blessedness and others to eternal fire, but his teaching was condemned at the Synod of *Quiercy in 849.

At the *Reformation J. *Calvin made the doctrine of Predestination a cornerstone of his system. Rejecting the univeral saving will of God, he maintained that Christ's atoning death was offered for the elect alone. He added to the gratuitous predestination of the elect the equally gratuitous and positive reprobation of the damned, to whom salvation is denied from all eternity without any fault on their part. Post-Tridentine RC theologians, on the other hand, in their formulations of the doctrine of Predestination, have sought to preserve the element of human consent and the reality of the Divine will that 'all men should be saved'.

PREFACE. In the Eucharist, the words which introduce the central part of the service. It begins with the '*Sursum Corda' and ends with the '*Sanctus'. The main part of it is an ascription of praise to the Creator in union with the worship of the angelic company. In W. liturgies part of it varies with the feast observed.

PRELATE. The term was originally of wide connotation, but it came to be restricted to Church officials of high rank. In the C of E it is reserved for bishops; in the RC Church it is also applied to a variety of officers attached to the Roman curia.

PREMONSTRATENSIAN   CANONS, also 'Norbertines' and, in England, 'White Canons' from the colour of their habit. An order founded by St. *Norbert at Prémontré, near Laon, in 1120. The basis of their rule is the so-called rule of St. *Augustine, with additional austerities. The order spread quickly over W. Europe and became powerful in Hungary. It became nearly extinct in the early 19th cent., but has re-established its influence.

PREPARATION, Day of. A Jewish name for Friday, i.e. the day preceding, and therefore employed in preparation for, the *Sabbath. The title may perhaps also have been used for the day before certain other great. feasts, e.g. the *Passover. All four Gospels record that the Crucifixion took place on the day of preparation.

PRESANCTIFIED, Mass of the. A shortened form of the Eucharistic Liturgy without consecration, a *Host consecrated at a previous Mass being used for Communion. In the E. Church it is ordinarily celebrated on the *Wednesdays and *Fridays in *Lent; in the W. it is restricted to *Good Friday. Acc. to the current RC rite the ciborium, containing Hosts consecrated on *Maundy Thursday, is brought from the Altar of *Repose to the High Altar; the priest says various prayers and then communicates himself and the people.

PRESBYTER. The earliest organization of the Christian Churches in Palestine resembled that of the Jewish synagogues, each of which was administered by a board of 'elders' (πρεσβύτεροι, i.e. 'presbyters'). Acts 14: 23 mentions the appointment of presbyters in the Churches founded by St. *Paul. At first the presbyters seem to have been identical with the 'overseers' (ἐπίσκοποι, i.e. 'bishops'), but from the 2nd cent. the title of bishop is normally confined to the presidents of these local councils of presbyters, and as such 'bishops' came to be distinguished, both in honour and prerogative, from the presbyters, who were held to derive their authority by delegation from the bishops. See also *Bishop* and *Priest*.

PRESBYTERIANISM. A form of ecclesiastical polity wherein the Church is governed by *presbyters. Its proponents in the 16th and 17th cents. regarded it not as an innovation but as the restoration of the apostolic model found in the NT, and many held it to be the only legitimate form of Church government.

The normal pattern of government of Presbyterian Churches is a hierarchy of courts: the *Kirk-Session, *Presbytery, Synod, and *General Assembly. These courts are representative bodies of ministers and elders based ultimately on popular election. There are differing views about the status of the elders: some see them as presbyters set apart for a ruling office in the Church; others regard them as laymen chosen to be helpers and administrators. Ministers are elected by the people, but their ordination is an act of the Presbytery. All Presbyterian Churches hold that the supreme standard of faith and practice is contained in the Bible, but most of them adopt the *Westminster Confession and Catechisms as subordinate standards. Their doctrine is traditionally *Calvinistic.

Presbyterian Churches are found in all Continents. The strongest concentrations are in *Scotland (the only Presbyterian State Church), the *U.S.A., *Hungary, *Holland, Northern *Ireland, Switzerland, and *France. The World Alliance of Reformed and Presbyterian Churches (founded in 1875) was merged in 1970 with the International *Congregational Council to form the World Alliance of Reformed Churches (Congregational/Presbyterian). Various Presbyterian Churches have been involved in regional unions, e.g. in *Canada. In 1972 the Presbyterian Church of England united with the greater part of the Congregational Church of England and Wales to form the *United Reformed Church.

PRESBYTERY. (1) The sanctuary or eastern part of the chancel of a church beyond the choir. (2) The residence of (esp.) RC priests. (3) Acc. to current *Presbyterian usage, the Church court which has oversight of and jurisdiction over a particular area. A Presbyterian minister is ordained by it (the ministerial members only joining in the imposition of hands) and is subject to it, and it is responsible for the oversight of public worship.

PRESENTATION OF CHRIST IN THE TEMPLE, The. In the BCP an alternative name for the feast of the *Purification of the BVM or *Candlemas (2 Feb.).

PRESENTATION OF THE BVM, The. A feast kept on 21 Nov. to commemorate the presentation of the BVM in the Temple when 3 years old, as related in the apocryphal 'Book of *James'.

PRESENTATION OF THE LORD, The. The title given in the RC Church since 1969 to the feast of *Candlemas.

PRESTER JOHN (i.e. 'Presbyter' John), legendary medieval Christian king of Asia. The story of a *Nestorian priest-king who had defeated the Muslims and would bring help to the Holy Land spread in Europe from the mid-12th cent. In 1177 *Alexander III wrote a letter 'to the King of the Indies, the most holy priest'; this was supposed to be addressed to Prester John, but it may have been meant for a real king of *Ethiopia, which was often confused with India. Another theory identifies Prester John with the Chinese prince, Gor Khan, who defeated the Sultan of Persia in 1141.

PRICE, RICHARD (1723–91), Nonconformist minister, moral and political philosopher. In *A Review of the Principal Questions in Morals* (1758) he defended a view of ethical action which had affinities with the teaching later expounded by I. *Kant. He held that the rightness and wrongness of an action belonged to it intrinsically and criticized the 'moral sense' view of ethics. By 1778 he was a *Unitarian.

PRICKET. A stand containing one or more upright spikes on which to fix votive candles.

PRIDE. The first of the *seven deadly sins, being the inordinate love of one's own excellence.

PRIDEAUX, HUMPHREY (1648–1724), Dean of *Norwich from 1702. His fame rested on two treatises, his *Life of Mahomet* (1697), really a tract against the *Deists, and *The Old and New Testaments connected in the History of the Jews* (1716–18), an account of the Jewish people in the last centuries before the Christian era.

PRIE-DIEU (Fr., 'pray God'). A small prayer-desk for private use, usually constructed with a sloping ledge.

PRIERIAS, SYLVESTER (1456–1523), Sylvester Mazzolini, opponent of M. *Luther. A native of Priero in Piedmont, he entered the *Dominican Order. His *Summa Summarum* (1515), an alphabetically arranged compendium of moral theology, became popular despite its small intrinsic merit, and in 1515 *Leo X appointed him 'Sacri Palatii Magister'. In 1517 he entered the lists against Luther. The Papal case suffered through not being in more competent hands.

PRIEST. The word 'priest' is etymologically a contraction of '*presbyter' (Gk.

πρεσβύτερος), but the traditional English versions of the NT render πρεσβύτερος by 'elder' and keep 'priest' and 'priesthood' for the purely sacerdotal terms ἱερεύς and ἱεράτευμα (Lat. *sacerdos* and *sacerdotium*). By the end of the Old English period 'priest' had become the current word alike for 'presbyter' and 'sacerdos' and so an ambiguous term.

The idea and institution of priesthood are found in almost all the great religions, usually connected with the conception of *sacrifice. Acc. to the OT the priesthood before the age of *Moses was patriarchal, but Moses was ordered to consecrate *Aaron and his sons 'to minister in the priest's office' (Exod. 28: 1); later priests were held to be descendants of Aaron, though various legal fictions mitigated this rule. The importance of the priesthood, and esp. of the *High Priest, increased with the enhanced position of the *Temple in later Judaism. His position as mediator between God and man came to be the predominant idea of the Jewish priesthood in the time of Christ. In the NT (esp. in Heb. 5) Christ Himself is seen as the culmination of the High Priesthood. By His Sacrifice as Priest He reconciles God to men, fulfilling what had been foreshadowed in the Jewish sacrifices. For the continuation of the offering of this Sacrifice, esp. in the Eucharist, a Christian priesthood was established in the Church.

The idea of priesthood as belonging to the Christian ministry was, however, a gradual development. While by the 3rd cent. presbyters were held to share in the episcopal *sacerdotium*, and could offer the Eucharist and receive penitents, it seems that these functions could be exercised only in the absence of the bishop and were regarded as delegated by him. With the spread of Christianity in the country and the establishment of parish churches, the presbyters adopted more fully the priestly functions of the bishop. As the parish priest became the normal celebrant of the Eucharist and customarily exercised the power of absolution, he came to be regarded increasingly as the representative of God to the people rather than the converse. His supernatural functions and powers were emphasized and he acquired a position outside the feudal hierarchy. He remained, however, entirely subordinate to his bishop, and the validity of his position depended on his ordination.

The tendency of medieval theology to see

the priesthood of the clergy almost exclusively in relation to the Mass led to its rejection by the Reformers. The term 'priest' was retained in the BCP apparently to make clear that *deacons were not to celebrate the Holy Communion. See also *Orders*.

PRIESTLEY, JOSEPH (1733–1804), *Presbyterian minister and scientist. His religious beliefs became increasingly unorthodox. In his *History of the Corruptions of Christianity* (1782) he denied the impeccability and infallibility of the Lord, views which he elaborated in his *History of Early Opinions concerning Jesus Christ* (1786). A violent controversy with S. *Horsley followed. In 1791 Priestley became one of the founder members of the *Unitarian Society. From 1794 he lived in America. As a scientist he is known for his 'discovery' of oxygen in 1774 and his work on *Different Kinds of Air* (1774–86).

PRIMASIUS (6th cent.), Bp. of Hadrumetum in N. Africa. His commentary on Rev. is valuable for the light which it throws on the history of the *Old Latin text of the NT

PRIMATE. The title of the bishop of the 'first see', usually the chief bishop of a single state or people. The Abp. of *Canterbury is 'Primate of All England', the Abp. of *York 'Primate of England'.

PRIME. The *Office traditionally appointed for the first hour, i.e. 6 a.m. It dates from c. 395 but was dropped from the 1971 *Breviary.

PRIMER or **Prymer.** A devotional book popular among the educated laity from at least the early 14th cent. It contained the *Little Office of the BVM, the *Seven Penitential Psalms, the 15 *Gradual Psalms, the *Litany of the Saints, and the Office for the Dead.

PRIMICERIUS. A title applied to the senior in rank of several classes of officials, both ecclesiastical and secular.

PRIMINIUS, St. See *Pirminius, St.*

PRIMITIVE METHODIST CHURCH. One of the *Methodist Churches which united in 1932. About 1800 Hugh Bourne began an evangelistic movement outside the official structure of Methodism near Mow Cop, Staffs., and here in 1807 Lorenzo Dow, an American Methodist, introduced the Camp Meeting. This form of meeting, held for a whole day in the open and designed for those not attracted by the ordinary work of the Church, was condemned by the Wesleyan Conference, and in 1810 both Bourne and William Clowes, who had carried Bourne's earlier evangelistic work to Tunstall, were expelled from the Methodist Church. In 1811 their followers united to form the Primitive Methodist Church, which soon engaged in widespread evangelism. In 1932 it united with the Wesleyan and *United Methodists.

PRIMUS. The title of the presiding bishop of the Scottish Episcopal Church.

PRIOR. Under *Benedictine influence the term came to denote the monk who ranked next to the *abbot and deputized for him. Later it was applied also to the heads of houses in the *mendicant orders and of small houses dependent on an abbey. See also *Priory*.

PRIORESS. The head or deputy head of certain houses of nuns. In general the prioress fulfils the same functions as the *prior in a male order. In the case of an abbey, she is second in command to the *abbess.

PRIORY. A religious house presided over by a *prior or *prioress. In some orders the priory is the normal unit. The *Benedictines distinguish between 'conventual priories' (self-governing houses) and 'obedientiary priories', which are dependencies of abbeys.

PRISCA. The name given to a 5th-cent. Latin translation of the canons of certain Greek Councils, incl. those of *Nicaea and *Chalcedon.

PRISCILLA, St. (1st cent.), also **Prisca**, an early Christian convert. She is mentioned six times in the NT and it is clear that she and her husband Aquila were prominent members of the primitive Church. The suggestion of A. *Harnack that they wrote Heb. has met with little favour. There are no sufficient grounds for identifying her with the St. Prisca whose relics are supposed to be enshrined in the church on the Aventine Hill in Rome known as the *titulus S. Priscae* or with the Priscilla of the 'Coemeterium Priscillae', one of the oldest *catacombs.

PRISCILLIANISM. A 4th–5th-cent. heresy of uncertain origin. Priscillian was the leader of an ascetic movement in Spain; despite condemnation of practices attributed to his adherents at Saragossa in 380, he became Bp. of Ávila soon afterwards. In 381 he and his followers were exiled. In Italy they got the decree of exile annulled by the secular authorities and, returning to Spain, won a large following. The new Emp. Maximus, however, sought the support of the Catholic bishops, and in 386 Priscillian was tried on a charge of sorcery, convicted, and executed. A Council of *Toledo in 400 decreed the deposition of those Priscillianist bishops who would not abandon the heresy, but the movement did not disappear until after its condemnation by the Council of Braga in 563.

In its developed form Priscillianism seems to have been a kind of *Manichaean Dualism, with *Docetic and *Sabellian elements. Its adherents taught a *Modalist doctrine of the Trinity and denied the pre-existence of Christ before His birth from the BVM as well as His real humanity; hence their fasting on Christmas Day and on Sundays. Angels and human souls were emanations of the Godhead, and souls were united to bodies in punishment for their sins, the body being the creation of the devil, who was not a fallen angel but the principle of evil. It is uncertain how far these tenets were inspired by Priscillian himself.

PRIVATE CHAPELS ACT (1871). This Act regulates the status of C of E chapels in schools, hospitals, and similar institutions, permitting the diocesan bishop to license a cleric to serve in such chapels.

PRIVILEGED ALTAR. An altar at which, acc. to RC canon law until 1967, a *plenary indulgence could be secured for a soul in *purgatory by the application of a Mass celebrated on it.

PRIVILEGED PRESSES, The. The Oxford and Cambridge University Presses, so called in respect of their right, shared only with the King's (Queen's) Printer, of printing the BCP and, in England, the Authorized Version of the Bible, which are perpetual Crown copyright.

PRIVY COUNCIL, Judicial Committee of the. See *Judicial Committee of the Privy Council*.

PROBABILIORISM. The system of *moral theology based on the principle that, if the licitness or illicitness of an action is in doubt, it is lawful to follow the opinion favouring liberty only when it is more probable than the opinion favouring the law. Though paramount in the early 18th cent., it has now been abandoned by most theologians.

PROBABILISM. The system of *moral theology based on the principle that, if the licitness or illicitness of an action is in doubt, it is lawful to follow the solidly probable opinion favouring liberty, even though the opposing opinion be more probable.

Probabilist principles were developed in Spain in the 16th cent., esp. by the *Dominican B. *Medina, and were accepted by both the Dominicans and the *Jesuits. The system was, however, recognized as being open to charges of *Laxism. In 1656 a conflict broke out. In that year the Dominicans adopted a system which came to be known as *Probabiliorism, and B. *Pascal, inspired by *Jansenism, attacked the morality of the Jesuits, with whom Probabilism had been increasingly identified. By the early 18th cent. Probabiliorism held sway. The subsequent rehabilitation of Probabilism is due esp. to the authority of St. *Alphonsus Liguori, who in 1762 expounded his own theory of *Equiprobabilism, which rests at bottom on Probabilist principles. Probabilism, with Equiprobabilism, is now the most generally accepted system in the RC Church.

PROBATIONER. In *Presbyterian Churches, one who, after examination and approval by the *Presbytery, receives a licence to preach. He may assist the minister but must not administer the Sacraments until he is ordained to a charge of his own.

PROCESS OF CANONIZATION. See *Beatification* and *Canonization*.

PROCESS THEOLOGY. A modern theological movement which emphasizes the processive or evolutionary nature of man and the world, and holds that God Himself is in process of development through His intercourse with the changing world. It originated in the U.S.A., esp. in the University of Chicago during the 1920s and 1930s. Its concept of God stresses His relationships with creatures, His capacity to 'surpass' Himself (but in respect of other entities to remain 'unsurpassable'), His 'bi-polar' nature, and His root attribute as love rather than uncreatedness.

PROCESSION (Liturgical). Processions may be festal or penitential. Acc. to W. use they take place before the principal celebration of the Eucharist on festivals; the ancient English use was for processions to be held after *Vespers. Processions are sometimes held in the open air as acts of witness, e.g. on *Good Friday. Other traditional processions include those on *Palm Sunday, the *Rogation Days, and *Corpus Christi.

PROCESSION (Theological). In Trinitarian doctrine, the attribute which distinguishes the Holy Spirit from the Persons of the Father and the Son. See also *Double Procession* and *Filioque.*

PROCESSIONAL. The book containing the text of the *litanies, hymns, and prayers formally prescribed for use in processions.

PROCLUS, St. (d. 446/7), Patr. of *Constantinople from 434. He won sympathy by his moderation in the cause of orthodoxy, and his popularity was enhanced by the solemn translation of the body of St. *Chrysostom (438). His works include the so-called 'Tome of St. Proclus' (Ep. 2) on the doctrine of the one Christ in two natures, directed against *Theodore of Mopsuestia.

PROCOPIUS OF CAESAREA (mid-6th cent.), Byzantine historian. He wrote a 'History of the Wars' (i.e. those which he had witnessed), 'De Aedificiis' (an account of the buildings of the Emp. *Justinian), and the so-called 'Anecdota' (or 'Secret History'), issued only after his death. His works are of great historical value.

PROCOPIUS OF GAZA (*c.* 475–*c.* 538), rhetorician and Biblical exegete. He was perhaps the foremost figure of the 'School of Gaza', a group of rhetoricians of the 5th–6th cent. His Biblical works consist mostly of extensive extracts from older exegetes.

PROCTORS FOR THE CLERGY. The elected representatives of the Anglican clergy who, together with the *ex officio* members, constitute the Lower Houses of the *Convocations of *Canterbury and *York.

PROFESSION, Religious. The taking of the vows of poverty, chastity, and obedience, necessary to the embracing of the 'religious life'.

PROHIBITED DEGREES. The relationships of blood or marriage which render it unlawful for two persons to marry. Blood relationships are called '*consanguinity'; relationships by marriage '*affinity'. Such relationships are called in canon law 'degrees'. Ecclesiastical legislation forbidding marriage between persons related in certain degrees is based on Lev. 18. In the C of E the prohibited degrees are listed in the Table of *Kindred and Affinity in the 1969 *Canons (B 31).

PROKIMENON. Verses from the Psalter sung before the *Epistle in the Byzantine Liturgy.

PROLOCUTOR. The title of the president of each of the Lower Houses of the *Convocations of *Canterbury and *York.

PROMISED LAND, The. The land of *Canaan, promised to *Abraham and his descendants (Gen. 12: 7 &c.).

PROMOTOR FIDEI (Lat., 'promoter of the faith'). The member of the Congregation of the Causes of Saints appointed to examine critically the alleged virtues and miracles of a candidate for *beatification or *canonization. He is popularly known as 'the Devil's Advocate'.

PRONE. The vernacular office attached to the sermon at High Mass on Sundays and feast days in the Middle Ages. It ordinarily consisted of such items as the 'bidding of the *bedes' (q.v.) and expositions of the Lord's Prayer and Creed, as well as notifications of ensuing feasts and fasts and *banns of marriage.

PRONOUNCEMENT STORIES. A name proposed by V. Taylor for those passages in the Gospels which M. *Dibelius terms

'*Paradigms' (q.v.).

PROPAGANDA. The *Roman Congregation concerned with missions to heathen countries and the administration of territories where there is no established hierarchy. It originated in the latter half of the 16th cent. to meet the spiritual needs of the newly discovered heathen populations. At first it was a cardinalitial commission; it was made a congregation in 1622.

PROPER. The part of the *Eucharist and *Offices which changes with the ecclesiastical season. The 'Proper of Saints' is the Proper for festivals of a fixed date; the 'Proper of Time' that for Sundays, *ferias, and *movable feasts. In the RC Church many saints' days share the same Proper with others; such Propers are printed once in a separate part of the *Missal or *Breviary under the heading '*Common of Saints'.

PROPHECY. From the earliest times Christians have believed that before the Incarnation God the Holy Spirit 'spake by the prophets' (*Nicene Creed), and it has generally been recognized that the prophets were the inspired deliverers of God's message not only about the future but also to their own contemporaries, to whom they declared His will.

In NT times the Jews applied the term 'the Prophets' to a large section of the OT Canon intermediate in authority between the ancient 'Law' and the more recent 'Writings'. In this connection it was customary to distinguish (1) the 'Former Prophets', viz. Jos., Jgs., 1 and 2 Sam., 1 and 2 Kgs., and (2) the 'Latter Prophets', viz. Is., Jer., Ezek., and the 12 (*Minor) Prophets. But the name of prophet could be applied in a wider sense, e.g. to *Moses.

The beginning of Hebrew prophecy can be traced to the early days of the monarchy. 1 Sam. 9 f. attests the existence of two types of prophet: the Seer, possessed of clairvoyance, like Samuel, who was able to show Saul the whereabouts of the lost asses, and the ecstatic, associated with a local shrine, who uttered words not his own, held to be God's (1 Sam. 10: 10 f.). Gradually the ecstatic features became of less importance and the delivery of a Divine message or 'word' became the dominating feature of prophecy.

It is in the prophets of the OT that most of the passages concerning the *Messiah occur. Christ Himself saw the fulfilment of OT prophecy in His own ministry, e.g. declaring that in His coming Is. 61: 1 was fulfilled (Lk. 4: 21). Similarly the Evangelists point to the fulfilment of a number of OT prophecies in the events they describe, and the appeal to OT prophecy was a constant feature of early Christian preaching (e.g. Acts 8: 26–35). It was only with the *Enlightenment and the rise of a critical approach to history that doubts began to be cast on the existence of any real anticipation of NT events in such texts as Is. 7: 14.

PROPHETS (Early Christian). There are some indications (notably the lists in 1 Cor. 12: 28 and Eph. 4: 11) that there was in the primitive Church a separate group of ministers known as 'prophets'. On the other hand it appears that the term 'prophet' might be applied to an elder, a deacon, or even a lay member of the Church (Acts 15: 32 and 21: 10). An itinerant ministry of prophets is described in the *Didache, but the value of this evidence is disputed.

PROPHETS (Old Testament). See *Prophecy.*

PROPITIATION. The general meaning of the word is the appeasing of the wrath of the Deity by prayer or sacrifice when a sin or offence has been committed against Him. In Christian thought the death of Christ has usually been regarded as a propitiatory sacrifice to the Father for the sins of the world. See also *Atonement.*

PROPRIETARY CHAPEL. In the C of E a chapel built by subscription and maintained by private individuals. The ministers of such chapels were normally granted episcopal licences, which could be issued only with the consent of the incumbent of the parish. Few, if any, still exist.

PROSE. An alternative name for the *Sequence (q.v.).

PROSELYTE. A convert to Judaism and, in a wider sense, a convert to any faith or sect.

PROSKOMIDE. In the E. Church, the elaborate preparation of the bread and wine for the Eucharist; it takes place before the beginning of the service.

PROSPER OF AQUITAINE, St.
(c. 390–c. 463), theologian. Prosper Tiro of
Aquitania was living at Marseilles when the
*Semi-Pelagian controversy broke out (426).
He wrote to St. *Augustine, and in 431 he
went to Rome to secure *Celestine I's support for Augustinian teaching. He was later
secretary to *Leo I. It appears that his theological views developed from the rigid
Augustinianism of his earlier controversial
writings to a milder view which rejected
predestination to damnation and affirmed the
will of God to save all men, though believing
in the reprobation of a great number. He
influenced the Carolingian theologians.

PROSPHORA. In the E. Church, the altar
bread. Traditionally five loaves are required;
they are solemnly cut up at the *Proskomide.
Part of each loaf is used for the liturgy; the
rest is not consecrated but is distributed later
among the congregation. The Greek Church
now uses one large loaf, but the Russian
Church continues to use five smaller ones.

PROTASIUS, St. See Gervasius and Protasius, Sts.

PROTESTANT EPISCOPAL CHURCH.
The Church in the *United States of America
which is in communion with the see of *Canterbury (since 1970, the Episcopal Church).
    The first Anglican church in America was
built at Jamestown, Virginia, in 1607; many
other congregations were established, all
under the jurisdiction of the Bp. of London.
It was only after the War of Independence
that the Protestant Episcopal Church became
an autonomous organization. In 1784 S.
*Seabury, who had been elected bishop by
the clergy of Connecticut, received episcopal
consecration from the bishops of the (Episcopal) Church of *Scotland. At a General
Convention in 1789 a constitution and canons were drawn up and the Prayer Book
revised. During the Civil War of 1861–5,
the Church in the southern states formed
itself into a separate body, but reconciliation
followed the peace of 1865. Since then the
Church has expanded at home and abroad,
establishing missionary dioceses in many
parts of the world.
    The constitution of the Protestant Episco-
pal Church provides for the laity a greater
share in administration at all levels than has

been customary in England, and bishops are
elected by a majority vote of the clerical and
lay orders in diocesan synods. In 1962 the
Protestant Episcopal Church joined with nine
American Protestant denominations in the
*Consultation on Church Union, but the Plan
of Union produced by this body in 1970 was
set aside in 1973.

PROTESTANTISM. The system of Christian faith and practice based on acceptance of
the principles of the Reformation. The term
is derived from the 'Protestatio' of the
reforming members of the Diet of *Speyer
(1529) against the decision of the Catholic
majority.
    The chief branches of original Protestant-
ism were *Lutheranism, *Calvinism, and
*Zwinglianism (qq.v.). The position of the
Anglican Communion is disputed, but in
popular parlance Protestantism in England is
taken to include both the C of E and most
Nonconformists.
    The chief characteristics of original
Protestantism, common to all its denominations, are the acceptance of the Bible as the
only source of revealed truth, the doctrine of
*justification by faith alone, and the univer-
sal priesthood of all believers. Protestantism
has tended to stress the transcendence of
God, laying corresponding emphasis on the
effects of the *Fall and *Original Sin and the
impotence of the unaided human intellect to
gain any knowledge of God; to minimize the
liturgical aspects of Christianity; and to put
preaching and hearing of the Word before
Sacramental faith and practice. While it has
rejected asceticism, it has upheld for the
individual a high, if at times austere, standard of personal morality. The principle of
'private judgement' in the interpretation of
Scripture accounts for the variety of sects
and Churches typical of Protestantism, in
which many shades of doctrine and practice
are found.

PROTEVANGELIUM, The. An alternative title for the 'Book of *James' (q.v.).

PROTHESIS. In the E. Church the word is
used of: (1) the table on which the solemn
preparation (*Proskomide) of the Eucharistic
gifts takes place; (2) the chamber to the left
of the apse of the church in which the table
stands; and (3) the Proskomide itself.

PROTO-LUKE. A first draft which St.

*Luke is supposed to have made of his Gospel. The theory was developed by B.H. *Streeter.

PROTOMARTYR (i.e. First Martyr). A title commonly given to St. *Stephen and occasionally to the first martyrs of different countries, e.g. to St. *Alban, the 'Protomartyr of England'.

PROTONOTARY APOSTOLIC. A member of the college of *notaries attached to the Papal court.

PROVERBS, Book of. This poetical OT Book is divided into 8 clearly defined sections, three of which are attributed to *Solomon. As it stands, the Book represents a compilation of various collections of proverbs, stemming from widely different periods and places, while the separate collections contain individual sayings of even more diverse origin. While some of the sayings may go back to Solomon, the tradition that he compiled the Book is prob. best explained by the fact that he was known to have uttered proverbs and to have made his court a centre of Eastern wisdom (1 Kgs. 4: 29-34).

PROVIDENTISSIMUS DEUS (1893). An encyclical on the study of the Bible issued by *Leo XIII. Its purpose was to give guidance, esp. to the clergy, in the new situation brought about by recent discoveries in archaeology and literary criticism. While it stressed the importance of the study of the new evidence, it condemned the use made of it in some quarters.

PROVINCE. A group of *dioceses, territorially contiguous, forming an ecclesiastical unit, so called because such groups were originally coincident with the Provinces of the Roman Empire.

PROVINCIAL. An official of a religious order, subject to the superior-general. He exercises authority over all houses of the order within a particular area. The office came into being with the *Mendicant Orders and was taken over by most modern orders and congregations. The provincial is normally elected by the provincial chapter for a given period.

PROVISIORS, Statutes of. Four English laws, passed in 1351, 1353, 1365, and 1389, intended to check the practice of Papal 'provision' or nomination to vacant benefices over the head of the ordinary patron. The practice of provision nevertheless continued until the Reformation.

PROVOST. In modern times, the head of an ecclesiastical chapter. In England the title is used in the newer dioceses of the head of a cathedral chapter where the cathedral is also a parish church. The title is used in a non-ecclesiastical sense for the heads of certain colleges.

PRUDENTIUS AURELIUS CLEMENS (348-c. 410), Latin poet and hymn-writer. A Spaniard by birth, he had a successful career in civil administration and spent his retirement in devout exercises and Christian writing. His apologetic poems exhibit distinction in abstract thought as well as in the imitation of classical models. Extracts from his hymns, which are composed in classical metres, are found in most W. *breviaries. Those in common use include 'Bethlehem, of noblest cities'.

PRUDENTIUS, GALINDO (d. 861), Bp. of Troyes from c. 843. He played an important part in the controversy on *Predestination between *Hincmar of Reims and *Gottschalk, defending the Augustinianism of the latter and denying the general saving will of God. In his *Epistola ad Hincmarum* he taught predestination to damnation as well as to salvation.

PRYMER. See *Primer*.

PRYNNE, WILLIAM (1600-69), *Puritan controversialist. He was severely punished after the publication of *Histriomastix* (1632), which was thought to contain veiled attacks on *Charles I and *Henrietta Maria, and he was again imprisoned when he wrote against the 'Book of *Sports' in 1637. His ideal of the supremacy of the State over the Church put him out of sympathy with the *Independents, whom he also attacked. When he gained a seat in the House of Commons in 1648, he opposed the King's execution. He was imprisoned for a time under the Commonwealth. *Charles II appointed him Keeper of the Tower Records, but his *Presbyterianism brought him into conflict with the reviving Anglicanism.

PSALMS, Book of (Gk. ψαλμοί, 'songs, accompanied by string music'). The 150 Psalms are variously enumerated; for the most part the Gk. and Lat. (Vulg.) versions are one number behind the Heb. counting (e.g. Ps. 90 AV is Ps. 89 Vulg.).

The Psalms are traditionally divided into five books, viz. 1–41, 42–72, 73–89, 90–106, 107–50, but there are indications of earlier groupings which point back to independently existing collections. Rubrics in the *Massoretic text and in the *Septuagint make it clear that in its present form the Psalter is a liturgical book; it has often been described as the 'hymn-book of the Second *Temple'. The popular belief that *David was the author of the whole Psalter can no longer be sustained. But though few, if any, of the Psalms can be assigned to David, there is no reason to doubt that many of them come from the early years of the Monarchy and in their original form may have been used in the worship of the First Temple. Uncertainty prevails as to the date when the various collections were made, but they were prob. all post-exilic.

Traditionally interpreted, the Psalms are held to cover the whole range of relations between God and man. This interpretation has been challenged at various points in the last 100 years, some for instance arguing that the 'I' of the Psalms commonly refers not to an individual but to Israel as a nation.

In the Church the Psalter has been used in public worship and in private prayer from very early times. In the Divine *Office of the RC Church, until the recent revision of the *Breviary, the whole Psalter was recited once a week; in the C of E the BCP provided for its recitation every month. See also *Psalters, Western*.

PSALMS, Imprecatory and Metrical. See *Imprecatory Psalms* and *Metrical Psalters*.

PSALMS OF SOLOMON. See *Solomon, Psalms of*.

PSALTER COLLECTS. *Collects recited in early times by the officiating priest after each Psalm. The recital of the collects was abandoned after the Carolingian age, except in Spain, where the composition of new collects continued until the 11th cent.

PSALTERS, Western. The earliest Latin Psalters were translated from the *Septua-gint. St. *Jerome in his preface to the *Gallican Psalter says that he had made an earlier translation of the Psalms from the LXX; this has traditionally been equated with the *Roman Psalter (q.v.). He made a fresh translation from the *Hexaplaric text of the LXX (the Gallican Psalter, q.v.) and a further one from the Hebrew (the 'Hebrew Psalter'). Conservatism prevented this last Psalter from replacing the older version.

The version of the Psalms in the BCP is based on M. *Coverdale's translation from the Vulgate, i.e. from the Gallican Psalter, and thus embodies many Septuagintal readings not found in the Hebrew. The authors of the 'Revised Psalter' (1964) tried to preserve Coverdale's style, while basing their translation on the Hebrew text.

PSALTERY. (1) An ancient and medieval stringed instrument. (2) The book which contained the Psalms (and often certain other matter) for recitation at the Divine *Office in the medieval W. rite. When their contents came to be incorporated in the *Breviary, Psalteries fell into disuse.

PSELLUS, MICHAEL (c. 1019–c. 1078), Byzantine philosopher, historian, theologian, and statesman. He held high office at the Imperial court, but fell from favour in 1072 and lived in obscurity. His Chronicle is an important source for the history of the period 976–1077. His other works include treatises against the Latin theologians and against the *Messalians, as well as commentaries on *Plato and *Aristotle.

PSEUDEPIGRAPHA. Writings ascribed to some other than their real author, generally with a view to giving them an enhanced authority. The term is used esp. of the pseudonymous Jewish works dating from the centuries immediately before and after the beginning of the Christian era, which are not included in the OT or *Apocrypha. Among them are the 'Books of *Enoch', the 'Assumption of *Moses', the later 'Books of *Baruch', and the 'Psalms of *Solomon'.

PSEUDO-CLEMENTINES; PSEUDO-ISIDORIAN DECRETALS. See *Clementine Literature* and *False Decretals*.

PSILANTHROPISM. The heretical doctrine that Christ was just a man and not God and man in one Person.

PSYCHOLOGY OF RELIGION. A modern field of study in which the concepts and methods of psychology are applied to religious experience and behaviour. One of the first to investigate such possible applications of psychology was W. *James; the topics he studied included the experience of well-being or of conflict in human response to God, and the experiences of religious conversion and of saintliness and mysticism. The early work of S. Freud (1856–1939) on psycho-analysis also contributed to the psychology of religion. Though his reductionist views of religion no longer command respect, his observations about the relations of certain religious practices and obsessional behaviour, and his speculations about patterns of early personal and religious growth, laid the foundations for later work. It is, however, generally agreed that merely psychological methods cannot fully answer questions about the validity of religious behaviour and experience, even if they can account for some aspects of both in non-religious terms.

PTOLEMAIC SYSTEM. The body of astronomical doctrines elaborated by Ptolemy (2nd cent. A.D.). It explained the apparent motions of the sun, moon, and planets on the assumption that the earth was stationary.

PUBLIC WORSHIP REGULATION ACT (1874). An Act designed to suppress the growth of ritualism in the C of E. The imprisonment of four priests for contumacy between 1877 and 1882 discredited the Act. It was repealed by the *Ecclesiastical Jurisdiction Measure, 1963.

PUBLICAN. The word used in the traditional English versions of the Bible to translate the Gk. term τελώνης (Lat. *publicanus*), a member of one of the financial organizations which farmed taxes in the service of the Roman government. In view of the abuses and corruptions to which the system led, the publicans were the object of widespread hatred.

PUDENS, St. A Christian of Rome, mentioned in 2 Tim. 4: 21 as sending greetings to *Timothy. Tradition makes him St. *Peter's host at Rome. There are no sufficient grounds for identifying him with the Pudens (prob. 3rd cent.) who gave his house (*titulus*

Pudentis or *ecclesia Pudentiana*) to the Roman Church.

PUDENTIANA, St. She is supposed to have been an early Christian Roman virgin, but her cult prob. rests on the mistaken notion that the 'ecclesia Pudentiana' in Rome, which is the church of St. *Pudens, presupposed a St. Pudentiana.

PUFENDORF, SAMUEL (1632–94), German professor of natural and international law. Developing the system of H. *Grotius, he divided law into natural, civil, and moral, and maintained that while moral law was based on revelation and civil law on the positive enactments of the State, natural law had its basis in the instincts of society, and therefore ultimately in human reason.

PUGIN, AUGUSTUS WELBY NORTHMORE (1812–52), architect and *ecclesiologist. He was the chief initiator and inspirer of the 'Gothic Revival'. His works include St. Giles', Cheadle, and St. George's (RC) Cathedral, *Southwark. He collaborated with C. Barry on the designs for the Houses of Parliament.

PULCHERIA, St. (399–453), E. Empress from 450. From 414 to 416 she was guardian of her brother, *Theodosius II. A stalwart supporter of orthodoxy, she induced him to condemn *Nestorius and in the *Monophysite controversy she was on the orthodox side. As Empress she arranged for a General Council to meet at *Chalcedon in 451.

PULLEN, ROBERT (d. 1146), theologian. He was one of the earliest known masters in the schools of *Oxford and he later taught in *Paris. He was made a cardinal in 1143–4 and *c.* 1144 he became papal chancellor. At Rome he used his influence against Peter *Abelard.

PULPIT. An elevated stand of stone or wood for the preacher or reader. They first became general in the later Middle Ages. Except in *cathedrals, the north side of the nave is considered the proper place for the pulpit. The workmanship is sometimes elaborate. Pulpits are also generally found in monastic refectories.

PURCELL, HENRY (1659–95), English composer. From 1680 he was organist at

*Westminster Abbey and from 1682 also at the *Chapel Royal. His most famous ecclesiastical work is the *Te Deum* and *Jubilate* in D (1694). He developed the verse anthem, foreshadowed by W. *Byrd; much of the music is elaborate and highly dramatic; the words are nearly always from the OT. Even more extensive are his secular compositions.

PURCHAS JUDGEMENT, The. The judgement given in 1871 by the *Judicial Committee of the Privy Council against the Rev. John Purchas that *Eucharistic Vestments, the *Eastward Position, the *Mixed Chalice, and Wafer *Bread were illegal. The decision meant that the ritualists were henceforth held to be law-breakers, but it was widely disregarded.

PURGATIVE WAY, The. The first stage of mental prayer, acc. to the scheme commonly adopted by *ascetic theologians. The chief activity of the soul at this stage is the eradication of bad habits, with repentance for past sins; to this end the imagination and intellect are called into play.

PURGATORY. Acc. to RC teaching the place or state of temporal punishment, where those who have died in the grace of God expiate their unforgiven *venial sins and undergo such punishment as is still due to forgiven sins, before being admitted to the *Beatific Vision. 2 Macc. 12: 39–45 is adduced in support of the doctrine, while Christ's words on the sin against the Holy Spirit which will be forgiven 'neither in this world nor in that which is to come' (Mt. 12: 31 f.) seem to imply a state beyond the grave where expiation is still possible. Without the conception of purgatory the practice of offering prayers for the *dead (q.v.) is held to be unintelligible.

The doctrine of Purgatory was developed systematically in the W., explicit teaching being evolved in order to avoid confusion of thought about the state of souls between death and the *General Judgement. Acc. to St. *Thomas Aquinas, the guilt (*culpa*) of venial sin is expiated immediately after death by an act of perfect charity and only the punishment remains to be borne; the smallest pain in Purgatory is greater than the greatest pain upon earth, but it is relieved by the certitude of salvation which establishes the Holy Souls in peace, despite their sufferings; and they may be helped by the prayers of the faithful

and esp. by the offering of Mass on their behalf. The official teaching of the W. Church was defined at the Councils of *Lyons (1274) and *Florence (1439); with a view to reaching agreement with the Greeks the Latins confined themselves to the existence of Purgatory and the usefulness of prayer and pious works offered for the departed.

The existence of Purgatory was rejected by the Reformers, who taught that souls are freed from sin by faith in Christ alone without any works, and therefore, if saved, go straight to heaven. The Council of *Trent reaffirmed the teaching propounded at Lyons and Florence, forbidding fanciful elaborations. The E. Church attaches importance to the practice of praying for the dead, but is less explicit about their exact status than the RC Church. There is no generally accepted teaching on the subject in the C of E.

PURIFICATION OF THE BVM. The feast kept on 2 Feb. in commemoration of the BVM's purification in the Temple (Lk. 2: 21–39); it is also known as *Candlemas (q.v.).

PURIFICATOR. A small piece of white linen used at celebrations of the Eucharist to cleanse the *chalice after communion.

PURIM. A Jewish festival celebrated in the spring. It commemorates the deliverance of the Jews from massacre under the Persian Empire (473 B.C.), as related in the Book of *Esther.

PURITANS. The more extreme English Protestants who, dissatisfied with the religious settlement of *Elizabeth I, sought a further purification of the Church from supposedly unscriptural and corrupt forms. They were influential, esp. among the mercantile classes. At first they attacked such things as church ornaments, *vestments, *surplices, *organs, the *sign of the cross, and ecclesiastical courts; from the early 1570s the more extreme Puritans attacked the institution of episcopacy itself. On *James I's accession they presented the *Millenary Petition (1603), which led to the unsuccessful *Hampton Court Conference (1604). The Great Rebellion (sometimes called the 'Puritan Revolution') in and after 1642 led to the temporary triumph of *Presbyterianism, but also to the proliferation of sects, and the term 'Puritan' ceased to be applicable after 1660.

PURVEY, JOHN (*c.* 1353–*c.* 1428), *Wycliffite preacher. His main achievement was a revision of the literal and almost unreadable English version of the Bible made by *Nicholas of Hereford. Begun in Wycliffe's lifetime, it was prob. completed at Bristol in 1388.

PUSEY, EDWARD BOUVERIE (1800–82), *Tractarian leader. From 1828 he was Regius Professor of Hebrew at Oxford and canon of Christ Church. At the end of 1833 he became formally attached to the *Oxford Movement by contributing one of the *Tracts for the Times*; with the withdrawal of J. H. *Newman in 1841 the leadership of the movement devolved on Pusey. His sermon on *The Holy Eucharist*, preached before the University in 1843, was condemned by the Vice-Chancellor and six doctors of divinity; the condemnation secured for it wide publicity and drew attention to the doctrine of the *Real Presence. In 1845 Pusey assisted in the foundation of the first Anglican sisterhood; from 1839 he had worked for the establishment of *religious orders in Anglicanism and throughout his life he encouraged efforts in that direction. In 1846 he preached another University sermon on *The Entire Absolution of the Penitent*, in which he claimed for the C of E the power of the keys and the reality of priestly absolution; the practice of private confession in modern Anglicanism dates from this work. As the principal champion of the High Church Movement Pusey frequently had to defend its doctrines, e.g. in the *Gorham Case, and from 1867 he took an active part in the Ritualist controversy. He wrote various works designed to promote union with the RC Church, but his hopes were disappointed when the *Vatican Council of 1869–70 defined Papal Infallibility.

PUSEYISM. A contemporary title for the *Tractarian Movement, from its leader E. B. *Pusey.

PYRRHONISM. Properly, the system of sceptical philosophy expounded *c.* 300 B.C. by the Greek thinker Pyrrho of Elis. In a wider sense the term is now used of any sceptical system of thought.

PYX. In official documents the term is used of any receptacle designed to contain the reserved *Host, but it is commonly applied esp. to the small gold or silver-gilt box which is used for carrying the Bl. Sacrament to the sick. For this purpose it is wrapped in a small *corporal and placed in a pyx-bag hung round the priest's neck.

Q

'Q'. The symbol (usually, perhaps wrongly, held to come from the German *Quelle*, 'source') for the hypothetical source of those passages in the Synoptic Gospels where Mt. and Lk. show a close similarity to each other but not to anything in Mk. (See *Synoptic Problem*.) The existence of such a document is still challenged, but the hypothesis is widely accepted.

Q.A.B. See *Queen Anne's Bounty*.

QUADRAGESIMA. Another name for the forty days of *Lent and, occasionally, for the first Sunday in Lent.

QUADRAGESIMO ANNO (1931). An encyclical letter of *Pius XI confirming and elaborating the theses of *Rerum Novarum* (q.v.).

QUADRATUS, St. (2nd cent.), *Apologist. About 124 in Asia Minor he wrote an apology for the Christian faith addressed to the Emp. Hadrian; a single fragment is preserved by *Eusebius.

QUADRIVIUM. The medieval name for the four sciences (music, arithmetic, geometry, and astronomy) which constituted the superior group of the *Seven Liberal Arts.

QUAKERS. A popular name for the Society

of *Friends.

QUANTA CURA (1864). The encyclical to which the *Syllabus Errorum* was attached.

QUARE IMPEDIT. In the C of E, a form of legal action which a patron may bring in a temporal court against a bishop who refuses to institute a presentee to an ecclesiastical benefice.

QUARLES, FRANCIS (1592–1644), religious poet. He was for a time secretary to Abp. J. *Ussher and later chronologer to the city of London. He published a collection of Biblical paraphrases under the title *Divine Poems* (1630) and two emblem-books. In his later years he wrote devotional prose; his *Enchiridion* (1640), a collection of thoughts on religion and morals, achieved great popularity. Though overladen with conceits and epithets, his poetry shows deep religious feeling.

QUARR ABBEY, Isle of Wight. In 1131/2 Baldwin de Redvers founded a monastery on the site, which was colonized from *Savigny; it survived until the *Dissolution in 1537. In 1908 the site was acquired by the *Benedictines exiled from *Solesmes, and a red brick abbey in Flemish style was built. The house is a centre of liturgical and historical study.

QUARTODECIMANISM. The custom of observing *Easter on the 14th day of Nisan (the day of the Jewish *Passover), whatever the day of the week, and not on the following Sunday. The tradition was rooted in Asia Minor. When St. *Polycarp, Bp. of Smyrna, visited Rome c. 155, Pope Anicetus refused to change his own practice but had no scruples about Polycarp's continuing to follow his custom. A more rigid line was taken by *Victor I (189–98), who tried to suppress Quartodecimanism. The Quartodecimans later organized themselves as a separate Church, surviving until the 5th cent.

QUATTRO CORONATI (i.e. 'the Four Crowned Ones'). A group of four martyrs to whom a famous basilica in Rome is dedicated. There is doubt as to which saints are intended.

QUEEN ANNE'S BOUNTY ('Q.A.B.'). A fund formed by Queen *Anne in 1704 to receive the firstfruits (*annates) and tenths which had been confiscated by *Henry VIII; they were to be used to augment the livings of the poorer Anglican clergy. The fund later received considerable parliamentary grants and private benefactions. In 1948 Q.A.B. was joined with the *Ecclesiastical Commissioners to form the *Church Commissioners for England.

QUESNEL, PASQUIER (1634–1719), French *Jansenist. He became an *Oratorian in 1657. In 1672 he issued the first edition of the work which became famous as *Réflexions morales*. As against the formalized methods of spirituality in the manuals, the work emphasized the value of close study of the Bible in increasing devotion. His edition of the works of St. *Leo (1675) was put on the *Index because of the *Gallican theories developed in the notes. In 1684 he refused to subscribe to an anti-Jansenist formula imposed by his superiors and went to Brussels; he was imprisoned in 1703 but escaped to Holland. His *Réflexions* was condemned in a brief by *Clement XI in 1708 and by the bull *Unigenitus (1713); among the doctrines censured were the theses that no grace is given outside the Church, that grace is irresistible, and that all acts of a sinner, even prayer, are sins.

QUICUNQUE VULT. An alternative name for the *Athanasian Creed.

QUIERCY, Synods of. Several synods were held at Quiercy near Laon in the 9th cent. Those of 849 and 853, which met under *Hincmar of Reims, condemned the extreme form of *predestination taught by *Gottschalk.

QUIETISM. The teaching of certain 17th-cent. writers, esp. M. de *Molinos (condemned in 1687) and to a lesser degree Mme *Guyon and Abp. *Fénelon; by extension the term is used loosely of any system of spirituality minimizing human activity.

The fundamental principle of Quietism is its condemnation of all human effort. In order to be perfect, a man must attain complete passivity and annihilation of will, abandoning himself to God to such an extent that he ceases to care even about his own salvation. This state is reached by a form of mental prayer in which the soul consciously refuses not only discursive meditation but any distinct act, and simply rests in the presence of God in pure faith. Once a man has reached this state outward acts are superfluous and sin impossible.

QUINISEXT SYNOD. See *Trullan Synod.*

QUIÑONES, FRANCISCO DE (d. 1540), cardinal. Of noble Spanish family, he became a *Franciscan in 1498; in 1523 and 1526 he was elected Minister General of the *Observants. After the Sack of Rome (1527) he mediated between *Charles V and *Clement VII, who made him a cardinal. On the Pope's instruction he compiled a new *Breviary, publd. in 1535; it is often called the 'Breviary of the Holy Cross', after the cardinal's titular church. It was widely used before it was proscribed in 1558, and it had considerable influence on the BCP.

QUINQUAGESIMA. In modern usage, the Sunday before *Ash Wednesday. In the RC Church the term was suppressed in 1969.

QUINQUE VIAE. The five 'ways' or arguments by which St. *Thomas Aquinas sought to prove the existence of God from those effects of His Being which are known to us, viz. (1) that motion implies a first mover; (2) that a sequence of efficient causes, and their effects, such as we find in the world, implies an uncaused first cause; (3) that the existence of things which are not self-explanatory, and therefore might logically not exist, implies some necessary being; (4) that the comparisons we make (more or less 'true', 'noble', &c.) imply a standard of comparison which is in itself perfect in all these qualities; (5) that the fulfilment by inanimate or unintelligible objects of an end to which they are evidently designed to work implies a purposive intelligence in their creation and direction.

QUIRE. An old spelling of *choir.

QUIRINUS. The signature over which a series of 69 letters on the *Vatican Council were published in the *Augsburger Allgemeine Zeitung* in 1869–70. Their author is now known to have been J. J. L. von *Döllinger.

QUMRAN. The site of some ruins at the NW. end of the *Dead Sea where the first of the *Dead Sea Scrolls was found in 1947, to be followed by further finds in later years.

QUO VADIS? (Lat., 'Where are you going?'). Acc. to a legend, first found in the Acts of *Peter, this question was asked by St. Peter when, fleeing from Rome, he met Christ. The Lord replied, 'I am going to be crucified again.' Peter turned back to Rome, where he was martyred.

QUOAD OMNIA. The name given to the Scottish parishes to which the ancient *teinds or tithes belonged. They were so called because they were provided *quoad omnia*, i.e. in respect of all things civil and ecclesiastical. Where new parishes were created, they were designated *quoad sacra*, i.e. as provided in respect of ecclesiastical affairs only; they were supported by modern endowments and the liberality of their members.

QUOAD SACRA. See *Quoad Omnia.*

QUODLIBET. An academic exercise in medieval universities. Originally it was a voluntary disputation in which a master undertook to deal with any question raised by any of the participants. The answers were afterwards drawn up in writing and published. In the 14th cent. its character changed and it came to be part of the exercise required of a bachelor seeking the licentiate.

R

RABANUS MAURUS (776/84–856), theologian. He was master of the monastery school at *Fulda, which under him became one of the most influential in Europe; from 822 to 842 he was abbot of Fulda. In 847 he became Abp. of Mainz. He carried forward the evangelization of Germany and to this end he furthered the learning of monks and clerics. He wrote a manual for the clergy, Biblical commentaries, and an encyclopaedic work *De Rerum Naturis*. He took part in the controversy which centred on *Gottschalk and he opposed the pronounced realism of the sacramental teaching of *Paschasius Radbertus. He was a prolific poet, and the '*Veni Creator Spiritus' has often been attributed to him.

RABBI (Heb., 'my master'). A Jewish title of respect given to honoured teachers by disciples and others. Soon after NT times it came to be added to the name of Jewish religious leaders as a title, e.g. 'Rabbi Johanan'.

RABBULA (d. 435), Bp. of *Edessa from 412. A leading figure in the Syrian Church, he opposed *Nestorianism and in particular attacked the writings of *Theodore of Mopsuestia. He may have compiled the *Peshitta text of the NT, but his part in this is disputed.

RACCOLTA. An officially approved RC prayer book containing all the devotions to which papal *indulgences were attached. It was supplanted in 1968.

RACOVIAN CATECHISM. The first statement of Socinian principles. Drawn up by Valentin Schmalz and Johannes Völkel on the basis of drafts by F. P. *Socinus, it was published in Polish in 1605 at Racow in S. Poland. German and Latin versions followed. It was not a formal confessional creed but a body of opinions which would point believers to eternal life.

RAD, GERHARD VON (1901–71), German OT scholar. His most important writings were concerned with *Deuteronomy, the analysis and interpretation of the *Hexateuch, and the theology of the OT. He did not attempt to construct a unified system of OT theology but expounded (1) Israel's confession of the *Heilsgeschichte* (lit., 'Salvation History') as proclaimed in the cult and transmitted in the historical traditions, (2) the searching criticism of the older traditions by the Prophets and their proclamation that new Divine acts were about to take place, and (3) the relationship between the OT and NT in terms of a modified *typological interpretation.

RADBERTUS, PASCHASIUS. See *Paschasius Radbertus*.

RADEGUNDE, St. (518–87), the Queen of Clothaire I, King of the Franks. His murder of her brother gave her an excuse to flee from court (*c.* 550). Soon afterwards she founded a convent outside Poitiers, where she spent the rest of her life. In 569 she obtained a fragment of the true cross, which inspired *Venantius Fortunatus to write the '*Vexilla regis'.

RADEWYNS, FLORENTIUS. See *Florentius Radewyns*.

RAHNER, KARL (1904–84), RC theologian. He became a *Jesuit in 1922 and held professorial chairs at Innsbruck and Munich. He was one of the editors of the new *Lexikon für Theologie und Kirche* (1957–68) and was a *peritus* (expert [adviser]) at the Second *Vatican Council.

His basic position was expounded in *Geist in Welt* (1939; Eng. tr., *Spirit in the World*, 1968). While interpreting in *existentialist terms St. *Thomas Aquinas's doctrine of perception as the grasping of intelligible being through the medium of the sensible species, he sees the human subjectivity as functioning within a horizon of being whose ultimate determinant is God. His pastoral writings are direct and forceful.

RAIKES, ROBERT (1735–1811), the founder of *Sunday Schools. The owner of the *Gloucester Journal*, Raikes was moved by the neglected condition of the local children and their behaviour on Sundays; he helped to establish a Sunday School in a neighbouring parish and in 1780 he started a school in his own parish, open on weekdays and Sundays, for the teaching of Scripture, reading, and other elementary subjects. His methods were followed by Hannah *More and others.

RAINOLDS, JOHN (1549–1607), Anglican divine. From 1598 he was President of Corpus Christi College, Oxford. At the *Hampton Court Conference (1604) he was the chief representative of the *Puritan cause. He had a prominent part in preparing the AV.

RAMBLER, The. A monthly RC periodical, founded in 1848, which became an organ of liberal English Catholicism. It was suppressed in 1864.

RAMÓN LLULL. See *Lull, Raymond.*

RAMSEY, ARTHUR MICHAEL (1904–), Abp. of *Canterbury 1961–75. He held professorial chairs at *Durham and Cambridge before he became Bp. of Durham in 1952. He was translated to *York in 1956. During his primacy *Alternative Services were authorized, *Synodical Government was inaugurated (in 1970), and there were extended negotiations on an *Anglican–Methodist scheme of union.

RAMUS, PETRUS (**Pierre de la Ramée**) (1515–72), French humanist. Despite his attacks on the system of *Aristotle and the university curriculum at *Paris, he became a professor at the Collège Royal in 1551. On becoming a *Calvinist in 1562, he went to Germany. He returned to Paris in 1571, but he was killed in the Massacre of St. *Bartholomew's Day. To Aristotle's system he opposed a mixture of logic and rhetoric which declared deduction to be the final scientific method.

RANCÉ, ARMAND-JEAN LE BOUTHILLIER DE (1626–1700), reformer of *La Trappe. At an early age he was provided with various benefices, including that of *commendatory abbot of La Trappe. He underwent a dramatic conversion in 1657; in 1662 he resigned all his benefices except that of La Trappe, where he introduced the *Cistercian Reform; he then entered the novitiate at Perseigne, emerging to be blessed as regular abbot of La Trappe in 1664. He added more stringent regulations to the existing rules of the Reformed Cistercians and made his community the model of what was later called the *Trappist Reform.

RANKE, LEOPOLD VON (1795–1886), German historian. His work was marked by the use of original sources, a fundamentally objective attitude, and an understanding of national tendencies in their relation to the history of their age. His 'History of the Popes' removed papal history from denominational polemics.

RANTERS. A fanatical sect of the 17th cent. They appealed to their inward experience of Christ and denied the authority of Scripture, Creeds, and the Ministry.

RAPHAEL, St., *Archangel. In *Tobit and *Enoch he figures as one of the seven archangels who stand in the presence of God. Acc. to Tobit (12: 15) he hears the prayers of holy men and brings them before God; in I Enoch (10: 7) he is said to have 'healed' the earth when it was defiled by the sins of the fallen angels.

In the C of E the Guild of St. Raphael was founded in 1915 to restore the Ministry of Healing as part of the normal function of the Church.

RAPHAEL (1483–1520) (**Raffaele Sanzio**), the most famous of the Renaissance painters. In 1508 he was summoned to Rome to decorate the Vatican 'Stanze' and in 1514 appointed chief architect of *St. Peter's. His works include the *Espousals of the Virgin* (1504; Brera, Milan), the *Sistine Madonna*, and the *Madonna della Sedia* (*c.* 1513–14; Pitti Palace, Florence).

RAPP, JOHANN GEORG (1757–1847), founder of the *Harmony Society (q.v.).

RAS SHAMRA TABLETS. A collection of cuneiform tablets with mythological poems and ritual prescriptions excavated at Ras Shamra (anciently Ugarit) in N. Syria from 1929 onwards. They prob. date from the 14th cent. B.C. or earlier and are in a hitherto unknown alphabetical script and a Semitic dialect akin to Hebrew. Their contents show some remarkable correspondences with the OT.

RASHDALL, HASTINGS (1858–1924), moral philosopher and theologian. He taught philosphy at Oxford from 1888 to 1917 and then was Dean of *Carlisle. *The Theory of Good and Evil* (1907) expounded an ethical doctrine which he described as 'Ideal *Utilitarianism'. *The Idea of Atonement in Christian Theology* (1919) upheld an '*Exemplarist' theory.

RASHI (1040–1105), Jewish Biblical scholar, so called from the initials of his name, Rabbi Solomon ben Isaac. His aim, in opposition to the current exegesis of his time, was to interpret the OT according to its literal sense. His commentaries were influential among Jews and Christians from an early date.

RASKOLNIKI (Russian, 'schismatics').

An alternative name for the *Old Believers (q.v.).

RATHERIUS (*c.* 887–974), Bp. of *Verona. He received the see in 931, but was soon removed; he was in possession of it again from 962 to 968. A man of refractory and ambitious character, he took a prominent part in the ecclesiastical life of his time.

RATIO STUDIORUM (Lat., 'the method of the studies'). The abbreviated name of the *Jesuit scheme of studies issued in 1599. It was based on the best pedagogical theory of the time, and the success of Jesuit secondary education from the 16th to the 18th cent. was largely due to it.

RATIONALE. The word has been used of the breastplate worn by the Jewish *high priest, of a liturgical vestment worn by some German bishops, of a gold ornament formerly sometimes worn by bishops celebrating Mass, and of a set of liturgical rules, e.g. those of W. *Durandus.

RATISBON, The Conference of (1541). A conference of three Catholic and three Protestant theologians convened by *Charles V at Ratisbon (Regensburg). Though doctrinal agreement was reached on most issues, the hostility of M. *Luther, as well as political rivalries, prevented any reunion being effected.

RATRAMNUS (d. 868), monk of *Corbie. His *De Praedestinatione* defended the doctrine of double *predestination, i.e. to good and evil. His most famous work was his treatise *De Corpore et Sanguine Domini*, in which he attacked the realist view of the Eucharist defended by *Paschasius Radbertus. In the 16th cent. he was claimed by several of the Reformers as supporting their own doctrines, though whether justly or not is disputed.

RAVENNA. Acc. to tradition the first Bp. of Ravenna was St. *Apollinaris (q.v.). After the city was chosen as the Imperial residence in 404, it grew in importance and wealth. In 493 it fell to *Theodoric the Goth, who introduced *Arianism. It was captured for the Byzantine Empire by Belisarius (540) and became the capital of the Exarchate until it fell to the Lombards in 751. It is unrivalled in its mosaics and other remains of early Christian art.

RAYMOND LULL. See *Lull, Raymond*.

RAYMOND NONNATUS, St. (*c.* 1204–1240), *Mercedarian missioner. The accounts of his life are late and unreliable. He appears to have been sent to N. Africa, redeemed many slaves, and when his funds were exhausted gave himself up in ransom; for some years he lived among the Muslims, converting many to the Christian faith. He was himself ransomed by members of his order.

RAYMOND OF PEÑAFORT, St. (1185–1275), Spanish canonist. He became a *Dominican in 1222. His *Summa de casibus poenitentiae* influenced the whole development of the penitential system. In 1230 *Gregory IX charged him with the collection and arrangement of papal decretals subsequent to *Gratian; the work was finished and promulgated in 1234. In 1238 he was elected General of his order; his revision of the Dominican constitution remained in force until 1924. From 1240 he devoted himself to the conversion of Jews and Moors.

RAYMOND OF SEBONDE (d. 1432–6), Spanish philosopher. He taught at Toulouse. His *Liber Naturae sive Creaturarum* or *Theologia Naturalis* achieved fame through M. de *Montaigne, who translated it in 1569. Its prologue, maintaining that it is possible for human reason to discover the contents of the Christian Revelation in nature alone, was put on the *Index in 1595. The book itself, however, was highly esteemed.

READER, Lay. See *Lay Reader*.

READERS. See *Lectors*.

REAL PRESENCE, The. In (esp. *Anglican) Eucharistic theology an expression used to cover several doctrines emphasizing the actual presence of the Body and Blood of Christ in the Sacrament, as contrasted with others that maintain that the Body and Blood are present only figuratively or symbolically.

REALISM. (1) Any form of belief which is chary of speculation and rooted in fact. In this sense Christianity is realistic.
   (2) The philosophical doctrine of the reality of the external world as against the

idealistic view that it is constituted by consciousness.

(3) In a more technical sense the doctrine that abstract concepts ('*universals') have a real existence apart from the individuals ('particulars') in which they are embodied. This was developed in the Middle Ages on the basis of *Plato's metaphysic and opposed by *Nominalism.

RECAPITULATION (Lat. *recapitulatio*, a 'summing up', 'summary'). The Greek equivalent in its verbal form is used in Eph. 1: 10, where God is said to 'sum up' all things in Christ, and from this passage the term was taken over by the Fathers. The conception of recapitulation was elaborated by St. *Irenaeus, who interpreted it both as the restoration of fallen humanity to communion with God through the obedience of Christ and as the summing up of the previous revelations of God in past ages in the Incarnation.

RECARED (d. 601), King of the Visigoths. He was associated with his father in governing the country (most of Spain) from 573 and succeeded him in 586. In 587 he abandoned *Arianism and became a Catholic. This step did much to unite the country, since the Catholics were more powerful than the Arians.

RECEPTIONISM. A form of Eucharistic teaching acc. to which, while the bread and wine continue to exist unchanged after consecration, the faithful communicant receives together with them the Body and Blood of Christ.

RECLUSE. A person who lives apart from the world, esp. for the purpose of religious meditation.

RECOGNITIONS, Clementine. See *Clementine Literature*.

RECOLLECTION. A term used by spiritual writers to denote the concentration of the soul on the presence of God. It involves the renunciation of all avoidable dissipations, and its use is habitually recommended to those who wish to lead an interior life. In a more restricted sense the word is applied to a certain stage of prayer, in which the memory, understanding, and will are held to be stilled by Divine action and the soul left in a state of peace in which grace can work without hindrance.

RECOLLECTS. The title of two separate religious orders:

(1) *The Franciscan Recollects*. A reformed branch of the Franciscan *Observants, started in France at the end of the 16th cent. In 1897 they were incorporated with the other Observants.

(2) *The Augustinian Recollects*. A reformed branch of the *Augustinian hermits, started in Spain. Their first house was founded in 1589. They were constituted an independent order in 1912.

RECORD, The. An Anglican weekly newspaper, begun in 1828. It was strongly *Evangelical. In 1949 it was amalgamated with the *Church of England Newspaper*.

RECTOR. In the C of E a rector, as distinguished from a *vicar, is a parish incumbent whose *tithes are not impropriate. See also *Lay Rector*.

RECUSANCY. Refusal to attend the services of the C of E, applied esp. after 1570 to RCs. Recusancy received a powerful impetus with the arrival in England of the *Jesuits and other priests from the Continent *c.* 1580. Elizabethan and Jacobean statesmen regarded it as a dangerous problem because of its tenacious roots throughout the social structure of some regions, e.g. in the North of England. Stiff penalties were imposed by various statutes, though their enforcement varied. By the *Catholic Relief Act of 1791 refusal to attend the services of the C of E ceased to be a crime, though RCs continued to suffer certain disabilities, which have now nearly all been removed.

REDACTION CRITICISM. The investigation of the editorial work done by Biblical writers on earlier material, e.g. of the use made of the Marcan material by Matthew and Luke.

RED HAT. The flat-crowned broad-brimmed hat traditionally distinctive of a *cardinal. Although cardinals are now invested with a red *biretta instead, the expression 'red hat' is still used for the cardinal's office.

RED LETTER DAY. An important feast or saint's day. Such days were often printed in red in ecclesiastical calendars. In the C of E the term is applied to the days for which the BCP provides a proper Collect, Epistle, and Gospel.

RED MASS. Acc. to W. usage, a *votive Mass of the Holy Spirit, so called from the red vestments in which it is traditionally celebrated.

RED SEA. The crossing of the Red Sea by the Israelites, recorded in Exod. 14 and 15, marked the end of their bondage in Egypt and was subsequently regarded as a turning-point in their destiny. The site of the crossing is disputed.

REDEMPTION. The idea of redemption is common to many religions, being based on the desire of man to be delivered from sin, suffering, and death. Christianity claims that in it alone has redemption become a fact through the Incarnation and Death of Christ. It is viewed by theologians under the double aspect of deliverance from sin and the restoration of man and the world to communion with God.

While the Greek Fathers stressed the restoration of man to the Divine life, the Latins gave primacy to the expiation of our sins through the sacrificial death of Christ and worked out their theology of redemption in direct connection with the doctrine of *Original Sin. Redemption is the free gift of God to fallen man, who could not have redeemed himself. Catholic theologians hold that man is nevertheless enabled to co-operate with *grace towards justification and sanctification. The Reformers denied the possibility of human co-operation except by faith alone, and placed exclusive emphasis on the forgiveness of sin and justification by imputation of the righteousness of Christ. In the 16th and 17th cents. some Protestant and RC theologians, influenced by the teaching of J. *Calvin and C. *Jansen, advocated the view that Redemption extends only to the elect; this was pronounced heretical by *Innocent X in 1653. See also *Atonement*.

REDEMPTORISTS. The common name for the members of the 'Congregation of the Most Holy Redeemer', founded by St. *Alphonsus Liguori in 1732. It was instituted for mission work among the poor both in Europe and among the heathen, and it has refused to engage in purely educational acti-

vities.

REFORMATIO LEGUM ECCLESIAS-TICARUM (Lat., 'the Reform of the Ecclesiastical Laws'), a book which was designed to provide a system of order and discipline for the C of E in place of the medieval *canon law. It was presented to Parliament in March 1553, but the death of *Edward VI prevented further progress.

REFORMATION, The. This loose term covers an involved series of changes in W. Christendom between the 14th and 17th cents. They may be said to have begun with the attacks of the *Lollards and *Hussites upon the hierarchical and legalist structure of the Church. The *Great Schism and the *Conciliar Movement weakened the authority of the Papacy and widespread discontent simmered against the worldliness and financial exactions that characterized the Papacy as an Italian power. Consequently, when M. *Luther protested against the corruptions of Rome and the abuses attending the sale of *indulgences in 1517, he was breaking no new controversial ground. Indeed, most of the Reformation movements laid stress, not upon innovation, but upon return to a primitive excellence. Study of St. *Augustine had led Luther to question the emphasis of later medieval theology upon 'good works'; later his theological reading raised doubts about the validity of the Papal claims to supremacy. From such traditionalist origins were derived his attacks upon *transubstantiation and clerical *celibacy, as well as his demands for the abolition of Papal power in Germany and for the radical reform of the religious orders. By 1530 or soon afterwards the rulers of Saxony, Hesse, Brandenburg, and Brunswick, as well as the kings of *Denmark and *Sweden, were won to the reformed beliefs, and they proceeded to regulate the Churches in their territories acc. to *Lutheran principles, which were also adopted by a number of the free cities in Germany.

In Switzerland H. *Zwingli, motivated at first by beliefs analogous to those of Luther, in 1523-4 captured the support of the civic authorities at Zürich and carried through anti-papal, anti-hierarchic, and anti-monastic reforms in the city. The movement spread through the Swiss cantons and much of SW. Germany. After Zwingli's death (1531) leadership of the Swiss Reformation passed from Zürich to Geneva. Here in 1541 J. *Calvin finally got accepted an elaborately organized theocracy. In his hands reforming opinion assumed a more explicitly doctrinal and revolutionary tone. A coherent theological system based upon the doctrine of *predestination was provided by his *Institutes* (1536). *Calvinism became the driving force of the Reformation in W. Germany, *France, *Holland, and *Scotland. In each case it was linked with political struggle.

The English Reformation was an insular process responsive to peculiar political and social forces. *Henry VIII, a convinced traditionalist in both doctrine and Church government, accomplished the overthrow of Papal power in England and the *dissolution of the monasteries largely in pursuit of a long-standing monarchical policy of extending the sovereignty of the central government in every department. See *Church of England*.

REFORMED CHURCHES. Though sometimes used to include all the Protestant Churches, the term usually denotes the *Calvinist bodies, esp. as contrasted with the *Lutherans.

REFORMED PRESBYTERIAN CHURCH, The. The small body of Scottish *Presbyterians who declined to accept the settlement of 1690 which established the Church of *Scotland. The Reformed Presbytery was formed in 1743. The majority joined the *Free Church of Scotland in 1876, but some remain as an independent body.

REFRESHMENT SUNDAY. The Fourth Sunday in *Lent, so called perhaps in reference to the traditional Gospel of the day relating the feeding of the five thousand (Jn. 6: 1–14), or perhaps because of the relaxation of the Lenten discipline allowed on this day. It is also known as '*Mothering Sunday' (q.v.).

REGALE. In legal language esp., the rights to the revenues of vacant bishoprics and abbeys and the presentation to their dependent benefices claimed by the kings of Europe during the Middle Ages. The claim was denied by the Papacy and became closely associated with the *Investiture Controversy. In England it is still enjoyed by the Crown over the temporalities of vacant sees (though the revenues are restored when the newly elected Bishop does homage).

REGENERATION. The spiritual rebirth which, acc. to traditional theology, is effected in the soul by Baptism (q.v.).

REGENSBURG, Conference of. See *Ratisbon, Conference of*.

REGIMINI MILITANTIS ECCLESIAE (1540). The papal bull instituting the *Jesuit Order.

REGINA COELI (Lat., 'Queen of Heaven'). The *Eastertide anthem to the BVM, so called from its opening words. Its authorship is unkown, but it prob. dates from the 12th cent.

REGINALD OF PIPERNO (c. 1230–90), *Dominican friar. He was the confessor and secretary of St. *Thomas Aquinas, and he compiled the Supplement to the Third Part of the *Summa Theologica* after his death.

REGIONARIUS. A name in use in the early Middle Ages for certain of the clergy of Rome.

REGIUM DONUM (Lat., 'Royal Gift'). A grant made from public funds to the *Presbyterian, *Baptist, and *Congregational Churches in England until 1851. It originated out of sums which *Charles II ordered to be paid to Presbyterian ministers after the *Declaration of Indulgence of 1672.

REGIUM PLACET. See *Exequatur*.

REGNANS IN EXCELSIS (1570). The bull of excommunication against *Elizabeth I, issued by Pope *Pius V.

REGULA MAGISTRI. An anonymous monastic Rule written by 'the Master' in Italy SE. of Rome c. 500–25. In part it is verbally identical with the prologue and chapters 1–7 of the Rule of St. *Benedict; the relationship of the two Rules has been the subject of much controversy, but most scholars now give priority to the *Regula Magistri*.

REGULAR. A general name for those clergy who are bound by the vows of religion and live in community. They are distinguished from the seculars, i.e. priests living in the world.

REGULAR CANONS; REGULAR CLERKS. See *Canons Regular*; *Clerks Regular*.

REGULARIS CONCORDIA. A code of monastic observance in England, approved by the Synod of *Winchester (*c.* 970). Acc. to *Aelfric, it would appear that the compilation was the work of St. *Ethelwold, though it was prob. inspired by St. *Dunstan, to whom it was long attributed. Its provisions generally follow the *Benedictine tradition.

REICHENAU. A small island in the western arm of Lake Constance famous for its *Benedictine monastery, founded by St. *Pirminius in 724. Its collection of MSS. (many now at Karlsruhe) was already established in the early 9th cent.

REICHSBISCHOF. The title adopted in 1933 for the office of the head of the united German Evangelical Church, incorporating all the provincial Churches.

REIMARUS, HERMANN SAMUEL (1694–1768), *Deist and Biblical critic. From 1727 he was professor of Hebrew and oriental languages at Hamburg. Between 1744 and 1767 he composed the treatise from which G. E. *Lessing published the *Wolfenbüttel Fragments* in 1774–8. The work, which Reimarus kept back from publication during his lifetime, rejected miracles and revelation, and sought to convict the Biblical writers of conscious fraud, innumerable contradictions, and fanaticism.

REIMS. Acc. to tradition the see was founded in the 3rd cent., but the first bishop of whom there is historical evidence was Imbetausius (or Bethausius), who took part in the Council of *Arles (314). The power of the see increased under St. *Remigius, who baptized *Clovis in 496, and under *Hincmar (d. 882). The right of the archbishops to crown the kings of France was recognized by *Sylvester II in 999.

The cathedral, one of the finest examples of French Gothic, was begun in 1211 and completed in the 14th cent. The famous west front was damaged in the 1914–18 War, but has been restored.

REIMS NEW TESTAMENT. See *Douai-Reims Bible*.

REINCARNATION. See *Metempsychosis*.

REINKENS, JOSEPH HUBERT (1821–96), *Old Catholic bishop. He became professor of Church history at Breslau in 1850. He was opposed to the definition of Papal Infallibility at the First *Vatican Council and in 1871 he joined in the *Nuremberg Declaration. After excommunication from the RC Church, he was elected the first bishop of the German Old Catholics in 1873 and consecrated by Bp. Hermann Heykamp of Deventer.

REITZENSTEIN, RICHARD (1861–1931), German philologist and historian of religion. In *Poimandres* (1904) he tried to show that NT phraseology and ideas were largely derived from *Hermetic sources and that the Christian Churches were modelled on Hermetic communities.

RELICS. In Christian usage the word is applied to the material remains of a saint after his death and to sacred objects which have been in contact with his body. From an early date the bodies of *martyrs were venerated; clear evidence comes from the 'Martyrdom of *Polycarp' (*c.* 156). At Rome the cult was linked with the *catacombs, where services were held at their tombs. Under the influence of the *Iconoclastic Controversy, the Second Council of *Nicaea (787) anathematized those who despised relics and ordered that no church should be consecrated without them. The veneration of relics was approved for the E. Church by the Council of *Constantinople in 1084, but it never held the same place as in the W. In the W the cult increased, esp. during the *Crusades, when quantities of relics, often spurious, were brought back from the Holy Land. They were kept in *reliquaries, carried in procession, and often gave rise to superstitious practices.

The theological foundation for the cult of relics was developed in the Middle Ages. Stress was laid on the special dignity of the bodies of saints as temples of the Holy Spirit destined to a glorious resurrection, and on the sanction given by the Godhead in making them the occasion of miracles. The doctrine was confirmed by the Council of *Trent against the Reformers. See also *Saints, Devotion to the*.

RELIEF ACTS. See *Catholic Relief Acts*.

RELIGIONSGESCHICHTLICHE SCHULE (Germ., 'History of Religion School'). A group of German Biblical scholars influential between 1880 and 1920 who advocated extensive use of the data from the comparative study of religion in the interpretation of Christianity. They reduced dogmatic considerations to a minimum and sought parallels to Christianity in Egyptian, Babylonian, and Hellenistic religious systems.

RELIGIOUS. A technical term for a member of a religious order or congregation.

RELIGIOUS DRAMA. See *Drama*.

RELIGIOUS ORDERS IN ANGLICANISM. The revival of religious orders in the Anglican Communion was one of the results of the *Oxford Movement. In 1841 E. B. *Pusey received the vows of Marian Rebecca Hughes, who in 1849 was to become the first superior of the Convent of the Holy and Undivided Trinity at Oxford, and in 1845 he founded the first community at Park Village, Regent's Park, in London which was later merged in the Society of the Holy Trinity, founded at Devonport by Priscilla Lydia *Sellon in 1848 and now at Ascot. Other communities followed in quick succession, including the Community of St. Mary the Virgin at Wantage (1848), the Community of St. John the Baptist at Clewer (1852), and the Community of St. Margaret at East Grinstead (1855). These were all 'active' or 'mixed' communities, combining the monastic life with a life of service, and they were among the pioneers in the care of the poor in the slums of great cities. In 1907, with the foundation of the first 'enclosed' community, the 'Sisters of the Love of God' at Fairacres, Oxford, the 'contemplative' life was revived.

The first religious order for men was the *Society of St. John the Evangelist, founded at Cowley by R. M. *Benson in 1865. It was followed by the Society of the Sacred Mission, founded in 1891, which went to Kelham in 1903, and the *Community of the Resurrection (1892). The English Order of St. Benedict at *Nashdom Abbey sprang from the Benedictine community at *Caldey. After the First World War an English *Franciscan Order was established.

From England the revival of the religious life spread to other parts of the Anglican Communion. After the *Lambeth Conference of 1930 an 'Advisory Council on the Relation of the Bishops and Religious Communities' was set up in England, and similar Councils have been established elsewhere.

RELIGIOUS TRACT SOCIETY. A society of Anglicans and Nonconformists founded in 1799 for the publication and dissemination of tracts and other evangelical literature. In 1935 it was absorbed in the *United Society for Christian Literature.

RELIQUARY. A receptacle for *relics. They have been made in various shapes, frequently of precious metals and richly decorated.

REMBRANDT (1606–69) (**Rembrandt Harmensz** or **Harmenszoon van Rijn**), Dutch painter. The son of a wealthy miller of *Leyden, he was famous for his portraits by the time he moved to Amsterdam in 1631. His wife died in 1642 and financial difficulties led to bankruptcy. His sufferings helped to deepen and spiritualize his art and to give him an understanding of the Passion, the theme of some 90 paintings and etchings. Characteristic was his treatment of light and shade out of which his human figures appear to grow, thereby producing an impression of a happening beyond space and time.

REMIGIUS, St. (*c.* 438–*c.* 533), also **Remi**, 'Apostle of the Franks'. He was elected Metropolitan of *Reims at the age of 22. In 496 he baptized *Clovis I, King of the Franks, together with many of his subjects. He directed missions to the Morini and the *Arians of Burgundy and is associated with the foundation of various bishoprics. Acc. to legend the *ampulla of chrism traditionally used in the coronation of French kings was brought by a dove in answer to his prayers at the baptism of Clovis.

REMIGIUS OF AUXERRE (*c.* 841–*c.* 908), philosopher. His most important works are his commentaries on Martianus Capella and on *Boethius' *De Consolatione Philosophiae*. In them the work of more original Carolingian scholars, notably Johannes Scotus *Erigena, was presented in a form that made their teaching assimilable in the schools.

REMONSTRANCE, The. The statement

of *Arminian doctrine drawn up at Gouda in 1610. Under five headings it sets out in positive form the leading Arminian doctrines on salvation. Among the *Calvinistic doctrines repudiated were both the *Supralapsarian and *Sublapsarian forms of *predestination, the doctrine that Christ died only for the elect, and the belief that the saints could not fall from grace. The Remonstrants were condemned at the Synod of *Dort (1618–19).

RENAN, JOSEPH ERNEST (1823–92), French philosopher, theologian, and orientalist. His *Averroès et l'averroïsme* (1852) established his reputation as a scholar. In 1860 he was sent on an archaeological mission to Phoenicia and Syria, and it was in Palestine that he wrote his *Vie de Jésus*. In this book he repudiated the supernatural element in Christ's life, ignored its moral aspect, and portrayed Him as an amiable Galilean preacher. Its publication in 1863 created a sensation.

RENAUDOT, EUSÈBE (1646–1720), French orientalist and liturgist. His two chief theological works are his *Historia Jacobitarum Patriarcharum Alexandrinorum* (1713) and his *Liturgiarum Orientalium Collectio* (1716). The latter contains the texts of many E. liturgies, with copious notes and commentaries, and is still indispensable.

RENUNCIATION OF THE DEVIL. The renunciation of Satan at *Baptism is attested in St. *Hippolytus' *Apostolic Tradition* and has been a regular part of almost all Baptismal rites, E. and W.

REORDINATION. The repetition of an ordination to the priesthood when it has been conferred either *extra ecclesiam*, i.e. by a heretical or schismatic bishop, or *intra ecclesiam* but not canonically, e.g. by a deposed bishop. Though a matter of controversy from the 3rd cent., reordination was often practised before the 12th cent., when the doctrine of the *Sacraments began to receive more precise formulation. Acc. to Catholic theology the Sacrament of *Orders is held to confer on the recipient an indelible *character, provided that it is conferred in the right form and with the right *intention.

REPARATION. The making amends for damage done to another. In moral theology it is generally used in a sense similar to *restitution (q.v.). In modern devotional language the term is also used for the amends made to God for offences against Him by means of prayer and penance. It plays a central part in the *Sacred Heart devotion.

REPENTANCE. The condemnation and abhorrence of one's own sins. It includes sorrow for the sin committed, confession of guilt, and the purpose of amendment.

REPINGTON, PHILIP (d. 1424), Bp. of *Lincoln from 1404 to 1419. In early life he supported the teaching of J. *Wycliffe; in 1382 he was excommunicated, but he soon recanted. He was several times chancellor of the university of Oxford and in 1399 he became confessor to Henry IV. Gregory XII made him a cardinal in 1408.

REPOSE, Altar of. An altar on which (acc. to W. usage) *Hosts consecrated at the *Maundy Thursday Mass are reserved for Communion on *Good Friday.

REPROACHES, The. A set of reproaches addressed by the Crucified Saviour to His unfaithful people, which form part of the *Good Friday liturgy of the RC Church. They are built up on OT passages, but their early history is obscure. They are sung during the *Veneration of the Cross.

REPROBATION. The act by which God condemns sinners to eternal punishment, and the state of this punishment. St. *Augustine used expressions which could be taken as meaning that God predestines some men to perdition, and in the 9th cent. *Gottschalk was accused of teaching this explicitly. This issue has been central to the controversies over *predestination (q.v.).

REQUIEM. A Mass offered for the dead, so named from the opening words of the *introit which, until recently, was used at all such Masses in the Roman rite. Many of the features previously characteristic of requiems disappeared in the 1970 Roman Missal: vestments, which used to be black, may now be any colour determined by national conferences of bishops, and unbleached candles are no longer required. On the occasion of a burial, the Mass is followed immediately by a final commendation.

REREDOS. Any decoration put up above and behind an altar. The earliest type were paintings on the walls against which altars backed. In the Middle Ages the reredos came commonly to be made of painted wooden panels, either fixed or in the form of a triptych, or of carved stone or alabaster.

RERUM NOVARUM (1891). An encyclical of *Leo XIII, intended to apply traditional Catholic teaching to the conditions created by the Industrial Revolution. On the ground that society originated in the family, it proclaimed private property a natural right and condemned socialism as infringing it; it upheld the ideal of a just wage, defined as 'enough to support the wage-earner in reasonable and frugal comfort' with a family; and it maintained that the natural place of women was in the home. The 40th anniversary of its publication was marked by the issue of *Quadragesimo Anno*; on the 80th anniversary in 1971 *Paul VI published an Apostolic Letter on Social Justice.

RESCISSORY ACT (1661). The Act passed by the Scottish Parliament which repealed legislation enacted since 1633. Its effect was to overthrow *Presbyterianism and restore episcopacy.

RESERVATION. The practice of keeping the Bread (and occasionally also the Wine) consecrated at the Eucharist, primarily for the purpose of Communion. At first the faithful kept the Bl. Sacrament in their homes or on their persons, but from the 4th cent. the churches became the ordinary places of reservation. The Sacrament was kept either in the sacristy or in the church itself, in an *aumbry in the wall, in a *pyx hanging over the altar, or in a *tabernacle on the altar, the last being the normal modern RC practice. A lamp is kept burning nearby as a sign of honour. In the E. a drop of the consecrated Wine is placed on the *Host, which may then be artificially dried.

In the C of E the 1549 BCP provided for reservation for the Communion of the sick, but the provision was dropped in 1552. In the 19th and 20th cents. the practice was revived in some places.

RESERVATION, Mental. See *Mental Reservation*.

RESERVED SINS. Bishops in the RC Church have the right to 'reserve' certain sins to their own jurisdiction. Some sins are reserved by a general law, others by a particular enactment. In normal cases absolution for reserved sins may be granted only by the authority making the reservation, his successor, superior, or delegate.

RESIDENCE. All clergy are under a grave obligation to reside in the place in which they are authorized to minister. Owing to frequent abuses, injunctions on the subject figure in *canons from early times; the duty is precisely specified in modern RC canon law and in the C of E canons of 1969.

RESPONSES. See *Versicles*.

RESPONSORY. A liturgical chant traditionally consisting of a series of *versicles and responses, the text usually taken from Scripture. The arrangement was designed for alternate singing of sentences or lines by different people. At Mass there were formerly responsories at the *Gradual (now replaced by a Responsorial Psalm sung by cantor or choir and people) and at the *Offertory. In the *Office there are responsories after the lessons in the '*Office of Readings' and a shorter form, the 'responsorium breve', follows the Little *Chapter in the other Offices.

RESTITUTION. In W. *moral theology, the act of 'commutative justice' by which an injury done to the goods or person of another is repaired. Theologians have elaborated on the degree of restitution required, depending on whether the injury was done in good or bad faith and, in the case of goods, whether they are still extant.

RESTORATION, The. A term used by English historians to describe the restoration of the monarchy under *Charles II in 1660, and the period immediately following this event.

RESURRECTION, Community of the. See *Community of the Resurrection*.

RESURRECTION OF CHRIST, The. That Christ, after His death and burial, rose again on the third day, is a fundamental tenet of the Christian faith. It was the basic element in the earliest preaching of the Gospel by the Apostles (see Acts 2: 22–36), and at a date before most of the NT Books were written St. *Paul testified that it was part of the Gospel that he had 'received' that Christ 'rose again the third day' and had been seen by many (1 Cor. 15: 1-17). By stating that Christ 'was buried' and then 'rose again' before listing His appearances, Paul pointed to an objective resurrection in which Christ's human body no longer remained in the tomb.

The Gospel records of the various appearances of Christ after His Resurrection are unclear over details of place and time. In Mk. and Mt. the disciples are bidden to go to *Galilee to meet the Risen Lord; in Lk. and Jn. Christ first showed Himself to His disciples in *Jerusalem. While the accounts of the Resurrection appearances in Mt. and Lk. might be read as referring to a single day, Jn. spaces the events over a week or more, and Acts fixes the period at 40 days, closing with the *Ascension. To these Paul adds the appearance to himself on the road to Damascus. But on the significance of the Resurrection as Christ's conquest over death and His entrance into His glory all the NT writers are agreed.

RESURRECTION OF THE DEAD. It is a fundamental Christian belief that at the *Parousia or 'Second Coming' of Christ departed souls will be restored to bodily life and the saved will enter in this renewed form upon the life of heaven. The Christian teaching on the resurrection of the dead differs from the Greek doctrine of the natural immortality of the soul in that it implies a restoration of the whole psychophysical organism, and it holds that life after death is wholly a gift of God. At some periods it has been maintained that the resurrection will involve revivifying the material particles of the dead body, but many theologians now argue that the resurrection body will be a body of a new order, identical with the earthly body only in the sense that it will be the recognizable organism of the same personality.

RETABLE. A structure placed at the back of an altar in the form either of a ledge on which ornaments may be set or a frame for decorated panels.

RETREAT. A period of days spent in silence and occupied with meditation and other religious exercises. As a formal devotion, retreats were introduced in the *Counter-Reformation period; retreat houses were established in the 17th cent. In the RC Church the practice of making an annual retreat became widespread in the 19th cent. In the C of E retreats were introduced under the influence of the *Oxford Movement.

RETZ, CARDINAL DE (Jean François Paul de Gondi) (1614-79), Abp. of Paris. He was made a cardinal in 1652 at Louis XIV's suggestion, but he soon fell from favour and was imprisoned. When his uncle died in 1654, his plenipotentiaries took possession of the see of Paris, which had been in his family since 1569, and a few months later he escaped from prison. After various adventures he returned to Paris in 1661, was reconciled to the king, and in 1662 exchanged his see for the abbey of *St.-Denis.

REUCHLIN, JOHANNES (1455-1522), German humanist. He studied Hebrew with the help of some learned Jews, and his most important work, *De Rudimentis Hebraicis* (1506), comprising a Hebrew grammar and lexicon, placed the scientific study of Hebrew on a new basis; it was also a powerful stimulus to the study of the OT in the original. The latter years of his life were troubled by a controversy with the *Dominicans of *Cologne on the destruction of Jewish books which Reuchlin opposed in the interests of scholarship. Though many of the Reformers took part in the controversy on Reuchlin's side, he remained a loyal Catholic.

REUNION. Desire for the visible unity of Christendom has increased in the present century, both on practical and on theological grounds. The problems involved vary with the different bodies between whom reunion is envisaged, but there has been growing doctrinal agreement between the major Christian denominations. In recent times there has also been a marked change in the attitude of the RC Church towards members of other communions; in the Decree on Ecumenism of the Second *Vatican Council they were described as 'separated brethren' rather than as outside the Church. Joint commissions of RCs with various other Churches have been established.

Reunion with the *Orthodox Church has frequently been attempted by W. Churches. After the short-lived union achieved by the Council of *Florence (1439), there were other less important *rapprochements*. Some

Orthodox Churches sent observers to the Second Vatican Council, and in 1965 the mutual anathemas of 1054 between the E. and W. Churches were lifted. There have also been various contacts with the Orthodox by the C of E and by the *Old Catholics.

Since the 17th cent. there have been aspirations for reunion between the C of E and the RC Church, notably at the time of the *Oxford Movement and at the *Malines Conversations (1921–5). There have also been intermittent efforts to unite the English Dissenters with the Established Church, beginning with the abortive attempt at the *Restoration to 'comprehend' *Presbyterians and Independents. The *Lambeth Conference of 1888 laid down four conditions for such a union. The *Kikuyu Conference (1913) showed a widespread desire among missionaries for federation and intercommunion without waiting for dogmatic agreement or uniformity in Church order. The main difficulty which emerged in conversations between the C of E and the Free Churches concerned questions of ministry, which figured prominently in the abortive *Anglican–Methodist Conversations (1955–1972). In other parts of the world unions in which Anglicans were involved with nonepiscopal Churches have been achieved, notably in *South India in 1947.

There have been a number of unions which represent the healing of past internal dissensions, and inter-confessional unions on a geographical basis. For instance, in 1900 the *Free Church of Scotland and the *United Presbyterian Church joined to form the *United Free Church of Scotland, which itself merged in 1929 with the Established Church of *Scotland. In 1925 the United Church of *Canada was established, including former *Methodists, *Congregationalists, and Presbyterians. There have been many such unions in the *United States of America. There a wider *Consultation on Church Union was set up in 1962, but the Plan of Union produced in 1970 has been shelved.

Plans for union on a confessional rather than a geographical basis were initiated in 1966 between the International Congregational Council and the World Alliance of Reformed and Presbyterian Churches; these came to fruition in 1970. Two years later the Presbyterian Church of England and the greater part of the Congregational Church of England and Wales united to form the *United Reformed Church. The union of two confessional organizations on a world-wide basis appears to be without precedent.

See also *Ecumenical Movement* and *Uniat Churches*.

REUSCH, FRANZ HEINRICH (1825–1900), *Old Catholic theologian. In 1870 he opposed the infallibility decrees of the *Vatican Council and in 1872 he was excommunicated on his refusal to subscribe. He then took a leading part in organizing the Old Catholic Church and in arranging the *Bonn Conferences of 1874 and 1875. When the Old Catholics abandoned clerical *celibacy in 1878, Reusch protested and retired into lay communion.

REVELATION. In Christian theology the word is used both of the corpus of truth about Himself which God discloses and of the process by which His communication of it takes place. Since it is commonly held that some truths about God can be learnt through man's natural endowments (e.g. His existence, which philosophers outside the Christian tradition have claimed they could establish), while others, e.g. the doctrine of the Holy *Trinity, are not knowable except by faith, Christian philosophers have distinguished between 'truths of reason' and 'truths of revelation'. Traditionally, Protestants have held that all revelation is sufficiently contained in the Bible, Catholics that part is also found in the *tradition of the Church.

REVELATION, Book of. The last Book of the NT and the only one that is *apocalyptic. Apart from the letters to the *Seven Churches of Asia Minor, the Book consists of a series of visions.

The author of the Book is described in the title as 'John the Divine'. In the W. he has traditionally been identified with St. *John the Apostle. Modern scholars have noted points of contact between Jn. and Rev., but regard common authorship as precluded by differences in outlook as well as of language. It is not unlikely that the author's name was John; he was an otherwise unknown Christian of Asia Minor.

Its hostile attitude to Rome indicates that the Book cannot be earlier than the persecution under *Nero in 64. It more probably dates from a later persecution, perhaps that of *Domitian (81–96).

REVEREND. An epithet of respect applied to the clergy since the 15th cent. Since the 17th cent. it has been used as a title prefixed to their names in correspondence. Archbishops are styled 'Most Reverend'; other Bishops 'Right Reverend', and Deans 'Very Reverend'.

REVISED VERSION OF THE BIBLE, The. See *Bible (English Versions)*, 4.

REVIVALISM. A type of religious worship and practice centring on evangelical revivals, or outbursts of mass religious fervour, and stimulated by intensive preaching and prayer meetings.

REVUE BIBLIQUE. A quarterly periodical published in Paris by the *Dominicans of the convent of St. Étienne at *Jerusalem. It was founded by M. J. *Lagrange and first appeared in Jan. 1892.

RHEIMS. See *Reims*.

RHENATUS, BEATUS (1485–1547), German humanist. He produced many editions of the classics and of the *Fathers and an excellent work on German antiquities. In 1540–1 he published the works of his friend D. *Erasmus. Like him, Rhenatus at first favoured the Reformers, but changed his attitude when the revolutionary character of Protestantism became apparent.

RHODES, Knights of. See *Hospitallers*.

RHODO (2nd cent.), anti-*Gnostic apologist. For a time he was a disciple of *Tatian at Rome; he wrote under the Emp. Commodus (180–92).

RHYTHMICAL OFFICE. A form of *Breviary office, popular in the Middle Ages, in which not only the hymns but also almost all the other parts except the psalms and lessons were put into metre or rhyme.

RICAUT, P. See *Rycaut, P.*

RICCI, MATTEO (1552–1610), *Jesuit missionary. He worked in *China from 1582. He gained the esteem of the Chinese by displaying and explaining to them European scientific instruments, esp. clocks and a map of the world, and he made many converts by adapting Christianity to Chinese

notions. After his death his methods gave rise to a protracted controversy on the legitimacy of *accommodation (q.v.), which was condemned in 1704 and 1715.

RICCI, SCIPIONE DE' (1741–1810), Bp. of Pistoia-Prato from 1780 to 1790. He took the lead in introducing into N. Italy *Josephinist doctrines and a higher standard of morals. He carried through a plan of reform at the Synod of *Pistoia (1786), but he was deposed in 1790.

RICHARD OF CHICHESTER, St. (c. 1197–1253), Bp. of *Chichester. He was born at 'Wych' (i.e. Droitwich) and hence is sometimes known as 'Richard of Wych'. He was elected Bp. of Chichester in 1244 and consecrated by *Innocent IV in 1245. He was a man of deep spirituality and an excellent administrator.

RICHARD OF MIDDLETON (born c. 1249), 'Richardus de Mediavilla', *Franciscan philosopher and theologian. It is disputed whether he was English or French, and little is known of his life. His chief works are a commentary on the 'Sentences' of *Peter Lombard, which is notable for its clarity and precision, *Quodlibets*, and *Quaestiones disputatae*.

RICHARD OF ST.-VICTOR (d. 1173), *Victorine mystic and theologian. A treatise *De Trinitate* was his most important work. Despite his mystical temperament, he insisted on the importance of demonstration and argument in matters of theology and the folly of being content with an array of authorities. He held that it was possible to arrive at the essentials of the Christian doctrine of the *Trinity by the process of speculative reasoning.

RICHELIEU, ARMAND JEAN DU PLESSIS (1585–1642), French cardinal and politician. He was made a cardinal in 1622 and in 1629 he became chief minister and virtual ruler of France. He aimed at the establishment of absolutism in France and the destruction of the Habsburg–Spanish power in Europe. In pursuit of the former aim he fought the *Huguenots, who were allied with the feudal aristocracy. They were defeated at La Rochelle in 1628 and their political privileges were abolished. In foreign policy he supported the Protestant German princes and

*Gustavus Adolphus of Sweden against the Emperor, thus impeding the work of Catholic restoration in Germany. Though an enemy of the *Jesuits, he opposed *Jansenism and dispersed the Solitaires of *Port-Royal in 1638.

RIDLEY, NICHOLAS (c. 1500–55), Bp. of London from 1550. From 1535 he had leanings towards the teaching of the Reformers, partly through reading *Ratramnus's work on the Eucharist, and with the accession of *Edward VI his Protestantism became more pronounced. On *Mary's accession he was deprived of his see. He was excommunicated in 1554 and burnt with H. *Latimer.

RIDSDALE JUDGEMENT. The judgement of the *Judicial Committee of the Privy Council in 1877 that the use of *Eucharistic Vestments was illegal in the C of E, but that the *Eastward Position was permitted, provided that it did not conceal from the congregation the *manual acts. The defendant in the case was the Rev. C. J. Ridsdale, vicar of St. Peter's, Folkestone.

RIEMENSCHNEIDER,   TILMAN (c. 1460–1531), German wood-carver and sculptor. In his altar-pieces he secured unity by focusing the design on a central point. In place of colour he achieved his effects by the play of light, the nature of his material, and the highly expressive faces of his figures. His work was long neglected but is now highly esteemed.

RIENZO, COLA DI (c. 1313–54), Tribune of the Roman people. The son of a Roman innkeeper, he gained the confidence of *Clement VI on a mission to *Avignon in 1343. When in 1347 he summoned the people of Rome to the Capitol and was invested with almost dictatorial powers, the Pope sanctioned his action, but he was driven from Rome later in the year. Nevertheless, in 1353 Innocent VI sent Rienzo to Rome with Card. Albornoz, and he entered the city in triumph in 1354. His cruelty and luxury again alienated the people and he was killed while trying to escape.

RIEVAULX (i.e. Rye Valley), N. Yorks. One of the earliest *Cistercian foundations in England. In 1131 William Espec provided the site for a colony of Cistercians sent by St.

*Bernard of Clairvaux. The abbey soon gained a reputation as a centre of devotion, learning, and agriculture. The buildings are in ruins, but part of the Early English church remains.

RIGORISM. In a technical sense the term is used as another name for the system of moral theology known as *Tutiorism. Nontechnically it denotes the cult of extreme asceticism and self-denial and rigid keeping of the letter of the law, and thus approximates in meaning to formalism.

RIMINI, Synod of. See *Ariminum and Seleucia, Synods of.*

RINGS. The ring is commonly considered an emblem of fidelity. Those in Christian use include:

(1) Episcopal rings. Rings are first mentioned as an official part of a bishop's insignia of office in the 7th cent. They now usually contain an amethyst.

(2) Nuns' rings. In many orders a ring is conferred at solemn *profession.

(3) Wedding rings. Originating in the betrothal rings used by the Romans, they were adopted by Christians at an early date. Customs regarding their use have varied. The current RC marriage ceremony envisages the use of a ring for both husband and wife.

(4) The 'Fisherman's Ring' is a seal-ring placed on the finger of a new Pope and broken at his death. Engraved on it is St. *Peter in a boat fishing, with the Pope's name round it.

(5) The 'Coronation Ring' in England is placed on the 4th finger of the Sovereign's right hand as 'the emblem of Kingly Dignity and of Defence of the Catholic Faith'.

RIPALDA,   JUAN   MARTÍNEZ   DE (1594–1648), Spanish *Jesuit. He was one of the most famous theologians of his time. His chief work is a treatise on the supernatural, *De Ente Supernaturali* (1634–48).

RIPON. About 650 Aldfrid, King of Northumbria, founded a monastery, of which St. *Wilfrid became abbot in 661; it was destroyed in 950. In the 11th cent. *Augustinian canons built a new church on the ruins. This foundation was dissolved by *Henry VIII, but was re-founded as a collegiate church in 1604. In 1836 the church became the cathedral of the new diocese of Ripon.

RITA OF CASCIA, St. (1381–1457), nun. She apparently married reluctantly, but made an exemplary wife and mother. After her husband's death she was admitted to the *Augustinian convent at Cascia in Umbria, owing (it is related) to supernatural intervention. She lived very austerely.

RITES, The Congregation of Sacred. This Congregation was established by *Sixtus V in 1588 to carry out the decrees of the Council of *Trent regarding uniformity of public worship. It was responsible for the direction of liturgy and everything to do with *canonization, *beatification, and the veneration of *relics. In 1969 it was divided into two Congregations, one for the Causes of Saints and the other for Divine Worship.

RITSCHL, ALBRECHT (1822–89), German Protestant theologian. He was professor of theology first at Bonn and then at Göttingen. He began his career as a disciple of F. C. *Baur and the *Tübingen School, but he came to abandon that position. He insisted on the irreducibility of religion to other forms of experience. We apprehend by faith, not by reason, and this faith rests not on the intellectual apprehension of facts but on the making of value-judgements. He further insisted that it was to a community, not to individuals, that the Gospel was, and still is, committed. It is in and through the community that justification is primarily achieved.

Ritschl's writings, and esp. *Die christliche Lehre von der Rechtfertigung und Versöhnung* (1870–4), exercised an immense influence on the theology of Germany in the late 19th cent. The so-called 'Ritschlian School' was characterized by its stress on ethics and on the 'community', and by its repudiation of metaphysics and religious experience.

RITUAL. Strictly, the prescribed form of words of a liturgical function. In common usage the word is also employed, often in a derogatory sense, of the accompanying ceremonial. In the 19th cent. the term 'Ritualist' was used of those who introduced medieval or modern RC ceremonial into the C of E.

RITUAL COMMISSION, The. The Royal Commission created in 1867 to inquire into the differences in ceremonial practice in the C of E. Its four reports dealt with *Eucharistic vestments (1867), *incense and lights (1868), the *lectionary (1869), and Prayer Book revision and other subjects (1870).

RITUAL MASSES. The Masses provided in the 1970 Roman Missal for use on the various occasions when Sacraments or other solemn acts are included in the Eucharist, e.g. at *Baptisms, weddings, or wedding anniversaries.

RITUALE ROMANUM. The official service book of the RC rite, containing the prayers and formulas for the administration of the Sacraments and other liturgical actions of a priest apart from the Mass and Divine Office.

RITUS SERVANDUS. The short title of two liturgical items relating to the traditional RC rite: (1) The rules about the customs and ceremonial of the Mass, now obsolete; and (2) A book containing directions and prayers for *Benediction of the Blessed Sacrament and certain other extra-liturgical services, now obsolescent.

ROBBER COUNCIL OF EPHESUS (449). See *Latrocinium*.

ROBERT, St. (*c.* 1027–1111), Abbot of Molesme. He became a monk when he was 15. In 1075 he founded a monastery at Molesme in Burgundy for some hermits who had asked to be placed under his direction. When divisions appeared in the community, Robert and some of the monks left Molesme in 1098 and founded the monastery at *Cîteaux. 18 months later the monks of Molesme asked to have their abbot back; Robert returned and Molesme became a famous *Benedictine centre.

ROBERT BELLARMINE, St.; ROBERT OF HOLCOT. See *Bellarmine, St. Robert*, and *Holcot, Robert*.

ROBERT OF MELUN (d. 1167), *Scholastic theologian. An Englishman by birth, he studied and taught at *Paris. In 1142 he went to Melun, where he directed a school. He became Bp. of *Hereford in 1163. His Trinitarian doctrine was influential. Acc. to him, power is to be esp. attributed to the Father, wisdom to the Son, and goodness to the Holy Spirit, without, however, robbing the other two Persons of the quality predicated in a particular way of the one. He used every device of dialectic to maintain a conservative position.

ROBERT OF WINCHELSEA. See *Winchelsea, Robert of.*

ROBERT, P. See *Olivetan.*

ROBERTSON, FREDERICK WILLIAM (1816–53), Anglican preacher. He had abandoned his earlier *Evangelicalism in favour of a *Broad Church type of theology before 1847, when he was appointed minister of Trinity Chapel, Brighton, a small *proprietary chapel. Here his influence as a preacher extended far and wide, embracing the working classes. His appeal lay in his manifest sincerity, his spiritual insight, and his capacity for analysing motive and character.

ROBINSON, HENRY WHEELER (1872–1945), *Baptist theologian. From 1920 to 1942 he was Principal of Regent's Park College and he was chiefly responsible for its transference from London to Oxford. His main interests lay in the fields of OT theology and the doctrines of the Holy Spirit and Redemption. His influence extended far beyond his own communion.

ROBINSON, JOHN (*c.* 1572–1625), pastor of the *Pilgrim Fathers. Though ordained in the C of E, he became a *Puritan, joining the 'gathered Church' at Scrooby Manor, Notts. In 1608 he and his congregation fled to Holland. From 1617 he interested himself in the plans of his community at *Leyden to emigrate to America, as their strict *Calvinism had brought them into conflict with the *Arminianism of which Leyden was a centre. Though he was prevented from sailing in the *Mayflower*, he encouraged the enterprise.

ROCH, St. (*c.* 1295–1327), healer of the plague-stricken. He is said to have stopped on a journey from France to Italy at the plague-ridden town of Aquapendente, where he cured many by the sign of the cross, and later to have performed similar miracles elsewhere.

ROCHESTER, Kent. The see was founded by St. *Augustine, who consecrated St. *Justus its first bishop in 604. The cathedral, which was served in early times by secular canons, was damaged by the Mercians and by the Danes. Gundulf (Bp., 1077–1108) began a new cathedral, and in 1082 replaced the secular canons by *Benedictines; this cathedral was consecrated in 1130. In 1343 the choir was rebuilt and a central tower added (replaced 1825–7). At the *Dissolution, *c.* 1541, the monks were replaced by a dean and canons.

ROCHET. A white linen vestment, resembling the *surplice but with tight sleeves, which is worn by bishops and occasionally by other ecclesiastical dignitaries. The rochet worn by Anglican bishops under the *chimere has wide lawn sleeves.

ROCOCO. A development of *baroque architecture and decoration, which originated in France and lasted from *c.* 1715 to 1750.

ROGATION DAYS. In W. Christendom certain prescribed days of prayer and fasting in the early summer, associated esp. with prayer for the harvest. The 'Major Rogation' on 25 Apr. was a Christianization of the pagan observance of the 'Robigalia', which took the form of processions through the cornfields to pray for the preservation of the crops from mildew. The 'Minor Rogations', on the Monday, Tuesday, and Wednesday before *Ascension Day, derived from the processional litanies ordered by St. *Mamertus of Vienne (*c.* 470), when his diocese was troubled by volcanic eruptions; they spread through Gaul and elsewhere. In the C of E the BCP of 1662 ordered the observance of the three (minor) Rogations as 'Days of Fasting and Abstinence'. In the RC Church the Rogation Days were replaced in 1969 by periods of prayer for the needs of mankind, the fruits of the earth, and the works of men's hands; these periods may be arranged at any time of year.

ROGERS, JOHN (*c.* 1500–55), editor of '*Matthew's Bible'. He became a Protestant in Holland, soon after meeting W. *Tyndale (d. 1536), and in 1537 under the name of 'Thomas Matthew' he published the first complete version of the Bible in English; his own share was confined to contributing prefaces and marginal notes. Returning to London in 1548, he was given preferment by the Crown, but under *Mary he was burnt at *Smithfield.

ROLLE OF HAMPOLE, RICHARD (*c.* 1300–49), English hermit and mystic. He appears to have been a native of Yorkshire and to have studied at Oxford. At the age of 18 he became a hermit; he spent the last years of his life near the convent of *Cistercian nuns at Hampole. He was widely venerated and attempts were made to secure his canonization.

His prolific writings on mystical and ascetical topics contain references to his own experiences (under the distinctive terms 'heat', 'sweetness', and 'song'), as well as a defence of his views on the value of the eremitical life. His best-known writings in English are his lyric poems, his commentary on the Psalter, and letters written for the guidance of others. His Latin treatises *Incendium Amoris* and *Emendatio Vitae* were later translated into Middle English.

ROLLS CHAPEL, The. A chapel which once stood on the site of the Public Record Office, London. The first chapel (begun in 1233) was part of a foundation by Henry III for the reception of converted Jews; this was destroyed in the 17th cent. After extensive rebuilding, in 1895 it was decided to pull down the crumbling walls of the Chapel and erect a museum.

ROMAINE, WILLIAM (1714–95), *Calvinist preacher. After following the scholarly traditions of the C of E in his early years, he came under the influence of G. *Whitefield in 1755 and became one of the chief representatives of rigid Calvinism. His preaching attracted vast crowds to St. George's, Hanover Square, where their presence was resented by the fashionable parishioners. After holding brief appointments at other London churches, Romaine became incumbent of St. Anne's, Blackfriars, in 1766.

ROMAN CATHOLICISM. The term, which denotes the faith and practice of Christians who are in communion with the Pope, is used esp. of Catholicism as it has existed since the *Reformation, in contradistinction to *Protestant bodies. Whereas in the early centuries the Church had to clarify the mysteries of the *Trinity and the *Incarnation and in the Middle Ages concentrated on the relation of God and man through *grace and the *sacraments, post-Tridentine theologians have been esp. concerned with the structure and prerogatives of the Church,

the position of the BVM in the economy of salvation, and the function of the Papacy. In recent years there has been some reaction against the positions adopted at the end of the 19th cent.; this movement is connected with the Second *Vatican Council, with its doctrine of the *collegiality of bishops, the use of the vernacular in worship, and a more liberal attitude towards Christians of other denominations.

From an external point of view RCism presents itself as an organized hierarchy of bishops and priests, with the Pope at its head. Supernatural life is normally mediated to individual Christians by members of the hierarchy in the *seven sacraments, which cover the whole life of RCs. The centre of this liturgical life is the Mass (or *Eucharist). Frequency of Communion has been encouraged in modern times, but it is required only at Easter. Attendance at Mass is obligatory on all Sundays and *Feasts of Obligation.

In post-Reformation Catholicism the religious life increased in scope and size. New orders, of whom the *Jesuits were the most influential, were founded to engage in teaching, nursing, and social work. The period since the Second World War has seen the growth of 'lay congregations', such as the 'Little Brothers' inspired by the ideals of Charles *de Foucauld, seeking to combine an element of contemplation with the discipline of earning their living, often in industrial society. Despite some changes of emphasis in recent years, the primary aim of the RC Church remains the sanctification of its members and the conversion of souls.

ROMAN CATHOLIC RELIEF ACTS. See *Catholic Relief Acts.*

ROMAN CONGREGATIONS. The executive departments of the Roman *curia responsible for the central administration of the RC Church. They were established by *Sixtus V in 1588. Since the reorganization of the curia in 1967, there have been nine congregations, most of them with modified titles and redefined competence.

ROMAN MARTYROLOGY, The. The official *martyrology of the RC Church. It was compiled by a commission of scholars, incl. C. *Baronius, and issued in 1584 to replace the various local adaptations of *Usuard's text which had been current since the Middle Ages. It has been subject to various revisions.

ROMAN PSALTER, The. The text of the Psalms used in Italian churches until the time of *Pius V (1566–72), when it was virtually replaced, except at *St. Peter's, Rome, by the '*Gallican Psalter' (q.v.). It has commonly been equated with the revision of the Latin Psalter which St. *Jerome says that he made hastily on the basis of the LXX, but this identification has been challenged. See *Psalters, Western*.

ROMANIA, Christianity in. See *Rumania, Christianity in*.

ROMANOS, St. (*fl. c.* 540), 'Melodos', Greek religious poet, the most significant composer of the *contakion*, the metrical sermon chanted to music. A Syrian by birth, he made his way to *Constantinople, where he achieved fame. Eighty metrical sermons have come down under his name, but not all are genuine.

ROMANS, Epistle to the. The longest of St. *Paul's letters and the most systematic theologically. It was prob. sent from *Corinth, *c.* A.D. 58, when Paul was about to leave for *Jerusalem at the end of his 'Third Missionary Journey' and was proposing to travel thence to *Rome.

Paul points to the universality of sin and concludes that man cannot be justified by any human effort at obedience. *Justification is given by the righteousness of God which is revealed in Christ, whom God 'set forth to be a propitiation' (3: 25) to reconcile sinful man to God. This free gift of God is to be appropriated by *faith. Paul then rebuts the suggestion that in such a situation we might as well 'continue in sin, that grace may abound' (6: 1); in reply he points to the change in character effected by *Baptism. Discussing the destiny of the Jews, who appear to have rejected the salvation offered, he emphasizes the sovereignty of God and suggests that the falling away of the Jews may be only temporary. He then deals with the practical obligations of the Christian life. He ends with greetings, the 'grace', and a doxology.

The integrity of the text has been much discussed. There is evidence that one ancient recension ended at 14: 23 and another at 15: 33, both followed immediately by the doxo-

logy. There are also texts which omit the name 'Rome' in 1: 7 and 1: 15. Apart from the textual evidence, many modern scholars have contended that the long list of personal greetings in ch. 16 suggests that this chapter was designed for a Church in which Paul had friends, rather than Rome, which he explicitly states (1: 13) that he had never visited.

Rom. has always been recognized as a primary contribution to Christian theology. Its teaching was esp. influential in St. *Augustine's anti-*Pelagian writings, and it has profoundly influenced the Christian outlook on *original sin, merit, and justification generally.

ROMANTICISM. The movement in literature and art reasserting passion and imagination in reaction from the classicism and rationalism which marked the 18th cent. The term is also used in a more exact sense of a school which flourished in Germany in the late 18th to early 19th cent., including Goethe, F. *Schlegel, and F. D. E. *Schleiermacher.

ROMANUS, St. A deacon and *exorcist of a church in *Caesarea in Palestine, who was martyred at *Antioch (*c.* 304) in the *Diocletianic persecution.

ROMANUS, St., 'Melodus'. See *Romanos, St.*

ROME (Early Christian). An early but not well grounded tradition asserts that St. *Peter reached Rome in A.D. 42. When the Epistle to the *Romans was written (*c.* A.D. 58), a large Christian community already existed at Rome. St. *Paul arrived between A.D. 59 and 61, and many scholars hold that his '*Captivity Epistles', as well as Mk., Lk., Acts, and 1 Pet., were written in Rome. The burning of the city under *Nero (A.D. 64) was the pretext for a general persecution of Christians in which it appears that both Peter and Paul were martyred. In the remaining part of the 1st cent. the Church grew and attracted persons of every social rank.

The early bishops of Rome were all Greek-speaking and mostly administrators rather than theologians. *Victor I (189–98) was the first Latin-speaking Pope, and his action in the *Quartodeciman Controversy reflects the growing importance of the see. A serious schism was caused by St. *Hippolytus's dispute with *Callistus I (217–22) on disciplinary and dogmatic matters. During the persecution of *Decius (249–51) *Fabian (236–50) was martyred and the see kept vacant for 13 months. Another rigorist schism, led by *Novatian, took place under *Cornelius (251–3). Persecution broke out again under the Emp. Valerian (253–60), who struck at the clergy and at the property of the Church, and in 258 *Sixtus II and all his deacons were martyred.

By this date the Roman Church was highly organized. Under Cornelius there were 46 *presbyters, 7 *deacons, and a large number of lesser ministers. The considerable property of the Church included private houses in the city for worship and burial-places outside the walls (*catacombs). The administration of the property and the relief of the poor fell to the deacons, each of whom had a district and staff under him.

After the *Diocletianic persecution (in which the Church's property was confiscated), conditions gradually eased until full toleration was granted by the so-called Edict of *Milan (313). In the period between 313 and the fall of the W. Empire in 476 the authority of the Bishops, or Popes, of Rome steadily increased. They consistently intervened on the orthodox side in the theological disputes of the time. *Julius I (337–52) and *Liberius (352–66) upheld the Nicene faith against the *Arians, *Damasus I (366-84) condemned *Apollinarianism, *Innocent I (402–17) *Pelagianism, and *Celestine I (422–32) *Nestorianism, while the '*Tome' of *Leo I (440-61) assisted the defeat of *Eutychianism at the Council of *Chalcedon (451). The Council of *Sardica (343) and the legislation of the Emps. Gratian (375–83) and *Theodosius (379–95) firmly established the Roman see as a court of appeal. The growth of Christianity in Rome in the period is reflected in the building of a large number of churches under *Sylvester I (314–35) and his successors, the restoration by Damasus of the tombs of the martyrs, the introduction of monastic life by St. *Athanasius and St. *Jerome, and the beginning of the latter's new translation of the Bible (*Vulgate).

Rome declined in political significance when the capital of the Empire was moved to *Constantinople (330), and even in the W. Milan and later *Ravenna became the effective capitals rather than Rome. In the 5th cent. Italy was invaded and Rome was sacked. The partial conquest of Italy by the *Arian Lombards and the decline of the Byzantine power led the Popes to assume political authority in Rome. Fortunately for the Papacy this crisis coincided with the pontificates of the able Pelagius II (579–90) and his greater successor *Gregory I (590–604). In the 7th cent. relations between the Papacy and the Byzantine Emperors, who were the nominal overlords of Rome, deteriorated. The beginnings of the temporal power of the Papacy may be seen in the Donation of Sutri to 'St. Peter' (729) by the Lombard King Liutprand, but the growth of Lombard power caused *Stephen II in 753 to appeal to the Frankish king *Pepin. The Frankish intervention led to the destruction of the Lombard kingdom, to the restoration of the Roman Duchy and the Exarchate of Ravenna not to the Byzantine Emperor but to the Papacy, and in 800 to the coronation in Rome by *Leo III of *Charlemagne as Roman Emperor.

See also Patrimony of St. Peter; also Lateran Basilica, The; St. Peter's, Rome; Santa Maria Maggiore, and St. Paul's outside the Walls.

ROMUALD, St. (c. 950–1027), founder of the *Camaldolese Order. A nobleman of *Ravenna, he entered the abbey of Sant'Apollinare in Classe through horror at his father's having killed a man in a duel. He subsequently retired to the marshes to practise more rigid asceticism. In his later years he founded various hermitages and monasteries, that at Campus Maldoli becoming the centre of the Camaldolese Order.

RONCALLI, A. G. See John XXIII.

'ROOT AND BRANCH'. The London Petition of 1640 demanded that the episcopal system 'with all its dependencies, roots, and branches, be abolished'. The Petition became known as the Root and Branch Petition; and the expression came to be used of any thorough-going policy.

ROSARY. The devotion to the Fifteen *Mysteries (q.v.) in which 15 '*decades' of *Hail Marys are recited, each decade being preceded by the *Lord's Prayer and followed by the *Gloria Patri. Ordinarily only a third part of the Rosary, the so-called *chaplet, is said on one occasion. To assist the memory, the prayers are commonly counted on a string of beads.

ROSCELLINUS (d. *c.* 1125), *Scholastic philosopher and theologian. He was accused of *Tritheism at a Council at Soissons in 1092, but he denied having taught it. He was one of the first and most outstanding defenders of *Nominalism. He stressed the universal *in voce* to the detriment of the universal *in re*, claiming to establish that a being can have no parts. These philosophical tenets led him to adopt a Tritheist position, on the ground that if the Three Persons of the Trinity were identical in substance, as orthodoxy affirms, the Father, in generating the Son, would generate Himself and, on the other hand, the Father and the Holy Spirit would have become incarnate together with the Son.

ROSE OF LIMA, St. (1586–1617), the first canonized saint of America. She lived in Lima, Peru. A vow of virginity and her strictness of life incurred persecution from her family and friends, and long illness and early death crowned her mortifications. She was canonized in 1671 and is the Patroness of S. America and the Philippines.

ROSE, Golden. See *Golden Rose.*

ROSETTA STONE. A basalt stele, discovered in 1799 at Rosetta, on the W. bank of the mouth of the Nile, which provided the key to the Egyptian hieroglyphics. It records in Egyptian (both hieroglyphic and demotic) and in Greek a decree of the priests assembled at Memphis in favour of Ptolemy V Epiphanes (reigned 204–181 B.C.).

ROSICRUCIANS. The name assumed by members of certain secret societies who venerated the emblems of the Rose and Cross as twin symbols of the Lord's Resurrection and Redemption. Early in the 17th cent. two anonymous writings in Germany (now assigned to the *Lutheran pastor J. V. Andreae) related the fabulous story of a certain Christian Rosenkreutz, who founded a secret society devoted to the study of the hidden things of nature and an esoteric kind of Christianity, which the author claimed was still in existence. The books, which were meant to be satirical, were taken seriously, and a number of societies with alchemistic tendencies came into being under this title.

ROSMINI-SERBATI, ANTONIO (1797–1855), Italian philosopher. His system is founded on the leading idea of indeterminate being, innate in the human soul. If analysed, this idea divides itself into a plurality of other ideas which are identical with those that are in the mind of God. He distinguished between degrees of being acc. to their completeness, God alone being absolutely complete. The being, however, which actualizes finite nature and which is the object of human intuition, is 'something of God', though not God Himself. Some of Rosmini's works were put on the *Index in 1849, though removed before his death, but 40 propositions from his writings were mildly condemned in 1887–8.

In 1828 he founded the congregation of 'Fathers of Charity', often known as 'Rosminians'. Its chief aim is the sanctification of its members, combined with such works of charity as they may be called upon to perform.

ROSSETTI, CHRISTINA GEORGINA (1830–94), poetess. She was a younger sister of D. G. *Rossetti, and closely associated with the Pre-Raphaelite Brotherhood. Her works include the carol 'In the bleak midwinter'.

ROSSETTI, DANTE GABRIEL (1828–1882), English painter and poet, and one of the founders of the Pre-Raphaelite Brotherhood. In his early years he was much influenced by *Dante, and in his own poetry of this period Christian themes abound, his ideal of womanhood being expressed by the BVM and Beatrice. His paintings, which include *The Seed of David* in *Llandaff Cathedral, try to recall the spiritual beauty of medieval painters, not entirely successfully. From *c.* 1863 religious motives disappear and his poetry and art are inherently sensual.

ROSVITHA. See *Hrosvit.*

ROSY SEQUENCE. Part of the hymn '*Jesu, dulcis memoria' (q.v.) used as a *sequence for the Feast of the *Holy Name in the *Sarum rite.

ROTA SACRA ROMANA. The normal tribunal for judging cases brought before the Holy See. It dates from the mid-13th cent.; its name appears to derive from the circular table used by the judges at *Avignon. In the 18th cent. its duties were limited to civil cases and hence ended with the cessation of the temporal power of the Papacy in 1870. Reconstituted in 1908, it tries all cases except those reserved for the Pope himself and is the court of appeal for cases tried in episcopal courts.

ROTHMANN, BERNT (*c.* 1495–1535), German *Anabaptist. In 1529 he was appointed chaplain of St. Maurice's church outside Münster; by 1531 he was openly preaching *Lutheran doctrines. In 1534 he became an Anabaptist. He took part in organizing communism and the burning of books in his 'New Jerusalem' (of which the Bible was to be the only law book) and in the introduction of polygamy. He died during the occupation of Münster by the troops of the Bishop and his allies.

ROUSSEAU, JEAN-JACQUES (1712–78), French author. He became a RC in 1728. In 1741 he went to Paris; here he was introduced to the circle of the *Encyclopaedists. He returned to his native city, Geneva, in 1754, and also to *Calvinism. In the same year he wrote his *Discours sur l'origine et les fondements de l'inégalité parmi les hommes*; on the gratuitous assumption that primitive man was a free and happy being, Rousseau alleged that human inequalities arose from the undue development of his social and proprietary instincts. In 1756 he settled near Montmorency, where he wrote his most famous works. In *Émile, ou de l'Éducation* (1762) he developed a Utopian programme of education far from the corrupting influences of society. He advocated a *Deism which, although similar to that of the *Philosophes* in affirming belief in the existence of God, the soul, and a future life, found its ultimate justification in the individual's sense of a personal relationship with God through the conscience, of which He is the source and inspiration. *Du contrat social* (1762) set out his theory of a just state, resting on the general will of the people. Here 'civil religion' forbids all dogmatic intolerance and admits only those religions which do not claim to possess absolute truth.

After his death Rousseau became one of the most powerful influences in Europe. His religious impact was the deeper as he offered man a substitute for revealed religion which was not only doctrinally simple and unelaborate in its moral prescriptions, but also addressed to his emotional as well as his intellectual needs.

ROUTH, MARTIN JOSEPH (1755–1854), President of Magdalen College, Oxford, from 1791. It was he who advised S *Seabury, when sent to Europe to inaugurate an episcopal succession for the American (Anglican) Church, to seek it from the Scottish Episcopal Church. Routh's *Reliquiae Sacrae*, an edition of scattered pre-Nicene patristic texts, appeared in 1814–18; a completely revised edition in 1846–8.

ROWITES. The disciples of J. McL. *Campbell, who was in charge of the parish of Row, near Cardross, Dumbarton, from 1825 to 1830.

ROWNTREE, JOSEPH (1836–1925), *Quaker philanthropist. The head of the great cocoa business of Rowntree & Co., he was a pioneer in the movement for securing for workpeople reasonable hours and conditions of labour, higher wages, and provision against old age and unemployment. He established three trusts to carry out some of his ideals.

ROYAL CHAPELS; ROYAL DECLARATION. See *Chapel Royal* and *Declaration of the Sovereign*.

ROYAL SCHOOL OF CHURCH MUSIC (R.S.C.M.). An organization founded in 1927 as the School of English Church Music, and granted its present title in 1945. Its work has consisted in advice to choirs affiliated to the School, provision of music, and the organization of choral festivals. The College of St. Nicholas, founded at Chislehurst, Kent, in 1929, to provide courses for organists, choristers, clergy, and ordinands, was moved in 1954 to Addington Palace, a former archiepiscopal residence near Croydon.

RUBRICS. Ritual or ceremonial directions in service books. The word originated from the fact that they were often written in red to distinguish them from the text of the services. See also *Black Rubric* and *Ornaments Rubric*.

RUCHERAT (or **RUCHRAT**), JOHN. See *John of Wesel*.

RUFINUS, TYRANNIUS or TURRANIUS (*c.* 345–410), monk, historian, and translator. Born near *Aquileia, he went to Egypt *c.* 372 and for some years he studied at *Alexandria under *Didymus the Blind. In 381 he was in *Jerusalem. With *Melania the Elder he founded a *double monastery on the Mount of *Olives. He returned to Italy in 397.

Though he was also an original writer, Rufinus is important mainly as a translator of Greek theological works into Latin at a time when knowledge of Greek was declining in the W. His free rendering of *Origen's *De Principiis*, the only complete text now surviving, was intended to vindicate Origen's orthodoxy. It involved Rufinus in bitter controversy with St. *Jerome, who criticized the tendentious character of the rendering. His commentary on the *Apostles' Creed gives the earliest continuous Latin text of the 4th-cent. form of the Creed, as used at Aquileia and Rome.

RUINART, THIERRY (1657–1709), *Maurist patristic scholar. In his celebrated *Acta Primorum Martyrum Sincera et Selecta* (1689) he admitted only those of the *acts of the martyrs which seemed to him authentic; some of the contents are no longer considered genuine.

RULE, GOLDEN; RULE OF ST. BENEDICT; RULE OF THE MASTER. See *Golden Rule*; *Benedict, Rule of St*; and *Regula Magistri*.

RULER. A name formerly applied to those who presided in cathedrals over the singing in choir.

RUMANIA, Christianity in. Roman Dacia, which roughly covered the present Rumania, received Christianity through Roman soldiers and colonists in the 4th cent. or earlier. Under Bulgarian rule its ecclesiastical affairs were placed under *Constantinople, and its worship gradually took on an E. character.

The country became virtually a self-governing state in 1862, and in 1885 the claim of her national Church for independence from the metropolitan jurisdiction of Constantinople was allowed. In the 1923 constitution the Rumanian Orthodox Church was recognized as the national Church. Since 1944, however, the Church has been closely controlled by the Communist government.

RUPERT OF DEUTZ (*c.* 1075–1129/30), theologian. At an early age he entered the abbey of St. Laurent in Liège. In his first work, *Liber de divinis officiis*, he used language about the Eucharist which provoked the accusation that he taught the doctrine later known as *Impanation. In 1116 a fellow monk returned from a period of study under *Anselm of Laon reporting that he taught that God willed that evil should happen. Rupert was scandalized and wrote a rejoinder, *De Voluntate Dei*. This created a storm and he had to retire to the monastery of Siegburg. The Abp. of Cologne secured his election as Abbot of Deutz (near Cologne) in 1120. The 16th-cent. Reformers tried to find support in his writings for their own doctrines.

RURAL DEAN. In the C of E the head of a group of parishes in a given area ('Rural Deanery'), appointed by the Bishop of the diocese. The office is ancient, but its duties were gradually taken over by the Archdeacon; it was revived in 1836. The Rural Dean is president of the Ruridecanal Chapter, i.e. the chapter of the incumbents and clergy licensed under seal in the Deanery, and co-chairman of the Deanery Synods established by the *Synodical Government Measure.

RUSKIN, JOHN (1819–1900), English art critic and social reformer. His fame was established by the first volume of his *Modern Painters* (1843–60). In this and later writing he expounded his spiritual interpretation of art; he held that the art and architecture of a people are the expression of its religion and morality. His *Stones of Venice* (1851–3) included the famous chapter on 'The Nature of Gothic' which became an influence in the growth of the Gothic Revival in architecture. After 1860 he devoted himself to social and economic problems. His early *Evangelicalism gave place to a vague *Theism, and his ideas for social reform included a plan for a completely dependent State Church with state-salaried officials and a minimum of dogma. In 1870 he was elected the first professor of fine arts in Oxford. Here his social programme was among the influences leading to the establishment of university settlements.

RUSSELL, CHARLES TAZE (1852–1916), founder of the International Bible

Students Association, generally known as '*Jehovah's Witnesses' (q.v.). A draper of Pittsburg, Pennsylvania, he assumed the title of 'Pastor' in 1878. He issued a number of books and published *The Watchtower* (1879 ff.), a magazine of his movement. In 1884 he founded the Watch Tower Bible and Tract Society. Despite various scandals in which Russell was involved, his sect flourished.

RUSSIA, Christianity in. Christian missionaries first preached extensively in Russia in the 9th and 10th cents. The Emp. *Vladimir was baptized *c.* 988 and established Christianity as the official religion in his dominions. At the *Great Schism of 1054 the Russian Church took the E. side. Monastic life began *c.* 1051 with the coming from Mount *Athos of the monk Antony, who established himself near Kiev; it spread rapidly. The monasteries supplied bishops, while the secular clergy were commonly married and unlettered.

In 1461 the Russian Church was divided between two Metropolitans, centred at Moscow and Kiev; the former was entirely Russian and rigidly Orthodox, the latter more exposed to W. influence. Russia rejected the union achieved at the Council of *Florence (1439) and in 1448 a Council of Russian bishops elected a Metropolitan of Moscow without reference to the Greek ecclesiastical authorities; in this way the Russian Church became *autocephalous.

In 1503 a famous dispute broke out over monastic ownership of property, the 'Possessors' being led by St. *Joseph of Volokalamsk and the 'Non-Possessors' by St. *Nil Sorski. The latter came into conflict with the Tsar and were largely suppressed. In 1551 the Council of the Hundred Chapters was called to reform the clergy. The Russian Church realized a great ambition with the creation of the Patriarchate of Moscow in 1589.

Since the Council of Florence RCs had been severely repressed in the Moscow Tsardom, but Russians in the metropolis of Kiev fell within the territory of *Poland and Lithuania and were under pressure from their RC overlords. A large number of Russian Orthodox in this area recognized the Papacy at the Synod of *Brest–Litovsk in 1596.

Within the Russian Church the liturgical reforms of the Patr. *Nikon (d. 1681) precipitated the schism of the *Old Believers, which greatly weakened the Church in Russia. The Emp. Peter the Great (1676–1725), anxious to subjugate the Church to his authority, abolished the office of Patriarch, and in his 'Spiritual Regulation' of 1721 replaced it with the *Holy Synod, whose members were nominated by the Emperor.

In 1917–18 a large council of bishops, priests, and laity met in Moscow and initiated a thorough reorganization of all aspects of Church life, in particular restoring the Patriarchate, to which *Tikhon was elected. The Revolution of 1917, however, brought into power a government which was not only committed to the materialist and anti-religious doctrines of Marxism, but also hated the Church as the instrument and associate of Tsardom. Public worship was not forbidden, but many church buildings were confiscated and secularized, and the teaching of religion to persons under 18 became a criminal offence. Intensive 'anti-God' propaganda was maintained throughout the 1920s and 1930s. On the outbreak of hostilities with Germany in 1941, a number of concessions were made; these included the opening of 8 seminaries for training the clergy. After the War the Orthodox Church in Russia retained a limited degree of freedom, but since 1960 the Soviet State has been more oppressive in its policy towards the Church.

RUTH, Book of. This OT Book tells the story of Ruth, a Moabitess, who married a Hebrew in Moab. After her husband's death, she returned with her mother-in-law to Judah; Boaz, a kinsman of her former husband, took her under his protection and married her. Though the incident is set in the later days of the Judges (before 1000 B.C.), the Book is not earlier than the Exile (6th cent. B.C.). The genealogy at the end (4: 18–22) indicates one of the apparent aims of the author, viz. to record the Moabite strain in *David's ancestry. Ruth is thus an ancestress of Christ (Mt. 1: 5–16).

RUTHENIAN CHURCHES. Certain *Uniat Churches mostly in Polish Galicia, Czechoslovakia, and Hungary, with colonies in N. and S. America. In 1595 the Metropolitan of Kiev and certain other bishops sought communion with Rome, which was achieved in the Union of *Brest–Litovsk. After the Partition of Poland (1795) most of the Ruthenians, except those of Galicia, passed under the sovereignty of Russia and were gradually absorbed into the Orthodox Church; in 1905, when toleration was granted to RCs in Russia, those who still survived passed to the Latin rite. The Ruthenians of Galicia came under Austrian rule. They enjoyed toleration in the 19th cent., but have suffered from the political troubles of E. Europe in more recent times.

A further Ruthenian community (the Podcarpathian Ruthenians) was granted a separate jurisdiction with the creation of the eparchy of Mukachevo in 1771. It was created to settle the disputes between the Ruthenian metropolitan north of the Carpathians and the settlement (dating from the 14th cent.) of Little and White Russians south of the Carpathians, brought into communion with Rome by the Union of Uzhorod in 1646.

RUTHERFORD, JOSEPH FRANKLIN (1869–1941), called 'Judge Rutherford', second head of the '*Jehovah's Witnesses'. He was given an attorney's licence c. 1892, and he frequently defended C. T. *Russell in the courts. He became a supporter of his sect and in 1917, after Russell's death, its head. Under his leadership it assumed a more revolutionary aspect.

RUTHERFORD, MARK, pseudonym of William Hale White (1831–1913), author. A civil servant for most of his life, he won recognition as a religious author by *The Autobiography of Mark Rutherford* (1881).

RUTHERFORD, SAMUEL (c. 1600–61), Scottish *Presbyterian divine. In 1639 he became professor of divinity at St. Mary's College, St. Andrews, and in 1647 principal. He was one of the Scottish commissioners at the *Westminster Assembly in 1643. His *Lex Rex* (1644), attacking monarchical absolutism, brought him repute as a constitutional theorist; it was publicly burnt at the Restoration (1660).

RUTILIUS CLAUDIUS NAMATIANUS (5th cent.), Latin poet. In 416 he returned to his native Gaul from Rome; in *De Reditu Suo* he described the journey. He was almost certainly a pagan. His poem throws light on the background of the Church in the period.

RUYSBROECK, JAN VAN (1293–1381), Flemish mystic. He retired to a hermitage at Groenendael, near Brussels, with two other priests in 1343. They were joined by others, and in 1349 the group became a community of *Canons Regular, with Ruysbroeck as prior until his death. Groenendael became prominent in the religious movement later known as *Devotio Moderna*. Ruysbroeck's mystical writings, in Flemish, include *The Spiritual Espousals, The Seven Steps of the Ladder of Spiritual Love*, and *The Sparkling Stone*.

RYCAUT, PAUL (1628–1700), also **Ricaut**, traveller and author. He was secretary to the British Embassy at *Constantinople and then consul to the Levant Company at Smyrna. His essay on *The Present State of the Greek and Armenian Churches* (1679) remains an important source of information. He also wrote on Turkey.

RYLANDS ST. JOHN. Part of a page of a papyrus codex, now in the John Rylands Library, Manchester, which has the text of Jn. 18: 31–3 on one side and 18: 37–8 on the other. Prob. dating from the first half of the 2nd cent., it is both the earliest known MS. of any part of the NT and also the earliest distinct evidence for the existence of St. *John's Gospel.

RYLE, JOHN CHARLES (1816–1900), first Bp. of Liverpool from 1880. A strong *Evangelical, he defended his convictions in a number of tracts which had a wide circulation.

RYSWICK CLAUSE, The. The clause inserted into the Treaty of Ryswick between the Emp. Leopold and Louis XIV of France (1697), modifying the general rule that the religious frontiers should revert to their position at the time of the Treaty of Nymegen (1679) in favour of the Catholic communities in those places where they had been re-established by Louis in the interval.

S

SA, MANOEL DE (c. 1530–96), Portuguese *Jesuit. In 1595 he published *Aphorismi Confessariorum*, a manual of *casuistry in dictionary form. It was placed on the *Index in 1603 for allowing confession and absolution to be made by letter, but in its corrected edition of 1607–8 it enjoyed great esteem.

SABAOTH. A Hebrew word meaning 'armies' or 'hosts' which is left untranslated in older versions of the NT and of the *Te Deum.

SABAS, St. (439–532), monk. A native of Cappadocia, in 478 he founded a large *lavra in Palestine. He reluctantly accepted ordination to the priesthood (not then usual among monks) in 490, and in 492 the Patr. of *Jerusalem made him superior of all the hermits in Palestine.

SABAS, St., Patron of Serbia. See *Sava, St.*

SABATIER, AUGUSTE (1839–1901), French Protestant theologian. He propagated the theories of F. D. E. *Schleiermacher and A. *Ritschl in France, applied the methods of historical criticism to the NT, and, esp. by his interpretation of Christian dogma as the symbolism of religious feelings, he exercised a profound influence not only on French Protestantism but also in Catholic theological circles.

SABATIER, PAUL (1858–1928), *Calvinist pastor and student of St. *Francis. He held two pastoral cures, but he was forced by ill health to give up the work; he devoted the rest of his life to research. His *Vie de St. François* (1893; Eng. tr., 1894) depicts the mission of the saint as a renewal of the medieval Church in the light of the 'pure Gospel'; it is brilliant in presentation and penetrating in its pyschological understanding. His later work continued to give impetus to Franciscan studies and brought to light new material.

SABATIER, PIERRE (1682–1742), *Maurist scholar. His monumental work was a virtually exhaustive collection of the material then available for the *Old Latin (i.e. pre-*Vulgate) text of the Bible. It was published posthumously.

SABBATARIANISM. Excessive strictness in the observance of the Divinely ordained day of rest. In its more rigorous form it is a peculiar development of the English and Scottish Reformation, being unknown on the Continent even among *Calvinists.

The beginning of 17th-cent. Sabbatarianism is connected with the publication of N. Bound's *True Doctrine of the Sabbath* (1595), which advocated strict enforcement on OT lines. The ensuing controversy assumed political importance when *James I issued his *Book of* *Sports* (1618), allowing sport on Sunday. The Puritan Sabbath was imposed by various Acts of Parliament, but somewhat relaxed at the Restoration. Under the influence of the *Evangelical Revival rigorism reappeared at the end of the 18th cent.; the Lord's Day Observance Act (1781) forbade the opening on Sunday of places of entertainment or debate to which admission was gained by payment. Relaxation has been progressive in England since the latter part of the 19th cent. See also *Sunday.*

SABBATH. The seventh day of the Jewish week. It served the twofold purpose of being a day set apart for the worship of God (Exod. 31: 13–17) as well as for the rest and recreation of man and cattle (Deut. 5: 14). The prohibition of work was regulated by minute prescription. It was one of the grievances of the *Pharisees against Christ that He was prepared to heal on the Sabbath (e.g. Mt. 12: 10–14). Though the primitive Church continued to keep the seventh day as a day of rest and prayer, the fact that the Resurrection took place on the first day of the week soon led to the substitution of that day (*Sunday) for the Jewish Sabbath on Saturday.

SABBATINE PRIVILEGE. An indulgence granted to the *Carmelite Order. On the basis of a bull ascribed to *John XXII (1322) members of the order and its confraternities were promised unfailing salvation and early release from *purgatory if certain conditions were met. The Privilege has been confirmed by modern Popes, but the original bull is generally regarded as spurious.

SABELLIANISM. An alternative name for the Modalist form of *Monarchianism (q.v.). It is so called after Sabellius, who was prob. a 3rd-cent. theologian of Roman origin.

SABINA, St. Acc. to her *acta*, she was a widow of Umbria, who was converted by her servant and martyred at Rome *c*. 126. It is unlikely that such a saint existed. The *acta* were prob. fabricated to account for the church of St. Sabina (*titulus Sabinae*) on the Aventine Hill at Rome.

SACCAS, AMMONIUS. See *Ammonius Saccas*.

SACHEVERELL, HENRY (1674–1724), High Church divine and pamphleteer. In 1709 he preached two sermons upholding the doctrine of non-resistance and emphasizing the dangers to the Church of the Whig government's policy of toleration and allowing *Occasional Conformity. The House of Commons condemned the sermons as seditious and Sacheverell was impeached, but the sentence imposed was so light as to be a triumph for the accused, and he became a popular hero.

SACRAMENT. Acc. to the BCP *Catechism, 'an outward and visible sign of an inward and spiritual grace given unto us, ordained by Christ himself, as a means whereby we receive the same, and a pledge to assure us thereof'; or, acc. to St. *Thomas Aquinas, 'the sign' of a sacred thing in so far as it sanctifies men'. In Christian theology the scope of what the word comprises has varied widely, as many as 30 Sacraments being sometimes listed. In *Peter Lombard's *Sentences* the *seven Sacraments which have become traditional are enumerated, viz. *Baptism, *Confirmation, the *Eucharist, *Penance, Extreme *Unction, *Orders, and *Matrimony. This sevenfold number was given formal definition at the Council of *Trent and is accepted in the E. Church. A special rank among the Sacraments has always been given to Baptism and the Eucharist. In the C of E Art. 25 of the *Thirty-Nine Articles differentiates between them as 'two Sacraments ordained of Christ our Lord in the Gospel' as distinct from the other 'five commonly called Sacraments'.

Acc. to traditional Catholic theology, a distinction is made between the 'matter' and 'form' of the Sacraments, the matter being the material element (in Baptism, water; in the Eucharist, the bread and wine) and the form the consecratory words (in Baptism, the pronouncement of the Triple Formula; in the Eucharist, the words 'This is My Body', 'This is My Blood'). The right matter and the right form, used with the right *intention, are necessary for the validity of the Sacrament, which is independent of the worthiness or unworthiness of the minister. Three of the Sacraments, Baptism, Confirmation, and Orders, are held to imprint an abiding mark or *character, and therefore cannot be repeated. In Protestantism the technicalities of sacramental theology are less developed, the main importance being attached to Baptism and the Eucharist or Lord's Supper.

See also the entries on the separate Sacraments.

SACRAMENT HOUSE. A shrine-like receptacle for the *reservation of the Bl. Sacrament. Sacrament houses were usually made in the form of a small tower, the central part of which was done in open-work. From the 16th cent. they were largely displaced by *tabernacles.

SACRAMENTALS. Certain religious practices and objects akin to the *sacraments (q.v.), but of less importance. They include the *sign of the cross, saying of *grace at meals, *vestments, palms, and ashes. Acc. to RC theologians, they do not convey grace *ex opere operato*, but *ex opere operantis ecclesiae*; by the Church's intercession they convey spiritual effects and by their aid various occasions in daily life are rendered holy.

SACRAMENTARY. In the W. Church, the liturgical book in use until the 13th cent. for the celebrant at Mass. It contained the *Canon of the Mass and the proper *Collects, *Prefaces, and other prayers for use throughout the year, but not the *Epistles, *Gospels, or those parts of the service which were sung. From the 10th cent. onwards Sacramentaries began gradually to be replaced by *Missals.

SACRED COLLEGE. The corporation of *cardinals in the RC Church. The chief duties of the College are to elect the Pope and act as his privy council, though a cardinal loses his right to take part in the electoral conclave when he reaches the age of 80.

SACRED HEART. Devotion to the physical heart of Jesus can be traced back to the Middle Ages, esp. among the mystics. In the

17th cent. an elaborate theological foundation was provided by St. John *Eudes, but it was the visions of St. *Margaret Mary Alacoque in 1673–5 which gave definite shape to the object of the devotion and its practices. Its most prominent feature was *reparation for the outrages committed against the Divine Love, esp. in the Bl. Sacrament. It became a popular RC devotion, though the Mass and Office for the feast were not authorized until 1765; it is observed on the Friday in the week after *Corpus Christi.

SACRED HEART OF MARY. Devotion to the heart of the BVM was fostered in the 17th cent. by St. John *Eudes, who linked it with the cult of the *Sacred Heart of Jesus. In 1805 *Pius VII allowed the observance of a feast, which in 1944 was made universal, to be kept on 22 Aug.; in 1969 it became an optional '*memoria'.

SACRIFICE. Sacrifice is fundamentally the offering to the Deity of a gift, esp. a living creature. It is a widespread feature of religion. Early in the OT there is the record of the sacrifices of Cain and *Abel (Gen. 4: 3–5), while the demand for the sacrifice of *Isaac (Gen. 22) underlies the need for the offering to be a costly one. Sacrifices were also associated with the making of *covenants, such as that of God with Israel at *Sinai (Exod. 24: 4–8). After the settlement in Canaan, sacrificial observances became more elaborate; from the 7th cent. B.C. they were restricted to the *Temple at Jerusalem. When the Temple was rebuilt after the Exile, sacrifice continued until its destruction in A.D. 70. The chief annual sacrifice was that of the *Paschal Lamb at the *Passover.

At the Institution of the Eucharist, Christ pointed to the sacrificial quality of His death (cf. Mk. 10: 45), speaking of the shedding of His Blood in a New Covenant. The Fathers developed the ideas of the NT, stressing the uniqueness of His sacrifice in that He was: (1) a voluntary victim; (2) a victim of infinite value; and (3) Himself also the priest. In the Middle Ages the relationship of Christ's sacrifice with the Eucharist was elaborated. Christian theology also commonly asserts that the individual's conscious obedience to the will of God may be a form of sacrifice.

SACRILEGE. Violation or contemptuous treatment of a person, thing, or place publicly dedicated to the worship of God. It is held to be a grave sin, unless the matter is trivial.

SACRING BELL. A bell, also known as a 'Sanctus bell', sometimes rung at Mass to focus the people's attention, e.g. at the *Elevation.

SACRISTAN. The term is used for either (1) a *sexton, or (2) the sacrist or official who has charge of the contents of a church, including the vestments and sacred vessels.

SACRISTY. A room (or suite of rooms) annexed to a church or chapel for keeping the sacred vessels and for the vesting of priests and other clerics.

SADDUCEES. A Jewish politico-religious sect, opposed to the *Pharisees. They stood for the interests of the priestly aristocracy and at the time of Christ they were important in *Jerusalem and in the *Temple. They rejected the oral tradition of interpretation and accepted the written Law only; thus they rejected belief in the resurrection of the body and the existence of angels and spirits. They appear to have taken a leading part against Christ and repeatedly attacked the Apostles.

SADHU, The. See *Sundar Singh, Sudhu.*

SADOLETO, JACOPO (1477–1547), cardinal from 1536. In 1537 he became a member of the special commission for the reform of the Church and the preparation of a General Council. He tried to win back both P. *Melanchthon and the city of Geneva to the RC faith. He was one of the most trusted advisers of *Paul III.

SAHDONA (7th cent.), spiritual writer. He was expelled from the *Nestorian Church because of his teaching on the Person of Christ. His 'Book of Perfection' is one of the masterpieces of Syrian spirituality.

ST. ALBANS. A church has existed at Verulamium on the site of the reputed martyrdom of St. *Alban at least since the time of *Bede; c. 794 King *Offa endowed a monastery which became famous. In 1077 Paul of Caen, the first Norman abbot, began to rebuild it. At the Reformation the church was bought from *Edward VI (1553) for use as a parish church. In 1877 a diocese of St. Albans was created and the abbey became the cathedral church.

ST. ASAPH. The foundation of the diocese, now a see in the Anglican Province of *Wales, is prob. to be ascribed to St. *Kentigern (c. 560), after whose disciple and successor, St. *Asaph, the see took its name. It was originally a monastic settlement of the *Celtic type. The present cathedral is largely the work of Bp. Redman (c. 1480); the choir was rebuilt c. 1770; and the whole restored by G. G. *Scott (1869–75).

SAINT-CYRAN, ABBÉ DE (1581–1643), Jean Duvergier de Hauranne, commendatory Abbot of Saint-Cyran from 1620, and one of the authors of *Jansenism. He was a close friend of C. *Jansen, and, attracted to St. *Augustine's writings, he sought to reform Catholicism on Augustinian lines. From 1623 he was associated with the *Arnauld family and with *Port-Royal; as spiritual director of the convent from 1633 he came to exercise great influence. From 1638 to 1643 he was imprisoned by Card. *Richelieu.

ST. DAVIDS. Acc. to tradition a monastery was founded by St. *David (6th cent.) at Menevia, which was thereafter called St. Davids. The early history is fragmentary. In 1115 Bernard the Norman was elected bishop and the see became suffragan to *Canterbury. The shrine of St. David was a popular place of pilgrimage. The present cathedral was begun by Bp. Peter de Leia (1176–98).

ST.-DENIS. The *Benedictine abbey at St.-Denis, 4 miles north of Paris, was founded c. 625 and contained the reputed shrine of St. Denis (see *Dionysius, St.* [3]). It became the regular burying-place of the kings of France and long enjoyed royal favour. It was dissolved and sacked at the Revolution (1792–3); the buildings are now a 'national monument'.

ST. GALL. See *Gall, St.*

ST.-GERMAIN-DES-PRÉS. An abbey in *Paris, founded in the 6th cent., it later assumed the name of its benefactor, St. *Germanus of Paris. In the 17th cent. it adopted the *Maurist reform and became famous as a centre of scholarship. Most of its buildings were destroyed in the French Revolution, but its fine collection of MSS.

was saved.

ST. JOHN LATERAN. See *Lateran Basilica, The.*

ST.-MAUR, Congregation of. See *Maurists.*

ST.-OMER. The Jesuit college of St.-Omer in Artois was founded by R. *Parsons c. 1592 for the education of the English RC laity. When the Jesuits were expelled from France in 1762, they moved their school to Bruges, and later to *Stonyhurst. The buildings at St.-Omer were used for the preparatory school of the English clergy at *Douai until 1795.

ST. PATRICK'S PURGATORY. A place of pilgrimage on Station Island in Donegal. Acc. to tradition St. *Patrick here saw a vision which promised to all who should visit the sanctuary in penitence and faith a *plenary indulgence for all their sins and, if their faith did not fail, a sight of the torments of the damned and the joys of the redeemed.

ST. PAUL'S CATHEDRAL, London. A church was built c. 607 by *Ethelbert, King of Kent, as a cathedral for *Mellitus, first Bp. of London. It was rebuilt in stone by St. *Erconwald between 675 and 685. This Saxon building was burnt in 1087. The new Norman cathedral was begun in the same year and completed in 1332. In the NE. part of the Close stood 'St. Paul's Cross', which became a national centre for religious and political proclamations, sermons, and disputations; it was destroyed in 1643. The cathedral, already ruinous, was burnt in the Great Fire of 1666. The present cathedral, designed by Sir Christopher *Wren, combines classical style with a traditionally Gothic ground-plan. It was completed in 1710.

ST. PAUL'S OUTSIDE THE WALLS, Rome (San Paolo fuori le Mura). The original structure, erected by *Constantine over the relics of St. *Paul (324), was rebuilt as a large basilica in the late 4th cent. This was destoyed by fire in 1823, only the triumphal arch and its mosaics remaining. The present church was consecrated in 1854.

ST. PETER'S, Rome. The present 16th-cent. building replaced an older basilican structure, erected by *Constantine (d. 337) on the supposed site of St. *Peter's crucifixion. *Nicholas V (1447–55) planned to replace it by a new church in the form of a Latin cross. Work began under *Julius II in 1506 and was continued by a succession of architects, who all made changes in the design. Under *Sixtus V the nave was lengthened to accommodate a vast congregation. The building was finished in 1626.

The traditional burial-place of St. Peter is the *confessio* under the high altar. Extensive excavations have revealed the remains of a shrine which, it is claimed, dates from the 3rd cent., if not earlier.

SAINT-SIMON, CLAUDE HENRI DE ROUVROY (1760–1825), exponent of French socialism. In a number of works he argued that only the industrial classes work for the moral and physical welfare of mankind and that they should be preferred to those who had hitherto been privileged. His *Nouveau Christianisme* (1825) maintains that the only Divine principle in Christianity is that men must behave as brothers; religion should therefore provide amelioration of the lot of the poorest, with dogma and cult as negligible accessories.

His teaching had little following in his lifetime but was influential later in the 19th and the early 20th cents.

ST. SOPHIA. See *Santa Sophia.*

SAINT-SULPICE, Society of. The congregation of secular priests founded by J. J. *Olier in the parish of St.-Sulpice, Paris, in 1642, with the aim of forming a zealous clergy, esp. suited to be directors of seminaries. The Society spread to *Canada in 1657 and it soon gained a profound influence on the ecclesiastical life of France. Despite various troubles, it still trains many of those destined for the French priesthood.

ST.-VICTOR, Abbey of. See *Victorines.*

SAINTE-CHAPELLE, The. The chapel in Paris built *c.* 1245 by *Louis IX to house the *Crown of Thorns and other relics of the Passion. It was finally secularized in 1906.

SAINTS, Devotion to the. The practice of venerating and invoking the saints has long been an element in Catholic devotion. Its justification rests on the beliefs that the saints are close to God (because of their holiness) and accessible to man (whose nature they share), and in the efficacy of intercessory prayer.

In the NT the gift of special privileges for certain people in the next world is held to be indicated in Christ's promises to the Apostles (Mt. 19: 28), while support for the idea that the dead may intercede for the living is found in the parable of Dives and Lazarus (Lk. 16: 19–31). But it is to the implications of the Pauline doctrine of the Church as the Mystical Body of Christ, rather than to specific texts, that the advocates of devotion to the saints appeal.

There is clear evidence of devotion to *martyrs in the 'Martyrdom of *Polycarp' (*c.* 156), and this was furthered by the growing cult of their *relics. From the 4th cent. the ranks of those accounted saints were enlarged by the addition of '*confessors' and virgins, on the ground that a life of renunciation and holiness might equal the devotion of those who had died for Christ. Thus ascetics such as St. *Antony were soon venerated in the E., and in the W. St. *Augustine was honoured as a saint at Carthage before 475. Theologians sought to rebut the charge of idolatry by drawing a distinction between the worship of God, expressed by the word '*latria', and the cult of honour and imitation due to saints, expressed in the term '*dulia'.

Liturgical developments followed popular devotion and the current of Patristic teaching. The mention of saints in the Mass is attested by Augustine, and from the 8th cent. the lives of saints were read at *Mattins. Councils often found it necessary to curb the excesses and superstition of popular devotion. Among the Reformers all cult of the saints was repudiated, esp. by the *Zwinglians and *Calvinists, on the ground that it was not explicitly recommended in Scripture.

See also *Beatification* and *Canonization.*

SAKKOS. In the E. Church an embroidered liturgical vestment worn by bishops. It is similar in form to the *dalmatic in the W.

SALAMANCA, School of. See *Salmanticenses.*

SALESIANS. The Society of St. *Francis de Sales was founded near Turin in 1859 by St. John *Bosco for the Christian education of boys and young men of the poorer classes, esp. with a view to their ordination. In 1846 he began to gather boys together in what he termed 'festive oratories' and night schools. A congregation of priests and teachers under the patronage of St. Francis de Sales came into being and in 1859 began to live by a rule drawn up by Bosco.

SALETTE, La. See *La Salette*.

SALISBURY. Bp. Herman united the dioceses of Ramsbury and *Sherborne in 1058 and transferred the see to Old Sarum in 1075. Here his successor, St. *Osmund, built a cathedral, constituted a chapter, and drew up offices, which perhaps formed the basis of the Sarum Rite (see the next entry). Richard *Poore moved the see to New Sarum or Salisbury in 1218 and laid the foundation of the new cathedral in 1220. The cathedral, completed in 1266, is a rare example of architectural unity. The spire was added between 1334 and 1350.

SALISBURY or **SARUM, Use of.** The medieval modification of the Roman rite used in the cathedral church at Salisbury. It was traditionally ascribed to St. *Osmund. The *Consuetudinary, i.e. the cathedral statutes and customs and a complete directory of services, was compiled by Richard *Poore (d. 1237). The 'New Use of Sarum' was a further (14th-cent.) revision. In the later Middle Ages the Sarum Use was followed in many other dioceses; it provided the main material for the First (1549) BCP.

SALMANTICENSES. The customary name for the authors of the *Cursus theologicus Summam d. Thomae complectens*, a group of Discalced *Carmelites who taught at Salamanca between 1600 and 1725. Their names are now known. The *Cursus* is a huge commentary on the 'Summa' of St. *Thomas Aquinas.

SALMASIUS, CLAUDIUS (1588–1653), Claude Saumaise, French classical scholar. In 1632 he became a professor at *Leyden. He wrote two works defending the compatibility of *usury with Christian principles and a defence of *Charles I which prompted a reply by J. *Milton.

SALOME. (1) A woman who followed Christ to Jerusalem. Matthew appears to identify her with the mother of St. *James and St. *John, the sons of Zebedee (Mt. 27: 56; cf. Mk. 15: 40). She is sometimes identified with the sister of the BVM (Jn. 19: 25). See *Marys in the NT* (4).

(2) The name given by *Josephus to the daughter of Herodias who is mentioned without a name at Mt. 14: 6 and Mk. 6: 22.

SALONICA. See *Thessalonica*.

SALT. Because of its preservative quality salt was a sign of purity and incorruptibility, esp. among the Semitic peoples. It served to confirm contracts and friendship, and its use was prescribed for every oblation (Lev. 2: 13). The offering of salt to *catechumens formerly formed part of the RC rite of *Baptism. Salt may also be used in the preparation of *holy water.

SALTMARSH, JOHN (d. 1647), preacher and writer. He was at first an ardent supporter of episcopacy and conformity; later he advocated complete religious liberty. In 1646 he became a chaplain in Fairfax's army.

SALTUM, Per. See *Per saltum*.

SALVATION ARMY, The. An international Christian organization for evangelistic and social work. It was founded by W. *Booth in 1865 and received its present form and title in 1878. It is organized on a military basis, with a 'General' at its head. Its religious teaching is largely in harmony with traditional *evangelical belief, but it rejects all Sacraments. Open-air meetings with brass bands characterize its method of presenting religion to the people.

SALVE REGINA (Lat., 'Hail, [Holy] Queen'). One of the oldest Marian *antiphons, sometimes recited in the W. Church at the end of the canonical hours. It is among the most widely used Catholic prayers to the BVM. Its authorship is unknown. The earliest MS. evidence is usually dated at the end of the 11th cent.

SALVIAN (*c*. 400–*c*. 480), of Marseilles, ecclesiastical writer. His *De Gubernatione Dei*, by contrasting the vices of decadent Roman civilization with the virtues of the victorious barbarians, uses the latter as a witness to God's judgement on society and as an incentive for Christians to purity of life and faith in Providence.

SAMARIA. The capital of the kingdom of *Israel, i.e. of the 'Ten [northern] Tribes', founded by King Omri (c. 880 B.C.) and in 721 captured by the Assyrians, who resettled the territory with pagans from other parts of their empire (2 Kgs. 18: 9-12 and chapter 17). Acc. to Jewish tradition, the Samaritans known to later Judaism and the NT were the descendants of these settlers. The hostility of the Jews to the Samaritans was proverbial. See also *Good Samaritan, The.*

SAMARITAN PENTATEUCH, The. A slightly divergent form of the *Pentateuch in Hebrew, current since pre-Christian times among the Samaritans and the only part of the OT accepted by them. Where it differs from the *Massoretic (i.e. the standard Jewish) text, it usually seems to be inferior.

SAMSON (prob. 11th cent. B.C.), Hebrew hero and traditionally the last of the great 'judges'. Acc. to Jgs. 13: 2–16: 31, he was endowed with prodigious strength and wrought havoc among the Philistines; when he fell victim to his passion for Delilah and revealed to her the secret of his strength, the Philistines put out his eyes, but he was granted his revenge in pulling down the pillars of the temple where 3,000 Philistines were assembled. His faith is commended in the NT (Heb. 11: 32). He is the hero of J. *Milton's *Samson Agonistes* (1671) and of one of G. F. *Handel's oratorios (1743).

SAMSON, St. (c. 490–?565), Bp. of Dol. A native of Wales, he gained such a reputation for piety and as a miracle-worker that he retired to Brittany in search of solitude. Having landed near Dol, he built a monastery and was made bishop.

SAMUEL, Books of. The two Books of Samuel were originally a single Book, which was divided for convenience by the compilers of the LXX, who also grouped the Books of Samuel with those of *Kings under the single title of the '[Four] Books of the Reigns'. The English Bible follows the Hebrew title. After relating the history of the prophet Samuel, the writer describes the reigns of Saul (c. 1025–1010 B.C.) and *David (c. 1010–970).

SANATIO IN RADICE (Lat., 'healing at

the root'). In canon law the process whereby an invalid 'marriage' is validated retrospectively, i.e. from the moment it was solemnized.

SANBENITO. The yellow penitential garment which the Spanish *Inquisition ordered those who had confessed heresy to wear.

SANCHEZ, THOMAS (1550–1610), Spanish *Jesuit. He became famous for his *Disputationes de sancto matrimonii sacramento* (1602), a comprehensive work on the moral and canonical aspects of matrimony which enjoyed high authority in the 17th cent.

SANCROFT, WILLIAM (1617–93), Abp. of *Canterbury. He became Dean of *St. Paul's in 1664 and collaborated with C. *Wren over the rebuilding of the cathedral after the Great Fire of 1666. He was made Abp. of Canterbury in 1677. On the accession of the RC *James II (1685), he altered the *Coronation rite so that the Communion could be omitted. He led the *Seven Bishops who opposed the *Declaration of Indulgence in 1688 and was imprisoned. In 1690 he was deprived as a *Nonjuror.

SANCTA SOPHIA. See *Santa Sophia.*

SANCTORALE. The section of a *Missal or *Breviary containing the Mass or Offices peculiar to the festivals of particular saints.

SANCTUARY. The part of a church containing the altar (or, if there are several altars, the high altar).

SANCTUARY, Right of. In medieval England this was of two kinds, ecclesiastical and secular. The former developed out of the usage that a criminal who had taken refuge in a church might not be removed from it, but was allowed to take an oath of abjuration before the coroner and proceed to a seaport. Secular and jurisdictional sanctuary relied upon a royal grant, and in theory at least might be held to apply to any franchise where the lord had *jura regalia.* This institution is frequently confused with ecclesiastical sanctuary, since criminals commonly repaired to a church in a franchise, esp. in the ecclesiastical liberties such as *Durham and *Beverley. In 1540 the privilege of sanctuary was restricted to seven cities. In 1623 sanctuary for crime was abolished, though it lingered for civil processes until 1723. Christ.

SANCTUS. The hymn of adoration which follows the *Preface in the Eucharist and begins with the words 'Holy, holy, holy'.

SANCTUS BELL. See *Sacring Bell*.

SANDALS, Episcopal. Low shoes with leather soles and the upper part of embroidery which may be worn by bishops in the RC Church at solemn Pontifical Masses and other functions (e.g. Ordinations) performed during them. Stockings of the liturgical colour of the day are worn with them.

SANDEMANIANS. See *Glasites*.

SANDERS, NICHOLAS (*c.* 1530–81), RC controversialist and historian. He left England after the accession of *Elizabeth I. In 1565 he went to Louvain, where he became professor of theology and engaged in the controversy aroused by J. *Jewel's *Apology*. He became consultor to *Gregory XIII on English affairs in 1572, and in 1579 he went to *Ireland as papal agent to stir up an insurrection. His unfinished *De Origine ac Progressu Schismatis Anglicani* (publd. 1585) is now admitted to be accurate in many of its controversial statements.

SANDERSON, ROBERT (1587–1663), Bp. of *Lincoln from 1660. He took a leading part in the *Savoy Conference and drafted the preface to the 1662 BCP. His *Nine Cases of Conscience* (1678) was one of the most notable contributions to moral theology in its age.

SANDYS, EDWIN (*c.* 1516–88), Abp. of *York from 1575. He was a fervent and learned opponent of Romanist practices, with personal leanings towards *Puritanism. He was one of the translators of the *Bishops' Bible.

SANHEDRIN. The supreme Jewish council and highest court of justice at *Jerusalem in NT times. Its origin is obscure, but it goes back before Roman times, when it was given a definite place in the administration of Palestine. It dealt with the religious problems of the whole Jewish world, collected taxes, and acted as a civil court for Jerusalem. It pronounced sentence of death on

SANKEY, I. D. See *Moody, D. L.*

SANTA CLAUS. An American corruption of the Dutch form of St. *Nicholas, Bp. of Myra (q.v.).

SANTA MARIA MAGGIORE, Rome. The church was founded by Pope *Liberius (352–66); the present structure was erected under Sixtus III (432–40). Acc. to a medieval tradition the site was indicated by the BVM, who one August night left her footprints in a miraculous fall of snow.

SANTA SOPHIA. The famous church at *Constantinople, dedicated to the 'Holy *Wisdom' (i.e. the Person of Christ), was built under *Justinian and consecrated in 538. Its chief feature is the huge dome which crowns the basilica; this dates from 562, the original low dome having collapsed in 558. In 1453 the Turks converted it into a mosque and the mosaics were covered up and partly destroyed. It is now a museum.

SANTIAGO DE COMPOSTELA. See *Compostela*.

SANTIAGO, Order of. A military order under the patronage of St. *James the Apostle, founded in 1170 for the protection of pilgrims and the expulsion of the Moors. Its constitution was modelled on that of the *Templars. Its knights were allowed to marry.

SARABAITES. A class of ascetics in the early Church who lived either in their own houses or in small groups and acknowledged no monastic superior.

SARACENS. A word used by medieval writers of the Arabs generally and later applied to the infidel and Muslim nations against whom the *Crusaders fought.

SARAPION, St. See *Serapion, St.*

SARAVIA, HADRIAN À (1531–1613), Protestant divine. As pastor at Antwerp he helped to draft the *Belgic Confession (1561); he was later professor of divinity at *Leyden. In 1585 he left Holland for England, where he held various benefices and became a zealous supporter of episcopacy. He was one of the translators of the AV of the Bible.

SARCOPHAGUS. A stone coffin, usually adorned with bas-relief. Until the Byzantine period sarcophagi were much used by both Christians and pagans. From the 4th cent. those of Christians came to be adorned with designs depicting a limited number of Christian subjects.

SARDICA, Council of (modern Sofia). A Council summoned c. 343 mainly to settle the orthodoxy of St. *Athanasius. The E. bishops refused to take part on the ground that Athanasius, whom the E. had deposed, was being regarded by the W. as a member of the synod; the W. bishops therefore met by themselves. They confirmed the restoration of Athanasius and passed some famous disciplinary canons; chief among these are the provisions constituting the Bp. of Rome a court of appeal for accused bishops in certain circumstances.

SARPI, PAOLO (1552–1623), *Servite theologian. In the struggle between *Venice and *Paul V (1606–7), he defended the interests of the Republic, which appointed him its theological consultor in 1606. He was excommunicated in 1607 but he continued to exercise his priestly functions until his death. His *History of the Council of Trent* (first publd. in 1619) is based on authentic material but, lacking objectivity, represents the Council as a conspiracy against the reform of the Church.

SARUM; SARUM RITE. See *Salisbury*; *Salisbury, Use of*.

SATAN. In Hebrew-Christian tradition, the supreme embodiment of evil, also called the *Devil (q.v.).

SATISFACTION. An act of reparation for an injury committed; in Christian theology esp. the payment of a penalty due to God on account of sin. St. *Anselm gave the term theological currency in reference to the *Atonement by interpreting Christ's death as a vicarious satisfaction for the sins of the world.

In Catholic theology satisfaction is held to be a necessary element in the sacrament of *penance. With the attenuation of penances and the practice of giving absolution before

satisfaction was made, the distinction between forgiveness of the fault and the satisfaction due to it after forgiveness was worked out clearly; the classic example adduced was the penance inflicted on *David after Nathan had pronounced God's forgiveness (2 Sam. 12: 13–14). Thus *satisfactio operis* came to be regarded as a necessary means of avoiding punishment in *purgatory after the sin itself had been remitted by sacramental absolution.

SATURDAY. The Jewish '*Sabbath' and the day of the week on which Christ's body rested in the tomb. In the W. Saturday was regarded as a fast day by the 3rd cent., but, except in *Lent and on the *Ember Days, the Saturday fast was finally abolished in 1918. On the other hand, in most E. Churches from the 4th cent. Saturday was distinguished by a celebration of the Liturgy, which in Lent is still confined to Saturday and Sunday. The connection of Saturday with the BVM in the W. is a medieval development. See also *Holy Saturday*.

SATURNINUS (2nd cent.), Syrian *Gnostic. He held that the origin of all things was to be sought in a Father, who created a series of angels and other supernatural beings who in turn created man. Man was a powerless entity who wriggled on the ground until a Divine spark set him on his feet. The God of the Jews was one of the creator angels, and the Supreme Father sent the Saviour to destroy this God and to redeem such as were endowed with the Divine spark.

SAVA, St. (c. 1176–1235), also Sabas, patron of *Serbia. In 1191 Rastko, a son of the Serbian king, went secretly to Mount *Athos and became a monk under the name of Sava. He returned to Serbia in 1208; as archimandrite of the monastery of Studenica he took an active part in the religious and political life of the country. He opposed the policy of his brother, who in 1217 was crowned king with the help of the Pope, and in 1219 he established an independent Serbian Church, being consecrated first archbishop in Nicaea.

SAVIGNY, Abbey of, in Normandy. In 1105 Vitalis of Mortain established a hermitage in the Forest of Savigny. When some of the hermits felt a call to follow the *Benedictine Rule in its primitive strictness, the abbey was established. It rose to high repute and daughter houses were founded. In 1147 they were integrated into the *Cistercian Order.

SAVILE, HENRY (1549–1622), Warden of Merton College, Oxford, and then Provost of Eton. In 1604 he was one of the scholars appointed to prepare the AV of the Bible. In 1610–13 he published his celebrated edition of the works of St. John *Chrysostom, which is still of value in determining the correct text of some treatises.

SAVONAROLA, GIROLAMO (1452–98), Italian preacher and reformer. He became a *Dominican in 1474, and in 1482 he was sent to the priory of San Marco in Florence. He attracted attention by his passionate denunciation of the immorality of the Florentines and of contemporary clergy. He also prophesied on the future of the Church, often in apocalyptic language. In 1491 he became prior. He supported Charles VIII of France in his Italian campaign of 1494–5, seeing in him the instrument of God for the reform of the Church, and he established a kind of theocratic democracy in Florence. His severity, however, made him enemies. He was summoned to Rome by *Alexander VI and excommunicated in 1497. The people turned against him and he was hanged as a schismatic and heretic. His character has been variously judged.

SAVOY CONFERENCE, The (1661). A conference of 12 bishops, 12 *Presbyterian divines, and 9 assessors from each party which met in G. *Sheldon's lodgings at the Savoy in London, to review the BCP. The Presbyterians sought means to enable them to remain within the Established Church, but in reply to their *Exceptions to the BCP the bishops made only 17 trivial concessions.

SAVOY DECLARATION, The (1658). A statement of *Congregational principles and polity of a moderate type, drawn up at a conference held in the Chapel of the Savoy in London by representatives of 120 Churches. It consists of a Preface, a Confession of Faith closely akin to the *Westminster Confession, and a Platform of Discipline declaring that all necessary power is vested in each individual Church.

SAWTREY, WILLIAM (d. 1401), *Lollard. A priest of Lynn, Norfolk, he was charged with heresy in 1399. Charged again in 1401, he was burnt on the ground that he had relapsed into heresies which he had abjured two years earlier.

SAXON CONFESSION, The (1551). The Protestant Confession of Faith drawn up by P. *Melanchthon at the Emp. *Charles V's request for the Council of *Trent.

SAYINGS OF JESUS, The. The name given by the first editors to the texts preserved in two *Oxyrhynchus papyri (Nos. 1 and 654). It is now clear that these texts, together with those in No. 655, if not part of the Greek original of the Gospel of *Thomas, are closely related to it.

SCALA SANCTA (also known as the **Scala Pilati**). A staircase of 28 marble steps near the *Lateran church at Rome. Tradition asserts that they were the steps descended by Christ after His condemnation to death and brought to the W. by St. *Helena from the palace of *Pilate at Jerusalem.

SCALIGER, JOSEPH JUSTUS (1540–1609), French scholar. He became a *Calvinist in 1562. From 1593 he was a professor at *Leyden. His editions of Latin authors marked an advance in the field of *textual criticism. His most famous work, *De Emendatione Temporum* (1583), established the modern science of chronology. His *Thesaurus Temporum* (1606) contains a brilliant partial reconstruction of the 'Chronicon' of *Eusebius of Caesarea.

SCAPULAR. A short cloak consisting essentially of a piece of cloth worn over the shoulders and hanging down in front and behind. It is usually 14–18 inches wide with its two ends reaching almost to the feet, and forms part of the regular monastic *habit. A garment of much smaller dimensions (known as the 'smaller scapular') is worn by people living in the world who have become affiliated to religious orders; important privileges have become attached to wearing the smaller scapular in the RC Church.

SCARAMELLI, GIOVANNI BATTISTA (1687–1752), *Jesuit spiritual writer. In his 'Ascetic Directory' (*Direttorio ascetico*, 1752), which has long been regarded as a classic, he examines the nature of Christian perfection and the means of attaining it.

SCETE. The southern part of the *Nitrian desert, celebrated as a centre of monasticism in the 4th and 5th cents

SCHAFF, PHILIP (1819–93), theologian and Church historian. Born in Switzerland, he was educated in Germany, and became a professor first of the German Reformed Seminary at Mercersburg, Pennsylvania (1844), and then in the *Union Theological Seminary, New York (1870). He saw through the press an immense body of theological literature, editing an American adaptation of J. J. *Herzog's *Realencyclopädie* and a series of patristic translations. He was an exponent of the '*Mercersburg Theology'.

SCHEEBEN, MATTHIAS JOSEPH (1835–88), RC theologian. From 1860 he was professor of dogma at the seminary at *Cologne. In various works he emphasized the rights of supernatural faith against the rationalist and naturalist tendencies of 18th- and 19th-cent. theology. He was an opponent of J. J. I. von *Döllinger and a passionate defender of Papal *Infallibility.

SCHEFFLER, J. See *Angelus Silesius.*

SCHELLING, FRIEDRICH WILHELM JOSEPH VON (1775–1854), German philosopher. In his early years he acknowledged only one reality, the infinite and absolute Ego, of which the universe was the expression. This abstract pantheism was soon modified in favour of his conception of 'Naturphilosophie', acc. to which nature was an absolute being which works unconsciously, though purposively. The problem of the relation of nature to spirit then gave rise to his 'Identitätsphilosophie': both nature and spirit are but manifestations of one and the same being, absolute identity being the ground of all things. In his attempt to reconcile Christianity with his philosophy he distinguished three elements in God: (1) the blind primeval necessary being; (2) the three potentialities of the Divine Essence, viz. unconscious will (material cause), rational will (efficient cause), and unity of the two (final cause of creation); and (3) the Three Persons who evolve from the three potentialities by overcoming the primeval being. He exercised a profound influence on German thought.

SCHELSTRATE, EMMANUEL (1649–1692), Belgian Church historian and canonist. He became Prefect of the *Vatican Library. He wrote in defence of the Holy See against *Gallican tendencies. His treatise on the *disciplina arcana* (1685) maintained that this was of Dominical origin and that it explained the relative weakness of the evidence for the doctrine of the Person of Christ as well as for the Sacraments in the primitive Church.

SCHENUDI. See *Shenoute.*

SCHISM. Formal and wilful separation from the unity of the Church. It is distinguished from heresy in that the separation involved is not doctrinal in basis; whereas heresy is opposed to faith, schism is opposed to charity. It does not involve loss of orders: a bishop in schism can ordain and a priest in schism can celebrate the Eucharist. See also *Ecumenical Movement* and *Reunion.*

SCHLATTER, ADOLF (1852–1938), Protestant theologian. He held that the only sound foundation of systematic theology lay in Biblical exegesis, and he also opposed all idealistic interpretations of the Christian faith. He thus anticipated the *Dialectical Theology of K. *Barth.

SCHLEGEL, FRIEDRICH (1772–1829), *Romantic author and Catholic apologist. He was one of the leaders of the Romantic Movement in Berlin. He became a RC in 1808. In lectures on history and modern philosophy at Vienna (1810–12) he defended the medieval Imperial idea against the Napoleonic State, and with C. M. *Hofbauer and others he sought to restore the national life of Austria and Germany on a Catholic basis. He later looked to literature and philosophy for a renewed Catholicism.

SCHLEIERMACHER, FRIEDRICH DANIEL ERNST (1768–1834), German theologian. He was Reformed preacher at the Charité in Berlin, professor of theology at Halle (1804–7), and later preacher at the Dreifaltigkeitskirche in Berlin and Dean of the Theological Faculty of the newly founded university. In 1799 he published his famous *Reden über die Religion* (Eng. tr., *Religion. Speeches to its Cultured Despisers,* 1893), in which he tried to win the educated classes back to religion. Contending that religion was based on intuition and feeling and independent of all dogma, he saw its highest experience in a sensation of union with the infinite. In his most important work, *Der christliche Glaube* (1821–2), he defines religion as a feeling of absolute dependence which finds its purest expression in monotheism; the variety of forms which this feeling assumes in different individuals and nations accounts for the diversity of religions, of which Christianity is the highest, but not the only true one. His emphasis on feeling as the basis of religion was a reaction both from contemporary German rationalism and from the ruling formalist orthodoxy. His influence on Protestant thought has been immense.

SCHMALKALDIC ARTICLES (1537). The doctrinal statement drawn up by M. *Luther for presentation to the projected General Council summoned by *Paul III. An assembly of Lutheran princes and theologians at Schmalkalden approved the Articles, as well as a more conciliatory appendix by P. *Melanchthon.

SCHMALKALDIC LEAGUE. The alliance concluded at Schmalkalden in 1531 between the Protestant groups in Germany. It united the *Lutherans and *Zwinglians, as well as N. and S. German princes.

SCHMIDT, B. See *Smith, B.*

SCHMIEDEL, PAUL WILHELM (1851–1935), NT scholar. He is best known for his attack on a small group of critics who denied the historical existence of Christ: on the basis of 9 passages in the Gospels, which could not be the invention of the primitive Church, he argued that the historicity of Jesus was put beyond dispute. He was, however, himself a radical critic.

SCHOLA CANTORUM (Lat., 'school of singers'). In the worship of the early Church all music was rendered by the clergy and congregation, but gradually the practice of having a body of trained singers was introduced. At Rome the Schola was established on a sound footing by *Gregory the Great (d. 604). The custom spread over W. Christendom.

SCHOLARIUS, GEORGE. See *George Scholarius.*

SCHOLASTICA, St. (*c.* 480–*c.* 543), sister of St. *Benedict. She established a convent at Plombariola, a few miles from *Monte Cassino.

SCHOLASTICISM. The educational tradition of the medieval Schools and, in particular, a method of philosophical and theological speculation which aimed at a better understanding of revealed truth by intellectual processes.

The theoretical foundations of Scholasticism were laid by St. *Augustine, who linked the need for understanding and belief, and by *Boethius, whose translations of, and commentaries on, *Aristotle and *Porphyry later introduced medieval thinkers to their first knowledge of logic. *Cassiodorus propounded a plan of studies which put the *seven liberal arts at the basis of all secular and religious learning; this programme prepared the way for the philosophical and theological speculation of the Middle Ages.

In the 9th cent. John Scotus *Erigena clearly stated the distinction between *auctoritas* (authority, i.e. Scripture) and *ratio* (reason). Scripture is still the main source of our knowledge of God, but it is the duty of reason, illuminated by God, to investigate and expound the Christian data supplied by authority. The study of the *trivium, esp. of dialectic, developed in the 10th and 11th cents. It gave rise to the controversy between the *Realists and the *Nominalists over *universals, but the service which dialectic could render to theology was widely recognized. At the end of the 11th cent. St. *Anselm asserted the right of reason to inquire into revealed truths, not in the sense that by rational reasoning we acquire the knowledge of faith, but because it seems reprehensible if, once established in the faith, we make no effort to understand what we believe. In the 12th cent. the development of '*Sentences' afforded the first systematic arrangement of theological questions and also a timid endeavour to use the argument from reason. More important was the appearance of the *quaestio*, with its argument for and against. *Abelard perfected this technique, unreservedly applying to theology the dialectical method, based on the *quaestio* and *interrogatio* and on the *disputatio*.

Of decisive importance was the introduction to the W. of the works of Aristotle and the Arabic commentators *Avicenna and

*Averroes. The so-called Augustinians refused to accept whatever they felt to be in opposition to Augustine. The Latin Averroists, such as *Siger of Brabant, adhered to Aristotelian doctrines as interpreted by the Arabian commentators, even when they were in opposition to Catholic doctrine. A harmony between Augustine and Aristotle was worked out by St. *Thomas Aquinas, whose *Summa Theologica is regarded as the crowning achievement of Scholastic theology. Following the usual method of presenting a doctrine in argument, counter-argument, and solution, he drew the line between faith and reason with the utmost clarity, securely establishing their connection and showing the completion of the one by the other. From this period Scholasticism declined. *William of Occam taught a Nominalism which undermined all belief in the possibility of objective knowledge. Such teaching was a factor in the dissolution of medieval Scholasticism, and some aspects of it exercised a decisive influence on the Protestant Reformers.

Interest in Scholasticism revived at the end of the 19th cent. and neo-Thomism held a central place in RC theology in the first half of the 20th cent.

SCHOLIA. Notes inserted in the margins of ancient MSS. They were introduced by Christian scholars into MSS. of Biblical and ecclesiastical texts.

SCHOOL OF ENGLISH CHURCH MUSIC. See *Royal School of Church Music*.

SCHOOLMEN. The teachers of philosophy and theology at the medieval European universities, then usually called 'schools'. See *Scholasticism*.

SCHOOLS, Cathedral and **Sunday**. See *Cathedral Schools, Sunday Schools*.

SCHOPENHAUER, ARTHUR (1788–1860), German philosopher. His chief work was *Die Welt als Wille und Vorstellung* ('1819' [really 1818]; Eng. tr., *The World as Will and Idea*, 1883–6). He held that the ultimate Reality was Will. Though he claimed to be at one with the Christian mystics in teaching that the extinction of the will by pity and mortification of the passions was the sovereign remedy for the evils of existence, his whole philosophy was one of pessimism; it was one of the chief anti-Christian systems in 19th-cent. Germany.

SCHÜRER, EMIL (1844–1910), German NT scholar. His 'History of the Jewish People in the Time of Jesus Christ' (original German, 1874) gives a detailed account of the history, customs, beliefs, and literature of the Jews from the time of the *Maccabees to the wars under Trajan; it is still a standard work.

SCHÜTZ, HEINRICH (1585–1672), German composer. Apart from secular works, he wrote much Church music, and he is famous for his Passion music. He exercised a profound influence on J. S. *Bach.

SCHWABACH, Articles of (1529), the first of the *Lutheran Confessions. The 17 Articles were based on those considered and, with one exception, adopted at the Colloquy of *Marburg.

SCHWARTZ, EDUARD (1858–1940), classical philologist and Patristic scholar. He held a succession of professorships in Germany. His main work, the *Acta Conciliorum Oecumenicorum* (1914–40), was a grandly planned edition of the Greek Councils; it provided, for the first time, a critical edition of the 'Acts' of *Ephesus (431) and *Chalcedon (451). His collection of papers on St. *Athanasius (1904–11) was also important.

SCHWEITZER, ALBERT (1875–1965), German theologian, physician, and organist. In *Das Messianitäts- und Leidensgeheimnis* (1901; Eng. tr., *The Mystery of the Kingdom of God*, 1925) he expounded the leading idea of his theological work, viz. that the Lord's teaching centred in His conviction of the imminent end of the world. The book caused a stir, and in 1902 Schweitzer was made a lecturer at Strasburg university. In *Von Reimarus zu Wrede* (1906; Eng. tr., *The Quest of the Historical Jesus*, 1910), he developed an interpretation of Christ's life on the basis of 'thoroughgoing eschatology'; he held that the Lord shared with His contemporaries the expectation of a speedy end of the world and, when this proved a mistake, concluded that He Himself must suffer in order to save His people from the tribulations preceding the last days. In 1911 he took a degree in medicine and in 1913 he went to

Lambaréné in French Equatorial Africa (now Gabon) to care for the sick and engage in missionary work. Having been interned in France in 1917, he went back to Strasburg in 1918. His *Kulturphilosophie* (1923) summed up his views on ethics as 'reverence for life'. In 1924 he returned to Lambaréné and restored his ruined hospital; this was his main concern for the rest of his life, though he continued theological writing. His work exercised a profound influence on Protestant theology.

SCHWENCKFELDIANS. The followers of the Silesian Reformation theologian Caspar Schwenckfeld (1490–1561). Schwenckfeld, who was a mystic by temperament, was impressed by the writings of J. *Tauler and M. *Luther. He soon found, however, that he could not give unreserved assent to many of the Protestant doctrines. He also came to hold a doctrine of the deification of Christ's humanity, and in 1540 he issued an account of his beliefs on this subject. A few years later he withdrew from the Lutheran Church. After his death a small band of disciples, calling themselves the 'Confessors of the Glory of Christ', continued to propagate his teaching.

SCIENCE, Christian. See *Christian Science*.

SCIENTIA MEDIA (Lat., 'mediate knowledge'). A term coined by L. *Molina in his attempt to reconcile God's foreknowledge with human freewill. It designates the knowledge which God has of 'futuribilia', i.e. of things which are not, but which would be if certain conditions were realized, and thus are intermediate between mere possibilities and actual future events.

SCILLITAN MARTYRS, The. Seven men and five women of Scillium in N. Africa who were executed in 180 for refusal to renounce Christianity and swear by the 'genius' of the Roman Emperor.

S.C.M. See *Student Christian Movement*.

SCONE, Perthshire. An ancient Scottish religious centre and once the capital of a Pictish kingdom. In 1115 an abbey of *Augustinian canons was settled here, and from 1153 the kings of Scotland were crowned at Scone. The Stone of Destiny was brought to *Westminster Abbey in 1296; it was traditionally believed to be that on which *Jacob laid his head at *Bethel (Gen. 28: 11).

SCORY, JOHN (d. 1585), Anglican bishop. He was a *Dominican before the *dissolution of the monasteries. He became Bp. of *Rochester in 1551 and of *Chichester in 1552. Under *Mary he was deprived of his see; he recanted but left England. He returned in 1558 and in 1559 he became Bp. of *Hereford. He assisted at M. *Parker's consecration and is thus held to be one of the channels by which the episcopal succession was preserved in the C of E.

SCOTISM. The system of Scholastic philosophy expounded by *Duns Scotus.

SCOTLAND, Christianity in. The first known Christian missionary in Scotland was St. *Ninian; he built a stone church at Whithorn (397) and conducted a widespread mission among the Picts. The next great evangelist was St. *Columba, who made *Iona the centre of his missionary labours (563–97). The Church which grew up in Scotland was *Celtic: it was monastic and missionary; the heads of its communities were presbyter-abbots, not bishops; it was independent of Rome and maintained peculiar customs such as a date of Easter different from that of the Roman Church. After the Synod of *Whitby (664) Roman usages were gradually adopted and the Scoto-Pictish Church eventually emerged as a united body under a national bishop. The Romanization of the Scottish Church was completed under the influence of Queen *Margaret (d. 1093) and her sons, esp. David I, in whose reign (1124–53) diocesan episcopacy was extended and Roman monastic orders introduced. Throughout the Middle Ages the independence of the Scottish Church against the claims of *Canterbury and *York to supremacy was constantly affirmed.

The first wave of the Reformation in Scotland was *Lutheran, the second *Calvinist. After the return of John *Knox in 1559, the Reformed Church of Scotland was established on Presbyterian lines in 1560. For more than a century, however, the fortunes of Scottish Presbyterianism ebbed and flowed owing to the determination of the Stuart kings to make the Kirk episcopal. The imposition of the Prayer Book brought the conflict between the Kirk and *Charles I to a head in 1637. In 1638 the Presbyterian *National Covenant was subscribed and Episcopacy was swept away. In 1643 the alliance between the Scottish Covenanters and the Long Parliament was cemented by the *Solemn League and Covenant, which was to impose Presbyterianism throughout the British Isles. The *Westminster Assembly then produced a number of documents which were formally accepted as standards by the Church of Scotland. After the Restoration (1660) Episcopacy was reestablished, but at the Revolution the Church of Scotland became Presbyterian again in 1690 and has remained so.

The Church of Scotland was weakened by a number of secessions in the 18th cent. and by the *Disruption of 1843, when nearly a third of its ministers and members left the Establishment and founded the *Free Church. Later there were unions between different Presbyterian Churches in Scotland, notably in 1847 (Secession and Relief to form *United Presbyterian), 1900 (United Presbyterian and Free to form *United Free), and in 1929 (United Free and Church of Scotland under the name of the latter).

Those who adhered to Episcopacy after 1690 formed the Episcopal Church of Scotland. This is in communion with the C of E, but is autonomous and has its own Prayer Book. The RC Church retains its hold on the descendants of those in the Highlands who were never influenced by the Reformation and on those of Irish extraction in the industrial Lowland areas.

SCOTT, GEORGE GILBERT (1811–87), architect. He worked mainly in Gothic style and largely on ecclesiastical buildings. He was architect to the Dean and Chapter of *Westminster Abbey from 1849, and he was entrusted with work in the cathedrals at *Ely, *Hereford, *Salisbury, and *Gloucester. His 'restorations' met with much resistance because of his preference for his own designs to original plans.

His grandson, GILES GILBERT SCOTT (1880–1960), designed the Anglican cathedral at *Liverpool.

SCOTT, ROBERT (1811–87), lexicographer. He was Master of Balliol College, Oxford, from 1854 to 1870 and then Dean of *Rochester. He collaborated with H. G. *Liddell on a famous Greek Lexicon.

SCOTT, THOMAS (1747-1821), Biblical commentator. His *Commentary on the Bible*, issued in weekly numbers between 1788 and 1792, had a huge circulation. It sought to find a message in each section of the Bible and persistently refused to shirk difficulties.

SCOTTISH CONFESSION, The. The first Confession of Faith of the Reformed Church of Scotland. It is a typically *Calvinist document. It was adopted by the Scottish Parliament in 1560 and remained the confessional standard until it was superseded by the *Westminster Confession in 1647.

SCOTUS, DUNS. See *Duns Scotus*.

SCOTUS ERIGENA. See *Erigena*.

'SCOURGE OF GOD', The. See *Attila*.

SCREENS. Partitions of wood, stone, or iron, dividing a church into two or more parts. Chancel or choir screens, dividing the choir from the nave, may be high, solid, and elaborate, or quite low; when surmounted by a cross ('rood'), they are termed 'roodscreens'.

SCRIPTORIUM. The room, esp. in a monastery, which was set apart for scribes to copy MSS.

SCROFULA, Touching for. See *King's Evil, Touching for the*.

SCROPE, RICHARD LE (c. 1346–1405), Abp. of *York from 1398. Though he assisted in forcing the abdication of Richard II in 1399 and took part in the enthronement of Henry IV, he grew discontented with the latter's government and favoured the Earl of Northumberland's revolt, to which his reputation for holiness gave weight. He led an army against the royal troops, but was tricked into surrender and irregularly sentenced to death. Miracles were believed to have taken place at his tomb.

SCRUPLES. In *moral theology, unfounded fears that there is sin where there is none.

SCRUTINY. In the early Church a term applied to the formal testing to which *catechumens were subjected before their baptism. The word came also to be used of the examination of candidates for holy orders.

SEA, Forms of Prayer to be used at. In the BCP, a small collection of prayers and anthems for use in various circumstances at sea.

SEABURY, SAMUEL (1729–96), first bishop of the *Protestant Episcopal Church of America. Ordained priest by the Bp. of *Lincoln in 1753, he worked in New Brunswick and later near New York. He was elected bishop in 1783. His inability to take the Oath of Allegiance, now that the United States was independent of Britain, precluded his consecration by English bishops, but arrangements were made for him to obtain episcopal *orders in Scotland. He was consecrated at Aberdeen in 1784.

SEAL OF CONFESSION. The absolute obligation not to reveal anything said by a penitent using the Sacrament of *penance. It admits of no exception.

SEBALDUS, St., patron saint of Nuremberg. His date (8th–11th cent.) is disputed and nothing certain is known of him. He is traditionally held to have lived as a hermit and preached near Nuremberg. His tomb is attested as a place of pilgrimage from 1072.

SE-BAPTISTS (Lat. *se baptizare*, 'to baptize oneself'). A name sometimes given to the followers of John *Smyth (q.v.).

SEBASTE, The Forty Martyrs of. Forty Christian soldiers of the '*Thundering Legion' who were martyred at Sebaste in Lesser Armenia, *c.* 320, by being left naked on the ice of a frozen pond, with baths of hot water on the banks as a temptation to apostatize. The place of one who gave way was taken by a heathen soldier of the guard, who was immediately converted.

SEBASTIAN, St., Roman martyr. Acc. to legend he was sentenced by *Diocletian to be shot by archers, recovered from this ordeal, and presented himself before the Emperor, who caused him to be clubbed to death.

SECKER, THOMAS (1693–1768), Abp. of *Canterbury from 1758. Converted from Dissent, he stood in high favour with Queen Caroline and achieved rapid preferment. He stood for tolerance and good sense in general. He favoured the dispatch of bishops to the American colonies.

SECOND ADAM. A title of Christ, the new head of redeemed humanity, as contrasted with the 'first *Adam', the original member and type of fallen man. The conception goes back to St. *Paul, whose expression, however, is not the 'second' but the 'last Adam' (1 Cor. 15: 45).

SECOND COMING. See *Parousia*.

SECRET. The name long given to the prayer recited by the celebrant at Mass after the offering of the bread and wine. Until 1964 it was customarily said silently; from this circumstance the name prob. derived.

SECRÉTAN, CHARLES (1815–95), Swiss Protestant theologian and philosopher. He was one of the leaders of liberal Protestant thought in Switzerland in the 19th cent. As his outlook matured he increasingly emphasized the moral significance of faith and the importance of freedom.

SECRETS OF ENOCH, Book of the. See *Enoch, Books of.*

SECTARY. The term was applied in the 17th and 18th cents. to Nonconformist Protestants in England. It is now occasionally used of those whose zeal for their own religious body is considered excessive.

SECULAR ARM. A term used, esp. in *canon law, to describe the State or any lay power concerned in ecclesiastical cases. Resort by individuals to the lay authorities to interfere with or hinder the process of ecclesiastical jurisdiction is punished by excommunication in the RC Church. On the other hand the Church has not felt justified in imposing penalties involving mutilation or death; when stern measures were felt necessary, esp. for heresy, after trial by an ecclesiastical judge the condemned prisoner was handed over to the secular authorities for punishment.

SECULAR CLERGY. Priests living in the world, as distinct from the '*regular clergy', i.e. members of religious orders.

SECULARISM. The term was coined *c.* 1850 to denote a system which sought to order and interpret life on principles taken solely from this world, without recourse to belief in God and a future world. It is now used in a more general sense of the tendency to ignore, if not to deny, the principles of supernatural religion.

SEDE VACANTE (Lat., 'the see being vacant'). The period during which a diocese is without a bishop.

SEDIA GESTATORIA. The portable throne on which the Pope is carried on certain formal occasions.

SEDILIA. The seats for the celebrant, deacon, and subdeacon, on the south side of the chancel. In medieval England they were usually stone benches built into a niche in the wall. On the Continent of Europe and in modern England wooden seats have been more common.

SEDULIUS SCOTUS (9th cent.), poet and scholar. A native of *Ireland, in 848 he went to Liège, where he established a centre of Irish culture. Besides numerous poems on religious and secular subjects, he wrote several theological works, incl. commentaries on Mt. and on St. Paul's Epistles. The Pauline commentaries are of interest because they draw on the genuine text of *Pelagius.

SEE. The official 'seat' or 'throne' (*cathedra) of a bishop. It normally stands in the *cathedral of the diocese; hence the place where the cathedral is located is also known as the bishop's see. See also *Holy See.

SEEKERS. A small early 17th-cent. *Puritan sect. They believed that no true Church had existed since the spirit of *Antichrist became uppermost in the Church, and that God would in His own time ordain new Apostles or Prophets to found a new Church; they did not think it right to hasten on this process.

SEELEY, JOHN ROBERT (1834–95), historian. From 1869 he was professor of modern history at Cambridge. He is famous for his book *Ecce Homo* (1865; q.v.).

SEGNERI, PAOLO (1624–94), Italian *Jesuit. He was a great preacher. His sermons combined vigorous and ordered argument with powerful emotional appeal.

SEISES, Dance of the. The religious dance performed in Seville cathedral in the course of the celebrations of *Corpus Christi and the Immaculate *Conception of the BVM.

SELDEN, JOHN (1584–1654), author of *The History of Tithes*. A moderate *Puritan, he became a member of the *Westminster Assembly in 1643. He was learned in both law and oriental studies. In his *History of Tithes* (1618) he upheld the legal, but denied the Divine, basis of the obligation to pay *tithes.

SELEUCIA, Synod of. See *Ariminum and Seleucia, Synods of*.

SELLON, PRISCILLA LYDIA (*c.* 1821–1876), a restorer of *religious orders in Anglicanism. In 1848, hearing a public appeal by H. *Phillpotts, Bp. of Exeter, she abandoned a plan to leave England in order to work among the destitute of Plymouth, Devonport, and Stonehouse. She was joined by others and created a community life; the Devonport Sisters of Mercy did heroic work in the cholera epidemic of 1848. In 1856 she united her community with the Sisters of the Holy Cross at Osnaburgh Street, Regent's Park, in London, and assumed the title of Abbess of the combined sisterhood of the 'Society of the Most Holy Trinity' (now centred at Ascot Priory, Berks.).

SELWYN, GEORGE AUGUSTUS (1809–78), first Bp. of *New Zealand from 1841 to 1867. He was a *Tractarian in his convictions. He had a marked effect on the future of the New Zealand Church, for whose constitution he was largely responsible. He became Bp. of *Lichfield in 1868.

SEMIARIANISM. The teaching of the theologians who gathered round *Basil of Ancyra from *c.* 356 and upheld a doctrine of Christ's Sonship intermediate between that of orthodoxy and *Arianism. Over against the term '*Homoousios' ('of the same substance'), they took as their watchword 'Homoiousios' ('of like substance'), but the whole tendency of the group was towards orthodoxy.

SEMI-DOUBLES. Feasts in the RC

calendar of an intermediate rank, which was abolished in 1955.

SEMINARY. The term is sometimes used to describe Anglican *theological colleges, but it is more usually kept for the corresponding institutions in the RC Church. The Council of *Trent ordered the establishment of a seminary in every diocese and this has remained roughly the rule in the RC Church.

SEMI-PELAGIANISM. Teaching on human nature which, while not denying the necessity of *grace for salvation, maintained that the first steps towards the Christian life were ordinarily taken by the human will and that grace supervened only later. The position was roughly midway between the doctrines of St. *Augustine and *Pelagius. The doctrine first took shape in the writings of *Cassian of Marseilles (c. 420) and received widespread support in Gaul. There were controversies in the mid-5th and early-6th cents., but after the condemnation of Semi-Pelagianism by the Council of *Orange in 529, the Augustinian teaching on grace was generally accepted.

SEMI-QUIETISM. The doctrines of Abp. *Fénelon and others who, though not sufficiently unorthodox to come under the censures attaching to *Quietism, manifest certain quietist tendencies.

SEMLER, JOHANN SALOMO (1725–91), *Lutheran theologian and Biblical critic. He was one of the first German theologians to apply the critico-historical method to the study of the Bible, and he reached some novel and unorthodox conclusions. He held, however, that Christian ministers should be required to make external profession of all traditional doctrine.

SEMPRINGHAM. The mother-house of the Order founded by St. *Gilbert of Sempringham (q.v.).

SENECA, LUCIUS ANNAEUS (c. 4 B.C.– A.D. 65), Roman moralist. He entered on a career at the bar, was banished to Corsica (41–9), and then became tutor to the future Emp. *Nero. In the early part of Nero's reign he exercised much influence; later he was charged with taking part in Piso's conspiracy and forced to take his own life. His writings represent *Stoicism at its best.

There is also in existence an apocryphal correspondence between Seneca (8 letters) and St. *Paul (6 letters). Their manner and style show that they cannot be the work of either writer.

SENS, Councils of. Many provincial Councils were held at Sens. The most famous was that of 1140 which condemned *Abelard for heresy.

SENTENCES. Short reasoned expositions of the main truths of Christian doctrine. The Latin word *sententia* originally meant any exposition of thought, but in the Middle Ages it took on a new technical meaning in relation to exegesis. Collections of *Sentences* were systematized compilations of opinions, of which the most famous was that of *Peter Lombard. By the 13th cent. *sententia* denoted an accepted theological proposition.

SEPARATISTS. A title applied to the followers of R. *Browne and later to the *Congregationalists and others who separated from the C of E.

SEPTUAGESIMA. The third Sunday before *Lent and hence the ninth Sunday before *Easter. In the RC Church it was suppressed in 1969; it previously marked a stage towards the Lenten fast, with purple vestments being worn from that day until *Holy Week. It is still so observed in the C of E.

SEPTUAGINT, The. ('LXX'.) The most influential of the Greek versions of the OT. Jewish tradition ascribes its origin to the initiative of Ptolemy Philadelphus (285–246 B.C.), who wanted a translation of the Hebrew Law and engaged 72 translators (hence the title 'Septuagint') for the work. The name was gradually attached not just to the *Pentateuch but to the whole OT. Internal evidence suggests that it was the work of a number of translators, working in different places and over a long period. It was prob. complete by 132 B.C.

The LXX differs from the Hebrew Bible both in the order of the Books and in the fact that it contains those Books known as the *Apocrypha in English Bibles. The text also differs in some places, e.g. the LXX of 1 Kgs. contains passages not in the Hebrew.

In the early Church the LXX was regarded as the standard form of the OT, from which the NT writers quote, and it was the basis of the '*Old Latin' versions. St. *Jerome's *Vulgate first provided Christians with a Latin text of the OT from the original and did much to dispel the belief that the LXX was verbally inspired.

SEPULCHRE, Holy. See *Holy Sepulchre*.

SEQUENCE. In the Liturgy, a rhythm sung on certain days after the last reading before the *Gospel. In medieval times a large number of sequences were in regular use, but in the current Roman Missal there are only five, including '*Victimae paschali' and '*Veni, Sancte Spiritus'.

SERAPHIC ORDER, The. Another name for the *Franciscan Order.

SERAPHIM. The supernatural creatures, each with six wings, which *Isaiah saw standing above the throne of God (Is. 6: 2–7). Christian exegetes have held them to be a category of *angels, counterparts to the *Cherubim.

SERAPHIM OF SAROV, St. (1759–1833), Russian monk and *staretz. At 19 he entered the monastery of Sarov in the Oka region of E. Russia. From 1794 to 1825 he lived in seclusion, first as a hermit close to the monastery and then enclosed in a small cell within the monastic building. In 1825 he opened the door of his cell; he then devoted his energies to the work of spiritual direction, receiving visitors from all parts of Russia.

SERAPION, St. (d. 211), Bp. of *Antioch from 199. Though he was one of the chief theologians of his age, little is known of him. Only fragments of his writings survive.

SERAPION, St. (d. after 360), Bp. of Thmuis in the Nile delta from *c.* 339. He had been a monk and companion of St. *Antony. St. *Athanasius chose him for a difficult mission to the Emp. Constantius and addressed to him a series of letters on the Divinity of the Holy Spirit. Serapion wrote against the *Manichees, and a *Sacramentary which has come down under his name is prob. his compilation.

SERBIA, Church of (in Yugoslavia). Systematic missionary work in Serbia was first undertaken by the Byzantines in the second half of the 9th cent., and by 891 Christianity was the official religion. The attachment of the Serbs to E. Christianity did not become definite until the early 13th cent. An *autocephalous Serbian Church was established by St. *Sava in 1219, and in 1375 the Serbian *Patriarchate was recognized by *Constantinople. In the Ottoman period the Serbs passed under Greek ecclesiastical control, but the Serbian Church became autocephalous again in 1879 and the Patriarchate was restored in 1920.

SERGIUS (d. 638), Patr. of *Constantinople from 610 and exponent of *Monothelitism. In an attempt to reconcile the *Monophysites with the adherents of *Chalcedonian orthodoxy, he began to teach that there were two natures in Christ but only one mode of activity. The matter was referred to Pope *Honorius I, who used the unfortunate expression 'one will'. Sergius then modified his teaching to affirm that there was one will in Christ and embodied this in the '*Ecthesis' promulgated by *Heraclius in 638. Tradition ascribes to him the authorship of the '*Acathistus'.

SERGIUS, St. (d. 701), Pope from 687. He resisted the attempt of the Emp. Justinian II to secure his support for the *Trullan Synod (692), and he introduced into the Mass the singing of the *Agnus Dei.

SERGIUS, St. (*c.* 1314–92), Russian monastic reformer and mystic. With his brother he founded the famous monastery of the Holy Trinity near Moscow, thereby reestablishing in Russia the community life which had been lost through the Tartar invasion. He exercised great influence over all classes in Russia, and founded 40 monasteries.

SERGIUS PAULUS. The proconsul of *Cyprus who, acc. to Acts 13: 4–12, invited St. *Paul and St. *Barnabas to preach before him and 'believed'.

SERMO GENERALIS. The ceremony at which the final decision in trials of heretics by the *Inquisition was pronounced, usually with great solemnity. The proceedings closed with the turning-over of the guilty to the *secular arm.

SERMON ON THE MOUNT, The. The Lord's discourse in Mt. 5–7 setting out the principles of the Christian ethic. It includes the *Beatitudes and the *Lord's Prayer.

SERVANT SONGS. Four passages in *Deutero-Isaiah (Is. 42: 1–4, 49: 1–6, 50: 4–9, and 52: 13–53: 12) describing the person and character of the 'servant of the Lord'. Whether the writer referred to the nation of Israel or to an individual is disputed. Christian theology has traditionally interpreted the passages as a prophecy of Christ.

SERVATUS LUPUS. See *Lupus, Servatus*.

SERVER. In the W. Church a minister in the sanctuary, esp. at the *Eucharist. His main duties are to make the responses, bring the bread and wine to the altar, and wash the celebrant's hands.

SERVETUS, MICHAEL (1511–53), heretic. From 1541 to 1553 he was physician to the Abp. of Vienne. His principal work, *Christianismi Restitutio*, appeared anonymously in 1553. In it he denied the doctrine of the Trinity and the true Divinity of Christ. His authorship was denounced to the *Inquisition and he was imprisoned. He escaped to Geneva, but J. *Calvin had him arrested and he was burnt.

SERVICE, Divine. See *Divine Service*.

SERVILE WORK (Lat. *opus servile*, Lev. 23, Num. 28 and 29, Vulg.), a term used of the work which is forbidden on the *Sabbath; in RC *canon law it is applied to work which may not be done on *Sundays or Holy Days. Various attempts have been made to define it.

SERVITES. A religious order founded in 1240 by 7 wealthy Florentines who had left the world 7 years earlier to devote themselves to the service of the BVM. They adopted the Rule of St. *Augustine, with some additions from the *Dominican constitutions.

SERVUS SERVORUM DEI (Lat., 'the servant of God's servants'). A title of the Pope used in official documents.

SESSION. See *Kirk-session*.

SETTLEMENT, Act of (1701). The Act which vested the succession to the British Crown in the Electress Sophia of Hanover, who was the granddaughter of *James I. It set aside the hereditary rights of the descendants of *Charles I, since the son of *James II was a RC. The Act also ordained that future sovereigns and their consorts should 'join in Communion' with the C of E.

SEVEN BISHOPS, Trial of the. When *James II decreed in 1688 that his *Declaration of Indulgence should be read in all churches, Abp. W. *Sancroft and six other bishops protested. They were imprisoned and tried on a charge of seditious libel, but the jury acquitted them.

SEVEN CHURCHES, The. The Churches in Asia Minor to which the letter incorporated in Rev. (1–3) was addressed, viz. *Ephesus, Smyrna, *Pergamum, *Thyatira, Sardis, *Philadelphia, and *Laodicea.

SEVEN CORPORAL ACTS OF MERCY. See *Corporal Works of Mercy*.

SEVEN DEACONS. The title traditionally given to the 'seven men of honest report' who, acc. to Acts 6: 1–6, were appointed to administer the temporal concerns of the Church. Their appointment has been held to institute the order of *deacons, and for many centuries the number of deacons at Rome was restricted to seven.

SEVEN DEADLY SINS. They are *pride, covetousness, lust, envy, gluttony, anger, and sloth (*accidie).

SEVEN LIBERAL ARTS. The group of sciences which formed the staple of secular education in the earlier Middle Ages, consisting of the elementary *Trivium (grammar, rhetoric, and dialectic) and the more advanced *Quadrivium (music, arithmetic, geometry, and astronomy). More was covered by the disciplines of the Trivium than their titles might suggest. Not until the student had completed his studies in the liberal arts was he held competent to proceed to theology.

SEVEN PENITENTIAL PSALMS, The. Psalms 6, 32, 38, 51, 102, 130, and 143.

SEVEN SACRAMENTS, The. *Baptism, *Confirmation, *Eucharist, *Penance, Extreme *Unction, *Orders, and *Matrimony. It was through the *Sentences* of *Peter Lombard (*c.* 1150) that the belief gained credence that these seven *Sacraments constituted a set different in kind from all other religious rites. Their sevenfold number was defined at the Council of *Trent and is also accepted by the E. Church. See also *Sacrament*.

SEVEN SLEEPERS OF EPHESUS. Seven Christian young men who are said to have been walled up in a cave during the *Decian persecution (*c.* 250) and to have been awakened under the Emp. *Theodosius II (d. 450).

SEVEN SORROWS OF THE BVM. Acc. to the Roman *Breviary, the sorrows were: (1) at the prophecy of *Simeon; (2) at the flight into Egypt; (3) at the loss of the Holy Child; (4) on meeting the Lord on the way to Calvary; (5) at standing at the foot of the Cross; (6) at the taking down of Christ from the Cross; (7) at His burial.

SEVEN VIRTUES, The. They are faith, hope, charity, justice, prudence, temperance, and fortitude.

SEVEN WORDS FROM THE CROSS. The 7 sentences which the Gospels record as spoken by Christ on the Cross. They are: (1) 'Father, forgive them; for they know not what they do' (Lk. 23: 34); (2) 'Today shalt thou be with me in paradise' (Lk. 23: 43); (3) 'Woman, behold thy son!... Behold thy mother!' (Jn. 19: 26 f.); (4) 'My God, my God, why hast thou forsaken me?' (Mt. 27: 46); (5) 'I thirst' (Jn. 19: 28); (6) 'It is finished' (Jn. 19: 30); (7) 'Father, into thy hands I commend my spirit' (Lk. 23: 46).

SEVENTH-DAY ADVENTISTS. One of the groups of *Adventists who originally expected the Second Coming of Christ in 1844. Later that year they began to observe the seventh day of the week as the *Sabbath, though the name 'Seventh-day Adventists' was not adopted until 1861. In England their beginnings as an organized community go back to a mission at Southampton in 1878. They are a staunchly Protestant body. They practise adult Baptism, require strict temperance, and observe the Sabbath from sunset on Friday to sunset on Saturday.

SEVERIAN (*fl. c.* 400), Bp. of Gabala in Syria. An opponent of St. *Chrysostom, he played an important part in the events leading up to the Synod of the *Oak in 403. He is important chiefly as a Biblical exegete of the *Antiochene school.

SEVERINUS, St. (d. 482), 'Apostle of Austria'. He was in early life a monk in the East. After the death of *Attila in 453, he came to Noricum Ripense, then overrun by barbarian invaders; he rallied the Church, founded two monasteries, and organized relief work.

SEVERUS (*c.* 465–538), *Monophysite Patr. of *Antioch. At *Constantinople he secured the support of the Emp. Anastasius (491–518) for the persecuted Monophysite monks, and in 512 he was made Patr. of Antioch in place of the deposed Flavian II. On Justin I's accession (518) he was deposed. He was the leading theologian of the moderate Monophysites. Many of his writings survive, mainly in Syriac translation.

SEVERUS, GABRIEL and SULPICIUS. See *Gabriel Severus* and *Sulpicius Severus*.

SEXAGESIMA. The second Sunday before *Lent and hence the eighth before *Easter. The name was suppressed in the RC Church in 1969, but it survives in the C of E.

SEXT. (1) In *canon law the sixth book of *decretals, promulgated by *Boniface VIII in 1298. It contains the decretals issued since the publication of the five books by *Gregory IX (1234).
(2) The Breviary *Office appointed to be said at noon, i.e. the sixth hour. See also *Terce*.

SEXTON. Traditionally the sexton was the assistant to the *parish clerk. His main duties were cleaning the church, ringing the bell, and digging graves. In the C of E he is now appointed by the minister and *parochial church council, who determine the nature of his duties and terms of employment (can. E 3 of 1969).

SEYMOUR, EDWARD. See *Somerset, Duke of*.

SHAFTESBURY, ANTHONY ASHLEY COOPER (1801–85), **7th Earl of,** social reformer. His main concern was with the amelioration of the conditions of the working classes, and he was largely responsible for the Factory Act of 1874. He was a fervent *Evangelical. For many years he was president of the *British and Foreign Bible Society.

SHAKERS, also 'The United Society of Believers in Christ's Second Appearing' or 'The Millennial Church', a communistic and pacifist body which originated during a *Quaker revival in England in 1747. The original leaders were succeeded by Ann Lee, known as Mother Ann, who came to be regarded as 'The female principle in Christ', Jesus being the 'male principle'; in her the Second Coming was fulfilled. In 1774 she led a small band to the U.S.A.; they settled near Albany, N.Y. Their numbers were increased in 1780 by converts from an independent religious revival near New Lebanon. By the 1950s only a few families remained and the sect is prob. now extinct.

SHAKESPEARE, JOHN HOWARD (1857–1928), British *Baptist. He became secretary of the Baptist Union in 1898 and made it a highly influential organization. He was largely responsible for founding the Baptist World Alliance (1905) and the Federal Council of the Evangelical *Free Churches (1919).

SHAMMAI, School of. The disciples of Shammai, a leading rabbinical teacher in the time of Christ. In contrast with the School of *Hillel, the Shammaites interpreted the Mosaic Law strictly and rigidly.

SHARP, JAMES (1613–79), Abp. of St. Andrews from 1661. He was rewarded by appointment to this office for his collaboration with General G. Monck from 1659 and his secret work for the restoration of episcopacy. As Archbishop he took severe measures to abolish Presbyterianism, and he aroused bitter resentment by his support for the oppressive policy of the Duke of Lauderdale. He was murdered.

SHARP, JOHN (1645–1714), Abp. of *York from 1691. As Dean of *Norwich he refused to read the *Declaration of Indulgence in 1688. In 1689 he took the oaths to

William and Mary, but announced that he would not accept any bishopric vacated by a *Nonjuror. His episcopate was marked by a high standard of duty.

SHAXTON, NICHOLAS (*c.* 1485–1556), Bp. of *Salisbury. He was a member of the committee appointed by Cambridge University in 1530 to consider *Henry VIII's divorce. He developed pronounced Protestant views. In 1535 he was made Bp. of Salisbury, but he resigned in 1539 in protest against the *Six Articles.

SHEER THURSDAY. An old name for *Maundy Thursday.

SHELDON, GILBERT (1598–1677), Abp. of *Canterbury from 1663. In 1660 he became Bp. of London and Master of the Savoy, and in 1661 the *Savoy Conference met at his lodgings. As Archbishop he worked for the re-establishment of W. *Laud's religious principles. He carried through the arrangement whereby the *Convocations ceased to tax the clergy (1664).

SHEMA, The. The confession of faith to be recited by Jewish men morning and evening. It consists of 3 Biblical passages (Deut. 6: 4–9, 11: 13–21, Num. 15: 37–41), preceded and followed by blessings.

SHENOUTE (d. *c.* 450), Abbot of Athribis in Egypt from *c.* 388. His community of monks and nuns grew very large. His government was severe and he added many austerities to the more humane rule of *Pachomius. In 431 he accompanied St. *Cyril of Alexandria to the Council of *Ephesus, where he opposed *Nestorius. His writings (in Coptic) deal mainly with monastic concerns and exhortations to virtue.

SHEOL. In the OT, the underworld, the place of departed souls. It is translated in the AV variously as 'hell', 'grave', or 'pit'. The notion reflects an undeveloped and shadowy belief in the future life which was superseded by more defined beliefs in later Judaism.

SHEPHERD OF HERMAS, The. The treatise of *Hermas (q.v.), so named from the angel who, in the form of a shepherd, is represented as having communicated to Hermas some of its contents.

SHEPPARD, HUGH RICHARD LAWRIE (1880–1937), popularly 'Dick Sheppard', vicar of St. Martin-in-the-Fields, London, from 1914 to 1926. His religious enthusiasm and personal attractiveness won the affection of innumerable people in all stations of life, esp. after the growth of broadcasting. From 1929 to 1931 he was Dean of *Canterbury. In his last years he was an ardent Pacifist.

SHERBORNE. St. *Aldhelm established the seat of the Bp. of W. Wessex here in 705. In 1058 the see was united with Ramsbury and in 1075 moved to Old *Sarum. At the *Dissolution in 1536 the abbey, a fine example in Perpendicular style, became the parish church. A bishopric of Sherborne, suffragan to *Salisbury, was founded in 1928.

SHERLOCK, WILLIAM (1641–1707), Dean of *St. Paul's. In the Revolution of 1688 he sided with the *Nonjurors. His *Vindication of the Doctrines of the Trinity and of the Incarnation* (1690) provoked a violent controversy, in which he was accused of teaching *Tritheism. In the same year he took the oath of allegiance to William and Mary, and in 1691 he became Dean of St. Paul's.

SHEWBREAD. The twelve loaves which, acc. to the practice of the Jewish *Temple, were prepared from the finest flour and, arranged in two piles, set out weekly beside the altar of incense. When they were removed for renewal at the end of the week, only the priests might eat them.

SHIBBOLETH. A word used by Jephthah as a test to distinguish the Gileadites from the Ephraimites, who could not pronounce it (Jgs. 12: 4 ff.). In modern usage it denotes a sectarian or party catchword.

SHORTENED SERVICES ACT. See *Uniformity, Act of, Amendment Act* (1872).

SHORTHOUSE, JOSEPH HENRY (1834–1903), author of *John Inglesant* (1881). The son of *Quaker parents, Shorthouse was baptized in the C of E in 1861. The delicacy and charm with which John Inglesant's spiritual pilgrimage is portrayed, its sympathetic understanding of the religious life of the 17th cent., and its vivid delineation of the community at *Little Gidding, made the book a powerful *apologia* for Anglicanism.

SHRINE. The word can designate a *reliquary (q.v.), a sacred image of special importance, or any holy place, esp one connected with *pilgrimages.

SHROUD, Holy. See *Holy Shroud.*

SHROVE TUESDAY. The day immediately before *Ash Wednesday, so named from the 'shriving', i.e. confession and absolution, of the faithful on that day.

SIAN-FU STONE. See *Sigan-Fu Stone.*

SIBYLLINE ORACLES, The. A collection of oracles imitating the pagan 'Sibylline Books'. The oracles, written in hexameters, are preceded by a prose prologue affirming that they are utterances of Greek Sibyls of various periods. Their genuineness was accepted by many of the Fathers, who drew from them arguments in defence of Christianity. Modern critics assign them to Jewish and Christian authors; for, though genuine Greek oracles are inserted in some places, the tendency of the whole is monotheistic and Messianic. The dates of the Jewish portions range from the *Maccabean period to the time of the Emp. Hadrian (117–38); the Christian additions seem to date from the 2nd cent. onwards.

SICARD (1160–1215), Bp. of Cremona from 1185. His *Chronicon*, a history of the world to 1213, is a primary authority for the Crusade of *Frederick I. His *Mitrale* throws light on contemporary liturgical practice. He also wrote a *Summa* on the Decretum of *Gratian.

SICILIAN VESPERS, The. A massacre of the French in Sicily in 1282, the signal for which was the tolling of the bell for *Vespers.

SICK, Visitation of the (BCP). See *Visitation of the Sick.*

SICKINGEN, FRANZ VON (1481–1523), German knight. Under the influence of U. von *Hutten he embraced the Reformation, defended J. *Reuchlin, and offered his castles as places of refuge for Protestants. In 1522 he led an army against the Abp. of Trier and was mortally wounded in a counter-attack.

SIDESMEN. In the C of E, persons elected to assist the *churchwardens. Their original function was to secure the attendance of parishioners at divine service; it is now their duty to promote the cause of true religion in the parish, as well as to assist the churchwardens in maintaining order and decency in the church and churchyard.

SIDETES, PHILIP. See *Philip Sidetes.*

SIDGWICK, HENRY (1838–1900), moral philosopher. At Cambridge he supported the movement for abolishing religious tests. His *Methods of Ethics* (1874), a study of moral philosophy on mainly *hedonistic lines, had considerable influence.

SIDONIUS APOLLINARIS, St. (c. 423–c. 480), statesman and bishop. About 450 he married a daughter of the future Emp. Avitus (455–6) and entered upon a successful political career. In 469, while prob. still a layman, he was unwillingly elected Bp. of Clermont. He was imprisoned when Clermont was occupied by the Visigoths in 475, but he was freed and reinstated in his diocese in 476. His poems show great technical skill; his letters are a valuable historical source.

SIGAN-FU STONE, The. A *Nestorian monument discovered in 1625 at Sigan-Fu (or Sian-Fu) in NW. *China; it was set up in A.D. 781. It records the arrival of a missionary from Tuts'in in 635 and gives an account of the fortunes of the Church to date. It is the main witness to the growth of Christianity in the Far East before the 13th cent.

SIGEBERT OF GEMBLOUX (c. 1030–1112), *Benedictine monk and chronicler. His two main works are the *Chronicon* (from 381 to 1111), which betrays lack of critical discernment but from 1024 relies partly on first-hand information, and *De Viris Illustribus*, an ecclesiastical literary history with an air of great erudition.

SIGER OF BRABANT (c. 1240–c. 1284), *Averroist philosopher. By 1266 he was teaching in *Paris. He was involved in the condemnation of 13 errors by the Bp. of

Paris in 1270 and in that year St. *Thomas Aquinas wrote his *De Unitate Intellectus contra Averroistas,* which was directed chiefly against him. In 1276 he was cited for heresy by Simon du Val, Inquisitor of France; he had already fled the country.

Siger's main works were commentaries and *quaestiones* on *Aristotle. He regarded it as his task not to conceal Aristotle's views, even if these were contrary to revealed truth. The chief doctrines in question were the eternity of the world and the unity of the intellect in the human race, which involved the denial of personal immortality and of rewards and punishments in a future life. Critics accused him of holding that some tenets might be true in theology and false in philosophy; this he would have disputed, though it is not clear from his writings how far he resolved the status of philosophical truths.

SIGN OF THE CROSS. From early times the sign of the cross has been used to sanctify actions in daily life, as an encouragement in temptation and trial, and as a means of mutual recognition in times of persecution. It is also employed in *Baptism and *Confirmation, and its use was extended to the liturgical blessing of people and things. It is now made by drawing the right hand from forehead to breast and then from shoulder to shoulder, returning to the centre afterwards.

SILAS, St. A prominent early Christian disciple. He was St. *Paul's companion on his first visit to Macedonia and *Corinth, and St. Paul associated him with himself and *Timothy in writing to the *Thessalonians, giving his name in the form 'Silvanus'. He is prob. to be identified with St. *Peter's amanuensis (1 Pet. 5: 12).

SILENCE, The Argument from. The deduction from the absence of any known reference to a subject in the extant writings of a particular author that he was ignorant of it.

SILESIUS, ANGELUS. See *Angelus Silesius.*

SILOAM, The Pool of. A pool or reservoir at *Jerusalem, mentioned in both the OT and the NT. It is almost certainly the modern *Birket Silwān.*

SILVESTER. See *Sylvester.*

SILVIA OF AQUITAINE. A relative of the Roman prefect Rufinus. She was at one time thought to be the authoress of the 'Pilgrimage of *Etheria' (q.v.).

SIMEON. (1) In the OT, one of the Hebrew patriarchs, the ancestor of the tribe of that name. (2) The aged and devout Jew who took the infant Christ in his arms in the *Temple at *Jerusalem, spoke the words now known as the '*Nunc Dimittis', and prophesied that a sword would pierce the soul of the BVM (Lk. 2: 25-35).

SIMEON, the New Theologian, St. (949-1022), Byzantine mystic and spiritual writer. Becoming a monk in 977, in 981 he was made abbot of St. Mamas in *Constantinople, but because of the fierce opposition aroused by some aspects of his teaching, he went into exile in Asia Minor in 1009. He assigned a central place to the vision of the Divine Light and exercised a formative influence on the rise of *Hesychasm. His appellation 'the New Theologian' prob. implies a comparison with St. *Gregory of Nazianzus, known in the E. as 'Gregory the Theologian'.

SIMEON OF DURHAM (c. 1060-1130), *Benedictine monk and chronicler. His *Historia Ecclesiae Dunelmensis* takes the history of the see of *Durham to 1096. He was prob. also the author of a general history of England.

SIMEON METAPHRASTES, St. (fl. c. 960), also known as **Logothetes**, Byzantine hagiographer. He owes his fame to his collection of saints' lives ('Menologion'). A few of the lives were simply copied from earlier collections, but most of them were worked over ('metaphrased'; hence his name) to make their style acceptable to the taste of the time. His work was added to in later times.

SIMEON STYLITES, St. (c. 390-459), the first of the *stylites or pillar saints. After some time as a monk, he spent several years as a hermit in N. Syria and then mounted a pillar, at first low but gradually increased to a height of 40 cubits (c. 20 metres); he lived on the top of it until his death. This novel form of austerity attracted a stream of pilgrims and was widely imitated.

SIMEON OF THESSALONICA (d. 1429), Abp. of *Thessalonica. Little is known of his life, but he was an influential author. His main work, a 'Dialogue against all Heresies and on the One Faith', consists of a short treatise on doctrine and a longer one on the Liturgy and Sacraments.

SIMEON, CHARLES (1759-1836), leader of the *Evangelical Revival. From 1783 he was vicar of Holy Trinity, Cambridge. His Evangelicalism at first met with hostility, but his pastoral zeal broke down opposition. He was one of the founders of the *C.M.S. (1799). He also founded a body of trustees (the Simeon Trustees) for securing and administering Church patronage in accordance with his principles.

SIMILITUDO DEI (Lat., 'likeness of God'). The element in man's being as originally constituted which he lost through the *Fall. See *Imago Dei*.

SIMON, St., 'the Less', Apostle. Nothing is known of his personal history, but from Lk. 6: 15 it may be inferred that he had been a member of the *Zealots. The apocryphal 'Passion of Simon and *Jude' relates the preaching and martyrdom of the two Apostles in Persia. In the W. they are always linked in the ecclesiastical calendar and in the dedication of churches.

SIMON OF CYRENE. A passer-by who was compelled by the Roman soldiers to carry Christ's cross on the way to the crucifixion (Mt. 27: 32 &c.). In modern times he has been claimed as patron by groups of people working among outcasts.

SIMON MAGUS. Acc. to Acts 8: 9-24, a sorcerer, who practised in *Samaria, was converted to Christianity and baptized; he was rebuked by St. *Peter for trying to obtain spiritual powers for money (hence the term '*simony'). A *Gnostic sect was supposed to have taken its origin from him. The founder of the sect, however, seems to have been a different Simon, a native of Gitta in Samaria, who lived in the 2nd cent.

SIMON PETER, St. An alternative designation for St. *Peter (q.v.), who was originally called Simon.

SIMON STOCK, St. (c. 1165-1265),

*Carmelite. One of the first Englishmen to join the Carmelites when they settled in Britain, he became General c. 1247. During his term of office the order increased rapidly, and he obtained Papal approval for its reorganization. The name 'Stock' perhaps derives from a legend that as a young man he lived a hermit's life in a tree-trunk.

SIMON OF SUDBURY (d. 1381), Abp. of *Canterbury from 1375. He seems to have been reluctant to take proceedings against J. *Wycliffe until ordered by the Pope to do so, and then he was not extreme in his measures. In 1380 he became Chancellor and was responsible for the imposition of a poll tax. He was killed in a general rising of the peasants.

SIMON, RICHARD (1638–1712), Biblical scholar. From 1662 to 1678 he was a member of the French *Oratory. His *Histoire critique du Vieux Testament* (1678), arguing from the existence of duplicate accounts of the same incident and variations of style, denied that *Moses was the author of the *Pentateuch. He is generally regarded as the founder of OT criticism.

SIMONS, MENNO. See *Mennonites*.

SIMONS IN THE NT. Besides (1) Simon *Peter, the Apostle, (2) *Simon 'the Less', Apostle, (3) *Simon Magus, and (4) *Simon of Cyrene, the NT mentions (5) Simon, one of the *Brethren of the Lord; (6) Simon the *Pharisee, in whose house Christ was anointed by 'a woman which was a sinner' (Lk. 7: 36–50); (7) Simon the leper, in whose house at *Bethany Christ was anointed by an unnamed woman (Mk. 14: 3–9); and (8) Simon, a tanner, with whom St. Peter lodged at Joppa (Acts 9: 43).

SIMONY. The term, which is derived from *Simon Magus (see Acts 8: 18–24), denotes the purchase or sale of spiritual things. The canons of the early Church show that simony became frequent after the age of the persecutions; there has been a continuous stream of legislation against it, esp. in connection with ecclesiastical preferment.

SIMPLE FEASTS. Feasts of the lowest rank in the pre-1960 RC calendar.

SIMPLICIANUS, St. (d. 400), Bp. of Milan from 397. He was instrumental in bringing about the conversion of *Victorinus; he prepared St. *Ambrose for his baptism and ordination, and he played a part in St. *Augustine's conversion. He succeeded Ambrose in the see of Milan.

SIMPLICIUS, St. (d. 483), Pope from 468. During his pontificate, which was marked by the fall of the W. Empire (476) and the spread of the *Monophysite heresy, he advanced the jurisdictional claims and the prestige of the Roman see. In the E. he successfully intervened in defence of the *Chalcedonian formula against its Monophysite critics.

SIMULTANEUM. The term was orginally used in 16th-cent. Germany for the authorization of two or more religious communions in the same territory; it came to be restricted to the simultaneous right of two religious congregations differing in their faith to use a single ecclesiastical building. Special provisions for this practice were made in the Peace of *Ryswick (1697).

SIN. The purposeful disobedience of a creature to the known will of God. In the OT it is represented as a constant factor in the experience both of God's people and of the world from the first transgression of *Adam and *Eve. *Ezekiel and *Jeremiah proclaim the personal responsiblity of each man for his sins. The Psalms, with their stress on the heart as the seat of sin, provide penetrating insights on its personal and emotional effects. In the NT the Lord emphasizes that the roots of sin lie in a man's character (Mt. 5: 21–5; 15: 18–20). St. *Paul explains sin as a breach of the *natural law written in the conscience of man (Rom. 2: 14–16) and asserts its universality.

Later theology has added little to what is implicit in the Bible. Among the influential factors in the development of this theology was St. *Augustine's rejection of the *Manichaean doctrine that evil was a substance and the created universe inherently wicked, in favour of the *Platonic view that sin is in essence a privation of good. The development of the *penitential system in the Middle Ages tended to foster an external view of sin. Rejecting this, M. *Luther preached *justification by faith alone. Under the secularizing influence of the *Enlightenment attempts were made to remove sin from its religious setting and to interpret it as moral evil; in the 19th cent. the notion of sin was largely eliminated from much popular religious teaching. In the present century there has been renewed emphasis on the gravity of sin (e.g. in *Dialectical Theology).

See also *Atonement*, *Fall*, *Original Sin*, *Penance*, and *Redemption*.

SINAI. The mountain in the desert between Egypt and Palestine where the Law was given to *Moses (Exod. 19: 1 ff.). The region of the traditional Sinai (now Jebel Katherina) was an early centre of Christian monasticism; the monastery dedicated to St. *Catherine of Alexandria claims to have been built on the site to which her body was miraculously transported.

The Church of Sinai is the smallest independent Church of the Orthodox communion. It is ruled by the 'Archbishop of Mount Sinai', who is abbot of the monastery of St. Catherine.

SINAITICUS, Codex. See *Codex Sinaiticus*.

SION. See *Zion*.

SION COLLEGE, London. Thomas White (d. 1624) left £3,000 for a 'college' for the clergy of London, with almshouses attached. The College, now on the Victoria Embankment, functions mainly as a library.

SI QUIS (Lat., 'If anybody'). The public notice issued on behalf of a candidate for a benefice, holy orders, &c., which requires any objectors to come forward.

SIRICIUS, St. (c. 334–99), Bp. of Rome from 384. His pontificate marked a stage in the development of Papal authority. His letter to Himerius, Bp. of Tarragona (385), advocating relatively lenient treatment of penitents, is the first Papal *decretal; and the disciplinary canons of a synod held in Rome in 386 were sent to the African Church.

SIRMIUM, Blasphemy of. The doctrinal formula issued by the Council of Sirmium (in Bosnia) in 357, setting out the teaching of the extreme *Arians. All mention of the term 'substance' in Trinitarian speculation was forbidden, and the subordination of the Son to the Father was asserted. It takes its name from St. *Hilary of Poitiers's description of it.

SIRMOND, JACQUES (1559–1651), French *Jesuit scholar. He is important for his editions of the Fathers. His attack on the identity of *Dionysius of Paris and *Dionysius the (Pseudo-) Areopagite provoked controversy.

SISTERS OF MERCY. (1) A name widely used in the 19th cent. of any (esp. Anglican) religious community engaged in nursing or similar work. (2) A RC sisterhood founded in Dublin in 1827.

SISTINE CHAPEL. The principal chapel of the *Vatican Palace, so called because it was built for *Sixtus IV (1471–84).

SISTINE MADONNA. A painting by *Raphael, depicting the Virgin and Child floating on the clouds of heaven, between St. *Sixtus II and St. *Barbara. It is now in Dresden.

SITZ IM LEBEN (Germ., 'place in life'). A term used chiefly in Biblical criticism, to signify the circumstances (often in the life of a community) in which a particular story, saying, &c., was either created or preserved and transmitted.

SIX ARTICLES, The. Articles passed by Act of Parliament in 1539 at *Henry VIII's bidding to prevent the spread of Reformation doctrines and practices. They maintained *transubstantiation and *communion in one kind, enforced clerical *celibacy, upheld *monastic vows, and defended private *Masses and *auricular confession.

SIX POINTS, The. The *Eastward Position, *Eucharistic Vestments, *Mixed Chalice, *Altar Lights, Unleavened *Bread at the Eucharist, and *Incense. Their introduction into the C of E followed a campaign, set on foot c. 1870, to restore these and similar ceremonial usages. See also *Purchas Judgement*, *Lincoln Judgement*.

SIXTUS II, St. (d. 258), or 'Xystus', Pope from 257. He resumed relations with St. *Cyprian and the Churches of Africa and Asia Minor broken off by his predecessor over the question of the validity of baptism by heretics. He suffered martyrdom and was highly venerated.

SIXTUS IV (1414–84), Pope from 1471. A *Franciscan, he became General of the order in 1464. With him the *nepotism of the Renaissance Popes reached its worst stage, implicating the Papacy in political intrigues with Italian cities and leading to confusion in the Papal finances. He founded the Sistine Choir and built the *Sistine Chapel.

SIXTUS V (1521–90), Pope from 1585. He put the Papal finances on a sound basis by the sale of certain offices, the setting-up of more '*montes', and additional taxes. Continuing the reform of the *Curia, he established the *Roman congregations. He built the *Lateran Palace and the *Vatican Library, had the cupola of *St. Peter's finished, and supplied Rome with drinking water. He also inaugurated an edition of the *Vulgate.

SLAVERY. A state of servitude by which a man becomes the property of another man. Although there is no specific condemnation of slavery in the NT, the spiritual equality of men and the charity demanded are ultimately incompatible with it. From *Constantine onwards Imperial legislation followed Christian sentiment and many mitigations were introduced; slavery was gradually transformed into the milder institution of serfdom, which slowly disappeared at the end of the Middle Ages. After the fall of *Constantinople in 1453, however, the Turks reduced large numbers of Christians to servitude, and in America the Spanish, Portuguese, and British settlers made slaves of the Indians and introduced slaves from Africa, despite the steady resistance of missionaries and the condemnations of successive Popes. In the 18th cent. the movement against slavery was taken up by the *Quakers and then by philanthropists such as W. *Wilberforce. The slave trade was made illegal in 1808 and slavery abolished in the British Empire in 1833. In the U.S.A. a constitutional amendment in 1865 prohibited slavery for ever.

SLEIDANUS, JOHANNES (1506–56), annalist of the German Reformation. He adopted Protestant views of a *Calvinist type before 1536. His *De Statu Religionis et Reipublicae Carolo V Caesare Commentarii* (1555; Eng. tr., 1560) contains documents which make it the chief contemporary source for the period, though its author's impartiality won him little favour from his contemporaries.

SLESSOR, MARY (1848–1915), missionary of the *United Presbyterian Church. In 1876 she sailed for the Calabar coast of W. Africa. Here she gained great influence with the native population and ended many tribal abuses (e.g. twin murder and human sacrifice). In 1905 she was invested with the powers of a magistrate.

SMART, PETER (1569–c. 1652), *Puritan. As a prebendary of *Durham cathedral he resisted the introduction of High Church ceremonial and preached a violent sermon on the subject in 1628. He was brought before the Court of *High Commission and in 1631 he was degraded and imprisoned. The Long Parliament declared his imprisonment void and restored him in 1641.

'SMECTYMNUUS'. The professed writer of a book published in 1641 defending the *Presbyterian theory of Christian ministry in reply to J. *Hall's *Humble Remonstrance*. The name was made up of the initials of the five authors.

SMITH, BERNARD (c. 1630–1708), called 'Father Smith', organ-builder. A native of Germany (his original name was Schmidt), he came to England before 1660. He built organs for *Westminster Abbey, *Wells, *St. Paul's, and *Durham Cathedrals, *Christ Church, Oxford, and Trinity College, Cambridge (this last finished after his death).

SMITH, J. (c. 1554–1612). See *Smyth, J.*

SMITH, JOHN (1618–52), *Cambridge Platonist. Under the influence of B. *Whichcote, he became one of the leading Cambridge Platonists, upholding spiritual religion against the acrimonious theological disputes of the age.

SMITH, WILLIAM ROBERTSON (1846–94), Scottish theologian and Semitic scholar. He was at the centre of the storm provoked by the *Higher Criticism of the OT. His articles in the 9th edition of the *Encyclopaedia Britannica* were severely criticized by a committee of the General Assembly of the *Free Church of Scotland as undermining belief in the inspiration of Scripture, and in 1881 he was removed from his chair at the Free Church College in Aberdeen. He spent the rest of his life in Cambridge. His lectures on *The Old Testament in the Jewish Church* (publd. 1881) popularized J. *Wellhausen's theory of the structure and date of the *Pentateuch and the development of Israelite religion; in *The Prophets of Israel* (1882) he expounded on this basis the life and teaching of the early Prophets.

SMITHFIELD, London. The place was formerly noted as the site of executions, esp. during the Reformation period. It is now a meat market.

SMYTH or **SMITH, JOHN** (*c*. 1554–1612), *Baptist. Ordained in the C of E, he became a *Puritan preacher at *Lincoln and later a *Separatist pastor in Gainsborough. He led a company of exiles to Amsterdam *c*. 1608 and there, after baptizing himself (hence his title, the '*Se-Baptist'), in 1609 he established the first modern Baptist Church. He came increasingly under *Mennonite influence.

SOBORNOST. A Russian term with no exact English equivalent. In modern Russian theology it denotes a unity of many persons within the organic fellowship of the Church, each person maintaining his full freedom and personal integrity. It is claimed as a special characteristic of the *Orthodox Church, contrasted with the juridical authority of the RC Church and the individualism of the Protestant communions.

SOCIALISM, Christian. See *Christian Socialism*.

SOCIETY FOR PROMOTING CHRISTIAN KNOWLEDGE; SOCIETY FOR THE PROPAGATION OF THE GOSPEL; SOCIETY OF JESUS. See *S.P.C.K.*, *S.P.G.*, and *Jesuits*.

SOCIETY OF ST. JOHN THE EVANGELIST (S.S.J.E.). An Anglican society of mission priests and laymen, popularly known as the '*Cowley Fathers'. It was founded in 1865 by R. M. *Benson and is the oldest Anglican religious community for men.

SOCINIANISM. See the following entry and *Unitarianism*.

SOCINUS. The Latinized name of (1)

LELIO FRANCESCO MARIA SOZINI (1525–62). Trained as a lawyer at *Bologna, he found his main interests in theology and was received by the Reformers in various countries. At Geneva he was challenged on the doctrine of the Trinity, but satisfied H. *Bullinger.
(2) FAUSTO PAOLO SOZZINI (1539–1604), his nephew. In 1562 he published a work denying the essential Divinity of Christ; by 1563 he had rejected the natural immortality of man. From 1579 he lived in Poland, where he did much to spread moderate *Unitarian doctrines among the upper classes. See also *Racovian Catechism* and *Unitarianism*.

SOCRATES (*c*. 380–450), 'Scholasticus', Greek historian. His 'Church History' was designed as a continuation of *Eusebius's work and extends from the abdication of *Diocletian (305) to 439. It is generally objective and lucidly written, if colourless.

SODALITY. In the RC Church a guild established for the furtherence of some religious purpose by common action or mutual assistance.

SÖDERBLOM, NATHAN (1866–1931), *Lutheran Abp. of *Upsala from 1914. He was a prominent supporter of the *Ecumenical Movement and the leading figure in the *Stockholm Conference on '*Life and Work' (1925); his aim was to organize practical co-operation between the Churches, esp. on social questions, without consideration of doctrinal differences. He encouraged the liturgical movement in the Swedish Church.
In *The Nature of Revelation* (1903; Eng. tr., 1933) he defended the position of *Higher Criticism; he criticized the dogma of the two natures in Christ as unacceptable to modern man, and he maintained that God's revelation is restricted neither to the Bible nor to the Church, but continues throughout history.

SODOM AND GOMORRAH. Acc. to Gen. 19: 24 f. two cities which were destroyed by fire from heaven because of their wickedness.

SODOR AND MAN. The present Anglican diocese of Sodor and Man consists of the Isle of Man. The original diocese of Sodor, which seems to date from the 11th cent., included also the Hebrides and other islands west of Scotland; the Scottish islands were detached in 1334. The termination 'and Man' was apparently added in error by a 17th-cent. legal draughtsman.

SOHM, RUDOLPH (1841–1917), German jurist and Protestant Church historian. He developed the idea that while the Church was wholly spiritual, law was wholly secular; hence the development of canon law ('Catholicism') was an abandonment of the primitive ideal of the Church, which was fundamentally a '*charismatic' body.

SOISSONS, Councils of. The two chief Councils were those of 1092, which condemned *Roscellinus for teaching *Tritheism; and 1121, which condemned Peter *Abelard's *Theologia Summi Boni.*

SOLEAS. In the E. Church the platform immediately in front of the *iconostasis.

SOLEMN LEAGUE AND COVENANT. The agreement between the Scots and the English Parliament of 1643. Its professed aims were the maintenance of the *Presbyterian Church of Scotland, the reformation of the Church of England and uniformity of the Churches in the British Isles, the preservation of Parliaments and the liberties of the kingdoms, and defence of the just power of the King. For a time the proceedings of the *Westminster Assembly took a Presbyterian turn, but after 1644 the Independents came to power and the Covenant was a dead letter in England.

SOLEMNITAS (Lat., commonly rendered in English 'Solemnity'), the name given since 1969 in the RC Church to feasts of the greatest importance.

SOLESMES. The seat of a famous *Benedictine monastery in France. It was founded in 1010, but in modern times its history goes back to Dom Prosper *Guéranger, who settled there with five other priests in 1833. It became a centre of the *Liturgical Movement, taking a notable part in the revival and development of liturgical music.

SOLIFIDIANISM. The doctrine of *Justification by faith alone (*sola fide*) proclaimed by the Protestant Reformers.

SOLOMON (d. *c.* 930 B.C.), King of Israel from *c.* 970 B.C., when he succeeded his father *David. The impression given in 1 Kgs. 1–11 is of an oriental despot, honoured for his wealth and wisdom. This reputation was responsible for the later attribution to him of the Books of *Proverbs, *Canticles, *Ecclesiastes, and *Wisdom. His reign marked the zenith of ancient Israel's prosperity; the *Temple was part of a grandiose building scheme intended to make *Jerusalem a worthy capital of the kingdom. To finance his projects he imposed a system of levies and forced labour; the resulting discontent led, after his death, to the secession of the ten northern tribes. See also the following entries.

SOLOMON, Odes of. This *pseudepigraphical work contains 42 short hymns of a lyrical character. They may be Christian adaptations of a Jewish work but are more probably wholly Christian in origin. If Christian they were almost certainly written in Syria or Palestine in the 1st or 2nd cent. A.D. It is disputed whether their original language was Syriac or Greek.

SOLOMON, Psalms of. A Jewish *pseudepigraphical collection of 18 Psalms. Though extant only in Greek (and a Syriac translation of the Greek), they were almost certainly written in Hebrew. They date from the post-*Maccabean age, prob. from the years 70–40 B.C. The last two Psalms predict the coming of a *Messiah of the house of *David.

SOLOMON, The Song of (also called 'The Song of Songs' or 'Canticles'), OT Book. It seems to be an anthology of love poems, ascribed to *Solomon and his beloved (the 'Shulamite') and their friends. It prob. dates from as late as the 3rd cent. B.C., though individual poems may be much earlier.

Both Jewish and Christian exegetes have interpreted the Book allegorically. In the *Talmud it is regarded as an allegory of God's dealings with Israel. Christians have seen in it a description of God's relations with the Church or with the individual soul.

SOLOMON, Wisdom of. See *Wisdom of Solomon.*

SOLOVIEFF, VLADIMIR (1853–1900), Russian philosopher and theologian. Until

1881 he shared the antipathy of many Slavophils for the RC Church; he later changed his attitude and carried on negotiations with J. G. *Strossmayer for a reunion of the Orthodox and RC Churches. His *La Russie et l'Église universelle* (1889) met with violent opposition in Russia, and in 1896 he became a RC. In his philosophical system he admitted *Gnostic elements and upheld the existence of a female principle, 'Sophia' (*Wisdom) or the world-soul.

SOMASCHI, The. An order of clerks regular founded in 1532 by St. *Jerome Emiliani at Somasca in N. Italy.

SOMERSET, Duke of (*c*. 1506–52), Protector of England, 1547–50. Edward Seymour was a brother of Jane Seymour, third wife of *Henry VIII. He was a leading figure in the Council when his nephew succeeded as *Edward VI. As Protector he pressed on the reforming cause in the English Church. He was deprived of office in 1550 and executed on a charge of conspiracy.

SON OF MAN. In the NT a title applied to Christ. With one exception (Acts 7: 56) it is found only in the Gospels and here always on the Lord's lips.
  The significance of the phrase is debated. There is reason to think that in the popular Aramaic of NT times it was used simply as a paraphrase for 'I'. The corresponding expression in the OT is often a synonym for man, i.e. a human being. On the basis of Dan. 7: 13, however, some scholars have argued that in the Gospels the term had a 'communal' sense and was indicative of the Messianic community. Traditionally 'Son of Man' is held to signify esp. the humility of Christ's incarnate manhood as contrasted with the majesty of His Divinity denoted by 'Son of God'; it also emphasizes His universalist role in contrast with the nationalist conceptions associated with the title 'Son of David'.

SONG OF SONGS, The. See *Solomon, The Song of*.

SONG OF THE THREE CHILDREN, The. A short Book of the *Apocrypha. In the LXX and *Vulgate (where it is inserted after Dan. 3: 23) the Song is part of the story of the three Hebrew exiles thrown into the furnace by Nebuchadnezzar. It includes the canticle of praise known as the *Benedicite.

SONGS OF ASCENT or **SONGS OF DEGREES.** See *Gradual Psalms*.

SONGS OF PRAISE. A 'national' hymnal designed for use by Christians of all denominations, first published in 1925. Theologically its standpoint was markedly liberal, and became even more so in the 2nd edition of 1931.

SOPHIA, St. See *Santa Sophia*.

SOPHRONIUS, St. (*c*. 560–638), Patr. of *Jerusalem from 634. His identity with Sophronius 'the Sophist' now seems beyond dispute. From 633 he was the chief opponent of *Monothelitism. He witnessed the capture of Jerusalem by the Saracens in 637.

SORBONNE. The most famous college of the old University of *Paris. It was founded *c*. 1257 by Robert de Sorbon, confessor of *Louis IX, for the education of advanced students aspiring to the theological doctorate. Its reputation became very great. From the late Middle Ages it favoured *Gallican tendencies, and its opposition to the bull *Unigenitus (1713) lost it Papal favour. It was suppressed in 1792 but re-established as the Theological Faculty of the University in 1808. The faculty was abolished in 1882, but the name 'Sorbonne' is widely used of the modern University of Paris.

SORROWFUL MYSTERIES, The Five. The second *chaplet of the *Rosary, consisting of the Agony in Gethsemane, the Scourging, the Crowning with Thorns, the Carrying of the Cross, and the Crucifixion.

SOTERIOLOGY. The section of Christian theology which treats of the saving work of Christ for the world.

SOTO, DOMINIC (1494–1560), Spanish *Dominican theologian. He was professor of theology at Salamanca. In 1545 *Charles V chose him as Imperial Theologian for the Council of *Trent, at which he expounded the *Thomistic doctrine on grace and free will.

SOUBIROUS, BERNADETTE. See *Bernadette, St.*

SOUL. The Bible is explicit only on the facts of the distinction between body and soul, the creation of the soul of the first man by the Divine breath, and its immortality.

Acc. to the teaching of St. *Thomas Aquinas, which has been widely accepted, the soul is an individual spiritual substance, the 'form' of the body; body and soul together constitute the human entity, though the soul may be severed from the body and lead a separate existence, as happens after death. As it is purely spiritual the soul is not, as *Traducianism affirms, a product of the generative powers of man, but each individual soul is a new creation of God (*Creationism). *Lutheran and *Calvinist theologians have commonly favoured some form of Traducianism as conforming more nearly to the Reformation tenet of the depravity of human nature.

SOURCE CRITICISM. See *Higher Criticism*.

SOUTH, ROBERT (1634–1716), English divine. His sermons, which were witty and often sarcastic, became exceedingly popular, but his outspokenness precluded him from high preferment. For several years he controverted W. *Sherlock's dubiously orthodox teaching on the Trinity.

SOUTH AFRICA, Christianity in. The first Christian missionaries to Africa south of the R. Zambezi were Portuguese. Their effect was very limited, and Christianity was really introduced by the Dutch, who began to settle in 1652. In the Napoleonic Wars the British occupied the Cape and they retained the colony in 1814.

The existence of a large White community led to the establishment of a settled Church, but, apart from a *Moravian mission to the Cape in 1737, there was practically no attempt to convert the Africans before the end of the 18th cent. The *L.M.S. arrived in 1799, and in the following period the immensity of the field, with the gradual opening-up of communications, gave scope for the missionary activity of religious bodies from almost every part of W. Christendom. The expansion of this activity in the later 19th cent. led to some overlapping and friction. The first *ecumenical organization in S. Africa, the General Missionary Conference, was founded in 1904.

In modern times relations between the South African Churches and the State have attracted attention. The Dutch Reformed Church, whose theology is not incompatible with the ideology of 'separate development', left the *World Council of Churches after the Sharpeville crisis of 1960. The other Churches have all more or less actively opposed the policy of the State, and some leading Churchmen have been deported. *African Independent Churches are more numerous in South Africa than elsewhere.

SOUTH INDIA, Church of. The Church inaugurated in 1947 by a union of: (1) the (*Anglican) Church of *India, Burma, and Ceylon; (2) *Methodists; and (3) the South India United Church, which had been formed by an earlier union of *Presbyterian, *Congregationalist, and Dutch Reformed bodies. One of the basic principles of its formation was the acceptance of ministers possessing congregational, presbyteral, and episcopal ordination into a united ministry, without requiring the reordination of any, combined with the introduction of an episcopate in the historic succession (from Anglicanism) and its maintenance for the future, and the assurance that all subsequent ordinations would be episcopal.

The 1948 *Lambeth Conference gave the union a measure of qualified approval and in 1955 a state of 'limited intercommunion' between the C of E and the Church of South India was achieved.

SOUTH SEAS, Christianity in the. In 1776 a RC mission was sent by the Viceroy of Peru to Tahiti, but withdrew after a few months. The *L.M.S. sent evangelists who started work in the Society Islands in 1796 and in Tahiti in 1797. The work of the L.M.S. in the area was more widespread and persistent than that of any other society, but many other bodies sent missionaries. Among RCs the work was entrusted particularly to the Picpus Fathers (approved in 1817), whose members included Father *Damien, and the *Marists. Difficulties of communication and the savagery of the inhabitants made the task of the missionaries a particularly hard one.

SOUTHCOTT, JOANNA (1750–1814), religious fanatic. A domestic servant, she joined the *Methodist Society in 1791 and in 1792 proclaimed that she was the woman of Rev. 12. She proceeded to 'seal' the 144,000 elect at a charge varying from 12 to 21 shillings. She had a habit of writing and sealing prophecies; R. T. *Davidson, when Abp. of Canterbury, was repeatedly asked to open a box said to contain them.

SOUTHWARK. The Anglican diocese was created in 1905. The church of the priory of St. Mary Overie ('over the water from the City of London'), founded in 1106, became the cathedral. It had been the parish church of St. Saviour, Southwark, since the *dissolution of the priory in 1539, but had fallen into disrepair.

The RC diocese dates from the restoration of the hierarchy in 1850; it was made an archdiocese in 1965.

SOUTHWELL. St. *Paulinus is said to have founded a collegiate church c. 630. A college of secular canons was dissolved by *Henry VIII in 1540, refounded in 1585, and again dissolved in 1841. In 1884 the church, which has a Norman nave and transepts, became the cathedral of the new diocese.

SOUTHWELL, St. ROBERT (c. 1561–1595), *Jesuit poet. A native of Norfolk, he was sent on the English mission in 1586. He was arrested in 1592, and after three years' imprisonment he was hanged and quartered as a traitor. He was among the *Forty Martyrs of England and Wales canonized in 1970.

Most of his poems were prob. written in prison. Designed to encourage Catholics under persecution, they express deep religious feeling and became popular with both Catholics and Protestants.

SOZOMEN (early 5th cent.), Salmaninius Hermias Sozomenus, Church historian. A lawyer at *Constantinople, he determined to continue *Eusebius of Caesarea's 'Church History' to his own day. His work covers the period 323 to 425. He drew on *Socrates, but reports some subjects, e.g. the spread of Christianity among the *Armenians, Saracens, and Goths, more fully.

SPAIN, Christianity in. Christian missionaries reached Spain very early. In the 5th cent. *Arian Visigoths overran the land, but in 589 their king, *Recared, accepted Catholicism. In the 8th cent. the Muslim Moors conquered Spain and in the 9th cent. the persecution of Christians began. The Christian reconquest, which began with the victory at Calatañazor in 1002, was completed only with the reduction of Granada in 1492. It was accompanied by strong French influence and the founding of religious houses. The later Middle Ages were marked by the introduction of the *Inquisition, which was fostered by the civil power as a means of checking the Jews. Under *Charles V (1519–55) Spanish power reached its peak: not only was its influence in Europe unparalleled, but in the New World it had won an empire equalled only by that of *Portugal. The adhesion of Spain to the Papacy in the conflicts of the 16th cent. was thus an important political factor. At the same time the moderating influence of the Spanish bishops at the Council of *Trent did much to shape the *Counter-Reformation. Under *Philip II (1555–98) the decay of Spanish power began, and it continued in the succeeding centuries. Political and religious liberalism appeared in Spain c. 1800; it never came to terms with the traditional Spanish spirit, which in both spheres is reactionary, and there have been long periods of unrest and strife. In these conflicts the Church has been on the conservative side. The Second *Vatican Council's teaching on religious freedom, political liberty, and social justice introduced new tensions in the Spanish Church.

There is a small Protestant minority, which has been tolerated since 1910.

SPALATIN, GEORG (1484–1545), humanist and Reformer. Georg Burckhardt was born at Spalt (hence his name), near Nuremberg. In 1509 he became tutor to the sons of the Prince Elector *Frederick III of Saxony. He was sent to *Wittenberg in 1511; here he became acquainted with M. *Luther. It was mainly through Spalatin's influence that the Elector was won over to Lutheranism.

S.P.C.K. The Society for Promoting Christian Knowledge. It was founded by T. *Bray and others in 1698 'to promote and encourage the erection of charity schools in ... England and Wales; to disperse, both at home and abroad, Bibles and tracts of religion', and generally to promote Christian knowledge. Through its agency many Church schools and teacher-training colleges have been built in Britain and in the mission field. It also has an important publishing house in London.

SPEAKER'S COMMENTARY, The. A commentary on the Bible, publd. between 1871 and 1881, at the instance of J. E. Denison, who was Speaker of the House of Commons from 1857 to 1872. Its object was to defend a conservative attitude to Scripture.

SPEIER, Diets of. See *Speyer, Diets of.*

SPENCER, HERBERT (1820–1903), the chief exponent of *Agnosticism in 19th-cent. England. He divided reality into the knowable (the province of science) and the unknowable (that of religion). He asserted that man could not only be conscious of the unknowable, but that knowledge itself was finally dependent upon the unknowable, and that the Absolute is the fundamental reality behind all things. Nevertheless the Absolute could not be known in the strict sense of the word.

SPENCER, JOHN (1630–93), English Hebraist. In his *De Legibus Hebraeorum Ritualibus et earum Rationibus* (1685) he sought to trace the connection between the religious rites of the Hebrews and those of other Semitic peoples. Though he had to rely on second-hand information, he can claim to be the founder of the study of *comparative religion. His work was taken up in the 19th cent.

SPENER, PHILIPP JAKOB (1635–1705), founder of German *Pietism. The influence of J. de Labadie (see *Labadists*) gave Spener's religion a personal and interior turn, and he became convinced of a call to revivify the *Lutheran Church. In 1666 he became minister at Frankfurt. Here he introduced 'Collegia Pietatis', devotional meetings which gathered twice a week in his house; and he issued his *Pia Desideria* (1675). When the ecclesiastical authorities became hostile, he went to Dresden as court preacher in 1686; in 1691 he became rector of the Nikolaikirche in Berlin. His movement, by then known as 'Pietism', made rapid progress, and in 1694 the University of Halle was founded, largely under his influence.

SPEYER, Diets of. (1) The Diet of 1526 marked a new stage in the consolidation of reforming influences in Germany. It determined that each Prince should order ecclesi-

astical affairs in his own State in accordance with his conscience.
(2) The Diet of 1529 was controlled by a Catholic majority. It passed legislation to end all toleration of *Lutherans in Catholic districts. Six princes and 14 cities made a formal 'protest'; henceforward the Reformers were known as 'Protestants'.

S.P.G. The Society for the Propagation of the Gospel in foreign parts. It was founded in 1701 by T. *Bray and others to provide the ministrations of the C of E for British people overseas and to evangelize the non-Christian races subject to the Crown. In 1965 it joined with the *U.M.C.A. to form the United Society for the Propagation of the Gospel.

SPINCKES, NATHANIEL (1653–1727), *Nonjuror. He was a prebendary and rector of St. Martin's, *Salisbury, when he was deprived on refusing to take the oath of allegiance to William and Mary in 1690. In 1713 he was consecrated bishop by G. *Hickes, but he took no title. In the dispute about the *Usages, he advocated retention of the BCP as it was. A man of considerable learning, he was revered for his personal piety.

SPINOZA, BARUCH (BENEDICT DE) (1632–77), Dutch Jewish philosopher. In 1656 he was expelled from the Synagogue and forced to leave Amsterdam. He earned his living grinding lenses. Most of his works were published posthumously.
Spinoza is the most thorough-going modern exponent of *pantheism. Since he held that the human mind is part of the Divine impersonal intellect, he denied both freedom and will, the permanence of personality, and immortality. The conceptions of a personal God and an immortal soul being ruled out, Spinoza's religious ideas are purely rational. His studies on the Bible, carried on from the same point of view, made him a precursor of modern historical criticism.

SPIRIT. In Christian theology the word denotes: (1) The intelligent and immaterial part of man or the human *soul in general, whether united with the body in life or separated from it in death, and esp. that aspect of it which is concerned with religious truth and action and is directly susceptible to Divine influence. (2) An order of being which is superhuman in the sense that it is not subject to the limits of time, space, and a bodily frame. (3) One of the creatures belonging to this order, whether good or evil, i.e. angels or demons. (4) The Third Person of the *Trinity (see *Holy Spirit, The*).

SPIRIT, Brethren of the Free. See *Brethren of the Free Spirit*.

SPIRITUAL EXERCISES, The. St. *Ignatius Loyola drafted this treatise at Manresa and revised and expanded it through most of his life. It contains a series of meditations and rules designed to lead souls to conquer their passions and give themselves to God. It contains a wealth of ascetic advice and is still widely used for *retreats.

SPIRITUAL FRANCISCANS. Before St. *Francis's death two groups of *Franciscans could be distinguished: (1) those led by *Elias of Cortona who wanted to mitigate the rule of poverty and remodel the order, and (2) the 'Zealots' or 'Spirituals', who wished to maintain the original way of life. The latter group became more apparent as the Franciscan rule was progressively modified, and under the generalship of *John of Parma (1247–57) their view was officially accepted. Subsequent attempts to reach a compromise were unacceptable to the Spirituals and in the 14th cent. the controversy threatened to create a schism in the order. *John XXII issued a series of bulls, culminating in one that declared the Spirituals' doctrine of the absolute poverty of Christ and the Apostles heretical (1323). The conflict continued, but in the face of persecution the numbers of the Spirituals declined. See also *Observantines*.

SPIRITUAL HEALING. Though sometimes used as a synonym for psychotherapy, the phrase is properly confined to attempts to heal the whole personality by prayer and sacramental means. Among the methods in general use are *unction and the laying on of hands. The patient is generally encouraged also to make use of medical skill, though some hold that spiritual means alone should suffice.

SPIRITUAL WORKS OF MERCY, The. Traditionally these are: converting the sinner; instructing the ignorant; counselling the doubtful; comforting the sorrowful; bearing wrongs patiently; forgiving injuries; praying

for the living and the dead. See also *Corporal Works of Mercy*.

SPIRITUALISM. A system of (often superstitious) beliefs and practices the purpose of which is to establish communication with the spirits of the dead. Necromancy is an element common to most primitive and many higher religions; an early example is recorded in 1 Sam. 28: 8. In its modern form Spiritualism dates from the occult experiences of the American Fox family in 1848; it spread to England and the Continent. It professes to make contact with the souls of the departed chiefly by means of mediums, accompanied by table-turning, automatic writing, and other devices. The practice of Spiritualism is condemned by all parts of the Church.

SPONSOR. A *godparent (q.v.).

SPOON, Liturgical. In the E. rites a spoon is used for giving Communion, a portion of the consecrated Host being dipped in the chalice and the two species being conveyed on the spoon to the communicant. In the RC Church the use of a spoon for administering the consecrated Wine was sanctioned in 1965. In the W. spoons have also sometimes been used to measure the water at the mixing of the chalice.

SPORTS, The Book of. A declaration defining the recreations permissible on *Sunday, first issued in 1617 by *James I for the use of magistrates in Lancashire, and extended in 1618 to the whole country. It was reissued by *Charles I in 1633. It permitted archery and dancing and was designed to counteract *Sabbatarianism.

SPOTTISWOOODE, JOHN (1565–1639), Abp. of St. Andrews and historian. Originally a strict *Presbyterian, he became an adherent of the royal policy and the chief agent of *James I in suppressing the political influence of the Kirk. He was consecrated Abp. of Glasgow in 1610; in 1615 he was translated to St. Andrews. At the General Assembly of the Kirk in 1618 he made himself Moderator without election and imposed the Five Articles of *Perth. In 1635 *Charles I made him Chancellor; as such he gave reluctant support to the introduction of the BCP in Scotland. When the *National Covenant was signed in 1638 he fled to Newcastle.

His *History of the Church of Scotland* [to 1625] (1655) is well documented; it reflects the author's position.

SPURGEON, CHARLES HADDON (1834–92), *Baptist preacher. In 1854 he went to Southwark; his sermons drew such crowds that a new church, the Metropolitan Tabernacle in Newington Causeway, was built. He estranged some members of his community by his rigid opposition to liberal methods of Biblical exegesis, and in 1887 he withdrew from the Baptist Union.

SPY WEDNESDAY. The Wednesday before *Good Friday, so named as the day on which *Judas Iscariot betrayed Christ (Mt. 26: 14–16).

SPYRIDON, St. (d. *c.* 348), Bp. of Tremithus in *Cyprus. He was a simple peasant who, acc. to tradition, had suffered in the *Diocletianic persecution. As bishop he is said to have attended the Council of *Nicaea; he was certainly present at that of *Sardica (*c.* 343). There are many legends attached to his life.

S.S.J.E. See *Society of St. John the Evangelist.*

STABAT MATER DOLOROSA. A Latin hymn of unknown date describing the Sorrows of the BVM at the Cross. It came into liturgical use in the later Middle Ages. The many English translations include 'At the Cross her station keeping'.

STABILITY. The vow taken by every monk under the Rule of St. *Benedict to remain until death attached to the monastery of his *profession.

STAFF, Pastoral. See *Crosier.*

STAINER, JOHN (1840–1901), organist and composer. In 1872 he became organist at *St. Paul's Cathedral, where he carried out reforms in the service music. He was professor of music in the university of Oxford from 1889 to 1899 and from 1900 Master of the Musicians' Company. His main works were oratorios and cantatas, among them *The Crucifixion* (1887).

STALLS. The fixed seats on both sides of the choirs of cathedrals and certain other churches. They are usually separated by high projecting arms, often richly carved, and sometimes surmounted by canopies. The seats can frequently be turned back, disclosing a bracket called a *misericord.

STANBROOK ABBEY. A house of enclosed RC *Benedictine nuns near *Worcester. The community was founded at Cambrai in 1625. After their property was confiscated in the French Revolution in 1793, the survivors came to England in 1795; they settled at Stanbrook Hall in 1838. The abbey is known for its fine printing.

STANISLAUS, St. (1030–79), Patron of Poland. Bp. of Cracow from 1072, Stanislaus came into conflict with King Boleslav II, whom he repeatedly reproved for scandalous conduct. Eventually he excommunicated the King, and acc. to tradition, Boleslav himself killed him while he was offering Mass.

STANLEY, ARTHUR PENRHYN (1815–81), *Broad Church divine. As Dean of *Westminster from 1864, he tried to make the Abbey a national shrine for all, irrespective of creed. He offended many Churchmen by inviting all the scholars who had produced the RV, including a *Unitarian, to receive Holy Communion in the Abbey.

STANTON, ARTHUR HENRY (1839–1913), *Anglo-Catholic priest. In 1862 he was ordained to the title of St. Alban's, Holborn, where he remained as curate for 50 years. He won the confidence of thousands of men in the roughest part of London, but, like many Anglo-Catholic priests at that time, he met with official opposition.

STAPELDON, WALTER DE (*c.* 1261–1326), Bp. of *Exeter from 1308. He helped to rebuild Exeter Cathedral and founded Stapeldon Hall, which became Exeter College, Oxford. As Lord Treasurer from 1320, he reformed the royal exchequer. He was murdered by the London mob for his association with the misgovernment of Edward II.

STAPLETON, THOMAS (1535–98), RC controversialist. He became a prebendary of *Chichester under *Mary in 1558, but fled to

Louvain on *Elizabeth I's accession. He taught in the universities at Douai and Louvain and became Dean of Hilverenbeck. He was an able and erudite controversialist and a prolific writer.

STARETZ. In the Russian Church, a religious leader who is sought out as a spiritual guide because of his exceptional personal holiness. He has no formal position in the ecclesiastical hierarchy.

STAROVERY. Another name for the '*Old Believers' (q.v.).

STATE PRAYERS. In the BCP, the prayers for the Sovereign and Royal Family towards the end of *Mattins and *Evensong.

STATE SERVICES. In the C of E, the services appointed to commemorate days of national rejoicing and deliverance. There were formerly a number of such services printed at the end of the BCP, but since 1859 only that commemorating the Sovereign's accession has been retained.

STATES OF THE CHURCH. Those parts of Italy and the territory of *Avignon and Venaissin in France which formerly acknowledged the temporal sovereignty of the Papacy. Some of these lands were also known as the '*Patrimony of St. Peter' (q.v.).

In 1791 the Papal territories in France were lost, and by 1861 the Papacy was left with Rome alone, all the rest having been absorbed into the kingdom of Italy. In 1870 Rome itself was lost and the Pope withdrew into the *Vatican. By the Law of *Guarantees (1871) Italy allowed the Pope a pension and declared the Vatican, the *Lateran, and the Papal villa at *Castel Gandolfo to be extra-territorial. The *Lateran Treaty signed by *Pius XI in 1929 contained an agreement on much the same lines and constituted 'Vatican City' a separate State.

STATION DAYS. Certain days on which the Pope formerly celebrated Mass in one of the so-called 'station churches' in Rome. The solemnity was enhanced by processions of clergy and people from one church, called *collecta*, to the station church (the Lat. word *statio* being from early times the term for the Christian assemblies of worship) where the Pope was to offer Mass. Acc. to tradition it was *Gregory I who assigned its special church to each of the station days. The number of these days was subsequently increased to 87. The Papal Station Masses fell into disuse, esp. during the exile of the Popes at *Avignon, but traces of the custom survive in the *indulgences attached to visits to the station churches.

STATIONS OF THE CROSS. A series of 14 pictures or carvings which depict incidents in the last journey of Christ from *Pilate's house to His entombment. They are commonly arranged round the walls of a church; it is a popular devotion to visit the stations in order, reciting prayers and meditating on each incident.

STATUTA ECCLESIAE ANTIQUA (Lat., 'The Ancient Statutes of the Church'). A document comprising a confession of faith, disciplinary canons, and a ritual for *ordination. It was compiled in S. Gaul in the second half of the 5th cent.

STEIN, EDITH (1891–1942), *Carmelite nun. Of Jewish family, she studied under E. Husserl and became a leading figure in the *Phenomenological School. She became a RC in 1922 and tried to interpret Phenomenology from a *Thomist standpoint. She joined the Carmelites in 1934. She was put to death by the Nazis in a gas-chamber.

STEINER, RUDOLF (1861–1925), founder of *Anthroposophy. Rejecting the Eastern associations of the *Theosophical Society, he founded the Anthroposophical Society in 1913. His aim was to develop the faculty of spirit cognition inherent in ordinary people and to put them in touch with the spiritual world from which materialism had estranged them. His teaching was based on acceptance of *reincarnation.

'STEPHANUS' (Estienne). A family of scholar-printers.

ROBERT ESTIENNE (1503–59), Printer to Francis I, King of France, is famous for his *Thesaurus Linguae Latinae* (1532) and for his editions of the Bible, incl. the OT in Hebrew and the NT in Greek. His annotations to his Bibles provoked attacks by the *Sorbonne, and in 1551 he fled to Geneva. The verse divisions which he introduced in his 1551 NT are still used.

HENRI ESTIENNE (1528–98), Robert's

eldest son, published editions of the *Fathers. His *Thesaurus Linguae Graecae* (1572) was indispensable to generations of Greek scholars.

STEPHEN, St. (d. *c.* 35), protomartyr and traditionally the first *deacon. He was one of those appointed by the Apostles to 'serve tables' in *Jerusalem (Acts 6: 5). He incurred the hostility of the Jews and, after delivering before the *Sanhedrin the discourse reproduced in Acts 7: 2–53, he was stoned, apparently without formal trial. He died confessing Christ and asking forgiveness for his persecutors (Acts 7: 59).

STEPHEN I, St. (d. 257), Pope from 254. He intervened in disputes in Gaul and in Spain. He also became involved in a bitter controversy with St. *Cyprian over the validity of Baptism by heretics, which Cyprian held to be null and void.

STEPHEN II (III) (d. 757), Pope from 752. (He is sometimes counted the third of his name, 'Stephen II' having died four days after his election.) When the Lombard king besieged Rome, the Pope turned in vain to the Byzantine Emperor for help; he then crossed the Alps to ask for assistance from the Frankish king, *Pepin. From Pepin Stephen obtained the much-discussed 'Donation' of Quiercy (754). See also *Patrimony of St. Peter*.

STEPHEN III (IV) (d. 772), Pope from 768. He held a synod at the *Lateran which excluded laymen from Papal elections, confirmed the veneration of images, and anathematized the iconoclastic synod of 754. He allied himself with the Lombards.

STEPHEN, St. (975–1038), first king of *Hungary. He became a Christian in 985 and on his accession to the Hungarian throne in 997 he set out to Christianize the country. In 1001 he obtained from the Pope a royal crown, part of which is incorporated in the crown preserved at Budapest.

STEPHEN HARDING, St. (d. 1134), abbot of *Cîteaux from 1109. The monastery was facing the danger of extinction when St. *Bernard and 30 followers joined the community in 1112. The sudden increase in numbers soon necessitated other foundations. In order to maintain the original austerity and uniform government, Stephen drew up the nucleus of the *Carta Caritatis*, which established the system of regular visitations and General Chapters in the *Cistercian Order.

STERCORANISTS. Persons asserting that the Bl. Sacrament is digested and evacuated by the recipient. Although they are written of as a sect, there appears to be no evidence that such a sect existed.

STERN, HENRY AARON (1820–85), missionary to the Jews. He was born of Jewish parents in Hesse-Cassel. Having entered on a commercial career he went to London, where he received Christian baptism in 1840. He was later ordained. He worked among the Jews in various parts of the Middle East, doing notable work among the Black Falasha Jews in Ethiopia.

STERNHOLD, THOMAS (d. 1549), versifier of the Psalms. He entered *Henry VIII's service and became a court favourite. He published a metrical edition of 19 Psalms in 1547; a second edition of 37 Psalms appeared posthumously in 1549. A third edition of 1557 had a further 7 Psalms by 'J. H.' (John Hopkins, a Suffolk clergyman, d. 1570). The collection, in a complete edition printed by J. *Day in 1562, became known as 'Sternhold and Hopkins'.

STERRY, PETER (?1613–72), *Puritan divine. He was a member of the *Westminster Assembly and from 1649 one of O. *Cromwell's chaplains. After Cromwell's death he devoted himself to literary pursuits. His theology was a mixture of *Calvinism and *Neoplatonism.

STICHARION. The liturgical tunic worn in the E. Church, comparable to the *alb in the West.

STICHERON. In the E. Church a brief liturgical hymn which is attached to a verse of a Psalm or other Scriptural passage.

STIGAND (d. ?1072), Abp. of *Canterbury. He became Bp. of *Winchester in 1047. When he was appointed Abp. of Canterbury in 1052, he retained the see of Winchester as well. He did not secure Papal recognition until 1058, and then from Benedict X, who was himself deposed in 1059.

Stigand was covetous and worldly, and his position provided a pretext for *William I's invasion in 1066. He was deposed in 1070.

STIGMATIZATION. The reproduction of the wounds of the Passion of Christ in the human body. Stigmata may be either invisible, when the pain is experienced without any exterior sign, or visible, in which case they normally consist of wounds or blood blisters on hands, feet, and near the heart, also on the head (Crown of Thorns) or shoulders and back (carrying the Cross and Scourging). They do not become septic and resist treatment. The first person known to have received the stigmata is St. *Francis of Assisi; since then cases have been numerous. The attitude of the RC Church has always been guarded.

STILLINGFLEET, EDWARD (1635–99), Bp. of *Worcester from 1689. He held *Latitudinarian views. His *Irenicum* (1659) advocated a union between *Episcopalians and *Presbyterians, treating forms of Church government as inessential. In 1664 he replied to the *Jesuit account of the controversy between W. *Laud and J. *Fisher in his *Rational Account of the Grounds of the Protestant Religion*. His *Origines Britannicae* (1685) deals with the sources of the British Church.

STOCK, St. SIMON. See *Simon Stock, St.*

STOCKHOLM CONFERENCE (1925). The Universal Christian Conference on *Life and Work which met in Stockholm to promote Christian influences on political, social, and economic life. It was attended by representatives of most of the larger religious bodies except the RC Church.

STOICISM. A Greco-Roman school of philosophy founded at *Athens by Zeno of Citium (335–263 B.C.). The system is a form of materialistic *pantheism. God is the immanent all-pervading energy by which the natural world is created and sustained. He is also the world reason or '*Logos' which manifests itself in the order and beauty of the world. To the Stoic the good man is the wise man, and his wisdom consists in conformity to nature, i.e. in living according to the law of the universe embodied in the Divine reason.

STOLE. A liturgical vestment consisting of a long narrow strip of silk. Its origin is doubtful. It has become the distinctive vestment of the *deacon, who wears it like a sash over his left shoulder. It is, however, also a regular vestment of the priest, who in the RC Church now always wears it round the neck with its ends falling straight down in the front, as does the bishop. Besides being used at Mass, it is worn when administering the Sacraments and generally when preaching. Its colour depends on that of the other vestments and the occasion, e.g. when hearing confessions the priest wears a purple stole. In the C of E the use of the stole was revived in the middle of the 19th cent.

STONYHURST COLLEGE. One of the largest RC public schools in England. Conducted by the *Jesuits, it traces its origin to the foundation of a college for English boys at *St.-Omer in 1592. It moved to Stonyhurst Hall in Lancashire in 1794.

STORCH, NICHOLAS (d. 1530), *Anabaptist. He became leader of the *Zwickau Prophets (q.v.) after T. *Münzer's flight. He later established an Anabaptist sect in Poland. He taught that since all godly men were under the direct influence of the Holy Spirit, a ministerial and sacramental Church was unnecessary.

STOUP. A basin near the entrance of a church containing *holy water with which the faithful may sprinkle themselves. Stoups are of various forms, either let into the wall or standing on a socle, and often richly decorated.

STRABO, WALAFRID. See *Walafrid Strabo*.

STRATFORD, JOHN DE (d. 1348), Abp. of *Canterbury from 1333. He advised Edward II to abdicate and in 1330 Edward III made him Chancellor. When Edward returned from an unsuccessful expedition to Flanders in 1340, a series of charges were brought against Stratford. He stood firm and obtained recognition of the principle that peers should be tried only by their equals in Parliament. He then retired from political life.

STRAUSS, DAVID FRIEDRICH (1808–1874), German theologian. His famous

Leben Jesu (1835–6) applied the 'myth theory' to the life of Christ. It denied the historical foundation of all supernatural elements in the Gospels, which were assigned to an unintentionally creative legend (the 'myth'), developed between the death of Christ and the writing of the Gospels in the 2nd cent. The growth of primitive Christianity was to be understood in terms of the *Hegelian dialectic. The book led to Strauss's dismissal from his post at Tübingen, but it exercised a deep influence on subsequent German Protestant theology.

STREET, GEORGE EDMUND (1824–81), architect. He worked for a time under G. C. *Scott and became a leader in the Gothic Revival. In 1850 he was appointed Diocesan Architect by S. *Wilberforce, Bp. of *Oxford. He was responsible for a large number of churches and ecclesiastical institutions.

STREETER, BURNETT HILLMAN (1874–1937), Anglican theologian and NT scholar. His research into the *Synoptic problem did much to win the consent of English Biblical scholarship to the priority of St. *Mark's Gospel and the existence of '*Q'. *The Four Gospels* (1924) set out his conclusions on the Gospels as a whole and also expounded some original ideas, notably his theses on the '*Caesarean text' and '*Proto-Luke'.

STREITGESPRÄCHE (Germ., 'controversial discussions'). In *form-criticism, R. *Bultmann's designation for a group of *apophthegms in the Gospels, introduced by a controversial statement by Christ's enemies. The Question on the Tribute Money (Mk. 12: 13–17) is a characteristic instance.

STRIGEL, VICTORINUS (1524–69), Reformation theologian. In 1548 he became professor and rector of the new school at Jena. Here, in opposition to the strict *Lutheranism of M. *Flacius, he expounded more moderate and conciliatory doctrines and defended a form of *synergism. He was later professor at Leipzig (1563–7) and then at Heidelberg.

STROSSMAYER, JOSEPH GEORG (1815–1905), Bp. of Diakovár in Yugoslavia from 1850. At the *Vatican Council of 1869-70 he opposed the definition of Papal Infallibility, and he caused a 'scene' at the Council by his ill-timed defence of Protestantism. After some delay he published the Vatican decrees in his official diocesan journal.

STRYPE, JOHN (1643–1737), English Church historian. His works deal mainly with the Reformation period. They include *Memorials of Thomas Cranmer* (1694) and *Annals of the Reformation in England* (1709–31). The wealth of documentation on which they are based renders them valuable, despite their bad arrangement, cumbersome style, and frequent errors.

STUBBS, JOHN (*c.* 1543-91), *Puritan fanatic. In 1579 he published *The Discovery of a Gaping Gulf*, attacking *Elizabeth I's proposed marriage with Henry, Duke of Anjou. Stubbs, his publisher and printer were all sentenced and the first two had their right hands cut off. In 1589 he became M.P. for Great Yarmouth.

STUBBS, WILLIAM (1825–1901), historian and bishop. He was Regius Professor of Modern History at Oxford (1866–84) and then Bp. of *Chester (1884–9) and of *Oxford (1889–1901). He was the greatest British historian of his time. Many of his works deal with ecclesiastical sources.

STUDD, CHARLES THOMAS (1862–1931), missionary. He was influenced by his father's conversion at a mission of D. L. *Moody and I. D. Sankey in 1877, and he volunteered for missionary work in *China. As one of the 'Cambridge Seven' his intention aroused great interest and laid the seeds of the Student Volunteer Movement. He worked successively in China, *India, and Central Africa.

STUDDERT KENNEDY, GEOFFREY ANKETELL (1883–1929), Anglican priest. As Chaplain to the Forces (1916–19) he won the affectionate title of 'Woodbine Willie', from a brand of cigarettes which he distributed. In 1922 he was appointed Rector of St. Edmund, King and Martyr, Lombard Street. He held unconventional views on various theological matters.

STUDENT CHRISTIAN MOVEMENT (S.C.M.). The British section of a world fellowship of students who 'desire to understand the Christian faith and live the Christian life'. It developed out of several independent movements at Cambridge and elsewhere in the 19th cent. It is an interdenominational body, with which many of the leaders of the *Ecumenical Movement have been associated.

STUDIOS. A monastery at *Constantinople, acc. to tradition founded in 463 by Studios, a former Roman consul. Its monks followed the rule of the '*Acoemetae'. They were driven from the monastery under the Emp. Constantine Copronymus (741–75), and few returned. St. *Theodore, who became abbot in 799, introduced a new rule, based on that of St. *Basil; manual work played a larger part and discipline was strict. Studios then became the model and centre of E. monasticism.

STUDIUM GENERALE. A name current from the 14th cent. for what is now a university.

STUNDISTS. Certain Russian evangelical sects which emerged in the Ukraine c. 1858–62, under the influence of *Lutheran and Reformed pastors and *Mennonite preachers. They became increasingly *Baptist in orientation.

STURM, JOHANNES (1507–89), Reformer and educationalist. Having become a Protestant under M. *Bucer's influence, he moved from Paris to Strasburg in 1537. Here he took an active part in furthering the Reformation. His interest in education did much to make the city one of the chief educational centres in Europe.

STYLITE. In the early Church a solitary who lived on the top of a pillar. The pillars varied in height and the platforms on the top were generally provided with a parapet against which the Stylite would lean for sleep. Food was usually provided by disciples or admirers. There are many instances of such ascetics from the 5th to the 10th cent., and isolated examples to modern times.

SUAREZ, FRANCISCO DE (1548–1617), Spanish *Jesuit. He taught in Rome and at Alcalá. In 1597 *Philip II summoned him to the university of Coimbra, where he lectured until 1616. He is accounted the greatest theologian of his order.

His *Disputatae Metaphysicae* (1597) became a standard textbook and exercised much influence; it abandoned *Aristotle's sequence of thought to give an independent systematic treatment of the subject. In a series of major works on *grace, he developed the system known as *Congruism; this sought to solve the problem of the relation between human freedom and Divine grace. Acc. to Suarez, God does not cause man's free acts, but, foreseeing them by His special knowledge (called *scientia media*), He brings about the salvation of the elect by giving them those graces of which He foresees they will make good use in certain given circumstances. This teaching provoked opposition but it became the prevalent doctrine among non-Thomist RC theologians. His *De Legibus* (1612), on the principles of natural and international law, has influenced jurists and legislators in Europe and America.

SUBCINCTORIUM. An ecclesiastical vestment resembling the *maniple, now worn only by the Pope. Its original purpose was to secure the *stole to the *girdle.

SUBDEACON. In the RC Church, until the office was suppressed in 1972, a person in the lowest of the *major orders. The office existed by the 3rd cent.; until the 13th cent. it was regarded as a *minor, not a major, order.

A subdeacon was one of the 3 sacred ministers at *High Mass, where his functions included that of chanting the *Epistle. In modern times, however, his part was often taken by a person in deacon's or priest's orders. In the C of E the subdiaconate was given up in the 16th cent. It survives as a minor order in the E. Church.

SUBIACO. A town c. 40 miles east of Rome, famous as the site of the grotto where St. *Benedict settled on his retirement from the world. It became the cradle of the *Benedictine Order.

SUBINTRODUCTAE. In the early Church, women who lived associated with men in spiritual marriage. The practice was forbidden by early 4th cent. councils.

SUBLAPSARIANISM, also known as 'Infra-' or 'Post-lapsarianism'. The form of the *Calvinistic doctrine of *Predestination that holds that it was only after the *Fall that God decreed the election or non-election of individuals to salvation.

SUBMERSION. The form of *Baptism in which the water completely covers the candidate's body. It is the method used in the *Orthodox and several other of the E. Churches and is one of the methods provided in the 1969 RC rite for the Baptism of Infants. It is widely supposed to have been the custom in the early Church.

SUBMISSION OF THE CLERGY. The act whereby the English *Convocations in 1532 surrendered to the demands of *Henry VIII. Its effect was to make the King supreme in ecclesiastical causes. In 1534 it was incorporated into an Act of Parliament.

SUBORDINATIONISM. Teaching about the Godhead which regards either the Son as subordinate to the Father or the Holy Spirit as subordinate to both. It was a characteristic tendency in much Christian teaching of the first three cents. The issue was explicitly dealt with in the conflicts with *Arianism and then with the *Pneumatomachi.

SUBSTANCE. (1) In philosophy the word has played an important part since the time of *Aristotle, whose distinctions were taken over by the *Schoolmen. In general, *substantia* was the permanent, underlying reality as contrasted with its changing and visible accidents.
(2) In the Christian doctrine of the Godhead, the word is used to express the underlying Being, by which all Three Persons are One.
(3) In the medieval teaching on the *Eucharist, the substance of the Eucharistic species was contrasted with their '*accidents' (q.v.). See *Transubstantiation*.

SUBUNISTS. The party in 15th-cent. Bohemia which defended the practice of Communion in one kind against the *Utraquists.

SUBURBICARIAN DIOCESES. The 7 dioceses in the immediate vicinity of Rome. The '*Cardinal Bishops' take their episcopal titles from these sees, but since 1962 they have not had pastoral charge of them. The dioceses are small but ancient; their bishops had the right to take part in papal elections

prob. as early as the 11th cent.

SUCCENTOR. In *cathedral churches of the 'Old Foundation', the title usually given to the deputy of the *Precentor. He is generally a *minor canon.

SUCCESSION, Apostolic. See *Apostolic Succession*.

SUDBURY, SIMON. See *Simon of Sudbury*.

SUETONIUS, Roman historian and secretary to the Emp. Hadrian (117–38). He is apparently one of the first pagan writers to mention Christianity.

SUFFRAGAN BISHOP. The phrase denotes: (1) Any Bishop in relation to his *Archbishop or *Metropolitan. (2) An assistant Bishop appointed to help the Bishop of the diocese. In the later Middle Ages such appointments were frequent and were made by the Pope. In England an Act of 1534 made provision for the appointment of suffragan Bishops, but the office lapsed in 1592. In 1870 suffragan Bishops of Nottingham and Dover were consecrated. There are now suffragan Bishops in most dioceses of the C of E.

SUGER (c. 1081–1151), Abbot of *St.-Denis, near Paris, from 1122. Though of humble origins, for much of his life Suger was an influential adviser to the French Crown; during Louis VII's absence on the Second *Crusade he was one of the Regents. His Life of Louis VI is a primary historical source. His new church at St.-Denis (choir consecrated 1144), of which he left an account, was a crucial step in the development of Gothic architecture.

SUICER, JOHANN KASPAR (1620–84), Swiss Reformed theologian. His *Thesaurus Ecclesiasticus e Patribus Graecis* (1682) is a work of great erudition and value.

SUIDAS (c. A.D. 1000), 'Greek lexicographer'. The supposition that the Greek lexicon which goes under this name was the work of a certain 'Suidas' is prob. mistaken; the word apparently means an armoury of information. The lexicon, completed c. 1000, contains some items of historical importance.

SULPICE, St. See *Saint-Sulpice*.

SULPICIUS SEVERUS (*c.* 360–*c.* 420), historian and hagiographer. He was an advocate in Aquitaine before his conversion to asceticism (*c.* 394). He then settled on an estate in S. Gaul where he wrote his Life of St. *Martin of Tours. A literary *tour de force*, this is a disciple's interpretation rather than a historical representation. He also wrote a Chronicle of sacred history from the Creation to A.D. 400.

SUMMA. Originally a title of reference books on various subjects, the term, as used by medieval writers, came to denote a compendium of theology, philosophy, or canon law. These compendia were used as handbooks in the Schools, much like the earlier *Sentences.

'SUMMA THEOLOGICA'. The chief dogmatic work of St. *Thomas Aquinas. The three parts treat respectively of God, of man's return to God, and of Christ as the way of man to God. The final sections, on the Sacraments and the Last Things, were left unfinished, the missing parts being supplied by *Reginald of Piperno.

SUMNER, CHARLES RICHARD (1790–1874), Bp. of *Winchester, 1827–69. He owed rapid preferment to George IV, but lost the royal favour by voting for the *Catholic Emancipation Bill in 1829. He was an *Evangelical in sympathy and opposed R. D. *Hampden's appointment to the see of Hereford. In his diocese he was a capable administrator.

SUMNER, JOHN BIRD (1780–1862), Abp. of *Canterbury from 1848. Though he disapproved of R. D. *Hampden's theology, he did not oppose his appointment as Bp. of *Hereford, and took part in his consecration. In the controversy over the *Gorham Case he denied that Baptismal Regeneration was a fundamental doctrine of the C of E. In 1852 he presided over the Upper House of *Convocation when it met for business for the first time in 135 years.

SUN, Canticle of the. See *Canticle of the Sun*.

SUNDAR SINGH, Sadhu (1889–*c.* 1929), Indian Christian and mystic. Born of wealthy Sikh parents, he was converted to Christianity by a vision and baptized in the C of E in 1905. He donned the robe of a Sadhu (i.e. 'holy man') in an attempt to present Christianity in a Hindu form. He travelled widely in India and made strenuous efforts to evangelize Tibet.

SUNDAY. Sunday replaced the Jewish *Sabbath mainly in commemoration of Christ's Resurrection on this day. Already in NT times St. *Paul and the Christians of Troas assembled on the first day of the week 'to break bread' (Acts 20: 7), and in Rev. (1: 10) it is called 'the Lord's day'.

The observance of Sunday as a day of rest began to be regulated by ecclesiastical legislation early in the 4th cent., and in 321 *Constantine forbade townspeople to work on Sundays, though permitting farm labour. From the 6th to the 13th cent. ecclesiastical legislation became stricter, also enforcing attendance at Mass; it was supported by the infliction of severe penalties by the civil authorities. From the 13th cent. *dispensations became common. Modern RC practice requires the faithful to hear Mass on Sundays and refrain from *servile work, except where either or both would cause grave inconvenience.

The Protestant Churches did not at first introduce special Sunday legislation, but the abuse of Sunday led to a reaction in some places. See *Sabbatarianism*.

SUNDAY LETTER. In ecclesiastical calendars that one of the seven letters A to G, allotted to the days of the year in rotation (1 Jan. = A, &c.) which coincides with the Sundays in a given year.

SUNDAY SCHOOLS. Schools, mainly for children, in which instruction, now primarily religious, is given on Sunday; they are usually held in conjunction with a parish or congregation. Although there are isolated earlier examples of schools for poor children on Sundays, the movement owed its success to R. *Raikes, who, along with the local incumbent, engaged four women in 1780 to instruct the children of Gloucester in reading and the Catechism on Sundays. In 1803 the Sunday School Union, an interdenominational body, was founded to improve methods, fill gaps, and help with supplies of books and material for Sunday Schools in the London area; similar affiliated associations were founded elsewhere. The desire of Anglicans to introduce more specifically C of E teaching into Sunday Schools led to the foundation of the Sunday School Institute in 1843; in 1936 this was incorporated into the *National Society. In 1966 the (National from 1921) Sunday School Union became the National Christian Education Council.

SUPEREROGATION, Works of. In RC *moral theology, acts which are not enjoined as of strict obligation, and are therefore not simply good as opposed to bad, but better as opposed to good.

SUPERINTENDENTS. In the reformed Church of Scotland, officials appointed under the *First Book of* *Discipline* (1560) to oversee districts roughly corresponding to the old dioceses. They would appear to have been temporary office-bearers chosen, because of the dearth of ministers, to settle and organize the churches under their care. In the *Lutheran Churches, officials of the same name were created from an early date for similar reasons and with similar functions; they were to be appointed by, and responsible to, the civil power. See also *General Superintendent*.

SUPERIOR. One who has authority over others by virtue of his ecclesiastical rank. The term is commonly used of the heads of certain religious orders or congregations.

SUPPER, The Last. See *Last Supper*.

SUPRALAPSARIANISM (or 'Antelapsarianism'). The extreme form of the *Calvinist doctrine of *Predestination which maintains that God decreed the election and non-election of individuals even before the *Fall of Adam.

SUPREMACY, Act of. The Act passed in 1534 confirming to *Henry VIII and his successors the title of 'the only supreme head in earth of the Church of England'. It was repealed by *Mary. *Elizabeth I's Act of Supremacy (1559) declared the Queen to be 'the only supreme governor ... as well in all spiritual or ecclesiastical things or causes as temporal'.

SURIN, JEAN JOSEPH (1600–65), French *Jesuit mystic and spiritual writer. In 1636 he was sent to exorcize some nuns believed to be possessed by the devil; in the event he experienced a series of mysterious trials lasting for 20 years, which were followed by a period of mystic exaltation. His writings insist on the need for purification by self-abnegation and suffering; they advocate the practice of the presence of God and the prayer of contemplation in which the soul, abandoned to the direction of the Holy Spirit, loses itself in the love of God.

SURPLICE. A loose white liturgical garment, with wide sleeves. It developed from the *alb, allowing room for warm clothes underneath. From the 12th cent. it came to be the distinctive dress of the lower clergy and was generally used by priests outside Mass. It is now worn by all clerics, and is also used by laymen, e.g. in choir.

Its use in the C of E was a matter of controversy in the reign of *Elizabeth I, but is now accepted. See *Vestiarian Controversy*.

SURPLICE FEES. Fees which are payable to the incumbent of a parish for marriages and burials, whoever performs the service.

SURROGATE. In ecclesiastical usage, the clergyman or other person appointed by the bishop as his deputy to grant licences for marriages without *banns.

SURSUM CORDA (Lat., 'Lift up your hearts'). In the Eucharist the words addressed by the celebrant to the congregation immediately before the *Preface.

SUSANNA, Book of. A short Book of the *Apocrypha, reckoned in the *Vulgate as Dan. 13. It tells of the false accusation of adultery brought against Susanna, her condemnation, and her final deliverance by the sagacity of Daniel. In the Christian era the incident became a symbol of the saved soul.

SUSANNA, St. (3rd cent.), Roman martyr. Acc. to legend she was put to death for refusing to marry a pagan relative of *Diocletian.

SUSO, HENRY. See *Henry Suso*.

SUVERMERIAN. A word applied by the Saxon Reformers to certain Swiss Protestant extremists.

SWAINSON, CHARLES ANTHONY (1820–87), Anglican divine. He wrote two important books on the Creeds and edited a collection of texts on *The Greek Liturgies* (1864), parts of which are still indispensable.

SWASTIKA. A symbol in the form of a cross of equal arms, each of which is bent back in the shape of a hook. It was prob. in origin a charm for attracting good luck and averting misfortune; it is found on vases dating from c. 4000–3000 B.C. In modern times it was adopted by the National Socialist Party in Germany.

SWEDEN, Christianity in. St. *Anskar (801–65) preached in Sweden, but his work was destroyed by civil wars. The systematic conversion of the country, largely from England, began in the 11th cent. and was completed in the 12th. In the later Middle Ages the position of the clergy was highly privileged and the Church amassed great wealth. The Reformation was gradual. In 1524 relations with the Roman Curia were broken off and Olaus *Petri (a pupil of M. *Luther) began to preach with the king's approval, but the ancient episcopal succession was deliberately maintained. It was only in 1593 that the Swedes adopted the *Augsburg Confession, so formally committing themselves to *Lutheran dogma. In the 19th cent. the Swedish Church suffered from a wave of *Latitudinarianism; this was succeeded by an *Evangelical revival which largely destroyed sacramental religion. In the 20th cent. there has been renewed recognition of the value of the historic ministry, the sacraments, and liturgical worship, but Lutheran doctrine is considered more fundamental than Church order.

SWEDENBORG, EMANUEL (1688–1772), originally Swedberg, Swedish scientist and mystical thinker. While employed at the Swedish Board of Mines (1716–47) he anticipated various later scientific discoveries and hypotheses, and he is claimed as the founder of crystallography. In 1743–5 his outlook underwent a sudden development. He became conscious of direct contact with the spiritual world and felt that he was commissioned to make known his doctrines to the world at large. The agency was to be the New Church, organized not as a body separate from the existing Churches, but a spiritual fraternity of all those, of whatever allegiance, who accepted his doctrines. He resigned his post and devoted himself to writing. His teaching was a mixture of pantheism and theosophy.

Among the earliest disseminators of his doctrines were two C of E clergymen in Lancashire, but the formal creation of the New Jerusalem Church was the work of five ex-Wesleyan preachers in London in 1787. In the U.S.A. the first congregation was formed in Baltimore in 1792. There are also bodies of Swedenborgians on the Continent of Europe and in Australia. They claim a world membership of c. 40,000.

SWETE, HENRY BARCLAY (1835–1917), Biblical and patristic scholar. From 1890 to 1915 he was Regius Professor of Divinity at Cambridge. He was concerned with the inauguration of a number of co-operative projects, incl. the *Journal of Theological Studies* and *A Patristic Greek Lexicon* (publd. 1961–8). His own works included an edition of the *Septuagint (1887–94).

SWIFT, JONATHAN (1667–1745), Dean of St. Patrick's, *Dublin, from 1713, and satirist. In politics he was a Whig, but he wrote against the *Occasional Conformity Bill in 1708, and he used his satirical power for religious ends in his *Argument to Prove the Inconvenience of Abolishing Christianity* (1708). He is popularly remembered as the author of *Gulliver's Travels* (1726).

SWISS GUARD. The military guardians of the Papal Palace. The corps, instituted by *Julius II (1503–13), consists of about 100 men, recruited from all the Swiss cantons.

SWITHIN, St. (d. 862), also 'Swithun', Bp. of *Winchester from 852. Little is known of his life, but he seems to have been the trusted adviser of Egbert, King of Wessex. Originally buried 'humbly' outside the walls of the minster, in 971 his relics were translated to a shrine in the cathedral. The popular belief that the weather on St. Swithin's Day (15 July) will be that of the next 40 days may have arisen from a similar attribution to the feast of Sts. Processus and Martinian, which coincides with the anniversary of St. Swithin's death (2 July).

'SWORD OF THE SPIRIT'. A RC social movement inaugurated by Card. A. *Hinsley in 1940. Its aims were supported by the Abps. of *Canterbury and *York and the

Moderator of the Free Churches, but the initial co-operation between RCs and other groups was restricted in 1941. In 1965 it became the Catholic Institute for International Relations.

SYLLABUS ERRORUM. A set of 80 theses, already condemned in earlier pronouncements of *Pius IX and promulgated as erroneous in 1864. They covered a wide area, including pantheism, rationalism, the Church and its rights, civil society and its relation to the Church, ethics, and modern Liberalism. The covering letter seemed to make the Syllabus dogmatically binding. Its issue aroused a storm of protest.

SYLVESTER, St., Bp. of Rome from 314 to 335. Little is known of him. Later legend asserts that he baptized *Constantine (cleansing him from physical leprosy) at the Baptistery of the *Lateran and established the Lateran church as the cathedral of Rome on land given him by the Emperor. He is also the reputed recipient of the *Donation of Constantine.

SYLVESTER II (c. 940–1003), Pope from 999. Gerbert is important both as a scholar and as a Churchman. It appears that in the school at *Reims he was the first master in Europe to use a substantial part of the logical works of *Aristotle and *Boethius as a practical system of education, and he wrote extensively on mathematics. He became Abp. of Reims in 991, Patr. of *Ravenna in 998, and Pope in 999. He owed these promotions to the Emp. Otto III, and his choice of papal name was in conscious imitation of *Sylvester I, who had long been regarded as the pattern of papal co-operation with the Emperor. As Pope, he opposed *simony and upheld clerical *celibacy, and did much to strengthen the Church in E. Europe. He established archbishoprics in Gniezno (Poland) and Esztergom (Hungary) and recognized St. *Stephen of Hungary as king.

SYLVESTRINES. A small religious order founded in 1231 by St. Sylvester Gozzolini. They follow a rule akin to that of St. *Benedict.

SYMEON. See *Simeon*.

SYMMACHUS (prob. later 2nd cent.), translator of the Gk. version of the OT reproduced in the 4th column of *Origen's *Hexapla. Hardly anything is known of his life. He preferred a readable style and palatable rendering to verbal accuracy, and he modified the anthropomorphic expressions of the Hebrew text.

SYMMACHUS, St. (d. 514), Pope from 498. He was opposed by Laurentius, whom the party of his predecessor elected against him, and whom *Theodoric allowed to return to Rome, even though the synod which he summoned in 501 declared Symmachus the rightful Pope. In 507 Theodoric withdrew his opposition. In the latter part of his pontificate Symmachus devoted himself to the defence of the Catholic faith against the *Henoticon and against the *Manichaeans, whom he expelled from Rome. He also introduced the singing of the *Gloria in excelsis* at Mass on Sundays.

SYNAGOGUE. It appears that the Jews introduced synagogues as regular meeting-places for worship during the Babylonian exile (6th cent. B.C.), when they could no longer take part in the *Temple worship at *Jerusalem. The worship of the synagogue has always been non-sacrificial; it consists chiefly of readings from Scripture, with prayers, canticles, and sometimes a sermon. Christ took part in synagogue worship and often preached or taught in the synagogue, and St. *Paul seems normally to have preached the Gospel in the synagogue of the places he visited before turning to the Gentiles.

SYNAPTE. In the E. Church, a prayer in the form of a *litany used in the Liturgy and other services.

SYNAXARION. (1) In the E. Church, a short account of a saint or feast appointed to be read at the early morning service (*Orthros); (2) the book containing these passages ('The Greater Synaxarion'); (3) another book which merely enumerates the feasts to be observed, with a reference to the appropriate Biblical lessons ('The Lesser Synaxarion').

SYNAXIS. An assembly for public worship. In the E. Church the term includes the Eucharist; in the W. it was used in early times esp. of non-Eucharistic services.

SYNCELLUS. In the Byzantine Church, an ecclesiastic who lived continually with a bishop, esp. in the capacity of a domestic chaplain and in order to bear witness to the purity of the bishop's moral life. In later times the word was used of a dignitary associated as counsellor with a prelate who subsequently succeeded to his office.

SYNCELLUS, GEORGE. See *George Syncellus.*

SYNCRETISM. The attempt to combine opposing doctrines and practices, esp. in reference to philosophical and religious systems. The term was applied in the 17th cent. to the teaching of G. *Calixtus (q.v.).

SYNERGISM. The teaching of P. *Melanchthon that in the act of conversion the human will can co-operate with the Holy Spirit and God's grace.

SYNESIUS (*c.* 370–*c.* 414), Bp. of Ptolemais. Brought up as a pagan, in 403 Synesius married a Christian wife. Having won the confidence of his fellow-Alexandrians by a successful embassy to the Imperial court, *c.* 410 he was chosen Bp. of Ptolemais in Cyrenaica, although prob. not even baptized. He was eventually consecrated, without engaging to give up either his wife or his philosophical doctrines. A series of domestic and other tragedies marked his episcopate. His writings all date from his pre-Christian period.

SYNOD. See *Council* and the following entry.

SYNODICAL GOVERNMENT. The system of government of the C of E introduced by the Synodical Government Measure of 1969. A General Synod took over all the powers of the *Church Assembly, which ceased to exist, and most of those of the *Convocations, which, however, remained in being. It is composed of a House of Bishops and a House of Clergy, comprising the Upper and Lower Houses of the Convocations, and a House of Laity of not more than 250 members elected by members of the Houses of Laity of the Deanery Synods. Matters concerning doctrinal formulas, church services, and the administration of the Sacraments can be approved only in terms proposed by the House of Bishops.

Diocesan Conferences were replaced by Diocesan Synods, consisting of the Bishop, a House of Clergy, and a House of Laity. Members of the last two are elected by the respective Houses of the Deanery Synods, which replaced the former Ruridecanal Conferences. The base of the structure is the *Parochial Church Council, whose functions are fundamentally unchanged.

SYNODICON. (1) An act of a synod or a collection of such acts. (2) A liturgical text used in the E. Church on the Feast of *Orthodoxy.

SYNOPTIC PROBLEM. The problem of the literary relations between the three 'Synoptic Gospels' (Mt., Mk., Lk.), which arises from the occurrence of a large amount of common subject-matter and often similar phrasing in more than one Gospel. Almost all scholars now hold that this parallelism is due to literary interdependence. There is wide, but less complete, agreement that: (1) Mk. is the earliest of the three Gospels and was used as a framework by both Mt. and Lk.; (2) the non-Marcan material common to Mt. and Lk. is derived from a single lost source, known to critics as '*Q'; (3) the authors of Mt. and Lk. used further sources for the matter peculiar to each of them. Whether these sources were written or oral, and whether each Evangelist had one or more than one source, is debated. Without prejudging these questions, scholars use the letters 'M' and 'L' to denote this material.

SYNTERESIS. A technical term used by *Scholastic theologians for our knowledge of the first principles of moral action.

SYRIAC. A branch of *Aramaic which was spoken in *Edessa and its neighbourhood from shortly before the beginning of the Christian era. It was used extensively in the early Church because of the active Christian communities in these parts. Most of the surviving literature is Christian and a number of Greek patristic works survive only in Syriac translation. It is still used in the liturgy of the *Nestorians and *Jacobites, but it became an artificial language when Arabic became the current vernacular. See also the following entry.

SYRIAC VERSIONS OF THE BIBLE. These are of special value to textual critics because of their early date and the natural accuracy of Syriac scholars. The chief versions of the OT were: (1) the *Peshitta, made for Jews in the 2nd cent. A.D. and revised under the influence of Greek Christians to harmonize with the *Septuagint; and (2) the Syro-Hexaplar, a close rendering of the LXX text in *Origen's *Hexapla, made at *Alexandria in 616–17 by Paul, Bp. of Tella in Mesopotamia.

The Gospels were known in a Syriac version of *Tatian's *Diatessaron and in a translation of the 4 Gospels separately, known as the *Old Syriac version. The latter is prob. not earlier than 200 and is independent of, and later than, the Syriac Diatessaron. It is generally held to be the basis of the Peshitta (q.v.). There were two further versions of the NT: the *Philoxenian in 508, and the *Harklean in 616.

SYRIAN CATHOLICS. A body of *Uniat Christians descended from the Syrian *Jacobites (*Monophysites). The present Church traces its existence to the accession of Mar Michael Garweh, who had become a RC, to the Abpric. of Aleppo in 1783.

SYRIAN ORTHODOX. The body of Orthodox Christians who trace their descent to that part of the Patriarchate of *Antioch which refused to accept the decisions of the Council of *Chalcedon on the Person of Christ. In the W. they are fequently described as *Jacobites or *Monophysites (qq.v. for their early history).

Their numbers were reduced in the 14th cent. by Mongol invasions, in the 18th cent. by the establishment of a separate *uniat patriarchate (see *Syrian Catholics*), and at the turn of the present century by massacres at the hands of the Turks. They now number c. 200,000 in the Middle East, c. 50,000 in N. and S. America, and perhaps a million in South *India (*Malabar Christians). Their liturgical language is *Syriac.

SYRIAN TEXT OF THE NT, The. The name given by B. F. *Westcott and F. J. A. *Hort to an edition of the Greek text of the NT which they held was made in or near Antioch in Syria c. A.D. 300, and of which *Lucian of Antioch was the probable author.

SYRO-CHALDAEANS. An alternative name for the *Chaldean Christians.

SYZYGY. A word used by the *Gnostics for a pair of cosmological opposites, e.g. male and female. It was held that the universe had come into being through the interaction of such opposites.

T

TABERNACLE (Jewish), also called the 'tent of meeting'. The portable shrine said to have been constructed under *Moses's direction during the wilderness wanderings. Theologically it was held to embody the presence of God in the midst of His people.

TABERNACLE (Christian). The word now denotes the box placed on the altar which contains the vessels in which the Bl. Sacrament is reserved in RC churches. Acc. to current legislation it may stand on the High Altar, but an altar in a side chapel is preferred.

TABLE, Communion. See *Communion Table*.

TABLET, The. A RC weekly founded in 1840.

TABORITES. The extreme party of the *Hussites, so named from Mount Tabor, their stronghold south of Prague. They gained ascendancy after the death of King Wenceslaus (1419) and, under their leader Zizka, began to spread the 'Kingdom of God' by force of arms. They split into two parties after his death (1424): the more moderate joined the Catholics after the Compactata of Prague (1433; see *Utraquists*); the radicals were defeated at Lipany in 1434 and disappeared from history.

TACITUS, CORNELIUS (c. 55–120), Roman historian. In his *Annals*, xv.44, he mentions the persecution of the Christians by

*Nero, who, he says, made them scapegoats for the fire of Rome (A.D. 64). The passage contains one of the earliest witnesses in non-Christian literature to the Crucifixion.

TAIT, ARCHIBALD CAMPBELL (1811–82), Abp. of *Canterbury from 1868. At Oxford in 1841 he was one of the Four Tutors who protested against Tract 90 (see *Tractarianism*), and as Bp. of London (1856–68) he withdrew the licence of Alfred Poole, curate of St. Barnabas, Pimlico, for hearing confessions. As Archbishop he used his gifts of statesmanship to secure the best possible terms for the disestablished Church of *Ireland. The *Public Worship Regulation Act (1874) was mainly his creation.

TAIZÉ COMMUNITY, an ecumenical monastic community founded in 1940 by Roger Schutz (b. 1915). Schutz became convinced of the need for some form of traditional monasticism within Protestantism; in 1940 he acquired a house at Taizé in SE. France, in which he sheltered Jewish and other refugees until 1942. With the German occupation he moved to Geneva and began living a community life with Max Thurian and others. In 1944 they moved to Taizé and the first seven brothers took solemn vows in 1949. The Rule of Taizé, composed in 1952, provides for a life similar to that of other monastic orders, except that the members dress as laymen and recite only three Offices a day. Their main work lies in the promotion of Christian unity.

TALBOT, EDWARD STUART (1844–1934), Anglican bishop. The first Warden of Keble College, Oxford (1870–88), and Vicar of Leeds (1888–95), he became Bp. of *Rochester in 1895. His main work here was the division of the diocese and the creation of the see of *Southwark, of which he became bishop in 1905. From 1911 to 1924 he was Bp. of *Winchester. He promoted moderate *High Church principles throughout his life.
     Talbot House ('*Toc H') was founded in memory of his son, Gilbert Talbot (1891–1915).

TALL BROTHERS, The. Four monks who led the *Origenist Movement in Egypt at the end of the 4th cent. In 399 they made their way from the *Nitrian Desert to *Alexandria and later went to *Constantinople, where they gained the support of St. *Chrysostom.

TALLEYRAND-PÉRIGORD, CHARLES MAURICE DE (1754–1838), Prince of Benevento. In 1789 he was made Bp. of Autun. He joined the cause of the Revolution and became a member of the Constitutional Assembly, taking the oath to the *Civil Constitution and consecrating persons prepared to do likewise to fill the vacated bishoprics. In 1791 he was constrained to resign his see and in 1792 he was excommunicated. He became Foreign Minister in 1796, took charge of the provisional government of France in 1814, and was French Ambassador to England from 1830 to 1834.

TALLIS, THOMAS (d. 1585), the 'Father of English Cathedral Music'. He was organist of Waltham Abbey before its dissolution in 1540 and soon afterwards became a Gentleman of the Chapel Royal. He received grants from Queens *Mary and *Elizabeth I His main compositions are vocal works; they are mostly set to Latin words but include a number of settings of the Anglican service.

TALMUD. The Jewish compilations which embody the *Mishnah, or oral teaching of the Jews, and the Gemara, or collection of discussions on the Mishnah. The two main forms of the Talmud, the Palestinian and the Babylonian, both date from the 5th cent. A.D., but include much earlier material.

TAMBARAM CONFERENCE. The missionary conference, convened by the International Missionary Council, which met at Tambaram, near Madras, in 1938. Its membership was drawn from 69 countries and all the more important non-RC communions.

TAMETSI. The *Tridentine decree of 1563 prescribing the formal mode of celebrating matrimony. It aimed at repressing *clandestinity. It was not normally published in Protestant countries and it was superseded in 1908 by the provisions of *Ne Temere.

TANNER, THOMAS (1674–1735), English antiquary and divine. His *Notitia Monastica* (1695) is an erudite account of the medieval religious houses in England and Wales. His *Bibliotheca Britannico-Hibernica* (publd. by D. *Wilkins in 1748) gives an account of British writers to the beginning of the 17th cent.; it long remained a standard work.

TANTUM ERGO. The last two verses of St. *Thomas Aquinas's hymn '*Pange lingua gloriosi', commonly used at *Benediction in the RC Church. The best-known Eng. tr. begins 'Therefore we, before Him bending'.

TARASIUS, St. (d. 806), Patr. of *Constantinople from 784. He sought to restore good relations with the W. Church and persuaded the Empress Irene to convoke a General Council in concert with Pope *Hadrian I; it met at *Nicaea in 787 under his presidency. He was later attacked for laxity by *Theodore of Studios.

TARGUM. The *Aramaic translations or paraphrases of the OT which were made from at least the 1st cent. A.D., when Hebrew had ceased to be the normal medium of speech among the Jews.

TARSICIUS, St. (3rd–4th cent.), martyr. Acc. to tradition he was killed in Rome by a mob while bearing the Bl. Sacrament rather than surrender it to profanation.

TARSUS. Pompey made this ancient city of Asia Minor the capital of the Roman province of Cilicia in 67 B.C. It became the seat of a *Stoic philosophical school and was the birthplace of St. *Paul. In Christian times it became an episcopal see.

TASSO, TORQUATO (1544–95), Italian poet. He entered the service of Card. Luigi d'Este in 1565, but he was able to devote much of his time to his great epic, *Gerusalemme liberata*, a poem on the first *Crusade, completed in 1574. He later suffered from religious scruples and persecution mania; he died shortly before receiving the crown of the Poet Laureate intended for him by *Clement VIII.

TATE, NAHUM (1652–1715), and **BRADY,** NICHOLAS (1659–1726), authors of the *New Version of the Psalms* (1696). Both were Irish Protestant clergymen. Tate became Poet Laureate in 1692. Brady was chaplain to William III, Mary, and Queen *Anne. The *New Version* is a versification of the Psalter according to the artificial taste of the period. It gradually supplanted the rendering of T. *Sternhold and J. Hopkins and was widely used until the early 19th cent.

TATIAN (born *c.* 120), *Apologist and rigorist. A native of Syria, he became a Christian in Rome between 150 and 165. About 172 he returned to the E., where he is said to have founded the *Encratites. His *Oratio ad Graecos* is a passionate defence of the antiquity and purity of Christianity, combined with a violent attack on Greek civilization. His chief claim to fame is his *Diatessaron* (q.v.).

TATTAM, HENRY (1789–1868), Anglican divine and scholar. He recovered from the *Nitrian desert several important Coptic and Syriac MSS., including a 5th-cent. codex of the *Old Syriac text of the Gospels.

TAULER, JOHANN (*c.* 1300–61), German *Dominican mystic. He became famous as a preacher and director, esp. of nuns. His surviving sermons emphasize the indwelling of God in the human soul, and describe in detail the Mystic Way, which he conceives as consisting chiefly in the practice of the virtues, esp. humility and abandonment to the will of God. Union is to be desired not so much for its own sake as for the results which it produces in the soul.

TAUSEN, HANS (1494–1561), Reformer, the 'Danish Luther'. He was a *Hospitaller, but came under the influence of M. *Luther at *Wittenberg. On his return to *Denmark he discarded his religious habit and, on becoming chaplain to King Frederick I (1526), he married and used Danish in Church services. In 1529 he secured the support of the Danish National Assembly. A Confession of 43 Articles was drawn up by Tausen and his supporters, but this was later set aside in favour of the more moderate *Augsburg Confession.

TAVERNER'S BIBLE. The English translation of the Bible issued in 1539 by Richard Taverner. It was a revision of *Matthew's Bible.

TAX-COLLECTOR, TAX-GATHERER. Terms used in modern English versions of the Bible to replace publican (q.v.).

TAYLOR, JAMES HUDSON (1832–1905), founder of the *China Inland Mission. A medical man who felt called to be a missionary, he sailed for China in 1853 under the auspices of the Chinese Evangelization Society. He returned to England in 1860 and in 1865 founded the interdenominational China Inland Mission. He went back to China, conforming as far as he could to Chinese habits of life.

TAYLOR, JEREMY (1613–67), Anglican bishop and writer. He was chaplain to *Charles I, rector of Uppingham, and then chaplain in the Royalist army. After a short imprisonment he retired in 1645 to Wales, where he lived as chaplain to Lord Carbery at Golden Grove. Most of his best works were written here. In 1660 he was appointed Bp. of Down and Connor and Vice-Chancellor of *Dublin University, and in 1661 he received the further see of Dromore. His fame rests on his devotional writings, esp. *The Rule and Exercise of Holy Living* (1650) and *The Rule and Exercise of Holy Dying* (1651). They are characteristic expressions of Anglican spirituality in their insistence on a well-ordered piety which stresses temperance and moderation. His theological works were less felicitous.

TAYLOR, JOHN (1694–1761), Dissenting divine. His *Hebrew Concordance* (1754–7) was designed to serve also the purposes of a lexicon and marked an important advance in the study of Hebrew roots. His *Scripture Doctrine of Original Sin* (1740), which circulated widely in Britain and America, by undermining the foundations of the *Calvinist system did much to prepare the way for the *Unitarian Movement in American Congregationalism.

TEACHING OF THE TWELVE APOSTLES, The. The full title of the work commonly known as *The*Didache* (q.v.).

TE DEUM. A Latin hymn to the Father and the Son, in rhythmical prose. Verses 22 ff. are suffrages, appended to the original at an early date. The ascription of the hymn to Sts. *Ambrose and *Augustine is rejected by modern scholars. Its use in the *Office is mentioned in the Rule of St. *Benedict. The BCP includes in *Mattins the Eng. tr. 'We praise thee, O God'.

TE IGITUR (Lat., 'Thee, therefore'), usually regarded as the opening words of the *Canon of the Roman Mass, and hence also the name for the first part of the Canon.

TEILHARD DE CHARDIN, PIERRE (1881–1955), French *Jesuit theologian and scientist. He worked for many years in China, where he gained a reputation as a palaeontologist; his last years were spent in America. His theological works appeared only after his death, beginning with *Le Phénomène humain* (1955; Eng. tr., *The Phenomenon of Man*, 1959). They made a powerful impression as a new synthesis of science and religion. The universe is seen as an evolutionary process in which the movement is always towards systems of greater complexity. Correlated with this movement towards complexity is the movement towards higher levels of consciousness. The whole process has included several critical moments or thresholds at which leaps to new levels have been made. Such thresholds were the emergence of life on earth and then the emergence of rational self-consciousness in man. This latter emergence has special significance, since it means that evolution no longer takes place in accordance with the laws of nature only, but that man now takes part in directing it. The whole process moves towards a fulfilment in which all things will be gathered up in God.

TEILO, St. (6th cent.), patron saint and Bp. of *Llandaff. He is credited with having been consecrated bishop at *Jerusalem while on a pilgrimage to Palestine and (a less unlikely tradition) with having visited St. *Samson at Dol. He is said to have succeeded St. *Dubritius in the see of Llandaff in 495.

TEINDS. The Scottish equivalent of *tithes. The system was ended by Act of Parliament in 1925.

TELEMACHUS, St. Acc. to *Theodoret, Telemachus was an E. monk who, seeking to end the gladiatorial shows at Rome, in 391 entered the arena to separate the combatants and was killed by the spectators.

TELEOLOGY. The science of ends or final causes, and esp. the doctrine that the universe embodies design and purpose. This doctrine forms the basis of the modern argument from design (known as the 'physico-theological argument' or the 'teleological argument') for the existence of God. In its classic form it sets out from the observation that every biological species is apparently designed to serve its own needs and argues therefrom to an intelligent Creator.

TELESIO, BERNARDINO (1508–88), Italian humanist. In 1566 he founded a scientific academy at Naples. His doctrines were based on an extreme empiricism, but he built up a speculative system in which the *Aristotelian doctrine of matter and form was replaced by one of matter and force.

TELESPHORUS, St. (d. *c.* 137), Bp. of Rome from *c.* 127. He is the only 2nd-cent. Pope whose martyrdom is well attested.

TEMPERANCE. Restraint of the appetites and passions in accordance with reason. It is one of the four *cardinal virtues. For the Christian, temperance in its physical aspects is linked with the need for self-control of the body, regarded as a 'temple of the Holy Spirit'. The 'temperance societies', founded to foster abstinence from alcohol, date from the 19th cent.

TEMPLARS, or 'Knights Templar'. The 'Poor Knights of Christ and of the Temple of Solomon', one of the two chief military orders of medieval Christendom. In 1118 Hugh de Payens, a knight of Champagne, and eight companions bound themselves by a solemn vow to protect pilgrims on the public roads of the Holy Land. They were given quarters on the site of *Solomon's *Temple. At the Council of Troyes (1128) approval was given to their rule, said to have been drawn up by St. *Bernard. They soon increased in influence and wealth, acquiring property in every part of Christendom. In the *Crusader states of the 12th and 13th cents. the professional forces of the Templars and the *Hospitallers played an increasingly important role.

The integrity and credit of the order led to its being much trusted as a banking house. Its wealth led to its ruin after the fall of Acre (1291). Philip the Fair of France coveted its riches; aided by a renegade Templar he brought charges of sodomy, blasphemy, and heresy against the order, and *Clement V suppressed it at the Council of *Vienne in 1312. The Templars' innocence is now generally admitted.

TEMPLE, The. Although the idea of a national shrine of the Jews at Jerusalem was conceived by *David, the first Temple dated

from the reign of *Solomon (*c.* 970–*c.* 930 B.C.). This building became the central sanctuary of Jewish religion, and here alone could sacrificial worship be offered. It was destroyed by the Babylonians in 586 B.C.. Its rebuilding (the 'Second Temple') was undertaken in 520 B.C. The grandest Temple building was put up by *Herod the Great. This was the Temple standing in Christ's time. With the destruction of Jerusalem in A.D. 70 the Temple worship ceased.

TEMPLE, FREDERICK (1821–1902), Abp. of *Canterbury from 1897. He was Headmaster of Rugby (1857–69), Bp. of *Exeter (1869–85), and Bp. of London (1885–97). At London he played an important part in the *Lincoln Judgement (1890) and he became involved in conflict with the *High Church party. His archiepiscopate was marked by the *Lambeth Conference of 1897 and the issue of the *Lambeth Opinions of 1899–1900.

TEMPLE, WILLIAM (1881–1944), Abp. of *York (1929–42) and of *Canterbury (from 1942). He was a son of F. *Temple. In 1923 he became a member (from 1925, Chairman) of the Commission which in 1938 produced the report on *Doctrine in the Church of England*. As Abp. of York he became prominent in national life, esp. through his concern with social, economic, and international problems. He presided over the *Malvern Conference in 1941. His time at Canterbury was overshadowed by the 1939–45 War; he joined with Card. A. *Hinsley and the Moderator of the Free Church Council in issuing a statement of principles which should guide a post-war settlement.

TEMPORALE. The section of a *Missal or *Breviary which supplies the variable parts of the services for the ecclesiastical year, except in so far as they are provided for in the *Sanctorale.

TEMPTATION. The etymology of the word suggests a neutral meaning of 'trying' or 'proving'. This primary sense is retained in the idea of God's tempting *Abraham (Gen. 22: 1). It may also be the meaning of the word in the traditional version of the *Lord's Prayer. In most passages of the NT and in common usage, however, it has the implication of incitement to sin. In this sense temptation seems to be part of man's experience, even before the *Fall; it is inherent in *free will and not sinful before consent. See also the following entry.

TEMPTATION OF CHRIST. In the account of the Temptation of Christ in the Wilderness after His Baptism, three particular temptations are described in Mt. 4: 1–11, viz. (1) to use His power as Son of God to turn stones into bread to satisfy His hunger; (2) to cast Himself down from a pinnacle of the Temple, i.e. to put God to an arbitrary test and to stage a spectacular miracle; and (3) to obtain from the devil power over all the kingdoms of the world by falling down and worshipping him, i.e. to desert His true mission for the sake of power unworthily obtained. In Lk. 4: 1–13 the last two temptations are related in the reverse order.

TEMPUS CLAUSUM (Lat., 'closed time'). Certain seasons in the Christian year in which, because of their solemn or penitential character, marriages were formerly not normally solemnized.

TEN ARTICLES, The (1536). The first Articles of faith issued by the C of E in the Reformation period. Adopted by *Convocation at the desire of *Henry VIII, they were superseded in 1537 by 'The *Bishops' Book'.

TEN COMMANDMENTS, The. See *Commandments, The Ten*.

TEN THOUSAND MARTYRS, The. The *Roman Martyrology commemorates two such groups: (1) on 22 June there is a reference to a legendary record of 10,000 soldiers crucified on Mt. Ararat; (2) on 18 Mar. an entry relates to a group who suffered at the beginning of the *Diocletianic persecution (303).

TEN TRIBES, The. On *Solomon's death (c. 930 B.C.), ten of the twelve Hebrew tribes separated to form the kingdom of Israel, while two formed the kingdom of Judah. When Israel was conquered by the Assyrians in 721, many of the more prosperous people were deported to Assyria (2 Kgs. 17: 1-6). The theory of the '*British Israelites' that these people were ancestors of the British has no solid basis.

TEN YEARS' CONFLICT, The (1833–43). The conflict in the Church of *Scotland which culminated in the *Disruption. It arose from the claim of some of the laity for a say in the choice of their ministers. In 1833 a motion in the *General Assembly that a majority of dissentient voices should veto the presentee of a patron was lost, but in the 1834 Assembly the Veto Act was passed. When the Act was tested in the courts, the House of Lords in 1839 ruled it *ultra vires*. The climax came in 1843, when about a third of the members and ministers of the Church seceded and formed the *Free Church of Scotland.

TENEBRAE. The popular name for the special form of *Mattins and *Lauds provided for the last three days of *Holy Week. Until 1955 it was sung by anticipation on the three preceding evenings. The name (lit. 'darkness'), prob. derived from the ceremony of extinguishing the lights in church one by one during the service.

TENISON, THOMAS (1636–1715), Abp. of *Canterbury from 1695. He revived the Archbishop's Court and took a prominent part in founding the *S.P.G. He fell into disfavour under Queen *Anne because of his pronounced Whig and *Low Church views.

TERCE, SEXT, NONE. The *Offices said at the third, sixth, and ninth hours respectively. They each consist of a hymn, three Psalms (or one Psalm divided into three parts) with *antiphons, a short reading from the Bible, a *versicle and response, and a concluding prayer. Since 1971 only one of these Offices is required, and the time of day at which it is said dictates which should be chosen.

TERESA OF ÁVILA, the commonly used name of **Teresa of Jesus, St.** (1515–82), Spanish *Carmelite nun and mystic. She entered the Carmelite convent of the Incarnation ('Mitigated Observance') at Ávila in 1535, but it was not until 1555 that she was finally converted to a life of perfection Her mystic life began soon afterwards with Divine locutions, her first ecstasy, and an intellectual vision of Christ. Despite opposition, in 1562 she founded the convent of St. Joseph at Ávila, where the primitive rule was observed. Here she wrote *The Way of Perfection* (for her nuns), having recently completed her *Life*, a spiritual autobiography.

From 1567 she was engaged in establishing houses of the primitive rule ('Discalced Carmelites') for both nuns and friars; in this undertaking she received much help from St. *John of the Cross. At the same time her own religious life deepened until it reached the state of 'spiritual marriage' (1572). She wrote *Foundations*, *The Interior Castle*, and some smaller books. Her influence as a spiritual writer was epoch-making, because she was the first to point to the existence of states of prayer intermediate between discursive meditation and ecstasy and to give a scientific description of the entire life of prayer from meditation to the so-called mystic marriage. She also combined mystic experience with ceaseless activity.

TERESA OF LISIEUX, St. (1873–97), *Carmelite nun. The daughter of a devout watchmaker, she obtained permission to enter the Carmelite convent at Lisieux at the age of 15. She was professed in 1890 and from 1893 was assistant novice-mistress. She died of tuberculosis.

The spread of her fame was largely due to the decision of the prioress of Lisieux to circulate to all Carmelite houses a revised version of Teresa's autobiography, *L'Histoire d'une âme*. Miracles were reported and by 1907 an account of these was appended to the autobiography. She was canonized in 1925. The popularity of her cult lay in its appeal to ordinary people: her life showed that the attainment of sanctity was possible not only through extreme mortification but through continual renunciation in small matters. In England she is popularly known as 'The Little Flower' from the subtitle of her autobiography.

TERMINISM. (1) The doctrine held by some *Pietists, that God has ordained a definite period or term in the life of every individual at the end of which he loses his opportunity of achieving salvation. (2) An alternative name for *Nominalism.

TERRITORIALISM. The theory that the civil authority has the right to determine the religious doctrines of its subjects.

TERSANCTUS. An alternative name for the *Sanctus.

TERSTEEGEN, GERHARD (1697–1769), German Protestant devotional writer. He underwent a conversion in a circle of *Pietists at the age of 20 and retired into solitude, earning his living as a ribbon-weaver. From 1728 he devoted himself entirely to directing souls and devotional meetings. He translated into German many French *Quietist works, but he is chiefly known for his hymns. Those translated into English include 'Lo, God is here!'.

TERTIARY. A member of a 'Third Order' (q.v.). The term 'tertiary' is popularly used only of those members living in the world (technically 'Secular Tertiaries', distinguished from 'Regular Tertiaries', who live in community). The most important are the *Franciscan, *Dominican, and *Carmelite Tertiaries. They make a novitiate and are clothed with the habit of the Order, which is, however, seldom worn, a *scapular under ordinary clothes taking its place. They observe a rule, recite an office, keep special fasts, and have their own spiritual privileges. For the practice of Regular Tertiaries, see *Third Order*.

TERTULLIAN, QUINTUS SEPTIMIUS FLORENS (*c.* 160–*c.* 225), African Church Father. Brought up in Carthage as a pagan, Tertullian may have practised as a lawyer. He eventually joined the *Montanist sect. The chronology of his life is disputed.

Tertullian wrote a large number of apologetic, theological, and ascetic works. In his *Apologeticum* (*c.* 197) he appeals for toleration of Christianity, attacking pagan superstition, rebutting charges against Christian morality, and claiming that Christians are no danger to the State but useful citizens. In moral and disciplinary works addressed to Christians he emphasizes the separation from pagan society which is needed to escape contamination from its immorality and idolatry. His theological works are mainly polemical in origin and form. In the early *De Praescriptione Haereticorum* he disposes of all heresy in principle: only the true Church possesses the authentic tradition and has the authority to interpret Scripture; it has no need to argue. Against *Marcion he defended the identity of the God of the Old and New Testaments and that of Jesus Christ with the *Messiah of prophecy. Against '*Praxeas' he tried to expose the unscriptural and unhistorical implications of *Modalism and to formulate a positive doctrine of the *Trinity. In *De Anima*, which advocated

*Traducianism, he prepared the way for the pessimistic doctrine of the *Fall and *Original Sin which came, through St. *Augustine, to dominate Latin theology. The rigorist strain in Tertullian, and the opposition which it evoked, took him into Montanism, and his rigorism is evident in his extant Montanist works.

TEST ACT, The (1673). The Act requiring all holders of office under the Crown to receive Communion acc. to the usage of the C of E, to take the Oaths of Supremacy and Allegiance to the Sovereign, and to make the '*Declaration against Transubstantiation'. It remained in force until 1829.

TESTAMENT, Old and **New**. See *Old Testament* and *New Testament*.

TESTAMENT OF OUR LORD IN GALILEE, also known as **The Epistle of the Apostles**. An apocryphal document, written c. 150, in the form of an *encyclical sent out by the Apostles. It purports to record conversations between the Apostles and the Risen Christ.

TESTAMENTS OF THE TWELVE PATRIARCHS, The. A *pseudepigraphical writing which professes to relate the message that each of the twelve sons of *Jacob gave to his descendants on his death-bed. It is a matter of dispute whether the work was Christian in origin or Jewish (in which case the obviously Christian passages are explained as an interpolation). If Jewish, it prob. dates from the 2nd cent. B.C.; if Christian, from c. A.D. 200.

TESTAMENTUM DOMINI. A short Christian treatise professing to be in the words of Christ. It contains detailed regulations on matters of ecclesiastical order and church building, and a liturgy. It prob. dates from the 4th–5th cent., was a private compilation, and does not represent the official practice of any Church.

TETRAGRAMMATON, The. The technical name for the four-lettered Hebrew name of God יהוה (i.e. YHWH or JHVH). Because of its sacred character, from c. 300 B.C. the Jews tended to avoid uttering it when reading Scripture and substituted 'Adonai' (i.e. the Hebrew word for 'Lord'), whence the rendering Κύριος of the LXX,

Dominus of the *Vulgate, and 'the LORD' of the AV and RV. When *vowel points were put into Hebrew MSS. those of 'Adonai' were inserted into the letters of the Tetragrammaton, and since the 16th cent. the bastard word 'Jehovah', obtained by fusing the vowels of the one word with the consonants of the other, has become established. The original pronunciation is commonly thought to have been 'Yahweh' or 'Jahveh' and both these forms are found in scholarly works.

TETRAPOLITAN CONFESSION, The. A Protestant Confession of Faith drawn up by M. *Bucer and W. *Capito at the Diet of *Augsburg in 1530 and presented to *Charles V in the name of four S. German cities.

TETRATEUCH. A name given to the first four Books of the *Pentateuch (Gen.–Num.). It is argued that these Books were compiled from the same sources and on the same editorial principles, and that the main dividing line in the earlier part of the OT is to be placed at the end of Num.; Deut. is then regarded as the first volume of a '*Deuteronomic History' extending to II Kgs.

TETZEL, JOHANN (c. 1465–1519), German *Dominican. In 1516, when the *indulgence was issued for the rebuilding of *St. Peter's, Rome, Tetzel was made subcommissary for the regions of Magdeburg and Halberstadt. He caused scandal by his commercialism and support for the popular idea that a money payment could be applied with unfailing effect to deliver a soul from purgatory. After hearing Tetzel, M. *Luther issued his Ninety-Five Theses in 1517.

TEUTONIC ORDER. The order of German knights grew out of a nursing community founded near Acre in 1190. In 1198 it was converted into a military order with the rule of the *Templars; in 1245 it received a rule of its own. The order, made up of knights, priests, and lay brothers, was active and richly endowed in Palestine and Syria, but soon sought to advance the frontiers of Christendom elsewhere. Duke Conrad of Masovia invited the knights to subdue the heathen Prussians and in 1226 *Frederick II conferred princely powers on the Grand Master and gave almost limitless rights over future conquests to the order. The Knights made great advances eastwards from Prussia, building castles, administering their territories, and colonizing them with German immigrants. When Lithuania accepted Latin Christianity in 1386 their crusading task lost its meaning. In 1525 the Grand Master, *Albert of Prussia, resigned his office, embraced *Lutheranism, and secularized his territory for dynastic ends. The order survived under the protection of the Habsburgs. From *c.* 1840 it found its vocation once more in hospital work, esp. in military hospitals, and in schools.

TEXTUAL CRITICISM. The critical study of the text of a writer whose work has come down from the period before the invention of printing. Few scribes can copy a text accurately; consequently the more often a text is copied and the greater the number of resulting MSS., the greater the variation there is likely to be between them. The task of the textual critic is to compare and evaluate the differences in the MSS. (known as different 'readings') in order to reconstruct the history of the text through its various stages and ultimately to establish the original text as it left the hands of its author.

The majority of the extant Hebrew MSS. of the OT have few variations. This situation is probably due to the establishment of the so-called *Massoretic text early in the Christian era and to its being subsequently copied with the greatest care. The *Septuagint Greek MSS., however, display differences among themselves, but there are a number of instances in which they agree in differing from the Hebrew. Critics deduced that the LXX translation was made from a different (and prob. earlier) text than that which has survived in the Massoretic text. This deduction has been confirmed by the discovery of the *Dead Sea Scrolls.

In the NT there are numerous variations between Greek MSS., some of them considerable, such as that involving the end of the Gospel of *Mark (q.v.). Study has revealed that very generally three types of text are to be distinguished; the evidence of the ancient versions (Latin, *Syriac, *Coptic, &c.) and quotations in the Fathers have made it possible to localize and date these types. They are: (1) a type associated with *Alexandria, which goes back to an early 2nd-cent. archetype; (2) a *Western type (so called because its chief witnesses are the Latin versions and Fathers), which can be traced to *c.* A.D. 150; and (3) a type associated with *Antioch and *Constantinople (the so-called 'Koine', *Byzantine, or *Syrian text), which appears to be a systematic revision undertaken towards the end of the 3rd cent. This type of text is found in the majority of extant Greek MSS. of the NT and was the text behind the first printed editions.

The works of early and medieval Christian writers have sometimes survived in one MS., sometimes in many. In these cases the problems confronting the textual critic and the methods used in dealing with them are similar to those encountered in the NT.

Modern editors of texts, whether Biblical or otherwise, are accustomed to print as the text of their edition either the text of a single MS. or a text which they have themselves constructed from the total material available; in either case it is usual to accompany the text with a statement of variant readings found in other MSS. or elsewhere (e.g. in versions and quotations). This is normally printed at the foot of the page and is known as a '*critical apparatus'.

The belief that textual criticism has radically altered the text lying behind the traditional translations of the Bible has been one of the factors prompting the production of modern versions. At least in the NT, the resulting changes are less fundamental than is often supposed.

TEXTUS RECEPTUS (Lat., 'the Received Text'). The Greek text of the NT ordinarily contained in printed editions until the later decades of the 19th cent. It is in substance the *Byzantine text contained in the majority of MSS. and underlies the AV. See *Textual Criticism.*

THADDAEUS, St. Mentioned in Mt. 10: 3 and Mk. 3: 8 (some MSS. read *Lebbaeus), he is usually identified with the Apostle *Jude (q.v.); sometimes with *Addai (q.v.).

THEATINES, religious order. The 'Clerks Regular of the Divine Providence' were founded in Rome in 1524 by St. *Cajetan and Gian Pietro Caraffa (Bp. of Chieti, or 'Theate'; later *Paul IV). The order spread in Italy, and into Spain and Central Europe; it played an important part in the *Counter-Reformation.

THEBAID, The. The upper part of the Nile

valley (named after its capital, Thebes). From the 3rd cent. it was the cradle of Christian monasticism.

THEBAN LEGION, The. The Christian legion from the *Thebaid which is said to have been massacred under the Emp. Maximian. See *Maurice, St.*

THECLA, St. See *Paul and Thecla, Acts of.*

THEISM. In current usage the word denotes a philosophical system which accepts a transcendent and personal God who not only created but also preserves and governs the world, the contingency of which does not exclude miracles and the exercise of human freedom.

THEMISTIANS. See *Agnoetae.*

THEOBALD (d. 1161), Abp. of *Canterbury from 1138. He had various disputes with *Henry of Blois, who was Papal Legate until 1143. When Theobald defied King Stephen and attended the Council of Reims in 1148, his property was confiscated and he was exiled; for a short time *Eugenius III placed England under an *interdict. In 1152 Theobald refused to crown Stephen's son Eustace and had to flee to Flanders In 1153, however, he reconciled Stephen and Henry of Anjou and on Stephen's death (1154) he crowned Henry king and recommended to him the future St. Thomas *Becket as chancellor.

THEOCRACY (lit. 'government by God'). The Gk. term was coined by *Josephus to denote the political organization of the Jewish people. Yahweh was regarded as the supreme ruler of the Hebrews; His laws constituted both religious and civil obligations. A theocratic form of government was known to many ancient peoples and is intrinsic to *Islam. An attempt to realize the theocratic ideal was made by J. *Calvin at Geneva.

THEODICY. That part of theology which is concerned to defend the goodness and omnipotence of God against objections arising from the existence of evil in the world. The word is sometimes used as a synonym for *Natural Theology.

THEODORA I (c. 500–47), wife of *Justi-

nian, crowned as co-regnant Empress in 527. Her sympathies were with the *Monophysite party and it was prob. mainly because of her influence that Justinian sought to conciliate the Monophysites, esp. in the dispute over the *Three Chapters.

THEODORE THE LECTOR (6th cent.), Church historian. His 'Tripartite History' is composed of extracts from the histories of *Socrates, *Sozomen, and *Theodoret. His own Church History continued to the time of Justin I (d. 527); only fragments remain.

THEODORE OF MOPSUESTIA (c. 350–428), Antiochene exegete and theologian. From 392 he was Bp. of Mopsuestia in Cilicia. In his Biblical commentaries he used critical, philological, and historical methods, rejecting the Alexandrian use of allegorical interpretation. His teaching on the Incarnation was condemned at the Councils of *Ephesus (431) and *Constantinople (553), but the recovery in modern times of some of his works preserved in Syriac has shown that he has sometimes been unjustly judged; his Christological terminology is imprecise.

THEODORE OF RAÏTHU (fl. c. 550), monk at the monastery of Raïthu on the Gulf of Suez. He wrote a *Praeparatio* defending the Christological formulas of St. *Cyril of Alexandria (d. 444) and of the Council of *Chalcedon (451) alike and attacking the doctrines of his contemporaries *Severus of Antioch and *Julian of Halicarnassus.

THEODORE OF STUDIOS, St. (759–826), monastic reformer. He became Abbot of Saccudium (in Bithynia) in 794. In 796 he opposed the adulterous marriage of the Emp. Constantine VI; he was banished but recalled a year later. In 799 he and most of his community went from Saccudium, which was exposed to Saracen raids, to the old monastery of *Studios (q.v.) at Constantinople; under Theodore it became the centre of E. monasticism. When Leo V became Emperor is 813, he revived an *Iconoclastic policy and exiled Theodore, its most vigorous opponent. After Leo's assassination in 820, Theodore was recalled, but as imageworship was prohibited in Constantinople, he spent most of his time on the peninsula of Tryphon. He is widely venerated in the E.

THEODORE OF TARSUS, St. (*c.* 602–90), Abp. of *Canterbury from 668. He was an Asiatic Greek, recommended to Pope *Vitalian by *Hadrian, who accompanied him to Britain. Theodore set about reforming the government of the Church by dividing dioceses and extending the episcopate. In 673 he presided over the first important synod of the English Church at *Hertford and in 680 he held another synod at *Hatfield. The 'Penitential' ascribed to him is of later date.

THEODORET (*c.* 393–*c.* 466), Bp. of Cyrrhus in Syria from 423. He soon became involved in the Christological controversy between *Nestorius and *Cyril of Alexandria. In a polemical work against Cyril, he maintained a duality in Christ and accepted the title of *Theotokos only in a figurative sense. Though he abandoned this position in a later confession of faith in 448, he was nevertheless deposed by the Council held at Ephesus in 449 (the *Latrocinium) and forced into exile. The new Emp. Marcian summoned him to the Council of *Chalcedon (451), where he reluctantly anathematized Nestorius. He apparently spent his last years peacefully administering his diocese. A century later his writings against Cyril were the subject of the '*Three Chapters Controversy' and were condemned at the Council of *Constantinople (553). His other works include the *Eranistes*, which is a treatise against the *Monophysites, a fine Christian Apology, and a Church History continuing the work of *Eusebius to 428. His exegetical works are among the finest specimens of the *Antiochene school.

THEODORIC (*c.* 455–526), King of the Ostrogoths from 475 and ruler of Italy from 493. He spent his boyhood and youth as a hostage in *Constantinople. In 487 he was commissioned by the Emp. *Zeno to overthrow Odoacer, then king in Italy. When he had achieved this end, he ruled virtually independently.

THEODOSIAN CODE, The. In 435 *Theodosius II instructed a commission to codify, with any necessary adaptations, all general constitutions enacted since *Constantine I. The Code was promulgated in 438. It was accepted as authoritative in the W., even after its supersession in the E. by *Justinian.

THEODOSIAN COLLECTION, The. The compilation of documents in the *Verona Chapter MS. LX (58) subscribed with the name of Theodosius the Deacon. It contains important material not found elsewhere.

THEODOSIUS I (the 'Great'), Roman Emperor from 379 to 395. In secular affairs he defeated and pacified the Goths. Ecclesiastically he founded the orthodox Christian State; *Arianism and other heresies became legal offences, sacrifice was forbidden, and paganism almost outlawed.

THEODOSIUS II (401–50), E. Roman Emperor from 408. The grandson of *Theodosius I, he is significant in ecclesiastical history for summoning the Council of *Ephesus (431) and enacting the *Theodosian Code. Politically he was incompetent.

THEODOTION (2nd cent.), translator of the Gk. version of the OT placed in *Origen's *Hexapla next after the LXX. Hardly anything is known of his life. From the 4th cent. the Church used his version of Dan. in preference to the LXX.

THEODOTUS (2nd cent.), *Gnostic. He was a follower of *Valentinus, known from fragments of his works preserved by *Clement of Alexandria.

THEODOTUS, the Cobbler or Leatherseller (2nd cent.), Adoptionist *Monarchian. He proclaimed that Jesus was a man who had been anointed with the Holy Spirit at His Baptism and thus became Christ. He was excommunicated by Pope *Victor.

THEODOTUS (d. *c.* 445), Bp. of Ancyra (modern Ankara). At first a supporter of *Nestorius, he became one of his most determined adversaries, taking a prominent part on the Cyrilline side at the Council of *Ephesus (431). His surviving works include two sermons for *Christmas and the *Purification, which are early witnesses to the existence of these feasts.

THEODULF (*c.* 750–821), Bp. of Orleans. He was appointed bishop by *Charlemagne before 798 and took part in the trial of *Leo III in 800. After Charlemagne's death he was accused of conspiracy and deposed in 818.

A leading theologian, he wrote a treatise on the Holy Spirit, in which he defended the *Filioque, and another on Baptism. One of his hymns, the 'Gloria, laus, et honor' ('All glory, laud, and honour'), became the *Palm Sunday Processional in the W. Church. There are grounds for attributing to him the authorship of the '*Caroline Books'.

THEOGNOSTUS (d. *c.* 282), *Alexandrian ecclesiastical writer. He was head of the *Catechetical School, prob. succeeding *Dionysius. He elaborated a system of theology on *Origenist lines in his *Hypotyposes*, of which an account is preserved by *Photius.

THEOLOGIA CRUCIS (Lat., 'theology of the cross'). The name given by M. *Luther to the theological principle that our knowledge of the being of God must be derived from the study of Christ in His humiliation and the suffering He underwent on the cross. He opposed it to a *theologia gloriae* ('theology of glory') which would maintain that a true knowledge of God can be obtained from the study of nature.

THEOLOGIA GERMANICA. A late 14th-cent. mystical treatise apparently written by a priest of the *Teutonic Order. It counsels poverty of spirit and abandonment to God as the means of transformation by love into participation of the Divine nature.

THEOLOGICAL COLLEGES (Anglican). In these Colleges candidates receive their final preparation for ordination. There were various attempts before the 19th cent. to establish theological colleges, but Edinburgh Theological College, founded in 1810, is the oldest surviving theological college in the Anglican Communion. Later in the century colleges were opened in the majority of English dioceses, but in recent years many have closed or been amalgamated, and some have joined with colleges of other denominations.

THEOLOGICAL VIRTUES, The. *Faith, *hope, and *charity (or *love), which are grouped together by St. *Paul as the bases of the Christian life. They are contrasted with the natural or *cardinal virtues.

THEOLOGY, literally the 'science of God'. In its Christian sense it is the science of the Divinely revealed religious truths. Its theme is the Being and Nature of God and His creatures and the whole complex of the Divine dispensation from the *Fall of Adam to the *Redemption through Christ and its mediation to men by His Church, including the so-called natural truths of God, which are accessible to mere reason. Its purpose is to investigate the contents of belief by means of reason enlightened by faith and to promote its deeper understanding.

THEOPASCHITES, 'those who hold that God suffered'. A group of 6th-cent. *Monophysite theologians. At *Constantinople in 519 they defended the formula 'One of the Trinity was crucified'. This was rejected by the Patr. of Constantinople and (with some hesitation) by Pope *Hormisdas.

THEOPHANY. An appearance of God in visible form, temporary and not necessarily material.

THEOPHILANTHROPISTS. A *Deistic sect founded in France at the end of the 18th cent. The three articles of its creed were belief in God, virtue, and immortality. It was given by the Directory the use of 10 churches in Paris, but it soon lost ground when Catholicism was re-established by the *Concordat of 1801.

THEOPHILUS, St. (later 2nd cent.), Bp. of *Antioch and *Apologist. The purpose of his 'Apology' was to set before the pagan world the Christian idea of God and the superiority of the doctrine of *creation over the immoral myths of the Olympian religion. He was also the first theologian to use the word '*Triad' of the Godhead.

THEOPHILUS (d. 412), Patr. of *Alexandria from 385. In the early years of his patriarchate he took an active part in suppressing the remnants of paganism in the city. His later campaign against *Origenism was encouraged by jealousy of the see of *Constantinople.

THEOPHYLACT (11th cent.), Byzantine exegete. About 1078 he was made Abp. of Achrida in the country of the Bulgarians. He wrote a series of commentaries on several OT Books and the whole of the NT except Rev. They are marked by lucidity of thought and expression and closely follow the text, while at the same time insisting on practical morality.

THEOSOPHY. In its wider application the term denotes any intuitive knowledge of the Divine and as such covers a number of religious and philosophical systems akin to pantheism and natural mysticism. In a more restricted sense it is applied to the movement instigated by H. P. Blavatsky, who, with Col. H. C. Olcott, founded the Theosophical Society in New York in 1875. In 1882 Adyar (near Madras) became their headquarters. Theosophists believe in the transmigration of souls, the brotherhood of man irrespective of colour and creed, and complicated systems of psychology and cosmology; they deny both a personal God and personal immortality.

THEOTOKION. In the E. Church a stanza of liturgical hymnography addressed to the BVM.

THEOTOKOS, the 'God-bearer', a title of the BVM. The word was used by the Greek Fathers from *Origen onwards and became a popular term of devotion. In 429 it was attacked by the *Nestorians as incompatible with the full humanity of Christ. It was defended by St. *Cyril of Alexandria and upheld at the Councils of *Ephesus (431) and *Chalcedon (451). Its orthodoxy was then generally accepted.

THERAPEUTAE. A pre-Christian monastic community of Egyptian Jews described by *Philo. Nothing is known of their later history.

THERESA, St.; THÉRÈSE, St. See *Teresa of Ávila, St.; Teresa of Lisieux, St.*

THERMARION. In the E. Church a vessel for the warm water mixed with the wine after its consecration in the Eucharist and used in washing altars at their dedication.

THESSALONIANS, Epistles to the. These two NT Epistles were prob. written by St. *Paul at *Corinth c. 51 and are prob. the earliest of his letters. In the First Epistle he assures his converts that at the Second Coming of Christ those who have died in the Lord will rise first and then, together with the living, be united with Him; he declines to pronounce on the time and circumstances of

these events. The Second Epistle reminds the Thessalonians, who, believing in the immediately impending *Parousia, were neglecting their ordinary duties, that the apostasy and the 'Son of Perdition' must come first, and teaches that there is still something or someone 'that restraineth' (2: 6–7). This may refer to the Roman Empire under Claudius; in the traditional view it refers to a supernatural power such as St. *Michael.

The authenticity of the First Epistle is generally accepted. That of the Second is rejected by some scholars on the grounds of the alleged incompatibility of the eschatological teaching of the two Epistles and their different tone.

THESSALONICA. The modern Salonica in Macedonia, it was founded c. 315 B.C. Under the Romans it became the virtual capital of the province. In A.D. 50 or 51 St. *Paul visited the city and founded a Christian community (Acts 17). For his letters to the *Thessalonians, see the previous entry.

THEUDAS. The leader of an unsuccessful insurrection mentioned in a speech attributed to *Gamaliel in Acts 5: 36. *Josephus describes an insurrection by a leader of this name in A.D. 45 or 46, but there are chronological difficulties in reconciling the two references.

THIERRY OF CHARTRES (d. after 1151), philosopher and theologian. He taught at *Chartres and *Paris. He became Archdeacon and Chancellor of Chartres in 1141. Some time between 1151 and 1156 he retired to a monastery, and nothing further is known.

He was a leading exponent of the Platonist tendencies of the school of Chartres. In his *De Sex Dierum Operibus* he interpreted the Genesis account of creation acc. to *Plato's *Timaeus*, regarding the Divine form as the form of all things. In the work of creation he assigned the four *Aristotelian causes to the Persons of the Trinity, the Father being the efficient cause, the Son the formal, and the Holy Spirit—also identified with Plato's world-soul—the final cause, whereas Divinely created matter was the material cause.

THIRD ORDERS. Religious organizations affiliated usually to one of the *Mendicant Orders, and so called to distinguish them from the First and Second Orders of fully professed men and women respectively. They live either in the world, and are then usually called 'Tertiaries' (q.v.), or in community. The latter, or 'Regular Tertiaries', arose from the desire of numbers of 'Secular Tertiaries' to lead a community life; they are now all under vows and, in the case of nuns, are often as strictly enclosed as their Sisters of the Second Order. The most important Third Orders are those of the *Dominicans and *Franciscans. For 'Secular Tertiaries', see *Tertiary*.

THIRD ROME. A name used by Russian Christians for Moscow.

THIRLBY, THOMAS (1506?–70), successively Bp. of *Westminster (1540), *Norwich (1550), and *Ely (1554). In 1549 he opposed the First Prayer Book of *Edward VI and the Act of *Uniformity, but accepted them when passed. Under *Elizabeth I he refused to take the Oath of Supremacy and was deposed and imprisoned.

THIRLWALL, CONNOP (1797–1875), historian and Bp of *St. Davids from 1840. He learnt Welsh, restored Church life in his diocese, and took part in the ecclesiastical questions of his day in a liberal spirit. He supported the removal of the civil disabilities of the Jews (1848) and urged the disestablishment of the Church of *Ireland (1869).

THIRTY-NINE ARTICLES, The. The set of doctrinal formulas finally accepted by the C of E. The first text was issued by *Convocation in 1563; they received their final form in 1571. They are not a statement of Christian doctrine in the form of a creed; rather they are short summaries of dogmatic tenets, each dealing with some point raised in contemporary controversy. Various interpretations have been put on some of them. Since 1865 the clergy have been required to affirm only a general assent; a more particular subscription was previously required.

THIRTY YEARS WAR, The (1618–48). A series of religious and political wars fought in Central Europe. The causes included the decay of the *Holy Roman Empire and the continued religious unrest after the Peace of *Augsburg (1555). The Bohemian Protestants rebelled in 1618 and set up Frederick V of the Palatinate in opposition to the Emp. *Ferdinand II. They were defeated by the armies of the Catholic League. In 1623 war broke out again in Lower Saxony. After victories by the Imperial generals in 1626, the Peace of Lübeck was concluded in 1629. In the same year Ferdinand ordered the restitution of all ecclesiastical property appropriated since 1552; this edict provoked much opposition. In 1630 *Gustavus Adolphus of Sweden landed in Pomerania; he was encouraged by Card. *Richelieu, who was pursuing an anti-Habsburg policy. In 1632 Gustavus won the battle of Lützen, but was killed himself. The Imperial and Bavarian troops gained a decisive victory at Nördlingen (1634), which led to the Treaty of Prague between the Emperor and most of the Protestant estates (1635). The Swedes, however, continued to fight and were openly joined by France. The French position became increasingly advantageous and in 1644 negotiations were opened, leading to the Peace of *Westphalia (1648). By this the ecclesiastical state of the Empire was restored to what it had been in 1624, except for the secularization of much ecclesiastical property which was distributed among the Powers in compensation for their part in the war. The decrees of the Peace of Augsburg were reaffirmed and extended to the *Calvinists.

THOLUCK, FRIEDRICH AUGUST GOTTREU (1799–1877), German Protestant theologian. His influential work, *Die Lehre von der Sünde und dem Versöhner* (1823) did much to check the spread of Rationalism in Germany. He was a representative of the *Vermittlungstheologie (q.v.), combining personal piety with wide disregard for dogma.

THOMAS, St., Apostle. He is mentioned as one of the Twelve in all four Gospels. In Jn. he appears in three episodes, viz. offering to die with the Lord on the way to Bethany (11: 16), interrupting the Last Discourse with the question 'We know not whither thou goest, how can we know the way?' (14: 5), and doubting the Resurrection (20: 24–8). After Christ's appearance he confesses his faith in the words 'My Lord and my God' and is thus the first explicitly to confess His Divinity. Acc. to one tradition he evangelized the Parthians, acc. to another he preached in *India. See also the following entries.

THOMAS, Acts of. An apocryphal book recounting the missionary activities of the Apostle St. *Thomas. Gundaphorus, an Indian king, sent a merchant to Syria to obtain a skilled architect. The merchant met Jesus, who recommended Thomas; Thomas agreed to go back with him. Gundaphorus and many others were converted. Thomas was eventually killed for persuading Mygdonia to cease marriage relationships with her husband. The Acts contain four poems, including a famous 'Hymn to the Redeemer' or 'Hymn of the Pearl' (108–13). The work is *Gnostic in origin, dates from before the middle of the 3rd cent., and was prob. written in Syriac.

THOMAS, Apocalypse of. An apocryphal eschatological treatise, prob. written by a *Manichaean at the end of the 4th cent.

THOMAS, Gospel of. An apocryphal Gospel of which a *Coptic version was found at *Nag Hammadi in 1945–6. The Greek original perhaps dates from c. 150, the Coptic from c. 400. It professes to be the work of St. *Thomas. It is not, like the canonical Gospels, historical in form, but consists of a series of pithy sayings and parabolic discourses of Christ; some of them have points of contact with the sayings in '*Q'.

THOMAS, Infancy Gospel of. An apocryphal writing which professes to record miracles performed by Christ in His childhood. The alleged miracles are primarily displays of power, without theological point or moral justification.

THOMAS AQUINAS, St. (c. 1225–74), 'Doctor Angelicus', philosopher and theologian. Of noble birth, he was educated at the *Benedictine school at *Monte Cassino, being destined by his parents for the abbacy. Despite opposition, he joined the *Dominican Order in 1244. From 1245 to 1248 he was at *Paris, where he came under the influence of St. *Albertus Magnus; he went with him to *Cologne. In 1252 he returned to Paris. He was sent to Italy in 1259 and taught in various Dominican houses there until he was recalled to Paris in 1269. Here he combated the teaching of *Siger of Brabant. In 1272 he went to Naples to set up a Dominican school. He died on his way to the Council of *Lyons.

The extent of his writing is immense. His philosophy is largely embodied in commentaries on *Aristotle, and indeed it received its characteristic shape under the influence of his newly recovered works. Much of his theology and spirituality is contained in his Biblical commentaries. His work found its culmination in two *Summae*: the *Summa contra Gentiles*, designed as a text-book for missionaries, and the *Summa Theologica*, the highest achievement of medieval theological systematization, which was unfinished at the time of his death. Several propositions from his writings were condemned in 1277, but in 1278 the Dominican General Chapter officially imposed his teaching in the order, and the RC Church has accepted the substance of it as an authentic expression of doctrine.

Fundamental in his teaching is a sharp distinction between reason and faith. If in a large area reason is paramount, many fundamental Christian verities (the *Trinity, the *Incarnation) lie beyond its province. Such doctrines reach us through *revelation, embodied in Scripture and in the teaching of the Fathers. As their province is that of faith, where primacy belongs to the will, not the intellect, their acceptance by the believer is a matter of moral decision.

In his theory of knowledge, he accepts the Aristotelian maxim that, since all knowledge presupposes an essential likeness between the knower and the known and man's nature is corporeal as well as intellectual, cognition necessarily sets out from sense-perception. This belief gave his arguments for the existence of God their characteristic shape. Also running through his system are the Aristotelian antitheses of potency and act and of *matter and *form.

His theology was less original, but equally thoroughly elaborated. The Incarnation and the *Sacraments claimed his special attention. Against the *Franciscans he maintained that the Incarnation would not have taken place apart from the *Fall and that the BVM was not *immaculately conceived. He held that all *seven Sacraments were instituted by Christ, that the Eucharist was the highest of them all, and that as the ultimate purpose of *Orders was the Eucharist, the Priesthood was the highest Order and the Episcopate not a separate Order. For elaborating the doctrine of *transubstantiation he employed the Aristotelian philosophy of *substance and *accidents. He is said to have composed the Office for the newly instituted feast of *Corpus Christi, but there is some doubt in this matter.

THOMAS BECKET OF CANTERBURY, St.; THOMAS BRADWARDINE; THOMAS OF CANTILUPE, St. See *Becket, St. Thomas; Bradwardine, Thomas;* and *Cantilupe, St. Thomas de.*

THOMAS OF CELANO (*c.* 1190–1260), first biographer of St. *Francis. He wrote two lives, one in 1228 and the other in 1246-7, and the *Tractatus de Miraculis S. Francisci* in 1250–3; in modern times their historicity has been challenged. He also wrote the 'Legend' of St. *Clare and, according to an uncertain tradition, the *Dies Irae.*

THOMAS CHRISTIANS. See *Malabar Christians.*

THOMAS OF HEREFORD, St. See *Cantilupe, St. Thomas de.*

THOMAS À JESU (1564–1627), Spanish spiritual writer. Influenced by the works of St. *Teresa, Díaz Sánchez de Ávila entered the *Carmelite Order in 1587. He was called to Rome in 1607. His writings on missionary theory contributed to the foundation of the Congregation 'De *Propaganda Fide'. His works on mysticism present the teaching of St. Teresa in the form of *Scholastic treatises.

THOMAS À KEMPIS (*c.* 1380–1471), ascetical writer and probably the author of the '*Imitation of Christ'. Thomas Hemerken was born at Kempen, near Cologne, educated by the *Brethren of the Common Life, and in 1399 entered the house of the *Canons Regular at the Agnietenberg, near Zwolle (a daughter-house of *Windesheim), taking the habit in 1406. All his writings are pervaded by a devotional spirit.

THOMAS OF MARGA (9th cent.), *Nestorian historian. He was Bp. of Marga in Iraq and later Metropolitan of Beth-Garmai. His *Book of Governors*, written *c.* 840, is one of the main authorities for the early history of the Nestorian Church.

THOMAS MORE, St. See *More, St. Thomas.*

THOMISM. The systematized expression of the (esp. philosophical) doctrines of St. *Thomas Aquinas.

THOMPSON, FRANCIS (1859–1907), RC poet. He was intended for the priesthood but later unsuccessfully studied medicine. In 1885 he went to London and spent three years in almost complete destitution. His first volume of *Poems* (1893) includes 'The Hound of Heaven', a poem almost autobiographical in its arresting description of the pursuit of the soul by God. In *Sister Songs* (1895) and *New Poems* (1897) the asceticism of the mystic and a sacramental conception of nature are blended.

THORESBY, JOHN (d. 1373), Abp. of *York from 1351. He was Chancellor of England from 1349 to 1356 and guardian of the kingdom in 1355. It was mainly through his instrumentality that the old dispute as to the respective privileges of *Canterbury and York was settled.

THORN, Conference of (1645). A conference of Catholic, *Lutheran, and *Calvinist theologians convened on the proposal of the king of Poland to bring about religious reunion. No result was achieved.

THORNDIKE, HERBERT (1598–1672), Anglican theologian. He was ejected from his living in 1643 and from his fellowship of Trinity College, Cambridge, in 1646. In 1661 he became a Prebendary of *Westminster. His chief work is *An Epilogue to the Tragedy of the Church of England* (1659). In this he looks for a united Christendom on the basis of the first six *General Councils, conceding a certain superiority to the Pope with prescriptive rights over the W. Church.

THORVALDSEN, BERTEL (1770–1844), Danish sculptor. His most famous religious work is the monumental group of Christ and His Apostles in the Frue Kirke at Copenhagen; the figure of the Risen Christ, His hands extended in blessing, has often been imitated.

THREE CHAPTERS, The. Three subjects condemned by *Justinian in an edict of 543–4, viz. (1) the person and work of *Theodore of Mopsuestia; (2) the writings of *Theodoret against *Cyril of Alexandria; and (3) the letter of *Ibas of Edessa to Maris.

The E. patriarchs assented, but Pope *Vigilius at first refused to approve the edict on the ground that it opposed the decrees of the Council of *Chalcedon. After the Fifth General Council at *Constantinople in 553 had condemned the Three Chapters, the Pope accepted the Council's decision.

THREE CHILDREN, Song of the. See *Song of the Three Children*.

THREE DENOMINATIONS, The. A title applied to the *Presbyterian, *Congregational and *Baptist Churches. Their ministers in London formed an association for joint political action in 1727.

THREE HOURS' SERVICE, The. A service held on *Good Friday during the hours of the Lord's Passion from noon to 3 p.m. It usually consists of seven sermons on the *Seven Words from the Cross, interspersed with hymns and prayers.

THREE WITNESSES, The. See *Johannine Comma*.

THUNDERING LEGION, The. When in the Danubian campaigns of *Marcus Aurelius a sudden rainstorm saved the Roman army from drought and defeat in 172, Christians attributed this to the prayers of the Christian members of the 'Legio XII Fulminata'. The mistranslation 'thundering' for 'thunderstruck' led to an elaboration that a thunderbolt had destroyed the enemy.

THURIBLE. A metal vessel for the ceremonial burning of *incense. The container is usually suspended on chains from which it can be swung during the incensation.

THURIFER. A person appointed to carry the *thurible at religious ceremonies and services.

THURNEYSEN, EDUARD (1888–1974), Swiss Protestant theologian. From 1913 he was intimately associated with K. *Barth, and he contributed to the elaboration of *Dialectical Theology; he was esp. concerned with its pastoral and social applications.

THURSDAY, Holy or **Maundy**. See *Maundy Thursday*.

THYATIRA, a city in N. Lydia. It is one of the 'Seven Churches' addressed in Rev. (2: 18–29); here it is upbraided for tolerating a 'Jezebel' who teaches Christians 'to commit fornication and to eat things sacrificed to idols' (2: 20). In the 3rd cent. it was a stronghold of *Montanism.

TIARA, papal head-dress. It attained its present shape, like a beehive, in the 15th cent. Until recently, it was worn by, or carried in front of, the Pope at important non-liturgical functions, such as papal processions, and at solemn acts of jurisdiction, such as dogmatic definitions.

TIELE, CORNELIS PETRUS (1830–1902), Dutch theologian. As professor of religious history at *Leyden university (1877–1901), he exercised great influence on the development of the study of comparative religion.

TIKHON (1866–1925), Basil Ivanovitch Belavin, the first Patriarch of the *Russian Church since 1700. In 1917 he became Metropolitan of Moscow, and later in the year the Panrussian Council elected him Patriarch. His courage and humility gave him moral authority. In 1919 he anathematized all who persecuted the Church and he imposed neutrality on the clergy in the civil war. He resisted the State confiscation of Church property in the famine of 1921–2 and was placed under arrest. In 1923 he signed a declaration professing loyalty to the Soviet Government; he was then allowed to live in a monastery in Moscow and to officiate in the capital.

TIKHON OF ZADONSK, St. (1724–83), Russian spiritual writer. In 1761 he was appointed assistant bishop in the Novgorod diocese, and in 1763 Bp. of Voronezh. He resigned in 1767, settling at the Zadonsk monastery in central Russia in 1769. He was much influenced by the West.

TILLEMONT, LOUIS SÉBASTIEN LE NAIN DE (1637–98), French Church historian. His *Mémoires pour servir à l'histoire ecclésiastique des six premiers siècles* (16 vols., 1693–1712) is a work of great erudition, tracing the history of Christianity to the year 513.

TILLICH, PAUL (1886–1965), Protestant theologian. He held university positions in

Germany, but had to leave the country in 1933. He settled in the U.S.A., and was a professor in turn at the *Union Theological Seminary, New York, at Harvard, and at Chicago.

Tillich was a prolific writer and exercised great influence. His aim was to bridge the gap between Christian faith and modern culture. To do this he employed the 'method of correlation', acc. to which the content of the Christian revelation is stated as answering the questions arising out of the cultural situation. This situation was interpreted by Tillich in terms of *existentialism, ontology, and Jungian psychology. Prob. the most important of his works was his *Systematic Theology* (1951–64).

TILLOTSON, JOHN (1630–94), Abp. of *Canterbury from 1691. He attended the *Savoy Conference (1661) as a watcher on the Nonconformist side. In 1689 he was made Dean of *St. Paul's. His archiepiscopate was undistinguished. His policy was based on dislike of the RC Church and a desire to include all Protestant dissenters, except *Unitarians, within the C of E.

TIMOTHY, St. St. *Paul's companion on his Second Missionary Journey and later one of his most intimate friends. He was entrusted by Paul with missions to *Thessalonica (1 Thess. 3: 2) and to *Corinth (1 Cor. 4: 17) and became his representative at *Ephesus (1 Tim 1: 3); acc. to *Eusebius he was the first bishop of that city. He is said to have been martyred in 97, when he opposed the festivities of Diana. See also the next entry.

TIMOTHY AND TITUS, Epistles to. The term 'Pastoral Epistles', under which these three NT Epistles attributed to St. *Paul are generally known, dates from the 18th cent. The chief subjects dealt with are the appointment and duties of Church ministers, and certain doctrinal difficulties. They shed valuable light on contemporary Church organization and discipline, which they show still in a fluctuating state.

Since the early 19th cent. the authenticity of the Pastorals has frequently been denied by NT critics on the grounds that they cannot be fitted into the framework of Paul's life as known from Acts, and that their vocabulary is different from that of the other Pauline letters. On the other hand, the existence of Pauline elements is so clear that some have suggested that a number of genuine Pauline fragments formed the basis on which a later editor worked, prob. at the beginning of the 2nd cent.

TIMOTHY (d. 517), Patr. of *Constantinople from 511. After some hesitation he defended *Monophysite doctrine, and at a synod in 515 he condemned the *Chalcedonian teaching. Introduction of the regular use of the *Nicene Creed in the Liturgy at Constantinople is ascribed to him.

TIMOTHY AELURUS (d. 477), *Monophysite Patr. of *Alexandria. He became patriarch in 457, but being unacceptable to the majority of bishops he was banished by the Emp. Leo I in 460. In exile he propagated Monophysitism, but also anathematized *Eutyches. He was recalled to Alexandria by the Emp. Basiliscus in 475 and died before another decree of banishment by the Emp. *Zeno could be carried out.

TINDAL, MATTHEW (1655–1733), a leading *Deist. His most important work, *Christianity as Old as the Creation* (1730) sought to show that the religion of nature is common to all creeds.

TINDAL, W. See *Tyndale, W.*

TINTERN ABBEY, in the Wye valley. It was founded in 1131 for *Cistercian monks from the Abbey of L'Aumône. The magnificent abbey church was built in the 13th cent. The ruins inspired a poem of W. *Wordsworth.

TIPPET. A broad black scarf worn by Anglican clergy in choir over the *surplice. It evolved, it seems, from the long ends of the academic hood which hung down from the shoulders in front, and was not originally confined to the clergy.

TISCHENDORF, CONSTANTIN (1815–1874), NT textual critic. From 1859 he was professor of theology at Leipzig. He visited many libraries in search of MSS., the most famous of his finds being the *Codex Sinaiticus (q.v.). Between 1841 and 1869 he published eight critical editions of the Gk. NT with full *critical apparatus of the variant readings; the last edition remains a standard work of reference.

TISSOT, JAMES JOSEPH JACQUES (1836–1902), French Bible illustrator. He was a painter of fashionable women. After an experience of conversion he devoted himself to illustrating the life of Christ. In his *Vie de Notre-Seigneur Jésus-Christ* (1896) he depicted the scenes of the Gospel in a fresh and unconventional style. His illustrations of the OT are inferior in quality.

TITHES. The clergy were maintained in early times by receiving one quarter of the offerings of the laity, the remaining three quarters going to the upkeep of the fabric of the church, the relief of the poor, and the bishop. This system was superseded by tithes, the payment of a tenth part of all the produce of the land. As the parochial system developed, the tithes of each parish were allotted to its own 'parson' and this allocation became a general law, enforced in England in 900.

Tithes came to be divided into the 'great tithes', those of the main crops (wheat, oats, &c.), and 'small', those of minor produce (lambs, chickens, &c.). An incumbent entitled to the whole tithes of a parish was termed a '*rector'. The tithes of some parishes came to be *appropriated to monasteries or *impropriated to lay proprietors or corporations, who were then bound to provide and endow a clergyman to reside in the parish and perform the ecclesiastical duties. The endowment of such a clergyman, called the '*vicar', usually took the form of part of the *glebe, together with the small tithes, which were difficult to collect.

Modern legislation has practically abolished tithe as a State land tax in England. While some have held that the payment of tithe is demanded by Divine law, being specifically ordered in the OT and implied in the NT, others have argued that it is for the Church to decide about methods of payment and that the Divine law is not broken if tithes as such are abolished, provided that there are offerings sufficient to maintain the practice of religion.

TITIAN (*c.* 1476–1576), Tiziano Vecellio or Vecelli, Venetian painter. His *Tribute Money* (*c.* 1515) is famous for the face of Christ, blending sweetness with majesty. The *Assumption* (Venice) is a monumental work of high craftsmanship; *Ecce Homo* and the *Crowning with Thorns* (Louvre) are fraught with tragic emotion.

TITLE. At least since the 3rd cent. the term has been used to designate the older churches of Rome. As several clergy were attached to each *titulus*, all of whom were provided with revenues for their maintenance, allocation to a 'title' at *ordination came to mean the provision of maintenance. Hence the term has acquired the general sense of a definite spiritual charge or office with guarantee of maintenance, without which a bishop may not ordinarily ordain a man unless he is prepared personally to support him until he can prefer him to a 'living'.

TITUS, St. A disciple of St. *Paul. He appears on the journey to the Apostles' Council at *Jerusalem (Gal. 2: 1); he went on missions to *Corinth (2 Cor. 8: 6) and was left in Crete to organize the Church (Tit. 1: 5). He is believed later to have become its first bishop. For the Epistle to Titus, see *Timothy and Titus, Epistles to*.

TITUS (4th cent.), Bp. of Bostra. He wrote a long treatise against the *Manichaeans. In the first part he gives the Christian solution to the problem of evil based on the ideas of Divine Providence and human free will; in the second he defends the OT and denounces the Manichaean falsifications of the NT.

TOBIT, Book of. This Book of the *Apocrypha was written in Aramaic or Hebrew, prob. *c.* 200 B.C. It relates the story of Tobit, a pious Jew of the captivity of Nineveh, who became poor and blind. He prayed and, remembering a debt due from a friend in Media, he sent his son Tobias there with a companion who later revealed himself as the angel *Raphael. With the angel's assistance Tobias rescued a kinswoman from the power of a demon and married her. Raphael recovered the debt and then enabled Tobias to heal Tobit of his blindness.

TOC H. A Christian fellowship which originated in Talbot House, a soldiers' club opened in Belgium in 1915 under the Rev. P. T. B. Clayton and named after Lt. Gilbert Talbot, son of E. S. *Talbot. In 1920 Toc H (the army signallers' method of pronouncing T H) was refounded in London and spread rapidly. The close fellowship finds its outlet in a variety of Christian social service.

TOKEN, Communion. See *Communion Tokens*.

TOLAND, JOHN (1670–1722), *Deistical writer. In *Christianity not Mysterious* (1696) he asserts that neither God Himself nor His revelation is above the comprehension of human reason, and he attributes the mystery of Christianity to the intrusion of pagan conceptions and the machinations of priestcraft. The book aroused great indignation. Further scandal was caused by a passage in his *Life of Milton* (1698), which was believed to cast doubt upon the authenticity of the NT; in his reply Toland said that he was referring to the apocryphal writings. Though not an original thinker, Toland was influential.

TOLEDO, Councils of. The many Councils held at Toledo include the 'First' (400), directed against *Priscillianism; the 'Third' (589), when *Recared renounced *Arianism; and the 'Fourth' (633), which issued important liturgical regulations.

TOLEDO, Rite of. Another name for the *Mozarabic Rite (q.v.), which is still used in one chapel of Toledo cathedral.

TOLERATI (Lat., 'tolerated persons'). The technical name for those *excommunicated persons with whom the faithful are allowed to have intercourse of a non-religious kind.

TOLERATION. Religious toleration is the leaving undisturbed of those whose faith and practice are other than one's own. It may arise from respect for the rights of another person to freedom of belief, or from indifference.

Christianity, with its claim to be the only true religion, is dogmatically intolerant. Dissent ('heresy') within its ranks has repeatedly been anathematized. In the Middle Ages, owing to the close association of Church and State, catholic and citizen became synonymous terms, and the State carried out sentences against heretics. The Renaissance, with its religious indifference, and the Reformation, by its revolt against the authority of the Papacy, established the conditions for the future development of toleration. The Reformers, however, were intolerant of dissentients, and the Peace of *Augsburg (1555) recognized one religion in a State to the exclusion of all others.

The most notable early instances of practical toleration were the colonies of Maryland, founded in 1632 for persecuted Catholics, which also offered asylum to Protestants, and Rhode Island, founded by Roger *Williams (q.v.). In England toleration was demanded, esp. by the *Baptists, *Congregationalists, and *Quakers. Except for RCs and *Unitarians, it was virtually granted in the *Toleration Act of 1689. In the 19th cent. it became the policy of most European governments. The RC Church remained authoritarian until recent years.

TOLERATION, Edict of (313). See *Milan, Edict of.*

TOLERATION ACT (1689). This Act granted freedom of worship to dissenters on certain conditions, but excluded RCs and *Unitarians.

TOLSTOY, LEO (1828–1910), Russian novelist and social reformer. After the publication of his two most famous novels, *War and Peace* (1864–9) and *Anna Karenina* (1873–7), he renounced literary ambition, though he continued to write on moral and religious subjects. He became critical of the formalism of the Orthodox Church, which excommunicated him in 1901. He tried to live in great simplicity, renouncing his property and the happiness of family life. His religious teaching in its latest phase claimed to be a following of the Gospel with the miraculous and other irrelevancies set aside: the key was to be found in the *Sermon on the Mount. He rejected the divinity of Christ and believed that men's greatest good consisted in loving one another.

TOME OF DAMASUS, The. A collection of 24 canons endorsed by a Roman synod (prob. in 382) and subsequently sent by Pope *Damasus to Paulinus, then recognized in Rome as the legitimate Bp. of *Antioch. Twenty-three of them are dogmatic, anathematizing the main Trinitarian and Christological heresies of the 4th cent. The ninth, condemning the *translation of bishops, was directed against *Melitius of Antioch.

TOME OF LEO, The. The letter sent by *Leo I to *Flavian, Patr. of *Constantinople, on 13 June 449. It expounds the Christological doctrine of the Latin Church, and was directed esp. against *Eutyches. It was given formal authority at the Council of *Chalcedon (451).

TOMMASI, Bl. GIUSEPPE MARIA (1649–1713), liturgical scholar. The eldest son of the Duke of Palma, he resigned his claims as heir and entered the *Theatine Order. Of his numerous publications, the editions of the ancient *sacramentaries and *missals are esp. valuable.

TONGUES, Gift of. See *Glossolalia* and *Pentecostalism*.

TONSURE. The shaving of all or part of the head, traditionally a distinctive feature of monks and clerics in the RC Church. It has no place in the 1972 Rite of Admission to the *Clerical State; monks now follow various customs in the matter.

TOPLADY, AUGUSTUS MONTAGUE (1740–78), Anglican divine and hymn-writer. He adopted extreme *Calvinist opinions in 1758; in *The Historic Proof of the Doctrinal Calvinism of the Church of England* (1774) he developed his subject from the *Apostolic Fathers onwards. He is chiefly remembered for his hymns, which include 'Rock of Ages'.

TORAH. The English equivalent of a Hebrew word usually translated 'Law'. It was pre-eminently the function of the priests to give 'torah' or instruction on the Will of God, and the word came also to be used of written collections of such priestly decisions, as well as of the *Pentateuch.

TORGAU ARTICLES, The. A memorandum summarizing the disciplinary and cere-monial demands of M. *Luther, P. *Melanchthon, J. *Bugenhagen, and J. *Jonas which was handed to the Diet of *Augsburg (1530).

TORQUEMADA, JUAN DE (1388–1468), Spanish *Dominican theologian. In 1433 he became Papal theologian at the Council of *Basle and he took an active part in the negotiations with the Bohemians and the Greeks. He was created cardinal in 1439, and for the rest of his life had a large share in ecclesiastical Papal policy. He wrote on canon law and on the nature of the Church.

TORQUEMADA, TOMÁS DE (1420–98), Spanish Grand Inquisitor. He entered the *Dominican Order at an early age. He was confessor to *Ferdinand and *Isabella of Spain. In 1478 they were allowed by *Sixtus IV to establish the *Inquisition in Spain, and in 1483 Torquemada became Grand Inquisitor. He set up tribunals in various cities and laid down directions for the guidance of Inquisitors. The number of burnings during his term of office, formerly exaggerated, is now given as about 2,000.

TOSEFTA (Heb., 'supplement'). A collection of early Jewish traditions of the same character as, and contemporary with, the *Mishnah, but not incorporated in it.

TOTAL DEPRAVITY. A term used, esp. in *Calvinism, to express the extreme wretchedness of man's condition as the result of the *Fall.

TOTAL IMMERSION. See *Submersion*.

TOUCHING FOR THE KING'S EVIL. See *King's Evil, Touching for the*.

TRACT (liturgical). A chant formerly sung or recited on certain penitential days in place of the *Alleluia after the *Gradual at Mass. It was suppressed in 1969.

TRACT (propagandist). A pamphlet, usually with a religious or moral purpose. The religious controversies of the 16th and 17th cents. stimulated the production of tracts, e.g. the *Marprelate Tracts. On the *Tracts for the Times*, see the following entry.

TRACTARIANISM. A name for the earlier stages of the *Oxford Movement, derived from the *Tracts for the Times* (1833–41) issued under its aegis. They secured a wide circulation and their influence was large. Their form gradually changed from brief leaflets to learned treatises. The storm provoked by J. H. *Newman's *Tract No. 90* (on the *Thirty-Nine Articles) brought the series to a close. Other authors included E. B. *Pusey and J. *Keble.

TRACTATUS ORIGENIS (Lat., 'Trac-tates of Origen'). A collection of homilies formerly ascribed to *Origen; they are prob. the work of *Gregory, Bp. of Elvira.

TRACTORIA. Originally a 'letter of sum-mons', the word was also applied to letters containing the decisions of Councils.

TRADITIO-HISTORICAL CRITICISM.
In Biblical criticism, the study of the development of texts and motifs (often with particular reference to oral transmission), the circumstances in the life of the community in which they were created and its cultural background.

TRADITIO SYMBOLI (Lat., the 'delivery' or 'handing over of the Creed'). In the early Church candidates for *Baptism were subjected to a long course of instruction; the latter part of this consisted of explanations of the Creed, known as the 'delivery' or *traditio*, by which the candidates 'received the Creed' into their own keeping. At their Baptism they were required to recite and profess the Creed, thus 'returning it' (*redditio symboli*) to the presiding bishop. The ceremony has been restored in the 1972 RC Order for Adult Baptism.

TRADITION. In the early Christian Fathers tradition means the revelation made by God and delivered by Him to His people through the prophets and apostles. It denotes something 'handed over', not something 'handed down'. From the 3rd cent. it was sometimes expressly identified with the Gospel record contained in Scripture.

In a more modern sense tradition means the continuous stream of explanation and elucidation of the primitive faith, illustrating the way in which Christianity has been presented and understood in past ages. It is the accumulated wisdom of the past. In the Reformation period the relation of unwritten tradition and Scripture became a matter of controversy between Protestants and Catholics. As against the Protestant belief in the sole sufficiency of the Bible, the Council of *Trent appeared to lay down that Scripture and tradition were to be received as of equal authority. The Second *Vatican Council minimized the distinction.

TRADITION OF THE INSTRUMENTS.
See *Instruments, Tradition of the*.

TRADITIONALISM. In its strict sense, a theory proposed by a group of 19th-cent. RC thinkers, acc. to whom all metaphysical, moral, and religious knowledge is based on a primitive revelation of God to man handed down in an unbroken tradition. Denying to human reason the power of attaining by itself to any truths, it makes an act of faith in a

revealed tradition the origin of all knowledge. It was condemned in a number of decrees and ruled out at the First *Vatican Council (1870).

The term is used less strictly by liberal theologians of what they consider unduly conservative beliefs.

TRADITORS. The name given in Africa in early times to Christians who had surrendered the Scriptures when their possession was forbidden in the persecution of *Diocletian.

TRADUCIANISM. The theory that the human soul is transmitted by parents to their children. The term is sometimes restricted to the crudely materialistic view that this happens in the physical act of generation. Though Traducianism was advocated by some of the Fathers to explain *original sin, *Creationism came to be generally accepted in the Middle Ages.

TRAHERNE, THOMAS (*c.* 1636–74), Anglican divine and poet. He is the least orthodox of the *Metaphysical poets, the elements of sin and suffering being largely excluded from his optimistic conception of experience. His poetry, which is remarkable for a penetrating sense of the glory of nature and childhood, is pantheistic in feeling. His poems were not published until 1903; they were followed in 1908 by *Centuries of Meditations*, reflections on ethics and religion.

TRANSENNA. In ecclesiastical architecture, a wall, usually of marble, pierced with holes in a regular pattern. Transennae were often used to surround the tomb of a martyr.

TRANSFIGURATION, The. The appearing of the Lord in glory during His earthly life, related in the Synoptic Gospels (Mt. 17: 1–13; Mk. 9: 2–13, and Lk. 9: 28–36). This vision of Christ, transfigured, with *Moses and *Elijah, was witnessed by Sts. *Peter, *James, and *John. It is described by the Evangelists as a historical event. The Feast of the Transfiguration, observed on 6 Aug., originated in the East.

TRANSLATION. In ecclesiastical usage: (1) the transference of the relics of a saint either from their original place of burial into an altar tomb or shrine or from one shrine to another; (2) the transference to a different day of a feast when a particular season (e.g. *Holy Week) prohibits its observance, or when a feast of higher rank occurs on the same day; (3) the transference of a cleric from one ecclesiastical office to another, esp. of a bishop from one diocese to another.

TRANSMIGRATION OF SOULS. See *Metempsychosis*.

TRANSUBSTANTIATION. In the theology of the *Eucharist, the conversion of the whole substance of the bread and wine into the whole substance of the Body and Blood of Christ, only the *accidents (i.e. the appearance of the bread and wine) remaining. Belief in transubstantiation was defined as *de fide* at the Fourth *Lateran Council in 1215; the elaboration of the doctrine found its classic formulation in the teaching of St. *Thomas Aquinas.

TRAPPISTS. The popular name for the main branch of the *Cistercians of the Strict Observance. The reform was introduced to *La Trappe in 1662 by A. J. Le B. de *Rancé, who added austerities of his own to the existing reformed rules. His constitutions, meant for domestic use, were adopted by other houses. Expelled at the time of the French Revolution, the community of La Trappe kept together until they could return in 1817. Rancé's prescriptions, somewhat stiffened, became the standard rule for most new or revived houses of the Strict Observance.

TRAVERS, WALTER (c. 1548–1635), *Puritan divine. In 1594 he became the first Provost of *Trinity College, Dublin. His main work, *Ecclesiasticae Disciplinae et Anglicanae Ecclesiae ab illa Aberrationis plena e verbo Dei et dilucida Explicatio* (1574), in which he defended the *Presbyterian form of Church government as of Dominical institution, exercised a determinative influence on the policy of the Puritan Reformers.

TRAVERSARI, AMBROGIO (c. 1386–1439), Italian humanist. He entered the *Camaldolese Order in 1400 and in 1431 became its General. Fired by the possession of a splendid collection of Greek patristic MSS., he translated many of the Greek Fathers into Latin. He also fostered movements

for reunion with the E. Church.

TREACLE BIBLE, The. A popular name for the '*Great Bible' (1539), from its rendering of Jer. 8: 22: 'There is no more *triacle* [AV: 'balm'] in Gilead'.

TRE FONTANE. The traditional site of St. *Paul's martyrdom, some 3 miles south of Rome. Acc. to legend, his head, on being severed from his body, rebounded from the ground at three points, from which issued the three springs which give the place its name.

TREGELLES, SAMUEL PRIDEAUX (1813–75), Biblical scholar. In 1838 he formed a design for a critical text of the NT which should replace the '*textus receptus'; he travelled extensively collating Gk. MSS. His NT (apart from Rev.) appeared in 1870.

TREMELLIUS, JOHN IMMANUEL (1510–80), Hebrew scholar. The son of a Jew, he was converted to Catholicism in 1540; in 1541 *Peter Martyr persuaded him to become a Protestant. He was King's Reader at Cambridge from 1549 to 1553. His main work was his translation of the OT and NT into Latin from Hebrew and Syriac respectively.

TRENCH, RICHARD CHENEVIX (1807–86), Abp. of *Dublin from 1863 to 1884. He strongly opposed W. E. *Gladstone's proposals for disestablishing the Church of *Ireland. His books on the *Parables (1841) and *Miracles (1846) created fresh interest in the Gospels in some quarters.

TRENT, Council of (1545–63). Reckoned by RCs as the 19th *Oecumenical Council, it embodied the ideals of the *Counter-Reformation and established a solid base for the renewal of discipline and spiritual life in the RC Church. The spread of Protestantism and the need for moral and administrative reforms had led to widespread demands for a General Council. Summoned by *Paul III in 1537, it eventually met at Trent in 1545.

Period I (1545–7). The Council reaffirmed the *Nicene Creed as the basis of faith; it upheld the validity of Scripture and *tradition as sources of religious truth, and also the sole authority of the Church to interpret the Bible; and it defined the theology of the *Sacraments in general. Its decrees on

*Original Sin and on *Justification and *Merit struck at the root of the Protestant system.

Period II (1551–2). Recalled by *Julius III, the Council reached important decisions on the *Eucharist, on *Penance, and on Extreme *Unction. *Transubstantiation was affirmed and the *Lutheran, *Calvinist, and *Zwinglian Eucharistic doctrines were repudiated. A revolt of the princes against *Charles V led to the Council's suspension.

Period III (1562–3). When the Council reassembled under *Pius IV, all hope of conciliating the Protestants had gone. The doctrine of *concomitance was affirmed, with the denial of the *chalice to the laity, and there were various definitions on the sacrificial character of the Mass. Other decrees dealt with *Orders and *Matrimony, established *seminaries in each diocese, and regulated the appointment of bishops. Various works recommended or initiated by the Council were handed over to the Pope for completion. These included the revision of the *Vulgate, publication of the *Catechism of the Council of Trent, and reform of the *Breviary.

TRENTAL. A set of 30 *Requiem Masses for the repose of a soul, whether said on a single or on successive days.

TRIAD. A word first used of the *Trinity in the Godhead by *Theophilus of Antioch.

TRIDENTINE. Having reference to the Council of *Trent.

TRIDUUM SACRUM (Lat., 'the sacred three days'). The last three days of *Holy Week, i.e. *Maundy Thursday, *Good Friday, and *Holy Saturday.

TRIERS, The. A body of commissioners appointed by O. *Cromwell under an Act of 1654 to approve preachers and lecturers before their admission to benefices.

TRIMMER, SARAH (1741–1810), authoress. She interested herself in the establishment of *Sunday Schools. Her Abridgements of the OT and NT (both 1793) were designed as text-books for charity schools. *The History of the Robins* (1786) was long a favourite children's book for the better classes.

TRINITARIAN. In modern usage, a person who believes in the doctrine of the *Trinity, as contrasted with a *Unitarian.

TRINITARIANS (Order of the Most Holy Trinity). The order was founded in 1198 by St. *John of Matha and St. Felix of Valois (d. 1212); its members are sometimes called 'Mathurins'. They devoted themselves esp. to the ransoming of captives. In 1596 a reform was started in Spain; these Barefooted Trinitarians alone survive and engage in education, nursing, and pastoral work.

TRINITY, Doctrine of the. The central Christian dogma that the One God exists in Three Persons (Father, Son, and Holy Spirit) and one substance. It is a mystery in the strict sense, in that it can neither be known by reason apart from revelation, nor demonstrated by reason after it has been revealed, but it is not incompatible with the principles of rational thought.

Though the word 'Trinity', in its Greek form τριάς, was first used by *Theophilus of Antioch (c. A.D. 180), the concept is held to be foreshadowed in various OT texts and to be explicitly taught in some passages of the NT, esp. in the Baptismal formula of Mt. 28: 19 and by the wording of 1 Pet. 1: 2 and 2 Cor. 13: 14. In the early Church the doctrine was embodied in creeds and doxologies. Where it was elaborated, the language was indefinite and not always free from *subordinationism. At the Councils of *Nicaea (325) and *Constantinople (381) the dogma was defined in the face of heresies. Against *Sabellianism the real distinction, and against *Arianism and *Macedonianism the equality and co-eternity, of the Three Persons were affirmed. The Persons differ only in origin, in that the Father is ungenerated, the Son is generated by the Father, and the Holy Spirit proceeds from the Father through the Son.

In the W. the doctrine developed somewhat differently. Latin theologians started, not from the difference of the Persons, as did many of the Greeks, but from the unity of the substance. The Procession of the Holy Spirit was attributed equally to the Father and to the Son, and so here the Trinitarian symbol was not a line (as in the E.), but a triangle. The generation of the Son was compared to an act of thinking on the part of the Father, and the Holy Spirit explained as the mutual love of the Father and the Son.

TRINITY COLLEGE, DUBLIN. The (one) college in the university of *Dublin, founded in 1591. Membership was long confined to Anglicans, but religious tests were abolished in 1873.

TRINITY SUNDAY. The first Sunday after *Pentecost or *Whitsun. Its observance as a celebration embracing God in all Three Persons was universally enjoined in the W. in 1334. In the *Sarum Missal and in the BCP Sundays are reckoned after Trinity and not after Pentecost as was usual in the Roman rite until 1969.

TRIODION. In the E. rite a liturgical book containing the variable parts of the services from the 4th Sunday before Lent until the Saturday before Easter.

TRIPLE CANDLESTICK. In the W. rite until 1955 a triple candlestick was used in the *Paschal Vigil Service to hold the three candles which were successively lit during the procession to the altar. In the E. Church a triple candlestick is used for episcopal blessings.

TRISAGION. (Gk., 'thrice holy'). The refrain 'Holy God, Holy and mighty, Holy and immortal, have mercy upon us'. It is a characteristic feature of Orthodox worship, chanted at most services. In the Roman rite it is sung as part of the *Reproaches on Good Friday.

TRITHEISM. The heretical teaching about the *Trinity which denies the unity of substance in the Three Divine Persons. The name is used esp. of the teaching of a group of 6th-cent. *Monophysites, incl. John Philoponus, the commentator on *Aristotle. By his identification of person and nature, Philoponus was led to affirm three Divine substances in the Trinity. Various medieval philosophers were accused of tritheism.

TRITHEMIUS, JOHANNES (1462–1516), abbot of Sponheim (W. Germany) from 1483 to 1506. He rapidly brought about the reform of the monastery, collecting a library of MSS. which made it among the most famous in Europe.

TRITO-ISAIAH. The last eleven chapters of Isaiah (56–66) or the author(s) of them.

TRIUMPHANT, The Church. The body of Christians in heaven.

TRIVIUM. The medieval name for grammar, rhetoric, and dialectic, which constituted the inferior group of the *Seven Liberal Arts.

TROELTSCH, ERNST (1865–1923), theologian and philosopher. He held professorships at Heidelberg (1894–1915) and then at Berlin. He was important for his examination of the place of religion in society.

TROPARION. A generic term used in the E. Church for a stanza of religious poetry.

TROPE. In the W. Church a short series of words added to amplify or embellish the text of the Mass or Breviary Office and sung by the choir. Tropes lost popularity in the 13th cent. and gradually went out of use.

TROPHIMUS, St. (1) A Gentile disciple who accompanied St. *Paul on part of his Third Missionary Journey and to *Jerusalem, where rumours of his introduction into the *Temple were the chief ground for a riot (Acts 21: 29). (2) The first Bp. of Arles.

TRUCE OF GOD. In medieval times, a suspension of hostilities ordered by the Church on certain days and during some seasons, e.g. in *Lent.

TRULLAN SYNOD. The synod of E. bishops held in 692 to pass disciplinary canons to complete the work of the Fifth (553) and Sixth (680) General Councils (hence its other name of 'Quinisext' or Fifth–Sixth Council). It sat in the domed room ('trullus') of the Emp. Justinian II's palace at *Constantinople. Its decrees were rejected by the Pope.

TRURO. The Anglican diocese of Truro, covering Cornwall, was created in 1877. In Anglo-Saxon times the Cornish Church had been independent; in 931 it was finally incorporated in the English Church and Cornwall became an English diocese. In 1027 it was annexed to the see of *Crediton and in 1050 the see of the united diocese was fixed at *Exeter.

TÜBINGEN. The university, founded in 1477, became a centre of *Lutheran orthodoxy when Württemberg was made Protestant by Duke Ulrich in 1534–5. The 18th-cent. 'Tübingen School' of theology was characterized by a 'Biblical Supranaturalism', which put the guarantee of Christ and the Apostles in the place of the orthodox Protestant doctrine of the inspiration of Scripture and regarded the Bible as the exclusive source and law book of Christianity, from which the tenets of the faith were to be derived by deductive methods. In the 19th cent. another school of theology was founded by F. C. *Baur (see *Tübingen School*). A Catholic faculty of theology, which became important, was opened in 1817; it has been characterized by its emphasis on the need to relate modern thought to the data of faith.

TÜBINGEN SCHOOL. A school of German NT theologians founded by F. C. *Baur. It tried to apply G. W. F. *Hegel's conception of development to primitive Christianity: the early Church was divided into 'Petrinists' (Jewish Christians) and 'Paulinists' (Gentile Christians), the cleavage between them being healed only in the later 2nd cent. ('Catholicism'). Most NT Books were regarded as a product of the 2nd-cent. synthesis and therefore as of practically no historical value for the period to which they refer. The influence of the school was at its peak in the 1840s; its position has been generally abandoned.

TUCKNEY, ANTHONY (1599–1670), *Puritan divine. In the *Westminster Assembly as chairman of committee he took a leading part in drawing up its doctrinal formularies. He held high academic office at Cambridge until the *Restoration.

TULCAN BISHOPS (Gaelic *tulachan*, 'little hillock'). A term contemptuously applied to the titular bishops introduced by the Scottish *Presbyterians after the Covenant of Leith (1572).

TULLOCH, JOHN (1823–86), Scottish theologian. From *c.* 1875 he was the most prominent member of the Church of Scotland and in 1878 he was elected *Moderator. He tried to awaken a spirit of liberal orthodoxy.

TUNICLE. In the W. Church the outer liturgical garment of the *subdeacon. It seems to have developed from the ordinary overcoat of the later Roman Empire. It became obsolete with the suppression of the office of subdeacon in the RC Church.

TUNKERS, also known as Dunkers and as German Baptists, and officially called the 'Church of the Brethren'. They originated in Germany in 1708 but were compelled by persecution to emigrate to America (1719–29). They reject infant Baptism, insist on total immersion, accompany the Lord's Supper with an *agape, and refuse to take oaths or bear arms.

TUNSTALL, CUTHBERT (1474–1559), Bp. of London (1522–30) and then of *Durham. In the divorce of *Henry VIII he was one of the counsel of the Queen. In the following years he was sympathetic to Catholic doctrine, but lacked strength of purpose, first opposing the Royal Supremacy and then accepting it. Under *Edward VI his position became increasingly difficult and he was deprived of his bishopric in 1552; he was reinstated under *Mary in 1554. On *Elizabeth I's accession he refused to take the Oath of Supremacy and declined to consecrate M. *Parker (1559). He was deprived of his see and kept a prisoner in *Lambeth Palace.

TURRECREMATA. An alternative form of Torquemada (q.v.).

TUTIORISM. The system of moral theology (also termed **Rigorism**), acc. to which in cases of doubt the 'safer opinion' (i.e. that in favour of the moral principle) must be followed unless there is a degree of probability amounting to moral certitude in the 'less safe opinion' (i.e. that against the principle). It was condemned in 1690.

TWELFTH NIGHT. The evening before the twelfth day (*Epiphany) after *Christmas, formerly kept as a time of merry-making.

TWELVE ARTICLES, The. The charter of the *Peasants' Revolt adopted at Memmingen in 1525. The Peasants' demands included the right to appoint their own pastors, control over *tithes, and the abolition of serfdom. M. *Luther expressed agreement with the Articles, though he opposed the attempt to achieve these ends by revolt.

TYCHICUS. A disciple of St. *Paul who accompanied him on his Third Missionary Journey and in his captivity. He was the bearer of the letters to the *Colossians and *Ephesians. Several cities claim him as bishop.

TYCHON, Patriarch. See *Tikhon.*

TYCONIUS (d. *c.* 400), *Donatist theologian. He seems to have been an important layman; he was attacked for his Catholicizing views and condemned by a Donatist Council at Carthage *c.* 380. His chief work was his *Liber Regularum*, which propounded seven rules for interpreting Scripture. They were incorporated by St. *Augustine in his *De Doctrina Christiana* and thus influenced medieval exegesis.

TYNDALE, WILLIAM (1494?–1536), translator of the Bible and Reformer. When C. *Tunstall, Bp. of London, refused to support his project for translating the Bible into English, Tyndale went to Germany. The printing of his first NT began at *Cologne in 1525 and was completed at Worms the same year. Tyndale spent most of the rest of his life in Antwerp, where he repeatedly revised his NT. He also published translations of the Pentateuch (1530) and Jonah (1531) and left Jos.–2 Chron. in MS. His translations, made from the Greek and Hebrew, were the basis of both the AV and RV. He was burnt for heresy.

TYPES. In theology the foreshadowing of the Christian dispensation in the events and persons of the OT. Just as Christ could refer to *Jonah as the symbol of His *Resurrection, so St. *Paul found in the Israelites' crossing of the Red Sea the 'type' of Baptism (1 Cor. 10: 1–6). Typology was much used in the early Church.

TYPICON. In the E. Church a liturgical manual indicating how the services are to be recited throughout the ecclesiastical year.

TYPOS, The. The Imperial edict issued by Constans II in 647 or 648 to supersede the *Ecthesis. It forbade anyone to assert either *Monothelite or *Dyothelite beliefs, and

required that teaching should be limited to what had been defined in the first five Oecumenical Councils.

TYRANNICIDE. The murder of a tyrant whose rule has become insupportable. Some Christians hold that it is unjustifiable on the ground either that all killing is forbidden or that force is invested by Divine authority in the *de facto* civil government. Most hold that rebellion, including tyrannicide, is defensible in conditions when, if the oppressor were an alien, war would be justified, and provided that the grievance is considerable and circumstances offer no milder means of redress.

TYRE AND SIDON. The two chief cities of the Phoenicians, on the coast of Lebanon. In OT times they carried on a lucrative trade. The inhabitants of the region are mentioned among those attracted to Christ (Lk. 6: 17) and He visited the district (Mk. 7: 24). Tyre was held by the *Crusaders, 1124–1291.

TYRRELL, GEORGE (1861–1901), English *Modernist theologian. He became a RC in 1879 and a *Jesuit in 1880. In 1896 he was sent to Farm Street, the main Jesuit church in London; here he was a sought-after confessor and made a name through his devotional writing. His friendship with F. *von Hügel led to his acquaintance with the writings of the Continental Modernists; this contributed to his increasing hostility towards *Scholasticism and his stress on the anti-intellectual and experiential aspects of religion. An article on hell, entitled 'A Perverted Devotion', in 1899 caused his retirement to the Jesuit mission house in Richmond, N. Yorks. He asked in vain for secularization in 1905, but he was expelled from his order in 1906 after the publication of an anonymous 'Letter to a Professor' in which he contrasted living faith with dead theology. He was excommunicated when two letters in *The Times* (1907) protested against the issue of *Pius X's encyclical 'Pascendi'. His posthumous work, *Christianity at the Cross-Roads* (1909) questioned whether Christianity was the final religion, and held out hope of a universal religion of which Christianity was but the germ.

U

UBAGHS, GERHARD CASIMIR (1800–75), the chief representative of the *Traditionalist *Ontologism of Louvain. He combined the belief that knowledge of metaphysical and moral truth is based on a primitive Divine teaching handed on by oral tradition, with the Ontologist doctrine of the direct contemplation of God by the intellect in the 'objective ideas'. His teaching was censured in 1864; he soon submitted.

UBERTINO **OF** **CASALE** (1259–c. 1330), *Spiritual Franciscan. He became a *Franciscan in 1273. In 1305 he wrote his main work, *Arbor vitae crucifixae Jesu Christi*, a collection of apocalyptic ideas on the Church and society. He was summoned to *Avignon by *Clement V in 1310 to defend the Spirituals in the controversy on poverty, and 1322 *John XXII asked his opinion on the question of 'theoretical poverty', then a matter of dispute between the *Dominicans and the Franciscans. He fled from the Curia in 1325 and was prob. among the Franciscans who accompanied Louis of Bavaria to Rome.

UBIQUITARIANISM. The doctrine held by M. *Luther and others that Christ in His human nature is everywhere present. Luther used it to uphold his belief in the Real Presence of Christ in the *Eucharist.

UDALL, JOHN (c.1560–92), *Puritan pamphleteer and Hebrew scholar. In 1588 he published anonymously a widely read pamphlet on *The State of the Church of England*, and he was suspected of complicity in the *Marprelate Tracts. In 1590, refusing to clear himself on oath, he was found guilty of the authorship of *A Demonstration of the Truth* … [1588], but the sentence of death was not executed. His *Key to the Holy Tongue* (1593) included a Hebrew dictionary.

UDALL, NICHOLAS (c.1505–56), Reformer and dramatist. His *Lutheran sympathies prob. forced him in 1529 to leave Oxford, where he held a probationary Fellowship. He became Headmaster of Eton in 1534, but was dismissed in 1541. In 1547 he was appointed to assist Princess (later Queen) *Mary in translating the *Paraphrases* of D. *Erasmus. He received preferment under *Edward VI and remained in favour under Mary. His own works include translations of Erasmus's *Apophthegms* (1542) and of *Peter Martyr's treatise on the *Eucharist (c. 1550). His *Ralph Roister Doister*, a Christmas comedy written for a London school, was recovered in the 19th century.

U.I.O.D.G. (or **I.O.D.G.**), i.e. the initial letters of *(ut) in omnibus Deus glorificetur* ('that God may be glorified in all things'), a motto of the *Benedictine Order.

ULLATHORNE, WILLIAM BERNARD (1806–89), RC Bp. of Birmingham. A *Benedictine monk of *Downside, in 1832 he volunteered for the mission in *Australia. He organized the RC Church there, working esp. among the convicts. He returned to England in 1840. On the restoration of the hierarchy in 1850 he became Bp. of Birmingham. He worked with Card. N. P. S. *Wiseman to bring about the fusion of the old Catholics with the recent Oxford converts and with the Italian priests of the new congregations. He resigned his see in 1888.

ULPHILAS (c. 311–83), Apostle of the Goths. About 341 he was consecrated bishop by *Eusebius of Nicomedia. Soon afterwards he returned as a missionary to the Goths, among whom he had grown up. He translated the Bible into *Gothic. Through his connection with Eusebius he was led into *Arianism, to which the Goths were long attached.

ULRICH, St. (c. 890–973), Bp. of Augsburg from 923. He is the first person known to have been formally *canonized by a Pope; John XV pronounced him a saint in 993.

ULRICH, St. (d. 1154). See *Wulfric, St.*

ULTRAMONTANISM. A tendency in the RC Church which favours the centralization of authority in the Papal *Curia as opposed to national and diocesan independence. It developed in the 17th and 18th cents. when national movements such as *Gallicanism and *Josephinism became discredited either as involved in definite heresy or as countenancing the liberal anti-Christian movements which found expression in the French Revolution of 1789. The main stages of the triumph of Ultramontanism were the revival in 1814 of the *Jesuit Order, which was the mainstay of curial as opposed to local authority; the publication in 1864 of the *Syllabus, in which Catholicism and liberalism were held to be incompatible; and the declaration of the *Vatican Council in 1870 that the Pope is infallible when he makes a solemn pronouncement on faith or morals.

U.M.C.A. The (Anglican) Universities' Mission to Central Africa. It was founded in response to an appeal by D. *Livingstone in Cambridge in 1857. After an expedition to Malawi, the Mission was moved in 1864 to the island of Zanzibar, then the centre of the slave trade, which the Sultan was persuaded to abolish in 1873. In that year work was reestablished on the mainland; it extended through Tanzania, Malawi, and Zambia. In 1965 the U.M.C.A. joined with the *S.P.G. to form the *U.S.P.G.

UNAM SANCTAM (1302). The Bull issued by *Boniface VIII in his quarrel with Philip IV of France, declaring that there was 'One Holy Catholic and Apostolic Church' outside which there was 'neither salvation nor remission of sins'. It contained nothing new, but it marked the zenith of the growing claims of the medieval Papacy.

UNCIAL SCRIPT. A form of majuscule script (similar to modern 'capitals') used for books in Greek and Latin from the 4th to the 8th cent. A.D.

UNCREATED LIGHT. In the *Hesychast system the mystical light of God's visible Presence which the soul was held to be capable of apprehending by submitting to an elaborate process of ascetic purification and devotion.

UNCTION. Anointing with oil, with a religious significance, usually by a bishop or priest, e.g. at the *Coronation of a monarch. In the RC and E. Churches Unction is used at both *Baptism and *Confirmation, but the word is most commonly applied to the Sacrament of Unction (or Anointing) of the Sick, long known as Extreme Unction.

In the NT anointing of the sick is mentioned in Mk. 6: 13 and Jas. 5: 14 f. There are various references in the Fathers, and from the time of *Peter Lombard (d. 1160) it was reckoned one of the *Seven Sacraments. Until c. 800 recovery from illness was expected to result. In the W., however, the rite became connected with the penitential system and was commonly postponed until death was approaching; bodily recovery was not ordinarily looked for. The 1972 RC Ordo again lays emphasis on healing. After prayer and the laying on of hands, the patient is anointed on the forehead and hands; normally oil blessed by the Bishop on *Maundy Thursday is used. In the E. Church the rite, called *Euchelaion* ('oil of prayer'), is celebrated in church by a number of priests. The primary end is said to be physical cure, but in fact it is often received as a preparation for Communion by those who are not ill. In the C of E a form of unction was included in the Order for the *Visitation of the Sick in the 1549 BCP, but was dropped in 1552. A 'Form of Unction and the Laying on of Hands' was approved for provisional use in 1935.

UNDERHILL, EVELYN (1875–1941), English exponent of the mystical life. In 1907 she underwent a religious conversion and turned to the study of the mystics. The comprehensive approach of her book on *Mysticism* (1911) made it a standard work. In 1911 she came under the influence of F. *von Hügel and about the same time she began to undertake individual spiritual direction. From 1924 she conducted retreats. *Worship* (1936) embodies her general outlook in a broad review of the subject.

UNIAT CHURCHES. The Churches of E. Christendom in communion with Rome, which yet retain their respective languages, rites, and canon law in accordance with the terms of their union; these usually provide for *Communion in both kinds and marriage of the clergy. The main groups are the *Maronites, *Syrians, *Malankarese, all of the Antiochene rite; the *Armenians; the *Chaldeans and *Malabrese of the Chaldean rite;

the *Copts and *Ethiopians, both of the Alexandrian rite; and of the Byzantine rite, the *Ruthenians, *Hungarians, *Melchites, and some Slavs and Greeks.

UNIFORMITY, Acts of. (1) The 1549 Act imposed the exclusive use of the first Book of *Common Prayer in all public services and laid down penalties for holders of benefices who failed to comply. (2) The 1552 Act ordered the use of the revised BCP of that year. Absence from church was punishable by ecclesiastical censure, and attendance at other forms of service by imprisonment. (3) The 1559 Act ordered the use of the 1552 BCP, with slight modifications. Absence from church was now punishable by a fine. (4) The 1662 Act required that all ministers should publicly assent to the 1662 BCP and ordered its exclusive use. Ministers not episcopally ordained were to be deprived. Some 2,000 *Presbyterian ministers who refused to conform were ejected from their livings.

The 1662 Act has been modified by subsequent legislation, esp. the *Church of England (Worship and Doctrine) Measure, 1974.

UNIFORMITY, Act of, AMENDMENT ACT (1872), known as the 'Shortened Services Act'. This provided for the optional use of shortened forms of Morning and Evening Prayer. It was repealed by the *Church of England (Worship and Doctrine) Measure, 1974.

UNIGENITUS. (1) *Clement VI's bull of 1343 approving the teaching that *Indulgences owe their efficacy to the Pope's dispensation of the accumulated *merit of the Church. (2) *Clement XI's constitution of 1713 condemning 101 propositions from P. *Quesnel's *Réflexions morales*.

UNION OF CHRISTENDOM. See *Reunion*.

UNION THEOLOGICAL SEMINARY, New York. An institution for the training of ministers founded in 1836 by the independent action of the 'New School Presbyterians' for 'men of moderate views' of any denomination.

UNITARIANISM. A type of Christian thought and religious observance which

rejects the doctrines of the Trinity and the Divinity of Christ in favour of the unipersonality of God.

Modern Unitarianism dates from the Reformation era. It attracted adherents among those of extreme reforming views, esp. among the sects. Early Unitarians included M. *Servetus and B. *Ochino. Organized communities became established in the 16th–17th cents. in *Poland, where F. *Socinus was their leader from 1579 until his death (1604) and where the *Racovian Catechism was issued in 1605, in *Hungary, and in England. J. *Biddle, who is reckoned the father of English Unitarianism, held conventicles in London in 1658–62. A century later Unitarian principles were defended by J. *Priestley, and in 1773 T. *Lindsey seceded from the C of E and for the first time formed a Unitarian denomination. Unitarianism was also widely accepted by Dissenting congregations, esp. among the English *Presbyterians. In the 19th cent. great influence was exercised by J. *Martineau, who insisted that 'Unitarian' could be only the name of the belief of individuals, not the restrictive title of a denomination. The early 20th cent. saw a swing towards more radical Unitarianism, and since 1925 the Unitarians in England have been a distinctive and organized denomination, though recently declining in numbers.

In America the beginnings of definite Unitarianism date from the later 18th cent. In the early 19th cent. Unitarianism was also adopted in *Congregationalist Churches. By the end of the 19th cent. American Unitarianism had become a liberal or rationalist movement, accepting scientific methods and ideas. In 1961 the American Unitarian Association (founded in 1825) joined with the Universalist Church of America to form the Unitarian Universalist Association.

UNITAS FRATRUM. A title of the *Bohemian Brethren (q.v.).

UNITED CHURCH OF CHRIST. A Church in the U.S.A. formed in 1957 by the union of the Evangelical and Reformed Church with the *Congregational Christian Churches. Both bodies were themselves the results of earlier unions, the former containing both *Lutheran and *Calvinist elements.

UNITED FREE CHURCH OF SCOTLAND. The Church formed in 1900 by the union of the *United Presbyterian Church and the *Free Church of Scotland. The greater part joined the Established Church of Scotland in 1929, but a minority remains outside this union.

UNITED METHODIST CHURCH. The branch of Methodism formed in 1907 by the union of the *Methodist New Connexion, the *Bible Christians, and the *United Methodist Free Churches (qq.v.). It was itself embodied in the *Methodist Church (q.v.) in 1932.

UNITED METHODIST FREE CHURCHES. An amalgamation of small communities which had broken away from Wesleyan *Methodism for constitutional, not doctrinal, reasons. The Protestant Methodists were formed in 1827; the immediate cause of their secession was the erection of an organ at Brunswick Chapel, Leeds. The Wesleyan Methodist Association was formed in 1835 as the result of a dispute about the foundation of a Theological Institution for the training of ministers; it was joined by the Protestant Methodists in 1836. The Wesleyan Reformers came into being after three ministers had been expelled from the 1849 Conference when they refused to answer questions about some anonymous fly-sheets. The Wesleyan Methodist Association and the Wesleyan Reformers joined in 1857 to form the United Methodist Free Churches. In 1907 this body became part of the *United Methodist Church.

UNITED PRESBYTERIAN CHURCH. The Church formed in Scotland in 1847 by the union of the *United Secession Church and the Relief Synod, a body formed in 1761 after difficulties over the patronage system. In 1900, apart from a small minority (the *Wee Frees) it joined the *Free Church of Scotland to form the *United Free Church of Scotland.

UNITED REFORMED CHURCH. The Church formed in 1972 by the union of the greater part of the *Congregational Church of England and Wales with the *Presbyterian Church of England.

UNITED SECESSION CHURCH. The Church formed in Scotland in 1820 by the fusion of the two groups into which the *Burghers had divided. In 1847 it was em-

bodied in the *United Presbyterian Church.

UNITED SOCIETY FOR CHRISTIAN LITERATURE. A Society formed in 1935 by the fusion of the *Religious Tract Society, the Christian Literature Society for India and Africa (founded 1858), and the Christian Literature Society for China (founded 1884).

UNITED SOCIETY FOR THE PROPAGATION OF THE GOSPEL. See *U.S.P.G.*

UNITED STATES OF AMERICA, Christianity in. The founding of England's colonies on the N. American mainland was bound up with religious thought and practice. The C of E, brought by the Virginia Company to Jamestown (1607), became established from Maryland southwards. But it did not flourish and, lacking American bishops, adopted a virtually congregationalist polity. In the central and northern colonies religion was a more live issue. The *Pilgrim Fathers, who established Plymouth Colony in 1620, were strict *Calvinists who had fled from persecution. In the decade after 1630 the *Puritan followers of W. *Ames and W. *Perkins migrated to Massachusetts Bay, where they developed the Federal or Covenant theology in its fullest form; later the spiritual rigour of the colonists gave way and led to the *Half-Way Covenant (1662). Roger *Williams, who had been forced to leave Massachusetts in 1635, founded the colony of Rhode Island (1636), which allowed wide religious toleration, and William *Penn established Pennsylvania (1682) as a refuge for *Quakers and others. Maryland began in 1634 with a strong RC population, passed through a Puritan period, and saw the C of E established in 1702.

In the 18th cent. the colonies moved towards greater stability and maturity. A new element of diversity, however, was introduced by immigrant groups with new ways of worship. The *Baptist, *Methodist, *Presbyterian, *Lutheran, and Dutch Reformed Churches became important, and religious pluralism emerged. The dominant note in American theology was evangelical, and revivalism developed as the chief means of achieving evangelistic goals. The First *Great Awakening (c. 1726–70) was perhaps the first real inter-colonial movement.

The Revolution (1776) brought the disestablishment of State Churches (C of E in the South, *Congregationalism in the North) and forced religion into a denominational mould. The C of E developed into the independent *Protestant Episcopal Church.

The period of the Second Great Awakening (c. 1795–1835) coincided with the opening of an era of social reform, including the anti-*slavery movement. *Millenarianism also became an influence in American theology after 1800. Theological divisions, slavery, and sectional conflict led to divisions among the Presbyterians, Baptists, and Methodists. In the later part of the 19th cent. religious Liberalism emerged as an attempt to relate American theology to such current ideas as evolution and *higher criticism. The attempt within Liberalism to relate religion to society gave rise to the Social Gospel Movement which flourished between c. 1890 and the First World War. Orthodox Evangelicals reacted sharply to the rise of Liberalism and American theology became a battleground between the defenders of the old order (sometimes called *Fundamentalists) and the Liberals (often described as Modernists). Denominations were riven and heresy trials multiplied. One of the fruits of the Neo-Orthodox theology which developed after 1920 was a return to Biblical theology. The period after the Second World War witnessed a surge of piety. It has also seen challenges to the meaning and importance of the Gospel in the so-called 'post-Christian' era and a decline in Church membership.

The rapid rate of social and cultural change in America accounts in part for the number of religious sects outside the main stream of Christian life. In the 19th cent. bodies ministering to those on the fringes of society included the *Disciples of Christ (1809), the *Mormons (1830), and the *Christian Scientists (1875), all of which matured into denominational form with the passage of time. In modern America the religions of the dispossessed have more often taken the form of *Holiness or *Pentecostal Churches. Though Negroes have always had some part in the White Churches, there has been a tendency in Protestant tradition to establish specifically Negro Churches. Their emphasis has been other-worldly and eschatological, though in the 20th cent. increasingly activist roles have been adopted.

Among Protestant denominations in modern times there have been a large number of mergers. In the 1960s a wider approach was embodied in the *Consultation on Church Union (q.v.). In 1970 it produced a Plan of Union, which has since been set aside.

While RCs worshipped in America almost from the beginning, they were few in number until after 1820 when their community was increased by Irish and German immigrants. The first RC bishop (J. *Carroll) was consecrated in 1790 and in 1829 the American bishops held their first provincial council at *Baltimore. In 1908 America was removed from the jurisdiction of the Sacred Congregation of the *Propaganda and its missionary status ended. After 1920 immigration restrictions terminated the influx of European RCs and as a group American RCs rose socially and economically. The election of President J. F. Kennedy in 1960 completed their integration into American political life.

The E. *Orthodox community is mainly of Russian and Greek extraction, derived from waves of immigrants since 1900. It is concentrated in Pennsylvania and around the Great Lakes.

UNITIVE WAY, The. The third and last stage of the spiritual life.

'UNIVERS, L''. A French newspaper which, under the editorship of L. *Veuillot, became an organ of extreme *Ultramontane views. It was finally suppressed in 1874.

UNIVERSALISM. (1) The anti-nationalist teaching of some of the later Hebrew prophets that God's purposes covered not only the Jewish race but at least some men of other nations. (2) Another name for Apocatastasis (q.v.).

UNIVERSALS. Abstract concepts, representing the common elements belonging to individuals of the same genus or species. The medieval doctrine of universals derived from Greek philosophy. According to their answer to the question whether universals were things ('res') or only names ('nomina'), philosophers subscribed to the system of *Realism or *Nominalism (qq.v.).

UNIVERSITIES' MISSION TO CENTRAL AFRICA. See U.M.C.A.

UNKNOWING, The Cloud of. See Cloud

of Unknowing, The.

UNLEAVENED BREAD. See *Bread, Leavened and Unleavened.*

UPPER ROOM, The. See *Cenaculum, The.*

UPSALA. Upsala became the head of an ecclesiastical province, separate from *Lund, in 1164,, and from the mid-15th cent. until the Reformation the Archbishop was styled 'Primate of Sweden'. The university, founded in 1477, in the 19th cent. became the home of a liberal theology as contrasted with the orthodoxy of Lund. The *World Council of Churches held its fourth Assembly in Upsala in 1968.

URBAN II (*c.* 1042–99), Pope from 1088. He was a monk of *Cluny, called to Rome by *Gregory VII. On his election he was faced by an antipope, who was backed by the Emp. *Henry IV,, and he could not at first enter Rome. In 1089 he held a Council at Melfi which promulgated canons against *simony, lay *investiture, and clerical marriage, and in 1095 he held two Councils at Piacenza and *Clermont, also concerned with the reform of the Church. At Clermont the '*Truce of God' was proclaimed a law of the Church; Philip of France, who had put away his Queen and remarried, was anathematized; and Urban launched the First *Crusade. He also tried to heal the E. schism.

URBAN V (1309–70), Pope from 1362. He was a *Benedictine monk and in many ways the best of the *Avignon Popes. He seriously tried to reform the Church, esp. with regard to the distribution of benefices. In 1367, urged by the German Emp. Charles IV, he moved to Rome, where he was enthusiastically received by the people. In 1369 he received the Greek Emp. John V Palaeologus into communion. Later in the year Perugia revolted and war broke out between England and France; despite the admonitions of St. *Bridget, Urban returned to France in 1370 and soon died.

URBAN VI (1318–89), Pope from 8 Apr. 1378. He was elected under pressure from the Roman populace, who demanded an Italian. Though he had previously been noted for his austerity and aptitude for affairs, his pontificate became a series of grave imprudences. In Aug. 1378 the French cardinals declared his election void as performed under duress, and in Sept. they elected the antipope Clement VII, thus beginning the *Great Schism.

URBAN VIII (1568–1644), Pope from 1623. Though Maffeo Barberini was essentially a 'political' Pope, he encouraged religious life by canonizing a number of saints and approving new orders such as the *Visitation (1626), and he promoted missionary efforts by founding the Urban College of *Propaganda (1627). His decrees on *canonization form the basis of the present law and his revision of the *Breviary remained in force until 1912. Under him G. *Galilei was condemned for the second time (1633) and the *Augustinus* of C. O. *Jansen declared heretical (1642). From 1625 he favoured the policy of Card. *Richelieu against the Habsburgs and deprived the Catholic League of subsidies, but he tried to prevent the alliance of France and Sweden.

URBI ET ORBI (Lat., 'to the City [i.e. of Rome] and for the World'). A phrase used esp. of the solemn blessing which the Pope imparts from time to time from the balcony of *St Peter's, Rome.

URBS BEATA HIERUSALEM. A 6th–7th-cent. hymn celebrating the Heavenly Jerusalem in terms suggested by Rev. 21. The many English translations include J. M. *Neale's 'Blessed City, heavenly Salem'.

URBS SION AUREA. A set of extracts from a work of St. *Bernard of Cluny in use as the well-known hymn 'Jerusalem the golden'.

URGESCHICHTE (Germ., 'pre-history'). A term used in *Dialectical Theology for events which, from the standpoint of faith, are seen to be God's direct supernatural revelation to man, though viewed from the human angle they appear merely as historical occurrences.

URMARCUS (Germ., 'primitive Mark'), a supposed early and long lost draft of St. *Mark's Gospel.

URSACIUS (*fl. c.* 335–71), Bp. of Singidunum (Belgrade). With *Valens (q.v.), a leader of the Arians in the West.

URSULA, St. The legend of St. Ursula and her 11,000 virgins grew out of the veneration of some nameless virgins martyred at *Cologne, attested in the 4th–5th cent. By the 8th–9th cent. several thousand virgins were said to have perished. Still later Ursula, whose name was attached to their leader, was described as a British princess who, accompanied by 11,000 virgins, went on a pilgrimage to Rome, and on her return was murdered with her companions at Cologne by the Huns.

URSULINES. The oldest teaching order of women in the RC Church. It was founded at Brescia in 1535 by St. *Angela Merici as a society of virgins dedicated to Christian education, but living in their own homes. Community life and simple vows were introduced in 1572. In 1612 *Paul V allowed the Ursulines of Paris solemn vows and strict enclosure; convents founded on these lines multiplied, esp. in France and Canada.

USAGERS. The section of the *Nonjurors who in 1719 accepted the Communion Service drawn up by J. *Collier and others. They were so named from the four 'usages' which the new rite contained, viz. the '*mixed chalice', prayers for the *dead, a prayer for the descent of the Holy Spirit on the elements (*Epiclesis), and an oblatory prayer.

USE. In liturgy, a local modification of the standard (esp. Roman) rite. In the W. such uses arose partly through the absorption of *Gallican features by the Roman rite as it spread through Europe, and partly through local developments in the Roman rite itself. They were often used over a wide area, e.g. the Use of *Salisbury. Most of them were abolished by the Council of *Trent.

U.S.P.G. The United Society for the Propagation of the Gospel, formed in 1965 by the amalgamation of the *S.P.G. and the *U.M.C.A.

USSHER, JAMES (1581–1656), Abp. of *Armagh from 1625. A scholar of vast learning, he was an authority on a wide range of subjects, including Biblical chronology and the early history of Ireland. He distinguished the seven genuine letters of St. *Ignatius from the later spurious ones, whose existence had previously discredited the whole collection. After the Irish rebellion in 1641 he remained in England.

USUARD, Martyrology of. The most widely circulated of the medieval *martyrologies and the basis of the '*Roman Martyrology'. Its compiler, Usuard (d. c. 875), was a monk of the Abbey of *St.-Germain-des-Prés at Paris. He seems to have based his work on the somewhat earlier Martyrology of *Ado of Vienne (d. 875).

USURY. The exaction of interest was forbidden in the OT in the case of Jewish debtors. In the patristic age clerics were forbidden to lend at interest and in the Middle Ages this prohibition was extended to laymen. It was justified by the medieval view of money as solely a means of exchange. With the rise of capitalism, money came to be regarded not as a barren means of exchange but as capital productive of wealth, and the exaction of a reasonable rate of interest is tolerated by the Church.

UTICA, The Martyrs of. A group of early African martyrs of uncertain date who suffered at the Massa Candida ('White Farm'). The name of the place, misunderstood as 'White Lump', gave rise to the legend that they were thrown into slaking quicklime and their bodies reduced to a mass of white powder. Acc. to St. *Augustine, the massacre took place at Utica, 35 miles from Carthage.

UTILITARIANISM. The doctrine in ethics which identifies the good with happiness and maintains those actions to be right which bring the greatest happiness to the greatest number.

UTRAQUISM. The doctrine that the laity, like the clergy, should receive Communion under the forms of both bread and wine. It was maintained by the followers of John *Huss. Communion in both kinds was conceded to the laity by the Compactata of Prague (1433) and maintained by the Bohemian Diet until 1567. See also *Communion in both kinds*.

UTRECHT, Declaration of. The profession of faith which is the doctrinal basis of the *Old Catholic Church. It was drawn up at Utrecht in 1889. While professing adherence to the beliefs of the primitive Church, it is mainly concerned with controverting specific doctrines of the RC Church, including the decrees on the Papacy of the *Vatican

Council of 1870, the dogma of the *Immaculate Conception of the BVM, and the *Syllabus of 1864.

UVEDALE. An alternative form of Udall (q.v.).

V

VAISON, Councils of. Two important Councils were held at Vaison in SE. France. (1) That of 442 provided, *inter alia*, that clergy should receive the *chrism at Easter from their own bishops, and it regulated the adoption of children. (2) That of 529 issued five canons of liturgical import.

VALDÉS, JUAN DE (?1490–1541), Valdesso, Spanish humanist and religious writer. From 1531 he lived in Italy. He became the spiritual centre of a group of prominent people anxious for reform and spiritual renewal within the Church. Though he remained a Catholic, he paved the way for Protestant ideas by his emphasis on religious feeling and his disregard for ecclesiastical authority; after his death many of his friends left the RC Church. He wrote a number of devotional books, many of them remarkable for their penetrating insight and charm of exposition.

VALDES, P. See *Waldensians*.

VALENCE, Councils of. Three important Councils were held at Valence in Dauphiné. (1) That of 374 issued four disciplinary canons. (2) That of *c*. 530 was directed against *Pelagianism and *Semi-Pelagianism. (3) That of 855 discussed *Predestination. Against *Hincmar of Reims and the Council of *Quiercy (853) it upheld 'Double Predestination' and rejected the view that the redemptive work of Christ extended to all men.

VALENS (4th cent.), Bp. of Mursa (Osijek in Yugoslavia). With *Ursacius, Bp. of Singidunum, he was an *Arian leader in the W. Pupils of *Arius, they became bitter enemies of St. *Athanasius. They attacked him or adopted a more compromising position in

accordance with changes in the policy of the Emp. Constantius.

VALENTINE, St. The commemoration formerly observed on 14 Feb. appears to refer to two Valentines: a Roman priest martyred on the Flaminian Way *c*. 269, and a Bp. of Terni who was taken to Rome and martyred. The traditional association of St. Valentine's day with courtship is connected perhaps with the pagan festival of Lupercalia (mid-Feb.) or with the natural season, not with any tradition concerning either saint of this name.

VALENTINUS (2nd cent.), an influential *Gnostic theologian and founder of the sect of Valentinians. A native of Egypt, he lived at Rome from *c*. 136 to *c*. 165, had hopes of being elected bishop, but was passed over, seceded from the Church, and later perhaps went to *Cyprus.

His writings may include the *Evangelium Veritatis*, but his main production was a systematic theology known only in the developed and modified form given to it by his disciples. The spiritual world or 'pleroma' comprises thirty 'aeons' forming a succession of pairs (*syzygies); these are said to have been originally conceived as aspects of the divinity, but in the later systems appear like distinct deities. The visible world owes its origin to the fall of Sophia, the youngest of these, her ultimate offspring being the *Demiurge, identified with the God of the OT. Redemption was effected by the aeon Christ, who united himself with the man Jesus (either at his conception or at his baptism) to bring man the saving knowledge ('gnosis') of his origin and destiny. This gnosis, however, is given only to the spiritual men or 'pneumatics', i.e. the Valentinians, who through it enter the 'pleroma'; other Christians (called 'psychics') by faith and good works attain only to the middle realm of the Demiurge; the rest of mankind is given over to eternal perdition.

VALERIAN, St. (d. *c.* 460), Bp of Cemele (now Cimiez) in S. Gaul. He was present at the Councils of Riez (439) and *Vaison (442), and he upheld the jurisdictional claims of the see of Arles against *Leo I. Theologically he seems to have inclined to *Semi-Pelagianism.

VALIDATION OF MARRIAGE. A marriage null by reason of defective consent or some *diriment impediment can be validated in canon law (a) by simple renewal of consent or (b) by *dispensation.

VALLA, LORENZO (*c.* 1406–57), Italian humanist. He proved the spuriousness of the '*Donation of Constantine' in a work which contained a bitter attack on the temporal power of the Papacy. He also undertook a critical comparison between the *Vulgate and the Greek NT. He was an opponent of *Scholasticism, and he denied the possibility of understanding the harmony of God's omnipotence with human free will. His *De Elegantiis Linguae Latinae* (1442) long remained a standard work on humanist Latin. His novel and audacious views had a deep influence on Renaissance scholars and on the Reformers.

VALLUMBROSAN ORDER. A religious order, so named from the mother house at Vallombrosa, *c.* 20 miles from Florence. It was founded *c.* 1036 by St. *John Gualbert and spread rapidly. There were reforms of the order in the 15th and 17th cents. The mother house was burnt by the soldiers of *Charles V in 1527, plundered by Napoleon's troops in 1808, and finally suppressed in 1866. The order still has a few houses in Italy. The rule is based on that of St. *Benedict, but with greater stress on austerity and penance.

VALOR ECCLESIASTICUS. The official valuation of ecclesiastical and monastic revenues made in 1535, popularly known as the 'King's Books'. It was necessitated by the legislation of *Henry VIII appropriating ecclesiastical revenues to the Crown.

VAMPING HORN. A species of trumpet used in churches for humming harmonies to fill out the insufficient body of sound from other instruments. It was in use from the later 17th until the 19th cent.

VAN DEN STEEN, CORNELIUS C. See *Cornelius a Lapide*.

VAN ESPEN, ZEGER BERNHARD (1646–1728), Belgian canonist. His most important work is *Jus Ecclesiasticum Universum* (1700). He defended *Gallican theories and was an ardent upholder of secular power against religious authority.

VAN EYCK, HUBERT (*c.* 1366–1426) and JAN (*c.* 1390–1441), Flemish painters. Hubert went to Ghent, where he began the altar-piece, *The Adoration of the Lamb*, for the cathedral of St. Bavon. Jan became court painter of Philip the Good of Burgundy in 1425 and settled in Bruges.

The *Adoration*, which Jan finished in 1432, combines the allegorical treatment of the Middle Ages with a hitherto unknown naturalism and delight in detail. The work, based on Rev., consists of over 200 figures, grouped on several panels round the central figure of the Lamb, standing on the altar and adored by processions of saints.

VAN MANEN, WILLEM CHRISTIAAN (1842–1905), Dutch Biblical scholar. His views attracted attention as curiosities rather than for their intrinsic value. He held, e.g., that all the NT writings belong to the sub-Apostolic period and that St. *Paul wrote none of the Epistles attributed to him.

VAN MILDERT, WILLIAM (1765–1836), Bp. of *Durham from 1826. The last bishop with palatine rank, he was one of the founders of Durham University.

VANE, HENRY (1613–62), English politician. In the Long Parliament he was a bitter opponent of W. *Laud and of Strafford, and he was one of the commissioners chiefly responsible for the *Solemn League and Covenant. He became President of the Council of State in 1652, but latterly lost influence. At the *Restoration he was arrested and was executed in 1662.

VANGEON, H. L. See *Ghéon, H.*

VATICAN. The main residence of the Popes in Rome since their return from

*Avignon in 1377. Little of the existing building is earlier than the 15th cent. Extensive rebuilding was planned by *Nicholas V in 1447 and completed by *Clement VIII (d. 1605). By the Law of *Guarantees (1871) the Vatican was granted extraterritoriality, and additional privileges were conceded in the *Lateran Treaty of 1929. The Vatican Library contains important MSS. For the basilica, see *St. Peter's, Rome*.

VATICAN COUNCIL, The First (1869–70), reckoned by RCs the 20th *Oecumenical Council. Convoked by *Pius IX in 1868, it was intended to deal with a wide variety of subjects. Even before the Council began, two bodies of opinion stood out: the *Ultramontane majority, who favoured the heightening of Papal authority and the definition of Papal *Infallibility, and the liberal minority.

The Council opened in Dec. 1869. It began by discussing the schema 'De Fide'. A revised constitution on Faith, 'Dei Filius', was promulgated on 24 Apr. 1870. It contains four chapters on God the Creator, on Revelation, on Faith, and on Faith and Reason. It was decided that the questions of Papal Infallibility and the Primacy of the Pope should be dealt with before other points in the schema on the Church. In the debate on the Primacy the minority particularly objected to the definition of the Pope's jurisdiction as ordinary, immediate, and truly episcopal. They also tried to get his Infallibility linked more closely with that of the Church. The constitution '*Pastor Aeternus', accepted on 18 July, disappointed the extremists on both sides. It clearly stated the Infallibility of the Pope, but restricted it to those occasions when, speaking *ex* *cathedra*, he defined a doctrine regarding faith and morals. The outbreak of war between France and Prussia on 19 July and the Italian occupation of Rome brought the Council to an end.

The definitions of the Council aroused serious opposition only in Germany and Austria. In these countries small minorities organized themselves as '*Old Catholics', and in Germany Bismarck's opposition to the consolidation of Papal power issued in the *Kulturkampf*.

VATICAN COUNCIL, The Second (1962–5), reckoned by RCs the 21st *Oecumenical Council. The decision to hold

a Council was apparently due entirely to *John XXIII; it was intended to renew the life of the Church and to bring up to date its teaching, discipline, and organization, with the unity of all Christians as the ultimate goal. After the First Session (Oct.–Dec. 1962), Pope John died. *Paul VI on his election announced that he intended to continue the Council. The Second Session (Sept.–Dec. 1963) promulgated a Constitution on the Liturgy and a decree on the Instruments of Social Communication. The Third Session (Sept.–Nov. 1964) promulgated a Dogmatic Constitution on the Church and decrees on Ecumenism and the Eastern Catholic Churches; and the Pope proclaimed the BVM to be the 'Mother of the Church'. The Fourth Session (Sept.–Dec. 1965) promulgated decrees on a variety of subjects, including the Bishops' Pastoral Office, Renewal of the Religious Life, and the Apostolate of the Laity. The Pope formulated the norms of the new episcopal synod which was to help him govern the Church and announced the beginning of the reform of the *Curia.

The legislation implementing the decisions of the Council was largely carried out during the pontificate of Paul VI (q.v.). Some of the liturgical reforms had been foreshadowed under *Pius XII, but the Council gave an enormous impetus to changes of attitude in the RC Church towards other bodies, both Christian and non-Christian, and to the world in general, and even more spectacularly to changes in its own life. These included the use of the vernacular in worship, a new liturgy, and a less authoritarian attitude, with the attendant tensions inherent in rapid change.

VAUDOIS. See *Waldenses*.

VAUGHAN, CHARLES JOHN (1816–97), Dean of *Llandaff from 1879. In 1860 he became Vicar of Doncaster. Here he began preparing graduates for ordination; by the time of his death over 450 young men, known as 'Vaughan's Doves', had gone through his training. His sympathy with Nonconformity won him influence in S. Wales, and he took part in the foundation of the University College at Cardiff (1883–4).

VAUGHAN, HENRY (1622–95), poet. He practised medicine in Brecon and from *c*. 1650 at Newton-by-Usk. A spiritual experience, due partly perhaps to the death of a brother and a serious illness, issued in a collection of spiritual poems, *Silex Scintillans* (1650–55). They are marked by an atmosphere of intense and sustained religious fervour. He is often numbered among the *metaphysical poets.

VAUGHAN, HERBERT (1832–1903), Abp. of Westminster from 1892, made Cardinal in 1893. Descended from an old English RC family, Vaughan bought the *Tablet* in 1868 and for three years acted as editor, championing the *Ultramontane cause. The most notable events of his archiepiscopate were his obtaining permission from the authorities at Rome for RCs to attend the ancient English universities, the building of *Westminster Cathedral, the discussions over *Anglican Ordinations, and his activities in connection with the Education Bill of 1902.

VAUGHAN WILLIAMS, R. See *Williams, R. Vaughan.*

VÁZQUEZ, GABRIEL (1549–1604), Spanish *Jesuit theologian. His main work was a commentary on the *Summa Theologica* of St. *Thomas Aquinas. In the current discussion on the doctrine of grace, he adopted a *Molinist position.

VEDAST, St. (d. 539), also 'Vaast'. He was deputed to prepare *Clovis I for baptism. About 499 he was consecrated Bp. of Arras, where he established Christianity; he was also put in charge of the diocese of Cambrai.

VEIL. (1) Christian headdress. The veil, which was worn by Roman matrons, from the 3rd cent. was given by the bishop to consecrated virgins as a symbol of their spiritual marriage to Christ; it later came to be considered the most important part of the religious *habit of women. In the C of E female candidates traditionally wear a white veil at *Confirmation.

(2) Liturgical cloths for covering various objects, e.g., the *chalice veil, *humeral veil (qq.v.), and the veil used for the *ciborium when containing the sacred species. In the W. Church it was customary to veil all crucifixes and pictures during *Passiontide and later throughout Lent. In current RC practice such veiling is not obligatory and is confined to *Holy Week.

VENANTIUS FORTUNATUS (c. 530–c. 610), Latin poet. Born near *Venice, c. 565 he went on a pilgrimage to the tomb of St. *Martin of Tours; he settled at Poitiers, of which he became bishop towards the end of the 6th cent. He wrote much occasional verse, a long metrical life of St. Martin of Tours, and prose lives of St. *Hilary of Poitiers, St. *Germanus of Paris, Queen *Radegunde, and various local celebrities, as well as the hymns which stand out as the true expression of his genius; they include '*Vexilla Regis' and '*Pange lingua gloriosi'.

VENERABLE. (1) In the RC Church, a title bestowed on a departed person when a certain stage in the process of *Beatification has been reached. It is also used of other persons of holy life, esp. the 'Venerable *Bede'. (2) In the C of E, the proper address of an *archdeacon.

VENERATION OF THE CROSS. A ceremony of the Latin rite for *Good Friday, also called **Creeping to the Cross**, in which clergy and people solemnly venerate a crucifix, usually at the entrance to the sanctuary.

VENI CREATOR. A Latin hymn to the Holy Spirit, prob. composed in the Frankish Empire in the 9th cent. It has been used at Vespers in *Whitsuntide since the 10th cent.; it is also used at the ordination of priests and bishops. The best-known English version is that of J. *Cosin, 'Come, Holy Ghost, our souls inspire'.

VENI SANCTE SPIRITUS. The *Sequence for *Whitsunday. Its authorship is now usually attributed to Stephen *Langton. English translations include 'Come, Thou Holy Paraclete'.

VENI, VENI, EMMANUEL ('O come, O come, Emmanuel'). The hymn is a versification of the *O-Antiphons (q.v.), but the origin of both the words and the music is obscure.

VENIAL SIN. In RC *moral theology, a sin which, though it disposes the soul to death and is the greatest of all evils except *mortal sin (q.v.), does not wholly deprive the soul of sanctifying grace.

VENICE. The see of Venice goes back to the bishopric founded in 774 on the isle of Olivolo, later known as Castello. Owing to the constant disputes between the see of Olivolo and the patriarchate of Grado, to which it belonged, both were suppressed in 1451 and replaced by the patriarchate of Venice.

The most famous church is that of San Marco. The original chapel, destined to receive the relics of St. *Mark, was completed in 883. Burnt down in 976, it was rebuilt (1063–71) on the model of the basilica of the Apostles at Constantinople. Its plan forms a Greek cross of equal arms, the centre and each arm being surmounted by a dome; the interior is richly decorated with marbles and mosaics. It became the cathedral of the patriarchate in 1807.

VENITE. Ps. 95 [Vulg. 94], so called from the opening word of its Latin version. From the time of St. *Benedict it has been used in the first *office of the day in the W. Church. From the *Breviary it came into *Mattins in the BCP. See also *Invitatory*.

VENN, HENRY (1725–97), *Evangelical Anglican divine and one of the founders of the *Clapham Sect. *The Complete Duty of Man* (1763) was very popular.

VERGER. Strictly the official who carries a mace or verge before a dignitary. The term is now commonly used for one who takes care of the interior fabric of a church.

VERGIL, VERGILIUS. See *Virgil, Virgilius*.

VERMIGLI, PIETRO MARTIRE. See *Peter Martyr*.

VERMITTLUNGSTHEOLOGIE. A school of 19th-cent. German Protestant theologians who tried in various ways to combine the traditional *Protestantism of the Reformation Confessions with modern science, philosophy, and theological scholarship.

VERNAZZA, BATTISTA (1497–1587), *Augustinian canoness and mystic. From 1510 until her death she lived in a convent at Genoa. She is believed to be the final redactor of the life and so-called *Works* of St.

*Catherine of Genoa and the writer of the 'Spiritual Dialogue' which they incorporate.

VERONA. The first historically attested Bp. of Verona is Lucilius, who took part in the Council of *Sardica (343). Its patron is St. *Zeno. An important synod was held at Verona in 1184; it introduced the episcopal inquisition. The 12th-cent. cathedral houses *Titian's painting of the Assumption, and the chapter library has a celebrated collection of manuscripts.

VERONICA, St. A woman of Jerusalem who is said to have offered her headcloth to the Lord to wipe the blood and sweat from His face on the way to *Calvary; He returned it with His features impressed upon it. The legend is first found in its present form in the 14th cent. The incident occupies a regular position in the *Stations of the Cross.

VERSICLE. A short sentence, often taken from the Pss., which is said or sung antiphonally in Christian worship. It is answered by a 'response' on the part of the congregation or the other half of the choir.

VESPERALE. (1) A liturgical book containing the Psalms, hymns, &c. used at *Vespers, with their chants. Those of *Compline are commonly added. (2) In the W. Church, the cloth spread over the altar when not in use to keep the white linen altar-cloths clean.

VESPERS. The Evening Office of the W. Church. It is of great antiquity. In its present form a hymn is followed by two Psalms, a NT *canticle, a short lesson, a short *responsory, the *Magnificat with *antiphons, and prayers. With *Lauds it is the most important of the Day Offices and is frequently chanted with great solemnity. The service of *Evensong in the BCP was partly formed on the model of Vespers, with additions from *Compline.

VESPERS, Sicilian. See *Sicilian Vespers*.

VESTIARIAN CONTROVERSY, The. A dispute about clerical dress which began under *Edward VI and under *Elizabeth I became one of the foundations of the *Puritan party. The question became acute in 1550, when John *Hooper, nominated Bp. of *Gloucester, at first refused to be consecrated in the *surplice and *rochet prescribed by the BCP. After Elizabeth's accession the restoration of vestments in the Chapel Royal excited opposition. M. *Parker's *Advertisements* (1566) required the use of a surplice in parish churches and a *cope in cathedral and collegiate churches. 37 London clergy refused compliance and were deprived. Serious disturbances followed.

VESTMENTS. The distinctive dress worn by the clergy when performing the services of the Church. It originated in the ordinary clothes of the world of antiquity and developed into a specifically priestly costume between the 4th and 9th cents., largely because the laity abandoned the use of long tunics and mantles. By the 10th cent. the main liturgical vestments and their use had been established in the W. From the 10th to the 13th cent. minor changes were made. The *surplice was substituted for the *alb on many occasions and the *chasuble came to be almost restricted to the celebration of Mass. Bishops also received additional vestments, such as *sandals, *mitre, and *gloves. See also *Eucharistic Vestments, Cope,* and *Ornaments Rubric.*

VESTRY. A room in or attached to a church in which the vestments, vessels, and other requisites for Divine worship are kept and in which the clergy vest. From the fact that it was here that parishioners formerly met to transact the business of the parish, the word came to be used both of the body of parishioners and of the actual meeting. Since 1894 the vestries of the C of E have lost most of their powers. In the *Protestant Episcopal Church of the U.S.A. every parish has a 'vestry', consisting of the incumbent, two wardens, and a number of vestrymen; it is responsible for the financial administration of the parish and exercises control over the appointment of the incumbent (subject to the bishop's approval).

VEUILLOT, LOUIS (1813–83), *Ultramontane French journalist. In 1843 he became editor of the *Univers,* a newspaper then of little importance, which increased in authority and gained an international significance through his defence of the Church; during the First Vatican Council he was so closely in the confidence of the Pope that the *Univers* became almost an official organ. In

his original stand for the freedom of Catholic teaching he was widely supported by French Catholics; much less so when he defended the temporal power of the Papacy and advocated Papal Infallibility.

VEUSTER, J. DE. See *Damien, Father.*

VEXILLA REGIS. The Latin hymn by *Venantius Fortunatus celebrating the victory of Christ on the Cross. It is sung at *Vespers in *Holy Week. The English translation, 'The royal banners forward go', is due to J. M. *Neale.

VIA DOLOROSA. The route in *Jerusalem which Christ is believed to have followed from the judgement hall of *Pilate to *Calvary.

VIA MEDIA (Lat., 'The Middle Way'). A term used esp. by J. H. *Newman and other *Tractarians for the Anglican system as a middle road between 'Popery' and 'Dissent'. This conception of Anglicanism is found in the 17th century.

VIANNEY, St. J.-B. M. See *Curé d'Ars, The.*

VIATICUM (Lat., 'provision for a journey'). The Holy Communion given to those in likelihood of immediate death to strengthen them with grace for their journey into eternity.

VICAR. In the C of E the priest of a parish where the *tithes have been appropriated (see *tithes*). As parish priest he holds exactly the same spiritual status as a *rector, and the forms of *institution and *induction are identical.

VICAR APOSTOLIC. The name given to a RC titular bishop in countries where the normal hierarchy is not established or the ordinary jurisdiction of the bishop is impeded.

VICAR OF CHRIST, The. A title of the Popes dating from the 8th cent.

VICAR GENERAL. An official whom a bishop deputes to represent him in the exercise of his jurisdiction. In early times his functions were mostly performed by the *archdeacons, but by the end of the 13th cent. the office was established and its duties defined.

In the C of E the office is ordinarily committed to the *Chancellor of the diocese. Each archbishop has a Vicar General who holds a court for the confirmation of bishops, where the validity of the election and the qualifications of the candidate may be challenged.

VICELIN, St. (*c.* 1090–1154), 'Apostle of Holstein'. Ordained priest in 1126, he was sent by Adalbero, Bp. of Bremen, as a missionary among the pagan Wagrians. From 1127 he worked in Holstein. After the unfortunate Crusade against the Wends in 1147 had destroyed his labours, he was consecrated Bp. of Oldenburg in 1149.

VICO,   GIOVANNI   BATTISTA (1668–1744), Italian jurist and philosopher. His main work was his *Principii di una scienza nuova d'intorno alla natura comune delle nazioni* (1725). Replying to R. *Descartes's attack on the value of historical study, Vico drew a distinction between the method and nature of natural science and those of history and maintained that mathematics was not a description of the general nature of reality but only the application of man-made rules; history, on the other hand, describes the behaviour of men and to that extent is amenable to human understanding. The two keys to understanding the past were, he held, the nature of language and the nature of ritual or myth. Myths were the means of conveying deep truths. He showed that much of the 'Natural Law' which philosophers tried to project back into primitive times was incompatible with the outlook of the early writings we possess.

VICTIMAE PASCHALI (Lat., 'To the Paschal Victim'). The Easter *Sequence in the W. Church, written by *Wipo.

VICTOR I, St. (d. 198), Pope from 189. In order to settle the *Quartodeciman controversy, he ordered synods to be held throughout Christendom. He threatened *Polycrates of Ephesus and other bishops of Asia Minor with excommunication if they refused to give up their practice of keeping Easter on 14 Nisan instead of the following Sunday, but he may have taken back the sentence.

VICTOR, St. (d. 554), Bp. of Capua from

541. His most celebrated work is a harmony of the Gospels, made on the basis of the *Vulgate text.

VICTOR (late 5th cent.), Bp. of Vita in N. Africa. Part of his history of the persecution of the Catholic Church in Africa by the *Arian Vandals, which was written *c.* 485, is based on contemporary material and the author's own experience. It provides a vivid picture of political and religious life.

VICTORINES. The *canons regular of the former abbey of St.-Victor at Paris. The house was founded by *William of Champeaux and built in 1113. Many famous scholars, mystics, and poets were found among the Victorines, esp. in the 12th cent., among them *Adam of St.-Victor, *Hugh of St.-Victor, *Richard of St.-Victor, and *Walter of St.-Victor. The abbey was secularized in the French Revolution.

VICTORINUS, St. (d. *c.* 304), Bp. of Pettau, near the Austrian-Yugoslav border. He is the earliest known exegete of the Latin Church, but nearly all his works are lost, prob. because of the *millenarianist tendencies which caused them to be condemned by the '*Decretum Gelasianum'. Of his commentaries only that on Rev. survives. The treatise *De Fabrica Mundi* is almost certainly his.

VICTORINUS AFER, CAIUS (or FABIUS) MARIUS (4th cent.), rhetor and theologian. A native of Africa, he taught at Rome. About the middle of the century he became a Christian, resigned his rhetorship in 362 (an event which excited comment and influenced St. *Augustine), and wrote theological works against the *Arians. The obscurity of his writing is largely due to the fact that he was translating philosophical Greek into Latin in an attempt to utilize a form of 4th-cent. *Neoplatonic metaphysics to elucidate and defend the Nicene doctrine of the Trinity.

VICTRICIUS, St. (*c.* 330–*c.* 407), Bp. of Rouen from *c.* 380. He entered the army, but on becoming a Christian renounced his military profession. As bishop he defended the faith against pagans and heretics and undertook missionary work in Flanders, Hainault, and Brabant. He was the recipient of a letter of *Innocent I on disciplinary matters.

VIDI AQUAM (Lat., 'I beheld water'). The anthem sung in the W. Church in Eastertide during the asperging of the congregation in place of the *Asperges sung during the rest of the year.

VIEIRA, ANTÓNIO (1608–97), Portuguese *Jesuit. He was brought up in Brazil. Returning to Lisbon in 1641, he soon won influence at court. In 1652 he was sent to refound the missions to the Maranhão and Grão Pará which had lapsed in 1649; his most notable achievement in this field was the conversion of the Nheengaíbas on the island of Marajó. His attempts to uphold the freedom of the Amerindians led to difficulties and he was arraigned before the *Inquisition. In 1669 he went to Rome to plead his case and he was exempted from the jurisdiction of the Portuguese Inquisition. In 1681 he returned to Brazil for the rest of his life.

VIENNE, Council of (1311–12). The 15th *Oecumenical Council, summoned by *Clement V primarily to deal with the question of the *Templars, who were being accused of heresy and immorality. The majority at the Council at first held that the evidence against the Templars was insufficient, but when Philip IV of France appeared with an army before Vienne, the Pope suppressed the order. The Council issued a number of miscellaneous decrees.

VIGIL. Nocturnal services of prayer, often ending with the *Eucharist, were common in the early Church. The vigil before *Easter lasted throughout the night (see *Paschal Vigil Service*); those before Sundays and other feasts normally comprised only the beginning (*Vespers) and the end of the night. From the latter the offices of *Mattins and *Lauds developed. Because of abuses the vigils of the people came to be restricted to the early hours, i.e. before nightfall, and then it became customary to anticipate the vigil. At first confined to the afternoon of the preceding day, fast, office, and Mass of the vigil were gradually moved back to the morning and the whole day became a 'profestum'. In the RC calendar of 1969 all vigils except that of Easter were abolished, but the 1971 *Breviary provides a short additional office for optional use on the eves of Sundays and great feasts.

VIGILANTIUS (*fl. c.* 400), presbyter of Aquitaine. A visit to St. *Jerome at *Bethlehem ended in a quarrel, and Vigilantius attacked Jerome as an *Origenist. Jerome replied with his *Contra Vigilantium* (406).

VIGILIUS (d. 555), Pope from 537. In the *Three Chapters Controversy he at first refused his assent to *Justinian's condemnation of the writings of *Theodore of Mopsuestia, *Theodoret, and *Ibas of Edessa. After he had been brought to Constantinople, he repudiated the Three Chapters in his 'Iudicatum' of 548, though not without reservations in favour of the Council of *Chalcedon. His capitulation met with great opposition in the W. and the Pope retracted his 'Iudicatum'. After the Council of *Constantinople in 553 had condemned the Three Chapters, Vigilius accepted its decision. The case was cited at the First *Vatican Council by the opponents of Papal *Infallibility.

VIGILIUS (*fl. c.* 500), Bp. of Thapsus. Banished from Africa by the *Arian king, Huneric, he fled to *Constantinople. His chief work, 'Against Eutyches', attacks *Monophysitism and defends the *Tome of *Leo and the *Chalcedonian Definition.

VILATTE, JOSEPH RENÉ (1854–1929), '*episcopus vagans'. A Frenchman by birth, in 1892, on the authority of an apparently forged bull, he was consecrated in Ceylon as *Old Catholic bishop in America by Abp. Álvares, a schismatic from the Church of Antioch. He himself consecrated a number of bishops who have not been recognized by any other Christian body.

VILMAR, AUGUST FRIEDRICH CHRISTIAN (1800–60), German *Lutheran theologian. He opposed all forms of rationalism, upholding dogmatic and confessional Lutheranism, and he defended the retention of the ancient creeds in worship.

VINCENT, St. (4th cent.), protomartyr of *Spain. Acc. to tradition he was a deacon and suffered in the *Diocletianic persecution.

VINCENT OF BEAUVAIS (*c.* 1190–1264), *Dominican encyclopaedist. He was in close relations with *Louis IX. His *Speculum Maius*, composed between 1247 and 1259, set out to be a compendium of the whole range of knowledge accessible in his time.

VINCENT FERRER, St. (*c.* 1350–1419), *Dominican mission preacher. Between 1399 and 1409 he made a series of journeys through Europe, collecting a crowd of followers, some of whom were stirred to severe forms of penance. He is credited with performing many miracles. He took a prominent part in the movement to end the Papal schism.

VINCENT OF LÉRINS, St. (d. before 450), *Semi-Pelagian theologian. He was a monk of *Lérins, and prob. the object of one of *Prosper of Aquitaine's controversial writings. His own *Commonitorium*, which was designed to provide a guide to the determination of the true Catholic faith, embodies the famous *Vincentian Canon (q.v.).

VINCENT DE PAUL, St. (*c.* 1580–1660), founder of the *Lazarist Fathers and of the 'Sisters of Charity'. Captured by pirates in 1605, he spent two years as a slave in Tunisia. From 1613 to 1625 he was tutor in the household of Count de Gondi, General of the galleys; he did much to relieve the lot of the prisoners. He founded the Congregation of the Mission, usually called Lazarists (q.v.), in 1625; 8 years later, with St. Louise de Marillac, he founded the 'Sisters of Charity', the first congregation of women without enclosure devoted to the care of the sick and poor. The 'Society of St. Vincent de Paul', founded in 1833, is a lay association for the service of the poor.

VINCENTIAN CANON, The. The threefold test of Catholicity laid down by St. *Vincent of Lérins. By the triple test of oecumenicity, antiquity, and consent, the Church is to differentiate between true and false tradition.

VINCI, LEONARDO DA. See *Leonardo da Vinci*.

VINCIBLE IGNORANCE. The converse of *invincible ignorance (q.v.).

VINEAM DOMINI SABAOTH (1705). The Constitution of *Clement XI against the French *Jansenists. It maintained that the Pope could determine questions of fact as well as doctrine and that such decisions must be accepted 'by the heart' of the believer and not merely received 'with respectful silence'.

VINEGAR BIBLE. A popular name for an edition of the AV printed in 1716–17, in which the headline of Lk. 20 reads 'The Parable of the Vinegar' instead of 'The Parable of the Vineyard'.

VINES, RICHARD (1600?–56), *Puritan divine. He was a member of the committee of the *Westminster Assembly which drafted the *Westminster Confession, and on the Parliamentary Committee of Accommodation he defended *Presbyterian ordinations. He was made Master of Pembroke College, Cambridge, in 1644. In 1649 he opposed the abolition of the kingly office and the House of Peers, and being ejected from Pembroke College and Watton Rectory he became minister of St. Lawrence Jewry.

VINET, ALEXANDRE RUDOLF (1797–1847), Swiss Reformed theologian. He was professor of practical theology at Lausanne from 1837 to 1847, when he attached himself to the newly constituted Free Church in the Canton Vaud. His conception of Christianity was individualistic, the seat of religion being the conscience and dogma important only in so far as it issued in moral action.

VIO, T. DE. See *Cajetan, T. de Vio*.

VIRET, PIERRE (1511–71), early Protestant Reformer. In 1533 he became G. *Farel's assistant at Geneva; he later worked mainly in Lausanne. In 1561 he went to France and took a leading part in the affairs of the French Reformed Church.

VIRGER. An alternative form of *Verger.

VIRGIL (70–19 B.C.), Roman poet. Publius Vergilius Maro was the son of a rich citizen of Mantua. He abandoned rhetoric and politics to study philosophy, to which he intended to devote himself when he had completed the *Aeneid*. He wrote ten pastorals, known as the *Eclogues* (i.e. occasional poems), the *Georgics*, on Italy and its agricultural wealth, and the unfinished *Aeneid*, an epic on the foundation of Rome by the exiled Trojan, based on Homer.

Virgil's language and style were widely influential. *Constantine tried to appropriate the Fourth ('Messianic') *Eclogue* as a prophecy of Christ, born of a virgin (l. 6: *iam redit et virgo*). Despite protests against the facile Christianization of Virgil, and although during the last period of serious pagan opposition at Rome the pagans regarded Virgil as a philosophical authority, later Christian writers accorded him a unique place among pagan authors.

VIRGILIUS OF SALZBURG, St. (*c*. 700–84), 'Apostle of Carinthia'. A learned Irishman, he went to the Continent in 743 and for some years governed the diocese of Salzburg without becoming bishop. St. *Boniface, who disapproved of this arrangement, in 748 accused him to Pope *Zacharias of heretical views about the spherical shape of the earth and the existence of the antipodes. Virgilius was, however, eventually consecrated to the see of Salzburg in either 755 or 767. He secured the conversion of the Alpine Slavs.

VIRGIN BIRTH OF CHRIST, The. The belief that Jesus Christ had no human father, but was conceived by the BVM by the power of the Holy Spirit, is clearly stated in the narratives of Christ's Infancy recorded in the Gospels (Mt. 1 f. and Lk. 1 f.), and has been a consistent tenet of orthodox Christian theology. During the last hundred years it has been challenged by some liberal theologians on such grounds as a general suspicion of everything miraculous and a belief that the LXX of Is. 7: 14, as an inexact rendering of the Heb., gave rise to, or at least promoted, the legend; the absence of reference to the Virgin Birth in other parts of the NT; and the contention that it would have been more congruous with the full Humanity of Christ for His Birth to be like that of other men. None of these points is unanswered.

The doctrine of the Virgin Birth is quite distinct from that of the *Incarnation, and acceptance of Christ's Divine Sonship is not theologically dependent on His not being the son of *Joseph.

VIRGIN MARY, The Blessed. See *Mary, The Blessed Virgin*.

VIRTUALISM. A form of *Eucharistic doctrine according to which, while the bread and wine continue to exist unchanged after consecration, the faithful communicant receives together with the elements the virtue or power of the Body and Blood of Christ.

VIRTUES, Cardinal and Theological. See *Cardinal Virtues* and *Theological Virtues*.

VISIGOTHIC RITE. An alternative name for the *Mozarabic Rite.

VISITANDINE ORDER. See *Visitation Order*.

VISITATIO LIMINUM APOSTOLORUM. See *Ad Limina Apostolorum*.

VISITATION, Episcopal. Episcopal Visitations are designed for the periodic inspection of those temporal and spiritual affairs of a diocese under the bishop's control. From the 6th cent. they have been regulated by ecclesiastical councils. In the later Middle Ages, when the work was already conducted by commissaries of the bishop, elaborate legal forms for the presentation of offenders were developed. In the C of E the Abps. of *Canterbury and *York have the right to visit the dioceses of their respective provinces.

VISITATION OF OUR LADY. The feast which commemorates the BVM's visit to *Elizabeth recorded in Lk. 1: 39–56. It originated in the 13th cent. It was kept on 2 July until in the RC Church it was moved to 31 May in 1969.

VISITATION ORDER, also known as **Visitandines,** the 'Order of the Visitation of the BVM'. Founded in 1610 by St. *Francis de Sales and St. *Jane Frances de Chantal, the order was designed to include women unable to bear the austerities of the older orders. Originally only the novices were enclosed and the professed sisters went out on works of mercy, esp. nursing the sick, but since 1618 the whole order has been enclosed and primarily contemplative.

VISITATION OF THE SICK, The. The 'Order for the Visitation of the Sick' in the BCP provides for prayers, exhortations, and blessing in the presence of the sick person; it includes an exhortation to confession with a form prescribed for priestly absolution. In the 1549 BCP provision was made for *unction, but this was dropped in 1552. The 'Communion of the Sick' provides for a celebration of the *Eucharist in the sickroom. For RC rite, see *Unction*.

VITALIAN (d. 672), Pope from 657. During the early part of his pontificate he kept on good terms with the E. and in 663 he received the E. Emp. Constans II in Rome. Later his name was removed from the *diptychs at Constantinople for his adhesion to '*Dyothelite' views.

VITALIS, St. St. *Ambrose relates that in 393 he discovered the bones of St. Agricola and St. Vitalis (Agricola's slave) in a Jewish cemetery at *Bologna, and that both had suffered death together. The cult of St. Vitalis then spread rapidly.

VITALIS, ORDERICUS. See *Ordericus Vitalis.*

VITANDI (Lat., 'persons to be avoided'). The technical name for those *excommunicated persons with whom the faithful are debarred from having any intercourse.

VITORIA, FRANCISCO DE (*c.* 1485–1546), Spanish *Dominican. From 1526 he was professor of theology at Salamanca. By substituting the *Summa Theologica* of St. *Thomas Aquinas for *Peter Lombard's *Sentences* as the theological textbook, he inaugurated a new school at Salamanca, which became the chief university in Europe for the study of Scholasticism in the 16th cent. Often regarded as the 'Father of International Law', Vitoria discussed the morality of the conquest of the Indies and laid down the conditions of a just *war.

VITUS, St. (d. perhaps 303), martyr. According to a late legend he was born in S. Italy of pagan parents and secretly brought up as a Christian by his nurse and her husband, all three being martyred under *Diocletian. He is invoked against sudden death, hydrophobia, and the convulsive disorder known as St. Vitus's dance.

VLADIMIR, St. (956–1015), the Apostle of the Russians and Ruthenians. In 978 he took Kiev from his brother and subsequently conquered large areas of White Russia. He helped the Emp. Basil II to quell a revolt and *c.* 987 married the Emperor's sister. Henceforth he was an ardent promoter of Christianity, which he imposed by force.

VOETIUS, GISBERT (1589–1676), Dutch Reformed theologian. At *Leyden he came under the influence of F. *Gomar, and he

took a prominent part in the Synod of *Dort. He opposed *Arminianism and defended uncompromising *Calvinistic predestinationism. In 1634 he became professor of theology and oriental languages at Utrecht.

VOLTAIRE, pseudonym of **François-Marie Arouet** (1694–1778), the most celebrated of the French 'Philosophes'. His *Lettres Philosophiques* (1734) was publicly burnt in Paris, and he fled to Lorraine. In 1758 he bought an estate on the Swiss border and lived as a country gentleman. Here he turned to positive social action, taking up the cause of victims of religious intolerance. He attacked atheism not, as is sometimes maintained, because he regarded belief in the existence of God and personal immortality as necessary simply for the government of the masses, but out of a pragmatic conviction that without these beliefs human existence would be one of meaningless anarchy.

VOLUNTARY. A piece of organ music, played usually at the beginning or end of a religious service.

VOLUNTARYISM. The doctrine that the Church should be independent of the State.

VON HARNACK, A.; **VON HOFMANN,** J. C. K. See *Harnack, A.*; *Hofmann, J. C. K. von.*

VON HÜGEL, Baron FRIEDRICH (1852–1925), RC theologian and philosopher. He had a cosmopolitan education and settled in England in 1867. He found himself in growing accord with the cultural and liberalizing tendencies in the RC Church and several of the leaders of the *Modernist Movement became his friends. In 1908 he published *The Mystical Element of Religion as studied in St. Catherine of Genoa and her Friends.* It was followed by an article on Jn. in the 11th edition of the *Encyclopaedia Britannica* (1911), *Eternal Life* (1912), *Essays and Addresses on the Philosophy of Religion* (1921–6), and *The Reality of God* (1931; part of a course of *Gifford Lectures which he was unable to deliver). He was concerned with the relation of Christianity to history, the place of human culture in the Christian life, and the significance of *eschatology. He saw the Institutional, the Intellectual, and the Mystical as the three abiding elements in religion. He became one of the chief religious influences in cultured circles in England, more so outside the RC Church than within it.

VORSTIUS (Konrad von der Vorst) (1569–1622), *Arminian theologian. In 1610, after the death of J. Arminius, he accepted a call to succeed him at *Leyden. In the same year he published his *Tractatus Theologicus de Deo*, which attracted attention because of its rationalist tendencies. F. *Gomar pronounced it heretical and *James I instructed the British ambassador at The Hague to oppose Vorstius's appointment. Vorstius was condemned as a heretic at the Synod of *Dort (1618–19) and banished from the territory of the States-General.

VOSS, GERHARD JAN (1577–1649), Dutch humanist theologian. He held various posts at *Leyden and was reluctantly involved in the disputes between the *Remonstrants and their opponents. In 1632 he became a professor at the newly founded Athenaeum at Amsterdam. He disproved the traditional authorship of the *Athanasian Creed and made solid contributions to learning in other fields.

VOTIVE MASSES. In the past Latin Missals have provided Votive Masses for a wide variety of occasions and objects, such as the restoration of peace and in honour of the Lord's Passion. In the 1970 Roman Missal there are 15. The Solemn Votive Masses ('for a grave cause') have been replaced by 46 Masses and Prayers for Various Occasions, while the *Ritual Masses (q.v.) provide for particular needs.

VOWEL POINTS. *Hebrew was originally written without signs for the vowels. Their absence was remedied first by using some of the existing consonants as vowel letters as well as consonants and later, when the language was no longer spoken and there was danger of the pronunciation being forgotten, by introducing 'vowel points'. These are dots or strokes superimposed on the consonantal text.

VOWS. Solemn and voluntary promises made to perform something not otherwise required but believed to be acceptable to the person to whom they are made. In the OT vows are sometimes explicitly dependent upon the performance of certain favours by God; others appear to have been made unconditionally. The obligation to fulfil a vow once made was very solemn. Christ, however, condemned the Jewish rule which enabled a man to escape his duty to his parents on the pretext of a vow (Mk. 7: 9–13). Acc. to Catholic moral theology a vow to be valid must be made freely by a person who has sufficient use of reason, be within the bounds of possibility of performance, and tending to some future good. With the development of *monasticism, the threefold vow of poverty, chastity, and obedience, taken on entering the religious life, came to occupy special prominence.

VOYSEY, CHARLES (1828–1912), Theistic preacher. From 1864 to 1871 he was vicar of Healaugh, nr. Tadcaster; his heterodox opinions led to his deprivation. He then founded the 'Theistic Church', with headquarters in London.

VULGATE. The Latin version of the Bible most widely used in the W. It was mainly the work of St. *Jerome, and its original purpose was to end the differences of text in the *Old Latin MSS.

Jerome began his work, at the request of Pope *Damasus in 382, with a revision of the Gospels which was completed in 384. It is unlikely that he revised the rest of the NT. In revising the OT he began with the Psalter. About 392 he completed the '*Gallican Psalter' (q.v.), using as his basis Origen's *Hexaplaric text of the LXX. He then decided that a satisfactory version of the OT could be made only with a fresh translation directly from the Hebrew. This translation occupied him intermittently for some 15 years and included a new translation of the Psalter (the 'Hebrew Psalter'), which never became popular. Both old and new versions of Scripture continued in use for some time, but the excellence of Jerome's work was gradually recognized. When (prob. in the 6th cent.) the various Books came to be collected into a single Bible (the Vulgate as we know it), it consisted of Jerome's translation from the Hebrew of the Jewish canonical Books except the Psalter, the Gallican Psalter, Jerome's translation of Tobit and Judith, Old Latin translations of the rest of the *Apocrypha, Jerome's revision of the Gospels, and a revised text of Acts, Epistles, and Rev. All that can be said with certainty about the revision of the latter part of the NT is that the earliest evidence for its existence occurs in quotations in the writings of *Pelagius and his circle.

W

WADDING, LUKE (1588–1657), *Franciscan historian. An Irishman, he joined the Franciscan Order in Spain. In 1618 he was sent to Rome to promote the definition of the *Immaculate Conception. He served on a number of Papal commissions and advised the Sacred Congregation of the *Propaganda on the reorganization of the Church in *Ireland. His chief works were the *Annales Ordinis Minorum* (1625–54), a monumental collection of material on the Franciscan Order to 1540, with its subsidiary *Scriptores Ordinis Minorum* (1650), and his edition of the works of *Duns Scotus (1639).

WAILING WALL, The, in *Jerusalem, known in Jewish tradition as the 'Western Wall'. It was originally part of the *Temple structure erected by *Herod the Great and has been venerated by Jews since the destruction of the Temple in A.D. 70.

WAKE. The name was originally applied to the all-night vigil kept before certain feast days, but it came to refer to the feasting and merrymaking on the holy-day itself and then to a fair held annually on the festival of the local patron saint.

WAKE, WILLIAM (1657–1737), Abp. of *Canterbury from 1716. From 1717 to 1720 he engaged in negotiations with *Gallican leaders, notably L. E. *Dupin, on a plan for reunion between the C of E and the French Church. Wake sympathized with Nonconformists and advocated changes in the BCP to meet their difficulties.

WALAFRID STRABO (c. 808–49), i.e. 'Walafrid the Squinter', abbot of *Reichenau from 838. He wrote a large number of works, both in poetry and prose, secular and religious. His *De Exordiis*, a handbook on matters of liturgical and archaeological interest, throws light on the religious practices of his time. The *Glossa Ordinaria* was long attributed to him.

WALBURGA, St. (c. 710–79), sister of St. *Willibald and St. Winnebald (d. 761). At the wish of St. *Boniface she went from England to help in his missionary work in Germany; on Winnebald's death she assumed direction of his *double monastery at Heidenheim.

WALDEN, ROGER (d. 1406), Abp. of *Canterbury. He rose to high office in the royal service, becoming Treasurer of England in 1395. On T. *Arundel's banishment in 1397 Richard II secured Walden's *provision to the see of Canterbury by the Pope. When Arundel returned with Henry IV (1399), Walden's property was plundered and his register destroyed. He became Bp. of London in 1405.

WALDENSES, also 'Vaudois'. This small Christian community, which survives in Piedmont ('Chiesa Evangelica Valdese'), originated in the 'poor men of Lyons', organized in the 12th cent. by Peter Valdes (formerly, but incorrectly, spelt Waldo), from whom it took its name. Attempts to link it with the primitive Church lack historical basis.

Valdes was a rich merchant of Lyons who died some time between 1205 and 1218. In or soon after 1173 he distributed his property among the poor and became an itinerant and mendicant preacher; he quickly attracted a following of men and women. They sought ecclesiastical recognition at the Third *Lateran Council (1179); *Alexander III approved Valdes's vow of poverty but forbade him and his companions to preach except by invitation of the clergy. Valdes soon ceased to obey this prohibition. Despite the orthodoxy of the profession of faith which he made to Cardinal Henry of Albano c. 1179–80, the Council of Verona (1184) placed the *Cathari and the 'poor men of Lyons' equally under the ban of excommunication. Valdes and his followers increasingly organized themselves apart from the Church, ignored its decrees and sanctions, and appointed their own ministers. Above all they insisted on the right and duty of preaching.

The Waldenses grew in numbers and spread in S. France and Spain, and then in Germany, Piedmont, and Lombardy. From the time of *Innocent III they suffered severe persecution and their numbers dwindled. In the 16th cent. contact was made with the Reformers. In 1532 a synod at Chanforans in the valley of the Angrogne adopted a new Confession of Faith which included the doctrine of *predestination; formally renounced all recognition of the RC Church; and accepted clerical marriage. For a brief space they enjoyed in Piedmont a measure of freedom. There were various later persecutions, but they received help from non-RC bodies, including active intervention on their behalf by O. *Cromwell. It was not, however, until 1848 that they had real political and religious freedom.

WALDENSTRÖM, PAUL PETER (1838–1917), Swedish Free Churchman. He put forward a theory of the *Atonement which was inconsistent with *Lutheran orthodoxy: man had to be reconciled to God, not God to man, and God sent His Son, not in wrath but in love. Waldenström founded the largest sectarian movement in Sweden.

WALES, Christianity in. The early history of Christianity in Wales is obscure; continuity from late Roman times has been suggested. In the 6th cent. there were several outstanding Welsh saints whose names are associated with large monastic foundations; from four of these communities (*Llandaff, *St. Asaph, *St. Davids, and *Bangor) the territorial bishoprics ultimately emerged. The Welsh Church long maintained closer links with the *Celtic Churches of *Ireland, *Scotland, and Brittany than with England, but the Norman conquest of England and the subsequent conquest of parts of Wales by Norman lords reopened the Church in Wales to English and Continental influences. The Welsh sees were gradually subjected to the supremacy of *Canterbury, and in the 12th cent. diocesan and parochial boundaries began to be defined. The system of *tithes was instituted, and by the end of the 13th cent. a judicial and administrative organization was in being. Latin monasticism also was introduced by the Norman invaders. In the later Middle Ages the Welsh Church suffered to a special degree from inertia, and the religious houses were seriously undermanned. The breach with Rome and the *dissolution of the monasteries aroused little opposition; the greatest upheaval was caused by *Mary Tudor's brief attempt to impose clerical *celibacy. *Elizabeth I appointed resident, active, Welsh-speaking bishops, who enforced the 1559 settlement, and a *Welsh Bible and Prayer Book were authorized by an Act of 1563.

The beginnings of Nonconformity in Wales are represented by the foundation of a 'gathered' Church at Llanfaches in 1639. Though by 1676 Nonconformists formed only 5 per cent of the population, the influence of the Church declined. The Welsh sees were poor and usually held by absentees, and lay appropriation of tithes ensured that most parish clergy were poor and ill-educated. *Methodism, preached by H. *Harris, spread rapidly, though its adherents remained within the Church until the *Calvinistic Methodists broke away in 1811. The Church failed to adapt to the large increase in population, Nonconformity grew, and a split developed: the landowners and many of the ironmasters were English-speaking, Anglican, and Tory; the tenant farmers and the new miners and industrial workers were Welsh-speaking, Nonconformist, and radical. Although there was an Anglican revival in the early part of the second half of the 19th cent., the disestablishment of the Church of *Ireland (1869) and the Englishness of the Church in Wales led to growing demands for disestablishment. An Act of 1914 eventually disestablished the Welsh Church; it took effect in 1920. A separate province was created; the bishops are nominated by electors representing various elements in the Church, and one of the diocesans is elected by his fellows Archbishop of Wales. The Church in Wales is no longer an 'alien Church'; services are conducted in Welsh as well as in English, and after 1920 it increased in numbers and influence. Welsh Nonconformity lost a unifying objective and Welsh nationalism turned to secular objectives. The Calvinist Methodists are still the most numerous of the Free Churches; the *Baptists and *United Reformed Church remain strong, but among the Wesleyans there has been a marked decline in numbers. The RCs are a small but vigorous community, recruited largely from Irish immigrant stock in the SE.

WALL, WILLIAM (1647–1728), Anglican divine. His *History of Infant Baptism* (1705), designed to combat the arguments of the *Baptists, has remained the English classic work on the subject.

WALSINGHAM, Norfolk. A replica of the Holy House at *Nazareth, said to have been built in the 11th cent., made Walsingham an important place of pilgrimage in the Middle Ages. The shrine was destroyed in 1538, but pilgrimages have been revived by both Anglicans and RCs.

WALTER, HUBERT. See *Hubert Walter*.

WALTER DE STAPELDON. See *Stapeldon, Walter de*.

WALTER OF ST.-VICTOR (d. after 1180), prior of St.-Victor (see *Victorines*). He wrote a highly controversial work, *Contra Quatuor Labyrinthos Franciae*, attacking the dialectical method of *Abelard and others.

WALTON, BRIAN (*c.* 1600–61), editor of the 'London *Polyglot Bible'. The *Biblia Sacra Polyglotta*, in six volumes, was completed in 1657. Nine languages are represented, but no individual Book of the Bible is printed in more than eight versions. The work, which has not been superseded, is esp. useful because of its lucid arrangement. Walton was appointed Bp. of *Chester in 1660.

WALTON, IZAAK (1593–1683), English author. He retired from business in 1644 and spent most of the rest of his life as a guest in the families of eminent ecclesiastics. His *Compleat Angler* (1653) breathes simplicity, charm, and gentle piety. His Lives of J. *Donne (1640), H. Wotton (1651), R. *Hooker (1665), G. *Herbert (1670), and R. *Sanderson (1678) were based on personal knowledge and extensive investigation.

WANDERING JEW, The. The Jew who, acc. to popular legend, taunted Christ on His way to crucifixion and was doomed to wander over the earth until the Last Day. The legend first appeared in a pamphlet published in 1602. Various meetings with the Jew have been reported.

WAR, Christian Attitude to. It has always been recognized that in a world wholly governed by Christian principles war would be ruled out; nevertheless, since Christians are members of a secular society in which the use of force is necessary for the maintenance of order, it is widely, though not universally, held that war and Christian participation in it are on occasion morally justifiable and even praiseworthy. The *Crusades are the classic example of warfare undertaken for supposedly religious ends. Medieval moral theologians came to distinguish between wars in which a Christian could or could not legitimately take part. St. *Thomas Aquinas lays down 3 conditions for a 'just war': that it must be on the authority of the sovereign; that the cause must be just; and that the belligerents should have a rightful intention. F. de *Vitoria (d. 1546) adds that the war must be waged by 'proper means'.

In modern times 'Absolute Pacifism', that is the doctrine that warfare is in all circumstances forbidden by the Gospel, has been upheld by various groups of people, including leading Churchmen. The main stream of Christian thought, however, has not supported the modern pacifist movements, on the ground that there are even worse evils than physical destruction.

WAR, Participation of the Clergy in. Since the Middle Ages clerics in *major orders have been expressly forbidden to take a direct part in the shedding of blood. Where, however, the power of the State compels them to undertake military duties, they are permitted to conform. The C of E generally upholds the medieval discipline.

WARBURTON, WILLIAM (1698–1779), Bp. of *Gloucester from 1759. His *Divine Legation of Moses* (1737–41) professed to uphold the Divine origin of the Mosaic Law against the *Deists by the singular argument that it contained no doctrine of eternal life: since the doctrine of future rewards and punishments is essential to the well-being of humanity, its absence in the OT can only be explained by Divine inspiration. He was involved in many controversies. He preached against the slave trade as early as 1766.

WARD, MARY (1585–1645), foundress of the '*English Ladies'. She entered a convent of the *Poor Clares in 1606. In 1609, wanting a more active life, with 5 other English-women she founded a religious congregation, the 'Institute of the Blessed Virgin Mary', on the model of the *Jesuit Order. Its freedom from enclosure and from episcopal control caused *Urban VIII to suppress the Institute, but she was later able to reopen her houses on slightly different lines.

WARD, SETH (1617–89), Bp. successively of *Exeter (from 1662) and *Salisbury (from 1667). He had earlier been Savilian Professor of Astronomy at Oxford and was one of the original members of the Royal Society. He was a determined opponent of dissenters and a vigorous supporter of the *Conventicle and *Five Mile Acts.

WARD, WILFRID (1856–1916), RC critic. The son of W. G. *Ward, he wrote lives of his father and of Cardinals N. P. S. *Wiseman and J. H. *Newman. Under his direction the *Dublin Review (of which he became editor in 1906) rose to distinguished rank.

WARD, WILLIAM GEORGE (1812–82), theologian and philosopher. A fellow of Balliol College, Oxford, he pushed *Tractarian principles to extremes, and in 1845 he was deprived of his degrees for heresy. He became a RC, supported the *Ultramontane party, and engaged in much controversial writing.

WARHAM, WILLIAM (c. 1456–1532), Abp. of *Canterbury from 1503. From 1504 to 1515 he was also Lord Chancellor. In 1527 he was T. *Wolsey's assessor in the secret inquiry into the validity of *Henry VIII's marriage, and in 1530 he signed the petition to the Pope asking him to grant the King a divorce. When in 1531 the English clergy were bidden to acknowledge Henry as the Supreme Head of the Church in England, Warham introduced the amendment 'so far as the law of Christ will allow'. In 1532 he formally though ineffectually protested against all Acts of Parliament prejudicial to the Pope.

WARTBURG. The castle in Thuringia where M. *Luther was hidden after being seized (with his own connivance) on his way home from the Diet of *Worms in 1521.

WATCH TOWER BIBLE AND TRACT

SOCIETY. See *Jehovah's Witnesses*.

WATER. See *Holy Water*.

WATERLAND, DANIEL (1683–1740), Anglican divine. He took part in the theological controversies of his time, esp. those on the Divinity of Christ and the Trinity, on *Deism, and on the *Eucharist. The Eucharist was, he held, a commemorative and representative service, which possessed a sacrifical aspect from the remembrance of Christ's death, and the sacramental Presence was to be understood as the virtue and grace of the Lord's Body and Blood communicated to the worthy receiver. This intermediate position was long widely accepted in the C of E.

WATSON, RICHARD (1737–1816), Bp. of *Llandaff from 1782. He was given a bishopric as a known opponent of the American War, but his proposals for radical ecclesiastical reform, including a redistribution of Church revenues, brought him into disfavour with the government.

WATTS, ISAAC (1674–1748), hymnwriter. He was pastor of the *Independent congregation at Mark Lane, London; from 1703 his health deteriorated and he resigned in 1712. In his later years he seems to have inclined towards *Unitarianism. His hymns did much to make hymn-singing a powerful devotional force, esp. in Nonconformity, where the use of music in worship had generally been regarded with suspicion. They include 'When I survey the wondrous Cross' and 'Our God, our help in ages past'.

WAYNFLETE, WILLIAM. See *William of Waynflete*.

WAZO (980/90–1048), Bp. of Liège from 1042. He defended the rights of the Emp. Henry III against Henry I of France, but in the incipient conflict between the Papacy and the Empire he upheld the superiority of the spiritual authority.

WEARMOUTH and JARROW. The twin *Benedictine abbeys between the Tyne and the Wear, founded respectively in 674 and 682 by St. *Benedict Biscop, soon became a centre of learning and culture; they became widely known through the writings of *Bede. Part of their site is occupied by the parish churches.

WEBB, BENJAMIN (1819–85), ecclesiologist. While still an undergraduate, with J. M. *Neale he founded the *Cambridge Camden Society for the revival of ecclesiology. He was himself a strictly moderate ceremonialist and never wore the Eucharistic vestments.

WEDNESDAY. From early times Wednesday, the day on which the Lord was betrayed, was together with *Friday a Christian fast day and long continued so in *Embertide.

WEE FREES. The minority of the *Free Church of Scotland which remained outside the *United Free Church founded in 1900.

WEEK. The week as a liturgical institution derived from the Jewish observance of the *Sabbath. The conception of a day of rest specially dedicated to God was taken over by the Christians, but transferred to the first day of the week (*Sunday) in honour of the *Resurrection. The Jewish fasts of Tuesday and Thursday were translated to *Wednesday, the day of the Betrayal, and *Friday, the day of the Crucifixion. Thursday as a day of rejoicing on account of the *Ascension and of the Institution of the *Eucharist came into prominence in the early Middle Ages, and *Saturday began to be dedicated to the BVM. See also *Holy Week*.

WEIGEL, VALENTIN (1533–88), *Lutheran mystical writer. His works, unknown until the 17th cent., consisted esp. of attacks on the 'Bibliolaters' and of cosmological speculations incompatible with dogmatic Lutheranism. They influenced J. *Boehme.

WEISS, BERNHARD (1827–1918), German NT critic. He distinguished in the NT a number of doctrinal systems which he analysed and classified under four heads (Teaching of Jesus, Original Apostolic Christianity, Paulinism, and Post-Paulinism). His critical foundations were on the whole conservative, though he upheld the priority of Mk. before it was generally accepted.

WEISS, JOHANNES (1863–1914), German NT critic. He was the son of B. *Weiss. His *Die Predigt Jesu vom Reiche Gottes* (1892) was the first attempt at a consistent eschatological interpretation of the Gospel,

defending the thesis that the central purpose of Christ's mission was to proclaim the imminence of a transcendental Kingdom of God, in which He Himself was to be manifested as the Messiah. He expounded for the first time the principles of *Form-Criticism in an article, 'Literaturgeschichte des NT', in *Religion in Geschichte und Gegenwart* (1912).

WELLHAUSEN, JULIUS (1844–1918), German Biblical critic and orientalist. His thesis on the relative dating of the component documents of the *Pentateuch completely transformed OT studies. It sought to establish the gradual development of Hebrew religion from a nomadic stage through that of the Prophets to the religion of the Law. In his later years he turned to a critical study of the NT on similar lines, but here his conclusions met with less ready acceptance.

WELLS. A church of secular canons is said to have been founded at Wells c. 705. In 909 this church became the cathedral of the newly created diocese of the Somerset people. After the see was moved to *Bath in 1088, the establishment at Wells fell into neglect, but Bp. Robert of Lewes (1136–66) refounded the chapter on the lines of St. *Osmund's constitution at *Salisbury and endowed 24 *prebends. The present cathedral was begun c. 1186 and the main structure consecrated in 1239. The magnificent 13th-cent. west front has over 370 figures and reliefs. The most striking interior feature is the inverted arches (14th cent.), by which the piers of the tower are strengthened. See also *Bath and Wells*.

WELSH BIBLE AND PRAYER BOOK. The NT first appeared in Welsh in 1567, the whole Bible in 1588. A revision was issued in 1620. A modern version of the NT was published in 1975; the OT is expected in 1988.

A Welsh translation of the English BCP of 1559 was issued in 1567; one lesson was still read in English. A full translation of the 1662 BCP appeared in 1664. In 1956 the Governing Body of the Church in Wales authorized for experimental use revisions of individual services. A new Prayer Book (in two parts) was issued in 1984–5.

WENCESLAS, St. (c. 907–29), Bohemian prince. Taking over the government from his mother c. 922, he worked for the religious and cultural improvement of his people. He was murdered by his brother and soon venerated as a martyr. The content of J. M. *Neale's 'Good King Wenceslas' is imaginary.

WERBURGH, St. (d. *c.* 699), abbess. The daughter of a Mercian king, she entered the *Benedictine abbey of *Ely, where she became abbess. She was later instigated by King Ethelred to reform the nunneries of his kingdom. In 875, for fear of the Danes, her body was removed to *Chester.

WESEL, JOHN OF. See *John of Wesel.*

WESLEY, CHARLES (1707–88), brother of John *Wesley. An active member of the Oxford *Methodists, he experienced conversion in 1738, engaged in itinerant preaching, and eventually settled in London. He remained faithful to the C of E. He was a gifted and indefatigable hymn-writer; all his collections professed to be the joint work of the two brothers. Favourite hymns include 'Jesu, Lover of my soul', 'Love divine, all loves excelling', and 'Lo! He comes, with clouds descending'.

WESLEY, JOHN (1703–91), founder of the *Methodist Movement. He was the 15th child of the Rev. Samuel Wesley, rector of Epworth, Lincolnshire, and from 1727 to 1729 his curate. At Oxford he gathered around him a group of devout Christians who became known as the 'Holy Club' or 'Methodists'. In 1735 he set out with his brother Charles on a missionary journey to Georgia, but he alienated the colonists and returned home (1737). After a visit to *Herrnhut, he experienced conversion in 1738 and determined to devote his life to evangelistic work. Finding the churches closed to him, he began preaching out of doors; his success led him to organize a body of lay preachers to follow up his evangelism. From 1742 he covered the whole of the British Isles, travelling very extensively. In 1744 he held a conference of lay preachers; this became an annual event, for which a legal constitution was provided in 1784. From small beginnings in 1760 the Methodist system gradually developed in America. The needs of this field induced Wesley to ordain Dr. Thomas Coke (1747–1814) Superintendent or Bishop, and to instruct him to ordain Francis *Asbury as his colleague.

Wesley himself still wanted the Movement to remain within the C of E, but an increasingly independent system grew up.

WESLEY, SAMUEL SEBASTIAN (1810–76), composer and organist. A grandson of Charles *Wesley, he was organist at *Hereford and *Exeter Cathedrals, Leeds Parish Church, and *Winchester and *Gloucester Cathedrals. His compositions include the anthems 'The Wilderness' and 'Blessed be the God and Father'.

WESLEYAN METHODISTS. See *Methodist Churches.*

WESSEL (*c.* 1420–89), Dutch theologian, also known as **Gansfort**. He taught at *Paris and later visited Italy. German Protestants regard him as a 'Reformer before the Reformation' since in his attitude to the Papacy, to the authority of the Church, and to the superstitious tendencies of his age, he shared many of the views of M. *Luther.

WESSENBERG, IGNAZ HEINRICH VON (1774–1860), *Febronianist reformer. Though he was only a subdeacon, in 1802 K. von Dalberg, Coadjutor Prince-Bishop of Constance, appointed him his *vicar general. He aimed at the creation of a National German Church, largely independent of Rome. At Rome his views aroused opposition and Dalberg was constrained to depose him. On Dalberg's death (1817) the Chapter elected Wessenberg as vicar general and administrator of the diocese. In open disobedience to the Pope he acted as administrator until 1827, when the diocese of Constance was incorporated into that of Freiburg. He retired into private life in 1833.

WEST AFRICA, Christianity in. The first Europeans arrived on the coast of W. Africa at the end of the 15th cent., but for the most part they were involved in the slave trade rather than in evangelization. The abolition of the slave trade in the early 19th cent. and the exploration of previously unknown parts of Africa was followed by sustained missionary activity by Churches of every denomination. The British Government expeditions up the Niger in 1854 and 1857 were accompanied by S. A. Crowther, who in 1864 was consecrated Bp. of the Niger Territory, the first African Bp. in the Anglican Communion. *Methodist missionaries were followed by *Presbyterians and *Baptists (originally from the U.S.A.). RC missions were established in the second half of the 19th cent. In French territory not only RCs were active, but also French Evangelicals, incl. A. *Schweitzer. In the present cent. in W. Africa as elsewhere there has been growing co-operation between the non-RC Churches, and since the Second World War national Churches have been established by most denominations. *African Independent Churches (q.v.) have also multiplied.

WEST INDIES, Christianity in the. The earliest evangelization was carried out by RC missionaries who came with the Spanish colonists from the end of the 15th cent., and a bishopric was established at San Domingo in 1511. When the aboriginal population was exterminated and replaced by Negro slaves from W. Africa, attempts were made to see that the slaves were baptized, but the brutality with which they were treated led to antagonism and revolt.

In the early 17th cent. the British began to settle in some of the islands and acquired others by capture. Here the C of E was established, but until the 19th cent. it made little attempt to evangelize the natives. Missionary work was, however, undertaken by the *Moravians, *Methodists, and *Baptists. In 1824 Anglican bishoprics were established in Jamaica and Barbados, and in 1883 the West Indies was constituted an independent Province of the Anglican Communion.

In those areas which were originally French or Spanish the RC Church remains predominant. After the liberation of the slaves (1833), there was an influx of Orientals, who resisted evangelization. In the 20th cent. all the Churches have tried to build up native ministries and there have been attempts by most non-RC Churches to join in *ecumenical discussions. There has been vast growth among the *Pentecostal Churches.

WESTCOTT, BROOKE FOSS (1825–1901), Bp. of *Durham from 1890. While he was Regius Professor of Divinity at Cambridge, he prepared, with F. J. A. *Hort, the celebrated edition of the Gk. NT, published in 1881; it was followed by his great commentaries on Jn. (1881), on the Epp. of Jn. (1883), and on Heb. (1889). In his diocese he made social problems his special concern, and he mediated in the coal strike of 1892.

WESTERÅS, The Ordinance of. The regulations passed by the Diet of Westerås in 1527, which carried through the Protestant Reformation in *Sweden.

WESTERN TEXT OF THE NT. An early form of the Gk. text of the NT, so named by B. F. *Westcott and J. F. A. *Hort because the chief authorities for it were of Western *provenance*, viz. some Graeco-Latin MSS., the *Old Latin, and quotations in the Latin Fathers. It reflects changes which the NT suffered before A.D. 150, and in some places it prob. preserves the correct text against other witnesses.

WESTMINSTER ABBEY. Acc. to a legend, prob. of 13th-cent. origin, a *Benedictine abbey was founded in Thorney Island in 616 and miraculously consecrated by St. *Peter. Rebuilding and restoration of the abbey was undertaken by *Edward the Confessor in commutation of a vow to go on a pilgrimage to Rome. Erection of the present church in Gothic style began in 1245; the eastern part was complete in 1269 and the nave finished c. 1505. The western towers, designed by C. *Wren, were completed between 1740 and 1750.

The Benedictine foundation of Edward the Confessor became one of the richest abbeys in England. In 1540 the monastery was dissolved and a *collegiate church established; the abbey became a Royal *Peculiar, retaining its independence from the see of London. In 1540 a bishopric was established; it was suppressed in 1550. Since the time of *William I the abbey has been the traditional place for the coronation of the sovereign; it has retained a unique position as a centre of the national life.

WESTMINSTER ASSEMBLY. The synod appointed by the Long Parliament in 1643 to reform the English Church. It consisted of 30 lay assessors and 121 divines of widely differing views; when the *Solemn League and Covenant was adopted it was increased by 5 clerical and 3 lay Commissioners from *Scotland.

The Assembly began by revising the *Thirty-Nine Articles, but with the appearance of the Solemn League and Covenant it turned to the production of a new formula, the *Westminster Confession (q.v.). It also prepared the Directory of Public *Worship (q.v.) and the two *Westminster Catechisms (q.v.). Although only partially and temporarily accepted in England, these documents were approved by the Church of Scotland and came into general use throughout the *Presbyterian world.

WESTMINSTER CATECHISMS. Two Catechisms compiled by the *Westminster Assembly and approved by Parliament and the *General Assembly of the Church of *Scotland in 1648. The Larger Catechism is a popular restatement of the teaching of the *Westminster Confession. The more important Shorter Catechism opens with the well-known Question and Answer: 'What is the chief end of man?' 'Man's chief end is to glorify God and to enjoy Him for ever.'

WESTMINSTER CATHEDRAL. The cathedral of the RC Abp. of Westminster, begun in 1895 and opened in 1903. It was designed in early 'Christian Byzantine' style and executed mainly in red brick.

WESTMINSTER CONFESSION. The profession of *Presbyterian faith drawn up by the *Westminster Assembly. It was approved by Parliament in 1648, having been ratified by the *General Assembly of the Church of *Scotland in the previous year. It immediately established itself as the definitive statement of Presbyterian doctrine in the English-speaking world.

WESTON, FRANK (1871–1924), Anglican Bp. of Zanzibar from 1908. Joining the *U.M.C.A. in 1898, he learned to live among Africans and to understand their point of view. He took the lead in opposing the proposals of the *Kikuyu Conference of 1913. In 1920 he largely inspired the appeal for Christian Unity put out by the *Lambeth Conference.

WESTPHALIA, Peace of (1648). Two treaties which ended the *Thirty Years War (q.v.).

WESTWARD POSITION. In some early churches (esp. *basilicas), the celebrant of the Eucharist stood on the far side of the altar from the people. The practice of celebrating the Eucharist from this position (normally facing westward) has gradually been adopted in the RC Church in modern times and is followed in some C of E churches.

WETTE, W. M. L. DE. See *De Wette, W. M. L.*

WETTSTEIN, JOHANN JAKOB (1693–1754), NT critic. From 1733 he was a professor at Amsterdam. His edition of the Gk. NT (1751–2) included in the critical apparatus many important variants hitherto unrecorded and also the *sigla* for denoting the MSS. in common use since then.

WEYMOUTH NEW TESTAMENT. The English version of the NT published in 1903 under the title *The New Testament in Modern Speech*. It was the work of R. F. Weymouth (1822–1902), a *Baptist schoolmaster.

WHARTON, HENRY (1664–95), medievalist. In 1688 he became domestic chaplain to Abp. W. *Sancroft; though he took the Oaths of Allegiance and Supremacy to William and Mary in 1689 he failed to find favour with the authorities. The first two volumes of his *Anglia Sacra* (1691) provide a history to the Reformation of the English sees whose *cathedrals were served by *regulars. They contain editions of medieval chronicles and other original texts, and remain indispensable. A third volume, intended to cover the cathedrals served by the *secular clergy, was unfinished.

WHATELY, RICHARD (1787–1863), Anglican Abp. of *Dublin from 1831. At Oxford he was one of the best-known of the '*Noetics', an anti-*Erastian, and an anti-*Evangelical; later he opposed the *Tractarians. In Dublin he took an active part in the religious and political life of *Ireland and did valuable work as a Commissioner of National Education.

WHICHCOTE, BENJAMIN (1609–83), *Cambridge Platonist. He became Provost of King's College, Cambridge, in 1644. He was ejected at the Restoration, but restored to favour in 1662 on accepting the Act of *Uniformity. He then held important cures in London.

Whichcote was averse to the pessimistic view of human nature prevalent among the *Puritans and exalted man as a child of reason. He saw in reason the test of Scripture, maintained that some matters on which good men disagreed were insoluble, and pleaded for freedom of thought.

WHISTON, WILLIAM (1667–1752), mathematician and theologian. In 1703 he succeeded I. *Newton as Lucasian Professor of Mathematics at Cambridge; his *Arianizing views led to his expulsion from the university in 1710, and in 1747 he joined the *General Baptists. He is remembered for his translation of *Josephus (1737; often reprinted).

WHITAKER, WILLIAM (1548-95), *Puritan divine. In 1580 he became Regius Professor of Divinity at Cambridge and in 1586 Master of St. John's College. A strict *Calvinist, he exercised a wide influence by his devotion to learning and his impartiality. He was mainly responsible for drafting the *Lambeth Articles.

WHITBY, The Synod of (664). The chief question settled at the Synod was the date of Easter (see *Paschal Controversies*). The Christians of Northumbria followed the Irish custom, whereas those of the South had adopted the Roman system. The Synod, led by King Oswy, decided to follow Rome. The *Celtic Churches hesitated for some time before accepting the decision.

WHITCHURCH, EDWARD (d. 1561), printer. He became an adherent of the Reformed doctrines and in 1537 he associated himself with R. *Grafton to circulate *Matthew's Bible (printed at Antwerp). In 1538 he and Grafton gave financial assistance to M. *Coverdale in printing his NT at Paris and in 1539 they published the *Great Bible in London. Under *Edward VI Whitchurch printed the BCP of 1549 and 1552.

WHITE FATHERS. The RC Society of Missionaries of Africa, founded by Abp. Charles Lavigerie at Algiers in 1868. It is composed of secular priests and coadjutor brothers living in community without vows, but bound by solemn oath to lifelong work in the African mission. They wear a white tunic and a mantle or hooded cloak, with a rosary round the neck.

WHITE FRIARS. The *Carmelite friars, so called from their white cloaks and *scapulars.

WHITE LADIES. A popular name, from their white habits, for (1) the Sisters of the Presentation of Mary, a teaching order

founded in France in 1796; (2) the *Magdalenes; (3) the *Cistercian nuns.

WHITE MONKS. The *Cistercian monks, so called from the colour of their habit, which was of undyed wool.

WHITE SISTERS. (1) The Congregation of the Missionary Sisters of Our Lady of Africa was founded by Abp. C. Lavigerie in 1869 to assist the *White Fathers (q.v.). (2) The Congregation of the Daughters of the Holy Ghost, called White Sisters from their white habit, was founded in Brittany in 1706. Their chief objects are the education of children and the care of the sick.

WHITE, FRANCIS (*c.* 1564–1638), Bp. successively of *Carlisle, *Norwich, and *Ely. He was a prominent anti-Papist disputant and in 1622 he was engaged by *James I to support W. *Laud in presenting the Anglican case in a formal dispute with the *Jesuit 'John *Fisher'.

WHITE, JOSEPH BLANCO (1775–1814), theological writer. Born in Spain of Irish parents, he was ordained to the RC priesthood in 1800. He suffered religious doubt, came to England in 1810, and later became an Anglican; he was well known among the *Tractarians. He finally became a *Unitarian.

WHITE, WILLIAM HALE. The real name of 'Mark *Rutherford' (q.v.).

WHITEFIELD, GEORGE (1714–70), *Methodist evangelist. At Oxford he came under the influence of John and Charles *Wesley; he followed them to Georgia, where he founded an orphanage. On returning to England soon afterwards, he began to hold large open-air meetings. His preaching met with remarkable response, though his activities were frowned upon by ecclesiastical authority, esp. as his markedly *Calvinist theology appeared less orthodox than that of the Wesleys. Through the patronage of Selina, Countess of *Huntingdon, he was able to open a tabernacle in London. He was the most striking orator of the Methodist revival, and often visited America.

WHITGIFT, JOHN (*c.* 1530–1604), Abp. of *Canterbury from 1583. He held high office at Cambridge, where his opposition to

T. *Cartwright brought him to the notice of *Elizabeth I. As Archbishop he used the Ecclesiastical Commission to repress *Puritanism (e.g. the *Marprelate Tracts), and he resisted the attempts of the extreme Puritans to impose upon the Church a *Presbyterian form of government in 1584–5. Theologically he was a *Calvinist.

WHITSUNDAY. The Feast of the Descent of the Holy Spirit upon the Apostles on the 50th day after *Easter (see *Pentecost*). It ranks, after Easter, as the second festival of the Church. In the W. the Vigil of Pentecost soon became a secondary date for *Baptisms, with a ceremony resembling that of the *Paschal Vigil Service. The association of the Vigil with Baptism survived in the RC Church until 1955.

WHITTIER, JOHN GREENLEAF (1807–92), American *Quaker poet, associated with the anti-*slavery movement. He wrote several well-known hymns, including 'Dear Lord and Father of mankind' and 'Immortal love, for ever full'.

WHITTINGHAM, WILLIAM (c. 1524–1579), *Calvinist. In *Mary's reign he supported J. *Knox at Frankfurt and then at Geneva, where he succeeded him as minister in 1559, apparently without receiving any ordination. In 1563 he was made Dean of *Durham. His iconoclasm and failure to conform to the BCP led E. *Sandys, Abp. of York, to try to deprive him on the ground that he had not been validly ordained, but he died before the proceedings were concluded.

WHOLE DUTY OF MAN, The. A devotional treatise published c. 1658 and formerly widely used. It has been attributed to H. *Hammond, J. *Fell, and (with most probability) to R. *Allestree.

WICHERN, JOHANN HINRICH (1808–1881), founder of the German *Innere Mission. In 1833 he founded an institute in Hamburg, the Rauhes Haus, to provide for the spiritual and material needs of neglected children. From 1844 he edited a periodical which became the central organ of all charitable undertakings in the German Protestant Churches; at his suggestion these were co-ordinated in the central organization of the Innere Mission at the first congress of the Evangelical Churches in 1848. He later

undertook prison reform and assisted those wounded in war.

WICLIF, J. See *Wycliffe, J.*

WIDOWS. In NT times widows had an acknowledged claim to the charity of their fellow-Christians, and they soon acquired a recognized status and privileges in the Church.

WIED, HERMANN VON. See *Hermann of Wied.*

WILBERFORCE, SAMUEL (1805–73), Bp. of *Oxford (1845–69) and then of *Winchester. He encouraged the building of churches and the formation of Anglican sisterhoods, and he founded Cuddesdon Theological College (1854). His effective methods of pastoral administration were widely imitated. One of the main achievements of his last years was the initiation of the revision of the AV.

WILBERFORCE, WILLIAM (1759–1833), philanthropist. He was converted to *Evangelicalism and dissuaded from taking Holy *Orders by advice that he could best serve Christianity in Parliament. He became a prominent member of the *Clapham Sect. His main concern was the abolition of the slave trade; after many vicissitudes the Bill to effect this became law in 1807. He then supported the movement for the abolition of slavery, achieved in 1833. He also helped in the foundation of the *C.M.S. and the *British and Foreign Bible Society, advocated the introduction of missionaries into *India, and championed the cause of *Sunday observance.

WILFRID, St. (634–709), Bp. of *York. He was educated at *Lindisfarne, but he became dissatisfied with the *Celtic way of religious life and as Abbot of *Ripon he introduced the *Benedictine Rule. At the Synod of *Whitby (664) he was largely responsible for the victory of the Roman party. Soon afterwards he was consecrated Bp. of York at Compiègne; he found his see occupied by St. *Chad, but he was put in possession of it by *Theodore, Abp. of Canterbury, in 669. When Theodore divided the see of York in 678, Wilfrid went to Rome to appeal. He was eventually reinstated in his see from 686 to 691. He then had to flee from York and a synod held in 703 called upon him to resign; after a further successful appeal to Rome, he agreed to resign in favour of St. *John of Beverley. He brought England into closer touch with the Papacy and succeeded in replacing Celtic usages in N. England by the Roman liturgy.

WILKES, PAGET (1871–1934), missionary. In 1897 he sailed for *Japan under the *C.M.S. Here he formed the idea of a Japanese Evangelistic Band which, free of ecclesiastical organization, would be directed towards aggressive evangelism; in 1903 the 'One by One Band' of Japan was established, with its centre at Kobe. Wilkes spent all his active life in Japan.

WILKINS, DAVID (1685–1745), editor of the 'Concilia'. He was Librarian of *Lambeth Palace. His *Concilia Magnae Britanniae et Hiberniae* (1737), a monumental collection of documents, is still a standard source for work on British and Irish ecclesiastical councils.

WILKINS, JOHN (1614–72), Bp. of *Chester from 1668. His chief interests lay in the furthering of science and philosophy, and when the Royal Society received its charter in 1662 he became its first secretary. At Chester he advocated the toleration of dissenters. He was a strong upholder of natural theology and maintained that the conflicting contentions of fanatics and sceptics were the main cause of unbelief.

WILLEHAD, St. (d. 789), Bp. of Bremen from 787. A native of Northumbria, he set out for missionary work in Frisia. In 780 *Charlemagne sent him to preach to the Saxons at Wigmodia near the North Sea.

WILLIAM I (?1028–87), Duke of Normandy and King of England ('the Conqueror'). The illegitimate son of Duke Robert I, William won and kept firm control over Normandy. In 1066, with the blessing of *Alexander II, he conquered England. His relations with Rome remained generally co-operative. There was no conflict over lay *investiture, which William continued to practise. The episcopate in England was largely Normanized, and in co-operation with Abp. *Lanfranc the king saw to the implementation of papal legislation on *simony, clerical immorality, and diocesan administration.

WILLIAM OF AUVERGNE (c. 1180–1249), philosopher and theologian. He became Bp. of Paris in 1228 and was influential at the court of *Louis IX. His prolific writings mainly form a vast philosophico-theological encyclopaedia, *Magisterium Divinale*. He drew on *Aristotelian material. He largely prepared the way for later *Scholasticism by teaching a moderate form of *Realism, being among the first Schoolmen to recognize a real distinction between essence and existence.

WILLIAM OF AUXERRE (d. 1231), *Scholastic theologian. He taught at *Paris. He was among the first to make use of the doctrines of the newly discovered writings of *Aristotle in his *Summa Aurea*.

WILLIAM OF CHAMPEAUX (c. 1070–1121), *Scholastic philosopher. He taught at the cathedral school in *Paris, whence he was driven (1108) by *Abelard's ridicule of his exaggerated *Realism. He retired to the priory of St.-Victor, apparently modified his doctrines, and by his lectures there laid the foundations of the *Victorine school. In 1113 he became Bp. of Châlons.

WILLIAM OF CONCHES (c. 1080–c. 1154), philosopher. He was a pupil of *Bernard of Chartres and sought to further his efforts to encourage the study of the profane sciences and literature in the interests of a Christian humanism. His writings deal mainly with natural philosophy.

WILLIAM OF MALMESBURY (c. 1090–c. 1143), historian. He appears to have spent most of his life in the monastery at *Malmesbury. His *Gesta Regum Anglorum* (1120) and *Gesta Pontificum Anglorum* (1125) deal respectively with the secular and ecclesiastical history of England. His *Historia Novella* continues the *Gesta Regum* to the year 1142.

WILLIAM OF MOERBEKE (c. 1215–1286), translator. A *Dominican, he was sent to Thebes (c. 1259) and Nicaea (1260), and then attached to the Papal Curia until he became Abp. of Thebes in 1278. His translations of *Aristotle include works not previously translated into Latin as well as revisions of existing translations on the basis of Greek MSS. He also translated a number of commentaries on Aristotle.

WILLIAM OF NORWICH, St. (1132–44), supposed victim of a Jewish ritual murder. An apprentice at *Norwich, he was enticed from his home on the Monday in *Holy Week 1144 and on *Holy Saturday his body was found with marks of violence. He is supposed to have been crucified by Jews during the Passover. His cult dates from 1151.

WILLIAM OF OCCAM (or OCKHAM) (c. 1285–1347), philosopher, theologian, and polemicist. A native of Ockham in Surrey, he joined the *Franciscan Order and taught at *Oxford. In 1323 he was denounced at *Avignon for teaching dangerous doctrines; a commission censured 51 propositions from his writings, but no formal condemnation followed. In 1327 the Minister General of the Franciscans charged him to examine the Papal constitutions in the dispute on Franciscan poverty; Occam concluded that *John XXII had taken up heretical positions. In 1328 he fled to Louis of Bavaria, under whose protection he remained until 1347. He wrote a series of polemical works against the Pope and was excommunicated and sentenced to expulsion from the order.

Occam was a vigorous, critical, and independent thinker, and he contributed to the development of formal logic. He eliminated the notion, then generally accepted, of the existence of *universals. Only individual things exist, and they are directly apprehended by the mind. On the theological side much of his thinking was determined by his resolute attempt to do away with anything that limited God's omnipotence and freedom. His radical criticism of *Realism and his rethinking of the relationship between theology and philosophy prepared the ground for a more scientific approach to reality. His theological influence was still felt in the 15th cent., and M. *Luther regarded himself as a follower of Occam. His political theories played an important part in the development of the *Conciliar Movement.

WILLIAM OF ST.-THIERRY (c. 1085–1148), theologian and mystical writer. He was elected Abbot of the *Benedictine abbey at St.-Thierry, near Reims, in 1119/20. He formed a close friendship with St. *Bernard, whom he would have liked to join at *Clairvaux. In 1135 he joined a group of *Cistercians establishing a house at Signy in the forest of the Ardennes.

In 1138 William wrote to St. Bernard urging him to refute Peter *Abelard's views on the Trinity and Redemption. He himself wrote against Abelard and against *William of Conches. His other works include two commentaries on the Song of Songs, his *Meditativae orationes*, and his famous *Epistola ad Fratres de Monte Dei de Vita Solitaria*, known as the 'Golden Letter' and often attributed to St. Bernard.

WILLIAM OF TYRE (c. 1130–85), historian. Born in Palestine of European parents, in 1167 he was appointed Archdeacon of Tyre by Amaury, King of Jerusalem, with an enhanced stipend on condition that he wrote the official history of the reign. In 1175 he was consecrated Abp. of Tyre. His *Historia Rerum in Partibus Transmarinis Gestarum* covers the period from 1095 (Preaching of the First *Crusade) to 1184. It is the primary authority from 1127, and is marked by insight, tolerance, and impartiality.

WILLIAM OF WAYNFLETE (c. 1395–1486), Bp. of *Winchester from 1447. In 1448 he obtained licence to found a hall in Oxford to foster the study of theology and philosophy; in 1457 it was refounded as Magdalen College. He was a favourite of *Henry VI, took a prominent part in public affairs, and was Chancellor from 1456 to 1460.

WILLIAM OF WYKEHAM (1324–1404), Bp. of *Winchester from 1367. He also became Chancellor in 1367, but, being blamed for the disasters of the French war, he was driven from office in 1371. He then devoted himself mainly to his diocese and to his plans for academic foundations. At Oxford he founded a college dedicated to St. Mary, but soon known as New College, and at Winchester he established a school for 70 poor scholars. As a member of the commission of regency appointed in 1386 and as Chancellor from 1389 to 1391, he tried to exercise a moderating influence.

WILLIAM OF YORK, St. (d. 1154), Abp. of *York. William Fitzherbert was elected Abp. of York in 1142, but as he was accused of *simony by the *Cistercians, *Theobald, Abp. of *Canterbury, refused to consecrate him. Pope Innocent II allowed his consecration in 1143, but when he went to Rome for the *pallium in 1147, *Eugenius III suspended him, and after his relatives had attacked *Fountains Abbey, where the rival candidate was abbot, he was deposed. Pope Anastasius IV restored him in 1154. He died a month later, possibly by poison. He was regarded as a martyr, and miracles at his tomb were reported.

WILLIAMS, CHARLES WALTER STANSBY (1886–1945), poet and theological writer. He wrote novels largely devoted to supernatural themes, a penetrating study of the Church under the title *The Descent of the Dove* (1939), as well as poems. He did much to commend Christianity in a sacramental form to many who would have been unmoved by conventional apologetic.

WILLIAMS, ISAAC (1802–65), *Tractarian poet and theologian. He wrote the famous Tract No. 80 on 'Reserve in Communicating Religious Knowledge'. This lost him the election to the chair of poetry in 1842 and led to his withdrawal from Oxford.

WILLIAMS, JOHN (1582–1650), Abp. of *York. Under *James I he received many benefices, including the Bpric. of *Lincoln (1621), and was made Lord Keeper. He was disliked by *Charles I and W. *Laud, but in the Long Parliament he headed a party of compromise and, recovering royal favour, was translated to York in 1641. After the Civil War he retired to Wales.

WILLIAMS, JOHN (1796–1839), missionary. He worked under the *L.M.S., sailing for the Pacific Islands in 1817. After years of successful work in the *South Seas, he landed at Dillon's Bay, Erromanga, where he was killed and eaten by the natives. News of his death caused a burst of missionary enthusiasm in England.

WILLIAMS, RALPH VAUGHAN (1872–1958), composer. Apart from active service in the 1914–18 War, his life was devoted to music. He composed works of every kind, including nine symphonies and six operas. He wrote hymn tunes, among them the notable *Sine Nomine* ('For all the saints'), *canticle settings and anthems, the *Te Deum* in G for C. G. *Lang's enthronement at Canterbury and a *Festal Te Deum* for the coronation of George VI. He was music editor of the *English Hymnal* and helped in the preparation of *Songs of Praise* and the *Oxford Book of Carols*.

WILLIAMS, ROGER (c. 1604–83), champion of religious toleration. He sailed for N. America in search of religious liberty in 1630. When he was ordered to leave Massachusetts in 1635, he took refuge among the Indians outside the state, founding a settlement which he called 'Providence' (1636). Here he established the first *Baptist Church in America. The constitution of the colony (later called 'Rhode Island'), included wide religious latitude, and when the *Quakers came to America in 1656 Williams granted them political toleration, though he attacked their doctrines.

WILLIAMS, ROWLAND (1817–70), Anglican divine. His essay on Biblical criticism in *Essays and Reviews* (1860) led to a prosecution for heterodoxy; the Court of *Arches sentenced him to a year's suspension, but the sentence was annulled by the *Judicial Committee of the Privy Council in 1864.

WILLIBALD, St. (700–86), Bp. of Eichstätt from 742. In 722 he set out from England on a pilgrimage to Rome; he then went on to the E. Mediterranean. After he had spent 10 years in retirement at *Monte Cassino, Gregory III sent him to Germany. He was ordained by St. *Boniface, to whom he was related.

WILLIBRORD, St. (658–739), 'Apostle of Frisia'. A Northumbrian, he was educated at *Ripon and then spent 12 years in an Irish abbey. In 690 he made his way as a missionary to W. Frisia. He gained Papal support and in 695 he was consecrated Abp. of the Frisians. *Pepin gave him a site for a cathedral just outside Utrecht, and in 698 he founded the monastery of Echternach in Luxemburg which became a missionary centre. His work extended to *Denmark, Heligoland, and Thuringia.

WILSNACK. A former place of pilgrimage in Germany. After a fire in the church in 1383 three consecrated *hosts were said to have been found unharmed, but marked with drops of blood. The alleged miracle, followed by other extraordinary events, drew crowds of pilgrims. In 1552 Wilsnack became Protestant and the miraculous hosts were burnt.

WILSON, THOMAS (1663–1755), Bp. of *Sodor and Man from 1698. He set himself to raise the standards of spiritual life and pastoral efficiency. His Ecclesiastical Constitutions of 1704 imposed public penance for slander, perjury, immorality, and other offences; their administration involved him in acrimonious legal disputes, as did his suspension of his archdeacon for heresy (1722). His devotional works long enjoyed a wide circulation.

WINCHELSEA, ROBERT OF (c. 1245–1313), Abp. of *Canterbury from 1293. He became Rector of the University of *Paris in 1267. Returning to England c. 1283, he studied theology at *Oxford, where he was Chancellor in 1288. His theological teaching was concerned with the doctrine of the Trinity. As Archbishop he was a staunch upholder of ecclesiastical rights and soon became involved in disputes with Edward I over taxation of the clergy. When Edward's vassal became Pope as *Clement V (1305), Winchelsea was suspended. After Edward I's death in 1307, he returned to his see, but was soon in opposition to Edward II.

WINCHESTER. About 670 the bishopric of Wessex was transferred from *Dorchester to Winchester. The political importance of the city and the fame of St. *Swithin (Bp. 852–62) assisted the growth in power of the see. St. *Ethelwold (Bp. 963–84) replaced the secular canons of the cathedral with *Benedictine monks. A new cathedral in Norman style was built by Walkelin (Bp. 1070–98) on a site adjoining that of the Anglo-Saxon church. Apart from the transepts this church has been gradually transformed from Norman to Gothic. The Lady Chapel and the retro-choir were built in Early English style; the Perpendicular nave was completed by *William of Wykeham (Bp. 1367–1404), who also founded Winchester College. The Hospital of St. Cross in Winchester was founded by *Henry of Blois (Bp. 1129–71), who also built six episcopal residences. The see of Winchester ranks fifth among the English bishoprics, and the

bishop always has a seat in the House of Lords.

WINDESHEIM, near Zwolle, in Holland. A house of *Augustinian Canons was established in 1387 by six of G. de *Groote's disciples under the direction of *Florentius Radewyns. With three other Dutch monasteries they formed the 'Congregation of Windesheim', which grew rapidly in the 15th cent. The Canons of Windesheim were the chief monastic representatives of the '*Devotio Moderna'. Their members included *Thomas à Kempis and G. *Biel. The Congregation, reorganized in 1573, survived in Belgium and the Catholic parts of Germany until 1802.

WINDSOR, St. George's Chapel. The 'Royal Free Chapel of Windsor' was constituted by Edward III to take charge of the shrine of the Order of the Garter (founded c. 1348); it received its statutes in 1352. The present Perpendicular chapel, with its elaborate stone vaulting, dates from 1475–1508.

WINDTHORST, LUDWIG (1812–91), German Catholic politician. He held high office in Hanover. After the union of Hanover with Prussia in 1866, he became a member of the N. German Diet and later of the German Reichstag. In 1871 he helped to found the *Centre Party; he was its leader until his death. He played a prominent part in the *Kulturkampf and had a considerable share in the negotiations for the repeal of the *May Laws.

WINE. Wine is frequently mentioned in the Bible and appears to have been in everyday use in Palestine in NT times. It has traditionally been held to be one of the essential materials for a valid *Eucharist. The words of administration imply that the consecrated wine conveys to the communicant the Blood of Christ, though RC theologians have held that both the Body and the Blood are present in each of the Eucharistic species. From early times it has been customary to mix water with the wine at the Eucharist. In the C of E the admixture was not ordered after 1552, but it was generally revived in the 19th cent. A conscientious abstinence from wine has led to the use of unfermented grape-juice by Nonconformists.

WINIFRED, St. (d. c. 650), patron saint of

N. Wales. Acc. to late legends, she was a fair maiden sought in marriage by Prince Caradog of Hawarden; refusing his advances, she was wounded (or killed) by him, but miraculously healed (or restored to life) by her uncle, St. *Beuno. A spring marked the scene, the present Holywell, Clwyd; here she established a nunnery and became abbess.

WIPO (d. 1050), hymn-writer. He was chaplain to the Emps. Conrad II and Henry III. His best-known work is the '*Victimae paschali laudes', the *sequence for Easter Day. His history of the reign of Conrad II (1024–39) is a primary source.

WISDOM. Wisdom, whether human or Divine, occupies a prominent place in the OT. Divine Wisdom is manifested in creation and in God's guidance of nations and individuals (Wisd. 10–19). It is more than a mere quality and tends increasingly to become a *hypostasis, so esp. in Prov. 8 and Wisd. 7: 22 ff. In the NT Divine Wisdom is incarnate in Christ, whom St. *Paul calls 'the wisdom of God' (1 Cor. 1: 24). Wisdom is also intimately linked with the Holy Spirit, one of whose gifts it is (1 Cor. 12: 8). Among the Fathers most use 'Wisdom' as a synonym for the Incarnate Word or *Logos, some for the Third Person of the Trinity. In *Gnostic thought, which saw in Wisdom a Divine emanation and a cause of the creation and redemption of the world, the conception played a central part. In some modern writers it has again become a subject of speculation in connection with the Deity.

WISDOM OF SOLOMON, The. A Book of the *Apocrypha. The first part (1: 1–6: 8) describes the different destinies awaiting the righteous and the wicked; the second part (6: 9–9: 18) contains the meditation on Wisdom which gives the Book its name; the last part (10–19) reviews the history of Israel to the *Exodus, with an excursus on idolatry in 13–15. The ascription of the Book to *Solomon is a literary device. It was almost certainly written by an *Alexandrian Jew, perhaps c. A.D. 40.

The Book has had great influence on Christian thought. It may have been directly used by St. *Paul. In later writers the terms used of the Divine Wisdom are freely applied to Christ.

WISEMAN, NICHOLAS PATRICK STEPHEN (1802–65), English cardinal. He was rector of the English College at Rome (1828–40) before he returned to England as coadjutor to the *Vicar Apostolic of the Midland District. When the RC hierarchy was restored in 1850 he became the first Abp. of *Westminster and a cardinal. A believer in *Ultramontane methods of devotion, he was opposed by the older school of English RCs.

WISHART, GEORGE (c. 1513–46), Scottish Reformer. He fled to England when charged with heresy in 1538 and travelled on the Continent. Returning to Scotland in 1543, he began active propaganda on behalf of the Reformed doctrines, being assisted by J. *Knox. He was arrested and burnt.

WITCHCRAFT. The malevolent exercise of preternatural power, esp. by women, attributed to a connection with demons. The narrative of the witch of Endor (1 Sam. 28: 7–25) and the condemnations of witchcraft in the OT (Exod. 22: 18) and NT (Gal. 5: 20) have sometimes been adduced as proofs of its existence.

In the early Middle Ages the persecution of witches, which had been a feature of Roman law, was officially discouraged, but popular superstition did not die out. Popes Alexander IV (1258) and *John XXII (1320) allowed the *Inquisition to deal with witchcraft if connected with heresy, and secular courts also took action. Mass persecutions began in the later 15th cent. The Reformers, with their often exaggerated belief in the power of the devil, further contributed to the evil, as did the unrest stirred up by the religious wars. The persecution of witches practically ceased in the 18th cent. under the influence of the *Enlightenment.

WITELO (b. c. 1230), philosopher and scientist. Born in Silesia, he studied at Padua and later went to Viterbo, where he became the friend of *William of Moerbeke. Of his later life nothing certain is known. His treatise on optics, *Perspectiva,* is based on the work of the Arabic scholar Alhazen. Its psychological doctrines are akin to modern views on association and the subconscious. Its metaphysical teaching is *Neoplatonist.

WITNESSES, The Three. See *Johannine Comma.*

WITTENBERG, the cradle of the *Reformation. At its university, founded in 1502, M. *Luther became a professor in 1508. In 1517 he affixed his 95 theses against *indulgences to the door of the Schlosskirche, and in 1522 Protestant public worship was celebrated for the first time, in the parish church.

WITTENBERG, Concord of (1536). An agreement on *Eucharistic doctrine drawn up by P. *Melanchthon and accepted by a large and representative body of *Lutheran and *Zwinglian theologians at Wittenberg. The Swiss Zwinglians, however, refused to accept it.

WOLFENBÜTTEL FRAGMENTS, The. The title under which G. E. *Lessing issued seven extracts (1774–8) from an unpublished work in which H. S. *Reimarus had attacked historic Christianity.

WOLFF, CHRISTIAN (1679–1754), German philosopher. He became a professor at Halle in 1706. In an attempt to systematize the principles of G. W. *Leibniz, he developed a comprehensive system of philosophy. His confidence in reason offended the *Pietists, who persuaded Frederick William I to expel him in 1723. He spent his exile at *Marburg. He was recalled on the accession of Frederick the Great (1740). His system was taught in most German universities in the later 18th cent.

WOLFGANG, St. (c. 924–94), Bp. of Ratisbon from 972. He was educated at *Reichenau, taught at Trier, and in 964 entered the *Benedictine Order at *Einsiedeln. He was an ardent reformer.

WOLSEY, THOMAS (c. 1474–1530), cardinal. He held a number of benefices under Henry VII and under *Henry VIII he rose rapidly. He became Abp. of *York in 1514 and a cardinal in 1515. A month later he was made Lord Chancellor. In foreign policy he skilfully held the balance of power between the Empire and France. In 1521, though he favoured friendship with France, he had to sign a secret treaty with the Emp. *Charles V, who nevertheless failed to use his influence to get Wolsey elected Pope. At home he made enemies, esp. by his ruthless methods of raising money for the French war. When in 1527 Henry began to take steps to obtain his divorce, Wolsey tried hard to further his wishes. His failure to obtain the Papal dispensation incurred the King's displeasure. In 1529 Wolsey pleaded guilty to a *praemunire, surrendered the Great Seal, and gave up his property to the King. He spent his last months in his diocese. In 1530 he was arrested on a charge of treason; he died on the way to London.

WOODARD, NATHANIEL (1811–91), founder of the 'Woodard Schools'. As a curate in East London he became convinced of the need for public schools which would provide a middle-class education on a definitely Anglican basis. In 1848 he outlined his ideas in his *Plea for the Middle Classes* and established the St. Nicolas Society for the realization of his plans. He received wide moral and financial support, esp. from High Churchmen, and many schools were founded, among them Lancing (1848) and Hurstpierpoint (1850). He became a Canon of Manchester in 1870.

WOOLMAN, JOHN (1720–72), American *Quaker preacher. From 1743 he led a long campaign against *slavery, travelling among the Quaker communities in America in support of Negro rights. His *Journal* describes his activities from 1756 until his death.

WOOLSTON, THOMAS (1670–1733), *Deistical writer. In 1721 he was deprived of a Fellowship in Cambridge and announced his intention of founding a new sect. He wrote in support of A. *Collins and maintained that the Virgin Birth and the Resurrection were allegories.

WORCESTER. The diocese was founded c. 680 for the tribe of the Hwicce when the diocese of Mercia was divided. The first cathedral was richly endowed by the Mercian kings. The secular canons who served it were replaced by *Benedictine monks under St. *Oswald, who also built a new cathedral (completed in 983). After this had been destroyed by the Danes, it was rebuilt (1084–9) by St. *Wulfstan, though little of his work survives. The cathedral, in which King *John was buried, was restored and reconsecrated in 1218. It has been much altered. The choir is Early English and the nave Perpendicular in style.

WORCESTER HOUSE DECLARATION (1660). See *Declarations of Indulgence*.

WORD OF GOD. See *Logos*.

WORDSWORTH, CHRISTOPHER (1807–85), Bp. of *Lincoln from 1869. He was a conservative High Churchman. He wrote a commentary on the whole Bible which had a wide circulation, and he contributed to the field of *patristics. He also wrote hymns, among them 'Songs of thankfulness and praise'.

WORDSWORTH, JOHN (1843–1911), Bp. of *Salisbury from 1885. The elder son of C. *Wordsworth, he was one of the best Latin scholars of his day. From 1878 he worked on a critical edition of the *Vulgate NT (Mt. to Rom. publd. 1889–1911; minor edition of the whole NT, 1911). As bishop he was an invaluable adviser to Abp. E. W. *Benson and an enthusiastic worker in the cause of reunion, esp. with the *Swedish and *Old Catholic Churches. In 1897 he composed the Latin *Responsio* sent by the Abps. of *Canterbury and *York in reply to '*Apostolicae curae'.

WORDSWORTH, WILLIAM (1770–1850), English poet. In 1798 he and S. T. Coleridge published *Lyrical Ballads*, which contains the famous 'Lines written ... above Tintern Abbey'. Wordsworth's aim in this collection was to bring out the deeper spiritual meaning in everyday persons and events. Among his later works were *The Prelude*, his spiritual autobiography (completed 1805), and *Poems in Two Volumes* (1807), containing the 'Ode to Duty' and 'Ode. Intimations of Immortality'. The great inspiration of his art was nature, which he invested with spiritual qualities; this process at times brought his thought near to *pantheism.

WORLD COUNCIL OF CHURCHES, The. The 'fellowship of Churches which accept our Lord Jesus Christ as God and Saviour', formally constituted at *Amsterdam in 1948. The organization arose from the fusion of two earlier movements, '*Life and Work' and '*Faith and Order'. A provisional organization was established at Utrecht in 1938, but because of the Second World War the formal constitution was delayed until 1948. The headquarters of the Council are in Geneva.

Apart from the RC Church and the *Unitarians, the Council includes all the main denominations of the W., nearly all the Eastern *Orthodox Churches, and *c.* 200 other Churches of the non-Western world, mainly in Asia and Africa. Since 1961 the RC Church has sent accredited observers to Assemblies and in 1968 it became a full member of the Faith and Order Commission. Most of the work of the Council is advisory, but it has a number of administrative units; the largest of these is the Division of Inter-Church Aid, Refugee and World Service.

WORLD EVANGELICAL FELLOW-SHIP. See *Evangelical Alliance*.

WORMS, Concordat of (1122). The agreement between *Callistus II and the Emp. Henry V which ended the *Investiture Controversy. The Emperor renounced all investiture by ring and staff. The Pope conceded that in the German kingdom (only) elections of bishops and abbots should take place in the presence of the Emperor, who should grant the regalia by investiture with the sceptre before consecration; in other parts of the Empire consecration was to precede investiture with the regalia.

WORMS, Diet of (1521). The Imperial Diet at which M. *Luther defended his doctrines before *Charles V. On the last day Luther's teaching was formally condemned in the Edict of Worms.

WORMS, Disputation of (1540–1). A colloquy arranged at Worms with a view to reuniting the Catholics and Protestants in Germany. After an agreed formula had been reached on *original sin, it was decided to end the discussions in view of the forthcoming Reichstag at *Ratisbon.

WORMS, Synod of (1076). The synod convened by the Emp. *Henry IV to defend his claims in the *Investiture Controversy. It issued a sharply anti-papal statement. *Gregory VII excommunicated Henry soon afterwards.

WORSHIP, Directory of Public (1645). The 'Directory for the Public Worship of God' was compiled by the *Westminster Assembly on *Presbyterian principles; it was designed to replace the BCP. In *Scotland it was accepted by the *General Assembly and became one of the standards of Presbyterianism. An Ordinance requiring its use in

England was passed by Parliament but was not long enforced.

WOUNDS, The Five Sacred. Though the Passion narratives of the Gospels expressly record only the opening of the Lord's side, the piercing of His hands and feet, a normal practice in contemporary crucifixions, is attested in the Resurrection appearances. Devotion to the Five Wounds developed in the Middle Ages. It was fostered by the *Stigmatization of St. *Francis of Assisi. Preference was soon given to the wound in the side; this gradually led to the cult of the *Sacred Heart.

WRATH OF GOD, The. An anthropomorphic phrase for the Divine attitude to sin. Wrath is predicated of God only metaphorically, as the human passions have no equivalent in the purely spiritual Divine substance. In the NT the wrath of God is particularly associated with the Judgement on the Last Day.

WREDE, WILLIAM (1859–1906), German NT scholar. He challenged the current view that Mk. was an unadorned record of historical fact. He also maintained that Jesus did not claim to be the *Messiah and that the Christian religion received its essential form largely through St. *Paul's radical transformation of Christ's teaching.

WREN, CHRISTOPHER (1632–1723), architect of *St. Paul's Cathedral. He was Savilian Professor of Astronomy at Oxford and a founder of the Royal Society. After the Great Fire of 1666 in London, he was one of the rebuilders of the city. Besides St. Paul's Cathedral, built between 1675 and 1710, Wren was responsible for 52 churches and 36 company halls.

WROTH, WILLIAM (c. 1575–1642), the first Welsh Nonconformist pastor. He became rector of Llanfaches, Gwent, in 1611, and after a sudden conversion in 1620 he became famous as a *Puritan preacher. In 1639, after he had ceased to hold his living, he established at Llanfaches the first separatist Church in Wales.

WULFRIC, St. (d. 1154), also 'Ulrich', anchorite. After a conversion attributed to an interview with a beggar, who told him the contents of his purse and prophesied a life of sanctity for him, c. 1125 he was enclosed in a cell at Haselbury, Somerset. He became famous for his prophecies and miracles.

WULFSTAN (d. 1023), Bp. of London, 996–1002, and Abp. of *York from 1002. He was a prominent royal counsellor and a distinguished writer in Old English. His numerous homilies are practical hortatory expositions of essential doctrine; his 'Institutes of Polity, Civil and Ecclesiastical' is mainly concerned with the duties of the different ranks and classes of society. He composed most of the legislation issued after 1008 by Kings Ethelred II and Canute and drafted or influenced various private lawcodes.

WULFSTAN, St. (c. 1009–95), Bp. of *Worcester from 1062. He had spent some 25 years in a monastery at Worcester, and accepted the bishopric reluctantly. He administered his diocese effectively and, together with *Lanfranc, suppressed the slave trade between England and Ireland.

WÜRTTEMBERG CONFESSION, The. A Protestant confession of faith compiled by J. *Brenz in 1552 for presentation to the Council of *Trent.

WYCLIFFE, JOHN (c. 1330–84), philosopher, theologian, and reformer. He was Master of Balliol College (c. 1360–1) and Warden of Canterbury Hall, Oxford (1365–7). He was also rector of Fillingham (1361–8), of Ludgershall (1368–84), and of Lutterworth (1374–84), but until 1381 he lived mainly in Oxford. He was in the service of John of Gaunt and the Black Prince after 1371, and thus saved from ecclesiastical censure.

Wycliffe's early reputation was as a philosopher. He reacted against the prevailing scepticism of Oxford thought, which divorced the spheres of natural and supernatural knowledge; in his *Summa de Ente* he argued that individual beings derived from God through a hierarchy of universals and were therefore in essence changeless and indestructible. His growing repugnance at the religious institutions of his time led him to elaborate a concept of the Church which distinguished its eternal, ideal reality from the visible, 'material' Church, and denied to the latter any authority which did not derive from the former. In his *De Civili Dominio* he argued that secular and ecclesiastical authority depended on grace and that therefore the clergy, if not in a state of grace, could lawfully be deprived of their endowments by the civil power. He later maintained that the Bible was the sole criterion of doctrine, that the authority of the Pope was ill-founded in Scripture, and that the monastic life had no Biblical foundation. He also attacked the doctrine of *transubstantiation as philosophically unsound and as encouraging a superstitious attitude to the Eucharist.

Wycliffe gradually lost support in Oxford. His Eucharistic teaching was condemned by the University in 1381, and in 1382 Abp. W. *Courtenay condemned a wide range of his doctrines and the persons of his followers, though not Wycliffe himself. Wycliffe retired to Lutterworth. His later influence in England, whether on the *Lollards or in general, is problematical. From c. 1380 his writings exercised a major influence on Czech scholars, notably J. *Huss. The 16th-cent. Reformers appealed to Wycliffe, but his preoccupations were largely different from theirs.

WYCLIFFITES. See *Lollardy*.

WYNFRITH, St. See *Boniface, St.*

WYTTENBACH, THOMAS (1472–1526), Swiss Reformer. He came under the influence of the Humanist movement at Basel, where H. *Zwingli was among his pupils. In 1515 he became pastor at Biel, and from 1523 he publicly supported the Reformation.

X

XAVIER, St. FRANCIS. See *Francis Xavier, St.*

XIMÉNEZ DE CISNEROS, FRANCISCO (1436–1517), Cardinal Abp. of Toledo. He was *vicar general in the diocese of Siguenza before he became an *Observantine friar. He attracted crowds of penitents and retired to a remote monastery. In 1492 he reluctantly became confessor to Queen *Isabella; his advice was sought on matters of state as well as spiritual matters. He became Abp. of Toledo in 1495; the office carried with it the High Chancellorship of Castile. On Isabella's death (1504) he accomplished the delicate task of establishing concord between *Ferdinand and his son-in-law, Philip of Burgundy, who succeeded to the throne of Castile. On Philip's death (1506), Ximénez virtually ruled Castile until Ferdinand returned from Naples, bringing for him a cardinal's hat (1507). When Ferdinand died in 1516, Ximénez was regent during the minority of *Charles V; he died, possibly by poison, on his way to meet Charles, who had landed in Asturias and virtually dismissed him. A great patron of learning, from his own resources he founded the university of Alcalá and commissioned the *Complutensian Polyglot.

XYSTUS. See *Sixtus*.

Y

YAH, an abbreviation of *Yahweh, used in poetical passages in the OT.

YAHWEH. The Hebrew proper name of the Deity. It prob. represents the correct original pronunciation of the *Tetragrammaton (q.v.).

YEAR, Liturgical. In the W. Church the Christian year is based on the *week and on the festivals of *Easter and *Christmas. It begins on the first Sunday in *Advent. Sundays have traditionally been numbered through Advent, after Christmas and after *Epiphany, through *Lent, after Easter, and after *Whitsunday or *Trinity Sunday. Acc. to the calendar introduced into the RC Church in 1969, after Epiphany the 'Sundays of the Year' are numbered consecutively, excluding the period from the beginning of Lent to Whitsunday. In the E. Church the year falls into three parts: *triodion (the ten weeks before Easter), *pentecostarion (the paschal season), and *octoechos (the rest of the year).

YEW SUNDAY. A medieval name for *Palm Sunday.

Y.M.C.A. (Young Men's Christian Association). An association founded in London in 1844 by George Williams. It has always been essentially lay and undenominational in character. Its object is to win young men and boys for Christ by uniting them in fellowship through activities designed to develop their powers of body, mind, and spirit. Much of the work is done in club buildings and hostels, but the Y.M.C.A. also provides services for members of the Forces, prisoners of war, and refugees, and runs training schemes and holiday centres.

YOM KIPPUR. The Hebrew name for the Day of *Atonement.

YONGE, CHARLOTTE MARY (1823–1901), novelist. When in 1835 J. *Keble became vicar of Hursley, she came under his influence. She determined to apply her talent as a storyteller to spreading the faith in fiction. Besides best-selling novels, she wrote lives of J. C. *Patteson and Hannah *More.

YORK. York was the military headquarters of the Romans in Britain. A Bp. of York is mentioned in 314. The original Christian community was destroyed by the Saxon invasions. St. *Paulinus, who was consecrated Bp. of York in 625, baptized the Northumbrian king *Edwin in 627 and received the *pallium in 631. In 633 there was another pagan invasion; Paulinus fled to *Rochester, and York came under the care of the *Celtic bishops of *Lindisfarne. The see was restored in 664 with the consecration of St. *Wilfrid, who reintroduced Roman

usages. In 735 under *Egbert the see was raised to archiepiscopal dignity and its archbishops became primates of the Northern Province, as *Gregory the Great had originally intended. Egbert also founded the famous school at York. Under the first Norman Abp., Thomas of Bayeux (1070–1100), the struggle for precedence between Canterbury and York began. It was finally settled by Pope Innocent VI (1352–62), who decided that the Abp. of Canterbury was to have precedence and the title 'Primate of All England', and that the Abp. of York should be styled 'Primate of England'. Either might carry his cross in the other's province.

Medieval York was important as a regional capital, and throughout the Middle Ages and later the Abps. of York took a leading part in governing the North of England. Before the Reformation there were over 40 parish churches and 9 religious houses in York. The Saxon cathedral was destroyed by the Normans during the rebellion of 1069. Abp. Thomas began and Abp. Roger (1154–81) completed the Norman church which preceded the present York Minster, rebuilt between c. 1227 and 1472. There were four restorations in the 19th cent. The foundations of the central tower and west front, which rest on Roman rubbish, were strengthened between 1967 and 1972.

YOUNG MEN'S (and **WOMEN'S**) **CHRISTIAN ASSOCIATION.** See *Y.M.C.A.* and *Y.W.C.A.*

YOUNG, PATRICK (1584–1652), Biblical and Patristic scholar. He was Royal Librarian under *James I. In 1633 he published from the *Codex Alexandrinus the first edition of *Clement of Rome's *Ep. I ad Cor.*

YULE. *Christmas and its attendant festivities.

Y.W.C.A. (Young Women's Christian Association). A movement similar to the *Y.M.C.A. Two organizations were founded in 1855, one by Miss Robarts and the other by Lady Kinnaird; they united in 1877.

Z

ZABARELLA, FRANCESCO (1360–1417), Italian canonist. Created cardinal by *John XXIII in 1411, he conducted the negotiations with the Emp. Sigismund for the Council of *Constance. His conduct at the Council contributed to healing the schism. His writings on canon law long remained standard works.

ZACCHAEUS. A *publican, he climbed a tree to see Christ, and was called by name to come down and give Him lodging in his house (Lk. 19: 1–10).

ZACHARIAH. The father of St. *John the Baptist. A Jewish priest, he received a vision in the *Temple promising him a son; he celebrated the birth of the child and the coming redemption of Israel in the '*Benedictus'.

ZACHARIAS, St. (d. 752), Pope from 741. He induced the Lombard king, Liutprand, to restore her patrimonies to the Church and to abandon his attack on *Ravenna. He supported the missionary work of St. *Boniface, confirmed the deposition of the last of the Merovingians, and had *Pepin anointed by Boniface. He denounced the *Iconoclastic policy of the Emp. Constantine Copronymus.

ZACHARIAS SCHOLASTICUS (d. after 536), *Monophysite Bp. of Mitylene on the island of Lesbos. His most important work was a Church history, valuable for the period 450–91. He also wrote lives of *Severus of Antioch, Peter the Iberian, and others, and works directed against the *Neoplatonists and the *Manichees.

ZADOKITE DOCUMENTS. See *Dead Sea Scrolls.*

ZAHN, THEODOR (1838–1933), German NT and patristic scholar. His standpoint was that of sober conservatism and his work was marked by erudition and thoroughness. His long series of studies on the NT *Canon contained much pioneer work. In the field of patristics he wrote on *Marcellus of Ancyra, St. *Ignatius, and on the Acts of *John.

ZARATHUSTRA. See *Zoroastrianism.*

ZEALOTS. A Jewish party of revolt. Acc. to *Josephus they were followers of John of Gischala who inspired the fanatical resistance in Jerusalem which led to its destruction by the Romans in A.D. 70. They have commonly been identified with (1) the followers of Judas of Gamala who led a revolt in A.D. 6, and (2) the Sicarii, who tried to achieve their ends by assassinating their political opponents and refused to surrender to the Romans at Masada. There is no good reason for either identification. The epithet 'zealot' applied to St. *Simon 'the Less' in Lk. 6: 15 may mean that he belonged to the Zealot party, or may merely describe his character.

ZECHARIAH, Book of. *Minor Prophet. Chs. 1–8, written by Zechariah, date from 519–517 B.C. An introductory prophecy is followed by an account of 8 visions. In one of these Zerubbabel, the contemporary head of the royal house of Judah, is exhorted to complete the restoration of the *Temple and is perhaps identified with the Davidic prince (see *Messiah*; 4: 6–10). In chs. 7–8 Zechariah asserts the need for righteousness rather than fasting, and prophesies the future glory of Judah when the Gentiles seeking God should voluntarily join themselves to the Jews. Chs. 9–14 contain two anonymous prophecies of a different style and reflecting the circumstances of a later age.

ZENO, St. (d. c. 375), Bp. of *Verona from 362. He was an African. His sermons (*Tractatus*) have affinities with the writings of *Tertullian and *Cyprian; they did not come into circulation until the early Middle Ages.

ZENO (c. 450?–91), E. Emperor from 474. His reign was marked by a series of disastrous wars, and his *Henoticon (482) did nothing to bring about the desired union of the *Monophysites with the orthodox.

ZEPHANIAH, Book of. *Minor Prophet. The Book announces the approaching judgement of all nations in the Day of the Lord, but holds out the hope of future conversion among the heathen and of a faithful remnant among the Jews. The prophecy claims to have been delivered in the reign of Josiah (d. 608 B.C.). The opening words of the '*Dies irae' are taken from the *Vulgate version of 1: 15 f.

ZEPHYRINUS, St. (d. 217), Pope from 198. Little is known of him. St. *Hippolytus charged him with laxity in enforcing discipline and failure to suppress the heresies (esp. *Sabellianism) prevalent in Rome, but he excommunicated *Theodotus the Cobbler and his disciple Theodotus the Money Changer who defended the cause of 'Adoptionist *Monarchianism'.

ZIGABENUS, EUTHYMIUS. See *Euthymius Zigabenus.*

ZILLERTHAL EVANGELICALS. A body of Protestants living in the Zillerthal, one of the valleys of the Tyrol, who seceded from the RC Church in 1829 and the following years. They were ordered to leave the country and settled in Prussia.

ZINZENDORF, NIKOLAUS LUDWIG, GRAF VON (1700–60), founder of the *Herrnhuter 'Brüdergemeine'. From 1722 he received on one of his estates Protestant emigrants from Austria, many of them descendants of the *Bohemian Brethren. He gave up his government post in 1727 and devoted himself to the care of the colony, called Herrnhut. He was attacked as an innovator by orthodox *Lutherans and exiled from Saxony from 1736 to 1747. In 1737 he secured *Moravian episcopal consecration. He founded communities in the Baltic provinces, *Holland, England, the *West Indies, and N. America.

Opposed alike to the unbelieving rationalism and the barren Protestant orthodoxy of his time, Zinzendorf proclaimed a 'religion of the heart', based on an intimate fellowship with the Saviour. Though he hoped to realize his ideals within the framework of the different Protestant Churches, he was forced to give his work a separate organization. His emphasis on the place of feeling in religion profoundly influenced 19th-cent. German theology.

ZION. The citadel of *Jerusalem, taken by *David from the Jebusites (2 Sam. 5: 6–7). The name came to signify Jerusalem itself (Is. 1: 27) and, allegorically, the heavenly city (Heb. 12: 22).

ZITA, St. (c. 1215–72), the patroness of domestic servants. At the age of 12 she entered the service of the Fatinelli family at Lucca, where she remained until her death. She was fervently religious.

ZONARAS, JOHANNES (12th cent.), Byzantine canonist and historian. He held high office in the Imperial administration before he retired to a monastery. His 'Universal History' preserves material which would otherwise be lost; it extends to 1118 and covers events which Zonaras witnessed. He also wrote a commentary on Greek canon law.

ZOROASTRIANISM. The doctrinal system ascribed to Zoroaster (Zarathustra) which became the dominant religion in Iran.

Zoroaster prob. lived c. 628–551 B.C. He taught that the world was made by one 'Wise Lord' with the help of his Holy Spirit and six other spirits or attributes of God. These spirits work against the Evil Spirit, who is helped by six other spirits. After the life on earth of a virgin-born Saviour, God will triumph over evil and all souls will pass over the 'bridge of decision' (from which some must first fall into purifying flames) and enjoy eternal bliss. His ideas are sometimes held to have influenced Christianity.

ZOSIMUS (d. 418), Bp. of Rome from 417. His pontificate was marked by blunders. The African Church, led by St. *Augustine, compelled him to retract his favourable judgement of *Pelagianism, and he was outmanœuvred when, citing as *Nicene a canon which belonged to the Council of *Sardica, he tried to quash the sentence passed on *Apiarius by the Bp. of Sicca.

ZOSIMUS (later 5th cent.), Greek historian. His history of the Roman Empire, extending to 410, is a primary source for the secular history of the 4th cent. Because of its anti-Christian bias, it serves as a corrective to the better-known accounts of ecclesiastical affairs in Christian writers.

ZUCCHETTO. A small round skull-cap used by certain RC ecclesiastics.

ZÜRICH CONSENSUS. See *Consensus Tigurinus*.

ZWICKAU PROPHETS. A group of *Anabaptists who sought to realize the rule of the elect in a community at Zwickau, an industrial town in Saxony. They moved to *Wittenberg in 1521, but were promptly put down by M. *Luther on his return in 1522.

ZWINGLI, ULRICH (1484–1531), Swiss Reformer. Ordained priest in 1506, he became pastor at Glarus. Here he devoted himself to humanistic studies. In 1516 he left Glarus for *Einsiedeln, where the pilgrimage abuses quickened his desire for reform. In 1518 he was elected People's Preacher at the Old Minster in Zürich. The rupture with ecclesiastical authority came gradually. The real beginning of the Swiss Reformation was Zwingli's lectures on the NT in 1519; they were followed by attacks on *purgatory, invocation of *saints, and *monasticism. His first Reformation tract appeared in 1522. Johann *Faber, sent to Zürich to deal with the situation, was silenced in a public disputation in 1523, when Zwingli upheld 67 theses. Acc. to Zwingli, the sole basis of truth was the Gospel; the authority of the Pope, the sacrifice of the Mass, times and seasons of fasting, and clerical *celibacy were rejected. The City Council supported Zwingli and the Minster Chapter was made independent of episcopal control. It was at this stage that Zwingli developed his characteristic Eucharistic teaching. In 1522 he still accepted a traditional view of the Eucharist, but by 1524 he upheld a purely symbolic interpretation. The ensuing conflict with M. *Luther led to the fruitless Colloquy of *Marburg (1529); the division was so deep that any union of Protestant forces was impossible. Meanwhile the movement had spread to other parts of Switzerland. It met with resistance in the Forest Cantons. In 1531 they made a sudden attack on Zürich and Zwingli was killed in battle.

CHRONOLOGICAL LIST OF POPES AND ANTIPOPES

Antipopes are indicated by indenting the names to the right in [ ]

until *c.* 64	St. *Peter	384–99	*Siricius
	*Linus	399–401	Anastasius I
	*Anacletus	402–17	*Innocent I
fl. c. 96	*Clement I	417–18	*Zosimus
	Evaristus	418–22	*Boniface I
	Alexander I	[418–19	Eulalius]
*c.*117–*c.*127	Sixtus I	422–32	*Celestine I
*c.*127–*c.*137	*Telesphorus	432–40	Sixtus III
*c.*137–*c.*140	Hyginus	440–61	*Leo I
*c.*140–*c.*154	*Pius I	461–8	Hilarus
*c.*154–*c.*166	Anicetus	468–83	*Simplicius
*c.*166–*c.*175	Soter	483–92	Felix III (II)
175–89	Eleutherius	492–6	*Gelasius I
189–98	*Victor I	496–8	Anastasius II
198–217	*Zephyrinus	498–514	*Symmachus
217–22	*Callistus I	[498, 501–5	Laurentius]
[217–*c.*235	*Hippolytus]	514–23	*Hormisdas
222–30	Urban I	523–6	John I
230–5	Pontian	526–30	Felix IV (III)
235–6	Anterus	530–2	Boniface II
236–50	*Fabian	[530	Dioscorus]
251–3	*Cornelius	533–5	John II
[251	*Novatian]	535–6	*Agapetus I
253–4	Lucius I	536–7	Silverius
254–7	*Stephen I	537–55	*Vigilius
257–8	*Sixtus II	556–61	Pelagius I
259–68	*Dionysius	561–74	John III
269–74	Felix I	575–9	Benedict I
275–83	Eutychianus	579–90	Pelagius II
283–96	Caius	590–604	*Gregory I
296–304	Marcellinus	604–6	Sabinianus
308–9	Marcellus I	607	Boniface III
310	Eusebius	608–15	Boniface IV
311–314	*Miltiades	615–18	Deusdedit or Adeodatus I
314–35	*Sylvester I	619–25	Boniface V
336	Mark	625–38	*Honorius I
337–52	*Julius I	640	Severinus
352–66	*Liberius	640–2	John IV
[355–65	Felix II]	642–9	Theodore I
366–84	*Damasus I	649–55	*Martin I[1]
[366–7	Ursinus]	654–7	Eugenius I

[1] After Martin's banishment his successor was elected and consecrated.

657–72	*Vitalian	896–7	Stephen VII
672–6	Adeodatus II	897	Romanus
676–8	Donus	897	Theodore II
678–81	*Agatho	898–900	John IX
682–3	Leo II	900–3	Benedict IV
684–5	Benedict II	903	Leo V
685–6	John V	[903–4	Christopher]
686–7	Cono	904–11	Sergius III
[687	Theodore]	911–13	Anastasius III
[687	Paschal]	913–14	Lando
687–701	*Sergius I	914–28	John X
701–5	John VI	928	Leo VI
705–7	John VII	928–31	Stephen VIII
708	Sisinnius	931–5	John XI
708–15	Constantine	936–9	Leo VII
715–31	*Gregory II	939–42	Stephen IX
731–41	Gregory III	942–6	Marinus II
741–52	*Zacharias	946–55	Agapetus II
752	Stephen II	955–64	*John XII
752–7	*Stephen II (III)	[963–5	Leo VIII]
757–67	Paul I	964–6	Benedict V
[767–9	Constantine]	965–72	John XIII
[768	Philip]	973–4	Benedict VI
768–72	*Stephen III (IV)	[974 & 984–5	Boniface VII]
772–95	*Hadrian I	974–83	Benedict VII
795–816	*Leo III	983–4	John XIV
816–17	Stephen V	985–96	John XV
817–24	Paschal I	996–9	Gregory V
824–7	Eugenius II	[997–8	John XVI]
827	Valentine	999–1003	*Sylvester II
827–44	Gregory IV	1003	John XVII
[844	John]	1004–9	John XVIII
844–7	Sergius II	1009–12	Sergius IV
847–55	*Leo IV	1012–24	Benedict VIII
855–8	Benedict III	[1012	Gregory]
[855	*Anastasius Bibliothecarius]	1024–32	John XIX
		1032–44	Benedict IX
858–67	*Nicholas I	1045	Sylvester III
867–72	Hadrian II	1045	Benedict IX
872–82	John VIII		[for the second time]
882–4	Marinus I	1045–6	Gregory VI
884–5	Hadrian III	1046–7	Clement II
885–91	Stephen VI	1047–8	Benedict IX
891–6	*Formosus		[for the third time]
896	Boniface VI	1048	Damasus II

1048–54	*Leo IX	1243–54	*Innocent IV
1055–7	Victor II	1254–61	Alexander IV
1057–8	Stephen X	1261–4	Urban IV
[1058–9	Benedict X]	1265–8	Clement IV
1059–61	Nicholas II	1271–6	*Gregory X
1061–73	*Alexander II	1276	Innocent V
[1061–72	Honorius II]	1276	Hadrian V
1073–85	*Gregory VII	1276–7	John XXI[2]
[1080, 1084–		1277–80	Nicholas III
1100	Clement III]	1281–5	*Martin IV
1086–7	Victor III	1285–7	Honorius IV
1088–99	*Urban II	1288–92	Nicholas IV
1099–1118	*Paschal II	1294	*Celestine V
[1100–2	Theodoric]	1294–1303	*Boniface VIII
[1102	Albert]	1303–4	Benedict XI
[1105 11	Sylvester IV]	1305–14	*Clement V
1118–19	Gelasius II	1316–34	*John XXII
[1118 21	Gregory VIII]	[1328–30	Nicholas V]
1119–24	*Callistus II	1334–42	*Benedict XII
1124–30	Honorius II	1342–52	*Clement VI
[1124	Celestine II]	1352–62	Innocent VI
1130–43	Innocent II	1362–70	*Urban V
[1130–8	Anacletus II]	1370–8	*Gregory XI
[1138	Victor IV]	1378–89	* Urban VI
1143–4	Celestine II	[1378–94	Clement VII]
1144–5	Lucius II	1389–1404	Boniface IX
1145–53	*Eugenius III	[1394–1423	*Benedict XIII]
1153–4	Anastasius IV	1404–6	Innocent VII
1154–9	*Hadrian IV	1406–15	Gregory XII
1159–81	*Alexander III	[1409–10	*Alexander V]
[1159–64	Victor IV[1]]	[1410–15	*John XXIII]
[1164–8	Paschal III]	1417–31	*Martin V
[1168–78	Callistus III]	[1423–9	Clement VIII]
[1179–80	Innocent III]	[1425–30	Benedict XIV]
1181–5	Lucius III	1431–47	*Eugenius IV
1185–7	Urban III	[1439–49	Felix V]
1187	Gregory VIII	1447–55	*Nicholas V
1187–91	Clement III	1455–8	*Callistus III
1191–8	*Celestine III	1458–64	*Pius II
1198–1216	*Innocent III	1464–71	Paul II
1216–27	*Honorius III	1471 84	*Sixtus IV
1227–41	*Gregory IX	1484–92	Innocent VIII
1241	Celestine IV	1492–1503	*Alexander VI

[1] No account was taken of the previous antipope, who had resisted for a very short time.
[2] No Pope bearing the name of John XX ever existed.

1503	Pius III	1676–89	*Innocent XI
1503–13	*Julius II	1689–91	*Alexander VIII
1513–21	*Leo X	1691–1700	Innocent XII
1522–3	*Hadrian VI	1700–21	*Clement XI
1523–34	*Clement VII	1721–4	Innocent XIII
1534–49	*Paul III	1724–30	*Benedict XIII
1550–5	*Julius III	1730–40	Clement XII
1555	Marcellus II	1740–58	*Benedict XIV
1555–9	*Paul IV	1758–69	*Clement XIII
1559–65	*Pius IV	1769–74	*Clement XIV
1566–72	*Pius V	1775–99	*Pius VI
1572–85	*Gregory XIII	1800–23	*Pius VII
1585–90	*Sixtus V	1823–9	Leo XII
1590	Urban VII	1829–30	Pius VIII
1590–1	Gregory XIV	1831–46	*Gregory XVI
1591	Innocent IX	1846–78	*Pius IX
1592–1605	*Clement VIII	1878–1903	*Leo XIII
1605	Leo XI	1903–14	*Pius X
1605–21	*Paul V	1914–22	*Benedict XV
1621–3	Gregory XV	1922–39	*Pius XI
1623–44	*Urban VIII	1939–58	*Pius XII
1644–55	*Innocent X	1958–63	*John XXIII
1655–67	*Alexander VII	1963–78	*Paul VI
1667–9	Clement IX	1978	John Paul I
1670–6	Clement X	1978–	John Paul II